Calendar Of Letters, Despatches, And State Papers Relating To The Negotiations Between England And Spain Preserved In The Archives At Simancas And Elsewhere: Henry Viii. 1509-[1546] 12 V...

Great Britain. Public Record Office

Nabu Public Domain Reprints:

You are holding a reproduction of an original work published before 1923 that is in the public domain in the United States of America, and possibly other countries. You may freely copy and distribute this work as no entity (individual or corporate) has a copyright on the body of the work. This book may contain prior copyright references, and library stamps (as most of these works were scanned from library copies). These have been scanned and retained as part of the historical artifact.

This book may have occasional imperfections such as missing or blurred pages, poor pictures, errant marks, etc. that were either part of the original artifact, or were introduced by the scanning process. We believe this work is culturally important, and despite the imperfections, have elected to bring it back into print as part of our continuing commitment to the preservation of printed works worldwide. We appreciate your understanding of the imperfections in the preservation process, and hope you enjoy this valuable book.

CALENDARS.

Instructions to Editors.

The Master of the Rolls desires to call the attention of the Editors of Calendars to the following considerations, with a view to secure uniformity of plan in the important works on which they are engaged :—

He is anxious to extend, as far as is consistent with proper economy and despatch, the utility of the Calendars of State Papers now publishing under his control : 1st. As the most efficient means of making the national archives accessible to all who are interested in historical inquiries; 2nd. As the best justification of the liberality and munificence of the Government in throwing open these papers to the public, and providing proper catalogues of their contents at the national expense.

The greater number of the readers who will consult and value these works can have little or no opportunity of visiting the Public Record Office, in which these papers are deposited. The means for consulting the originals must necessarily be limited when readers live at a distance from the metropolis; still more if they are residents of Scotland, Ireland, distant colonies, or foreign states. Even when such an opportunity does exist, the difficulty of mastering the original hands in which these papers are written will deter many readers from consulting them. Above all, their great variety and number must present formidable obstacles to literary inquirers, however able, sanguine, and energetic, when the information contained in them is not made accessible by satisfactory Calendars.

The Master of the Rolls considers that, without superseding the necessity of consulting the originals, every Editor ought to frame his Calendar in such a manner that it shall present, in as condensed a form as possible, a correct index of the contents of the papers described in it. He considers that the entries should be so minute as to enable the reader to discover not only the general contents of the originals, but also what *they do not* contain. If the information be not sufficiently precise, if facts and names be omitted or concealed under a vague and general description, the reader will be often misled, he will assume that where the abstracts are silent as to information to be found in the documents, such information does not exist; or he will have to examine every original in detail, and thus one great purpose will have been lost for which these Calendars have been compiled.

As the documents are various, the Master of the Rolls considers that they will demand a corresponding mode of treatment. The following rules are to be observed :—

1st. All formal and official documents, such as letters of credence, warrants, grants, and the like, should be described as briefly as possible.

2nd. Letters and documents referring to one subject only should be catalogued as briefly as is consistent with correctness. But when they contain miscellaneous news, such a description should be given as will enable a reader to form an adequate notion of the variety of their contents.

3rd. Wherever a letter or paper is especially difficult to decipher, or the allusions more than ordinarily obscure, it will be advisable for the Editor to adhere, as closely as is consistent with brevity, to the text of the document. He is to do the same when it contains secret or very rare information.

4th. Where the Editor has deciphered letters in cipher, the decipher may be printed at full length. But when a contemporary or authorised decipher exists it will be sufficient to treat the cipher as an ordinary document.

5th. Striking peculiarities of expression, proverbs, manners, &c., are to be noticed.

6th. Original dates are to be given at the close of each entry, that the reader may know the exact evidence by which the marginal dates are determined.

7th. Where letters are endorsed by the receivers and the date of their delivery specified, these endorsements are to be recorded.

8th. The number of written pages of each document is to be specified, as a security for its integrity, and that readers may know what proportion the abstract bears to the original.

9th. The language of every document is to be specified. If, however, the greater part of the collection be in English, it will be sufficient to denote those only which are in a different tongue.

10th. Where documents have been printed, a reference should be given to the publication.

11th. Each series is to be chronological.

12th. The Prefaces of Editors, in explanation of documents in the volume, are not to exceed fifty pages, unless the written permission of the Master of the Rolls to the contrary be obtained.

⁂ Editors employed in foreign archives are to transcribe at full length important and secret papers.

CALENDAR

OF

LETTERS, DESPATCHES, AND STATE PAPERS,

RELATING TO

THE NEGOTIATIONS BETWEEN ENGLAND AND SPAIN,

PRESERVED IN

THE ARCHIVES AT SIMANCAS, VIENNA, BRUSSELS, AND ELSEWHERE.

Vol. VIII.

HENRY VIII.

1545–1546.

EDITED BY

MARTIN A. S. HUME.

PUBLISHED BY THE AUTHORITY OF THE LORDS COMMISSIONERS OF HIS MAJESTY'S TREASURY,
UNDER THE DIRECTION OF THE MASTER OF THE ROLLS.

LONDON:
PRINTED FOR HIS MAJESTY'S STATIONERY OFFICE
BY MACKIE AND CO. LD.

And to be purchased, either directly or through any Bookseller, from
EYRE AND SPOTTISWOODE, EAST HARDING STREET, FLEET STREET, E.C.; or
OLIVER AND BOYD, EDINBURGH; or
E. PONSONBY, 116, GRAFTON STREET, DUBLIN.

1904.

CONTENTS.

	PAGE.
INTRODUCTION	v
CALENDAR 1545–1546	1
ADDENDA	561
ERRATA AND INDEXES	614

INTRODUCTION.

The papers calendared in the present volume cover the last two years of the reign and life of Henry VIII., a period hardly equalled in importance by any other of similar length in modern history, since it saw the ranging of the forces for and against the Reformation, and the development of the new divisions created by the religious affinities which had run athwart traditional international alliances. In England the failing health of the old King, and the growth of the Protestant influence in his councils, were already foreshadowing the regime of Seymour and Dudley, and gradually and reluctantly widening the rift between England and the Emperor. The secret clauses of the treaty of Crespy, which bound Francis to aid Charles in the giant task he had set himself to overcome the Protestant Reformation on the continent, drew together temporarily the two interests upon whose antagonism the welfare, even the safety, of England depended; whilst the rallying of the Farnese Pope to the side of his old enemy the Emperor, and the conclusion of a long truce with the Turk, placed the Emperor in a position, for the first time, to plan his crushing blow at the Schmalkaldic League, with the object of grinding the Protestant princes under his heel, and perhaps of securing to his Spanish son Philip the reversion of the Empire with world-wide supremacy. The plan, as was afterwards proved, was too vast a one and affected too many interests, to be carried out in its entirety, but during its inception and early success in the period covered by this volume it served to increase the tendency of the English rulers towards an anti-Catholic policy, whilst it rendered more urgent than ever the subjection of Scottish foreign relations to English influence, and created a new bond of interest between the Protestant German princes in arms against their suzerain in alliance with the Pope, and the great enemy of the papacy across the North Sea.

Throughout the letters in the present volume, however, there is traceable the deep distrust and falsity that characterised the alliances arising out of the new circumstances of religious division. To serve the interests of his family Paul III. with many groans unlocked his treasure chest, and became the servant of the Emperor whom he had always hated; he even consented at last to the meeting of a great Council of the Church at Trent in the Imperial dominions; but his distrust of the Emperor was invincible, and he ever tried to take away with one hand what he gave with the other, wrangling and haggling, as will be seen in the correspondence, over every demand of his ally, until the inevitable split once more for a time threw the papacy on to its ancient lines of policy. The attitude of Charles towards Rome was an exactly similar one. He needed for the purpose of suppressing Lutheranism the money and moral support of Farnese, as well as his influence in keeping France quiet, and was obliged to feign a submission to the pontiff that the violent and insulting expressions used by himself and his agent in their confidential correspondence when speaking of the Pope show to have been but skin-deep. But although Charles was thus driven by religious necessity into unholy alliance with the papacy and France, his traditional enemies, his instinctive desire, as exhibited in the correspondence now before us, was to keep intact his old friendship with Henry of England, who was at open war with France, and embodied the defiance of the papal authority.

Between the Emperor and Francis the new union was just as insincere. The main provisions of the Treaty of Crespy were still unfulfilled on both sides. In principle it had been decided by the Emperor that of the two matrimonial alternatives left to him in the treaty, he chose the marriage of the Duke of Orleans with a daughter of Ferdinand King of the Romans, with the dowry of Milan or Flanders (*see* Vol. VII. of the Calendar); but there was apparently no intention whatever of carrying the union into effect, and the reclamations on both sides were made in a purely retaliatory spirit. The religious affinities created by the new spirit of the Reformation were indeed on all sides, as yet, not strong enough to over-ride for long the international interests that had been the growth of centuries. Both Charles and Francis were desirous of crushing Protestantism; and their union for the purpose seemed necessary; but to the Emperor and his brother Ferdinand the surrender of Flanders or Milan seemed too large a price to pay for doubtful French neutrality; whilst to Francis—and more especially to the Dauphin Henry—the making of a French prince a vassal of the Emperor would appear a poor return for the claims of the French sovereign to Milan, which if successful might eventually lead to his election to the imperial throne. Henry VIII., on the other hand, who had much reason for anger with the Emperor for his shabby betrayal of him in making peace separately at Crespy, and whose religious leanings would naturally dispose him to sympathise with the German Protestants, was bound by his old diplomatic traditions to the extent of limiting his intervention in their favour to acrimonious verbal protest to the Imperial ambassador, much less effective aid than the ample supplies of money secretly contributed to the Protestant cause by the Emperor's Catholic ally and brother-in-law Francis. The whole of the important and interesting correspondence in the present volume thus exhibits the strange spectacle of a series of imperative new alliances in which none of the parties were sincere, each national interest pursuing its own ends to the detriment of the rest, under cover of mutual agreements with other objects, and yearning still to continue the old international connections which had been deranged by the growth of religious revolt from the papacy.

The last volume of the Calendar ended with Henry VIII. still at war with France, sore and angry at the trick that his ally had played him by making peace alone and leaving him face to face with the enemy. The excuse made by Charles for his desertion was, as is related fully in the introduction of the last volume, that Henry had told the Bishop of Arras (De Granvelle), who had been sent to Boulogne by the Emperor to see him on the subject, that his Imperial master was at liberty to make peace if he pleased, so long as no clauses detrimental to his (Henry's) claims were introduced into the treaty. Henry continued subsequently to disclaim, with great violence and anger, the expression attributed to him by Arras; but there seems to be no doubt that he did hastily say something of the kind. which provided De Granvelle with the pretext he sought. The Emperor, indeed, had already practically agreed to a separate peace before Arras saw Henry at Boulogne; and Henry himself was at the time in close negotiation with the French with a similar object. Each of the two allies was, in fact, endeavouring to get the start of the other in making peace, and Charles succeeded, thanks mainly to Francis' mistress, the Duchess of Étampes, who had more to gain from the Emperor than from Henry.

Finding that his indignant remonstrances by his ambassador, Dr. Wotton, were unavailing, Henry had sent in October his two principal councillors, Stephen Gardiner, Bishop of Winchester, and Edward Seymour, Earl of Hertford, to Brussels, for the purpose of claiming from Charles the fulfilment of a clause of the treaty of alliance which, it was alleged, bound him to declare war anew against France, in consequence of the French "invasion" of Henry's new conquest of Boulogne. An account of their abortive embassy will be found in the last volume of this Calendar, but their obvious discontent at their departure, and the imperious need for Charles to mollify Henry whilst maintaining his recently-concluded alliance with France, prompted him to send back to the English Court the man who, of all others, had learned to manage Henry in every mood. Eustace Chapuys, for nearly sixteen years, during the most critical periods of the Schism of England, and the divorce and death of Queen Katharine, had dexterously contrived to prevent an open rupture between

Henry and Charles. It was a great achievement of diplomacy, and the Emperor concluded that the man who had effected it would be able, better than another, to tide over the present difficulty. Chapuys was old and ill, and had frequently implored his master to relieve him. His mission, therefore, was understood to be only a temporary one, and with him as joint ambassador went the diplomatist whom Charles had destined to be his successor, François Van der Delft, a Flemish knight, who after he had gained confidence by a few months' experience in his new post, proved himself in subtlety, dexterity and boldness, to be a worthy follower in the footsteps of his predecessor.

Chapuys and Van der Delft arrived in London on Christmas eve, 1544, and on Sunday morning, 28 December, 1544, at Greenwich, they had their first audience of the King. Chapuys noticed that though Henry boasted that he had never been better in his life, he had become much broken since his return from Boulogne. But the ambassadors soon found that, however feeble he might be in body, his spirit was as high as ever. He had "whipped" the French well at sea, he said; had made them "pay scot" to a good tune by captures of their victuallers and wine ships in the Channel. This was touching a sore point, for one of the Emperor's main objects in consenting to the hard terms of the peace of Crespy was to restore to his half-ruined Flemish subjects their lucrative traffic in fish and other provisions with France; whereas the English King insisted upon regarding all victuals for the French as contraband of war, and had embargoed great quantities of herrings and other food destined for France in Flemish bottoms, on the assumed ground that the cargoes belonged to French subjects. Parallel with the great international questions dealt with in the correspondence, there runs incessantly this irritating secondary dispute of the seizures, and later of the open piracy that arose out of them. As will be noticed in due course, retaliatory measures, much special diplomatic negotiation on both sides, and more than one attempt at arbitration, produced but little result in the way of redress, and in most cases the merchants found finally that they could make better terms for themselves by compromise with the captors than by diplomatic action that was hampered by the commercial claims being used to obtain political concessions.

Chapuys was the spokesman when, after attending Mass with the King, saluting the Queen (Catharine Parr) and Princess Mary, and dining with the Privy Councillors, the two Imperial ambassadors were formally received in the presence chamber at Greenwich. With due circumlocution the old ambassador set forth once more the arguments against the re-entry of Charles into the war, which had already been discussed *ad nauseam* with Hertford and Gardiner at Brussels. Henry listened impatiently, changing colour now and again with anger; but when Chapuys in justification of his master repeated the assertion that had been contradicted so often about Henry's remark to Granvelle, the King fairly flew into a passion, and dared any man to assert that he had unconditionally said any such thing. Chapuys insisted that he himself had heard him with many others; and, with what looks like malicious pertinacity, elaborated this strong point against the King. "The King was intensely annoyed and irritated at this, and told me quite openly that it was a great lie."[*] Henry was too angry to be a match in dialectics with the subtle ambassador, who soon involved him in a mesh of inextricable confusion and self-contradiction; and the interview ended with hot passion on the one side and dignified resentment at the King's rough language on the other; the subject being relegated to further discussion between the ambassadors and the Privy Council on the following day. When the demand had first been formulated in Brussels by Hertford and Gardiner, the Emperor had, with the hope of tiding over the difficulty without giving a flat refusal, taken a period of ten weeks in which to give his official reply. Of this period some

---

[*] p. 5.

INTRODUCTION. xi

eight weeks had already passed; and angry though Henry was at being contradicted and his word called into question, he, and especially his councillors, could not afford to offend the Emperor or alienate his ambassadors before the reply due in a fortnight was given. It does not, indeed, seem to have entered the head of the English King and his council that Charles could fail to make some sort of declaration against the French sooner or later, which at least would give moral strength to the English cause and hamper injuriously French commerce.

When, therefore, after a day or two's delay, owing to the feigned diplomatic illness of Chapuys, Hertford, Gardiner and Paget waited upon the ambassadors as a deputation of the Council, for the purpose of discussing the whole business, the English councillors made great efforts to palliate and explain away the King's strong language. Chapuys had already gained a point by assuming the position of an aggrieved party, and made the most of it. There was too much talk, he said, in England, to the effect that the Emperor had failed in his obligations towards the King, and the vindication of his Majesty's reputation should be public, such talk not being allowed, to the injury of a friendly sovereign. The King, continued Chapuys, had become excited when he had addressed him; and it had been impossible for him, Chapuys, to conclude his address. "Certain unpleasant passages had "occurred between the King and us . . . and I thanked "God it had not happened to any other of your Majesty's "Ministers instead of to me; for I was not sure whether any "other would have put up with it. But I, who knew the "King's humour so well, and so ardently desired the "continuance of his friendship with my master, would avoid "reporting if possible any event which could injure the good "feeling."* Then, after deprecating passion in diplomacy, Chapuys once more set forth the whole of the arguments with which we are familiar with the object of excusing his master

* p. 10.

xii   INTRODUCTION.

from complying with the clauses of the treaty providing for his coming to the aid of the King of England against an invading force. But he carried the argument somewhat further than previously, and threw the English Councillors into a fright by alleging that Henry himself had first broken the treaty by his conduct of the war. Gardiner did his best to defend his master, but Chapuys, according to his own showing, refuted him at every point; and then, carrying the war into the enemy's camp, complained bitterly of the English seizures of Spanish and Flemish property at sea. Gardiner alone attempted to make a stand against the avalanche of accusation, by saying quite truly that the King of England's aid in the war had certainly promoted the Emperor's objects. "I (Chapuys) "immediately replied that he was too fond of repeating such "things; and he forced me to say what otherwise I should not "say; namely, that his constant repetition of this point took "the form of a reproach;" and this allowed the ambassador another chance, of which he availed himself to the full, for the exaltation of the Emperor, and the depreciation of all things English. It is quite evident, however, that the Councillors only regarded this scolding as an excuse for minimising the Emperor's inevitable concession. "They "seemed convinced that your Majesty would raise no difficulty "in making the declaration (against France) after the "expiration of the ten weeks; but I extricated myself by "saying that I had no knowledge of your Majesty's intention, "but was sure your Majesty would not fail on that or any "other point to do what was proper and incumbent upon "you."†

Neither Henry nor his Councillors could convince themselves that Chapuys had been sent to England with his colleague merely for the purpose of repeating the old arguments and statements which had been discussed several times already; and finding that all their attempts to draw from the imperial ambassadors in the formal interviews any declaration

---

* p. 15.   † p. 17.

of what was believed to be their secret mission, Hertford and Gardiner sought Chapuys privately, in order, as they said, to chat with him without witnesses, evidently for the purpose of obtaining from him, if possible, some inkling of how far Charles was prepared to go in acceding to the English demands. In the long interview that followed the English Councillors were apologetic for their King's rudeness, and they made great efforts to come to close quarters with their cunning interlocutor, but with little effect. Henry, they said, could easily be brought to a yielding and friendly attitude if appearances of humouring him were kept up, "anyone who " knew how to manage him might do almost as he liked with " him." If the Emperor would only write a few amiable words himself to the King, the pending questions might be harmoniously settled. What sort of words? asked Chapuys. "They said that your Majesty might assure the King of your " perfect, sincere and inviolable amity, and of your absolute " intention to observe all engagements and promises." Chapuys saw plainly that this general declaration was not the real object aimed at, and replied that similar professions had already been made by the Emperor through his ambassadors. " But the King would like it better," replied the Englishmen, " if it were written;" and then, somewhat clumsily, they came to the main point; which, after all, was an absurdly transparent attempt upon such an experienced diplomatist as Chapuys, to deprive the Emperor of the most dreaded and efficacious weapon in his armoury as against the English King. "In addition to the two professions above mentioned the letter "should contain a third clause, saying that your Majesty was " perfectly satisfied with all the King had done in the enter- " prise, and that it was your Majesty's intention to fulfil " punctually the terms of the Treaty. I laughed when I heard " this, and said I was surprised that they did not add a demand " that your Majesty (the Emperor) should ask the King's " pardon. For my own part, I would never advise the " Emperor to concede the last-mentioned clauses; for, to say " the plain truth, my own opinion was that the King had "broken the Treaty."[*] Chapuys having by this bold stroke reduced the English councillors to a defensive position, again pushed his advantage to the utmost. The declaration by the Emperor against France, he urged, would be worse than useless to England. France would care nothing for it, whilst it would ruin the Emperor's Flemish subjects to have their trade suddenly stopped again. Then he in his turn brought forward, although unofficially, what he knew was the Emperor's object. Why not, he asked, take advantage of the arbitration clause purposely inserted in the Emperor's treaty of peace with France, and ask his Imperial Majesty to arbitrate between France and England? But as this course would have involved the recognition of the treaty itself by Henry, who would thus lose his claim upon the Emperor for renewed aid in the war by virtue of his alliance, the English Councillors were reticent, though not repellant, in their reception of Chapuys' hint.

The details of the two first interviews of Chapuys and Van der Delft with Henry and his ministers have been set forth here somewhat fully, because the whole of the subsequent discussions proceeded on the same lines of argument. It was of the highest importance to Charles that the English King should be kept in hopeful suspense as long as possible, in order that he might not be driven to a sudden coalition with his enemy Francis to the Emperor's detriment; but it would have been fatal to the great projects that were already maturing in the Emperor's mind to be drawn into a violation of the Treaty of Crespy of which the ink was hardly dry. As we have seen in Chapuys' management of the political controversy, the method adopted was to shift the ground, and turn Henry from a claimant to a defendant. The English King demanded the fulfilment of the clauses of the Treaty of Alliance negotiated by Gonzaga in 1542; he was met with the answer that not only had he put himself out of court by his verbal consent to Granvelle that the Emperor should make peace separately, but that he himself had been the first to violate the Treaty by his

---

[*] p. 19.

INTRODUCTION. xv

conduct of the war; and these points must be investigated before he could claim under the Treaty. He was thus, to his intense indignation, forced to vindicate his own action before calling into question that of the Emperor.

Exactly the same method was followed in the commercial dispute, arising out of the English wholesale seizures of Flemish and Spanish ships, under the pretext that they carried French property liable to seizure, or contraband of war in the form of food for France. Henry had begun by expressing indignation that his late ally, immediately after his separate peace with France was signed, should allow his subjects to carry on an active trade in provisions with the French, whose power of resistance and aggression against the English was thus increased; and, on the pretexts already mentioned, a large number of Flemish ships, with their cargoes, were seized and carried to English ports, to the deterioration or destruction of the perishable food stuffs, and to the utter disorganisation of the recently reopened traffic. We have seen that, in this respect also, Henry was promptly driven to assume a defensive position, by the forcible protests and demands for explanation by the Emperor and his sister, Mary of Hungary, Governess of the Netherlands. But a much stronger move with the same object was made suddenly and unexpectedly in Flanders almost simultaneously with the arrival of Chapuys and Van der Delft in London; the effect being not only to reduce the English to the position of defendants at all points, but also to make Henry a suppliant, rather than a claimant demanding his rights. The step in question was the seizure of all English ships, property and subjects in the Emperor's Netherlands dominions on the 5th January, 1545,[o] and the despatch to England of a special envoy, M. de Tourcoing, to demand of Henry the fulfilment of the Treaty of Alliance, providing for the right of Flemings to trade without molestation from England. If the embargoed Flemish and other ships were not immediately released in England the Emperor would

---

[o] p. 21.

reluctantly be compelled to deal with Henry's subjects in Flanders as the Emperor's subjects were treated in England, and as a first step an embargo was placed on their property. The excuse that the Flemish ships carried food for France was to be regarded as of no avail. If the Emperor's subjects had done wrong it was for their own sovereign to punish them; not the King of England, whose duty it was to complain to the Emperor.

Before Tourcoing arrived in London the news of the seizures in Flanders had reached Henry at Greenwich, and at daybreak on the 9th January the King hastily and urgently summoned the Imperial ambassadors to the palace. It is evident that the English were aghast at the blow that had been dealt them, for amongst the property seized in Antwerp was a mass of valuable merchandise, in the hands of Henry's agents, destined to raise funds for the repayment of loans advanced by certain merchants there to the King of England.° When Chapuys and Van der Delft reached Greenwich, having been opportunely joined by Tourcoing on the way, they found the English Council in a state of great indignation. Surely, said they, the King of England might be trusted to do justice if requested, without such violent and scandalous coercion as this; and thereupon the whole of the grievances on both sides were once more set forth at interminable length; but, to the great glee of Chapuys, the strong action taken in Flanders "rendered these people as supple and tractable as possible;" and Tourcoing was hurried back to Flanders the next day bearing with him a note pledging the English Government to the immediate and complete release of all the property seized, simultaneously with a similar release of English property on

---

° A letter (3 March, 1545) in the R.O., German Correspondence, from Secretary Paget to Secretary Petre, quoted in Burgon's Life of Gresham, throws a curious light upon the effects of the seizure on English merchants. "Some, indede, shall wynne by it; as William Lok, Sir Richard Gresham and his son, and William Gresham, with such others for the most part that occupy sylkes, who owe more than they have here (*i.e.*, in Flanders). But Mr. Warren, Mr. Hill, Chester, and divers others a greate nombre are like to have a great swoope, having much here and owing little."

INTRODUCTION.

the other side. Chapuys had accepted the solution thus offered in the interests of peace, and for the furtherance of the more important political objects of his mission; but the Emperor was extremely angry with him and his colleague for doing so; and, with quite unusual warmth, reproved him for exceeding his instructions.[°] Charles was evidently desirous of holding the English property he had seized as a pledge for Henry's future good behaviour, and with utter bad faith, and on the flimsiest excuses, evaded his part of the bargain made for mutual release.

Finding it impossible to extract from Chapuys and his colleague the slightest hint upon which a compromise might be based, in the matter of the warlike aid demanded by Henry against the French, the English councillors themselves advanced certain requests, two of which they doubtless thought would be readily conceded by the Emperor as a means of avoiding a general declaration of war, which it was clear he could not make. These requests were presented almost simultaneously in London to Chapuys, and in Brussels by Dr. Wotton, the English ambassador to the Emperor. First, as a matter of form, the Emperor was once more asked to declare war upon the French, now that the ten weeks taken for consideration had expired. To this Charles replied with a temporising plea, whilst blaming Henry for the delay. The second demand seemed much more reasonable; namely, that the agreement to release the English property seized in Flanders should be fulfilled; but to this also the Emperor only replied that he would have the request considered; and he advanced a host of new obscuring conditions, evidently intended to justify his intended evasion of the undertaking made by his ambassadors.[†] The third request, which doubtless was that upon which the English thought a compromise might be effected, was that the Emperor would allow the passage through his territories of German and Italian mercenaries, whom Henry desired to recruit for his coming spring campaign

---

[°] p. 27. [†] p. 27.

in the north of France; but even to this request Charles was irresponsive. He could not, he said, violate his recent treaty with France by showing special favour to England in the war; the French were asking for similar concessions which he refused; besides, the King of England had previously used his mercenaries so badly, and Flanders had suffered severely in the previous year by the disorderly bands in the English service passing through to France. It was therefore, he said, preferable for the mercenaries to be sent by sea; a course which the Emperor knew perfectly well was impracticable for Henry, to whom this reply gave great offence. It must have been evident to the latter, indeed, that he had been outwitted at all points by the more unscrupulous diplomacy of the Emperor; for, whilst nearly all the Flemish property detained in England had been released unconditionally, the English goods seized in Flanders were still impounded; and bland professions of affection for him on the part of the Emperor were all the satisfaction that Henry could get from Chapuys and Van der Delft in reply to his demands for restitution and for the fulfilment of the terms of the alliance. That he should be treated with no more consideration than the King of France, with whom he had gone to war on the Emperor's account, galled Henry beyond measure; and there was hardly an interview between him and the Imperial ambassadors in which the King did not fly into a rage, and blurt out undiplomatic expressions which afterwards had to be palliated or smoothed away by his leading councillors; for whilst he was at war with France he dared not quarrel with the Emperor; and at war with France apparently he must remain, unless he gave up his new conquest of Boulogne, which he swore he would never do. On the other hand, there was nothing that suited the Emperor better than that the war between France and England should linger on, with Henry always in hope that, sooner or later, his former ally would help him.

In order to end the deadlock, which grew ever more dangerous to him as the spring approached, Henry, at the end of February, 1545, determined to send Secretary Paget to

Flanders to negotiate with the Emperor direct. Sir William Paget was one of the staunchest of the Imperial partisans in the English council, and as a pensioner of the Emperor he was ensured of an amiable reception personally at Brussels; but he found Charles V. and his councillors more than ever inclined to make hard terms, now that the need of Henry was becoming greater, and the embargoed English property in Flanders was still unreleased. It is fair to say that in the long disputes with the Imperial councillors and the subsequent interviews with the Emperor himself, Paget stood his ground manfully, and pressed the English case with the utmost assiduity; sometimes with a show of indignation at the sudden assumption by the Emperor of an almost prudish neutrality in the war which he himself had provoked. A new cause of complaint, moreover, had sprung up since the agreement for the mutual release of the seizures was made in London; and Paget found himself confronted therewith when he urged the immediate raising of the embargo on English merchandise in Flanders. Certain ships conveying to Spain time-expired men in the Emperor's service had put into English ports through stress of weather and lack of provisions. Henry, as we have seen, was greatly in need of mercenaries for the coming campaign in France, and, as the story is told in this correspondence, the soldiers, of whom there were about 1,000, being tired of the sea and desirous of earning the good wages offered by the King of England, were ready to seize upon any excuse for disembarking, and remaining in his service. The Emperor was extremely indignant when the mere hint of such a thing was conveyed to him; and in the settlement which Paget, after much clever fencing, was able to conclude with the Flemish councillors, with regard to the freedom of commerce and navigation, he was obliged to agree to a clause binding his master to abstain absolutely from receiving the Spanish soldiers into his service[*]; which clause Henry succeeded in evading, as,

---

[*] The history of the Spanish mercenaries has been told in full by the editor in The Spanish Chronicle of Henry VIII. (1889) and more recently in Spanish in his volume "Españoles è Ingleses en el Siglo XVI." (1903).

indeed, both he and the Emperor appear to have done in the case of all clauses with which compliance was inconvenient to them.

Although this carefully-worded agreement was settled with Paget for the mutual release of the commercial seizures on both sides, against cautionary security being given for their value, pending the investigation by a joint commission of the complaints and claims alleged by the subjects of both sovereigns, the English Secretary made no progress on the main point of the military aid claimed from the Emperor against France. When it became evident to him that if he pressed for a decided answer on this point, the result would be a negative, he told the Flemish Councillors that his instructions on this subject were only to discuss it and not to receive the Emperor's decision. Chapuys and his colleague were probably right in their opinion that the underlying object of Paget's mission was, if he judged that the Emperor could not be drawn into the war again, to endeavour to re-open the negotiations for peace with France.° The war, indeed, was pressing very heavily upon England, and now that Francis was free from danger on the Emperor's side, it was evident that Henry would have to make a greater effort than ever in the coming campaign of 1545, if he was to retain his conquest of Boulogne, or even obtain favourable terms of peace from his enemy. During his first conference with the Flemish Councillors Paget deplored the favour that was being shown to the French in Flanders. "It appeared to him that, since the peace, no effort whatever had been exerted here to help the English to obtain a favourable peace, and he begged the imperial Commissioners to bear this in mind."† To this the Flemish ministers replied that, although the Emperor had never wavered in his desire that peace might be made, he "did not wish to meddle beyond what was agreeable to the King," and suggested that perhaps the arrival of a Scottish envoy in Flanders, David Paniter, soon afterwards Bishop of Ross,

---

° p. 56.   † p. 49.

might afford the Emperor an opportunity of opening negotiations for peace if the King of England desired intervention. Paget referred the question to his master in London; and on 20 March, 1545, Paget and Dr. Wotton conveyed the reply to the Emperor's Council. This is set forth at length in the important State Paper calendared on page 65. As was to be supposed, Henry rejected the idea of making the Scottish envoy the intermediary, and requested the Emperor to act directly; but the terms suggested by the English were at once seen by Charles and his councillors to be impossible of attainment. Henry, indeed, abated nothing of his claim, and requested the Emperor to propose the same conditions that were to be put forward by England before the separate peace had been negotiated. " And if the French would not agree to them all, they might accept some of them. If they (the French) talked about Boulogne, the Emperor should say that having regard to the great expense the King had incurred in conquering, fortifying and holding the place, he would never surrender it, but with God's help hoped to maintain it against any force."° The Emperor had some days previously sounded the French ambassadors on the subject, and they had been equally emphatic in their declaration with regard to their sovereign's determination to regain Boulogne. "The Emperor then asked them (*i.e.* the French ambassadors) how therefore it was possible for him to settle affairs if the King of France insisted upon recovering Boulogne, and the King of England insisted upon keeping it. Even if he were Solomon, he said, he could not ask them to divide Boulogne, as Solomon had decided in the case of the disputed child."† Although the negotiations dragged on for a time with suggestions of a long truce and other expedients, it is evident that, a *modus vivendi* with regard to the freedom of maritime traffic having been settled with Paget, the Emperor was not particularly desirous of bringing about peace between France and England, especially as he had contrived to convey

---

° p. 66.   † p. 67.

clearly to Paget that he had no present intention of being himself drawn again into the war.

As instancing the bad faith prevalent on all sides, it is curious to note that whilst Paget was at Brussels he appears to have sent two Englishmen secretly to Paris in order to sound Francis through Chastillon as to his willingness to make peace with England and form a coalition with Henry against the Emperor.[°] Almost simultaneously the Duchess d'Etampes, the famous mistress of Francis I., sent two gentlemen to the English commandant at Boulogne with similar tentative overtures[†]; and the Admiral of France, Claude Annebaut, suggested to the Admiral of England, through his secretary, that peace might be made on certain conditions.[‡] But, though the first of these attempts was baited with the attractive offer of marrying Henry's eldest daughter Mary Tudor to the Duke of Orleans, with Boulogne as a dowry, the whole of the overtures fell through owing to the irreconcilable difference as to the possession of the conquered territory. A similar inconclusive result attended the arbitration commission which met at Bourbourg, near Gravelines, to dispose of the claims raised by the subjects of the Emperor and King Henry respectively for seizures and embargoes on property. This almost abortive arbitration commission was the last official duty in which the veteran Chapuys was actively employed; but although the dishonesty on both sides with regard to the seizures prevented the success of the arbitration, the great diplomatist took advantage of his almost daily conversations with Dr. Thirlby and Sir William Petre at Bourbourg to carry considerably further than before the preliminaries for an agreement between the Emperor and Henry with regard to the aid claimed by the latter against the French. Chapuys' letters on the subject to the Emperor and to Van der Delft contain passages which prove that the latest official acts of his career were inspired by the subtlety that had characterised the whole of his official conduct in England. His advice was that the

---

[°] p. 77. [†] p. 94. [‡] p. 99.

claim advanced by Henry might be safely conceded in principle, but surrounded by limitations and conditions; since he did not conceive it to be possible that the French could invade English territory in the force, or for the time, necessary for the Emperor's contingent to be demanded and furnished; and that, even if such were the case, at the last moment the aid might be commuted by a cash subsidy. The hard conditions laid down by the Emperor of such acceptance in principle of Henry's claim were that the King of England should recognise unreservedly the peace treaty between the Emperor and France, that he should be satisfied with the amount of aid stipulated in the treaty itself, and not ask for more; that the subvention should take the form of a money payment; that the Emperor's subjects should be free from all molestation from England; that all property seized on both sides should be restored, and that no peace should be concluded between England and France without the Emperor's consent.[*] Chapuys, whilst approving of these conditions, endeavoured in his letters to soften them somewhat in appearance, in order to prevent Henry from breaking away and joining France. It is evident, indeed, that the principal reason that prompted the Emperor and his councillors to go even so far as they did in their concessions, was their desire that the war between England and France should not be too rapidly ended with the combatants unexhausted. Chapuys, writing to Lois Scors, President of the Flemish Council, on July 4, 1545, puts this point quite plainly. "You know better than I can tell you the importance of keeping this King (*i.e.* of England) friendly; more especially in view of the distrust and inconstancy of our neighbours, the French . . . It would be advisable, therefore, to avoid giving the King of England cause for suspicion of the Emperor, or to drive him to think of other combinations, which he threatens to do—although his threats are of no great consequence, because, even if he comes to terms with France, he will not enter into any

---

[*] p. 181.

plans against the Emperor. . . It would be better for his Majesty's interests that the arrangement (between France and England) should not take place too soon."*

Van der Delft was instructed to bring forward the proposals for an understanding only if he were imperatively obliged to do so by reason of pressure of the English demand; the Emperor's desire being to delay the matter as long as possible. When, therefore, Van der Delft saw Henry on the 29th June, 1545, he opened the interview by complaining bitterly of certain fresh seizures of Flemish and Spanish cargoes by the English. Henry, probably unaware of the real object of this diversion, fell into the trap and was drawn into a long and angry wrangle as to the way in which he and his subjects were treated. He would stand it, he said, no longer. English property had been seized in Spain now, and he knew that a new embargo was pending in Antwerp. He protested that he had been played with long enough; and he hinted very broadly that if the Emperor failed to fulfil the treaty with him to the full he would form a coalition with the French.† Van der Delft, whilst openly most conciliatory, artfully added fuel to the King's rage by once more bringing up the statement, so often contradicted, that the Emperor had made peace by the King's special permission; and in Henry's passion the specific question of the re-entry of Charles into the war was thus forgotten and passed over, to the secret glee of the Fleming.

Henry's hints that his patience was well-nigh exhausted, however, were not without effect. These hints were repeated to the Emperor himself shortly afterwards by the English ambassador in Flanders (Dr. Wotton), and although Charles once more went over all the old arguments and complaints, he was sufficiently impressed to order Van der Delft to seek immediate audience with Henry and to suggest that the Emperor might endeavour to effect a reconciliation between the two combatants, if the latter were willing; but, as to the

---

* p. 161. † p. 155.

aid demanded in the war, that must be considered jointly with other pending questions. This was merely procrastination for the purpose of keeping Henry in play; but the circumstances were nevertheless such as to render much further delay difficult. The siege of Boulogne by the French was being pressed vigorously, and the English resources were strained to the utmost; but, what was of much more urgent importance, a powerful French fleet had been mustered in the Channel, including the war galleys usually stationed in the Mediterranean, and a maritime engagement, perhaps an invasion of England itself, was seen to be imminent, in which case there could be no doubt of the Emperor's obligation to help his ally. Henry and Dudley had for weeks previously been busy organising a sea-force to resist the threatened attack; and by the end of June had collected over a hundred sail of fighting ships at Spithead. The weakness of the French position was that, owing to lack of capacious harbour accommodation on the northern coast of France, the items of the fleet were scattered in various ports, and had to be concentrated for the purpose of united action. In order to prevent this, a number of English ships were despatched from Spithead early in July with instructions to burn the main body of the French fleet by means of fire ships. When Chapuys saw Thirlby and Petre at Bourbourg on the 14th July, they told him that, although the English fleet had encountered the French galleys, it had been unable to attack them for want of wind; whilst the galleys had not dared to approach the English great ships for fear of the artillery; and both forces had returned to harbour without serious damage. This was practically a defeat for the English, as whilst their ships returned, considerably damaged by a subsequent storm, to Spithead to refit, Claude Annebaut was able to form a junction between his great ships and the French galleys under Paulin Baron de la Garde, and to complete his preparations for a descent upon the English coast.

Although the object in view seems hardly to have been thoroughly understood at the time, it is evident from the nature and disposition of his force that the French Admiral did not contemplate effecting a serious invasion, and subsequent events proved that the raid upon English soil was merely a bold diversion, for the purpose of enabling the French to finish unmolested the forts they were erecting upon their coast to command the mouth of Boulogne harbour; and thus to prevent the revictualling of the town by sea. In the circumstances it was evident to the Emperor that to avoid being drawn into the war he must promptly come to an understanding with Henry in regard to the aid, or else that peace or a truce must be talked about between the combatants, since it would have been fatal to the great plans which he was maturing for Charles to have offended the English King beyond conciliation. The letter of the 9th of July, 1545, instructing Van der Delft to come to closer quarters with the King upon the main questions at issue, contained also for the first time indications that the Emperor was in earnest in his desire to effect a settlement between England and France.° The letter overtook the ambassador whilst he was on his way to Portsmouth to join the King, who had gone thither to review the fleet; and on Van der Delft's arrival there on the 17th he at once asked for audience. An interesting account is given by him of his entertainment by Dudley at dinner on board the "Great Harry," and of the naval preparations which he saw.†

When he was conducted to Henry and broached the subject of peace, he found the King in no very gentle mood. He was sore and indignant at the treatment of his subjects and himself, and, in answer to Van der Delft's request that he would furnish him with a hint that might form a basis for peace negotiation, he angrily retorted that the initiative must come from others. He had taken Boulogne and meant to hold it, but if terms were proposed to him he would consider them; beyond this he would not go. On the next day whilst Henry sat at dinner on the flagship, the alarm was given that the French fleet was in sight; and Van der Delft, who was an eye-

---

° pp. 163-4.   † p. 187.

witness of the stirring events that followed, gives a valuable and graphic account of the landing of the French on the Isle of Wight, the loss of the Mary Rose in harbour, and the subsequent retirement of the invaders.[*]

On Thursday, 23 July, the ambassador sought audience of the King, but only saw the Council, who gave him the reply to the Emperor's message. Henry, they said, was determined to vindicate his power, and punish the insolence of the French. Out of respect for the Emperor's overtures he was willing informally to say that if the French would accede to all his demands and pay the whole cost of the war—the amount to be left to arbitration—he would enter into negotiation: "with regard to Boulogne, however, he would never surrender the place to force. If they wanted it they must induce him by other means." Then came the real message that was meant to be conveyed to the Emperor. The invading enemy was now in England, and the King demanded that the contingent to be furnished by the Emperor in such circumstances should be sent forthwith[†]; a demand which the English ambassador in Flanders was to urge upon his Imperial Majesty simultaneously. Soft-spoken temporising would seem to have come to an end of its efficaciousness; and, in accordance with his orders, Van der Delft hinted to Paget the next morning without prejudice that it might in any case be well to commute the aid demanded by a money payment. To his delight he heard a few hours later that the King had no objection to that course being taken; the aim of the English doubtless being to draw Charles into this technical breach of neutrality, if nothing better could be done, with the hope of widening the breach between him and the French later.

But the Emperor had not yet come to the end of the resources of procrastination. After he had listened to Dr. Wotton's demand he wrote to Van der Delft, on the 17th July,[‡] instructing him to obscure the main issue by a cloud of complaints about the seizures, and the breach of Henry's

---

[*] p. 191.   [†] p. 192.   [‡] p. 175.

obligations under the Treaty; and then to "offer to come to some elucidation of the difficulties which must necessarily be examined and settled before we can resolve about the assistance requested by him in the event of invasion;"° and the rigid conditions upon which aid could be given, as already recited, were also, if necessary, to be laid before the English King. The interview at Portsmouth between Henry and Van der Delft consequent upon these instructions resembled many that had preceded it. All the old contentions on either side were repeated, angrily by the King, and with suave insistence by the ambassador. The Emperor was unquestionably bound to declare war against France at once, urged Henry, now that England itself had been invaded, and there was no need for further talk about it; but at length he consented to waive his extreme claim if a money subvention was promptly sent, the embargoed property of subjects on both sides being simultaneously released.† In the meanwhile the Imperial ambassadors in France were also making overtures to Francis I. with regard to a reconciliation with England. Francis was rapidly hastening to the grave; and extremely curious, not to say repulsive, details of his condition are contained in the letters of St. Mauris to the Emperor.‡ He was earnestly desirous, at the instance of his mistress, to effect a peace before he died; but, even so, he dared not sacrifice his claim for the surrender of Boulogne, though he was ready to pay a ransom for it. But as on this point of the retention of Boulogne, Henry was inflexible, especially now that the Emperor had been obliged to some extent to make common cause with him again against the French, the negotiations for peace dragged on as ineffectually as before.

To prolong these negotiations, one of the Emperor's principal councillors, Cornelius Scepperus, Sieur D'Eick, was sent to England in August; and whilst he was in the midst of his efforts to persuade Henry to a reconciliation with Francis through the Emperor's mediation, news came that the young

---

° p. 181.   † p. 208.   ‡ pp. 196 and 219.

Duke of Orleans, the second son of Francis, had died of fever. This greatly changed the situation. The Duke's marriage to a nominee of the Emperor, with the dowry of Milan or Flanders, had been the main provision of the peace of Crespy; and although, as we have seen, each of the parties had shown great reluctance to fulfil the provisions of the treaty, the premature death of the Duke brought distinctly nearer the chances of war between the Emperor and Francis, lessened the Emperor's desire to see the combatants at peace, and inspired Henry with fresh hopes of being able to gain effective assistance from his Imperial ally.

As soon as the Emperor received the news he hurriedly wrote to Scepperus and Van der Delft in England, sounding a note of alarm lest the French and English might suddenly join their forces and attack him.* Henry was to be addressed in widely different terms to those previously employed. Now that the Duke of Orleans was dead the Emperor was more than ever inclined " *pour faire quelque bonne œuvre:*" "and such is the constant and perfect friendship between us, that we confide absolutely in him not to treat, or consent, to anything to the prejudice of ourselves, our states or our subjects which may be proposed to him by the King of France. We hope, on the contrary, that he will have due regard to our amity, and to the faithful observance of the treaties between us. To this you will add all the fair words that you may think appropriate, according as you may perceive the King's tendency and the chances of a treaty of peace (*i.e.* with France) being negotiated to our prejudice."† Even on the sore point of the passage of Henry's mercenaries through the Imperial dominions to France, almost conciliatory language was now to be used towards him.

Up to this point every shift and device had been seized upon by Van der Delft to delay a final arrangement with respect to the subsidy to be contributed by the Emperor to the English war expenses, notwithstanding the constant demands of the

---

* p. 245. † p. 245.

English for a definite understanding; and the hollow peace negotiations through the Imperial ministers had furnished a new excuse for shelving the inconvenient subject. But the death of the Duke of Orleans revived Henry's hopes of a much more efficient aid from his ally than a mere money subvention, and on the very day that he received the news of the Duke's death he sent Scepperus hastily back to Flanders, ostensibly with a reply to the peace suggestions, but really with a secret mission to propose a meeting between the Emperor and the King of England. No sooner had he gone than another grave source of irritation occurred. Henry had raised a large sum of money on loan from the Fuggers of Augsburg for the payment of German mercenaries, and, on the pretext that it was intended to export the specie, the whole amount was embargoed by the authorities at Antwerp. The indignation of Henry and his councillors knew no bounds, and when his complaints were met with lame excuses he bitterly reproached his ally with his want of straightforwardness.[o] But far more alarming than his reproaches was the hint that the emissaries of the Protestant German Princes had approached both him and Francis with proposals for peace and a league between France and England, which he, Henry, said he had rejected, preferring to stand by his alliance with the Emperor, unless the latter drove him to act otherwise.

Charles was placed in a difficult quandary by the desire of his English ally to celebrate an ostentatious meeting between them. It was impossible for him to risk offending Henry by refusing point blank; but his plans for dealing a treacherous and fatal blow at the Reformation through his Lutheran subjects were now (September, 1545) practically complete; and he himself was to attend the fateful Diet of the princes at Ratisbon in the opening days of the new year, 1546. To have been drawn into a new and intimate alliance with a Schismatic King to the detriment of the Catholic Monarch of France would inevitably have alienated from him, not only the latter,

[o] p. 251.

INTRODUCTION. xxxi

but also Paul III., the cunning old Farnese, whose ambition for his house, after long enmity, had led him to provide the help without which the Emperor's plans against the Protestants could not have been undertaken. Dissimulation was once more the Emperor's only course, and Scepperus was sent back to England with professions of a warm desire on the part of his Imperial master to meet his dear friend and uncle the King of England. Letters patent, even, were conferred specially upon Scepperus authorising him to settle the preliminaries of the meeting°—but he was instructed to dwell upon the risk that Henry would run in crossing the sea in the late autumn, especially as the English territory in France was crowded with unsanitary soldiers and scourged by the plague. Still, if Henry insisted upon it, the Emperor was willing to halt on his Artois border on his way to Germany in October and meet his ally; but this must be on condition that the King of France would agree to a suspension of hostilities. The whole of the subjects to be referred to at the interview must, moreover, be exhaustively discussed and settled beforehand; so that at the actual meeting "there should be no question between us but of good cheer and kindly greeting."† Charles had apparently no intention of meeting the King at all; but it was obviously to his advantage to pretend that he had, and to learn if possible the proposals that Henry was so anxious to bring forward.

After some trouble, Francis was prevailed upon by the Emperor's ministers to consent to a truce for six weeks, ostensibly for the purpose of holding a conference between his representatives and those of Henry, in the Emperor's territory, with a view to peace negotiations. Before this truce was conceded by the French King, however, Scepperus delivered his specious message in England. Henry was ready to agree to everything and to run all risks of crossing the sea; only that, as it was then the 8th October, and, so far as he knew, the truce with France had still to be negotiated, the meeting

---

° p. 258.   † p. 254.

must be deferred for a short time. He set forth, however, for the Emperor's benefit the subjects he desired to settle at the meeting; and if Charles had at any time really entertained the idea of the interview, the knowledge he now gained that Henry's only object was to bind him tighter by treaty,* must have banished all intention of meeting the King of England.

When Van der Delft next saw Henry alone (13 October) after Scepperus had gone back to the Emperor with the answer referred to above, he told the King of the six weeks' truce consented to by Francis. What was the use, exclaimed Henry angrily, of a six weeks' truce? It was to his disadvantage, and was all a trick of the French to gain their own ends. A six months' truce he would listen to, and, if before that time the meeting with the Emperor could not take place, he did not want a truce at all. With much reluctance, eventually, and only for appearance sake, Henry at last consented to send Bishop Gardiner to Flanders to meet the envoy sent by Francis, Admiral Annebaut; but there was from the first no intention whatever on Henry's part of concluding a cessation of hostilities, unless the interview with the Emperor was to take place. Henry indeed saw clearly that, unless he could draw Charles into closer union with him against France, the truce would allow his antagonist fresh breathing time, beset as he was with poverty, famine and pestilence; whilst his own mercenaries were standing idle, consuming his substance. When therefore, with much pretended regret, the Emperor finally pleaded the impossibility of delaying his voyage to Germany for the purpose of meeting Henry, the insincere peace negotiations of Gardiner in Flanders, though still long protracted, were foredoomed to failure.

It became evident at length to the English, if not to the French, that the Emperor and his ministers were rather a hindrance than a help in the attempts to effect a reconciliation. So long as the negotiations could be carried on in Flanders under the eye of the Imperial ministers, they could be delayed

---

* p. 262.

almost indefinitely by the latter; the question of the English demand for aid being shelved in the meanwhile, and both combatants depleting their resources by keeping their armaments standing. Recognising this, Henry, at the end of November, 1545, sent Paget himself to Calais to negotiate for peace through the envoys of the Protestant German princes, whose advent in London with suggestions of mediation in September had greatly disturbed Van der Delft, and deepened the suspicions of the Emperor.° But neither of the combatants was yet completely exhausted, and the incompatible claims to the possession of Boulogne still stood in the way of a peaceful settlement. The early spring of 1546, therefore, saw vigorous new preparations on both sides for a prosecution of the war.

In the meanwhile Charles' great plot against the Reformation was gradually approaching fruition. The correspondence printed in the last volume of the Calendar and the present one exhibit admirably the patient cunning and tact with which the Emperor and his Flemish ministers had paralysed possible inimical action on the part of England and France. Both countries were now well nigh tired of war, and impoverished by the expenditure and waste of resources entailed by the protracted hostilities. Francis I., and even more so his son the Dauphin Henry, were, it is true, restive and discontented to see that the secret understanding into which they had been drawn to make common cause with their late enemy for the suppression of religious liberty, was intended solely to benefit Charles and his house; but they were powerless at present to act against the Emperor, because apart from the strain of their war with England, they found themselves deprived of their mainstay as against the house of Austria, namely, the Pope, who had for the time been drawn completely to the side of the Emperor.

The curious process by which the Farneses were alternately lectured or cajoled into submission is laid bare in the papers

---

° p. 249.

calendared in this volume more clearly and pungently than elsewhere.* In November of the previous year (1544) Paul III had consented in principle, being urged thereto by both the Emperor and Francis, to the holding of a great council of the Church in an imperial city. This of itself was a great concession, for it brought distinctly nearer the time when the vague uncertainty as to the doctrines and practices of the Church, which alone prevented a decisive armed struggle for religious freedom, would be brought to an end, and the sole alternative to submission would be for the Protestant princes of Germany to oppose their suzerain in arms. With many misgivings the Pope had gone thus far, but having done so he doubtless considered that he had a right to make capital out of his concession for the benefit of his family. In the last volume of this Calender (Vol. vii., p. 464) the Emperor's letter to his ambassador in Rome, Juan de Vega, recites that Cardinal Poggio, the Nuncio, whilst congratulating him upon the secret clauses of the Peace of Crespy, had hinted that if the Emperor would befriend the Farnese family the Pope might easily be persuaded to contribute a considerable sum of money towards the expenses of a war against the Turks and the subjugation of the heretics.

Charles had seized the opportunity and instructed Vega to speak plainly to the Pope. There must be no vague generalities. The treasure known to be in the hands of the Church for the conquest of the Turk, might with equal merit and good conscience be applied to a war against the Lutherans. But if the Pope would not provide a large sum, say 500,000 or 600,000 ducats, for the purpose of such war, the Emperor must dissemble with the heretics and make the best of it. If, on the contrary, the Pope would aid him heartily he would befriend the Farneses and secure for ever the supremacy of Rome. In the present volume (page 34) the Emperor puts the matter even more frankly in a letter to his friend and

---

* See also Von Druffel's "Kaiser Karl V. und die Römische Kurie" 1544-6 (Münchner Academie).

adviser, Francisco de los Cobos, who was acting as financial mentor to the young Regent Philip in Spain. To him there is no obscuring talk about a war with the Turk; it is the Protestants alone who are to be attacked, and not only must the Pope dip his hands into his treasure chest handsomely, but "much money should be obtained from prelates and churches in Spain; and we desire you to take the preliminary steps which shall enable us in due time to realise such contributions easily and promptly. This must be done with the greatest secrecy; for if the prelates learn beforehand that they are to be thus taxed some of them might betray the matter to the Protestants in order to prevent the execution of the measures intended." From this letter, which is dated 17 February, 1545, to the end of the story, the correspondence between Charles and his son, and Cobos, in the present volume throws a vivid light upon the financial methods of the period. From Castile alone could the Emperor draw funds at his own good will; for the defeat of the Commons at Villalar twenty years before had struck a death blow to the independence of the Castilian Cortes; and Spain was plundered and despoiled to utter exhaustion to satisfy the Emperor's needs. Cobos, over and over again, protested despairingly that no more money could be wrung out of the suffering country. Young Philip, in a letter most remarkable for its wisdom and frankness, pleads for mercy for the Spanish people.° The Emperor was adamant; money he must have to crush the Lutherans, and though he wept, as he says, at being forced thus to afflict his Spanish subjects, his aims were those of God and His Church; and all other considerations must be placed in the background. Cobos and Philip dutifully did their best to obey, and their expedients were as ingenious as they were desperate, such as suddenly pouncing upon all the gold and silver coin in Seville, 200,000 crowns, and shipping it to Genoa for the Emperor;† but their letters in this volume plainly show that they gravely disapproved of a policy which

---

° pp. 78, 550, &c.   † pp. 478, 490.

wrought such misery and suffering to the Spanish people over whom they were placed to rule.

With the resources of his lay Castilian subjects Charles could do as he pleased; but when he sought to lay hands upon the property of the clergy he had to deal with the Pope, and a most interesting series of letters in the present volume, passing between the Emperor and his agents in Rome, exhibit the means adopted to persuade or compel Paul III. to accede to the almost insatiable demands of the Emperor for funds, both directly from the Pope and from the ecclesiastical property in Spain and Flanders. Charles attended the Diet at Worms in May, 1545, and he found the princes in deep distrust and suspicion of him. John Frederick of Saxony and others had refused to attend unless the religious questions were to be settled not at a council of bishops at Trent, but at a free Christian assembly uncontrolled by Rome; the Lutherans obstinately refused to vote a subsidy for the war against the Turk unless they were assured of freedom of molestation, no matter what conclusion might be arrived at by the bishops at Trent. Charles' plans had been shrouded in the most profound secrecy, but that something extraordinary was afoot was clear to the German Protestants, and from this period, the spring of 1545, the breach between them and the Emperor widened daily. The person that had been indicated by Charles as a fit intermediary to conclude a secret alliance between himself and the Pope was the youthful Cardinal Farnese, the grandson of Paul III. He was inexperienced as well as ambitious; and it was thought might easily be influenced to the Emperor's advantage. To Worms, therefore, Cardinal Farnese travelled to meet the Emperor in May, 1545, ostensibly to bring a Papal subsidy of 100,000 crowns contributed to a war against the Turk; but really to conclude the treaty by which Paul III. pledged himself to finance a campaign against the Protestants. Charles' bold demands somewhat alarmed the young Cardinal, and he dared not concede all that was asked, but he went back to his grandfather the Emperor's eager servant, and, with the aid of the

Imperial agents at Rome, finally persuaded the Pope to grant a money subvention of 200,000 ducats, and to provide and pay a contingent of 12,000 foot and 500 horse for the war; and hopes were also held out that, in certain circumstances, 100,000 ducats more might be contributed. A Bull was given, moreover, granting to the Emperor for the war half the ecclesiastical first fruits of Spain, and a sum of 500,000 ducats to be raised by the sale of the Spanish monastic manors.* The details of the latter subsidy and its proposed commutation by a sum to be raised by the sale of the portable property of the monasteries led to a long and acrimonious dispute with the Pope, from whom, after the first flush of confidence in Charles had passed, every concession had to be wrung painfully, with infinite bickering, by the Imperial agents. The letters of Juan de Vega in this volume, especially, show the hollow nature of the exaggerated verbal professions of respect paid by the Emperor and his ministers to the Pontiff. Paul III. is represented throughout by Vega as a crafty, garrulous curmudgeon, whose word was worth nothing, and whose religion itself was a consideration secondary to his greed. The agreement with the Pope took so long to settle that Charles was obliged to defer the opening of hostilities until the following year, 1546, and in an important letter written by him after his return to Flanders, 16 February, 1546, to his son Philip, he sets forth all the considerations that had moved him to adopt the critical resolution to which he was pledged, to commence war against his own subjects in the summer.†

During the early spring and summer of 1546, whilst the interminable wrangling with the Pope was going on, Vega endeavouring to exact to the utmost every promise given, and Paul III. himself haggling over every item, striving to retract and minimise as much as possible, the war between France and England lingered on; and the same system of wearisome hairsplitting and procrastination was continued by Van der Delft and Scepperus in England, to avoid the settlement

---

* p. 268.   † p. 307.

of the vexed question of the subsidy to be contributed by the Emperor to the war against France. Another diversion to lead Henry to overlook the subsidy was made by the Emperor through Van der Delft and Scepperus in March, namely, the proposal for a marriage between the young Prince of Wales and a daughter of the Emperor's brother Ferdinand. There was, of course, no intention really of effecting such a match; but it served its turn by keeping Henry quiet for a time, whilst the blow against the Protestants was being planned, and was artfully utilised as a means of exacerbating Henry's irritation against the French. Scepperus told Henry[*] "that the French intended to circumvent and deceive him by means of a marriage treaty between his son and a daughter of Scotland. By this means they would recover Boulogne, with a peace or a long truce. They would get the Queen of Scotland (*i.e.*, Mary of Guise) to consent to this marriage treaty with her daughter, letting her know that the undertaking would . . . . not be binding." Henry had learnt by means of his own ambassador that Ferdinand proposed only to give his daughter a dowry of 100,000 crowns, and he probably understood the insincere nature of the proposals. He consequently received Scepperus' bland assurances very stiffly, and suddenly burst out, "When shall I have the aid?"

It was evident that Henry was by this time undeceived with regard to the Emperor's friendship, and his patience was nearly at an end. He could not, he knew, go to war with his late ally, either to help the German Protestants or for any other object, for his resources were greatly depleted; but he cannot avoid having felt the annoyance which he frequently showed at the way in which he had been outwitted and deceived all along by the soft-spoken generalities of the Imperial ministers. His main object for the time was to retain Boulogne, at almost any cost compatible with peace. Every request he made to the Emperor or his sister the Stadtholderinn, either for the passage of mercenaries, the

---

[*] p. 331.

exportation of foodstuffs for his army, the transit of arms or ammunition through Flemish ports, or permission to raise a loan in Imperial territory, was met by meticulous objections, and either refused altogether or minimised and delayed so as to be of little use.

In these circumstances, aided by the ever-growing distrust both of Francis and himself at the Emperor's proceedings in Germany and Italy, it was inevitable that Henry should at length recognise the wisdom of attempting to come to terms with France. Through Italian intermediaries sent to England by the Duchess d'Etampes, at length a meeting was arranged at the end of April, 1546, between Lord Admiral Dudley (Lord Lisle) and Admiral Annebaut at Ardres, and terms highly favourable to England were conceded by the French. Henry was to retain Boulogne for eight years and surrender it upon payment of the vast sum of 2,000,000 sun crowns in gold. Henry boasted that this was equivalent to the permanent retention of the conquered territory, since France would never be able to raise such an amount as that mentioned, whilst the French ministers affected to be pleased at their bargain, because the fortifications erected by the English at Boulogne were to be given up intact at the end of eight years, and these, they said, represented an expenditure equal to the ransom to be paid.[o]

To the great delight of the subjects on both sides, half ruined as they were by the war and the consequent interference with trade, peace was finally concluded in July, 1546; and Henry was free to turn his attention to the urgent problems that faced his country and the cause of religious emancipation from Rome which he had embraced. It was high time; for though the war into which he had been cleverly cajoled and deserted had left him, as well as Francis, too much exhausted to oppose the Emperor's dangerous plans abroad, yet Henry's rapidly-failing health, and the profound divisions opened amongst his ministers by the impending change, as well as by

---

[o] pp. 392, 394, 397, 399, 404, 409, 419.

the renewed acuteness of the religious question, rendered it necessary that affairs in England itself should be dealt with firmly, unless a heritage of revolution, perhaps disintegration, was to be left to the child who was to succeed to the throne.

The forces for and against the consummation of religious reform were ranging themselves in the English Court, Gardiner and Paget, with the tacit support of Winchester, Wriothesley and the Howards on the one side, contending for mastery with Seymour and Dudley on the other. In the absence from court of the two latter nobles persecution of the "heretics" in England was rampant in the summer of 1546,[*] to the delight of the Imperial ambassadors, who foresaw but little difficulty in reconciling Henry to the Emperor's religious war in Germany whilst Gardiner and Paget were paramount in his councils. Intrigue and distrust, however, prevailed everywhere. Duke Philip of Bavaria was running backwards and forwards from Germany to England on mysterious missions; Sturmius and Dr. Brun, the Lutheran envoys, obtained audience with Henry himself;[†] and, although England and France were now ostentatiously friendly, Paget, and even Henry, hinted frequently to Van der Delft that overtures were being made to them by the French for a coalition to strike a treacherous blow at the Emperor; whilst the Imperial ambassadors were full of suggestions to Henry that the French intended to betray him. On the whole it is evident that Henry himself, though naturally distrustful of the Emperor's proceedings towards the German Protestants, as the Emperor was of him,[‡] was firmly resolved to stand by the traditional Imperial alliance, and to regard his friendship with France as a measure of temporary expediency.

By the end of June, 1546, the Emperor's intention to submit to the arbitrament of the sword the right of his German subjects to choose their own faith could no longer be treated as a secret. His alliance with the Pope, and all the

---

[*] p. 426.   [†] pp. 464, 467.
[‡] p. 454 et alia.

details of the papal aid, had been babbled abroad from Rome long ago; the contingent of troops to be commanded by Ottavio Farnese, the Emperor's son-in-law and the Pope's grandson, was already mustering; but even at this late hour the duplicity of the Emperor's methods were as apparent as ever. The proceedings at the Diet at Ratisbon, and the intrigues to secure at least the neutrality of Maurice of Saxony and the Duke of Bavaria, had convinced all the world that the Emperor's objects both in the Council of Trent and in the coming war were the unification of religion, in order to render his house politically supreme; but, whilst he ceaselessly urged upon the penurious and distrustful Pope the exclusively religious character of the crusade, for which ecclesiastical treasures were being so profusely bled, he took care to impress upon other potentates the obviously specious view that he had only to deal with disobedient and rebellious subjects, like John Frederick of Saxony and Frederick of Hesse, who had defied his authority in the matter of the captive Henry of Brunswick.

When Charles instructed his ambassador to congratulate Henry upon the conclusion of peace between England and France (21 June, 1546),* the following passage of his letter contains the first direct intimation that was conveyed to the King of England of the Emperor's intentions. "We presume that rumours will have reached England that we are mustering an army; and perhaps the Protestants, even those who are ignorant of the object we have in view, may use great efforts to persuade the King of England to help them. You will, therefore, be very vigilant to obtain information of what goes on; so that when a fitting opportunity occurs, and in the way you may think best, you may inform the King that it is impossible for us to ignore the proffered support and exhortations of the Catholics and honest folk of Germany, urging us to bring to reason certain princes who wish to pervert the common peace and justice of this country, and who wish to

---
* p. 410.

tyrannise over and oppress ecclesiastics and nobles on the pretext of religion. We trust that, in regard of our friendship, the King will refuse to lend ear to such people, or to countenance them. By so doing he will demonstrate the affection he has always so emphatically professed towards us." More precise still was the letter of Charles' sister, the Stadtholderinn, to Van der Delft, of the same date, ordering him to assure Henry of the purely secular nature of the enterprise. "The Emperor, having made every possible effort to bring the affairs of Germany to concord and tranquillity by conciliation and an avoidance of force, his Majesty recognising that the Duke of Saxony and the Landgrave incessantly oppose his authority by keeping Duke Henry of Brunswick and his son prisoners, and occupying his territories, whilst refusing to attend the Diet . . . which, as vassals of the empire, they were bound to do, has come to the conclusion that no further hope can be entertained that the two princes will be brought to submission by mildness; and his Majesty has consequently raised his forces . . . to bring them to obedience. . . . . As many people are trying to make out that this enterprise is not directed against the Duke and the Landgrave, but is really undertaken on religious grounds, you may assure the King *that his Majesty's intention is not to meddle with the religious question at all, but simply to punish the disobedience of the Duke and the Landgrave, in the hope that he may thus bring Germany to unity. You will report what answer the King makes, and what he seems to think of the enterprise, and also the rumours current about it in England.*"[o] Considering that from the first letter from Charles to his son (p. 34) on the subject, the solely religious aim in view had been dwelt upon emphatically, both to the Pope and the Spaniards, and that the Lutherans and Protestants throughout Europe were perfectly aware of it, the euphemistic falseness of the Emperor's professions could hardly have deceived Henry or anyone else at this late period.

---

[o] p. 411.

INTRODUCTION.

In effect, when Van der Delft saw the King on the 5th July with the Emperor's message,[°] Henry made no secret of his annoyance. "The reasons alleged by me, he said, were mere shadows; it was really the Pope's money that had induced the Emperor to do as he had done; and he feared that his Majesty would find himself deceived after all. The real origin of the war was perfectly well understood, and it was quite probable that those who pretended to be on his Majesty's side now would be against him some day."[†] In a subsequent interview with the Emperor's tools, Paget and Gardiner, Van der Delft primed them well with the Imperial view; and "as these councillors are those most in favour with the King, I doubt not that they will be good instruments for maintaining the existing friendship, and for preventing the Protestants from gaining footing or favour here. They (Gardiner and Paget) have confidently promised me this."

Only distant echoes of the Schmalkaldic campaign, so far as regards the Emperor's personal part in it, reach us through the documents calendared in the present volume; but much more detailed and interesting matter will be found in the letters of Juan de Vega and other Spanish ministers with regard to the share of the Pope and his grandsons in the war, and of the straits to which Charles was reduced for money, in consequence of old Farnese's tergiversation. Some extremely curious lights are thrown, moreover, upon the purely political view taken by Charles and his ministers of the Council of Trent, especially in the letters of the famous Spanish writer, Diego Hurtado de Mendoza, the Imperial ambassador in Venice, and the Emperor's agent in the Council[‡]: and a letter from Titian to the Emperor, sent from Venice through Mendoza,[§] is valuable as fixing the date and the circumstances under which the famous portrait of the Empress Elizabeth now in the Museo del Prado at Madrid was painted.

[°] p. 424.
[†] This was a curiously correct forecast of what happened with Maurice of Saxony.
[‡] pp. 515, 521, 529, etc.   [§] p. 258.

Whilst the interminable discussions between the Imperial ambassadors and Henry's ministers with regard to the restitution of the commercial property seized on both sides still went on, and the almost equally acrid negotiations were in progress as to the inclusion of the Scots in Henry's peace with France, the old King's health daily declined. Van der Delft saw him at Oatlands on the 7th December, 1546, when the Emperor's campaign was on the point of reaching a triumphant conclusion. The King was ailing, but he was as mentally alert as ever. After some of the usual generalities about the falsity of the French, Henry told the ambassador that he desired to have a chat with him. He had, he said, always been a good friend of the Emperor, and was somewhat hurt that he had not sent him more frequent news of his proceedings, since he (Henry) was full of good wishes for his success. "But," he continued, "I am afraid that he will allow himself to be seduced by the Pope." The ambassador assured him that no treaty made by the Emperor with the Pope would be to his (Henry's) prejudice. "I know," replied the King, "that the Pope has not fulfilled the promises he made to the Emperor;" and he then suggested that a peace with the Protestants should be made by his mediation, and that a strong coalition between himself and the Emperor, with the Lutheran princes and Denmark, should be made to humble France and her allies (*i.e.*, the Pope, &c.), "who are awaiting an opportunity to play their own game."[*] At another interview a few days later, also at Oatlands, Henry again urged a reconciliation of Charles with the Protestants and a new alliance against the French. It is clear to see that this fresh solicitude on the part of the King for the Protestants indicated a rise in the Seymour influence at court; and the arrest of Norfolk and Surrey,[†] which Van der Delft records in the same letter (14 December, 1546) marks the complete predominance of the party which ruled Henry in the last few weeks of his life.

---

[*] p. 524.   [†] pp. 527, 531, 533.

Van der Delft writes on the 24th December, 1546: "I do not know what to suspect. Although the King recently told me, as an excuse for not receiving me when I sought audience, that he had suffered from a sharp attack of fever, which had lasted in its burning stage for thirty hours, though he was now quite restored, his colour does not bear out the latter statement; and he looks to me greatly fallen away. . . . Sire, I do not think in any case that I ought to conceal my opinion of affairs here, which change almost daily. Four or five months ago great enquiries and prosecutions were carried out against the heretics and Sacramentarians, but they have now ceased since the Earl of Hertford and the Lord Admiral have resided at Court. The public opinion, therefore, that these two nobles are in favour of the Sects may be accepted as true; and also that they have obtained such influence over the King as to lead him according to their fancy. In order to avoid this some of the principal councillors, to whom I had pointed out the evils and dangers threatened by these Sects, unless they were vigorously opposed, requested me to address the King to this effect. I find them (*i.e.*, the councillors) now of a different aspect, and much inclined to please and entertain the Earl and the Admiral, neither of whom has ever been favourable towards your Majesty's subjects. This being the case, and since those who were well disposed have changed, it may be assumed that these two (*i.e.*, Seymour and Dudley) have entirely obtained the favour and authority of the King. A proof of this is that nothing is now done at court without their intervention, and the meetings of the Council are mostly held at the Earl of Hertford's house." The ambassador continues that, though the King during his lifetime will not change his policy, yet that "strange acts and constitutions" would be adopted when he died. Already, indeed, Van der Delft found it more difficult than ever to deal with the Council now that it was dominated by Seymour, and he beseeches his master to consider the best means of protecting his interests when the King shall have passed away.

In reply to this Van der Delft was instructed to set forth his own opinion on the matter; and for the last time the aged Chapuys, now living in invalid retirement at Louvain, was called upon to give to his master the benefit of his unrivalled experience of English politics.

The final State paper penned by the diplomatist whose letters have filled so many volumes of the series of Calendars of which this is the last, is inspired as usual by the cautious moderation, the suave patience that waits upon events rather than attempting to force them. He deprecates value being attached to his opinion, because he has lost touch of the English people: "who are so changeable and inconstant that they vary, I will not say from year to year, but every moment; and no other set of affairs, in my opinion, so urgently needs personal consideration on the spot, or upon which an opinion is so likely to be wrong if given without recent observation."[*] But, withal, in compliance with his master's orders, Chapuys' knowledge of Henry's imperious character was once more utilised to give wise but hopeless advice. If the King, he says, gives countenance to the stirrers-up of heresy, the Earl of Hertford and the Lord Admiral, which it may be feared he does, for the reasons stated by Van der Delft, and because the Queen, influenced by the Duchess of Suffolk, the Countess of Hertford and the Admiral's wife "is infected with the sect;" which she would not favour openly if the King was not tending the same way, it would be quite useless to attempt to turn him from his fancy by words and exhortations; even if they were addressed to him in the name of the Emperor. "On the contrary, they would be more likely to give him a pretext for hurrying on the enterprise, and harden him in his obstinacy, in order that he might show his absolute power and independence of anyone. It again might bring about a certain irritation or coolness on his part, which, at the present time, is undesirable in the interests of Christendom."[†] If, however, the slightest signs of wavering be shown by Henry,

---

[*] p. 555. [†] p. 555.

Chapuys was of opinion that Van der Delft, in accord with Paget and the Imperial party in the Council, might put before the King unofficially the danger of religious innovations; though it was to be feared, he continued, that even the friendly Councillors would now be disinclined to "join in the dance, or to undertake anything against the Earl and the Admiral, seeing the violent and injurious words used recently by the former towards the Lord Chancellor (Wriothesley), and by the Admiral towards Winchester" (Gardiner). "In order to hold a candle to the devil," he continues, Van der Delft might repeat his discourse to Seymour and Dudley. "It is out of the question, of course, that he could convert them, their malady being one of those incurable mental ones into which they have fallen by natural inclination. With Norfolk in prison, the Catholic councillors cowed, and the episcopal property threatened, there was nothing to stand in the way of Seymour's plans. The Emperor, hints Chapuys, having let slip his opportunity for striking a blow to vindicate years before the position of Queen Katharine of Aragon and her daughter the Princess Mary, heresy had become strong and deeply rooted : "and nothing his Majesty says now will have any effect upon them. On the contrary they will turn it to their own profit and advantage."

As a counsel of despair, Chapuys suggests that in the, not unlikely, event of the King's death being followed by disturbances, Van der Delft on the spot might take advantage of them for the Emperor's ends; and the irritation of the English commercial class against the new Government might be augmented by a fresh seizure of all English property in Flanders and Spain, on the pretext that the injuries done to Imperial subjects had not been redressed. "There is no doubt that the Government would be much perplexed by such seizures, since the King (Henry) himself was so much upset by them the last time, and by the complaints of his people." Beyond this feeble remedy Chapuys could advise nothing. If Parliament were free as it used to be, something might be done, he said, by remonstrance there; but now "no man present at the sittings dare for his life's sake open his mouth, or say a word without watching the will of the King and Council." "In conclusion, I beg to say that, in my opinion, it would at present be advisable for his Majesty, the Emperor, to avoid any further action either spiritual or temporal. . . The aphorism of physicians, with regard to certain maladies, should be borne in mind. They say that the best and quickest cure that can be adopted is to leave the evil untouched to avoid irritating it further."[o]

These weak and futile words, the last recorded of the ambassador whose period of office had witnessed the vast change in international relations which had arisen from Henry's defiance of the papacy, fittingly mark the utter impotence to which the new religious divisions had condemned the Emperor. For centuries the balance of power in Europe had depended upon the close alliance of the rulers of Flanders and Spain with the ruler of England, as an offset to the secular friendship between France and Scotland. When Henry broke the allegiance of his country to the papacy, and Charles assumed the position of prime champion of the traditional Roman Church, the problems of European politics changed. But with French ambitions in Italy and Flanders perennially alert, with the Turks on one flank and the French another, the Emperor had not dared to drive his Schismatic ally into alliance with his ancient enemies. Injury and indignity to the Spanish Queen of England, disinheritance and insult of her half Spanish daughter, defiance of the papal authority of which Charles had constituted himself the defender, and attacks upon the Catholic Church which was the mainstay of the Spanish power; all these had been condoned and glozed over by Chapuys by his master's orders during a long series of years, because the Emperor dared not allow religious considerations to override the political needs which bound him to England at any cost. We see in Chapuys' hopeless words quoted above how it had ended. England strong in the knowledge

---

[o] p. 558.

of the Emperor's straits had gone her King's way, and was drifting every year further from the foreign influences which had for so long swayed her. Once for a brief space after the peace of Crespy it had looked as if the two great Catholic monarchs might forget their secular enmity, and jointly attack England on religious grounds; but in the correspondence in this volume may be traced the process by which this short-lived co-operation for the suppression of heresy gave place to the old jealousy and distrust between France and the Empire, upon which the immunity of England had always depended. Once again, when the Catholic Mary succeeded, and married her cousin Philip, the ancient hold of the house of Spain and Burgundy upon England seemed secure; and well-nigh universal domination under the Emperor's son as probable consequence. It was but a last flicker, to die down completely when the daughter of Anne Boleyn became Queen of England. In the period covered by the eight volumes of the present Calendar the process of England's emancipation from foreign influence was practically completed, and the power of Spain and the Empire doomed to the slow decay of which Chapuys' final words are the first distinctive signs.

MARTIN A. S. HUME.

SPANISH CALENDAR,
HENRY VIII.

VOL. VIII.

1545.
1 Jan.
Vienna
Imp. Arch.

1. MARY OF SCOTLAND to the EMPEROR.

Sends David Paniter,* her Councillor, to congratulate the Emperor on the conclusion of the peace with France; and begs him to remain friendly with Scotland. Stirling; Kalends of January, 1545. Signed Jacobus Arranis Comes.

3 Jan.
Vienna
Imp. Arch.

2. CHAPUYS and VAN DER DELFT† to the EMPEROR.

We travelled hither with all possible speed, and arrived very late the day before Christmas-eve. The next morning we advised the Council of our arrival, whereat they appeared pleased; and took in good part our message, to the effect that, owing to the holidays, we would not importune the King for an audience; but would leave it entirely to the convenience and pleasure of his Majesty. On the following day, which was Christmas Day, the King sent the Secretary of the Council to visit and welcome us, and to offer to provide anything in the way of lodging or otherwise that we might require. His Majesty, moreover, sent word to say that, whenever we chose to go to Court we should be heartily welcomed. On the day after Christmas Day, we requested an audience, which was granted for the next day (*i.e.*, Saturday) or Sunday. As we saw that Sunday would be the more convenient day for the King, we agreed to go on that day after dinner; but on Saturday evening the Bishop of Winchester and Mr. Bartlett‡ (Bertellet) came to say that the King would greatly prefer that we should go in the morning, and that they were instructed to conduct us. We readily agreed to this, considering that doubtless the King not only desired that we should witness the festivities at Court, but even more that the people should see us; for the reasons already conveyed to your

---

* David Paniter was Arran's Secretary. He was prior of St. Mary Isle, Abbot of Cambuskenneth, and subsequently, until his death in 1558, Bishop of Ross. During the year 1545 he not only went on this embassy to the Emperor, but also proceeded on a mission to the King of France.

† For the instructions of Chapuys and Van der Delft *see* p. 447 of the previous voume of this Calendar.

‡ This was doubtless "Mr. Bartlett of the King's Chamber."

A. 3999. Wt. 22059/285. M.

1545.

Majesty. We met the King just as he came out to go to Mass, and after saluting him, and conveying to him your Majesty's good wishes I, Van der Delft, handed to him your Majesty's letters, which he took but forgot to make the usual enquiries as to your Majesty's health and well-being. We thought this arose rather from his anxiety to greet us personally, and from his haste to go in to Mass, than from any other reason; although he also forgot the enquiries after dinner, perhaps through his attention being taken up in answering and refuting us.

When the King had entered his oratory we were conducted, without the slightest hint of a desire on our part, to the oratory of the Queen, who shortly afterwards herself entered. We conveyed to her your Majesty's greeting, and thanks for the good offices which she had always exercised towards the preservation of friendship between your Majesty and the King; and also thanked her for the favour she showed to the Lady Mary. The Queen answered very graciously that she did not deserve so much courtesy from your Majesty; and what she did for Lady Mary was less than she would like to do, and was only her duty in every respect. With regard to the maintenance of friendship, she said she had done, and would do, nothing to prevent its growing still firmer: and she hoped that God would avert even the slightest dissension, as the friendship was so necessary and both sovereigns were so good. We afterwards saluted Lady Mary, and gave her your Majesty's greetings; for which she was humbly thankful. We were then conducted to the King's oratory; and on the conclusion of the Mass, when his Majesty came out from his pew he addressed us very heartily, saying that I (Chapuys) did not look so well as when I was at the camp at Boulogne, where he said I was better in health than he had ever seen me. He also, he said, was ten times better there than he had been since. There is no need for him to insist greatly upon this point, for he is evidently much broken since his return. He then added, speaking very loudly, that those people—meaning the French—had been well whipped both by land and sea, and had paid their scot lately; by reason of the great quantity of wine seized by his (Henry's) ships of war, besides over fifty French ships having been captured by his subjects on the west coast. The men of Rye, also, had not been backward in damaging the enemy. The French, he said, raised a great outcry at first, when they heard that he had ordered his ships to return to port to refresh: but when they learnt that they were putting to sea again, the Frenchmen soon retired in a great fright; for if they had only waited a couple of days longer they would have been destroyed.

After we had dined with the Councillors we took the opportunity of praying them, in the name of the Queen Dowager of Hungary, to use their influence with the King to have certain Frenchmen sent to Flanders. These Frenchmen had been captured off Dunkirk by an English ship of war at the instance of your Majesty, in order that they might be capitally punished for having attacked a Zealand ship off the coast of Zealand, which ship they would have sunk or captured if assistance had not arrived. The Councillors answered that they would speak to the King on the subject and

1545.

let us know his decision. We also remonstrated with them on the loss and damage inflicted on your Majesty's subjects by the embargo at Dover of eighteen or twenty vessels loaded with merchandise destined for France. The Councillors replied that some of the ships were loaded with herrings, the exportation of which could not be permitted, in view of your Majesty's prohibition of the conveyance of victuals to France. They, the Councillors, believed that most of the remaining merchandise in the vessels was the property of Frenchmen, under cover of the names of some of your Majesty's subjects; and it was only just that the ships should be detained here until it was ascertained whether the said merchandise belonged to French subjects or not. We were able to assure them that the bills of lading and the merchants' marks testified to whom the merchandise belonged, and said that it was unjust to detain the goods in the absence of certain proof to the contrary. It was, we added, "Corinthian law" to sentence first and enquire afterwards; and, as for the herrings, if there was any violation of your Majesty's orders it was for you, and not for the English, to punish it, both on the persons and the property of your subjects. But, withal, we could get no reply but that it was necessary to hold the matter over for the present. We suspect, from the look of the Chancellor, when he whispered something to the Earl of Hertford, that there is but small appearance of the releasing of these vessels until a decisive answer is received from your Majesty with regard to the demands made by the Earl of Hertford and the Bishop of Winchester.[*] Besides the above mentioned vessels, they have embargoed here ten or twelve of the ships that have brought goods from Antwerp, though we imagine that their object is to make use of the crews. During our conversation with the Council we were summoned to see the King, who received us very graciously, and was courteous enough to insist that I (Chapuys) should be seated before he was. Before he took his seat again he repeated to us the contents of your Majesty's letter to him, and said that he was ready to hear our credentials. As your Majesty will see further on he made me (Chapuys) pay dearly for this piece of politeness on his part.

In accordance with the arrangement which we (*i.e.*, the two ambassadors) had made together I, Chapuys, addressed the King; commencing by saying that your Majesty had been much surprised that the Earl of Hertford and the Bishop of Winchester were not satisfied with the answers given to them by your Majesty respecting the subject of their mission, notwithstanding all the arguments that your ministers had used to convince them. Your Majesty, I said, believed, nevertheless, that he (the King), thanks to his virtue and prudence, would consider the reply reasonable, sufficient and to the point; but if he still remained dissatisfied with it your Majesty had instructed us to repeat to him the arguments already brought forward, and others which have subsequently occurred to your Majesty. The King replied that he willingly believed what we said,

---

[*] For particulars of Seymour and Gardiner's mission to the Emperor in order to claim his aid against France by virtue of the treaty of alliance with England, *see* the preceding volume of this Calendar.

1545.

but had no doubt that he could so convincingly answer our arguments that we should not have a word more to say. I (Chapuys) then set forth carefully the three points of your Majesty's reply, beginning by saying that even if the greater part of the statements made by the said ambassadors (*i.e.*, Seymour and Gardiner) had been correct, there was still no cause for dissatisfaction with the reply, for the reasons stated to his ministers; which reasons I repeated briefly to him. It appeared to us, moreover, that the demand itself was confused and general, the English ambassadors basing it upon various clauses of the treaty, which did little to support their case; and the letter which the King had recently written to your Majesty saying that the demand was well-founded, and setting forth the details of his claim was equally uncertain and general. To tell the truth, I could not make out exactly what declaration he really demanded. It could not be a question of defensive action (against the French) for the reasons set forth to his ambassadors; and that, all hostility having ceased, I could not understand how, even if your Majesty was inclined to declare yourself, he, the King, would consent to it; as such a thing would redound greatly to your Majesty's discredit, whilst he, the King, would not profit by it in the least. The treaty of peace (with the French) had, moreover, been so recently concluded, the French having done nothing since to violate it nor given your Majesty any reason for a hostile declaration, that it would be impossible to close people's mouths if such a course as that requested were taken. The object aimed at by the King as the result of such a declaration was, I said, not that which was professed, but was really the prohibition of trade between the subjects of your Majesty and the French, the effect of which would be in every way to make war rather upon the former than the latter. He, the King, I said, had seen that even during the heat of the war between your Majesty and France, trade was allowed to be carried on by means of safe-conducts, of which the King had not complained. It is true that inconvenience arose out of this system to the poorer sort of people, who could not afford to obtain the safe-conducts; and consequently that the profit was made by the rich and by those who needed it least.

I then proceeded to say that, as the peace between your Majesty and France had been made by his, the King's, consent, there was but slight ground for his urging your Majesty to make this declaration, since it was obvious that his consent to the conclusion of peace must be understood to extend to the subsidiary points, without which the peace could not be concluded at all. On hearing this the King, who had changed colour several times during my speech, now did so more markedly than before; and speaking angrily and excitedly, said that it was not true that he had ever given his consent, except on condition that he was satisfied, in the form laid down and sent by him to his ambassador with your Majesty. He dared any man to tell him that this was not true. There were other witnesses besides Messieurs Arras, Courrières and myself;[*] namely the

---

[*] An account of the interview mentioned here, and the King's alleged speech to the Bishop of Arras consenting to the peace, will be found in the preceding volume of this Calendar.

1545.

Dukes of Alburquerque and Suffolk;* and none of us three had any credence from him to convey such a report to your Majesty. His own ambassador was properly accredited and should be better believed. Our reply was that no letter of credence was needed, since there were a sufficient number of witnesses present and we were satisfied to have learnt his decision. I also reminded him minutely of his words to M. d'Arras, in order to convince him that we were right; but he continually interrupted me angrily; saying that he should like to know if any body would dare to assert that he had distinctly declared his willingness that your Majesty should treat with France, even though he (the King) was not satisfied on his side. I replied that, since he insisted that his consent was conditional upon his claims being satisfied, I would not contradict him; but unless I was asleep or out of my mind at the time, I clearly heard him use the expressions which Messieurs d'Arras and de Courrières had reported to your Majesty, and I had written to the Queen (Dowager of Hungary). As to his assertion that he had not expressed his willingness that your Majesty should treat unless he was satisfied, I could positively affirm that he did not limit his consent by any such reservation. If it had been otherwise it is obvious, I said, that he would have complained at once after he had received news that peace was concluded † just as readily as he made other complaints to M. de Courrières and me. During the whole time that he remained at Boulogne he had not contradicted what he had said to M. d'Arras; nor had he referred to the matter in any way whatever. Whilst I was thus setting forth my arguments and points to prove his free and unconditional consent to the negotiations, he endeavoured constantly to confuse the issue, saying that I was dwelling upon several things that had nothing to do with the matter and bidding me keep to the main point. I continued, however, to state the case as I thought best; and amongst other things I said that, not only had he declared his wishes to M. d'Arras in the matter, but at the request of Cardinal du Bellay and his colleagues he had despatched a courier, who went with Secretary L'Aubespine, to inform your Majesty that you might proceed with the treaty of peace with the King of France as he (the King of England) had good hope of being able to obtain the conditions which he was demanding of the French. The King was intensely annoyed and irritated at this, and told me quite openly that it was a great lie; but he did not attempt to refute the main assertion, confining himself to a dispute as to the time when the

---

* The participation of the Duke of Alburquerque in the campaign before Boulogne will be found fully detailed and explained in the Spanish Chronicle of Henry VIII., edited by the present writer. The original author of the Chronicle is believed to have been Antonio de Guaras, a Spanish merchant living in London who appears to have accompanied Alburquerque to Boulogne as interpreter. His account of the fateful interview with Arras, in which Henry rashly gave away his case, agrees with that given by the other subjects of the Emperor present. It will be seen that during the whole of the subsequent negotiations Henry was fruitlessly struggling to free himself from the consequences of his thoughtless speech, of which the youthful Bishop of Arras, the future Cardinal de Granvelle, saw the importance as soon as it was pronounced.

† By reference to page 364 of Vol. 7 of this Calendar it will be seen that Henry did complain to Chapuys through Gardiner when he learnt of the conclusion of peace.

occurrence I mentioned took place. He tried to make me believe that I had said that the courier had been despatched before M. d'Arras; and he then began to recount the comings and goings both of the Cardinal (du Bellay) and M. d'Arras, until, either through his anger or forgetfulness, he got into a complete confusion, and no one could set him right. He could not, however, deny what had taken place between the Cardinal (du Bellay) and the Council in the presence of Courrières and myself. I replied to his arguments without fear or surprise; saying that, not for all the possessions of your Majesty and himself, would I tell an untruth; as he from long experience of me should know. If he found otherwise, I said, I would renounce my ambassadorial privilege, and would willingly undergo punishment. It might, I said, have been expected of him, to judge from his actions hitherto, that he would have taken it in good part, and even considered it a great service to him, that I should speak thus frankly to him in so important a matter as this; but if he desired it I would abstain from proceeding further; though I should be much disappointed at the result of the voyage, which I had undertaken solely in the hope of doing him service. He softened somewhat at this, and I led him on to repeat what he alleged that he had said to M. d'Arras. According to his account, after blaming those who had advised your Majesty to advance so far into France and place yourself in so difficult a position, he said that he was willing that your Majesty should negotiate with France, and that he would convey his views more fully to your Majesty through his ambassador; but his consent was only meant, he said, after the conditions which he had forwarded to his ambassador had been accepted (i.e., by the French). I pointed out to him that nothing could have been concluded on his side in this way, since neither your Majesty nor his ambassador was empowered for the purpose; but he denied the latter point, saying that his ambassador was empowered. I questioned this, and told him that, even if it were so, your Majesty was fully justified; because the ambassador had never exhibited or mentioned such powers. The King replied that there was no occasion for him to do so; as probably before M. d'Arras left on his mission, or soon afterwards the treaty was concluded between your Majesty and the King of France.* Though I tried to convince him to the contrary, and pointed out to him that your Majesty had subsequently captured Soissons, the King would not alter his opinion, and distinctly contradicted me with regard to Soissons.

With regard to my point that he had not complained at Boulogne (i.e., of the conclusion of a separate peace) the King made no reply at the time; but he subsequently referred to it, and said that the reason why he had made no complaint was that I had given him to understand from letters I had received from the Queen (Dowager of Hungary) that your Majesty was negotiating for him as well as for

---

* That this was practically the case, though the document was probably not signed until after Arras' return to the Emperor, is shown in the Introduction to the preceding volume of this Calendar.

1545.

yourself. I replied that the Queen wrote that she did not know the particulars of the treaty; but he would not be convinced, until I reminded him that an hour or two after Courrières and I had been with him, the Bishop of Winchester and the General of the Forces[*] had come to our lodgings to inform us that as soon as we had left the King's presence Cardinal du Bellay had visited him and informed him of the conclusion of the peace, and of the submission of the King of France to arbitration with regard to the pensions and overdue payments to England; asking us whether we had received any such advice, to which we had replied that we had not. I had on that occasion disputed with the Bishop of Winchester, saying that, even without the said submission by France to the arbitration of your Majesty of the question of the payments due to the King of England, your Majesty was justified in concluding peace. The altercation had lasted some time, as Courrières and the General could testify. This I said was very different from what the King asserted I had given him to understand; and I also reminded him that when I received letters from your Majesty telling me of the treaty and of the submission to your arbitration of the question of the payments, I sent and informed him of it. At that time he made no objection whatever, nor had he done so at the time of his departure from Boulogne, when de Courrières and I had conversed with him at length on these matters. In the face of so many facts, the King could not hold out, and said that even if all this was the case, as I said, the truth remained unchanged. Seeing that he could find no more arguments to convince us, as he had boasted at first that he could do, he changed his tack, and said that all this wrangling was waste of time, as affairs were dressed up afterwards to suit our purpose. When we wanted to negotiate with him in future it would be better to put everything in writing, and he would reply in the same way, otherwise he would not negotiate with us at all. As we said that we were not authorised to do this, he would despatch to your Majesty a special mission. He tried to persuade me that he had never negotiated State affairs except in writing; although I told him that during the fifteen years and a half that I had been here, I had never written to him a single word of any negotiation I had conducted. I said that this affair, moreover, needed no writing, as it consisted simply of the three points which I had laid before him; but if it was the intention to have adopted this procedure, his ambassadors should have commenced it, they being the initiators; to which he replied that it was not their place. After explaining the three points, I said that it appeared to me that he, the King, had better reason to be pleased at the conclusion of the treaty of peace than your Majesty; since (as he said) having formerly surrendered some of his claims for the sake of peace, he now returned to his original demands. And yet your Majesty

---

[*] It is not quite clear who is the person referred to here as le general des guerres. In Chapuys' account of the event, written at the time to the Queen Dowager, he calls the person who accompanied Gardiner on the occasion *le tesorier des guerres*; and Senor Gayangos assumes that Sir Thomas Cheyne was meant. Page 363, Vol. 7, of this Calendar.

1545.

had in your own treaty with the King of France stipulated for the points which had influenced him (the King of England) in favour of the treaty with France, namely that the King of France should withdraw his friendship from the Turk, which was provided for in your Majesty's treaty : secondly the submission to arbitration of the question of the pensions ; and, thirdly, the abstention of the King of France from joint action with the Scots against him, which point could doubtless be arranged without difficulty, an agreement on other points being arrived at. The King did not attempt to answer these arguments, but turned the matter aside : but finally he let fall a confession that he had made certain that the French would have accepted his conditions. I did not neglect to remark thereupon, that this fact, together with other reasons, had moved him to consent so frankly and freely to your Majesty's negotiating with the King of France. He replied that there would not have been the slightest objection to that, if your Majesty had been a little stiffer (eust tenu ung peu bon). He said, also, that he must remind me that the first time I spoke to him at the Camp at Boulogne, when he repeated to me the offers brought to him by Framoiselles, I had said that it would not do to go to sleep or depend much upon the Frenchmen's talk ; and that a lasting and honourable peace could only be made sword in hand. I admitted that I had said this, and had added that it was necessary to follow up the enemy actively. If, I had said, it was to be a question of making peace, your Majesty and he could entrust the negotiations to the Queen Dowager of Hungary, who was in a good position to communicate with both, and had means for conducting the negotiations successfully, Warlike operations were so dangerous and sudden : he and your Majesty were too far apart for rapid communication, and it was important for your Majesty to learn his decision early, for your guidance ; since you were (not) in a position to retire easily, as he could, who was near his own territory. To this the King had replied that it was much the best way for those directly interested to manage their own affairs, instead of referring them to a third party. He admitted that he had said this, and I then continued that what I had said about following up the enemy actively was for the purpose of inciting him to pursue the voyage to Paris. He said that I had not expressed anything of the sort, and had even praised his action before Boulogne ; but this I flatly denied, saying that no one would testify that I had done so. I said it would have been most unfortunate for me to have taken such a course, for I knew that the siege of Boulogne was hopelessly against the agreement made by treaty, and prejudiced the main object aimed at. I had, I said, complained to his ministers that the terms of the treaty were not being complied with. He retorted that he was quite sure that none of his ministers would testify to this, and ended by saying that your Majesty should bear in mind that in many countries, nay, nearly all over the world, people were murmuring that your Majesty had made peace without him ; and that if this action was not redressed in the way he had requested, it looked as if no trust could ever be placed in treaties between princes.

No power in the world could prevent people from talking. To

1545.

escape from us he seized upon our proposal that, if he wished for our points in writing we would repeat them and others to the Council, who could take them down; and he accordingly referred us to the Councillors, asking us very graciously when we should be at leisure to confer with them. In the meanwhile, he thought that as it would be inconvenient for us to return from Greenwich at night, it would be better that we should meet the Council next morning.

The Council duly awaited us as arranged, but we thought better to send an excuse that we were both indisposed, whereupon the Councillors, taking it in good part, offered to be ready to receive us whenever we liked to go. To say the truth, it seemed best to us thus to show a little resentment of the rudeness of the previous day, although we clearly perceived by various indications that the King himself was sorry, to have used us as he did. Although he stormed (bravé) at first, it was easy to guess that he was not altogether displeased at the delay proposed in your Majesty's name, with regard to the declaration,° for the reasons set forth : the main point with him being his anxiety as to the intentions of your Majesty after the delay had expired, which he calculated would be in eight or ten days, counting from the time that the answer was given to his ambasssadors.

We thought well to remind the King of what he had said with regard to the terms which M. d'Arras had conveyed to him from your Majesty, namely that they would have been hard and inacceptable even if their object was to release your Majesty from prison : whereupon he began very passionately and vehemently to declaim about the two marriages.† He said it was a most unwise condition, and the more he thought of it, the more astonished he was that your Majesty should ever have condescended to such a thing.

Since writing the above, yesterday, we sent to the Council to say that for various reasons we had been unable on Sunday to explain fully the points of our mission, and that as the matter was important we were sorry that our indisposition had prevented us from waiting upon them. We therefore requested them to move the King to send to us some of his Councillors versed in the matter, with whom we could confer, and who could report to him. They conveyed this message to the King and he immediately instructed the Earl of Hertford, the Bishop of Winchester, and Secretary Paget to wait upon us this morning. We thought best to take this course, in order to confirm the excuse we had sent ; and to avoid having to discuss before such a turmoil of Councillors.

The said deputies came this morning, and, as we had agreed, I, Chapuys, discoursed with them. I began by regretting our indisposition, both on account of the trouble we had given them to come,

---

° This was a delay of ten weeks taken by the Emperor in which to give his decided answer to Henry's requisition that he should furnish the armed contingent stipulated by the treaty of alliance in case of the invasion of English territory. It will be seen later that Charles declined to recognise the "invasion" by the French of the County of Boulogne, as this territory did not belong to England at the time that the treaty was signed and was not comprised in it.

† This refers to the terms actually agreed upon by Charles and Francis (*see* Vol. VII.); the two marriages in question being that of the Duke of Orleans with the daughter or the niece of Charles.

1545.

and also because we were so desirous of discussing with the Councillors the affairs in hand; which appeared to us to be of unprecedented importance, both to your Majesty and the King, and might entail, unless well understood, results of the highest consequence, and matters difficult to stomach. It therefore seemed to my colleague and myself that our discourse should not only be listened to by the Councillors, but that, so to speak, it should be heard by the nation at large for your Majesty's justification, if what several of them said was true: namely that it was common talk in the realm that your Majesty had failed in your obligations towards the King. We did not believe that the King himself, or they, would allow such talk; which, moreover, did not redound to the King's own honour; and the public would be pleased to know that he was on good terms with your Majesty. This would be greatly prejudiced if the people were persuaded to the contrary, and I had thought well to mention this matter to them in the interests of the honour of both princes, and in order that they might take what steps were necessary. When we had produced to them your Majesty's answer we protested that it was not our intention to say anything inconsistent with that; and we had supported it by several arguments addressed to the King. Finding, however, that he was somewhat excited we had been unable to conclude our address or to ascertain the King's decision with regard to your Majesty's reply. Certain unpleasant passages had occurred between the King and us, which they (the Councillors) probably heard, and I thanked God that it had not happened to any other of your Majesty's ministers instead of to me, for I was not sure that any other would have put up with it. But I, who knew the King's humour so well, and so ardently desired the continuance of his friendship with my master, would avoid reporting, if possible, any event which could injure the good feeling. I ascribed what had passed to the familiarity with which the King had always treated me, and I would, I said, condone everything he said to me in consideration of the honour with which he had formerly treated me. He might confidently believe that no subject or servant of his own was more anxious for his welfare or more desirous of serving him than I. I repeated that the matter at issue was most important, and it was consequently necessary that it should be considered maturely and without passion. Saving the King's acquiescence, the matter mainly depended upon two points. The first was whether, in view of the King's consent to your Majesty's making peace with France, it was incumbent on your Majesty to make the declaration demanded by the Earl of Hertford and the Bishop of Winchester on behalf of the King. For the reasons given to the Earl and the Bishop when they were with your Majesty, and subsequently sent to the King, we thought not, and we besought the Councillors, as good and virtuous ministers, to consider deeply the points already brought forward, and those we should add thereto. The second point was one that we were extremely loath to approach, since it was the very unpleasant assertion of the violation of the treaty (*i.e.*, by the King of England), and we were convinced that your Majesty

1545.

would not renounce the rights which the said violation gave you, nor would any of your Councillors advise you to do so.

I then repeated in substance the discussion that had taken place between the King and us, and the Councillors had no reply to make. With regard, however, to the King's consent (to the peace) given to M. d'Arras, and reported by the latter, the Councillors wished to make out that before the return of M. d'Arras the whole of the conditions of peace between your Majesty and the King of France were agreed upon—or practically so—the signature only being wanting. They said that there was already some softening of the war in the matter of burning; and the Admiral of France was with your Majesty. This had been reported by the English Ambassador, and had not been denied by M. de Granvelle. I replied to this in the terms which your Majesty wrote to M. de Courrières and myself from Soissons, and they had no more to say.* The Bishop of Winchester also dwelt somewhat upon the letter of the Queen (Dowager of Hungary) mentioned in your Majesty's despatches; but after I had reminded him of what had taken place at Boulogne he dropped the subject. He maintained that even if the King had done no more than reserve the maintenance of existing treaties; which reservation indeed, was provided for in the treaty of peace between your Majesty and France; it would be sufficient to oblige your Majesty to declare against France, since at a period subsequent to the said treaty of peace, the King of France had violated the reservation by invading English territory. The King of France, he said, was informed by the preamble of the arbitration clause that your Majesty could not conclude peace unless the King of England's claims were satisfied; and by binding himself to the observance of the treaty with this reservation he (Francis) tacitly bound himself also to satisfy the King of England. I replied that, even if this were so, no right would accrue to their master under a treaty which he had refused to acknowledge; and they themselves (*i.e.*, Hertford and Gardiner) had refused even to see. The preamble to the arbitration clause, which they had refused to accept, was, moreover, limited by the presumption that it would become operative by the consent of their master (Henry); and this must be understood to apply not only to the principal point but also to the subsidiary articles, such as are usually inserted in all treaties. One of these ran, "Friend of the friends, and enemy of the enemies." The King had expressly consented to your Majesty becoming the friend of the King of France, who was then his (Henry's) open enemy, and had so continued to be. The invasion of English territory had not made him (Francis) more of an enemy than he was before, and the fact of the continuance of the same enmity that existed when the King of England gave his consent to the peace, was no reason why your Majesty should again declare yourself against France. With regard to the so-called invasion in the neighbourhood of Guisnes: it ought not to be so considered, since legists held that the principal intention,

---

* This letter is not now to be found, but the point referred to, namely the vigorous prosecution of the war whilst the peace negotiations with France were pending, is fully dealt with in Arras' instructions written at the same time. *See* Vol. VII., p. 328.

1545.

and not the incidental or occasional acts, should be regarded. If, I added, they would examine closely the treaty of friendship (*i.e.*, between Henry and Charles) they would find that the mutual defence clause, where it said that on the retirement of the enemy the assistance might be withdrawn, did not mean that the prince whose territories were invaded could renew a claim for aid for the purpose of following the enemy into their own territory again, and so prevent a repetition of the invasion. It might be said that the French had come principally for the purpose of raising the siege of Montreuil and recovering Boulogne; and with this object it might be desirable for them to drive the English as far away as possible, which they had done by following them to Calais, and other places belonging to England. Finding themselves between Calais and Ardres the famished and desperate (French) soldiers had done some damage, and had endeavoured to recover some victuals. I said that it would be necessary to clear up articles 6 and 18 of the said treaty of friendship; since it appeared that in their opinion, in case of invasion, and aid being rendered to them, the invader was to be held as a common enemy until peace was made by common consent; even though the invasion itself might have ceased. I said that, in my opinion, the clauses in question were intended to refer only to the period during which the invasion lasted. I gave several legal reasons for this; and said that otherwise such absurdities would follow as I felt sure your Majesty would never admit. Up to the present, in your desire to please the King to the utmost, you had accepted their interpretations; but it was not reasonable to expect your Majesty to continue your attitude of hostility against Scotland; since there was no appearance of an arrangement between their master (Henry) and the Scots; and it would not be right to deprive your Majesty and your subjects, for this reason, of trade with Scotland to their great injury. It would be unjust, also, that they (*i.e.*, the Netherlanders) should be expected to forego the herring fishery of the Scottish coasts, or to be bound to burden themselves by equipping war ships. The deputies replied that the clause in question meant the aid to be sent before the invasion, in order that the dignity of the allied princes might be safeguarded. An invasion might be sprung upon them, in which case it would be easier to prevent than to remedy when it had taken place. I said that their argument was a very thin (maigre) one. The text to the treaty only mentioned the aid being given after the invasion; and if it were necessary for it to be known that your Majesty and the King were making common cause, and that any invader of either territory would have to deal with both sovereigns, some means of making this understood could be found during the invasion. With regard to the declaration (against France), for which they had pressed your Majesty, I said that such a demand could hardly have been made with full knowledge: because, in addition to the proofs which had recently been shown to the King of how little he would profit, and how much your Majesty and your subjects would lose by such a declaration, it must be remembered that it would throw all Christendom into turmoil. The war would recommence between

1545.

your Majesty and France; the door would be opened for the Turk to work his will on the frontiers of Hungary and Germany; and even if strictly your Majesty were bound to make such a declaration, it seemed that you would fulfil all that could be fairly expected of you, if you continued, as heretofore, to divert victuals from the French, and weakened them to the extent of their 600 men-at-arms and 10,000 infantry, which by your treaty with France you have at your disposal against the Turk. I added that they (the English) were powerful enough to resist the French for the whole of next year if necessary, as it was impossible for the French to encamp in the Boulognais for want of forage and other victuals; and, therefore, the English ought not to ask, or even allow, your Majesty to make the declaration, seeing the injury it would cause you. They (the deputies) replied that, whatever appearance of reasonableness there might be in our contentions, it was not strong enough to justify the breaking of the formal alliance with them, and leaving them in the lurch. In any case, the world would not think well of such a proceeding.

The deputies subsequently endeavoured to justify the King, their master, in respect to the non-fulfilment of the treaty,* by saying that in laying seige to Montreuil and Boulogne, he had only followed the example set by your Majesty in besieging St. Disier. It looked as if your Majesty was desirous of coming to terms with France, and had deliberately placed yourself in a difficult position. If, they said, the King their Master had wished to make peace with France, he might easily have played a trick whilst your Majesty was before St. Disier; such, for instance, as to lead his army across the Somme, and to send someone to your Majesty, as you sent M. d'Arras to him, to give you notice that unless you raised the siege, and at once marched to his aid, he would be obliged to make peace. The object of the deputies in saying this was to lead us to conclude that this was the interpretation which the people had placed on your Majesty's action. We gave them, however, such a reply that we think they were sorry for having broached this suggestion. I reminded them that, even before the King left England, I had on two occasions urged him in the presence of the Council to pursue the main intention of advancing on Paris, and I had found him very cool about the enterprise, raising all manner of difficulties, most of which must have existed when the Viceroy of Sicily was here. † I had also found the same lukewarmness existing in the Council; and the last conference I had had with the members on the subject had been peremptorily closed by one more subtle than the rest, in order that your Majesty should not learn that the King

---

* As one of the strings to their diplomatic bow it was considered advisable to retort to Henry's demand for armed aid under the treaty, that he had himself failed to fulfil the obligations he had undertaken in the treaty arranged with Gonzaga in London (see Vol. V. part 2) for the conduct of the war. It will be recollected that instead of joining the Emperor on the Somme, as agreed and advancing with him on Paris, Henry had tarried before Boulogne and Montreuil. Henry pointed out that neither had Charles fulfilled his part of the bargain by staying to besiege St. Disier. These wearisome *tu quoques* continued throughout the whole subsequent negotiation.

† The plan for a junction of the English and Imperial armies and a joint advance on Paris had been agreed upon by Henry and Gonzaga, Viceroy of Sicily, as the Emperor's representative. *See* Vol. VII.

had no intention of carrying out the main part of the plan. That this was the case has since been made obvious by events, and the King himself had not concealed it, for he had declared repeatedly that he would a hundred times rather capture Boulogne than Paris. It had, moreover, been clearly proved since, and pointed out to them by your Majesty's ministers, that the capture of Boulogne and Montreuil was not necessary for the purpose of advancing into France. They (the English) might have marched on your Majesty's frontier as easily as on their own soil, being abundantly furnished with supplies from your territories, if they had appointed commissaries in time, as recommended by the Viceroy (Gonzaga), and had arranged for the proper treatment of the contractors. It was quite otherwise with your Majesty, who had to depend upon Lorraine for your supplies, which was the same as depending upon France itself, and it was positively impossible for you to obtain victuals, unless you captured St. Disier. To tell them the plain truth, I said, even if the siege of Boulogne and Montreuil had been allowed by the arrangement, it would not have excused them from fulfilling the main plan; for the slackness and bad management were such as to make the sieges simply a farce, more especially that of Montreuil. As they themselves had always said, they were fighting at Montreuil without a chance of winning; for they could not surround the place, and it suited them to leave one of the gates free. Their bombardment had never been worth a cabbage (*ung choux*) and they had made no effort to carry the place. In fact, the siege was nothing but a sham, for the purpose of gaining time and serving their own ends without going too far away from their head quarters at Boulogne. At the latter place also, they seem to have purposely wasted time, to avoid having to advance further; for after the first short bombardment, the breach effected was, in the opinion of soldiers, as nice and easy of assault as ever was seen. If the King had even ordered an assault and tried his luck, as your Majesty did at St. Disier, it would have been some excuse. If the sole object of the campaign had been Boulogne, and there was no obligation to advance on Paris, the King might well have temporised to avoid losing his men; but, seeing that he was bound by the arrangement with your Majesty, he should have acted otherwise. The councillors could find no fit answer for this, but the Bishop of Winchester said that when the Council conferred with M d'Arras in the presence of M. de Courrières and myself, he (the Bishop of Winchester), speaking for his colleagues, had asked M. d'Arras whether he was instructed to complain of the non-fulfilment of the treaty by the King; to which question a negative reply had been given, and consequently that he (the Bishop of Winchester) had concluded that your Majesty was satisfied in this respect. I easily upset this contention: and pointed out, unofficially and under reserve, that if your Majesty had known that the King did not intend to fulfil the arrangement, as agreed upon, it would have been enormously to your advantage, and worth a vast sum of money to you, that the King should have remained neutral. Your Majesty, without having to wait for anyone else,

1545.

might then have pushed forward on the main enterprise, choosing a much more convenient route to Paris than that by Champagne, which route you had adopted at the urgent request of the King, though it was the worst and most difficult that you could have chosen. The object of this was to leave to him the choice of all other routes, with the Netherlands as his base of supply. Besides this, your Majesty had taken into your service the forces, both horse and foot, which had been raised for the King, and had incurred the cost of the 2,000 men you kept at sea, entirely in the interests of the King, for during other wars your Majesty had never maintained such a force. It is certain that in such case your Majesty would have been able to carry all before you, and would have brought the King of France to reason. Besides this, your Majesty would have been the richer by the 200,000 crowns which the Netherlanders would willingly have paid to exempt themselves from furnishing ships, and, above all, from supplying waggons for the English forces. Indeed it would have been to the advantage of the Netherlanders to have paid double as much for exemption, for they have lost a great deal more. Not only would this money not have been lost, as it has been, but it would have been an enormous help to your Majesty in the enterprise. The Netherlands also had suffered very serious injury from being unable to send their merchandise to France; and especially herrings, which will not keep good whilst a safe-conduct is being obtained. Even when safe-conducts had been granted by your Majesty and the Queen Dowager, the English had plundered the ships. It could be proved positively that, since the declaration of war with France, the English had captured from subjects of your Majesty, principally Spaniards, property worth 150,000 ducats; whilst even shortly before the declaration of war 40,000 crowns worth belonging to certain merchants of Burgos was seized at the port of Southampton. Not only had these merchants failed to obtain restitution, but they had been unable to get even an enquiry into their claims. The deputies boasted a great deal of the greatness of their armies, but they had been of no use or service whatever to your Majesty; for as the King himself had said several times to M. de Courrières and myself, in spite of the English armies, all the French soldiers on the frontiers, except the garrisons, had gone to fight your Majesty's forces, the garrisons themselves only being prevented from moving because of the (imperial) troops which remained behind (*i.e.*, on the Flemish frontier) under the command of the Duke of Arschot and the Count de Roeulx.

We begged the deputies to consider well and lay before the King all we had said, as they were far better able to do than we.

Thereupon the Bishop of Winchester repeated what he said to your Majesty's ministers at Brussels; namely that the friendship and aid of his master had greatly promoted your Majesty's interests. I immediately replied that he was too fond of repeating such things; and he forced me against my will to say what otherwise I should not say: namely that his constant repetition of this point took the form of a reproach. If the friendship of the King had been advantageous to your Majesty, that of your Majesty had been no less fortunate for the King. It was true that God had granted success to your Majesty during the alliance, but His divine goodness had not deserted you when you were the King's enemy, but had even granted you one of your greatest victories, namely, when M de Lautrec was defeated.* If it was needful, I said, to go back further still, they (the English) might recollect that before the alliance with the house of Spain this country (England) had been in terrible combustion and revolt, not only on account of the Scots, but by Peterkin Warbeck, the Marshal of the West and others, but since the alliance everything had been peaceful. As for the capture of the King of France (i.e., at Pavia) the English had no reason to boast in that matter, for after Master Russell no one knew better than I what became of the broad-angels which the King (Henry) was then sending (i.e., to Italy). One portion of the money at the time was at Genoa, another portion at Rome, and a small sum was handed to M. de Bourbon for his expedition in Provence.† We were astonished also that they (the English) should assert that the troops they had sent to Landrecis were the cause of the submission of the Duke of Cleves to your Majesty. I doubted very much whether the Duke or the Gheldres-men even knew of the coming of the English; but even if they did and the English had been ten times as numerous, the Gheldres-men would have taken no notice of them. It (i.e., the submission of the Duke of Cleves) must be ascribed to the goodness of God and the battle of Daren, where no Englishmen were present. All three of the deputies interrupted me here, and appeared vexed that they had opened up this matter; and finally confessed that, as I said, the alliance had been to the advantage of both parties. With regard to the excuse for not supplying waggons, when I had repeated all that had passed in the matter, and had stated the efforts made by the Queen (Dowager) they had nothing more to say; and especially when I pointed out to them the discourtesy shown, not only on the part of private persons, but also by the King's agents in exporting all the best mares from the Netherlands, under the pretext of using them for the enterprise, instead which they sent them to England for breeding. The King himself had sent over 200 besides those exported by private persons clandestinely from Holland and elsewhere with the carts that were sent for the English army transport.‡

Up to the present we see no signs that the King is carrying on any negotiations with France. Far from it, his mind seems quite taken up with plans for the fortification of Boulogne and

---

* That is to say the campaign of Lombardy in 1521—the year after Henry's meeting with Francis on the "Field of the Cloth of Gold"—when the Milanese was lost to France.

† A most minute and curious account of the disposal of the money-subvention paid by England to the Emperor is given in a letter from the Bishop of Bath (John Clerk) Henry's ambassador in Rome, to Wolsey, dated 6 April, 1525, shortly after the battle of Pavia (MS. Cotton Vit. B. 7 and printed in Ellis). If Clerk's accounts be trustworthy Chapuys would appear to have had no other cause of complaint than that the money was paid after the victory instead of before it, and that Clerk in Rome and Sir John Russell in Milan spent or retained a comparatively small sum for expenses. The imperialists however were to be paid 45,000 Suncrowns instead of 50,000, and Clerk says that "they be ryght well contented to take this in this manner and gevithe the Kynges Highnes harty thankes therefor." In the same volume are letters from Sir John Russell to Wolsey respecting the subsidy, particularly with regard to Constable Bourbon's demands.

‡ All these petty points of contention are dwelt upon fully in Vol. VII. They were deliberately kept alive by both parties as sets-off one against the other.

1545.

the furnishing of victuals and stores, of which great quantities have already been sent. Every day fresh pioneers and other troops are being sent to Boulogne; and the King has recently retained in his service M. Loys de l'Arme, a Bolognese, and the Count Bernard de St. Boniface, a Veronese, as well as another man named Philip Prince of Bucharest. They have been sent to Venice to look out for Italian soldiers, but they are not yet authorised to engage any, until the Queen's secretary joins them with instructions to pay the necessary money. This secretary is to go first to the Diet of Worms, and, in accordance with what he hears there, will, we believe, either go on to Italy, or else look for troops in Germany. The king has decided to send someone to the King of Denmark. We knew this some days ago, but as Secretary Paget has now informed us of it we communicate it to your Majesty.

Our interview (with the deputies) was brought to an end with a request on our part that they would consider all we had said; and together with their colleagues, use their influence with the King that he might be satisfied with the explanations in justification of your Majesty. They replied, that they would do so willingly; and the Earl of Hertford and the Bishop of Winchester, especially, rose and approached me with the assurance they would do their very best, if only in return for the treatment accorded to them when they went to your Majesty. They seemed convinced that your Majesty would raise no difficulty in making the declaration (against France) after the expiration of the ten weeks; but I extricated myself by saying that I had no knowledge of your Majesty's intentions on the subject, beyond what I had said; only that I was sure that your Majesty would not fail on that, or any other point, to do what was proper and incumbent upon you. They promised, as they departed, to convey to us as soon as possible the King's decision; but they previously besought us very earnestly to tell them if we bore any other fresh message on the matter, as the King thought we did, in view of what your Majesty had said in the conference with Hertford and Winchester. This was to the effect that your Majesty would send hither ambassadors to satisfy the King: but they said that they had not hitherto seen any justification or satisfaction whatever, beyond what had already been given to them (*i.e.*, to Hertford and Winchester on their embassy to the Emperor). We replied to this that, even though they (the deputies) might not be authorised to accept the justification as satisfactory, the King would do so.

London, 3 January, 1545.

4 Jan.
Vienna
Imp. Arch.

3. CHAPUYS to the EMPEROR.

Since the enclosed letters jointly from my colleague and myself were written, the Earl of Hertford, the Bishop of Winchester and Secretary Paget sent word to me that, as they had to come to town (*i.e.*, from Greenwich) to-day, they would not fail to come and chat with me privately and without witnesses. They came immediately after dinner; and began at once to apologise for the behaviour of the King towards me on Sunday last. They assured me of the

1545.

great affection that the King bore me, using many expressions which it would be tedious to repeat. They then went on to say that neither the King nor they could believe that, considering my ill-health, I had come to England unless on some more important mission than that which I and my colleague had disclosed. Otherwise, they said, surely it was not necessary for me to come, simply to repeat the same statements that had been already fully debated at Brussels. I replied that I had no private mission whatever. The mission upon which I had come was important enough to justify the coming of a more able person than myself, as they would admit if they considered the contentions laid before them the day before yesterday. It was true that the matter had been fully discussed at Brussels; and if they (Hertford and Winchester) had thoroughly mastered and understood it, my coming might to some extent have been unnecessary. I then laid before them certain letters which the Queen Dowager of Hungary had written to my colleague and myself complaining of the excesses of the English troops not long ago near Arras; and also of the insults, pillage and illtreatment, by them of the people of Dunkirk, Nieuport and Ostend and others. I said that this was a fresh proof, in addition to those already set forth, of the truth of my contention, that the neutrality of the King would have been greatly to the advantage of your Majesty's subjects;[*] and I expected they would shortly hear of numberless complaints of the same sort. A Spaniard only this morning told me that he would furnish me with a written statement of the losses that had been inflicted on Spaniards, which exceeded the amount I had mentioned the day before yesterday. They (the English Councillors) blankly looked at each other, but had not a word to say in reply to this.

I then asked them if they had reported to the King what had passed at our conference, and what he thought of it all. They answered that they had reported summarily, but I ought to know the character of the King sufficiently well to be sure that he was always anxious to reciprocate; nay even to exceed, any friendly approaches made to him and that any one who knew how to manage him might do almost as they liked with him, if he could be satisfied that his friendship would be returned. They (the Councillors) thought that if your Majesty were pleased to write a few amiable words to the King, they would have more influence than anything else in appeasing and settling matters. I asked them what sort of words they meant. They said that your Majesty might assure the King of your perfect, sincere, and inviolable amity, and of your absolute intention to observe all engagements and promises. They did not venture to proceed any further; and I pointed out to them that what they suggested had already been emphatically declared to them by your Majesty, and subsequently by my colleague and myself to the King. They insisted a little, however, saying that the King would like it better if it were written to him; and after they had dwelt upon this for a time, they came to the real matter which touches them. They

---

[*] That is to say that it would have been more advantageous for the Emperor and his subjects, if England had stood aloof from the war altogether, than to have entered into it and then to have conducted it independently for her own ends.

1545.

haggled a good deal over saying it; I am not quite sure whether in consequence of their being half ashamed of it, or from their anxiety to wrap it up nicely: but when it did come out, it was that, in addition to the two professions above-mentioned, the letter should contain a third clause, saying that your Majesty was perfectly satisfied with all the King had done in the enterprise, and that it was your intention to fulfil punctually the terms of the treaty. I laughed when I heard this, and said I was surprised that they did not add a demand that your Majesty should ask the King's pardon. For my part, I said, I would never advise the Emperor to concede the last clauses they mentioned, for to say the plain truth, my own opinion was that the King had broken the treaty. Since, as they said, all the world was talking in a manner unfavourable to your Majesty in the matter of this peace with France, and they themselves, against all reason, raised doubt about the consent (given by the King to the peace between Charles and Francis) conveyed by M. d'Arras to your Majesty, it would be necessary for us to let the world know what really had happened. I made clear, as I had done the day before yesterday, that what I said was quite unofficial; as I knew no more of your Majesty's intentions than what I had told them. I then proceeded to ask them what the King would do, if your Majesty consented to write as they wished: to which they replied that the King would consent to the delay that your Majesty had taken.* I replied that, though, frankly, I had no idea how far your Majesty might consider that a favour from them, I thought that, even though the delay was conceded, and it was three times as long as it was, your Majesty would not be under the slightest obligation to them for it; bearing in mind what had passed in the matter of the declaration against Cleves and Denmark which the King had been requested to make, but which they (the English) would never admit that they promised, until they learnt that your Majesty had made friends with the Duke of Holstein.†

After some more talk, I repeated that, whatever they might say, I did not believe that the King was so bad a friend to your Majesty as to ask you to do a thing derogatory to your honour, and to lay yourself open to the blame of the whole world, besides, as I had already said, throwing all Christendom into turmoil and danger, without any benefit to the King, and even to his disadvantage. So long as your Majesty remained at peace with France the strength of the latter would be reduced by the French contingent against the Turk. There was, moreover, another point to be considered. The Netherlanders had spent immense sums over this war, and the only benefit they had derived from the peace was the opening of trade,

---

* *i.e.*, the period of 10 weeks that Charles had taken in which to reply finally to the demand for aid.

† By reference to the correspondence contained in the preceding volume of this Calendar it will be seen that the allies had in the previous year persistently endeavoured to gain advantage over each other. England by forcing the Emperor to declare war against Scotland and the Emperor by extorting from Henry a similar declaration against the usurping King of Denmark and the Duke of Cleves, the brother of the divorced Queen of England. The declarations in both cases were delayed until circumstances had rendered them of little service.

1545.

upon which riches of their country depended. If, I said, after all their sacrifices, they saw themselves deprived of the benefit in order to serve the interests of others, and with no advantage either to your Majesty or to themselves, they would at once cry murder; for they are very free of speech: and your Majesty would in future be unable to obtain any aid from them. If they (the English) imagined that the King of France would care very much for the declaration they requested, they were making a great mistake; for he did not care a cabbage for it.* I begged them to point this out to the King, and to direct his attention to the various considerations I had set forth. I said, if they would reflect well on the whole matter—admitting the King's consent to the negotiations with France—there was, in my opinion, not the slightest question that their demand that your Majesty should make the declaration was unwarranted. They wanted to dispute this, but after a short time they departed, promising to lay the contentions before the King more fully than heretofore. Seeing the complexity, as well as the importance, of the affair, I thought well to give them a hint, if they needed it, which might lead to a settlement; by saying that, in my opinion, they had acted, and were acting, unwisely in pressing your Majesty to make the declaration. Even if your Majesty did not avail yourself of the King's own non-fulfilment of the treaty, which was as clear as the sun at noon, your Majesty was not in the slightest degree bound. There were, I said, other, and more legitimate, means for obtaining the object they sought. They begged me eagerly to tell them what these means were; and after a show of hesitation, and a protest that I was speaking in confidence; hoping that your Majesty would not be informed of what I said, I told them that they must be aware, as I had recently declared to the King, that your Majesty had not obtained and accepted the arbitration (*i.e.*, of Henry's claims against France) from any desire of your own to adjudicate on the question, but with the objects already explained to the King. Your Majesty had, I said, considered that, however advantageous it was to adjudicate between two enemies; and so to gain the friendship, at all events, of one of them, it was a thankless office to adjudicate between two friends, and thus turn one into an enemy. It nevertheless seemed to me that the best means of arriving at a settlement would be for the King to endeavour to have the arbitration carried through: and I pointed out to them fully the advantages which they might derive from it, besides avoiding the difficulties I had mentioned. They ruminated for some time on it, and said much which need not be repeated, but they finally approved of the suggestion. I do not know whether I was overbold in bringing it forward; but in such case I crave your Majesty's pardon, and beg that my fault may be attributed to my desire to serve your Majesty.

London, 4th January, 1545.

---

* That is to say that the stoppage of commercial intercourse, which would be the main outcome of the declaration requested, would only slightly injure the French, whilst it would ruin the Flemings, &c.

1545.
5 Jan.
Vienna
Imp. Arch.

4. Minute of Letters Patent.

Charles, etc. Whereas complaints have been made to us that certain subjects of the King of England have for some time past been arresting vessels loaded with merchandise of great value belonging to our subjects, both Spaniards and Netherlanders. In order that due steps may be taken for the indemnification of our subjects we have informed the English ambassador resident in our Court of the matter;* but, pending the reply and redress for the injury inflicted, we have, at the request of our subjects, decided to arrest the persons, property and ships of the King's subjects here. In order that this decree may be executed with the gentleness and moderation due to our friendship with the King, we have decided to entrust the task to a person faithful to us; and one in whose diligence, tact, loyalty and virtue we have full confidence. We have therefore appointed you; our well-beloved and trusty councillor and Master of Requests, M. Charles Boissot, doctor of laws, who are hereby instructed to proceed to our cities of Antwerp and Bergen, and there to seize and place at our disposal all the persons, ships, merchandise and other property, belonging to the subjects of the King of England; which persons and property will be safely guarded and remain absolutely intact, until our further orders: and this shall be your full warrant therefor. All our officers and subjects are hereby ordered to obey, assist and forward the fulfilment of this warrant and to give such aid thereto as the holder may request.

Ghent, 5th February, 1545.

5 Jan.
Brussels
Neg. Aug.
B.M.
Add. 28,594.

5. Instructions from the Emperor to his Gentleman of the Mouth, Mde. Torquen,† for his mission to England.

You will proceed with what diligence you may to England, addressing yourself in the first place to our ambassadors, Eustace Chapuys and François Van der Delft, to whom you will deliver your letters and show them this instruction. You will explain your mission to them, and obtain and follow their advice as to your bearing towards the King and his Council. You will then, acting under their direction, present to the King our letters of credence, with our very affectionate greeting, and tell him that we have been several times informed that his people have captured a number of ships, some loaded with goods, provisions, etc., of great value, and others in ballast, belonging to our subjects both Flemish and Spanish. The pretext given for these seizures is that the ships

---

* On the 3rd January Dr. Wotton (the English Ambassador with the Emperor) wrote to Henry VIII. that M. d'Arras (Antoine de Perrenot) and Dr. Boissot had called upon him to complain bitterly of the seizure of Flemish ships in England (especially on the West Coast, Fowey, Dartmouth, etc.), and threatened that unless these ships were instantly released and the owners indemnified the Emperor would decree the seizure of all English subjects and property in his dominions. State Papers R.O. Vol. X.

† The name of this envoy is spelt in an extraordinary variety of ways, Turcoin, Torquain, Tourcaigne, Torquen, Turkuin, Tourcoigne, etc. He had been sent on a temporary mission in the previous year, 1544. His real name was Baudoin de Lanoy, Sieur de Tourcoing, and he was descended from the famous Charles de Lanoy, Prince of Sulmona and Viceroy of Naples.

were about to load or discharge in France, and the men on board have been detained. Our subjects have grievously complained of this; and in accordance with our duty to protect them, and provide redress for the injuries done to them, we have on several occasions remonstrated against the damage thus inflicted since the treaty of friendship was signed. No redress has hitherto been forthcoming, although quite recently we informed the King's ambassador here of the great complaints we were constantly receiving from our subjects, of the losses that were daily being inflicted upon them by Englishmen. These losses already reach a large amount, and we laid the claims before the ambassador, in order that some effort might be put forth on the King's part to make restitution of the property seized. The complaints however, continue and increase every day; and being unable to refuse protection to our subjects, we have acceded to their prayers, and have ordered the seizure of all English subjects, ships and merchandise here. This has been done as moderately, and quietly, as possible; and the persons interested have been given to understand that the sequestration has only been ordered for the reason set forth above, and pending a reply from the King, on receipt of which we will act in accordance therewith. We trust his reply will be such as is demanded by the close friendship between us: and we now despatch you to him for the purpose of making this statement to him, and to beg him to conform to the treaty of alliance, and release the property seized, whilst allowing our subjects in future to pass by sea without molestation. If the contrary be the case, we shall not be able to avoid treating his subjects as he treats ours, though this would cause us great regret, and we would fain avoid it if possible. We have despatched our councillor Charles Boissot to inform the English merchants of the cause of the arrests, and the course we propose to take, in order that they may not think that more harshness than is necessary accompanies the measures, but that our object is solely to provide for the indemnification of our subjects.

You will set this forth to the King, with all possible modesty, and in kind words, such as you may see will induce him to consent to the release of the seizures. You will act throughout in conformity with the advice of our ambasssadors, and go and return from your mission with all possible speed.—Ghent, 5 January, 1545.

P.S.—It is possible that the King may seek to explain the seizures by saying that the ships were loaded with victuals, etc., for for conveyance to France, and consequently that they were good prizes. If this line be taken, you will say that, even if that were the case, it was not for him to arrest our subjects, but that he should have informed us of the matter, and we would have taken such steps as were necessary. To proceed thus forcibly against these subjects of ours was in direct violation of the treaty of alliance, and you will therefore persist in demanding the release; using the gentlest words possible, but at the same time letting the King know that, failing the release of the property seized in England, we shall be obliged to seek the redress and indemnification of our subjects by other means.

1545.
11 Jan.
Vienna
Imp. Arch.

6. CHAPUYS and VAN DER DELFT to the QUEEN DOWAGER of HUNGARY.

Your Majesty will learn, both by the verbal report of M. de Turquin, the bearer of the present, and from the letters we are writing to his Majesty, of the decision which has been adopted respecting the complaints made by your Majesty through us. The people here are much annoyed that the news of the embargo of English subjects and property in the Netherlands should have anticipated the courtesy and conciliation they wished to show to your Majesty. They gave us to understand that on the same day that the news arrived, but before its reception, the Earl of Hertford and Secretary Paget were coming to tell us that your Majesty's complaints should all be redressed, as you desired. Nevertheless we are very glad that his Majesty (*i.e.*, the Emperor) took the step he did; not only in respect of the present matter but to prevent a repetition of such affairs. We hope it will make these people more tractable for the future.

London, 11 January, 1545.

11 Jan.
Vienna
Imp. Arch.

7. CHAPUYS and VAN DER DELFT to the EMPEROR.

On the 9th instant at daybreak the King sent a very pressing and affectionate message to us, begging us to visit him at Greenwich, as he wished to communicate to us a matter of great importance. Just as we were setting out M. de Turquin arrived very opportunely and delivered to us your Majesty's letter, and in the barge on the way down the river we learnt the particulars of his mission. When we arrived at Greenwich, the Councillors began by saying that the King was exceedingly astonished to learn that, instead of your Majesty doing as you promised the Earl of Hertford and the Bishop of Winchester you would do: namely send to a minister here to satisfy him (the King) with regard to his claims, strange and scandalous news had reached him that your Majesty had arrested the persons, ships and property of his subjects in the Netherlands; even his own agents who were there on his business of obtaining payment of a considerable sum of money which he had ordered to be raised in Antwerp.* This was prevented by the embargo mentioned, to the great injury of many and to the loss of credit by the King, which ought to have been considered; especially as the arrest was effected without reason, justice or law, and in violation of the treaties. It was impossible to plead as a reason for it that certain Flemish vessels had been embargoed here; for surely the King's honour and justice, and those of the ministers, might be trusted to the extent that they would not embargo vessels belonging to the Emperor's subjects without good and legitimate cause. This was the case with the cargoes of herrings, which, like all other victuals it was prohibited to supply to the enemies of a friendly state. They (the Councillors) were notified from various quarters that the greater part of the merchandise in question belonged to Frenchmen, and had been fraudulently shipped in the names of

---

* Apparently, from the context, money to be raised for the purpose of repaying advances made to the King by Antwerp bankers.

1545.

certain subjects of your Majesty. For this reason, and in the ordinary process of law, the ships were subject to arrest; and consequently the seizures made in Flanders were iniquitous and insulting. They said that the other day they had submitted to the King the statements of the plaintiffs,* which he had handed to them; and his Majesty had ordered the case to be considered by the whole of the Council. As a consequence, he had yesterday instructed the Earl of Hertford and Secretary Paget to inform us that the ships would be released. We replied to this in accordance with the instructions brought by M. de Turquin; adding that they might recollect that, when two or three English ships were arrested in Flanders, at the time when M. de Bossu† had come to despatch the vessels for the expedition against the Turk, the arrest in that case being quite legitimate and in accordance with the treaty, the King had immediately ordered the seizure of all the Flemish ships in English ports. With regard to the pretext they (the Councillors) alleged for the stoppage of the vessels here, there was no ground for it whatever, as was clearly proved by the fact that they had hitherto not been able to prove any of their allegations. To speak frankly, it seemed to me that reason and honesty should have led the King in the present ambiguous and questionable relations between the countries, to have sent an envoy specially to your Majesty as you had sent M. de Turquin to explain the whole matter, if he went so far as to seize, as he had done, a whole fleet of vessels belonging to your Majesty's subjects. It was impossible for your Majesty to have proceeded more moderately than you had done, in overlooking for so long without resentment such action as theirs, in the belief that the King would order the release of the ships. Even if the merchandise did belong to Frenchmen and it was necessary to seize it, there was surely no reason for preventing the sailing of the ships that were empty. The King complained of the seizure (in Flanders), on the ground that the merchants whom he had ordered to pay the money in Antwerp, had been prevented from doing so, but he should also consider how many poor merchants might suffer in credit, honour and property, by the stoppage of the ships here. As we had already told them, in order to avoid Corinthian justice (*i.e.*, execution first and trial afterwards—Jedburgh justice) they ought to have their proofs complete before they carry out their sentence. During the five weeks that these ships had been detained here there had been plenty of time to have ascertained their intentions; and, as for the statement of the Earl of Hertford and the Bishop of Winchester, that they had heard as they passed through Dunkirk from natives of the place that the French came there to buy herrings, which your Majesty's subjects carried to France, there is no sufficient evidence of its truth. It may have been said by worthless scamps simply to please them: on the other hand the seamen's books and the merchants' marks prove that the allegations were untrue, and the arrests ought not to have been made. If they (the Councillors) knew the bitter complaints that

---

*That is to say the claimants to the Flemish vessels and goods seized in England.
†Adolph de Bourgogne, Sieur de Beures, called de Bossu, Admiral of Flanders (d. December, 1540).

1545.

reached your Majesty from your subjects about it they would not be surprised at your Majesty's action. The Flemings say that it would be more profitable for them if a state of open war existed than to continue long in this way; for in case of war, either they would not sail at all, or they would provide for their protection: in any case they would escape this present miserable ill-treatment. After some further conversation, the Chancellor and the Duke of Suffolk went to report to the King, and on their return after they had conferred at length with the rest of the Council, we went to dinner and subsequently resumed the discussion. The King, however, sent for M. de Turquin, saying that if we liked we might accompany him. For several reasons we thought better not to do so, since the mission was not an intricate one, and we had no doubt that M. de Turquin would fulfill it fittingly; besides which we thought that the King would speak more freely with M. de Turquin alone. We considered we should be better employed by gaining time and continuing the discussion with the Councillors. We were with them until four o'clock in the afternoon, when they went to the King. On their return they brought us in substance what is contained in the note which accompanies this, signed by the Bishop of Winchester and Secretary Paget, who came to us on the following day, in order to write the note. The note, however, was not settled without some altercation, as the draft they brought with them was sufficiently punctilious and vain, as your Majesty will learn from M. de Turquin, together with the other particulars of his negotiation with the King. Amongst other things, the Bishop (of Winchester) and Paget gave us notice that the King had ordered the Deputy of Calais to remedy the excesses committed (by the English) in the neighbourhood of Arras, and the King prayed your Majesty to be good enough to order that the French should not be allowed to convey victuals through your territory, as they do daily from Theurosane to Ardres; and in case your Majesty did not think fit to do this, that the English should be permitted the same privilege as the French. We willingly agreed to make the representation requested and promised to convey the reply to the King.

Under correction, it seems to us that it would be well to please the King and avoid difficulties by immediately ordering, if it so please your Majesty, that no victuals should be conveyed to France, even by sea; and also by proclaiming by placard or otherwise, that no person shall convey under cover of his name, and especially by sea, any goods belonging either to English or French subjects; in the same way that this King did some years since when he was neutral. There is another thing that we must not forget to say; namely, that the Councillors urged us to beg your Majesty to order your officers not to give occasion in future for such scandalous proceedings; and they (the English), on their side, would do the same. They begged that if by chance at a future time their naval forces misbehaved themselves, and committed any offence upon your subjects, your Majesty would bear in mind, that these fighting men are accustomed to do such insolent acts; but that as soon as the offence is known here the King will immediately cause the sufferers to be indemnified, and the delinquents fittingly punished.

1545.

Your Majesty will have seen by our previous letters that we could wish for nothing better than the step that your Majesty has taken. It has rendered these people as supple and tractable as possible, as M. de Turquin will report.

The Bishop and Paget also said that, as the English were now alone in the war, and the French were boasting that, not only would they invade Boulogne, but also Calais and Guisnes, the King would need many more troops, both horse and foot, than he had. It was impossible to convey them to the places he held in France, except through your Majesty's dominions, no matter whether they were Germans or Italians or both; and as time was getting short, he was obliged without delay to engage such soldiers. The money and time in raising them would, however, be wasted unless he was assured of your Majesty's goodwill; and could depend upon obtaining such safe-conducts and passports as, and when, he needed them. He (Paget) begged us, in the King's name, to write to your Majesty and do our best to obtain this assurance. To tell the truth we do not doubt that he will very soon endeavour to procure these passports, more for the purpose of publishing both in Italy and Germany the fact of his having got them, and to arouse the jealousy of the King of France, than to make use of them. We pray your Majesty to tell us what answer we should make.

London, 11 January, 1545.

Docketed, "From the ambassadors in England, 11th January, brought by M. de Torquoyn and received at Brussels, the 17th of the same month."

27 Jan.
Vienna
Imp. Arch.

8. The EMPEROR to CHAPUYS and VAN DER DELFT.

The English ambassador resident here has addressed us on three points: first that we should declare war against France, inasmuch as the period of delay which we had taken for our decision, 10 weeks, had expired: secondly that, in accordance with the agreement made by you with the King's representatives, we should raise the embargo (*i.e.*, on English subjects and property): and thirdly that we should issue authority and safe conducts for the passage of the troops they wish to bring into their service, both Germans and Italians. With regard to the first point we have replied that, subsequent to the departure of the Earl of Hertford and the Bishop of Winchester from here, we sent you Messieurs Francis Van der Delft and Eustace Chapuys to England, together, in order that you might communicate more fully with them, before any final decision was adopted on the points debated here with the English ministers. Matters, however, still remained in suspense owing to the action of the King and his ministers; and consequently what we had said respecting the declaration must also be considered to remain suspended. In any case, it was necessary that a settlement should be arrived at in England. He, the ambassador, only replied that he would communicate this; and if you are spoken to on the subject it will be well for you to answer in the same way

---

* *i.e.*, in embargoing the English property in Flanders.

1545.

with regard to the delay. On the second point we replied that we would have the demand examined; but we gave the ambassador clearly to understand that we had been very badly treated in this matter by the King, with regard to the violent seizure of the ships and merchandise of our subjects. It was necessary for the due preservation of friendship that good offices should be mutual and equal. We had not been able to avoid ordering the embargo of English subjects and property in the face of so many well founded complaints made by our people. He gave a general excuse, and intimated that the King had already decided to restore the vessels embargoed by his people, before the arrival of M. de Torquoin in England. At the same time, he said, on his own account, that he had written about it as soon as he knew of M. de Torquoin's mission. He hardly knew how to get out of this, or to get over the fact that the King's intended release was really decided upon in consequence of the embargo decreed on this side. We ended by saying that we would have the matter looked into, and would reply more fully in due course.

With regard to the passports and safe conducts for troops, we pointed out the difficulty in the matter, inasmuch as it was necessary for us to avoid giving to the French any reasonable cause for asserting that we were breaking the conditions of the treaty of peace, made with them by the express consent of the King of England, and on this subject, also, we promised him a decision later.

Referring to the abovementioned agreement, made by you with the English ministers, we may say that it is considered here extremely prejudicial to our subjects. We do not know whether you have actually signed and delivered it to the English, as the copy you send hither is only signed by them: but it would seem from what you (Chapuys) write to the Bishop of Arras that the agreement has been executed. If this be the case, in order to give due credit to your signature, we have decided to reply that, although you had no instructions to conclude such an arrangement, and it is to some extent informal, since the place and time of execution is omitted, yet we are willing that the release should be effected in accordance with the agreement. Since, however, the agreement was made in England, it was only right that the embargo should immediately have been raised there, as is distinctly set forth in the writing: but as up to the present we have no information whatever that this has been done, we see no reason why we should decree the release on this side. The embargo here was decreed for very urgent and legitimate reasons, and if it were raised on such terms our Netherlands subjects would be driven to despair; for, such has been the ill-treatment they have suffered in many ways from the English, without being able to obtain redress from the King and his ministers, that they would at once conclude that they would never receive restitution or redress. Nevertheless, if the English subjects who have been embargoed here will give security to satisfy the claims of our subjects in like case, the embargo on them shall be raised. We have ordered this reply to be sent to the English ambassador; and at the same time have stated that several Portuguese merchants have complained of injury being done to them in

England since the beginning of the war, the amount of their losses being over 100,000 florins, as you will see by the claim herewith. You will press their case and endeavour to obtain satisfaction and redress for them.

With regard to the request of the English that they should retain the herrings and other victuals on paying a reasonable price for them, we have already seen from experience that when this point is conceded, the English want to fix the price according to their own fancy; and in that case they get the goods at less than cost price, to the great injury of our subjects. If, however, you have conceded it, we suppose you will know those who will fix the price; and that it will be done honestly by persons above suspicion, whereby our subjects may not suffer loss, but make a fair profit. You must press this actively, both for the present and future, so that our subjects may not be cheated as they have been.

With respect to the pitch and tar, the merchandise, so far as we understand is free, since neither of the articles is on the prohibited list. Our subjects therefore have the right to trade in them freely, in accordance with the treaties. In this matter also they (*i.e.*, the English) must bear in mind the favour shown here to English merchants; and must extend to our subjects similar treatment.

The request of the English that, if any of their people chance to commit violence on our subjects at sea, we should refrain from reprisals, and only claim redress, may be answered by you as we have answered the English Ambassador here; namely that the English can easily distinguish both by land and sea the Netherlands merchants and subjects; and the King is so well obeyed that if he pleases he can take such measures as to render reprisals unnecessary. If he will do this, no attack shall come from this side, but otherwise it is impossible to avoid allowing our subjects to have their revenge.

Touching the passport and safe-conduct for the Italians and Germans, we have also ordered a reply to be given, to the effect that, in addition to the consideration already mentioned as to the observance of the treaty with France, the French themselves are asking us for similar safe-conducts and other concessions prejudicial to the English concerning the war; which we intend to refuse. In addition to this, our territories here suffered so severely last year from the passage of the horse and foot soldiers raised in Germany for the King of England, that the subjects of our patrimonial dominions, and those of the empire, might be stirred even to rebellion; and grave consequences might ensue if we allowed a similar thing to occur now. If the King wants Italians, he can bring them by sea from the Mediterranean; whilst Germans could be had by way of Hamburg and West Friesland. There is still another reason against the request which I mention for your information: namely that, considering the way in which the King of England has hitherto used his troops, and the recent seizure of our ships, we have good reason for declining to allow him to bring through our territory a strong body of soldiers in his service. We are sending you this expressly, before replying to the English

1545.

ambassador; in order that he may not anticipate you as he generally does.—Brussels, 27 January, 1545.

5 Feb.
Vienna
Imp. Arch.

9. CHAPUYS and VAN DER DELFT to the EMPEROR.

On the 30th ultimo we received your Majesty's letters of the 27th, and on the following day the Councillors, who had also received the English ambassador's despatch on the same subject, sent to ask us, in case we did not think of coming to court the next day, whether we would kindly name an hour when some of their number might come and speak with us. We excused ourselves, as we were both very unwell, and the matter was not very pressing. The day before yesterday the Council again sent to beg us to make an appointment to meet some of them, protesting that their business with us would be so soon finished and they would not weary us. We thought well not to refuse this time; and, accordingly, at 3 o'clock yesterday afternoon the Master of the Horse* and Secretary Paget came to us. They began by condoling with us in the King's name for our indisposition, for which reason he had sent them to visit us; and also to point out to us that although the King had done so much in the matter of raising the embargoes of ships and merchandise here, he perceived no signs of reciprocity on the other side. We were aware, they said, that the sailors who remained here had been freely restored to their ships, to the full satisfaction of the parties; and that the rest of the goods and merchandise, of which the owners could not be found, had been at our request placed in the hands of a Genoese merchant Angelon Salvaglio, with authority to sell the herrings at the best price obtainable on account of those to whom they might belong; whilst the tar and pitch had been restored to the owners that they might do as they pleased with them. They (the Councillors) thought there was nothing more for the King's Council to do, but if we thought otherwise and would tell them, they would at once do it. They again touched upon the King's annoyance if the seizures in Flanders prevented him from keeping his word with the Antwerp merchants to whom he owed money. Paget went so far as to say nevertheless, that if what was said was true, the King would not pay a single penny, since the very men who were to receive the money were amongst the principal promoters of the seizures; naming specially Jehan Carlo and Jaspar Duchy.†

We replied that there was no ground for surprise that your Majesty had not yet released their people and property; as probably you had not been apprised of the fulfilment of the conditions by the embargoes being raised on this side. To tell them truth, I said, I did not consider, moreover, that the King had yet completed his part; since there still remained 18 vessels despoiled, which the sailors had been obliged to leave and return to Flanders. The merchandise also had not been formally returned to its owners, as the latter, owing to the ill-treatment they received from the King's officers, were forced to absent themselves and appeal to your Majesty.

*Sir Anthony Browne.
†The names of these Genoese bankers appear to have been Giovanni Carlo, and Gasparo Dolci.

1545.

We had no authority to accept what had been done as a full reparation, but we would let your Majesty know exactly what had happened, and perchance you might be satisfied therewith. We did not omit to set forth the great injury and loss that had been suffered by your Majesty's subjects through these arrests, and also that since the "note" had been written, the King had tried to limit it with regard to the pitch and tar; and he had specifically broken the agreement by refusing the restitution of certain Rhine wines belonging to a citizen of Bruges, although the Councillors had expressly assured us that they should be restored without fail. The Councillors had confessed this since, saying that there would have been no difficulty about these wines, if they were in other hands than those of the King. The latter sent word to us a week later, saying, that if we did not consider the agreement contained in the "note" fulfilled without the restitution of these wines, he would regard the whole arrangement as at an end; and requesting us to reply decisively, that he might proceed accordingly. With regard to the restoration of the wines, what he required was that a judgment should be given, as to whether or not they were a good prize, and he demanded no privilege whatever in the hearing of the case, other than that enjoyed by a private individual.

So far as we can judge, the difficulty in the restoration of the wines arises from the fact there was captured with them some ten or twelve thousand crowns worth of gold, silver and silk tissues, belonging to Italians, which the King has retained as a good prize, and has already arranged with the parties interested; who might consider themselves wronged if the wines were restored; since both things were captured first by the French in an English harbour, and six hours afterwards recaptured from them by an English ship-of-war. In consequence of this, the French capture not having been a good one, the King could not legally appropriate the prize. The Councillors concluded by begging us very earnestly to move your Majesty to raise the embargo on the other side; and they showed by their words how alarmed they are at the delay in doing so. They probably fear that your Majesty may hold the property seized as a sort of set-off to the King's violation of the treaty made with the Viceroy of Sicily.[*]

We humbly thank your Majesty for having deigned to honour us by accepting the "note" of agreement; but we should deeply regret if the acceptance caused any prejudice to your Majesty's subjects, since the agreement was made without reference to the fundamental rights, and mainly for the purpose of conciliating the merchants here and to bring them to their former goodwill.

With regard to the passport and safe conduct for troops, mentioned in your Majesty's letters, we have done our best to soften the King's resentment at your Majesty's having placed him in this respect on the same footing as the King of France; since, in accordance with your last treaty with France, they (the English) observe that you are not bound to allow the passage of French

---

[*] That is to say the agreement made with Gonzaga in London between Henry and the Emperor for the joint prosecution of the war with France. *See* Vol VII. and also Vol. VI., part two, for particulars of this treaty.

1545.

troops; a privilege which this King asserts that you are bound to in his case by the treaty of friendship with him. We put this aspect aside, and pointed out the evident impossibility of such permission being given, saying at the same time that the Mediterranean route was open to him or Italians, and that the Germans could be brought from Hamburg and West Friesland. They (the English) replied that even then they would need your Majesty's passport, which we said was not the case; whereupon they retorted that we seemed to stand out as stiffly about granting the safe conducts as we did about the rest of the difficulties raised. They afterwards touched, as if incidentally, on the point of the declaration of your Majesty against the French; but we soon closed their mouths on that subject and left them without a word to say for themselves. They then went on to remark that your Majesty had told the English ambassador that, ever since our arrival in England, we had been pressing ceaselessly for a decisive reply to certain points, but had been unable to obtain any satisfaction. We asked them if any special point had been mentioned; to which they replied in the negative; and we said that we would read carefully through your Majesty's letters again, to see what point you referred to; besides which we would write to your Majesty about it.

We have not failed to request that their troops shall be prevented from injuring your Majesty's subjects, both for the sake of justice and to avoid difficulties that may result. Touching the seizure effected at the beginning of the war, of certain property belonging to citizens of Burgos, the Councillors professed surprise that these old claims should be mixed up with the present questions. If, they said, the release of the ships and property now embargoed by your Majesty was to be deferred until all outstanding claims were settled, it would mean that the release would never be given. We replied that we were quite uninformed, as to whether your Majesty intended to defer granting the release until outstanding claims were settled or not; but as the points at issue could be settled in a couple of hours, and were of great importance, we begged the King to have the affairs adjudicated upon. They promised to bear the subject in mind.

London, 5 February, 1545.

7 Feb.
Paris
Arch. Nat.
K. 1,485.
B.M. 28,594.

10. St. Maurice to Francisco de los Cobos.

I send you herewith a statement of occurences here since my arrival as the Emperor's ambassador resident, knowing that by doing so I shall be serving the Emperor and pleasing M. de Granvelle. I wrote to you previously by M. de Silly and do not repeat what I said, only to pray you to order the couriers on their way back to Spain to seek me, so that you may be kept informed of what goes on at this Court.

I send you duplicate of the salary-warrant the Emperor has deigned to grant me whilst I am here, in order that the amount may be paid in Spain. As you are the person upon whom my payment mainly depends, I humbly pray you to help me to obtain it without great delay, which would cause me serious prejudice. Expenses here are excessive owing to an incredible dearness of living, etc. . . .

1545.

I send you an ancient prophecy which has recently been rediscovered in this realm with respect to the war these people are preparing against the English.

Melun, 7 February, 1545.

(Spanish translation of summary of the news contained in the above and subsequent letters, 7 and 28 Feby. and 24 and 31 March.)

The long and perilous illness of the King Francis I.

The preparations being made in France for the war against England, and the extremity to which Ardres is reduced; although, on the other hand he heard that the French wished to make a truce with the English, in order to bring his Majesty (i.e., the Emperor) the more readily to the fulfilment of the agreement (i.e., the marriage arranged in the treaty of peace).

A talk of a marriage between the Prince of Piedmont and Madame Margaret.*

What was occurring in the matter of Captain Guzman.

The talk about the Ambassador who was sent by the King of France to the Turk.

That the Emperor was summoning the Prince of Piedmont to his Court.

News from the Turk.

The Duke of Orleans was getting ready to go to Worms.

About the reprisals.

About the Duke of Alburquerque.

The matter of the restitution of the territories comprised in the treaty of peace.

Vigilance advised on the Perpignan frontier.

31 March.

Joy of the King of France at the good health of Prince and Princess Philip, and the pregnancy of the latter.

Scotland requests aid against England.

The English have captured a castle near Ardres.

Rumours that the King of England desired peace with France by means of a marriage of the Princess of England (i.e., Mary) with the Duke of Orleans.

Arrangements for the Council (of Trent).

Respecting the troops promised by the Pope to the King of France, and the King's angry reply.

The King (of France) sent to Rome the friar who negotiated the peace, to urge the Pope to write to his Majesty (i.e. the Emperor) asking him to declare war against England.

The restitution of Stenay. Illness of the Duke of Lorraine and the succession of his States.

The King (of France) is increasing the number of his galleys.

The King wants to avoid giving the aid against the Turk.

The plague.

13 Feb.
Vienna
Imp. Arch.

11. François Van der Delft to the Emperor.

I humbly acknowledge receipt of letters of 20th January, respecting three vessels loaded with merchandise belonging to

---

* Margaret of France, daughter of Frances I. She eventually married Emmanuel Philibert (then Duke of Savoy) years afterwards.

1545.

citizens of Burgos seized by English subjects at the beginning of the late wars. In accordance with your Majesty's instructions, that I should take an opportunity of pressing the King and Council for restitution, I addressed the latter at my next interview with them; saying that I had letters of credence from your Majesty to the King, and orders to address the Council on a subject of importance; and desired to know when I could see the King for the purpose of delivering my message. I then opened the question to the Councillors; and they expressed surprise, and thought it unreasonable, that, as we had not previously made any such claim, we should come at this time of day to complain, when their subjects and property were still under embargo in Flanders—a morsel which sorely sticks in their throats. I replied, as I thought fitting, alleging the constant appeals made to your Majesty for some time past by the merchants. Your Majesty and the Queen (Dowager of Hungary) had, I said, written so often about it, as to prove how well founded the complaints were. With regard to the claims in question not having been pressed: that had been caused out of consideration for them (the English), and even at their instance, as I had heard from M. Chapuys; and also because there were at the time other matters of greater importance demanding attention; but which now should not further prejudice your Majesty's subjects. When the Councillors had conferred with the King, I was told that if I would return on the following day I should have audience. I did so, and was at court early in the afternoon, when I was at once summoned to the King. I presented my letter, with due respect, repeating modestly the contents, and claiming the restitution of the property referred to. The King made a wry face at it, and began to re-open several matters that had happened at Boulogne, the same as he had dwelt upon to M. Chapuys and myself when we first arrived here, and of which due account was written to your Majesty at the time. He came round to the credence, however, of his own accord; saying that the capture was a perfectly good one, made from the French. It was, he said, the first exploit performed by him in the alliance against them: and the sailors on the ships had all declared that the property belonged to French subjects; although, even without that, the presumption was strong enough. He was, however, convinced that if your Majesty were correctly informed in the matter you would not press this claim for the benefit of Frenchmen; though it seemed very strange, now that his subjects were under your Majesty's embargo, you should come after so long an interval, and spring such a demand upon him. He had never hitherto heard of any complaint in the matter: and he then called his Chancellor and the Duke of Suffolk, who were on the other side of the room (after they had led me to the King) in whose presence he repeated what he had said; adding that in proceeding thus, we were not regarding the treaties, according to which an agreement should be arrived at without this formal demand for restitution. I pointed out to him, as I had done to his Councillors, that he ought not to take it in this light, knowing as he did your Majesty's intention and good will to adhere strictly to the perfect friendship between you and him. Your Majesty, however, was obliged to safeguard the interests of your subjects, to whom really this property would be proved to belong. It was not necessary in this case to adopt the procedure under the treaties; the justice of the matter being so evident that, with the merest glance at the facts, the question settled itself; in addition to which we had the most convincing proofs, which I trusted would lead him to consent to justice being done, as was also confidently hoped by your Majesty. After all this, he replied that he would write to his ambassador about it, in order that he (*i.e.* the ambassador, Dr. Wotton) might represent to your Majesty that when his subjects in the Netherlands were disembargoed he would take care that no wrong was done by your Majesty's subjects, but that every favour should be shown to them. He asked me to move your Majesty to raise the embargo, and showed great annoyance that it was being, as he said, more delayed than if no agreement had been made between his ministers and us. With regard to the case in question, he would be inclined to refer the decision to commissioners here, who would see that justice was done. This was all I could get from him in the matter.

London, 13 February, 1545.

17 Feb.
Simancas
E.F. 501
extract

12. LICENTIATE VARGAS° to FRANCISCO DE LOS COBOS.†

The Pope is liberal of fair words, but sparing of good deeds respecting the enterprises against the Turks and the Protestants. He is saying now that he cannot allow the sale of the monastic property (in Spain) without conferring on the subject with the consistory of Cardinals.

His Holiness expresses his firm intention to assist the King of France against the English, as he says that a war with the King of England is as praiseworthy as a war with the Turks. Juan de Vega‡ writes that the Pope is determinedly hostile to the Emperor and will do nothing in his favour "until the water rises as high as his mouth" (*i.e.* until he is in danger of being drowned).

Brussels, 17 February, 1545.

17 Feb.
Simancas
E.F 501.

13. THE EMPEROR to FRANCISCO DE LOS COBOS.

You will learn the state of current politics by reading the letters addressed to the Prince, but, for your further private information, we send you a copy of the despatch forwarded to Juan de Vega respecting the negotiations with the Pope, and also a summary of the communications with the Nuncio Poggio, and with Sfondato,§ touching the assistance to be furnished by the Pope in a war against the Turks and Protestants.

°Vargas was one of the Emperor's Spanish secretaries, and was subsequently sent with the imperial ambassador to the Council of Trent, of which he wrote an account in a series of letters to de Granvelle the younger (Bishop of Arras).
†Francisco de los Cobos. High Commander of Leon in the Military order of Santiago, was the political guide and mentor of the young Regent Prince Philip in Spain, especially in financial matters.
‡ Juan de Vega was the Emperor's ambassador in Rome.
§ Giovanni Poggio Bishop of Tropea and the Cardinal Archbishop Francisco de Sfondrato were the Papal Nuncios to the Emperor.

1545.

The Pope's representatives have promised us in general terms his assistance in such a war; but we have decided not to undertake anything, especially against the Protestants, until we see clearly that the Pope is ready to assist us, not by words alone but by deeds. The danger of utter ruin with which the heretics threaten Christendom is so great that the Roman See must help us with a considerable sum of money in the enterprise against the Protestants. Prelates and ecclesiastics should in our opinion contribute most liberally to the expenses of efforts to suppress heresy. From prelates and Churches in Spain much money should be obtained; and we desire you to take the prelimnairy steps which shall enable us in due time to realise such contributions easily and promptly. This must be done with the greatest secrecy; for if the Prelates learn beforehand that they are to be thus taxed, some of them might betray the matter to the Protestants, in order to prevent the execution of the measures intended.

Brussels, 17 February, 1545. (*Spanish Draft.*)

Endorsed. "The last despatches taken by Don Bernardino from Brussels to Spain."

21 Feb.
Vienna
Imp. Arch.

14. CHAPUYS and VAN DER DELFT to the EMPEROR.

The bearer of this is Secretary Paget; who in order to prove that he has no desire to slip away unnoticed, has sent to ask us for letters to your Majesty, and to assure us that, if his occupations and the haste in which he is, had allowed him, he would greatly have liked to come personally and inform us of the details of the mission entrusted to him. We expect, from many indications, that the instructions given to him will be more moderate, and his powers more ample, than those given to the Earl of Hertford and the Bishop of Winchester.[*] Whatever they may be, however, we are quite sure that he will do his best to preserve and increase the friendship between your Majesty and the King, in view of his (Paget's) previous attachment to your Majesty's interests. He not only exerts himself to the utmost to help and favour your ministers, but extends his efforts to the wellbeing of all your subjects; and we think well to give your Majesty notice of this, in order that he may be received favourably, and thus be spurred to still greater devotion and service, which his position enables him to render.

London, 21st February.

21 Feb.
Vienna
Imp. Arch

15. THE EMPEROR to CHAPUYS and VAN DER DELFT.

We have received your lettters of 5th instant, informing us of the conversation you had with the Master of the Horse and Secretary Paget, especially about the raising of the embargo. By your letters, and also by the reports of our subjects, we understand that the

---

[*] Paget's instructions are in the Record Office, State Papers, Vol. X, p. 295. Paget also carried letters from Henry VIII. to the Queen Dowager of Hungary—Regent of Flanders, and to the Emperor's Secretary de Granvelle, dated 20th February. These letters are in the Imperial Archives at Vienna (Hof Coresp. Fasc Varia No. 1), but as they are merely introductory and recommendatory, they are not reproduced here.

restitution in England has not been effected properly. This is the case with the ships belonging to our subjects, which are still in England by the fault of the English, and also with the herrings, which have been sold there without the owners' consent, and without redress: besides which, other property has been retained in England. Although we presume that you will have made proper representations about all this, we wish you had sent us fuller information on the subject, saying if the property still detained is of great value, and giving your views as to the manner in which the restitution was being carried out; and also your opinion with regard to the release on this side, justly demanded by the King of England through you, and most importunately urged through his ambassador here. The ambassador strives his utmost to convince us that all the property in England has been restored, fully and generously; and we desire you, as early as possible, to enlighten us on the matter, without omitting reference to the Burgos property, and to the other of our subjects who have been injured, and have had their property seized since the beginning of the late year. In order to please the English ambassador, after saying that we had certain knowledge that the restitution had not been fully effected in England, especially in the case of the ships still there, and the herrings, we told him that we were willing to give up all the English ships, on this side, and also to begin to raise the embargoes on English property, on their giving security, which they could easily obtain, pending the completion of the restitution on the other side. With regard to the Burgos claim, we said the fact of the seizure having been made so long ago as the commencement of the war, only made the claim stronger, as the redress had been so long withheld, and gave another reason against further delay. We added that it was very necessary that some measure should at once be agreed upon, to protect, in future, subjects of both monarchs from these molestations, seizures and detentions, from which our subjects have suffered so severely: and that henceforward friendship, good-neighbourship and reasonable equality should be observed.

The ambassador thereupon insisted with much earnestness in his enquiry, as to whether it was intended to defer the release on account of the Burgos and other claims arising out of seizures during the war, or only until the above-mentioned security could be obtained. He was informed, as before, that we were ready to begin to raise the embargoes on goods claimed by those who gave security, and on the ships and sailors here: but that, as you very well pointed out, the Burgos and other similar claims could be settled very easily and promptly, whilst the arrangement for the future security of subjects on both sides was being discussed. You will keep both these points in hand, the measure for future protection being especially important to our subjects, and necessary in order to avoid troubles which may otherwise arise.

With regard to the request for safe-conduct for the passage of German and Italian soldiers for the English service, the ambassador has on several occasions pressed the matter vehemently and rudely, unconvinced by any arguments of ours; such as we wrote to you, showing that we are not bound to grant such safe-conducts by the

1545.

treaty, and pointing out the vast damage and danger suffered by our territories and by Liege, last year from Landenberg's horse and foot, and other bands for the King of England. But the ambassador has never been convinced; nor has he suggested any way of avoiding a repetition of the same evils in the future. We told him, moreover, that the Electors, Princes and the States of the Empire, were endeavouring to renew the edicts prohibiting the raising of mercenaries in Germany, owing to the need for soldiers against the Turk: but we said if his master really wanted the troops, we had indicated how he could get them, and had told him that we would look the other way; which was more than we would do for the French. We tell you this for your guidance in talking of the matter there. Touching what was said to you by the English about the declaration against France, urged so pressingly lately by the Earl of Hertford and the Bishop of Winchester, whose mouths, as you say, you so promptly closed, it would have been well for you to write telling us the arguments you employed, and how you closed their mouths. The mere statement of this fact gives us no information; and the matter is of the highest importance, and was the principal reason for our sending you M. Eustace Chapuys to England. The ambassador here is pressing us very hard on the matter; and has gone so far as to say that it is necessary that his master should have an answer yes or no, in order that he may proceed accordingly. As the Earl and the Bishop spoke similarly, it will be well for you to keep your eye on the point. We have always avoided dealing with the requisition; and with this object we sent you and M. Van der Delft to carry on the communication, and to endeavour to satisfy the King with our reasons, and such other arguments as appeared desirable. It would be well for you to write as soon as possible, telling us everything you have heard on the subject, with your own opinions. In the meanwhile, you will do your best to excuse and postpone the declaration, but with all possible dexterity, whilst signifying to the King and his ministers that our intention is to observe faithfully the treaty of friendship, so far as it is possible honestly for us to do so, consistently with the treaty we have now made with France, by the King (of England's) consent. At the same time you must keep to the point of the non-fulfilment of the agreement on the part of England; and you must appear not to know that the English ambassador has been pressing for our final decision, and endeavouring to discover if there is any possibility of our abandoning the French, and declaring war against them. The ambassador approaches us sometimes softly, with the assurance that his master will remain friendly with us through thick and thin, and sometimes roughly. The reply given has been, that we desire sincerely to remain friendly with the King, and to fulfil the treaty of friendship, in so far as is possible, without breaking our treaty with France. Brussels, 21 February, 1545.

25 Feb.
Vienna
Imp. Arch.

16. CHAPUYS and VAN DER DELFT to the EMPEROR.

We received yesterday your Majesty's letter of the 21st instant. With regard to what has passed in the matter of the restitution of

1545.

the ships and merchandise seized here, as we recorded in our previous letters, the King and Councillors have displayed great diligence and care in fulfilling the promise of redress. They have amply indemnified the sailors who have lodged complaints, and also the merchants who have produced evidence of their rights. It is, however, the case that very few merchants have hitherto claimed restitution; and the King consequently requested us to appoint a person to whom the property unclaimed in London might be delivered in order that such property might be retained or sold on account of the owners. We did so; nominating Angelon Salvaglio, a Genoese merchant, a man of credit and substance; who after waiting for some time, and finding that no one came to claim the merchandise; not even the herrings which were being injured by keeping, sold them at the highest price obtainable—as good, indeed, as the owners could have got; so that the owners have no ground for complaint, though no one has come to claim the money. It is true that the quantity of herrings is small in comparison with that demanded by the Flemings; not exceeding 140 lasts. The rest of the merchandise, which chiefly consists of pitch and tar, amounting to about 150 lasts, of which a memorandum* is sent herewith, could only be sold here at a loss, and Salvaglio has consequently done nothing with it, pending the arrival of the owners here. The greater part of the merchandise detained must still be at Dover, Calais and Boulogne and we have no means whatever of obtaining an estimate of its value. We are much astonished that those to whom the property belongs have not come to make their claims.

With regard to our opinion as to whether the restitution has an appearance of being carried out honestly here, we reply that we have not the slightest doubt of it, on condition that the embargo on the other side is retained as the King and everyone else here are so much perplexed at the embargo, and so desirous of getting it raised. It is certain that the prolongation of the embargo would cause scandal and be extremely prejudicial to the English; and in our opinion it would be advisable to raise it, but it should be done with the caution (*i.e.* security) mentioned in your Majesty's letters. This is reasonable and really necessary, not only on account of the pending claims of the Burgos merchants, but also because the greater part of the property seized, both ships and goods, still remains here. The excuse for further delay in the matter of the Burgos claims, is that the King awaits the reply to his letters to your Majesty demanding that the matter shall be decided by the procedure laid down in the treaty of amity; namely by a conference of arbitrators chosen by himself and your Majesty; as I (Van der Delft) informed your Majesty in my recent letters. This would mean that we should never get to the main business, as we have no doubt that your Majesty in your wisdom will see, and will have regard to the justice and reparation due to your subjects.

With regard to the safe-conducts for the German and Italian troops, your Majesty's reasons for declining to grant them are so

---

* The note of the goods is still attached to the original letter at Vienna, but is not reproduced here, as the detail is of no importance.

1545.

cogent and unanswerable, that no further justification is needful. We will, however, not fail to re-state the reasons when opportunity offers, both to the King and Council.

In the matter of the demand so persistently and importunately pressed by the King and his ministers, that your Majesty should declare yourself against France, your Majesty will have seen by our letters of the 3rd and 4th January that the King refused to be satisfied with the reply given by your Majesty to the Earl of Hertford and the Bishop of Winchester. We repeated the arguments to the best of our ability; and the King, unable either to meet or controvert our contentions, flew into a passion and angrily alleged things which had already been contradicted, and others which damaged his own case, remaining to the last obstinately unconvinced. Your Majesty will also have learnt that in our two conferences with the Earl of Hertford, the Bishop of Winchester and Secretary Paget, we repeated our conversation with the King, and that they also were unable to extricate themselves, or controvert what we said. Since the two conferences in question the councillors have not referred to this matter, except incidentally, and in a joking, semi-shamefaced, fashion. This was the case recently with Secretary Paget, in the presence of the Master-of-the-Horse, and we replied to him that, as they only referred to this point in jest, we had somewhat passed it over; but if they were in earnest we thought they were wrong in continuing to talk about it after the unanswerable arguments and reasons we had laid before them. Paget retorted that no person could know better than I (Eustace Chapuys) who had drafted the treaty; and he would like to know if the King of France, who had consented to the reservation of the treaty of alliance between your Majesty and the King of England, had not violated his engagements towards your Majesty by invading English territory; and consequently whether the King of France had not therefore forfeited the benefit of the said treaty. He (Paget) would also be glad to learn if the treaty of friendship between your Majesty and both Kings did not provide that, in case of the invasion of the territory of one of them by the other, the third party to the treaty was bound to declare against the invader. In reply, I placed before Paget the principal arguments which had already been stated; and, with regard to the latter portion of his remarks I said, that, in the absence of a special clause to that effect, the third party was not bound to declare against the invader. With respect to his (Paget's) first point, I said that, even if the treaty between his master and your Majesty had been specially reserved in your Majesty's treaty with the King of France, his (Paget's) master could not claim any advantage from it, since the King (of England) had from the first refused to acknowledge the Emperor's treaty with France. If, I added, he (Paget) wanted to take so literally the reservation of the treaty (*i.e.* between Charles and Henry) his master might on the strength of it claim France, and a good many other things mentioned in the treaty, besides the declaration of your Majesty. The reservation of the treaty, I said, must be understood only in so far as it did not clash with the treaty of friendship agreed upon between your Majesty and the King of

France, which treaty was made with the consent of the King (of England); the King of France becoming a friend of your Majesty, but still remaining an enemy of the King of England. At the time the King (of England) gave his consent to the treaty the King of France was as much his enemy as he is now: occupying (according to the pretension of the King of England) the latter's realm of France and injuring him in other points of far more importance than the invasion upon which the English now founded their claim for your Majesty's declaration. It could not be said that the invasion complained of made the King of France more of an enemy than he was before. If the King (of England) therefore, was willing, notwithstanding this enmity, to consent to a friendship between your Majesty and the King of France, it was clear that such consent carried with it the customary clauses for the maintenance of the amity thus established, the King of France being no more of an enemy to England than he was before. Paget could only gape at this, and seemed half confused, not saying a single word in reply. We afterwards remarked that we almost believed what several of the courtiers were saying; namely that the King wished to drag your Majesty into war again, not because he needed your present assistance but out of jealousy at the friendship between your Majesty and the Christian King; and in order that he (Henry) might himself slip out of the war and leave your Majesty in the lurch. We repeated more than five or six times, that if each of the allies had fulfilled this part of the agreement for the joint enterprise, there would have been no dispute about Boulogne nor any of these affairs; for a secure and advantageous peace would have been made. They made no answer to this, either, but the Master of the Horse kept shrugging his shoulders all the time, as if to admit what was said, though at the end of the argument he remarked that there was still time to do it. I replied that there was very little chance of it now for many reasons. The King of France was more strongly fortified than ever, and could do more in his defence for a penny than the aggressors for a hundred times as much. However rich their master might be, we said, he would probably be sorry to incur again such an expenditure as he faced last year. Perhaps, indeed, it would be impossible for him to provide for nearly so much. They said nothing in reply, which surprised us, as the Master of the Horse is immoderately inclined to exalt the great wealth of his master.

Since your Majesty seeks a good pretext for delay in the matter of the declaration, we think there will be no necessity for us to press for a decisive reply from the King, as we are quite certain that any such reply would be curt and obstinate. After all is said, there is but small chance of bringing him to reason, except by means of complaint as to his having failed to fulfil the arrangement (i.e. for the conduct of the war); and we have been careful to keep that point unimpaired. It is only necessary for us to speak to him or his ministers on the point, to prolong affairs. Even if such were not the case, we think it would be better not to press forward the matter of the safe-conducts until we are informed of the particulars

1545.

of Paget's mission, in order to preserve our liberty of action with regard to his demands; which we doubt not will be more modest and softer than before. We beg your Majesty to instruct us how we are to proceed; and also concerning the steps to be taken to protect your Majesty's subjects in future from insult, pillage and oppression at the hands of the English. The management of this is beyond us, seeing the difficulties which the English will raise in order to continue their usual custom.

London, 25 February, 1545.

25 Feb.
Simancas
E.F. 505.
extract.

17. THE EMPEROR to JUAN DE VEGA (Ambassador in Rome).

Regrets that the Pope° has created so few Cardinals of his party, and especially that the hat has been refused to Don Pedro Pacheco, Bishop of Jaen. Notes Vega's remark that the Pope is much alarmed at the Council (of Trent), and even more alarmed at the Diet (of Worms), and the Emperor approves of Vega's device to keep his Holiness in the same mind, neither banishing his fear nor increasing it. Vega must endeavour to bind the Pope to help the Emperor with a large sum of money, and he (the Pope) also ought to send a Nuncio to the Diet, and correspond with M. de Granvelle who is going to Worms to make the necessary preparations. "With regard to the aid which the Pope declares he will give to the King of France against the King of England, you have done well in not openly opposing it, but in taking your principal stand on the importance of resisting the Turk, and redressing religious evils. You will continue the same course until the matter is discussed by the German States, and we see what steps are best to be taken."

Brussels, 25 February. (*Spanish Draft.*)

Feb. S.D.
Simancas
E Roma 872.

18. Draft of letter to be written from the EMPEROR to JUAN DE VEGA (Ambassador in Rome).

You will have learnt by the summary of the treaty of peace we sent you from Cambresis, details of the stipulations made respecting the marriage of the Duke of Orleans with our daughter the Infanta Maria taking with her the States of Flanders and Burgundy, or with the second daughter of our brother the King of the Romans, carrying the duchy of Milan as her dower. As the matter was of vast importance, we consulted our son the Prince and the Council of State who advise him, and also our sister Queen Maria and the Flemish nobles, communicating likewise on the subject with our brother the King of the Romans by letter and confidential envoys, since my indisposition prevented me from visiting him personally, as I had intended. The result has been that which you will see by the enclosed declaration,† which we send you in a Spanish translation from the French for your

---

° The Pope was Paul III (Farnese), who with his family had hitherto been bitterly opposed to the Emperor's policy in Italy.
† The full text of the declaration was included by error in the last volume of this Calendar dated December 1544. See Vol. vii. p. 474.

guidance. We doubt not that you will study its form and contents closely. The declaration has not yet been sent to the King of France, as he has not hitherto restored Stenay to the Duke of Lorraine, as he is pledged to do; and for the same reason we are detaining the hostages, giving them to understand that though the declaration is ready we are deferring its presentation for that reason. As we learn that Stenay is shortly to be restored, we have thought well to inform you of our intention. You will see by the wording of the declaration, that our device is to keep the King of France still hopeful, that if the bid for Flanders was raised, we might still be willing to come to terms about it.* The object of this is to see what the next step of the French will be, and to gain time. The declaration also mentions the various defaults made in fulfilling the terms of the treaty, and the things still undone, which, although not formally set forth as conditions, were tacitly understood to be so; and notification is given that, unless the terms are carried out in their entirety, we shall have to reconsider our position. We have thought well to inform you of this in the strictest secrecy, because, according to their usual manner, the French as soon as they receive our declaration, will at once try to make capital out of it to gain over the Italian Republics, etc., which are, as we know by long experience, apt to welcome novelties, and to give credit lightly to anything that is told them. If, therefore, we send this declaration (to the King of France) it will be advisable that it should at once be known all over Italy. You will, with all due dexterity, inform the Pope of it, without mentioning the considerations set forth above or those that follow, but simply saying that we are honestly anxious to fulfil our part, and doubt not that the King of France will do the same in the interests of peace, which is the thing we most ardently desire. It is the more necessary that we should thus dissemble with the Pope, because of what you say about (his) confidential negotiations with the French. By the wording of the declaration you will see, that all we have to do is to stick to the Milan solution, without going any further; the purpose being to gain time, and see what the French will do. You will see that nothing is said yet about the express consent of the daughter of the King of the Romans, and other means and conditions which would be necessary to consider before giving up possession of the State of Milan. As, moreover, the French have not fulfilled the terms of the treaty within the stipulated period; and, in their usual fickle way, they will be sure to commit fresh breaches, even if they do not enter into plans to upset the whole treaty of peace, it may well happen that cause may be given for us to question or postpone the fulfilment on our part. There is some talk, too, of the ill-feeling between the two brothers; though some people deny it. Still it would not be surprising if this gave rise to some reason for preventing the carrying out of the conditions. Besides this, the investiture is only to be in the male line, and the fortresses of Milan and Cremona are to be retained in our hands, all the commanders of fortresses to be chosen

---

* That is to say what increased endowment Francis would give to his young son with the object of persuading the Emperor to choose the other alternative marriage, namely that of his daughter Maria with the coveted dower of Flanders.

1545.

by us. These and similar conditions will have to be discussed and settled at length, and the negotiation will necessarily be delayed. But as the matter is very delicate, we do not wish on any account that there should be the slightest suspicion that we desire to depart from our pledges, except for urgent and legitimate reasons. For public reasons, also, it is most necessary at present, in view of the remedying of religious evils by the Council, and the aid in the war against the Turk, that no ground should be given to the French to hold aloof from these things on the ground that we have failed to carry out our promises, and cast the blame upon us. Above all the most complete secrecy must be observed about this.

Worms, S.D.

The draft declaration which accompanied the above letter is at (Simancas, E. 67) and sets forth, first that the Emperor for various reasons regrets that the marriage of his daughter the Princess Maria with the Duke of Orleans is not convenient, and that he has consequently chosen the clause stipulating for the marriage of the daughter of the King of the Romans (Catharine) with the Duke. In accordance with the summary given in the letter to Vega, the document then hints that the King of France, if he desires it, may still make fresh proposals for the other alternative marriage: "but he (the Emperor) wishes to say in all friendship that the portion of the Duke of Orleans might well be larger for either of these two marriages."

The restitution of Hesdin is claimed* in accordance with the treaty, and that of Charlerois is demanded. The delay in the restoration of Stenay† to Lorraine is complained of, and a great grievance is made of the unreasonable and imperious bearing of the French commissioners at Cambrai for the settlement of the details of the peace. Amidst constantly reiterated professions of a desire to fulfil the terms of the treaty, a cloud of small doubts and questions are raised, such as the depredations of the French on Portuguese shipping, the delay in the restitution of Spanish and Flemish property plundered at sea; and the King of France is finally exhorted to remedy these evils. The whole tenour of the document (8 pages) is admirably calculated to fulfil the Emperor's design of keeping the King of France in suspense as to the prize of Flanders or Milan for his son, until the Turks were rendered harmless, and the Protestants were dealt with by the Council of Trent, or if necessary afterwards by force of arms. As will be seen later, the death of Francis I. and of the young Duke of Orleans soon afterwards put an end to the suggested marriages and relieved the Emperor of his anxiety in this respect.

---

* According to the terms of the treaty of Crépy, the town and bailiwick of Hedin which had been claimed as part of the Artois dominion of the Emperor for many years was to be surrendered by the French. For the text of the treaty of Crépy see "Recueil de Traités."

† The place of Sténay had been surrendered by the late Duke of Lorraine to France, and this was considered by the Emperor to be an infringement of the feudal rights of the empire over this portion of the Duke's dominions. The town was therefore to revert to Lorraine by the treaty though according to the text it does not appear that this could be exacted until the territory to be ceded by Charles to the bride of the Duke of Orleans had been transferred to the latter. When this was done, also, the Piedmontese territory occupied by the French was to be restored to the Duke of Savoy.

1545.
N.D.
Feb. (?)
Vienna
Imp. Arch

19. CHAPUYS and VAN DER DELFT to the QUEEN DOWAGER.

Since our arrival here we have received several letters from your Majesty concerning the assaults, pillage and violence committed by the English upon his Majesty's subjects, in the neighbourhoood of Arras and upon sailors from Nieuport, Dunkirk, and Ostend. Upon these and innumerable other complaints, and also upon the daily seizure of ships, we have addressed full remonstrances to the Council, and demanded redress. Up to the present we have obtained no satisfaction. We were expecting a definite reply yesterday, when we were informed by the Council that orders had been sent to the admiral to enquire into the matter, and to adopt such measures as he found necessary. No prompt decision can be expected from him; and it is very certain that if no other step but this be taken, his Majesty's subjects will suffer notable injury. The only reply sent to us with regard to the Arras* complaint is that it shall be considered.

London, N.D.

8 March
Vienna
Imp. Arch

THE QUEEN REGENT to CHAPUYS and VAN DER DELFT.

This is to inform you that Secretary Paget arrived here on the 27th ultimo. After stating his mission, and complaining bitterly of the seizures of English persons and property here, he requested the Emperor to raise the embargoes; having regard, as he said, to the fact that the King had entirely released everything seized in England, although he maintained that the merchandise embargoed there was legally stopped, not as belonging to the Emperor's subjects, but as the property of Frenchmen.

He also requested the Emperor to declare war against the French, in accordance with the treaty of alliance.

The Emperor† caused the answer to his demands to be communicated to him (Paget) in the presence of the resident ambassador, Nicholas Wotton; and pointed out to them the urgent reasons which had dictated the seizures, the object not being to injure Englishmen, but to avoid greater troubles. The Emperor had not refused to raise the embargoes, if they (the English) would begin by doing the same; and of their having done so he had received no news. All that he had learnt was that 150 lasts of herrings had been released, and 50 lasts of pitch and tar; which was not by any means all that had been embargoed. On the contrary, there was a great quantity of property still detained at Boulogne and Calais; and fresh complaints were constantly reaching us of new seizures being made every day by the English of ships and goods belonging to the Emperor's subjects. Besides all this, some ships equipped in Zeeland to carry Spanish infantry to Spain had

---

* That is to say the complaint of the Emperor's subjects on the Flemish border near Arras at the incursions and outrages committed upon them by the soldiery in the English service in France.

† The Emperor was in Brussels at the time, having been ill of gout there since his arrival on the 1st February. He was "following a regimen of Indian wood" for the cure of his malady until 15th March.

been stopped*; and these his Majesty wished released without loss to him.

With regard to the declaration against France, the causes which exempted his Majesty from the obligation of acceding to their request had already been fully explained to the Earl of Hertford and the Bishop of Winchester, and there was no need to repeat them. Even if the Emperor were bound to make this declaration under the treaty there were several grave reasons why it was inconvenient at the present season to enter anew into war with France; and the Emperor was under the impression that the King, their master, had been convinced and satisfied in this respect, as he had reason to be.

Secretary Paget appeared downcast at so strong a reply being given to his demand; and cried out that his master had entered into the war at the instance, and for the advantage, of the Emperor; and that now he was deserted and left alone, without help or support. Since the treaty of peace with France had been signed no attempt, he said, had been made to bring about peace for him. Even when the Bishop of Arras and other ambassadors were present at Calais at the time that the negotiations were being carried on with Cardinal de Bellay, they had made no effort to smooth matters between France and England.† With regard to the seizures, he, Paget, maintained that the King had good reason to seize victuals that were being carried to his enemy; and although it could be proved that the owners were French, he (the King) had released everything, and consequently it was only right that the embargo should be raised on this side.

On the point of the declaration (against France) he, Paget, and all his colleagues on the Council held it as notorious and unquestionable that the Emperor was bound to make the declaration. The reasons alleged by his Majesty which made it at present inconvenient to do so, had, so far as he was aware, never yet been set forth. The Emperor's commissioners replied that it was perfectly well-known that his Majesty was not bound to make the declaration; for the reasons already stated on other occasions; and if the matter were pressed and a definite answer demanded, these reasons would again be set forth so plainly that everyone would acknowledge that his Majesty was free from any obligation. With regard to the considerations which rendered it unadvisable for his Majesty to make the declaration, even if he were bound to do so by treaty, they were so evident, and had been alleged so often, that there was no need to insist upon them. Nevertheless, in order to satisfy the Secretary (Paget) two of these considerations might be mentioned to him. First; did he consider it reasonable, after his Majesty had made a treaty with France, that he should forthwith break it again; and whether, if he did so, the Emperor would not suffer in reputation before the world? Secondly; since news comes from all sides of an intended descent of the Turk next season, whether it is

---

* The whole story of the detention of the Spanish infantry and its taking service under the English flag is told in the Spanish Chronicle of Henry VIII., edited by the present writer.

† See details of these negotiations in Vol. VII. of this Calendar.

1545.

not more fitting for Christian princes to seek peace with each other than to re-open war: and whether the Germans would not have good cause for resentment if they were deprived of the aid against the Turk promised by the King of France. His Majesty had done no small favour to the King of England by stipulating for the employment of French forces against the Turk, and thus diverting them. Since, however, a definite answer to the request was demanded by England, his Majesty would consider it, and give such a justification of his action as would put put him right with the King.

The Secretary (Paget) then declared that he only asked for a definite reply in the matter of the seizures. The reasons alleged for deferring the declaration against France were weighty: and he would refrain from discussing them. But he sincerely hoped that he would be able to carry back with him a favourable answer. Otherwise he would be the most unhappy man in the world: for he had always favoured the Emperor's party.

The Emperor having received a report of the above conversation, decided to give the reply, of which a copy is enclosed herewith, referring only to the question of the seizures. This reply was repeated to the (English) ambassadors on the 4th instant and Paget was very much dissatisfied with it. After much discussion on both sides, Paget begged that a more favourable reply should be given. On consideration, his Majesty decided to adhere to this reply, and by his orders we repeated it to Paget in the presence of the two English ambassadors here[*]. Paget again remonstrated, but finally seeing that he could get nothing further, he advanced as if of his own accord certain expedients in the interests of a settlement. If, he said, his Majesty would release everything seized the King would do the same: and with regard to the old disputed claims of those who alleged illegal seizures in England, such as the Burgos merchants and Jasper Doulchy and others, a day could be fixed for hearing the cases, commissioners could be appointed by both princes, and restitution should be effected according to their decision.

With respect to the measures for the future, the King of England would undertake to allow Netherlanders to frequent France, on condition that they did not carry victuals or munitions of war, pending such time as the question of the declaration of the Emperor against France remained undecided.

These expedients having been considered by the Emperor, who did not desire to reject them entirely, the ambassadors were informed that his Majesty would be willing to come to an understanding on this basis, if he had the prior assurance from the King, or from Paget in his name, that they would be confirmed. Paget was at first quite shocked at this; saying that he had not brought forward these expedients officially, but simply as suggestions of his own, and he could not enter into negotiations upon them. His mission was to beg for a reply with regard to the release of the seizures. After much discussion, however, he finally consented to listen to

---

[*] Dr Nicholas Wotton accredited to the Emperor, and Dr. Layton accredited to the Queen Dowager of Hungary, Regent of the Netherlands.

1545.

what was to be said about his suggestions, but without binding himself in any way. The Emperor's commissioners had put in writing the conditions which seemed necessary for the acceptance of Paget's suggestions, and exhibited a copy to Paget (copy of which writing is also adjoined) at whose request a copy was handed to him on the understanding that the writing was not authorised by the Emperor or binding, but was only a suggestion made by the Commissioners.

During these discussions a secretary named David Paniter arrived here from Scotland bringing letters of credence to us, in virtue whereof he set forth the ancient friendship that had existed unbroken between Scotland and the Netherlands for 150 years. Scotland, he said, had given no reason now for breaking this amity, but the efforts of their old enemy had caused his Majesty last year to declare against the Scots, who wished to remain friendly with him. The envoy begged us to obtain for him audience of the Emperor, and to use our influence in favour of the continuance of friendly and neighbourly relations.

The (English) ambassadors were at once informed of this. The Emperor, they were told, had no quarrel with the Scots; and was at war with them solely at the instance of the King of England. He wished therefore the ambassadors to consider what answer could be given to the Scottish envoy, since his Majesty did not intend to deal with Scotland, except jointly with the King of England.

The ambassadors tried several times to get out of it, on the ground that they had no instructions; but at last said that, in their opinion, the envoy might be told that the Scots would do well to come to terms with the King of England. When they (the Scots) had done this, they would be reconciled with the Emperor. The commissioners undertook to convey this advice to his Majesty.

As Secretary Paget had remarked that no favour had been shown to his master since the signature of the treaty of peace with France, with the object of bringing about peace for England as well, the imperial commissioners said, as if of their own accord and in the interest of friendship, that his Majesty desired nothing better than that the King of England should also be at peace. The only reason why he had not hitherto made any move in that direction, was that he did not wish to meddle beyond what was agreeable to the King. But as soon as his Majesty thought that his intervention would be acceptable, he would willingly offer it. They (i.e. the ambassadors and Paget) could consider whether the coming of this Scottish envoy might not offer an opportunity for setting some negotiations afoot, either for peace or a truce, without giving any indication that they originated with the King of England. It so, the imperial commissioners offered their good offices in the matter. The English ambassadors thanked them and promised to consider it; subsequently asking for a further delay, until they could communicate to the King the writing (i.e. about the seizures) already referred to. They begged that you (i.e. Chapuys and Van der Delft) should not be informed of their negotiations until they received a reply from England. They sent off their special courier to-day; but as it is possible that they may have sent him for other purposes than those avowed, we

1545.

have thought well to advise you precisely, so that you may watch closely what goes on there, and see whether anything further is attempted, either in the way of holding the seizures more strictly, or effecting new ones: informing us with all diligence, but without appearing to know anything about Paget's negotiations here, unless you consider necessary.

Brussels, 8 March, 1545.

21. A report to the EMPEROR of what passed with SECRETARY PAGET on the 2nd March, 1545.

First he declared that he had been sent about the release of the property seized here, since the King had already released all ships and merchandise that had been arrested in England, notwithstanding that the arrests had been made for good reasons, the property really belonging to Frenchmen, and not to his Majesty's subjects, as he could prove by means of some of the richest merchants in Antwerp. The second object of his mission was to obtain the declaration against France, in accordance with the treaty, the delay claimed by his Majesty having long ago expired.*

He (Paget) was informed that the Emperor had already set forth to the Earl of Hertford and the Bishop of Winchester the reasons why his Majesty was not obliged to make the declaration; and even if it were otherwise, public affairs rendered it unadvisable to make such declaration, and this should be accepted as a sufficient excuse. With regard to the seizures, the Emperor had not been able to avoid complying with the clamour of his subjects. The allegation that the property belonged to Frenchmen was highly improbable, as it had been shipped here or owned by his Majesty's subjects. If fraud was discovered, there was no desire to shelter French property, but this must not be taken as an excuse for detaining all goods from here. Nothing is more desirable than that release should be effected on both sides, and that steps should be taken to avoid such troublesome occurrences in future; but as quite recently a fresh seizure had been made (in England) of nine Biscay vessels there was no appearance of a cessation of the seizures on the part of the English. On the point of the declaration against France, the Secretary (Paget) replied that, according to the treaty, it was notorious that the Emperor was bound to make it; and as for the suggestion that, even if that were so there were certain considerations which should cause the King to refrain from pressing the point, he (Paget) had never been informed what those considerations were.

With respect to the seizures, the treaty provided that in the case of a seizure being effected by one party, the other should not adopt reprisals, but that the matter should be settled by an arbitration court held for the purpose. Besides this, it would be shown that the goods seized really belonged to Frenchmen, and that the ships were consequently good captures by law, as laid down by the Vice Admiral of Flanders in a similar case, where victuals were being conveyed to the French, then their enemies, and the ships

---

* That is to say the ten weeks taken by Charles in which to give his final reply to the demand presented by Seymour and Gardiner.

1545.

were seized and held to be legal captures. Nevertheless, the King, in order to preserve friendship, had released everything, and promised in future to do all that was necessary; for which reason he requested a similar release of the seizures on this side. In future when anything of the same sort occurred it should be settled not against the treaty by reprisals, but by special joint arbitration, as stipulated. As to the fresh arrests alleged, he was unable to speak; but it might be that the King had detained the ships not as prizes, but for the purpose of himself making use of them in the war.

Paget then confidentially, and as a constant partisan of the Emperor, went on to say that all English subjects lamented that so much favour was shown to the French here, whilst it seemed that Englishmen were ill treated and abused. It appeared to him that since the peace no effort whatever had been exerted here to help them (the English) to obtain a favourable peace also; and he begged the imperial commissioners to bear this in mind, and do their best in the interest of the maintenance of friendship.

The Commissioners replied in the first place, that since the peace with France, there had been no cessation of effort to favour the English in every possible way. With this object it had been forbidden to convey food to the French camp from the Emperor's dominions, whilst food had been supplied to the English troops. The French had always been informed that it was intended to observe the treaty with England; and nothing had been permitted in infraction of that treaty. His Majesty desired nothing better than that they (the English) should be as completely at peace with France as he now was, but he had not meddled because he did not wish to go further than was agreeable to the King of England. So far as concerned the maintenance of friendship, the Commissioners promised their best offices, as they knew the Emperor wished the same.

Touching the declaration demanded against France, it was held to be unquestionable that his Majesty was not bound thereto, for the reasons stated to the Earl of Hertford and the Bishop of Winchester, which there was no need to repeat. The considerations which should make the King refrain from pressing the point had also been set forth, and had doubtless been conveyed to the King by the Ambassadors of the Emperor. Nevertheless, as Paget stated that he had not heard them, and asked for a definite reply, some of these considerations would be repeated to him.

First: the demand was made about two months after the peace with France was signed; and it was neither reasonable nor honest to break a treaty so suddenly. To do so would be unworthy of the Emperor.

Secondly: the Emperor had been moved to make this peace in the hope of bringing about a pacification of all Christendom, in order to resist the invasion of the Turk; as since last year it was known that preparations were being made for a Turkish descent upon Germany; and adequate resistance would have been impossible if the Emperor had remained at war with France; in addition to which the promised assistance of the King of France against the Turk would have been lost. For this reason the peace was so popular in Germany. His Majesty, moreover, had by this stipulation not only provided for the general interests of Christendom, but had also greatly benefited the King of England by diverting the French forces.

In the matter of the seizures, we had learnt that the vessels (in England) had been released, and the same had been done on this side. The merchandise, however, had been only partially released; and above all new seizures had been effected, which could not be excused on the ground that the King wished to employ the ships, because these vessels were loaded here for the voyage to Biscay, and were merely passing the English coast. It would have been a different thing if the ships had either loaded or discharged in England. To avoid such annoyances for the future some arrangements must be made, as well as redressing the present case.

The Secretary (Paget) finally declared that he had not demanded a definite reply in the matter of the declaration against France; but only with regard to the raising of the arrests. The considerations which had been alleged for not making the declaration were weighty, and he would not discuss them. He did not quite understand what was meant by making arrangements for the future; because if the declaration was made against France there was no need for providing for the future, since relations (*i.e.* between France and the Emperor's dominions) would cease. Perchance the meaning was that some arrangement other than the special arbitration courts might be made (*i.e.* to avoid future trouble in the matter of seizures) for the period during which the Emperor was considering about the declaration. The reply given to this was, that there was no intention to refer to the period during which the Emperor considered about the declaration; but it was desired to know what were the views of the King of England on the point of whether the subjects of the Emperor should frequent France or not; as your Majesty's decision would be guided by his answer. With regard also to the special arbitration courts, it was desirable to know the details of the procedure proposed. The Secretary (Paget) replied that he had no instructions as to future regulations; and it would be advisable to communicate with the King. The Commissioners undertook to report all this to the Emperor.

8 March.
Vienna
Imp. Arch.

22. Note of the EMPEROR'S reply to PAGET'S representations respecting the seizures of merchandise.

The Emperor having considered the report of the communications with Sir William Paget, councillor and first secretary to the King of England, his good brother and perpetual ally; and having maturely weighed all the arguments alleged on both sides in the matter of raising the embargo placed upon English property here, has ordered the following reply to be given to the secretary. The Emperor's object in ordering the seizures was not in the slightest degree to injure or ill treat English subjects, whose presence in his dominions he welcomes, and whom he desires to treat with all favour, as they have been treated for many years past; but solely

1545.

to satisfy the clamour of his subjects, who complained unceasingly of the ill-treatment, pillage and oppression, suffered by them at the hands of the English since the conclusion of the recent treaty with France; and declared that they would prefer to be considered openly as enemies, in which case they could take steps for their defence, and would be on their guard, rather than be thus despoiled and outraged, without being able to protect themselves, out of respect for his Majesty, who had ordered them strictly to observe friendship and good neighbourship towards the subjects of the King. They alleged that, not only were they seized in England itself, but the poor fishermen out at sea were despoiled of everything they had by the English ships of war.

The merchant ships also sailing to France or Spain have been obliged to enter English ports, and the men on board have there been pillaged, not only of all their cargoes but also of their ships' furniture and stores, and even of their own clothes and money. Out of pure poverty and need, therefore, they have been obliged to abandon everything and take to flight.

Our said subjects alleged that the King of England's officers were not content with seizing a ship here and there, but seized every ship they met at sea, and our subjects begged for permission to adopt reprisals. In view of difficulties which this would have brought about, his Majesty, to satisfy his subjects, was constrained to decree the seizure of the persons and property of English merchants here. But this was done with such moderation and civility that no one had cause to complain; since no merchandise was moved, but simply placed under embargo where it was, and no loss was suffered except for the time being. On the other hand, the Emperor's subjects not only suffered in this way, but incurred enormous losses by being forced to discharge in England, and sell at a vile price, the cargoes which they had consigned to France and Spain; added to which their property was seized, and to a large extent sold, in their absence, and against their will.

As soon as the seizures were decreed here his Majesty informed the English merchants that the only reason for the measure was that already referred to: and that as soon as the property of his subjects was released in England, a similar release would be effected here. A message to the same effect was sent by him to the King by M. Tourquoyn.

After this an undertaking was made to release the property on both sides, but the conditions were such that the Emperor's subjects were in no sense satisfied; and were still unable to obtain restitution of their property.

Notwithstanding this, as soon as his Majesty was informed that the Flemish ships had been released, he ordered a similar release of all English ships and sailors here. His Majesty, however, is still without intelligence that all his subjects' property has been fully restored; although his ambassadors have written that a certain quantity of herrings have been released and sold in England, and also some pitch. No mention, however, is made of the herrings and other merchandise which had already been sold before the order of release was given; nor of the property seized off Calais and

Boulogne, for which the Emperor's subjects allege that they can obtain no redress whatever.

In addition to this, his Majesty learns that the vessels which he fitted out here for the purpose of conveying a portion of his Spanish infantry to Spain, on board of which ships several gentlemen of his household, Spanish merchants and others, had loaded a great quantity of their property, for the purpose of carrying it with greater safety, have been detained in England, on the pretext that the King wished to employ these ships for the war. By this means the Spanish infantry will be obliged to remain in England; and his Majesty will be deprived of their services for the protection of his coasts against the infidel, for which purpose he was despatching them to Spain. In this case, therefore, not only are the merchants prejudiced by the detention of their goods in transit; but his Majesty himself is seriously injured by the loss of the pay of these soldiers, for which he must be indemnified for the time that their presence in Spain is hindered.

There is moreover no excuse whatever for detaining these ships in the King's service; since they were neither equipped nor destined for an English port; and though certain artillery and munitions of war were loaded on board, they were intended for delivery in Spain, and the King of England has no right to use them.

For these reasons his Majesty would have ample grounds to continue the embargo here; but in order to please the King of England, he is willing, fully and completely, to release all the property detained here, against good cautionary security that a similar release will be effected of all ships and property belonging to his subjects detained in the possessions of the King of England, on both sides of the Channel, and that the owners of the merchandise already sold shall be indemnified. In addition to this, the King of England must undertake to restore the ships which carried the infantry, in the same state and condition in which they were when they entered an English port; and place them on the high sea, in order that they may proceed on their voyage to Spain, as his Majesty ordered them to do; the King of England not retaining either men, goods, artillery or munitions. The said cautionary security shall be held until the Burgos merchants have been satisfied in their claims, and also until Jasper Doulchy's claim is settled for herrings, which he alleges were captured last year, in spite of the safe-conduct obtained by him; or otherwise until such time as representatives of the two sovereigns shall have decided upon the claims of the above-mentioned merchants and of Jasper Doulchy.

In future the King must undertake not to hinder the voyages of his Majesty's subjects to France, either directly or indirectly, so long as his Majesty may desire that his subjects should enjoy the effects of the peace with the King of France.

A conference is to be appointed for the consideration of complaints of subjects of both princes, in accordance with the treaty; and for the devising of such measures for the future as may be desirable in the interests of inter-communication between the peoples.

When the King of England takes steps which shall ensure to the subjects of the Emperor the enjoyment of peaceful trade in England

1545.

and elsewhere, the Emperor will undertake to preserve the subjects of England here in tranquillity and security.

The draft agreement referred to in the Queen Dowager's letter of 8th March.

In order that the embargoes, both in England and in the dominions of the Emperor, placed upon ships, merchandise and subjects, should be raised; and the loss and injury arising therefrom avoided; and also in order that subjects on both sides may in future enjoy favourable treatment as in old times, the representatives (Commis) of the Emperor and the Ambassadors of the King of England, France and Ireland, have agreed upon the following points:—

1. The two monarchs will raise all embargoes which have been placed upon persons or goods by them or their officers since the commencement of the last war. This shall be done on both sides fully and completely, in good faith and without fraud; and in the case of merchandise already sold, the owners thereof shall be recompensed for the value of the same at a reasonable price: it being, however, understood that in cases where the King or his officers allege that the property belongs to French subjects, and is consequently a legal capture, the two contracting princes will appoint Commissioners to enquire and decide upon the matter. For this purpose such Commissioners shall be furnished with ample powers, and also to enquire into and decide all other complaints of the subjects of both monarchs on either side, and to order what may be just in relation thereto. Both monarchs will undertake, as their representatives now undertake in their name, to comply with the decisions which the afore-mentioned Commissioners may agree upon. As in some cases it may be necessary to take evidence, the Commissioners may delegate their powers for this purpose, as they may consider advisable.

The King of England shall release and place in entire freedom the ships equipped in Zeeland for the purpose of conveying certain Spanish soldiers whom his Imperial Majesty is sending to Spain, and also all property and merchandise in the said ships. The King of England shall not retain in his service any of the said soldiers, either with their consent or otherwise; since those who abandon his Imperial Majesty's service are considered as rebels, and as such cannot be harboured or retained in the realm of England. In case the ships shall have sailed without the soldiers the King will provide other vessels for the conveyance of the men to Spain.*

In order to obviate for the future similar unpleasant occurrences it is mutually agreed that the subjects on either side shall be at liberty to navigate freely wheresoever they will, without let or hindrance from the other. Always provided that in the case of his Majesty's subjects sailing for France (which it shall be licit for them to do, without hindrance, pending further orders) they shall not carry

---

* Reference to the writer's Spanish Chronicle of Henry VIII. will show how this stipulation was evaded by Henry; and how the Spanish Companies entered the English service.

any food, victuals, or munitions of war to be landed in France; but only such quantities of the same as may be really needful for the use of the ships themselves.

10 March.
Vienna
Imp. Arch.

23. EUSTACE CHAPUYS to Secretary JOOS BAVE.

As we have only just learnt of the pending departure of this courier, we cannot write to their Majesties (the Emperor and the Queen Regent of the Netherlands), and in default thereof I write a few lines to you to say that these people (the English) appear somewhat cooler than before in the matter of the restitution of the property detained here. They are already beginning to lament that the King, as they say, should have spent from his own pocket nearly 4,000 ducats in the matter, and the Councillors have during the last few days refused on three occasions to receive the Ambassador's (Van der Delft's) people and mine, who had gone to lodge the complaints, which had been sent to us by the Queen (Dowager of Hungary). Our people also mentioned to them the case of the farmer (censier) detained at Calais, and the Ostend complaints. The Council had already written to the Deputy of Calais about it, but no satisfaction has been obtained, and the Council has made no further move in the matter. From this it is easy to see what sort of redress will be obtained, in cases which may still remain pending after the embargo is raised on our side. The excuse the Council gives for declining to entertain fresh complaints is that the whole affair must be settled by the procedure specified by the treaty. If we liked to pay them in their own coin (rendre de tel pain souppe) we might tell them, that as they consider the seizures on our side to be an infraction of the treaty, the same procedure might be adopted in both cases.

With regard to the going of the Scottish ambassador to Flanders, respecting which the Queen (Dowager of Hungary) wrote to us, there has been no need for us to give the King any explanations about it, as he was satisfied with what his Ambassador wrote to him on the subject.

I learn that these people (the English) have sent to Brussels a Frenchman who is married and settled here, for the purpose of arranging something with Morette,* with whom he is friendly; and I am told that English Ambassadors resident there (in Brussels) are constantly visiting the French Ambassador. The King of England's people, who had gone on a foray over the Scottish border, have received a terrible thrashing. They have lost 2,000 horsemen, and one of the best and bravest of their captains, the son of the Warden of the Marches whose name I forget. They say that the Earl of Douglas was at the head of the Scots, at least the King believes so, though he (the King) in order to minimise the affair will not admit that more than 1,500 of his men fell. The fact is, however, that not one escaped death; and for the further advantage of the Scots the Englishmen dismounted to fight, so that all the English horses fell intact into the hands of the enemy. It is true that fortune

---

*Charles Solier de Morette, French ambassador to the Emperor.

1545.

somewhat softened this blow by the capture by the English, a week ago, of two Scottish ships on their voyage from France, with munitions and other valuable property. There are many Italian and Spanish captains here, and among others Gamboa* who has been made Colonel (Maestre de Campo) with 150 ducats a month pay. London, 10th March, 1545.

11 March.
Vienna
Imp. Arch.

24. CHAPUYS and VAN DER DELFT to the QUEEN DOWAGER.

We received yesterday at noon your Majesty's letter of the 8th instant, with the enclosures informing us of what had passed there between the Emperor's Commissioners and the English Ambassadors. With regard to it we have only to say that the Emperor's case was presented admirably, and we shall be greatly aided by it. For the present we will obey instructions and exhibit no knowledge of the conferences in question.

With regard to the main reason which moved your Majesty to send the special courier to us, namely the desire to know whether the English Ambassadors had sent their messenger hither for any other purpose than that which they pretended, and if peradventure there were any new seizures being made, or the previous seizures were being rendered more strict, we beg to inform your Majesty that the Ambassadors appear to have acted straightforwardly in what they have written hither. After the Councillors yesterday had read the despatch brought by Paget's man (who arrived at the same time as our courier) and had discussed it for some time, they came out of the Council Chamber gayer and in better spirits than they had been for a long while. They shortly afterwards sent the Secretary of the Council to tell us that the King had heard that his Majesty raised some difficulty about his (Henry's) retaining in his service the returning Spanish soldiers; and in order to learn the Emperor's final decision on this point, he (the King) had sent a special post five or six days ago; his intention being to dismiss all these soldiers if the Emperor so wished it, as he did not desire to displease his Majesty in this, or in anything else. As it would be difficult for the soldiers to find means of transport, if the vessels in which they came were to set sail, he (the King) begged very earnestly that we would do him the favour of sending one of our men, in company with one of his officers, to the commanders of the ships, to inform them of the position, and to beseech them, if it was in any way possible, to await the Emperor's reply, and to re-embark the soldiers if his Majesty desired it. The King would, he said, be happy to defray the expense which might be incurred by the delay. Not only did the King desire that our man should be sent for the purpose referred to, but also that he might bear witness that the said ships had not been seized, and that by his (the King's) orders, all good treatment was being extended to them. We thought best not to refuse to send the man as the King

---

*Pedro de Gamboa, who distinguished himself greatly and was knighted by Somerset at the battle of Pinkie. He was murdered by one of his compatriots in St. Sepulchre's churchyard outside Newgate in January, 1550. (*See* Spanish Chronicle of Henry VIII.

1545.

wished, and he left with the King's officer this morning; but we are very much afraid that, with this favourable wind blowing for their voyage, he will find that the ships have sailed. We cannot learn that any fresh seizures are being made, unless it be that of a ship loaded in Lisbon by one Antonio de la Torre, which the English assert that they found abandoned and derelict off Dieppe; and it is therefore held by the Council to be a good prize, both because it had been abandoned, and because it was a French ship. In order to justify this, the Council sent us to-day certain letters and documents found in the ship, which letters, etc., we have not yet had time to examine. The Council also sends us word that, when we have leisure to consider the matter, they will make us judges of it. We observe no appearance, either, of any increase of stringency in the old seizures. On the contrary, there seems a desire to make absolute and complete restitution; although a day or two ago there appeared a little less zeal about it; as they (the English Council) seemed very much annoyed at the complaints we made to them by your Majesty's orders in the matter of the farmer (censier) seized at Calais, and the sailors taken belonging to Ostend and Antwerp. They (the Council) have not yet sent us any reply to these complaints, although we have twice requested them to do so. As the matter, however, is of small importance and not pressing, we have not thought necessary to be too importunate about it; especially as they say they are busy and the result of Paget's mission is still pending. Paget has acted very well hitherto, and we believe that these people will do their best to complete the restitution, even with the security demanded.

We are of opinion that, no matter what the ostensible object may be, the real purpose of Paget's mission is to open up some negotiation for peace. We judge this from several things said by the Secretary of the Council, who came to us yesterday on the above-mentioned matters with more amiability and apparent pleasure than ever before, and told us that he had no doubt that these warlike affairs would very soon have a favourable issue. Paget is probably authorised to initiate this. Peace is certainly extremely necessary for Christendom at large, but more especially for this country, which is wondrously oppressed; and will be so to an insupportable degree if it has to sustain a long war, both on account of the excessive exactions it will have to pay and of the scarcity of food.

With regard to the arrival of the Scottish Secretary there, as mentioned in your Majesty's letters of 23 February (8 March?) this King (i.e. of England) was already satisfied about it by the advices which reached him through his ambassador Wotton; and he will be the more pleased at the intelligence of the way in which Paget has been dealt with in the matter. No further explanations therefore need be given to him.

Although it is quite unnecessary to add anything to the note handed (i.e. in Brussels) to the English ministers, yet as your Majesty orders us to give our humble opinion, we venture to say that we think the first clause ought to express more specifically than it does what is meant by the words "since the commencement of the last war"; whether since the King of France commenced war

1545.

against the Emperor, or only since the latter and the King of England jointly waged war against the King of France. If the former is meant the Burgos merchants' claims and the jewels will be comprised, but not otherwise. Under correction, we think that in such case, these affairs and that of Doulchy ought not to be submitted to a joint arbitration court (diette) as the facts are notorious, and the parties have already lost heavily by the delay. The reference to a joint arbitration court (diette) would enormously extend this delay, as the procedure is extremely dilatory: besides which the cases are important, and there is a great deal of feeling here about them; so that not a person in England, whatever his powers are, would dare for his life's sake to decide otherwise than in favour of the King's contention. To the King alone, therefore, should the demand for redress be made; and the same may be said in the case of the jewels, as this depends upon the declaration that he (the King) must make respecting the passport he granted. It will be advisable for the representatives of these three claims therefore to be here; as otherwise we think there will be no conclusion reached in the joint arbitration court; as little, indeed, as the result obtained by the one held about three years ago at Calais and Bourbourg, for the purpose of improving intercourse. This is even more necessary now, in consequence of the various innovations introduced by the English. Under correction, also, we think that mutual indemnity for subjects on both sides might be stipulated for, in order that claimants might not be forced to waste time and money. The monarchs should be bound to make good the damage committed by their respective armed forces—even those at sea—upon the subjects of the other: the ground for this being that the monarch ought only to entrust force to well conducted persons; and that the captain of a ship who injures others should be punished, or at least dismissed from his command. It might also be stipulated that neither of the princes should equip (ships?) without giving sufficient security not to offend the subjects of the other; so that a more prompt redress might be obtainable, without scouring the sea in search of the evil doer.

London, 11 March, 1545.

12 March.
Vienna
Imp. Arch.

25. CHAPUYS and VAN DER DELFT to the QUEEN DOWAGER.

After we had closed the letters written yesterday, and were about to dispatch the courier, the Secretary of the Council came to tell us that this morning at eight the Earl of Hertford and the Bishop of Winchester would come and communicate something to us. We therefore detained the courier until we had heard what they had to say. They came as appointed, and began by thanking us for having sent our man to the ships that had brought the Spanish soldiers; after which, they said, they were instructed to inform us of all that had taken place respecting the said soldiers. For this purpose they had brought with them, by the King's orders, a gentleman of his chamber named Master Philip Aubyn, who, in the King's justification and his own, gave us to understand that the King, having heard that the ships had arrived in the Downs short of provisions, and

1545.

that there was some talk of the soldiers wishing to leave the vessels and enter his service, had sent Aubyn to give orders in the ports of the West that the ships were to be welcomed and well treated. When Aubyn arrived at Plymouth he had found there one of the ships that had separated from the others, and had run aground near the harbour. He did his best to get the ship into a condition to sail after the others, which she did, and Aubyn then proceeded to Falmouth, where he found the rest of the vessels and soldiers. The latter were dying in numbers daily, both on account of the travail of the sea, and more especially by reason of the hardship and absence of food. In accordance with the King's orders, he (Aubyn) had caused the people of the country to treat them kindly, and to lodge in their houses those who were ill. He had said nothing to the soldiers but to express his pleasure at the good friendship existing between the Emperor and the King of England, who hearing of their need had sent him to succour them and help them on their way; and also to give them some money, if peradventure any one or two of them wished to enter his service. This led the soldiers to declare to him the misery and need in which they were. The provisions that had been brought on board the ships were all consumed, and they (the soldiers) had even spent the fortnight's wage that had been given to them to pay their way from the Spanish port to their homes. They had, they said, been dismissed, with leave to return to their own houses, and without any obligation to go to any other place in the Emperor's service. Upon this, Madame, we greatly extolled this good and kindly action of the King, begging the Earl of Hertford and the Bishop of Winchester to thank his Majesty in our names; and to assure him that we would convey to the Emperor the intelligence of his goodness; for which, we were sure, his imperial Majesty would feel obliged, and if opportunity offered would reciprocate. The Earl of Hertford then went on to say—as he affirmed entirely on his own account, and without instruction from the King—that when he was last at Boulogne and Calais, and more recently in London, he had heard from people coming from France, and even from Italians who were passing over constantly, that the King of France had in his service over 400 Spaniards. Since the Emperor allowed this to the Christian King, with much greater reason should he give a similar privilege to the King of England, and allow him to retain such of these Spanish soldiers as were willing to enter his service; especially having regard to the terms of the treaty existing between the Emperor and the King of England.

We replied, also unofficially, that in truth, we also had heard that there were a certain number of Spanish soldiers in France; but a much smaller number than they said: but they (*i.e.* the English Councillors) must surely have heard that most of these soldiers, who had been on their way home through France, had been absolutely obliged by sickness to remain there. The King of France had acted very kindly towards them, sheltering them in Paris and elsewhere, and having them cured of their ills, the soldiers could not avoid without ingratitude entering into his service. They must also bear in mind that the greater number of the soldiers who remained in France were such as his Majesty (the

1545.

Emperor) did not care to retain in his service; and, moreover, when he dismissed them, he did not expect to require so many troops for the defence of Spain, as his Majesty had not then learnt for certain either of the surprise of Los Gelves by the Turks, or of the preparations being made by Barbarossa, of which news now came from all sides. As a consequence of this, the Emperor will have to provide for the defence of La Goletta, and his other fortresses in Barbary, as well as for Sicily, Sardinia, Majorca, Minorca, and other islands, and all the seaboard of Spain. They (the English Councillors) replied that there was no indication that the soldiers in question were being sent to Spain for any such purpose; since they were not consigned to any particular place on his Majesty's service, but were simply going to their homes; but we answered that soldiers in want of money said all manner of things to get themselves out of their need; and his Majesty's word must be taken before theirs. If, however, what they said was true, and they were on the way to their own homes; it was simply that his Majesty could not decide where he needed to employ them, until the enemy's designs were known, when he would use them where they might be wanted. They (the English Councillors) surely could not think that the Emperor was so bad a manager as to pay wages before he wanted the men. If he sent men home it was in order that they might be ready at his call for service when needed. Even if, as they alleged, the treaty allowed the King to engage subjects of the Emperor for his service, it was of course understood to mean only in case the Emperor did not require them for his own purposes; and certainly did not authorise the taking of men whom the Emperor had specially retained and assembled, as in this case. They had seen that, since he made peace with France, the Emperor had raised no objection at all to the King's retaining Spaniards in his service, and had instructed M. de Buren to remain as long as the King wished.° We felt sure that the Emperor would greatly prefer the Spaniards that are in the French service to be on the side of the English; though his Majesty could not well recall them, as the treaty with France did not enable him to recall rebels as the treaty with England did.

Hertford and the Bishop made no reply to this, and only remarked that, if such were the case, the King had no wish to do otherwise than he had sent them to say, namely, to conform entirely to the wishes of the Emperor in the matter: but still they might tell us that the King would have good reason to be offended, if it was seen subsequently that these soldiers were not being sent to Spain for the purposes alleged. We said we could only hope to God that the need for thus employing them in the Emperor's service might not arise; and we thought that the King would rejoice if the enemy of the faith refrained from making an attack which would necessitate resistance. The King's wisdom, we said, would show him that, in view of the current rumours about the Turk, the Emperor could not avoid making timely provisions for defence.

° That is to say the small Spanish contingent that had entered Henry's service for the French war.

1545.

Hertford and Winchester then informed us that yesterday the King had told them that a letter had reached him from Paget, saying that the Council in Flanders had positively assured him, that when they (Hertford and Winchester) went to the Emperor to request the declaration against France, they were utterly unable to answer the arguments opposed to them, and would have given way on every point if they had had powers to do so. Hertford and Winchester felt that this was charging them, not only with ignorance, but also with being bad and unfaithful ministers. For their own part, they said, they thought they had justified the demand they had made to his Majesty, and had sufficiently replied to all the objections which had been urged against it. They felt certain from the answer given to them in his lodging by M. de Granvelle, and afterwards in the presence of the Emperor, that the latter would not fail to make the declaration after the expiry of the ten weeks which he took to consider the matter.

We replied that, if any member of the Flemish Council had said what they alleged, we thought it was not by the order, or with the knowledge, of his Majesty, who had instructed us to lay all the arguments before the King; not doubting that the latter, as a good and prudent prince, would see the reason of our contention more readily than they (Hertford and Winchester) had done. No doubt Paget must have mistaken what was said, as he does not understand French very well. Perhaps what was really said was, that such a reply was given to them as ought to have satisfied them; and the opinion expressed that they might have admitted that they were satisfied if they had had power to do so.

The Bishop of Winchester then began the old contentions about the declaration; dwelling mainly upon the point that, as the King of France was generally bound in the treaty of peace to respect the treaty of friendship between the Emperor and the King of England by reason of the special reservation contained in the former treaty, it could not be urged that he had not violated the treaty, both by the attempt of the Dauphin on Boulogne, and by Cardinal du Bellay's statement during the negotiations in which M. d'Arras and I (Chapuys) took part, to the effect that he would enter into no peace negotiations until Boulogne was surrendered; whereas the treaty of friendship provided that that town should come into the hands of the English. We replied to this, as we have done on other occasions, that they could not allege rights under the treaty of peace which they refused to recognise. With regard to the clause inserted by the King of England in the treaty of friendship, to the effect that he was to have Boulogne to hold as security for the future payment of the pensions, they had only to look at the treaty to see that the King could only claim this in case the King of France submitted at the first demand. If he refused to do so (as he did), the King of England was to have Guyenne and Normandy; and it would be a very strange contention to say that the King of France was bound by his treaty of peace to accept the treaty of friendship in this particular, or any other point opposed to the tenour of the peace treaty itself. With regard to the wording of the clause in the treaty of friendship by which the

1545.

Emperor bound himself not to treat for peace until the King of England was satisfied: apart from the fact that they could not invoke the treaty for the reasons already explained, the point would not help them much if they bore in mind the alternative, which they omitted to quote, namely, "without the consent of the King." There was no ground for them to question that such consent had been given freely and fully by the King. It did not rest alone upon the word of M. d'Arras; for M. de Courrières and I also bore witness to it. The contention of the Earl of Hertford, that the word of the King must be taken before that of M. d'Arras, because the report of the latter (to the Emperor) bore every indication of being worded to please and serve his sovereign, was absolutely groundless and unreasonable; since M. d'Arras and the others who were present claimed nothing by virtue of the report, and would indeed be wretches thus to burden their consciences, without the slightest profit or object. The probability was quite the other way.

They (Hertford and Winchester) then went on to say that it seemed incredible that the Emperor, after having advanced triumphantly so far into France, should have been forced to accept peace; and that the alleged necessity was simply a pretext. We replied that if they recollected the mission entrusted to M. d'Arras they would acknowledge that the Emperor had no desire to enter into the peace, if the King (of England), on his side, had carried out the terms of his engagements. It was perfectly true that the Emperor had made the most exhausting efforts, as had been set forth by M. d'Arras; and we were astounded that they should assert that his Majesty was not in need to accept the peace; seeing that he had obtained nothing for himself by it. He had, indeed, done more for the advantage of the King (of England) than for his own, as had been demonstrated to them frequently. We felt sure that if they repeated what they said in the presence of the King he would contradict them. The Bishop of Winchester let slip a thing which we must not fail to report. He said that before M. d'Arras returned to the Emperor peace had been made.[*] We refuted this sharply, and requested him to refrain in future from saying such things, as they were neither handsome nor honest, and could not be tolerated, being untrue and injurious to the honour of the Emperor. He tried to excuse and explain away what he had said, but he did it so ineffectually as not to satisfy even the Earl of Hertford, who begged him to keep clear of such matters.

We repeated also to them what we had formerly said to Paget; namely that, as the King had consented to the amity between the Emperor and the King of France, with whom he (the King of England) remained at war; and whose enmity therefore did not increase thereafter but continued the same, there was no ground for asking the Emperor to declare war anew, as no fresh fact had occurred since. There is not very much importance in this argument; but the only answer they could make to it was, that by the same rule his Majesty might have revoked the declaration against

---

[*] This was unquestionably true (See Vol. VII. of this Calendar) although the documents do not appear to have been actually signed until a day or two after Arras met the Emperor.

1545.

Scotland; whereas the continuance by him of the state of war with the Scots proved the continued validity of the treaty of friendship, and the same course should have been followed in the case of France. We replied that they must not draw any consequence to his Majesty's prejudice from his superabundant desire to please the King; besides which the two cases were entirely different, since the King had not consented to the Emperor making any peace or truce with Scotland, as he had done in the case of France. Nothing more was said and the interview ended.

At this moment the Secretary of the Council has come to inform us from the King that he had learnt that recently there had been detained at Flushing a Scottish ship which had been captured by one of his captains. The Flushing people had not only detained the ship and captain, but had used towards the latter defiant and opprobrious words, quite inconsistent with friendship and good neighbourship. He begged me to ask your Majesty to have the matter attended to, and especially to consider amongst other things how well the soldiers and ships of the Emperor had been treated in this country.

London, 12 March, 1545.

13 March.
Vienna
Imp. Arch.

26. CHAPUYS to the SECRETARY of the EMPEROR'S COUNCIL.

Knowing that all English affairs are promptly communicated to you, I have refrained from repeating them in letters addressed to you, and have consequently been debarred from the need for writing to you, though my goodwill to do so has not failed etc. Since closing the letters addressed to the Queen, I have called to mind something that I have omitted. This was that the Bishop of Winchester appeared to lay some stress upon the King's consent to the peace with France having been conditional upon his (the King's) being satisfied therewith, in accordance with the conditions which he had written to his Ambassador. We told him (the Bishop of Winchester) that there was never any question of such a reservation. Even if there had been, since the King had not sent to his Ambassador authority to treat, as we had often asked him to do, and M. d'Arras had told them (the English) that there could be no more delay or reference, they could not take their stand on it. But even beyond this, if we might say so, it could be sustained that the King had no right to allege the pretended reservation, nor the reservation which the Emperor had inserted in his treaty with France,* since he (the King of England) had declined to acknowledge or even to read the treaty itself. Thus it was that on the one hand there was no reservation in the treaty operative in the King's favour, and on the other the King's consent to the treaty was unconditional. I just write you this in confidence.

London, 13 March, 1545.

* That is to say the clause in the treaty of peace which reserved in vigour the treaty of alliance between England and the Emperor.

1545.
14 March.
Simancas
E.F. 501.

27. LICENTIATE VARGAS to FRANCISCO DE LOS COBOS.

The Pope is displaying but little goodwill. He is afraid of religious matters being dealt with at the Council (of Trent) and still more of their being discussed at the Diet (of Worms). The King of France is urging him very strongly to aid him in the war against England, and the King (of France) frankly declares that unless the 6,000 foot soldiers promised to him are forthcoming, he will confiscate all the church property in his realm. The Pope is angry and alarmed; and we may probably soon see the effects of this in his actions.

Brussels, 14 March, 1545. (*Spanish Draft.*)

15 March.
Simancas
E.F. 501.

28. THE EMPEROR to FRANCISCO DE LOS COBOS.

Thanks for the information sent respecting the sending of French captains to Bayonne and the enlistment of soldiers there. It is possible that they may be needed to fight the English; but on the other hand it may be that, notwithstanding the peace, the French have other intentions, and it would therefore be advisable to see that our frontiers are furnished with troops. There must be, however, care taken not to arouse the suspicion of the French.

Brussels, 15 March, 1545. (*Spanish Draft.*)

15 March.
Vienna
Imp. Arch.

29. CHAPUYS and VAN DER DELFT to the QUEEN DOWAGER.

In previous letters we related that a ship from Portugal loaded with merchandise belonging to certain Burgalese had been captured, the Councillors here informing us that it was found deserted and derelict, which we now understand is not true. In order to justify the capture, the Council sent us many pretty messages, and said they would let us decide the validity of the capture. They submitted to us the charter-party and other documents, which ill supported their case, but retained the principal evidence, such as the cargo book etc. Trusting in their fine promises, we were moved to write to your Majesty, saying that there was an appearance of the affair being settled honestly and promptly. We have, however, since seen that things are very different from what we expected; since the Council have declared the capture to be a good one; and have allowed the merchandise to be sold, without consenting to hear the person authorised to claim the same on account of the owners; notwithstanding that he offered to take over the goods, paying in cash the price at which they had been appraised. He also offered to pay down to the merchants who have bought the goods the profit they might make on the transaction, unless he could prove positively and promptly that the goods belonged to subjects of his Majesty. These offers have been refused, in spite of all our remonstrances and representations to the Council, and the Councillors have treated our messengers most rudely, having even gone so far as to accuse us of exceeding our duty in assisting such claims, which is a most outrageous thing. We think right to inform your Majesty of this, in order that we may not be blamed for having written as we did. To tell the truth, it is a very poor indication of future friendly relations with his Majesty's subjects, who, unless some different course is adopted here, will be great gainers if they abandon navigation altogether; for it is certain that no ship will be allowed to pass without some molestation from these people, on the pretext that it carries French property. It is well that your Majesty should know, in order that you may understand the tricks of these people, that the merchandise in question which was worth fully 8,000 ducats, was sold for less than half that sum. To make the matter worse, the capture was made by a fisherman, who has no property and gives as his sureties men of the same class as himself; so that, even if the capture be adjudged illegal the merchants will have difficulty in recovering anything. We have also to report that these people have not released a ship belonging to Jasper Doulchy, and loaded with woad owned by Doulchy and Antenori. The latter is one of the two men in whose favour your Majesty recently wrote to us. We pray your Majesty will take up this matter, in order that these merchants may be indemnified, and also that for the future these people (the English) may be restrained from committing even worse acts than this. We are in a position now for making some such arrangement, as we have in hand a sufficient counterbalance of theirs.*

London, 15 March, 1545.

19 March.
Vienna
Imp. Arch.

30. Draft reply to the points raised by PAGET on the 16th March, the reply being given to him on the 20th.

The answer given to the English Ambassadors was, that with respect to the English ship arrested at the Sluys, there was very good reason for her arrest there, since she had been embargoed at Zeeland and had evaded the embargo. Nevertheless, as the Emperor had no wish to make a point of this, he would, in consideration for the King, release the said ship; on the understanding that, if the ship in question had committed any damage to those who demanded her arrest, the master should be held responsible on giving bail. They (the Ambassadors) had asserted that she had done no damage; and consequently M. de. Praet† and his son should be instructed to release the ship.

With regard to the declaration demanded, against the French, and the request that the Emperor would say whether, apart from the question of past events, his Majesty would observe the treaty for the future; the answer given was, that his Majesty would observe it so far as he was bound to do; which he had already replied to the Earl of Hertford and the Bishop of Winchester.

Paget remarked with reference to this, that when the treaty was quoted by them to support their contentions, they were told that the Emperor was not bound by it, whilst they maintained to the contrary. If, he asked, the King had consented to the negotiations, which, however, he asserted was not the case, was the Emperor for

---

* That is to say in the English property under embargo in Flanders.
† Louis de Flandre Sieur de Praet. one of the Emperor's Council, Governor of Sluys.

HENRY VIII. 65

1545.

ever exempt from declaring against France, though he still continued at war with Scotland? The reply given to Paget was that the Emperor was exempt from making such declaration during the course of the present war, but in the event of peace being made (*i.e.*, between France and England), and a fresh war afterwards breaking out, the case would be altered. The consent given by the King was subsequently debated by Paget and he was told that if he wished to reopen that point, he had better go over all the reasons alleged by the Emperor to prove that he was not bound to make the declaration, and if he was a good servant to the Emperor he would acknowledge that there was no obligation. He thereupon swore that if he were a servant of the Emperor, he would advise him to send word to the King that there was no reason for him at present to make the declaration; but that if France continued the war, his Majesty would prove to the King (of England) that he was his friend, and would declare against France. He was told that if perchance he did give such advice he would find himself alone, and all the rest (of the Emperor's advisers) of a contrary opinion.

20 March.
Vienna
Imp. Arch.

31. MEMORANDUM of the NEGOTIATIONS* for a PEACE between FRANCE and ENGLAND, and of the DISCUSSION with the ENGLISH AMBASSADORS.

The English Ambassadors announced that they had received replies to their letters, and had instructions to answer his Majesty. First they requested that, as the King had released all the seizures on his side, the Emperor should do the like, and in this they persisted. They were willing to agree to the appointment of a joint Court of Arbitration, to adjudicate on the claims of subjects, and also to arrange the conditions upon which the Netherlanders might trade with France for the future. The King thanked the Emperor for his action with regard to the Ambassador from Scotland, and begged that the latter might be promptly dismissed, with the reply that the Emperor had declared war with Scotland at the instance of the King of England, and when the Scots made peace with the latter they would be at peace with the Emperor.

The King also thanked the Emperor for the wish he expressed that the King might be at peace, and for his Majesty's promise to strive to that end. The King prayed the Emperor to bear in mind the great advantage accruing to the common enemy of the faith, the Turk, by the continuance of the war between France and England. The King from the first had entered into the war in alliance with the Emperor, with the object of attaining more promptly a general peace; and so to present a stronger resistance to the Turk. The peace was very needful for all Christendom; but since it had been suggested that the mission of the Scottish ambassador might be used to open negotiations, the King was of opinion that matters

---

* This refers to the suggestion thrown out by the Emperor's representatives in response to Paget's hints (*see* the Queen Regent's letter of 8th March, p. 47) that the Emperor might mediate between England and France. It will be recollected that Paget had referred to London about this; and had sent thither the unofficial draft agreement for mutual restoration of property seized and arbitration of disputed claims.

1545.

should not be commenced by that means. The King thought that it would be much better that the Emperor should open negotiations himself, and the King hoped he would do so.

He suggested that a beginning might be made by bringing forward the conditions which the Ambassador Wotton had exhibited after the return of M. d'Arras; and if the French would not agree to them all, they might be induced to accept some of them. If they (the French) talked about Boulogne, the Emperor should say that, having regard to the great expense the King had incurred, not only in conquering the place, but in fortifying and holding it, he would never surrender it, for his reputation's sake, but, with God's help, hoped to hold it against any force.

No reply to this was given on the part of his Majesty; the Emperor's deputies merely repeating the three points in order to have them quite correct. After which they asked the ambassadors how the Netherlanders were to carry on their relations and trade with France pending the decision of the proposed joint arbitration court. They (the English) replied that the King could not consent to such trade being carried on, without prejudicing his case in the matter of the declaration of war which he demanded against France; but Paget was willing to undertake that the King would, during the interval in question, connive at the continuance of the trade. They finally handed us a document in draft founded upon the note handed to them by the imperial Commissioners (see page 53) by which the King agreed to release the seizures. The Commissioners took charge of it and promised to report.

The Ambassador then broached the subject of the time and place for holding the proposed joint Arbitration Conference. The imperial commissioners asked what were the King's wishes on the subject. They were told that he had not named any particular place, but they (the Ambassadors) thought that Calais would be a fit place for the meeting, and that the day might be fixed for the 1st May. They also wished to know what personages his Majesty thought of sending, so that the King might send men of a similar position.

On the evening of the same day the President of the Privy Council and M. D'eick were with Secretary Paget, and told him that they had reported to his Majesty the conversation of the morning. His Majesty had sent them to tell him, confidentially, that he had expected the King of England's reply to be such as it was, and three days ago, in conversation with the French Ambassadors he had mentioned incidentally that he wished they were at peace with England, and he would willingly aid in bringing about such a result, if he thought there was a good chance of success. The Ambassadors praised his good-will, and said that a peace would be very advantageous for Christendom at large: they would be very glad to help it forward and would not reject any approaches. The Emperor then asked them what could be done about Boulogne. and they answered that the King of France would never abandon Boulogne. The Emperor asked how therefore it was possible for him to settle affairs, if the King of France insisted upon recovering Boulogne, and the King of England insisted upon keeping it. Even if he were Solomon, he said, he could not ask them to divide

1545.

Boulogne, as Solomon had decided in the case of the disputed child.

As one of the (French) Ambassadors is shortly going back to the King, and the Emperor is now informed of Paget's message with regard to the opening of peace negociations, his Majesty thinks that the best course will be to take up the negotiations where they were discontinued. The French had replied to the King's note, but no answer had yet been given by the King of England to their representations.[*] Secretary Paget might therefore give some response to the French reply, somewhat moderating the King's original note.

As the King of France insists so positively in recovering Boulogne, and the King of England will not give it up, his Majesty had an idea that perhaps a truce might be arranged, in order to gain time for considering some means for settling about Boulogne.

Secretary Paget replied, that he had no instructions to write anything, or to moderate the King's note; but the King was willing, on condition of his keeping Boulogne, that his Majesty should see whether he could moderate the terms of the note, and the King would adhere to what the Emperor considered reasonable. He (Paget) had also no authority with regard to a truce, but in his private capacity. he might say that if his Majesty could induce the French to consent to a truce, he was of opinion that his master the King would accept it; and on his (Paget's) return he would use his influence in that direction.

On the 21st March, the next day, the President (of the Council) and M. D'eick visited the French ambassadors, and informed them that his Majesty, having thought over the conversation that he had had with them about England at their last audience, was of opinion that, in order to put an end to the war and bring about a general peace, it might be advisable to arrange a truce to gain time, during which some means might be devised for settling the question of Boulogne, one way or the other. His Majesty feared that the King (of France) might consider it hard to grant a truce which might be utilised by the English for fortifying Boulogne; but nevertheless the Emperor is so desirous of attaining a general peace, that he had authorised us (i.e., the President of the Council and M. D'eick) to tell them (the French ambassadors) the reasons why in his opinion the King of France ought to be moved to agree to the truce.

In the first place, he should consider the welfare of Christendom at large, which generally suffers from this war, and that the common enemy is greatly encouraged to invade Christendom by the war. If a truce were agreed upon it might be hoped that God would find means to attain to a good peace, and to prevent the further shedding of Christian blood.

Secondly, they (the French) should ask themselves if affairs are now propitious for besieging Boulogne, and capturing it by force, considering the lack of victuals in the neighbourhood, and that the place is very strongly fortified and amply supplied with everything necessary. And again, whether the English who hold it, are not likely to stand out obstinately to the death rather than give it up: and if, in short, there is not a very small chance of the French being able to capture it by arms.

---

[*] This refers to the negotiations of the previous year at Calais and Boulogne.

1545.

To make an attack upon England itself in order to drive the King to surrender Boulogne is fine to talk about, but the result would be very uncertain. The English would take measures to guard their country; and unless the French army occupied the whole realm it would return weaker than it went, and the King of England would become more obstinate than before. There are other hazards and perils which an army may expect, and especially a sea force, which is more exposed to accidents than is a land army.

The English, moreover, are bringing great pressure to bear upon his Majesty to help them, in accordance with the treaty, in case the King of France invades the realm or the territories included in the terms of the treaty. It will be difficult for the Emperor to avoid doing this, without breaking the treaty, which he does not wish to do, but desires to keep his promise to all parties.

It will be wise also, to bear in mind the condition of the two monarchs (*i.e.*, of France and England); the King of France being a man of strong constitution, who may live long; and when it shall please God to take him no change will occur in the State, as the Dauphin is a man capable of ruling. It is, however, quite otherwise with the King of England, who is a prince of short life, and on his death the realm will descend to a child. For many reasons the King of France may then obtain Boulogne cheaply.

In addition to this, it is reported that Ardres is in great danger from famine and pestilence, and the place may be saved by a truce. This is a very important point for the future recovery of Boulogne.

Notwithstanding all this, the Emperor has no desire to interfere in the matter beyond what may be agreeable to the King (of France); and his only motive is his anxiety to obtain a general peace.

The (French) ambassadors extolled the Emperor's kindness, but said they had no instructions on the matter. They would, however, willingly communicate to the King what had been said, and would do their best to forward such an arrangement as that suggested. On the 22nd the President of the Council and M. D'eick saw the English ambassadors, and informed them that the Emperor had considered the documents for the release of the seizures, which they had handed in; and as the period to be covered by the agreement is different from that mentioned in the draft delivered to them (*i.e.*, the English), the Emperor wishes to know how they propose to deal with the seizures effected before the period mentioned. They replied that it was not proposed to release such seizures, but to refer them for decision to the joint arbitration of representatives of the two monarchs.

It was also pointed out to them that their document undertook to release the ships fitted out in Zeeland for the conveyance of the Spanish infantry, with all the property on board of such ships; but nothing whatever was said about the soldiers, who would also have to be sent on. They replied that they did not think the Emperor would insist upon this, seeing that the ships were already released and despatched, and only about 400 soldiers had remained. Surely his Majesty would not refuse their master so small a thing as this. Besides, a portion of the troops had been sent across the Channel,

HENRY VIII.

1545.

and having deserted the (English) service were killed in France.*
The imperial commissioners would not give way on this point, but
insisted that the soldiers should be included in the agreement. The
ambassadors refused to agree to it, and said that it would be better
to leave out the whole clause, as the ships had already sailed.

They were next reminded that they had omitted from their
document the general clause for obviating difficulties for the future,
the imperial commissioners insisting that this clause must be re-
inserted. This the ambassadors refused, saying that the King
would not consent formally to the Netherlanders carrying on communications with France; although Paget agreed that the King
would connive at it. This we were willing to agree to on our side,
by means of a general clause providing that his Majesty's subjects
should be at liberty to frequent the sea without molestation; no
special mention being made of France. Paget's assurance for the
King was therefore accepted on condition of the article being worded
generally to avoid prejudice as follows: "In order to preserve and
increase the amity which has always existed between the two princes,
their respective subjects meeting each other at sea shall behave as
good friends are bound to do." This the ambassadors refused, insisting that the free navigation of the sea by the Emperor's subjects
should depend upon Paget's word, which, however, he was willing to
pledge in the presence of his Majesty and the Council.

They were then told that they had added to the clause prohibiting
the conveyance of victuals and munitions of war to France "or any
other thing serving for equipment." This was so general that the
clause would make it impossible for anything to be conveyed to
France without risk of seizure. It was already forbidden on this
side to export victuals and munitions, and it was understood that
this clause of the agreement must cover the same articles as are
comprised in his Majesty's prohibition here. It will therefore be
advisable that an understanding should be arrived as to the
merchandise to be included in the prohibition. They (the English)
consented to this without much difficulty.

Finally, with regard to the joint arbitration, they stood out for
1st May as the date, and Calais as the place of meeting; but after
they had heard the objections against the fitness of Calais, they
consented to the meeting taking place at Gravelines, Dunkirk,
Bergen, St. Omer or Bourbourg, the choice being left to them.

March.
Vienna
Imp. Arch.

32. ORIGINAL DRAFT of the ENGLISH AMENDMENT of the PROPOSED AGREEMENT between ENGLAND and the EMPEROR, referred

---

*The story of the desertion of Captain Juan de Haro and two other captains with their companies of Spaniards to the French will be found fully related in the Spanish Chronicle of Henry VIII. Haro himself and 25 of his men were killed by the English, who pursued him; but when the other deserting Spaniards met their countrymen in the English service during the truce which preceded the peace between England and France, they were so stung by the reproaches addressed to them for having deserted, that a duel was fought by captains on both sides. The English champion on the occasion was the afterwards famous Julian Romero. Colonel Gamboa's account of the desertion of the Spanish companies will be found in a letter addressed by him to the King (14th April, 1545) in the Hatfield Papers, part 1. Hist. MSS. Com.

to in the preceding memorandum, with the marginal notes added during the conference between the IMPERIAL COMMISSIONERS and the ENGLISH AMBASSADORS.*

Whereas arrest have been made both† in the realm of England and the Emperor's Netherlands, of ships, goods and merchandise of the subjects of both monarchs: and in order to avoid the injury which may result therefrom; and further in order that the subjects on both sides may hereafter be favourably treated as they were for so many years previously, the commissioners of the Emperor and the ambassadors of the King of England, France, etc., have agreed as follows:—

1. The two monarchs will immediately raise all arrests made by them or their officers of the persons, property, goods and merchandise, belonging to the subjects on both sides, since‡ the entry of the two princes and their armies into France. The release shall be full, free and in good faith, without fraud or innovation on either side; and in the case of any of the property having been sold, and being impossible of restitution, the owners shall be recompensed for the value of their property at a reasonable appraisement. It is understood that if the King or his officers claim that any of the goods are the property of Frenchmen, and consequently fair capture, the two monarchs will appoint commissioners to enquire and decide according to right and justice.

To this end the commissioners shall have full power to examine and take cognisance of§ all other complaints of subjects on either side, and to adjudicate upon the same, according to justice. The two monarchs mutually agree, and the said commissioners and ambassadors now agree on their behalf, to carry out and fulfil the decisions at which the said (arbitration) commissioners arrive.

The commissioners shall meet ‖(on the 1st May next at Calais and Gravelines, or at Gravelines and Marcke, as they may agree). The King will agree that the ships fitted out in Zeeland to convey certain Spanish soldiers to Spain shall be free to depart at their pleasure with the goods and merchandise found on board of them, without loss to his Majesty.

It is agreed that the Emperor's subjects shall not convey to France or to any enemies of the King any victuals, munitions of war or other equipments.¶

---

* Marginal note in original "Since these articles were written the marginal additions have been made."

†The following addition is written in the margin "in the realms of Spain and other territories of the Emperor, and in the realms and countries under the dominion of the King of England." The probable main object of this addition was to secure precedence for mentioning the Emperor's dominions, which, it will be noted in the English draft, were placed after those of the King of England.

‡ Marginal alteration in the original "Since the 20th June last."

§ Marginal addition in original "the complaints and claims of the merchants of Burgos in Spain who say that certain ships of theirs were seized in England and."

‖ The words in brackets are written in another hand, the draft having evidently come from England with this clause in blank, in order that Paget might settle the time and place of meeting.

¶ Marginal addition in original. "except such as may be necessary without fraud for the purposes of their own ships."

HENRY VIII.

1545.

For the preservation and increase of the amity which has always existed between the two monarchs, their respective subjects meeting at sea shall behave towards each other as good friends and allies are bound to do.

It is understood that nothing in this agreement shall be interpreted as a derogation of the already existing treaty between the two monarchs.

The above clauses having been agreed upon by us, the commissioners and ambassadors on behalf of the two sovereigns promise that they shall be duly observed and respected. Brussels, 6th April, 1545.*

24 March.
Simancas.
E.F. 501
extract.

33. LICENTIATE VARGAS to FRANCISCO DE LOS COBOS.

The health of his Majesty has improved: he intends to leave here for Antwerp on the 13th or 14th proximo and starts for Worms on the 20th.† The King of the Romans arrived at Worms on the 14th and the sittings of the Diet have begun.

Cardinals Santa Croce and Monti, who are commissioners to the Council, have arrived at Trent. The Germans, however, think that the Council will not take place, and that the Pope is only appearing to acquiesce for the look of the thing. They are confirmed in this idea by the fact that the Cardinal of England (i.e. Reginald Pole), who had been appointed one of the commissioners, has refused to accept the office, giving as his reason that he was in fear of Ludovico delle Arme, who is enlisting troops in Italy for the King of England. In order to overcome this difficulty the Pope ordered the arrest, in Bologna where he lives, of the father of Ludovico. It is expected that his Holiness will exact a large sum of money from the prisoner.

Brussels, 24 March, 1545. (*Spanish draft*).

25 March.
Simancas.
E. 69.

34. FRANCISCO DE LOS COBOS to DE GRANVELLE.

Acknowledges receipt of letters written as Granvelle was departing for the Diet (of Worms). Praises his self-sacrifice in going thither for the service of God and his Majesty. Personal compliments and good wishes. Has no remark to make as to his Majesty's decision in the matter of the alternative marriage, only to urge that it should be carried through promptly, so that the peace may be firmly established, and all occasion for suspicion banished.‡ I note what some intemperate persons are saying about the terms of peace; and Idiaquez and others had told me the same. I recognise that in the circumstances we could not avoid doing as

---

* This agreement copied fair, and signed by Schore (the President of the Council), Cornelius Scepperus, Bave, William Paget and Nicholas Wotton is also in the Imperial Archives.

† The Emperor left Brussels on the 7th April for Baren Malines and Antwerp and then at the end of April by slow stages proceeded to Germany. *See* Vandernesse's itinerary in Bradford's correspondence of Charles V.

‡ It will be seen by this that even Cobos was not informed of the Emperor's intention to avoid, if possible, the fulfilment of the conditions of peace, so far as regarded the marriage, either of his daughter or his niece with the Duke of Orleans.

1545.

we have done, or even making peace on worse terms. Hesdin does not matter much, in comparison with the rest, especially if the other Flemish and Piedmont territories are restored: seeing that his Majesty's resources are so exhausted. I can judge of the rest of his dominions from what I see here in Spain. It is very fine to grumble about the terms of peace; but they are always complaining of the war. All things considered, you may well be satisfied with what has been done, and need not trouble yourself about the murmurs of the discontented; for all those who really understand affairs, and especially those who like myself have to deal with them, and see the great necessity that exists everywhere, approve of the peace. The state of affairs here is such that no more aid can possibly be obtained. What has been got already is more than could be afforded: and having this in view, his Majesty's action should be deeply considered. Do not let them deceive themselves, for this is the very truth; and as we have reached this extremity, notwithstanding the peace, you can judge what the state of things would be if the war continued. Urgently prays that the terms of peace may be fulfilled. Seeing that I cannot do as his Majesty orders, I am in great trouble and would fain leave here, for perhaps others in my absence might do better.° I am writing to his Majesty, praying for permission to serve him elsewhere. Pray do not think I say this with any ulterior views, for in truth I have no other object but his Majesty's service.

With regard to the Duke of Alba, I have always been of opinion that nothing could be done until the decision as to the alternative marriage was arrived at, and the question of the Diet settled. If his Majesty's resolution about Milan is carried out, I think he (Alba) would go thither. He appears more willing to serve his Majesty abroad than here, either against the Turk or otherwise, as he thinks the Emperor is very short of company. He will be greatly missed here in his important office, but he is of opinion that he would be more useful with his Majesty. Granvelle's patent of Knighthood (*encomienda*) has been despatched. Congratulates Granvelle upon the Pope's intentions towards the Bishop of Arras. The dignity will be well bestowed.†—Valladolid, 25 March, 1645.

25 March.
Simancas.
E. 69

35. PRINCE PHILIP to the EMPEROR.

Received letters of 27th ultimo by Bernardino de Mendoza and 3rd instant. Congratulations on improvement of Emperor's gout, which has caused writer much anxiety. Hopes the wood water (*agua de palo*)‡ will cure it entirely, for the mere truce is not

---

° This refers to the Emperor's continued demand for fresh money to be raised in Spain. In the Cortes of Valladolid of the previous year a pitiable story of the state of the country had been told; but the members were unwillingly forced to vote the ordinary tri-annual subsidy of 300 millions of maravedis, and an additional 150 millions payable in three instalments in December 1544, June 1545 and December 1545, that is to say three years extraordinary subsidy within twelve months. (*See* Danvila y Collado. El Poder Civil en España.)

† Probably even thus early there was an idea of making Antoine de Perrenot a Cardinal.

‡ Vanderness mentions that the Emperor went through a five weeks' course of "Indian wood" for his malady.

1545.

enough. Kind regards from the Princess, who though suffering somewhat from her pregnancy, is fairly well and hopeful. Notes the decision arrived at with regard to the alternative marriages. He approves, and has never had any other object than the service of his Majesty and the general good; no personal end of his own. Earnestly prays that the resolution may really be carried out, and no ground given to the French to complain of non-compliance. It was well you deferred answer till Stenay was restored, and the captured ships surrendered. The subjects here have been begging me for redress in this latter affair; but I have referred them to your Majesty and to the ambassador in France. It will be just for you to favour these claims, for there was no excuse for seizing these ships after peace was signed. Notes with approval the Emperor's plans for resisting the Turk, who threatens Vienna, and for the subjection of the Protestants, the settlement of German questions, and the holding of the Council. Any one of these subjects is sufficient to cause anxiety, but the whole coming together is of tremendous importance. God knows how all of us here are ardently wishing and praying for success in these just and holy matters; and how ready we are to sacrifice even our blood to forward them; but for so many years past we have been seeking means in every direction that everything here is absolutely exhausted. To such extremity are we reduced that nothing can be obtained by any device. As your Majesty knows our only ways of getting money in Spain is by sale-tithes (*alcabalas*), the sale of "Crusade" indulgencies, our share of the ecclesiastical tithe (*tercias*) subsidies and grants; and as your Majesty has been informed several times of the state of these sources of revenue, there is no need to repeat it here. All the subsidy and "Crusade" revenue is pledged and anticipated; and already the poor people are burdened with two ordinary and two extraordinary grants up to the year 1548.* There is no way of getting more money from them, for your Majesty knows that, even with your own presence here, it was impossible to extract from the people any sort of excise (*sisa*) or other tax whatever. As to loans, notwithstanding all our efforts, the infliction of many vexations, and the imprisonment of those who might lend money, the utmost that could be got was 30,000 ducats, and the whole of the people are desperate. I must not omit to mention that the comparisons your Majesty draws between the grants that the French people have voted for their King, and those obtained from Spain, are misleading. The great fertility of France enables her to bear such taxes as are impossible in sterile Spain. One bad year here leaves the people so crushed with poverty that they are unable to hold up their heads again for many years. And, besides, every nation has its customs, and it has always been usual in France for such grants to be made, whereas here they would not be tolerated. Regard must be had to the peculiarity of nations, and the character of the peoples, and the treatment of them must vary accordingly: and it must be borne in mind that last year Spain voted 450 million maravedis, which is a vast sum. What with this and the other ordinary and

---

* *See* note to preceding letter, Cobos to Granvelle

1545.

extraordinary taxation, the common people who have to pay the grants are reduced to the lowest depth of calamity, many of them going naked with nothing to cover them. So universal is the poverty that it not only afflicts your Majesty's vassals, but also and even to a greater extent the vassals of the nobles, for they are utterly unable to pay any rents. The prisons are full and ruin impends over all. Believe me, your Majesty if this were not the case I would not dare to write it.* Your Majesty, says that, although we write to you from here that on no account is it advisable at present to summon Cortes, for reasons stated, you consider it too long to wait for your coming before obtaining fresh supplies and request that in the present circumstances a different decision should be adopted. I assembled the Council of State in my presence on various occasions, together with the President of the Royal Council and Dr. Guevara † to consider this point. It was discussed in all its bearings and the great difficulties in the way, as already explained to your Majesty, were again considered. The former Cortes (*i.e.* of 1544) was convoked with great misgiving as to the good issue, against the opinion and vote of the Royal Council and others, and having been so recently held and having voted a larger sum than ever before, even greater fear must be entertained now; especially in view of the universal poverty of the common people, who pay these taxes. Bad harvests, and one trouble after another, have produced a state of things that makes it impossible to believe that further ordinary supply could be obtained or that those who are not accustomed to pay would consent to do so now. (Details at great length other reasons which make the convocation of Cortes, or the imposition of fresh taxation impracticable and highly dangerous. Even if the Cortes voted the supply, the people would not and could not pay. Similar reasons are given, also at great length, against summoning the Cortes of Catalonia, etc., and a fervently worded assurance is given that night and day Philip and his Council are endeavouring to find some other means of raising money by loan or otherwise.)

Notes letter of Emperor to Juan de Vega respecting the aid promised by the Pope's Nuncios against the Turks and the Protestants. His Holiness might at least do thus much; but from what I hear it will all end in generalities. I spoke to the Comendador Mayor (Cobos) about your Majesty's idea that a considerable subsidy might be got from the bishops. By his advice I secretly consulted the Council of State, the Cardinal Archbishop of Seville; and the President of the Royal Council.§ They thought no good would come of speaking of the matter to the bishops, as the latter would at once tell the clergy, and all manner of difficulties

---

* This bold and statesmanlike letter, though it can hardly have been entirely indited by the young Regent of 18 years, must nevertheless have represented his own opinions, after hearing those of Cobos, Alba, and Cardinal Tavera.

† D. Antonio de Guevara, a Franciscan monk and a famous legist and historian, the official chronicler of the Emperor. His political and didactic works had a great vogue throughout Europe and especially in England. He died during this year 1545.

‡ Cardinal Garcia de Loaysa. President of the Council of the Indies.

§ Cardinal Tavera of Toledo, one of Philip's principal mentors. He died in this year 1545.

1545.

would be raised, an appeal to Rome made, and after all we should get nothing. The bishops at present pay very little, and most of them are in need. They would try to excuse themselves on the ground that they have to pay the pensions, and those who are going to the Council will be put to heavy expense. (These and many other reasons are adduced for recommending the Emperor to desist from the idea of exacting a subsidy from the bishops.) It would be better that your Majesty should obtain from the Pope another concession similar to that of the half first fruits, which expires next year. The Cardinals of Seville and Toledo are in favour of this and the Nuncio also will do his best. We have also discussed about the property of the churches, but it is thought that very little would be got from that source, as with the exception of Toledo and a few others, they are mostly very poor, and the recent rains have ruined and brought down many of the walls. They are indeed, asking us for help. Nothing could be done with the monasteries without the Bull we have asked for.

(Discusses and approves of the nomination of prelates, etc., by the Emperor to proceed to the Council of Trent.)

The pay for Andrea Doria's galleys shall be attended to. We have already paid him 5,000 ducats in gold and silver from the Indies for last year, and 2,100 ducats of the same for January and February of this year; so that we only owe him now for the month of March. We have not yet investigated with his representatives the amount payable to him for interest on overdue instalments. Will try in future to keep the payments up to date, but it will be difficult. He (Doria) is asking again for an increased interest, but we will put him off with soft words. If he is paid punctually in future he ought to be satisfied.

With regard to your Majesty's remarks about the increase of offices here; no more appointments shall be made in the judicial, accountants, or revenue services. Your Majesty will see by former letters that this was always the intention, and we will try and get as much as possible from this source. It is the least prejudicial way of obtaining means.

Your Majesty should again write to Rome urgently about the Spanish monasteries and the Moriscos of Granada, and great diligence will be necessary in the matter. It will be also very advisable to have the (Papal) briefs about the recently converted people of Valencia, for which we have waited so long, sent without further delay, as it is of the highest importance in the service of our Lord and the peace of these realms. We have not yet effected the disarmament of the Moriscos, as we have been waiting for these briefs which will facilitate the operation, and also for the report from the Duke Don Fernando (of Aragon) as to the financial measures necessary for raising there the troops which we shall want for the purpose, as we have none available here.

(Summary of news from South America. Greatly regrets the events that have occurred in Peru.)

Gives an account of the measures adopted for the fortification of Barcelona, and the defence of the Catalonian frontier.

Refers at length to many domestic affairs, such as the quarrels between the Bishop of Cordova and his Chapter, the affairs of the

1545.

Duke of Gandia, those of the Count de Puñonrostro, the indebtedness of the Duke Don Fernando of Aragon, in consequence of his income from the Sicilian revenues not having been paid, etc.

Several Navarrese captains, etc., ask for permission to accept the King of France's offer to employ them. Asks the Emperor's decision on the point. Philip is strongly of opinion that Navarrese especially should be forbidden from entering the French service. If any Spaniards are allowed to go, they should be Castilians.

Diego Ortiz Melgaredo[*] has been imprisoned in accordance with the Emperor's orders. His confession is enclosed. He is wounded in both legs by harquebuss shots fired at the taking of St. Disier, and as the doctors say his close confinement would be very injurious to his health, he has been relieved of his fetters, and has given bail to keep within the prison bounds. Begs the Emperor to send instructions. From his confession Ortiz does not seem much to blame and he asks for a reward.

Postscript.—From Guipuzcoa I learn that in addition to the ship from the Indies captured by the English, as related in the report of the Council of the Indies, they have plundered another vessel belonging to St. Sebastian. Full report herewith. Begs for instructions.

Rejoices at later news of the Emperor's recovery and ability now to travel.

Valladolid, 25 March, 1545 (27 *pages*).

31 March.
Paris
Arch. Nat.
K. 1485.

36. ST. MAURIS (Imperial Ambassador in France) to FRANCISCO DE LOS COBOS.

Letters of 21st February received. Surprised you have not the cipher, as the Emperor told me all the principal officers had it. It is true I have since added certain disguised names, of which I send copy, and also of the cipher itself. Many thanks for obtaining payment of my salary. Rejoices at health of Prince and Princess; and prays for safe delivery of the latter.

Health of the King of France. The surgeons have closed four of the five issues that existed in his abscess, leaving the other open for the elimination of the infected matter. By this issue the King usually urinates, instead of by the natural passage, and this makes some of the surgeons think that his bladder must be ulcerated. As the wound is incurable the patient cannot last long, and he follows no regime, but lives according to his fancy. Others say that they have seen people thus afflicted live for a long while, but they one and all agreed that the King's body must be very corrupt. He is obliged to be carried in a litter, in order not to ulcerate the wounds, which he insisted upon having closed up.

I answer the Prince direct with respect to the two matters he entrusted to me. With regard to the occurrences here, I may say that the preparations for the invasion of England next summer still

---

[*] Diego Ortiz was an ensign in the Emperor's service (*see* Vol. VII, p. 266) but the offence he had committed is not known.

HENRY VIII.

1545.

continue, the commander of the fleet having already been chosen,* as he himself tells me. He expects to have 30,000 men, of whom 6,000 will be cavalry. Captain Paulin† left court a fortnight ago for Marseilles, to conduct the King's galleys to the open sea, this Paulin being the lieutenant of the person mentioned. He will hold the sea, whilst the troops are on land.

Under Paulin there will be the Prior of Capua‡, who has been retained here to serve in this war; although he begged for a long time to be allowed to retire from the French service, and claimed a large sum of money, which he says the King of France owes him for money he spent in Italy during the last war. They are making great preparations of shipping on the coast; and at Rouen the King has had six galleys constructed, and six vessels have arrived from Scotland to aid the French.

Three weeks ago there arrived here a Scottish ambassador to inform the King that the English had a force of men and ships ready to invade and ruin Scotland; and that unless French aid was promptly forthcoming, the Scots would be obliged to come to terms with the English. This King thereupon despatched M. de L'Orge§ with 2,500 foot and 600 horse, of whom 100 are Scots, to Scotland. But according to all accounts, this force cannot arrive before the end of April. He is only to carry with him 60,000 crowns to raise Scottish troops; and the said ambassador is therefore in despair of the aid. It is even feared that M. de L'Orge may be encountered at sea by the English.

The English have recently captured a castle near Ardres from the French. It is a place of importance, as the possession of it will enable the victualling of Ardres to be prevented. Ardres is in great need and the King is sending as many men as possible towards Abbeville in order to endeavour to revictual the former town.

About ten days since there was at this Court an Englishman named Tout‖ Lotges, a merchant living in London, who was accompanied by another Englishman, without whom he was unable to negotiate. He addressed himself to M. de Chastillon¶, the Maitre d' Hotel of the Queen of France, as they were old friends. He told Chastillon that a Secretary of the King of England whilst he was at Brussels had sent him specially to him (Chastillon) in order that he might convey to the King of France the King of England's wish for peace, and his desire to abandon the friendship of the Emperor, as the latter had made peace without

---

* There is a cipher sign to indicate who is the person referred to, but the key does not contain the sign, which was one of the private marks referred to in the first paragraph of the letter. The person chosen was Annebaut, Admiral of France.

† Paulin Baron de la Garde, General of the galleys of France, who brought the galleys from Marseilles to the Channel, and commanded them when the attack was made upon the English coast. *See* Brantome's curious life of him.

‡ Leone Strozzi, Prior of Capua, Admiral of the galleys of Rhodes. His memoirs are also included in Brantome.

§ Jacques de L'Orge de Montgomerie, who was himself of Scottish descent.

‖ The name is thus spelt in the original. The person referred to was perhaps Thomas Lodge, a famous London merchant-banker, who was afterwards knighted, and was sheriff in 1559, and Lord Mayor in 1563.

¶ Chastillon had been ambassador in England, and this would explain his acquaintanceship with the London merchant.

1545.

him, and was only seeking the ruin of both of them. He was ready to cement a firm peace by the marriage of the Princess of England with the Duke of Orleans, giving to the Princess as a dower that which otherwise would depend upon the fortune of war. He added that the little Prince of England was of weak constitution, and if he died the Duke of Orleans would become King. The King of France, having been informed of this, replied through Chastillon that he would listen to no proposals for peace until Boulogne was first restored. Tout Lotges answered that perhaps some expedient might be found; and he then returned to obtain the King's decision about Boulogne, promising to return in a fortnight. He saluted the King of France before he left, the King receiving him in State surrounded by his courtiers, for the purpose, apparently, of showing that he was not dead yet. I have informed the Emperor of this.

The French have chosen a number of prelates and other learned men to go to the Council; but have decided not to send a multitude. They make no show of starting. There is a rumour that the Protestants will take no part in the Council, unless they are assured first that the Hungarian enterprise and the driving back of the Turk are to be persevered in.

The Pope had undertaken to furnish the King of France with 6,000 men against the English, but now informs him that he can only send 3,000, as he must send some to Hungary; and he will be put to great expense by the Council. The King is furiously angry about this, and has sent word to the Pope by his ambassador in Rome for his Holiness to send a legate to Lyons to issue the Papal indulgences for France, and that the money thus gained should be applied to the war against the English. The Pope proposed that he should give permission to the King of France to raise three tenths from the clergy, two tenths being for him, and the other tenth being applied to maintain the troops he was to send. The King replied that he was no subject of the Pope to need his permission for levying tenths in his realm, and if his Holiness did not help him he would take care that the contributions from France did not reach Rome. They are thus fencing with each other, and the Pope resents the pressure daily exerted upon him from here to grant unreasonable things. The enmity is increased by the desire of the King of France to dispose of the benefices of Savoy and Piedmont[*]; which the Pope says belong to him. His Holiness is also very angry that the King of France should treat for peace without informing him of it, and should refuse, as he did, to admit to the negotiations the legate sent by the Pope to take part in them.

The Spanish Jacobin friar who intervened in the peace negotiations was recently sent to Rome by the King of France, to exhort the Pope to write to the Emperor, begging him to declare against the English; as otherwise the King of France would find it difficult to attend both to the war and the Council (of Trent). The Spaniard has not yet returned. As these people are pressing for the

---

[*] It will be recollected that a considerable portion of the Duke of Savoy's dominions was now occupied by the French.

1545.

Emperor's decision as to the alternative marriage, his Majesty has insisted upon the production of the original letters of conveyance of Stenay to France from the late Duke of Lorraine. There was much difficulty about this for a time, as the letters are said to be lost; but at last they were discovered in the house of M. de Longueval* who had maliciously hidden them. The new Duke of Lorraine† has been ill but is now out of danger. His uncle, being executor, is going to Lorraine to put him into possession of his States.

The King of France is counting upon Milan being given to the Duke of Orleans, but thinks that the bride will be our Princess. With this object, they are trying to endow the Duke better and more quickly than before, as the King of France says he would rather have one princess in rags than the other richly dressed.‡

The King of France has increased the number of his galleys by a quarter, and has caused proclamation by trumpeters throughout his realm that money must be provided for him. I know on good authority that he will try all he can to avoid furnishing this year the contingent against the Turk stipulated in the treaty of peace. News has just arrived that the Pope will send 4,000 soldiers against the English, but he wishes to furnish the men and officers himself, whilst the King of France wants the money. So they are still in dispute.

The Paris merchants have news that the son of the Turk has allied himself with the Sophi, and that they are entering Egypt in force; so that the Turk is obliged to go and defend his dominions.

A gentleman whom the King of France sent to the Turk has just returned. He says the Turk is still at Adrianople, making preparations for war; but it was not known whether it was for Vienna or Egypt.

The Emperor instructed me to negotiate with the King of France to obtain a return of the property taken from the Duke of Alburquerque.§ The only result I have been able to gain is that the King has consented to refer the matter for decision to his Council whereas previously it had always been dealt with by the Admiralty Court. Such is the inclination of these people, however, that I fear the Duke will never get anything.

The King arrived here three days ago, and proceeds by Tours to Normandy.

---

* The name is thus spelt in the original, but probably the person meant is M. de Longueville (Duke de Longueville) the son of Mary of Lorraine, Queen of Scots, by her first husband.

† The "new Duke of Lorraine" was Francis formerly Marquis de Pont à Mousson and Duke de Bar who had succeeded his father Antoine le Bon in the previous year. He was an invalid and died a short time after this was written. His uncle was the elder Cardinal Lorraine.

‡ That is to say he would rather that his son the Duke of Orleans should marry Mary of Austria daughter of the Emperor poorly endowed than Catherine daughter of Ferdinand King of the Romans, with a large dowry. Mary eventually married her cousin Maximilian and became Empress whilst Catherine married the Duke of Ferrara.

§ The Duke of Alburquerque (Beltran de la Cueva third Duke) had acted as principal military adviser to the King of England in his campaign before Boulogne. When Henry returned to England he insisted upon the Duke crossing at the same time. His followers, in a hurry and determined not to be left behind, hastily shipped the Duke's and their own horses and portable property and treasure at Calais and Dunkirk. A considerable portion of this was captured by a French ship on the way across to the Thames, and the loss appears never to have been made good. *See* Spanish Chronicle of Henry VIII.

1545.

They say here that Ardres is still provisioned for six weeks; but they hope to succour the place and are sending the most of their men-at-arms well mounted to carry victuals thither.

The plague is spreading in Paris, Lyons and Picardy and great scarcity reigns in Paris.

The Secretary of the Ambassador Morette has arrived here to say that the Emperor will send his declaration as to the alternative marriage without fail by the end of this month. Morette is coming hither post with the Emperor's envoy, but will return to his embassy after Easter.

Amboise, 31 March, 1545.

31 March.
Paris
Arch. Nat.
K. 1485.

37. ST. MAURIS to FRANCISCO DE LOS COBOS.

I wrote to you fully by the Emperor's courier and have now only to add that I have made his declaration to the King, saying, in effect, that the former decided to choose the alternative marriage of the second daughter of the King of the Romans with the dower of Milan; but still holding out hopes that if the Duke of Orleans be better endowed by the King, a marriage with our Princess might be possible. The King and everyone else here is pleased with this declaration, and the King is sending one of his secretaries of commandments, named L'Aubespine, to the Emperor with the answer, which has not been communicated to me. I am told that he (the King) has been advised to accept Milan for the present; but still saying that in time the other marriage might be arranged. I am, however, of opinion that people here will never advise or allow any of the territories of the Crown to be alienated.* I have sent to ask what the answer is and will inform you as soon as I learn. The King's ministers have asked me to write to you begging for the surrender to the abbot of .a certain member who has fled to Roussillon from a monastery in France. As this is in accordance with the treaties, and the French do so for us, I beg you will kindly have the order sent to me.

I send information about the two ships sunk by the French. I hear that two armed caravels are putting to sea to commit similar acts.

I am told that 600 horses are being brought from Spain, mostly from Aragon and Fuentarrabia.

There are a great number of Spanish doubloons in France.—Amboise, 31 March, 1545.

Accompanying the aforegoing letter is a note (2 folios) giving details of the capture of certain Portuguese ships by two French vessels belonging to Rochelle. The prizes were made in the West Indies, and much of the cargoes belonged to subjects of the Emperor. One of the ships was declared officially by the captors to contain 600 marks of gold, and a great quantity of round pearls; but it was supposed that the treasure on board greatly exceeded that amount. It was asserted that all the captures had been made two months after the declaration of peace; but as only Portuguese ships had

---

* That is to say in order to increase he endowment of the Duke of Orleans.

1545.

been brought into port as prizes, it was suspected that the captors had sunk all the Spanish ships they had met. The Emperor should be informed that the French seize every Portuguese vessel they encounter, and their judges invariably declare them good prizes. The men on board are sent to the galleys and those who are worth it are held to ransom.

6 April.
Vienna
Imp. Arch.

38. L. SCHORE (President of the Emperor's Flemish Council) to the EMPEROR.

Your Majesty may say to Paget that since his coming you had informed him, that in order to avoid disagreements in future between your subjects and those of England, it would be necessary to take measures whereby your subjects might navigate the sea, even for the purpose of going to France without molestation from the English. Paget had replied that the King could not consent to this, so far as regarded their going to France, but he would connive at your subjects going to that country without molestation, on condition that they carried no victuals or munitions of war; and he would give you his assurance to this effect by the King's authority. Your Majesty had consented to this, supposing that no difficulty would be raised to a general clause being inserted, providing that your subjects might frequent the sea without hindrance, since the King is bound to this by the treaty. Without such a clause your subjects would have no security, and any objection to it appeared captious; since no mention whatever is made of France, and you are willing that the article should be so worded as to avoid prejudicing any of the King's pretensions.

Paget excuses himself from agreeing to this, on the ground that he has no authority, but your Majesty may tell him, that as he sent to England the draft we gave him here, which contained the general clause, the King's objection to it was only so far as regarded the part relating to France, respecting which part we are now agreed; and that the King cannot refuse that to which he is notoriously bound to consent by treaty.

6 April.
Vienna
Imp. Arch.

39. MEMORANDUM of AGREEMENT concerning CONTRABAND of WAR.

The commissioners of the Emperor and the ambassadors of the King of England having this day, 6 April, 1545, agreed that during the war between England and France the subjects of his imperial Majesty are not to be allowed to convey to France or other countries inimical to the King of England any munitions of war or victuals; the said commissioners and ambassadors, in order to avoid all misunderstanding, have agreed that the subjects of his imperial Majesty shall not convey to France or other inimical country any of the following articles.

Armour. Iron or steel mail, mail or woollen jackets.

Lances. Pikes. Halberds. Falcon beaks. Mallets. Swords. Daggers. Poignards or any other fighting blades.

Military saddles. Headpieces (*i.e.* for horses).

1545.

Steel or leather bards. Targets or Roundels.
Artillery, either of wrought or cast-iron. Harquebusses.
Culverins or any fire-arm.
Crossbows or bows.
Copper or other metal which may be used to forge or cast artillery.
All sorts of gunpowder. Saltpetre and sulphur.
Bullets and projectiles of iron.
Pitch, etc.

It is agreed that in the prohibited victuals shall not be included Spanish or other sweet wines, spices, sugar, succades and other drugs, nor any syrups or other compositions of honey or mead. (Signed) Schore, Cornille Scepperus, Bave, William Paget, Nicholas Wotton.

N.D.
April?
Vienna
Imp. Arch.

40. L. SCHORE (President of the Flemish Council) and SCEPPERUS (M. D'eick) to the EMPEROR.

We went yesterday to see Paget who said that he had no authority to alter the note formerly handed to your Majesty,* but that the King would be willing (on condition of his retaining Boulogne) that your Majesty should make whatever arrangements you thought best. He showed us the King's letters to this effect. Paget also said that he had no instructions about a truce; but he was of opinion that if your Majesty would induce the King of France to accept a truce, the King (of England) would consent thereto and he (Paget) would do his best with that object.

This morning we went, by order of the Queen, to see the French ambassadors and persuade them to put an end to this war, and we suggested that it would be well to agree to a truce; urging upon them several reasons in favour of this course. At the same time we assured them that your Majesty had no other end to serve than that of the peace of the world, and would not interfere further, until you heard the King's pleasure on the point. They (the ambassadors) took it in very good part, promising to convey what we had said to the King; and if they found him at all inclined to it, they would endeavour to bring about an understanding. They had, however, received despatches which made it necessary that they should ask for audience; and they trusted that your Majesty would be willing to listen to them, as their mission did not touch the King's interests but those of your Majesty, in which the King was as much concerned as if they were his own.

Morette afterwards said that they would speak to your Majesty of another truce, which makes us think that their business may be about the Turk. They said the affair was pressing and begged your Majesty to signify an appointment.

7 April.
Imp. Arch.

41. PAGET's verbal undertaking that the KING will connive at the carrying on of trade between the Netherlands and France.

Sir William Paget, knight, Councillor and First Secretary to the King of England, has declared in the presence of the Queen

---
*This refers to the note handed to the Emperor by Wotton during the negotiations for peace in the previous year setting forth Henry's claims against France.

1545.

(Dowager of Hungary, Regent of the Netherlands), and certain members of the Emperor's Council, that the King, his master, is willing, for the sake of his imperial Majesty, to connive at the subjects of the latter carrying on navigation, traffic and business to and in France, without hindrance or injury; on condition that they may not convey to France any victuals or munitions of war. This he declared in the presence also of M. de Sempy, knight of the Order (*i.e.* the Golden Fleece), Loys de Schore, knight, President of the Privy Council, and Cornille Sceppernus, knight, Councillor of State to his Majesty, on the 5th March, 1545, before Easter.

This day the 7th April, Secretary Paget read this memorandum, and confessed that he had made to the Queen the declaration set forth herein, in the presence of the undersigned. Schore, Cornille Sceppernus.

10 April.
Vienna
Imp. Arch.

42. The Queen Dowager to Chapuys and Van der Delft.

Since our letters of the 8th ultimo and receipt of yours of 11th, 12th, and 15th of same, Secretary Paget, in an audience requested by him before he received the King's reply concerning his negotiations here, complained of the arrest of an English ship by the captain of the Sluys, the said ship having broken the embargo placed upon it in Zeeland. The arrest was afterwards raised, although the master of the ship was liable to serious consequences. During this audience Paget said that he had power from the King to ascertain from the Emperor whether, placing aside past events, his Majesty would in future observe the stipulation of the treaty of friendship. As the point was a purely captious one, brought forward simply to justify the King's demand for the declaration against France, Paget was told frankly and openly, that if he asked the question for the purpose of leading up to the declaration against France, his Majesty had no intention whatever of placing aside any past events; but on the contrary would keep them fittingly in view. He would, nevertheless, observe the said treaty, so far as he was bound to do, as he had already replied to the Earl of Hertford and the Bishop of Winchester. Paget thereupon broke out into great lamentations, saying that his Majesty was bound by the treaty to make the declaration, no matter what was said to the contrary; and even if the King had consented to the treaty with France (which the King still insisted that he had not done), was it to be understood that the Emperor was for ever exempt from making the declaration or from fulfilling the article in the treaty (of friendship) which dealt with the subject? He was told in reply, that if he wished to persist in the demand for the declaration, it would be better to go over past affairs, and such explanations would be given to him as should satisfy him. To conceal nothing from him, we might say that the Emperor did not consider that after he had arranged with France with the King of England's consent, he was bound, or to be expected, to declare against France during the present war; and so to violate the treaty of peace, to which the Emperor is as much bound as he is to his treaty with England; although the latter treaty provides for a closer alliance between the parties. His

1545.

Majesty has always declared that he would comply with all his obligations towards both powers, but if after this present war was over, another war should break out, the Emperor would act in a way which would satisfy the King of England. Finally the Secretary (Paget) endeavoured to persuade us that the Emperor should, in order to please the King of England, send word to him that, although the present state of Christendom rendered it inadvisable for him now publicly to declare himself against France, yet if the war continued, he would show his friendship for the King of England by declaring against France later. The Emperor's commissioners did not like this suggestion, and declined to convey it to his Majesty; as they were sure he would not listen to it.

After Paget had received the answer from his master, he had a second audience, and declared that the King, having been informed of the communications that had passed, thanked his Majesty for his kindness and goodwill to bring about peace for England. If his Majesty could induce the King of France to come to terms, the King of England would also willingly do the same; and he suggested that with this object the conditions formerly laid before the Emperor by Wotton might be brought forward again.

Having regard to the expense incurred in conquering, and subsequently in fortifying, Boulogne, the King could not, out of respect for his own reputation, surrender the place, and he begged the Emperor, as a good ally and true friend, to satisfy the French.

He also thanked the Emperor for the intimation sent to him of the mission of the Scottish envoy and of the answer given thereto. The King begged that the envoy might promptly be sent back.

Touching the release of the seizures, after expressing sorrow at the delay that had taken place in the release on this side, and saying that it was not necessary to draw up any documents on the matter; since the King of England had already released everything, he (Paget) finally produced a paper founded upon the draft which had been handed to him here (and of which duplicate was sent you). Some alterations had been made, and the mention of free navigation for his Majesty's subjects had been omitted. This Paget explained by saying that the provision was contained in the treaty of friendship, and the King could not consent formally to the Netherlanders trading with France. The imperial Commissioners were not satisfied with this, and maintained that after all the wrongs and troubles that had been inflicted upon us in violation of the treaty, the seizures could not be released until we had some assurance for the future that our people would be better treated, and allowed to sail the sea without molestation. We were ready to omit all special reference to France, on receiving the verbal assurance which Paget had formerly proposed.

Paget replied that he had no orders to change the terms of the document sent from England; but he was quite willing to declare on behalf of the King in the presence of the (Flemish) Council and anyone else that the King of England would not hinder the subjects of the Emperor in their navigation, and would even connive at their going to France. He was told by the commissioners that this was not sufficient. They insisted upon the general clause

1545.

assuring unmolested navigation being inserted in the agreement. Paget complained bitterly of this, taking his stand on the point of honour, and resenting the refusal to accept his word; given, as he said, in the King's name in virtue of his credentials. The Emperor himself then sent for Paget, and told him that the agreement could not be accepted without the insertion of the said general clause; Paget's reply being that he could not agree to this without further instructions. He begged that, pending the receipt of these, the persons of English subjects might be released: but seeing the objections which his Majesty raised to this, he asked that certain merchandise might be released, these goods he said having been sent for the purpose of repaying the loans which he had raised in Antwerp. His Majesty consented to this.

Having communicated with England, Paget received further instructions, and finally the agreement, of which a copy is enclosed, was made with him. By this, apart from the prohibition of the conveyance of food and munitions to France, the subjects of the Emperor are in future secured against molestation at sea. An agreement has also been made with him as to the articles coming under the head of munitions of war, and the articles of consumption of which the export to France is permitted. In order that no future misunderstanding shall occur with regard to the liberty of the subjects on this side to sail to France, we have drawn up a statement of the words pronounced by Paget, which statement has been shown to him and confirmed by him, as you will see by the document enclosed.* After Paget had seen the orders given for the release, he departed in apparent contentment. You will see that all seizures made subsequent to the 20 June last are to be released, if anything else remains. This was the best we could get from Paget.

With regard to the intervention between France and England, his Majesty, having heard Paget's message, as given above, replied that he feared that the French would insist very strongly in the recovery of Boulogne, and would probably decline to entertain any negotiations, until that point was conceded. His Majesty therefore considered that the best way to open negotiations would be to treat for a truce, during which the King of England would not be prejudiced, because he held Boulogne and could even in the meanwhile strengthen his position there. Paget replied that he had no instructions respecting a truce, but he would willingly inform the King of the suggestion. He subsequently announced that the King approved of the Emperor's advice, and would be glad to agree to a truce for such period as his Majesty thought best.

His Majesty also caused the French ambassadors to be sounded, with the object of inducing the King (of France) to accept a truce with England; and several reasons were given to them why the King of France should not refuse. If he (the Emperor) learnt that the King (of France) was inclined thereto, he promised to approach the King of England and endeavour to obtain his concurrence. The ambassadors promised to communicate with their King; and

---

* All the documents referred to will be found in the preceding pages.

Morette, on his departure from here with the declaration as to the marriage alternatives, promised to speak to the King about the truce and to send word hither. No communication from him has yet arrived.

The agreement taken by Paget provides for the meeting on the 1st May of the representatives of both monarchs, for the purpose of enquiring into and arbitrating upon all questions and claims at issue made by subjects on both sides. This is understood to refer, not only to assaults at sea or to the seizures, but also to all other complaints and grievances, as to the infraction of the treaty of commerce and the wrongs daily committed in England in violation of the treaty. You will therefore inform us of what you can ascertain of the ill-treatment of our people by the English, in order that instructions may accordingly be drawn up for the Commissioners who are to be sent. We think of sending to the joint arbitration some gentleman and two masters of requests, as we informed Paget before he left.

With reference to what Paget wrote about a remark which he said had been made to him by some of the Councillors here, to the effect that the Earl of Hertford and the Bishop of Winchester had been unable to find any reply to our arguments about the declaration against France, and that they would have agreed if they had had power, we understand that the remark was not made in that sense. Paget was told that if the King intended to persist in his request for the declaration, it would be necessary for us to repeat the arguments we addressed to the Earl and the Bishop; which reasons were sufficient to demonstrate that the Emperor was under no obligation to make the declaration, whatever might be said to the contrary.

These arguments had subsequently been repeated to the King who had not yet given his decision on the subject; and it had consequently been concluded that he was satisfied and convinced. Nothing was said about the Earl and the Bishop not having been able to reply; but it was certainly said that the arguments they urged were not sufficient to induce his Majesty to make the declaration. As to the Earl and the Bishop's assertion that they felt sure that at the expiration of the 10 weeks his Majesty would make the declaration, we can only say that they must have very badly understood what was said to them to have gained such an impression. You know well from your own instructions that his Majesty never had any intention of declaring war against France, and thus suddenly to violate the treaty which he had only just made with the consent of the King of England. The Scottish ambassador is still here. Although no answer has been given to him beyond what was communicated to you, and you can assure the King of England of this if he mentions it, still we are desirous of so dealing with the (Scottish) ambassador, as to prevent our relations with Scotland from growing more unpleasant than they are; and to enable the subjects here to sail the sea without molestation from the Scots, so long as we abstain from active hostilities against them. This is the reason for the ambassador's continued sojourn here; and we inform you in confidence, knowing

1545.

that you will keep the secret. If you hear that people on that side are offended at the ambassador's stay here, you must let us know, so that we may instruct you what excuse to make. Brussels, 10 April, 1544.

12 April.
Paris
Arch. Nat.
K. 1486.

43. EXTRACT from LETTERS from the EMPEROR'S AMBASSADOR in FRANCE (ST. MAURIS) to the EMPEROR.

Your Majesty enjoined me to enquire closely whether the French galleys returned to Marseilles, if the intention of sending them out still continued, and if so who was to command them. I have done so and learn that, if peace is not made with the English, the galleys will not go to the Levant this year, but will proceed to the port of Etaples, which the King is having deepened to receive them, in accordance with the plan I have already sent to your Majesty. From this port they will attempt to prevent the revictualling of Boulogne. The King of France reckoned that, taking into consideration the garrison that the English were maintaining at Boulogne, they could not put into the place more than three months' provisions, after which time further supplies would have to be sent. They (the French) therefore decided to send the galleys thither about the middle of May, with 20 armed vessels to hold the passage and hinder the revictualling. The galleys will accordingly go to Etaples for this purpose, so as to be near Boulogne, and the King of France does not intend to send them to the Levant unless this war (i.e. with the English) ceases. Even after that he will retain them (the galleys) outside the Mediterranean; saying that they are too much knocked about to go so long a voyage, and he will rather break them up, keeping about half-a-dozen for his own needs, and sending the convicts overland by way of Lyons, near which place on the Rhone they will take the water again. The King has fitted out nine new galleys at Marseilles, though they are not yet armed. In order to secure the coast in that direction, a certain Genoese named Fiesco had bought, or was to buy, the Pope's ships, and bring them into the French service. All this depends upon whether peace be made or not between England and France, but as soon as I learn that such a peace is settled I will endeavour to discover what is to be done with the galleys. Some of them have already left (Marseilles) and I learn on good authority that they are all to be at sea by the end of April; but only for the purpose of scouring the seas and committing their usual pilfering and depredations. It is positively asserted here that, as nothing was settled at Cambrai about maritime matters, when the French commissioners returned the captains of the galleys were told that they might continue their captures as before, and that, if necessary, aid should be given to them. The Admiral was quite willing; and indeed had endeavoured to bring this about, as he receives a tenth of the value of the prizes. This, Sire, is a matter of so much importance to your poor subjects, that I have thought necessary to bring it before you, in order that, in some way or another, it may be remedied. Truly I think these people are more bent upon this passion for plunder than ever I saw them before, as they have a lively recollection of their past gains from it. To judge by their own talk, it will be very difficult to persuade them to modify their orders. In case they capture prizes it will be useless for us to depend upon my remonstrances or claims, here, as they insist upon referring everything to the Admiralty, to be dealt with according to their maritime laws, which are iniquitous. I write thus minutely to your Majesty, because I have, of my own action, already declared to the Chancellor and the Admiral that by some means or another their orders must positively be reformed. I have, however, got nothing from them, but remarks that clearly show their intention to sustain and protect these people in their robberies. It is true that if peace were to be declared all these difficulties would cease, but so long as the war continues, and your Majesty's subjects have no safety in their navigation, they will be treated as badly as can be by these people, who bear them no goodwill.

With regard to your Majesty's observations respecting the Scottish pirates, I beg to say that these pirates after having worked their will in the ports of Normandy upon your Majesty's Flemish subjects retired to Brittany when they found that the merchants were prosecuting them at law for the return of their property. They subsequently committed some fresh depredations on the Spaniards frequenting the Brittany coast. I complained of this to the King, without waiting for special instructions to do so, as the matter was so pressing and outrageous, and the French had received the Scots so differently from what the King had assured me they would. The King replied that he had sent the Scots to Brittany, in order to drive away the English, who were committing all sorts of incursions there, but that he had prohibited the Scots from touching your Majesty's subjects or their property, on any account, and had not heard that they had done so. In conversation with me on the subject, he admitted that they could do much more damage at sea on the Brittany coast than off Normandy, as they could command a certain Strait, by which every ship sailing between Flanders and Spain must necessarily pass; and he added that, if he chose to construct a fort near this Strait, he might command the whole high sea. He said that on your Majesty's voyages to and fro, you had passed through this Strait. After all this, he told me that he considered these robberies of the Scots to be perfectly scandalous and pernicious, and so he had declared to M. de L'Orge, who had endeavoured to excuse them, when the King told him it was quite enough for Scotland to be at war with England, without seeking to quarrel with your Majesty as well. The King ended by promising to write at once to M. d'Etampes, ordering him to lay hands on all the ships captured by the Scots from your Majesty's subjects, and return them to the owners immediately, forbidding these pirates from doing such wrong for the future, and punishing them severely if they disobey. I know for certain that those letters have been written, the King having in my presence given directions about them to the Dauphin, to whom he complained of such proceedings, and told him that it was for him (the Dauphin) to provide redress, as he exercised the sovereignty of Brittany. The Dauphin replied that he knew of two Spanish

1545.

ships having been captured by these pirates, but as soon as he heard of it he had ordered the vessels to be restored, and he believed this had been done. He would, moreover, take steps to prevent such outrages for the future, and I earnestly begged him to bear the matter in mind. I know he has done so, and I believe that M. d' Etampes will scrupulously carry out the orders sent to him. I have also written to M. d' Etampes to the same effect. I feel sure that when your Majesty lets the King know that the Governor (*i.e.*, of Scotland)* disavows these pirates, he (the King) cannot avoid doing the same, and turning them out of his ports or at least taking care that they do nothing against your Majesty's subjects, and insisting upon the restitution of their plunder, of which hitherto little has been recovered. As soon as they took their plunder into the Norman ports they sold it to Frenchmen, with whom they had already arranged. I hear from worthy merchants that their plunder off Normandy was worth thirty or forty thousand crowns, of which hardly anything will be recovered, unless the Governor (*i.e.*, of Scotland) requests this King to seize it. But if peace is declared all these troubles will cease.

Melun, 12 April, 1545.

17 April.
Simancas
E. 1377.

44. THE EMPEROR to FIGUEROA (Ambassador in Genoa).

Yours of 28th ultimo received. The object of the present is to inform you that the French ambassador here has assured us from his master, that the latter learns from good authority that the King of England is making some agreement with the Duke of Savoy; and has sent him 150,000 crowns to begin war against the King of France in Piedmont. The Marquis del Guasto and Prince Doria have also, he says, been together a great deal; and in constant confabulation with you. He (the King of France) thus wishes to intimate that they not only intend to aid the Duke of Savoy, but are even planning a descent upon Marseilles by sea. He also speaks of the Sienese and ———† and others who are plotting together, and intend to raise 2,000 infantry to advance on Pigneroli and Montcalieri, and finally to raise war from the State of Milan, with the object of aiding Savoy. The King of France says that he has ascertained that this is not being done by our orders, but he has been informed that, at least, it is with our knowledge; and he begs us very earnestly, having regard to the condition of our relations, and the trust he reposed in our word, that we will take steps to prevent it, and will punish the Duke of Savoy. We have replied that, not only has the Duke of Savoy not informed us of this—which is perfectly true—but that we do not believe that the English King has been so liberal to him as to send him the sum mentioned; seeing how little the Duke could do. We do not, moreover, think, for many reasons, that the things the King mentions are being done, and we feel sure that, even if the King of England were to approach the Duke, the latter would enter into no arrangement without previously consulting us and learning our wishes.

* The Regent Earl of Arran.
† Blank in original.

1545.

As to the Marquis del Guasto, Prince Doria, the Sienese* and the others, we said that we did not believe that such a thing had entered their heads; but even in the highly improbable case that it had, we were certain that neither the Marquis nor Doria would move a step in such a business without our knowledge and consent. The King of France, we said, might calm his fears, and depend absolutely upon our word; which would be kept as it always had been. We were positive that no minister of ours had ever thought of, or dealt with, such a plan as that spoken of, and the truth of this would easily be proved on investigation. The Ambassador enquired in case the Duke of Savoy promoted the war, as it was suspected he would, whether we would join the King of France in punishing him. To this we replied that, although we were always of opinion that the Duke would not stir in such a business without first informing us, yet if such a thing were to happen, the King of France would have no need to trouble himself or interfere at all; for we ourselves would fittingly punish the Duke, and the King would have no cause to complain. We judge that all this is of less importance than the French make out, and that the suspicions may have originated from your going to Milan, in order to inform the Marquis del Guasto of what we wrote to you about the alternative marriage, and from the subsequent communications between the Marquis and the Duke (of Savoy). In accordance with their usual character, the French need very little ground upon which to found their suspicions, and they talk as lightly as they think; but as things are in their present condition, it will be advisable to avoid all occasion for distrust. We wish to show by our actions the absolute straightforwardness of our proceedings throughout, and for this reason we have thought well to inform you of the above for your own guidance; and in order that you may convey it to the Marquis del Guasto, verbally if he be there, or by a confidential messenger, and also write it to the Duke of Savoy. He is the principal person of whom they complain, and it will be wise for him to take great care to avoid any communications or negotiations which may give rise to suspicion, or provide the French with a handle they may seize. You will avoid meeting as much as possible, and will, with such dissimulation as you may, produce the impression upon the French that they were misinformed upon the whole thing, and so do away with this constant distrust.

No doubt when we arrive at Antwerp we shall have received the Marquis del Guasto's letters to which you refer, and we will then answer yours.

Since writing the above we have received the letters of which we enclose copy from our ambassador in France. Inform the Marquis of the contents.

Malines, 17 April, 1545.

19 April.
Vienna
Imp. Arch.

45. CHAPUYS and VAN DER DELFT to the QUEEN DOWAGER.

On the 15th we received letters of 10th, with enclosures, informing

---
*Probably Ottavio Farnese is meant.

1545.

us fully of the negotiations with Paget. His own good and sincere report of the same negotiations was extremely well received by the King and all the Councillors, who are marvellously pleased at Paget's success, as they informed us to-day. On the day after Paget's arrival here, which was the 10th, the Council declared to the mayor, sheriffs and burgesses of London, that the relations of amity between the Emperor and the King were never better than at present, and that they (*i.e.*, the citizens) might freely, and without misgiving, ship their merchandise, and trade in his Majesty's dominions. Although we were gratified at this indication of the King's favourable tendency, we were not altogether satisfied, as neither the King nor the Council had given us any information whatever, or even mentioned, Paget's mission or his return. For this reason, and to learn fully what had been agreed upon; and also to ascertain whether any offence had been taken at the stay of the Scottish Ambassador at Brussels; to discover whom they were going to send to the joint arbitration; and further to ask for the release of certain ships which were still detained here, we thought it advisable to ask for an audience of the Council. They begged us to postpone it until this morning; and, both before and after dinner, we communicated with them on several private claims, such as that of the Burgos merchants, the jewel claim and several others. At length, we dwelt upon the case of the detention of a ship belonging to Thomas Barbain, loaded with woad from Bordeaux, and after much discussion obtained its release. With regard, however, to the ship of Albroz Pardo and his partners, of which we have written to your Majesty, they (the councillors) raised difficulties, in consequence of the goods having been sold. As they could not answer our arguments, they told us that we ought not to stand upon so small a thing, especially in view of the liberal and full release of the rest of the property by the King. Even during the last few days they had released 8 or 10 ships loaded with Bordeaux-wine bound to Flanders, although they thought that a portion of the cargo belonged to Frenchmen. The Council had informed us about the capture of these ships some six days before, with the desire of excusing the Captain of the Isle of Wight, who had mistaken them for enemies, and had discharged several cannon shot against them, but doing no more damage than piercing one ship in an unimportant spot. The King has chosen as his representatives at the joint arbitration Dr. Petre,[*] a companion of Secretary Paget, Dr. Trigoult (Trigway?), and for gentleman of the short-robe Master Vaughan,[†] who was formerly ambassador to your Majesty, and also Master Chamberlain. They will arrive there on the 4th or 5th May with the necessary powers and instructions and with full information as to the injuries which they allege have been suffered by Englishmen; and for the excuse and defence against the claims made upon them. The Councillors have been marvellously diligent and dexterous in this matter, sending information privately to the trades and merchants of all sorts.

---

[*] Sir William Petre, Secretary of State.
[†] Stephen Vaughan.

1545.

The Council has not mentioned to us the long stay of the Scottish ambassador in Flanders; although our conversation was such as would have admitted of some reference being made to it. They said nothing about it even when they came to tell us from the King that he was informed that the King of France intended shortly to send a number of troops to Scotland, and a large sum of money to move the Scots to invade England; in which case, they said, the Emperor was bound by the treaty of friendship to help the English with men and money. They begged us to advise his Majesty to this effect, in order that he might make timely provision to aid if required. We promised to do so, but went no further in the matter.

Touching the wrongs constantly committed by these people upon the Emperor's subjects, we presume that your Majesty and the Councillors will be fully informed of the details of most, or all, of them. We will, nevertheless, obey the orders sent to us, and mention a few points. Although it is provided in the treaty of intercourse that the subjects on both sides may visit and sojourn in either territory, and trade freely as in their own country, these people, during the last few years, have expelled innumerable Flemings from England, refusing to allow them to live here, unless they take out letters of neutrality which cost a large sum of money. These letters of neutrality are outrageous, as they contain an oath of allegiance (fidelité) as if to a natural sovereign, besides which the foreigner is obliged to acknowledge the constitution as it exists here, and those who have houses or live here are obliged, not only to take out these letters of neutrality, but are assessed to pay double the taxes paid by Englishmen. Besides this, for the last 12 or 13 years, they have had to pay to the Mayor and chiefs of the city certain dues they call "*carage,*" a most injurious tax, which was formerly not paid. For some time past, too, they are prohibited from exporting wheat, cheese and most kinds of undressed cloth, so that there is nothing left for the Netherlanders to export from here but tin, lead and certain sorts of cloth; and lead has been lately on the point of being prohibited, in consequence of a design of the King to monopolise the export trade in the metal, of which he has great quantities.[*] Nothing more has been said about the complaint of the Earl of Hertford and the Bishop of Winchester, mentioned in your Majesty's letters. They appeared quite satisfied with our original explanation. We are strongly under the impression that Secretary Paget never wrote anything of the kind, and that it was merely an excuse for coming to see us.

When Paget's penultimate letters reached here the King ordered the biscuit-bakers and other provision dealers not to hurry much with their orders, and it was also proposed to release certain Venetian and Aragonese vessels which had been detained here to serve in the war. But a few days afterwards the embargo on the

---

[*] It is mentioned elsewhere in these papers that Henry's great stores of lead came from the roofs of the dismantled monasteries.

1545.

ships was confirmed, and a number of men in the neighbourhood have been warned for service. This looks as if the King was not now so hopeful of the truce (*i.e.*, with France) as he was when Paget wrote.

London, 19 April, 1545.

NOTE.—Attached to the above letter, there is a small strip of paper, apparently written afterwards, containing the following in cipher. "It is true that the prohibitions mentioned would be bearable if there were any necessity for them; but such is not the case, for every day they allow such merchandise etc. to be exported by means of licenses which cost a great deal of money."

25 April.
Vienna
Imp. Arch.

46. THE EMPEROR to CHAPUYS.

In accordance with the arrangement effected with Paget, of which you have been informed, it will be necessary for us to send some worthy personages to Gravelines next month, to meet those appointed by the King of England to represent him. Considering the long experience you have had of English affairs, and of the English way of negotiating, we have decided that no one more fitting than yourself could be chosen for one of these personages. It will therefore be necessary for you to make preparations for taking leave of the King and setting forth on your journey. Your further stay in England is, moreover, unnecessary, having regard to the arrangement made with Paget; and M. Francis Van der Delft will be able to fulfil the other parts of the mission, in accordance with our instructions from time to time, and those of the Queen Dowager.

We enclosed in recent letters to you from the Queen two memorials in Spanish, detailing certain seizures and robberies committed by English ships upon our Spanish subjects on their homeward voyage from the Indies, and also upon others from Biscay. In return for these robberies, our said subjects have used reprisals before informing us of them. You will request the restitution of the property seized, in accordance with the treaty made with Paget; and if they speak to you about the reprisals, you must make the best excuse you can, saying that they were effected without our knowledge; and that, as soon as we learn of the restitution being made, we will make a similar restitution on our side.

Antwerp, 25 April, 1545.

26 April.
Vienna
Imp. Arch.

47. CHAPUYS and VAN DER DELFT to the QUEEN DOWAGER.

Two days since we received your Majesty's letter of the 20th. With regard to the choice of the English Commissioners for the joint arbitration at Gravelines, your Majesty has already been informed by the English ambassador, and by our former letters. The Councillors, up to yesterday, had made no change, but Paget told our man this morning that the Council were going at once to see the King, for the purpose of obtaining the nomination of Dr. Carne, the resident ambassador to your Majesty, in the place of the Court Master (Chamberlain?) or of Vaughan. He sent word to us at the same time that he was willing for the meeting to be postponed until the 8th May but not longer.

1545.

Nothing further has been said about the stay of the Scottish ambassador in Flanders, but, in accordance with your Majesty's instructions, I will, if a good opportunity offers, endeavour to draw them to the subject.

With regard to your Majesty's information as to the despatch from here of the Duchess d' Etampes' secretary, we took a fitting opportunity of mentioning it to Secretary Paget. He replied that it was true that an Italian was recently sent to the French Court respecting the exchange of some English prisoners. Whilst he was there he was approached by several personages, to learn whether there was any possibility of inducing this King to surrender Boulogne on reasonable terms. The Italian had raised great difficulties, but had gone no further in the matter, as he was not empowered and knew nothing about it. Madame d' Etampes had thereupon despatched a gentleman to Boulogne to see Lord Poyns the Governor, under the pretext of exchanging prisoners. This gentleman had had several conferences with Poyns, respecting a peace between the two countries and the restitution of Boulogne; and when the King (of England) was informed of this by Poyns, he replied that on no account in the world was such a thing as the surrender of Boulogne to be discussed. Since then, Paget said, the King had heard nothing more about such a proposition, and we believe this to be the truth. If any person had come from France upon such an errand, we could not fail to have known of it; and no one has come from France for a long time past, except a certain yokel who calls himself a gentleman and says he was in the service of M. d'Enghien, but has come hither in consequence of the illtreatment he met with in France. It appears to us that, no matter how clever a negotiator they may send hither, the French will find it very hard work to persuade the King to the demolition or restoration of Boulogne. On the contrary, he is more likely to make that his principal advantage by the war, for reasons which your Majesty will understand better than we do.

With regard to the capture of 60 French vessels mentioned by the English Ambassador, it is true that the news reached the King recently from several quarters; but as the matter was not entirely believed, we thought better not to advise your Majesty of it until it was confirmed. We took an opportunity that offered, however, of writing of it to Secretary Bave: though we do not know whether he has received the letters. After all is said, this grand talk has mostly ended in smoke; as the only captures are 9 or 10 small boats of little value, which were seized off the coast of Brittany. The English force however descended thence upon an island called Belle Isle which they ransomed for 1,500 or 2,000 crowns paid by the inhabitants, notwithstanding which, the English sacked the place and treated the people very cruelly; though all they have brought home from there is a little wheat and some chattels. With regard to the alleged arrest of the Zeelanders and their ships, we can hardly speak of the matter, unless the parties complain to the Councillors, who will not fail to take fitting measures if the statements are proved. We do not however believe that anything of the sort has taken place, as no claim has been made. With

1545.

reference to the Spanish ships mentioned in the documents sent to us by your Majesty, the Council have taken steps to secure the ship and merchandise captured by Renegat, and they assure us that the restitution shall be made without fail, on condition that a similar release is effected in Spain of the ships seized there belonging to Renegat. The Council also promise to enquire into the contents of the document in Spanish, and to take measures accordingly.

The King has recently sent the Earl of Arundel and other gentlemen to the West coast opposite France, in order to raise ships and men for the defence of that coast. He has also made three very large musters of ships and men, to send to Scotland; whither he is sending all the Spaniards and Italians he has in his service. The Earl of Hertford is to go in command; and we think that their design is to restore a castle which they demolished last year, standing near the sea in the middle of a river. By this means, the King could keep Scotland in submission, as the castle stands in the most commodious place for the purpose. They did not venture last year to undertake the fortification of this place, in consequence of their haste to return and accompany the King to Boulogne, and also because they had not at hand the necessary material, with which they are now amply provided.

We doubt not that your Majesty will have learnt that the Marquis de Palavicini has arrived here with a good company of men, and with some experienced Italian captains. So far as we can understand, however, the man is greatly disappointed in the promises they held out to him, that he should be in chief command of all the Italians in the King's service. Judging by the small sum of money which the King has advanced to him, and certain remarks of the ministers, he even fears that they look upon him with suspicion, and he would be very glad if he and his company were elsewhere. Still, as they have entered into the dance, they will have to go through with it, with what patience they may.

London, 26 April, 1545.

Postscript.—At this moment as we were closing the letter Paget has sent us word that to-morrow afternoon the Bishop of Winchester and himself will come and visit us.

27 April.
Vienna
Imp Arch

48. CHAPUYS and VAN DER DELFT to the QUEEN DOWAGER.

The messenger who should have left yesterday with our letters postponed his departure, which has given us the time to write the present letter to add to the packet. The Bishop of Winchester and Paget have only just left us. The first object of their visit was to assure us of the King's unreserved and sincere desire to comply fully with the agreement entered into through Paget with the Emperor; and to lose no time in settling the whole affair. It must, they said, be borne in mind, however, that there were certain points which could not be decided off-hand; such as the two claims contained in the Spanish statement mentioned in our last, into which an enquiry would have to be made, and the matter verified. The same was the case with the capture made by

1545.

Renegat, which they seek to explain and justify by the seizure and retention of some of his ships in Spain. They (the English) have nevertheless sequestrated all Renegat's property; and have sent to summon him hither, in order to examine into the matter. They have also sent for a captain who recently seized certain Spanish ships, and, as is asserted, forcibly extorted from the masters a statement that the cargoes belonged to Frenchmen. The councillors said that the King was greatly annoyed that such insolence should be committed, and, in order to remedy such a state of things, he had thought necessary to recall and prohibit the sailing of all privateers (navires aventurières). We praised this decision; but begged them also to use their influence to have the King's own forces enjoined to behave in accordance with the agreements made, and as friendship and good neighbourship demanded. They (the councillors) then asked us if we had no news on the matter of the proposed truce between France and England, to which we could only reply by saying that his Majesty (the Emperor) had not yet heard from the King of France on the subject, and that some people ascribed the delay in the response to the sending of the gentleman of the Duchess d' Etampes to Boulogne. Secretary Paget confirmed this, and stated to us more fully than we previously knew it, the information conveyed to your Majesty in our last letter, about the said Secretary (of the Duchess d'Etampes) and the French intrigues. He (Paget) then disclosed to us, although he had commenced the above conversation unofficially, that the matter had been broached to us by the orders of the King, who was greatly astonished that no reply had been sent. We assured them that, in our opinion, the Emperor would be no less displeased, seeing how anxious he had been to bring about peace. They (the Councillors) then asked what we thought about the proposed truce, and whether we had any hope of it, to which we answered that we could not avoid having good hope of it, seeing that the Emperor had intervened in the matter. This reply did not satisfy them; and they pressed us at once to give them our real opinion about it. After much hesitation, and many excuses for our boldness in venturing to give a personal opinion on the affairs of so wise a prince who was blessed with such prudent counsellors, we were constrained to cede to their importunity, and to tell them, that in our opinion, the making of a simple truce could only redound to the advantage and credit of the King of England; and to the discredit of the French; who would not be likely to consent to a truce, unless it contained some condition favourable to them. They, the French, did not fear the invasion of their country by the English, as they did not believe they would advance beyond Boulogne; and therefore judged it to be more advantageous for them, to let the King of England go to the expense of holding Boulogne against an enemy, than to allow him to save money by means of a truce. It was, we said, a very difficult matter to devise a scheme for reconciliation on this point of Boulogne; since the English were absolutely determined to keep the place, and the French were just as determined to recover it. We proceeded to

1545.

say, lightly and almost jocosely, in order that they might not think we spoke officially, that if they thought to leave the question of Boulogne in suspense until the pensions were paid, it seemed to us most unlikely that the French would listen to such a thing; for it was evident that if they (the French) impoverished themselves first by paying the pensions, they would have less chance of recovering Boulogne than they had at present. Winchester and Paget made no reply to this; but, judging from their demeanour, they seemed to think that it would be no small favour to the French to allow them to defer the payment of the pensions until after the truce had expired.

We put all the pressure possible upon them (Winchester and Paget) to ascertain to what extent the King was disposed to give way; but we could get nothing out of them. On the contrary, they talked much of the great preparations the King had made for the expedition to Scotland; and said that, even if the King of France sent the 30,000 or 40,000 men to this coast, they (the English) did not care. On the other hand, the King (of England) had so thoroughly provided for the defence of his frontiers, that no matter what force the King of France might send, it could do no harm. We thought best not to contradict any of this, but simply observed that, nevertheless, peace would always be welcome, and would be much better than continuing the war. Princes, we said, were mortal, the same as other folks, and as God had made them tutors and administrators of their people, they could do nothing more honourable or appropriate than to pray to God for their peace and welfare. We mentioned, incidentally, that if the King (of England) remained long in the present state of things, he would spend an enormous treasure on the defence of Boulogne, without any advantage or recompense whatever. They seemed to admit this by saying that the King, having considered all points, including the repose of Christendom, was desirous of coming to an understanding for peace on honourable and reasonable conditions. We remarked that they appeared to us to adhere too closely to the conditions which had been proposed in the negotiations between the English ministers and Cardinal du Bellay. To this Paget replied, that he had spoken to the Emperor on that subject, and had proposed that his Majesty should adopt these conditions, or others, which he might be able to arrange.

They told us that, in addition to Dr. Carne, mentioned in our former letter, the Bishop of Westminster[a] who belongs to the Privy Council is to take part in the Conference of Gravelines, as commissioner; so that they will have four doctors on their side. They have said no more about sending Vaughan or the Court-master (Danvers?) and we forgot to enquire whether they are to go to the Conference.

London, 27 April, 1545.

7 May.
Paris
Arch. Nat.
K. 1485.

49. St. Mauris to Francisco de los Cobos.

Letters of 4th and 17 April received. With regard to the preparations here against England, it is certain that they have

---

[a] Dr. Thirlby, afterwards Bishop of Ely.

1545.

decided upon war both by land and sea. The plan is for the French to send to sea 300 ships and 25 galleys, with five galleasses and 10,000 men, in order to make incursions on the island of England, where they intend to make a fort on the coast avoiding proceeding inland. When this is done, they will land their men near Boulogne, where the King of France expects to be able to force the harbour with wooden booms, and to construct a fort on the beach like that which was demolished by the English.* The object of this will be to prevent the English from re-victualling the place. They (the French) intend to have a large number of pioneers to fill the moat and enter over the walls. This is the exact plan of the French up to the present time. The fleet from Marseilles was to leave port on the 1st of this month.

Touching the declaration of the alternative marriage, neither the Duke of Orleans, who has been with the Emperor, nor the Secretary who preceded him, had done anything further than to thank the Emperor for his goodwill. This, I am informed by the Emperor himself, although many things to the contrary were said here; and I am of opinion that the King of France still thinks we shall seek him for a marriage with our princess, in which he is much mistaken.

The English are only besieging Ardres from the neighbouring places where they have garrisons, and consequently victuals are constantly being introduced into the town under cover of night. The place is thus able to hold out. It is to be revictualled on the 20th of this month.

If a man be sent here to claim the two ships seized, I am promised that he shall be referred to the pilot and sailors of the ships, in order that he may be able to learn exactly what happened. I have obtained an order from the King of France that the property seized is all to be embargoed, and an inventory made of it.

The only thing I have to write about the intelligence between the Pope and this King is that everything is going smoothly again, because his Holiness has undertaken to furnish the cost of a contingent of 3,000 men against the English for four months, the money being supplied instead of the men. It is true that the French still demand 4,000 men; and I am told that Cardinal Farnese has arrived at Worms in relation to the settlement of some misunderstanding between the Pope and the Emperor. There is, I am assured, good hope that he will succeed. The Cardinal is afterwards to come hither, for the purpose of inducing the French to send representatives to the Council (of Trent).

---

* This was an ancient Roman tower surrounded by entrenchments, standing on the coast near the mouth of Boulogne harbour. It was called by the French the Tour d'Ordre, and by the English the Old Man; and after it had been captured and dismantled by the English, the Duke of Alburquerque urged Henry to establish a strong modern fort on the opposite side of the harbour, predicting that otherwise the French would do so and make it a point d'appui for an attack upon Boulogne. Henry laughed at the advice, with the result seen in these letters. There is no doubt that the principal object of the French Naval attack upon England was to divert Henry's forces and especially the shipping, in order that the fort above mentioned and another which the Spaniards called St. Jean de Rus, north of Boulogne, should be the more easily constructed.

1545.

The negotiations between the English merchant and Chastillon have been broken off, as the French insist upon recovering Boulogne, and the English insist upon keeping it. The Admiral of France recently sent his secretary to discuss the matter with the Admiral of England, and to offer an increased pension (*i.e.*, national tribute) part of it to be paid in ready money, if they would surrender Boulogne. The English admiral replied that they had better reduce the pension and let English keep Boulogne.

These people (the French) are using every means to influence the Duke of Savoy in the marriage of his son.* But he replies that, however much he may desire it, he will never consent to any match without the goodwill of the Emperor. The Prince of Piedmont is now going to visit his Majesty. News given by the Venetian ambassador to the King of France about the Turk. The latter is making great war-preparations, and has imposed a special war tax. Still hopes continue to be entertained of a truce, by means of the King of France. The Emperor will send a man with the French envoy to Turkey. When the embassy was decided upon, the King of France sent a message to inform the Turk, and to obtain passports for our envoy, who will go direct to Ragusa. The object of the King of France in seeking the truce is to avoid giving the contingent he has promised the Emperor against Turkey; but the Emperor has only consented to the truce, on condition that he does not waive his claim to the contingent, and I have negotiated to this effect.

I have nothing more to say as to the plot about Perpignan; but certainly these people are finely anxious to get the place back. One of them said lately that it was a wound that would never stop bleeding. The Dauphin, especially, wishes to recover it to retrieve his lost honour. I have no doubt M. D'Albret is just as anxious to regain Navarre; but he is much too weak, and he is now sending to pray the Emperor to give him some compensation for his rights. He is desirous that the political rights and privileges of Navarre (fors) shall be respected. He wishes the Emperor to propose a marriage between his daughter† and the second son of the King of the Romans. He (D'Albret) has spoken to me about it, but I told him that he ought not to enter into any negotiation unknown to the King of France; to which he replied that, if the Emperor took the initiative, the King would not be displeased. All this is with the object of getting something at present; or at least that he should be allowed to retain the title of King of Navarre. The Carmelite

---

* That is to say to persuade Emmanuel Philibert, afterwards Duke of Savoy, to marry Margaret of France, which he eventually did many years afterwards.

† It will be recollected that the Spanish kingdom of Navarre had been seized by Charles' grandfather, Ferdinand of Aragon; and that the house of Albret, in which the Navarrese Crown was vested, were now practically reduced to the position of feudal princes of France, in virtue of their Bearnese and other territories north of the Pyrenees. Charles somewhat later thought (as indeed he had done years before) of marrying his own heir Philip with the young Queen Jeanne d'Albret and so to regulate the relations of his house towards the kingdom of Navarre. It need hardly be mentioned that Jeanne subsequently married Antoine de Bourbon, Duke of Vendome, a prince of the house of France, and that on the extinction of the Valois dynasty (1589) her son Henry of Navarre became King of France and ancestor of the present family of Bourbon.

1545.

friar, who intervened in the peace, has returned from Rome and brings a brief by which the Pope requests the Emperor to declare against the English. The reply of the Emperor to this was that as he was an honourable prince, he intended to keep his word to both monarchs. Another reason why he could not declare against the English was that he was engaged against the Turk, but he would endeavour to bring about peace between them (*i.e.*, the French and the English) if possible. The Carmelite was authorised (by the Emperor) to declare to the King of France that, if the latter would consent to a truce he (the Emperor) would negotiate it, Secretary Paget having told him that his master was willing if he was allowed to retain Boulogne. The Carmelite is now being sent back to Rome by the King, to pray the Pope to write to all Christian princes, calling upon them to aid France against the King of England; as it is now a question of executing the sentence of the Apostolic See against a Schismatic. The King of France declares that he will never negotiate a peace which does not restore Boulogne to him. In the meanwhile, the Emperor is determined not to allow the supply of victuals from his dominions to either of the combatants; and a general prohibition has been issued in Germany against any persons leaving the country to enter the service of either prince. But still the King of France expects to obtain 8,000 lansquenets. With reference to this, M. Leyton has informed me that he learns on good authority that two or three thousand Spaniards have gone over to the King of France's service from the Biscay provinces, travelling in bands of 400 by way of Fuentarrabia. There is a Spaniard here in the French service named Salcedo, who says that these Spanish troops are expected. I willingly send notice of this, because these people (the French) ceaselessly endeavour to embroil us with the English, and to make the latter believe that our people are helping the French. For this purpose they are making use of this Carmelite, who is a Spaniard, and the Emperor has ordered him not to accept any more commissions from them without his permission.

A fortnight ago there arrived here a Genoese of the family of Fiesco requesting the aid of the King of France, in order to render the latter paramount at Genoa, and to drive away Prince Doria. He says he has brought the plot to a point, and holds out hope that the people will favour it, if they see themselves supported from here. The plan, however, did not commend itself to the King, to the great disgust of the Dauphin, who urged that the offer should be accepted. This shows his ill-will towards us.

Count William (of Nassau?) is still a prisoner, as the Prince Roche sur Yonne refuses the ransom offered of 20,000 crowns, of which the Emperor is to pay 5,000. The sum originally demanded was 35,000. The King refuses to moderate the demand, though I have begged him from the Emperor to do so. I have no news yet of the reply given by the Protestants to the two points submitted to them, namely religion and aid against the Turk, but these people (the French) say that the Protestants will not consent to the Council, unless it be free, or in other words that decisions shall rest in other hands than in those of the princes of the church. They write to

1545.

me, however, that the presence of the Emperor will greatly influence a favourable reply, which will be given as soon as his Majesty arrives at Worms. I expect that will be in three days from now, as he left Antwerp seven days ago, after he had dismissed the Duke of Orleans, to whom he gave the choice of following him to Worms or returning to France.* The King of France thought that his son ought to come hither to take part in the campaign at Boulogne; whilst the Duke wished to go to Germany on account of the Turk, and to frighten the Protestants out of their evil inclinations. It is certain, however, that the Emperor was not at all anxious for him (the Duke) to go to Germany. So everybody was satisfied.

The French have not sent anyone yet to the Council. They say that this is because the Lutherans are so cool about it, and they (the French) are waiting to see whether they will agree to it. Their intention is to send a number of prelates, amongst others M. Du Bellay, Bishop of Rennes, and the Bishop of Arles, the rest of the prelates being given leave to go if they please.

News comes from the King of Portugal that the Turk intended to send a strong force against the Indies. Negotiations between the writer and the French ministers for the revocation by the France of the letters of marque against Portugal, and the settlement of the claims on both sides.

The statement that the Duke of Savoy intended to commence hostilities against France in Piedmont is now proved to be a lie. The statement that Martin Varotten, the Bastard of Geldres, and Duke Maurice of Saxony, were raising troops for the English has also been found untrue.

The King has made his Keeper of the Seal, Grand Chancellor; the late Chancellor Poyet being deprived of his offices, and declared for ever incapable of holding any position. He is condemned to a fine of 100,000 francs, and five years' imprisonment in the Bastille. Count William is in the same prison, and came to the gate to receive him and bid him welcome.

On Easter Day the young Princess D'Albret made a public declaration in a chapel in the palace of Plessy, where the King was present, to the effect that she had never wished to contract marriage with M. de Cleves; and she swore this by the body of God of which she had that day partaken, and by the holy gospels. I have sent a written copy of this declaration to the Emperor, and it will come in very apposite, for I expect the Duke (of Cleves) will now marry one of the daughters of the King of the Romans.

The Duke D'Albret arrived here to-day, and sent to salute the King and Queen, he said by the orders of the Emperor. I think he will not mention his rings here, so small is his hope that they will return them to him, the King still being of opinion that the whole matter should be decided by his Privy Council. The Venetian ambassador has news that the envoy sent by the King of the Romans to the

---

* Vandernesse says that the Emperor left Liers for Diest on his way to Germany, on the 31st April, whilst the Stadtholderinn (Queen Mary of Hungary) went to Brussels with the Duke of Orleans, who then returned to France for the purpose (it may be added) of taking part in the campaign against the English, during which he caught the plague and died.

Turk died of fever on the very day fixed for his first audience. The Hungarians have made every preparation possible to resist the Turk.

They say that the Duke of ———— * has taken the field with 4,000 men and has entered the territory of Cologne against the aged M. de Cologne, who has married in his old age. There is also a rumour that the Duke of Saxony and the Landgrave of Hesse are arming, though it is said to be only because they fear to be taken unawares.

The King of France requested by the Secretary he sent to the Emperor, that his Majesty would sign the declaration of the alternative marriage. The reply given was that the declaration exhibited was the one which he (the Emperor) had ordered to be written, and as I was his ambassador here, no further signature was necessary. His Majesty has since written ordering me, if I am asked to do so, and not otherwise, to certify at the foot of the declaration that it is the document sent to me.

It has been agreed that the Scots and the Netherlanders may trade with each other, under safe conducts.

The Marquis del Guasto is at Genoa awaiting the Marchioness, who comes from Naples by sea.

The King of France is fortifying seven places near St. Disier.

The Cardinal of Lorraine returned from Nancy two days since, having made the division of the patrimony between his two nephews, M. de Lorraine and M. de Metz.† The latter obtained for his share 15,000 crowns; and the Duchess of Lorraine has given him 10,000 francs worth of furniture. Some lordships have also been given to M. de Guise, to increase his portion, so that they are all well provided for.

M. de Gragnan, who was sent to Worms by the King of France, has declared to M. de Granvelle that he had been sent for three objects: to induce the Protestants to agree to the Council, to prevent the Duke of Lorraine from again receiving the Dukedom of Bar as a fief of the Empire, as the King was informed he intended to do, to his, the King's, prejudice; and thirdly to recover a sum of money owed by the Duke of Bavaria to the King of France. The real reason of his going, however, is believed to be simply to traverse all our plans, and come to an understanding with the Protestants. With reference to this, a prince-elector, I know not which, sent recently to the King of France, to say that the latter ought not to trust in the Emperor at all, as he was sure his Majesty would not keep his word: and advising him (the King of France) not to abandon his old friends in Germany, whom he would always find faithful.

The King of France has proposed a re-trial of Poyet, who, he says, has not been condemned to a sufficient punishment. It is said that this is done at the request of Madame d'Etampes, who wishes to obtain the rest of Poyet's property.

---

* Blank in original.
† i.e., between the Duke Francis of Lorraine and the Bishop of Metz, Jean of Lorraine, afterwards the younger Cardinal of Lorraine.

1545.

The said person (Madame d' Etampes*) is now tracking down Cardinal Tournon, and has already caused his chief secretary to be arrested. She charges the Cardinal with peculation in the penultimate war, when he was Governor of Lyons.

These people here are delighted at a defeat inflicted by the Scots upon the English. They assert that 4,000 men were killed, including the commmander, and many nobles captured.†

M. de L' Orge is being pressed to embark as soon as possible to succour Scotland. It is said that the English are awaiting him on the Irish coast to attack him. I know for certain that the (French) galley fleet left Marseilles on the 30th April last.

Sends documents for the payment of his salary in Spain. Don Enrique de Toledo has passed through here and was very kindly received by the King. He went with M. D'Albret to salute the King; and the latter made them both kiss all the ladies in the French fashion. The ladies were assembled in the saloon to receive them after the King's supper. There was a great deal of astonishment at this.

The writer will have to appoint a representative in Spain to receive his salary, etc., but as he knows nobody there, he prays Cobos to recommend someone. The writer suggests Secretary Gonzalo Perez.

Blois, 7 May, 1545.

7 May.
Paris
Arch. Nat.
K. 1485.
extract.

50. ST. MAURIS (Imperial Ambassador in France) to the REGENT PRINCE PHILIP.

According to the treaty of peace between Spain and France, only such captured vessels are to be restored to their owners as were seized after the conclusion of the treaty. The King of France has now issued a decree prohibiting vessels of all kinds from conveying victuals or munitions of war to England. Since the publication of this order, a Biscay-ship loaded with hides, belonging to English subjects, and other merchandise, the property of Spaniards, sailed from Ireland for Spain. On the high seas she was captured and confiscated by the French, who in justification of their action, quote the old law, which declares neutral ships and neutral goods to be subject to confiscation, if a portion only of the cargo belongs to the enemy. This appears to be a very strange and unjust contention, as free commerce between Spain and England was expressly reserved by the last treaty of peace made by the Emperor with France; whereas, if this French law now evoked be really operative, such commerce would become impossible. Has remonstrated to this effect with the French Government.

Blois, 7 May, 1545 (Spanish translation in the handwriting of Gonzalo Perez).

9 May.
Vienna
Imp. Arch.

51. CHAPUYS to the EMPEROR.

On the 3rd instant I received your Majesty's letters of the

---
* The famous mistress of Francis I.
† These reports of great defeats of the English on the Scottish border were doubtless distorted and exaggerated echoes of the unsuccessful movements of Lennox, etc.

545.

25th ultimo; and I immediately sent to Court to request audience, in order to take leave of the King, in accordance with your Majesty's instructions. The King fixed the audience for the next morning at 10; but I anticipated the appointment by an hour. When I had entered the back door of the King's apartments, having traversed the garden facing the Queen's lodgings, and arrived nearly at the other end, close to the (principal) entrance of the King's apartments, my people informed me that the Queen and the Princess were following us quickly. I hardly had time to rise from the chair in which I was being carried, before she (Queen Catharine Parr) approached quite near, and seemed from the small suite she had with her, and the haste with which she came, as if her purpose in coming was specially to speak to me. She was only accompanied by four or five women of the chamber; and opened the conversation by saying that the King had told her the previous evening that I was coming that morning, to take my leave of him. Whilst on the one hand she was very sorry for my departure, as she had been told that I had always acted well in my office, and the King had confidence in me, on the other hand she doubted not that my health would be better on the other side of the water. I could, however, she said, do as much on the other side as here, for the preservation of the amity between your Majesty and the King, of which I had been one of the chief promoters. For this reason, she was glad that I should go; and although she had no doubt that so wise and good a monarch as your Majesty, would realise the importance and necessity of maintaining this friendship, of which the King, on his part, had given so many proofs in the past; yet it seemed to her that your Majesty had not been so thoroughly informed hitherto, either by my letters or otherwise, of the King's sincere affection and goodwill, as I should be able to report by word of mouth. She therefore begged me affectionately, after I had presented to your Majesty her humble service, to express explicitly to you all I had learned here of the good wishes of the King towards you; and likewise to use my best influence in favour of the maintenance and increase of the existing friendship. She asked me very minutely, and most graciously, after your Majesty's health and expressed great joy to learn of your Majesty's amelioration, adding many courteous and kind expressions. I then asked to be allowed to salute the Princess, which was at once accorded, she, the Queen, being anxious, as it seemed to me, that I should not suffer from having to stand too long. She withdrew seven or eight paces, so as not to overhear my conversation with the Princess. The latter, however, appeared unwilling to prolong the interview, in order not to do detain the Queen, who stood apart regarding us. The Queen would not allow me to accompany her back to her apartments. The conversation with the Princess was confined to my assurance of your Majesty's good wishes towards her, and her humble thanks for the same. In default of power to repay your Majesty in any other way, she said she was bound to pray constantly to God for your Majesty's health and prosperity. When the Queen saw that I had finished my talk with the Princess, she returned immediately to me, and asked if, perchance,

1545.

some of the gentlemen who accompanied me had come from your Majesty. She then many enquiries as to the health, etc., of the Queen (Dowager) of Hungary, to whom she desired to be most affectionately remembered. She said that the King was under great obligation to her Majesty for having on all occasions shown so much goodwill towards him; and she (the Queen of England) continued with a thousand compliments on the Queen (Dowager's) virtue, prudence and diligence. After some other conversation, the Queen returned to her lodgings without allowing me to stir from where I was.

When I left the Queen, I went to the Councillors and repeated to them the contents of your Majesty's letter, both in relation to my departure and the reason for it, and the other points (such as that of Carceres, the restitution of the ship captured by Renegat, and the restitution of the ship from St. Sebastian taken by Windham). The Councillors expressed regret at my departure, for reasons similar to those stated by the Queen; but entertained the same hope with regard to it as that expressed by her. With respect to the second point, they promised me to do their best to discover the whole of Carceres' proceedings and said they would report fully. Referring to the two remaining points, they assured me that there should be no failing in the entire restitution of the ships and goods mentioned; in the assurance that similar steps would be taken in Spain, in accordance with right and justice. There was no need for me to excuse the reprisals effected in Spain, as they did not refer to the matter in the least. When this subject was finished the Chancellor* and the Duke of Suffolk† came to me, for the purpose of talking privately: and after a great prologue about the friendship the King had always shown towards your Majesty, and the importance of maintaining it, the mutual good feeling of the subjects on both sides, and the responsibility and expense the King had incurred for the sake of his love and goodwill to your Majesty; they begged me very earnestly to inform your Majesty fully of everything, and to strive, to the extent of my power, for the maintenance of the friendship, which had not only been advantageous but necessary for your Majesty. They expressed an opinion that the King of France would not be very long before he re-opened the war against your Majesty; to judge, they said, from their (the English) experience of French good faith. If your Majesty would help the King (of England), even with a few men, waggons and victuals, he thought he would be able, not only to keep the French quiet, but to benefit all parties. They then asked me what I had heard of the truce proposed by Your Majesty, and what expedient could be adopted to arrive at a peace or a truce. I replied that I believed your Majesty had received no reply respecting the truce; and I suspected (as I had told them before) that this arose from the confidence with which the French had been inspired by the sending of the Secretary of the Duchess d'Etampes. With regard to the means or expedient about which they asked, I said that that was a subject upon which I could not venture to speak in the presence of such prudent

---

* Wriothesley.
† Charles Brandon, who died soon afterwards.

1545.

personages. I had no doubt that both the King and they had already well ruminated on the matter; and if they cared to open any point to me, I would submit it to your Majesty, either on their behalf, or as of my own motion. They replied that up to the present there did not appear to be much chance of anything being settled, since the Christian King insisted upon the recovery of Boulogne, which place the King, their master, had not the slightest intention in the world of giving up. They repeated that they did make much account of the friendship of the King of France; and especially if your Majesty would agree to give them the assistance above-mentioned. After some further conversation on this, and other points, we went to dinner.

After we had finished dinner the Chancellor and Suffolk repeated almost entirely what they had said before, and begged me very earnestly to give them my opinion as to the expedient which might be adopted to bring about peace or a truce. I excused myself, as before; but in order to escape their importunity, I said (after making due reservation), that I saw no other means at present than to find some person to whose custody Boulogne might be confided during the truce. They asked me whether I meant that the place should be held by your Majesty; to which I replied that I was not speaking of your Majesty, or of any other specific person; but of any sufficient and suitable person. They appeared somewhat pensive at this; and said that there would be a good deal of trouble to find any such sufficient and suitable person. They asked me not to mention this conversation to the King, nor would they, and they begged me to believe that what they had said was entirely on their own account, and without the King's knowledge. He was, they said, not so anxious for peace as many people might think. After having assured them of your Majesty's great affection and goodwill towards the King, I went on to say, that, since the hearts of the two monarchs concurred in true and sincere amity, it was surely unnecessary to wrangle over the words of the treaty, and would be better only to regard the honesty of both sides. If, I said, there was anything that need be added to or substracted from the treaty, in order that all possibility of disagreement should be banished, it would be well that it should be done, the treaties in their entirety remaining. For my own part I wished the matter to be so clear that in future no man of the long robe should ever have an opportunity of meddling with it; and I should have the honour of having, not only commenced, but carried through and finally established affairs upon a sound basis. They expressed their pleasure at this; and asked me to say in what particular I thought the clauses required elucidation. I replied that it appeared to me, that as your Majesty always desired to comply with the tenour of the treaties, and had taken up so well-founded a position, the declaration requested of you was out of the question. It was for them (the English) to consider the matter, and moderate their demands in accordance with reason. The only reply they made to this was that I spoke wisely; and that when matters came to that point, they hoped that I would use my best efforts, as I had done in the past. After a word or two about the long stay of the Scottish ambassador in Flanders, they (the

1545.

Councillors) called Secretary Paget to come and talk with me, whilst they (Wriothesley and Suffolk) seated themselves a little lower down in order to leave room for Paget and myself to communicate the more freely. After Secretary Paget had recited to me the whole particulars of his negotiations in Flanders, and had even repeated several notable and praiseworthy discourses which he had heard from your Majesty, of all of which, he said, he had made full and kindly report to the King, he went on to say that he was infinitely perplexed and troubled to see that, since his departure from Flanders, things had not progressed there as he had hoped. He had intimated to the King that he had very good reason to feel aggrieved at this, especially in the case of the Scottish ambassador, whose immediate expulsion from (the Emperor's) Court he (Henry) might have demanded under the treaties, but which ambassador was still with your Majesty, greatly to the King's regret. Secretary Paget continued that he was also much perplexed, because he had assured the King that there would be no difficulty about the export of the arms and munitions that he (the King) had gathered in Antwerp. These arms, &c., had been brought from Italy and Germany, without the slightest detriment to your territories, and, but for his confidence in your Majesty's affection, he would certainly have sent them by some other route; although nothing but profit could accrue to your Majesty's dominions by their carriage, and to the merchants who had the business in hand. Notwithstanding this, your Majesty was stickling about granting the licences for the exportation of the things. At least, in such case, your Majesty, he said, ought to order that the King should be released from the bargain he had made with regard to them with Erasmus Brusquel; and he (Paget) begged me sincerely—as he again did on my departure—to write most urgently to your Majesty about it, in order to avoid giving offence to the King, both on account of your Majesty's self, and also in regard to his (Paget's) assurance to the King of your Majesty's great affection for him.

After some further conversation Paget went to the King; and shortly afterwards summoned me to the presence. The King received me most graciously, and after he had said some kind things about my convalescence and my departure from England, I gave him an account of the contents of your Majesty's letters. His answers to the various points were in agreement with those already given to me by the Council, except in the matter of Carceres,[*] who he said at once, he did not think was a spy. By the report of certain theologians whom he (the King) had sent at Easter-tide in case the man (Caceres) wished to confess, he (the King) learnt that there never was a person so repentant as he for his evil life, or who wept more bitterly his now detested vices. He did not deny that he had behaved very badly, both towards your Majesty and the King of France, whom he

---

[*] This was a man to whom several short and obscure references are contained in the previous correspondence. He appears to have been a Spaniard who was ostensibly a spy in France, and had fled to England on the conclusion of peace between Francis and Charles. His surrender was now demanded by the Emperor.

endeavoured to deceive, as he did other princes, in order that he might get money to maintain his detestable life. With regard to the rumour that Caceres was a priest, the King said that the man had married in Spain, and was so much worried by his relatives, and especially his mother-in-law, that he left the country. Some time afterwards he heard from Spain that his wife was dead; and he had then taken it into his head to become a priest: but just as he was about to take orders he learnt that his wife was still living and well. He had therefore proceeded no further with his intention. To tell the truth, he (the King) had no great reason for punishing him, because, although the King of France had sent him hither to undertake some plot to his (King Henry's) detriment, yet the intention of Caceres always was to enter the service of England, and to obtain some honest preferment here. When he found himself unable to obtain this preferment, he decided to suborn as many of the Spanish and other soldiers who were in the English service as he could. Up to the present it did not appear that he had effected or proposed any evil practice; and had deferred those he had in his mind until his return to Calais. Seeing the King's tendency in this matter, I thought it better not to press him further, but simply remarked that I thought that your Majesty would be more displeased that Caceres should have plotted against him, than for any plots the same man might have made against yourself, who I believed would be very glad to hear of the man's innocence.

The King subsequently repeated the complaint about the long stay of the Scottish ambassador near your Majesty, touching upon the same reasons as those mentioned by Paget. I pointed out to him that this was more to his advantage than otherwise, as he might have learnt from Paget, to whom I had communicated the whole of the said ambassador's mission; and something might be understood to his profit by means of his ambassador. The King replied that this was all make believe. Nothing of importance had been communicated to Paget; and he (the King) had learnt from Scotland (which he almost held in his hand) and also by certain letters he had captured, that the said ambassador was treating for a marriage with one of the sons of the King of the Romans;* which was a very extraordinary thing. I assured him that there had never been any mention of such a marriage, and he replied that he placed as much reliance in my assurance as he did in the note which the ambassador Van der Delft and I had signed for the release of the seizures. It did not look well before the world to see the Scottish ambassador so kindly treated in your Majesty's court; and your Majesty's recent attitude towards the Duke of Orleans on his arrival was equally open to objection. He (the King) thought decidedly that all this was in contempt of him. I replied that as for the reception of the Duke of Orleans, your Majesty could not do otherwise than order your subjects to welcome him honourably;

---

* That is to say a marriage with the infant Queen of Scots. Needless to say that such a marriage at this time was never contemplated The remark was probably a feeler from Henry, who was determined if possible to marry his own heir to the infant Marie Stuart.

1545.

bearing in mind that the honour in such case redounds more to the giver than to the receiver, and that it behoved your Majesty to repay the respect shown to you on your passage through France. He replied that the honour was excessive, having regard to the person of the Duke of Orleans; besides which, it was not worth while thus to endeavour to conciliate the King of France, who was apparently mortally ill at the time, and could not take any notice of it. It was true, he said, that the King of France was probably as desperately ill as was alleged; because the Duke (of Orleans), although he came on so important a business, brought no letters from the King, notwithstanding his pretence of seeking them, and saying that he had forgotten them. I thought better to say no more about the (Scottish) ambassador, seeing what I had said to Paget on the matter; namely amongst other things, that Morette had told him (*i.e.* the Scottish ambassador) on his (Morette's) departure, on no account to leave your Majesty until his (Morette's) return, or until he heard from him. To this I added an expression of surprise that he (Paget) should make so much of the matter, seeing that there was nothing in the treaties which restrained either sovereign from receiving an ambassador from the enemy of the other, providing that everything that passed should be faithfully communicated to the other Sovereign. It was the more permissible for your Majesty to listen to the Scottish ambassador, I said, since his (Paget's) master had the power of giving safe-conducts to Scots to trade in Flanders.

The King also complained to me that three French galleys and a galliot had been welcomed in Dunkirk harbour, to which complaint I replied that he might be sure that your Majesty did not know of this. You would certainly not allow French armed vessels to frequent or stay in your ports and seek opportunity to injure English subjects, both on account of your Majesty's friendship for him, and because of the prejudice it might bring upon your own people; but I was of opinion that, in case of necessity, such ships might legitimately take shelter in Flemish ports; as, indeed, his Council had frankly admitted.

Speaking on the subject of the peace or truce between England and France, the King observed that he would very much prefer a settled peace to a truce, as the latter gave but little definite result or assurance; but, after all, if your Majesty would aid him, in accordance with the treaty, he did not care very much either for a peace or a truce with the French. They were, in fact, so short of men, victuals and money, that they could neither injure him nor resist him, as had been proved by the successful exploits of the English on land and sea against them. Even during the last ten days the English privateers not in his service had captured 23 French vessels, and shortly before as many more had been sunk, burnt or captured; so that he calculated that his people had taken no less than 300 French ships since the beginning of the war. He thereupon begged, and even supplicated me, as one knowing better than anyone else, the importance of the treaty of friendship, and also his own loyal goodwill towards your Majesty, that I would report very fully, and use my best endeavours, in every way, to induce your

1545.

Majesty to declare against the French, in accordance with the said treaty. I replied that there was no necessity whatever to urge your Majesty to fulfil your obligations under the treaties, as you were quite resolved to do so. With regard, however, to the declaration referred to, he had heard so many cogent reasons justifying your Majesty's attitude on the matter, that there was no need for further discussion. I had, moreover, I reminded him, not come now for that purpose; and I could not sufficiently express my surprise that he had not accepted the reference to the arbitration of your Majesty, which the King of France had consented to abide by. By this means, I said, he might either weaken his enemy legally, by obtaining the arrears of the pension, or else excite your Majesty's resentment against the King of France in consequence of the non-fulfilment by the latter of the treaty (*i.e.* of peace); which might furnish an honourable opportunity for your Majesty to make some such declaration as that requested. The King replied that your Majesty had made no approaches to him in this matter; which I admitted was true; as I thought that your Majesty had accepted the arbitration knowing full well the danger of judging between two friends, one of whom is sure to be offended by the decision, and sometimes both. When I said two friends, the King began to shake his head, and afterwards said that your Majesty put a great deal of trust in the King of France, which surprised him (Henry) very much, having regard to all that had happened. Your Majesty also had solicited the King of France to send an ambassador accompanied by a representative of your Majesty to the Turk, for the purpose of obtaining peace or a truce for eight years; but he had no doubt that the King of France would rather hinder any such agreement than help it, so that he might always keep your Majesty apprehensive on that side, and in constant need of his intercession.

The King then went on to say that there seemed some prospect of progress being made in the matter of the Council summoned to Trent, and he was very much surprised that your Majesty was willing for the Council to meet before the affairs in Germany had been placed on a better footing. By this he clearly indicated that he was not pleased with the Council. Finally, he once more urged me to use my best offices with your Majesty, for the effect already mentioned, both on account of my duty towards your Majesty, and also because I had almost forced him to consent to the treaty by my multitudinous arguments and representations. He repeated a great many of these, and told me that he still had the silver pen which I had sent him to sign the treaty.

I forget to say that the King did not confirm the statements made by his Council to the ambassador Van der Delft and myself about the Secretary of Madame d'Etampes; and it is my opinion that, no matter what dissimilation the King and his people may adopt regarding peace, there is really nothing they more desire.

Gravelines, 9 May, 1545.

9 May.
Vienna
Imp. Arch.

52. CHAPUYS to the QUEEN DOWAGER of HUNGARY.

I have only to add to the letter I am writing to his Imperial Majesty about English affairs, copy of which is enclosed, that I

1545.

have refrained from dwelling fully upon the very kind and complimentary expressions used by the Queen of England towards your Majesty, not from my own wish, but because I believe your Majesty has no appetite for these things. But I must not forget the very affectionate messages entrusted to me for your Majesty by the King and Queen, nor the humble regards sent by the Princess (Mary) who is quite well, and is well-treated by the King and Queen.

Gravelines, 9 May, 1545.

Postscript.—I have brought from England with me a thoroughbred dog sent by Paget. I will forward it shortly to Brussels.

13 May.
Simancas.
E. Genoa.
1377.

53. ANDREA DORIA to PRINCE PHILIP.

Congratulations on the pregnancy of the Princess, his wife. Has no direct news from the Emperor. The twenty galleys which are to serve him (Philip) are in good order. Sends him a letter from the ambassador of the King of the Romans forwarded to him by the Viceroy of Sicily.

Seventeen galleys, two galleasses and 20 transports have sailed from Marseilles with 2,000 Gascon soldiers. It is said that this fleet is bound for Normandy; but others assert that its destination is England. Particulars of the expedition are not known, but it is said that Pietro Strozzi is on board one of the galleys.

Genoa, 13 May, 1545.

[*Italian, original.*]

19 May.
Vienna
Imp. Arch.

54. CHAPUYS to JOOS BAVE, Flemish Secretary of State.

I take the opportunity of this messenger leaving for Brussels to write you a few words. As you will have heard, the English have captured a French galliot and have driven a galley ashore near Boulogne but without loss of life by drowning, although the whole crew fell into the hands of the English. The latter assert that they have during the last few days captured the place of Ardellot in which were a considerable number of men holding it for the King of France. These men marched out by arrangement, and the English count upon keeping the place. If they do they will have to exercise more care than they have at Guisnes, where about a week ago they allowed to pass about a hundred sheep convoyed by a small number of Frenchmen who took them into Ardres; and on the following day, in order still further to improve their soup, the soldiers in Ardres raided a hundred and fifty head of cattle from Guisnes. Two days afterwards the French passed through so large a number of waggons and men as to revictual Ardres.

With regard to this arbitration conference (diette) we have had no meetings yet, except one at Calais and one here, the former of which I could not attend; but when all is said and done, even though the English representatives may have full powers and increase them by words, it looks as if they wanted to draw out matters indefinitely, to judge by the innumerable complaints they have brought forward. Many of these complaints are very old, and some of them have been already dealt with by legal process in Spain and elsewhere. It appears that they propose only to make restitution to our people *pari passu* with the decision of these old claims. They have not omitted to include in their claims the one per cent. tax imposed at Calais during the late wars, and on this account the English claim no less than 30,000 ducats. I doubt not that his Majesty and the ministers who represent him in this conference will resolutely refuse to go into these old complaints, for the examination and decision of which a century would not suffice. God send that all may be satisfactorily arranged. In consequence of the uncertainty of this messenger and the absence of really important matter, I have not cared to trouble our patron[*] or Monseigneur d'Arras, to both of whom pray commend me.

Gravelines, 19 May, 1545.

13 May.
Simancas.
E. 1377.

55. The Emperor to Figueroa.

Yours of 27th and 28th April received. In answer to your enquiry as to what is to be done with the galleys this year and the stay of the Prince at Genoa on the occasion of the declaration upon the alternative marriage, we refer you to our last letters. With regard to the French suspicions about negotiations between the Prince Doria and the Marquis del Guasto, although we had already understood here that there was not much foundation therein, we are still glad to know that the truth of the business has come out; and that no cause of complaint has been given in this or anything else.

Our ambassador in France has informed us that a certain Genoese called "Something" de Fiesco, a man of credit and position in Genoa, has been with the King of France recently, pressing him to aid his brother the Governor of the city. He professes to have already won over the populace and says that, as soon as they see a certainty of French support, they will declare themselves. The King of France rejected the overtures and replied that he had no desire to break friendship with us, as the city was not only under our protection, but had also been included in the treaty of peace. It is said that the Dauphin had exerted great pressure upon his father to aid this Genoese, on the pretext that Prince Doria intended to make himself master of Genoa. Though this business seems to be as groundless as the others, yet as sometimes inconvenience is caused by not striking at the root of such rumours, we think best to let you know, so that you may, in the manner you may consider advisable, speak to Prince Doria about it, and discover secretly if there is such a man in Genoa as the person mentioned as having been in France lately, and as being the brother of the Governor; and any other particulars you can learn. If you find there is anything in it, take such measures as may be necessary to stop it.

Worms, 30 May, 1545.

30 May.
Simancas.
E. 1377.

56. The Emperor to Prince Doria.

Letters of 26th and 27th April received. Thanks for notes of

---

[*] Probably the Imperial Secretary of State, the elder de Granvelle.

1545.

measures necessary for the defence of Sicily against invasion, and for suggestion for relieving Milan somewhat by sending a portion of the Spanish infantry now in Lombardy to Sicily. When we are sure of the Turk's intentions etc. your suggestions shall be considered. We need say no more here about what is to be done with the galleys, as we are sure that you will act in accordance with what we wrote to you in former letters; namely to have the galleys ready to go out and join the others as soon as possible, in order that the combined force may do what may be considered necessary. Glad to be assured of the groundlessness of French suspicions. We never thought you or the Marquis (del Guasto) would do anything of the sort without our knowledge.

Cardinal Farnese has come hither from the Pope, with a great show of friendship and desire for a complete understanding between his Holiness and us. He makes very liberal promises, and says that the Pope wishes to act in entire accord with us in all public affairs, and to place his house and people under our protection and guidance. We replied fittingly, saying that there should be no lack of reciprocity on our part. In accordance with this, we have considered the question of resisting the Turk, for which object he, (Farnese) brought a bill of exchange for ———— crowns which has been duly deposited. We have also discussed at length the subjects of the Council, religion, and the obstinacy of and difficuties raised by, these protestants, together with the measures which may have to be adopted in regard to them. The Cardinal found that matters were more perplexing than his Holiness had imagined, especially owing to the obstinacy of the protestants in refusing to accept or take part in the Council. They still remain obdurate about the Council in the discussions at this Diet; and the Cardinal, although he seemed to wish to stay here longer, has accordingly decided to return to his Holiness to inform him better of the position, and to consider what had better be done. The King of France informed us that he had opened negotiations for a truce with the Turk, and suggested that we might send a person to accompany his envoy, to endeavour to bring about repose to Christendom, and thus to free ourselves from this obstacle, so that we could the better attend to other affairs, notably that of religion and the faith; which we always wished to take in hand and now more than ever, seeing the present peril. We have therefore, with the approval of our brother the King (of the Romans), decided to send a person with instructions to conclude a truce, which shall include all Christian potentates.

Worms, 30 May, 1545.

1 June.
Vienna
Imp. Arch.

57. VAN DER DELFT to the QUEEN DOWAGER.

Your Majesty's letters of 24th ultimo received; by which I learn that you had been informed by the ambassador Chapuys of the King of England's resentment at the long stay in Flanders of the Scottish ambassador, and that the King had been advised that the business he had in hand was a marriage between one of the sons of the King of the Romans and the young Queen of Scotland.

1545.

Your Majesty instructs me, if any such discourse is addressed to me, to assure the King of the truth. I will do so without fail if occasion arises; but up to the present I have heard no whisper of the matter, although ten days since I was with the lords of the Council about certain outrages committed here upon the Emperor's subjects. It is true that about three months ago a vulgar rumour was current, originating, as I discovered, from a merchant's servant, that the ships were ready in Zeeland to go over and fetch the Queen of Scotland. I caused the varlet who had spread the news to be reprehended and forbidden to disseminate such lies for the future. When Chapuys returned from taking leave of the King, he told me that the latter had complained on the subject; and added that the King had also said that he had news that the Emperor had sent an envoy to the Turk. Your Majesty will know how much truth there is in this. As I do not know whether Chapuys omitted to convey this to you as well, I have thought best to mention it. With regard to the answer which your Majesty orders me to give if anything is said to me about a treaty with the Scots: I will obey as usual, and will keep the secrecy required. I have received from your Majesty the duplicate of the instructions given to the Commissioners who are to meet at Gravelines, and it will be useful for me to learn from them (the Commissioners) occasionally what progress they make.

There is no occurrence here with which I need detain your Majesty, except that yesterday morning early an English courier arrived at this Court from that of the Emperor, despatched, I suppose, by the English ambassador resident there. He reported that he had left the Emperor at Worms, and that Cardinal Farnese had arrived there, of which I had previously been advised. He reports also that the Emperor had forbidden the doctrine of the country to be preached there (i.e., at Worms). I do not know what to say, except that these people (the English) appear to be very anxious and doubtful to see what will happen about the Council (i.e., of Trent). They are also greatly offended that their ships and goods have been arrested in Spain; as they think that they have done all they need do for Spanish complainants, when they send them to the Admiralty. The Spaniards will not consent to this method of treating their claims, and, under correction, I think they are right, as the cases are thus prolonged indefinitely.

They have news here that there are a great number of French galleys at sea, some of which have been sighted near Calais. They say that they (i.e., the French) are expecting 17 more large war ships. There is also a rumour of some defeat of the English at Boulogne. There is nothing new from Scotland, whither they have sent their Italians and Spaniards.[*]

London, 1 June, 1545.

3 June.
Vienna
Imp. Arch.

58. The Emperor to Van der Delft.

We have had no news from you for a long while; indeed not since the departure (from England) of Chapuys, who in his letter from

---

[*] The writer of the Spanish Chronicle of Henry VIII. says there were 800 Spaniards sent to Scotland at this time.

1545.

Gravelines fully informed us of what had passed with the King of England and his Council when Chapuys took leave of them. We send this letter to request you to let us know, as soon as you can, what is happening there, and what war preparations are being made both in England and France, with all concomitant details you can obtain. Inform us also what is the tendency of the English in the matter of a truce or peace with France. We must recommend you very emphatically to keep us continually advised on these points, as it is especially necessary at this time; and we will from time to time communicate with you what we consider advisable for our service.

Worms, 3 June, 1545.

3 June.
Vienna
Imp. Arch.

59. The Emperor to Chapuys.

We have received your letters reporting your arrival at Gravelines, and your leavetaking with the King, Queen and Princess of England, and of the lords of the Council. We note the various conversations you had with each of them, and fully approve of your action. As we have had no news for a long time from your successor, who remained in England, we are sending him special instructions to keep us well posted in all that passes there, as it is extremely necessary at this time, with affairs in their present position between England and France; both armies standing ready. We are ordering him (Van der Delft) to be on the watch for any expedient or opportunity which may offer for effecting a peace or truce between them. It will be advisable for you during your stay at Gravelines to do the same, and to write daily to your successor telling him how you think he should act, recommending him to write to us as frequently as possible, and yourself doing the same.

Worms, 3 June, 1545.

4 June.
Simancas.
E. C. de C.
72.

60. Juan Martinez de Recalde* to Prince Philip.

The English on the one hand and the French on the other plunder every Spanish ship they encounter on the Spanish and Portuguese coasts. They take from them guns, munitions and merchandise to the value of a hundred or two hundred ducats each vessel, and in the Flanders Channel similar robberies are perpetrated. The English are said to be much worse than the French.

[Endorsed in the handwriting of Gonzalo Perez: "Copy of letters concerning the French and English navies. Summary of what Juan Martinez de Recalde writes 4 June 1545."]

11 June.
Vienna
Imp. Arch.

61. Chapuys to the Emperor.

Your Majesty's other deputies and myself were in communication with the King of England's commissioners yesterday, after the

---

* This was a famous Biscay seaman who had charge of the King's maritime interests on the coasts of Northern Spain. He commanded the Biscay squadron which escorted Philip across the Bay to marry Mary Tudor; and in his old age was one of the principal commanders of the ships of the Armada, dying with grief at the catastrophe and worn out by hardship immediately after his return to Spain (October, 1588).

1545.

receipt of your Majesty's letters of the 3rd instant. Being desirous, in accordance with your Majesty's instructions, of ascertaining something of the King's feeling respecting a peace or truce with France, it occurred to me when we had finished our business, to say to the Bishop of Westminster and Dr. Petre (both members of the Council and attached to your Majesty's interests) that your Majesty had been extremely gratified to hear from me of the kind and friendly expressions used by the King and Queen, as well as by the Council, towards your Majesty, when I took my leave. I added that your Majesty had approved of my assurance of reciprocal feelings on your Majesty's part, and that on the point of the suggested peace or truce, respecting which I had had some conversation with the King and the Council, your Majesty would be very glad to hear of some means by which your good offices might be made available. I had, I said, been instructed by your Majesty to inform you if there was any appearance of such a possibility; and doubtless the ambassador Van der Delft had received similar instructions. I therefore begged them (*i.e.*, Thirlby and Petre), if they thought I could be of any service to the King in this matter, to do me the honour to tell me; so that I might in this way endeavour to repay in part some of the many favours the King had shown to me. The bishop and the doctor thanked me warmly for my goodwill in reporting as I had done to your Majesty, and for my desire to serve the King; and they promised to write specially to his Majesty on the subject, reporting to me in due course his reply.

After dinner to-day the said bishop (*i.e.* Thirlby, of Westminster) came to me for the purpose, as he said, of hearing more clearly the remarks I made yesterday to him and Dr. Petre. In my opinion however, his real object was to learn whether there was anything further in your Majesty's letters on the subject, beyond what I had said. I repeated my previous remarks, and begged him to tell me if there was any means by which a peace or truce with the French might be attained; but I could extract nothing from him, as he assured me that he had not heard in the Council any mention of such means, and he himself had not wit enough to initiate so important a matter.

At the request of the bishop and his colleagues, your Majesty's other commissioners and I wrote to the Queen (Dowager of Hungary) in Flanders touching the arrest of English subjects and property in Spain (the release of which has not yet been effected, notwithstanding the agreement made with Paget at his departure); and also to beg that the sailors of Blanckenburgh, and others, should not be allowed to undertake the conveyance of French troops, or serve as pilots for them, as the King (of England) had been informed on good authority they were doing. But in addition to this, the bishop now begged me to write on these points direct to your Majesty praying you to order the release of the seizures (in Spain) and to forbid any favour, help, council or guidance, being given to the French by Flemings; and furthermore that when there were indications of the approach of the French fleet to the Flemish coast, orders should be given prohibiting the fishermen of the country from putting to sea, so that they might not be taken

1545.

and compelled to act as pilots for the French. I submit these subjects to your Majesty accordingly. I wrote to the Ambassador in England (Van der Delft) as instructed by your Majesty, and will continue to do so whilst I am here. For the present I had nothing to say, except to report the procedure and progress of this arbitration conference (diette); of which your Majesty will have been fully informed by the despatches written by my colleagues and myself to the Queen Dowager of Hungary.

Bourbourg, 11 June, 1545.

Endorsed:—"From Chapuys 11 June, received at Worms the 18th of the same month, 1545."

12 June.
Vienna
Imp. Arch.

62. Van der Delft to the Emperor.

Since the departure of the ambassador Chapuys for the conference of Gravelines nothing has occurred here with which I thought it necessary to trouble your Majesty; all pending questions, except two, having been either settled before he left, or else referred to the said conference. One of the claims still pending was that of Martin Sanchez de Miranda, which your Majesty ordered me to press prior the departure of Chapuys, and the other was the affair of Antonio de Guaras, a Spanish merchant resident in the city of London.° We had long previously been fully instructed to press the matters by the Queen Dowager, and in both cases have demanded the restitution of the property seized by the English on the pretext that it was owned by Frenchmen. I have used every possible effort to forward the claims, but with the only result up to the present that the Council have sent to me the captains of the two merchants concerned.† The first was Guaras' man, a certain Renegat,‡ whose name I believe will be known to your Majesty as having been the cause of the seizures (of English property) in Spain, by reason of his depredations upon your subjects on the coast of Andalusia, whose harbours he violated, spoliating everything he came across at sea, and even plundering a ship from the Indies, which, I am informed, carried some treasure belonging to your Majesty. I entered into conversation with him and found his statements to be mean

---

* This man, who lived as a merchant in London for more than forty years, was, in my opinion, the author of the Spanish Chronicle of Henry VIII. already mentioned. He wrote an account of the accession of Queen Mary to the English throne, which was printed; and an English version of it has been published with a sketch of Guaras' life, by Dr. Richard Garnett, C.B. For about five years. 1572-77, during the suspension of regular diplomatic relations, he acted as Spanish Chargé d'Affaires in England, but was imprisoned and finally expelled from England for his participation in the plots against Elizabeth. A large number of his letters will be found in Vol. II. of the Spanish Calendar of Elizabeth. This very case of Renegat was quoted thirty-five years later both by the English and Spanish in the disputes relating to Drake's plunder. *See* Spanish Calendar of Elizabeth, Vol. III., pp. 55 and 94.

† Although this is the exact wording of the original, the context makes it clear that the two captains referred to (Renegat and Wyndham) are those who had seized the property respectively of Guaras and Miranda.

‡ This was Robert Renneger or Ronnyger, who was apparently the first English seaman to capture a Spanish treasure coming from the Indies. The gold he brought to London was lodged in the Tower and it was eight years before the Emperor's ambassador obtained partial restitution, though as will be seen in the correspondence the real owners of the treasure never got anything at all, the gold being confiscated by the Emperor, as it was shipped without declaration in violation of the decrees.

and shameful; but he kept obstinately to them. I could not avoid tearing his miserable case to pieces, reproving his disgraceful conduct towards your Majesty's subjects, in spite of the close friendship that existed between the two sovereigns, and pointing out to him the audacity of his violent proceedings without any legitimate excuse. I told him that he would never do any good; and that it would be much better for him to take to some other trade than the sea, for he was rendering no good service either to his sovereign or to himself by his present courses. The excuse he gave was that he had been wronged by your Majesty's subjects; and also that a person had informed him that war was to take place between his King and your Majesty, which had caused him to do as he had done. But he refused to admit that he was wrong, and insisted upon colouring his action by frivolous excuses. On his leaving me, those who accompanied him begged me to take the affair in good part, and I promised them that I would do my best to smooth the matter over, but that I was nevertheless anything but satisfied with the man.

Some time afterwards, four or five days ago, a doctor who is the brother-in-law of the Chancellor here (Wriothesley) came to me with the captain who had seized Miranda's property. This captain's name is Wyndham, and he was accompanied by two other men, who endeavoured to convince me that the goods in question belonged to Frenchmen, as all the sailors, they said, had confessed before the Justice of the Peace at Plymouth; and even Miranda himself had acknowledged in writing. As we had asserted that this writing had been obtained from Miranda by force, they had brought a witness who, they said, would prove to the contrary. This witness turned out to be the very man who had given a certificate to Miranda, to the effect that the writing signed by the latter in Plymouth had been extorted by force. After much examination and argument on both sides, Miranda himself being present to facilitate the enquiry, the fault of the captain was made manifest by his own statements. But he still persisted in colouring the facts; saying that the witness referred to had certified that Miranda's written declaration had been extorted from him, in consequence of the urgent prayers of Miranda, who told him he would be utterly ruined if he did not obtain the certificate in question, and would never dare to return to Spain. Much discussion arose out of this, but finally, unaided by any evidence beyond their own admissions and general probability, I sent them away almost convinced.

I thought necessary to go to the Council for the purpose of informing them what had passed at the enquiry held at my house, and especially as in the interim they had referred Guaras' case to the Admiralty, although it had already been so long delayed. I thought we had reason to complain of this, as according to the recent arrangement with Paget they could not take this course. I had also continued to send them a number of fresh complaints from your Majesty's subjects, to which no answer had been given. I therefore sent to ask for an appointment, for the purpose of concluding the affairs of Miranda and Guaras, as

1545.

well as other complaints, which I said it behoved them to redress speedily, in order to avoid the multiplication of such claims, and the consequent recrudescence of the troubles from which we are only just emerging.

When my man gave them this message, they began to declare again that the goods claimed by Miranda belonged to French subjects, as, they said, was the case also with the other claims, and they had decided to send them all to the Admiralty; as in future they intended to do with all similar complaints. It was, they said, no business of theirs (*i.e.*, the Councillors) to decide questions which appertained to the regular Admiralty tribunals. They had quite enough to do with affairs of State and the war, in which they were now engaged alone against France and Scotland, and they knew not whom else. I presume they meant by this last, our holy father the Pope, as I understand they now look upon it as certain that his Holiness will have sent some galleys and money to the King of France. My man replied that he had simply been sent to their Lordships to request an interview for a couple of hours on any day convenient to them. The Chancellor thereupon asked if I had received letters from your Majesty, in which case I should be welcome; but that if I proposed to come simply about the merchants' claims there was no more to be said on that subject, and he begged me to be easy on the point, as they had referred them all to the Admiralty. If there was any point still pending and I would advise them, they would see to it.

I was rather irritated at such a reply as this; seeing that in covert words it was a refusal to give me audience, even for so short a time. But nevertheless, in order to fulfil my instructions to the best of my scant ability, I considered necessary to go to the Council; and so to make the first advance, notwithstanding the answer, which I thought entirely at variance with the agreement made with Paget. It seemed to me, moreover, that they could not avoid taking my visit in good part, seeing that it was for the purpose of giving them information which might prevent difficulties otherwise impending from the multiplication of merchants' claims, the reference of which to the Admiralty, was, I knew, for many reasons unsatisfactory to the claimants.

With this object, after I had thoroughly examined the various claims, I went on the following day to the Council, arriving early, before the whole of the members had assembled. I was received civilly, but, it seemed to me, not very cordially; and when they were all present I explained my coming, as having been prompted, not only by my duty in my office, but also by my anxiety to see matters on a good footing. There was at present, I said, some little acerbity through their fault, which I would help them willingly to banish. After expressing some annoyance at the answer they had sent me about the audience, I then came to business, repeating what had passed in the enquiry I had held in the cases of Guaras and Miranda, and requesting them to examine the evidence and compare it with the captain's statements, so that they might give a decision in the matters. They replied that they considered me so sage and discreet that they expected I should have regard to the great affairs which occupied them, would avoid importuning them on matters purely judicial; whereupon they repeated their message of the previous day, to the effect that these cases appertained to the Admiralty. I said that I held the Admiralty tribunals in due respect, and had no desire whatever to depreciate them, but I nevertheless begged their Lordships to fix an hour to examine the cases for themselves, the evidence being so clear that if they would consent to look at it, they might dispose of all the complaints in two or three hours. This I said, moreover, was, as they were aware, the procedure to which they are pledged by Paget's agreement, and any other course would be an infraction of it. They replied that it was we who had failed to fulfil the said treaty: for when the embargo on English property was raised in Antwerp they were obliged to give security, of which no mention was made in the treaty. I said that this was not the proper way to look at it. The security was only exacted pending our claims on this side being satisfied. Besides, they said, the English were in all other countries submitted to the admiralty jurisdiction, even in Flanders; and furthermore, observed the Bishop of Winchester, when he was last with the Emperor at Brussels a question was under discussion, in which the King of England himself was interested, and that was referred to the Admiralty (in Flanders). In Spain, he said, they were referred to the Council of the Indies, and notably in the case of the present seizures (in Spain). I excused these seizures, saying that they were effected without your Majesty's knowledge. They made a great ado about it, saying that it was a violation of international intercourse, and of the treaty of friendship; to which I replied that if they considered it so very bad how could they excuse the efforts made here to defend Captain Renegat, who had so shamefully outraged your Majesty's subjects, in violation of all treaties and rights? According to their own doctrine, I said, they ought to punish him in exemplary fashion as a pirate, instead of which, so far as I could see, he was being made quite a hero of here for his fine piece of work.[*] For the good of both parties, I said, I wished he might never see either England or Spain again, for he was a man who would never act well anywhere, and I was quite at a loss to understand how they could tolerate such acts from a like person, whilst we on both sides were striving incessantly to increase the old amity between the crowns. We disputed thus for a long while, until dinner time.

As one councillor after the other rose, the Chancellor approached me, and made a long complaint about their being abandoned thus in the war against two or three princes, without aid or ally. Considering the trouble he (Wriothesley) had taken to bring his master to the alliance with your Majesty and the small advantage they had derived from it, he grieved greatly at their condition. It was quite true, he said, that they did not doubt your Majesty's wish to fulfil the treaty of friendship, but he nevertheless wished that it were somewhat more clearly evinced. All this he expressed in very

---

[*] Both Renniger and his brother commanded ships against the French during this year.

1545.

many involved words, sometimes slipping in an observation about peace or a truce, but always so obscurely that I could make nothing more of it; though it seemed to me as if he desired that I should write to your Majesty about it. When he had finished his discourse, he and the rest of the Councillors pressed me to stay to dinner with them, which I did. My answer to him was short, as we went to wash, and I limited myself to assuring them of your Majesty's affection for the King, his realm and his subjects; for all of which your friendship could not be exaggerated. With that we went to table.

After dinner I endeavoured to obtain some more satisfactory reply to your subjects' claims than a reference to the Admiralty Court; saying that there was scant hope of obtaining justice there, since they (the councillors) in referring the cases to the Admiralty prejudge them, and roundly state that the goods in question belonged to Frenchmen; and it was quite certain that the members of the court would not contradict their masters, however clear the evidence might be on the other side. I therefore urgently begged them to have the evidence examined on their own behalf; and I went so far as to propose that if, as they said, they could not examine it themselves, they should appoint some honest persons to aid one of the councillors to make the enquiry and confront the witnesses on both sides, weighing the balance of probability in doubtful points; and deciding as they thought just. They remained quite obdurate however, and I could obtain no concession on the point; nor would they consent to release the property against security, which I proposed. I supported this suggestion by saying that not only would this be just on the merits of the case, but since the merchants depended entirely upon their Lordships' wisdom and integrity, though they (the councillors) said the goods in question were French property, the complainants were quite content to abide by their judgment, if they would only consent to examine the evidence. I used every persuasion I could think of to induce them to grant some concession which should restrain the merchants from again laying their complaints before your Majesty; which, as I said, they (the councillors) would understand would by no means forward the release of the seizures in Spain, although the latter were effected without your Majesty's knowledge. But withal, Sire, I could get nothing whatever from them.

I would also have proposed that these cases should have been referred to the arbitration conference (diette) but I thought better not to take this course just yet, as that will be easy to obtain, and may be left as a last resource. I shall be glad to receive your Majesty's instructions on this point; but I am not altogether certain about the result of this reference to the arbitration conference, seeing how ready these people are to refer everything thither, as if they were sure that nothing would be achieved.

I must not omit to mention that, as I was leaving, Paget entered into conversation with me, and complained bitterly that they had been unable to obtain from your Majesty permission for the export of certain munitions of war which they had ordered. He said it was a trifling matter in itself, but the King was so much annoyed and offended at it, that if he (Paget) were a rich man, and money could have got over the difficulty, he would willingly have sacrificed half his fortune to have avoided the rebuff. He also complained that if they needed a captain (a Spanish mercenary?) it was necessary for him to pretend to be going (from Flanders) to France, and then to come from St. Omer hither. It was true, he added, that plenty of smooth words were given to them; and especially lately to the English ambassador with your Majesty at Worms, but the King was anxious to see some deeds to match. I replied that I was much astonished to hear such talk, since he himself had told me when he returned from his mission to your Majesty, that he had been so well treated, and had taken leave of your Majesty so joyously and well satisfied. He had, I said, apparently forgotten all this. When I departed, however, I confirmed the assurance of your Majesty's entire affection, which I said would always lead you to gratify the King, his realm and his subjects, in accordance with the ancient amity and inviolable alliance. I left the chamber with the ordinary salutation, and was honourably and courteously conducted to the outer precincts of the Court by the King's Master of the Horse (Sir Anthony Browne) notwithstanding my protests.

When I had returned home, and considered the merely negative results which I had obtained from my interview with the Council, I thought before writing to your Majesty I had better send to Paget again, which I did the next day; saying that I had conveyed the reply of the Lords of the Council to the merchants, and that the latter had declared that rather than go to the Admiralty Court to prosecute claims to their property for three or four years, without being able to obtain possession of their goods against security, they would almost prefer to abandon the claims altogether. They (the merchants) saw that their only chance of redress was to appeal to your Majesty, and had requested me to give them letters to the Emperor with a statement of the case; but I was in some doubt and perplexity about writing to your Majesty on a point that had been so unfavourably and obstinately dealt with on their side. I therefore thought best to appeal to him (Paget), trusting to his affection and his invariable desire to interpret affairs in the most friendly way. I held out hopes to him that, if he could arrange for the merchants to obtain possession of their goods against security, I would endeavour to withhold the complaints, and prevent the merchants from appealing to your Majesty, whom otherwise I must fully inform.

Paget replied that, with regard to my perplexity about writing to your Majesty what had passed between the Council and myself, he knew me to be so sage and discreet that he was sure I should take the best course, as he also was certain that your Majesty and the (imperial) Council would be satisfied with the reply that had been given to me. This reply he repeated, saying that the Lords of the Council begged to be excused from dealing with cases which appertained strictly to the Admiralty jurisdiction. They (the Councillors) were too busy with affairs of State to occupy themselves with matters which should be settled by ordinary judicial process. They had done so previously (referring to the seizures at Antwerp) because on that occasion the claims in question were influencing State affairs, but no precedent must be formed from it. With regard to releasing the goods on security, Paget replied that if they (the councillors) chose to believe the allegations of the English merchants, they would arrest all Spanish merchants here; but having the assurance that the seizures in Spain were effected without the knowledge of your Majesty, they preferred not to listen to the prayers of the merchants; especially as your Majesty had personally assured him (Paget) of your intention to respect inviolably the friendship and alliance, and to cause the subjects on both sides to be treated with absolute equality. This intention had been entirely frustrated in Spain, and the treaty itself violated. Admitting, he said, that some offence or violation may have been committed by one of their private captains, it was still illicit for the other side immediately to effect a seizure in reprisal; and he doubted not that your Majesty would promptly order a release.

This was the reply brought back by my man, and your Majesty is now in possession of everything that has passed. Pray forgive me for making so long a story of it; and deign to instruct me how to proceed, for I am now completely checked, with the Council obstinately immoveable, though in violation of the treaty, on one side, and your Majesty's wronged and dissatisfied subjects on the other. The reasons why the merchants are so much afraid of the Admiralty Court was conveyed to your Majesty some time ago. I am told that everything is settled by two persons, of whom one is generally absent. Your Majesty may perhaps consider whether some favourable influence might not be exercised. Several persons have told me that they have seen good effects from it. But, withal, the procedure is so slow as to be unending.

Under correction, it seems to me to be necessary in any case that your Majesty's subjects should be able to obtain possession of their goods on giving security, both in present and future cases; for it looks as if these people meant to seize everything they meet at sea on the pretext that it is French property; and then refer all claimants to the Admiralty. No matter what bills of lading the mariners produce, they are asserted to be false; and the masters are told that they have a double set. This procedure will be more profitable in the end to the English than a counter seizure would be, whilst they can always glose it over by pretending that they are doing strict justice to your subjects in the Admiralty Court; the property in the meanwhile being sacrificed at wretched prices.

I am sending a duplicate of this long letter to the Queen Dowager. Again under correction, I beg to state that in my opinion this difficulty in promptly redressing the claims of your Majesty's subjects does not arise from any change from their (*i.e.*, the English) former devotion to your Majesty; but perhaps rather because they may find a cooling in the hopes they entertained of being able, through you, to obtain a peace or truce with the French. They let this be seen by their conversation, saying that formerly your Majesty replied to them to the effect that it would be better that the first approaches for a peace or truce should come from the

1545.

French; but in the meanwhile time is going on, and they see that nothing is being done in the matter.

Great diligence is being used here in the arming and equipping of ships, which are being sent to sea one after the other. A few days ago the admiral[*] with 23 or 24 vessels was ready to sail; but the wind did not serve for leaving harbour until the day before yesterday. There are a great many more ships which will follow him; so that, they say they will have 120 or 130 ships, well supplied with guns and men. The Duke of Norfolk, Lord St. John, Master of the Household, and Sir Anthony Browne, Master of the Horse, recently returned from the north and west countries, whither they had gone to put the country and harbours in a state of defence so that, as they told me, they fear not the coming of their enemies.

There is nothing fresh from Scotland, whither they recently sent the Italians and Spaniards that they have in their service, but there is no news of their having done anything yet. The Earl of Hertford and Master Knyvett are their chiefs. The bearer of the present is fully able to give information with respect to his case to any person appointed by your Majesty to hear him. As other merchants also may be on the way with their evidence, I do not trouble your Majesty further on the subject, except to repeat that I have done my best for them, but that they are all referred to the Admiralty Court.

London, 12th June, 1545.

13 June.
Vienna
Imp. Arch.

63. VAN DER DELFT to the QUEEN DOWAGER.

Since my last letters I have never ceased to press upon the Council the claims and grievances of his Majesty's subjects. These claims increase from day to day, and have now accumulated to such an extent, by reason of the delay in dealing with them, as to threaten to fall into utter confusion, the merchants after lengthy proceedings finding themselves most unsatisfactorily referred to the Admiralty Courts. Seeing that this course was not only unfavourable to the parties, but was in contravention with the agreement recently made with Paget, I thought well to see the Councillors, in the hope of persuading them to do justice promptly to the various claimants. I was however quite unable to move them, and they persist in their resolution to refer all such claims present and future to the Admiralty, where foreigners cannot hope for a favourable issue. I am now fully informing the Emperor of this, as will be seen by copies of my letters to him herewith; and I humbly beg your Majesty to consider the consequences which may arise, and devise some remedy. It is to be feared that if these people gain their point this time, and send all complaints to the Admiralty, they will seize everything they find afloat, on the pretext that it is French property, and the only redress will be to proceed in the Admiralty Court. It looks, indeed, as if they had already made up their minds to do this, for no matter what bills of lading are shown to them, they always

---

[*] John Dudley, Lord Lisle, afterwards Earl of Warwick and Duke of Northumberland

1545.

say they are false and that double sets of bills of lading are signed. In the meanwhile, the claims of the Emperor's subjects grow in number, and at the present moment I have received two new complaints, in addition to those which the complainants have referred to his Imperial Majesty for redress. To say the truth, Madame, I am much perplexed to see the evil inclination of these people (*i.e.*, the English Council) towards the proposals I have made to them, whilst his Majesty's subjects remain still without redress. Even if the Council were to decide upon the claims, as we request, I doubt not that the Emperor's subjects would lose considerably. I await the orders of the Emperor and yourself, with regard to the advisability of speaking of the reference of these claims to the arbitration conference.

Under correction, Madame, in any case I think it very necessary that every effort should be made for the merchants to be able to obtain possession of their goods on giving security, and so to continue their voyages. Otherwise their loss will ruinous, considering the character of these people here, who during the progress of the case value the goods and sell them immediately, often for half their real value; and then if the decision is given in favour of the merchant, they will only pay him the amount of money they have received for the sale. Even this can only be got by great pressure. I can assure your Majesty that this is true.

As I was dispatching this letter I received your Majesty's instructions to assist certain merchants of Bruges to obtain from this King a safe conduct to trade with Scotland, similar to those granted to them by the Emperor. I will obey: but I cannot refrain from mentioning that there was to-day a rumour on 'Change here that peace had been proclaimed with the Scots in Antwerp. If the Council mention the matter to me, I will answer in accordance with your Majesty's previous instructions.

London, 13 June, 1545.

13 June.
Vienna
Imp. Arch.

64. The EMPEROR to VAN DER DELFT.

About a fortnight since the English Ambassador addressed us on several points, and especially regarding the rendering of the assistance stipulated in the treaty of alliance, in case of invasion. You will learn the details of our answer from the copy herewith of a letter we have written on the subject to the Queen Dowager of Hungary: and from it you will understand the difficulty and perplexity which surrounds either the giving or refusing of the aid requested. In view of the copies we send you, you will be able to consider and adopt the best means you can devise for successfully dealing with the subject, which may be summarized under seven heads for your guidance.

First: we must avoid an infraction of the terms of our treaties with England and France, and must give no excuse for either of them to allege any violation on our part.

Secondly: we must not admit, either expressly or tacitly, that the King of England has fulfilled his part of the treaty; and must continue to insist that the arrangement we made with the King of France was made with his (the King of England's) full consent.

Thirdly: the King of England must be made to understand that if we give him the aid required, it must not be inferred that for the same reason we can give him any further assistance, or forbid our subjects from trading with France.

Fourthly: admitting that the terms of the treaty bind us to give the aid in case the King of France should invade the realm of England with the forces stated in the treaty; it must be borne in mind that at the present time the object of any invasion would be solely for the recovery of Boulogne, the defence of which place is not comprised in the treaty, and the King of France has always been willing to conclude peace if Boulogne were restored to him. Our efforts should rather be directed to this latter object, than to aid either party to continue the war.

Fifthly: The difficulty in our furnishing aid in the form of men is increased by reason of the ill-treatment meted out to our subjects who entered the King of England's service ashore and afloat last year, the violence committed on them subsequently, and the opprobrious words and bad behaviour used towards them in England.

Sixthly: In accordance with reason, and in fulfilment of the treaty of alliance, the King of England should fully and honestly restore to all our subjects, Flemish and Spanish, the ships and property belonging to them still detained by him and his people. There can be no excuse now for his not doing this, as the facts of the detention are notorious; and the procedure stipulated by the treaty has been adopted; although his representatives refuse to be reasonable, or to be guided by the evidence. And above all, the injuries inflicted on our subjects during the war last year by Landenberg's troops and the Englishmen must not be forgotten, as we reminded the Earl of Hertford and the Bishop of Winchester when they came on their mission to us.

Seventhly: There is a rumour that the King of England is negotiating with the Protestants of Germany for the purpose of forming a confederacy with them. This he cannot do without our consent, by the terms of the treaty, and it is of the highest importance to us, both as touching our imperial authority and for other reasons. We are sure that if the war goes on between France and England; and especially if the latter be invaded, either from France or Scotland, the King of England will continue to press for the aid he now demands from us through his ambassador, and we have therefore decided to place the negotiations in your hands. We presume that the English ambassador is merely instructed to press us to grant the assistance without debating the pro and contra: and as you were present in Brussels when the matter was discussed with Hertford and Winchester, and in conjunction with your colleague Chapuys have dealt with it since your arrival in England, we think you will be better able than another to take the negotiations in hand, and to proceed as you think best in our interest, having in view the progress of the war, the relations between the combatants, and the greater or less pressure that may be exercised by the King of England to obtain the aid he requests.

Your main object will be to temporise as long as possible, and to endeavour to avoid our granting the aid, seeing the difficulties thereto set forth in the copies of letters enclosed. You may obtain an opportunity of coming to some final understanding with them, in accordance with what you heard in Brussels, and the instructions to Chapuys and yourself when you left for England. Such settlement has hitherto been avoided by the English, although it was the principal reason for our sending Chapuys thither.

As was pointed out to the Earl of Hertford and the Bishop of Winchester, even if we consented to waive the point of the non-fulfilment of the treaty by the King of England, and also that the sole object of the war now is the recovery of Boulogne (which place was not included in the treaty, for which reason the King of France might greatly resent the granting of aid to England), it will be absolutely necessary, in any case, before we come to any decision in the matter of the aid, that the King of England shall approve of our treaty of peace with France, which treaty was concluded with his consent. It is quite true that we were at liberty to make the treaty without his acquiescence, since he declined to send his troops to join us as he had agreed to do; and in reply to our requisition that he should send them said that he could not do so as they were engaged in an enterprise of his own, having nothing to do with the principal object of the war.

In any case, it will be necessary for him to be satisfied with the aid to be sent him, and he must not demand anything further, either from ourselves or our subjects, which might directly or indirectly infringe upon our treaty of peace with France. Our subjects also must be allowed freely to communicate, frequent, and trade, with France and other countries both by land and sea, without any hindrance or opposition from the King of England or his people.

For the reasons fully explained in the letters to our sister, and lightly touched upon above, the aid must take the form of a money payment.

Besides this, the restitution of our subjects' property must be fully effected as a preliminary measure, and at once; and we must be assured that the King of England has not made, and will not make, any treaty with the Protestants or with anyone else, even with the King of France, without our knowledge. This is in conformity with the treaty, and when the latter is confirmed by the King of England he must fulfil its clauses, absolutely, in all matters touching us or our subjects.

You must always take particular care not to say or admit anything which will allow the King of England or his people the slightest pretext for alleging that, either overtly or tacitly, we have condoned the non-fulfilment of the treaty by him. This is a most vital point, as you were informed prior to your departure from Brussels. The various conditions mentioned above must not be brought forward by you in a way which may imply that if they are accepted the aid will necessarily be granted. You will put them before the King, in order that he may give his decision upon them, which you will communicate to us; and we will then resolve with regard to the granting of the aid. This was the main purpose of your mission and that of Chapuys, and the King and his

SPANISH STATE PAPERS.

545.

Council must be made to understand that, until the above-mentioned questions are settled, we cannot come to any decision with regard to their request; as the Earl of Hertford and the Bishop of Winchester were previously informed, though they persisted that we were bound to declare war unconditionally against France, and all they demanded simply tended to that end. The King and his Council may still pretend that we are so bound, notwithstanding any aid we may give—or even in consequence thereof—but this must not for a moment be admitted.

With regard to the allegation of the Earl of Hertford and the Bishop of Winchester, that on their departure we consented to grant the aid demanded in case of the invasion of England, you may reply—as we say in our letter to the Queen (Dowager)—that the only expression we used was that in such case we would fulfil our obligations. This, moreover, was in continuation of what we had said on other points, touching the treaty and its observance, without contravening the other treaty with France. If the King of England wants to apply what we said upon these points to the granting of the aid, he can only do so by accepting with it the various other conditions and limitations contained in the same and previous speeches, which were always referred to. And at the same time also you must keep in view the nonfulfilment of the treaty (by England) subsequently, as for instance in the redress and restitution to our subjects.

You will always take great care to set forth the views we have stated in the most gracious and courteous manner possible, dwelling constantly both to the King and his Council upon our desire scrupulously to preserve the kindly peace, and sincere and perfect friendship which exists between us and our peoples; and likewise upon our anxiety to do all we can to bring about a peace between England and France. You must, however, be careful not to say anything about France which may be used by the English King or his people to breed discord between us and the French.

If you find the King and his people violent and unreasonable, you must still not break off the negotiations, or give them an excuse for saying that we have refused the aid. You will confine yourself to the ground that all your statements are preliminary, and for the purpose of gaining information which will be conveyed to us, to help us in our final decision; and that you are confident that our resolve in this, and all else, will be with reason and honesty to fulfil everything to which we are bound. You will make them understand that what you are negotiating on that side is not for the purpose of delaying our decision, but rather to expedite it. It will be highly necessary for you to let us know all you are doing, and the conversations you have with the King and Council, as well as the progress of the war; whether there is any appearance of negotiation between the English and the French, the attitude of the English towards the Scots, the means by which the King of England is obtaining resources for the war, the feeling of the English people generally about the war, and other particulars which you may consider merit description.

It will be advisable for you to keep up a continual correspondence with M. Eustace Chapuys whilst he is conferring with the English

1545.

Commissioners, communicating with him as often as you can, and consulting him as need may arise and time will allow, both upon the matters set forth above, and other points of your mission. We are sending this dispatch through him, in order that he may master the contents and give you his advice on the whole subject. We also instruct him to take such steps in the matter with the English Commissioners as he may consider advisable, and to keep you informed.

Worms, 13 June, 1545.

Postscript.—We must not omit to inform you that the English Ambassador has not returned a second time to speak with us on the points referred to above; but we expect he will soon do so, as we deferred our reply to him until we had received advices from the Queen our sister. When he renews his application we will refer him to the instructions we have given to you to conduct the negotiations in England, and will go no further with him. We doubt not that he will then immediately inform the King, who will at once, either personally or through his Council, speak to you about it. Until this happens you need make no sign, but it is well that you should be preadvised.

13 June.
Vienna
Imp. Arch.

65. The Emperor to Chapuys.

We are sending this special courier to our ambassador in England, M. Van der Delft, for the reasons which you will see by our letters to him, of which copies are enclosed. We have ordered the courier to go first to you (supposing you still to be at Gravelines) and you will have the various documents deciphered, and will consider the whole matter. You will then write fully to Van der Delft, giving him your views as to how he should proceed, as your long experience in England will enable you better than any other to judge the best manner of carrying on the negotiation. We have instructed him in our letters to follow your advice, and to keep in communication with you on this and other parts of his mission, whilst you are occupied with the arbitration conference. We are confident from our knowledge of your continued zeal in our service that you will keep in touch with Van der Delft and advise him for the best.

Worms, 13 June, 1545.

14 June.
Vienna
Imp. Arch.

66. Van der Delft to the Emperor.

I have received your Majesty's letters of the 3rd instant, rebuking me for my long silence, and ordering me to keep your Majesty informed continually with regard to events and opinions here. I pray your Majesty to pardon my silence, which arose from the absence of matter with which I thought worthy of troubling your Majesty, especially since the departure last month of my predecessor M. Chapuys. Nevertheless, the letters from me now on the way to your Majesty contain a full account of affairs. To them I have at present only to add that there is a rumour here that the French are gathering for the purpose of attacking Boulogne and Calais, and that the King is shortly to go ten or twelve miles from here towards Dover. With regard to a peace or truce, your Majesty will learn by

1545.

my other letters that it seems still their hope that they may obtain peace or a truce through your Majesty's intervention, though your Majesty appears to have told them recently that you thought the approaches should first come from France. In future I will keep your Majesty constantly advised as you order.

London, 14 June, 1545.

18 June.
Vienna
Imp. Arch.

67. VAN DER DELFT to the EMPEROR.

Since writing the earlier letters which accompany this (such letters having been written to be sent by the first opportunity), I have learnt on good authority that a Secretary of the Queen of England named Richard Butler is in some part of Germany, where he must have been a month or six weeks before your Majesty left Brussels. His mission is to solicit secretly the German princes to form a league with this King, which seems to me, Sire, to be a point of the highest importance, as touching the religious question. I have thought well, therefore, to advise your Majesty of it at once by the bearer, who is going also for the purpose of complaining to your Majesty of the seizure and detention of his merchandise, the same answer having been given to him as to the others, referring him to the Admiralty Court. As he was ready to depart, I have begged him to lose no time, for the reason stated above.

The merchants on 'Change here have news that 24 or 25 French galleys, with about 40 great warships, have come to Brittany. Fresh ships are constantly being sent to sea here to join the admiral, who they say, will have 20,000 men, without counting victuallers. The Dukes of Suffolk and Norfolk depart to-day, but I know not whither. Warning has been given here to all gentlemen burgesses and peasants, to be ready with arms to join the standards when the beacons are lit, as is the custom here, on the hill-tops, towers, and other eminences every three miles. By this organisation they say they can muster 25,000 or 30,000 men within two hours; and even in a very short time they can have the whole country under arms. Whatever side, therefore, an enemy approaches, they have a great muster of men ready to receive him, and they are very confident of their strength in consequence of this, being delighted to see their enemy near.

London, 18th June, 1545.

Endorsed:—"From the ambassador in England 18 June received at Worms on the 25th of the same month.'

18 June.
Vienna
Imp. Arch.

68. VAN DER DELFT to the QUEEN DOWAGER.

I am writing to the Emperor as per copy enclosed; and as the matter is so important, I cannot avoid likewise advising your Majesty. I also wish to say that I have been informed from two quarters that the King is secretly warning his subjects and merchants abroad to secure their property in good time, whilst those who are in England are forbidden to export any merchandise. As this is a dangerous thing to write, unless it be true, I have not ventured to touch upon it in my letters to the Emperor, until I have been able to make further enquiries as to its correctness. I have, however, thought

1545.

well to inform your Majesty, who may perhaps discover if it be true by enquiring in Antwerp or elsewhere, and inform his Majesty if you consider advisable. I will communicate to your Majesty what I can learn further on the point.

London, 18 June, 1545.

18 June.
Vienna
Imp. Arch.

69. VAN DER DELFT to the BURGOMASTER and CORPORATION of BRUGES.

Your letters of 9th instant received by bearer, and I have, in accordance with your request, given to the bearer all the help I could for the fulfilment of his mission. But withal, the only reply he bears is to the effect that Secretary Paget (who is the principal adviser of the King) having read the request I had attached to the visé of the safe conduct you sent me, simply shrugged his shoulders, and gave the documents back to your man. I am not surprised at this, for I predicted it when I saw that your man was only authorised to ask this King to grant a safe conduct similar to that which you sent. So much importance is attached to such a matter here, that even if half the Councillors had been gained to support the request, I doubt whether you would have succeeded with the King himself. As it depends entirely upon the special grace of the King, and must proceed from his own mouth, the only way is to gain friends about him. With regard to your request that I should intercede with the King, you must know, gentlemen, that on no account whatever can this be considered a part of my duty, and I could not undertake to do such a thing, until I had fuller instructions from the Queen (Dowager) than are contained in the letters she writes to me, ordering me only to give such assistance as I could, which I have done. You may consider whether there is any other service I can do you, and if there be, and you will inform me of it, I will do the best I can according to my abilities.

London, 18 June, 1545.

18 June.
Vienna
Imp. Arch.

70. CHAPUYS to the EMPEROR.

I received yesterday morning your Majesty's letter enclosing the despatches for the ambassador in England; and as the deciphering of the despatch took a long time I have hardly yet been able to master its contents. I should have liked to have time to consider maturely the whole question before writing to the ambassador, but as I understand the King shortly intends to visit the sea coast facing France, and in that case the ambassador could not proceed with the negotiation I thought better not to delay the courier. The dispatch, moreover, is so full and circumspect that, neither I nor any man living could in my opinion add anything to it, and it would have been not only waste of time but a great piece of rashness for me to have attempted to do so. Besides this the ambassador is not only clever but has already a better knowledge of the English mode of proceeding than I have. Nevertheless, in my desire to be considered rash or foolish rather than disobedient, I have written hastily to the Ambassador to the effect contained in my letter to M. de Granvelle.

After dinner to-day I was again with the Bishop of Westminster and Secretary Petre, and took the opportunity to speak of two ships belonging to Quintana de Done, that had been seized in England, and certain other private affairs. After some discussion I assured them that, considering how important it was that peace and unity should continue to exist between your Majesty and their King, in the interests of their successors and of the subjects on both sides, I, who had been the instrument for establishing this friendship, would not cease night or day to seek means to increase it, and to extirpate every cause for dissension or suspicion. This, I said, had moved me to recollect the request which had been addressed to Van der Delft and myself on behalf of the King, that we would pre-advise your Majesty to make provision for furnishing the aid stipulated in the treaty of alliance, in the event of the French joining the Scots for the purpose of invading England, as the rumour now ran that they intended to do. I had considered that perhaps the King might one of these days make the request, in consequence of the news of the great muster of forces the French were making for the recovery of Boulogne; and, influenced by the feelings which I had stated, I thought well to point out to them that, if the King had any such intention, it would be advisable that matters should be so managed that your Majesty and your advisers should have no legitimate reason for refusing it. I was quite sure, I said, that your Majesty was still determined to fulfil honourably, and to the utmost, your obligations under the treaty, and would be sorry to have to decline their request, but, to be frank with them, it seemed to me that the delay that had occurred in redressing the injuries done to your Majesty's subjects did not exhibit the good faith of which Secretary Paget had so emphatically assured your Majesty. Still less auspicious were the seizures recently made, and those that were daily taking place, which seemed to me most extraordinary, and quite at variance with the agreement made with Paget. I had, moreover, heard it said, though I did not believe it, that the King was seeking to make some arrangement with the protestants of the Empire; which would be contrary to the treaty as well as to common honesty.

I went on to say that the King would be wise to recognise the treaty of peace which your Majesty had concluded with France by his consent (which was the real truth) and that steps should be taken to prevent their people, even courtiers, from being so froward as to rail at the treaty of peace. It is true that not much importance need be attached to what such people said, since your Majesty's virtue and integrity were justified before the world, but the worst of it was that it gave rise to the presumption that these people would not dare to speak as they did, if they were not aware that the King thought in the same way, and would be pleased at what they said. This might give your Majesty reason for resentment; and my own opinion was that, not only was the King's recognition of the treaty of peace necessary, but also his express approbation of it, since the French were ceaselessly importuning your Majesty not to consider yourself bound to aid the King of England, on the ground that the reservation in favour of the King of England introduced into the

1545.

treaty of peace was nullified by his refusal to recognise the treaty itself.

Furthermore, I said, touching the reason for my return to England, that it appeared to me that the King had been more anxious to settle the matter respecting which he had sent the Earl of Hertford and the Bishop of Winchester to Flanders, than to verify his contention with regard to his consent to the treaty of peace.* From the first interview that my colleague and I had with him, besides addressing me in very strange fashion, he had told us that he did not intend to negotiate with us, except in writing, and if we had no instructions to that effect he would send a special courier to obtain them from your Majesty, which he had not done; nor had he subsequently made any appearance of a desire to discuss matters. It is true that two days afterwards, the Earl of Hertford, the Bishop of Winchester and Paget had come to us, but that was at our request, in order that we might repeat to them the rest of our instructions, which we had not recited to the King. Their coming was owing to no action of the King, who simply gave them instructions to listen to what we had to say; and after it was communicated to him and the affair had been debated, we were never spoken to on the subject, except incidentally and by way of pastime. The demands made upon your Majesty by the Earl of Hertford and the Bishop of Winchester were certainly most extraordinary; namely to declare war (against France) and to interdict trade between your subjects and the French. The latter prohibition would have been especially grievous to your Majesty's subjects, already so greatly prejudiced by the recent wars, and the trade in question in no wise injured the King of England, whose action, in pressing for the prohibition of trade, could not be imagined to proceed from any friendly motive; even if your Majesty, in virtue of the treaty of alliance, had furnished him with the aid stipulated.

I said nothing to them about commuting the armed contingent for a money subsidy, in the belief that the King will take it very badly; especially for the reasons mentioned in the letters to the Queen. According to my poor foolish fancy, I think we ought to leave that to the very last, as it will make the King very discontented and indignant; and perhaps without reason, as the French forces may be deterred by fear of the English from going to Scotland, where, moreover, in any case, they could not maintain themselves, owing to the great scarcity of victuals existing. If they intend to waste time by besieging Boulogne, your Majesty is not bound in the slightest degree to aid in its defence. With regard to a French attempt against Calais, the English themselves have no misgiving on that point, both on account of the (French) lack of victuals, and because they believe your Majesty would not allow the French to pass by way of Gravelines. If, on the other hand, they undertake the siege of Guisnes, they can only do it by exhausting your Majesty's adjoining territories of provisions; and even then they would be

---

* That is to say, that he had been more desirous of again drawing the Emperor into war with France than of defending his contention that the peace between the Emperor and France had been made without his expressed consent.

short of victuals. But supposing that there is an appearance of the aid really having to be furnished, your Majesty is not bound to grant it until six weeks after the actual invasion, and the consequent demand of the King, so that you would then have plenty of time to suggest the commutation. On the other hand, if the ambassador (Van der Delft) mentions the suggestion, now, even as if of his own accord and unofficially, they (the English) are so suspicious that they would be sure to think it came from your Majesty, or at least it would give them an opportunity of guessing your Majesty's intentions, which they might try to frustrate by alleging that your Majesty promised the King to raise troops in Germany for his service whom your Majesty could pay.

The bishop (Thirlby) and Secretary Petre thanked me warmly for my good offices on the King's behalf, and assured me of the King's great desire to maintain friendship with your Majesty. The bishop then began to apologise very emphatically for having somewhat warmly denied at a meeting of the Conference yesterday that the conclusion of peace between your Majesty and France had been with the consent of the King of England. It was impossible, he said, for him to help denying it, as the assertion was made so publicly, and he might have been blamed if he had remained silent. For his part, he continued, he spoke of such matters unwillingly, but it might be supposed that, not only in England, but throughout Christendom, it would be said that your Majesty had drawn the King into war, and had then cast upon his shoulders the whole of the burden. As to seeking an understanding with the Protestants, the King had never thought of doing such a thing; and had now no representative in Germany to undertake such a negotiation. With regard to the redress of injuries done to your Majesty's subjects, he had not up to the present learnt of any injury having been done to them that had not been redressed; and he doubted not that, if there was any vessel now detained in England in contravention of Paget's agreement, proper steps would be taken in the matter. They both of them assured me of this, and said that your Majesty's subjects had no such ground for their lamentations as the English had against the subjects of your Majesty, especially against Spaniards, as had been proved by the claims and complaints which they (Thirlby and Petre) had produced. To say the truth, they have brought forward a large number of such complaints; but they are all old grievances, and have already been dealt with judicially. They (Thirlby and Petre) said that they had heard that reprisals had been authorised in Spain against the English, which they thought very strange; and the King would have much reason to be offended at it. He would have equally great cause for resentment if he heard that his subjects' testimony was not admitted in courts of law in Spain, on the ground that they were heretics, and that their claims were thus forfeited. They gave no answer of importance to the other points upon which I had touched; but said, with reference to my remark about the King's conversation with me, that however that might be, the King had never had a bad opinion of me, and that he still

1545.

retained his regard for me was proved by the fact that, when they took their leave of him, and expressed their insufficiency for the mission entrusted to them, in this conference, owing to their inexperience in such affairs, the King replied that there was no danger, since I should be here, well informed of the matter, and would tell the pure truth, against no matter whom. I believe this was invented by the bishop and the secretary; for I am decidedly of opinion that the King had no wish that I should be present when these affairs were debated. With regard to the existence of any sign of negotiation between the Kings of England and France, I beg to say that I can perceive none whatever. It is true that from the conversation related above, it would seem that the King of England would be willing to listen to overtures, from a desire to restore repose to Christendom, rather than from any fear of the French; for whom he did not care a button. The Secretary (Petre) said that very likely, before many days had passed, the French would be too busy looking to the defence of their own country to think of invading that of another King. The King (of England) he said, had, or soon would have, quite 300 ships at sea, carrying 20,000 soldiers; whilst the land forces, on any side the French might attack, would not be inferior in numbers. For this purpose the King had despatched to various parts nearly all the lords that surrounded him; the Duke of Suffolk going to the Midlands, the Duke of Norfolk to his own country, the Earl of Hertford to the Scottish Border, Lord Privy Seal (*i.e.*, Lord Russell) to Essex, Lord St. John and the Master of the Horse (Sir Anthony Browne) to Southampton and Chichester. By this means not a port was left undefended; besides which the King has for the purpose of resisting the French fleet, and to send across the sea, four or five thousand men who are already beginning to embark. Although there had been a talk of 30,000 men for Scotland (to be raised by Scotland?) very few had really been raised, even since the news that the French fleet had passed the Straits of Gibraltar[*]; and the bishop and the secretary (*i.e.*, Thirlby and Petre) think that the Scots are very short of food.

The English are daily strengthening the towns of Guisnes with the intention of holding it, their only fear being the lack of victuals, of which their supply is not large, even of wheat there and at Calais, as the whole of their stores are destined for Boulogne.

Touching the public opinion of the English regarding the war; so far as I can learn—and I have heard it from innumerable people—there is not a soul with any wit in England who does not blaspheme at the war, and most of them have christened Boulogne by the name of "the new Milan,"[†] which will bring about their destruction. The money for the prosecution of the war has been raised by the King since his return from Boulogne, by means of a subsidy exacted from his subjects under the name of a benevolence, and the bishop and the secretary assert that the proceeds of it exceed

---

[*] The French galleys with, it was said, a strong Papal contingent coming from the Mediterranean to re-inforce the French fleet in the Channel.

[†] Referring doubtless to the terrible consequences which had ensued to Francis from the occupation of Milan.

400,000 ducats. I expect he (the King) will have sold some of the church revenues, as he began to do when he crossed the Channel last. It is said that he has drawn great profit from the abasement of the coinage; but withal, there is an appearance of money being short; for, as I hear, the garrisons have not been paid for some months, and the King is being dunned to pay his other debts. I say nothing of the conclusions that may be drawn from the King's desire to raise 400,000 ducats in Antwerp, for the security of which he has a large quantity of lead from the ruined churches. There was a talk also of taking the revenues of the collegiate churches; of which I doubt not your Majesty will be fully informed by the ambassador in England.

Bourbourg, 18th June, 1545.

Endorsed:—" Chapuys, from Bourbourg 18th June, received at Worms 2nd July 1545."

18 June.
Vienna
Imp. Arch.

71. Chapuys to Van der Delft.

I received this morning the enclosed dispatch from his Majesty, which was not deciphered until between 5 and 6 o'clock in the afternoon; and a considerable portion of the time which remained for me to consider the dispatch, was occupied in discoursing with M. de Roeulx and the Chancellor of the Order, who came to visit me. I have therefore lacked leisure, I will not say to meditate, but even to give proper consideration to the very important matter contained in the despatch. I am extremely sorry for this, although the despatch itself has been so carefully and wisely drafted by his Majesty and M. de Granvelle, that the need for my consideration was not very pressing; particularly also as it is addressed to you, who have no need for my trifling advice. If his Majesty had not desired it—ut sub Minervam, etc.—it would have been superogatory even to have addressed the document through me; for the matter is of such great importance as to be beyond not only my advice, but even my comprehension. Although anyone would consider it a great honour, I do not rejoice very much at it myself, for fear that it will only show up my own incompetence, and lower the opinion in which hitherto his Majesty has held me. Well; leaving aside these prologues, I may say that in view of the wording of the dispatch, his Majesty might repeat what Cato said in speaking of Cæsar and Pompey, " Quem fugiam video, quem sequar nescio," though in my poor foolish judgment I hope that in the end his Majesty's great good fortune will enable him to come out of the main business without inconvenience and to the satisfaction of the parties. On the side of Scotland there is not much appearance that the case for demanding the aid will arise, seeing that they (the Scots) have been badly punished, and are so disunited and suspicious of each other. The great desire will only be for peace, and they are neither able nor willing to keep at war. Even if they were at their best, they would hardly be able to invade England in the force needful for the Emperor's aid to be demanded under the treaty. With regard to the French army on this side, no matter what noise the French may make, it would be utterly impossible for them to keep the field for six weeks, owing to their want of victuals. This is notorious, and has been repeated by divers soldiers who have left the French camp from pure famine. If this is really the case, the French will be gone before his Majesty is bound to furnish aid, either in men or money. I confess that this argument is a very uncertain one, and I should take care not to use it to anyone but you, who I know will, for friendship sake, excuse it. If one could be a wizard to know the truth beforehand, it would be an excellent reason for promptly and confidently granting the King's demand, without any risk of being called upon to fulfil our promise. But verily, as we cannot know the future, it will be necessary, as his Majesty prudently says, to keep the thing in general terms so that no distrust (of us) may be felt.

As our principal object in the meanwhile is to gain time, my opinion is that it will be best not to hurry in opening the matter to the Council, but to let them make the first approaches. They will not fail to do this when you are with them; and you might seek opportunities to visit them. There would have been no necessity for me to have given you this advice if before writing it I had read the latter part of his Majesty's letter, where he expressly instructs you to the same effect.

It appears to me also, that we should for the present avoid mentioning the substitution of the armed aid by a money subsidy, as the King will be very much annoyed by such a suggestion, since he attaches more importance, as he says, to the official assistance being given than to the money. As matters are not so very pressing, and it may yet happen that the aid may not be needed, there will be time afterwards to bring forward reasons for our not sending the aid in the form of troops. There is another reason for deferring the mention of a pecuniary aid. It is quite possible that when the Kings of France and England are in arms, the Emperor may consider it necessary, for the safety of his own frontiers, to assemble an armed force, and this fact may cause the Kings of France and England to be more inclined to peace. In this case and the aid demanded by the King of of England being unnecessary the Emperor might in accordance with the treaty, cast upon the King the whole or part of the expense he had incurred in raising these troops, on the excuse that they were intended for him.

His Majesty has very wisely laid down the conditions he requires before he grants the aid, as otherwise his Majesty's expense would be useless, since they (the English) would find as many pretexts for haggling afterwards as they do now. With regard to his Majesty's demand that the King of England should ratify his (the Emperor's) treaty of friendship with France, it seems to me unadvisable to convey the idea to the English that the point is of vital importance to the Emperor himself. Since his Majesty made peace with France by consent of the King of England the latter should recognise the treaty in order to deprive the English courtiers of a pretext for speaking strangely and untruly about it, and also to stop the French from alleging with good reason, that the King of England cannot claim the benefit of the clause inserted in the treaty by the Emperor in his favour, unless he recognises the treaty itself. This is all that occurs to me to say with regard to the dispatch, which itself is so well drafted that any addition or alteration to it would be vain. I doubt not, moreover, that you will conduct everything as dexterously and prudently as need be. You will, I am sure, also, take thought and counsel as you go on (*in arena*), and if you choose to consult me I shall take it as a favour, and will write you my poor advice, since this is the will of our master, which will excuse my temerity to you who know my ineptitude.

You will note what I and my colleagues write to you about this arbitration conference. I have only to add to it that the English deputies have recently produced certain affidavits made in London on the 3rd instant, by which they try to prove that the Spaniards who are represented by Carrion* have been recompensed for their losses by the King of France out of the English property at Rouen. In view of this, Carrion has left here for Rouen to obtain evidence to the contrary.

With regard to the books mentioned in the letters, M. de Bonvise can help you better than anyone.

Bourbourg, 18 June, 1545.

19 June.
Vienna
Imp. Arch.

72. The EMPEROR to the CHANCELLOR OF BRABANT.

We are receiving daily complaints of the depredations committed by the English upon our Flemish and Spanish subjects, for which neither restitution nor redress can be obtained. The exportation of merchandise from England to our dominions has also been prohibited, and English property is being openly withdrawn from our territories.† As our sister the Queen Dowager, to whom we are now writing, is at present far away in Friesland, and delay may be inadvisable, we command you, as soon as you receive this, to proceed to Antwerp, and make secret enquiries there as to whether there are any signs that the English are directly or indirectly withdrawing their property and merchandise from Antwerp, Bruges, Bergen or elsewhere. If this be the case, you will take such measures as may be possible to prevent it, and if this cannot be done without the knowledge of the English, you will tell them that your action is owing to the complaints and grievances of our subjects, who have been plundered, and for their indemnity, until such time as we or our sister shall order otherwise. Inform us of what you do. We enclose a letter to the rentmaster of Zeeland, ordering him to follow your instructions to a similar effect.

Worms, 19 June, 1545.

(20?) June.
Vienna
Imp. Arch.

73. The EMPEROR to CHAPUYS.

You have already heard of the fresh depredations committed by the English on our subjects both Flemish and Spanish, without

---

* These were certain Spanish merchants of Burgos, Santander, etc. The signatures to Lope de Carrion's power of attorney are those of Juan de la Peña, Pedro de Porres and Diego Pardo. Some curious references to Lope de Carrion, who was a Spaniard established in London, will be found in the "Spanish Chronicle of Henry VIII."

† It will be noted that this is a great overstatement of the case. Both Van der Delft and Chapuys only suggested that a secret movement was talked of, by which as much English property as possible should be kept out of the dominions of the Emperor, in consequence of the insecurity of it against arrest. Chapuys in his letter to the Chancellor of Brabant, and to Granvelle (25 June) pages 141 and 142, seems to have got frightened at the effect of his news.

1545.

justification, release or redress. In order, in any case, to obtain some sort of indemnity for our people, we are writing to our sister the Queen Dowager, and to our Chancellor of Brabant, the letters of which you will find copies enclosed. It will be well for you to inform our ambassador in England of this, and at the same time write to him your own advice on the subject, as you know best the character of Englishmen, and the way in which the ambassador should bear himself. We also enclose for him a letter written yesterday of which we send you a copy. We urge you again to fulfil the task with which we have entrusted you. We have received your letters of 11th instant, for which we thank you.

Worms, — June, 1545.

21 June.
Simancas
E. Castilla.
72.

74. Dr. Molon to the Emperor.

The Inquisitor General, the Cardinal of Toledo and the Council have appointed the writer Inquisitor at Seville. With great difficulty he accepted the post for the service of God and the Emperor. He arrived in Seville at the beginning of the year and found the Inquisition very inert. God allowed him to discover the offences which were being committed against his Divine Majesty in this province; and so as early as was possible, which was to-day, there was an auto de fé in which many heretics, Jews and some Lutherans, etc., were led out, as is set forth in the statement enclosed. God grant, in His divine mercy, that this may redound to His glory, and the exaltation of the faith. Commends his services in this for the Emperor's approval. Humble Vassal and Chaplain,

Castle of Triana, 21 June, 1545.   Doctor J. Molon.

The Statement enclosed contains the names of two men only as having continued obstinate, Francisco de Morales of Toledo, a new Christian of Jewish race, and Francisco de la Plata, a silversmith convert of Seville. Of those reconciled there are 36 men, of whom 17 are Moriscos, and the rest new Christians, Lutherans, Jews and others unspecified. Among them there are four Flemings, and one English Lutheran called "Robert." In addition to these there are 14 women, seven of whom are Moriscas; and a supplementary list of two women and one man "penanced with the habit," and eight men, of whom one is a Portuguese friar, "penanced without the habit." There is a transcript of this paper in the B.M., Add. 28594.

21 June.
Vienna
Imp. Arch.

75. Henry Garbrand to Jehan Lobel and Gerard de Has.

I beg to inform you that the Secretary here (Paget) has received letters from the English Commissioners at Bourbourg respecting the presentation of your claim for the goods and wine taken at Plymouth in William de Resesta's ship. I have to advise you that the said Secretary has indemnified me fully for the merchandise in question, on behalf of you, Anthony Rouze, and all other interested parties, from whom I held ample powers for the purpose. You will therefore withdraw your claims from the deputies, in order that they may see that you are satisfied with what I have done here. I was very much ashamed when I saw the letter making the claim on your behalf, although I had on my passage through Bourbourg begged Thomas Gamay not to make any such claim, as I had settled the matter here.

Greenwich, 21 June, 1545.

Addressed to Jehan de Lobel and Gerard de Has, winemerchants, Lille, Flanders.

Attached to the above is a letter of the same date from the writer at Greenwich to Thomas Gamay at Bourbourg, asking him for the reasons stated above to withdraw the claims referred to.

23 June.
Vienna
Imp. Arch.
Hop. Cor.

76. HENRY VIII. to the EMPEROR.[*]

We doubt not that by this time you will have been informed of the great preparations which the French have made by sea and by land for the purpose of invading our realms, and that the King of France has enlisted a large number of your Majesty's subjects with that object, and for the purpose of avenging himself, if possible, for the attack we as your ally made upon him. In accordance with the terms of our alliance we consider it necessary to inform you of these warlike preparations, and to request you forthwith to prepare the aid stipulated in case of invasion of the dominions of either of us by a third power, in order that immediately you are informed from us by our ambassador and Councillor Dr. Wotton that such invasion of our realm has taken place, you may send the assistance stipulated in the treaty; as we for our part have done towards you. You will, thereby, not only do us great pleasure, but will also demonstrate strongly the firmness of your friendship.

Dartford, 23 June, 1545.

25 June.
Vienna
Imp Arch

77. CHAPUYS to the EMPEROR.

Whilst I was in conference this morning with the English deputies I received your Majesty's letters of the 19th instant with enclosures, etc.; and after I had finished my other business with the deputies, I conveyed to them as a final tit-bit the contents of the letters in question, and those written by your Majesty to your ambassador in England. I set forth at length the greater part of the injuries, outrages and oppressions, committed on your Majesty's subjects since the agreement made in Brussels with Secretary Paget, as well as the seizure, shortly before the date of the agreement, of two ships which have not yet been restored. I added unofficially, that in my opinion, notwithstanding your Majesty's singular affection for their King, and the whole English nation, unless some remedy was found for such intolerable insolence, loss and injury, as were constantly inflicted upon your Majesty's subjects, you would be compelled to take steps to prevent your dominions from being utterly ruined. Your Majesty's peoples, I said, mainly depended upon their commerce and merchandise, and especially the mariners, of whom there were vast numbers, both in Spain and in these parts, living solely by seafaring. The deputies were astonished to hear that since their departure from England, such things had been going on, and also that the merchandise detained had not been restored to the

---

[*] There is in the Record Office (State Papers. Vol. X., p. 478) the original draft of this letter by Paget, differing slightly in wording from the document at Vienna given above.

1545.

owners against security: and they themselves affirmed that your Majesty's subjects ought not even to be burdened by having to find security, unless there was a strong presumptive indication that the property seized belonged to Frenchmen.

They had already three or four days ago written at my request to England about it, but they promised to write urgently again, and to do their best in the matter. They excused the delay that had taken place in remedying the evils, by saying that nearly all the Lords of the Council are absent from Court in various parts of the country, organising the defence, whilst the few who remained were so overwhelmed with business connected with the war, that they had no time to attend to anything else.

The deputies then went on to say, that your Majesty had not nearly so much cause for resentment for the matters referred to above, as their King had for the seizures effected in Spain of the property of Englishmen, which property had not yet been released. They complained even more bitterly that reprisals against Englishmen had been authorised (in Spain) without any enquiry being made into the cases, although they (the English) had not refused to do justice or to punish the man whose acts had given rise to the grievance. To this I replied that it was true that they had promised several times to punish the offender—one Renegat—and to make him give restitution, but it all ended in words, for Renegat had been welcomed at Court, and had swaggered about everywhere.

I seized an opportunity for saying that their people were quite in a hurry to withdraw from the Flanders trade. They replied that it was not to be wondered at, as the King had raised a fleet of fully three hundred sail, and it was probable that all the English ships, or at least all the English seamen, had gone for the King's service; so that it was impossible that the merchants could carry on their maritime trade as usual. The deputies (one of whom is the Courtmaster Danvers) swore that they knew of no Englishman who had withdrawn from Flanders any merchandise, either by land or sea; although the Bishop of Westminster let slip twice over that it was quite true that their merchants were very doubtful whether some rupture might not take place between their King and your Majesty, seeing what was being done in Spain against them.

When I had heard this excuse and assertion, I thought well to write to the Chancellor of Brabant that he should keep in suspense the arrest, about which your Majesty recently wrote to him, especially in view of the hope given by these deputies that your Majesty's subjects shall be indemnified; and I tell him (the Chancellor) that unless he sees imminent danger of the withdrawal of English property, it will be better to temporise and take no step, until we have news from England, or your Majesty orders otherwise. I have advised the ambassador in England of my colloquy with these Englishmen.

Bourbourg, 25 June, 1545.

25 June.
Vienna
Imp. Arch.

78. CHAPUYS to the CHANCELLOR OF BRABANT.

I received this morning letters from the Emperor, dated 9th instant with copy of his Majesty's last letter to you, respecting the enquiry into,

1545.

and embargo of English goods. His Majesty orders you to explain that he has effected the arrest for the purpose of indemnifying certain Spaniards for the seizure of three ships belonging to them in England. The English deputies here for the arbitration conference give me some hope that these ships may be restored; and although I doubt not that your wisdom and discretion would lead you in any case to consider maturely before you acted in a matter of so much importance, I have thought well to write to you, to say that, unless there is imminent danger in so doing, it would be better to temporise and avoid decisive action, until his Majesty has news from England as to the course there adopted respecting the restitution. I am writing to this effect to his Majesty from whom you may hear before you have finished your enquiries.

Bourbourg, 25 June, 1545.

25 June.
Vienna
Imp. Arch

79. CHAPUYS to DE GRANVELLE.

Your lordship will see by my letters to his Majesty all that I have to say on the points respecting which he wrote to me; and I write this short note only to express my astonishment that in his Majesty's letter to the Queen (Dowager) I should be quoted as the authority for the news that the English were secretly withdrawing their property from Antwerp. This must be a blunder of my man, whom I told to write the intelligence that trade with Spain had been prohibited in England; and that I heard that the commerce of the English with Flanders was daily diminishing. Although Jehan de Quintana Done explicitly assured me that he had seen between Gravelines and Bruges over twenty wagon loads of English merchandise coming from Antwerp, yet as the author of this news was somewhat open to suspicion, by reason of his interest in the matter, I had no intention of causing it to be conveyed to his Majesty. I now enclose copy of a letter I have written to the Chancellor of Brabant, and beg you to overlook my simplicity, and fault if such there be, and attribute the latter to my ardent desire to serve his Majesty. I also enclose extract from letters written yesterday by M. de Roeulx to the Chancellor of the order. If the intelligence contained therein be true, his Majesty may avoid for this year, at least, having to grant the aid requested by the English. Still I am doubtful whether the news be not mere hearsay, although there is nothing unlikely in it; and I have held for a long time past that the French will repent of having brought their galleys up here. Even if there was no danger from enemies or pestilence, they can be of no service to them here, and as they will have to winter in these climates not a convict will survive the change of air from that of the Levant. The number of the Germans mentioned in the extract (although the French say there are 10,000) do not reach 8,000.

Bourbourg, 25 June, 1545.

Extract of letter from M. de Roeulx[a] referred to in the above:—
The said man informed him that they (*i.e.*, the French) are in great

---

[a] M. de Roeulx was the Flemish officer who remained with his contingent in the service of the King of England at Boulogne by permission of the Emperor after the latter had made peace with France. He was Adrian de Croy, Count de Roeulx, brother of the Duke of Arschot.

1545.

fear lest the Emperor should return with the English. If he does so, France will be ruined, as the country was never in such poverty as at present. The Germans were in Champagne unpaid, and committing all sorts of disorder. They had resolved to march to Noyon, and not to leave there until they were paid in full. There is no means of raising the money to pay them, and even if they (*i.e.*, the French) could succeed in doing so, it would be still impossible for them to march against Boulogne for want of victuals. Their own (French) cavalry and infantry are unpaid, the nobility is impoverished and the people ruined, at which they are much surprised. In revictualling Ardres they have only done harm to the Emperor, as they have wasted all the wheat on the way from the river Falkenberg as far as Tournchen and they are constantly committing outrages in the neighbourhood. The said deponent was at Crotoy where he saw a galley entirely abandoned by its crew, most of the slaves having died of the plague. The captains of the French galleys are half distracted in the fear that a similar fate may befall their vessels; besides which they do not see a chance of their galleys being able to do anything.

25 June.
Vienna
Imp. Arch.

80. CHAPUYS to DE GRANVELLE.

This morning the English deputies again brought up the question of the reprisals authorised in Spain; and at my request they showed me the order given in the name of the Prince (*i.e.*, the Regent Philip) which I almost forced them to admit was not really a decree for reprisals, since it only ordered the seizure of English goods to the value of Renegat's depredations in Spain. I told them openly before the Chancellor of the Order and my other colleagues, that it seemed to me that they had no great reason to make so much ado about this seizure. It might be said, indeed, that they ought to be ashamed to press the point as they were doing, for it seemed to infer that they were willing to give greater license to Renegat than to the Prince; since the former, a mere private individual, had commenced these reprisals (if such they could be called) and yet they would not suffer his Serenity by just means to obtain indemnity for them in a much more modest fashion than Renegat had acted. The latter, moreover, as the Prince had probably heard, had been welcomed in England, and he still retained the property of which he piratically plundered Spaniards. In view of this, and the tardiness with which the restitution of the property previously seized from Spaniards was being conducted, naturally his Highness, as a good prince, could not overlook the injury inflicted by Renegat, or avoid taking due steps for obtaining an indemnity. The deputies, after some altercation, and severely blaming Renegat, who they said was worthy of punishment, showed annoyance at having brought the matter forward, and appeared more satisfied about it than they had previously been.

Bourbourg, 25 June, 1545.

29 June.
Vienna
Imp. Arch.

81. CHAPUYS to the EMPEROR.

After dinner to-day the Bishop of Westminster and Secretary Petre came to visit me, and in the course of conversation I took an opportunity to repeat some discourse which I had addressed to them on a previous occasion, respecting the matter of this arbitration conference. I pointed out to them how necessary it was that redress should be given to your Majesty's subjects for the loss and injury they had suffered. They (Thirlby and Petre) confirmed the hope, which they had previously held out to me, and in proof of what they said they handed me two letters, stating that a quantity of wine belonging to some merchants of Lille had been restored at their intercession.* This is a good beginning, as is also the release, against security, of a ship belonging to Quintana de Done, a merchant of Burgos; and the same owner had hopes that his principal vessel, about which your Majesty wrote to the ambassador, might be released on similar conditions. There seems, therefore, a chance of matters being remedied without resorting to the counter-arrest, or other unpleasant measures. The principal difficulty lies with the three ships belonging to Burgos merchants seized before the war; as they, the English, thought that they were quit of responsibility in that case, because they got the merchants themselves to testify that they had been indemnified out of the English goods seized at Rouen. Now, however, that we have obtained authentic documents from Rouen, we find that such is not the case, the goods there having been adjudged to other persons holding letters of marque. This greatly confuses and surprises them. After some conversation, they (*i.e.*, Thirlby and Petre) gave me to understand that Secretary Paget had written to them saying that he had laid before the King, the conversation I had recently had with them; and that his Majesty had taken it all in good part. He had also thanked me for my desire to maintain and strengthen the friendship existing, and to serve him. Paget had also told them that he was much surprised that your Majesty's ambassador had not broached any conversation about peace or a truce between England and France; since I had said that your Majesty desired nothing better, and that you had instructed me to adopt every means to forward that object. Doubtless, they said, your Majesty had given similar instructions to the ambsssador, and that I had done the same. I told them that the ambassador had refrained from opening the subject, in consequence of his not having been expressly ordered to do so, but only to watch and advise if any opportunity presented itself. In my opinion, your Majesty had deferred, and was still deferring, the bringing forward of the matter, until you saw a favourable opportunity, and some prospect of bringing it to a good issue to the contentment of the parties concerned. Otherwise, I said, your Majesty's intervention would only result in a slight to your own dignity. Besides, I continued, affairs were not yet in a very critical position; and they (the English) might be sure that your Majesty had not neglected to instruct your ministers in France to watch for a chance of influencing the King of France. But as your Majesty had found there no serious basis for negotiation, you had decided to let matters mature somewhat, until there appeared to be a fair opportunity. This opportunity I said, in my opinion, was at present, and it should be

---

*See letter from Garbrand to these merchants on page 139.

1545.

taken advantage of in order that the evils and uncertain result of a battle might be avoided; and I prayed them to let me know if they thought that anything could be done to forward the matter; or if, on the contrary, they thought it too late now to speak of it. They replied that it was not at all too late; and, as I had remarked that this was the best season to bring about a settlement, I ought to forward the matter with your Majesty. With regard to the other means I had spoken of, they said that their wit did not reach so far as to understand them; and I knew the temper of their master as well as they did. I answered that recently, before my departure from England, the Chancellor and the Duke of Suffolk had conjured me to give them my opinion; and I had suggested that it (Boulogne ?) might be placed in the keeping of a third party, at the joint expense of France and England. They (*i.e.*, Wriothesley and Suffolk) had rejected this, and had only expressed curiosity as to who the third party could be. I had not thought proper to mention your Majesty, as I did not know whether you would approve of the suggestion; but I myself was still of the same opinion. They (Thirlby and Petre) gave me no reply; on the contrary, the secretary (Petre) changed the conversation, with the excuse that he must not forget to tell me that Paget had written that he did not understand my purpose in bringing forward the statement that the King ought to ratify the Emperor's treaty of peace with France. I replied that, admitting that what had been done was with their King's consent, it was to his advantage to recognise the treaty, because he was one of the principal parties interested in it and because it was necessary in order to avail himself of the reservation in his favour stipulated by the treaty, and of the reference to the Emperor's arbitration of his (Henry's) claims against France. I continued, that he would by this course also shut the mouths of the French, who were trying to persuade your Majesty that you were in no wise bound to the King of England, failing the confirmation by the latter of the treaty of peace. Reverting to the main point, they (Thirlby and Petre) said that, although their master doubted whether the French had done anything; and there was every appearance of his being able to prevail more and more against them, yet he would not refuse any honourable conditions of peace. As for the restitution of Boulogne, however, the King would not consent to have it even mentioned, both on account of the advantage they (the English) look for, through the possession of the place, and as a point of personal honour; as the King thought that he could not surrender it without discredit to his prestige. The world would conclude that he gave it up through fear if he did so.

I said I knew, to some extent, the greatness of heart and power of their King. He was quite puissant enough to defend himself against the French, and yet from the time his predecessors had conquered Calais, I thought that they had had their hands full in holding and guarding the place. It was true, I said, that the former Kings of England were not so powerful as their (Thirlby and Petre's) master, the present King, but at the same time it must be recollected that the old Kings of France could not be compared in strength with the present one. It was unquestionable that the possession of Boulogne would be, as they said, a great advantage to England, if it could be held peacefully; but it was to be feared that, if the King of France found that he could not recover the place, he might fortify other places in the neighbourhood, and keep in them a strong force of soldiers, who would prevent the English from making any use of Boulogne and the surrounding country, which would thus prove a costly burden to them and no profit at all. All this, and other discourse to the same end, I placed before them (Thirlby and Petre) by way of conversation; in order to discover something of the King's feeling about the retention of Boulogne: but I made quite clear to them that the talk was confidential; and that I had neither instructions to mention the matter, nor the slightest desire to persuade or dissuade them in the restitution or retention of Boulogne. They thanked me for the confidence I had reposed in them; and I gathered the impression finally from their words and demeanour, that it will be possible to bring the King to surrender Boulogne, if a reasonable compensation be given to him; especially if the request comes from your Majesty; and his vain glory is satisfied by its being represented to him, that your Majesty and Christendom at large will be under a great obligation to him for his condescending to this peace, for the purpose of uniting the Christian Commonwealth and repelling the common enemy. In order to get on to the subject of the King of England's resources, I mentioned to them (Thirlby and Petre) that the French had conceived some hopes from the rumour that the King (of England) was short of money, since he had raised a loan in Antwerp at so high an interest at the very beginning of the war, and before his departure from London, he had compelled the citizens to buy certain revenues of his, the price of which did not exceed 100,000 ducats. I had, I said, heard from several quarters the talk that was going on amongst Frenchmen about it; but for my part I thought the King had quite as good an excuse for borrowing as the French had when they borrowed such vast sums from the Florentines and other merchants at Lyons, and of the Swiss, at the time that your Majesty's election to the Empire was afoot. The French had alleged then that they had not borrowed the money out of poverty, for the treasury of France was inexhaustible, but they had raised the funds at Lyons in order that the Fucars* and other German companies should not get hold of it and use it in your Majesty's interests, and the loans from the Swiss were for the purpose of attaching them to the French interest. They (Thirlby and Petre) admired this clever dexterity on the part of the French, but declined to be drawn into any conversation with regard to their own resources. They changed the subject by begging me to write and exert my influence that the ambassador in England should resume the talk about peace or a truce, in his conversation with the King or Council. They had no doubt in such case, that an opportunity might be found upon which negotiations could be based. They repeated their complaints that the English in Spain had been excluded from the tribunals as heretics; and that even the King, their master, had been vilified

---

* The Fuggers, the great German banking house, the Rothschilds of the 16th century.

1545.

there with the same title; which, they said, was not to be tolerated, even in the case of such friends as your Majesty and the King.

As I had heard that information had come from M. de Roeulx that the secretary of Madame d' Etampes had arrived at Boulogne, and that Cardinal Médon (Meudon?) was also expected there in a few days, I said to them (Thirlby and Petre) that I had hoped they were going to give me some good news, upon which I could have congratulated them, about the personage who had arrived at Boulogne on behalf of the King of France, to treat for peace, and about the other personage who was expected shortly. I said that your Majesty would greatly rejoice at the news. They replied that, on their faith and conscience, they had heard nothing in the world about such a thing; and trusted that it would not hinder your Majesty from taking the matter in hand.

Bourbourg, 29 June, 1545.

Endorsed:—From Chapuys 29 June: Received at Worms the 8th of same month (*sic*) 1545.

29 June.
Paris
Arch. Nat.
K. 1485.

82. St. Mauris to Francisco de los Cobos.

I send you an account of all that has happened here since my last of 15th June from Argentan.

Thirty Flemish mercantile hulks sailing from Rochelle towards Normandy in company with the French fleet, sighted a great fleet of Englishmen coming against them. They (the Flemings?) fired a signal which at sea indicates friendship. The Flemings then joined the French fleet which was near to them, and together they presented so formidable a front to the English that the latter were forced to retire. The King assures me that the English would have defeated the French if it had not been for these hulks, and in such case the French sea force would have been broken up for this year. The King is delighted with the attitude of these Flemings and has thanked the Emperor for it. Shortly afterwards three French galleys left Rouen to carry victuals to Étaples. Two of them were driven by stress of weather into Dunkirk, and the people of the place supplied them with a little fresh food but not so much as they requested. The other galley went aground and foundered off Boulogne, as did a ship that attempted to help her.

Ten thousand crowns have been melted and mixed with copper and other metal here, and forged into 150,000 crowns which have been delivered to Captain de L'Orge to pay the men-at-arms he takes to Scotland. I obtained possession of one of these base crowns, which I spent. Warn people not to be cheated by them. I hear that the Emperor has already sent a warning to Spain.

It is said that L'Orge has started for Scotland, taking the route by Ireland° after spreading the rumour that he would go through the Straits of Calais, where consequently the English fleet awaited him.

° The French force approached Scotland from the West and landed at Dumbarton. *See* Diurnall of   rrents.)

The King has issued an order that all French mariners meeting the subjects of the Emperor at sea are to treat them as friends, and aid them in every way.

The final decision of the King with regard to the conduct of the war with England, is to hold the sea, and thus prevent the victualling of Calais and Boulogne. He will not attempt to land in England but will attack it from Scotland, and he intends to construct two forts on the sea shore from which he may molest Boulogne.° He is going to ship an immense quantity of stones in six vessels, and have them discharged in the mouth of Boulogne harbour so as to obstruct the passage. A design of these two forts is enclosed.

The French, with very few troops have thrown a great quantity of food into Ardres, without any resistance from the English, most of whom had then gone to England.

It is said that Captain Dampierre, Governor of Ardres lost a considerable number of men in a skirmish near Guisnes and 30 men at arms were left on the field.†

Whilst Paulin was yet in Provence the King instructed him to disperse a number of Lutherans in the neighbourhood of Avignon. After some pursuit he dispersed them and executed some of them by burning: but since Paulin's departure the Lutherans have again assembled at the same place. The sect grows in number daily, most of them being women.

In deference to the King (of France) the Emperor has consented to the Scots trading in the Netherlands under safe conduct; but although the King used great pressure, the Emperor refused to include them (the Scots) in the treaty of peace. The King also tried very hard to get the Count de Mirandola‡ included in the treaty, but the Emperor refused absolutely, and insisted that, come what might, the Count would have to surrender to justice and answer the charge of homicide against him.

The King has consented that Count William (of Furstenberg?) should be free within the city of Paris, upon his giving security for the payment of his ransom, the King giving him a guarantee that he shall be safely conveyed out of the realm, when the Emperor places at ransom the Prince of Roche sur Yonne. With regard to the latter, Don Francisco (d'Este) is being asked to take 15,000 crowns for his ransom.

° This intention was carried out mainly during the feint attack upon the English coast. One of the forts at the south entrance of Boulogne harbour, "opposite the Old man," was constructed by M. de Chastillon, Captain of Montplaisir, and after him called Chastillon's garden. The other was at St. Jean on the sea shore to the north of the town. An extremely curious story is told of the King's message sent to Lord Grey de Wilton by Sir Thomas Palmer respecting Grey's suggestion that he should attack Chastillon's garden. By letter we are told Grey was forbidden to attack, and by word of mouth he was urged to do so. (Lord Grey de Wilton, Camden Society.) An exactly similar story is told respecting the castle of Hardillot, the capture of which has been mentioned in these letters: only that in that case Peter Carew was the messenger.

† Doubtless this was the gallant exploit of Lord Grey de Wilton, then Governor of Guisnes and described by Hollingshead. A further reference to the engagement is made in a later letter in which Hollingshead's account is supplemented by further details. Dampierre himself was killed in the fight.

‡ Galeotto Pico de la Mirandola Count della Concordia. His castle in the territory of Mantua was a position of importance, and his strong French sympathies during, and before, the late war had drawn upon him the resentment of the imperialists.

1545.

The King has got from Germany 6,000 lansquenets to serve against the English. He is sending them to Picardy to join 6,000 French infantry and about 4,000 horse, and to go against Boulogne under command of the Dauphin. It is said that the King himself will be there for a few days to see the forts made ready.

The King has sent six learned men to the Council (of Trent). When he knows that the Council is to proceed he will send most of his bishops, and the 12 personages he has assembled at Melun to discuss their action at the Council.

The King has for the present refused to allow the publication of the papal bull, forbidding the imposition or collection of tithes without the Pope's permission. The French say that their King is authorised to levy tithes, by special indult given to his predecessors in return for services performed for the Holy See.

M. Hannebault the Admiral and Marshal of France, has been appointed to command the fleet against the English. Peter Strozzi left Marseilles for the high seas some time since, and it is said that with only his own galley he captured three English ships, carrying goods, munitions and victuals belonging to the English. He was able to do it because the ships were becalmed. Peter Strozzi has been condemned in his cause against the King in the Parliament of Paris for 56,000 crowns, which he says he spent of his own money on the King's service in the last wars in Italy.

Cardinal Ferrara has arrived here and is made much of, as it was owing to his efforts that the Venetians and Genoese lent this King several vessels.

It is believed that when the King has seen the embarcation of his troops on the fleet, he and all his household will proceed to Abbeville with his reserve militia (*arriere ban*). He will not make use of his gendarmerie, in order, as he says, to relieve his people: but the real reason is that the "*arriere ban*" will serve him without pay, whereas he would have to pay the gendarmerie, to whom already 15 months' wages are owing.

When the Emperor had arrived at Worms M. de Grignan declared to him that he had been sent by the King (of France) to assure the German princes of the perfect amity which reigned between the King and the Emperor; and to beg them not to decide anything in the Diet to the King's prejudice, and especially in the matter of the Duchy of Bar.[*] M. de Grignan reports that the Emperor directed M. de Granvelle to ask him whether he was instructed to say anything to the Princes about the re-union of Christendom and to urge them to consent to the Council. He replied that he had no such instructions, but would write to the King about it. The Emperor thought this very strange, and instructed me to express surprise at it here. The reply given to me was that the envoy had been instructed to address the Princes exactly as the Emperor might wish and to assure them that the King of France would, in the matter of the Council, be guided by the Emperor's wishes.

---

[*] The Duchy of Bar, part of the territories of Lorraine, was held as a fief of the empire, whereas Lorraine itself was feudatory to France. The position of the Duke was thus rendered difficult and on the succession of each Duke a protest was made by France on the subject.

1545.

By the Emperor's orders I have urged them to an agreement for the surrender of Hesdin against a reasonable compensation, in accordance with the treaty of peace. They reply that it was arranged that the compensation should be decided by the King of France, and the King assures me that he instructed his representatives at the peace negotiations to break off the treaty, rather than consent to the restoration of Hesdin.* I said that, in effect, the Emperor might consider that the treaty had not been fulfilled unless the town was restored in return for a reasonable compensation : and his Majesty now formally demanded the surrender on those terms.

The King has republished decrees to the effect that all English property found at sea or in the ports, and any ships wholly or partially loaded with English goods, shall be confiscated to the King's use ; and also all goods and persons found in the said ships, even though the ships and remainder of the merchandise belong to the subjects of the Emperor or others. The Emperor, however, refuses to allow this, as a violation of the treaty of peace, and the Flemings complain that it amounts to a stoppage of their trade with England altogether.

After much effort I have obtained a suspension of the letters of marque against Portugal for six months, during which period the King of Portugal is to undertake to see justice done to the French claimants. I have accepted this, but after I communicated with the Portuguese ministers they thought that I ought to stipulate that the letters should be revoked altogether, or at least that during the suspension it should be agreed that justice should be done on both sides reciprocally. This the French consider a rejection of the understanding arrived at with me, and the letters of marque are consequently still in operation.

It has been decided here to recognise the succession to the principality of Orange, as it was bequeathed by the late Prince Renè. The case has been a long one.†

The Prince of Piedmont has arrived at the Emperor's Court, whereat these people are not pleased.

Don Diego Calvaja sent hither by our Prince tells me that he learnt on the way that the Scots had seized three Spanish ships in the harbour of Bordeaux. I have complained of this here, and was told that nothing was known about it, but that M. L'Orge and

---

* By the treaty of Crépy the fortress of Hesdin, which was claimed by the Emperor as part of his territory of Artois, was to be surrendered by the French on reasonable compensation being given for it. As will be seen, this compensation according to the French contention, was to be fixed by the King of France ; which of course meant that Hesdin would not be surrendered at all. This is one of the many proofs that neither Charles nor Francis really meant to fulfil the conditions. Both needed peace in the face of the rising power and cohesion of the protestants ; but each one thought to cheat the other out of the price.

† Renè of Nassau, the young Prince of Orange (by right of maternal descent) had been killed at St. Disier, leaving his petty French principality to his first cousin, the child William of Nassau, who inherited also the vast Flemish possessions of his house, and became in after years famous as William the Silent. The Flemish lordships were subject to the suzerainty of Charles ; whilst the principality of Orange-Chalons was claimed as feudatory by France (though the claim was always contested). Hence the difficulties raised by the King of France to recognising an adherent and feudatory of the Emperor as Prince of Orange.

1545.

M. Bury should be written to urging the immediate restitution of these ships if they had been so captured. As no complaint has been made to me by the parties interested, I also am ignorant if the report is true, and I am therefore holding my hand in the matter.

M. D'Albret recently sent to the Emperor, asking him to come to some agreement as to the Kingdom of Navarre. The Emperor instructs me to get quit of the matter as best I can. I am to tell him (D'Albret) that after a decision has been arrived at in the main affairs, this matter shall be dealt with.*

The Duke of Savoy has sent a gentleman hither to justify him to the King in the matter of the rumour about his intention to move war against the King. The latter replied that he never thought that the Duke, a virtuous Prince whom he looked upon as a kinsman and a friend, would think of such a thing. The Dauphin said the same. The only thing I have been able to obtain in the business of the Duke of Alburquerque† is the appointment of a commission to enquire into the capture of the property. The three points referred to them are; first if the ships upon which the property was loaded belonged to subjects of the Emperor; secondly if the vessels were exclusively freighted for the Duke and his household; and thirdly, if the said ships carried any property belonging to English subjects. The Duke's man has left here to obtain the declarations on these points, and a substitute will attend in the case when the information is submitted. From what the Duke told me, I should think these three points could easily be proved in his favour; and they will be obliged to restore his property, unless they invoke the decrees mentioned above.

Don Diego has left here with authority from the King to enquire into the seizures which were the cause of his coming. It is certain that if the enquiry brings anything to light the King will do prompt justice, as he has promised Don Diego. I, for my part, will also press the matter to the utmost.

It is asserted that the Turk left Adrianople for Constantinople, after he heard that the ambassadors of the Emperor and the King were coming to him to treat of the truce. The ambassadors have left Venice. Before doing so they compared their respective instructions, and the French envoy considered those of the imperial ambassador somewhat strange on one point; namely where it speaks of the Turk having shown an inclination towards the truce. The Frenchman said that this might offend the Turk, who is naturally insolent; and he (the French envoy) said that he would carry on the principal negotiations with the Turk, and would lead matters in a way that would secure the object aimed at; our ambassador simply having to sign the treaty when it was made.

I received your letters of 7th instant with the packet addressed to the Queen, which I delivered safely.‡ I have already answered the contents of the said letters in the aforegoing paragraphs, and have only to add that on the 4th July, the (French) sea force is to

---

* *See* note, page 99.
† *See* note, page 79.
‡ Eleanor of Austria Queen Dowager of Portugal, sister of the Emperor and the second wife of Francis I.

1545.

embark at Havre de Grace for the enterprise against England. It is asserted that the force will land on the island of England itself and will join the Scots forces in order to penetrate as far as possible inland. In addition to this, the King intends to go in person to the camp before Boulogne for the purpose of constructing the two forts, of which I sent a plan to our Prince, the intention being to reduce Boulogne by famine. There will also be another force of 15,000 men, who will be kept at sea.

(The writer's salary. He will endeavour to find a merchant to cash at Antwerp his drafts on Spain. Claims compensation for loss of exchange. For his first payment he received 600 crowns worth only 36 placks each, so that there is a difference of 80 crowns from the amount in ducats.)

I have now learnt from Germany that M. de Gragnan has declared to the States that the King (of France) desires the holding of the Council, and his statement was made in words satisfactory to the Emperor. I am informed that no decision has yet been arrived at with the Protestants; but it is hoped that they may be brought to reason, especially when they see that the Turk will not attack this year, and that the Emperor and the King are united against them. It appears that they (the Protestants) would rather refer the questions that are to be discussed at the Council, to the Emperor than to the Pope.

Caen, 29 June, 1545.

2 July.
Vienna
Imp. Arch.

83. VAN DER DELFT to the EMPEROR.

Your Majesty's letters of 13 June were delivered to me by the bearer of the present on the 19th. From them I learn of the pressure exerted by the English ambassador upon your Majesty in the matter of the aid, and I note the instructions by which I am to be governed when the matter is broached to me here. Your Majesty's dispatches, and also the copies sent to me of the Queen Dowager's letters, treat so fully and wisely of this important question, that my small understanding and new experience are now amply furnished with guidance. I will take pains to carry out your Majesty's intentions, with the participation and advice of M. de Chapuys as you command; and with this object on receipt of your Majesty's letters enclosed in a letter from him, I sent back the bearer to Chapuys, to beg for the further elucidation of certain points touched upon by him. This has been one of the principal reasons for the long delay in the return of the bearer, but I have also kept him back from day to day, in expectation of being summoned to court on this matter.

In the interim I received your Majesty's letters of the 17th, which came to hand on the 28th June, ordering me to lay before the King and Council the injury done to some subjects of yours, merchants of Burgos, by the seizure and detention of their property, and to demand prompt restitution, or at least the release of the merchandise against security. On the following day, accordingly, I saw the members of the Council by appointment; having judged it advisable thus to hurry my interview, as there was a rumour that the King was to leave in a day or two to visit the coast—which journey they

1545.

now say will be postponed for three or four days. I was with several of the members from eight o'clock in the morning until long after ten, but we did not enter into the discussion of my business, as some of the councillors (for whom they sent several times) were absent. At last, when it was getting late, Paget came in, but shortly afterwards he was sent to the King by the Council, and on his return he told the members in English that the King wished to see me, at least so it seemed to me from my small knowledge of the language, though they made no sign of such a thing to me, probably as I think, because it was just dinner time.

After I had dined with them, I was told that if I liked to speak to the King he would give me audience. I replied that I had not come to trouble his Majesty, but since he wished it, I was greatly honoured thereby. And so, Sire, without further trouble, I came to the King's presence. He received me very politely, and I excused myself for my boldness in thus troubling him personally, which had not been the object of my coming. He replied that it was no trouble, and he wished to chat with me. He then caused a stool to be brought, and, notwithstanding my excuses, insisted upon my being seated exactly opposite and quite close to him. I then began to set forth the substance of your Majesty's letters, using the sweetest words I could, and modestly asked that redress should be given to your Majesty's subjects, so many of whom had been wronged and injured by his. He displayed great astonishment, and said he could not understand how we could come and complain of him and his people, to whom such great damage was being done by us, in violation, not only of all reason and justice, but also conspicuously against the friendship and treaties existing. This was especially the case with these last seizures in Antwerp, and now by those just made in Spain; in addition to the ill treatment of the claimants in the Spanish tribunals, where they were denied all hearing and christened by the opprobrious name of heretics. If all this were not enough, reprisals had now been authorised in Spain. He would, he said, put up with these things no longer; he had gone too far now to be treated like a slave; for he was as good a sovereign-prince and King as another; and rather than tolerate such slights he would exert all his strength of body and purse. "I have been," he said, "a good friend of the Emperor, and I still will remain so; but let him treat me like a friend, and in accordance with the treaties between us. Just recently I asked leave to export from Brabant a quantity of powder which I had bought, and I have not been able to obtain even so little a thing as that."

These words were pronounced with extreme anger, whereupon I interrupted him, and asking him to pardon me, begged him to listen to what I had to say. I pointed out to him that affairs should not be looked at in that light, since your Majesty had never given him reason for dissatisfaction in the slightest degree. On the contrary, you had sought to increase and continue the perfect and ancient amity between him and you, which was inviolable. With regard to the seizure in Antwerp, he knew, I said, how that happened; and that your Majesty was forced thereto by the previous seizure of so many ships by the English. He replied that he had very good reason for seizing them, as they were carrying victuals to his enemies. I said that a large number of them carried no victuals at all, and some were empty, and he could have no reason for seizing them.

As for the seizures in Spain, they had been effected without your Majesty's knowledge; and in reprisal for injuries in which I could not believe that he had any part, and of which I was loath even to speak. "You know very well how to make up for them," he said. "Are these friendly things to do? They are quite the contrary. I wish all these professions and interpretations of amity were dropped, and that I could see some practical effects of friendship." I replied that no one in the world could reproach your Majesty in that respect: for you had done, and would do, everything to which you could reasonably be held to be obliged. As to "interpreting" the friendship to him, that was a thing in which I did not care to waste time, for I knew that it was so clearly recognised on both sides, and so indissoluble, that no doubt need exist about it.

He caught up my word "obliged" and said: What do you mean by obliged? There is a treaty between us; and that should either be binding or declared nul. He then referred to your Majesty's treaty of peace with France, and complained bitterly that he was deserted, and thus left alone at war. I replied that he knew very well that the peace was made by his express consent, but he struck in at once, saying that that would never be found true; and that there was no one in the world who could say it with truth. He would answer for that; for it touched his own honour. I persisted as well as I could, referring to the conclusions about it which had been given to the Earl of Hertford and the Bishop of Winchester at Brussels, and also to Chapuys' arguments on the subject in conversation with the King himself. I added also that he (Henry) had deserted your Majesty, and had left you in great necessity in France, without any help on his side, his excuse being that he was engaged before Boulogne. He replied that I knew nothing whatever about it; and continued to repeat that he had never given his consent. Besides, he said, even if he had, that was no reason why the two monarchs (*i.e.* Henry and Charles) should fall out about it. If there was any fault, either on the one side or the other, the ministers could arrange the matter. If it was found that he had been to blame in anything he would willingly compensate for it twice over. If we wished to keep to the treaty let us do it: otherwise say so. These words, Sire, were pronounced with so much vehemence, that I thought it wisest not to say what your Majesty writes in your letter: namely, that you might have treated for the peace without his consent, if you had chosen to do so. I did not wish to excite him to further rage; but still I replied that your Majesty had in no respect infringed the treaty, and had no wish to do so. On the contrary, you were resolved to respect it, so far as you could without violating the treaty you had made with France, which treaty must also be considered, since it was made with his (Henry's) consent. He immediately exclaimed again that no consent was given. Your Majesty, he said, had neither his letters, nor his seal, nor his signature, nor his word to vouch for it. As for the treaty

1545.

with France, whatever it might be, it could not alter or lessen the prior treaty with him, which, he said, should be valid, according to all its force and tenour, for it was attested with word, signature, seal and oath. He kept reverting to the expression that he would not be thus cajoled (*mené*) with these "interpretations." It was necessary to speak out. So far as he was concerned, he was a good friend and would remain so; but he wanted to see friendly deeds, not friendly words; and if that did not suit us, and we did not wish to keep to the treaty, let us say so, and he would then know how to act. He conveyed the impression that, if he were forced to it, he would do what otherwise he had no will for, persisting always with many words, which he used at his good pleasure, that he would not consent to be treated thus any longer. For affairs of merchants, he said, princes should not break friendship with each other, or go beyond their treaties; as had been done in the matter of the seizures in Spain. I again repeated what I had said before; setting forth the prior injuries that had been inflicted on your Majesty's subjects, and the seizures which still continued to be made daily here, not a ship being allowed to pass unmolested, notwithstanding the agreement made so lately with Paget. I said they (the English) arbitrarily asserted at their caprice that such and such ships were loaded with goods belonging to Frenchmen, and adjudged them to be good prizes, in spite of all proofs to the contrary. It was, I said, against all right and reason that they should detain property belonging to a friendly people, without allowing it to be released against sufficient bail. When the King heard this, he said he had heard nothing about bail. I replied that, on the contrary, it was the point we had always pressed. He thereupon summoned the councillors, and repeated to them in substance what I had said, and more particularly his own part of the conversation, getting once more angry as he went on.

There is, he said, a treaty in existence between the Emperor and myself, and I wish to know frankly what is the Emperor's intention as to keeping it or not. If he wishes to maintain the treaty he will find in me a constant and sincere friend; but if on the contrary he thinks to cajole me with his "interpretations," whilst I am being treated as I am, I will not endure it. If I undertake a thing I shall have means to carry it through; and you (*i.e.*, the Emperor's subjects) are wrong to trust Frenchmen as you are doing. Finally, as a reply to my demand, he added:—"let the Emperor fulfil the treaty and raise the embargo on my people, and I will release his." —He then left me, referring me to the council for the rest of my business. He communicated with the councillors, and took leave of me with a good countenance, saying that he depended upon my good offices in all things, as he considered me an honest man. I then went downstairs with one of the councillors, and waited in their chamber for the rest of them almost a quarter of an hour. When they arrived and we had discussed my conversation with the King, we entered into the business of the merchants. I pointed out to them, amongst other things, that it was in my opinion entirely outside the treaty of friendship for them to arrest all ships,

545.

on the assertion that they contained French property; and I told them that I was instructed by your Majesty to demand the release of such as belonged to your Majesty's subjects, at least on the owners furnishing sufficient security.

The Councillors declared that they had always striven to maintain the friendship, and accordingly, since my leaving the King, they had used such influence with him that he was pleased to consent that the merchants should have possession of their merchandise, on condition of their giving security here that the property of English subjects seized in Spain should be released. This did not appear to me to be acceptable. The merchants, I said, were quite ready to give security that their merchandise seized here did not belong to Frenchmen, but could not consent to be made responsible for other things as the English demanded. They (the Councillors) however knew already, I said, and might further be assured for me, that when they had released the property of your Majesty's subjects here. the seizures in Spain would also be raised. The Councillors insisted nevertheless, that they must have the security of the merchants to this effect, as they said it was necessary for them to have something to satisfy their own people, who are complaining constantly of the seizures in Spain.

I replied that they could not claim any redress as against our ships here, as the seizures in Spain had been effected without your Majesty's knowledge ; whilst our ships here were detained as prizes belonging to Frenchmen. It seemed now that they (the English) wanted to hold this property as a security for the release of the seizures in Spain ; and I therefore required to know on which pretext these ships were seized, whether as French prizes or as a set off against the arrest of English property in Spain.

They replied : "Take it which way you like. You heard what the King told you : have the seizures in Spain released and Spanish property will be released here ; " although, they said, we are able to prove that some of this property really belongs to Frenchmen. I said that if that were the case, we should never demand it, and only wanted our own. I laid before them the great injury and wrong that were being done to our people, who were losing their property. which the people here were wasting and selling for half its value, whilst the English property arrested in Spain was kept intact. After much argument, they seemed to be inclined to admit the justice of my demand, and sent twice to consult the King : but finally the answer I received was that the King intended to safeguard the interests of his subjects as well as other sovereigns did theirs, and he would not restore or release the property of Spaniards seized here, unless the property of Englishmen arrested in Spain was also released, or the Spaniards here gave security to that effect : or otherwise that they (the Spanish merchants) would permit their goods here to be detained under embargo, until the arrests in Spain were raised. For the future, however, the King had given orders that no molestation or hindrance should be offered to your Majesty's subjects in their voyages.

I replied that they well might give such an order, for they were already assured to double the amount of the English goods seized

1545.

in Spain. As for the Spanish merchants here giving permission for their property to be detained under embargo, that meant nothing at all, for their property had already been seized, and was held by force in defiance of all right.

The whole Council thereupon began vehemently to repeat and approve of the King's answer—to such an extent, indeed, that they did not appear like the same men; and the Council then rose.

As they evidently regarded the Spanish property they have seized more in the light of a set-off against the seizures in Spain than as a prize taken from French owners, I again asked them before I left on which ground they held it; to which they replied on both, and I might take my choice. When I took my departure they begged me to interpret in good part what had passed, as they trusted entirely in me to perform such favourable offices as I could. They had no doubt, they said, that I should bear in mind that princes when they talked sometimes were apt to show their authority. Notwithstanding plenty of fine words of this sort I do not refrain from informing your Majesty truly and fully of everything.

I am quite surprised, considering the manner in which they spoke, that they made no mention of the assistance they demand, except in very general terms when the King said he wished to know whether your Majesty intended to fulfil the treaty or not. With regard to the King's expression that, if he was treated like this he might be driven to what he otherwise would not willingly do; I do not understand it, unless he has some commencement of an understanding with the French; even though it may be only verbal. But in any case, Sire, they seem to me rather more haughty than they were. Under correction, it looks as if they wanted to be run after, and that they will release nothing until English property is first liberated or assured; since they are certain now of not losing anything. Amongst my many other arguments on the point, I said it was expedient, at least, to release the property of our subjects upon security being given; and they at once seized upon this word "expedient." We know very well what you mean by "expedient," they said; you are thinking of the dispatch that has been sent to Brabant ordering the seizure of English subjects and property there. "Let it be done, if it is not already done," they said; just thus, Sire, as if they had no property there at all. I quite believe that this may be so; for, as I wrote lately to the Queen (Dowager) and to M. de Granvelle, they have caused their merchants' goods everywhere to be sold or placed in surety, whilst they have forbidden the exportation of merchandise from here. I see now that this has been done as a means of getting the English property in Spain released without proceedings on their part. Pray pardon me, your Majesty, for repeating so many times some of the things written above. For brevity's sake I might have omitted them, but as they repeated in speech even oftener than I have written them, I have thought well to give your Majesty a full account.

I have nothing further to add to my three letters recently despatched, and now doubtless in your Majesty's hands, except that the Admiral has left with the greater part of the fleet for the coast

1545.

of France, for the purpose of trying to perform some exploit, before the French fleet appears. The Admiral is afterwards to bring the English fleet to the port of Portsmouth, where the whole navy is to muster on the 13th or 14th instant, and the King intends there to inspect the forces, which it is said will reach 200 sail.

The only news from Scotland is that the King of France has sent thither 2,000 infantry, 500 horsemen, and a considerable sum of money.

It is asserted that the Duke of Lauenberg with six or eight hundred horse is in the service of this King, and is to come to Calais shortly, passing by way of Liege and Haynau (Hainault). The payment of the last instalment of the benevolence due at Michaelmas is to be anticipated, and is payable at once, but there is no talk of any fresh demand, though the subjects are very doubtful. At all events, it is evident that nothing will be refused to this King; such is the fear in which they hold him, and their eagerness to see their enemy humiliated.

I do not know whether your Majesty has been informed that a Spaniard named Caceres, who is said to have served as a spy against your Majesty before Landrecy, and was recently arrested here as a French spy, has been liberated, for the purpose, I think, of doing the same sort of work elsewhere. In order that your Majesty may the earlier have advice from the Queen (Dowager) and M. Chapuys I am sending them copies of this letter.

London, 2 July, 1545.

2 July.
Vienna
Imp. Arch.

84. VAN DER DELFT to the QUEEN DOWAGER.

Since my last to your Majesty, I have received two letters from the Emperor, one of which contained copy of yours, touching the question of the aid demanded by the English. His Majesty instructs me how I am to bear myself in dealing with the point, and that I am to gain time, and not to broach the subject until approaches are made to me. Even when this occurs, I am to take care to say nothing that shall give the English any ground for arriving at a conclusion, either as to the granting or the refusal of the aid. The other letter from the Emperor orders me to take the first opportunity of strongly remonstrating with the King and Council against the daily outrages and wrongs being committed by the seizure of merchandise belonging to the Emperor's subjects on board ships, and to demand, at least, the release of the property against security. In accordance with these instructions, I went to Court and there had with the King and Council the conversations which I relate fully in my letters to the Emperor, of which I enclose copies. I cannot describe the annoyance displayed by the King at his not being able to obtain the license to export from Antwerp a quantity of powder, which he has bought. He cannot swallow the refusal of so trifling a request, seeing that he is constantly being assured of the great affection and perfect amity of the Emperor towards him. If it were possible to gratify the King in this, it would have a great effect; and I therefore venture to write as I have done, craving your Majesty's pardon for my boldness.

1545.

Whilst I was in conference with the Council, I gathered distinctly that Jasper Doulchy's claim, which is before the arbitration conference, will be favourably settled, for certain reasons not mentioned by the Councillors. I deduced from this that the other cases were not so hopeful.

London, 2 July, 1545.

4 July.
Vienna
Imp. Arch.

85. Chapuys to the Emperor.

I received this morning letters from the ambassador in England, dated the 2nd instant, and enclosing me copies of dispatches which he was sending to your Majesty of the same date. At the same time the Bishop of Westminster and Petre received letters sent by the King of England to his ambassador with your Majesty; the courier who brought them having accompanied the bearer from England.

After I had read the ambassador's letter and the copies, I went to our place of meeting, where I found that the English deputies had arrived some time before, and much earlier than usual, in order that they might have an opportunity of conversing with me. As soon as I entered the room the bishop (Thirlby) and the secretary (Petre) left their companions and drew me apart, saying that they had received letters from England informing them that the King wished to fulfil most scrupulously everything compatible with the good and perfect amity existing between him and your Majesty, and to banish all misgiving or ground for dispute. As an earnest of this, he would at once concede the claim of Jasper Doulchy, especially as Doulchy had acted very honestly in leaving the matter entirely in his (the King's) hands. Secretary Paget and the other councillors were of opinion that it would be extremely advisable, out of respect for the King, and for the satisfaction of the parties, that I should use my influence for the claim for the jewels and the Antenori claim to be dealt with similarly.

I promised to do my best in this, and also for the arrangemen of all unimportant or doubtful claims made by your Majesty's subjects. I asked them (*i.e.*, Thirlby and Petre) if they had any other news, but they feigned not to know anything about the King's having written to the ambassador with your Majesty; but thought that the courier had come over specially to them, in order that they might send to the ambassador an account of what they were doing here.

I thought the opportunity a propitious one for carrying matters further, and in the course of conversation, I said that at this period there was a greater need than ever before for your Majesty and their King to be served by wise ministers, in order to redress the complaints of subjects on both sides, and to avoid the unpleasant effects that might arise from them. Your Majesty's ambassador in England, I said, would certainly do his best, as he always had done in every case, but I noticed just now a special desire on his part to favour conciliation; because, although some angry words had passed between the King and him (of which he had confidentially informed me) he had made no mention of it in the letters he had written to

1545.

your Majesty. The object of hiding from them that your Majesty's ambassador had written everything to you, was that they should not imagine, if your Majesty thinks proper to concede their request, that you have been moved by their bragging, but on the contrary had been influenced solely by friendship and goodwill. I added that, so far as I was concerned, they might rest assured that there was nothing in the world that I desired more than the continuance and strengthening of the friendly alliance; and I begged them to tell me what I could do with that end. They replied that they were of opinion that in the matter of these seizures, declarations of release should at once be made by both parties. They were quite sure that the King would in future take such measures that none of his people, for the sake of the lives, would disturb or molest any of your Majesty's subjects. You ought not, they said, to take in ill part the King's desire to be assured of the release of his subjects' property, since, as a good prince, he was bound to safeguard their interests; especially as he found them ready constantly to give him prompt aid in purse and person. For their satisfaction he had caused mention to be made of the bail referred to in the letters written to your Majesty by your ambassador.[*] To tell me the truth, they thought that this bail might also be given (*i.e.*, by the Spanish merchants in London) out of some regard for the King's honour (of which he was very jealous) so that it might not be said that he had been intimidated into doing everything that your Majesty wished. The rest they were content to leave to me, as I knew better than anyone the importance of the affairs; but they wished to remark that, as the King was open and outspoken, he wished your Majesty would act towards him in a similar spirit, letting him know frankly, in the case of your being unable or unwilling to do anything to help him. It would be very rash of me to intrude my opinion on so important a matter, were it not in obedience to your Majesty's orders. Under correction, therefore, I venture to suggest that if at the present time there were in your Majesty's dominions a great quantity of English property and many Englishmen of substance (as was the case when your Majesty made the former seizure in Flanders), it would be an excellent step to decree a counter seizure against them: because, let the King of England boast and covertly threaten as he may, he will not on any account undertake any fresh enterprise. Now, however, as I understand that the English property in Spain is hardly sufficient to cover the depredations of Renegat, and there cannot be much in Flanders, it would, in my opinion, be better to dissemble for the present, and either by means of the solution suggested by the King of England, or some other which will occur to your Majesty, to bring about a mutual release of property seized on both sides. Otherwise the English will continue their captures at sea, and will take very good care to send no merchandise to your Majesty's dominions, except under

---

[*] That is to say the security which was demanded by Henry from the Spanish merchants claiming goods in England, not only that the property they claimed did not belong to French subjects, but also that the merchandise of English subjects seized in Spain should be released.

1545.

cover of other nationalities. In case it should please your Majesty to accept the suggestion of the King of England; and, in addition, to make it clear that the seizures in Spain were not effected by your Majesty's orders, but that you were displeased with them, the English will re-commence their trade as before. If thereafter it should be necessary, your Majesty will have plenty of English goods in your dominions to indemnify the merchants, and in the event of affairs reaching the extreme of a claim being made upon England for the non-fulfilment of the treaty, a part of the indemnity could come from the same source.

Bourbourg, 4th July 1545.

4 July.
Vienna
Imp. Arch.

86. CHAPUYS to LOIS SCORS (President of the Flemish Council).

The reasons which have prevented me from writing to the Queen (Dowager) have caused me to treat you similarly. Pray pardon my silence and believe my assurance that I am desirous of serving you etc. etc.

You know better than I can tell you the importance of keeping this King (*i.e.*, of England) friendly, more especially in view of the distrust and inconstancy of our neighbours (*i.e.*, the French) and for other reasons. It would be advisable therefore to avoid giving him (*i.e.*, the King of England) cause for suspicion of the Emperor, or to drive him to think of other combinations, which he threatens to do—although his threats are of no great consequence; because, even if he comes to terms with France, he will not enter with any plans against the Emperor. According to my poor foolish fancy, however, it would be better for his Majesty's interests that the arrangement (*i.e.*, between France and England) should not take place too soon. It will be preferable that they should both tire somewhat, and become more tractable than they are. As the English profess to be about to take steps for preventing in future all hindrance or molestation to navigation, I have thought well to send you enclosed a draft, upon which some sort agreement for that purpose may be based, the clauses of which you might arrange to meet the various cases of cruelty and outrage of which the English have been guilty.

Bourbourg, 4 July 1545.

4 July.
Vienna
Imp. Arch.

87. CHAPUYS to the QUEEN (Dowager) of Hungary.

Since my return from England I have been very ill; but in spite of that I should have written to your Majesty giving you an account of events if the Chancellor of the Order had not been good enough to undertake to do so. I have therefore refrained from troubling your Majesty, even about English affairs, as I supposed you would be fully informed of these from his imperial Majesty. I have intended on each occasion that I wrote to the Emperor to send your Majesty copies of the letters, which I had made for the purpose, but the fear of troubling your Majesty has always prevented me from actually dispatching them. The same fear would restrain me now, but for the fact that the Chancellor of the Order informs me this morning that your Majesty, even though you were fully advised from other sources, would be glad to receive this further proof of my goodwill. I therefore send your Majesty enclosed copies of all my letters to the Emperor, and beg to be pardoned for my tardiness, as well as for the simplicity of my letters.

Bourbourg, 4 July 1545.

7 July.
Vienna
Imp. Arch.

88. CHAPUYS to VAN DER DELFT.

Your letter of 2nd instant, with copy of what you had written to his Majesty, duly received. On the same day I despatched the courier with the letter from me to his Majesty, of which you will find copy enclosed. I have little to add to it, except to say that you have very prudently and discreetly laid the whole matter before his Majesty. This has been a great pleasure and consolation for me. With regard to your following the King or not, no person can speak more confidently than Secretary Paget; but since you ask my advice I may say that if the King's voyage is a private one, he will only wish his own people to accompany him; but if he goes with some appearance of state, and has to pass through important towns, I should think he would be glad of your company; which you might offer when the next affair of importance takes you to Court. Your discretion will dictate to you what will be best in view of circumstances. It is a pleasure for me to hear that the King holds me in such high esteem as you say. God grant me power to match my goodwill to do his Majesty service in return for his innumerable favours to me. I can well suppose that Secretary Paget does not fail occasionally to say a good word for me to the King; for which pray thank him, and remember me to him, as often as you have an opportunity of doing so. Be also my pledge to him that I will not fail to do the best office I can in all that touches the King's service.

Bourbourg, 7 July 1545.

9 July.
Vienna
Imp. Arch:

89. The EMPEROR to VAN DER DELFT.

We have received your letters of 12th and 13th ultimo, and have heard what you wrote to Granvelle on the same date, about the claims for restitution of our Spanish subjects who were robbed at sea, and whose ships are still detained. We approve of what you have said and done on the subject; and we have again discussed the matter here, and have spoken very plainly about it to the English ambassador. Matters came to this point, because the ambassador at once began to talk about the aid with which the King pretends we are bound to furnish him in case his realm is invaded. He asserts that the French and Scots are now in force; and it is considered certain that they will invade England, even if they have not already done so. His master the King therefore gives us notice, in order that we may have our contingent ready, and says that the sooner we are ready the greater will be his obligation to aid us, if similar need should ever arise on our side. We replied in the way you will see; and we repeat to you what we said, in order that you may communicate it also to the King, and

1545.

act as circumstances may dictate. We intended, we said, to justify ourselves completely with regard to the aid; but we thought it very strange that at such a time these outrages should be committed on our merchants, in utter violation of the treaty of friendship between his master and us. We begged him that the treaty should be more closely observed in the future, and that prompt redress and indemnity should be given to our subjects. The ambassador promised to use his influence to this end; although he tried to excuse the seizures and to throw the blame on our subjects. We rebutted this with the same arguments which you used; and you will, therefore, persist in demanding the restitution and redress claimed. You will also speak to the King and Council about the aid, in accordance with the instructions given in our former letters, if you have not already done so by the advice of Chapuys; and you will proceed generally on the lines laid down in our letters, and Chapuy's correspondence; consulting him by letter on any point which may arise out of the negotiations in England, and informing us and our sister as often as possible of all that passes.

With regard to the irritation displayed by Paget at our refusal of the licence to export war munitions (from Antwerp), we can only say that he has no reason whatever to be offended. His master should consider that, in every respect where it is decently possible, we are favouring his side, to the great annoyance of the French, who complain frequently about it. You can refer them to the explanation already given to Paget, and to the English ambassador on this side.

Enquiries have been made here about the Queen of England's secretary mentioned by you as negotiating with the Protestants, but nothing can be discovered about him. Make careful enquiries, and let us know the result, and also inform us of the condition of affairs generally in England.

You did well in informing the Queen (Dowager) of what you heard about the withdrawal of English property from the Netherlands, and the secret prohibition of the exportation of goods from England thither. We heard the news from another quarter also, and our sister will act in the matter as seems best. Keep her fully advised. We have spoken very earnestly to the English ambassador here about an arrangement between his master and the King of France, and have offered to use our utmost endeavours to forward it, if we could see any way of doing so. We have recommended the ambassador to write to his master on the subject, as we promised to do to you, in order that you might also address the King. We have also written to our ambassador in France, and we undertook to speak to the French ambassadors here, which we have done. They, on their part, have promised to address their master to the same end; and if we see the slightest sign that anything may come of it, we will use extreme diligence in forwarding it. This will have the effect of extricating us from this Diet (diette), and will enable us, in any case, to return to Flanders for so good a work, whilst it will obviate the difficulties that may arise from this war, of which the continuance, and the bad blood it breeds, displeases us greatly. You must do your very best to convey this to the King,

1545.

for which purpose we are sending you a letter of credence. You will communicate with Chapuys and our sister what you can learn of the King of England's wishes in the matter.

Worms, 9 July, 1545.

Note.—The draft of a letter of credence from Charles to Henry in favour of Van der Delft is attached to the above, asking the King to allow the ambassador to express to him the earnest desire of the Emperor to bring about a pacification between England and France.

9 July.
Vienna
Imp. Arch.

90. The Emperor to Chapuys.

We have received your letters, and have heard from Granvelle the advice you have given to your successor in England, respecting the contents of our recent despatches sent through you, touching the assistance claimed by the King of England, in case of invasion of his realm. We approve of all you say, which is marked by your accustomed prudence and devotion to our service. We beg you affectionately to continue to advise the ambassador whenever you consider necessary, and to write to us plainly and frankly what you think should be done in the matter for the future, in view of the way in which his action may be taken in England.

We also highly approve of what you wrote to Granvelle, about (your) endeavouring to bring about peace between England and France, which we really desire. We had already spoken on the subject to the French and English ambassadors here; but up to the present have got nothing but general words. You will see what we have written to your successor in England about it, and this will serve for your guidance in your communications with the English deputies and others, to make clear our wish to strain every effort in favour of peace.

Worms, 9th July 1545.

10 July.
Vienna
Imp. Arch.

91. Van der Delft to the Emperor.

Since my last of 2nd instant, nothing has occurred with respect to the merchants' affairs mentioned in your Majesty's latest letters, except that some of the merchants, moved by the great expense they were put to, and the heavy loss sustained by the seizure of their property; and seeing that my appeal to the King availed them nothing, have taken the course of themselves of soliciting individual members of the Council for the release. They have been answered that, if they would give bail to the full amount of the value of this property (which would be appraised for the purpose) against any and every claim of the King, the embargoes should be raised. As this reply seemed to be substantially the same as that which had been given to me, and which I would not accept, because the bail was to secure the release of the seizures in Spain, I thought better not to meddle further with the matter, until I received fresh orders from your Majesty. I have therefore stood aloof, and have allowed the merchants to make their own agreements, with the effect that some of their property has already been appraised. After the valuation had been made, one of the merchants

1545.

went to present his bail, but it was rejected by the Chancellor, who said that they understood that the whole of the merchants together were to give the bail.* I will advise you of what happens further in this matter and beg for instructions as to how I should proceed. There is no news here of the proceedings of the troops in Scotland, except that the Scots are said to have requested the English Commander-in-Chief, the Earl of Hertford, to abstain from further injuring them, as they were conferring among themselves as to the means for coming to an agreement. The English, however, looked upon this simply as a subterfuge, although it is unquestionable that a certain Scottish Archbishop is greatly at feud with the Cardinal (Beton), which is causing them much trouble. They are also very short of food in the country where the English have planted themselves, according to the Spaniards who are arriving from there daily.

With regard to the besieging of Boulogne (by the French) of which there is a rumour here, I have no doubt that your Majesty is amply informed by those on the spot. If these people (the English) make this a ground for speaking to me about the aid to be furnished by your Majesty under the treaty in the case of invasion, I will take care to answer them fittingly, being guided by the arguments contained in your Majesty's letters, and especially depending upon the point that the invasion has only for its object the recovery of Boulogne, which country is not covered by the treaty.

The measures adopted here to receive and combat the enemy are said on all sides to be excellent. These lords (of the Council) and great gentlemen are again distributed in all directions, in order to superintend matters. The King himself left on Saturday last to visit his ports and harbours; and I thought it was necessary out of politeness to offer to accompany him and swell his train if he wished it. I conveyed this to Secretary Paget before the King's departure, and he replied that I should be very welcome, and the King would be pleased if I came. I have therefore made preparations to follow him, and am departing to-morrow to join the King at Portsmouth, where he is to arrive on the 15th instant, and to stay, so it is said, for ten or twelve days, to inspect his fleet.

The day before yesterday the Venetian ambassador resident here came to converse with me, and amongst other discourse, he said that he was assured positively that an Italian captain named Ypolitus Mazinus, who was on the side of the French and was captured and brought here; being afterwards released on parole to go and seek his ransom, was again here recently on a mission from Madame d' Etampes, to make overtures for peace. He appears to have done this; but as the English saw that the first point demanded was the restitution of Boulogne, they refrained from proceeding further with him, and he went back without doing anything. I do not know whether the King was referring to this when he told me lately that, whenever he chose to do a certain thing he would have means of extricating himself from his annoy-

---

* That is to say jointly and severally, so that the whole of the property in England would be answerable for the seizures in Spain.

ances; or whether he meant to refer to the mission of a French gentleman, who has several times gone to Boulogne to communicate with the English; as I have since heard was the case.

I understand, also, that some captains, subjects of the Landgrave of Hesse, were recently with the lords of the Council, for the purpose of offering their services, boasting that they can bring a large number of men-at-arms, both horse and foot, for the King's service. They are, it is said, to come to Calais by passing through your Majesty's territory of Hainault. Others assert that the intention is to form an army, for the purpose of annoying the French on that side (*i.e.*, on the frontier of Hainault). If this be true, and these captains have been dispatched very promptly whilst others have been kept sueing so long, it certainly raises a suspicion that some understanding may exist between the King and the protestants, which is greatly to be feared and distrusted for the sake of religion.

There is a rumour here amongst the merchants, both English and foreign, who do nothing but murmur and shake their heads about an imminent rupture of friendly relations between your Majesty and this King. I am kept busy assuring those who speak to me on the subject that the friendship will continue; but I see that the English merchants who used to trade at Antwerp are returning hither ten or twelve at a time, whilst all our ships here are under arrest, and complaints of this kind are constantly reaching me. I thought best to send about it to the Chancellor, who still remains in London, and he replied that with regard to the ships arrested, they had been detained by the King's orders, as he wished to employ them when opportunity served to carry over a number of troops, horse and foot, against the French. Doubtlesss the hope is that he may be able to raise the fresh army above referred to. On the point of the retirement of the English (merchants) from Antwerp, the Chancellor replied to my message that it was not to be wondered at, seeing that the Chancellor of Brabant had recently come to Antwerp to enquire of the English merchants as to the quantity of merchandise they had, and its value. This, he said, was the reason of the withdrawal of the English, as they feared a seizure, the order for which was already in the hands of the Chancellor of Brabant. He (Wriothesley) made great complaints about this, and about the way in which they were constantly being treated by having their property seized, in direct violation of the treaty; and said that he wished these dark clouds were banished, for the good of both parties. The King, he said, was never so well disposed to be friendly with your Majesty as at the present time; but he looked for some reciprocity, and doubted not that when your Majesty learnt what he (the King) had recently said to me by word of mouth you would incline with your old friend to what reason and justice demanded for the ending of this bitterness, the continuation of a good understanding and the maintenance of the treaty of alliance, which was his and his people's sovereign desire. They had, he (Wriothesley) said, such entire confidence in your Majesty, that if affairs were placed before you as they were recently explained to me by the King, they were certain of a good and amiable reply, which they most earnestly

1545.

desired. Neverthless, if the reply were otherwise than as they anticipated, they must be patient and make the best of it.

This agrees, in effect with what I wrote fully to your Majesty recently, and the matter is of so much importance that I have used every possible means to ascertain their motive and reason for sticking so obstinately to the point of wanting to know decidedly whether your Majesty will, or will not, keep to the treaty. The only reason I can imagine is that the knowledge might guide them in their negotiations with the French. Their great solicitude to know one way or the other, certainly arouses a suspicion that they may have in hand some opening of negotiation with the French, of which, however, I can obtain no positive intelligence, beyond what I have written above. Now that I am going with the Court, I shall have a better opportunity of enquiring, and I will not fail to inform your Majesty of what I can learn.

London, 10 July 1545.

Postscript.—Just as I was closing this letter I learnt that the passage from Dover to Calais was stopped, in order, so they say, to prevent the French from receiving news of their movements. I was therefore obliged to send to Court for a passport for the courier, which is the cause of the delay.

Endorsed: Received at Worms, 22 July 1545.

10 July.
Vienna
Imp. Arch.

92. VAN DER DELFT to the QUEEN DOWAGER.

This letter contains in substance the same news as that conveyed in the letter to the Emperor above. As the variations are simply verbal or unimportant the letter to the Queen is not reproduced.

11 July.
Vienna
Imp. Arch.

93. VAN DER DELFT to CHAPUYS.

I received to-day yours of 7th instant with copies of two letters from you to the Emperor, for which I thank you sincerely; and especially for expressing so favourable an opinion of me to his Majesty. Your affection for me causes you to exalt my scant experience and great ignorance, *candidissimo tuo calculo et quamvis rerum tuarum sublimitas nullo adminculo indigeat, numquam tamen applausu suffragio omniques officio illi inserrire desinam.* I note your circumlocutions with the English deputies, whom you have brought to approve of the suggestions you made for peace; and I doubt not that his Majesty will be greatly pleased thereat; and also the King of England when the whole matter has been considered.

I do not know how to thank you for your many favours to me and especially for having given me advice as to whether or not I should follow the King in his progress. As time did not, however, allow me to await your answer, I decided to send to Paget, as you will see by the copies of my letters to the Emperor, which I enclose you, in order that you may kindly reform my faults and point them out to me, that I may correct them for the future.

I am now ready and equipped to follow the Court; though it has been at considerable expense, as I wished to be as handsomely furnished as possible, out of respect for my office, and especially because it behoves me to shine brilliantly in these gloomy times. Please God, I shall start to-morrow or the next day; and when I arrive at Court I will not fail to signify to the lords your ardent desire to put an end to this sour bickering and to confirm the ancient and inveterate friendship between these two princes, although the lords know it well already, especially Master Paget, to whom I will commend you as you desire. I cannot express my astonishment at not having received any letter from the Emperor or the Queen (Dowager) for so long a time. I have had nothing since the Queen wrote telling me to be guided by the instructions contained in the Emperor's letter of 13 June, and to act in accordance with your advice. This is very old history, considering that affairs are now in a different position, since these people will not listen any longer to our oft repeated arguments, and request a categorical statement of our intentions with regard to their demand for aid. They have got the whip hand of us now (*ils nous ont maintenant par la bride*). It seems to me that there is nothing more to say until the Emperor's reply comes.

London, 11 July 1545.

12 July.
Vienna
Imp. Arch.

94. CHAPUYS to VAN DER DELFT.

I received this afternoon by the bearer letters from his Majesty dated 9th instant, with other letters from his Majesty to you of same date. It would be a slight upon you for me to attempt to add anything to these; particularly as they have already passed muster before such wise and experienced captains. But still, to obey his Majesty's orders, and to comply with your request, as a friend should do, I will just say a word or two of my opinion. First with regard to the demand for the raising of the embargo on Spanish merchandise, and the probability of the English at once meeting you with a counter-claim for the release of the last seizures in Spain; I think they might be told that the first seizures in Spain were duly released, in accordance with the agreement with Paget, and the said agreement had been fulfilled on his Majesty's part: whilst the King of England has not fulfilled it, since he still retains certain ships which were covered by the agreement. The two captured by Master Winter are such; or at least one belonging to Jehan Symon, respecting which we spoke to Winter; and after the last time you and I were with the Council the Chancellor told us that since so many other ships had been released, we might well await the release of this one until the arbitration conference met, when Winter would be able to prove that he was in the right. Up to the present, however, though we have pressed the English deputies about it, and they have written requesting that Winter's proofs should be produced, nothing more has been heard of it. The same thing may be said about the claims of Antonio de Guaras, Antenori and others. It is greatly to be regretted that when his Majesty had in his hands ample property to indemnify his subjects he should have consented to listen to the importunities of the English; and should have taken for granted the good faith of the King, who promised to fulfil the agreement. This was a

1545.

very great mistake, as is proved, not only by the matter just referred to, but also by the claims under discussion here; and respecting which, it is impossible to bring these deputies to reason. There is, moreover, no ground for hope in the two important claims of Carrion and the jewels, as I predicted frequently to you would be the case. I should like to be just for one half hour with Secretary Paget, to ask him in a whisper what honesty there was, and what a show of confidence, in withdrawing their subjects and property secretly from his Majesty's dominions, whilst they still retained the vessels of his subjects, after we had depended upon their good faith. But still, I should only say it jokingly when opportunity presented itself.

With regard to the last arrest (in Spain), Renegat gave ample cause for it, and as I wrote to you before, surely it should be more permissible for princes and ministers of justice to decree reprisals for indemnity than for a private individual to begin and give the first cause for it by taking the law into his own hands. If they (the English) reply that such things done by public authority are the more blameable, it were better that they held their tongues; for, as someone has said "*si amici ricia cum toleras facis tua.*" The law, too, says "*princeps cum subdite flagitia connivet nec protestate urciscitur, facit sua*"; and it is as certain as can be that if, on Renegat's arrival, they had arrested him and punished him, as he deserved, the seizures in Spain would have been immediately relaxed; although with justice all that Renegat himself owned there might have been retained. The seizure in question, moreover, should cause no great surprise in England, in view of the provocation given by the illegitimate procedure there. The shifty way in which the release of the goods seized in England was being conducted was perfectly well known in Spain, and, if you have an opportunity, it could do no possible harm for you to point out that these stipulations for the good treatment of subjects and the redress of injuries are as much a part of the treaty of alliance as the clauses relating to aid in mutual defence against attack. It may be said, even, that still greater importance should be attached to the former stipulations than to the latter, considering that they were the subject of recapitulation with Paget; and measures should have been taken in anticipation for their fulfilment, as they had been long a subject of discussion, and concerned the welfare and mutual harmony of the peoples. With regard to the assistance formally demanded by the (English) ambassador, I still persist in my foolish opinion that, after all, it will not be necessary; and I hope that before you receive this, affairs may have somewhat developed in the way I mentioned in my former letter, and as his Majesty assumes may be the case. Although matters may be somewhat perplexing, as so many things are mixed, I have no doubt you will dexterously manage them to his Majesty's advantage and satisfaction. For my own part, I have only these few words to add with regard to the above subjects.

With respect to the promotion of peace between England and France, I have already written to you the conversation I had with the English deputies here, and consequently I need not repeat it.

SPANISH STATE PAPERS.

545.

It is true that, in order to sound them I discussed the pro and contra of the surrender or retention of Boulogne, but there was less danger in doing so on this side of the water, than perhaps would have been the case in England. I have no doubt you will bear this in mind, in accordance with the instructions given to us by the Emperor, and will be able to find out their views without irritating them—to diagnose the malady without hurting the patient.

I can assure that since I have been here, I have done my very best to preserve the friendship between the two sovereigns, and never so heartily and hopefully as at the present moment, seeking, as I do, every means of extirpating all causes of bitterness. Not the smallest of these is the affair of Carrion, which his Majesty, for his own dignity's sake, as well as for justice and conscience, cannot allow to drag without entirely abandoning the indemnity of his subjects. But on the other hand, bearing in mind the obstinacy of those people (the English), who, on a former occasion, went so far as to say that they would rather lose his Majesty's friendship than give up the said property, I have proposed to the deputies here a means by which the matter may be arranged without loss of prestige to his Majesty, and greatly to the advantage of the King of England. My suggestion is that the King should lend a sum of money, equal to the amount claimed by Carrion's people, with interest and a little over, to be repaid in two or three instalments within twenty or five and twenty years. As the King will not care to disburse the whole sum in money, pressed as he is with the expenses of the war, a part only need be advanced in coin, and the rest in the form of lead. Although this suggestion is made by me personally, without the assent of the parties interested, I have no doubt that I could induce them to accept it; for which purpose, if necessary, I would invoke his Majesty's authority, as well as that of M. de Granvelle and M. d' Arras, who have great influence with the parties and are well disposed towards the King's interests. The deputies appear to be delighted with the suggestion; not only personally, but in the name of the King, who they say is much obliged to me for it. This confabulation took place on Friday morning, before we entered into the conference, and the deputies left immediately for the purpose of sending a special message to the King about it. I tell you this, in case they should speak to you about the matter. I am not sure that you would forward the affair by speaking of it first yourself, for they are so suspicious and ready to interpret everything to their own advantage: but I leave that to your own discretion. If the deputies have written in the sense that I have said, and according to their promise to me, have reported in favour of Carrion's claim, I have no doubt that the King will accept the arrangement; but please keep it secret until we see the tendency one way or the other.

My colleagues and I have received a letter from the Queen (Dowager) written at Werde, capital of Friesland, dated the 2nd instant, saying that her Majesty is willing that the registers, books and accounts of the custom houses (*tollieux*) of Zeeland and Brabant, for the last ninety or hundred years should be shown to

1545.

the present and future ministers or agents of the King of England, who may be accompanied by as many merchants as they like, and may cause correct copies to be made, on condition that the King will allow a similar privilege to us in the case of London dues. We are to write to you, in order that you may choose some fit and proper persons to inspect these registers. In accordance with what I wrote to you on a former occasion, I doubt not that you will already have communicated with Mr. Antoine Bonvise, who can tell you better than anyone in England what to do, and whom to appoint for this purpose; as he will do also with regard to other old books touching the same business.

The Queen also writes that seeing the small appearance there is of anything being done in this conference (*diette*) we need not waste any more time, and can take our departure, after making the necessary remonstrances, as to the treatment of his Majesty's subjects, in order for the English to avoid being dealt with in a similar way by us. I think therefore that my colleagues and I will leave here on Thursday next; my intention being to go straight to Antwerp and thence without stopping to proceed to Louvain, unless his Majesty or the Queen Dowager should be expected shortly at Brussels.

Bourbourg, 12 July 1545.

15 July.
Vienna
Imp. Arch.

95. CHAPUYS to the EMPEROR.

On the 12th instant I received your Majesty's letters of the 9th, with those enclosed from your Majesty to the ambassador in England. After having read these I forwarded them at once, with merely a few words from myself, of which I send copy to M. de Granvelle. On the following day, as I was on my way to visit the Bishop of Westminster and Secretary Petre, to talk over these affairs, I met them at the place where the conference usually assembles. I told them what I thought necessary, and they displayed great joy at your Majesty's goodwill towards the King, and your desire to bring about peace, whilst they thanked me also for my good offices with the same object. They had, however, for the moment only to say that your Majesty would find your friendly feeling fully reciprocated by the King; and they were very sorry that the courier, who had no doubt been dispatched by the English ambassador with your Majesty, had not yet arrived, as they could otherwise have spoken more openly and fully on these matters. I repeated to them some of the observations I had made to them on a former occasion (set forth in my letter of 29th ultimo to your Majesty) whereupon they expressed regret at these seizures in England, and the other reasons which might retard your Majesty from sending to them the aid they requested; but the Bishop of Westminster nevertheless said that, as the request was based on a clear and unquestionable clause, it should not be met with an objection founded upon compensation for uncertain injuries, and still *sub judice*, as was the case with the ships still detained. This he said, however, as if in pastime, adding that one must say something; and that I knew very well that he never meddled with matters in which

SPANISH STATE PAPERS.

he was not authorised. But, he said, as I had associated with them so long, I could judge almost as well of their feelings by their silence as by their words. I took the opportunity of his mentioning compensation, for saying that the point to which they referred (*i.e.*, the question of the aid) was not more important nor more obligatory than the restitution of the ships and other property belonging to your Majesty's subjects, still detained in England; for in addition to the fact that the treaty itself expressly provided for the liberty, good treatment and indemnification of subjects, these points had been directly dealt with by your Majesty's ministers and Paget, and a separate confirmatory agreement entered into with him. They had no answer to this, except to say that they regretted these unpleasant things, and would do their best, for their part, to avoid future cause of complaint.

I received this morning letters from the ambassador in England, written on the 10th and closed on the 12th, with copies of his dispatches to your Majesty of same date. With regard to the paragraph relating to the bail demanded from the merchants subject to your Majesty, as a condition of the release of their property: namely that they shall hold themselves liable to be legally called upon at any time the King may choose, I think the ambassador did well in dissociating himself from the matter. It is not only a contravention of the agreement with Paget, but will prevent these subjects of your Majesty from finding anyone to deal with them, except for cash; besides the danger there is of unjust judgments against them. For this reason, I think that the best course would be that which I wrote to your Majesty in former letters;[*] unless, indeed, the seizure in Spain had any other object than that of obtaining restitution of the property seized by the English.

Touching the news from Boulogne, I have not heard of the occurrence of anything important, except that the Bishop and the Secretary told me—as also did the captain of Calais Castle—that Lord Poyns recently sallied from Boulogne to skirmish with the French, forty of the latter, and six or seven Englishmen being killed, Poyns himself having his horse killed under him. On the same day Lord Grey, whilst he was returning from Boulogne whither he had led some of his soldiers from Guisnes, met on the way some (French) light horse of whom he captured five and killed nine without loss on his side. Late last night the Bishop and the Secretary sent to tell me—and they confirm it this morning—that a number of the King's ships had encountered the French galleys, but in consequence of the calm the ships could not attack (*ruer sur*) the galleys, as the English wished. However great the calm might be, the galleys did not dare to approach the great ships, for fear of being destroyed by the vast quantity of ordnance on the latter. They tried to combat the small ones; but no damage was done on either side, except that one ship was pierced, and was at once repaired; and the galleys were finally obliged to retire to New Haven, whither

---

[*] Namely that the seizures in Spain should be released.

1545.

the ships could not follow them for want of wind. As some compensation, the English sighted a large number of French ships following the galleys, and captured seven or eight of them, most of the rest ran on the sandbanks, from which the English thought they could not be saved.

They (*i.e.*, the bishop and the secretary) report that the French are working with great energy to construct the fortress which was commenced in February last by M. de Biez, having at work on it over 600 pioneers. A little lower down they have prepared a place from which they can batter the mouth of the harbour (of Boulogne) and the whole of the banks, so far as they are opened out to them. If they achieve what they have begun it will be very difficult for the English to revictual or replenish Boulogne from the sea. I am told, indeed, that two days ago a ship loaded with victuals was sunk at the mouth of the harbour by the French artillery; the other ships that accompanied her returning to England in consequence. I doubt very much that they have victuals enough in Boulogne; as the bishop and the secretary told me the other day with very piteous countenances, that it had been thought that Boulogne was victualled for a long time, but that a part of the stores had gone bad. The people in the place are suffering from another difficulty; the plague, which is making cruel ravages; though they (*i.e.*, Thirlby and Petre) make out that the French camp is no better in this respect.

In my discourses with the bishop and the secretary I can discern no signs from them whatever of any negotiations for peace between England and France, and I fancy that what the Venetian told the ambassador in London is only an echo of what Paget mentioned to us before I left England, and the King confirmed when I took leave of him. Of course it is possible that something may be going on, but honestly I do not believe there is, for the King is so outspoken and boastful that he would not have refrained, when he told the ambassador that he had means for putting an end to annoyances, from saying that he was being pressed warmly with favourable conditions, as he did before when Lange, Framoiselles and other French intermediaries came to him. My poor opinion is, that we ought not to draw any such inferences from the anxiety of the King to obtain a categorical declaration from your Majesty as to the aid; because, from the very commencement, he pressed for the same through Hertford and Winchester. I think that one of his principal reasons for haste to obtain a decided answer is his fear of the completion of the marriage arranged with the Duke of Orleans. He has always dreaded and detested such a marriage; and he hopes that if he can pledge your Majesty sufficiently to give him the aid, and to prohibit intercourse between your subjects and the French, as he desires, the French will take offence, and the marriage will be broken off. He fears that if the wedding is carried through, all grounds for quarrel between your Majesty and the King of France will be banished, and the friendship between you become too intimate to suit him and his realm. He went so far once as to say to me, that he had no fear of being annoyed or troubled by anyone in the world, so long as a perfect amity did not exist between your Majesty and the Christian King.

1545.

Touching the discourse of the Chancellor (Wriothesley) to the ambassador, respecting the King's wish to keep friendly with your Majesty, and that all causes of dispute were abolished, I may say that the bishop and the secretary have addressed similar language to me here. Yesterday, for instance, during the conference, when all the deputies on both sides were present, the bishop repeated several times that it would be well to restore everything that still remained intact, and to pay compensation for the remainder, and say no more about it.

The bishop and the secretary expressed sorrow at the recent detention in England of five ships loaded with goods owned by Spaniards, and by Jehan Carlo, and they have written very earnestly, asking that they shall be released. God grant that their intervention may be effectual.

Notwithstanding all the trouble we have taken in this conference, we have gained nothing worth mentioning in the matter of private claims; and with regard to public policy only some declarations of secondary importance as to intercourse, have been adopted. The principal outcome of our labours has been to obtain the privilege of inspecting the old registers of the customs dues on both sides, in order to reform them, in accordance with the treaties. As we saw that we could come to no conclusion, we have, in accordance with the Queen's orders, mutually resolved to close the conference to-morrow, and depart in as friendly a manner as possible.

Bourbourg, 15 July 1545.

16 July.
Vienna
Imp. Arch.

96. FRANCISCO DE LOS COBOS to the EMPEROR.

Last Thursday, the 9th instant, the Prince (Philip) wrote to your Majesty by Ruy Gomez the happy news of the delivery of the Princess of a son, mother and infant both progressing favourably, and I also wrote, as your Majesty will have seen. Subsequently the Princess, although somewhat feverish all Friday, appeared very bright and strong; and we thought that all was well until Saturday morning, when the fever increased with occasional spasms and trembling fits, as the bleeding had ceased. This state of things increased all day, and by the evening the Princess was intermittently delirious. The night passed thus, and on Sunday morning, seeing that the malady had now become so grave as to be almost hopeless, the physicians decided to bleed the patient at the ankle. This was done, and the Princess again became conscious, and seemed somewhat better. The improvement, however, lasted but a very short time, and the attack became so severe that in a few hours extreme unction was administered at the Princess' request. The attack still increased until God took her to Himself on that day (Sunday) between four and five in the afternoon, amidst universal grief, such as your Majesty may imagine. Her end was tranquil and Christian; and she left a will and codicil, made before her illness. The Prince was so extremely grieved, as to prove that he loved her; although, judging by outward demonstration, some

1545.

people thought differently.* He at once decided to go the same night to the monastery of Abrojo, where was a fairly good lodging for him in the house they have repaired. He is so sad that he will allow no one to visit or see him. The Comendador Mayor of Castille, Don Antonio de Rojas and Don Alvaro de Cordova are with him. The Prince being in this trouble, has written to your Majesty very briefly; but sent for me, and directed me verbally to send your Majesty all the details.

Valladolid, 16 July 1545.

17 July.
Vienna
Imp. Arch.

97. The Emperor to Van der Delft.

Since our letter of 9th instant, the English ambassador here has addressed us respecting the communications that had passed between you and the King as to the seizure and detention of the ships, and the maintenance of the treaty between us. He was subsequently referred to M. de Granvelle; in order that we might consider and decide upon his representations, which were very lengthy. We here set down the details for your guidance.

With regard to the first point (*i.e.*, the seizures) the ambassador endeavoured to justify generally the seizure of the vessels, by alleging that our subjects had first commenced to use violence without cause, and that what had been done on the King's part had been occasioned by the injuries received by them (the English); and to prevent the furnishing of victuals to their enemies by our subjects. If seizures, he said, had been effected on their side, it was because they were necessary for indemnification; and he complained of the seizure decreed last year in Flanders, where they (the English) were the sufferers. For a long time past, moreover, he alleged, the seizures in England had been stopped; and not only were letters of marque now refused, but the privateers who were at sea had been recalled, although this measure was not approved of by the King's ministers, considering the service the privateers might have rendered to the King against the enemy, at all events in stopping the supply of victuals. As to the recent seizure of two vessels, this had been done by the King on an undeniable complaint of one of his subjects named Renegat, who having captured a French ship at sea, and learning that it contained certain goods belonging to our Spanish subjects, had voluntarily given up those that could be recognised as such. One person, however, made an unreasonable claim for certain goods, which he, Renegat, would not concede; and, as a consequence, the French prize had been seized in a Spanish port. Renegat, seeing this, and hearing that he, too, was to be detained, sailed with his own ship; and

---

*The young couple (Philip and his bride were barely 17) had only been married in November, 1543; and even thus early whispers of his liaison with Doña Isabel de Osorio were heard. This remark in the letter seems to add an authority to the rumours which they have hitherto lacked, though it is almost certain that after his wife's death he lived with -even if he did not secretly marry—Doña Isabel. Philip, however, always decorous, and it may be added always tender hearted when his successive wives were concerned, retired into the monastery for three weeks after Maria's death. The infant whose birth is here recorded was the unhappy Don Carlos.

when again on the high seas he fell in with a vessel homeward bound from the Indies; from which he took, as a pledge, only as much property as represented the value of the French prize. The property thus captured was duly checked, and a certificate given for it, except for the gold, which the master of the Indian vessel refused to inventory, because he had shipped it without the legal declaration, and expected to have it confiscated, and that he himself would be punished. This circumstance had caused the seizure in Spain of several (English) vessels: and the result of this, again, had been the detention in England of two Spanish ships belonging to Quintana Dueñas and Miranda, of which the cargoes had remained intact. The King, he said, was willing to release these vessels against bail, if the same course was adopted in Spain, without any mention being made of the restitution of the property taken by Renegat from Indian ship, of which the gold certainly belonged to us.° The ambassador dwelt much upon the seizure in Spain, which he said was in open violation of the treaty of alliance laying down a regular procedure for the settlement of these private quarrels without the adoption of reprisals.

He was answered that no further justification for our action was necessary than what had been given on several occasions already. It was notorious that the whole trouble had arisen from the acts of the English, for which our subjects had given no provocation whatever. Not only was it impossible for anyone to accuse them of anything, but up to the present, not the slightest evidence had been produced against them. We had, in fact, been compelled by the constant and urgent complaints of our subjects, who had been unable to obtain restitution of their ships or merchandise, to order the detention of the property of Englishmen in our dominions. We pointed out to the ambassador how modestly and moderately this had been done, as we had conveyed to the King himself, but we refrained from dwelling at length upon the honesty of the conduct on our side, from first to last, because it was sufficiently demonstrated by all that had happened before Paget came to Brussels; and by the agreement we made with him, which fully proved that our object was solely to provide for the security of our subjects.

Referring to the matter of Renegat, we said that you had already sufficiently debated the point, and had proved clearly that the seizure of the two ships (in England) had been without due cause. The manner in which the affair had been treated in England was monstrous; and we could only refer the ambassador to what you had said about it. It was a scandal that such a man as Renegat, having committed such a violent act of piracy, should be publicly welcomed, and made much of in the King's Court, instead of being punished. This, and other similar outrages upon our subjects, had given motive for the seizures in Spain by way of reprisal. The inexcusable nature of Renegat's act was demonstrated by the ambassador's own statement of the case, and as a consequence, that

---

° The gold belonged to "us," *i.e.* the Emperor, because in order to escape the heavy export dues upon the precious metals and the danger of its being seized for the use of the Government on its arrival in Seville, it had been shipped secretly without declaration; and was therefore held to be confiscate to the Emperor.

1545.

the seizure of the ships (in England) was effected without cause; since the first ship captured by Renegat was a Frenchman, and was taken into one of our ports, where a dispute arose with a subject of ours with regard to certain goods claimed by him. He appealed to the law to enforce his claim. Renegat does not even allege that any wrong or injustice was done to him or his ship; and it is obvious that he had not the slightest pretext for violently taking the matter into his own hands, and seizing from the Indian ship property belonging to our subjects. On this ground, the King of England had no right to arrest the two ships in question, and his having done so is a direct infraction of the treaty on his part, instead of on ours, as the ambassador wished to make out. If the King had desired to proceed according to the stipulations, he should have borne in mind that no violence had been offered to Renegat; he was only being proceeded against by ordinary legal procedure; and the matter should have been dealt with amicably, as is provided in the treaty. The (English) ambassador had no reply to this; except to say that the custom of navigation did not admit of a foreign ship in a friendly port being subjected to the local jurisdiction. We refuted this. The case was so clear as to need no further discussion, since custom could not override common law, and it was in accordance with strict equity that justice should be administered where it was invoked, and where the parties were. Renegat might freely have sailed away, if he had chosen to give bail, and if the affair had appeared as if it would be protracted.

With regard to the point of the maintenance of the treaty, the ambassador took the same line of argument as that adopted at Brussels by the Earl of Hertford, the Bishop of Winchester and himself. He urged that the treaty should be interpreted literally; the words being that one party should not make peace without the other, and that in case of invasion by a third party, the latter should be declared an enemy of both: it is also laid down that in such case the specified aid should be given by the party not attacked, who would undertake to forbid his subjects from entering the service of the invader, and to prevent the passage of troops through his dominions and the supply of munitions to the enemy. Furthermore it was specified that, even if the King of England wished to invade France we were bound to furnish him with men, victuals and other things on payment for them: and last year when the King of France invaded the country of Guisnes with a larger force than that specified in the treaty, the ambassador contended that we ought to have declared war against him, and have provided the assistance stipulated. We had, he said, not done so; but had given excuses to the King's (of England's) ambassadors, taking a period of ten weeks to consider our resolution. His master confidently expected that at the expiration of this period we should have granted him the aid demanded; but in spite of all his efforts, by means of his ambassador and otherwise, we still delayed the matter with generalities. We had, moreover, he said, refused leave to our subjects to enter the King's service, and had not permitted the passage through our territories of troops which he had raised elsewhere, or the export of munitions for him. On the other hand, we had allowed the passage of French troops; and the revictualling of Ardres had only been possible by this means. He (the ambassador) said his master wished to know whether we held the treaty to be valid or not, in order that he might proceed accordingly. If we did consider it valid, he begged us as a prince of honour to tell him frankly if there was any reason to defer the declaration (against France) any longer: if there was no such reason, we should take up arms with him against France. This, he said, was the time finally to bring the King of France to reason, as his realm was impoverished to the last degree of desperation, and the task would not only be an honourable one for us, but the fulfilment of our duty. With regard to the other treaty which we had made with the King of France, it should not, he said, in any way be allowed to prejudice the prior treaty with England; and we ought not to take our stand upon his (Henry's) reported consent to the conclusion of the treaty of peace, for he had never given such consent, except on the condition that his demands were granted by France. It would, he said, be too grievous and scandalous to give credit to the reports of private persons, and the talk of servitors, to the prejudice of an allied prince, and for the abrogation and contravention of a solemnly executed treaty. On the contrary, the assertion of his master, the King, should be accepted in preference, seeing his great qualities; besides which there was an honourable personage who was ready to maintain that the King had never given the alleged consent, except with the reservation above mentioned. Our answer to all this, was that the ambassador's preamble and arguments, claiming the maintenance of the treaty between his master and us, were identical with those set forth at Brussels (*i.e.*, by Seymour and Gardiner) which had been completely refuted in detail, both as to the observance of the treaty, and as to the assistance demanded. As the ambassador himself had been on that occasion one of those to whom our communication had been made, there was no need for us to repeat what we had said. It is true that we had taken a period of ten weeks in which to decide the course we should adopt, for various reasons which we gave at the time, but more especially to enable us to set forth our views to the King in the meanwhile, as we had stated them to his ambassadors; and, after a due consideration of the whole of the circumstances, thereafter to send him a decided answer. With this end, we again sent to him M. Eustace Chapuys, and also you, whom we had already appointed to succeed him. Chapuys having been so long concerned in English affairs and having negotiated the treaty, it was thought that he, better than anyone else, would be able to clear up the differences which had arisen out of the King's demand; but he had stayed a long time in England without any understanding being arrived at on the part of the King. The same thing was said to Paget when he was recently in Brussels, who replied that he could not at that time discuss the question of the declaration (against France). When the ambassador himself recently addressed us on the subject of the assistance, and warned us to make ready in anticipation of the event of its being necessary, we wrote to you very amply on the subject; this having been the reason why you had opened the discussion about it with the King; which discussion you had refrained from continuing, for fear of further angering him, after his references to the seizures of the ships. We added that the ambassador ought to consider, as we had no doubt his master would, that as we had made peace with France, especially by his consent, affairs must be so dealt with as to enable us to act sincerely, and in good faith, towards both. For this reason, we should be held bound to either treaty only so far as was compatible with the terms of the other, and we desired that a clear understanding should be come to on this point, in order that the difficulties which we had discussed with the ambassador, but which still remained unsolved, might be finally settled. With regard to the King's denial of his consent to the peace with France, we could only refer to what has already been said upon the subject. On some occasions it had appeared from the words of the King himself and his ministers that they did not insist upon their denial that such consent had been given. They mentioned some personage, who was ready to contradict what we said on the point, but up to the present his evidence had not been produced; and before it was produced they would have to prove that he was present when the King spoke to M. d'Arras and our ministers; and also that he was near enough to hear what was said. The ambassador had nothing to reply to this, or to our reference to Chapuys' mission, except that he was not aware of its express object. In reply to his contention that the assertion of the King's consent ought not to suffice to abrogate a solemnly signed treaty, we said that the circumstances of the case must be taken into consideration, and the state of affairs at the time. We were plunged far into an enemy's country, and in the position explained to the King, whilst he was detained before Boulogne and Montreuil, and by other matters of his own; and it was no season for long communications and capitulations or for the delay of M. d'Arras. On the contrary, the King ought rather to thank us that we left no effort untried on our part to include him. He was unable to do his part in the joint enterprise, as he confessed by the negotiation he was carrying on with France; and he entertained the firm hope of promptly bringing them to a successful conclusion. In these circumstances, he rightly and honestly consented to our negotiating with the French on our side, in accordance with the arrangement previously made that each one should treat for the settlement of his own demands; although, as was pointed out at the time to the ambassador, the King not having done his part in the joint enterprise by failing to send his army along the banks of the Somme against Paris, or entering France with 30,000 men before the 10 July, as he had agreed to do, we were at liberty to make peace separately with France, without his consent, on the receipt of the King's answer that he could not send his contingent to the joint enterprise, as he was detained before Boulogne and Montreuil. The terms of the treaty of peace, moreover, signally justify us; for the King of England is expressly and honourably reserved in it, and the friendship with him strictly respected. The King should consider all this, and our moderation throughout in the references we have been obliged to make to his failure to fulfil his part in the joint enterprise.

With regard to the remark of the ambassador, about not entertaining his master with generalities on the question of the aid requested, we said that it might easily be seen, by the fact that we had sent (Chapuys) specially to England to elucidate matters, and had since instructed you to communicate with the King with the same object, that our intention was not to delay affairs. The delay, indeed, was rather on the side of the King, and when he chose to speak frankly he would find that we were ready to agree to anything reasonable, and would perform what it might be decided that we were bound to. On the subject of the ambassador's allegation that we had refused to allow our patrimonial subjects to enter the King's service, we replied that the ambassador had never requested such a thing; but had only spoken of the subjects of the Empire. As we thought the ambassador was now trying to confuse the point, we told him that he knew he had never asked for anything but the free passage of the troops through the Netherlands; and that his Majesty, notwithstanding the prohibition, had given permission for Germans to enter the King's service. If he, the ambassador, had spoken of "patrimonial subjects," another reason would have been given to him that of the inability of his Majesty to over-ride the decrees of the Empire. The assertion that the French have been more favoured than the English is contrary to the fact. They had been absolutely refused permission to employ subjects of the Empire, much less our patrimonial subjects; and every effort had been made both in the Netherlands and Spain to prevent our subjects from* entering the French service. We have, indeed, some captains still in prison, who are being detained for punishment for their disobedience in this respect, though the French are importuning us to release them.

The French, moreover, are complaining greatly and constantly that we are favouring the English; and that whilst we refuse the French, men, munitions and other things, we are even now allowing the English to obtain large quantities of powder, armour and stores from the Netherlands. Referring to the English ambassador's assertion that the French march their armies through our territory, we said that we had not heard that such was the case, nor did we believe it. It is true that M. de Rega (?) had recently passed the borders of Hainault and had done some damage; but it had been followed by a representation from us to the French ambassadors openly demanding redress and punishment for the offence. If any other Frenchmen had crossed the frontiers at any point on their way to revictual Ardres, we had no knowledge of it, and in such case it must have been done suddenly, and was impossible either to prove

---

* The distinction was between the subjects of Charles as successor to the Duke of Burgundy, etc. by right of his father Philip and the subjects of the empire to which crown he had been elected. The sophistry of the answer is seen, when it is recollected that the complaint of the English ambassador really referred to the refusal of the Emperor to sanction the engagement of Spanish infantry (which however had entered Henry's service in spite of their Sovereign's prohibition). As Charles had inherited the crowns of Spain from his mother his use of the word patrimonial enabled him to confuse the issue and verbally put himself in the right.

or prevent. The ambassador at once said that for this alone we ought to declare war against France, and we replied that we should do so if the King of France or his ambassadors approved of the act. They, however, blamed and disavowed it, and promised that the King would do all he could to redress it. This point led us to mention the possibility of agreement between the Kings of England and France, in continuation of what we had recently said to the ambassador. The latter replied that he expected shortly an answer to the special despatch he had sent to England on the subject.

We carefully weighed and considered all the aforegoing, in view of the present state of Christendom, and the relations between France and England; bearing in mind the objects that each power may seek by continuing the war, and the possibility of a long delay of our decision giving the King of England a cause of grievance, and perhaps driving him to join the French against us; we replied to the English Ambassador, that we had already instructed you to endeavour to clear up the difficulties; and we promised to write to you immediately, ordering you to take the matter in hand promptly. It would not be our fault, we said, if everything was not settled as soon as possible, for us to act towards the King in accordance with what might be our obligations. We also would use every possible effort to return to the Netherlands, so as to consider whether some arrangement could not be effected between England and France.

We promised also to direct both you and Chapuys to try and devise some suitable means or expedient, by which the troubles about the seizures of ships on both sides might be settled, and similar accidents avoided for the future.

You will, accordingly, seek audience of the King as early as possible, and offer to come to some elucidation of the difficulties which must be necessarily examined and settled before we can resolve about the assistance requested by him, in the event of invasion. You will proceed in this, as softly as you can, in accordance with the instructions already given to you. The substantial points which should be determined are: first, that regarding the confirmation of our treaty of peace with France; secondly, that the King of England must be satisfied with the amount of assistance laid down in the treaty, and must not press us, or our subjects, to do anything in opposition to our treaty with France; and thirdly that the aid should assume the form of a money subvention; the claim for aid which was pressed last year when the French invaded Guisnes being abandoned. The said subvention would be furnished only in the event of England itself being invaded, either on the part of the Scots or the French, by the forces mentioned in the treaty; the inhabitants of our Spanish, Flemish and other dominions being assured of immunity from molestation, though the war between England and France should continue. The ships now detained must be released on both sides, and steps must be taken by which such differences may not occur again. The King of England must undertake not to treat with France, or any other power, except in accordance with the treaty of alliance, which stipulates that he can only do so by our express consent. If any treaty has already been made by him in contravention of this clause,

1545.

it shall be considered nul as regards anything to our prejudice. The non-fulfilment of the treaty (*i.e.*, by England), which we have always alleged, shall not be considered as condoned, at least in the case of the rupture of the treaty. You must exert all the dexterity you possess to convey to the King that our intention and desire in endeavouring to settle these points promptly, is to keep in perfect friendship with him, and to deal honestly and straightforwardly in all things; but without violating our agreement with France. You will repeat to him the reasons, stated above, which compelled us to make the treaty of peace; and will show him that, in reason and honesty, we cannot break it. He must consider, also, that, unless he recognises this treaty, and refrains from asking us to do anything against it, a reciprocal assurance being given by both of us that its provisions, so far as they concern each of us, shall be strictly respected, we (*i.e.*, the Emperor) might incur the enmity both of France and England; and our territories opposite England would certainly not be secure. We need not repeat the arguments on this point, as they have been already stated in former letters to you. In accordance with your advices, we will instruct you as to the decision we may arrive at. You will not fail to write about the peace, if you see there is any chance of it, and about anything else that may occur.

We send you a copy of what they write to us from Spain about the seizures of the ships, which will prove that the procedure there has been mild. You will seek means to have all the seizures released, our subjects duly indemnified, and some provision made for the future avoidance of these occurrences. Especially endeavour to get the ships seized in England released, even against bail, and the same shall be done in Spain; Renegat should restore what he took from the ship from the Indies at once, and lodge in your hands the gold he captured, as it is confiscate, and belongs to us,* whilst he should submit to the verdict of the tribunals in the matter of the French ship. We will order the case to be dealt with straightforwardly and promptly, and will hold in abeyance the seizure decreed (against Renegat) in Spain; unless he defaults, in which case the seizures will stand as before.—Worms, 17 July, 1545.

19 July.
Simancas.
E. 872.

98. Document Endorsed: "News to be sent to his Highness."

The following is what we hear from Rome up to to-day, 19th July. News from Ragusa to 30th June says that the Turk is peaceful, and there is no rumour of war, the Pope has news from the Levant to 28th ultimo confirming this.

Barbarossa is at present not in much favour with the Turk, and is at issue with those who govern.

The news contains nothing about Mustapha Pasha, the son of the Turk, but the love of the latter for the Sultana increases daily, and her power with it. All business is brought before her and everyone tries to please her.

---

* The gold, which reached a large amount, was lodged in the Tower of London and no portion of it was restored to Charles until the reign of Mary.

1545.

The Venetian ambassador here says that the Turk will not conclude the truce with his Majesty, except on condition that the peace with the King of France shall continue. This is denied by others, whose advices from the Levant say that the arrival of the ambassadors to make the truce is anxiously expected.

Some distrust has existed in Italy, and particularly in Siena, of the force which the Pope was arranging to levy; but this has now ceased. News comes from France that a number of prelates have left for the Council. Some also are preparing to go from Germany, but with some fear of the Lutherans, especially in his Majesty's absence. Frederick, the Count Palatine, has sent to the Pope, to say that he suspects that his Holiness will have been told certain things about him in matters of religion; but he supplicates him not to believe them lightly, and to rest assured that he is a good Catholic Christian, who intends to live and die in the faith. The Pope is proceeding against the Bishop of Cologne by peremptory deprivation.

There is intelligence that the King of England is treating with Luis de Gonzaga, lord of Castiglione, for the latter to enter his service and hold a territory in Italy where troops can be raised, as the French have done in Mirandola. His Holiness, however, is fully prepared to prevent the carrying out of this plan.

The Duke of Ferrara is sending his eldest son to France.

The Marquis del Guasto and the Prince of Piedmont have gone to his Majesty's court.

Cardinal Armignac says that the Duke of Orleans will go to the Emperor's court, and they say that if his Majesty proceeds against the infidels the King (of France) will not fail to contribute the 10,000 foot and 500 men-at-arms stipulated by the treaty, notwithstanding his war against the English.

It is said that Madame d'Etampes has again sent her secretary to England to treat for peace, although the answer given to him before was unfavourable.

A. Doria has taken out his own galleys, and those of Don Garcia (de Toledo) in search of Dragut Reis, of whom he had some news. John Antonio Doria has gone with the Prince's galleys to Sicily. The season is a good one in Italy, though bread is still dear in Rome.

The Pope has been deeply grieved by the death of his daughter Constance, though he hides it and appears cheerful. He is much consoled by the good relations now existing between him and his Majesty.

A Bishop who, it is said, is of Mirandola, has been imprisoned in the castle (of Sant' Angelo), on suspicion of poisoning; but it is stated that nothing has yet been proved against him.

20 July.
Simancas.
E. 872
extract.

99. JUAN DE VEGA[*] to PRINCE PHILIP.

It has been decided that the Pope will contribute to the enterprise against the protestants 500 horse and 12,000 foot, with 300,000 ducats, and the tenths from Spain; and he also gives the authority,

---

[*] Spanish ambassador in Rome.

1545.

which we requested some time ago, to sell the vassals of the monasteries. He has consented to these contributions with a readiness that contrasts strongly with his previous ill-will with regard to the two last concessions (*i.e.*, the cession of the tenths and the sale of the monastic vassals). Whilst we were negotiating this, M. Dandolo arrived to point out to his Holiness the difficulties which present themselves to the enterprise this year, and promising that it shall be undertaken next year. The Pope accepts this, although he would have preferred the enterprise to have been effected at once. Now that this alteration has been made, I am not sure what will be done in the other pending matters, though I think that the business of the first fruits will be despatched, and that the 300,000 crowns, or at least 200,000, will be deposited; the Pope continuing in his firm friendship with his Majesty; as he is quite aware of the troubles that may happen to him otherwise. His understanding with the Emperor has already so greatly raised his prestige that, amongst other things, the offices which were quite unsaleable before for want of purchasers, are now difficult to be obtained, as no one will sell them and their value has increased ten per cent. As I have every hope of getting the concession of the half first fruits, and the sale of the monastic vassals, it will be well for your Highness to have the matters considered, and arrangements made beforehand; so that no time shall be lost when the briefs are despatched.

Rome, 20 July, 1545.

21 July.
Vienna
Imp. Arch.

100. CHAPUYS to VAN DER DELFT.

Just as I was mounting my coach this morning at Malines to proceed to Louvain, I received the enclosed letters from his Majesty, but as my deciphering clerk was already at Louvain, I brought the courier hither with me; though I did so to my great regret, seeing the haste with which he had been sent, and the time he had already lost in seeking me. When finally I arrived here, and read the dispatch, I was the more sorry that I had not sent him straight on without delay, for I have nothing to add or substract to the contents. I am, moreover, greatly afflicted with the toils of the journey, which have moved the humours in such a way that the gout has seized my shoulders; and, what is worst, I cannot sit. I consequently refrain from saying anything more about the arrangements for the future security of navigation for his Majesty's subjects; but the draft I sent you before, with the copy of the convention made with Paget in Brussels, will serve as a basis for negotiation on the matter. I am delighted to hear that his Majesty has consented to the release of the seizures made in Spain, in the way stated in his Majesty's letters. I did not fail to write specially about this in my last letters to M. de Granvelle, saying that you would be very much perplexed at no mention of this most important subject having been made in his Majesty's former letters, and that I myself was very anxious, for fear that my bold and frank advice to his Majesty had given offence. Thank God, however, his Majesty's letters has relieved both of us; and there is no need for me to give my opinion of the manner in which the release is to be effected, since his Majesty fully states it, and the English are quite ready to accept the arrangement.

HENRY VIII. 185

1545.

With regard to the fresh denial given by the English Ambassador that the peace treaty with France was concluded by his King's consent, you know what I said to the King about it, and repeated in my memorandum written to you from Gravelines. Even after the peace was made, when M. de Carrières and I spoke with him (Henry) at Boulogne three times, he never expressed the slightest annoyance about it. I need only refer you on this point to the memorandum I sent you; but I must say a word in refutation of the King's argument that in the case of a treaty so solemnly executed as the alliance between the Emperor and the King, it is not reasonable to make any alteration in it on a mere verbal report by a subject. In addition to the reply given by his Majesty to the ambassador on this subject, it might be gently pointed out to the King, that it was clearly laid down in the treaty, that neither of the parties should enter into negotiations with the common enemy, without the consent of the other; and yet the King thought that each one might seek his own end, as seemed best to him. He had, indeed, been the first to listen to French overtures,[*] and had even arranged certain conditions with them, before he knew for certain the Emperor's wishes on the matter. And yet, in accordance with the clause of which he makes so much, the King was bound to ascertain what were his Majesty's views. If you find an opportunity, you might use this argument; but it should be borne in mind that it should be pressed lightly, and not dwelt upon sufficiently to give the King a chance of entering into fresh disputes; as it is the Emperor's wish that matters should be settled amicably.

I have nothing to add to the cipher despatches, excepting to say that I do not attach much importance to obtaining a declaration that no claim or demand shall be made upon his Majesty on account of the invasion of Guisnes last year; since it is unquestionable that, for several reasons, his Majesty was not bound on that occasion to provide the aid requested; and especially, as the siege did not last. With reference to the demand that his Majesty should declare himself still at at war with France, and prohibit his subjects from trading with that country, that point has been so convincingly discussed that Paget made no difficulty in agreeing in his master's name, that the Emperor's subjects should trade with France, on condition that they did not carry thither munitions of war or victuals.

As we are on the subject of the security of navigation, I thought well to say these few words, although doubtless you will have appealed to Paget's agreement to effect the release of the ships seized since it was made; my remarks consequently being confined to the ships taken previously.

Louvain, 21 July, 1545.

23 and 24 July.
Vienna Imp. Arch.

101. VAN DER DELFT to the EMPEROR.

I wrote on the 10th that I was on the point of leaving London,

---

[*] It has been pointed out in the Introduction to the last Volume of this Calendar that one of the reasons for the Emperor's eagerness to make peace for himself, was the fear that Henry would do so before him; and leave him in the lurch. It was, in fact, a game of cunning between the two Sovereigns as to which should be made arbiter of the claims of the other.

and I accordingly set out to follow the King. It happened that on the 14th the Chancellor (Wriothesley) and myself had to pass the night at the same village; and as I had long sought an opportunity of having a conversation with him, I was determined to seize so good a chance of doing so. I therefore had a watch set upon him very early in the morning, and contrived to start a quarter of an hour before him. I rode on gently, in order that he might overtake me, which he soon did, and after some civilities, we rode together all day and had much interesting discourse. As it is impossible to repeat all this in detail, I will only touch upon what is essential. This may be summarised under two heads, namely the redress to be granted to your subjects, and the promotion of the peace negotiations.

With regard to the first, I will only say that in my opinion we shall gain little or nothing, unless the seizures in Spain are released.

With reference to the question of peace which I discussed with him, I said that my greatest regret was to see the two monarchs at war, and I knew how glad your Majesty would be to see them reconciled. I had, I said, long been desirous of speaking to him, in order to assure him of your Majesty's desire to be of use for the promotion of peace; and I then pointed out to him that, since peace must be made sooner or later, it was better that it should be sooner, so that the evils and hazards of war might be avoided; and it behoved us to cast about for some means by which peace could be attained. He took this in good part, but still showed some annoyance that your Majesty had not intervened otherwise, and that hitherto nothing but words had been achieved. I replied that the fault was on their side, because they neither gave any indication of their wish for peace, nor ceased to treat your Majesty's subjects harshly. This, I said, was not calculated to increase your Majesty's good-will or desire to serve them.

When we arrived in the evening at the village where we were to sleep, he asked me to sup with him; he himself coming to my lodging to invite me. After supper he resumed the conversation that we had had on the road about the peace, and concluded by saying that he hoped I should do my best in the matter; and, for his part, he knew of no other means, except for your Majesty to send an envoy to the King of France, to show him the terms of the treaty of alliance you have with England, and to inform him that you could not avoid fulfilling these terms, unless he consented to agree to peace. With this a courier arrived with letters for him, and the Chancellor took leave of me.

When I arrived at my lodging, I found awaiting me the bearer of this letter, bringing me your Majesty's letters of 9th instant, with a credence for me to express to the King your Majesty's extreme displeasure at the continuance of the war; and your wish to aid actively in a reconciliation. This letter came most appositely, and I thought well to inform the Chancellor that I had received it. This I did on the morrow; and he expressed much pleasure at the news, asking me to use my best influence in the interests of peace. If, he said, the King perchance let slip any angry words, he prayed

1545.

me not to notice them. This was in confidence, and in accordance with my request that he would speak frankly to me, after which he thanked me, both for Majesty's goodwill and my own, and I then left him, as he was going to visit some other places and villages of his, whilst I continued on the road to Portsmouth.

On the morning of my arrival there, namely on the 17th instant, I sent to secretary Paget to ask for audience of the King. His Majesty's answer was that if the matter was very important I could come at any time, but that he would prefer the following Sunday. I was glad of this, as I inferred from it that the Chancellor had informed the King of my mission. In the meanwhile the King sent to me the Queen's Chancellor, to show me the fleet which is in this harbour. He afterwards took me on board the flagship called the "Great Harry."[*] The admiral[†] received me very civilly, and asked me to dinner for the following day, where I was very handsomely entertained with three or four Knights of the Garter.

The fleet did not exceed 80 sail, but 40 of the ships were large and beautiful, and they said they expected from the west country about sixty more.

After dinner the admiral told me that he had the King's orders to take me to his Majesty, as he would rather see me that afternoon, in consequence of the whole of his time being occupied the next day visiting his ships and dining on the flagship. I approached the King with the usual obeisance and handed to him your Majesty's credence; proceeding then to express your Majesty's desire to bring about peace, and your regret at the recrudescence of the war. I then recited at length what your Majesty had written to me. The King took it very well, but at once fell to the old complaints, which I refuted as well as I could: though I thought better that I should not dwell too much upon this part of the subject, or dispute about the point of the assistance demanded, as I considered that these questions would disappear if peace were concluded. But still I persisted as to the redress due to your subjects, who have been so rudely and unjustly treated; and I made in this respect a full and pertinent statement of claim. Reverting again to my credence, I assured the King of your Majesty's wish for peace, both for the sake of Christendom at large, and on account of your ancient amity with the King. Your Majesty, I said, was most anxious to be of use in the matter, but did not know how to take the first step; and if the King would confide in me, I pledged myself to maintain the discretion necessary for his honour and profit, as if I were his own subject; and I assured him that he might believe me, seeing how earnest was your Majesty's wish to obtain a peace which should redound to his advantage. With these and similar gentle words, I endeavoured to soften his angry remarks, and persisted in my

---

[*] The Great Harry was a vast old-fashioned, over-gunned ship of 1,000 tons burden, with two tiers of ordnance on the lower decks and a third tier on her half-deck and forecastle. Drawings and full descriptions of all the ships in the navy at this period will be found in Anthony's parchment rolls in the Pepysian Library at Magdalen College, Cambridge; the roll containing the galleases being at the British Museum. Add. 22047.

[†] Viscount Lisle. John Dudley, afterwards Earl of Warwick and Duke of Northumberland.

request that he would give me some indication of his goodwill, in order that I might do my best in the matter. He seemed much pleased at this, saying that if your Majesty's anxiety was such as I assured him, it would doubtless be shown in deeds, and that you would do him a friendly turn, as you knew how he had entered into this war. At my repeated suggestions that he would give me a lead for the opening of negotiations, he said that the lead should not come from him. His desire for peace was good; and he had not refused any conditions, as none had been proposed to him. When I said that the war was now being waged for Boulogne—though I did not persuade or dissuade him in the matter of its restitution—he replied that he had it, and would hold it, by right of conquest. As for the rest; if the overdue pensions were paid, and he was reimbursed for the cost of the war, he was willing to consent to peace. With this end he was willing to submit the question of the amount of indemnity to your Majesty's arbitration; but if he was expected to surrender Boulogne your Majesty could do nothing for him. If he would consent to give up Boulogne he could make peace without any intercession, for in such case he might dictate his own terms to France, and choose his hostages. We ought not, he said, to trust so much to the French as we did; which made me think that there might be some negotiations for a settlement between them; and indeed, under correction, I am of opinion that your Majesty ought now to move actively in the interests of peace, and become the means for bringing it about, for various reasons, especially as the King might otherwise become better friends with the French than with your Majesty. Pray pardon my boldness in thus stating my own view. To resume: I added that your Majesty was willing and ready to send (to France) such personages as might be considered fitting to forward the negotiations if the King wished: whereupon the latter asked me rather tartly whether the embassy suggested would only go to the King of France and not to him. I replied I was not advised on that point; but that my personal opinion was that the embassy would go to both sides, and this answer pleased him. When I saw this, I at once proceeded to beg him to consider what he could suggest in the interests of peace; but he rejected this, repeating that the first steps should not come from him. I then said, amongst other things, that, although it did not behove me to exceed my instructions, yet if he was willing to listen to me, and would pardon my boldness, I would give him my own opinion. He told me to speak my mind; and after many arguments showing how injurious it was to Christendom that the war should continue for such a town as Boulogne, I said that his magnanimity should make him consider how praiseworthy an action it would be to put an end to the contest. He had, I said, on a former occasion displayed such noble and virtuous liberality, not in surrendering, but in giving towns of great importance like Tournai; and though I did not presume to advise him, one way or the other, about surrendering Boulogne, I yet begged him to weigh and consider well, even if Boulogne was worth the trouble of fighting about. For my own part I thought it was not; and that if he could obtain in another form all his demands from

1545.

France, he might well act regarding Boulogne as his magnanimity might dictate, for the French did not like losing their own. He replied that Boulogne was not the first town that the French had lost. With regard to Tournai and Thérouanne, he had, he said, not acted as I seemed to think, but he would tell me what had happened. He then went on to say that he had held Tournai for about three years after peace had been concluded; and on the occasion of making a new and closer alliance with France, he had surrendered the town, the King of France doing him a good turn at the same time;° whilst Thérouanne was demolished before he gave it up. In short, Sire, it seems to me that he might by some means be induced to yield Boulogne if he could safeguard his prestige, by keeping the place for a certain time, or by some other such device. Finally, after much kind discourse he referred me to his council.

In the course of conversation he asked me about the mission of Secretary Veltwyck to the Turk with the French ambassador; the secretary, he said, having been sent by your Majesty. I denied this, and maintained that he had gone as the representative of the King of the Romans; but both the King and myself persisted in our respective views, the King finally saying that at least the ambassadors themselves had declared what he asserted, to the Seigniory of Venice.

When I left the King, he bade me farewell more amiably than he had ever done before, and I at once went downstairs to the Council, to whom I repeated what I had said to the King. We conferred and disputed for a very long while; in the first place about the indemnification of your subjects. The Councillors continued to plead as a set-off the seizures effected in Spain, and displayed great resentment at the letters of reprisal granted there, of which they offered to show me copies. They were equallly offended at the orders sent by your Majesty to the Chancellor of Brabant, which, they said were a violation of all treaties. I answered them as seemed fitting, pointing out to Paget the unjust way in which we were treated. Your Majesty, I said, had on his (Paget's) bare word released all the seizures at Antwerp, whereas the agreement he had made had not yet been fulfilled with regard to a ship belonging to some merchants of Burgos, whose property had been sold at Rye.

After much disputation they asked me to put in writing the remaining claims of your Majesty's subjects here, which claims they promised me should be disposed of in a day or two, justly and to my satisfaction: and they begged me at the same time to use my influence to get the seizures released in Spain.

Coming to the question of the peace, they complained that they had thus been left alone at war with France by your Majesty. I replied that your Majesty had not left them, or failed them in any way. You were obliged to observe your treaty with France, which had been made by their consent. They gave the same reply to this

---

° This was in the peace treaty between Francis and Henry, when the latter in 1526 determined to repudiate his promises made by the treaty of Madrid after the battle of Pavia; and Wolsey secured Francis temporarily to his master's side in his resentment against the Emperor.

that the King had done; namely that, even if he had consented—which was not the case—the treaty of alliance with them (*i.e.*, the English) over-rode all other treaties past and present. The very treaty with France, they said, showed this, as it recognised the obligation of your Majesty towards this King. I maintained that the consent of the King annulled all objections, as was demonstrated to them at Brussels; and, as to the treaty with France, I was not in a position to reply, as I had no copy of it and was ignorant of the clauses: whereupon they offered to lend me a copy whenever I liked.

In speaking of the peace mediation, they suggested that your Majesty might send the two personages to each of the princes, and request a cessation of hostilities; the King of France being constrained thereto, by showing him the terms of your Majesty's treaty with England, which, they said, would bring him to reasonable conditions of peace. I replied that this course was not desirable; but I thought, speaking quite unofficially, the King of England ought to recognise your Majesty's treaty with France, in order to avail himself of the arbitration clause contained in it. This, in my opinion, was the most friendly and advantageous procedure; but they rebutted this view, and so we remained without deciding anything, except that they would talk the matter over again with the King.

On the following day, Sunday, whilst the King was at dinner on the flagship, news came that the French were only five short leagues away. This turned out to be true, for within two hours their fleet in great force was seen in front of this port, and the King hurriedly left the flagship. The English fleet at once set sail to encounter the French, and on approaching them kept up a cannonade against the galleys, of which five had entered well into the harbour, whilst the English could not get out for want of wind, and in consequence of the opposition of the enemy.[*]

Towards evening, through misfortune and carelessness, the ship of Vice-Admiral George Carew foundered, and all hands on board, to the number of about 500, were drowned, with the exception of about five and twenty or thirty servants, sailors and the like, who escaped. I made enquiries of one of the survivors, a Fleming, how the ship perished, and he told me that the disaster was caused by their not having closed the lowest row of gun ports on one side of the ship. Having fired the guns on that side, the ship was turning, in order to fire from the other, when the wind caught her sails so strongly as to heel her over, and plunge her open gunports beneath the water, which flooded and sank her. They say, however that they can recover the ship and guns.[†]

---

[*] An interesting account of the hostilities off Portsmouth on this occasion will be found in Du Bellay's Memoires. *See* also the Spanish Chronicle of Henry VIII.; the Grafton and Wrothesley Chronicles and the Introduction to "Drake and the Tudor Navy" (Corbett).

[†] The loss of the Mary Rose, with the Vice-Admiral Sir George Carew, is described in exactly similar terms to this in the Spanish Chronicle of Henry VIII., the probable author of which (de Guaras), if he did not accompany the ambassador in his journey to Portsmouth, certainly obtained his information from the same source.

1545.

On Monday the firing on both sides went on nearly all day, and could be plainly witnessed from here. Some people say that at nightfall the English did some damage to a French galley.

Apparently the French fleet consisted of over 300 sail, without counting the 27 galleys they had; but still these people here seem determined to give battle, as soon as they get their ships together and the wind is favourable.

On Tuesday the French landed some men on the Isle of Wight, opposite this town. They set fire to four or five places, as we saw from here, and it is said that they burned ten or twelve small houses; after which they had several skirmishes with the English, who held the entrance to a strait, and who repelled the Frenchmen twice with some loss. At length the number of Englishmen kept on increasing until they reached 3,000 or more, and the Frenchmen were obliged to fall back and take refuge in a small earthwork fort.

A large force was sent against them, so that the English have now no fear whatever of the French, as there are now 8,000 English soldiers ready to resist their enterprise, and they say it will be easy to do so, as the island is covered with woods and hedges.[*]

Yesterday, Wednesday, and the previous night nothing could be heard but artillery firing, and there was a rumuor current that the French intended to land at another point. In view of this, and the fact that neither the King nor the Council had said anything to me about the assistance, I thought it advisable to sound their feeling on the matter without delay, for your Majesty's information. I therefore sent to the Council to ask for audience, saying that it was already four days since they had promised me an answer to my last communications to the King, and I wished to have something to send to your Majesty. I was ready, I said, to bring them the memorandum of claims made by your subjects here; and I wished therefore to speak with some of the individual Councillors, as I was aware that Council itself was so busy with the war. After communicating with the King, they sent me word that I might come to them to-day at about 9, and they would then tell me what the King had ordered.

I kept the appointment, and they at once gave me their message; to the effect that the King had considered my conversation with him, first on the point of your Majesty's wish to reconcile the two princes now at war, which assurance had been given to them on several previous occasions, although nothing more had come of it. Now, when the enemy was actually at their doors, direct proposals are tardily made. As things had been allowed to go so far, the King, as a prince of virtue and courage, was determined to show his power and to see what fortune might bring him. Nevertheless, as I had so urgently pressed him for some opening towards peace negotiations, and out of respect for your Majesty's good-will, which I had so emphatically asserted, the King had instructed them to tell me in confidence that if his overdue pensions were paid and

---

[*] This is a more closely chronological account of the events related than has hitherto been known. The local details and the strategy employed may be best understood by reading Du Bellay's account and the Introduction to "Drake and the Tudor Navy" (Corbett). *See also* letter from the Lord Admiral to the King, Hatfield Papers, part 1, Hist. MSS. Com. (*in extenso* in Haynes).

punctual payment assured for the future, the cost of the war—which had been increased by his being left so long to fight alone—being reimbursed to him, the amount to be left to the arbitration of your Majesty, he would enter into negotiations for peace. With regard to Boulogne, however, he would never surrender the place to force. If they wanted it they must induce him by other means. As I myself was witness, the councillors added, that the enemy was now in England, the King was despatching instructions to his ambassador with your Majesty, to demand the assistance stipulated in the treaty of alliance, and they begged me to write to your Majesty to the same effect.

I replied that, as to your Majesty's goodwill, that was as earnest as ever, and more so than I could express; but I reminded them that when I spoke to the King there was no knowledge of the coming of the enemy. I sincerely thanked the King for the confidence he reposed in me, but I could perceive no amendment in the terms they recited to me to those mentioned by the King when I saw him. Since I had so openly endeavoured to incline the King to peace, I was bound to say that as in my opinion Boulogne was not so necessary to his realm as to be worth keeping up the war for it, they ought also to have made similar efforts to discover some expedient that would have given your Majesty a chance of initiating a peace. I found, on the contrary, that I was frustrated. They made no answer to this, and did not even mention the proposal that your Majesty should send envoys: this omission, I think, being intentional, in order that your Majesty might send the personages on your own motion; depending as they (*i.e.*, the English Councillors) did upon my good offices in the matter.

As to the assistance demanded, I said I would willingly write what the King ordered: but as I descried at present some difficulties which might cause your Majesty to hold back, I thought it would be better for us to examine and discuss the question here, if they (the English) were anxious to advance it. I knew your Majesty wished to settle everything on a reasonable footing; but you had ample reason first to require that redress should be given to the large number of your subjects who had been so inequitably treated. Following this line, I recapitulated the points contained in your Majesty's letters on the subject; and I pointed out firmly that the war was being waged solely for Boulogne, which place was not comprised in the treaty which they invoked; asking them finally, if under these circumstances your Majesty thought fit to give the aid, what form they considered it ought to take. But, Sire, they refused either to listen or reply; saying that they were sure your Majesty would not raise such difficulties as I did. There was nothing, they said, to examine or discuss; and the King was determined to know one way or the other. For that purpose he was now sending to his ambassador to obtain your Majesty's reply. If your Majesty excused yourself on the ground of the sequestration of your subjects, or otherwise, they (the English) must make the best of it; but if on the contrary your Majesty fulfilled your treaty obligations, your subjects, now and in future, should be treated in a way which would please them and me. They promised me to release

1545.

all goods claimed by such subjects, on security being given for the value of merchandise suspected of being owned by Frenchmen; but before doing anything, the King desired to have your Majesty's reply about the aid. When that comes everything would be released. They understood very well, they said, that my words were well intended; but they had no further instructions, and hoped I would take it in good part and do my best.

Seeing that they refused to entertain my replies, I took my leave, and returned to my lodgings to draft this letter, as they are sending off their courier, and mine must accompany him, in order to ensure his passage, the ports being closed, as I wrote in my former letters. I therefore write somewhat hurriedly, so that your Majesty may be preadvised. I have decided once more to discuss fully the whole of the subjects to-morrow with Secretary Paget, who is in the highest favour here, and appears the best inclined to settle matters justly and honestly. If I can manage to delay the couriers until after my conversation with him, I will do so; and in such case will add to this the particulars of my interview; but if the couriers start before then I will send another specially to your Majesty.

Portsmouth, 23rd July, 1545.

Postscript.—Sire. They said they were ready yesterday, but their despatch was not so forward as I thought. I have therefore had time to speak to Secretary Paget before the couriers started. I did so early this morning, my principal object being to learn whether they would be satisfied with a pecuniary subvention, of which some slight hint had been thrown out yesterday by the Bishop of Winchester: my second object being to discover if they were of opinion that your Majesty, as a consequence, should prohibit commerce between your subjects and France. I opened the conversation by saying that, in accordance with their request of yesterday that I should use my best efforts with respect to the reply they had given me, I had been thinking all night, but could devise no excuse or ground for assuring your Majesty that your subjects should be indemnified; since they (*i.e.*, the English Councillors) gave me no earnest of such a step; but that on the contrary all ships, loaded and in ballast, were still detained in English ports. He (Paget) replied that, as to the redress, there would be no failing in that respect, but at the present time, and with this pressure upon them, they were not able to settle the matter. With regard to the ships detained here, they had no necessity to make known the cause of the arrest to the sailors and others; but in confidence he would inform me of it. This was solely that the King was quite determined to give battle to the French, and if the worst came to the worst, and the English were defeated, he intended to make use of these ships. To come to my point, I remarked that I fancied I had understood the Bishop of Winchester to say yesterday that the King required the aid in the form of money; but before writing to that effect to your Majesty, I wished to know what was their meaning. I said that if matters went so far as for your Majesty to consent to give the aid, it was impossible for them to think that you would re-commence your war with France in consequence, since peace had been made with their consent; or even that you would forbid your subjects to trade with France. I added that in saying this I was not moved by any doubt on the point, but merely to let them understand that if they thought otherwise they would waste their time and trouble. It was perfectly clear and obvious that your Majesty was bound to fulfil implicitly your treaty with France, and they evidently understood this, because they had told me in the King's name that henceforward your subjects trading with France should not be molested, unless there was a well-founded suspicion that they were conveying French property, in which case they might be boarded for the purpose of inspection, and if there was still any doubt, the merchandise should be released against security, as was agreed with him (Paget) in Brussels. He replied that, with regard to the Bishop of Winchester's mention of pecuniary aid, he (Paget) had no instructions from the King; and, for the rest, he hoped your Majesty would not desert them, in so far as you were bound to the contrary; seeing them in such extremity as they were. He made a long harangue, going over the old ground already so often repeated, the only conclusion of it being that the King would never withdraw from what he had once agreed to. This, I understood to refer to the commercial question; and it looks very much as if the only thing they demanded was the assistance, which I have always held in suspense, whilst they seem quite sure of obtaining it. Whilst we were thus talking, Paget was summoned to the King and we parted. Since then I sent to ask the Secretary when his courier was to leave. He said early to-morrow morning, and I sent him the name of the bearer to insert it in their courier's passport. This led him to say that he had spoken to the King about our conversation of this morning, and the King was quite content to leave to your Majesty, the decision as to whether the assistance should assume the form of men or money, but that in any case he begged that it might be sent promptly. With respect to the question of trade between your subjects and France, he said that I could well understand the meaning of what he had told me. It was plain enough.

Nothing fresh has happened here in the war. Both fleets still face each other, but to-day the two flagships approached somewhat nearer together. The French flagship, however, with the whole of the fleet drew away, of which the King sent me word. The wind has continued throughout in favour of the French, who they say have with them 500 light horse.

24th July, 1545.

Postscript.—They assert here that they have sunk one of the French galleys, and that the Chevalier D'Aux of Provence was killed on landing in the Isle of Wight.

Endorsed:—Received at Worms the last day of July 1545.

23 July.
Vienna
Imp. Arch.

102. VAN DER DELFT to the QUEEN DOWAGER.

Since my last of 10th instant, I have received letters from the Emperor, enclosing a credence for this King; and your Majesty may learn by the accompanying copies of the letters I now send to the Emperor what has passed here in relation thereto. I send

1545.

these letters through Chapuys, as I have not time to make a separate copy for him, it being extremely important that his Majesty should be informed of what I learn here respecting the assistance demanded before, or as soon, as the English ambassador, to whom they (the English Council) are now sending a courier. I have consequently enjoined my man to make no less haste than the English courier, and to go straight on to the Emperor, unless he finds Chapuys on the road. I am uncertain where he is just now, as he wrote that he was going to Louvain; but if he be still at Bourbourg or Gravelines, my man will send these letters to him from Dunkirk, and if at Louvain he will forward them from Brussels.

It looks as if this King were desirous of coming to an arrangement for peace, and would be glad of the intervention of the Emperor and your Majesty in his favour. This would be advisable for many reasons: it is certain that whilst the war lasts the Emperor's subjects will not be allowed to sail the seas without being robbed and spoliated by one side or the other. This is recognised already by some of the subjects here, as they complain of the French as much as they do of the English.

Portsmouth, 23 July, 1545.

25 July.
Vienna
Imp. Arch.
Hof. Cor.

103. HENRY VIII. to the EMPEROR.

Is recalling his ambassador and councillor, Dr. Wotton, from the Emperor's court, and sends in his place the Bishop of Westminster (Dr. Thirlby) as ambassador, whom he recommends to his Majesty's favour.

Portsmouth, 25 July, 1545.

27 July.
Paris
Arch. Nat.
K. 1485.

104. St. MAURIS to FRANCISCO DE LOS COBOS.

Yours of 10th received, acknowledging mine of 14th June, but not that of 30th June. You will since have received the latter enclosing plan of two forts that the King (of France) had constructed before Boulogne.

I send summary of news here since 30th June. You will not previously have learnt of the death of the Duke of Lorraine,* who had been seriously ill for the last two years; though some people say he was poisoned by these people. The administration of the States of Lorraine and Bar and the guardianship of the children are in dispute between the Duchess and M. de Metz.† The Duchess claims to be sole administratrix; whilst M. de Metz demands to be associated with her as administrator and controller. By the Emperor's orders I have urged the King to induce M. de Metz to abandon his claim to administer. The King promised to do his best to bring about an agreement, and I doubt not the question will soon be settled. Cardinal Lorraine‡ has already drawn up a draft

---

* Duke Francis, who had succeeded his father, Antoine le Bon, less than two years before.

† Jean de Lorraine, Bishop of Metz and Archbishop of Rheims, the elder Cardinal Lorraine, uncle of the late Duke of Lorraine.

‡ Charles de Lorraine, the younger Cardinal, brother of the Duke of Guise and of Mary, Queen Dowager of Scotland.

agreement. In case of continued contention, the King says he will have the matter decided, so far as concerns the Duchy of Bar, of which he claims to be sovereign.

I have pointed out to the King by the Emperor's instructions that the County of Charolois should be considered a sufficient compensation for Hesdin, but both the King and his ministers repudiate this and persist that they must have a place of equal importance and strength to Hesdin; and one that will be useful to them against the English. This, however, is impossible. The English recently seized a Spanish ship at sea, but as they were taking their prize to an English port, a dense fog came on; under cover of which the Spanish ship escaped and entered Havre de Grace; having only lost her artillery, which the English had taken out, and the principal owners of the ship who had been arrested.

Up to the present the Scots have refused to restore the 400 crowns they took from the Spanish ship, about which I wrote to you, and I expect now they never will do so, as they have gone back to Scotland. The ambassador of Florence has retired from France, because the King gave precedence to the ambassador of Ferrara. In reply to the remonstrances of the Florentine the King said that the Duchy of Ferrara was the more ancient, as Florence was no longer a republic.

The King of France has a vein ruptured and decayed *au plus profent (profond) dessoutbz les parties basses*, which makes the doctors despair of his long life, *per ce mesmes qui la dicte reynne respont au principal de ses parties*. This vein, according to the physicians, is the one upon which the life of a man depends. If it is ruptured it suffocates him. The King continues to urge the Pope to aid him against the King of England; and his Holiness has replied that he will furnish such aid willingly, on condition that no peace negotiations are undertaken with England without his (the Pope's) participation and co-operation. The King of France roundly refuses this, so that his Holiness has not yet contributed anything. The King intends to send to Rome as his ambassador a gentleman of the short robe and he hopes the Pope will also send a similar envoy to him. With regard to the Diet and the reply of the Germans, people here say that the recess will be for the purpose of allowing the Emperor to appoint twelve persons, of whom the protestants will nominate six, and the protestants will also appoint twelve others, of whom six will be chosen by the Emperor. These two deputations, with certain presidents to be agreed upon, will meet and discuss the whole of the questions raised by the protestants with regard to the Council, giving an account of their deliberations to the first Diet of the Empire; which will meet in December and will accept the decisions arrived at. I believe that something of the sort will be done; but I am not sure yet of the particulars. These people (*i.e.* the French) would have liked the Council to have proceeded against them (the protestants) for contumacy, and that hostilities had resulted.

Count William had agreed that his ransom should be promptly paid in Paris, if they would allow him to be at liberty within the city. The Emperor, however, at the request of the Count's relatives has refused to promise this, except upon the King of

1545.

France's undertaking that when he surrenders the prisoner, he will guarantee that he shall be safely conveyed out of the country. This the King declines to do, until the Prince of Roche sur Yonne be ransomed, which I expect will be soon, as the King has written to Franceso d' Este asking him to reduce the ransom.

By orders of the Emperor I have been urging the King to pay a beneficial pension to Cardinal Carpi. The King refuses, saying that all pensions are to be abolished, but he will allow the Cardinal to resign all his benefices in France in favour of French subjects to his, the King's, satisfaction.

I have also renewed my demand to the King that title deeds of the country of Burgundy in the archives of Dijon should be sought and handed to the Emperor, in accordance with the treaty of peace.

I am likewise pressing the King to take steps in the matter of the robberies recently committed by his troops in Artois. He replied that when he had proved that such pillage had taken place he would punish it severely, as he had never intended that injury should be done to his Majesty's subjects, and had instructed his commanders to that effect, forbidding them strictly even to pass over his Majesty's territories.

The King and the Duke of Orleans are trying their utmost to attain a marriage with our Princess, the King declaring that if the Emperor will consent to it, the Duke's portion shall be increased to any reasonable extent at the Emperor's own discretion, and that they (the French) will be satisfied with the duchy of Milan.

Secretary Gérard and M. de Moluc have arrived at Ragusa and great hopes are entertained that they will be successful (*i.e.*, in arranging a truce with the Turk). The Seigniory of Venice caused a large number of galleys to escort them to Ragusa. (Hopes of obtaining revocation of letters of marque against Portugal.)

The Emperor sent Dandolo to Rome to salute the Duchess (*i.e.* of Camerino) but the French suspect that it is for the purpose of explaining the recess of the Diet of Worms to the Pope.

There are many Lutherans in this country, which is sadly infected by them. Guienne and Normandy are especially contaminated; and when the King of France attempts to stifle the fire in one place it blazes out more fiercely than ever in others. Most of these Lutherans are sacramentarians; and it will be necessary in consequence of them for the King of France himself to promote the holding of the Council.

Before the King's fleet was ready to sail for England, the English with 40 or 50 ships appeared off Havre de Grace, at half a league's distance, and fired several cannon against the place. These people here were greatly alarmed at this; and the King especially was in great fear for his own person, as he was only three leagues away from the English, and his fleet was still unready for defence. He had all his baggage prepared for flight at midnight, and, but for one of his captains, he would have fled in great disorder.

On the 15th instant when the fleet in Havre de Grace was ready to sail, a great carrack, the principal vessel in the fleet caught fire. She contained all the baggage of the Admiral of France and of the nobles who are following him in the war. Although the carrack

545.

was already at sea and the fire spread rapidly they managed to bring her into port, although before they did so more than 200 persons were drowned throwing themselves into the sea, some gentlemen amongst them. Only the artillery and the gold and silver were saved, the ship being entirely burnt, to the great grief of the King.

On the 17th instant the fleet sailed from Havre against England, two hundred sail strong, twenty-three of them being galleys. The Admiral of France is in command. Three or four days afterwards the admiral sent back to Havre the finest and strongest ship of the fleet; his own flagship, called the Mistress. She was disabled by being run aground, but is being repaired with all speed to sail again.

A few days afterwards the fleet descended upon the Isle of Wight, which place the French burnt and destroyed, the Chevalier D'Aux being killed by the English. The King was very sorry for this, as he was one of the best and bravest captains in the fleet.

Captain L'Orges informs them (the French) that he has been warmly welcomed in Scotland, and that the Scots were to take the field to the number of 30,000 or 40,000 men on the 28th instant, promising to do their duty bravely for the King (of France). But L'Orges says he can do nothing without money; and sent a special messenger in haste to the King to tell him so.

They assert here that the King of England is seeking peace, offering to surrender Boulogne, if the rest of his claims are treated favourably. For this purpose he is to send his representatives to Boulogne, and the King of France his to Ardres, and the meetings will take place in one of those two places under safe conducts. The French say that the King of England wishes to arrange a marriage between his daughter the Princess and the Duke of Orleans, or between his son the prince and Margaret the daughter of the King of France. I have intervened in this matter by means of an Italian; and they (the French) reply that neither marriage will take place. By orders of the Emperor, I have asked the King if there was not some means by which peace could be arranged, but I find him resolute to obtain the surrender of Boulogne as a preliminary, though he is willing to leave all other points to his Majesty's discretion.

They are also convinced that the Prince of Piedmont, who is now with the Emperor, will pass through France on his way home; and they think this will give them an opportunity to induce him to consent to a marriage with Madame Margaret the daughter of this King. But he who reckons without his host sometimes errs in the reckoning.

The number of Spaniards going into the service of the King of France against England is only 500 men. The King wishes to give charge of them to his maitre d' hotel, Mendoza, who, however, is unwilling to accept the appointment.

Caudebec, 27 July, 1545.

1545.
27 July.
Paris
Arch. Nat.
K. 1485.

105. ST. MAURIS to PRINCE PHILIP.

Has conveyed to King, Queen, Dauphin, etc. the news of the accouchement of our princess of a son. King's congratulations upon the birth of the Emperor's first grand child. He (Francis) had the start of the Emperor in this respect, but, as he (Francis) was a few years older, this was only right.

Two days after, I was summoned to the Privy Council, and a complaint was made to me that Frenchmen were prevented from purchasing iron in Spain for exportation to France. The Council pointed out that by the treaty of peace commerce was to be permitted on both sides, and that Spaniards are allowed to purchase here wood for galley-sweeps, and pitch, of which there is very little in Spain. They requested me to write to your Highness, begging you to revoke the decree forbidding the exportation of iron.

They are also making a great ado that Don Bernardino de Mendoza[*] has captured some of their pilots and sailors whom they (the French) require for their war against England, and they complain that he is treating these men very harshly. I asked them why Don Bernardino had taken the men. They replied that he had done so as a reprisal for what Paulin had done when he passed Spain with the King of France's galleys. Some of the Emperor's convicts had voluntarily surrendered to him, saying that, in accordance with maritime usage, they had regained their liberty the moment they set foot on a foreign vessel. The Council made a great complaint about the outrage, as they called it, which resulted in their spoliation. We ought, they said, have made a claim upon them here for the convicts. I replied that, although I had no knowledge whatever of the fact, it seemed to me that we had every right to detain their people since they (the French) had began by taking ours. It was perfectly justifiable, I said, to retaliate in this way for an act of violence first committed. They had first chosen this form of proceeding and we had simply continued it. It was in no sense a reprisal. They insisted, nevertheless, that I should inform the Emperor and your Highness and when I asked them if they would give up the slaves, they replied that as they had been spoliated we should first give up their subjects; and afterwards justice should be done to us. If, they said, the King liked to be as rigorous as we were he would have already arrested our subjects, but he had not done so, because it would not have been in accordance with the friendship now existing. I replied that, if your Highness consented to give up their subjects reason demanded also that they should surrender the convicts. I have no doubt they will do so if their people are restored to them.

Caudebec, 27 July.

28 July.
Vienna
Imp. Arch.

106. VAN DER DELFT to the EMPEROR.

I have received your Majesty's letters of the 16th instant, informing me of the representation made by the English ambassador asking for your Majesty's decision respecting the observance of the

---

[*] Don Bernardino de Mendoza was a brother of the Marquis of Mondejar, hereditary Governor of Granada. He commanded the Spanish galleys in the Mediterranean.

545.

treaty, a declaration of war against France, and the aid stipulated in case of invasion. I note also the reply given him, and the orders that I am to seek audience of the king, and endeavour to clear up the points detailed in the letters referred to. In accordance therewith, I demanded and obtained audience; and having declared my mission to the King, I entered upon the principal point; namely that in case your Majesty contributed the aid requested, you could not be expected to declare formal war against France, or forbid commerce to your subjects. The King replied that if that was our view, it did not agree with the treaty. It was incompatible, he said, to give aid to one of the parties in a war, and still remain friendly with the other side. I replied that there was no incompatibility in it at all, since the peace your Majesty concluded with France was by his consent, although your Majesty might have concluded it independently of him (and here I repeated all your Majesty wrote on the subject) and thus I was led to touch upon the question of his own non-compliance with the terms of the treaty. He replied that the treaty made by the Viceroy (of Sicily) was a separate matter altogether,[*] which in no wise could derogate from the original treaty of alliance; and your Majesty yourself had not fulfilled it, as you had not entered France on the day fixed. What he had done before Boulogne had always been praised and approved of by your ambassadors, who said that they did so by your Majesty's orders. I replied that, so far as I understood, your Majesty had in every respect fulfilled your part; and the blame must rest upon him, both with regard to the Viceroy's (i.e. Gonzaga, Viceroy of Sicily's) treaty, and to the agreement made with Paget subsequently. I felt sure that the ambassadors in their congratulations had not departed from any point of the treaty; and I was extremely surprised to find this contention raised by him, and that at the same time he was requesting the declaration against France. I had, I thought, completely convinced him in the matter of this declaration; and even recently when his Council addressed me, ostensibly in his name, respecting the aid, they made not the slightest allusion or demand with regard to the declaration of war against France. On the contrary, it was I who had first raised the question, in order to have the point cleared up; and the Council had made no reply; which indicated, as I thought, that there was no difference of opinion about it. I was confirmed in this idea by the assurance of the Council that the King had ordered that the subjects of your Majesty should be allowed to trade freely with France without hindrance, and that navigation should be absolutely unmolested, this being a tacit withdrawal of the demand for a declaration of war against France. The King became very angry at this, saying that he looked for the aid accompanied by the declaration of war, as provided in the treaty, and that his Council had no instructions from him but to that effect. If he was willing, he said, to allow trade to continue, he did not on that account waive for a moment his demand for the

---

[*] This contention was quite true: Gonzaga's treaty negotiated in London in 1543 related simply to the conduct of the war. Its non-fulfilment by Henry still left the original treaty intact.

1545.

declaration: and he thereupon summoned the Councillors and addressed them very harshly in his own tongue, as I could perceive by his expression, though I did not understand the words. At last he became calmer, and asked to see the treaty, which his Councillors had with them. He read the clause referring to invasion, and requested me to explain it, since that was my mission. I replied that quite lately I had explained it to him by the same arguments as were addressed to his ambassadors at Brussels. The Bishop of Winchester then related the reply given to his last mission to your Majesty: namely, that some consideration ought to be had for your Majesty's present position, as you had so recently emerged from the war; and that regard for your Majesty's honour, as well as for the King's interests, ought to prevent them (the English) from pressing your Majesty so urgently to make this declaration. He (the Bishop of Winchester) made a long speech about his conferences at Brussels, and I replied that, although I had not been present at the time, I was well informed as to what had passed, and he had omitted one of the principal points; namely, the complaint made of the non-compliance with the treaty on the part of the King. The latter then at once demanded whether I regarded the treaty as broken; because, if so, I had better say so at once. I replied that your Majesty would not willingly proceed to that extremity, and wished to maintain perfect amity, and to carry out the treaty, so far as was fairly and honestly consistent with your treaty with France, made with his (Henry's) consent. The King then again took up the question of his consent, and the other points to which he always turns, and which I have fully detailed to your Majesty in former letters, with my replies. I begged him not to take my contentions in evil part; for it was not I who called into question the word of a prince. It was a part of my instructions, upon which your Majesty laid special stress; as you did also upon the fact that he had not succoured you in your need, in accordance with the treaty. He took this very well, saying that he knew I was only acting in obedience to my instructions, and seeing that I kept to the point he said, "Well, let us suppose that the case is as you say; would you therefore contend that if the King of France invades my realm the Emperor would never be bound to declare war against him?" To this I replied that, having regard to the fact that peace had been made by his consent, reason did not demand that you should again become the enemy of the man you had made your friend by virtue of his, Henry's, permission. His consent, I said, weakened the provisions of the treaty, to the extent of relieving your Majesty from the obligation of declaring war (against France), for otherwise the consent would have had no effect at all. He asked me if I was not ashamed to advance such an opinion, which was contrary to all law and equity, to which I replied that I could only say what my reason dictated, and, even if I were not a subject or officer of your Majesty, I could come to no other conclusion. The whole of the Councillors then began to talk. Ergo, said they, the Emperor means that the King would still be bound to oppose all the Emperor's enemies, whereas the Emperor is exempt in this case from helping the King. I repeated that your Majesty, having come to terms with France by his consent, had thus gained a point more than the King. The latter denied this. They were, he said, and still remained, equally liable under the treaty: *in eo pares sumus* was his expression, and he then asked me, in the case of his now making peace with France, and the King of France subsequently invading the Emperor's dominions if he (Henry) would be liable to be called upon to declare war against France and furnish aid on your Majesty's demand. I answered that he could not by the terms of the treaty negotiate with France without the express consent of your Majesty. On this point he appeared to want take his stand on your Majesty's last letter of credence, in which I am commanded to represent to him your regret at the recrudescence of this war. He interprets this to be a consent for him to come to an agreement with his enemy. Finally he wished to know from me whether we intended to keep to the treaty or not; and again if he was for the present satisfied with the aid alone, whether in a similar case in future your Majesty would be satisfied with his aid alone, without the declaration of war on his part. If you were satisfied with this, he thought it might be some day a disadvantage to your country. I replied that I had no instructions to discuss future eventualities; but it seemed to me that he (the King) would be bound in such case to declare war, as your Majesty would be, if it had not been for his consent to the peace, which gave us an advantage. With regard to any other enemies (than France) I thought that your Majesty would not fail to fulfil what was decided to be your obligation, and I instanced your enmity with Scotland on the King's account.

As the King and Council remained obstinately of opinion that your Majesty was bound to declare war under the treaty, and continued to repeat the same arguments, whilst I replied with the same retorts, I begged the King to pardon me for saying the same things so many times over. I told him that, as I found my contentions reasonable, I must continue to press them; but I prayed him to give me another and a more favourable reply, although I hoped that all these difficulties would soon disappear, by means of an honourable peace, which might be made by your Majesty's intervention, if you knew what were the King's intentions on the subject. I said that your Majesty had in your latest letters again instructed me to do my best, and to endeavour to find some means by which your good offices might be made available to bring about the peace you so ardently desired. The King took this in good part; but complained that your Majesty had been so tardy in doing what he said you easily could have done, namely in pointing out to the French your obligations towards this King, which had even been mentioned in your treaty with France. As I have no copy, and have not seen one, of this treaty, I could not say anything to this, except to repeat what I had replied on a former occasion, to the effect that your Majesty had no means of knowing the King (of England's) views on the matter, but you had never failed in your desire to be of service in it.

He then began to complain that your Majesty was showing favour to his enemies, but I demonstrated to him that such was not the case. Your Majesty had, I said, forbidden any of your subjects

1545.

from entering the French service, and held two captains prisoners awaiting sentence for having disobeyed this order. Both the King and Council displayed great pleasure at this.

With these and such like sweet words, I besought him to be more reasonable with regard to the declaration of war; for I was, I said, perplexed at having written so fully to your Majesty in my last letters, in the hope and belief that this point was quite disposed of, since they had only mentioned the question of the assistance. I was at a loss how I could excuse myself to your Majesty, but I should be obliged to confess my rashness and frivolity in writing as I did, seeing that the point was again brought forward acutely; and I prayed the King to come to some better resolution about it.

The King then with a cheerful countenance spoke of the old friendship with your Majesty, which still continued; and proceeded to say that, if your Majesty would write to me, saying that for certain good reasons your affairs did not allow you to recommence war and make the declaration requested; and asking him (Henry) to be satisfied with the aid alone, he would give such a reply as would be pleasing to your Majesty. As I could get nothing beyond this I undertook to write to your Majesty on account of what had passed; and I begged him (Henry) to see to the release of all the arrests of your subjects' property. Your Majesty, I declared, was willing to raise the sequestrations in Spain, on condition that the property captured by Renegat should be restored, the gold seized by him on the Indiaman delivered to me, as it was legally confiscate to your Majesty, and your subjects indemnified. He said he had ordered this to be done, and it would be done without fail. He then referred me to the Council.

During my conference with the Council they conceded the entire release of the seizures, the only condition being that those goods which were suspected to belong to Frenchmen should be released against security. Touching Renegat, they thought we might have a little patience, as the man was at sea, and no doubt the property was still intact; but in accordance with your Majesty's instructions I pressed that the matter might be disposed of, and the gold placed in my hands. They assured me that they had taken such measures that in future your subjects should be unmolested in their navigation; and in this respect, since my last letters they have made a good beginning. In addition to having now favourably disposed of all claims, they have put in prison the mayor of Plymouth and another citizen of wealth and reputation, for having dealt illegally with the goods of the Quintana Dueñas, a Spanish merchant, who will have to be fully indemnified before the prisoners are released, as I am assured by the Chancellor. Whilst I was busy with this letter Secretary Paget sent to say that he wished to talk with me. He came and told me that the King had spoken about me to him to-day. The King said he thought that I was displeased and melancholy when I took leave of him yesterday. He believed the reason was, because, as I said, I had written to your Majesty only about the aid; but still he thought I had no reason to be offended at that. If I had written what had passed with the Council on that occasion there was no harm done: I could now write an account of

1545.

my conference with the King; who (said Paget) now acknowledged that he had not instructed his Council to mention to me the matter of the declaration of war. He would not, indeed, have done so now, but for the purpose of clearing up the pending questions with which his ambassador informed him I was entrusted. Since the subject came up, he could not avoid showing that he had the right to demand the declaration; but I had nevertheless understood what the King meant when he said that your Majesty could write and ask to be excused from making the declaration, which declaration, I had said, might well be waived if they (the English) would only look upon the matter reasonably. After having discussed this, and all the aforegoing points, Paget finally told me that he wished to speak in confidence and quite independently of our respective official positions. He knew the King to be so well-meaning and open-hearted, that if he were treated justly and straightforwardly anything might be done with him; but it behoved us to look out that we did not lose him. I pretended not to think it possible that he should leave us; having no cause or reason to do so, but as I saw that Paget would not continue on these lines, I begun to talk of the peace. He asked me if your Majesty was of opinion that the King should give up Boulogne, to which I replied that I had no knowledge of that, but that I was sure that if your Majesty was instrumental in bringing about peace, your desire would be that it should redound to the honour and advantage of the King (of England). I asked him if I had done wrong the other day in saying to the King unofficially that Boulogne was not worth fighting about, or necessary for his realm. Paget replied that I was not wrong, and he appeared pleased that I had said what I had to the King. Seeing this, I said that if the King of France chose to discuss peace without the restoration of Boulogne, there was no doubt that it might be successfully concluded. Paget liked this, and agreed with it readily; soon afterwards taking his leave and returning to the Court.

On the same day that the courier left here with my last letters, the French departed from the Isle of Wight, and put to sea; the English fleet still remaining at anchor where it was. Soon afterwards the French landed between this place and Dover, at a point about 36 or 40 miles from here, about 1,500 men, harquebussiers and pikemen. As there was no suspicion of an attack at this point, there were but few preparations for defence, and the French burnt five or six poor cottages; but the people in the neighbourhood assembled about 300 men, including 20 archers, who bore themselves in such sort that they drove the French back to their ships, and this in such haste that, between killed in fight and drowned in the sea, they (the French) left a hundred men behind them; and these people (the English) have plucked up great courage.[*]

There is no news of Scotland, which is very strange, seeing that this King has in that quarter so large an army of English, Spaniards and Italians.

---

[*] This second descent of the French somewhere in the neighbourhood of Shoreham does not appear to be mentioned in the Chronicles.

1545.

The King leaves here to-morrow to continue his progress. I will not fail to report to your Majesty what happens.

Whilst writing this, I learn that the Channel passage, which was closed, is now open; and that your subjects may sail freely whithersoever they please. Verily, Sire, it is a marvellous thing to see these people so suddenly come to reason, after the way in which they have been talking lately. I do not know whence proceeds so great and rapid a change.

Portsmouth, 28 July, 1545.

28 July.
Imp. Arch.

107. Van der Delft to the Queen Dowager.

Just as the courier who carried my last letters was mounting, another arrived with his Majesty's letters of the 16th instant, addressed to me through M. de Chapuys. As the latter was not at Gravelines the courier followed him to Malines and Louvain, whence he came hither; this being the reason why the letters were so long delayed. If we could do something to please this King, and keep him in our favour, or could bring about peace, it appears to me that it would be a great and good act. Otherwise I greatly doubt whether he may not shortly take a step which may sooner or later turn out to our great disadvantage. Doubtless your Majesty is exerting all necessary vigilance.

Portsmouth, 28 July, 1545.

28 July.
Paris
Arch. Nat.
K 1485.

108. St. Mauris to Francisco de los Cobos.

The King and Council have settled the question of the letters of marque against the Portuguese, in the manner set forth in the enclosed memorandum, which, it appears to me, is tantamount to an entire revocation.

The King promises that Carvajal's[*] affair shall be promptly settled. The King at the same time told me that he had now ascertained the truth about the convicts that some of his captains had captured in Spain, and he was greatly scandalised thereat. He would punish the captains, and would immediatly order these convicts to be surrendered, being confident that the Emperor would also order his people to be given up to him (the King of France). So far as I can understand, the intention is to give the convicts up to me; but I think it would be better to devise some other method, for convicts are no game for my bag. I have also pointed out to the King, by the Emperor's orders, that certain of his ships are being fitted out to go to Peru with armed force. The King replied that his people might still go there to trade, but he was desirous of pleasing the Emperor in the matter and he would at once issue orders that no one should go thither on pain of death. I am following them up constantly to get this decree sent to the ports.

The French fleet has retired from the isle of Wight, having been unable to seize the harbour, and is now at Dieppe, whence it is

---

[*] Don Diego Carvajal had been sent by Prince Philip to demand restitution of certain Spanish ships seized by French privateers after peace was signed.

1545.

said that an attack will be made against Boulogne, or another descent attempted upon England itself. There is a rumour here, originating from some merchants of Rouen, that our Princess is dead. God grant that it be not true.

Caudebec, 28 July, 1545.

August (?)
Paris
Arch. Nat
K. 1486.
(*See* Note, page 243.)

109. ST. MAURIS and NOIRTHOUDT to the EMPEROR.

As soon as we received your Majesty's letter of the 2nd instant, we obtained audience of the King, for the purpose of laying before him the message entrusted to us. Before the audience the Admiral (Claude Hannebault) took us into his own chamber, until the King was ready to receive us. As he was anxious to know the object of our coming, we told him our instructions, which were to express to the King the Emperor's pleasure at his inclination towards peace. The Admiral thereupon endeavoured to draw from us the reply that the King of England had given to the Emperor to a similar message. We told him that the only answer we had heard was that the King of England was quite willing to negotiate for peace; and he (Hannebault) said that news had come from England that the King was not only very desirous of doing so, but was willing to surrender Boulogne in return for a sum of money, if his honour and dignity were safeguarded. We replied that we knew nothing about that, and that nothing of the sort had been said to your Majesty. We were then summoned to the King. Neither he nor Cardinal Tournon made any mention to us of what the Admiral had said; and we judge that the Admiral's object was only to draw some admission from us. In the audience with the King, I (St. Mauris) repeated what your Majesty had written, as to the pleasure you felt at his good inclination towards peace, etc., and also told him that, with regard to his offer to pay a sum of money for the surrender of Boulogne, as he had not mentioned any amount, we thought it would forward matters if he declared his views as to how much he was willing to pay. We stated to him, in accordance with your Majesty's instructions, that you doubted whether the King of England would be very ready to respond to such a proposal, even if the amount of the compensation was stated.

The King replied that the question of amount would have to be considered. It was a great concession, even to have discussed the giving of compensation at all, and it would be difficult to fix an amount; unless people were sent to Boulogne to see for themselves the outlay the King of England had incurred in fortifying the town, as he (the King of France) had never intended that the compensation should include the cost of the war itself. He would, he said, not stand out for the matter of 15,000 or 20,000, or even 30,000 crowns; besides which the question of amount might be left pending whilst estimates were being made.

We also laid before the King what your Majesty says about the inclusion of the Scots (in the proposed treaty of peace), in order to learn from him on what conditions this could be done. He replied that he could hardly say what conditions, except those that usually subsisted between them (*i.e.*, the English and Scots) when they were

1545.

at peace and amity. He knew, he said, that the King of England wished to subject Scotland to him, and with this object sought the marriage of the Princess of Scotland with his son. This was a very strange proceeding, and one to which he (Francis) would never consent. He thought, however, that it would be a very good work for anyone to reconcile the English and Scots, and put an end to their quarrels; but persisted that the inclusion of the Scots in the peace should be on the same conditions as were in existence in former years when they were at peace.

I mentioned the point of the payment of the overdue pensions (*i.e.*, subventions to England) in order to discover in what form he intended to pay them, and said that your Majesty wished to be informed as to his views on these points, so that you might be able to promote the peace negotiations actively and not allow them to drag. He replied that he would have the matter considered and the treaties examined in order that he might know for certain what his obligations towards England were.

Thereupon, Sire, I (Noirthoudt) told the King that your Majesty desired to have his opinion, as to whether he considered it advisable to propose a conference, to which French and English representatives, fully authorised and instructed, should be sent; such conference to be held at your Majesty's Court or elsewhere to discuss the differences existing. I declared that your Majesty would willingly send your representatives to the place chosen.

The King replied that he approved of this suggestion, and seemed very much delighted with it. He thought that it would be better to hold the conference in your Majesty's Court; using these words: "Where else better could I desire to hold it than in the presence of my good brother and great friend the Emperor?" If that could not be arranged, he said he would be willing to consent to another place; mentioning Gravelines or any similar place in your Majesty's dominions. He said that he would send his ambassadors fully instructed and empowered on the three points we had mentioned.

After dinner on the same day we went to Cardinal Tournon to whom we declared the substance of our mission, and told him that we would have given the same information to the Admiral, only that he was with the King. We also repeated to the Cardinal the conversation we had had with the King. He replied that he had already heard it from the King, and in his opinion the King had answered very well, as he had accepted the suggestion of a conference, which for his (the Cardinal's) part he thought should assemble in the presence of your Majesty. He thought this would be of the greatest advantage for the success of the negotiations, and was very firm on the point.

With regard to the inclusion of the Scots, the Cardinal replied exactly in the same way as the King had done. The question of the overdue subvention, he said, would have to be settled by an inspection of the treaties between France and England, which would demonstrate the obligation of the King; and the payments might be made in accordance therewith. The question should be referred to the proposed conference.

So far as we could judge, the King and his ministers would have preferred us to postpone our enquiries as to their views on the three

1545.

points named, until the result of M. d'Eick's negotiations was known. They think that the design is to get as much out of them as possible, and make them appear to be taking the first step in advance. We noticed signs of this feeling, especially in our conversation with the Cardinal, and we endeavoured to get over it by saying that your Majesty's only object was to carry through the negotiations successfully. We said that the same diligence to attain that end was being employed in England as well as here; and that what we had told him about M. d'Eick's having found the King of England willing to come to reasonable terms, should convince him that it was only after the latter had been approached that we asked the King of France to state his views, in order the further to promote the negotiations. When the conversation about the peace was finished, the Cardinal spoke about the lansquenets that the King of England is raising; and said that the French considered it very strange that your Majesty should allow these lansquenets to pass through your territories, considering the friendship at present existing. He said that your Majesty had given the King reason to hope that you would never allow such a thing to be done. In order to show us how much distrust had been caused by this passage of troops, he (the Cardinal) told us that M. de Gragnan had written, telling the King that your Majesty had replied to him on the subject that it would be very difficult for you to prevent the passage of these troops, now that they were already mustered. The Cardinal added, however, that the King cared very little for the entrance of these troops into France; so long as they did not pass through your Majesty's territories to Calais. That, he said, would indeed be out of harmony with the present sincere friendship, and he trusted your Majesty would take care not to allow it. He begged us to write to your Majesty on this subject, not, as he said, that the King had instructed him to do so; but that he and the Admiral had decided to make this request to us, in furtherance of their wish that the present friendship should continue without any cause for distrust. He assured us that the King would observe the friendship loyally to the end; and we promised him to write to your Majesty as he requested.

After this we heard that the Duke of Orleans was very much better than he had been two days before, and we thought it would be advisable for us to visit him in your Majesty's name, and congratulate him on his convalescence. We did so, and he approved to be very much gratified by the attention. He told us he was much better, and that he would have been sorry to die before he had done some great and signal service to your Majesty.

June and July to 2 August.
Simancas.
E. 641.

110. NEWS CURRENT in the EMPEROR'S COURT, written by PEDRO HUESCA to GONZALO PEREZ.

The Princes of the Empire have not come to the Diet, and there is but little hope that they will come; although their lodgings await them.

The Duke of Lorraine died about a week since. The Emperor sent Dandolo to visit the Duchess (*i.e.* of Camerino), and the King of France sent another personage.

HENRY VIII.

1545.

The King of France has assembled a great fleet of 37 galleys and numerous ships at Thérouanne, and the King of England has ready another fleet of ships to defend his Channel and coasts from the French, which they say he will do.

The English have two armies in Scotland, and the French have one. Both forces were strengthening themselves sturdily for hostilities. Boulogne is held in strength by the English, but constant skirmishes were going on in the neighbourhood.

The English have captured 300 loaded French ships from Brittany. They have also seized two vessels loaded with merchandise from Spain, the pretext being that they were the property of Frenchmen; but it is said they will be restored.

The French have captured a Spanish ship bringing gold from the Indies.

The King of England has sent a man to Italy to raise the troops he requires.

The Emperor will not stay here long, but will shortly return to Flanders.

Queen Mary (the Queen Dowager of Hungary) is in Friesland and will shortly go to Brussels.

It is hoped that the truce with the Turk will be concluded. It will be convenient for many respects.

The Turk will not raise a fleet or an army this year. It is said that the cause of this is the following. The Sultana sent a Pasha; ostensibly to pacify her eldest son, but really with orders to kill him. The son having learnt this took time by the forelock, killed the Pasha, and joined his forces with the Sophi. For this reason the Turk fears this year to leave his dominions to attack the Christians. The reason seems a good one.

Names of Spanish nobles expected to arrive at Worms.

Some people assert that the negotiations for peace between England and France are proceeding favourably. Personally I see but slight signs of it. We shall see.

The Landgrave (of Hesse) places in the Emperor's keeping the States of the Duke of Brunswick, in order that his Majesty may decide the dispute between them. But they say that the Landgrave wishes to impose some unreasonable conditions. The Lutheran princes are in arms with 80,000 men, it is said not without some fear of the Emperor. The Christian princes are also in arms for his Majesty's service, in case the Lutherans should attempt any movement.

The person sent by the King of France to visit the Duchess of Lorraine is M. de Guise, who takes with him a company of men-at-arms. It is said that his master (the King of France) advances some claim on the duchy of Bar, which is held by the Duchess.

Latest letters from Adrianople assert that the truce with the Turk will be concluded by the envoys of the Emperor and the King of France. The son of Barbarossa was going as Governor of Algiers with six galleys.

The Turk with the Sultana and all the Porte were leaving (Adrianople) for Constantinople very much pleased.

The Venetians cannot make up their minds whether the truce with the Turk will be a good thing for them or not.

1545.

The vessels leaving, or to leave, Constantinople were 25. They will go as far as Rhodes.

They say that the Council (of Trent) will adjourn to Metz, Mayence or Cologne. I learn that the Pope is on excellent terms with the Emperor now, and that in future he will do everything he can to please his Majesty.

It is asserted that the Turk designed to make King of Hungary a son of his by the present, second, wife.

Nicolo Seco, who is going as ambassador from the King of the Romans to the Turk, left Vienna on his journey with 25 horsemen well mounted and armed. He received for his expenses on his nine months' mission 9,000 gold ducats, and he is said to carry with him 25,000 ducats for presents to the Pashas.

Secretary Gérard arrived at Venice on the 3rd instant. He with the French envoy and Don Diego de Mendoza[*] visited the Seigniory. The two former personages were to leave for Constantinople on the 14th or 15th instant.

The Marquis del Guasto had not yet left Milan to come hither up to the 9th instant, but was expected to set out immediately. It is said that some of the Spanish theologians had arrived at Trent. The Council was suspended until All Saints day.

Worms, 22 June.

Subsequently we hear that as Dragut Reis was retiring to Los Gelves he was killed by the Arabs. If this be true, it is good news indeed. They write from Naples that Don Garcia de Toledo and Doria have captured on the coast of Calabria two cutters (*fustas*) and two rich galliots, carrying a famous Corsican corsair, whom Don Garcia hanged from the prow of his galley.

Marquis del Guasto has now left Milan, and will arrive here with the Viceroy of Sardinia on the 12th instant.

The Count Palatine left here the other day, for the purpose of obtaining the influence of the Duke of Saxony to persuade the Landgrave of Hesse to restore the States of the Duke of Brunswick. He will at the same time urge that the Council shall be held at Cologne or Metz; and in order to endeavour to induce the Pope to consent to this, it is said that Dandolo went to Rome. He left on the 7th instant. The recess of this Diet will, it is believed, commence at the end of this month.

The Vaivode of Buda and the Captain-General of the King of the Romans have effected a new truce for three months, and it is hoped that it will be followed by a cessation of hostilities for some years, as a consequence of the negotiations with the Turk. The envoys to the Turk have now left Venice.

The Prince of Piedmont is coming hither, but has fallen ill on the road.

The relations between the Emperor and the Pope grow in warmth.

On the 5th instant 40,000 crowns were sent to the Spanish infantry in Hungary by the Quartermaster Iñigo de Peralta. On

---

[*] The Spanish ambassador at Venice was the famous writer Don Diego Hurtado de Mendoza, author of the history of the Wars of Granada and it is believed also of the first picaresque novel Lazarillo de Tormes. He was associated with the Granvelles, father and son, in the representation of the Emperor at the Council of Trent.

1545.

the same day there came news of the death of the Queen of Poland, the daughter of the King of the Romans.

The Emperor is expected to leave here for Flanders in the middle of August.

Dated on the 7th July; but as no opportunity has offered of sending it the letter is now continued.

2 August.

You will already have learnt that Juan Zapata de Cardenas had been sent by the Emperor to Naples to arrest Don Garcia de Toledo.* This was done and Don Garcia is now a prisoner in Castelnuovo, and it is said that his galleys have been entrusted to Antonio Doria. The Marquis del Guasto is acting towards Don Garcia as a father with the Emperor. It is said that the reason for Don Garcia's imprisonment is the affair that lately happened at Malines to the Duke of Ferrandina, who, however, made no request that he should be arrested. On the 30th ultimo, the King of the Romans and his son Prince Maximilian left here. Don Fernando, the second son, remains with the Emperor. Whilst the King was hunting on the way, he received the news of the death of the Princess; and he returned to see the Emperor, again setting out for Bohemia the next day. The Emperor leaves here for Flanders with his Court on the 6th. They say he will go part of the way by water.

The Marquis del Guasto is in high favour with the Emperor, and is greatly feasted by all the Court. He is very glad to be able to set out for Milan before the Emperor leaves here. We have no news of any hostilities between the French and English armies in Scotland; but we learn that the two fleets encountered each other off an English port. Although the French fleet was superior, and a fine opportunity presented itself for the French to attack the English, they did not dare to do so. Whilst the English fleet were endeavouring to enter port an English carrack foundered with 300 men.

The Diet is suspended until December or January. There is to be a conference of 12 persons in Ratisbon or Nuremberg, six chosen by the Emperor and six by the Protestants for the purpose of reforming, so far as they can, the matter of the faith in these parts, pending the assembly of the Council. Don Juan de Figueroa is bearing this letter. He is going to condole with the Prince on the death of the Princess, which has caused the Emperor great grief. It is said that attempts will soon be made to marry the Prince again.

Worms, 2 August, 1545.

2 Aug.
Simancas.
E. 641.
Extract.

111. The Emperor to Francisco de los Cobos.

With regard to the ships that the English and French have captured and the damage which has been done by them and by the (French) galleys which left the Mediterranean for the Atlantic, I refer you to my letters to the Prince. I wish to speak especially of

---

*Don Garcia de Toledo was the able but turbulent Spanish Viceroy of Sicily, whose ambition and pride more than once caused him to be suspected in after years.

545.

the ship called the San Salvador from Santo Domingo, the master of which was Francisco Gallego. She was captured by the English, and, as is officially admitted by the English ambassador here, the English captain (*i.e.*, Renegat) who made the capture alleges as a pretext that our subjects had taken a ship from him. He therefore declares that he resorted to force, and having captured one ship, which he says did not contain sufficient value to compensate him, he fell in with this other one carrying the gold. The captain of the ship told him that the property on board belonged to us; and he had therefore better not touch it. The Englishman replied that he could not avoid doing so; but that he would give him (the Spanish captain) a certificate of the amount he took for his compensation. The master replied that he did not want the certificate, as it would prove that he had brought the treasure on board without registering it, and he would incur heavy punishment. In view of this, we wrote to our ambassador in England, instructing him in case of the restitution of the ship and contents, to embargo them as being our property, for the reason set forth. We let you know this, that you may inform the Council of the Indies; and have an enquiry made, for the purpose, if necessary, of proceeding against the culprits. Do not neglect this, and communicate the result to us.

Thanks for your good arrangements about the bills of exchange and the measures you have taken to keep faith with the merchants, and induce them to be satisfied with the instalments already agreed upon, without insisting upon the calculation of the interest at the end of each year. This is, as you say, a most important advantage, present and future. My sister, Queen Mary, writes that the Flemish merchants interested have agreed willingly, as you will have heard from them, as well as from the Queen. Of the bills for 150,000 ducats which you sent us 50,000 have been paid to the merchants in Flanders on the 1st July; and, at the end of the account they will be debited with the interest on the sum thus paid in advance. The warrant for the 36,477 crowns, at the rate of 67 groats each, will cover the last bill entirely. Thanks for sending us the bill for the other 50,000 ducats, payable either here in Germany or in Flanders. Most will be taken in Flanders.

Thanks for letter from the Infantas, telling us of the grave condition of Count Cifuentes.[*] If he dies you must consider who will be best to put in his place. Most of those suggested are married, and this is undesirable, as we should have to provide for their wives, etc. See what fitting widowers there are. With regard to the price of bread, as the year is a spare one and the common people will be in need, you will order the bread stuffs not to be kept back, but will have them sold at once to the town councils, but not to private persons so as to avoid forestalling and speculation. They may be sold for a real less per fanega than their value, so that they may be sold publicly in the shops at the same price that they cost, and no more. This will lower the price of bread: and that this shall be known, it will be well to publish the fact well. Take such measures that the poor shall receive the benefit, that being our intention.

---

[*] He was the Governor of the Emperor's young daughters Maria and Juana.

1545.

The emeralds and precious stones from Cartagena you will have sold, and also the pearls; and have the sum drawn against them paid. I am sure you are glad, as you say, that these stones and the gold came just in time to provide for the payment of Prince Doria and other necessary things.

Worms, 2 August, 1545.

2 Aug.
Simancas.
E. Flanders.
501.

112. The EMPEROR to PRINCE PHILIP.

You will have heard that Cardinal Farnese came hither from his Holiness, ostensibly to discuss religious matters and the resistance to be offered to the Turk, but really to palliate past events, and to promise emphatically his goodwill for the future, as well as that of the Cardinal and all his family, which they desire to place for ever under my protection.[*] The Cardinal added that his Holiness intended to act in accord and co-operation with us, in remedying the public affairs referred to, and others, especially with regard to the holding of the Council; and he brought a bill of exchange for 100,000 crowns to be employed as might be needful in resisting the Turk. A fitting answer to all this was given to the Cardinal; and it was especially pointed out to him that affairs here were in a most dangerous condition, and above all in relation to religion. There was evidence, we said, that the ruin of the faith in these parts would be consummated, unless his Holiness bestirred himself greatly; and the trouble would not end here; for there were signs that it would spread throughout Christendom. The Cardinal acknowledged this unhesitatingly; for he had the testimony of all the ecclesiastics, and even of the Nuncios who are, and have been, here; all of whom had studied the question for years. He expressed himself greatly surprised, and said that the Pope had no idea that the matter had gone so far as it had. This caused him to return to Rome by the post; for the purpose of laying the matter before his Holiness, and to show him how urgently it was needed that something should be done. He subsequently wrote to us, saying that the Pope was determined to devote himself to this; and to aid in money, to the extent of his power. He also consented to concede the bull for the half-first fruits of ecclesiastical revenues in Spain, and that for the sale of monastic property, on condition that the whole of the proceeds shall be devoted to the resistance (to the Turk) and the re-integration of the faith. As this is very important, and we are unwilling to lose the opportunity offered by his Holiness' good inclination, we thought well to dispatch Dandolo, ostensibly for the purpose of visiting the Duchess of Camarino, who is pregnant; but really in order that we may learn clearly what his Holiness' intentions are; and, if possible, assure ourselves as the extent of

[*] It will be recollected that the Farnese Pope's son and grandson were being kept out of their principality by the Emperor. Now that Francis had made peace with Charles, and the latter was supreme in Italy, the Farneses saw that they would have to eat humble pie and bribe the Emperor if ever they were to gain their possessions. This was the first indication of it; but Paul III. had to humble himself much more; and still further deplete his treasury before the Emperor consented to give to his natural daughter Margaret the duchies of Parma and Piacenza as a dowry on her marriage with Ottavio Farnese.

1545.

the aid we may expect from him. It is undoubtedly the case that affairs look so ominous here as to portend the utter destruction of religion, unless a prompt remedy be found. It is not Germany alone that has to be considered, for the rest of Christendom also will be contaminated, since these errors are already spreading into many parts of the country. We therefore await Dandolo's return with great anxiety, and will inform you if he arrives before we close this despatch.

In the meanwhile, we have discussed with the States of the Empire, and particularly with the mistaken protestants, as favourably as circumstances would allow; but they (the States, etc.) have been, and are, so stubborn that they not only demand that the decisions of the Council, which is to meet at Trent, shall be approved of by them, but expressly insist that they (the States, etc.) shall be assured by the catholic States and by us against any action of the Council. They say that, in any other case, there will be no peace for Germany; nor can we secure its loyalty. Up to the present it has been impossible to come to terms, but we have consented to the assembly of another conference, to see whether some harmonious settlement can be devised. We have agreed to the summoning of another Diet for next year, if peace continues, without any special mention being made of the Council. We have borne in mind, however, that this new conference will not interfere with the progress of the Council: and in the meanwhile we shall see what his Holiness is disposed to do, and the attitude assumed by public affairs generally. The holding of this new Diet at the time fixed will allow of such measures relating to religion, as may be possible or expedient, being dealt with in it, and will also enable us to return to Spain. As soon as we have closed matters here, we shall go to Flanders; and will set affairs in order there, arranging the Government in the way we have already discussed with some of the principal personages of Flanders. This will allow us to leave the Netherlands without being forced to return thither; hoping that, with the arrangements we shall make, the country will remain in good order. News from the Turk show that he will not move this year in a way which will necessitate resistance on our part. His garrisons may make a few raids on the frontiers of our brother (the King of the Romans) and steps are being taken to deal with these; but it is hoped that a truce for four or five years may be agreed to. In any case, care will be taken to make some provision against attack before we set out for Spain.

The King of France is so much embarrassed with his war against England, that he seems to be growing slack and careless. His people are raising difficulties and delays in fulfilling the conditions necessary prior to the alternative marriage, these conditions being of great importance. In addition to this, his subjects have been committing outrages at sea, off the Spanish and French coasts, to the detriment of our people. We have made the needful remonstrances against these acts; and our ambassador in France has been active in showing that there is no disinclination on our part to clear up the pending matters, and has pressed that these injuries shall be redressed.

HENRY VIII.

1545.

This will cause the postponement of the alternative marriage, and it may be supposed that the French will not take offence at this postponement; for the same, or similar, reasons caused the delay in the presentation of our declaration (*i.e.*, decision as to which marriage was chosen). As we wish to have the Duke of Alba here at the time, and to utilise his great experience in affairs etc., we have written to him to start as soon as possible, and come to hither with all speed. You will also order him to do so.

The King of England has demanded our assistance in his war against France, as stipulated by the treaty is case of invasion. There have been several long conferences with his ambassadors about this since we returned from the French expedition. The special ambassadors were in Brussels for some time on this business and we consequently sent Dr. Chapuys back again to England, with the new ambassador who had been appointed to succeed him, in order that he might come to some understanding about it. The negotiations on this side were therefore suspended for a time, with the consent of the English, and full instructions were given to our ambassadors as to the points that must be cleared up with the King; in order that we might keep faith with the French, whilst fulfilling our treaty obligations with England, so far as the two things were compatible. This was, and is, our intention: first to come to a clear understanding, which is quite possible to be done, and then, in case of the invasion of England, to give the King such aid as we agreed to contribute. We could not, however, consent to be bound to help in the case of Boulogne, since the clause only provides for the defence of such territories as were possessed by the King at the time the treaty was signed. We shall even be willing to waive the non-fulfillment by the King of his agreement with regard to the invasion of France, where he left us to bear the whole burden. We are, however, ceaselessly urging the French and English ambassadors here to come to some settlement; and we have instructed our ambassadors to work for a similar end. We have given out that we are hastening to close this Diet, and intend to set out on our return to Flanders, so as to be able to employ our good offices in the interests of peace. We shall be guided on our arrival by the position of the combatants, and by the need for preventing our dominions from being injured by the armies and fleets they have assembled. The Marquis del Guasto is here; and we are considering the means we shall adopt to pay the Spanish troops in Lombardy, and their maintenance for the future, as well as those in our pay in Hungary. We must see where we can send them to, in order to stop the harm they are doing, and make some use of them; since, in the present state of public affairs, we cannot think of dismissing them. If we wanted them, we should not be able to raise them again. Some fresh measures will also have to be taken for the government of Milan, where disorder has become rife during the war. We hear from Italy that Barbarossa is sending his son with 12 galleys to take possession of the King of Algiers. They are to start soon; and though we have taken such steps as seemed necessary in this direction, we think well to let you know; so that you, too, may look to the coast defences if Don Bernardino[*] went

---

[*] De Mendoza, the general of the Spanish galleys in the Mediterranean.

1545.

to the Goleta as was arranged, and has not returned. With relation to the depredations and captures of ships by the French and English, and the damage on the coast committed by the French galleys, we have been fully informed by your letters, and the reports of the (Spanish) Council. In compliance with our duty to protect our subjects, we have taken all necessary steps to demand from the Kings of France and England restitution of the property seized, whilst we promise to see that the claims of their subjects shall be dealt with similarly by us. Otherwise, we have informed them, we shall not be able to refuse to take other steps for the redress of our subjects. They (*i.e.*, the Kings of France and England) have always replied that our claims should be attended to; and Diego de Carvajal wrote hither recently that the matter was proceeding favourably, the King of France appearing extremely willing, and promising prompt justice. The English say that they will restore everything, if we do the same in Spain; and we have written to our ambassador instructing him to press for this to be carried into effect, whilst we have spoken very energetically about it to the ambassadors here, telling them of the constant complaints we continue to receive, and demanding the immediate return of the ships and merchandise seized. If this be not done, we say, we shall be obliged to adopt the steps already mentioned. In good faith and under the protection of peace, our subjects have carried their trade upon the sea: we cannot allow them to be molested and plundered in the exercise of this right, and we shall be forced to allow them to arm and compensate themselves. At the present time it is unadvisable to adopt reprisals, and to give letters of marque, as the English and French have strong forces at sea; and it might give them a ground for settling their own differences. Besides this, it would take a long time to get a sea force of any strength ready in Spain, as we have seen by experience, and in any case it would be too late to do anything; thus only disturbing matters without any result, and giving ground for suspicion that we had armed because the English and French had their fleets in commission. For these reasons we have decided that, as if of your own accord, and without any appearance of having acted by our instructions, you will cause an account to be made of the ships and merchandise captured by the French since the conclusion of peace, and of the damage done on the Spanish coast by the French galleys on their passage (*i.e.*, from Marseilles to the Bay of Biscay); and you will then, as gently as possible, sequestrate property belonging to Frenchmen in Spain to a similar value. The goods thus seized should be deposited in the hands of persons of credit; so that they may remain intact; and when the property captured from our subjects has been restored, and the claimants satisfied, then the goods sequestrated may be returned to their owners. Our subjects will thus have reason to be contented, and the others will have no cause to complain. With regard to the English, you write that you have already sequestrated property of theirs for the Indian ship plundered by that captain (*i.e.*, Renegat). The English ambassadors hold out good hopes of prompt restitution of the plunder, on condition of the same course being followed by us. The main part of the English seizures being thus secured, we

1545.

think it will be best not to embargo any more of their property, until we see how they act. Let us know what you do in both cases. The French have published a decree, pronouncing legal prizes all ships carrying any victuals or munitions for the English; their contention being that by ancient custom they have this right; not only as regards Spain, but also Flanders. This is so important as a general principle, that due representations are being made to the French against it, and these shall continue until the matter is altered. If this were permitted by us it would amount to a prohibition of the trade with England which the treaty of peace permits. We have no doubt that when the French see their their property in Spain sequestrated, they will moderate their tone and come to reason.

As soon as you sent us the information of the ships which were being fitted out in Brittany to sail to Peru, on the pretence of carrying merchandise thither, we caused the French ambassadors to be spoken to about them, and I personally mentioned the matter to them subsequently. They excused themselves by saying that they did not believe the information was true, but I warned them that it must be remedied, and also instructed our ambassador in France to press the complaint to the King. We have no answer yet. If you hear any more let me know, and say what it is considered will be the best measures to adopt about it.

Worms, 2 August, 1545.

6 Aug.
Vienna
Imp. Arch.

113. Chapuys to de Granvelle.

As I was on the point of departure from Malines on the 20th ultimo to come hither, I received the letters of his Majesty dated 16th, addressed to his ambassador in England; but in consequence of my grievous illness, I was unable to give to the ambassador any further advice concerning them than what you will see by the copies of the letters I wrote to him. I have since received from the ambassador copy of the letter he has written to his Majesty, with a letter to myself; but as I was at the worst point of my malady, and was unwilling to delay the forwarding of the copy in question to the Queen (Dowager), to whom it was addressed, I was only just able to glance hastily through the contents. As the ambassador seems to have conducted affairs very cleverly, both with the King and Council, and matters were taking the proper course, I thought it was unnecessary to add anything, especially as his Majesty had in his letters of the 16th foreseen and provided for every point, both with regard to the aid and the release of the seizures.

I have now just received other letters from the ambassador, dated 28th ultimo, with duplicate of what he was writing to the Emperor; from which I gather that affairs are progressing better and better. I am of opinion that everything will turn out well, if a little willingness is shown in humouring the temper of the King, which you know so well. It appears now that really the only point still open is that of the declaration of war against France, in case the aid is given (to the English). According to my poor foolish fancy, and under your Lordship's wise correction, it seems to me, that in this respect we might take advantage of the King's suggestion, and that his Majesty might please to write to the ambassador, saying that his Majesty, for the reasons so often repeated and so well known, desires not to be held to the declaration of war; and even if he might be so held, he trusts in the great goodness and honesty, and the ancient, sincere friendship of the King, that the latter will not place him in a position which will not benefit the King, and yet will grievously injure his Majesty and his Flemish subjects. The principal reasons given may be those already set forth, namely the need for the continuance of trade; and his Majesty might add that having regard to this, he sincerely begged the King to desist from his demand (for a declaration of war) at the present time, and thus to ratify the agreement already made between his Majesty's ministers and Secretary Paget. It seems to me that this would not be at all a bad course to take, because, in case of a rupture between the Emperor and France, his Majesty might demand a declaration of war from the King (of England) against France; whereas if his Majesty were now roundly to declare that *he* was not bound to make such a declaration, it would form a precedent for the King to do the same. I am very glad to hear that his Majesty has consented to give the assistance, and your Lordship will see by the Ambassador's letters what a change has taken place in the King. I am still strongly of opinion that the Emperor will not have to disburse a penny, for when once his Majesty really sets his hand to the promotion of peace, it will be quite possible to conclude some sort of suspension of hostilities before the expiration of the six weeks. Both parties must be already tired of the expense and trouble of the war, and even if this were not so, the galleys, the principal hope of the French fleet, will be obliged to withdraw and the rest cannot keep the sea without them. It appears to me, however, that the ambassador has omitted to broach one of the most important points; namely, the recognition or ratification (*i.e.*, by the King of England) of the Emperor's treaty of peace with France. I spoke at length on this subject to the Bishop of Westminster and Secretary Petre at Bourbourg, and they did not fail to advise the King of what I said, with the result that Paget wrote to tell them to find out my meaning, and for what purpose the request was made, as I informed the Emperor at the time. If his Majesty still requires the ratification, it would be well to remind the ambassador about it.

I can sincerely assure your Lordship that he (*i.e.*, the ambassador) might just as fairly have demanded the release of the property claimed by poor Carrion as any other goods detained in England, as the case in question is so very clear, and the injustice shameful. It is true that, as it was somewhat hard for them (the English) to swallow, the ambassador may have feared that it would have prevented the settlement of the other claims if he had made a firm stand about it; but it may perhaps seem advisable to your Lordship to slip a word or two about it into the Emperor's letters to the Ambassador, saying that his Majesty had not pressed Carrion's claim with the rest, because he understood that I had made some proposal for the settlement of it, and that the Bishop of Westminster and Petre had held out hopes of a successful agreement. The Ambassador might be instructed to do his best in the matter.

Since I have been here, I have no other recreation but to listen to the praises of the virtue and wisdom of your sons here. Verily, it is almost miraculous. I saw them this morning, the first time I had been out for a fortnight. They are very well, thank God.

Louvain, 6 August, 1545.

6 Aug.
Vienna
Imp. Arch.

114. The Emperor to Van der Delft.

We have received your letters of 24th ultimo and note the communications you had had with the King of England, his Chancellor, the Council and Secretary Paget, touching the means for forwarding a peace between England and France, the release of the ships under detention, and the contribution of the assistance stipulated by the treaty between us and England. You have very cleverly conducted the whole of these affairs. The ambassador has addressed us here in conformity with your letter, and as the full details of our answer to him have been forwarded to our sister, the Queen (Dowager), and our decision on all points, as you will see by the copy enclosed, we need not repeat what we say therein. You will, therefore, be guided in your dealing with the King by the contents of the letter, and the orders you may receive from our sister.

Inform us of what passes, as often as possible, and also keep us advised as to the progress of the war.

Worms, 6 August, 1545.

1545.[*]
Paris
Arch. Nat.
K. 1485.

115. Intelligence sent by the Imperial Ambassador in France.

The Christian King has been ill for a long time past, the commencement of his indisposition being a slow fever that he caught. This troubled him several times, and came on suddenly without any premonition, lasting on one occasion for five days. In addition to this fever it was discovered that he had a gathering under the lower parts, which distressed and weakened him so much that he could not stand, and he had to keep his bed. For the cure of this gathering the most expert doctors and surgeons of Paris were summoned. After purging the King they applied a cautery to the abcess, in order to open and destroy it. This treatment was continued until the abcess broke: but instead of discharging in one place only, as they expected, it broke out in three, in very dangerous positions: and there is at present no assurance that he will live. He has even fallen into extreme fainting and exhaustion, but he has always retained consciousness and still does so. The malady proceeds from a similar illness to that from which the King was suffering when the Emperor passed through France on his way from Spain. As the abcesses did

---

[*] The copy of this document in the Archives Nationales bears the date of 7 December, 1545. This cannot be correct. The intelligence contained it appears to be condensed from several communications sent by St. Mauris to the Emperor late in June and early in July, the present summary having been forwarded to Spain for the information of Prince Philip. This is probably the "long letter" referred to by St. Mauris in his letter to Cobos of the 7th August, and for this reason it is inserted here.

not discharge properly, the physicians have applied three fresh cauteries, and this has caused three issues, whence infected matter flows in great abundance. In order the better to recover from his malady, the King has commenced a course of Chinese wood, which his physicians say he must continue for 20 days. All the medical men are of opinion the malady proceeds from "the French sickness"; and for the eradication of this, the Chinese wood will aid greatly, unless, as is feared, the bladder is ulcerated. The King expects to be able shortly to go into the country in a litter, going first towards Blois and thence to his native place, Cognac.

The French have set afloat the intelligence that they will recommence the war against the English. They talk of raising three armies, one to go against Boulogne by land, principally with the object of preventing the victualling of the place; the second for Scotland, under the command of M. d'Enghien, who will have 20,000 foot and 400 men-at-arms, without counting the Scots raised in the country itself; and the third will be a naval force to muster in Normandy and attack England, capturing the first port they can with the object of marching inland thence and giving the English battle. The English will be obliged to fight or lose their country, as there are no fortresses except on the coast. Three millions of francs are to be raised from the French people for the commencement of the war, of which Captain Paulin has already received 90,000 to fit out ships and galleys at Marseilles, which he intends to send round to Normandy. They are also raising what vessels they can to aid the expedition, in Brittany and at Rochelle. The worst of it is, however, that the French recently lost fifty or sixty ships loaded with goods, which the English captured by force, and quite recently 17 more have been captured by the English. It is reported that the English have already about 80 to 100 armed ships, so that their fleet is very much stronger than the French. It must be borne in mind also, that the French army bound for Scotland will have to pass between Dover, Boulogne and Calais, and may find its passage disputed. In Boulogne there is ordinarily a garrison of 4,000 men who make many raids on their enemy both to Ardres and to Montreuil, burning everything as they go, in order to render victuals scarce. The King of England has recently constructed a new bastion adjoining Boulogne and the port, so that the harbour is now entirely dominated by the English, and they can introduce as many victuals as they please. They have accumulated in the place great quantities of provisions, artillery and munitions of war. They have recently captured by force a castle in the Boulognais, where they killed the 200 men who defended it. They afterwards tried to prevent the French from constructing a bulwark, which on the advice of a Venetian they had commenced to build quite near Boulogne harbour, with the object of stopping the English ships from approaching. For the constructing of this bulwark the French have already 6,000 footmen in the field, and a large number of horse. But really these people (the French) are withdrawing as much as they can from the war with England, having by means of intermediaries arranged for the Emperor to negotiate a truce between them and the English. The Dauphin will not consent to a truce, as he says it would be too shameful;

1545.

and no one knows at present what will happen. It is said that the truce is being sought, in order that they (the French) may be the better able to put pressure upon the Emperor to fulfil the clauses of the treaty of peace (of Crépy): but the distress in the country is very great, and the result to be expected from the war doubtful and dangerous. M. de Vendome with a good force recently revictualled Ardres and also Thérouanne, where the need was very great. As Vendome's force was the stronger, the English could not prevent this.

Intelligence arrives here that in Scotland the nobles and the people are at issue, the nobles for the most part siding with the English, whilst the people at large are in favour of the French and the Queen (of Scots). There is hope of a settlement being arrived at with the English, and the King of England goes so far as to propose a marriage between his son the Prince and the Princess (*i.e.*, Queen) of Scots, the prince to be held by the Scots as a pledge. Whatever he may negotiate, however, it is not believed that the King of England will ever give up his son.

This King has caused to assemble at Melun twelve of the wisest men in his realm, to discuss the opinions of the protestants, in order that they may subsequently attend the Councils General. These personages entered upon their dispute six weeks since, after the celebration of Mass; and they displayed outwardly great signs of devotion.

The King of France has brought forward the marriage of the Prince of Piedmont* with Madame Margaret, holding out hopes to the Duke of Savoy that he shall be favourably dealt with afterwards, and that all subjects of dispute between them shall thus be overcome. The King and Queen of Navarre† have again arrived at this court, and are still pressing the King (of France) to treat for a marriage between the Prince of Savoy and their daughter. They hope, in this case, that the daughter of France (*i.e.*, Margaret) may marry the eldest son of the King of the Romans. In order to render the chances of both suitors equal, it is said that the Emperor is summoning the said Prince of Piedmont to his side.

Count William of Furstenburg‡ has been put to ransom for 30,000 crowns, and it is said that the Emperor has fixed for the Prince of Roche sur Yonne the same ransom. People here resent this very much, as they say the Prince is poor; and yet they have never admitted the force of the same reason with regard to the Count.

---

* Emanuel Philibert, afterwards Duke of Savoy. The match took place many years later. At the time this letter was written, a considerable portion of Piedmont was occupied by the French, but by the treaty of Crépy, some fortresses were to be returned to Savoy after the Duke of Orleans had entered into possession of the Duchy of Milan.

† Marguérite of France, sister of Francis I., had married Henry d'Albret, titular King of Navarre. Their daughter here mentioned was the famous Jeanne d'Albert who up to the time of the peace of Crépy had been nominally betrothed to the Duke of Cleves. She afterwards married Antoine de Bourbon, Duke of Vendome, and by him became the mother of Henry IV. of France.

‡ In an earlier page of this volume it was suggested that Count William might have been one of the Nassaus. After the proof had been sent to press this was found not to be the case. Furstenberg had been captured by the French as he was attempting to guide the imperial forces across the Marne below Chalons.

1545.

Forty five warrants have recently been issued to as many captains to raise 500 footmen each, so that they may be ready when they are wanted, by which they mean the war with England if it recommences.

There has been in the Court of France a Spanish captain named Guzman, who solicited for a long time employment in the French service against the English, for which purpose he offered to bring 2,000 Spaniards, either those who were sent to Hungary for the King of the Romans or the others who were on their way home to Spain from Flanders by sea. He was long delayed without a reply, but his offer has now been accepted; and he has gone to raise the Spaniards. The French complain that many Spaniards who should have gone home to Spain by sea have remained in England; and they cannot avoid supposing that this was with the consent of the Emperor.*

It is said that the Emperor will furnish the King (of France) with 25,000 crowns a month in aid of the war against the English whilst the war lasts or else Italian infantry to a similar value. The commander of this infantry will be the nephew of the Pope, who is at present in the Court of France.

The Counts of Brienne and Roussy, brothers, who were taken prisoners at Ligny, recently proclaimed by sound of trumpet in Paris, that if any person denied that they had done their duty for the defence of Ligny, or otherwise impugned their honour, they would meet him in combat. Up to the present no one has accepted the challenge. Since the peace was signed the King of France sent a gentleman of Avignon to the Turk, to inform him that it was not a peace that he had concluded with the Emperor but only a truce, which he (the King of France) was obliged to grant by reason of the presence of two powerful (foreign) armies in his dominions. The recall of Barbarossa he said had given a great advantage to his (the French King's) enemies. The Turk, however, had been informed to the contrary and has imprisoned the ambassador, granting letters of reprisal against the French.

News has arrived here, confirmed by advices from Venice that the Turk recently left Constantinople for Adrianople, and before his departure, as an indication that he intended to undertake some notable enterprise, he visited the mosques, where he offered many sacrifices of animals, and worshipped at the shrines of his ancestors. He also took with him most of his treasure; and it is concluded from all this, that he will this year go against Vienna. It will, however, be necessary for him first to subdue the island of Komorn, where the King of Hungary has placed seven or eight thousand foot-soldiers to defend the point, which is of the greatest importance to him. There is a rumour that M. D'Orleans is to go to see the Emperor at Worms when the King has recovered. The prince is already making ready.

The Admiral of France and other captains have been very busy lately studying the marine charts, it is said planning the attack on

---

* A consideration of the earlier pages of this Calendar, and of the Spanish Chronicle of Henry VIII. will show that the mercenaries entered the English service against the wish of the Emperor. There were fully as many in the French service as in that of England.

1545.

England. But the Admiral has since fallen ill of gout, and is much troubled by an abcess behind the right ear. It has been necessary to make an incision and he is now better. But for the King of France's illness, the Spanish Jacobin friar who intervened in the peace* would already have been sent to the Pope to urge the latter to influence the Emperor to declare against England, and abandon his alliance with a King who is in rebellion against the church: and if the war with England is continued the friar will go.

The King ordered the captain who surrendered Boulogne to be arrested, but he escaped to England, the archers who were sent to arrest him having by mistake addressed themselves to his father-in-law, M. de Biez, and in the meanwhile the captain fled. He is accused of betraying the town; but withal, he defended it for 9 weeks without a bullet or a pound of powder, after having received 140,000 cannon shots.†

Notwithstanding all the (imperial) ambassador's efforts to obtain a revocation of the (French) letters of marque and reprisal against the Portuguese granted before the war, his efforts have been unavailing. The King of France has been informed on behalf of the Emperor that these letters of marque are a violation of the good understanding arrived at in the treaty of peace, as they can only be rendered effectual by force; though the King of Portugal is included in the treaty of peace, and should have the benefit of it.

After the conclusion of the peace the French took two vessels belonging to the Duke of Alburquerque; and the (imperial) ambassador has been pressing for a long time by orders of the Emperor for the restoration of these ships and their contents. He has however only been able to obtain the reference of the question to the Admiralty. The pretext adopted for the capture is that at the time the Duke was in the service of the King of England; and could not depart therefrom in consequence of the oath he had taken. The Duke denies this, and says that his intention was simply to pass through England on his way to Spain, his arrangement with the English having been made by express command of the Emperor.‡ By the treaty of peace the Princess D'Albret had to sign in authentic form the protest she made that it was not her intention to marry the Duke of Cleves.§ Immediately afterwards she accordingly sent the protest duly signed by her and others and witnessed by two notaries. The Duke of Cleves is not satisfied with this, and has insisted in the name of the Emperor that she should solemnly make her declaration in the presence of some Cardinals, and this has now been consented to by the King of France.

---

* This was Martin de Guzman, a monk of Soissons and a relative of the Emperor's confessor. He had been the instrument of the Duchess d'Etampes in approaching the Emperor through de Granvelle.

† This was Vervins, who although he escaped to England on this occasion, was, on his return to France in the following reign, executed for his surrender of Boulogne, which had greatly enraged the Dauphin (Henry II.)

‡ The engagement of the Duke of Alburquerque as adviser to Henry during the siege of Boulogne and the loss of his baggage and horses here referred to is fully described in the "Spanish Chronicle of Henry VIII."

§ It was important to Cleves and his new friend the Emperor that his engagement with Jeanne D'Albret should be formally cancelled, as he was about to become betrothed to a daughter of Ferdinand King of the Romans. Charles' brother and successor as Emperor.

1545.

The ambassador has also been pressing the King of France for the surrender of Stenay to the Duke of Lorraine, in accordance with the treaty, as the King, who might demand the demolition of the fortifications, wished to demolish them after he had surrendered the place. To this the imperial ambassador replied that the demolition must take place before the town was given up; so that the surrender might be complete and unconditional. The King of France at length consented to this, but the Duke of Lorraine complains that the old buildings have also been destroyed, which they should not have been; and the matter is now at a stand; the Duke refusing to accept Stenay in its present state. The Emperor has sent a gentleman thither to inspect and report.

There is also a dispute about the surrender of the town and castle of Cahors, in Piedmont near Pigneroli, which the Emperor says were captured after the truce of Nice, whilst the King of France insists that he was master of them before the truce. They say here that the French case will be proved before the Tribunal of accounts of Piedmont.

With regard to the Duke of Cleves' affair, mentioned above; when the Emperor had been informed of it he declared that he would be satisfied if the Princess made her protest before a bishop. This has been accepted on this side, and the protest will accordingly be made when the Princess returns to this Court, where she is shortly expected, she having been summoned from Alençon, where she was. The King and Queen of Navarre are already here.

The rumour runs here that the Emperor was making great preparations both in Spain and Italy for his expedition against Algiers, and Count de la Mirandola was in great fear that some soldiers who were in Lombardy were sent for the purpose of besieging his place. The King of France has consequently been making great efforts to get the Count included in the peace. At last, only six days ago, the Emperor wrote to the King that he was willing to refrain from attacking the Count, until it was decided by legal progress whether or not he held Mirandola by right. It is therefore expected that the matter will shortly be decided in the presence of Commissioners to be sent by the Emperor.

M. de Sedan, heir of the late Robert de la Marche, and the Queen of Scots, for her realm, are also begging to be included in the peace; and the King (of France) is urging these petitions on his Majesty, who has not yet decided one way or the other. With regard to Scotland, however, he says that as a preliminary, the injuries and losses suffered by his subjects at the hands of the Scots must be made good, they having been the cause of the war that was declared against Scotland.

The English some time since arrested several ships belonging to the Emperor's subjects, and all English property in the Netherlands had accordingly been embargoed. It is now understood that restitution has been made on both sides; and a new treaty has been signed, ensuring unmolested navigation to the subjects of both princes.

The French are at present putting into the field six or eight thousand infantry with a number of horse, to defend a bulwark

1545.

that they are raising just near Boulogne harbour, to prevent the revictualling of the place by the sea.*

During the last week it is again announced here that the war against the English will be recommenced this year. The chief commander is to be the Admiral, who they say will go to Scotland with 14,000 French infantry, 8,000 lansquenets with a good number of Swiss, and 3,000 Spaniards they expect to obtain through Captain Guzman and another Captain called Bartolomé del Real. The latter was appointed a gentleman of the (French) King's chamber a fortnight ago, and left court ten days since for Bilbao, in order to obtain as many ships as he can, and to load them up with Spanish wine and other provisions, as well as a number of foot soldiers, all of which he will take to join the French when they are at sea against the English. He (del Real) is an extremely tall man with a red face. He has promised to send men to England to report what forces the King (of England) can muster to resist the French. The Emperor has already been informed of this. The Emperor will shortly summon the Prince of Piedmont to his Court, and this may frustrate the plan of those Frenchmen to marry him. The Queen of Navarre also wants him for her daughter.

Those who have been deputed to go to the Council (of Trent) have taken leave of their congregations, and are making ready to go to the Council.

Rançon's nephew arrived here last week from Constantinople. He reports that the Turk was preparing for the expedition against Vienna for this year. The King (of France) is sending this news to the Emperor. But other reports say that the Turk is still in doubt, in view of the peace, and will only send troops to Hungary for defence.

The King left Fontainebleau yesterday for Blois, whither he will go by short stages. His health is still doubtful, and it is said that some time ago an abcess was cut from his lower parts.

No date.†
Simancas.
E. A. 641.

116. STATEMENT OF AFFAIRS sent by SECRETARY IDIAQUEZ (to Spain).

Cardinal Farnese has returned to Rome. He acted well with regard to the matters discussed with him.

The Pope is strongly in favour of the employment of force against the Protestants, and highly praises his Majesty's intentions in this respect. He agrees to help with 200,000 crowns in money, and gives hope of providing 100,000 more, and will contribute also 12,000 foot and 1,500 horse in his pay.

He will also grant to his Majesty the half-first fruits of Spain, and power to sell the monastic vassals (manors?) to the amount of 500,000 ducats; but he raised great difficulty about the latter, saying that it would be necessary to consider the recompense for the revenue which must be as secure as at present; and care must

---

* This would appear to have been "Chastillons garden," a fort on the south side of the harbour.

† The document at Simancas bears no date, but its contents point to its having been dispatched in the first days of August from Worms, as it contains the intelligence belonging to the month of July.

1545.

be taken not to interfere with the sites of the monasteries themselves.

This decision was accepted, and his Majesty undertook to make arrangements as soon as he left here (Worms?) for that was the most necessary of all things, since he was now in the midst of Lutherans, and must go to Ratisbon and Bavaria before they (the Protestants) learnt what was being arranged. They are already very suspicious, as they hear of the necessary preparations being made. It is true that the season is already very far advanced to undertake the affair this summer; but his Majesty did not care to raise difficulties (*i.e.*, to the Pope's envoy), and answered that, so far as he was concerned, there would be no shortcoming, as soon as his Holiness had provided his part. The Cardinal then left. He was urged that the Pope should at once deposit the 200,000 crowns, which would be necessary at the commencement, pending the raising of funds by his Majesty, by means of bills, and advances on the half-first fruits, and sale of the monastic manors. He was also reminded of the further 100,000, and was told, that if the war lasted longer than was at present provided for, the Pope must maintain his aid for the time of its duration. Juan de Vega[a] was also written to that he must use the utmost diligence in getting the Bull for the first fruits and the monastic manors sent off without delay; so that money may be raised on them immediately they come.

When Farnese had gone to Rome with this, it was seen, on consideration, how difficult, and indeed impossible, it was to raise the money needed in time. No bills could be obtained nor could funds be so speedily raised on the ecclesiastical concessions, and without funds, of course, nothing could be done. Even if the Spanish infantry in Italy, and the Pope's contingent could arrive in time, and Germans could be got, the cavalry, which would have to be brought from Gueldres and the Low Countries, would necessarily be long delayed; and, in no case, could the army be got together before the middle of September; and after that the wet and cold weather would stop warlike operations in this country (Germany). To begin the enterprise without being able to carry it through would be simply to waste what it cost, whilst the enemy would be put on the alert; and would gain courage, and become more obstinate and irrepressible than ever.

His Majesty did not like this view of the question at all, but was forced to admit its justice, and Dandolo was sent, on the pretext of visiting the Duchess of Camerino, and congratulating her on her pregnancy, his mission really being to convey the above views to the Pope, and to ask his opinion, whilst at the same time assuring him that, if there was time and possibility, his Majesty was willing to begin the enterprise at once. It was suggested that it would be best to draw up a regular treaty between the Pope and his Majesty, to be passed by the Consistory; so that we might be sure, in any case: and as their own interests—or rather those of the house of Farnese—are most likely to influence them, his Majesty has promised always to favour and protect them (*i.e.*, the Farneses), especially in the matter of Parma and Plasencia (Piacenza),

[a] Spanish Ambassador in Rome.

5.

which the Pope was anxious to transfer to the Duke of Camarino, as fiefs of the Church, without any allegiance to the Empire. Juan de Vega has been instructed to slacken or tighten the rein on the part of the Emperor, in this respect, in accordance with their behaviour in the other matter.*

The Pope's reply has now been received. His Holiness would have preferred that the enterprise should have been carried through this summer, but admits the justice of the difficulties raised to this, and it is therefore deferred to next year. In the meanwhile, he was preparing the Bulls. Before the Pope's reply came, as it was seen that the enterprise was impossible for this year, the question of the suspension of the Diet was considered. It was decided to arrange a recess, appointing a colloquy for ———† or All Saints; and to summon a Diet for the Sovereigns later, at which his Majesty would be present. There is a hope also of being able to alienate from the Lutherans the two or three of the principal cities. As soon as the recess is agreed upon, his Majesty will return to Flanders to set matters in order there, which is said to be necessary, though it is inconvenient for German affairs that he should be absent from here.

The King of the Romans and Hungary will have plenty to do. Even during these negotiations for a truce, the Turks have over-run Styria from Dalmatia, and have done a good deal of damage. The Duke of Lorraine died recently, leaving sons, though a brother of his wishes to take charge of the government of the State. He openly confesses that he will appeal for French aid, and the Emperor took measures, even before the late Duke died. It is a troublesome business, but it is hoped that a settlement may be arrived at, for otherwise difficulties may arise; and on his way to Flanders his Majesty will see to this.‡

With regard to France there is nothing to say; except that both French and English are hard at it, by land and sea, whilst both of them plunder Spanish shipping. Redress is scanty: but his Majesty is taking measures to bring about a settlement, and thus to ensure himself.

(The rest of the communication, 2 pages, is occupied by Italian affairs and others with no relation to England or Protestantism.)

---

* The sudden rallying of Paul III. and the Farneses to the Emperor's friendship, after many years of enmity, was solely prompted by the family ambition. The Pope desired to secure to his son Pier Luigi the sovereignty of the duchies of Parma and Piacenza, independent of the imperial suzerainty. The Emperor's troops occupied a considerable portion of the territories in question; and the Farneses tried by cunning to gain what it was evident they could not win by force. Pier Luigi Farnese was to be succeeded in the duchies by his second son Ottavio Duke of Camarino, who had married Margaret the illegitimate daughter of the Emperor (afterwards the famous Duchess of Parma, governess of the Netherlands). Pier Luigi was murdered in 1547 by the Emperor's friend and Viceroy Gonzaga: and when the Pope's estrangement from the Emperor was again complete, the new Duke Ottavio rallied entirely to his father-in-law's side; the new Pope Julius III. confirming him in his duchy, to which his son Alessandro Farnese eventually succeeded.

† Blank in original.

‡ *See* note page 195.

1545.
No date.*
Simancas.
E. F. 501.

117. PRINCE PHILIP to the EMPEROR.

Many thanks for informing me of the state of public affairs, and especially of the arrangement with the Pope. Delighted to see the goodwill of the latter to aid your Majesty, particularly in the submission of the Protestants, so necessary as it is to Christendom. Your Majesty, I am sure, will have duly considered the difficulties of so great and arduous an enterprise. From here (Spain) we can do no more than beseech Our Lord ardently to grant to his Holiness and your Majesty the means and forces necessary for gaining so immense a boon; and to pray your Majesty to take care, as we doubt not that you will do, that what you undertake in this matter must be undertaken with forces sufficient to ensure success. For its success, amongst other things, it will be necessary, as your Majesty says, to make use of the aid and support promised by the Pope. But these things sometimes fail, and, in such case, the whole weight and responsibility would fall upon your Majesty.

We have noted and considered here the discussions in the States of the Empire, the delay that has taken place on the part of the King of France with regard to the alternative marriage, and your Majesty's efforts to mediate between the Kings of France and England, and to bring about an honourable peace, whilst preventing the injury suffered by your dominions by the war. Everything has been done with your Majesty's customary prudence and judgment: and we may hope that all will, by God's grace, go on well, in order that your Majesty may be free to employ your holy zeal in His service. Your Majesty has been wise in summoning the Duke of Alba; for his ability and experience in affairs and his ardent desire to serve your Majesty well, cannot fail to make his presence with you advantageous; although he will be missed here; especially now that the Cardinal of Toledo† has died. But German affairs at present are more important, and the Duke is leaving, in order to arrive by the time your Majesty indicates. It is unnecessary for me to supplicate your Majesty to favour him, as he merits. Personally my obligation to him is great for the care he has displayed in matters here, both public and private.

With regard to the ships and merchandise captured by the French and English, your Majesty's instructions shall be followed, your Majesty's communication having been handed to the Councillors for their guidance. Still it would be well for your Majesty to keep your hand in the matter there, expressing annoyance at the injury done to your subjects, and endeavouring to obtain redress. No more has been heard about the ships which it was said the French were fitting out for the Indies; but if anything further is learnt we will let your Majesty know. The ambassador in France gave us due advice of what he wrote to your Majesty on this matter, and with regard to his negotiations with the King and Council about the convicts captured by Don Bernardino de Mendoza.

---

* The draft at Simancas bears no date, but as the contents are a reply to the information contained in the Emperor's letter of 2nd August (p. 213), the present letter must have been written early in the same month.

† Cardinal Tavera, who had been appointed with Cobos Philip's mentor in the Regency, when Charles left Spain in 1543.

HENRY VIII.   229

1545.
No date.°
Simancas.
E. F. 501.

118. Francisco de los Cobos to the Emperor.

With regard to affairs of State I refer your Majesty to his Highness' letter of reply: but I am very anxious about the position of affairs, more especially with regard to the remedy to be applied to Germany and the Protestants. As they are so numerous and obstinate great trouble will be experienced in any case, unless God in His mercy subdues them. I am quite convinced that before your Majesty decided upon the course you indicate, you will have considered maturely the great difficulties which will have to be encountered.† His Highness is also answering your Majesty about the ships that the French and English have captured, and about other warlike matters. With this and the Duke of Alba's report, your Majesty will be fully informed; and I therefore do not enlarge upon these points. It has seemed to me very necessary that the Duke of Alba should go to your Majesty. He will, it is true, be missed here, both in war preparations and ordinary business. If we were at war his presence here would be more necessary than it is. But still it is important that he should serve your Majesty there (*i.e.* in Germany) which he will do with prudence, experience and zeal. His needs are still great; and since your Majesty's departure he petitioned to be allowed to sell 200,000 crowns of revenue secured on his estates. He has had difficulty in raising funds to start on his journey, but is now departing full of zeal to serve your Majesty.

7 Aug.
Paris
Arch. Nat.
K. 1485.

119. St. Mauris to Francisco de los Cobos.

I wrote you a long letter recently by a man sent by the Portuguese ambassador resident here. I have since received your letter of 17 July, informing me of the death of our Princess‡; which intelligence I conveyed at once to the King (of France). He said he deeply regretted the sorrow that had fallen upon the Emperor and the Prince; but, since it had been sent by the will of God, it behoved us to turn this misfortune to some good account.§ This was repeated several times in general terms: God rest the soul of our good Princess.

Nothing of importance has happened here, except that the Admiral is at present with the fleet in Boulogne-roads, between Calais, Boulogne and Dover, thus preventing succour from reaching Boulogne. Up to the time of his (the Admiral's) coming thither the English had always had free entrance to, and exit from, Boulogne both by land and sea. It is said that they (the English) have discovered a new approach, and that the fort that is being constructed on this side cannot do them much damage. But still,

---

° The document bears no date, but it was evidently written at the same time as the preceding letter from Philip.

† It is evident from the tone of this letter and of the preceding one from Philip to his father, that the Emperor's decision to take up arms for the purpose of crushing Protestantism was not approved of by Cobos, upon whom would fall the burden of providing from already exhausted Spain the vast sums needed for the Emperor's project.

‡ Maria of Portugal the young wife of Prince Philip, who had died in childbed after the birth of the unhappy Don Carlos.

§ The meaning of this was that already Francis was thinking of a marriage between Philip and Margaret of France.

230 SPANISH STATE PAPERS.

1545.

the English dare not face the French fleet at sea, so they keep in their harbours. The Emperor is to leave Worms on the 10th instant.

Caudebec, 7 August, 1545.

10 Aug.
Vienna
Imp. Arch.

120. VAN DER DELFT to the QUEEN DOWAGER OF HUNGARY.

Just as I was mounting to go from this place (Petworth), where the King has been staying for three days, to visit the house of the Master of the Horse,* whither the bishop of Winchester and Secretary Paget were courteously taking me for a pleasure trip, the King sent to inform me that one of his servants who usually purchases harquebusses for him had recently had 408 (harquebusses) sent from Italy. They arrived at Antwerp some months since, consigned to another of his servants named Pedro Paulo Bezana, and were packed first in cases and then in great barrels; being declared in the Customhouse by the consignee as barrels of sugar. The fraud was discovered and the director of the Custom house confiscated the harquebusses in consequence, refusing to listen to any proposal for restitution. As, continued the King's message, he had permission from the Emperor and your Majesty to transport through the Emperor's dominions such harquebusses, on condition that it was done in such secret fashion that the French should not know of it, for this reason the arms had been declared by his people as barrels of sugar, as had been done before to the extent of 3,000 harquebusses, and he (the King) therefore begged me to mention the matter to your Majesty, in order that you might give instructions for the restitution of the sequestrated arms and their passage hither with 5,000 more that are ready for despatch. In accordance with the King's request I submit the point to your Majesty's pleasure.

Petworth, 10th August, 1545.

14 Aug.
Vienna
Hof. Cor.

121. HENRY VIII. to the QUEEN DOWAGER OF HUNGARY.

The writer is despatching to Flanders "Sir Ralph Fane knight, lieutenant of our Gentlemen Pensioners, and Master Francis Hall, controller of the town of Calais, together with the governor of our merchants, and two other gentlemen of our household," as his commissioners for the management of a certain matter there. Begs the Queen to aid and favour them in the performance of their mission.

Our Manor of Petworth, 14 August, 1545.

17 Aug.
Vienna
Imp. Arch.

122. VAN DER DELFT to the EMPEROR.

Since my last, written from Portsmouth, I have still continued to follow the King in his progress. His Majesty has done me all possible honour, inviting me several times to accompany him in hunting, which invitations I have always accepted; and have received many proofs of favour and affection from the King, who constantly holds kind and familiar conversation with me. On my arrival at this place (Guildford) I received your Majesty's letters of

---

* Sir Anthony Browne.

1545.

the 6th instant, with the enclosure touching the three points dealt with in my previous letters: namely, the raising of the embargo on the ships, the negotiations for peace, and the aid demanded as a consequence of the French invasion. Enclosed with your Majesty's letter I also received one from the Queen Dowager of Hungary, ordering me to use every means to obtain further enlightenment as to the feeling of the English with regard to these points, pending the dispatch by her of the personage who is to come hither to exhort this King to conclude peace. By this means it was hoped that, when the personage in question arrived here, he might be the better informed as to the course he should take. Your Majesty's despatch arrived opportunely, as the King had on the same day sent to invite me to accompany him in hunting. I duly attended the appointment, and took care to refer to the contents of the aforementioned letters, in the first place to Secretary Paget, who is the most influential person here, and afterwards to the King himself. They were both very well pleased with your Majesty's decision to furnish the aid, and to send the personage hither; but when I came to the ratification (i.e., by Henry) of your Majesty's treaty with France, they raised the difficulty mentioned in your Majesty's letter as having been brought forward recently by the English Ambassador; so that, as they said, they did not see their way to accept the said treaty of your Majesty with France with the reservation mentioned in it of your treaty with England. I did not know what reply to make on this point, as I was not acquainted with the scope of the reservation clause, not having in my possession a copy of the treaty and being ignorant of its provisions, as I recently informed your Majesty. I said, however, that speaking unofficially, I thought that your Majesty intended the King to approve of the treaty with France, in order that he might be in a position to benefit by the reservation contained in it as regards the aid: and that your Majesty's treaty with England would remain in full force against all powers, in so far as it did not run counter to your treaty with France.

To this he replied that he did not understand which treaty I was referring to, as if to signify that he thought your Majesty had several treaties with France.[*] It was finally agreed that our views should be put in writing for the King's information, and he would reply. We then entered into discourse about the peace, seeing that the cessation of this war would banish all the scruples.

I remarked that I thought it opportune and necessary that peace should be discussed; and that your Majesty was earnestly desirous of bringing about a settlement, your Majesty's ambassadors being already on the road both to him (Henry) and to the King of France; and every effort should be made, in the interests of Christendom at large, for the salvation of their respective subjects, and in order to avoid a further effusion of human blood. I urged the King to think over the means and preliminaries that might tend to that object, so that the ambassador might the sooner be despatched, and the great

---

[*] There was a secret treaty accompanying (and really explaining) the treaty to Crépy by which, as in the subsequent treaty of Cateau Cambresis. bound both monarchs to mutual aid for the extirpation of Protestantism. Henry and the Protestants already had an inkling of this.

1545.

boon of peace attained: and on these lines I continued, as opportunity occurred on the way, in order to sound the inclinations and views of the King and the Secretary as to an understanding. But I could gain no further guidance, beyond what I wrote in my former letters; except that I learnt, in strict confidence, that they were already in treaty with France through Mme. D'Etampes, who was managing the affair. The proposals the French made were the payment to the King (Henry) of his subsidy (pension) with the arrears, and 100,000 crowns as a ransom for Boulogne. But as the indemnity was very small and no mention was made of the cost of the war; and also, as I gathered, because the French in their last communication wished to include in the terms something about Scotland, the King (Henry) had cooled in the matter, and the negotiations had fallen into abeyance. The man who travelled backwards and forwards on these negotiations was one Bartolomé Compagni, an Italian merchant in London, who formerly came to see me about the affairs of Jasper Doulchy, and is at present at this Court. I do not know if he is waiting for some despatch. Anything further I can discover in the matter I will communicate to your Majesty.

With regard to the raising of the embargoes and the satisfaction of your subjects, the English are becoming every day more reasonable; and nearly everything has now been despatched.

Whilst looking on at the hunting I chatted with the Queen (Catharine Parr) who was very kind and gracious with me. She mentioned the death of the Princess of Spain (whom God rest), as also the King and Secretary Paget had done; but as I had no intelligence of the sad event, except the common rumour here, I replied that I had received no news.

With regard to the progress of the war since my last letters, I may report that the King's force put to sea, having, amongst others, 120 good fighting ships well equipped, firmly resolved and determined to give battle to the French; and it is announced here that they encountered them and a skirmish took place with the galleys, in the course of which the English sank a foyst[o] (fustè) and carried away the poop of a galley, without any loss on their side. The conflict was brought to an end by darkness; and the combatants lay to at night about two miles distant from each other. When morning came, however, and the English were preparing to renew the fight, they found no Frenchmen in sight. They had retired under cover of darkness, the English know not whither.[†]

In Scotland also the two armies have come in sight of each other. The Scots, seeing that these people (i.e., the English) to the number of 14,000 were ready to meet or pursue them (leur tenoyent myne et piedt) turned aside and avoided an encounter. Seeing this, the English appeared to have followed them up, and fallen on their rear, defeating a portion of them, the foreign troops in the service of this King being the principal actors in the scene. I know not,

---

[o] The foyst was a very long narrow galley with two masts carrying lateen sails. It was provided with 18 or 20 oars, and was manned by a crew of about a hundred.
[†] Lord Lisle (Dudley), Lord Admiral, had 84 ships under his command. The fleets met on the 15 August, in mid-Channel somewhere off Shoreham. See Lisle's own account of the engagement, State Papers Henry VIII., i 819, which agrees with this statement; and also that given by Lord Herbert of Cherbury.

1545.

Sire, when this will reach you, as the passage is difficult; but I thought best to write, pending the coming of the personage who is to represent your Majesty.

Guildford, 17 August, 1545.

August.
Vienna
Imp. Arch.

123. Letters patent from the Emperor in favour of the Councillor Cornelius Scepperus, ordering all the imperial officers to aid and forward him in every way on his voyage to England in the Emperor's service.

19 Aug.
Vienna
Imp. Arch.

124. CORNELIUS SCEPPERUS to PRESIDENT LOYS SCORS.

When I had arrived at Antwerp, as yet uncertain as to the road I should take to come hither (England) I learned from a sure source that it would not be possible for me to pass by way of Calais, as no passenger boat had left there for three weeks, in consequence of the close blockade maintained by the French galleys. Finding, however, at Antwerp a vessel loaded with sundry merchandise ready to sail for England, I made an arrangement with the master with the intention of coming over in her. In order not to lose any time, and as there was no wind blowing, I got into a little barge from Malines, and came to Flushing to await there the arrival of my ship from Antwerp, whilst I was making my arrangements for the voyage. Seeing, however, that the vessel was still delayed owing to the lightness of the wind, and there seemed to be no probability of my being able to come hither in her speedily, I took a boat on Sunday 16th instant; and, though there was no wind, we made some way that night with the tide; finally catching some wind from the N.N.W. about 10 o'clock on Monday. We then made such good efforts that on the same day we came to the English coast, and yesterday we arrived in this town of London, after suffering many troubles and annoyances, in consequence of having to lower our sails and give an account of ourselves to all sorts of warlike craft in the King's service guarding the Thames. There are many of them spread about in different directions, and we were consequently considerably delayed: and to make matters worse, when I arrived here I did not find the ambassador nor his wife nor anyone to represent him, at which I am annoyed (*que me vient mal à point*). I do not even know for certain where the King is, some maintaining that he is in the neighbourhood of Southampton, whilst others assert that he is elsewhere near Guildford, which is 25 miles from here. I shall go thither to seek him as soon as I can get post or other horses, which at present are not easily procurable, as there is so much demand for them; and the country and rivers are covered with soldiers coming and going.

I have no news I can write, as we saw at sea no fighting ships, either English or French; but on the river Thames and the coast many ships and small craft loaded with soldiers going towards Boulogne. I am informed that the Earl of Hertford left here very hurriedly by order of the King, but it is not known whither. The same thing is said about the Earl of Surrey. I find everyone very desirous of peace; but I do not know how it will be with the leaders. The others must dance to *their* tune. They say that on the 16th instant their ships of war put out from the harbours where they were lying, with the intention of seeking the French; and we were asked if we knew anything of the result. They are confident that an encounter has taken place; their only fear being the galleys, against which they are powerless, even when the weather is such as it is now. I will not fail to advise the Emperor of all that passes as soon as I can, and I beg you to excuse me to the Queen (Dowager) for not writing to her Majesty; having nothing to say.

London, 19 August, 1545, 7 o'clock.

21 Aug.
Vienna
Imp Arch.

125. CORNELIUS SCEPPERUS to the QUEEN DOWAGER.

I hope that your Majesty will have learned from the letter I wrote to the President (Scors) of my arrival in England, and I now proceed to report to your Majesty what has happened since. Just as I was about to mount horse the day before yesterday with the object of seeking the King, an Englishman came to me; one of those who last year went to the muster of Landenberger's troops at Liege. He had been despatched from the Court and was on his way to Flanders; and expressed great delight at my coming, only regretting that he could not remain here to entertain me. I asked him which way he was going, he answered, straight through to Antwerp, and thence to the muster of German troops near Siegen in the country of Westerwolt, adjoining Hesse, Cologne and Mayence, about four leagues from Confluence. There were, he said, 30 standards of foot-soldiers and 4,000 horse, with some pieces of artillery, to insure their passage from their mustering ground to the service of the King; and they had been paid beforehand. These forces, the gentleman in question was ordered to lead over French territory without touching the Emperor's dominions, to Calais or Boulogne; and, if by chance he was obliged to touch the Emperor's territory, it would only be for a very short time, and on a very small portion of it. He would, moreover, do no damage there, in any case, and would pay well for everything: that being the strict orders of the King and his ministers, besides his own wish. I asked him the name of the Captain of these mercenaries. He replied that it was one Frederick von Reissenberg: and when I told him I knew Frederick very well, which is true, and thought he was rather young for so important a command (my intention being to find out who had advanced him, and to learn if it had been managed by the Protestants), he, the gentleman, replied that Frederick had been well recommended by the Landgrave of Hesse, and had so well stated his case to the King and Council, that seeing that they had been cheated and abused by other Captains, such as the Bastard of Gueldres, who had not been recommended by any potentate, the King had decided to engage von Reissenberg. I asked the gentleman if the King and his Council had requested the Landgrave of Hesse to send them this or any other Captain for them to engage; to which he replied that they had not. The said von Reissenberg had simply brought a letter of recommendation from the Landgrave, stating, in effect, that he was a soldier, and was capable of leading into the king's service a considerable body of men, if it was desired. Otherwise he (i.e., the gentleman) knew nothing of

1545.

him, except that he spoke good Latin, which had helped him greatly here. I asked the gentleman which road these troops would take. He replied that von Reissenberg had told the King he knew of a road by which he could lead them in three days from Siegen into French territory, without touching the Emperor's dominions; though they would have to pass one portion of the territory of Liege, and bivouac twice in it only. I told him it was impossible; and he confessed that he himself knew nothing of the nature of the country; but said as it was not their intention to touch the Emperor's territories, they were assured of their passage, and would find guides and conductors with this end, determined that, where they did not get through by friendship, they would get through by force, following the example of Martin Van Rossem. I did not debate or question his assertions, in the first place because he told me all this as a great secret, and secondly because I was not well informed of the state of affairs here, as I shall be by and bye; but I could not omit to inform your Majesty of it. Frankly, I expect they will find themselves cheated by this Frederick; as they have been by the others; besides which, in my opinion, he is not a man capable of carrying through such an enterprise as that spoken of. Your Majesty will see by our other letters what the King replied to the exhortations of the Emperor's ambassador and myself in favour of peace.

Guildford, 21 August, 1545.

21 Aug.
Vienna
Imp. Arch.

126. SCEPPERUS and VAN DER DELFT to the QUEEN DOWAGER.

I, Scepperus, arrived at this place (Guildford) on the 19th instant, where I found the King staying. The bishop of Winchester and Sir William Paget, first secretary of the King, came and said that they had been authorised by the King to bid me welcome on his behalf. I asked them when his Majesty would accord us an audience; to which they replied whenever we desired one. I said, the sooner the better, and they seemed pleased, sending word to us an hour later fixing the audience for the next day at noon. We were duly received at the hour appointed, by the bishop of Winchester and Paget, who are the principal members of the Council, the Chancellor being absent and the Duke of Suffolk ill. They conducted us to the King, who received us very graciously with great demonstrations of delight. After I, Scepperus, had repeated to him your Majesty's affectionate messages, which he received kindly and wished your Majesty were in this country, that he might entertain you with hunting etc. etc. ......; I repeated to him the particulars of the mission with which I had been entrusted by the Emperor and your Majesty, in accordance with my instructions. I was careful to place clearly before him that which is set forth as the principal point of my mission in the instructions: namely that though his Imperial Majesty had no desire to press the King beyond his desires and inclinations; I exhorted him, for the reasons laid down in my instructions, to afford some opening by which peace might be concluded, and told him that the Sieur de Noirthoudt had been instructed to address the King of France in similar terms, both of us having been dispatched specially for the purpose.

1545.

He appeared to take it cheerfully and in good part, and replied that he thought he had lived hitherto in a way that would prevent anyone from saying that he was inordinately inclined to war, quite the contrary, indeed. He was not ignorant, either, of the troubles entailed upon Christendom by the war, and he bitterly regretted them; but we must bear in mind that he had been assailed, and his territories invaded by the King of France at Guisnes, Calais, and in this, his own island; and he was obliged to defend himself; defence, in such case, being permitted by every right, human and divine. He made a long speech at this juncture, reciting in detail the days and places upon which the French had descended upon his territories, and had been beaten with but little or no loss on his side. He found his own people, he said, determined and eager to fight the enemy wherever they could find him, and expressed himself delighted at the goodwill and affection of his people. So little had he feared the enemy, he continued, that he had not interrupted his accustomed pastimes and the pleasure of the chase, depending, as he did, upon the grace of God in his just quarrel, and upon the valour and affection of his subjects. It would also be found that after he had taken Boulogne which he had attacked out of consideration for the Emperor, his good brother (as he would always call him), he had made no further advance or invasion into French territory, and had given no further provocation to the enemy to assail him and invade his territories on all sides, as the French and their allies had done. He therefore thought that there was no special need for the Emperor and your Majesty to urge him to peace, since he had not sought war, but that the exhortation should rather be addressed to the King of France. He repeated that, up to the present, he had withstood the efforts and assaults of the King of France, and hoped shortly to be able to pay him back in similar coin, but more effectually; and he trusted with a better result than the French had obtained against him. He knew, he said, that the King of France was very short of money and men, and had been compelled by sheer necessity to abandon his enterprise, notwithstanding the weather that had been so favourable to him that it had been vulgarly called the "French God." As he (Henry) had witnessed the small result that had been attained by the King of France and his allies, with all their forces assembled, he no longer had the slightest fear of them: and, he added, if the Emperor had made any appearance of helping him (Henry) when the French were invading his Guisnes dominion (as he considered his Majesty was bound to do under the treaty of alliance, which was not prejudiced by the subsequent treaty between the Emperor and the King of France, even though he Henry had consented to it; which he maintained he had not done, notwithstanding the assertion of the bishop of Arras, about whom he muttered between his teeth) the King of France would not have dared to attempt what he had done, and his Imperial Majesty could easily have obtained from the King of France an absolution of the promises of marriage and territorial concessions made in the treaties. For, he said, there was more than one treaty as he knew very well, although he believed that we (*i.e.*, the ambassadors) were not aware of it. But he was perfectly certain that on account of those treaties some persons had been very heavily bribed with presents and money. As he said this he made signs with his hands and head as if he was counting money, manifesting sorrow at such a thing; and that by such means the King of France should have been able to free himself from apprehension of his Imperial Majesty. The latter, he said, would not attempt anything against these treaties, however just it might be to do so, although his Imperial Majesty would have the realm of England on his side, and, so to speak, at his disposal, a realm that had never failed him, and whose subjects were ready to risk their bodies and their possessions for him. This point brought him (Henry) on to his treaty with the Emperor, but he suddenly cut short that subject after a few words, saying that he would thresh that out with me, Van der Delft. He then reverted to the point now mainly under consideration, namely the peace negotiations, saying that he had no desire to hide from us that a discussion on the subject had taken place between him and the King of France, through Mme. D'Etampes, and it had advanced so far as for the King of France to promise to pay him (Henry) his pension and the arrears, together with a reasonable recompense for the recession of Boulogne, which should be satisfactory to him. But he (Henry) learnt afterwards that this recompense was only to be 100,000 crowns in one payment, which he said, half laughing, would not be enough for the pages; besides which conditions had been proposed to him concerning Scotland which were neither agreeable nor acceptable to him, and the negotiations were therefore entirely brought to a close. As for the future; the season was already so far advanced, and the galleys can no longer be of any service in these seas, that the winter itself would make peace; and he hoped that neither the Emperor his good brother, nor your Majesty, his good sister, having these facts in view, would urge or advise him to hand over to the King of France his conquest of Boulogne, which he had taken with great honour and heavy expense. He added that he could not make any suggestions for peace overtures. They should come from the French, who had assailed him and invaded his dominions, as the Emperor and your Majesty should recollect. For his part he was not yet tired of defending himself; and he expressed great joy that he had been able to measure his strength against that of his enemy. He continued, that if the Emperor liked, he (Henry) was quite sure that the King of France might again be brought so low as to be forced to consent to anything: but it could only be done by not allowing him time to regain his breath. He asked us to convey his answer to your Majesties. I, Scepperus, then replied to him, saying that he might be assured of the entire affection of the Emperor and your Majesty towards him, and that the intention of your Majesties was that in any peace negotiations his honour and prestige should be safeguarded. The principal reason which had moved the Emperor to send me to exhort him to peace was regard for the common welfare of Christendom, and more especially for the tranquillity of him (Henry) personally and of his realm and subjects; and the King of France had been addressed in similar terms. He (Henry) took this in very good part, and thanked the Emperor and your Majesty, in whom he seemed to have full confidence.

In view of this, even though he persisted that he could make no peace overtures, I, Scepperus, as if of my own motion, suggested whether, in order to promote such a peace and to give the Emperor more time to consider the best means of bringing it about when his Majesty arrived in Flanders, whither he was going principally with that object, he (Henry) would consent to a truce? He replied certainly not: he would either have peace or continued war, as he knew beyond question that the money provided by the bishops to his enemy the King of France was all spent, and a truce would not in any way advance the cause of peace. Finally, after further conversation, when we saw that we should get nothing from him beyond that which he had already said, we asked him if he wished us to communicate to the Emperor and your Majesty the reply he had given. He said yes; and begged us to do so. We have therefore thought well to report to your Majesty everything that passed, in order that we may not be blamed for omission in case the King should have sent a full report to his ambassador in Flanders. In conclusion, the King said he had not refused, and would not refuse, reasonable and honourable condition of peace; taking in very good part the expression we repeated to him, to the effect that the intention of the Emperor was not to put pressure upon him, or to favour one side more than the other.

By the above, Madame, your Majesty will perceive the change that has come over this country owing to the various successes they have gained over their enemies. In very truth, according to the judgment of the Spaniards, Italians and other foreigners, who have seen the musters of the English against their enemies, they deserve the highest praise and honour. The King himself took care to say as much, calling me, Van der Delft, to witness that the Admiral of France had not dared to await the approach of the English Admiral, but had retired after having made a demonstration of attacking.

Besides this, he said, on Friday last his (*i.e.*, the English) Admiral had found himself towards evening about a mile away from the French fleet, which he intended to attack on the morrow, but the French had slipped away secretly and fled during the night; so that at dawn, although his Admiral had made great efforts to find them, he could not see a single French ship. This has made them (the English) all very confident and they are not so much inclined to seek peace as they were when I, Van der Delft, sent my despatch of the 23th July to the Emperor, which was exactly the time when they were in fear of the result of the war, and distrustful of the power of the French fleet, which had appeared at the mouth of Portsmouth harbour, the King being on the flagship, and as he himself told us, not expecting the coming of the French.

We desired to have sent to M. de Noirthoudt an account of the King's reply in accordance with the arrangement made in your Majesty's presence and by your command, but we found the King so determined to prevent any excuse being given to the French, no matter from what quarter, to hint anything to the detriment of his reputation, such as might arise from the first message about peace going hence to France through us, that we thought it best to send our advice only to your Majesty.

1545.

With regard to Boulogne, we find that at the present time he (Henry) has no intention of giving it up; and will not listen to any proposal of a ransom. Indeed in conversation he called Boulogne "his daughter," and said she was not so hard pressed by pestilence and foes as I, Scepperus, had been informed on my road hither. The Councillors say that, in any case, they have 8,000 men on the other side of the sea ready to succour the place, without mentioning the troops coming to them from Germany. This is apparently the foundation of the king's expression that he would pay the French back in similar coin to their own, and with a better result than they obtained against him.

Touching the former negotiations for peace carried on by Bartolomé Compagni, which I, Van der Delft, have already reported to the Emperor in mine of 16th instant, I, Scepperus, recollected to have heard that a short fat man from Antwerp had been mixed up in the negotiations: and we found at this Court an advocate from Antwerp named Master Ringolt who is a short, fat man in the habit of frequenting the house of Bartolomé Compagni. According to our secret information the latter had suddenly left for France on the day that I, Scepperus, arrived at Court. But the day afterwards when we were returning from the Court we met him in the street, and we believe his voyage must have been abandoned; as Secretary Paget confidentially assured me, Van der Delft, that it had been. Paget said that the negotiation had not been commenced from any desire of theirs to come to terms with the French, but simply to cool the efforts of the latter against Boulogne, around which place, instead of five fortifications which the French said they were going to construct, only one has been commenced. The negotiations referred to were therefore considered to have been advantageous to the English, although the King himself, as he also informed us, had had nothing to do with them.

The King leaves Guildford to-day for his house at Hampton Court, 6 miles away. He is well. I pray your Majesty to instruct me, Scepperus, what further service I can do.

Guildford, 31 August, 1545.

21 Aug.
Vienna
Imp. Arch.

127. CORNELIUS SCEPPERUS to PRESIDENT LOYS SCORS.

By the accompanying letter from the Ambassador (Van der Delft) and myself to the Queen you will learn what has passed between the King and us; and you will see how little or no hope there is of peace overtures from this quarter. If such overtures do not come from their enemies, we are of opinion that nothing will be done. One good thing is that these folks do not love the French, and there is no sign of any secret understanding to the exclusion of the Emperor. This is certainly a great advantage. I have even heard from a source independent of the ambassador (Van der Delft) that the English Councillors are fully aware that the Emperor's dominions are so necessary to their welfare that they could not exist without them, and they believe that England is just as necessary to us.

The short fat man of whom you spoke to me before my departure is at this Court, and has not condescended to visit us once, although we saluted him, and he was opposite the ambassador's lodging when

I arrived. But, in any case, the whole intrigue has fallen through. I understand that this King's naval force consists of 16,000 men very well equipped, and it is increasing every day both in men and ships. They say the French fleet has completely withdrawn.

The efforts of the French on the Scottish side do not amount to much. It is true that the Scots raided into England and stayed for six hours only; but the English King's forces made such a show, that the Scots thought wise to go back, as they did with loss and shame. This King has his partisans in Scotland, both amongst the people of position and amongst the savages, of whom 8,000 have voluntarily entered his service. He therefore attaches little importance to the French being on the side of the Scots. There is news, too, that his troops have again beaten the Scots soundly, although the number of them was not large. All this puts his subjects in good heart to continue the war. The King ordered me to thank you on his behalf for the good offices you have done in his affairs, and I now do so, although I have no doubt he will also write letters of his own to the same effect. He has withdrawn to one of his pleasure houses, where there is neither a town nor a village for us to lodge in; and the ambassador and I have therefore come to this village of Mortlake (Maloch), where the ambassador has his residence very appropriately situated on the Thames, seven miles from London. We here await the good pleasure of the Emperor and the Queen (Dowager). I have written specially to the Queen, respecting the troops mustered near Confluence. They would be quite capable of crossing the Rhine and going through the territory of Cologne to Liege, thence touching a corner of Hainault, and so entering Artois; or else they might go round by the Ardennes, crossing the Meuse at Givey, and then entering Hainault, along the banks of the Somme; and thence towards Hesdin, so cutting off the French supplies of victuals. The French are in no condition to be able to contend with 30 standards of foot and 4,000 cavalry, besides having the English on their shoulders as well, unless they have been well forewarned and forearmed. Even then, they will have as much as they can do. I expect you know in Flanders the particulars of all this better than we do here, but I have thought well to send all that I have learnt for the information of her Majesty. The Councillors are keeping this matter strictly secret, and do not think that I know it. I prompted the ambassador to broach the subject to them, but they would not tell him the name of the colonel or commander of the Germans, and led him on a false scent.

I have not been able to learn that this King has allied himself with the Protestants, and in my opinion, he is very tractable and manageable with fair words. In all his conversations he has mentioned the Emperor and the Queen very respectfully; but he is not pleased with the treaty between the Emperor and the King of France, as you will understand when you have read our joint letter to the Queen. The merchants and rich citizens are very desirous of peace, but neither the common folk nor the gentry show any signs of such a wish. They are very well equipped and their artillery is much better than I could have believed if I had not seen it. Mortlake on Thames, 21 August, 1545.

HENRY VIII.

1545.
24 Aug.
Vienna
Imp. Arch.

128. CORNELIUS SCEPPERUS to PRESIDENT SCORS.

The Duke of Suffolk is dead,* and the Lord Admiral (Dudley) is increasing in influence. I understand that the Duke of Luxemburg, whose name is Francis and who was in the service of the Emperor before Cambresis, is to come hither shortly. They appear to be confident with regard to the passage of the Germans I spoke of. In addition to the man I referred to in my letter to the Queen they are sending over another commissioner named Ralph Fane, who was in Brussels last year about the Landenberger affair.†

For various good reasons, which I need not set down here, you will do well to have secretly seized and placed in safe keeping the person of Antonio Musica (?), a Spaniard whom you know. I understand that he is at present in Antwerp and writes constantly about things which he ought to avoid.

Mortlake, 24 August, 1545.

P.S.—We are here awaiting her Majesty's reply to our letters of the 21st. The King is in a solitary place. We propose to go to him as soon as we have anything to say.

31 Aug.
Vienna
Imp. Arch.

129. The EMPEROR to HENRY VIII.

Having heard that you have been pleased to recall your Councillor, Dr. Wotton, your ambassador to us, in order to employ him elsewhere, and that in his place you are sending the bishop of Westminster (Dr. Thirlby), we very willingly agree to this; although the former has always been extremely welcome to us, and has done his duty well and honestly. The bishop has been well received, and shall be duly respected in the discharge of his mission.

Brussels, 30 August, 1545.

1545.
Vienna
Imp. Arch.;

130. Memorandum headed: Suggestions that may be proposed to the King of England's ministers to attempt to bring about peace; or, failing that, a truce of long or short duration.

As the principal cause of dissension is Boulogne which the King of England will not abandon and the King of France insists upon obtaining, the following means of compromise may be suggested. The King of England might consent to retain Boulogne only until the King of France paid him in one sum 1,000,000 crowns of the arrears of pension. The King of France might undertake to pay from time to time the pensions as they become due and the balance of the arrears besides the million mentioned.

---

* Charles Brandon, who had been married to Henry's sister Mary, Queen Dowager of France. He had subsequently married Catharine Lady Willoughby D'Eresby, who survived him.

† For particulars of Fane's mission in 1544 and the discontent of the mercenaries under Landenberger, see Vol. VII. of this Calendar, pp. 209-215.

‡ The copy of this memorandum at Vienna is mis-dated 1538. It evidently, however, belongs to the period prior to the dispatch of the English and French plenipotentiaries to the Emperor and is consequently inserted here.

By these means Boulogne would practically remain for ever in the hands of the English as it is unlikely that the King of France could ever raise a complete million in addition to the current payments, for the restitution of the place, having regard to the state of his realm, and that his poor subjects have sustained the burden of this long war. The King of England might refuse to return Boulogne, or could take any other course that might appear advisable on the failure to pay any current instalment.

If the King of France insists upon the restoration of Boulogne it might be suggested that the above means would enable him to boast that he could have the place back whenever it pleased him.

If the King of France refused this suggestion, he might be induced to listen to the proposal that he should pay all the arrears up to 2,000,000 crowns in one sum or in short instalments, and give security to pay the current pensions as they fall due. If the King of France failed to pay the 2,000,000 in gold the King of England would retain Boulogne.

Another proposal is to try to induce the King of France to cede Boulogne in perpetuity to England in exchange for the abolition of the hereditary pension of 4,000 crowns: the life pension only being paid in future. If neither of these suggestions is at once acceptable to the princes, time might be gained for discussion by the arrangement of a truce. The princes should therefore be requested to give powers and instructions to their ambassadors resident with his Majesty (the Emperor) or others to be sent, to come to terms on this point if possible.

To induce the French ministers to listen, the most suitable way would be cautiously to point out the improbability of their being able to recover Boulogne by force and that the plan of attacking England through Scotland or otherwise is of doubtful result. In case of the invasion failing, the French would be burdened by the increased claims of the King of England, as well as the two pensions and arrears. The English fight well and would rather die than not defend their realm. All this must be considered, as well as the weakening of the Christian cause, to the advantage of the enemy of the faith. The loss of so many good lives on both sides, the harass and danger that must always attend war, fortune being so uncertain, make it advisable for the King of France to accept one of the above suggestions.

If nothing better can be done, efforts should be directed towards a truce. The French may be held that there is little appearance of their taking Boulogne by force, and a truce would be all in their favour as they would gain time by it, whilst affairs were proceeding and God ordained how the realm of England should fare after the death of the present King, who cannot live long and would leave a child to succeed him. Boulogne might then be recovered from his guardians with less difficulty than from the present King, who sets his heart on keeping the place as his own conquest. The truce also would save Ardres, which is in great danger from famine and plague. If Ardres be taken the English will be more obstinate than ever.

1545.
2 Sep.
Vienna
Imp. Arch.

131. The EMPEROR to SCEPPERUS and VAN DER DELFT.

We have deferred answering the joint letters you wrote to the Queen, our sister, on the 21st ultimo, until we had received news from the Sieur de Noirthoudt as to his proceedings with the King of France, in compliance with the instructions given to him, and especially in view of the fact that the King of England would make no overtures for peace on his side. On receipt of Noirthoudt's letter,* of which copy is enclosed with our reply to the same, we have decided in conformity therewith, that you should go to the King (Henry), and tell him it has given great pleasure to us and to the Queen, our sister, to learn of his good will and inclination towards peace, which further confirm our own; and will encourage us the more in our efforts to attain so desirable an end, for the good of Christendom at large, and by reason of the perfect amity which we bear towards the King. With this object we have informed you that the King of France had replied to our envoy M. Noirthoudt, setting forth the points stated in the letters enclosed, as a basis of peace negotiations. You will pray him (i.e., the King of England), since the King of France has thus made the first advance by stating his opinions as to the terms, that he (the King of England) will consider the various points and pronounce his views, in order that the negotiations may the better be promoted according to his wishes. You will obtain a clear expression of the King's views, as far as you can, upon each separate point, and even discover, if possible, whether he will listen to the retrocession of Boulogne, in exchange for a money indemnity, and if so of what amount. If you find he raises great difficulty in accepting a money payment you will suggest that it might be advisable to agree to an arrangement, by which Boulogne should remain in his hands for a certain fixed period, he binding himself to restore the place to the French after the expiration of the time, on the payment to him of an indemnity to be agreed upon. You will, however, be careful not to push this point so far as to give the King an excuse for saying that we advised him to accept a money payment. By the same rule, if you see any chance that the King will listen to a proposal for the surrender of Boulogne against a cash indemnity, you will make no mention of the above suggestion of leaving the place in his hands for a fixed period; but if either he or his Councillors bring such a proposal forward you will agree to convey the suggestion to us for transmission to the King of France. You will similarly ascertain, as far as you can, the King of England's views with regard to Scotland, and whether he wishes the King of France entirely to abandon the Scots; or if there is any means of including Scotland in the peace negotiations and upon what conditions. You will also inform yourselves as to the real point at issue between the King and the realm of Scotland, as we greatly doubt if the King of France would consent to abandon the Scots entirely.

If, peradventure, the King should raise any difficulty in declaring his views on the points, on the ground that they are

---

* Doubtless the letter without date from St. Mauris and Noirthoudt, tentatively ascribed to "August," and inserted on page 206 of the present volume.

1545.

too general in terms, you will point out to him that it will be extremely difficult for us to induce the King of France to be more precise, unless we can show some inclination towards an overture on the part of England. In order that we may effectually promote the negotiation we hope that, notwithstanding the general terms of the points submitted, he will give his views upon them; because the King of France having made the first approach, it will only be right that he (Henry) should make a reciprocal move, in order that the affair may be carried forward another stage. As soon as you have been able to ascertain that there is hope of a successful issue, you will see whether the King will consent to a conference, to which both monarchs would send ambassadors with full powers and instructions, either to our dominions or elsewhere; whither we ourselves, in the interests of peace, would willingly send our representatives as friendly mediators upon those points which were difficult of agreement. This, in our opinion, would be the best and shortest way to bring the peace to a successful issue. You will advise with all speed of what you can discover with regard to the King's views, and we will let you know what we can learn of the inclinations of the King of France.

Brussels, 2 September, 1545.

3 Sep.
Simancas.
E. R. 872.

132. SUMMARY OF INTELLIGENCE FROM ROME to the 3RD SEPTEMBER.

Cardinal Tournon writes to Cardinal Trivulciis* on the 17th ultimo, that the Duke of Orleans was going to Flanders to see his Majesty; and would bring back intelligence without further loss of time as to what would be done in Milan.† In the same letter and others, it has been stated here by the French that the King of England had sent to ask for peace; but from other advices from Flanders and Germany of the 13th, it appears that, although it is true that he was negotiating through a Florentine merchant called Bartolomé Compagni, there was no hope of a good issue, as the King's (of England) terms are very hard. The French greatly blamed the Admiral of France for the recent occurrence, when the English and French fleets were face to face. They say he might have done far more than he did.‡ The Pope learns from Cardinal Farnese that the French fleet has already withdrawn, and that the King of England had sent funds to raise 4,000 German horse; by the aid of which, and his English forces, he hopes to be able to compel the King of France to raise the siege of Boulogne. They are talking very ill here (Rome), and all over Italy, about the Pope, in relation to the Parma and Plasencia (Piacenza) affair; especially the French and Venetians. Neither Cardinal Armaignac, the former French ambassador, nor Cardinal Trivulciis attended the Consistory when the affair was discussed. The bishop of Burgos openly expressed his opinion in the Consistory with regard to Parma and Plasencia (Piacenza); saying that his Holiness ought not to do

---

* Cardinal Trivulcio was the French ambassador in Rome at the time.
† That is to say the Emperor's decision as to the alternate marriage and dowry.
‡ This was the encounter in mid Channel on 15 August, of which an account has already been given.

HENRY VIII.

1545.

as he proposed. He (the bishop of Burgos) gave reasons for his opinions, and was the only person present who spoke out thus clearly, although some others did not vote in favour of the proposal.

A courier on his way from Constantinople with letters of 13th and 14th July was stopped, and the letters he bore for the Seigniory of Venice alone were intercepted. This was effected by three or four unknown men, who met the courier three days' journey from Adrianople, and took the letters without injuring him in any way. The Seigniory is much annoyed and very suspicious.

11 Sep.
Vienna
Imp. Arch.

133. The EMPEROR to SCEPPERUS and VAN DER DELFT.

My Ambassador resident in France has informed me to-day for certain that the Duke of Orleans died on the 9th instant° at three in the afternoon and that as soon as the King of France learnt the news he ordered the ports and passes to be closed. There was a rumour that on the following day Cardinal Tournon and the Admiral of France were to leave hurriedly for the camps before Boulogne to be able to treat with the English from there. As both the parties have their forces mustered ready, they might perhaps make some agreement to our detriment, or to that of our Flemish dominions, especially as they know we are not prepared to resist them. We have therefore considered it necessary to send this courier with all speed to advise you, in order that you may, dexterously and by all possible means at your command, ascertain what chance there is of any such arrangement as that above suggested being made; and if so on what conditions. If you find that negotiations for an agreement are in forward progress you will declare confidentially to the King that we have been informed of the Duke of Orleans' death, and we are therefore more disposed than we have hitherto been to do something effectual (*pour faire quelque bonne œuvre*); and such is the constant and perfect friendship between us that we confide absolutely in him (Henry) not to treat or consent to anything to the prejudice of ourselves, our States, or subjects, which may be proposed to him on behalf of the King of France. We hope, on the contrary that he will have due regard to our amity, and to the faithful observance of the treaties between us. To this you will add all the fair words that you may think appropriate, according as you may perceive the King's tendency, and the chances of a treaty of peace being negotiated to our prejudice.

You will take careful notice of the King's expressions, and of the terms he and his Councillors employ in replying to you, giving us full information of everything by this courier. You will also ascertain, so far as you can, what the King intends to do with the troops he has in the neighbourhood of Confluence; and by what

---

° He died at Forêt Moutier near Abbeville, it was said of malignant fever or plague, but in this Calender it is stated in consequence of drinking cold water when he was heated. He had gone to Picardy with his brother the Dauphin to resist the passage of the German mercenaries in Henry's service under Von Reissenberg to raise the siege of Boulogne. The death of Charles of Valois, Duke of Orleans completely upset the arrangements made in the peace of Crépy, by which thanks to the Duchess D'Etampes, he was the principal gainer. It is evident from the Emperor's letters in this Calendar that he was anxious to avoid carrying out the stipulations in any case and the death of the young prince gave him a perfect excuse for doing so.

1545.

route he is going to send them. If you find that they are to pass by our territories, or through any corner thereof, you will lay before the King the injury that will be done to our subjects by the passage, and point out that there are other routes by which they could go to enter the enemy's country. You will say that we have full confidence that the King will not allow the troops to pass through our territories, and you will use such expressions in this respect as you may see necessary and efficacious; taking care, however, neither to consent nor altogether to refuse the passage of the troops by our lands. You must let the matter remain in terms that we are quite sure that the King will have the necessary regard for our friendship and the treaties between us. Send all the news you can, speedily.

Brussels, 11 September, 1545.

15 Sep.
Vienna
Imp. Arch.

134. VAN DER DELFT to the EMPEROR.

As, at the cordial and very pressing request of the King, M. D'Eick (*i.e.*, Scepperus) is now returning thither, your Majesty will hear from him fully and in detail the state of affairs here, both with regard to the subject of his own mission, and in respect of the other events and occurrences on this side. I do not therefore consider it necessary to trouble your Majesty with a long letter; but will only add that whilst M. D'Eick and I were in communication yesterday morning with the Councillors on the peace negotiations with France, the said Councillors declared that the reply to our representations, and the King's decision on the points and conditions submitted, would be given to us by the King personally after dinner. But nevertheless, they said the point at issue was not so much that; but rather the question of the aid which was to be furnished by your Majesty, in accordance with the treaty of alliance. The period had already passed by which the contingent should be here, counting from the time when the demand had been made, and they asked us if we had no news of its coming. M. D'Eick declined to enter upon the subject as it formed no part of his mission, but I replied that it was true that your Majesty had written to me the communication made to you by the English ambassador at Worms, and the answer given to him. I had myself discussed the matter fully with the King, laying down the conditions upon which your Majesty had consented to furnish the aid requested, one of which conditions was that they (the English) should confirm your Majesty's treaty with France, respecting which the King had replied to me that he did not know which treaty I referred to; but anything we wished him to do or approve of must be put in writing, and he would answer it. I had informed your Majesty of this on the 17th August, but had not yet received any reply, nor did I, indeed, expect one, as we had entered upon the discussion of this other matter (*i.e.*, the peace) which had quite changed the appearance of affairs. I made this an excuse for shelving the question; but they persisted, saying that the only conditions they knew anything about were those contained in the treaty of alliance, which took precedence of all others, past and future. They added that, since they had decided to pursue their enemy, who

1545.

had invaded their territories, no excuse could be alleged on behalf of your Majesty for not furnishing the aid until after the expiry of the four months stipulated in the treaty, which they offered to produce and show me. After some disputation I undertook to submit the matter to your Majesty, and I have therefore written these few lines, praying that after your Majesty has heard the full report of M. D'Eick, I may receive your commands on the subject. In the meanwhile it has seemed advisable to retain here the courier who has brought us the letters of your Majesty of 11th September conveying the news of the death of the Duke of Orleans (respecting the contents of which letters and the King's inclination thereon, M. D'Eick will report fully) in order that I may be able to communicate to your Majesty with speed any change that may be observable, and all other events that may occur.

Windsor, 15 September, 1545.

15 Sep.
Vienna
Hof. Cor.

135. HENRY VIII. to the EMPEROR.

During his conferences with the Emperor's special envoy, M. D'Eick, some suggestions of great importance have been broached. The writer has entrusted to M. D'Eick the mission of laying these before the Emperor; and he begs the latter to give to them his best consideration in the interest of the friendship and alliance that exist between the two princes.°

Windsor, 15 September, 1545.

15 Sep.
Simancas.
E. F. 501.

136. NEWS sent from FLANDERS by DON LUIS DE AVILA.

When the French fleet had left Boulogne the French who were before that place arranged with M. Dampierre, the Governor of Guisnes, the following plan. The garrison of Ardres, a French fortress, were to march up to the defences of Guisnes, which is held by the English, in order to induce the garrison of that fortress to sally and attack them. In the meanwhile it was arranged that the French army before Boulogne should place themselves in ambush and cut off the English garrison which was to sally from Guisnes. The force from Ardres marched out, as agreed upon, and the English from Guisnes duly sallied, as was expected, but as the force from the Boulogne army had not arrived the English garrison routed the men from Ardres and killed M. Dampierre, driving the fugitives back to Ardres.† As the English were returning in triumph they met the French troops from Boulogne who had at length arrived. The English were worsted in the ensuing fight; and the Guisnes men, after all, were contented with the day's work. Whilst the French army from before Boulogne had marched to Guisnes, the

---

° The secret negotiation with which Scepperus was sent backwards and forwards several times was the arrangement of a meeting between Charles and Henry. When the former found that the object was to pin him more tightly to the clauses of the treaty of alliance, which he had hitherto so cunningly evaded, he found excellent reasons, as will be seen in the documents, for declining the proposed interview. The whole negotiation is an excellent specimen of the insincere and selfish nature of the Emperor's diplomacy.

† An interesting account of this exploit by Lord Grey de Wilton will be found in Hollingshead.

1545.

English troops in the former town made a sortie, and entered the trenches of the fortress that the French are constructing, killing the sappers and 300 Swiss and Germans. They would have captured the fortress itself, if prompt reinforcements of French had not arrived.

The English fleet is still the master of these waters. It has burnt some French villages and sixteen French vessels. The English have thus still their foot on the neck of the French.

[*Spanish holograph.*]

18 Sep.
Vienna
Imp. Arch.

137. VAN DER DELFT to the QUEEN DOWAGER.

At this instant, supper time, the bishop of Winchester and Secretary Paget came to me and said that they had received the worst possible news that could come to them. They then proceeded to relate it to me, commencing by saying that, as I knew, they were at war at great expense; and as their coin was not current at the face value they were obliged to make use of their friends in Flanders. The King had accordingly agreed with the Fuggers in Antwerp to raise a certain sum of money by exchange, for the purpose of paying the German troops who had been engaged by him. He had already sent to order these troops to pay for everything down to the last penny and to march without doing the slightest damage or wrong to any subject of the Emperor or other friends; promising them (the troops) that money would be provided for them. And now just as they (the English) intended to utilise the money delivered by the Fuggers, the Margrave of Antwerp, by order of your Majesty, had embargoed the funds. Their own people, they said, had seen the order. They are very much aggrieved at it, especially at the present juncture and make great ceremony and complaint about it; saying that the King of France himself could not have devised any obstacle more annoying to them than this is, besides being so contrary to the confidence they had in us. They had, they said, come to me on the King's behalf to request me to write instantly to the Emperor or to your Majesty as above, requesting that the embargo should immediately be raised, and this obstacle removed; preventing them, as it did, so unjustly, from making use of their own money, which is a thing that would not be done to anyone in the world. Every merchant, however small, they said, raised money by exchange at his pleasure, and it seemed very strange that they (the English) should be thus troubled in such a matter, especially as it was known some time ago that the transaction was being conducted through Jasper Doulchy; and if there had been any objection to it, they (the English) ought to have been informed that it would not be allowed and they would adopted other means of obtaining the funds. It seemed to the King as if we had waited for the opportunity of seizing it just at this point when the greatest inconvenience would be caused; and they (Gardiner and Paget) then made the same request to me a second time in the name of the King and Council. Madame: in order to please the King I replied at once that I would write on the spot as I was requested, but begged them not to take the matter so much to heart (*prendre la*

HENRY VIII.   249

1545.

chose si hault); perhaps things were reported worse than they were. I did not believe that it had been done without giving to their people in Flanders some explanation or reason for it, whereupon they replied no good or reasonable reason had been alleged: and with that they left me.

I therefore send back the courier I had detained here with this letter to your Majesty, as they said that the seizure had been effected by your orders.

Nothing has happened here since M. D'Eick left, except that the Chancellor has arrived at Court with the principal officers of Chancery and the doctors of London. The admiral comes to-morrow. I know not what is the business in hand.

Windsor, 18 September, 1545.

21 Sep.
Vienna
Imp. Arch

138. VAN DER DELFT to the QUEEN DOWAGER.

Since I wrote on the 18th instant certain Germans have arrived here who are styled the ambassadors of the Landgrave of Hesse, respecting whom I am writing more fully to the Emperor by the bearer of the present, who is my own servant. Your Majesty will be able to understand by this whether it will not be advisable that the Emperor should entertain the proposal of which M. D'Eick was the bearer thither, in order to frustrate such intrigues as these, from which may arise serious troubles.

Windsor, 21 September, 1545.

21 Sep.
Vienna
Imp. Arch.

139. VAN DER DELFT to the EMPEROR.

Since the departure of the courier with my last letters of the 18th instant to the Queen Dowager, certain Germans arrived here; and being desirous of discovering who they were and the object of their coming, I went to the King's Council to request audience, on the pretext of dealing in some private claims made by your Majesty's subjects. In the course of conversation the Councillors asked me what news I brought. I replied that I had none, but that they must have something to impart to me, as I had heard that they had ambassadors there from France or I knew whence—wishing to dissemble that I knew they were Germans. The Councillors made no reply to this, and I saw that they wished to keep the matter secret and lead me astray. I therefore took every means to investigate in other directions, especially as these Germans were being welcomed and made much of. At last I have learnt from a good, though secret, source that the Germans have brought letters to the Chancellor and Secretary Paget, closed with five or six seals bearing the arms of the Landgrave of Hesse, the Duke of Saxony and the Duke of Wurtemberg; and in their talk it appears they also include the elective King of Denmark. Their names are Johannes Scledanus of Strasburg, Ludwig von Bombach, Marshal of the Landgrave, and the other is a young man named Philip, but whose surname I cannot discover. These three personages, together with two others, one of whom is called Sturmius and the other is the father of Philip, came to Metz and Lorraine where they are very well received;

1545.

continuing their journey to the King of France, with whom Sturmius and the other man remained, whilst the remaining three came hither. On their way through Abbeville they say that they supped in the Chamber of the Duke of Orleans the day before he died, and came thence by Montreuil and the camp before Boulogne, being escorted from there to Calais by a French trumpeter. I cannot ascertain particulars of their mission, except that they boast that for the last hundred years no embassy has arrived here with a more advantageous and favourable mission for the interests of England. To-day Scledanus and the marshal dined with the Council, and directly after dinner they were led by the bishop of Winchester, Secretary Paget, and Dr. Petre, into the King's presence, where they remained a full hour. As I heard that they were to have audience after dinner, I thought advisable also to ask for audience with the King, which I did the moment they entered the presence as I have described. I did this because they had been in such retirement and had thought to hide them from me; and also because I wished to endeavour to discover after they had seen the King something about their mission and the King's reception of them. I intended to tell the King that I had heard certain Frenchmen and Germans had come from France to treat with him, and in these circumstances I could not omit to remind him of the treaty of alliance he had with your Majesty, by the terms of which he was debarred from making any treaty without the knowledge and acquiescence of your Majesty; not doubting that he continued in his usual good inclination and friendship towards your Majesty, as he had recently assured M. D'Eick and myself was the case. But withal, Sire, my audience has been postponed until the afternoon of the day after to-morrow, as they say the King is going to dine to-morrow three or four miles from here. Nevertheless, seeing the importance of this affair, and that if the King enters into any agreement with these Germans your Majesty's territories there may be surrounded by allies, I have thought necessary to report to your Majesty without delay by a man of my own. I will not fail to advise of any arrangement entered into by the King.

Windsor, 21 September, 1545.

23 Sep.
Vienna
Imp. Arch.

140. VAN DER DELFT to the EMPEROR.

In accordance with what I wrote to your Majesty the day before yesterday I went to see the King this afternoon, making my pretext for seeking audience the rumour that Cardinal Tournon and the Admiral of France were to visit the camp before Boulogne for the purpose of negotiating with the English, and also that I had heard that certain ambassadors had arrived here from France, who were said to be Germans (and as they themselves confessed Protestants). In view of this, I said, I could not avoid repeating to the King the assurance of the friendship towards him entertained by your Majesty, and your confidence that he would not negotiate or consent to anything that might prejudice your States or subjects; but would always bear in mind the fulfilment of the treaties between him and your Majesty and all else that would tend to the maintenance of the perfect amity between you. The King answered me by dwelling

1545.

upon my word amity. I wish, he said, it was as sincere on the side of the Emperor as it is on mine. I have always borne him true affection and do so still, but I am being badly treated and at the present time even they are detaining my money; so I do not know what to think of it. I replied that I hoped very shortly to lay before him such reasons for the stoppage of the money as would satisfy him. How satisfied? he asked. I know all their reasons and they do not satisfy me at all. Some creature has told them that I wish to take the money out of the country. That is the reason. With that, Sire, he leant against a window, bidding me to be covered and stand by his side. He then repeated that he could not understand how your Majesty had thus deserted him on the mere word of a minister who bore neither letter nor credence from him.[*] He had, he said, always refused to enter into negotiations with France, however favourable the conditions offered to him (including the cession of Ardres and the payment of arrears of pension) unless your Majesty was first satisfied. He greatly exaggerated these two points and reminded me that he was getting an old man, having been King forty years, and no person could ever truly say that he had acted otherwise than sincerely and straightforwardly. He had, he said, done everything openly and had never gone about seeking secret intelligence or underhand intrigue to the prejudice of anyone. He would rather die than act otherwise. He had never broken his word and he would not hide from me that the Germans had been to see him, and had declared that they had been sent by certain German princes, who had sent a similar mission to the King of France to urge both to make peace. He (Henry) had replied that he was the person who had always loved peace, and still did not desire war; he was simply defending himself against French invasion. The French would not consent to peace unless Boulogne was restored; but he had honourably won the place at the sword's point and he meant to keep it. In effect he repeated the same words that he had addressed to M. D'Eick and me; adding that these Germans intended to stay here until they received news from their colleagues in France. He then asked me if I had not heard of the arrival (in Flanders) of M. D'Eick and if I expected him soon; to which I replied that I doubted not that your Majesty would dispatch him without delay. Finally, Sire, he repeated that this was the very opportunity to make quite sure of the French. They were, he said, in extreme necessity, all their frontier towns were badly provided, they had raised their Camp before Boulogne for the purpose of sending a portion of the troops to Savoy, which would not be to your Majesty's advantage, and the other portion was to invade his territory of Guisnes. As, therefore, the period for furnishing the aid under the treaty had now expired and he knew your Majesty had mustered your bands, he begged your Majesty to grant him the use of at least some of them to aid him in resisting the invasion of Guisnes, which was included in the treaty. He then spoke of the death of M. de Vendome and of the news

---

[*] That is to say the bishop of Arras, who had reported to Charles a hasty expression of Henry, which was eagerly construed into a consent for the Emperor to make a separate peace with France. *See* Vol. VII. of this Calendar.

1545.

he had received of the illness of the Dauphin, of the fortune of M. de Guise's son, and of the death of our holy father the Pope, which he still considered doubtful.* I then took my leave, apologising for having importuned him for audience without pressing cause. To this he replied in very gracious words that I was always welcome, and could come whenever I liked even without any business at all.

All this, Sire, passed without any show of anger although very coldly, and in set formal words which I could not help suspecting. But after I left the King, as the bishop of Winchester and Secretary Paget escorted me I entered into discourse with them, reproaching them for having tried to conceal from me the other day the mission of these Germans, which moreover was notorious. They excused themselves; and I pointed out to them that, if they intended to make any treaty with the Protestants, it would mean abandoning liberty and purchasing servitude. I made a little speech on this subject to convince them that no good result could possibly come from any such arrangement; and I plainly perceived that there had not been any mention of a treaty yet. They said that everything rested with your Majesty, and they hoped M. D'Eick would bring good news.

Windsor, 23 September, 1545.

26 Sep. (?)
Vienna
Hof. Cor.

141. The EMPEROR to HENRY VIII.

Has received the King's letter of credence brought by Eick, who has repeated to him verbally the message entrusted to him. M. D'Eick will in a similar manner convey to the King the Emperor's reply.

Brussels, 25 September, 1545 (?).

27 Sep.
Brussels.
Neg. Ang.

142. INSTRUCTIONS for you MESSIEURS CORNELIUS SCEPPERUS and FRANCIS VAN DER DELFT, for your mission to the KING OF ENGLAND, whither we are now sending you, SCEPPERUS, again.

In the first place you, Scepperus, will return to the King of England with all speed; and, after cordially saluting him, you will tell him how much we rejoice to learn that he was in good health, and we hope frequenty to receive similar news from him.

We have heard fully your report of his answer to the three principal points tending to peace, proposed by the King of France; and we have, in your presence, communicated the same to the French ambassadors who have undertaken to convey it to their master. We should have been glad if the King of England had made some counter proposals, in order that the matter might be carried a step further, as we are so desirous of bringing it to a good issue, both in the interests of Christendom at large, and in those of the two princes themselves, and their realms and subjects.

We have likewise learnt the principal object of your journey hither, namely to press upon us the desire of the King of England to have an interview with us and the Queen of Hungary our sister; for which purpose he is willing to cross the sea within a month

---

* This news was of course untrue; Paul III. did not die until four years afterwards.

from the day he learns of our desire with regard to the interview. On this point both of you, or either one if the other be indisposed, will convey to the King the following reply.

We are delighted to learn of the King's wish; knowing that it can only arise from the great love and affection he bears us. You will thank him warmly for this on our behalf. We have taken care to keep the suggestion secret, in order to guard his prestige and dignity, and have only communicated it to a few of our most confidential ministers. He need, therefore, be under no apprehension that it will ever be divulged to his prejudice.

Although we are desirous that such an interview should take place, in consideration of our love for the King, we cannot omit to point out two matters that might stand in the way of it; or, at least, defer its realisation. The first is the risk the King would incur personally, seeing that the season is far advanced, and the King's dominions on this side of the sea scourged by epidemics and crowded by soldiers, whose proximity is be avoided. In addition to this we have promised the States of the Empire to be present by the 6th January, at the place indicated for the assembly, which is at Regensburg, a long way from his dominions, and, on our way thither, we are desirous of visiting our territories of Gueldres and Utrecht, for which purpose we shall have to begin our journey very shortly. Notwithstanding these reasons, and bearing in mind the King's singular affection for us, which we are anxious to reciprocate, we shall be willing, if he still desires the interview, to approach our Flemish-Artois frontier to meet him, on condition that he be there during the month of October, as you, Scepperus, have assured us that he would be. It will be impossible for us to defer our journey towards Germany beyond that month; and secondly that the King of France will consent to a suspension of hostilities. Considering that the forces of both monarchs are so close to our borders, it will be impossible to agree to the interview unless the suspension be arranged. With this object, we have instructed our Ambassador resident in France to induce the King of France to consent to such a suspension of hostilities, and to agree to a peace conference in some part of our dominions, in order to give us a pretext for approaching our frontiers.

In order to assure the King (of England) of our intention, we have acceded to his request, and have dispatched letters-patents, conferring power on you to conclude in principle with the King or his Councillors the holding of the interview; and in the meanwhile to negotiate and promote it, and the matters dependent upon it, as will be necessary in a matter of so much importance.

You will especially learn from the King the place where the interview can most conveniently be held, having regard to the fact that plagues and sickness are prevalent in many quarters, whilst other places are much distressed by the effects of the war. Besides this, the long voyage we have to make renders it necessary that we should not go outside the limits of our territories of Flanders or Artois. For this reason, it seems that no places would-be more appropriate for the interview than the towns of Bruges, Nieuport, Bergen, St. Winnoc, Dunkirk, Gravelines, Bourbourg, or St. Omer; whichever the King may prefer. You will give us prompt advice of his choice, in order that we may have lodgings prepared and

1545.

provisions made for his safety and our own, with the ministers, train and suite who must accompany us.

If the King of England desires to know to whom the Emperor has communicated these your instructions, you may reply as follows:—Considering that the interview can only last for a few brief days—for the reasons above specified—it will not be convenient for the meeting to take place without an understanding being previously arrived at, as to the objects in view. For this reason we deem it highly necessary that the principal points for discussion at the interview should be thoroughly debated, settled, and fixed beforehand by the most confidential ministers on both sides; in order that at the actual meeting there should be no question between us but of good-cheer and kindly greeting, as is usual amongst princes. You will, accordingly, ask the King to enlighten us on these principal points beforehand, either by one of his own most confidential ministers, or through you, Scepperus, who will convey the same to us in cipher, which information shall reach no person but those whom we trust implicitly, and who will keep the secret inviolate. If the King desires it, you, Scepperus, may again cross the sea, to inform us verbally, so that we may, before the meeting takes place, decide upon the whole question. This is of great importance for the favourable issue of the said interview, and if it be not done, will not only render the meeting useless, but prejudical to the state of affairs, and dangerous to the ministers who have intervened in the matter, as you, Scepperus, may well consider, and will take opportunity of pointing out to the King and his ministers. It is of the first importance that we should be advised promptly on this point.

If they broach the subject of the aid, which, in virtue of the treaty of alliance, the King of England has demanded, you may say that the King will not fail to see that, since we are making such strenuous efforts to bring about peace, it would not be honest for us in the meanwhile to help one side against the other. But when we see how things are decided, either for peace or war, we shall be free to act if necessary. Even if during the interview, it be decided that we are bound to furnish the aid demanded, we shall willingly do so; since it is only a question of a money subsidy.

Finally, you will keep in hand that matter of the gold, which the English corsair Renegat seized in a Spanish ship bound from the Indies, and get the gold delivered into the hands of you, Van der Delft. You may assure the King and his ministers that, when this has been done, there will be no failure to release at once the ships embargoed in Spain, as a consequence of Renegat's action, as you have already been fully informed.

Brussels, 27 September, 1845.

October ?
Paris
Arch. Nat.
K. 1485.

143. St. Mauris to the King of the Romans.

I send enclosed copies of the joint letters of M. Noirthoudt and myself to the Emperor and the Queen of Hungary, giving reports of all that he and I have been able to do in the matter of a peace between England and France. To this I can only add that I have heard from M. D'Albret that the King of France is endeavouring to

1545.

bring about the peace, by means of a marriage between M. de Vendome* and the Princess of England; but he always sticks to the point of Boulogne, which the King of England insists upon retaining; or, at least, that it shall remain to his daughter on her marriage; which the French will not hear of. They are, however, very desirous of arranging a truce, and are putting it forward by various intermediaries and indirect means, whilst, at the same time, they publicly declare that they do not want it, and if the English seek it they (the French) will not grant it. The truth is, that pure necessity is driving them to it. They are very short of money, the sinew of war, and their people are so weak that if the war goes on and they have to contribute for another year, certainly half of them will abandon their property altogether. I may add that the day after the death of the Duke of Orleans, the Admiral went to the camp before Boulogne, it was said to discuss terms of peace with the English; or, at least, to agree upon a truce, which the French were willing to grant, so long as their fort before Boulogne remained in a state of defence. By means of it, and the war material they will introduce into it, they say they will be able to prevent the English from penetrating further into France; and Boulogne will therefore be useless to them (the English). They think that by concluding such a truce only the township of Boulogne will remain to the English, whilst the French will hold all the rest of the Boulognais. But, Sire, in this they are counting without their host.

I am enclosing with the present a copy of the medical report of the illness of the Duke of Orleans, who is greatly mourned here. The truth is that he died of pleurisy caught by drinking cold water whilst he was heated. God rest his soul. I think also the copy of my negotiation with the King (of France), with regard to the aid to the King of England, will also go enclosed.

I will summarise my other news of events here, so as not to weary your Majesty.

About a fortnight since the English with about 40 armed ships attacked Tréport in Normandy, burning the town and killing all the men and women they could catch. The King of France sent M. de Nevers, M. D'Aumale, and M. de Boissy, but the enemy had retired to sea when they arrived. The English now dominate the sea, as the French fleet is broken up. They talk of commissioning at once 40 armed ships to protect the (French) coast until a truce or a peace be concluded. As to the galleys, the season condemns them to stay in the corner of a harbour to serve as food for rats.

Sire, these people (the French) have no good news as to the success of their army in Scotland. The Scots are said to be blaming them for not sending money. Two days since an ambassador from Scotland arrived here, to arrange for the defence of Scotland, as they fear that during the winter the English will send a force against them, as they (the English) have men and ships ready.

The Jacobin friar who busied himself about the peace, was sent a few days since by the King of France to the Emperor, to inform him that the protestants have offered the King the restitution of

---

* This was Antoine de Bourbon, father of Henry IV.

1545.

Boulogne, if he (the King of France) will join with them against the Emperor in the matter of the Council (of Trent). The King of France rejected such a proposal, and would much rather obtain Boulogne by the intervention of his Majesty than otherwise. The friar is also to say that the King is sending to request the Pope to declare the King of England schismatic, and to exhort all Christian princes to attack him.

The French some time ago took the Marshal of Calais prisoner near that town, whilst he was out rabbit hunting. He is being detained here, and they expect to get a great ransom from him.* On the 20 August Count William (Furstenberg) paid his ransom of 30,000 ducats. I think he was brought to it by the persuasions of the Secretary, Jean Jaques, a German, in the hope that the King of France would freely deliver him after the ransom was paid, which the King has firmly refused to do; saying that the Count must not leave the city of Paris until the Prince of Roche sur Yonne is put to ransom. Count William is so desperate at this that he has fallen into a frenzy. If he had followed the advice of the Emperor he would have been in very different case.

Ten days ago, in the presence of the King, Paulin and the Strozzis had a dispute arising out of Paulin having said that the Strozzis had charged him with neglect of his duty against the English at sea, on the occasion that the Admiral was present with the (French) fleet. The Strozzis declared that they had not imputed the blame especially to Paulin, but they said that several good opportunities had been missed during the voyage of effecting notable exploits against the enemy. In support of their assertion they drew up a written statement of the events of the voyage, describing in detail the opportunities that had presented themselves. The King finally told them, however, that he wished them (i.e., the Strozzis and Paulin) to remain friends as he held them all as good servants of his own, and everything that had been done in the voyage had been by his own special orders, given for sundry reasons. Thus, Sire, the Admiral of France was exonerated from the fault imputed to him by everybody, namely that he had conducted the expedition extremely badly, which has made him very unpopular with the French.

The Emperor had requested the King to allow Cardinal Carpi to resign an abbacy he holds in France, in favour of a Frenchman; but the King refused, solely in consequence of the Cardinal having done many good offices for the Emperor against France, as is openly declared here: though the Frenchman who was to have succeeded to the preferment was agreeable to the King. This reply was given to the Ambassador before the death of the Duke of Orleans.

---

* This was Sir Thomas Palmer, Knight-Porter of Calais. He was beheaded for complicity in the Duke of Northumberland's treason.

† Paulin Baron de la Garde on the occasion in question (15 August), in command of the galleys, begun the action by manœuvring for the wind with the English oared boats. The wind, however, was very light, and Hannebault, with the French great ships, could not come up for some hours; and by that time the breeze had shifted in favour of the English, but was still too light for the great ships to be used advantageously against the French galleys. The fleet consequently anchored some distance apart as evening fell: and for some reason, not quite clear, the French sheered off in the night.

1545.

The Pope has contributed nothing hitherto to aid the war against England because he wished to stipulate that he should pay the money only on the condition that the King of France should not treat with the English without including the Holy See in the arrangement. This the King flatly refused, as he said he declined to pledge himself to an impossible condition.

The King of France is very much displeased that the Pope should have transferred Parma and Plasencia (Piacenza) to his son for the Duke of Camerino. The King of France says, as he did, indeed, whilst the Duke of Orleans was living, that this could not be done, to the prejudice of the Duke of Milan.° He (the King of France) alleges that the right had previously been acquired by him. Since the death of the Duke of Orleans they add that, even if the Emperor, as Duke of Milan, consented to the transfer, the latter could only be effected subject to existing rights.

The prior of Capua† and his brother have made many captures at sea from the Emperor's subjects, and have put some Spaniards into the galleys: going so far as to say that it was the Spaniards they were after. The Ambassadors of Venice and Ferrara were recently in a village through which at the same time were passing about 50 footmen who had been dismissed from the fleet. The soldiers attacked the lodgings of the Ambassadors with the intention of sacking and pillaging, as they would have done if the village-folk had not come to the rescue. It is not known whether the act was prompted or not. The matter is being investigated, and the troops are in prison.

Several Spaniards who had taken the field with many Normans have been captured in Normandy; amongst them two Spanish captains in the pay of the King (of France). They have asked me to beg the King to pardon them, but I have not ventured to do so without the Emperor's orders.

The French are deeply grieved that the Emperor has not surrendered Busque in Piedmont, as they now despair of getting it, the Duke of Orleans being dead. ‡ The King made great demands of money on the people of Paris two months ago. They begged to be excused on the ground that they had already furnished large sums. They remained obstinate for some time, and the King was exceedingly angry with them; but they have at last consented to lend six score thousand francs, and the King has granted them an impost to raise the amount. By this means he will be quit of the obligation to pay them back, and they will be not much out of pocket by the contribution.

Since the death of the Duke of Orleans I have done nothing in connection with the fulfilment of the treaty of peace (*i.e.* of Crépy) and I have therefore been unable to report to your Majesty whether these people look upon the treaty as at an end or not. I have been long plagued with fever and all my people have been ill, or I would have sent your Majesty the above information earlier. I will be more punctual in future.

° That is to say the Duke of Orleans who was to receive Milan as a dowry with his Austrian wife, Milan being a fief of the Empire, with certain alleged rights over Parma and Piacenza.

† This was Pietro Strozzi.

‡ The Piedmont settlement arranged in the treaty of Crépy was only to take effect after the Duchy of Milan had been handed over to the Duke of Orleans.

1545.
5 Oct.
Simancas.
E. V. 1318.

144. DIEGO HURTADO DE MENDOZA (Imperial Ambassador in Venice) to the EMPEROR.

News from Constantinople enclosed. I have in my company Dr. Zorilla, a man of sufficient learning and good life, whom I left at Trent, in order that he might report to me as need might arise. By the enclosed relation, your Majesty will see what has occurred there up to the present. M. de Clairmont, one of the French bishops, is here, and wishes to go and see Rome and Naples. The Council will not suffer much from his absence.

The portraits are sent with the present letter, the small one I have specially ordered to be carried with care. Titian is old, and works slowly. He has done his best; and I have told him as much as I could recollect. He says that your Majesty ordered him to be given other particulars, to enable him to do the work more perfectly: but he wishes that no other hand should touch it, or it will be spoiled. He has painted another picture of fancy for your Majesty, which is said to be his best work. Your Majesty granted him many years ago 300 loads of timber in Naples, and they now ask him three ducats a cartload for cutting; so that it produces no profit to him. I pray your Majesty make him another grant, that may bring him some advantage, or else order that the 300 carts shall be paid to him as your Majesty granted them.

The new Duke of Plasencia (Piacenza) has sent an envoy hither to thank the Seigniory for sending to greet him. The same person came to me to place the life and states of the Duke at your Majesty's disposal. I have thanked him.

Venice, 5 October, 1545.

5 Oct.
Simancas.
E. V. 1318.

145. TITIAN to the EMPEROR.

Don Diego Hurtado de Mendoza has forwarded the two portraits of the Empress, upon which I have exercised all the skill (diligentia) that I possessed. I should have wished to carry them myself, if the length of the journey and my advanced age had not made it impossible. I pray your Majesty to have your opinions and commands sent to me, and return the portraits that I may amend them, in accordance with your Majesty's desires. But pray your Majesty, do not allow another hand to touch them. With regard to all else touching my affairs I refer your Majesty to Don Diego's letter, and humbly prostrate myself at your Majesty's feet.

Venice, 5 October, 1545. Signed Titiano.
(*Holograph.*)

6 Oct.
Vienna
Imp. Arch.

146. The EMPEROR to SCEPPERUS and VAN DER DELFT.

We received yesterday letters from our ambassador in France, in reply to that which we wrote to him about your (Scepperus) action in England, your journey hither, and your return mission: touching also the suggestion of a cessation of hostilities for six weeks and the holding of a conference of English and French plenipotentiaries to endeavour to come to terms. After a good deal of discussion between our ambassador and the King of

1545.

France the latter has consented to this suspension of hostilities for six weeks, during which he will send duly authorised representatives to us, in order that the terms of peace may be discussed. But he lays down the condition that the negotiation is to take place in our territory, and not otherwise. In order to demonstrate his respect for us he will send the most confidential and dignified personages in his realm to represent him at the conference, mentioning expressly Cardinal Tournon or the Admiral. We have since heard from the French ambassadors here that the Admiral was shortly to leave on his journey hither; the King being under the impression that you will already have obtained from the other side a similar agreement for a suspension of hostilities and the meeting of plenipotentiaries. We are sending you this by special courier, in order that you may take steps accordingly to obtain from the King of England his acquiescence in this, and his consent to send amply instructed representatives as soon as possible. Advise us also by this courier in case your continued presence there is necessary, what action you have taken upon this and other points of your mission. Our ambassador in France also reports that during his communication with Cardinal Tournon and the Admiral on the subject of the suspension of hostilities and the meeting of the conference, the Cardinal remarked that the suspension would be greatly to the disadvantage of the French, as both their land and sea forces were ready; and besides this, to hold the conference without absolutely knowing whether the King of England would give up Boulogne or not, would be incurring a vast expense without the slightest hope of result, as his master the King of France was quite determined to make no terms unless Boulogne were restored. You will therefore sound the King of England on this point of the restitution; but you need not press it; your first effort will be to request him to send his representatives amply instructed with the object of concluding peace on reasonable conditions.

Brussels, 6 October, 1545.

8 Oct.
Vienna
Imp. Arch

147. REPLY of the KING OF ENGLAND to the REPRESENTATIONS of the EMPEROR'S COMMISSIONERS on the 4th October, 1545.

First the King thanks the Emperor and the Queen Dowager for their kind greetings, etc., etc.

Whereas the Emperor has communicated to the French Ambassadors resident at his court the King of England's reply respecting the three points proposed by the King of France, and the said ambassadors expressed a wish that the King of England himself had made proposals, the King recognising the obstinacy of his adversaries refers them to his former reply, to which he declines to add anything.

The King thanks the Emperor for communicating to him a certain letter revealing an intrigue to his detriment. He is convinced that the Emperor's action in this matter arises from his fraternal affection which the King will not fail to reciprocate.

The King is also gratified at the Emperor's expressed desire that an interview should take place between them, notwithstanding the Emperor's approaching departure for Germany; and he thanks him also for the solicitude shown for his safety, and his consideration with regard to the sea passage.

With regard to the final decision of the King as to the interview. The King desires of all things that it should take place if it can be done without giving too much trouble to the Emperor.

But, inasmuch as the Emperor informs him that he is willing to undertake it, if it can take place during the month of October; as the Emperor cannot well remain in Flanders beyond that time, owing to the assembly of the States of the Empire at Regensburg and the long voyage he has to make through Utrecht and Gueldres; the King replies that he cannot possibly cross the sea in October. Since the proposed interview spoken of by the Commissioners does not appear to have been finally determined upon by the Emperor, but is made conditional on the establishment of a truce, which the Emperor is urging through his Ambassador in France; and that if the truce is not made the interview cannot take place; and furthermore bearing in mind the short interval between now and the end of the month of October, the King finds it impossible to make the voyage so soon. But provided that the truce be effected and the Emperor be willing to defer for a few days his voyage to Germany (the King being informed that it is not absolutely necessary to appear at Regensburg on the exact day fixed) the King hopes with God's help to be able to be at Calais within one month after he learns that the truce is effected.

The King desires that the truce should extend to land and sea during six months; the places in the Boulognais not to be fortified by either side in that time, although they may be revictualled. The truce shall be proclaimed on the English side at Calais, Guisnes, Boulogne, London, Dover, Rye, Southampton, and Plymouth; and on the French side at Ardres, Montreuil, Abbeville, Paris, Amiens, Dieppe, Rouen, Brest, La Rochelle, and Bordeaux, and within ten days thereafter, at most, all hostilities shall cease by land and sea. Any warlike acts that may be committed after the expiration of that time shall be considered illegal; and restitution and reparation shall be made for them on either side. To conclude this the King will send powers to his Ambassador the bishop of Westminster.

The King out of consideration for the Emperor intends (in the event of the truce being effected) to send representatives, or to give powers to those already in Flanders, to enter into communication with the French commissioners, if they are of the same mind, for the purpose of arranging terms of peace in accordance with the instructions which the King will give to his Commissioners. With regard to an appropriate place for the interview between the Emperor and the King, the former has proposed several for the King's choice and, in order to please the Emperor and not to take him too far away from his road to Germany, the King would be very glad to meet him in one of those places: but unfortunately he finds it will be difficult or impossible for him to do so, in consequence of lack of horses for his train, which at this time of the year cannot be sent across the sea soon enough; nor can adequate preparation of fodder be made. The King therefore begs the Emperor to come as far as Calais, which town he promises to make so clean and fit that their two Majesties may stay there at their pleasure without fear of sickness or infection.

1545.

The Emperor has very prudently suggested that before the meeting takes place the principal points and articles which are to be the subjects of the interview should be mutually discussed and settled; in the first place because the time they can be together is very short, and secondly in order that there should be no question between them but of good cheer and kindly greeting, as is usual when princes meet. The King highly approves of this suggestion and, in order to carry it into effect has requested Scepperus to go to the Emperor, and, in addition to the above, to tell him that the object of the proposed interview is not in the least to importune the Emperor; but the proposal is principally prompted by the great affection and desire felt by the King to see the Emperor once again before his departure, as peradventure so appropriate an opportunity may not occur in future.

Another reason is, that it may be made manifest that, in spite of some suspicion and jealousy between them set afloat by the lying reports of certain ill-disposed people, the King and the Emperor are, and intend to remain for the future, perfect friends, allies and confederates, both in their own persons and in those of their children, heirs and successors to their realms and subjects, in accordance with the treaty of alliance: which the King holds to be inviolable, so far as he is concerned, and trusts that the Emperor also will regard it in the same way.

Since their Majesties entered jointly into the war with France, however, certain questions have arisen with regard to the substance of the treaty, and the King considers it highly advisable for the repose of the Emperor and himself, and the welfare of their respective countries, that these questions should be amicably settled. In any case, he has thought well to make the proposal to the Emperor, to obtain his Majesty's decision, in order that he, the King, may proceed accordingly, as his interests require.

To particularise the questions referred to: the 6th clause of the Treaty provides that the Emperor should hold as his enemy anyone who assails or supports the invasion of the lands and provinces of the King as set forth in the treaty, and should forbid his subjects to associate or trade with the subjects of the invader. The King of France has on three occasions openly and notoriously invaded the territories of the King, and the latter desires to learn from the Emperor how he proposes to deal with the said article of the treaty in these circumstances; and also with article VII. since the invasion has been made with the number of troops specified in the Treaty; and the Emperor's allegation that all this has been done for the recovery of Boulogne is not considered by the King to be either satisfactory nor sufficient. On similar grounds the King of France might cover any future invasion of the Emperor's territory by alleging that the object was the recovery of Milan, Naples, Sicily, or any other land to which the King of France might lay claim. By that rule the King of England might consider himself absolved from complying with the clause in question, which he thinks would redound more greatly to the disadvantage of the Emperor's countries than to his own. The articles are, moreover, unconditional in their tenour, and no mention is made of the reasons that may be alleged for an invasion. With regard to the

1545.

King's alleged consent to the Emperor's treaty with France, reported by the bishop of Arras, the King rebuts and denies it as a thing utterly untrue. But in any case, even if he had consented, it would not override clauses 6 and 7 about the invasion, which provide for the declaration of the invader as a common enemy and the furnishing of a specified aid to the invaded. The fourth clause, moreover, specially provides that neither prince shall treat with the King of France or any other, to the prejudice of the terms of the Treaty, so that whatever subsequent Treaty might be made, it could not be to the detriment of this one. The King maintains that the treaty made by the Emperor with France can in no way derogate from that previously made between the Emperor and himself, even though the King had consented as is pretended by the bishop of Arras. The King wishes also that clause 24 which lays down that whenever he wished to convey troops through the Emperor's country to go against France, he should be assisted by the Emperor with waggons, boats, victuals, munitions of war and other requisites against payment, should be better observed in future than it has been in the past.

Finally, for better assurance, and in the interests of the maintenance without further scruple of the friendly alliance, the King desires the Emperor to make a special declaration binding upon himself and his successors that he and they shall never seek absolution from the oath he has taken to observe the treaty: and the King on his side, immediately after these points have been settled will bind himself and his successors to fulfil the treaty exactly, and not to enter into any treaty or alliance with any other prince or potentate without the consent of the Emperor, to the prejudice of the terms of this treaty as is laid down in clause 14. Such consent must bear the hand seal of the consenting prince.*

Windsor, 8 October, 1545.

8 Oct.
Vienna
Hof. Cor.

148. HENRY VIII. to the EMPEROR.

M. D'Eick is now returning and it is therefore unnecessary to write at length. Bespeaks the Emperor's sympathetic consideration of M. D'Eick's communication; and he (Henry) has likewise instructed the bishop of Westminster to lay before the Emperor what we have thought desirable in order to bring about the realisation of our mutual affair (*i.e.*, the proposed interview).

Windsor, 8 October, 1545.

9 Oct.
Vienna
Imp. Arch.

149. VAN DER DELFT to the EMPEROR.

On the return hither a few days ago of M. D'Eick we communicated together touching the powers and instructions your Majesty deigned to send us; and in accordance therewith, we used every effort both with the King himself and with the principal members of his Council. As M. D'Eick is returning to your Majesty at once

---

* It is obvious now that, with the Emperor's great plot against the protestants in contemplation, to which every other consideration for the time was subordinated, nothing was further from Charles' intention than to allow himself to be bound down anew to the letter of his treaty with Henry.

he will convey verbally and fully the result of our action, and I need not therefore trouble your Majesty with a long letter. I will however add, on the subject of the gold seized by Renegat, that the Lords of the Council have conceded my demand and assure me of its restitution as soon as Renegat, who is still at sea, shall return. When he arrives I will not fail to press diligently for its delivery to me in accordance with your Majesty's pleasure. In the matter of the demands preferred by private citizens I have done and will do everything in my power, hoping that in time things may right themselves and the claimants receive justice, as, indeed, some of them have already done. On this point, on Scottish affairs and upon occurrences here M. D'Eick will also report.

Windsor, 9 October, 1845.

9 Oct.
Vienna
Imp. Arch.

150. VAN DER DELFT to the QUEEN DOWAGER OF HUNGARY.

I have received your Majesty's letters, referring to the seizure of this King's money in Antwerp, and, in accordance with your instructions, I have repeated both to the King and his Councillors the excuses contained in the letters, whereupon they showed no very great annoyance. Touching the various other special letters your Majesty has written to me on the subject of the restitution of the property taken from certain subjects of the Emperor by the English, I may say that I have done my best with these Councillors to obtain redress for the complainants. The Councillors have promised me to do strict justice; and have already taken the matter in hand. M. D'Eick who is going to Flanders will report on this and all else. I will not slacken in my efforts in favour of the claims referred to.

Windsor, 9 October, 1545.

10 Oct.
Vienna
Imp. Arch.

151. The EMPEROR to SCEPPERUS and VAN DER DELFT.

This is to inform you that the troops retained for the service of our good friend, cousin and perpetual ally the King of England and raised in the neighbourhood of Confluence and Treves, have done inestimable damage there; and afterwards came towards the city of Aix, passing thence through our territories on the other side of the Meuse doing very great damage in them. They then came before the town of Wesel on the Meuse belonging to our cousin the bishop of Liege, where the burgesses closed the gates against them. But nevertheless they forced their way over the walls, which were more ruinous than they ought to have been, and broke down the gates; their intention being to cross the Meuse there, and penetrate into our dominions in violation of the promise given to you by the King, and also of the assurance of his resident ambassador here. We do not know what to think of this, seeing that the agents and commissioners of the King are with these troops. Although they say they have orders not to pass though our territories, except one corner of them, they undisguidedly act in violation of the assurance so frequently given to us by the King. If they continue their course as it is rumoured amongst them that they will do, by the main road (Chausée) they will, in addition to passing, as they have done,

1545.

through our country on the other side of the Meuse, traverse our territories of Brabant and Hainault, in which case you may well consider how it will please our subjects and the damage and loss that will be suffered by the latter.° Even though the troops say they will pay what they have, if they pay at all they do so at their own discretion and not in accordance with the expense they really incur, and they pay nothing to the horsemen for fodder. We have caused this to be represented to the King of England's ambassador here, but he was only able to reply that he would convey the remonstrance to his master. But in the meanwhile our subjects and those of the bishop of Liege will suffer injury and we are anything but contented thereat. You will jointly lay this matter before the King, if Scepperus be still there; and if, as we suppose, that the assurances given to us on the subject have come from the King. You will point out, in such case, that his agents have exceeded their authority, and should be severely chastised in order to prevent others from thus perturbing the good relations that we wish to maintain with the King; and you will intimate to the King's ministers that the French are rejoiced at this sort of proceeding. They are spreading the rumour that the understanding between us and the King of England is not cordial.

We have also received a reply from the Sieur de Noirthoudt on the latest instruction we sent him at the time that you, Scepperus, left here. It is to the effect that the King of France is willing to appoint the Commissioners on his side to treat for peace and with that object will consent to a suspension of hostilities for six weeks. We now only await your report to effect the suspension and then to determine about our voyage (*i.e.* to Germany) in accordance with the result of your action with the King respecting the last mission entrusted to you. Time is passing quickly and the season is already advanced. Report as speedily as possible.

Brussels, 10 October, 1545.

14 Oct.
Vienna
Imp. Arch.

152. Van der Delft to the Emperor.

Since the departure of M. D'Eick from here the courier with your Majesty's letters of the 6th inst. arrived on the morning of the 12th, having, as he says been so long on the road owing to the storm delaying him in Calais. I received the letters in London, whither I had gone to inspect a house belonging to the King, formerly occupied by the ambassadors of France but which his Majesty has now given to me, as he knew I was badly lodged. I immediately came hither to the King and informed him that on the penultimate dispatch of M. D'Eick your Majesty had received news from your ambassador in France that the Christian King had, out of considera-

° The German mercenaries had intended to pass into French territory over the borders of Champagne, but were checked and delayed by a French army at Meziéres. The time thus lost, and the difficulty in passing through the imperial territory against orders, rendered another month's payment to them due. When this was not immediately forthcoming they mutinied, refused to advance, and subsequently riotously returned to Germany. Henry was almost invariably cheated and ill served by his German mercenaries; and this explains his eagerness to obtain, and his high opinion of, the Spanish and Italian infantry in his service.

1545.

tion for your Majesty, accorded a suspension of hostilities of six weeks, and also had agreed to the sending of plenipotentiaries in the meanwhile to treat for peace, etc. He replied that touching these points, he referred them to his ambassador with your Majesty, who had power to deal with them and also to the mission with which he had entrusted M. D'Eick. The truce or suspension for 6 weeks only would be a great disadvantage to him, as he had in his service so large a number of Germans to whom he had promised three months' pay. Your Majesty, he said, would understand that notwithstanding the great expense of these Germans, they would be unable to do much service after the first six weeks had been wasted. I replied that the King of France had agreed to this truce and the peace conference out of consideration for your Majesty and that some of the French ministers considered that it would be a disadvantage to their side as they were well prepared now by land and sea. He (Henry) replied that the case was quite otherwise. He knew very well that the plague was raging amongst them and they were in great want of victuals and money. The great ships had retired to Brest in Brittany; and he said he would not hide from me, and I could secretly report to your Majesty alone, that he hoped in a few days to perform a notable exploit in the Boulagnais, even to capture their fort and raze the rest of their fortresses. All the talk about the truce, he said, was simply with the object of attaining the end known to your Majesty. For that reason he would listen to a truce for six months; and if before that time the thing known to your Majesty could not take place (*i.e.* the interview) he did not want a truce at all. With regard to a peace conference, if the power that was now on the road for his ambassador was not sufficient, he would grant one according to your Majesty's wishes, and he instructed me to say that he referred the point to your Majesty's decision.

I then left the King, but bearing in mind that in any case politeness demanded that the English should send a fit personage of quality, since even the Admiral of France was designated to go to your Majesty on this peace question, I saw the bishop of Winchester and Secretary Paget, the King's most influential ministers, and told them what I thought it was incumbent for them to do on their side as regarded the envoy. They approved of what I said and undertook to speak to the King about it again. They brought me a reply that the King trusting to what I had said of the coming of the Admiral of France to your Majesty, had decided to reciprocate by sending to your Majesty shortly the bishop of Winchester, who would treat of the question of peace.

In speaking of the German troops the King complained bitterly of them, saying that they were ungovernable hot heads. He had sent letters and orders for them not to injure or offend in any way the subjects or territories of your Majesty. He seemed greatly annoyed that they had caused your Majesty any trouble, which he said he had heard from his ambassador that they had done, though I was quite ignorant of the matter.

I hear from a secret source that the ambassadors from the Protestants who left here two days ago obtained no other decision but that a certain deputy would be sent from here to them; the real

1545.

object being to keep the matter in suspense until they see how they will get on with your Majesty.
Windsor, 14 October, 1545.

15 Oct.
Vienna
Imp. Arch.

153. SECRETARY DE GRANVELLE to VAN DER DELFT.

M. D'Eick on his return hither from England duly reported to the Emperor everything that you and he jointly had arranged with the King of England. His Majesty (the Emperor) had some time ago decided to depart to-day and we were all ready to follow him, but recognising the pressing importance of the matter dealt with in this letter, he has ordered that the President (i.e. Lois Scors, president of the Flemish Council), M. D'Eick (i.e. Scepperus) and ourselves should remain here for this day, in order that we may communicate with the English ambassador.* I will not waste time by repeating here in detail the mission entrusted to M. D'Eick touching the truce and settlement between England and France, and the question between the King of England and the Emperor, but will limit myself to saying that after his Majesty had heard the report of M. D'Eick he decided that the most necessary point was to arrange a cessation of hostilities between the French and English. We therefore proposed this to the English ambassador, saying that the Emperor had received a reply from his resident ambassador in France, that the Christian King was willing out of consideration for his Majesty the Emperor to accept the proffered intervention of the latter for the conclusion of peace and the arrangement of a truce; the negotiation having been so far conducted by us with due consideration for the dignity of the King of England. The English ambassador finally asserted that he had no authority to consent to a truce, unless he was certain that the interview between the Emperor and the King of England would take place. It was pointed out to him that the Emperor having intervened in the interests of peace between the two Kings, by means of the envoys sent by the Queen Dowager of Hungary to France and England respectively, and his Majesty, having as usual, proceeded in perfectly good faith, he could not avoid persisting in his efforts to secure peace by every means in his power. If he succeeded it would be for the benefit of both sides; but he nevertheless did not intend to neglect the elucidation of the points concerning the treaty of alliance between him and the King of England, as well as the consideration of the various other matters confidentially entrusted by the King of England to M. D'Eick. In any case it appeared to his Majesty that, for the purpose of carrying out his good offices between the two Kings, and

---

* Vandenesse (Itinerary) says that on the "15th October the Emperor went from Brussels to Vaure, remaining at Mechlin from the 17th to the 22nd, and thence to Termonde till the 28th when he went to Ghent, remaining there till the 2nd November. On the 3rd November he was at Bruges, where he received Dr. Thirlby bishop of Westminster, who came to treat with the French plenipotentiaries under the auspices of the Emperor. The admiral and the chancellor of France having arrived on the 7th November negotiations were carried on daily in presence of de Granvelle, de Praet and President Scors till the 16th when his Majesty went to Alost, on the 17th to Vanlo and on the 18th to Antwerp. The Ministers .... followed his Majesty until the 24th, when the French Commissioners took leave of his Majesty and returned home without having been able to come to any agreement."

1545.

also for the other objects mentioned, the first necessary step was to agree upon the cessation of hostilities, as M. D'Eick had understood was the King of England's intention. His Majesty was of opinion that the sooner such a truce could be settled the better, and he had authorised us to press the English ambassador, and to urge similarly the ambassador of France, to avoid the evils and inconveniences produced by the continuance of war, of which the issue is always doubtful; and especially as an agreement might be rendered more difficult, and perhaps the private settlement between the Emperor and the King of England rendered impossible, by the gaining of a signal advantage by one side over the other at the present time. The Emperor was expecting letters from the King of the Romans, and from his ministers in Germany in a few days and on their receipt he would be able to give a more decided answer with regard to the best means of settling the private matter between the King of England and himself; and especially whether it will be possible for his Majesty to defer his departure; and if an interview can be arranged. No time will be lost by his Majesty in deciding these points; but still he is strongly of opinion that the first and most necessary thing to be done is to agree to the truce, and the rest can then be more advantageously dealt with. As the English ambassador persisted in his statement that he could not alter his previous reply, we decided in agreement with him that he shall send a special courier to his master, and that we would speak to the French ambassador here in order that he may obtain powers to settle the truce, and final instructions from his master with regard to the conditions demanded by the King of England; namely that the truce should be operative on land and sea for six months, during which period neither party may fortify any place in the Boulognais, though places may be revictualled: the truce to be proclaimed within a certain number of days in the neighbouring cities; and after the expiration of 10 days from the proclamation that all captures and acts of war shall be redressed and restored. As this is a matter of so much importance, it will be advisable for you to use your best efforts both with the King and his Council to induce the former to send his final decision with regard to it, and as soon thereafter as possible you shall have instructions on the other affairs. I am writing this hastily, as you may imagine since we only arrived here yesterday, so I will only add that I have received your letters sent by M. D'Eick; and I fully reciprocate your kind messages.

Brussels, 15th October, 1545.

15 Oct.
Vienna
Hof. Cor.

154. HENRY VIII. to the EMPEROR.

The writer has been informed by the imperial ambassador in England that the King of France intends to send his Admiral to the Emperor, with the object of treating for a peace or truce with England. As the Emperor thinks it desirable that he (Henry) should also send envoys for a similar purpose he has decided to entrust the bearer, the bishop of Winchester, with the mission; and he bespeaks for him the Emperor's credence and consideration.

Windsor, 15 October, 1545.

1545.
15 Oct.
Vienna
Hof. Cor.

155. HENRY VIII. to the QUEEN DOWAGER OF HUNGARY.

The bishop of Winchester is being despatched on a mission to the Emperor; and through him to communicate with the French envoys. Begs the Queen to aid and favour him.

Windsor, 15 October, 1545.

22 Oct.
Vienna
Imp. Arch.

156. VAN DER DELFT to the EMPEROR.

Since writing my letters of the 14th instant I have received those of M. de Granvelle, informing me that by your Majesty's commands he and M. D'Eick had dealt with the English ambassador at Brussels in the matter of the truce, and also that the French ambassadors there had asked him whether the King of England intended to include the Scots (in the truce). He (Granvelle) instructed me to use every possible effort to sound the people here on these points.

I have, Sire, been unable to ascertain anything, beyond the fact that the negotiations for the truce, so far as these people are concerned, are solely directed to the particular point which your Majesty knows of.* There is really no question of any truce with the French, much less with the Scots; though in my opinion if they (the English) were assured on the private points referred to they might be induced to agree to it, although affairs in Scotland are very favourable for them, as is confirmed by all the captains and soldiers who come from there.

I suppose that the bishop of Winchester will already have arrived there to negotiate with the French representative. The folks here are extremely curious to know about the arrival of the latter and they never fail to ask me for news on the subject. I am writing similarly to M. de Granvelle, but more in detail so it will not be necessary for me to weary your Majesty further.

London, 22 October, 1545.

23 Oct.
Simancas.
E. F. 501.

157. SECRETARY IDIAQUEZ to FRANCISCO DE LOS COBOS.

Dandino† and Marquina have arrived here with the Bull of the Pope concerning the half-first fruits and the sale of the monastic manors. One clause of the treaty, as it is now worded, is to the effect that if the war against the protestants does not take place, the half-first fruits shall be restored to the churches, and the manors revert to the monasteries. The Emperor objects to this clause. The Pope undertakes to pay to the Emperor a subvention of 200,000 ducats, and to provide a contingent of 12,000 foot and 500 horse to aid the enterprise against the protestants. The draft treaty now brought, however, makes no mention of the further 100,000 ducats, which the Pope was to pay. It is stipulated also that the papal contingent is only to remain with the Emperor for

---

* That is to say the proposed interview between Henry and Charles for which the former was so anxious, and which could not take place unless a cessation of hostilities was arranged. This was the confidential mission with which Henry had sent Scepperus back to the Emperor.
† Bishop of Caserta, the Pope's envoy.

four months. The Emperor demands that they shall be at his disposal for the duration of the war. The reply of the Pope to these objections is daily expected. The negotiations between France and England remain without change since my last. The Emperor has taken up the matter in order that he may be able to mediate between them. The German troops engaged by the King of England have already entered French territory and are marching towards Calais. The French have not yet made any definite offers to the English. They evidently wish to conclude peace, but do not like to be the first to propose it. It is expected that the King of France will shortly send an important personage to the Emperor.

(Ghent) 23 October, 1545.

23 Oct.
Simancas.
E. F. 501.

158. The EMPEROR to PRINCE PHILIP.

(The first two pages are occupied with the discussion of the details of the Papal concessions, recently made by the Pope for the purpose of raising funds from ecclesiastical sources in Spain. The Bulls, etc., had not been delivered, as the papal envoy Dandino (bishop of Caserta) insisted upon settling finally at the same time the details of the convention between the Emperor and the Pope, by which the latter was bound to aid the former in his already projected campaign for the suppression of the German protestants. These points after discussion with Dandino had been again referred to the Pope). (See previous letter, page 268.)

With regard to the opening of the Council (of Trent) we replied that his Holiness might pronounce it open whenever he pleased. Dandino represented that, owing to the smallness, dearness and unhealthiness of Trent, it would be advisable to transfer the Council elsewhere; and he pressed us to consider this.

The inconvenience of such a change was pointed out to him, and he was told that we were of opinion that it could not be entertained on any account. We have already informed you that one of the reasons for our return hither from Germany, was our desire to find some means of bringing about peace between France and England; in which were determined to do our best. With this end we wrote to our sister the Queen of Hungary, asking her to send envoys to both parties, to persuade them to concord by every possible means. This was done and the result was that both sides expressed their willingness to treat for peace on honourable conditions, although it was impossible to get them to agree about the restoration of Boulogne. The King of France has made up his mind to obtain the place, and the King of England is just as determined to retain it; though, as he says, out of consideration for us, he is willing to pay a money indemnity for it. In view of this, we have again instructed our resident ambassadors to persevere in their efforts, and bring about, at least, a suspension of hostilities for six weeks, pending which time both sides might send ambassadors hither with full instructions and powers; and we might consider by what means a peace might be effected. The King of France has informed our ambassador that he will accept the truce, and will send his plenipotentiaries as requested; and there are indications that one of the latter will be the Admiral. But the King of England has not

1545.

replied, though his answer is expected every day. When it arrives we will consider the whole matter, and will let you know what is decided.

With regard to the restitution of the ships and merchandise taken from our subjects in France during this war, Carvajal came hither and gave us full details of all that had been done. He was sent back again without delay; and we wrote at the same time very urgently to our ambassador, telling him to spare no effort in the matter. The last advices we have received, is that the King of France is willing to restore everything that still remains in being, and it is said that part of the property has already been given up. This, however, is an insufficient redress, as most of the property is no doubt already dispersed amongst many different holders; and we have, therefore, again written to the ambassador, and have spoken to the French (ambassadors) expressing great annoyance at the ill-treatment suffered by our subjects. We shall continue to do so until our subjects obtain redress.

With regard to England also, efforts have been, and will still be made, to a similar end. The King's reply is expected, and the person we have sent thither is instructed to follow the matter up diligently. It may be hoped that when the envoys come to the conference some good result may be obtained. With regard to the ships which the French are said to be fitting out for the Indies, nothing has yet been heard here. On the contrary, when the King of France was recently spoken to about it, he was anxious to give us the most perfect assurance. If we learn anything further on the point we will let you know.

Ghent, 28 October, 1545.

26 Oct.
Brussels.
Neg. Ang.

159. INSTRUCTIONS given to you CORNELIUS SCEPPERUS and FRANCIS VAN DER DELFT, knights and councillors, for the representations to be made by you to the KING OF ENGLAND, our good brother, cousin and perpetual ally, to whom you, SCEPPERUS, are now returning.

After cordial greetings, you will tell the King that you Scepperus have fully reported to us the conversations you had had with him, both on the subject of the proposed interview with us, and as regards the truce or a peace between him and the King of France. We have also been informed of the despatch of powers to the English resident ambassadors here, of the need for clearing up and settling certain secret points in disputes contained in our treaty of alliance, before the proposed interview takes place, in accordance with the terms of the instructions given to you on the 20 September. We have deeply considered these matters; and, as the King has, both through his own ambassador and through you, Scepperus, expressed a desire to learn, as soon as possible, our decision with regard to the interview, and the place fixed upon for it, in order that he might make his preparations, we have thought well to send you back at once to convey the following message to him.

First, having heard from you, Scepperus, when you first returned from England, of the King's great wish to cross the sea, for the purpose of seeing us, if we would approach our Flanders-Artois

1545.

frontier:—We, after weighing the present state of our affairs, are as anxious to see the King as he is to see us; and, with that end in view, we at once sent a special courier to our brother the King of the Romans, and to some of our confidential ministers, in order to learn from them whether our presence at the States of the Empire on the 6th January, could be deferred for a time, without too much injuring the interests of the Empire.

We have now received a reply, to the effect that, in order to keep our promise to the States, and to avoid giving an excuse for them to delay their attendance on the date fixed; to redress the disturbances that may arise there owing to the death of the Archbishop of Mayence, the first elector, and owing to the war raised by certain princes such as Duke Henry of Brunswick and his adversaries; and, above all, to enable us to make timely preparations to resist the Turk, the truce or peace with whom is very uncertain, no news of our ambassadors with him having been received; and for several other reasons, it is of the greatest importance that we should not fail to be present at the Imperial Diet on the day fixed; or earlier if possible.[°]

In view of this reply, which is weighty and reasonable, and of the fact that the King's voyage across could not be made so soon, or before the truce with the French was arranged, which truce has now been delayed by the difficulty raised by the English ambassador, who, in virtue of the powers sent to him, would not negotiate for a truce unless a peace was to be negotiated jointly with it; the interview, as the King very prudently points out, being impossible without a truce: having regard also to the weather, which henceforth will be unsettled as the winter is approaching, the days short, and the sea rough, and dangerous to the person of the King, which should not be put in peril: and also, as we are informed, the King is sending to us one of the most confidential of his Councillors, the bishop of Winchester, by which it may appear that he (the King) is not now so pressing for the interview, and the business that it was intended to transact in it may be done by the bishop, a person so competent and confidential: and finally that the matter may be kept secret until the proper time comes we are of opinion that only with the greatest difficulty could such an interview be arranged at the present time, desirous of it as we both may be.

In order to extinguish the flame of war raised amongst the princes of the Empire, which war, but for our presence, will spread and may cause the entire ruin of the German nation: and also in order to take our measures against the Turk, who will probably, as usual, not allow this opportunity to pass of making war on the side of Hungary, knowing of the troubles, dissensions and intestine war in Germany, we are more than ever urged to depart from these dominions; and, with the greatest speed we can command, we purpose travelling to Germany. We feel sure that when these considerations are laid before the King, he will, in his affection for us, approve of the course we have indicated. Otherwise it would have given us great pleasure to have awaited his coming; and to have seen him, even if the delay had been longer than that mentioned by

---

[°] The Emperor is careful not to mention his principal reason, namely the gathering of his army and the surprise of the German Protestant princes by an overwhelming force.

1545.

him. You will, on our behalf, pray him to take this in good part; and avoid further troubling himself personally in the hope of bringing about the interview, which, however, may, with God's help, yet be effected on a better opportunity than the present.

With regard to the specification of the secret clauses in the Treaty of alliance, which, in any case, it will be well to elucidate: since the King has sent so competent a person as the bishop of Winchester, who informed you of these secret points to be discussed, it may be concluded that the bishop will be sufficiently authorised by the King to deal with them; in which case we will give him our final decision before we leave these dominions. In case the bishop of Winchester is not bringing such powers, you will request the King to send them to him, in order that these affairs may be well settled. He will find that in this, and other respects, we shall always be anxious to please him, as is demanded by our good friendship and alliance; and we hope that on his side a similar feeling exists.

Up to the present we have no reply to the communication made to the English ambassador in Brussels, which communication he undertook to convey to the King, touching the truce with France. As the bishop of Winchester will probably know the King's intentions in this respect, you will go to him (i.e. Gardiner) and speak to him on the matter. You will urge that the truce should be concluded as speedily as possible, for the reasons given to the (English) ambassador. You, Scepperus, have seen letters from our ambassador in France, saying that the King of France had already chosen the Admiral, and that the latter was deferring his departure until the time had been agreed to. You will therefore on this and other points, use such arguments as you will find effective to induce the bishop of Winchester to favour the conclusion of the truce, which is necessary for all reasons, as the King of England himself has acknowledged. If you find you cannot prevail with the bishop of Winchester, you will use your efforts with the King, to get the truce considered, as soon as possible.

When you have set forth the above matters to the King, and have done what else you can to the same effect, you, Scepperus, will return to our sister the Queen of Hungary, whilst you, Van der Delft, will remain at your post, reporting to us all events of importance, in accordance with your previous instructions.

Ghent, 26 October, 1845.

26 Oct.
Vienna
Hof. Cor.

160. The EMPEROR to HENRY VIII.

M. D'Eick duly delivered the King's letter, and he is now ordered to return to England and, jointly with the resident ambassador, to convey a verbal message from the Emperor to the King.

Ghent, 26 October, 1545.

26 Oct.
Vienna
Hof. Cor.

161. The EMPEROR to the BISHOP OF WINCHESTER.

Is glad to hear of the bishop's arrival in Flanders, and has instructed M. D'Eick, who is now returning to England, to call upon the bishop on his way and confer with him.

Ghent, 26 October, 1545.

HENRY VIII.

1545.
26 Oct.
Vienna
Hof. Cor.

162. The Emperor to Van der Delft.

I have seen your letter written in answer to that of de Granvelle from Brussels (*i.e.* of 15 October). Scepperus is again returning to England and carries with him our instructions for you both, with regard to the latest mission with which he was entrusted by the King of England.

Ghent, 26 October, 1545.

27 Oct.
Vienna
Imp. Arch.

163. Scepperus to de Granvelle.

I expected to have found the bishop of Winchester at Bruges, but since Saturday and up to the present time he has remained in this town of Nieuport, not really on account of any bodily indisposition, but rather because of the delay that has taken place in the arrival of the Admiral of France by the side of the Emperor, although I have explained to him that the delay has arisen through the lack of a decision in the matter of the truce proposed in the interests of both parties. You will see the reply he gave me on the point, in my letter to the Emperor.

I also understand from him that his King will not retain in his service the Germans who are at Calais and elsewhere. He is dissatisfied with them, and is going to complain to the Emperor about those who were under the command of Frederick Von Reissenberg.

Nieuport, Tuesday, 27 October, 1545.

27 Oct.
Vienna
Imp. Arch.

164. Scepperus to the Emperor.

In accordance with your Majesty's instructions I have simply pointed out to the bishop of Winchester, who is now here at Nieuport, how important it is in the interest of his master the King that the truce with the French should be concluded as speedily as possible. In support of this I adduced several reasons and arguments which he admitted were of great weight; but he nevertheless assured me distinctly that he had no authority from the King to discuss or negotiate any such truce, unless your Majesty will consent to the interview desired by the King here, and not otherwise. The sole object of his (*i.e.* Gardiner's) coming to your Majesty he says, is to negotiate peace. He expected to have found the Admiral of France here for a similar purpose, otherwise he would not have hurried as he has done.

I find also that he has no power to treat with your Majesty on the secret points, which I submitted to you. The only course, therefore, is to request the King of England to grant such powers; and this I will do as soon as I arrive there, sending your Majesty due report of this and the rest of my mission.

Nieuport, 27 October, 1545.

29 Oct.
Simancas.
E. R.
872.

165. The Emperor to Juan de Vega (Ambassador in Rome).

(Highly approves of his discourse to the Pope and Cardinal Farnese, about the death of the Duke of Orleans and as to the Emperor's desire to continue at peace with the King of France. His thanks to the Pope and Cardinal for their expressions of

1545.

adhesion to the Emperor's interests were discreet: but he is not to go beyond them, or to admit any suggestion of theirs to intervene in the discussion of affairs (with France) "for matters are not yet in a position to be carried so far.") The Kings of France and England had agreed to treat for peace, and to send their envoys hither to us for this purpose; but the matter has been at a stand, as the King of France raises a difficulty about sending the Admiral, whom he needs for the war, and, moreover, the Admiral could not come, because of the German troops, which the King of England was bringing down, and which had already entered French territory. We learn now, however, that these troops have been dismissed and sent away; although they still keep with them the King of England's Commissioners, and their Colonel, until another month's pay has been given to them. We are in hopes, therefore, that the plenipotentiaries will soon be here, the bishop of Winchester, for England, being already near Bruges; and the Admiral of France may come in a few days. When they have arrived we shall see whether they are willing to come to terms. This being the condition of affairs, it does not seem advisable that the Pope should take any steps, or move in the matter at all. We have sent you this information confidentially, in order that you may arrange accordingly, and prevent the coming of the Cardinal (Farnese), or any other person they may want to send, to interfere, until affairs change, of which we will advise you. We have received no letter from the Cardinal. You may explain and apologise to him as you please.

It was well to send the Brief about the newly converted Moriscos of Granada, which was very necessary. Your care and diligence in the matter are highly approved of. (The rest of the letter (1¼ pages) is occupied entirely with Spanish ecclesiastical matters.)

Ghent, 29 October, 1545.

30 Oct.*
Vienna
Imp. Arch.

166. The EMPEROR to SCHEPPERUS and VAN DER DELFT.

The French ambassador resident here has informed us to-day that, notwithstanding the answer the King gave to our ambassador, to the effect that the dispatch of the Admiral of France would be deferred until the truce with the King of England had been arranged; since he had now learnt of the dismissal of the Germans who were near Liège for the purpose of invading his dominions, he (the King of France) had decided to send hither his admiral and his chancellor to discuss his differences with the King of England. We think necessary to inform you of this, and have also declared it here to the English ambassador for the information of the bishop of Winchester. We are leaving here on Monday next for Bruges to exert our influence as we may see advisable.

Ghent, October, 1545.

---

* The letter bears no date, but as the Emperor did not arrive at Ghent until the 28th or 29th of October, it must have been written on one of the last three days of the month.

HENRY VIII.

1545.
7 Nov.
Vienna
Hof. Cor.

167. HENRY VIII. to the EMPEROR.

He has received from M. D'Eick and the resident ambassador a full account of their mission. D'Eick will personally convey the King's answer to the Emperor; and the English ambassadors at the imperial court are also instructed on the matter.

Windsor, 7 November, 1545.

11 Nov.
Vienna
Imp. Arch.

168. VAN DER DELFT to the EMPEROR.

On the 14th October, I sent by your Majesty's courier a letter reporting that the bishop of Winchester was going to Flanders and giving an account of conversations I had had with the King. I had hoped that this courier would promptly have reached your Majesty, but I now learn that something has befallen him on the road and no one knows what has become of him. I will have proper enquiries made; and in the meanwhile send herewith copies of the letters he carried, although your Majesty will have learned through M. D'Eick full details not only as regards the past, but also with respect to the statement he made in my presence to the King, on his (Scepperus') return, and also the reply given by the King. With regard to Renegat I have not been able yet to obtain the restitution to me of what he captured from the Indies ship but the Councillors promise me faithfully to deliver it to me intact, although they bitterly complain of the seizure of English property effected in Spain. They thought some time ago that this would be annulled, or at least that the property seized would be disembargoed against security, especially as I am ceaselessly insisting that captures made here, however suspicious the circumstances, should be released on security being given. I am greatly afraid that I shall find difficulty in obtaining this in view of the course adopted in Spain; because they immediately begin to lag, and say that the reason why they entertained the suggestion was that they thought that the arrests (in Spain) would be raised some time since, at least against security; whereas they hear from the merchants that the contrary is the case; as your Majesty will learn more amply from M. D'Eick. I will nevertheless employ my every effort to obtain restitution of Renegat's plunder.

With regard to the complaints of your subjects—Spaniards and others—who have suffered injury from the agents of this King I have done my best, and have jointly with M. D'Eick spoken on the matter to the Chancellor of England begging that justice might be done.

London, 11 November, 1545.

16 Nov.
Simancas.
E. F. 501.

169. The EMPEROR to ST. MAURIS (Imperial Ambassador in France).

Thanks for diligence in reporting occurrences in France, and especially as regards the mission of the Admiral and Chancellor, the negotiations for peace with England, and the suggestion about marriage (*i.e.*, of Prince Philip) with Madame Margaret of France. The French plenipotentiaries arrived on the 7th instant, and we have been in conference with them and the Bishop of Winchester

1545.

and other English envoys daily. Up to the present however, it has been utterly impossible to come to any conclusion. The French demand the immediate surrender of Boulogne, in return for which they do not offer the smallest concession of territory. They offer to pay the arrears of "pension" to the King of England, and to give him 100,000 soldi as an equivalent for the works which the English have executed in Boulogne. They would, as a last concession, consent to pay a further 50,000; and have left to our arbitration the fixing of the sum within these limits, this being included as a clause in the treaty. The English, on the other hand, are resolved to retain Boulogne itself, or else to obtain for it a territorial indemnity elsewhere. The greatest concession which the English might be induced to make, although they have not yet declared themselves on the point, would be to surrender Boulogne to the French, after the whole of the arrears due to the King of England had been paid; and on the undertaking of the French to pay to him a life annuity of 100,000 soldi, and on his death to pay an annuity of 50,000 to his successors in perpetuity. This being the state of the negotiations, there seems nothing more for us to do than to await the return of the ambassador,* and see the intelligence he will bring. It will perhaps be best to negotiate a suspension of hostilities first.

It is said that the Protestants who intervened in the negotiations for peace between England and France have declared that they have good reasons for hope that Boulogne will be restored and Scotland included in the treaty. But the bishop of Winchester and the other English envoys swear roundly that, neither their master nor any of his servants, have ever hinted at such a thing; and that there is not the remotest probability of such a solution having been considered. You will, however, avoid all reference to, or appearance of knowing anything about these Protestant negotiations. The French have declared that they are ready to fulfil the clauses of the treaty of Crépy, and are at the same time pressing urgently for the marriage of our son (Prince Philip) with Madame Margaret, in order to ensure perpetual peace between us and the King of France. We have assured them that we, too, are quite willing to carry out the treaty of Crépy, and have spoken in great praise of the suggested marriage: but we have insisted that the Duke of Savoy should be restored to all his former possessions, that Hesdin should be surrendered against a reasonable indemnity, and that our subjects should be reinstated in the possession of the property of which they have been deprived.

Bruges, 16 November, 1545.

(Spanish translation in the handwriting of Ruy Gomez, evidently made for the use of Prince Philip.)

---

* The word ambassador in the original is underlined, and a note of interrogation is placed against it in the margin, showing that the recipient of the copy in Spain did not understand who was meant. It is probable that the Emperor was referring to Scepperus, who, as will be seen in a previous page, had been again sent to England to urge the conclusion of a truce late in the preceding month of October, and had apparently not yet reached the Emperor on his return, though he left London on the 12th November, four days before this letter was written.

HENRY VIII.

1545.
19 Nov.
Simancas.
E. Genoa.
1377.

170. PRINCE ANDREA DORIA to PRINCE PHILIP.

(First paragraphs concern the galleys in the Mediterranean.)

The Emperor is, according to my last advice of 31st ultimo, in good health, and is endeavouring to bring about a peaceful settlement between France and England.

The Landgrave (of Hesse), who was authorised by the King of England to raise a body of troops for him, has employed them to deprive the Duke of Brunswick of his States, and has taken him and his son prisoners.

Genoa, 19 November, 1545.

21 Nov.
Vienna
Hof. Cor.

171. HENRY VIII. to the EMPEROR.

Bespeaks friendly consideration and credence for the bishops of Winchester and Westminster, who are instructed to convey an important communication to the Emperor.

Westminster, 21 November, 1545.

25 Nov.
Simancas.
E. F. 501.

172. The EMPEROR to ST. MAURIS (Imperial Ambassador in France).

Left Bruges on the 16th and arrived at Antwerp on the 18th instant, at the same time as the French and English plenipotentiaries arrived there. The French ambassador at first avoided all reference to the business that brought them hither, either the peace negotiations with England, or the private negotiations with us. At last, however, on Monday they said they had heard that the English ambassadors had received the answer from their master, and asked us whether there was any chance of the negotiations being resumed. We replied that we had just heard from the English ambassadors the answer they had received from the King, and we promised them (*i.e.*, the French ambassadors) that we would communicate the intelligence to them after dinner. The French ambassadors and our commissioners being assembled, the latter said that the English ambassadors had received from their master strict and imperative orders to make it clear that he intended to retain Boulogne, which he had won by the sword in a great and righteous war, and which had cost him the blood of many of his best subjects. The English ambassadors added (said our commissioners) an expression of their great surprise that the King of France could imagine that Boulogne could be given back to him on the pretext that his honour demanded it. The King of England highly prized the possession of the place, and if it were returned to the King of France the latter would forget all about the debts due to the King of England, and would pay neither the arrears nor the future instalments. It would, moreover, only be an encouragement for the French to launch into future wars inconsiderately, and involve the English in vast expenditure. When the English had by great sacrifices of men and money gained a place from the French the latter would simply make peace and expect to regain without the surrender of any equivalent, the territory they had lost. It was not reasonable. The French ambassadors continued as resolute as before in demanding the restoration of Boulogne, whilst the English remained as determined to hold it.

278   SPANISH STATE PAPERS.

1545

With the acquiescence of the English we then proposed to the French that the English should retain Boulogne on paying to the French a money indemnity; which however was to be kept distinct from the pension payable to the King of England; but the French rejected this proposal.

A truce was then proposed; and the French expressed their willingness to accept it, if the request for it came from the English, but they themselves would never ask for it. The English made a similar declaration: they would accept a truce, out of respect for the Emperor's efforts, but they would not seek it. All expedients for bringing about a settlement being thus exhausted, the French ambassadors asked when they might be allowed to take leave of us. They were reminded that there were other negotiations to be completed, concerning the peace between us and the King of France. They replied that all possible concessions on their side had been made, and that all that was due to the Duke of Savoy and the Empire had already been granted. On this and all other outstanding points we could obtain nothing but general and evasive answers from the French ambassadors, who suggested that the further negotiations might be conducted by the resident ambassadors or by special plenipotentiaries appointed for the purpose.

When the conference had thus been brought to an end, the Admiral of France took M. de Praet and M. de Granvelle aside to a corner of the room, and proposed to them the immediate agreement for a marriage between the Prince (Philip) and Madame Margaret of France, leaving until later the settlement of the Duke of Savoy's affairs. Messieurs de Praet and Granvelle excused themselves from the course suggested, alleging the duty the Emperor owed to the empire, of which Savoy was a part.

The King of France has replied to our invitation that he should attend in person or by proxy the next assembly of the order (of the Golden Fleece). In communicating the King's reply, the Admiral of France added that when the King learnt of the failure of the peace negotiations between France and England, he had declared that no further action was to be taken in the matter. Although the English are disinclined to make peace at the present juncture, they will be glad to do so by and bye. But, continued the Admiral, his reason for coming hither was not to make any declaration respecting the English, but to inform the Emperor that the King of France really wished for the conclusion of a marriage between the Prince and Madame Margaret, which marriage would be a guarantee of perpetual peace between the two Houses.

(The rest of this letter, four pages, is occupied entirely with the affairs of Piedmont and the claims of the Duke of Savoy.)

Antwerp, 25 November, 1545.

(Spanish translation in the handwritings of Ruy Gomez and Idiaquez, evidently for the perusal of Prince Philip.)

25 Nov. (?)
Simancas.
E. F. 501.

173. News sent by SECRETARY IDIAQUEZ (apparently to the DUKE OF ALBA).

The Emperor has been negotiating in Bruges with the French and English plenipotentiaries; but as no settlement could be

1545.

arrived at; they came to this place (*i.e.*, Antwerp) where the negotiations are continued.

The Emperor has entered into negotiations on his own account with the French; but it has not yet been found possible to draft the articles of a treaty, as the French raise many difficulties, and would raise many more if the Emperor's attitude towards the English did not enable him to conclude an alliance with the King of England immediately the negotiations with France were broken off. The Landgrave (of Hesse) has forced the Duke of Brunswick to make peace with him. No answer has arrived from Rome to the points conveyed thither by Marquina. (*See* page 269.)

No news of the truce with the Turk.

30 Nov.
Vienna
Imp. Arch.

174. VAN DER DELFT to the EMPEROR.

Since the return thither of M. D'Eick, who carried with him my last letters, nothing has happened here worthy of writing to your Majesty, except that whilst M. D'Eick was still here there was some talk of sending the first secretary Paget oversea (we understood to your Majesty); and he started some days since accompanied by the bishop of Durham, but they have not left the King's dominions as they still remain at Calais or the neighbourhood.* This has rendered me very suspicious as he (Paget) gave me no indication of his departure as is usually done by personages here who are sent to your Majesty. As it seemed advisable that I should discover as far as possible the meaning of this voyage of the secretary to Calais, especially as the protestant envoys are still tarrying there, and the place is so near the French, I have made strenuous efforts to obtain some intelligence on the subject. The only thing, however, that I have yet been able to learn is that the voyage may be to meet certain French envoys, some people say the bishop of Soissons and the president of Rouen, who have been for the last eight days at Ardres. I have no doubt that your Majesty has better information of this than I, both by means of the ambassadors with you, and by advices from the neighbourhood of Gravelines. Still I have thought well to let your Majesty know.

A few days ago, when the King was at the opening of Parliament, the Chancellor made his speech, setting forth the invasion effected by the King of France and his allies, of this realm, and at divers points both by land and sea. The King of England (the Chancellor continued) was obliged to resist and defend himself, which he had done without loss and greatly to his honour, as all men knew. He therefore desired parliament to bear in mind that this had not been without incurring great expense. Secondly he set forth that there were certain bishops in the realm who are usurping and exercising prerogatives belonging to the King; and that this evil must be remedied, allowing the said bishops to remain in possession of their property and estates whilst the King enjoyed his own. On these points, and others depending upon them, parliament meets every

---

* It will be seen later that these direct negotiations with the French were more successful than previous attempts to come to terms, a three months' truce being arranged early in the following year, and a peace subsequently.

day, the King being often present in person; the people in general showing good will to contribute, owing to the hopes they have of peace.

Sire, four days since, out of compliment to the position I hold here as representing your Majesty, I was invited by the Lord Admiral to stand sponsor to a daughter of his, *the godmothers being Lady Mary in person and the widowed Duchess of Suffolk.† As the time we were assembled was somewhat long, Lady Mary, after showing me much honour and compliment, entered into conversation with me in various languages which she speaks very well. She said much of her great affection for your Majesty and of the joy she felt to hear of your health and prosperity. I replied appropriately, giving her similar assurances on behalf of your Majesty, with which she appeared much pleased and seemed really to enjoy her chat with me, which though rather long was of no importance, except that she said that all her wishes and constant prayers to God were that the present good and perfect friendship between your Majesty and the King might continue. I assured her absolutely that such would be the case, so far as your Majesty was concerned. I have thought well to report this pleasant conversation to your Majesty and pray for pardon if I have gone beyond my province in doing so.

London, 30 November, 1545.

15 Dec.
Simancas.
E. F. 500.

175. The EMPEROR to FRANCISCO DE LOS COBOS.

You will probably have already been informed of the negotiations which have taken place at Bruges and Antwerp, between our Commissioners and the plenipotentiaries of England and France. Notwithstanding the assurances given to us on that occasion, it is said by persons coming from France that the war will soon break out again. We do not think that this will be the case; but nevertheless, the frontiers of Spain towards France must be held by forces sufficient to defend them, if necessary. Bois le Duc (Herzogenbusch), 15 December, 1545.

18 Dec.
Simancas.
E. F. 501.
extract.

176. News sent to Spain by the Emperor's Spanish Secretary, IDIAQUEZ.

The French are very desirous of the marriage and will soon renew the negotiations for it.‡ It will, however, be taken in hand not by the ambassadors but by other persons. The English ambassadors are staying there (Brussels?) and amuse themselves as best they can. It is impossible for them to come to an understanding with the French, except through the mediation of the Emperor. The fact that the Emperor can, at any time he thinks fit, arrive at a perfect

---

* This was Lady Catharine Dudley who married Henry, third Earl of Huntingdon.
† This was Catharine Lady Willoughby in her own right whose mother had been the favourite Spanish friend of Catharine of Aragon. She subsequently married Francis Bertie and fled from the Marian persecution to Germany.
‡ That is the marriage that had been proposed by the Admiral of France (Hannebault) at Antwerp late in November, between the recently widowed Prince Philip and Margaret of France.

1545.

agreement with the English, is one of the principal means to bring the French to listen to reason. M. Gerard, who has gone with the French ambassador to conclude a truce with the Turk, has written that an agreement has been made to suspend hostilities for four years.

The (known) friar has returned from France. He brings the same news as that which the Admiral had already communicated; with the addition that the French are desirous of bringing about the marriage of the Prince of Piedmont with the daughter of D'Albret.

(*Endorsed*:—Political news sent by Secretary Idiaquez, Brussels, 18th December, 1545.)

20 Dec.
Vienna
Imp. Arch.

177. The Emperor to Van der Delft.

The ambassador of Portugal resident here has informed us that his King was sending to the King of England a gentleman of his to treat with him of certain affairs set forth in the letters of credence given to the envoy. The said gentleman fell ill on the road, and finding himself in danger of dying of his malady whilst in France, he sent his credentials, etc., to the said ambassador. The latter recognising the pressing nature of the mission is sending to England with the same credentials another gentleman, who is the bearer of the present letter, and he begs us to write desiring you to introduce him and help him with the King. We request that you will do so, giving him all the assistance you fairly can.

As the bishop of Winchester is still at Utrecht, in communication with our sister the Queen Dowager of Hungary and our representatives, and as the gout from which we are suffering has prevented us from going to Utrecht, we are unable to write you anything as to the decision that will be arrived at with the said bishop. We are, however, now much better; and hope to depart as soon as the Christmas holidays are over, and to go to Utrecht. From there we will write you fully as to the negotiations with the bishop of Winchester and all other points. 20 December, 1545.*

21 Dec.
Vienna
Imp. Arch.

178. Van der Delft to the Emperor.

This day the Lords of the Council have sent to me as they say by command of the King to inform me that there lately arrived here a Spanish comendador with letters of recommendation from the Duke of Alburquerque in order that this King might receive him in his service. The letter also stated than in consequence of a dispute he had had with another gentleman of your Majesty's household, he had found it advisable to leave your service, he having filled an office in your chamber; and in consequence of your Majesty's displeasure he had been commanded to live on his commandery in Spain. As he had not found favour with the Prince (Philip) he had withdrawn himself from Spain and had come hither. It appeared to the Council that this letter was a forgery; as

---

* The place from which place this letter was written is not clear, but it must have been Herzogenbusch, where the Emperor was laid up with gout from the 4th December until the 28th, when he left for Utrecht (Vandenesse. Itinerary).

1545.

the comendador had called himself by divers names, Don Pedro Pacheco in one place, Don Pedro de la Cueva in another, and Herrera in a third, his own servants not rightly knowing what to call him; and the Council consequently did not know what to think of him. Their doubt was increased by the fact that a French gentleman, who has recently joined this King's household, named M. de Bertheuille, otherwise Fontenay, had advised them that when your Majesty was before St. Disier, this comendador had carried on intelligence with him (Fontenay) and certain other Frenchmen; giving them much secret information about your Majesty's camp. The Councillors therefore gave me the above information in order that I might tell them my opinion about it. The King was inclined to send him back whence he came as he was a subject of your Majesty; only that he feared by this information that he might have done some other disservice or disloyalty and he therefore preferred, if I approved of it, to keep the gentleman by fair means, until I had time to report to your Majesty. I replied thanking the King and Council, who I said were so sage and prudent that they well knew the sort of person this must be. I had, I said, some knowledge of this comendador, who although he had only come to see me two or three times, I soon found to be shaky in his words (*vacillant en ses parolles*) and I thought the King would easily find as good servants as he would be. With regard to their intention to keep him till I reported to your Majesty, I approved of it and I would write on the subject. I now humbly do so and beg for your good commands.

In case the person of this comendador may be unknown to your Majesty in consequence of change of name, I may say that in the course of conversation he told me that he was sent twice by your Majesty to the King of France about the ransom of Count William of Furstenberg. I also gathered from his talk that he had long lived in France.

London, 21 December, 1545.

(June?) Simancas. E. 72.

179. EXAMINATION of JUAN ORTIZ DE LA REA, junior, a native of Castro Urdiales, before the ALCALDES RONQUILLO and CASTELLO in the royal prison at Valladolid.*

The prisoner deposes that he, being a soldier by profession, of sixteen years' service, was in Flanders last July, having gone to Antwerp with the intention of joining the Emperor's forces. But hearing that the Lorrainers were killing those who attempted to pass through their country, and he being alone and afraid, he decided to go to the King of England's army then before Boulogne. He was moved to this by hearing that the Duke of Alburquerque was with the English by his Majesty's orders, and the Duke had written to the deponent in Spain saying that he wished some gentlemen to go and join him there (*i.e.*, before Boulogne). The deponent took a servant with him called Juan Sangentes of

---

* The manuscript here summarised consists of twenty closely written pages; but as the legal form and phraseology are extremely involved and redundant, the important points alone are given here, in a condensed narrative shape.

1545.

Somorrostro. As soon as deponent arrived before Boulogne he went to salute the Duke of Alburquerque and offered his services. The Duke thanked him and asked him if he would accept a Captain's Commission to raise Spanish soldiers for the English service. He replied that he had no means of doing this, as there were no Spanish soldiers in Flanders: but he would rather serve as a private soldier with a pike over his shoulder and a corslet on his breast, than as Captain, as he had no men to begin with. The Duke approved of this and sent deponent with a servant of his called Inestrosa to speak with a gentleman named Henry Knyvett, a favourite and chamberlain of the King of England, who served as interpreter between the King and the Duke. The Duke and Knyvett afterwards spoke to the King about the deponent's wages which were fixed at 20 ducats a month as man at arms during the time of the war. The deponent then kissed the King's hand, and was in his pay and service until the camp was broken up, when he asked Knyvett whether he should remain at Boulogne or not. He was told that it was no good staying there as no Spanish men at arms would remain, but he had better return with the King to England. He did so, carrying his arms, horses, servants, etc., with him, and accompanying the Duke and Knyvett. He remained in the King's court for three or four months receiving there the wages of 20 ducats a month for the time he was on the campaign and for that he passed at court, minus 13 days; but he received no grant or gratuity for his journey to England or for his voyage from and return to Spain. He asked the Duke of Alburquerque to favour him by asking the King to give him a place in his household; but the Duke said that he would not advise him to try for that as Spaniards were not well treated in England; for even whilst he (the Duke) was there they were being unjustly used, and things would be worse in this respect when he had gone. The Duke told him that he could not remain in England with a clear conscience, for if he was overtaken by death there was no one there to confess him, and as he was married it would be much better that he should go home and not think of staying in England. The Duke afterwards told him to ask Knyvett to beg the King to give the deponent a pension in his own house in Spain where he might serve the King as he might be ordered to do. If you do this said the Duke, I will help you with the King and give you a good character. The deponent immediately went to Knyvett and offered to serve the King in Spain or elsewhere out of England. Knyvett replied; the Duke has already spoken about you to the King and says you can serve him with a ship or two. The deponent said yes, he could do this if the King obtained the Emperor's license for him to do so, but he could not bring ships without it. After Knyvett had again spoken to the King he told the deponent that he had better draw up a memorial to his Majesty, which he did; and Knyvett afterwards said to him, "Juan de la Rea the King is willing to maintain you in your own home, on condition that when an English Ambassador goes to Spain you accompany him to Court, and help him as may be needed; and also that you continue to write to the King carefully all that may happen at the Spanish Court. The King will pay for the messengers; and will be glad to

1545.

know how much you ask for this service." The deponent replied that he would leave that to the King. Knyvett then entered the presence chamber and the deponent went to tell the Duke of Alburquerque what had passed. Knyvett afterwards told him that the King was not enamoured of the suggestion but he would speak to his Majesty again about it. Subsequently Knyvett told the deponent that the King would make a present to him simply out of goodwill towards him, and in recognition of what he had done. The deponent was pleased at this, and went to receive the present which was 37½ angels equal to 60 ducats. He had already received 40; so that the 100 represented really only the 5 months and three days pay for the time he had served. The deponent went to the Duke and told him what had passed, whereat the Duke was displeased. The deponent then said to Knyvett. "Sir: the King has given me no present as your worship promised. He has not even paid me for the whole time I have served him, or given me anything for my journey hither and my return. The deponent then asked Knyvett to obtain leave for him to return to Spain, which he did, the license being signed and sealed by the King himself. With this he embarked at Dover for Calais, where he left his passport according to the regulation, and received in return a warrant to pass the guards. With the deponent from London there came Friar Juan de Ludeña, a relative of the Duke. He went by Bruges, and when on his way to Ghent was told that the Emperor was that very day leaving for Antwerp; so the deponent went direct to the latter place where he awaited his Majesty for some days. As he saw that the Emperor's arrival was delayed by the gout, he went to Ramua to see certain relatives of his there, and to embark some property belonging to him which he wished to send home by sea. He returned to Antwerp and thence to Ghent, where he stayed for some days in the hope of speaking to the Emperor on a certain matter interesting to deponent; but seeing that his Majesty continued unwell and could not receive him, the deponent started for Spain by land through France. Being asked whether he went to the French Court, whom he saw there and what he did, the deponent confessed that he went to Fontainebleau where the King of France was, and he remained there 15 days. He there spoke with Don Pedro de Guzman, whom some people call Don Pedro de Noche (Night), with whom he kept company during his stay and gave him an account of his doings in England. Don Pedro Guzman told him that if he liked he would get him into the service of the King of France, who was then at peace with the Emperor. The deponent thanked him and said he would be very glad to serve the King, without prejudice to the Emperor, against the King of England, who had so badly remunerated his services and treated him so scurvily. The deponent being a soldier begged Guzman to speak to the Admiral and the Duke of Orleans for him. They both went with covered faces to speak to them, and the Admiral promised to see the King about it. The principal secretary afterwards told the deponent that the King was ill, but the Admiral had said that the deponent was to receive 300 French livres a year and a Captain's commission to raise infantry. The deponent said he

1545.

could not do this without license from the Emperor and asked whether his appointment was to be made officially at once. The secretary replied no, as the King was ill; but when his Majesty recovered it would be done, so that he might look upon it as certain. But the deponent seeing that the affair was dragging, departed from the French Court and came to Spain. Before he left he gave an account of all this to Don Pedro de Guzman, and to other Spaniards there, but he received neither passport, nor warrant, nor money, nor a commission to raise troops, nor anything else; except only that the secretary made him a present of 50 crowns to buy a horse and help him on the way, as the deponent said he was in need. He came straight from the French Court to his own house by way of Bayonne and St. Jean de Luz, tarrying nowhere. He was asked whether at St. Sebastian or any other place he spoke to any soldiers or others to the effect that he had a commission to raise troops for the King of France. He replied that he had no reason to say such a thing, as he had no commission or authority whatever to raise men. It is true that in Castro Urdiales some of his kinsmen and friends asked him how he had got on; and he told them what had happened to him at the Court of France and in the English service. He was asked whether he had promised to any of these persons money or anything else if they agreed to serve the King of France, and he replied that he had not. He was asked what money had been given or sent to him by the French for raising troops and he said none whatever, nor had he received any communication from them since he left. Had he since he left the French Court spoken or written to any soldiers or others asking them to join him in serving the King of France? No, he had not; except that since his arrival at Castro Urdiales he had written one letter to Gaspar de Otañez his cousin, who had been a soldier at Pamplona, telling him of his arrival and afterwards another letter to the same cousin addressed to his native place, Otañez asking him to come and see him for pleasure, and at this very time he was arrested and he neither saw nor spoke to his cousin except in the town prison where the deponent was confined. All this he solemnly swears is true. Had he ever returned to the French Court after his arrival at his home? No, never; but a servant of his had been drowned in the ship in which he had embarked his property in Flanders. In this ship there had come Captain Tarifa and many other Spanish soldiers, who were drowned when the ship was lost off St. Jean de Luz, and the deponent had gone to that place to see whether he could recover any of his property. He stayed there about four or five days, but recovered nothing, and then returned home without speaking about any other business. He came to his house in company with the master of the ship that had been wrecked, and as he was leaving St. Sebastian fell in with certain Spanish soldiers who were on their way to France. They asked him if he was raising men for the King of France, as they had been told he was. He replied no for he had no authority to do so, but he hoped soon to receive his commission for that purpose. He gave to one of the soldiers, whose name he does not know, a memorandum written and signed by him, saying that the troops which the deponent was to

1545.

raise for the King of France were to be engaged in France, and were to be free from military duty in the Emperor's garrisons. He was asked if since he had been in the royal prison or in the keeping of the Corregidor of Biscay he had informed the King of France, the Admiral, or even the Duke of Alburquerque, of his arrest. He replied that when he was in the town prison of Bilbao he sent by the Emperor's post letters to the Duke of Alburquerque and other Spanish gentlemen telling them, and begging them to favour him. He also wrote to the Admiral of France and to the Chief Secretary saying that he was in prison at the request of the King of England, who had complained of him to the Emperor, but he knew not for what. He had prayed them to ask the Queen of France to write to the Emperor on his behalf; and that he should be brought before judges. He did not write to the King of France, nor to anyone else that he recollects. He was asked whether he endeavoured to buy any ships or galleys, especially the great galley of Don Alvaro de Bazan, and replied that he had never thought of such a thing. Did he bring from France or had he received from there monies to buy arms or other warlike stores? No, such a thing had never even been mentioned to him. Did they not send or bring him from France 10,000 ducats or crowns, or some other amount of money for the purposes named? No. Nothing passed or happened beyond what he has already said. But (he was asked) had he not already confessed to some person that what is suggested in the last question was the case; and had he not said that he had a salary of six reals a day from the King of France during the time both of peace and war? No. He recollected no such thing, nor of anything beyond what he has already deposed to have happened at the French Court. He was asked whether since he was lodged in the town prison at Bilbao any soldiers or other persons came to speak to him, and if so what passed with them? No, he replied, no soldiers had come to see him except the aforementioned Gaspar de Otañez, his cousin, who came to visit him, as did many other persons, but he had no conversation with them except on the subject of their visit. He recollects nothing else.

1546.
No date
(1 Jan. ?)
Paris.
Archives
Nationales.
K. 1486.

180. St. Mauris to the King of the Romans.

(Negotiations between the King of France and the Turk.)

The gentlemen here are much annoyed that the Admiral of France should have been sent to the Emperor to negotiate without some preliminary consultation being held. They think his going very inconsiderate, and are of opinion that prior to any negotiation with the Emperor being undertaken, the differences with England should have been settled. They understand perfectly that henceforward the English will be more difficult to deal with than ever, nothing having been arranged between the French and the Emperor. They (the French courtiers) hint that they know well whence proceeds the evil council. The King of France professes to be anxious to fulfil the last treaty and to maintain friendship with the Emperor, and to say the truth, Sire, he speaks from sheer necessity, as he fears lest the Emperor should enter into a close union with England. In any case, Sire, his real

1546.

feelings towards the Emperor are as bad as can be. He would, if he could, keep his Majesty in suspense by dissimulation, whilst he (the King of France) forwarded his usual pernicious practices and prepared for war.

He says sometimes that if he learns that the Emperor aims at breaking the treaty he (the King of France) will avenge himself by arranging with the English the question of Boulogne and the pensions, will consent to the English marriage in Scotland; and will then, with the aid of the English, attack the Emperor's Flemish dominions.

(An account of several conversations with the Dauphin and other persons in the French Court, respecting the projected marriage of Prince Philip with Princess Marguerite, the recession of Piedmont, etc.)

Eight or ten days ago the protestant commissioners returned here from Calais, having done but little towards concluding a peace or truce. But as they were legates they were sent back almost instantly post haste to Calais with instructions to proceed from there to England, if necessary, in order that they might, as if of their own action, bring every pressure to bear upon the English to agree to a truce. They were instructed simply to say that the King of France, in their own opinion, would accept a truce: the idea of people here being that during a years' cessation of hostilities they might finish their fort near Boulogne, and perhaps erect others from which to attack the place. On the other hand, it is asserted that the English claim that they must hold at least that portion of the Boulognais between Calais and Ardres, some ten or twelve leagues of territory, and they absolutely refuse to evacuate it, or allow another fort to be built. They will not consent therefore to a truce of more than four months during the winter; so they are very far from a settlement yet. They will be everlastingly at issue about the said fort as the King of France claims to occupy the whole of the Boulognais which belongs to him, whilst the English swear they will retain it by right of conquest. These people here at first said that in order to thwart the Emperor they would rather agree with the English and surrender Boulogne. The English now reply that they have captured Boulogne in fair fight and mean to keep it, demanding in addition the payment of the overdue pensions, and an assurance for the future. This is quite a different attitude from what the French expected. Sometimes when they are excited they say that they are not bound to pay the pensions, in consequence of the English having broken the treaties that stipulated for the payment. In short, Sire, the French are astounded at the spirit of the English, who are driving them hard by sea, and have caused them such tremendous losses. Amongst their other losses is that of the herring fisheries, to which they dare not go this year, this being the principal livelihood of the Normans. They are therefore less able than ever to contribute to the needs of the war this year. They are, in fact, so distressed and impoverished, that if they are pestered much more this year with impositions, the majority of them will have to abandon the land, as the King of France has been told by many persons. A short time since the King was

1546.

warned that people were murmuring in several parts of the country at the intolerable burden of the taxes, and he was advised to be moderate if he wished to avoid provoking a general rising. It appears as if this year, therefore, he may refrain from further burdening them, but if so, it will only be for the purpose of increasing the taxes next year, and of continuing to demand what he has imposed in the past. They are saying here that in the year 1546 his subjects will rise in rebellion against him in consequence. Except what he may now gather, he has not a single sou for himself, and he even tried to borrow some money of Lyons merchants, some Italians, and some Germans, offering them good security for as much as they would lend. In order to tempt them to do this he recently repaid them some sums he had borrowed from them for the war against the English. If they are wise, however, they will be very cautious how they deal with him in future. It is true that in time the King may get plenty of money, if he likes to extract it from the people; but it will come too late, and he is at present quite destitute.

(The rest of this letter (7 pages) is mainly concerned in Italian and French affairs, the King of France's intrigues against the Emperor, etc., the only matter of moment being a remark upon the great increase of Protestantism in France and the probability of a religious rising.)

7 Jan.
Vienna
Imp. Arch.

181. The EMPEROR to VAN DER DELFT.

We have received your letter of 21st ultimo, and have heard what you wrote to Granvelle in conformity therewith, respecting the Spanish personage referred to. Having considered your communications on the subject, it appears to us that, in any case, the King of England has acted kindly and straightforwardly in informing you through his Council of their impressions of the individual. Having regard to the prevarications of the man, his going thither cannot be otherwise than suspicious; and also that the letter he has presented from the Duke of Alburquerque must be false; since it cannot be possible that the duke would recommend one of our subjects to undertake anything away from our jurisdiction and without our knowledge. If the personage in question be a gentleman, as he affirms, and he says that we had cause to be displeased with him, and consequently ordered him to remain under arrest in the monastery of his order, it would seem as if it must be Don Pedro Portocarrero; who, having committed an outrage on a Spanish gentleman, was ordered by us to be carried a prisoner to the monastery of Uclés. His relationship with the Cuevas and the Herreras, may have given him an opportunity of changing his name; but his statement that he was sent by us to France respecting the release of Count William of Furstenberg is absolutely untrue, with regard to Portocarrero or any other Spaniard. It is obviously impossible in the case of Portocarrero; because he was made prisoner long before we entered France. It is also untrue what you are told by the Frenchman Bertheuille, who is in the King of England's service, to the effect that he obtained information in the French interest, from the personage in question, respecting what went on

HENRY VIII. 289

1546.

when we were before St. Disier. We write you this in detail to put you into possession of all the problems touching this man; and we have thought well to send to England a Spanish alguacil, who is acquainted with Portocarrero, to ascertain whether this man be he, or not. Whoever he is, he has given ample reason for detaining and interrogating him, to discover his identity. Whilst thanking the Council for the kindness and uprightness shown by the King and themselves in the matter, you will beg them on our behalf to arrest the man, and have him examined in your presence, so that the questions that you consider advisable may be put to him, in view of what we have written above. If he turns out to be Portocarrero you will arrange for the Spanish alguacil to be allowed to hand him the letter he bears, and to command him in our name to return to the monastery. If he proves to be some other person, let him be detained until you have communicated his replies to us; and ask the lords of the Council to let you have the letter he presented from the Duke of Alburquerque; so that we may know whether it is a forgery or not. You will do whatever else you consider necessary in the matter.

Utrecht, 7 January 1546.

P.S.—Since writing the above we are assured that the Spanish gentleman, who has gone to England, is not Don Pedro Portocarrero, but a certain Don Pedro Pacheco; who is a tall, thin, dark person. It is asserted by a man formerly in the Spanish infantry, who has recently arrived here, that this Don Pedro Pacheco passed through France from Spain. We have therefore decided not to send the Spanish alguacil, but we despatch the above letter to enable you to make up your mind as to which of the two persons mentioned is the one in question. If it be Portocarrero you will hand him the letters for him we now enclose. You can obtain information about him from Colonel (Maistre de Camp) Guevara,* who is said to be in England; or from some other of the Spaniards there. You will let us know what you can learn, and the reason for the going of this personage to England.

9 Jan.
Vienna
Imp. Arch.

182. VAN DER DELFT to the EMPEROR.

In accordance with the instructions contained in Your Majesty's letters of the 20th ultimo, I have given to the bearer thereof, the gentleman sent hither by the King of Portugal, all the support and assistance I am able; and I understand that he will be successful in his mission. Since I wrote to your Majesty on the 21st ultimo, respecting the Spanish Comendador, who has come hither, about whom the Council communicated with me and proposed to secure him, the person in question has been placed in good safe keeping. I have also spoken with the French gentleman Bertheuille, who accuses him, from whom I have learnt that the Comendador gave him information of all that passed in your Majesty's camp before St. Dizier, and that shortly afterwards the Comendador solicited

---

* Don Carlos de Guevara. The strange story of this mercenary soldier, his murder of Sir Pedro Gamboa, his rival colonel, on Snow Hill in January, 1550, and his execution at Smithfield will be found in "The Chronicle of Henry VIII." translated and edited by the present writer.

him for an allowance from France. The Comendador was captured by a troop of light horse, his own horses being burdened with his baggage; and, after having been conducted before the Admiral of France, was at once set at liberty. I have thought necessary to inform your Majesty of this, pending your Majesty's instructions on the matter, for which I am daily asked.

(Marginal note for reply written opposite the preceding paragraph. "He has already been informed that enquiries are being made in Spain respecting this Spaniard. It does not appear likely that it can be Don Pedro Portocarrero, and especially after what Bertheuille affirms. But, nevertheless, it is important that full investigation should be made. It will therefore be necessary for him (*i.e.* Van der Delft) to hold his hand and keep the person under detention until he receives further instructions from us. We have spoken to the English ambassadors here on the subject, and we suppose they will have written about it.")

Since the departure of M. D'Eick I have made several complaints respecting the disappearance of your Majesty's Courier with my letters, but no tidings of him can be obtained, except that he never arrived at Gravesend, for which place he started at night in a small boat. I will employ every effort to obtain further information, and the chancellor is rendering me great assistance,

(Marginal note, opposite the preceding paragraph. "It is a good work.")

Secretary Paget returned the day before yesterday, it is said, without having arrived at any settlement with the French. I hear from a secret source that this King's commissioners made advances towards the French Commissioners through the protestant envoys, to the effect that in order to commence negotiations for peace and the retrocession of Boulogne, the King of France should deposit in the hands of the German Princes (presumably the protestants) a sum of money to pay the overdue pensions to England, and the cost of the war; which they say would mean over three millions in gold. For the purpose of moderating these demands and bringing about some sort of settlement, one of the protestant envoys has been sent several times from Calais to the King of France, but without success; and the whole of the Commissioners, protestants French and English, have now all departed. Those people here who are in the secret have therefore lost all hope of peace, except it be through your Majesty's efforts. For the same reason I perceive that the conditions proposed by the English were drafted more for the purpose of giving some appearance of satisfaction to the protestants than to bring about a settlement.

(Marginal note to the preceding paragraph: "He will do well to obtain all the information he can about this.")

On Christmas eve Renegat came to see me, sent, as he said, by the Chancellor to justify himself. I told him he need not trouble himself, as I had so frequently and so publicly demonstrated that he was in the wrong. Finally he said that everything he had taken was still intact; and he was willing to submit the whole matter to the arbitration of the Chancellor and myself. I have sent to-day to the Chancellor about it, he (*i.e.* Wriothesley) having arrived here yesterday morning. He, however, appears unwilling to meddle in

1546.

the matter—as he was before—the said Renegat being in his service; but says that in the interests of justice he will give such orders as shall satisfy me; and that he is sure I shall only demand what is reasonable. So, Sire, on the first opportunity I will press the matter to an issue.

(Marginal note to the preceding paragraph: "He must persist to the end that everything captured must be restored.")

The Council recently sent to me certain English merchants who complained of the Inquisition in Spain. One of them whilst he was at San Sebastian saw an English captain thrown into prison because a new Testament was found in his ship, with some other books in English. The captain being asked whether he considered his sovereign the King of England a good Christian, replied that he did. All this is more fully set forth in their complaint, which I am sending to M. de Granvelle.

(Marginal note to the preceding paragraph. "The rescript has been handed at once to the Spanish council, in order that it may be forwarded to Spain, with instructions that English subjects are not to be molested, and no questions are to be asked about the King, as has already been ordered, unless Englishmen begin by saying anything scandalous about the Pope.")

The Parliament here has risen, though the conclusions they have arrived at are kept secret. I hear, however, that in addition to the subvention of eight groats in the pound of this money on all property real and personal, which comes to about half a quarter of the capital value, they have granted to the King for his use all the colleges, academies, and chantries founded for the souls of the departed, the value of which, they say, is very great.* In addition to this, he is to have the plate, money and rents of all the "Halls," which are the common houses belonging to the trade guilds. The bishops remain still in their positions, but the matter touches them closely; and they may feel what they fear at the next parliament,† which is fixed for November.

(Marginal note to the preceding paragraph. "He does well to enquire about this, and especially on the religious part of it, since he mentions the foundations for the departed, which are to be interfered with.")

Captain Conrad Penninck, who was in command of the town of Venloo for the Duke of Cleves, has arrived at this Court with leave of the elective King of Denmark, and of the town of Hamburg, to which he is under an obligation. Other Germans also have been here from the Duke of Lauenberg and certain counts,

---

* This last parliament of the reign, which had only met on the 23rd November previous, suppressed the whole of the chantries and pious foundations in England, for the benefit of the crown; and gave the King the right to seize the revenues of the Universities and Corporations on his pledge that nothing should be done but for the glory of God and the profit of the realm.

† This paragraph refers to the legalisation by this parliament of the, more or less forced, surrenders of houses and properties belonging to the Sees, made by Cranmer and other bishops to the crown in exchange for a guaranteed salary. Such of the superior clergy who still held in trust ecclesiastical property might well dread the result. Henry closed the legislature on the 24 December in a haughty and violent speech.

1546.

neighbours of the Duke of Brunswick, but they did not meet with the same amount of favour as is shown to Conrad Penninck. I will enquire how they (the English) are going to employ him.

(Marginal note to the preceding paragraph. "He must always endeavour to discover everything he can about Penninck, and must report to President Scors and M. D'Eick.")

London, 9 January 1546.

13 Jan.
Simancas.
E. R. 873.

183. JUAN DE VEGA to PRINCE PHILIP.

Your Highness will have learnt that since the Admiral of France and his companions left the Emperor's Court, Friar Gabriel de Guzman has made two journeys thither, and the Emperor has again recently declined the proposal made by the French, which, in good truth, is almost the same as the previous one. The French are generally admitted to be weak and overburdened by their war with England: although it is believed that his Holiness is encouraging them with words and promises, upon which, in my opinion, they do not place much reliance. Speculation is accordingly now busy as to how these matters are going to end; although the Pope is very anxious at the way the Council (of Trent) is proceeding. The last time I was with his Holiness, quite recently, he pressed me to give him my opinion, as to what course he ought to take. I excused myself, because until Marquina comes back I am uncertain as to the Emperor's wishes; and also because it is sometimes advisable to keep the Pope in suspense. I expect your Highness will have been advised of the truce with the Turk after the arrival of the Ambassadors who went to Constantinople.—Rome, 13 January 1546.

13 Jan.
Vienna
Imp. Arch.

184. VAN DER DELFT to the EMPEROR.

Doubtless your Majesty will have received my letters of the 9th instant. Nothing of importance has happened since, except that news has come of a defeat of the English in Scotland, in which I am informed about fourteen hundred men were lost, the reason being that the Germans and Spaniards in the King's service there were absent from the frontier, and in quarters at York and Newcastle. It is also asserted that there has been a great engagement between the English and French at Boulogne, where the English have lost about 1,200 foot-soldiers, with 8 English and 4 Italian captains. The Earl of Surrey* has consequently lost greatly in reputation, and there is considerable discontent at these heavy losses. Your Majesty may perhaps be more fully informed on these points, but I have thought well to report them.

London, 13 January 1546.

---

* This seems to have been a night surprise, when 3,000 Frenchmen attacked and temporarily captured the lower town of Boulogne. The garrison with two companies of Spanish mercenaries rallied in the high town and repelled the French with great slaughter. The losses on the English side as given above are probably much exaggerated; though a contemporary writer speaks of the great slaughter of French prisoners by the English in this fight.

HENRY VIII. 293

1546.
17 Jan.
Vienna
Imp. Arch.

185. The EMPEROR to VAN DER DELFT.

We received yesterday your letters of 11th instant. You did well in assisting the gentleman sent to England by the King of Portugal; and we recommend him to your further good offices if he should need them.

With regard to the Spaniard, who styles himself a comendador, we have written you our instructions. The more enquiries we make here about him, the more certain it appears that he cannot be Don Pedro Portocarrero; and it will be necessary, therefore, to look more closely at the assertions made by Bertheuille, and to endeavour to get to the bottom of the mystery. You will keep the matter in hand, and cause the Spaniard to be detained until you receive our reply to your communication touching the contents of our former letter. We have caused the English Ambassador here to be spoken to on the subject; and we suppose that he will already have written about it, and will do so again. You will do well to make all possible enquiry about the courier who has been lost; and also to let us know everything you can discover respecting the treaty between England and France. We shall be very glad of all the information you can send on the subject.

With regard to what you say about Renegat and his submission, you had better stand firm to the last in your positive demand that he shall restore everything he has taken. We have without delay caused to be referred to the Spanish Council the remonstrance drawn up by the English merchants complaining of the Inquisition. It will be at once sent to Spain with letters from us, giving directions that no injury shall be done to English subjects, or any infraction be committed of the promises we have recently made to the King of England, so long as the English make no scandalous allusions to the Pope.

We shall always be very glad to learn what you consider is likely to be done in England respecting religion; and more especially in relation to the alterations enacted by the last Parliament, concerning the services for the dead.*

Let us know also continually how they treat Capt. Conrad Penninck† and where, and in what, they employ him.—Utrecht, 17 January 1546.

19 Jan.
Vienna
Imp. Arch.

186. VAN DER DELFT to the EMPEROR.

I have received to-day your Majesty's letter of the 7th instant, enclosing a note instructing me to obtain further information, about the Spaniard detained here, respecting whom I wrote to your Majesty; and to discover whether he be Don Pedro Portocarrero or Don Pedro Pacheco. I will do so with all diligence, and will duly report to your Majesty. As, however, this Courier is about to start, I think well to inform your Majesty, that the description of the personage named Don Pedro Pacheco, who passed through France, differs

---

* That is to say the suppression of the chantries and the endowment of masses.
† This man is subsequently referred to more frequently as Kurtpenninck or Curtpenninck, but for the sake of uniformity the original form of the name has been preserved throughout.

1546.

entirely from that of the prisoner here; although the latter assumes the same name. The prisoner is a man of medium height, rather short than tall, and stout, with an ordinary colour, without being very dark. In order to learn the appearance of Don Pedro Portocarrero I have just sent to the Spanish Colonel (Maestre de Campo) named Gamboa,* whose description of him agrees somewhat closely with that of the prisoner. It will therefore be necessary to examine him, as your Majesty orders. Whether he be Portocarrero or not, it is certain that once when the Frenchman Bertheuille and he came to dine with me, he (the prisoner) stated in conversation, without contradiction from Bertheuille, many things that happened in the French camp whilst your Majesty was before St. Disier; and Bertheuille frequently appealed to him for confirmation as an eye-witness of matters he related, he having been in the camp after his capture by the French. But your Majesty will learn the truth by my next letter.

On the 13th instant I informed your Majesty of the defeats the English had suffered at Boulogne and in Scotland, but it is now affirmed that the engagement in Scotland was not nearly so disastrous as was at first reported; and they talk now of only two or three hundred men having been lost.†

These people are greatly astonished about Boulogne, and are very anxious, as they foresee the difficulties that may arise. Two days since the King consulted the whole Council, and summoned his Captains, English and foreign, the decision, as I learn, being to send to Boulogne the Earl of Hertford, and the said Colonel Gamboa, who, indeed, immediately started by post for the Scottish border to bring his men to Boulogne.‡

Captain Conrad Penninck has no command here, but I expect they will not let him go without giving him something to do, as they have detained him so long.

London, 19 January 1546.

19 Jan.
Paris.
Archives
Nationales.
K. 1486.

187. St. Mauris to Cobos.

I write to you from Compeigne by a Portuguese gentleman. I send you now five ciphered reports of what has since been done in my office. I will add that I recently received letters from M. Joos (Bave), dated 18th instant, saying that the Emperor had held a chapter of his Order (*i.e.* the Golden Fleece); but that the new knights had not been announced.§ His Majesty was in bed with the gout, but the great pain had left him two days before; and at the time, he was resting easily at night and would answer certain letters of mine as soon as he could attend to business.

---

* For a full account of Sir Pedro Gamboa and his murder by one of his compatriots, see "The Spanish Chronicle of Henry VIII."
† Even this appears to have been an exaggeration, as no battle of such magnitude at the time is recorded.
‡ This was done, the object being to prevent the strengthening of the French position at St. Jean between Boulogne and Calais.
§ No chapter of the Golden Fleece had been held since 1531 and no less than 22 vacancies in the order were filled up in the chapter here referred to.

HENRY VIII.

1546.

The King of France has again fallen ill of his usual malady, abscess. If the game lasts much longer he may cease playing altogether. The Pope also is said to be very ill. The English were recently repulsed by the French in an attempt to revictual the fort of Boulogne. The mercenaries serving in France had mutinied.°

The French have been unable to agree to a peace or truce with the English; and they have consequently resolved to make war on them in the neighbourhood of Boulogne about July next, before the Emperor again joins in the war. The English have fifty well-armed ships scouring the coasts of France.

The peace question still remains in suspense, and the marriage only talked about because the French will not let go their hold on Piedmont.†

M. de Granvelle informs me that the Emperor has instructed you to advance me as much money as you can on account of my allowance. I pray you therefore to deliver to Gonzalo Perez 1,500 Spanish crowns, which is less than half what is owing to me; or ducats if you like. If you could let me have the amount to come by the first courier I should be for ever obliged to you. The courier will find me at Paris or Melun, as the King will not be able to go far away.

Chalons near Paris, 19 January 1546.

25 Jan.
Vienna
Imp. Arch.

188. VAN DER DELFT to the EMPEROR.

As I informed your Majesty on the 19th instant I received on that day your Majesty's letter of the 7th respecting the Spaniard detained here, and on the morrow I sent to the Council, who were at Hampton Court, nine miles from here, where the King has been staying since Christmas, to say that I had received a reply from your Majesty and I should be glad if the prisoner were examined in my presence. I should therefore thank them to inform me when and where they wished the examination to take place, either at Hampton Court or here in London. I would attend at either place; and would have now gone personally to see them and thank them for their kindness in this matter, in accordance with your Majesty's orders, only that I did not wish to trouble them, especially as I know the prisoner was not at Hampton Court but in London. They replied that they had several charges against the prisoner, both on behalf of your Majesty and of that of their own King, and as they had only two days before placed him in greater security (I understand in the Tower of London) and the King was returning to London this week, they thought it would be better to defer the

---

° Much ill-feeling existed among the foreign mercenaries, giving rise to bitter recriminations. In April 1545 a number of Spaniards under Captains Mora and Aroe had deserted the English service at Boulogne and had joined the enemy, another body under Captain Haro being stopped by their compatriots in an attempt to do likewise, Haro and 25 of his followers being killed. All this led to the famous duel—to which subsequent reference will be made—between Julian Romero and Mora. (*See* Hatfield Papers, Hist. MSS. Com., Part 1. p. 45.)

† That is to say the permanent peace between the Emperor and France, the marriage which was to have cemented it being impossible owing to the death of the Duke of Orleans, and the unwillingness of both Charles and Francis to make the surrenders agreed upon.

examination until they arrived in town. I will act in the matter as your Majesty orders, and will duly report as soon as the examination takes place. Since taking the above step I have received your Majesty's letters of 17th instant, replying to mine of the 9th, and I note your Majesty's orders that I should press to the last for the restitution of everything captured by Renegat. I will act accordingly, but the scruples I encounter in the matter are duly set forth in my letter to M. de Granvelle, in order not to trouble your Majesty with them.

I will also not fail continuously to advise your Majesty of all occurrences here, as your Majesty commands. But, up to the present, nothing fresh has happened with regard to the religious question, and the interference with the foundations for the departed, beyond what I have already written.

Concerning Conrad Penninck I have learnt to-day that he has been received into the King's service, and is directed to bring ten standards of infantry into the service, on condition that they be not high Germans nor men infected by the Anabaptist or Sacramentarian sect. It is said that they will be men drawn from Bremen, Hamburg, Lubeck and the surrounding country; and a large number of them have already been assembled.

Great preparations are being made here to supply Boulogne, since they have heard that the King of France is raising a large body of Germans (and as the English say) with the full favour and aid of the protestants. Your Majesty will know what truth there is in this better than we. All the war ships are being put in order for the gathering of the fleet, and the Lord Admiral is shortly leaving court for this purpose.

London, 25 January 1546.

189. Van der Delft to de Granvelle.

Nothing of importance since receipt of last letters, and despatch of mine of 19th instant. The day before yesterday, I received his Majesty's letters of 17th ordering me to persist to the end in obtaining restitution of all the property captured by Renegat. I venture to ask your Lordship to instruct me how I can best carry out the wishes of his Majesty. I have always insisted to the utmost upon the restitution being made; but on every occasion when the matter seemed assured of a prompt solution I have found myself perplexed by the orders his Majesty wrote me from Worms on the 16 July, to the effect that I was to press for the release of the property and ships of Spaniards embargoed here, as well as for the restitution of the gold and other property captured by Renegat. When this was effected his Majesty would raise the embargo decreed in Spain. I proposed this and assured the King and Council of its performance, whereupon they raised the embargoes here, and promised me the restitution of what Renegat had wrongfully seized when he should return from sea. They have nevertheless frequently complained to me that the embargoes have not been raised in Spain, although they (the English) have done their part. I have always replied that they only had themselves to blame; as they had deferred giving satisfaction with regard to Renegat's plunder, and when

1546.

this was done the embargoes in Spain would be raised. The matter being now so far advanced as for Renegat to offer to give an account of all he has taken, and to place in my hands everything that appertains to his Majesty, I have no doubt that the Council will demand the fulfilment of my undertaking, that the embargoes in Spain shall be raised. As I do not know how matters stand in Spain, or even if his Majesty's intentions still remain the same, I have thought best not to press the affair too urgently, especially as Renegat in his communications affirms that what belongs to his Majesty is of small value, which I doubt. On the contrary, I suspect that they wish to put me off with just what Renegat thinks proper to surrender, as I have no detailed instructions as to the amount of gold I am to demand. I beg therefore that your Lordship will favour me with your advice, in order that I may be enabled to carry out his Majesty's intentions.

Pray forgive me for the prolixity of this letter: and in due time bear in mind the great expenses I am obliged to support here, which, God knows, are far beyond my capability.

London, 25 January 1546.

30 Jan.
Simancas.
E. A. 642.

190. The EMPEROR to PRINCE PHILIP.

His Holiness has hitherto rejected all my requests that he will grant me the brief authorising the sale of the monastic manors in Spain before I sign the treaty of alliance with him. The true intention and mind of this man (*i.e.* the Pope) will be demonstrated by the decision he now adopts. God grant that it be such as this most important business demands. He (the Pope) has proposed to the Venetians the formation of a defensive league. The Seigniory have however refused to listen to him. He is actuated by his fears about Parma and Piacenza. France and England remain on the same terms as when I last wrote. The Council (of Trent) proceeds but slowly. Its fourth sitting is to be held on Friday after Whitsuntide.—Utrecht, 30 January 1546.[*]

7 & 10 Feb.
Vienna
Imp. Arch.

191. CORNELIUS SCEPPERUS to LOYS SCORS.

I beg to inform you that I am tarrying here for the purpose of negotiating with the English ambassadors respecting the subsidy demanded by them for last year, upon which point they are very persistent. I have informed M. de Granvelle of this, and have to-day received a reply from him by a special courier. I do not know how they (the English) will take it, as the line adopted is that the Emperor denies his obligation to provide the subsidy in question: but I will report to you what passes. The courier informs me that the Emperor was in some pain yesterday night, and consequently did not leave for Zutphen, but was to do so to-day; and the Queen

---

[*] The above letter is included in a long letter in French from the Same to the Same and of similar date, relating entirely to the order of the Golden Fleece, to which so many new appointments had just been made.

1546.

(Dowager of Hungary) was to await him at Arnheim.* The man did not know whether his Majesty was going from Zutphen to Deventer. Orders have been issued to-day in this town forbidding all chapters to keep concubines, and enjoining them to eject such women from their houses, and live according to the Christian law. M. de Praet is still ill with gout.

Utrecht, Sunday, 7 February 1546.

P.S.—I thought this courier was to leave on Sunday; but he did not do so. I advise you that the Emperor arrived yesterday at Nimiguen. With regard to the affair with the English ambassadors, it is a stinking business, and they persist in their demand.

Utrecht, 10 February 1546.

15 Feb.
Vienna
Imp. Arch.

192. SCEPPERUS to LOYS SCORS.

You will understand by the verbatim Latin report I have sent to M. de Granvelle what passed between the English Ambassadors and myself respecting the ratifications exhibited on that occasion. There is, therefore, no need for me to repeat the account here, but I will not conceal from you that, after considering maturely your suggestion that a gentleman of the long-robe should be sent to England, I have arrived at the opinion that your advice is sound; and I have written to that effect to M. de Granvelle. As you are well aware, the two principal points upon which I am going thither have no connection whatever with the merchants or their disputes, although, as in duty bound, I will give them every support and assistance in my power; besides which it is agreed that the Emperor shall send someone to co-operate with his resident ambassador in the settlement of the disputes in question, in conjunction with two similar personages appointed by the King of England for the purpose. The third person, myself, accordingly, cannot intervene in the negotiation unless the King of England's Commissioners—who are already appointed—are willing. The difficulty which occurred to us was the choice of the jurist, to whom the task might be entrusted; and I mentioned to you Dr. Hermes, as having been one of those who were present at the Bourbourg Conference. I have since thought of Master Adolf van Pamele. I do not know whether either of these could be spared from the (Flemish) Privy Council, but I can suggest no one else, as I do not know any member of the Council at Malines fit for the task, or even whether the time is ripe for you to take such steps as you consider proper for the redress of these merchants. I think well to mention, however, that on my way to Bruges I recollected Master Leonard Casimbrot *eschevin* of this town (Bruges) a very decent (mectable) man who is active in settling disputes amongst merchants here. He is discreet, elderly and modest, though it is true that he is not in royal service, but in my opinion he would be very appropriate for the business if it is decided to employ anyone but an ordinary councillor, as I think might well be done in this English matter.

* Vandenesse says the Emperor travelled from Utrecht to Wagewing on the 3 February; to Arnheim on the 4th, to Zutphen on the 7th, back to Arnheim on the 8th, and to Nimiguen on the 9th.

1546.

You can consider the whole question. In the meanwhile I have said nothing about it to Casimbrot,* but I have no doubt he will do as he is ordered. He has been innumerable times in contact with English people, when he went backwards and forwards to Scotland; but he always bore himself so honestly that everyone considers him a worthy man. The King of England's ratification is in my hands, and I thought to have placed it in yours on Sunday evening, the day after I received it. But, as you had started before I arrived, I kept it, and will have it delivered to you securely closed, the bearer of the packet being ignorant of its contents. The copy of the treaty is in the possession of Master Joos Bave,† as it is right that he should have it. The corrected minute is in the keeping of the German secretary Christophe, who made the fair copy of it. The letter, signed and sealed, by the English Ambassadors, containing the promise of the ratification, with the articles touching the disputes of subjects and complaints of merchants, is in my coffer, and will be sent to you at the same time as the original of the ratification. With regard to our letters, they have been sent to England to be kept there, as I have seen by a special letter from the Council there. I should like to have got our letters back, but the ambassadors assured me that they had not possession of them, and that we might retain those that they had signed in exchange.

Secretary Christophe wishes to be treated like the other sacretaries. He is a good correspondent in Latin and German and fair in Spanish. He writes as good a hand as any of the others. I shall be pleased if you can take into consideration the petition he is forwarding to you.

Please also bear in mind the ambassador Van der Delft, that he may receive what is due to him, and have a special receiver appointed to obtain payment of his allowance in future as it falls due.

I shall await my dispatch here or in Zeeland, as I am unwilling to go by way of Calais for several reasons. Besides, the way by Flushing is shorter, for unless the wind is entirely contrary I can reach English territory in ten or twelve hours, with much less danger from the galleys and ships of war than by the other route. The wind at present blowing is very favourable, and it promises to continue for some time longer.

With regard to the suit commenced against Von Reissenberg,‡ I think that in the absence of Vice Chancellor Naves, Dr. Viglius might draw up the case, as Secretary Christophe has all the documents, which are not voluminous and a day or two would suffice to exhibit them all.

Bruges, 15 February 1546.

---

* Probably it was this man, a brother of Count Egmont's secretary, who subsequently became a prominent minister on the Protestant side during the revolt of the Netherlands. He came to England on a mission from the Prince of Orange and the Protestant Princes of Germany in 1572, when he was described as Secretary of the city of Bruges.

† He was Secretary of the Flemish Privy Council.

‡ This was the German mercenary leader who had raised troops for Henry and had, as was asserted, committed much violence on his passage through the Emperor's territories.

1546.
16 Feb.
Vienna
Imp. Arch.

193. SCEPPERUS TO DE GRANVILLE.

I wrote you briefly what had passed between the English ambassadors and myself on the 13th instant at Bois le Duc, with respect to the ratification; but as the more I think of the expressions used by the Bishop of Winchester on the occasion, the more suspicious they seem to me, I have thought well to set down these expressions in writing, in order that you may consider and discuss them, and penetrate the objects at which the English are aiming, in case they should repeat these expressions in conversation with the Emperor or elsewhere. In truth, Monseigneur, so far as I could understand from the Bishop of Winchester, there seems but small chance of negotiating with the King on the question of the marriage,* or on that of the merchants and subjects of the Emperor, unless some expedient can be found to deal with the subsidy they (the English) demand; either by entirely rejecting their demand, on the ground that they have not fulfilled the treaty, nor accepted the conditions laid down by the ambassador Van der Delft: that their troops have during the years '43 and '44 done more damage to the Emperor's dominions (without mentioning the Liège complaint), than would be represented by the amount of the subsidy; or else by delaying a definite reply as to the subsidy, on the pretext that the Emperor would be willing to overlook the past, and would accede to their request on certain conditions to be agreed upon with the Council, with regard to the period for which they demand the subvention. So far as I could judge, the Bishop of Winchester would stomach this answer better than a blank negative. Or some other expedient might be devised by you to avoid alienating the English altogether from us, and throwing them into the arms of their enemies, of which they would afterwards (though too late to be of any good to us) repent; if it be desirable for his imperial Majesty's objects, of which I am ignorant, that the friendship with England should be maintained.

For these reasons it will be advisable, before I depart for England, whether the Bishop of Winchester has a prior interview with the Emperor or not, that I should be distinctly informed and instructed as to his Majesty's resolution (*i.e.* as to the subsidy); since this question will be the first thing brought forward. I am the more convinced of this, since I learn here in Bruges that the King (of England) has recently taken into his Privy Council Dr. Nicholas Wotton, formerly his Ambassor to the Emperor, who, as you know, is naturally and by habit a harsh (agyre) man; and it may be feared will press hard this point of the subsidy.† I am also informed that the Earl of Hertford and the Biscayner Colonel Gamboa have returned from Boulogne to England; and that Conrad Penninck, the captain

---

* The marriage of Edward, Prince of Wales, with a daughter of the King of the Romans.

† Dean of Canterbury and York, son of Sir Robert Wotton of Bockton Malherb, Kent. He was employed in no less than 13 foreign missions under four sovereigns. He was offered the Archbishopric of Canterbury by Elizabeth, but refused it. He died at the age of 70, in 1566, and was buried at Canterbury. Lloyd (State Worthies) mentions his inflexible firmness and quotes one of his maxims to ambassadors as follows:—"Resolution: I made often as if I would fight when they knew my calling only allowed me to speak."

1546.

of low Germans, has been commissioned to raise as many as ten standards of infantry; or at least to bespeak them. From what I can understand great war preparations are being made in England, and the King has refused to admit into his service Count Rithberg or any of those who have served Henry of Brunswick, on the ground that they are well disposed to the Holy See. This incident, together with the long stay of the Bishop of Winchester on this side, and the expressions he made use of during my recent interview with him, make me suspect that there may be some other negotiations going on besides those with the Emperor; and I think necessary to advise you of this.

As it is possible that you will have to deal with the last treaty, I have had the copy of it delivered to Jacques, the clerk of Secretary Bave With regard to the original of the ratification, as I am afraid to send it across country, I will deposit it in a safe place, and will have it delivered into the hands of the president of the privy Council (*i.e.* Loys Scors).

I may also mention that I have been three times to England without knowing what remuneration I am to receive, and I pray you to inform me on this point before you leave. I have had my past allowances set down in writing and given to M. Vincent, financial commissioner, and have received at Utrecht, on account, 400 livres of forty groats. This, however, is much less than the amount due, and is not for the future. It is important I should know for my future guidance.

To put in order some little affairs of my own, I shall remain here at Bruges, or at the sea side, pending the Emperor's orders and such despatch as his Majesty chooses to send me. On receipt thereof I will start (for England) at once.

Bruges, 16 February 1546.

16 Feb.
Paris.
Archives
Nationales.
K. 1486.

194. ST. MAURIS to PRINCE PHILIP.

Answering your Highness' letter of 22 January, I beg to say that the King of France is at present well, but a month ago his abscess in the lower parts returned, and produced so much fever that his surgeons decided to open and cleanse it. Just as they were about to do so the wound opened of itself, and discharged so much septic matter that the King was greatly relieved; and the surgeons are keeping the issue open in the hope that he will benefit thereby. He still takes his pastime of hunting, being carried in a litter. He has just been for a fortnight's chase, with a very small following, leaving the Queen and court at St. Germain, whilst he went some ten or twelve leagues away, travelling by village roads to avoid being followed, his only object being to enjoy his pleasure, and the company of Madame Margaret* and Madame d'Etampes.†

The Dauphin is also with him. He is very well and living in great obedience to the King. He recently held a tourney on foot, he being one of the challengers; and not one of the troop who fought on foot bore himself more dexterously or more actively than

---

* Margaret of France, the favourite daughter of Francis, and afterwards wife of Emanuel Philibert Duke of Savoy.
† The King's mistress, formerly Mademoiselle d'Heilly.

he. The Queen of France* is in perfect health, being now much relieved of the malady which usually troubles her. Her Majesty endeavours by every means to obviate it so far as she can. The Dauphiness is also well and is expected to be brought to bed towards the end of March at Fontainebleau.† In answer to your Highness' enquiry I beg to say that the truce with the Turk has certainly only been agreed upon for one year. If it had not been for Monluc, who was sent to the Levant by the King of France, the Turk would have signed a truce for five years. The Turk wants the King of the Romans to surrender to him a fortress in Hungary and to pay him 12,000 ducats a year tribute. Monluc went to the Emperor to give him an account of his mission, and he was told that it would be communicated to the King of the Romans at the coming Diet at Regensberg (Ratisbon). Monluc said here that the truce would not last any longer than pleased the King of France, and that the Turk would not consent to a longer truce than one year after he had learnt of the death of the Duke of Orleans, as he said he wished to see how the Emperor treated the King with regard to the claims of the latter. The Admiral of France tells me that the Turk expected to have an immediate reply to the conditions he has brought forward, and wishes the King of France to mediate in the dispute with the King of the Romans. They think, Sir, that by this talk they will alarm the Emperor, who however, knows them well. What is still worse is that the King of of France has informed the Protestants that he will do all he can to prolong the said truce; which, in truth, he has very little intention of doing. The object of this is to make the Germans with the Emperor and the King of the Romans (i.e. the Catholics) think that no arrangement has been made with the Turk.

In reply to your Highness' enquiry as the present state of relations between the Emperor and the King of France I beg to inform you that everything is at a stand with regard to the further duration of peace, in consequence of the insistence of the King of France in retaining Piedmont, to which the Emperor will not consent. The King of France proposes that Piedmont should be divided into two parts, that bordering upon Milan to go to the Emperor, and the other part to France; for which portion the King offers a compensation to the Duke of Savoy. The Emperor will not agree to this; and the King consequently has garrisoned all his frontiers, and has provisioned the towns as plentifully as possible: his excuse being that he fears the Emperor may join the English in making war upon him. The despatch of his troops to the frontiers has produced so much sensation that the Emperor's subjects on the borders are in fear that the King of France may intend to begin the war himself, as he is always ready to do when he sees that it is to his advantage to take his enemies by surprise. But really, Sir, whilst he is at open war with England there is not much probability of his attacking the Emperor this year. He is no

---

* Eleanor of Austria-Burgundy, sister of the Emperor and Queen Dowager of Portugal, who had been married to Francis as one of the conditions of the peace concluded in 1526, when Francis was a prisoner in Madrid.

† Catherine de Medici. The child thus born was Elizabeth of Valois, who became the third wife of Philip II.

1546.

doubt in fear that his Majesty may attack him. But still it is safest to keep a good watch on the frontiers without going to useless expense; and thus to provide against a surprise. So far as I know, this is the Emperor's intention. Though it is certain that the King does not trust the Emperor, he always swears emphatically to me that he means to keep in peace and amity with his Majesty as long as he lives. My own opinion is that he will keep his oath until it suits him to break it.

Finally, I beg to inform your Highness that the King of France aims at bringing about by his means a marriage between Scotland and the Prince of England, in return for which England will restore Boulogne to him, and withdraw from alliance with the Emperor. He thinks to trick the English with this negotiation; his desire being to make the marriage matter simply a verbal promise for the future, the Princess of Scotland remaining in her own country, and thus to mock the English. If this intrigue succeeds not, the King of France intends to re-commence his war against the English this year.

Paris, 16 February 1546.

16 Feb.
Simancas.
E. A. 642.

195. The Emperor to Prince Philip.

Just as the Chief Postmaster (Tassis) was leaving, we received your letter of 26th ultimo and other despatches, and we must say how glad we are to hear of your good health, and of that of the Infantas my daughters and of Don Carlos. By other letters you will have learnt of my own health. Since writing, I still continued, with some inconvenience, on my journey, as far as this place (Nimiguen) where I suffered another attack in various parts. The next day, however, by means of a purge, I recovered; and am now, thank God, well again. If my improvement continues I shall leave here to-morrow, going by Venlo and other towns of this State to Maestricht in five or six days.* If I have time there, I will look into the matters about which you write, only the more important points being dealt with in this letter in order to save time.

With regard to financial affairs the Comendador Mayor (Cobos) wrote to us at length, and sent us a detailed account of the amounts that must of necessity be raised for ordinary expenditure this year. In these sums are included the expenses of our household, guards, galleys, frontier-forces for Africa and Spain, etc. and other items, with a statement of the sources from which Cobos thinks a portion of the funds may be drawn. We have already written that we are perfectly aware of all this; and it may well be believed that there is nothing we wish for more than to find a way to remedy or alleviate the distress in Spain, as far as possible. After we had finished our last journey, which was so necessary and produced such advantageous effects, we always kept this matter in view; and we will still do our best to avoid unnecessary expenditure: but affairs are in such a condition that every effort must be made on all hands, such as we are making here, in the Netherlands, and in Naples and Sicily. We must by no means lose

---

* The itinerary is given in Vandenesse.

1546.

sight of the future; either the King of France may attack us (though that is not probable this year, as he has England to cope with) or he may make it up with the King of England, seeing that he has, as we know, an understanding with the German protestants, as well as intrigues in Italy. In any case, it is of the highest importance that all these things should be kept in view, to avoid great difficulties; and especially considering the state of Spain, and of the obligations incurred there, must efforts be made in that country to raise the money necessary to meet the demands. This is all the more necessary, since, by Cobos' statement we see that the former first-fruits revenues, the Crusade revenue, and those of the military orders with other similar sources of supply are spent or pledged up to the end of the year 1548.° What is left of the revenue will have to meet the expenses of the Queen's household, your own and the Infantas' expenditure, the Councils, governors, judges, posts, and other claims that cannot be dispensed with. We have thought over and discussed this matter thoroughly, and have come to the conclusion that you might draw a considerable amount from a fresh grant from Aragon, Catalonia and Valencia. The period for which they granted the last supply has expired, and you had better consider about convoking their Cortes. We can see no reason here why this should not be done.†—Nimiguen, 16 February 1546.

16 Feb.
Simancas.
E. A. 642.

196. The EMPEROR to PRINCE PHILIP.

By the courier dispatched from Bois le Duc a reply was sent to you only on the most pressing points, in consequence of my indisposition there: and from Bomel we wrote a letter to the Comendador Mayor (Cobos) to be carried by a Portuguese who was on his way thither, in which we gave the directions which, after consultation with you, he, Cobos, was to follow. After I had arrived here and had just finished the celebration of the Golden Fleece I had another attack of gout, which plagued me all over; and I was for some days in great pain. It pleased God, however, after I had purged myself, and adopted other remedies, to relieve me, and I am now well, although somewhat weak, and was obliged to stay in Utrecht longer than I intended, in order to restore my strength. I am now going on my way, visiting as I pass certain towns of the state of Gueldres; and, with God's help, I hope to be at Ratisbon by the middle or end of March. In the meanwhile those appointed for the conference will discuss and endeavour to come to some arrangement about the religious question, in order that no time may be lost; and I have thought well to send the chief postmaster Raymundo de Tassis to inform you of our health, and to answer the various questions still pending.

° The Crusade revenue, so called, was a great source of profit to the sovereigns of Spain. It consisted in the right granted by successive Popes to them to sell the Bulls for indulgences to their subjects. The estates of the great military orders Calatrava, Santiago, Alcantara and Montesor had been appropriated by the "Catholic Sovereigns," the Comendadors being thenceforward paid a fixed allowance in money from the royal treasury.

† The Cortes of the Kingdoms of Aragon stood firmly upon their constitutional rights, and always drove a very hard bargain in voting supplies. The Cortes of Castile had already lost to a great extent their power of resisting royal demands.

1546.

First, you have already been informed of what passed with regard to the enterprise planned against the Protestants last year, for the purpose of bringing them back to the true faith, and making them abandon their opinions; all other means of doing so having failed, though we endeavoured to avoid taking this course. You have also learnt the aid offered to this enterprise by the Pope and our request to him about the concession of the half-first-fruit-Bulls, and the sale of the monastic manors to defray some of the expenses we should have to incur, and we informed you of the various difficulties and discussions which have arisen in the matter. Subsequently Marquina arrived here with his Holiness' decision; and we, having listened to the representations and requests of the Nuncios, to the effect that the capitulation binding us to commence the enterprise should be drawn up and signed at once, we resolved to delay the same until we should arrive at Ratisbon, giving as a reason for the delay the necessity of consulting again the King of the Romans. The Nuncios were satisfied with this, and have agreed that the Bull for the first-fruits, which was already here, should be sent to Spain at once, and this is now being done. The Bull for the sale of the monastic lands is also being drawn up in the form required, and Juan de Vega has been instructed to send it to Spain with all speed, in order that measures may be devised to raise the needed money from both sources, and arrangements made for obtaining advances upon it. But assurance must be given that none of the proceeds shall be actually collected, nor shall any official steps be taken to carry out the Bulls, until the capitulation has been signed; and also that the money so raised shall only be spent in the way stipulated by his Holiness. The Nuncios insisted that they had no authority to give their consent to the course ordered, but said that they had no doubt his Holiness would approve of our resolution, and of the reasons we gave for delaying the signature of the capitulation till the time stated and also of our measures to secure the employment of the funds raised only for the purpose intended. We have already communicated on the matter with the King of the Romans, and will do so again; and will also bear well in mind what you write to us from Spain, as to the importance of the business we have undertaken. In view of all the circumstances at the time, we will resolve the best course to be taken; so arranging matters that, one way or another, we shall be in Spain as early as possible.

Venlo, 16 February 1546.

Feb. 16.
Simancas.
E. A. 642.

197. The Emperor to Prince Philip.

In the other letter we tell you why we are sending this courier. The present will contain what seems to be the most important.

With regard to the enterprise against the Protestants you will see by the other letter what has passed with the Nuncios sent by his Holiness, and we have replied (*i.e.* to the Papal envoys) in conformity with what we say there, namely deferring the final decision until we reach Ratisbon. We have excused ourselves from signing the capitulation here, in the first place because secrecy is so necessary and we wished to avoid all chance of anything happening which might cause the Protestants more uneasiness than they have already displayed, in consequence of their mere suspicions and conjectures past and present, which might result in their taking up arms and make our presence at the Diet difficult; and in the second place, in case any of the Princes on the road should ask us about this matter, as we believe they will do, we shall be free to answer them satisfactorily, and assure them that nothing has been done that need render them uneasy. But, although we have generally made it understood that we have delayed the matter until we shall have arrived at Ratisbon, the following considerations occur to us. The religious question is in such a position, and the confusion of Germany so great, that there is little hope that the Protestants, of their own accord, will abandon their errors and return to the communion of the church. This has been proved by the experience of the past, and recognising now how greatly the evil has spread and daily continues to increase, it is evident that unless a prompt remedy be found, great difficulties and troubles may result, amongst others the dangers to which these Low Countries would be exposed by their proximity and connection with Germany. The matter, moreover, is signally for the service of Our Lord, the increase of His holy Catholic faith, and the quietude and repose of Christendom, to which we are so especially bound by the dignity to which God has elevated us. And, although we have exerted ourelves to the utmost to remedy the evil, exposing our own person to many troubles thereby, nothing has yet been effected, owing to their (*i.e.* Protestants') obstinacy, and to the efforts of certain persons, who, for reasons of their own, have obstructed us. It seems to us, therefore, that as this contingency arises in our time, it is our duty to deal with it, if for no other reason, in order that we may be freed from the anxieties arising from these countries (*i.e.* Germany, Flanders, &c.), and be able to go and repose in Spain. Otherwise you will see how great and constant would be the anxiety and trouble we should experience. Besides this the opportunity that now presents itself should be taken advantage of. We have not only settled the truce with the Turk, but the French have their hands full with the English, besides being in great poverty; and our position towards them is such that it is not probable they would attempt in Germany what at another time they might. We are, moreover, well armed and prepared for whatever may happen; this being a most important point. On consideration of all these reasons and others; and in view of his Holiness' offer of aid, he having granted us the Bulls for the half-first-fruits, and the sale of the monastic manors, which will produce a large sum, we conclude that the amount promised by the Pope, with some other funds which we hope to obtain, will be sufficient to cover the estimated cost of maintaining the army for the necessary period. We have weighed the whole question as carefully and as maturely as its importance demands, and discussed it at Worms with our brother the King of the Romans; as well as with servants and adherents of our own; and, in view of all the circumstances, we have decided, with God's help, to undertake the enterprise this year, if we obtain the funds referred to; and, even if we cannot obtain all, to undertake it with such resources as we have; unless, indeed,

1546.

something should intervene to make it impossible. When we arrive at Ratisbon, which will be at the middle of March, and after signing the capitulation between his Holiness and ourselves, we will at once set about making the provisions necessary for the army. The season, it is true, will be rather advanced; but the number of foot and horse that will have to be newly raised, in addition to the Spanish infantry that is now in Italy and Hungary, can be obtained easily; and there will be plenty of artillery and munitions. It is believed, also, that no difficulty whatever will occur about the victuals; as they will be gathered in such an abundantly supplied country as that surrounding Ratisbon, which is near the Duke of Bavaria's country, with the Archduke of Austria's dominions, the county of Tyrol: besides which there are other Catholic princes and free cities, who will necessarily have to help in a matter that so deeply concerns them. Bearing this in mind, and also the division that exists amongst Protestants, not only as regards peoples, but also between households, we confide in God, whose cause it is, that He will so direct the affair that it may end more quickly than we expect, and with less trouble than might be anticipated. Good care will be taken to ensure the Pope's fulfilment of his promise; and also in the case of other persons who will share in the enterprise. It may be reasonably hoped that with the army we shall collect, the rapidity and dissimulation with which it will be done, and the support we may find in some of the inhabitants themselves, though we do not depend very much upon that, the Protestants will not be able, for all their leagues, to gather forces sufficient to enable them to stand or defend themselves. It is thought that by capturing some territory and inflicting exemplary punishment, such as they deserve, the whole of the Protestants will submit, to the great service of Our Lord, and to the increase of our prestige, for having brought to a good issue so great and important an enterprise; thus securing the safety of our dominions, especially of Flanders. It will enable us to settle not only the religious question, but also to arrange affairs in Germany, so as to stop the intrigues that have hitherto been going on there, and other matters injurious to our repose. We therefore send you herewith the Bull for the half-first-fruits, and we are writing to Rome, asking them to dispatch promptly that for the sale of the monastic manors in due form. Juan de Vega is instructed to send you the Bull direct from there; for it will be necessary to get the money from both the sources mentioned without loss of time. We desire you to inform of this only the High Commander of Leon (*i.e.* Cobos) and instruct him to speak, with all dissimulation, and with some other pretext to lead them astray, with the persons he thinks fit, about an advance of funds. Let him consider the best way to get money quickly, but he must try, if possible, to make the clergy pay for the interest on the advances; so that the proceeds of the half-first-fruits may be received in full as they fall due. The clergy ought to do this, as the matter is one in which they are so closely concerned. Although the proceeds of the first-fruits will be a long while coming in, and it is impossible to say what will be the result obtained from the monastic manors, the securities are so good that no doubt favourable terms made be made for loans. It must be borne in mind that the money will be needed as early as possible this year, and it should be provided in Genoa, Milan, or Venice, and those parts, whence it may most easily be brought to Germany; because it is not advisable to deal in this matter with the Fuggers and the Belzares, as they live in Augsburg, and there is no certainty of their ability to provide the money. The same may be said with regard to the Flemish financiers; for the money could not be conveyed with safety from Flanders. It must also be provided that the money shall be such as is current in Germany. After you have discussed and considered all this, without concluding anything, you will send us a report of it by special courier, telling us the amount that can be obtained, and when. You will not, however, carry into effect the Bull for the half-first-fruits until further notice.

o o o o o o o o

We had written thus far when we received your letter of 26th ultimo. The points mentioned in it are replied to in my other letter. We will only say here that the High Comendador (Cobos) writes us the condition of financial affairs there (in Spain) and sends us a full report of what money could be raised for the purpose referred to. But nevertheless, we again repeat that we are still in the same mind as regards this enterprise against the Protestants, because it is so necessary, and, indeed, vital, for the good of Christendom; and also for our personal welfare, and that of our States, for our bodily repose, and for the settlement of Spanish affairs; as well as those of these dominions. Without effecting this, you may believe us when we say that things cannot go on. There are many difficulties, it is true, but there are also great advantages to be gained; but we need not dwell upon the subject further than to say that we are convinced that in the present state of affairs it is the last possible remedy. It will therefore be necessary to deal diligently and carefully in the raising of money for the enterprise on the Bulls for the half-first-fruits and the sale of the monastic manors. With this, and such funds as can be obtained from other sources which we are now seeking, we hope we shall have sufficient. With regard to the funds needed for Spain, and for our household, you may consider if it would be well to assemble the Cortes of Aragon,[*] and if so to do so at once. We do not see any objection whatever to this course. Their subvention, and the revenue from the grand masterships will have to be considered, and also the raising of a loan on the Bull of St. Peter; although this will only be preached at the end of next year. The other resources mentioned in Cobos' report must likewise be taken in hand; and we hope that any other expedient for obtaining funds that may occur will be taken advantage of. No doubt all this will be

---

[*] This was done at Monzon in the following year, 1547. The Cortes of Castile had voted their three years' supply at Valladolid in 1544, and were not due to meet again till 1548, but as will be seen by the letters from Cobos and the Prince, the condition of the country was so disastrous that they more than hinted at the unwisdom of the Emperor's policy in incurring so vast an expense in provoking a great religious war for which Spain was to pay. The present letter is an answer to these doubts.

1546.

sufficient not only to meet the ordinary expenditure in Spain for this year but also to send us a contribution to the enterprise into which we shall have entered. In such case it is only just that no opportunity should be missed of aiding and promoting it.

Venlo, 16 February 1546.

Feb. 17.
Vienna
Imp. Arch.

198. VAN DER DELFT to DE GRANVELLE.

On the 25th ultimo I wrote to you about Renegat; and as the Chancellor (Wriothesley) was anxious to bring the matter to an end, complaining in the meanwhile that the property of English subjects still remained under embargo in Spain without its being released even against security, I venture to pray your Lordship to instruct me how I am to act in the matter. As Renegat is in the Chancellor's service the latter declines to take any part in the decision, in order to avoid all suspicion; and has requested Sir William Paget to come to an agreement with me about it, which Paget says he is at once willing to do.

There is a Biscayner here named Martin Sanchez, who on his way from Spain to Flanders with his merchandise was plundered by the English. He previously brought letters to me from his Majesty about his claim, and I have accordingly done my best to obtain redress for him. As, however, the whole of the Council was very hard he returned to his Majesty at Spires and has again come hither with a second letter. After much pressure and controversy the matter was so thoroughly exposed that the whole of the Council could not avoid admitting, in the presence of Scepperus, that the man had been wronged. But still we cannot obtain any restitution, though in November last I received fresh letters from his Majesty and your Lordship to press the claim. The cause of this is that the Lord Privy Seal* has a share in the business, and stands in the way. I therefore see no other remedy than to lay the matter before the King personally, if the Emperor thinks fit to give me express orders to do so. Pray bear a hand in the matter for the rescue of this poor man, who for more than a year has sought redress here, and has grown desperate at seeing so many others sent before the Lord Admiral (who at present is dealing well and promptly with our claims) whilst all our efforts in the Council are fruitless. I do not think that an appeal to the King will be equally so.

London, 17 February 1546.

199. VAN DER DELFT to the EMPEROR.

Since my last letters of 25th utlimo the King, having returned from Hampton Court to Greenwich, the Lords of the Council ordered one of their secretaries to examine in the Tower the Comendador, who is a prisoner there. The various interrogations were first submitted to me by the Secretary, and as I saw that they were based on statements of the Frenchman Bertheuille, as to what had passed between them to the prejudice of your Majesty before St. Dizier, I thought well to precede them by an enquiry as to the man's name, quality, parentage and birthplace, his reasons for

---
* John Lord Russell.

1546.

coming hither, the length of time he was in your Majesty's service, and with what object he had told me that he had been sent by your Majesty to the King of France about the ransom of Count William (Furstenberg). One of my people was present at the examination. The prisoner replied to the first question that his name was Don Pedro Pacheco, son of Don Juan (Pacheco) of Toledo, his mother being a la Cueva*. He said he had been a comendador of Santiago for ten years, and had come hither to serve the King. He had been a gentleman of the table to your Majesty for about six years, and of the chamber three years afterwards, until he had a combat in your Majesty's Court with one Gerard Caralcero. In reply to the question whether he knew Don Pedro Portocarrero, he said that he did; and that Don Pedro was now in Spain. With regard to his statement to me about Count William, he said he did not recollect it. In reply to the interrogations of the Secretary he denied everything alleged, and said that he had no acquaintance with Bertheuille before he was taken prisoner. I therefore asked the Lords of the Council what they intended to do. They replied that they intended to confront him with Bertheuille; and that I should be pre-advised of what was done. They would also have handed me the letter from the Duke of Alburquerque (which they believe to be a forgery), but the man who had charge of it is absent. When he returns I will send your Majesty the letter in question; and report what takes place with Bertheuille.

I was at Court a few days since, in order to discover the cause for the coming of an ambassador from Poland who had been received both by the King and the Queen with great welcome, and as the King came from mass he acknowledged my salutation with a very joyful and smiling visage. He asked me whether I had not the authentic draft of his Ambassador's negotiations with your Majesty, and on hearing that I had nothing, he continued: "The Emperor, my good brother, has left Utrecht, and it is said that he intends to make war against the protestants." I replied that I had heard nothing about it, and I was sure your Majesty would not do anything that was not for general welfare of all christendom. With this the conversation ended, and I had no opportunity of learning, either from the King or the Council, the reason for the coming of this ambassador, except that on his way hither he had stayed some time at your Majesty's Court. The war preparations are being made with great activity; and every day German captains come to offer their services: but it appears to me that owing to the fault of von Reissenberg they (i.e. the English) do not require any more Germans beyond those that are to be brought by Conrad Penninck and some Westland (Oestlandt) horse. I hear that some Italian captains have left, and M. Louis de l'Armet (Loys de L'arma) is also to go to raise troops in Italy. I am informed secretly that they have delayed de l'Arme's departure, in order that may get

---

*This was the family of the Duke of Alburquerque, who had accompanied Henry in the war, and from whom the prisoner had ostensibly brought a letter of introduction.

†Luigi delle Arme was a famous Italian Condottiere in the service of England, and several references to him are made in the correspondence.

1546.

Luigi di Gonzaga, a member or ally of the house of Mantua, as chief of the Italians. For this reason, it is said the King has nominated him a Knight of the Garter. All the Spaniards (*i.e.* the mercenaries) have embarked for Boulogne, and the Lord Admiral who had gone thither has now returned. They are talking of the assembly there of a great land army.

London, 17 February 1546.

Feb. 21.
Vienna
Imp. Arch.

200. SCEPPERUS to LOYS SCORS.

I send you the duplicate of the two articles, which the English ambassadors say have been accepted by the King; and the instructions to the person who is to be appointed commissioner will now have to be drafted at once. Rumour here says that this will be Master Adrien Van der Burgh, a worthy and learned man; but I do not know how true this may be. Verily, whoever he may be, he will need the habergeon of patience, and the possession of a good steady brain to endure the clamour of so many people who will daily trouble him. As for myself, so long as the other affairs allow me to do so, I will aid to my best ability in this matter, at least whilst the two English commissioners put up with me; for the articles only provide for the appointment of one person to co-operate with the resident ambassador. I will send you by a safe hand the original of the treaty signed by the English ambassadors, and of the ratification similarly signed. I dare not send them lightly across country.

Bruges, 21 February 1546.

Feb. 22.
Simancas.
E. 1318
Extract.

201. DIEGO HURTADO DE MENDOZA[*] to the EMPEROR.

With regard to the Pope's aims and objects, I can only refer your Majesty to my former letters. Your Majesty may, however, be sure of one thing: if the Pope desires to obtain more power, spiritual or temporal, even though it be to the prejudice of your Majesty or another sovereign, he will try to do it in this Council (*i.e.* of Trent) and by the votes of the bishops; in which case no one can withstand him, as he does exactly as he likes with them (the bishops) and really disgraceful things take place. I therefore trust that national councils may be arranged, or else that this Council may be rendered unfruitful, although without allowing your Majesty's hand to be seen too openly.

With regard to the first point, of the title to be assumed by the Council; whether it will declare itself the representative of the universal church or not, I have written my opinion; and send a copy thereof herewith. As to the question of who is the true superior, I draw my view from the ancient and modern councils, and from other writers. This is that the Council is superior to the Pope: for the very canonists deprive the Pope on the one hand of what they concede him on the other. I am prepared to state my reasons for this opinion when necessary; and when your Majesty has time to see them I will send them written in Spanish.

---

[*] This was the famous man of letters, presumably the author of the first picaresque novel Lazarillo de Tormes. He was Spanish ambassador in Venice and the Emperor's special envoy to the Council of Trent, of which he wrote a history.

1546.

Touching the second point, I am of opinion that a beginning should be made on the general ground of the faith, the question of reform being considered afterwards. After this should be set forth the special doubts that arise in the christian religion. This is the order adopted from the Council of Nicea° until the present time. I can also send the bases upon which I found this view, and also as to the usurpation by the Pontiffs of temporal jurisdiction for the last eleven hundred odd years against both Emperors and peoples.

Venice, 22 February 1546.

Feb. 26.
Vienna
Imp. Arch.

202. The Emperor to Van der Delft.†

We have deferred replying to your last letters, which we received at Arnhem at the time that we were about to despatch M. D'Eick to the King of England, respecting the communications that had passed between us and the Bishop of Winchester and the other English ambassadors here, and also to salute the King on our behalf, and to inform him of our departure (*i.e.* to Germany). As you will learn everything by the letters we are now writing to M. D'Eick on his mission to England, he having instructions to communicate the same to you, we need not dwell upon business in this letter further than to request you to inform us that you have been able to ascertain as to the confession of the Spanish prisoner, and to continue to press for the restitution of the property captured by Renegat. We are ignorant of the exact amount of this property, but have written to Spain, asking for full particulars, which we will communicate to you as soon as we receive them.

Maestricht, 26 February 1546.

Feb. 26.
Vienna
Imp. Arch.

203. The Emperor to Scepperus.

We have heard what you wrote to Sr. de Granvelle on the 16th instant; and also the contents of the document referred to in your letter, with regard to the discourse you had had with the Bishop of Winchester and the other English ambassadors and the opinions you had formed as to their intentions in the matter of the aid, which they have claimed so persistently, in the drafting of the clauses of the explanatory agreement recently signed between the King and ourselves. We also note the conclusions you have arrived at as to the state of affairs existing between the Kings of England and France. After due consideration of all the points, we caused MM. de Granvelle and President Scors to confer with the English ambassadors, taking the opportunity of the latter having requested permission for the passage through these dominions of certain troops that Conrad Penninck has undertaken to bring into their service, and for the license to export from here some leather, saltpetre, harquebusses and pikes. Both on account of the importance of these

---

° The Council of Nice, A.D. 325, first authoritatively summarised the doctrines of the church, especially as regarded the Trinity. Mendoza's view with regard to the papal aggression in temporal affairs was that mainly acted upon by the stronger Spanish monarchs, who strove persistently for centuries to make their church a national one, depending upon the Sovereign.

† This draft reply is written on the letter from Van der Delft to de Granvelle of 25 January (page 296).

1546.

petitions themselves and with the object of seeing whether some arrangement could be made with the ambassadors respecting the aid, as well as in regard of your proposed voyage to England[*], it was decided that the above-mentioned interview should take place. Our commissioners having heard the particulars of the ambassadors' instructions and other subsequent observations respecting our projected voyage, replied to them that we were very anxious and desirous to accommodate their master as far as was possible, both on account of the treaty of alliance and in respect of the friendship that existed between us. But it was incumbent upon us to see that our own countries did not suffer injury, and to avoid the contravention of our treaty with France. We must obviate, moreover, similar requisitions on their (*i.e.* the French) part. With regard to Penninck and the troops he wished to lead through our dominions, it was desirable that Penninck himself should be seen here; so that he might say by which road he wished to take his men; because, although the ambassadors said that he would bring only a little troop, it was necessary for us to ascertain from him positively that they should not be increased in number in these countries nor be allowed to make a disagreeable sojourn. We must see also that the passage should be effected in such a way as to give as little cause for complaint as possible to the French; and as soon as Penninck came arrangements should be made with him and a speedy decision given. As the King had taken Penninck into his service, the latter might come hither with perfect security: but we may privately remark to you that the principal reason why we wish him to come is to ensure ourselves absolutely from him that he will neither directly or indirectly do anything to our prejudice. We do not believe that he will raise any difficulty about this, from what we hear from Martin Van Rossen. As regards the leather they wish to export, the license was conceded to them on condition that the export was managed with as little noise as possible, and occasion avoided for arousing the jealousy of the French. Similarly the harquebusses, the saltpetre and the pikes should be placed at their disposal so far as was compatible with the needs of these dominions themselves. Having arranged these points with the ambassadors, the latter declared themselves well satisfied.

As the ambassadors did not make any fresh allusion to the aid they had demanded they were then addressed on the subject of your proposed voyage to England, following up what had been said on the point at Utrecht, and your various communications with the ambassadors jointly and severally since then. They replied at once that, in their opinion, your going thither could only be productive of good; the object being to salute the King on our behalf and inform him of our departure for Germany: and also to discourse of the marriage of our niece with the Prince of England. In order, if possible, to draw them out somewhat farther, it was remarked that we were still of the same mind to send you to salute the King and inform him of our departure; but that as for the marriage

---

[*] It will be seen by the correspondence that the mission of Scepperus (M. D'Eick) to England was really to sound Henry as to the marriage of Prince Edward with a niece of the Emperor and to watch his attitude.

they had not referred to the matter for some time, and we did not know whether it had cooled or not. The Bishop of Winchester replied that he had received no letter from his master since the last conversation, but was expecting daily some instructions respecting his return. He was asked if he thought it would be better that we should defer our departure until his letters from England arrived, but he and the rest of them all answered at once that they thought not.

The Bishop of Winchester, still referring to the letters he was expecting, asked what route we intended to take, and whether we should pass through Metz; and he was told that we should first go to Luxemburg, and would there consider the road for the rest of the journey, as we could not decide before then. He pointedly asked what news there was of the conference, and if it was going forward, adding that he heard that the Council (of Trent) was progressing. He was told in reply that it was believed that the conference in question was assembled at the present time, and that all parties, so far as was understood, desired a peaceful understanding on the questions touching religion. When we arrived at Ratisbon we would see whether some good work could not be effected. With regard to the Council, some commencement had been made, and the matter now under consideration was as to whether the reformation should be proceeded with at once, or the correction of errors immediately discussed with it (*si l'on procederoit en premier lieu a la reformacion ou si incontinent l'on tracteroit avec ceste reformation des erreurs*). The ambassadors had already been assured that care had been, and would be, taken on our part not to enlarge the papal authority or to concede to the Council more power than it could fairly claim by right and reason, and it was emphatically repeated to them (the ambassadors) now, in order that they might not be persuaded to believe otherwise. They then asked what intelligence there was from France, and whether great war preparations were not going on there. They understood that the French were utterly tired of the expense and burden of maintaining the war. There was, we replied, much talk about preparations, it was true; but from what we could hear the French were more anxious to provision their forts near Boulogne, Ardres and Therouanne, which were in great need.

It was considered advisable at this point to remark that there were many rumours in France of an agreement with their master, whereto they replied that they had received no recent news from England, and their last information was that mentioned above.

Although the discourse lasted a long while the ambassadors made no allusion whatever to the aid they had requested, nor did they evince any sign of dissatisfaction. When they were leaving M. de Granvelle took the Bishop of Winchester aside, and remarked to him that it would be conducive to good relations if when they received any fresh news from England they would communicate it to us, in the interests of the alliance: hoping that the bishop would exert his good offices in the matter. The bishop took this in good part and promised to do so.

1546.

After the above interview had been maturely considered by us at Utrecht, together with the remarks respecting your journey to England, it was decided that the best course will be for you to pursue your voyage thither as speedily as possible. This course is the more necessary because, although there is every indication of close negotiations for peace between France and England, our intelligence from France convinces us that the French do not trust the other side, but are making every possible effort to secure and muster troops, whilst the English are acting in a similar way in the preparations already referred to. The talk of peace has on several occasions been even more prevalent than it is now, but has ended in nothing. Although it may certainly be concluded that both of the parties desire peace, the differences and claims on both sides are very great, and an arrangement will not easily be effected, as we have already seen. Perchance your going to England, and the assurance thus attained of our continued friendship for the King, together with the settlement recently made by M. de Granvelle with the Bishop of Winchester at Utrecht, may at least prevent the King of England from entering into any negotiations prejudicial to us.

You may, moreover, tell the King secretly and in confidence, that we have received advice from a trustworthy source that the French propose to deceive and circumvent him by means of a marriage which they will suggest between the Prince his son and the daughter of Scotland; a peace or long truce being effected, and Boulogne restored to them. They will endeavour to persuade the Queen (Mother) of Scotland to consent to the marriage of her daughter, whilst giving her to understand that her pledge or promise to that effect will not be binding, in consequence of the King of England being, as they say, schismatic; and no pledge given to such a person would hold good; or would not at once be annulled by the Pope. In addition to this they say a separate protest might be secretly made in the name of the girl. We have thought well, you may say, to inform him of this intention in confidence; and to warn him through you to keep his eye on the matter, although he is wise, and is so well aware of the sort of people he has to deal with, that we are sure that he and his prudent councillors will not allow themselves to be taken in.

When you arrive in England you will take such discreet means as you may, in order to learn how the King is inclined towards a marriage between our niece and the Prince; and in accordance as you may find him you will address him, more or less significantly, on the subject. You may, in any case, say that we have been much gratified to hear from the ambassadors that he bore so much goodwill towards such a match; and that our pleasure thereat is shared by our brother the King of the Romans, whom we have informed of what had passed in the matter. We presume that the ambassadors will have communicated to him (King Henry) the reply we gave to them: and you will advance or retire in your conversation on the subject, according as you may see advisable.

If there is any mention made about a dowry, you can refer to it in the sense already decided upon: the object being to induce the King to be satisfied with such dowry as the King of the Romans may be able to give to his daughter, and such as he gives to his other daughters; and to prevent any larger endowment being demanded in this case, either from our brother or ourselves, for the reasons which were fully discussed and you will recollect.

If you see that the King or his ministers persist in demanding a larger dowry, but still demonstrate a goodwill towards the marriage in principle, you may say that you have no further instructions on the point than those above-mentioned: but that we and our brother cannot believe that the King, who is so great and wealthy a prince, would take his stand upon such a matter. Nevertheless you will gladly inform us of what they say, though without the slightest hope on your part that our brother will be induced to give a larger dowry, or that we will consent to help him to do so, for the reasons already set forth.

In case you recognise that the King is well disposed towards the marriage, and is desirous of arranging it, you may ascertain how and when he would like to negotiate; and let us and the King of the Romans know at once, assuring the King of England that we will not fail on our part to reciprocate. You will also discover whether the King would be content for the negotiations to be entrusted to the English ambassadors who may be accredited to us at Ratisbon. This, truly, would be the most convenient and decorous way, as the father of the girl will be there with us. If, on the other hand, you find that the King of England does not wish for the match, or has already advanced with the treaty for a Scottish marriage, you may signify that the discussion on the matter here and your references to it in England have simply originated in a desire on our part to reciprocate the proposals made by the King through you for a closer alliance, and the Bishop of Winchester's remark to us at Antwerp respecting the marriage of our niece, to which, as you know, he said his master would willingly listen. However the King or his ministers may answer you on this subject, you will behave graciously towards them, saying that in any case we desire to keep on terms of sincere friendship with him, the prince his son, and all his realm.

If the King's councillors press you on the subject of the aid requested you may make the best shift you can to explain the reason for its not having been accorded, using the arguments already brought forward, particularly since the last agreement. But you will deal with the matter very moderately, taking care not to press more hardly upon the Bishop of Winchester and the other ambassadors than you find really necessary; although, in good truth, it is quite inexcusable that they made not the slightest mention of the aid for more than three weeks before the ratification of the agreement; and this, in fact, entirely exonerates us from furnishing the aid. Even after the ratificaton they said not a word about the aid until they received letters from England on the subject. There are, moreover, many other reasons which justify us, and prove conclusively that the aid cannot be granted.

If, notwithstanding everything, you find that the King or his ministers insist that we should pay the said subsidy, you may say, as if of your own accord, that we had no idea that the matter would be pressed by them; because, putting aside the many ample and

HENRY VIII.

1546.

peremptory reasons for our attitude, we could not think that the King of England would make a point of so trifling a thing. You will sound them at the same time as to the nature and duration of the aid they want: and you may signify to them that in no case could it be given, except during the continuance of the invasion formally specified in the treaty between the King and ourselves, and even then only after the notification had been given to us in the form often discussed. When you have heard all they have to say you may promise to convey to us the claim they make, with an assurance of your belief that we shall do everything in reason, though you will not express any approval of their claims.

If the questions of the Diet and the Council (of Trent) be mentioned, you will say what is written in a previous paragraph on those subjects, and you may add to the King the substance of what we replied to his ambassadors on the other points mentioned above, reconciling it all with your instructions as you may see necessary.

This letter will also be for our resident ambassador in England, and you will jointly do your best to carry out the mission entrusted to you. In addition to this you will make every effort to secure the redress due to our subjects, Flemings and Spaniards, for the injuries inflicted upon them; and also for the restitution of what Renegat has captured at sea from our subjects and belonging to us.

With regard to your allowance, etc., concerning which you have written to M. de Granvelle, for the frequent voyages you are making and have made, we have given orders for 400 florins more to be handed to you on account, for the expenses of the present voyage, and on your return the Queen, our sister, will look to the rest and provide what is fitting.

Maestricht, 26 February 1546.

Feb. 27.
Vienna
Imp. Arch.

204. VAN DER DELFT to the EMPEROR.

I have nothing very important to communicate to your Majesty; but, as I have the convenience of this courier, I think well to inform you that the King sent one of his secretaries to me a few days ago to learn the truth of the rumour that a public prohibition had been issued at Gravelines forbidding any victuals passing from there to the English, which, he said, seemed to be against the treaties, especially against that lately confirmed by your Majesty, and, he feared, would encourage his enemies. I replied that I had heard nothing about it, but I knew that great scarcity existed there (*i.e.* Gravelines) and your subjects were obliged to look after themselves. When the secretary saw that I had nothing to say about it he expressed a hope that there was no truth in the rumour. He told me that they were expecting daily the arrival of M. D'Eick, and asked me what news I had of him. I replied that I had none at all except the current talk of this Court that M. D'Eick was coming hither, and also a commissioner to settle the complaints and claims of subjects of both sovereigns.

The preparations for war are well advanced, especially by sea. The King has had constructed eight galleasses, which he considers much more advantageous than galleys, as each one will carry two cannons at the bows, and three, or if it is desired five, on each side,

1546.

and one on the poop. A great number of Irishmen are expected here to be sent to Boulogne. The talk is that the Marquis (*i.e.* Henry Grey, third Marquis of Dorset) and the Earl of Essex (*i.e.* Sir William Parr, afterwards Marquis of Northampton) will have command of the troops, which are being made ready. There are no foreign soldiers now remaining on the Scottish border, the German cavalry being all dismissed.

Sire, I am confused and apprehensive to have to inform your Majesty that there are rumours here of a new Queen, although I do not know why, or how true it may be. Some people attribute to it the sterility of the present Queen, whilst others say that there will be no change whilst the present war lasts.

Madame Suffolk is much talked about, and is in great favour; but the King shows no alteration in his demeanour towards the Queen, though the latter, as I am informed, is somewhat annoyed at the rumours.º

I have made enquiries respecting the mission of the Polish Ambassador; but I can discover nothing, except that it is publicly asserted that the object is to negotiate a marriage between his master and Lady Mary. I heard also from a person who was present that the Queen on one occasion twitted Lady Mary about it. The Polish Ambassador has been knighted by the King, who at the same time in open Court placed a golden collar round his neck.

London, 27 February 1546.

Feb. 27.
Simancas.
E. 374.

205. LOPE HURTADO DE MENDOZAº to PRINCE PHILIP.

(In a letter mainly respecting Portuguese affairs, the Inquisition in Portugal, and the famine in the country, the following passages relating to England occur.) The King (of Portugal) has received information from France that no peace has been made with England, and also that no negotiations were proceeding between his Majesty (the Emperor) and France. They write that small hope of peace exists.

With regard to the letters of marque given (by the French) against this country, the King (of Portugal) would not accept the suspension for a year except on certain conditions, which the ambassador in France writes that the King of France will not concede. Letters of marque and reprisal had therefore been conceded by the King of France, limited by the appointment of judges at Bruges and Lisbon, who are to decide as to the legality of the captures.

Armed English ships are doing as much damage as they can, which is a great deal. It is said that they have captured I know not how many ships loaded with wheat bound for Lisbon. The King of Portugal has sent an envoy to the King of England. I will duly advise the reply he brings back. The Portuguese are being

---

* Catharine, Baroness Willoughby D'Eresby in her own right was the god-daughter of Henry's first wife, her mother being Queen Catharine's close friend and compatriot Maria de Sarmiento, daughter of the Count de Salinas. By the death of her father, Lord Willoughby, in her childhood, her wardship fell to the King, who married her to his recently widowed brother-in-law, Charles Brandon, Duke of Suffolk, who had died shortly before this letter was written. The Duchess soon afterwards married one of her esquires, Francis Bertie.

† Spanish Ambassador in Portugal.

1546.

much harried at sea; and it is said that even Spaniards will be molested by the numerous armed ships that are out.

Almerim, 27 February 1546.

March 2.
Vienna
Imp. Arch

206. SCEPPERUS to LOYS SCORS.

I have informed you of the dispatch I have from the Emperor, with which I am now going to England.

Recommends to him certain law suits of his own and of his friends. Asks for an appointment for his bailiff at Eick, and a place as Flemish councillor for M. Cornelius Meunicx, advocate of Ghent. Sends the ratification of the King of England and two other documents securely enclosed by the hand of his wife, not daring to entrust them to anyone not absolutely sure. She will arrive at Brussels in the first week in Lent.

Bruges, 2 March 1546.

March 2.
Vienna
Imp. Arch.

207. The QUEEN DOWAGER to VAN DER DELFT.

You will learn from the letters taken by M. D'Eick, and from him personally, all that has passed with the Bishop of Winchester since he arrived here, both with regard to the confirmation of the treaty of alliance and to the aid demanded last year by the King of England up to the time of the Emperor's departure from Maestricht on his voyage to Germany. The bishop at the same time took the opportunity of presenting letters to us from the King of England, and of requesting us, in virtue of the same, to allow him to draw from the town of Antwerp the sum of four hundred thousand crowns in gold without hindrance from us, and also that we will permit the subjects of the Emperor here to carry victuals to England, and supply waggons for the King's service. We thought best not to give a decided answer on these points until we had consulted his Majesty upon them, the Emperor being then in this town (Maestricht) and the reply has consequently been delayed until now. The resident ambassador, Carne, has been informed that, having regard to the large sums of money drawn last year by the King of England from Antwerp, we should have had ample reason for refusing his request in this respect; particularly seeing how very strict they are in such matters in England; but in order to please the King we will consent to his drawing a sum not exceeding 200,000 crowns, providing that the money be not of the Emperor's coinage. With regard to the supply of victuals, Carne has been informed that, before we can make any concession in this respect, we wish to know from the King how he proposes that the subjects here should carry victuals to England. A general permit would obviously be tantamount to the abrogation of the prohibition of such traffic now in force, so far as regards England; in which case all other neighbouring countries would feel aggrieved. In addition to this the lack of victuals here is so great that we cannot reasonably do as he requests. If, however, his wish is simply to obtain some victuals for the sustenance of his troops only, we will endeavour to do all we can reasonably to meet his wishes, and so far as the scarcity here will permit: although the

1546.

subjects here will be sure to complain bitterly of the passage of the infantry the King is raising under Penninck, whose transit through his territory the Emperor has tacitly consented to allow in small bodies only, on the assurance of Penninck, who has not yet been here to confer with us.

With regard to the waggons, we also ask for information as to how the King proposes to make use of them. For the subjects here to be ordered to undertake to provide them would be extremely difficult, and also unreasonable considering the bad treatment they experienced in the year '44, which the Flemish representatives affirm cost the country of Flanders more than one hundred thousand crowns: whereas for us merely to consent to such of the subjects as pleased voluntarily supplying waggons would produce only a small number and of poor quality. It would also be necessary to watch very closely the passage of horses and mares, in order to prevent the pretext of employing the waggons being made use of to strip the country on this side of serviceable horses and mares, as the English tried to do in '44. Carne left here for Antwerp with this message, the Bishop of Winchester being doubtless still in that town. We have thought advisable to inform you of this, so that you may know how to reply if on the return of the bishop to England you are addressed on the subject. Carne also drew our attention to the mustering of French troops to revictual Ardres; with the intention, as he says, subsequently to invade the English towns on this side. He begs us to prevent their transit through the Emperor's country.

(Maestricht or Brussels?), 6 March 1546.

March 13
Vienna
Imp. Arch

208. VAN DER DELFT to the EMPEROR.

I heard to-day that the King has been indisposed with a fever for two or three days, but it cannot be dangerous, as he passes the time playing at cards with the Lord Admiral and other intimates. I do not know what will come of it, as his principal medical man, Dr. Butts, died this winter. I will enquire daily and report to your Majesty. There is no more talk about the Irish, who they said were to cross the sea nor about the Marquis (i.e. of Dorset) and the Admiral. I expect the latter will put to sea, the rumour being current that the French have already sailed with sixteen well-fitted ships, and have captured fifteen or sixteen vessels loaded with provisions sent from here for Boulogne, most of them (i.e. the vessels) being the property of your Netherlands subjects. They (the English) are afraid that the Spaniards who were embarked in the North country for Boulogne may also fall into the hands of the French. The preparation of ships here is therefore being pushed on very actively, and the King has ordered to Dover the largest vessels which were at Portsmouth.

Although these people are very tired of the war, they still show great determination to sustain it, on account of the King's desire to keep Boulogne, though from what I hear their preparations are more directed to defence than offence.

London, 10 March 1546.

1546.
March 12.
Simancas.
E. R. 873.

209. Report on JUAN DE VEGA's letter of 12 March.

Marquina and Dandino both arrived in Rome on the 23rd February. Three days afterwards Vega spoke to the Pope, urging upon him the need for despatching the Brief for the sale of the monastic manors. Although he appeared much pleased with the kind messages and assurances which Vega gave him on behalf of his Majesty, etc., he did not fail to refer to the sending of the Bull for the half-first-fruits to Castile, arguing that it was to some extent a violation of the letter sent by Cardinal Farnese to the Emperor's confessor.* Vega had done his best to satisfy the Pope on this point; and his Holiness promised that he would do what he could, asking Vega to give him a memorandum of the form in which he wished the Brief to be drawn up, and it should be duly considered. Vega had given this memorandum to Cardinal Farnese, and Cardinals Sfondrato and Cresencius were to consider it. Vega was sorry that Cardinal Arsinguelo was not to intervene in the affair, as he has always been very devoted and diligent in the Emperor's interests. Vega will not cease his efforts until the business is settled, which he expects will be done favourably, unless the Pope changes his mind, as he is apt to do.

(In the margin, the note for the reply to this paragraph runs as follows: "His Majesty doubts not that everything will have been done with due diligence and will await the result.")

The French are continuing their negotiations with the Pope through one Nicholas, who was formerly secretary to the King of France in Rome, a person of no very good qualities. The Pope is offended with Cardinal Trivulciis and other French cardinals, especially Salviati, as he learnt that during his recent illness they discussed the succession to the pontificate. This has greatly annoyed him.

Although the Pope's friends give out that the French are on his side in the matter of the Council (of Trent) and the rest, it is evident that his Holiness is not so confident about it. On the contrary, he manifests his opinion that there is little stability in French affairs, which he considers badly managed.

Salviati and Trivulciis are at loggerheads, and Juan de Vega thinks that in their discussions about the pontifical succession they must both have discovered that each of them aims at being the next Pope. If this should turn out to be the case it will greatly weaken the French party, which will thus find itself divided.

Salviati says that Trivulciis is opposed to peace being made; whilst he (Salviati) is in favour of it, and he makes a long speech about the ruin which otherwise threatens the King of France.

(Marginal note for reply: "With regard to the pontificate, Vega must bear in mind what has been written to him, and must keep a sharp look out, letting us know what occurs.")

---

* It will be seen by the Emperor's letter to his son of 16 February that the authority for the half-first-fruits of ecclesiastical patronage had been sent to Spain in order that measures might be taken at once for raising loans on security of it. This was considered by the Pope to be an evasion of the understanding that no action should be taken for obtaining funds from church sources until the treaty binding the Emperor to undertake the religious war was actually signed.

1546.

So far as can be judged, the Pope is not well pleased about other things besides the affairs of the Council, in which latter business he would have liked to obtain enlightenment as to the Emperor's intentions: Dandino having brought no decision about certain private affairs of his.[*]

But still the Pope hides his chagrin with great dissimulation, and raises no objections against what is asked of him, as it is his custom to do. This proves that the French must be very weak.

(Marginal note for reply: "They (*i.e.* the Pope's private affairs) were replied to and dealt with at the time in the best way possible in the circumstances: and in future they shall be attended to in accordance with the progress of events, and with the Pope's own procedure.")

Since the talk of Cardinal Farnese's going to the Emperor ceased, Juan de Vega has been informed that the King (of France's) agents in Rome have been pressing very urgently that he (Cardinal Farnese) should go. As they were formerly against his going the Pope's friends are shocked at their change of front. They (the French) were also against the going of the Emperor to Ratisbon, which renders them very uneasy.

The Pope really in his heart would prefer that the enterprise (against the Protestants) should not be executed, however much he may profess in words to the contrary; but Juan de Vega thinks that, just in the same way that he consented to the Council against his own inclination, he will fulfil his promises with regard to the enterprise, and perhaps even more than fulfil them, though he likes it but little. The enterprise and the Council will both be means for forcing the Pope on to the road your Majesty wishes him to take; and if your Majesty chooses, whilst pressing him on either point to give him hopes of his private ends, Juan de Vega thinks it would not be unadvisable to do so; at least until the Council and the enterprise are both well advanced. The talk about receiving Peter Strozzi and the so-called prior of Capua, his brother, into the Papal service has ceased; and the sale of the galleys to Count Fiesco has been completed and the galleys delivered. Vega has therefore done nothing in either matter.

(Marginal note for reply: "This is well as it is done; although as the Pope knew that he (Fiesco) was a pensioner of his Majesty it would only have been decent to have refrained from negotiating with him until he had paid his Majesty the compliment of mentioning it. Do not, however, let the Count (Fiesco) know that his Majesty is displeased.")

There is talk of Duke Ottavio (Farnese) coming to Germany. Vega learns that the Pope has been greatly annoyed at the rumours that have arisen amongst those barons in the territory of Piacenza, to the effect that they are feudatories of the Empire. A member of the house of Palavicini

---

[*] Namely the confirmation of his son Pier Luigi Farnese in the dukedoms of Parma and Piacenza; for which, as will be seen in the correspondence, the Emperor was determined to drive a hard bargain. It was claimed by the imperial party that the duchies were an appanage to the territory of Milan, a fief of the Empire.

1546.

has gone to Venice, but avoided Piacenza, whither the Duke Pier Luigi had summoned him. He had left a castle of his manned and provisioned, and the Duke wished to attack it, sending troops and cannon for the purpose, only that the Pope—as it is asserted—thought better that nothing should be done, and the matter has hitherto been dissembled.

(Marginal note for reply: "He does well to advise this, for the Marquis del Guasto* has written nothing about it.")

The Pope's displeasure has been increased by the address of a letter from the Emperor to the Duke Pier Luigi, in which he is not called Duke of Parma and Piacenza but simply Duke of Castro. They are, however, keeping this also very secret, though they do not hide their belief in the instability of the new State, which in their talk amongst themselves they say cannot last.

(Marginal note for reply: "There is nothing fresh to say about this. Vega knows what passed in the matter when Cardinal Farnese was at Worms and the mission sent by Dandolo. In accordance with this it is thought best not to make any change in Pier Luigi's style, in the letters written to him, having in view the rights of the Empire, at least until it was decided what would be the best course to adopt in the matter.")

It is said that the Pope was sending an envoy to push his negotiations with the Swiss, and Vega hears that the Pope is dealing with the Duke of Urbino to enter his service, as it is asserted that he is not satisfied with the Venetians. Juan de Vega thinks for many reasons, however, that the only object of all this is to make people think that he (the Pope) is prepared to appeal to force if necessary in the matter of Parma and Piacenza.

(Marginal note for reply: "We know here that the Duke (of Urbino) has agreed with the Venetians. There is not much ground for the talk about the Swiss.")

Don Juan de Luna went thither (to Rome) after the events that had happened at Siena, but had already departed. From what Vega could gather Don Juan was more determined not to return to that city than anything else. Either from his desire to serve Madame, or because he did not understand the artfulness of these people, he (Don Juan de Luna) conferred with the Duchess and Cardinal Farnese with regard to giving Siena to her Excellency; and Vega thinks that Don Juan and the Pope discussed the same question when the former went to take leave of his Holiness.† Vega thinks that no doubt Don Juan spoke of this matter, believing that it would be conducive to the Emperor's interests, but he did so without Vega's connivance.

---

* The Governor of Milan for the Emperor.
† Don Juan de Luna commanded the small imperial garrison in the republic of Siena, in which city French and Papal intrigue was busy stirring up strife and a rising had occurred. It will be seen by this and other letters that Margaret of Austria, the Emperor's natural daughter, who had married Ottavio Farnese, Duke of Camarino, the Pope's grandson, was made use of by the papal party to enable the Farneses to obtain a footing in Siena.

1546.

(Marginal note for reply: "His Majesty had already learnt of Don Juan de Luna's going to Rome, and supposed that he and Juan de Vega had conferred as to a remedy for the disturbance and troubles in Siena. No news, however, has been received from Don Juan, and his Majesty therefore defers for the present the measures necessary for settling the matter. Vega did well in cutting short the hopes of Madame of getting Siena. The place being a prey to turbulence his Majesty has no other present intention than to pacify it. This is conveyed to Vega, in order that he may discreetly deal with the question there.")

The Duchess (of Camarino), taking advantage of what Don Juan de Luna had said to her about Siena, spoke to Juan de Vega on the matter, by the Pope's orders, and treated it more seriously on her own behalf than she had previously done. She had children, she said; and dwelt at great length on the disorders that had taken place in the State, concluding by saying that it was necessary that some wise course should be adopted, and the wisest would be to place the State in the hands of those who were so loyal in your Majesty's service as she and her sons. Juan de Vega replied that your Majesty had always considered it extremely difficult to dispose of the Sienese Republic, in consequence of its ancient attachment to the Holy Empire and to the crown of Castile. Although your Majesty loved the Duchess as your daughter Vega had seen no inclination on your Majesty's part towards such a course as that which she proposed; but he thought that your Majesty's views on the matter might be considerably influenced by the Pope's trying to please you or otherwise. Vega said this because he thought that it might be useful to let them deceive themselves to some extent, as they are apt to do.

His Holiness is endeavouring by every possible means to raise money; and he is especially making arrangements that the tax he put upon flour in the year '40 shall last for 12 years. He is negotiating with the people of Rome for them to assure the tax to him for this period, in order that he may sell or farm it. Although they (the Papal court?) have hitherto made out that they had not much money, they are now pleased that people should say that they have.

March 14.
Vienna.
Imp. Arch.

210. SCEPPERUS to the QUEEN DOWAGER.

After I had received my dispatch from the Emperor I was informed for certain that the French with thirteen ships of war were in the Straits between England and France, and had already taken some English vessels. I therefore considered that it would be safer for me to go by sea, and I consequently went to Zeeland, putting thence to sea in fairly favourable weather. But very shortly it took an evil turn, so that only after very great suffering and danger, having been eight days at sea, and once obliged to take shelter in Dunkirk, did I finally arrive in England on Thursday last, coming to this city of London on the 13th instant, and finding the ambassador much rejoiced at my arrival. With regard to our mission, it is impossible for us to obtain audience of the King owing to the indisposition which for the last three weeks has

1546.

troubled him. He is now somewhat better, as we were informed yesterday by Sir William Paget, his chief secretary, who begged us, nevertheless, to have patience for four or five days longer, at the end of which time he would arrange to give us audience. The only course we could take was to condole with him on his illness, which arises from a malady in his leg. In conversation with Paget and elsewhere we gathered that there was not the slightest signs of peace between France and England, although they (the English) are very desirous of it. The preparations being made are very great, as I could perceive as we entered the Thames. As regards Scotland, negotiations are proceeding by means of Frenchmen for the marriage of the daughter of the King of Scotland who recently died and the son of the Regent (*i.e.* Arran). In good truth it appears to be the most probable arrangement, for the Scots love very much more to be ruled by their own countrymen than by foreigners. Besides which such a marriage as that suggested would probably extinguish the danger that the son referred to might at some future time raise opposition to the princess (*i.e.* Mary Stuart), he being a very near heir to the crown. However, as the girl is an infant, matters may change. There is no talk of a great war between the English and the Scots; on the contrary, it looks as if there was some sort of connivance between them. The Scots will not move unless money from France causes them to do so, for they much prefer to receive French aid in money rather than in men.

We are detaining here the Emperor's courier until we have had audience of the King, as until then we have nothing of importance to write.

London, 14 March 1546.

March 14.
Vienna.
Imp. Arch.

211. SCEPPERUS and VAN DER DELFT to the QUEEN DOWAGER.

This afternoon Sir William Paget, first secretary to the King, came to us, and amongst other conversation, of which an account will be given to your Majesty in our next letters, he requested us to beg your Majesty to allow transit through your territory of certain grain purchased at Amsterdam by a Commissioner of the King, one John Dimock. We asked him (Paget) if the grain was from Westland (Oestlandt) and what was the quantity, but he was unable to give us a precise answer. In the belief, however, that your Majesty will be fully informed on these points we have thought well in the present circumstances to advise you of Paget's request.

London, 14 March 1546.

March 14.
Vienna.
Imp. Arch.

212. VAN DER DELFT and SCEPPERUS to LOYS SCORS.

We have been requested by Sir William Paget, first secretary to the King, to beg the Queen (Dowager of Hungary) to be good enough to allow transit through Flanders of certain grain purchased at Amsterdam by John Dimock, and we do so with pleasure. The Secretary (*i.e.* Paget) also asked us to give him letters to you, in favour of the same request, and we did not like to refuse him. We therefore pray you to give your favourable consideration to the matter, so far as circumstances may render desirable and the maintenance of good friendship with this King may demand.

London, 15 March 1546.

1546.
March 17.
Simancas.
E. A. 642.

213. THE EMPEROR to PRINCE PHILIP.

(In a long letter of this date acknowledging Philip's letter of 18th February, and dealing fully with numerous questions concerning the internal Government of Spain and relations with other countries, the following passage alone refers to England.)

"With respect to England, the ambassadors of the King give us many assurances of his friendship towards us; and we are giving him all the facilities we well can in the large provision he is making for the continuance of the war. We have also sent thither our Councillor Scepperus to assure the King of our goodwill and, if opportunity offers, to speak of a marriage between the Prince of England and one of the daughters of our brother the King of the Romans, in accordance with a suggestion made by the Bishop of Winchester when he was leaving Maestricht on his return to England. Scepperus and another envoy sent by our sister Queen Mary are also instructed to obtain redress for the injuries inflicted by the English on our Spanish and Flemish subjects, and to devise some means for preventing the continuance of these depredations."

(The following paragraphs referring to the Protestant Reformation are also of interest.)

"All that can be said at present with regard to German affairs is that the seceders from the faith, and even some other States that have a similar inclination, are in great fear that we may at once commence war against them; and the three secular electors,* the Palatine, Saxony, and Brandenburg, sent their Ambassadors, as did the Protestants and the Bishop of Cologne, to Maestricht, where they awaited our arrival. Having listened to what they had to say we gave them the reply which we send herewith. This will also place you in possession of their demands; and we believe that the tenour of this reply, together with the steps we had already ordered the Chancellor of the Empire to take and the fact that we are travelling only with our ordinary guard have calmed them, and that they are all now manifesting a desire to come to some agreement about religion. As, however, they have on several previous occasions expressed a similar wish, and have afterwards become more obstinate than ever, we cannot count upon anything beyond what we see. But everything possible shall be done to attain so holy an end, though we doubt much as to the result, even though the Pope may not hinder this agreement, as he has done hitherto, and the King of France, at least underhand, do not interfere in the matter. When we have arrived at Ratisbon, where the Diet is to be held, we shall very soon see by appearances what we have to expect. In the meanwhile you must not neglect what we have already written, but must employ the utmost diligence; because we are certain that if any good result is to be attained it will be by reason of the fear of superior force by the seceders from the faith. Without this neither virtue nor goodness can be expected of them, for they are growing worse every day, and their

---

* The ecclesiastical electors were the Prince Archbishops of Mayence, Cologne, and Treves.

1546.

sensuality, already great, is gaining ground: this being the case in most of the other States as well. You shall be kept constantly informed of what may occur, and you must send us frequent advices from Spain.

You will bear in mind that, having regard to the scarcity of horses for the guards in Spain, in consequence of the large number lost in Algiers, and the need for providing in this respect, we recently conceded a certain number of licenses for mules to be used for riding purposes, notwithstanding the pragmatic forbidding such use, the proceeds to be used for the mounting of the guards. We have learnt that the wages of the guards are still owing for the last third of the year 1544, and the first third of 1545 and since. In view of the distress that this has caused them, and that the forces are breaking up in consequence of the impossibility of the men maintaining themselves, victuals being so dear, we have decided, in the absence of any other means of prompt succour, to grant a thousand more licenses in Spain for using mules for riding, notwithstanding the pragmatic. We send you herewith the authority, in which the reason is only lightly referred to, without descending to particulars."

Luxemburg, 17 March 1546.

Mar. 17 (?)
Simancas.
E. A. 642

214. Summary of news from the IMPERIAL COURT, apparently from DE GRANVELLE to COBOS.[*]

Since Marquina left with the despatch advices have been received from Rome to the effect that so great is the Pope's fear of the Council (of Trent), which he thinks is going further than he originally intended, that he is greatly upset and is making a thousand speeches about it. Some cooling even is noticeable in his attitude towards the German enterprise, of which he and his friends expressed so much approval. They are now hinting at the desirability, and even the necessity, of diverting it elsewhere, such as to England, fearing that if the German plan is carried through, the Emperor will, either by force or arrangement, bring the Protestants to consent to the celebration of the Council, which the Pope dreads, especially if the end is attained with his money, which is his ultimate resource. We are in hope that when Marquina arrives we shall learn the real facts, and so be able to arrange in accordance therewith the Diet of Ratisbon and other pending matters.

The Pope has expressed a wish to send legates, or even Cardinal Farnese himself, to discuss with his Majesty the question of peace with France, but as we have seen by experience what small results these embassies produce, his Holiness has been informed that under the present circumstances it is not considered desirable. In the course of these negotiations the Pope, as usual, suggested neutrality, hinting that under this guise he can best serve his Majesty; but by all his actions it is evident that he has not changed in the least

---

[*] The decipher in the Archives from which the above is translated bears the docket: "Vargas, 17 March 1546." This, however, would appear to be the date of the last advices from Rome contained in the document.

from his usual bent. You will have heard that the Siena people are disturbed, and have recently gone so far as to rise in rebellion, 20 people being killed and as many wounded. The Duke of Florence* at this juncture adopted his usual attitude towards the Emperor's interests, gathering his militia and approaching the Sienese frontier, and this prevented the revolt from going further. Since then we have news by way of Milan that they (the Sienese) had decided to send away the Spanish guard commanded by Don Juan (de Luna), on the ground that it would not fight on the day of the disturbance, and that they intended to send to the Marquis del Guasto for 100 soldiers, under another captain. We are hourly expecting reports from Don Juan, giving us details, and we shall take steps according to them. It will be necessary to inflict exemplary chastisement to curb their insolence and disrespect for his Majesty.

Your worship will know the position of French matters. Although the French are fortifying themselves and making a noise in Piedmont and elsewhere, and giving an appearance of intending to break with the Emperor, and the King of France has set out for Lyons to push matters forward, it is very unlikely that they will attempt anything of the sort; nor are they, indeed, in a position to do so. Their object probably is to benefit by the prestige which they think to gain.

It is announced that the English are determined not to make peace with the French, and each side is busy in forwarding its own aims. This is exactly what suits us best at present. The principal object of sending Scepperus to England, though the pretext was to visit the King, was really to keep an eye on his proceedings. The bishop who came from England to negotiate with the French (*i.e.* Gardiner, Bishop of Winchester) returned from Maestricht. Matters between his Majesty and the King of England remain in *statu quo ante*, certain questions respecting the interpretation of the Treaty having been answered by us. The English lodged protests, to the effect that our interpretation, and the confirmation of the Treaty in that sense, was not to be understood to prejudice the claim they made for his Majesty's aid last year. A reply explaining our reasons having been given to them they expressed themselves satisfied and withdrew their protests.

The coming of the ambassadors from the Protestants (*i.e.* to Maestricht) had more noise than substance in it. The only two points presented were, first, to pray his Majesty not to proceed against the Bishop of Cologne so severely as intended, but to refer his justification to the coming Diet of Ratisbon, where he might be heard by the other Princes of the Empire, and a decision arrived at; the second part was to set forth that rumours and apprehension existed amongst them, aroused by many different indications that the Emperor intended to raise war in Germany. The Princes marvelled much at this, for they had always offered to consider a remedy for the present differences, and they would for their part willingly agree to anything reasonable. They therefore humbly prayed the Emperor to consider the position well, and not to allow

---

* Cosmo de'Medici, who held his dukedom mainly owing to the Emperor's goodwill.

1546.

during his time that German blood should be shed by foreign troops. They added other things in this tone for their own justification, and his Majesty replied to them with the suavity and truth that your worship will understand from the condition of affairs.

We are going straight to Spires in seven stages; and it is expected that near there the Landgrave of Hesse will come out to justify himself to the Emperor, and to assure his Majesty of his goodwill, and that of the Protestants. Brunswick is still under arrest, pending the settlement of his business at Ratisbon. The King, and it is thought also the Queen, of the Romans will go thither.

Your worship will be informed direct from Trent with regard to the Council. His Holiness and his friends are not very well pleased with the Cardinal of Jaen, and would like to see him far away from there, as they know that he is as brave and zealous as befits his high dignity and office.

March 18
Vienna.
Imp. Arch.

215. SCEPPERUS to the QUEEN DOWAGER.

Since my last letter nothing new has happened here, except that the Earl of Hertford leaves to-day for Boulogne with five or six thousand Englishmen dressed in three colours. It is said that the intention is to encamp between the new town and Marquise, in order to prevent the French from making their fort at the latter place. The King is not yet well, and I have consequently not been able hitherto to obtain audience. This, at all events, is the reason given by Sir William Paget; but peradventure he (the King) is awaiting the return of the Bishop of Winchester, in order to learn what has passed between your Majesty and him (*i.e.* Gardiner) before he sees me. In any case I must have patience. The ships of this King are all ready, armed and re-victualled. In my opinion the war for this year will be more defensive than offensive on this (the English) side, and they (the English) will be satisfied with the number of lanceknechts which Conrad Penninck is commissioned to raise, at least until St. John's tide. I have written to this effect to M. de Granvelle. All the Italians, Germans and Spaniards who were sent against the Scots are now being brought to Boulogne. The Spaniards number from 1,600 to 1,800 men, good fighters, who have behaved well in the Scottish campaign. The principal nobles of the realm are not at present with the King, some being at Dover and Sandwich arranging about the victualling, and others elsewhere in divers places raising the troops to be furnished by the towns, boroughs and villages.

London, 18 March 1546.

March 22.
Vienna.
Imp. Arch.

216. SCEPPERUS and VAN DER DELFT to the EMPEROR.

I, Scepperus, having received your Majesty's dispatch for England, and hearing that the French were between Dover and Calais with 13 warships capturing all craft that appeared in the Straits, both those belonging to your subjects and others, whilst no English ship was there to guard the passage, I decided to cross over by the high sea from Zeeland, and so to avoid the Strait.

1546.

Having accordingly set forth with a favourable wind I encountered a sudden change, and was thus kept at sea between Flushing and England for seven days, being driven on one occasion as far down as Dunkirk. Finally, however, without encountering any Frenchmen, I arrived in London on the 13th instant, where I found the courier who carries this letter with certain communications from M. de Granvelle. I at once made my arrival known to the King's Council, and asked for audience of his Majesty. On the following Monday the King sent Sir William Paget to bid me welcome but to say that in consequence of his indisposition he was unfortunately unable to give me audience, begging me to have patience for four or five days. I could only say in reply to this that your Majesty would greatly deplore his illness when you heard of it, and I would await the King's good pleasure. As the King had been willingly informed by one of his most confidential ministers of the subjects upon which I had been instructed to address him, we both of us (Scepperus and Van der Delft) thought better to say a word or two about it to Secretary Paget, especially as your Majesty orders us by your letters of 26 February to endeavour to discover by every possible means whether the King would be favourably inclined to a marriage with your niece (*i.e.* with the Prince of Wales), in order that we might be guided in addressing the King on the subject. We sounded Paget, who was of opinion that we should open the matter with the King, although his Majesty considered the dowry proposed a very small one and not at all proportionate to the grandeur of the future King of England. As to the Scottish affair, he said there was nothing in that. On the contrary, a marriage was being arranged between the daughter of the late King of Scotland and the son of the present Regent of the realm (*i.e.* the Earl of Arran). On the subject of Conrad Penninck, he assured us that the latter had only authority to raise for him three thousand lansquenets, although he spread the rumour that the number was six thousand. Not more than ten, twenty, or at most thirty, would pass through your Majesty's territory together; and he (Paget) then asked us laughingly when your Majesty was going to furnish your contingent. We answered him in a similar strain that your Majesty was not bound to furnish any aid on account of past events; but we did not dwell upon this point, wishing to reserve it for a more fitting opportunity. From Monday until the following Friday we remained without any news from the King, but on the latter day a gentleman came from him to say that we might hold ourselves ready for Sunday. As we were on our way to the Court on Sunday we met one of the Bishop of Winchester's followers, who told us that his master had arrived in London early that morning and that we should find him at Court. This was the fact, and before we arrived at the King's lodgings the bishop himself came and stopped us, as he had not yet presented his respects to the King, and we therefore were not able to obtain access to his Majesty until after the bishop had seen him. The King received us kindly, and, anticipating our address, asked us to excuse the delay in giving us audience as it had arisen from his indisposition. He had, he said, had a burning fever for several consecutive days, and subsequently the malady had

1546.

attacked his leg, which was still somewhat affected; but his strong and robust constitution enabled him to stand illness. We replied that your Majesty would have been greatly grieved if you had known of his illness, but since he was now convalescent you would have reason for rejoicing. He said he had taken good care that his sickness should not be known; and verily, sire, his visage clearly shows that his malady was more severe than he makes out.

After this, I, Scepperus, saluted him on behalf of your Majesty; and said that you had not wished to leave your Netherlands dominions without first sending to visit him, and assuring him of the continuance of your goodwill towards him. I was also to assure him that your Majesty's voyage to Germany was undertaken for the public good, and if possible to pacify the troubles there, banishing the distrust entertained by the Protestants that your Majesty intended to make war upon them, the more especially that you had heard from your ambassador (Van der Delft) then present that he (i.e. King Henry) had advised your Majesty, as a true friend, to avoid entering into war with the Protestants. He (the King) replied that he thanked your Majesty for the visit, and wished you happy and good success in your voyage. He also would continue in the goodwill and friendship, which had prompted his remark to me, Van der Delft, about the Protestants. He desired the aggrandisement of your Majesty, and not the enfeeblement of your power or the ruin of your States. Although he did not seek overmuch the friendship of others, or concern himself with their affairs, he did not repel them, and he had been positively warned from several quarters that, in case of war against the Protestants, your Majesty would not only go against those who openly confessed themselves such but also against the rest, and even against those who showed themselves good and obedient subjects to you, together with their friends and allies in this quarrel. The Protestants, he said, would never allow the Bishop of Cologne to be driven out; but would defend and assist him, as all the rest of Germany would; but at the same time, he said that no doubt your Majesty would know how to conduct the matter better than he (Henry) could advise you.

After this, Sire, we broached to him the subject of the marriage, saying that your Majesty had heard with great pleasure the kind expressions used by his ambassadors on his behalf towards you, as also had the King of the Romans when they were conveyed to him. But the matter, we said, had gone no further, his (Henry's) ambassadors not having further pursued it. Your Majesty however, had heard from a trustworthy source, and had instructed me, Scepperus, secretly and confidentially to inform him that the French intended to circumvent and deceive him by means of a marriage treaty between his son and the daughter of Scotland. By this means they would recover Boulogne with a peace or a long truce. They would get the Queen of Scotland[*] to consent to this marriage treaty for her daughter, letting her know that the undertaking would, for several reasons, not be binding: and I set forth these reasons, in accordance with my instructions. Your Majesty,

---

[*] Mary of Guise, the Queen Mother.

1546.

however, knew him (Henry) to be so prudent, and to be so well aware of the character of the people with whom he was dealing, that you were sure that he and his wise Council would not be misled. Your Majesty had, nevertheless, instructed me to learn his pleasure with regard to this marriage (*i.e.* the marriage suggested by the Emperor, between Edward Prince of Wales and the daughter of Ferdinand, King of the Romans) and to ascertain whether he would listen to it. In accordance with his reception of this idea, I was to pursue or desist in my negotiations with regard to it; but that, in any case, your Majesty desired to keep on good terms and hearty friendship with him, his son, and his realm. The King nodded his head joyfully upon hearing this last sentence about your Majesty wishing to remain at peace with him, and then replied that, with regard the Scottish business, there was nothing in it: the French had enough to do without meddling with the marriage of his son or interfering in Scotland. He (Henry) had good hope that as regards Scotland he would have entirely his own way, perhaps even in spite of the French. He was not, he said, so light as to carry on negotiations with two parties at once for the same end, although, he added, he knew of some people who were in the habit of doing so; and doubtless we thought he might resemble them. This, however, was not the case, and we should judge him otherwise. But with regard to this marriage, of the prince his son with your Majesty's niece, really the proposal had cooled. His ambassador had, in accordance with their instructions, at the very commencement of their negotiations, requested the hand of one of the Emperor's daughters for the Prince his son, but it had been refused and one of the daughters of the King of the Romans had been offered instead, the Emperor's councillors saying that his imperial Majesty would regard the princess as a daughter of his own. He (Henry), being informed of this, and cordially approving of it, had instructed his ambassadors to learn further particulars as to the conditions proposed. As, however, they (the English ambassadors) finally heard that the dowry to be brought by the Princess was only 100,000 crowns, he considered the offer repulsive to his expectations, as such a sum was no fit dowry for an Emperor's daughter, or for a bride accepted as such, and he (King Henry) interpreted it as a slight and an affront to his son, who was a future King, when God should summon him (Henry), and was worthy of being held in no less respect and honour than a Duke of Orleans, who had been offered a very different dowry. For this reason, seeing that so little account was made of him (Henry), he had instructed his ambassadors to speak no more about it, and he had no intention of doing so. With this he began to get angry, and said that we came to him with nothing but empty words. He was not so lacking in sense as not to understand it perfectly well: for a long time past we had treated him in this way, which was not a fit return for the attachment that he had shown to us. If his ambassadors had not been told that the Emperor would regard the girl as his own daughter, he (Henry) would never have entertained the idea of simply a daughter of the King (of the Romans). His son was to be esteemed higher than a Duke. Although the King's remarks gave us ample matter for reply, and at the commencement we intended to answer him, when we saw he was so angry we thought better to smooth him down, in accordance with our instructions, and not to enter into a dispute with him. But I, Scepperus, bearing in mind that in my instructions I am enjoined to give no hope that the King of the Romans might be induced to increase the dowry, or that your Majesty might supplement it, remarked to the King that our instructions did not extend to the point in question, but that we would report his observations to your Majesty if he wished. I then asked, as if of my own accord, whether he (Henry) thought opportune, on the occasion of the Emperor's journey to Regensburg (Ratisbon) to send an envoy of his own to your Majesty, since the King of the Romans, the father of the girl, would be there; or otherwise whether he would instruct his ambassador to continue there the negotiations for the marriage. He replied that he would send no one, and declined to proceed further in the matter, unless his son were to be treated as well as it had been intended to treat the Duke of Orleans, and we might inform your Majesty of this. He then launched into complaints of the bad treatment that his subjects were receiving everywhere, especially in Spain, in violation of the promises made to him. He mentioned the two points of the release of his subjects and their ships, and the imprisonment of several of the former by the Inquisition, which treated them as heretics. I, Van der Delft, replied that, so far as regarded his subjects imprisoned by the Inquisition, I had forwarded to your Majesty the same petition which had been presented to him here, and had since heard that the prisoners in question had been liberated; which he might learn from his own subjects. I said if he knew all he would acknowledge that your Majesty's subjects had much greater reason to complain than his, since the arrests made in Spain did not amount to ten thousand crowns. The King then changed the subject and, with an appearance of great displeasure, turned his words against your Netherlands subjects. "You people," he said, "are supporting my enemies the Scots, especially in the principal towns." We replied that the Scots were doing us a great deal of harm, and we had complaints against them every day; we knew of no kindness being shown to them, except to a few who had safe-conducts. To this he retorted that the safe-conducts themselves were a violation of the treaties. Then, changing his tone and addressing me, Scepperus, he asked: "When shall I have the aid? My ambassador tells me that you have instructions to speak to me about it." I said it was true that I was instructed to address his Majesty on the subject when he wished, or those he might appoint, to hear me, and would afterwards report to him. This answer satisfied him; and in good truth, Sire, it was high time for us to get clear of him just then, in order to avoid offending him or irritating him further, having regard to his malady, and to postpone the question of the aid and our reply to his other complaints until another opportunity. With regard to occurrences here, there are already five or six thousand picked men (gens d'élite), well armed and clothed, sent from here to Boulogne; and as many more are to go from the other principal ports in the country. The Earl of Hertford is going to Boulogne as general, and was to have left

1546.

five days ago, but he told us yesterday for certain that he was departing to-day. The Lord Admiral is also going to the coast to send off the armed ships to convoy the staple wool fleet to Calais, wherein lies the wealth of this country. These armed ships will number forty, some of them fine and well-manned with soldiers, in addition to the 10,000 men above mentioned who are being sent to Boulogne. So far as we can ascertain from the remarks of the King and his Council and others, there seems to be no negotiation for peace between them and the French.

London, 22 March 1546.

March 22.
Vienna.
Imp. Arch.

217. SCEPPERUS and VAN DER DELFT to the QUEEN DOWAGER.

Your Majesty will be fully informed of what passed between the King and ourselves by the enclosed copy of our letter to the Emperor, and it will not be necessary to repeat the intelligence here. It may be advisable, however, to inform your Majesty, in addition, that he opened conversation respecting the wrongs and injuries which he alleged were being constantly inflicted upon his subjects. Although we had ample material for reply, we avoided doing so on this occasion, for the reasons set forth in our letter to the Emperor; and limited ourselves to saying that these matters might be settled with the whole of the rest of the subjects in dispute. He asked us if the doctor entrusted with the settlement of these subjects had arrived yet, as he (the King) was quite ready on his side to begin the work. We replied that we were expecting the arrival of the Commissioner from one day to another, and prayed his Majesty to continue in his good will in the matter. He took this in good part. We have, however, no news at all of Councillor Van der Burgh.

•London, 22 March 1546.

March 23.
Vienna.
Imp. Arch.

218. SCEPPERUS to the QUEEN DOWAGER.

In addition to what the Ambassador and I have written to the Emperor (duplicate enclosed) I beg to inform your Majesty that the King has fifty of his own ships equipped for war, without counting others belonging to his subjects and to foreigners, which he may use on payment. He is sending ten thousand Englishmen, the sturdiest, picked men of all his realm, to Boulogne; and shows every indication of an intention to continue the war. Conrad Penninck has only authority for three thousand men. Captains Martin von Hard of Guedelenbourg and Gheert Henricx, the Frisian, have done nothing yet, but are ordered to wait until the month of June, when they will be employed if they are needed. M. du Biez, marshal of France, has gone to the court of France; and I suspect that he may bear some commission from this side; because, although he is a worthy man and a loyal subject of his master, he is on good terms with the English and mixes in intrigues. I have decided to set out on my return journey as soon as I have made my statement to the King respecting the aid demanded by him, as otherwise these people (the English) will assume that the Emperor is willing to listen to the marriage suggested on the conditions mentioned in our joint letter; and this is quite at variance with

1546.

one of the clauses of my instructions, which I propose to follow *au pied de la lettre*. I have written a few words on the subject to M. de Praet. In my simple opinion time will show many things; and our surest course will to put our trust in God, and such forces as His divine mercy deigns to place in our hands, to maintain the Emperor and your Majesty in the possession of your governments and inheritance, without depending over much upon leagues and alliances with others, which are things that lightly change and are but little to be trusted. I shall be able on my return to demonstrate this more fully to your Majesty, and pray you humbly to pardon me for speaking thus.

London, 23 March 1546.

March 23.
Vienna.
Imp. Arch.

219. SCEPPERUS to DE GRANVELLE.

Athough you will be fully informed by the letter which the ambassador and I are writing to the Emperor of everything that passed between the King (of England) and us, yet I cannot omit to inform you that the King has a fine and powerful fleet ready, including fifty great ships belonging to himself, in addition to those he has taken for his service from the Emperor's subjects and other foreigners; so that he will have a stronger naval force than he had last year. He is also having built four galleasses, which are to be ready by Lent, and six new galleons of a very excellent sort, well fitted and armed.[*] For the present forty ships of war are going to convoy the wool fleet of the staple as far as Calais, whilst the rest are making ready. From what we write to his Imperial Majesty you will also perceive that it will be inadvisable for me to remain here any longer, as my tarrying might cause these people to hope that the Emperor would negotiate for this marriage on the conditions demanded by the King, which would be contrary to the tenour of my instructions. For this reason, as soon as I have laid before the King or his Council my statement with regard to the aid demanded, and have thoroughly discussed the same with them, I have determined to return to the Queen (Dowager of Hungary) and await his Imperial Majesty's further orders, leaving here the ambassador and Councillor Van der Burgh to settle the claims of the Emperor's subjects in conference with the King of England's Commissioners.

London, 23 March 1546.

---

[*] This change of naval policy on the part of Henry, indicated by the construction of galleasses and galleys for Channel fighting on the English side, appears to have been adopted in consequence of the helplessness of the English sailing ships in a light wind when the French galleys appeared in the Solent in the previous year. For some years the tendency in England had been to depend more and more upon sails for fighting ships, and this creation of an oared squadron was distinctly a retrograde step, which, however, was not long persevered in, as it only answered a passing need. In Dudley's letter to Paget on the subject (State Papers Henry VIII., Dom. I, 805) the following order is given: "Whereas the King's Majesty's pleasure is to have certain of his ships brought to pass to row to keep company with others of that sort to attend upon the French galleys."

1546.
March 23.
Vienna.
Imp. Arch.

220. SCEPPERUS to LOYS SCORS.

I have read the letter you wrote to the ambassador about the coming of Councillor Van der Burgh, who I hope will arrive here before my departure, and I will, as in duty bound, do my best in the business in the meanwhile. (He states his reasons for not prolonging his stay in England as in previous letter to Granvelle.) There is no news here, except the departure of the forty fine, powerful English war ships to convey the staple wool fleet to Calais. The provisioning of so many wool ships, etc., is causing great scarcity here. The provisions for the fortresses of Guisnes and the Boulognais and for the several armies are taken from the country without order or regulation of any sort; and you may well imagine what a great amount is wasted and spoilt. What usually costs here one shilling now can hardly be obtained for three or four. This applies to all sorts of victuals for man and beast, and also to the purchase of cattle and horses. The greatly increased cost of living moves the ambassador, Van der Delft, to crave consideration, with regard to his emoluments; as, unless the amount paid to him is increased, neither he nor his successors could possibly support the expense, especially as the King intends this year to visit the extreme ends of this realm, and the ambassador will have to accompany him in the interests of the Emperor and his subjects. The latter—mariners and merchants—are daily captured, plundered and molested by the English ships of war; and if they were deprived of refuge and protection with the ambassador they would lose everything instead of a part only of their property, as they do now. Besides this, whilst the ambassador accompanies the King he is the better able to discover and understand the intrigues that may be carried on. Our neighbours the French perceive this perfectly well, and act upon their knowledge; very often gaining the ear of the English for their own ends. The ambassador, Van der Delft, will, however, be quite unable to accompany the King on his progress without spending three times as much as he usually does, considering that he must change his lodging nearly every day, and incur the cost of carriages, etc. etc. Besides this he cannot leave his residence in London without an adequate guard to protect it, or on his return he would find it empty. No comparison can be drawn between the amount paid to the present ambassador and that formerly credited to M. Chapuys, as the latter gentleman for several years after his arrival here was aided by the late Queen (i.e. Catharine of Aragon) with large sums of money, as these people are very fond of relating, and he never went anywhere; staying sometimes a year or two in his own lodging without budging a step, not even going to Court, but doing all his business through his secretary. When the King wished to communicate anything to him, or to obtain information from him, he used to send one of his Council, as the King himself told me, so that Chapuys was not obliged to travel or incur any expense whatever, beyond his maintenance, which, in good truth, from what I hear, was handsome enough. He had, moreover, ample means in the form of pensions, etc., one of which—on the Neapolitan revenues—amounted to a

1546.

thousand ducats, and other income. I am not writing this out of envy or ill will towards him, for, thank God, such a feeling is far from me, but to justify the present ambassador's complaint and to show that it is not made without good reason. Recommends also a petition of his (Scepperus') son-in-law, Jerome Lanwerin.

London, 23 March 1546.

March 23.
Simancas.
E. R. 873.

221. Extracts from Letter from Juan de Vega to the Emperor.

In my letter of 12th instant I informed your Majesty of affairs up to that date, and especially of my interviews with the Pope respecting the Brief (*i.e.* for the sale of the monastic manors in Spain). The minute of our conversation was, as I mentioned, handed to Cardinal Farnese to be considered by the Cardinals appointed for the purpose. This was done and they have reported that, as the Brief contains absolute and unconditional authority for the execution of the measure, it should not be conceded by his Holiness.* Our answer was that, if it were drafted in any other form it would not be of any use for the object your Majesty had in view. It was suggested also by us that the Pope might perhaps grant another Brief, addressed to the Commissioners to whom the first Brief was entrusted, instructing them not to execute the latter until fresh orders were received from his Holiness. His Holiness would therefore be quite assured that the Brief would only be executed as intended; whilst your Majesty's demands would be complied with. If he would not consent to this I asked for a prompt and decisive reply, in order that your Majesty might take measures accordingly. Farnese undertook to propose this compromise to the Pope, and was of opinion that it ought certainly to be accepted. He now informs me that the Pope has replied that he must have time to consider the point. I have pressed him for a decision, and will send it to your Majesty as early as possible, unless I can obtain it before this courier leaves.

In the Consistory held on Monday, 15th instant, it is said that the Pope flew into such a rage with Salviati as never was seen before. Salviati himself sent me word that after the Cardinals were seated and the Consistory closeted, the Pope in great perturbation, and in a loud voice, summoned him, and told him he was not doing his duty, casting upon him the blame for the Duke of Florence's treatment of the friars. He said that Salviati when he was in Florence received presents from the Duke, who at the same time was turning the friars out of their monastery. He went on a long while in this strain, saying that the Duke was no duke or anything else† and refusing to allow Salviati to say anything in his defence, or at least to listen to what he said. Salviati begged that an enquiry should be ordered on the subject; and if he was found to be in fault that

---

* The meaning of this is that if the Brief were dispatched to Spain the manors might be sold and the proceeds appropriated by the Emperor, even if the latter did not carry out his intended crusade against the Protestants.

† It will be recollected that Cosmo de' Medici had shortly before this (1543) provided a large sum of money for the Emperor's need, and the consequent withdrawal of the imperial garrison from Florence and Leghorn had secured Cosmo in the dukedom of Florence with the Emperor's goodwill and protection.

546.

he should be punished, or otherwise that he should be absolved. At length, seeing the Pope in such a state of excitement, Salviati managed to leave him as decently as possible, and returned to his place. Other Cardidals who were present have confirmed to me this account of what passed.

It is asserted that the Pope held in his hand a statement sent to him by an uncertain author, presumably a friar. This he handed to Rodolphi to read aloud, which he did. It was to the effect that the Duke (of Florence) had deprived the monastery of its alms and other things, and the present inmates were unable to subsist; praying his Holiness to obtain justice for them. When the reading of the statement was finished the Pope made the most of the matter, and repeated that Salviati did not do his duty, ordering that a vote should be taken on the subject. Most of them (the Cardinals) spoke sensibly, especially Cardinal Farnese; although some of them did their best further to incite the Pope's anger. It may be held as certain that the Pope's demonstration was increased by the hatred he has conceived against Salviati, since he learnt of the intrigues it is understood he initiated for the succession to the Papacy when the Pope was ill lately. Doubtless his Holiness thought to counteract his advantage by means of the statement, and took the opportunity of humiliating Salviati under cover of the Duke's proceedings. Since then, on the 18th instant, Tuesday, at four o'clock in the night, they arrested a man who was here as secretary for the Duke with Everardo Seristori, his ambassador. He was here on business for the Duke, and was negotiating, especially with me. They have seized his papers, which proceeding is disapproved of by many persons. I also took this view, and on the Friday sent Pedro de Marquina to Farnese, to tell him from me that I had a letter from your Majesty in favour of the Duke, in the matter of the friars, in which I was ordered to speak to the Pope. I had, I said, deferred doing so, as the letter had reached me after the Duke had complied with the Pope's Brief; and I had rejoiced that I was thus saved from a duty which might be unpleasant to his Holiness. But in view of what had now happened it would be necessary that I should fulfil the mission intrusted to me and express to his Holiness your Majesty's interest in the Duke's affairs. I greatly regretted this, as the Pope was not well pleased with the Duke : his Holiness' health, moreover, was not so good as I should like it to be; and I feared, consequently, that my conversation on the matter might upset him. I suggested, therefore, that, in order to avoid these inconveniences, and to allay any suspicion on the part of your Majesty that others might be inciting the Pope to anger against the Duke for the purpose of raising troubles in Italy, his Eminence (Cardinal Farnese) who was so much attached to your Majesty, might see the Pope on the matter first, and advise me as to the best course to pursue when I had to speak to his Holiness myself. The Cardinal first of all swore to Marquina that he knew nothing whatever of this arrest until the day after the man was taken; and he had been very sorry to hear of it, as the course taken by the Pope and the Duke was not conducive to your Majesty's interests. Our remarks, he said, were wise; for the Pope would certainly be

1546.

vexed at your Majesty's taking the Duke under your protection, particularly as they (the Farneses?) had served your Majesty. As, however, he (Cardinal Farnese) was ignorant of the cause of the man's arrest he did not know how to advise me at present; but he would speak that night to the Pope, and would afterwards let me know how things stood.

The next day he sent Dandino to me, and the effect of what he said was that the Cardinal had had a long conversation with his Holiness on the matter, but had been unable to get any clear understanding about it. He would, however, still persevere and would try to extract from the Pope what the latter had refused to say in his last interview. He would let me know the result to-day, but in the meanwhile he thought best that I should not see his Holiness.

I let Dandino understand that I was not satisfied with his message, but said that I did not blame the Cardinal. He endeavoured to justify the arrest, but I told him that there was no possible justification for seizing the papers of the Duke's man. I said it was an extremely strange proceeding, and I should be obliged to address the Pope on the subject. I intend to do this without waiting any longer for Farnese's dallying, as it is all their cunning and base trickery, suggested by their hatred against the Duke of Florence.

There are many different opinions about the arrest of the man; but the prevailing view is that the Pope, seeing himself driven into a corner with the Council, and owing to intelligence which they say he has received on another subject, would like to raise any disturbance in the world to counteract it, just as a person might take poison to avoid a threatened greater evil. The intelligence to which I refer is that the King of England is showing a greater kindness towards religion; his enmity being mainly against the pontiffs personally, and especially against the present Pope: and also that the Protestants have sent ambassadors to your Majesty to pray that the Council (of Trent) should be transferred to Augsburg, as well as other news that he (the Pope) does not like. It is quite possible to believe this of his Holiness, who I hear from a certain source is in great confusion since the arrest of this man. Up to the present time the prisoner has not been examined, nor can we learn of any steps being taken with him. His Holiness has not communicated with anybody. He is, moreover, greatly concerned about his private affairs, and is a very sensitive person, whose natural failing has been increased by old age. He is much irritated about the Duke's retaining these prisoners of his, and withdrawing his ambassador from here, and very suspicious of the Duke's activity in the business of Siena, which touches the Pope so closely. All this has driven him to desperation; and just as he burst out so violently the other day against Salviati, he has done the same over this new matter. His rage is increased by his belief that the Duke thought that he was dead; and he is as much angered at this as if it was an injury to a person to look upon him as mortal. But still, I expect that by this time he is sorry for having done as he did.

His Holiness has recovered from the indisposition that prostrated him some time ago, which was a flux of blood; but he is not yet in his usual health. On the contrary, we are informed by the doctors

1546.

that he is troubled with his stomach, sometimes purging himself excessively, and sometimes the opposite. He is consequently at times incapacitated; and refuses to attend to business, at least other people's business.

Rome, 22 March 1546.

Postscript.—23 March.—I have thought best to detain this courier until I have seen his Holiness and can report fully on this matter to your Majesty.

From a perfectly trustworthy source I learn that his Holiness has summoned to Rome that famous scholar called Alciati, a native of Milan, who is now at Ferrara. The Duke of Ferrara has been requested to allow him to come hither. From the same authority I learn that Alciati has been summoned about the affairs of Parma and Piacenza.

March 24.
Vienna
Imp. Arch.

222. The QUEEN DOWAGER to VAN DER DELFT and SCEPPERUS.

This is to inform you that shortly before the departure from Maestricht the Bishop of Winchester, with the other ambassadors from the King of England, handed us letters from their King, and in virtue thereof made to us the three requests mentioned in the said letters: namely that the King should be allowed to raise by loan, exchange or otherwise, in Antwerp, a sum of 400,000 crowns to be taken to Calais: secondly that the Emperor's subjects here should be permitted to carry victuals to England, and thirdly that we would assist the King's commissioners to obtain here such waggons and warlike stores as the English might require. We deferred replying definitely to these points until we had consulted the Emperor, who was at the time in Maestricht. This we were unable to do until the moment of his Majesty's departure, and consequently the reply had to be deferred until our return to Brussels. Carne pressed so urgently for a reply, however, that we told him that, having regard to the large sums of money drawn by the King from Antwerp last year, we found the Bourse here poorly supplied with specie; the Emperor's business being hampered in consequence. This would have been, we said, a sufficient reason for refusing the King's first request, especially considering how very strict they are in England in prohibiting the export of specie from the realm; we were, nevertheless, anxious to please the King, and would consent to his raising and drawing not more than 200,000 crowns, not of the Emperor's coinage[*] but in English, French or Italian specie. With regard to the supply of provisions, we replied that he was well aware of the great scarcity of all sorts of victuals on this side, famine only having been averted by the prohibition of the export of food stuffs, and other intolerable evils having barely been avoided as a consequence; and it behoved us to watch the subject very closely. We could not, we said, give a general permission for the conveyance of food to England, for such a concession would be made an excuse for stripping the country of all food; and we should be unable to prevent a like export to France, where a similar scarcity exists.

[*] It will be noted in a previous letter from the Emperor to his son that the former stipulates that the sums to be raised by loan must be in money current in Germany.

1546.

This would be to the prejudice of the King of England, as the French are making great efforts to obtain permission to take supplies from here; though we have adopted such measures as to prevent them from doing so. Nevertheless, out of a desire to please the King (of England) we promised that we would do our best to assist him with the food he required for the supply of his troops on this side of the water, on condition that he informs us what victuals he desires, and that the amount be moderate enough for us, in view of the prevalent poverty here, to supply without unduly distressing the subjects of the Emperor.

Replying to the third request, about the waggons and munitions of war, we said that the King was well aware how we had helped him in this matter previously, but the subjects here had been so badly treated on that occasion by the English that they would rather be killed outright than go again to serve with his troops. The Flemish people said that they had suffered a loss of over a hundred thousand livres in the horses and waggons they had furnished for the English service, besides the number of their men who had been killed. We therefore did not see how we could compel the subjects to return to the English service; but if the King would let us know the number (of waggons) he required, we would endeavour to satisfy him to a reasonable extent. Carne went to Antwerp to carry this reply to the Bishop of Winchester, and on his return he said that it had all been communicated to the King; at the same time showing us the enclosed note, requesting permission to draw from here 1,200 lasts of wheat, besides the other victuals specified therein. This demand seemed so exorbitant that we were at a loss for a reply; and we have thought well to advise you of it and to direct you to point out to the King the unreasonableness of his request, seeing that each last contains 27 muids and the 1,200 lasts would consequently equal 32,400 muids of wheat; the withdrawal of which would suffice to increase very gravely the scarcity of food here. We are therefore quite unable to grant his request; and, even if we did, it would be impossible to supply such a quantity. Although the ambassador maintains that there is plenty of wheat in Julliers and Cleves, it is certain that we are greatly in want of it here; and the *virtal* of wheat, which usually cost 10 or 12 sous, is now worth 36 sous and more; three times its former price. According to the terms of the treaties, requests for supplies of victuals should be made dependent upon the fertility or sterility of the country, and the need existing for retaining its produce. If this principle is to be carried out strictly, it would lead us to refuse to allow any foodstuffs to be exported at all, but we are unwilling to give such an answer in this case, out of respect for the King. Since we gave this reply to Carne the latter has brought hither the man who, he says, has been authorised by the King to purchase the wheat, and requesting a passport for 80 lasts of wheat, which he says have been sent from Cleves; and a part of which they have already shipped at Dortrecht. We declined to grant the passport, for under such a pretext as this all the wheat in the country might be sent out, and incalculable evils result. We have, however, consented to his exporting from Amsterdam 100 lasts of wheat from Oestlandt, which will be

1546.

sufficient to feed his troops and to provision the fortresses. We have likewise given permission for them to send out 100 tubs of butter, 100 *libures sceppents* of cheese, each of which libures is equal to 300 lbs; and 2,000 hams. The ambassador, however, seemed to be far from satisfied with these concessions, which to us appeared to be very liberal indeed, considering the great scarcity here. Indeed, we were only moved to make them out of consideration for the King.

The Bishop of Winchester requested the Emperor, before his departure from Maestricht, to allow the passage through his territory of the infantry raised for the King of England's service by Conrad Penninck. He was told in reply that his Imperial Majesty was extremely desirous of pleasing the King; but that, having regard to the injuries and losses sustained by his subjects in the two last years from the troops raised for the King by Landenberger and Von Reissenberg, the Emperor desired that Penninck should first come to see us, and make arrangements for the passage of his men. The ambassador Carne now tells us that he has received letters from the King's Commissioners with Penninck, saying that, having learned from the Bishop of Winchester that his Majesty had given his consent to the passage of the troops, they intend to pass the muster of the men at Nieuhausen in the territory of Munster, and send them thence in small bands through this country before Penninck could possibly come to confer with us, as the muster cannot take place in his absence. This arrangement is entirely at variance with the terms of the Emperor's consent, and may give rise to very great injury to the subjects. We are consequently obliged to take measures to avoid the evils which we have experienced on other similar occasions, and we have asked the ambassador to direct the Commissioners to send Penninck with all speed to us here; otherwise if these troops plunder the Emperor's subjects, or make themselves objectionable, they may find themselves hindered on the road; as the subjects will not tolerate such a nuisance every year, and it is quite impossible for soldiers to travel through a country without doing damage, no matter how much care be taken. If this happens it will be the fault of the English Commissioners, and no blame can be attached to us; as we cannot prevent the subjects from ill-treating those who want to injure them and take their substance without paying for it. We have requested Carne to convey this to the King, in order that the latter may be well informed of the facts.

We have dispatched Master Adrian Van der Burgh, who is on his way from Utrecht, and on his arrival in London he will convey to you his instructions, in order that you may co-operate with him in forwarding his mission. We understand that someone is to be sent hither from England to the same effect. You will please inform us who is coming and when he leaves.

Binche, 24 March 1546.

1546.
March 25.
Vienna
Imp. Arch

223. Scepperus and Van der Delft to the Queen Dowager.

After dinner yesterday the Bishop of Winchester, the Master of the Horse and Secretary Paget came to us for the purpose of laying before us the following matters. The first was that they had been informed that the French intended to cast themselves upon the army under the Earl of Hertford, which left here on Monday last, before a junction had been effected with the other English troops and before Penninck's levies had joined. This would, they said, greatly injure the English and perhaps might frustrate their whole undertaking. They had learnt that your Majesty desired to see Penninck before you would promise to allow his men to pass through the Emperor's territory; and that from the 17th instant he (Penninck) had been prevented from mustering his men near Nieuhausen, where in all probability he is still held in suspense. It will, therefore, be almost impossible for him to go to your Majesty without delaying the levies, or at least without furnishing him with an excuse for not fulfilling his undertaking to place his men in Calais within a stated time. They (the above-mentioned councillors) begged us to write asking your Majesty to favour the passage of Penninck and his men in every way possible. They will not pass in a large body, but in groups of about thirty, and will pay for everything; and as their prompt arrival (in Calais) is important to the King's service, it is urgently requested on his behalf that they may not be hindered. The second matter was that they (the English) have 400 lasts of grain already loaded at Dortrecht, grown outside the Emperor's territories in such places as Westland (Oestlandt), Julliers, Cleves, etc., two hundred lasts being rye, and two hundred wheat. They beg to request your Majesty to allow transit for this grain, which is intended for the sustenance of their army; as otherwise they will be unable to keep their forces together, and confusion will result, and even the destruction of their army and the complete ruin of their prestige. They promise faithfully that, if the Emperor's Flemish territories need a similiar quantity of grain, they (the English) will provide it within six weeks as they have already agreed with Erasmus Schetz and two other merchants for the provision of a large further quantity of grain, grown outside his Majesty's dominions, and out of this the quantity for which transit is now requested may be made good. A portion of the further consignment is already embarked, so that the quantity now in question may be looked upon simply as a loan for six weeks. We beg your Majesty to consider this, as, in good truth, the reasons they give are really peremptory. We are aware that there is great scarcity of grain on the other side (*i.e.* in the Netherlands), but, as M. de Granvelle wrote to me (Scepperus) on the 4th March, that the Westland people might be allowed to supply the English, whose enterprise might otherwise entirely fail, we have thought well to pray your Majesty to give favourable consideration to the request. During this communication we found them (*i.e.* the English councillors) much more amiable than the King was in our audience on Sunday. We attribute his irritation on that occasion to his malady; but there was nothing settled: it was simply conversation,

1546.

as we will relate fully in another letter when anything is done, especially as this letter is passing through their (the English) hands and is being carried by their courier.

London, 25 March 1546.

March 26 and 27.
Vienna Imp. Arch.

224. SCEPPERUS and VAN DER DELFT to the QUEEN DOWAGER.

From the duplicates of our letters to the Emperor, your Majesty will learn what passed yesterday and to-day between us and some of the King's councillors. In addition to what we say there, however, we think well not to conceal from your Majesty that Secretary Paget told us in strict secrecy that the King holds your Majesty in such high esteem that there is nothing he would not do for you. He also told us of the present the King was sending to your Majesty, and suggested that in your letter thanking him for the present your Majesty might slip in a single word, saying that you would be pleased if this marriage were proceeded with. This, he said, would greatly aid the matter and would much gratify the King. Failing this, Paget suggested that your Majesty should authorise us, or someone else, to express a similar sentiment on your behalf. We could plainly see that the King would have been glad if your Majesty had entrusted me, Scepperus, with a letter of credence to him, as you have done on other occasions when I came hither, whereas this time I brought a letter from the Emperor alone. We replied to him (Paget) that we considered it quite certain that your Majesty was very desirous of this alliance, which on consideration would be found to be the best thing for both countries. Your Majesty, I said, had on other occasions spoken to me, Scepperus, in such terms of the proposed alliance as to prove that you were greatly in favour of it, but that on this occasion I had not been specially instructed by your Majesty to address the King on the subject, nor did I bear letters from your Majesty. He (Paget) thereupon changed the conversation to the allegation that the Emperor's subjects were constantly supplying the French in the neighbourhood of Ardres with victuals and fresh meat, etc., with the exception of grain, whereas it is forbidden for the Emperor's subjects to carry any provisions to Calais for the English. This, he said, was not impartial or fair; especially as the Calais people were our old friends, and the French were only recently reconciled enemies. Besides that, during the recent revictualling of Ardres by the French, several carts and waggons belonging to the Emperor's subjects have been employed by the French to carry provisions into the town; and herrings and other food are every day taken by such subjects to France by sea. In some cases, even, the vessels employed in this traffic had managed to escape the embargo placed upon them by the King's (Henry's) officers, and had put to sea, carrying with them the English officials who had been placed in charge. This, he said, was not in accordance either with reason or friendship, and your Majesty would do well to redress such complaints. You would gain an incredible amount of affection, not only from the King but from all his subjects, if you would sometimes allow them to purchase a few trifles. "For instance," he (Paget) said, "when the Bishop of Durham and I were

1546.

at Calais, we could not obtain from the Emperor's country any fresh vegetables, poultry, conies, or other similar trifles, which ought not to be put into the list of prohibited victuals, the intention of the prohibition being to avoid the denudation of the country of the food necessary for the sustenance of the inhabitants themselves. It was never intended to apply to fresh vegetables (freschures) or delicacies which are not intended for the common people (le menu peuple)." He (Paget) stated all this very modestly and civilly, expressing at the same time his strong desire to maintain and increase the friendship between the Emperor, your Majesty, and his master the King, and that of the respective subjects: assuring us that our people would always find preferential help and assistance from him (which assurance we reciprocated); and we therefore promised to report to your Majesty the substance of his remarks, begging you at the same time to bear it in your favourable consideration, in the interests of the friendship and alliance.

Madame,—It is apparent to me, Scepperus, that the King would resent my departure from here before the receipt of a reply from the Emperor or your Majesty with regard to the marriage, and the consequent indication that we had lost hope of anything better being done in the matter than at the first interview; and I have therefore decided to delay my departure for a few days, until the receipt of the first letters from the Emperor or your Majesty, if I see any likelihood of good coming from it.

London, 27 March 1546.

Note.—Another letter of the same date from the same writers to the Queen simply encloses a copy of the letter of introduction given by them to the "brother of the Lord Admiral" (Dudley) who carried a present from King Henry to Mary of Hungary. The Admiral is said to have on several occasions favoured the subjects of the Emperor, and the Queen is asked to thank him through his brother, the bearer of the original.

March 27.
Vienna
Imp. Arch.

225. Scepperus and Van der Delft to the Emperor.

Yesterday afternoon there came to visit us the Bishop of Winchester, the Master of the Horse and Secretary Paget, for the purpose of asking us to beg the Queen Regent of the Netherlands not to place any obstacle in the way of Conrad Penninck and his troops on their passage through your Majesty's dominions. They would travel ten, twenty or thirty at a time, without gathering in large bodies or doing any damage, and the three councillors mentioned personally pledged themselves to make good any damage if such there might be. They were anxious that Penninck and his men should have no excuse for not fulfilling their undertaking with the King, and they had learnt from a good source that the French intended to attack the Earl of Hertford before he had assembled all his forces. They were therefore in very great need of Penninck's men to safeguard the Earl of Hertford and the rest of his army. They also begged the Queen to be kind enough to allow them to export (from Flanders) for the sustenance of the army at Boulogne 400 lasts of wheat and rye which they have bought outside your

1546.

Majesty's dominions and have now shipped and ready to sail. They undertook positively that if a similar quantity was wanted on the other side (i.e. in the Netherlands) they would provide it within six weeks, they having contracted to that effect with Erasmus Schetz and two other merchants, who are to provide them with a further considerable quantity of these grains, grown outside your Majesty's territories; from which quantity they were willing that these 400 lasts should be made good, if needful, and thus it would only mean a loan of that amount of grain for six weeks. We did not like to refuse them, and have accordingly written to the Queen (Dowager of Hungary), who will act as she thinks best in the matter. When this matter was disposed of the councillors spoke about the aid demanded by the English Ambassador when your Majesty was at Worms some time ago. We replied maintaining that we were not bound to furnish the said assistance, for several reasons, amongst others that they (the English) had not accepted the conditions upon which alone the aid was promised, always provided that it should be decided that your Majesty was liable to furnish it at all under the circumstances. The councillors answered this by saying that the whole matter depended upon the decision as to whether the aid was due or not. If it was due under the treaty it should be furnished without any conditions or restrictions; and their acceptance or otherwise of conditions imposed had nothing to do with it. As it was growing late, and the Master of the Horse wished to return to the King the same evening, they told us that, since the question could not be settled off hand, they would defer its further discussion for another opportunity. The Bishop of Winchester and the Master of the Horse thereupon took me, Scepperus, aside and Paget similarly took me Van der Delft, and they respectively asked us how we had got on with the King. I, Scepperus, replied that I had concluded with his Majesty the two first points of my instructions; namely to visit and salute him on your Majesty's behalf, to which the King had kindly and graciously responded, and secondly the matter of the marriage, to which he would not listen unless his son the Prince was to be offered a similiar dowry to that which had been offered to the Duke of Orleans. The King, I said, was greatly offended that so small a dowry as a hundred thousand crowns should be suggested; and that being his decision we had informed the Emperor of it; but that nevertheless, even though the marriage did not take place, your Majesty was determined to keep on terms of friendship with the King, his son, and his realm, as we had told the King at the time. I could not, I said, see what more I could do in the matter; and I had therefore decided to return to Flanders as soon as the question of the aid had been settled. The councillors appeared discontented and sad at this, and said that the King did not look at the matter in this way. He was, they said, very well disposed towards the marriage, and I ought not to leave here like this, especially as the Bishop of Winchester had been told that I was authorised by your Majesty to treat of this marriage. I said that my mission did not extend to that which the King demanded, but if his Majesty had any wish to continue the negotiation I had unofficially suggested to him a means of doing so; namely to send one of his confidential ministers to Regensburg (Ratisbon) or to

1546.

instruct his ambassador there to speak to your Majesty and the King of the Romans, the father of the Princess, on the subject of the marriage, and to set forth the points to which the King objected. The matter would thus be kept afoot, and I should have fulfilled my mission. The conversation which took place between Secretary Paget and me (Van der Delft) was to almost the same effect as the above; only that I told him I considered it strange that they should be so scrupulous about the dowry, seeing how advantageous the marriage would be for both countries. To this Paget replied that your Majesty had said that you would regard your niece as your daughter, which you showed no signs of doing by offering so small a sum of money with her. I remarked that I did not know what dowry your Majesty would give to the Princess your daughter; perhaps it would not be so much. He (Paget) laughed at this and left me; and then the three of them together told us that the matter must not be dropped in this way, but both sides must join hands to promote the marriage. And so they left us.

Secretary Paget came to us this morning and showed us a letter which the Master of the Horse had written to him, relating that on his return to the King last evening he had conversed with him on their interview with us here, and especially on the marriage; and his Majesty had remarked that there was no alliance that he would prefer for his son to that with a Princess of your Majesty's house; but always on the condition that affairs should be dealt with reasonably. If, he said, we had written to your Majesty in any other sense we had misunderstood his meaning, and in such case we should immediately send off a courier to the Emperor correcting the impression. He (*i.e.* Browne) was to instruct Paget to tell us this. We replied that we had perfectly understood the King's reply to be such as the Master of the Horse now reported; and we had written nothing to your Majesty contrary to this. It is true, we continued, that this was his (*i.e.* Henry's) first reply, and we had hoped that he would not insist upon it: for, to speak frankly, we should never have thought that he would have made a point of the amount of the dowry, which in such cases was a secondary consideration to the great advantage accruing to the respective nations by like alliances. Your Majesty, the King of the Romans, and the Queen Regent had been delighted to hear at first that he (*i.e.* Henry) was favourably inclined to the marriage, but it never occurred to them that the matter could fall through on the question of the amount of money to be brought by the bride of so great a monarch. He (Paget) replied that he had understood that I, Scepperus, was authorised to increase the amount of the offer. I assured him that I had no desire to mislead him or anyone else; and, in good truth, that my powers did not extend to this point, as I had told the King himself. Speaking to him (Paget) as friends, we could plainly perceive that in the interests, and for the safety, of this realm, no better alliance than that now proposed could be adopted, unless it was that with Scotland, if the latter match were the means of submitting Scotland to their rule. We mentioned this latter point to hear what he (Paget) would say about it. He replied that the Scottish matter would not be settled by a marriage: it was almost impossible for the English to keep

1546.

Scotland, even if they conquered it, except as far as the river (Forth?) in consequence of the lack of food in the rest of the country beyond the river. There was, therefore, only this marriage with your Majesty's niece to be thought of; and he (Paget) begged us to do our best in the matter, praying me, Scepperus, to remain here. They, on their side, would act in the same way. We promised that we would do everything in our power. We have thought well to inform your Majesty of this.

London, 26 March 1546.

Postscript.—Sire,—As we were about to despatch this letter to your Majesty yesterday we heard a rumour that the Count Palatine Philip of Bavaria was expected to arrive here, having travelled by the Rhine as far as Dortrecht and thence to England incognito.* We therefore deferred despatching the letter until to-day and in the meanwhile to learn what truth there was in this. We have heard that they have sent to meet him and he will arrive at Court this evening. Some people say also that the Lord Admiral, who was to have left this morning, has postponed his departure for two or three days by order of the King. We will keep your Majesty informed.

We also learn that the English have captured seven ships loaded with wheat, which they say were bound from Zeeland to France. We do not know whether this wheat belonged to the King of Portugal.

London, 27 March 1546.

March 28.
Vienna
Imp. Arch.

226. SCEPPERUS to LOYS SCORS.

You will see what the ambassador and myself are writing to the Queen (Dowager of Hungary) and we have nothing of importance to add, except some details of the coming of the Count Palatine Philip, who was honourably received yesterday. It is evident that he has come for one of three objects: namely to get married, which is the general opinion, as the representative of some of the German princes, or else to obtain some command in the war. Lady Anne of Cleves has been for some time at Court, well received and treated. She left yesterday.

This King has arrested the son of de Lolme of Antwerp and others who escaped from prison in Antwerp. This was done without any request on our part, as we knew nothing about it, except from public rumour. The ambassador is much surprised that the authorities of the town of Antwerp should have neglected to inform him, especially as it is notorious that this realm is the refuge of all the rogues from our place (quod hic regio est asylum omnium malorum ex nostratibus). Some of them, however, will find themselves deceived; for this King is fitting out a galley, which is already

---

* Duke Philip of Bavaria, nephew of the Count Palatine, had been secretly betrothed to the Princess Mary six years previously on the occasion of his first visit to England (December, 1539) though Henry's sincerity in the matter may be questioned, as any intimacy between England and the Protestants in Germany made the Emperor desirous of pleasing Henry. On his present visit in 1546 Duke Philip agreed to a marriage contract, binding him to transport his bride within three months, receiving with her a dowry of 12,000 florins for the costs of the voyage, etc., and 40,000 florins in gold, half down and half in a year. The contract was never formally signed and is in State Papers, Henry VIII., C.C. 1. Record Office.

1546.

afloat, and it may serve as a lodging for some bad boys. We have heard nothing from Councillor Van der Burgh, and do not know where he is. The poor claimants who are here will rejoice at his coming, for everything here is grievously dear, double the usual price, and taxes increase daily. Two days ago they put a new tax of three scoters a barrel on beer.

All the war-ships have left the river, numbering about fifty sail of the King's own ships, fine and beautiful craft.

The Earl of Surrey, formerly captain of Boulogne, arrived at Court yesterday, but was coldly received and did not have access to the King. The Duke of Norfolk, father of the earl, is absent from Court. I do not know what is in hand, for they decide nothing, but keep in suspense several of their captains who have been commissioned to raise troops, but who are not dispatched: an evident sign that they (*i.e.* the English Government) are waiting for something, we know not what, unless it be some reply from M. du Biez, as I wrote to the Queen in my previous letters. They have dispatched certain other German captains of my acquaintance, with instructions to wait until the month of June, and in the interim they (the English) will let them know whether they will employ them or not.

Lent is very strictly observed in this country, quite as much or more so than with us, and nobody ventures to buy or sell meat. The ceremonies also are similarly kept up, according to the ancient ordinances of the Church.

The King is coming to-morrow to Westminster, which is a sign that some important business is to be decided—perhaps the marriage of the Count Palatine Philip. Time will tell.

London, 28 March (Six o'clock in the morning) 1546.

March 30.
Simancas.
E. R. 873.

227. JUAN DE VEGA to PRINCE PHILIP.

(The greater part of the letter is occupied with small financial and ecclesiastical points of no importance; but the following paragraphs, concerning the Protestant Reformation and the Council of Trent, etc., are interesting.)

"On Friday, 19th instant, his Holiness resolved in Consistory that the legates should be written to, giving them full authority to discuss in the Council the question of universal reformation. Very divergent views exist on this matter, some people believing that the authority has been given in order to prevent the Council from dealing with the question on its own account, whilst others think that it is an inspiration from heaven (juyzio de Dios).

"From a perfectly trustworthy source I learn that the French are extremely desirous of, and in need of, peace, but I do not know if they will be able to obtain it."

Rome, 30 March, 1546.

Postscript.—"The Pope and the Duke of Florence are on bad terms. The quarrel is an old one: the Duke having expelled from their monastery in Florence I know not how many Dominican friars on the ground that they were disturbers of his State. The Pope sent a Brief ordering the Duke to restore them to their monastery, which the Duke claims to have obeyed and the Pope

1546.

insists that he has not. Other subjects of dispute have arisen between them to exacerbate this ill feeling; and on the 18th instant, at 4 o'clock in the morning, they arrested here a man whom the Duke had here as secretary, with Everardo Seristori his ambassador, and seized his papers. I spoke very emphatically to the Pope about it, dwelling especially on the seizure of the papers. I pointed out to him that the present was no time to raise fresh troubles in Italy; and although the Emperor wished everyone to obey the Pope, including the Duke of Florence, he desired that the latter should be treated benignantly by his Holiness."

March 30.
Simancas.
E. A. 642.

228. THE EMPEROR to PRINCE PHILIP.

Before we left Luxemburg we wrote you what had occurred up to that time. We arrived at this place on the 22rd instant, in good health, thank God, and have remained here until to-day, to rest the men-at-arms who accompany us and because we also needed repose. We have also been delayed by the coming hither of the Bishop of Mayence, the Count Palatine and the Landgrave of Hesse. We are leaving here to-day and hope to arrive at Ratisbon without passing through Nuremburg or Ulm, within twelve or thirteen days. We send you this to inform you of our health, and of the news herein contained. Keep us continually advised as to your health, etc., and, if you have not already done so, answer our letter sent from Venlo.

We have discussed with the Count Palatine* especially German matters, and generally the question of the Diet. The Princess, my niece, accompanied him; and on the following day the Landgrave arrived. The only thing that could be done was to confirm what had been said at Maestricht to the envoys of the electors and the Protestants, with regard to my coming and its object. No more light could be gained as to what can be done in the Diet, except that the Count (Palatine) expresses a very great wish that some accord should be agreed to about religion, and that peace and justice should be re-established in this province. He offers his best services to this end, and the Landgrave has done the same, although no means for attaining the object has been mentioned, except a general desire that he may be of service. But from all he says it is very evident that an agreement will be extremely difficult. In any case, with God's help, we shall go on to Ratisbon without embarrassment, and shall use every possible effort, both on the road and after our arrival, to see how things are likely to go, and what can be done; taking every opportunity of conversing both with Catholics and Protestants with that object. We are urging our brother the King of the Romans to hasten thither with all speed, and in the meanwhile we await your answer to our letters.

We learn through our Ambassador in France that there was an intention of recalling to Marseilles the galleys that the King had in the western sea, and that on one occasion orders were given to this effect. The King, however, after postponed the execution of them to see whether he could not use the galleys against the

---

* The Count Palatine Frederick, who shortly afterwards openly espoused the Reformation.

1546.

English, or for the protection of his coasts and frontiers round Boulogne. He no doubt feared also that the galleys might be molested on our coast in return for the damage they did to our subjects on their outward voyage. This fear also led him to talk of dismantling the galleys and sending the rowers and officers overland; but the French are so fickle; and as they may still make up their mind to send the galleys back through the Straits, we think well to inform you of the possibility, and to say that, although we are well aware of the desirability of preventing these galleys from passing into the Mediterranean, we do not see how it can be done without an open rupture and full preparations beforehand. It will be very unadvisable to make a demonstration of illwill, without doing any effectual service; and it would be equally imprudent to endeavour to embarrass them in other ways, such as advising the ports to resist in case the galleys should put into any of them, because the ports are not well provided with artillery, and are not adapted for preventing entrance by force: besides which the galleys would always be stronger. The latter, moreover, could obtain water and victuals in many places without difficulty, and by force if they were in real need; but if they make the voyage they will be sure to be so well provisioned as, in all probality, not be driven to such extremity; and if they were, they would certainly find no difficulty in getting what they required in Portugal. We are of opinion, therefore, that the only thing that can be done will be to seize them, in case they are driven on our coast by bad weather and crippled, and, even then, unless we can take them all, or most of them, it will be unadvisable to attack them. For all these reasons we have decided that advice should only be sent to the ports, and not ostensibly by our orders, that no such damage as was inflicted by the galleys on their outward voyage must be suffered from them on their way back. Don Bernardino (de Mendoza)* must be also informed of this, so that he may keep a look out, and may put his galleys in order, without making public his reason for doing so. We are not writing to him directly, as we have no cipher with him. We are sure that if these measures are taken the French will not dare to send the galleys, as they are already doubtful about doing so. If, on the other hand, they decide to dismantle them and send the crews and fittings overland it will be very difficult for them to fit out the galleys again to be of any service this summer. To sum up: your object will be to make the French believe that the people on our coasts have of their own accord and in consequence of what happened before, decided not to welcome the galleys or provide them with anything.

It appears that by the express consent of the King of France they are still fitting out ships to send to the Indies, on the pretext that they are bound for Brazil, notwithstanding what was said on the matter to the French ambassadors, and the efforts made by our ambassador in France. We think well to advise you of this also, so that steps may be taken accordingly. We learn from Sicily that certain of the principal personages of that realm have been discovered to be contaminated by the evil sect of Luther. For this

---

* General of the Spanish galleys, brother of the Marquis de Mondejar.

1546.

reason the lack of an Inquisitor is much to be regretted, and if the matter is not remedied soon it may lead to still greater evils. No doubt the Brief for the Inquisitor-General will already have reached the Cardinal of Seville.* Let the above information accordingly be conveyed to him, in our and your names, in order that an Inquisitor may at once be appointed for Sicily, duly endowed with the necessary learning and experience for such a post, especially now that this new tendency is noticeable there.

Above all we again beg you to fulfil the order already given for meeting the bill of exchange for the breadstuffs sent from Sicily to Spain. It is most necessary that there should be no failure in this.

Spires, 30 March 1546.

March 30.
Simancas.
E. 73.

229. PRINCE PHILIP to the EMPEROR.

Your Majesty's letter of 16th instant received, and your decision with regard to the enterprise against the Protestants etc. duly noted. All the reasons alleged for deferring the signature of the treaty (with the Pope) until after your arrival at Ratisbon are most wise and prudent. Since your Majesty signifies your determination to carry through the enterprise this year, with such resources as you may have, there is no more to be said on that head. Your Majesty has been moved to this by saintly zeal, and I can only hope in God that the result may correspond with the object; which is so purely in His service. Your Majesty's aim being exclusively to redress evil in matters of faith, and reduce to submission those who have wandered from it, I pray that He may grant your Majesty the forces necessary for so great and difficult an enterprise. There is, however, one point which I should like to mention; namely that such security should be obtained for the aid promised by the Pope that it shall not fail you when it is most needed. This would be the greatest difficulty that could happen. I should wish also to remark that it seems to be the general impression, that as soon as the Protestants learn of your Majesty's resolution, they will approach closely to the King of France, in which case they may be able to offer a very strong resistance. But what is worse still, people fear that the King of England, seeing that your Majesty is suppressing the Protestants by force of arms, may think that when you have finished with them, the arms of your Majesty and the Pope may be turned against him and may make up his mind to ally himself at once with the Protestants and, perhaps even, with the King of France. The latter might take advantage of the circumstances to bring the King of England to consent to the conditions he so much desires. I am sure, however, that your Majesty will have considered this, and the many other difficulties which present themselves; and after having done so has come to the conclusion that the best course will be to carry through the enterprise. I heartily pray therefore to our Lord that it may be as rapidly concluded as your Majesty says, and as successful as I would have it be. I did not communicate what your Majesty wrote to me about it to anyone but the Comendador Mayor (Cobos),

---

* Garcia de Loaysa y Mendoza, Grand Inquisitor since February 1545. He died three weeks after the date of this letter.

1546.

and I instructed him to carry out diligently your Majesty's orders with regard to enquiring what bills of exchange can be obtained, and at what usance; and also that the payments should be made as your Majesty directs. He has taken the matter in hand with the needful secrecy, and with his usual care for your Majesty's service. He will write to your Majesty direct on the matter in detail, although in the other letter I send to your Majesty I give you a general account of all the sources from which funds may be obtained. Your Majesty may rest assured that the utmost possible effort shall be exerted here to supply your Majesty with what you need. It has been impossible for me to send the account until the present, because I have had to confer so many times with the Council of Finance, the Council of State, and the Council of Aragon. They have also been obliged to discuss the matter apart, and afterwards in my presence. All other matters will be treated in the general letter.

Madrid, 30 March 1546.

No date (March?)
Simancas.
E. A. 647.

230. Document headed "Opinion of the Confessor on the enterprise of Germany."

Although the strength and obstinacy of the Protestants should rightly be deeply considered, and the preparations of his Majesty be fully adequate, in case he decides to attack them; yet there are weighty reasons which convince me that the Protestants will be weak in the war. The following are those that occur to me.

1. The poverty of the princes, which is certainly very great, and their subjects and the cities are tired of furnishing them with money.

2. The great division and dissatisfaction amongst them. This is first noticeable in the cities, where there are many people Catholic at heart; others that are doubtful, now that they witness the fickleness and vanity of their doctors; others who out of pure mischief, and even against their conscience, have plunged into the business to obtain the liberty they desire. All these, when they see that they will have to risk their lives and property will be in great fear. Other people, and a great number who have joined the Protestants, are tired of the doctors, and resentful of the tyranny of the princes; and, like travellers who have for a long time followed the wrong road, have fallen out amongst themselves, casting upon each other blame for the error; and so enmity and dissension have arisen and each man goes his own way with stiffnecked pride, writing and speaking against his fellows. All this may be utilised against them; and although the evil has grown greatly, yet it is destroying itself. The abscess is so ripe that it seems now full time for it to open. Much dissension also exists amongst the princes, and advantage may be taken of this also, not only with the Catholics, but one prince might be tempted with the idea that he could obtain what belongs to another.

It would appear advisable therefore, that the first thing to be done should be to send to the cities a very firm but mildly worded ultimatum, telling them clearly and authoritatively how grave is the offence they have committed towards God, their ancestors, the nobles, the church and his Majesty; and offering them pardon if they will return to obedience; but if not declaring them and their princes as traitors. I think this would give rise to great perturbation amongst them. Perhaps also some Catholics might be consulted to see whether by means of some pious deceit, or through the carelessness of the defenders, some city might not be captured.

3. Another thing that constitutes their weakness is that as all the cities are commercial and business centres, the stoppage and hampering of their traffic, by closing the roads, navigable rivers, etc. would soon deprive them of their wealth. It would therefore seem advisable that his Majesty should, at least, sequestrate all the property of the (Protestant?) merchants in his territories; and though the property in question might quite justly be confiscated, his Majesty would adopt the course he considered best with regard to it. This measure would have to be executed suddenly, and without giving the merchants an opportunity of learning of it beforehand.

4. Their want of a leader; for if the Landgrave failed there would be no one: and I am of opinion that if his Majesty had hold of one of their principal men the rest would all take fright. By means of spies and in other ways something of this sort might be done.

5. The halfhearted way in which hitherto they have carried on their wars. I heard in Spires from many Catholics that the war they (the Protestants) had with the Duke of Brunswick, was conducted very weakly by them. The disorder was so great that, although the campaign only lasted a month, they (the Protestant troops) were without either food or money for half the time; and only did what they did because there was no resistance.[*] They say that the cities spent 700,000 florins, and this only proves how complete the disorganisation must have been; for the officers and nobles must have kept the money. The second war confirms this view, for the Duke of Brunswick very promptly recovered most of what they had taken from him, mainly owing to his own previous want of foresight. Finally, the Landgrave [†] has never done anything worth speaking of, and he is the sole cock of the German walk (*el solo es el gallillo de Alemania*).

6. The steadiness and joy with which the Catholics will fight being sure of their cause and of good conscience. They will be able to say to the Protestants as the King Abias said to the Israelites.

With regard to the treaty with the Pope, I believe three objections are raised: first that his Majesty is greatly bound down by it, and impeded in making an arrangement with the Protestants; because the treaty prevents him from treating with them on any

---

[*] Henry of Brunswick, whose dominions were held in sequestration by the Emperor until his differences with the confederates of the Smalkaldic league should be adjusted, had shortly before this undertaken to raise a mercenary army for the King of France. Having done this at the expense of Francis, Brunswick broke faith with the latter and threw himself upon the territories of which he himself had been deprived, with the hope of regaining them by force. The Landgrave (Philip) of Hesse and Maurice of Saxony on behalf of the Smalkaldic Confederation easily routed him however, and imprisoned both Brunswick and his son. As will be seen in the course of these letters the Emperor took advantage of this quarrel for his own ends, and espoused the cause of Brunswick, who had played false towards the King of France and the Protestant princes.

[†] Philip the Magnanimous.

1546.

matter of faith or the constitution of the church without the express consent of his Holiness or his legate. It is advanced as quite certain that they (*i.e.* the Pope and the churchman) will never consent to any abatement of their preëminence, and it is equally certain that the Protestants will never re-enter the union of the church, unless many customary and received usages are abolished, and many abuses remedied. It is thus made to appear that the Pope effectually prevents the Emperor from endeavouring to reform (the church), and makes him the defender of its abuses. He also, it is asserted, ties the Emperor's hands in temporal matters, since the latter is not to be allowed to treat upon a point which really touches the substance of the enterprise itself, and may not abandon or retard the execution. The second objection to the treaty is that the Pope gives but little, whilst he holds the Emperor to much; since his Holiness only binds himself to give a specified subsidy; and if the war is of long duration, which is quite probable, as the interests at stake are great, the Emperor may find that he has to bear the whole burden, and the Pope is under no obligation at all. The third objection is the small reliance that can be placed in the Pope; first, on account of his age; and if he were to die after the commencement of the enterprise neither the College of Cardinals nor the new pontiff would be bound; secondly, on account of his ill-will and bad intention towards his Majesty's greatness. This may lead him to bear no love to the enterprise; and he may serve his bad ends by allowing his troops, ostensibly raised for the enterprise, to be turned to other uses, or to fight on the side of his Majesty's enemies, and perhaps even to betray his Majesty into the hands of these heretics. The following answers may, in my opinion, be given to these objections:—

To the first. Premising, as is admitted by theologians and jurists, that all obligations entered into between men include not only the licit provisions contained in them, but an implied, if not expressed, understanding that they do not prevent the attainment of a greater good in the same direction, nor give a pretext for greater evil. It may be said, that by the treaty his Majesty is only bound in regard to spiritual questions and on the constitution of the church, so far as he has hitherto been; because, for instance, if the Protestants are to offer to return on condition that certain freedom was given to them, or that certain recent abuses should be abolished, his Majesty, even without the treaty, could not grant such conditions himself, but could insist upon the Pope and the Council granting them; and, under the treaty he could proceed in the same way, But I go beyond this. If the Protestants offered to submit on reasonable concessions being made, and on the abolition of things that were not essential; such conditions, in short, as learned and prudent men approved of, and the Pope refused, the Emperor would be no longer bound, for his Holiness would, in such case, be obstructive, and, by his refusal of reasonable terms, would hinder the return of the seceders to the church. His Majesty in such circumstances would be free to act independently of the treaty, and as if the latter did not exist. With regard to the third objection, I am of opinion that, though we may well believe that the Pope will do his best for his family and heirs, I certainly see no reason for

1546.

supposing that he will be so diabolical as to sacrifice the faith for the purpose of driving the Emperor into a corner. When the peace with France had been arranged, we witnessed that he at once expressed his willingness to contribute this subsidy; and had prepared it, so far as he could, when Dandolo was sent. I may also remark that the Pope's only fear is that the Emperor may abandon the enterprise; and his conditions are directed more to the prevention of this than for the purpose of hindering the execution. And, judging from outward appearances, he has good reasons for this, as many persons think, even the most devoted servants of his Majesty.

I may add that the Pope expects that, if he does as his Majesty wishes, due thanks will be given to him, and he is quite right in this. He complains that the papal profits in Spain and elsewhere are sequestrated and intercepted, and to all appearance his complaints are not unfounded.

I conclude by saying that, if his Majesty intends to carry through this undertaking and the Pope gives what is asked of him, the reasons for these fears and complaints should be banished; and, in all sincerity, fair promises and hopes should be given to him. If this course is taken it may be presumed that, either out of goodness, greed, or necessity, he will carry out his obligations in the treaty, and fulfil the promises he makes in addition. We must not be too hard on the Pope, for we are not quite blameless ourselves.

March (?)
Simancas.
E. 73.

231. Report of the Prior, the Consuls and other persons of the University of Burgos* etc., in reply to the letter of Prince Philip addressed to them, with regard to the measures that should be taken to protect Spanish shipping at sea from the depredations hitherto inflicted upon it by the English, Scots and French.

With regard to his Highness' question, as to whether arrangements should be made for the flotillas sailing outward from Spain to Flanders, to time their departure so as to enable them to meet at sea the flotillas homeward bound from Flanders to Spain: the opinion is that this cannot well be done, nor would it be advantageous or effectual if it could; for the following reasons. First it would be almost impossible to contrive the simultaneous sailing of the flotillas, because the cargoes sent from Spain are ready at a different season from those loaded in Flanders. To detain the respective merchandise for the purpose of simultaneous dispatch would inflict great damage upon his Majesty's territories on both sides. Even if this were done, and the flotillas were to meet at sea, it would be of little good, as one flotilla would be going one way and the other the opposite way; besides which difficulty, the flotilla from Flanders needs a different wind from that required by the ships coming from Biscay or Andalucia. For these reasons, and for the delay which would arise, they are of opinion that the method suggested should not be adopted. In addition to this, the custom of the University of Burgos for a long time past is to ensure the

---

* That is, the guild of merchants of Burgos.

1546.

safety of their merchandise in time of war by the following means. They send a flotilla fully armed and prepared for defence to Flanders with their goods; and the same flotilla is bound to bring a return of freight of Flemish merchandise to the Biscay ports. By thus sending their ships together and well armed they have always gone safely, and this same method will be continued in future.

The persons consulted are of opinion that his Majesty should send orders to the whole of the ports; especially those in Biscay and Guipuzcoa from San Sebastian to Santander, as well as to Cadiz, Seville etc., forbidding any ship to sail alone and without company into the western sea, either to Flanders, England, or France: the smallest number of ships to sail together being six. If there should be a larger number of vessels in those ports than six, they should all sail together, waiting for each other, as the delay could not be long; and it would be more than compensated for by the increased security.

His Majesty should also order that all the ships should carry such men, arms and munitions, as to be able to defend themselves, or even take the offensive if provocation was offered to them. The warlike material each ship would carry would depend upon her size, and would be regulated by a general order to be issued by his Majesty, the carrying out of the regulations being entrusted to the justices of the respective ports, who would insist upon strict compliance; as otherwise the ship-masters would evade the provisions for the purpose of gaining a larger profit on the voyage.

His Majesty should order, that if in any one port there were not enough ships to make up a flotilla, they should join those in neighbouring ports and sail in company; one captain being chosen as commodore, with such authority as his Majesty may dictate, who will have command of the flotilla during the voyage. No ships should be allowed to sail except under these conditions.

The persons consulted are of opinion that there would be no difficulty or disadvantage in the ships thus sailing together: on the contrary, great benefit would accrue from it, since their own experience shows that when ships sail thus they escape pillage, and can only be attacked by an armed national fleet, which would not commit the outrages which are committed by individual corsairs. Even if a national fleet were to capture a flotilla of several ships, it would be obliged to convey them to England; and could not conceal the capture; so that, as the matter would be an open and important one, a remedy could at once be applied. When the captures are small and isolated there is no redress. The greatest injury that the French and English have done to us in this war has been inflicted on solitary ships, which having encountered on the high seas they have boarded and plundered and abandoned the vessels, whose crews have had no opportunity of even knowing who had plundered them. For this reason it has been impossible to recover the booty, which has amounted to a vast sum. If the above recommendation be adopted this will be avoided, and no private freebooters would be able to cope with our armed flotillas.

With regard to ships loaded in the Galician ports, his Majesty should give similar orders; but, as the merchandise in that realm

1546.

is insufficient for the loading of many vessels, the orders referred to for so many to go together cannot be so rigorously enforced there, but as many as possible should sail in company.

All ships loaded in Flanders for whatever destination, should also go armed and in flotillas, in accordance with the suggestion made above. This will be easy there, as many ships sail from the Flemish ports, and they are well fitted etc.

The vessels loaded in Grand Canary are so few that it will be difficult to make up a flotilla; but his Majesty should instruct the justices of the islands to cause the ships to sail in company as much as possible, and well armed with men and cannon. They should also call in at Cadiz or Lisbon to join company with such ships as may be there and continue the voyage together. In these ports they will generally find ships loading for all parts.

His Majesty should cause the armed ships sailing either from Spain or Flanders, to give security that they will do no harm to the subjects of the Kings of England and France.

With regard to the ships to and from the Indies, especially those that bring the bullion (for the English and French dare to plunder everything they come across) his Majesty should order that the ships bringing gold should so far as possible sail in company as far as Havana; and that they should not sail thence alone, but in strong companies and well armed. If this be impossible the gold should be detained there until ships of war are sent from Seville to convoy them. The expense thus incurred will be less prejudicial than for them to sail alone and unprepared; because, as the English and French corsairs are now familiar with the voyage, they are much to be feared. They sail round the Indies for the purpose of plundering these ships. His Majesty's subjects load ships in France, both for Spain and Flanders; and as they sail from a country at war with England, and it is impossible to make up a flotilla of such ships in France, the English fleet may plunder them as they leave port with impunity, on the pretext that the King of England has forbidden the Emperor's subjects to ship their merchandise in French bottoms. His Majesty should therefore, provide that his subjects' goods shipped in Spanish or French ships should not be liable to capture, if such goods are really not the property of Frenchmen. His Majesty should order that ships bound to Bordeaux, Rochelle or Rouen, from Spain, should sail in company and well armed, to protect the Spanish property they carry from being plundered by English corsairs.

His Majesty should take steps that ships belonging to his subjects should not be detained in England, and that prompt justice should be done to them. He should also provide that no flotilla should sail from England, without its giving security not to molest his subjects; and if they did so that the value of the plunder should be made good. Security should also be given that all their captures from any source should be handed over to the justice of the first port they enter in England, with the bills of lading, manifests, and ships-papers they may have taken from the prizes. Until such prizes are adjudged to be fair none of the proceeds of them should be disposed of under heavy penalties. This would be a great

1546.

remedial measure, and would enable his Majesty's subjects to obtain redress for property really belonging to them. This is only just, and the English will grant it, if it is preceded by his Majesty's order that his own subjects shall give security as suggested above.

His Majesty should also give orders to the Spanish ports, that when an English fleet arrives, and the men land, they should be obliged to give security to do no harm to his Majesty's subjects; besides which they should not be allowed to remain in the neighbourhood of those ports where, as experience shows, they usually lie in wait for the ships to put to sea, for the purpose of robbing them; as they do without fear and without respect to their being the property of his Majesty's subjects. They should, moreover, not be allowed to make prizes within Spanish ports, as they have done recently. His Majesty should endeavour to get the King of England to give to the subjects of the former a safe-conduct whenever it may be requested, without any fee being expected for it. It is seen that the English armed vessels respect ships that bear such safeguards. His Majesty should also try to get the King of England's consent that the subjects of the former should be at liberty to load their goods in French bottoms, without their being liable to confiscation, according to the English statute. This would be a great benefit to the Biscayners, as it would enable French ships to bring the victuals they require, as they usually did, but are now prevented from doing.

The persons consulted are of opinion that the means of defence that ships in future should carry are as follows:—

A ship of 100 tons. 25 men, in addition to six ship-boys, and two cabin-boys, two of the men to be bombardiers.

 2 Great bombards. (Bombardas gruesas.)
 4 "Pasamuros."
 12 demi-Culverins. (Versos.)
 12 Harquebusses.
 2 Quintals of gunpowder.
 12 Crossbows and pikes, javelins, fighting screens and waist clothes.*

Ships either larger or smaller than 100 tons to be manned and armed in the same proportion. The tonnage of each ship must be inspected by the justice of the port, and its compliance with the above provisions certified. It may be provided as a penalty for non-compliance that no freight shall be recoverable in case of infraction of these rules. In order to prevent masters from putting to sea unarmed, his Majesty should order public proclamation to be made in every port; so that the masters may not allege the excuse of ignorance.

1 April.
Vienna.
Imp. Arch.

232. The QUEEN DOWAGER to VAN DER DELFT and SCEPPERUS.

The English Ambassador resident here has just handed us your letters of 25th March, and in accordance therewith has requested us to consent to the transit of the infantry under Penninck, without the latter being constrained, for the reasons mentioned in our

---

* That is, shields to cover the freeboard of a ship during an engagement.

1546.

former letters, to come hither to see us. We replied to the effect that the Ambassador himself was aware of the damage that the subjects here had suffered—and also those of Liège—in the last two years through the soldiers under Landenberger and Von Reissenberg, without any service being rendered to the King (of England) by the men who did it. This, we said, might have been avoided if the King's officers had consented to listen to people here; and as experience of the past makes us wise for the future, the Emperor before his departure from Maestricht gave orders, that before allowing the passage of the troops in question, Conrad Penninck was to come and see us, and satisfy us that the troops in their transit would do no damage to the poor country folk on the road. We were both unable and unwilling to contravene the orders of the Emperor in the matter; but out of consideration for the King's urgent request; whilst we must insist that Penninck shall come to us, we will so handle the matter that no delay shall be incurred by reason of his doing so, and Penninck shall not be taken two days away from his straight road. We will, indeed, despatch him so promptly that no complaint shall be made in that respect. We inform you of this, that you may convey it to the King's principal ministers, making them clearly understand that our wish is to please the King; but that we must, nevertheless, do our duty and see that the poor subjects on this side are not injured, especially in this time of extreme need and famine. Apart from this, they (the English ministers) may rest assured that we will do all we reasonably can to preserve the perfect amity between the Emperor and the King, and will serve the latter in every way.

With regard to the second request that we will allow transit of 400 lasts of grain, which they say they have loaded at Dortrecht, the produce of Cleves and Julliers; the ambassador before the receipt of your letters had already urged for permission to ship 80 lasts of wheat loaded at Dortrecht coming, as is alleged, from Cleves and Julliers. We were unable to grant his request, for the reasons set forth in our previous letters, which we hope you have received, and also because of the great scarcity now existing here. As this is increasing daily we are compelled to retain the wheat in transit from Cleves and Julliers, which can only be exported through these dominions. This is the only means we can devise to minimise the great dearth of wheat here; and although further supply be obtained, it would be at so excessive a cost that the poor people would be unable to pay for it. In addition to this, if the exportation of the Cleves and Julliers wheat is allowed, it would be impossible to keep the grain of the home harvest here, the quantity and appearance of the wheat being just the same. The Emperor before his departure, moreover, refused permission to the King of Portugal to export 20 lasts of such wheat; and we do not allow it even to the Spaniards, his Majesty's own subjects. You may therefore well consider if we could, or should, grant such a concession as that requested by the Ambassador, and especially for so large a quantity as 400 lasts, which would suffice to increase the already high price of grain here. Nevertheless, out of consideration for the King, we gave permission for the transport of

1546.

100 lasts from Oestlandt, which would serve as well as other wheat for the victualling of the fortresses, and the feeding of the troops in the field. When the conditions here improve we will not fail to aid to the utmost of our power, but until the new harvest comes forward we shall be compelled to keep a sharp eye on the transit of grain; unless, indeed, we want to see the poor people crying for bread, and dying by the roadside for want of it. If this were to happen from any oversight or neglect of ours, we should find it hard to answer for it to the Emperor and to the country. These seem to us sufficient reasons for our refusal, if they are fairly considered.

The English ambassador also informed us that four horses belonging to an Albanian captain who was going to join the King's service have been seized at Gravelines, and that certain Germans on their way to the same service had been stopped. We replied that the officers at Gravelines had only done their duty in preventing the passing of the said horses; for otherwise the pretext of going to serve the King of England would be made a cover for taking out all the horses from this country; which could not be allowed here, as it certainly would not be allowed in England. It did not appear, moreover, if the horses were raised in these dominions or not; although it was the rule that armed men should not pass through a prince's territory, without giving the authorities information as to their destination. Otherwise the men might just as well be going to join the King of England's enemies as to join his army. We felt displeased that they made no declaration at all until they found their way barred: and they deserved punishment rather than favour for their disrespect of the authorities of these dominions. With regard to the Ambassador's contention that by the last agreement of Utrecht the transit of horses and harness for the King's service was to be allowed, we replied that we were willing to carry out the agreement fully, but that we could not in virtue of it allow horses to pass, except for the King; due declaration of them being previously made, and the proper formalities complied with, in which case they would meet with reasonable compliance here. But the declarations etc. must be made before the horses and stopped by our officers. We have great ground for complaint that since the stoppage, the officers of the King have pushed the matter as if they were the aggrieved party, wishing to throw the whole of the blame upon us, and acting as if they had a right to command us. We cannot believe that this is in accordance with the King's wish; and you may confidentially say thus much to some of his ministers, in order that they may look to it for the future; as we cannot put up with such behaviour. If they make demands with regard to wheat already shipped and stopped, or to horses and other warlike stores under embargo, they will find us much more unyielding than if they had addressed us previously to the stoppage.

We have had delivered to the Ambassador a note sent to us by the Count de Roeulx, respecting some vessel taken by Lord Grey's people from Flemish subjects.° We enclose you a copy of the note.

° William Lord Grey de Wilton had just been appointed Governor of Boulogne on the recall of the Earl of Surrey. Count de Roeulx had commanded the Flemish imperial auxiliaries with the English army during the war and still remained in the service with a certain number of Flemings; but was mainly employed in safeguarding the Emperor's interests.

He (Count de Roeulx) has been unable to obtain satisfaction, and he considers that Lord Grey is acting more harshly towards his Majesty's subjects than to others, and no redress can be got from him. You will make the matter known in England so that Lord Grey may be specially instructed to settle the claim for this vessel, and to order his people for the future to avoid pillaging the subjects of his Majesty. They (the English) may rest assured that Count de Roeulx will request nothing from them for the benefit of their enemies. Lord Grey justifies the capture on the ground that the vessel was bound for a French port: but this is unreasonable, as it is permissable for the subjects here to communicate with the French, as well as with the English. Moreover, the strong places on the frontier are entirely destroyed and the lands ravaged; and the poor subjects of Artois being utterly ruined, have to maintain themselves as best they can with their boats; and it is most unjust to capture the latter. Master Adrien Van der Burgh left Malines eight days ago, and we hope that he will have arrived in England by this time. He has, however, but slight instructions with regard to the embargo placed upon English subjects etc. in Spain; so that you, Van der Delft, will have to instruct him, in accordance with the information that may have reached you on the subject.

With regard to the conversation that the King held with you, we can only refer you to the Emperor's letters. The King would not be displeased to obtain terms (*i.e.* for the marriage of his son) similar to those given to the Duke of Orleans; though we think he would be better pleased with something (*i.e.* a territorial dowry) nearer to his own realm, rather than Milan, which would be far too distant for him to hold safely.°

Whilst this letter was being made ready for despatch we received two letters from the Emperor's Council in Gueldres, dated the 26th ultimo: and saying that, notwithstanding their having written to Conrad Penninck telling him not to bring his infantry into his Majesty's territory, and especially not to go to Alten, which is attached to Gueldres, although it belongs to the Abbess, and is subject to his Majesty, Penninck had arrived at Alten with eight standards of foot, his intention being to pass his muster there. Penninck had sent representatives to the Council of Gueldres to request their permission to remain at Alten for a day or so, but they had refused, as they were bound to do, and wrote to him ordering him to depart immediately. They fear, however, that this will be fruitless, and that Penninck will pay as little attention to their second letter as he did to their first. We have complained indignantly of this to the English Ambassador here, and have told him that the King's Commissioners are going on in the same way now as they did in the two previous years with Landenberger's and

---

° This, as will be seen, was a rather disingenuous interpretation of Henry's words. His claim was of course not that the duchy of Milan should be given as a dowry with his son's bride, as was promised in the case of the Duke of Orleans, but that his son, the heir of England, should not be worse treated than the younger son of the King of France. The whole matter was evidently a feint so far as the Emperor was concerned, designed to prevent an arrangement with France based upon the marriage of the Prince of Wales with the infant Mary Stuart.

1546.

Von Reissenberg's levies. We shall take the necessary steps to protect the subjects under our rule, and will not permit the transit of these troops; since they (the English) have not fulfilled what they had always promised voluntarily; namely that the men should not pass in a body through his Majesty's dominions, but in small bands without doing any damage. The only reply given by the English Ambassador was that Alten was not in his Majesty's territory; and he tried to raise a dispute with us, as to the limits of the dominions under our rule. We had several altercations on this subject with the Ambassador, in which, as in the last two years, after the troops were assembled and feeding on the country he would give no further assurance that they would pass without doing damage, except to say that they had promised to this effect; which does not satisfy us. Finally we insisted that he should immediately order Penninck to withdraw his soldiers from the Emperor's territories; or otherwise we should direct—as we have now done—the four bands of horsemen in the neighbourhood; namely those of Count de Hochstadt, Sieurs Brederode, Du Praet, and the Marshal of Gueldres, to form a junction and cast themselves upon the said infantry if it attempts to advance before Penninck comes hither to see us, or any depredations are committed on his Majesty's subjects; and in the meanwhile we left it to the Ambassador to take such steps as he considered best in the interests of his master. We inform you of this, in order that you may state it to the King and his principal ministers: saying at the same time that the course we have been compelled to adopt is an unpleasing one to us, our desire always being to please the King; but it has been entirely brought about by the fault of the King's officers, who have prevented us from carrying out our wishes in this respect. From the beginning of the war they have refused to credit any of the advice given to them; although they have discovered that by going their own way they have erred. In addition to the expense they have incurred, the King has received no service at all from the troops they have brought. The disposition of soldiers is often bad enough, but these men are incorrigible in their fault of refusing to listen to the natives of the country, and wishing to play the master wherever they pass, entirely disregarding their promises to avoid injuring the poor subjects. If the King's service is retarded by this untoward proceeding we shall be sorry, but if in his wisdom he looks at the matter with due consideration and will remember the manner in which the poor subjects of this country and of Liège were treated in the last two years; he will acknowledge that our duty towards God, the Emperor, and his people, compels us to provide for their protection, and to prevent the passage of troops in the same style as in the previous years. The King's officers have from the first failed to fulfil their promises; and consequently, unless Penninck comes previously to see us, the infantry he commands will be opposed in any attempt they may make to advance; and the blame must not be imputed to us, but to the obstinacy of the King's officers. The Count de Roeulx declares that it would be very good if the King of England were to order that no pillage was to be taken from the subjects of the bailiwick of Hesdin,

1546.

which belongs to the Emperor, although the King of France occupies the fortress.* It would be a great benefit to the county of Artois, as well as for the subjects of Hesdin itself; and from the latter folk the King might obtain some good service, as they are not well disposed towards the French. We have asked the English ambassadors to write to some of the Councillors on this point, and we believe he will send to Paget. If the King would send someone to discuss the matter with Roeulx he might perhaps find it to his advantage to do as is requested. We should be glad to hear of it, as the people consider themselves subjects of the Emperor, and might be useful to the King. Sound Paget about it if you can, and carry the matter through, if it can be done without making a noise. —1 April 1546.

1 April.
Paris.
Archives
Nationales.
K. 1486.

233. St. Mauris to Cobos

On my departure from this place to join the court at Melun, I think well to inform you that the King (of France) continues his tendency towards peace (*i.e.* with the Emperor) as I informed you was the case in my last letters. Whilst the Emperor was on his journey recently to Ratisbon, the King, through his ambassador, intimated to his Majesty his earnest desire to carry through the marriage already under discussion, and that a new alliance should also be effected in the persons of the Infante of Spain and the daughter who might be born to the Dauphine.† He insists also, that he (Francis I.) and his Majesty should recompense the Duke of Savoy for Piedmont, but makes no new offers beyond those he formerly made. The Emperor replied to the same effect as before, namely that Piedmont must be restored, the King of France retaining for the safety of his realm some strong places belonging to Savoy on this side of the mountains. With regard to the suggested new alliance, his Majesty replied that the more alliances the better, but without carrying the matter any further. The fact of the matter is that the King and his ministers think they will deceive his Majesty with talk of this sort.

A Venetian merchant now resident in London has had an interview with the King (Francis I.). He was sent hither by the Lord Admiral of England to sound the Admiral of France, and see if there was any way of reconciling the two sovereigns; hopes being held out that some arrangement might be made with regard to Boulogne, after a settlement had been effected on the points of the indemnity, the security for future payments etc. These people are listening to the suggestion; and the negotiations are now proceeding. I will report the result. If no conclusion is arrived at, the French are determined to direct the war this year exclusively to the recovery of Boulogne, without attempting to carry on hostilities in Scotland or England. I am trying to get a copy of their plans.

---

* This was one of the places that had to be surrendered by the French under the treaty of Crespy, but was still held by them.

† That is to say between the unfortunate Don Carlos, only son of Prince Philip, then a newly born infant, and the Princess (Isabel de Valois) to whom he was afterwards betrothed, and his father married. The Dauphine, of course, was Catherine de Medici.

1546.

I spoke recently to the King of France about the Spanish ships that were captured in November last by a Rochelle vessel, respecting which the Royal (Spanish) Council wrote to the Emperor. I have been unable to get any other satisfaction than that if the claimants will come hither their cases shall be adjudicated upon. This is only meant to embroil and delay matters. Commissioners appointed by the Emperor and by the King of France have met at Cambrai for the purpose of settling maritime affairs and the question of these armed ships; but the French would not agree to restore any of the plunder they have illegally captured since the peace. It will therefore be necessary to warn Spanish merchants trading in England not to carry any English property in their vessels, for in such case everything will be confiscated; and to take care they bring their manifests in the ships with them. The Emperor has also written to me that he will order Spanish ships in future to sail in flotillas for greater safety. If they do not do so they will be captured every day. It will also be necessary to stop the Scots in their depredations. I am told that at present they are lingering in the Breton ports for the purpose of molesting Spaniards. I intend very shortly to make a representation to the King of France on this subject, requesting him to take steps in the matter. The said Scottish corsairs have already been turned out of the Norman ports at my request.

The French and his Holiness are still at issue, and the prelates appointed to go to the Council (of Trent) are not leaving France until after the recess of the Diet of Ratisbon.

(Begs for the 500 crowns promised by Cobos to be sent to Melun). Paris, 1 April 1546.

5 April.
Vienna
Imp. Arch.

234. SCEPPERUS and VAN DER DELFT to the QUEEN DOWAGER.

We were invited by the principal Lords of the Council yesterday to visit them, and we were with them this afternoon at Westminster, where the King is at present staying. An hour before our interview we received your Majesty's letters of the 1st instant, but had not time to decipher them fully, though we gathered their substance. We found a numerous assembly of councillors; and the Bishop of Winchester addressed us, to the effect that they had been informed of two things: First, that your Majesty raised great difficulty in allowing the passage of Conrad Penninck and his troops through your Majesty's jurisdiction, a cavalry force having been ordered to oppose them. In addition to this, certain threatening and harsh words had been used to the King's Commissioners, who had been sent to request permission for these troops to pass, towards the person of Penninck and his men, and it was said also that when Penninck appeared before your Majesty he would be forced to take certain strict oaths, that might cause the entire undoing of his force, which had been assembled at great cost to the King, and was already at the place of muster. The second subject was your Majesty's refusal to allow transit for the grain now at Dortrecht, bought by the English at Cleves, Julliers and other markets outside of the Emperor's own territories. They (the Councillors) considered both these facts extremely strange, and not in accordance with the treaties made with the King or with the interpretation recently agreed upon with regard to the clauses. They therefore desired to learn from us what they had to expect with regard to these points, and expressly requested a prompt reply. If Penninck's men, to the number previously stated, were not allowed to pass, and the grain necessary for their sustenance refused transit, notwithstanding the English undertaking to replace in the Netherlands a similar quantity within six weeks, the King would take his own course.

We replied that, with regard to the first point of Penninck's troops, we were greatly astonished that he had changed the place of muster, which he had first designated at Nieuenhausen, and afterwards had altered to Alten, an abbey in the duchy of Gueldres, or, at all events, under the protection and keeping of the Duke of Gueldres; this change having been adopted without any notice being given to your Majesty, or rather to the Count de Buren or Count Hochstadt, the governor's of the emperor's dominions nearest to Nieuenhausen. Penninck, moreover, had not condescended to present himself to your Majesty once, to arrange in accord with you the road to be taken by his men, notwithstanding the dearness of provisions, and the almost utter desolation of the country. Without some such accord, if it had been allowed for Penninck's men to go by whichever road they liked, certain of the Emperor's subjects and others would have committed outrages under cover of them, and then have fled to France, to the prejudice of the King (of England). For this reason the Emperor had wisely ordered before his departure, that Penninck should be summoned to discuss and decide the route to be followed by his men, and to avoid their spreading all over the place. We could not believe that either he or his men would be forced to take any oath prejudicial to the friendship between the Emperor and the King; but that is necessary to prevent the subjects of the Emperor from being despoiled and ruined, since the King paid these troops so liberally. We concluded that the fault was to be imputed entirely to Penninck, a mercenary man who had served in several countries, and could not be ignorant of the fact that if he wished to pass through the territory of any prince, much less that of the Emperor, it was only right that he should agree beforehand with the sovereign as to which road he should follow. If he had neglected to do this, the fault was his own, and must not be attributed to any hindrance opposed by your Majesty. With regard to the second point about the grain : some of the councillors had informed us eight or ten days ago, that the said grain had been purchased outside the Emperor's dominions, which made it probable that no such great objection would be raised to their request, as would be the case if it had been grown in the imperial territory. We had, however, been informed that your Majesty had granted transit for 100 lasts of grain from Westland (Oestlandt) to be sent from Amsterdam, instead of the 400 lasts requested by the English Ambassador. This, we said, was a good beginning. With regard to the 400 lasts at Dortrecht, a considerable quantity of this grain had been harvested in the Emperor's territory, which was greatly pressed with famine and dearness. The King therefore, ought not to take any offence at this matter for, charity begins at home (*charitas incipet a se*

1546.

ipsa). Their reply to this was that they desired to know what our opinion was on both points. If Penninck was not to be allowed to pass, the King would have to consider what course he should take with regard to him before incurring further expense on his account. As to the grain they (the English) could not do without it, and they considered that the offer they had made to replace it with a similar quantity in six weeks was a very reasonable one, and their request could not be refused without violating the clauses of the treaty of alliance. We assured them that we felt certain that no obstacle would be placed in the way of Penninck's passage, when he had arranged with your Majesty the road he should take; and with regard to the grain, that everything that could be possibly done to please them should be done. We promised to report to your Majesty the discourse on both points, and to beg you to bear them in favourable consideration. Under correction, Madame, we really think you should do so, especially in the present state of affairs, and the possibility of great changes arising out of this business, as we recently wrote to your Majesty. It is worthy of close consideration, and we urgently beseech your Majesty not to overlook it, for many good reasons, some of which with other points of importance we write to your Majesty by a special courier; this present letter, in order to accelerate the passage of Penninck, being sent, at the request of the Councillors, by their own courier, as they say that an hour's further delay of Penninck may ruin their entire undertaking, and cause them immense loss, the blame for which they will afterwards attribute to your Majesty.

London, 5 April 1546.

5 April.
Vienna,
Imp. Arch.

235. The EMPEROR to VAN DER DELFT.

We duly received your letter of the 10th ultimo, and the joint letter of yourself and M. D'Eick of 22nd ultimo. Having considered them and M. D'Eick's communication to M. de Granvelle respecting his (D'Eick's) return, we find that you have done very well, and have followed your instructions, both with regard to our desire to continue our friendship with the King, and in the matter of the marriage of the Prince of England. We consider that you gave good and fitting answers to the King's council, and especially in regard to our justification, in the contention that we are not bound to provide the aid they request, and the depredations, embargoes and other points comprised in your instructions. We suppose that M. D'Eick will have already left England, and we therefore again depend upon you to press these points as you see fitting; but without again referring to the matter of the marriage. If they approach the subject in conversation with you, you will confine yourself to the expressions contained in the instructions of M. D'Eick, and to those employed by him in reply to the English councillors. You will remind them that they were to write to their ambassador here on the subject; and if they ask you to write, you may say that you will use your best offices, but that you have no further instructions. If you see a good opportunity in discourse with the Bishop of Winchester, you may say that M. D'Eick was specially instructed to mention the marriage, in consequence of his (the Bishop of Winchester's) remark that he thought it advisable that the matter should be discussed. With regard to the war preparations, and other occurrences you mention in your said letters, we thank you for your advices, and shall be glad if you will send information as often as possible to us or to the Queen Dowager.

Dunkelspiel, 5 April 1546.

236. Schepperus and Van der Delft to the Queen Dowager.

6 April. Vienna. Imp. Arch.

Your Majesty will have learnt from the recent letters addressed by us to your Majesty and to the Emperor, details of our intercourse with the principal ministers of the King, respecting the two main questions dealt with in your Majesty's letter of 24th ultimo, namely the passage of Penninck's troops, and the transit of grain, also mentioned in your Majesty's letter of 1st instant, received at noon yesterday. As our letter to you of yesterday was handed to Paget for transmission, we think well to describe afresh certain points and expressions which occurred in the course of the negotiations, and other events. We beg to inform you that a Venetian named Francisco Bernardi, the master of a large Venetian ship, has been for some time past in the service of the King,° and has been employed by the ministers in conducting secret communications between France and England, without the knowledge of the Venetian secretary (Zambon) who is here for the seigniory. At least, so the secretary swears to us, and we have always hitherto found him a truthful man. This Francisco has already been to France once and returned immediately hither. The object of this can only be one of two, namely to agree upon some truce or peace between the two realms, or else to hoodwink the French with the hope of some such arrangement, and so to cause them to slacken in their undertaking, as was the case last year. It is, in our opinion, quite true that the Seigniory has no wish to see any increase of the Emperor's power in Italy; and that the aggrandisement of Sir Pierre Loys† is regarded by them (*i.e.* the Venetian Seigniory) with distrust; but still we cannot believe that the Seigniory would enter into any league or alliance to the prejudice of the Emperor. We have sounded the Venetian Secretary on this subject, and he is of the same opinion. But, however that may be, these people (*i.e.* the English) are evidently not without hope that something important is impending, either by means of Bernardi or otherwise. We saw this very plainly by the expressions used towards us during yesterday's conference; such, for instance, as that if Penninck was not to be allowed to pass, the King must take his own course; and that he thought it very strange that so little account was made of him

---

° Doubtless the great "Galeazza di Londra," which had been requisitioned by Henry for his service in the war. The envoy was a nephew of the Venetian noble Ser Mafio Bernardo, who was accused later in the year 1546 of divulging State secrets, and fled to Ravenna, where he was murdered by the connivance of his other nephews, the Erizzi and the envoy of England, Ludovico delle Arme who was beheaded for the crime.

† That is Pier Luigi Farnese, the Pope's son, Duke of Castro, and nominated Duke of Parma and Piacenza. The Pope's vehement desire to secure Italian sovereignties for his son was a constant menace to all the States, and was, as these letters show, the keynote of the policy of Paul III.

1546.
(Henry) by us, as he got nothing from us but hollow words, and he saw, even so soon as this after the agreement as to the interpretation of the treaty had been made, that things were going on in the old way. The Councillors expressed more surprise than at anything else, that we should say that we must take care not to offend the French, and that if we gave them (the English) permission to draw the supplies they required from the Emperor's territories, we could not deny the French a similar privilege. They (the English Councillors) regard it as a great injustice to them to compare them with the French, the ancient foes of Flanders, of which they (the English) have always been the friends. They (the Councillors) could not conceal the annoyance they feel at being left alone in this war; and some of them appear greatly displeased that the King has refused to ally himself with the Protestants, by means of whom they hoped to obtain the troops and supplies they needed, and to be able to gather their men where they pleased, instead of being, as now, hindered and obstructed. They attribute the latter trouble to Penninck's change of place for his muster. He originally fixed upon Nieuenhausen, but afterwards changed the place to Alten, as he had written to them (i.e. the English) that the Protestants had warned him not to muster any men in their country, or they would come and dislodge them. He was therefore obliged, he said, to go to Alten; which was a place not belonging to the Emperor's patrimony, the abbess of Alten having given her consent to the muster taking place there. They (the Councillors) considered it extremely strange when they heard that it was your Majesty's intention to force the men to retire from there, before your four bands of cavalry, and to capture Penninck himself. This, they said, was quite contrary to the good hope and confidence they had reposed in your Majesty, who, they had thought, would promote and aid their master's interests, rather than obstruct them. They (the Councillors) used quite vehement words on this point; and we failed not to reply suitably to them. If, we said, Penninck had been so careful to respect the wishes of the Protestants, he should also have respected those of the Emperor, and not have assembled his men on Gueldres territory, Alten being attached thereto for many years, and being entirely surrounded by towns and villages belonging to Gueldres, with the exception of one point where it abuts upon Cleves. When musters of men are made the whole surrounding country is affected by them, far more than by the mere passage of a larger number. By this we inferred that neither Penninck nor their commissioners had done their duty, and that the only remedy for the matter that occurred to us was for Penninck to be sent to your Majesty, if he had not already gone thither. We were, however, quite unable to satisfy or appease them, even though they thought that Penninck had already gone to your Majesty, as they fear that on the appearance of the four bands of cavalry, the foot soldiers that they (the English) have engaged and paid for a month, will disperse and carry their wages with them, either with or without the connivance of Penninck himself, who makes this his excuse for breaking his engagement. Thus not only will the King their master suffer a dead loss but the whole of his plans will be upset. We did our best to allay

1546.

their anxiety, saying that we had good hope that Penninck would easily settle with your Majesty as to the road he and his men should take, and the matter would thus be accelerated. We used the fairest words we could, in order not to drive them to utter despair: for they took good care to repeat that they had entered upon this war for the Emperor's sake; and reason demanded that they should be better treated than they are. Reverting again to the matter of the grain, etc., they maintained that under the treaty it was licit for them to convey through the Emperor's territory, in transit, all sorts of grain, etc., purchased elsewhere; either in Westland (Oestlandt), Cleves or Julliers. With regard to the bread stuffs from the Emperor's own territories, the treaty lays down that, according to the circumstances and seasons of the countries in question, the English are to be supplied at a reasonable price; and M. de Granvelle, and the President (*i.e.* the President of the Flemish Council, Loys Scors) had also held out hopes of this being done at their meeting with the Bishop of Winchester and his colleagues at Maestricht; always having regard to the needs of the Emperor's own territory, in accordance with the axiom which we laid down that charity begins at home. At this point certain of the principal and best-disposed of the Councillors, desirous of serving the Emperor's interest, said that, in order that it might not be thought that they wished to importune your Majesty for anything unreasonable, for the purpose of feeding their troops across the sea, they had agreed amongst themselves to reduce their own table expenses, and to send what they could spare for the maintenance of their forces. At the same time they trusted that, at all events, some help would be given to them on the other side (*i.e.*, in Flanders, etc.) in accordance with the treaty. They were willing, they said, to pay the present current prices, which they knew were high; and they reminded us again that they only asked for the export of the 400 lasts from Dortrecht as a loan for six weeks, as we wrote to your Majesty before, Erasmus Schetz and two other merchants undertaking to deliver a similar quantity for the use of the Emperor's subjects. They (the Councillors) said they wished to know, in few words, what they had to expect, adding these words in Latin "*Aliquid dat qui cito negat*"; and showing a good deal of displeasure. We took our principal stand on the scarcity and dearness on the other side, avoiding entering into dispute on the details, as we thought that the time for that had not yet come, and that it was inopportune for us at the present juncture to drive these people to despair, they being folks who rush from one extreme to another without stopping on the middle course. We know, to some extent, how important it is for the interests of his imperial Majesty and of his countries, especially the Netherlands, etc., to gain the present summer season with as little loss to the subjects as possible; and we pray your Majesty to take our proceedings in good part, bearing in mind that these people cannot be held much longer by words.

With regard to the other points, no opportunity has yet occurred for us to speak upon them; but we will do our duty in this and all other respects. Duke Philip of Bavaria has not come hither (as we are directly informed) for the purpose of getting married, but

1546.

to offer his services to the King. It is rumoured that he is to have charge of 25 standards of infantry and a considerable body of cavalry. Other people say that Duke Maurice (of Saxony) is to have command of a large army to lead it against France, and that the Marquis Albert of Brandenburg, son of Casimir, is authorised to join with 2,500 horse. We learn this from private people, having been unable to gain intelligence of it from other sources, which does not appear to be a peaceful sign. But still, measures do not seem to be so rapidly conducted here as would be necessary in such case; and we are of opinion that it may all be a feint, with the object of raising their prestige in the eyes of their enemies and of putting the latter to more expense.

Your Majesty will know better than we what they (the English) are doing on the other side of the sea, in St. John's roads, and in the flying siege which they say they have now placed before Ardres. It is certain that their forces in the field are daily increased by the joining of gentlemen of the King's household, both English and foreigners, in his service, especially Spaniards, soldiers of renown. With regard to Scotland nothing of importance is being done, both sides simply watching the frontiers.

Councillor Adrien Van der Burgh arrived here yesterday week, and we informed the King of his coming. Nicholas Wotton, formerly ambassador to the Emperor and an intimate councillor of the King, has been appointed with Dr. Petre to confer with us on this negotiation, and we hope to make a beginning to-morrow. We do not yet know, however, who is to represent the King in conjunction with the ambassador Carne, as a worthy man named Dr. Barbe, who had been nominated for the mission, died six days ago.

With respect to the aid demanded by the English, and the negotiations for the marriage of your niece and the prince, not a word has been said since Paget spoke to us about them. We suppose they want us to speak first about the marriage. We will be ruled on this point by the letters we expect from your Majesty. I. Scepperus, remain here as you command me. London, 6 April, 1546.

April 6.
Vienna.
Imp. Arch.

237. SCEPPERUS and VAN DER DELFT to the QUEEN DOWAGER.

After the present courier had started and was already on the road we learnt from a trustworthy source that this King had agreed with the Protestants to provide them with a certain sum of money, which he assures them. It appears that this negotiation has been in progress for some time, but the Protestants asked for an altogether excessive sum; which demand they afterwards moderated by means of the Count Palatine, Elector. This probably was one of the principal motives for the coming hither of Duke Philip of Bavaria, Count Palatine, in addition to the idea of the marriage which he desired, and which no doubt encouraged him to take the journey. For the final conclusion of the business Secretary Mason, now the King's postmaster, was to go thither. He has hitherto been considered a worthy man, and, so far as can be judged by outward appearance, has a hatred of innovations. This information caused us to delay the courier for a tide, and in the meanwhile we had weighed

1546.

the subject carefully. I, Scepperus, have often on former occasions, by command of your Majesties, visited persons of various sorts and conditions; and it occurs to me that this negotiation may possibly have been carried out for the purpose of enabling the King to make use of the Protestants, or at least to make his neighbours think that he may do so, for the reasons mentioned in our letters referring to the Venetian's (*i.e.* Bernardi's) intrigue. I am confirmed in this view by my recollection that I heard some time since that the Protestants had decided to receive him (the King of England) into their league, on his depositing in their hands a sum of money, in the same way that they received the King of Denmark for forty thousand gold florins* under certain private reservations and conditions. The report, whether true or false, may originate with the coming of a courier hither yesterday from Germany, the holding of a secret conference to-day in Duke Philip's chamber, and the search by Mason for four or five footmen speaking our language; although this, too, may be all a contrivance to deceive people, as your Majesties will understand. Nevertheless we have considered it our duty to send this report.

London, 6 April 1546.

Note. Accompanying the above letter (of which, according to an endorsement, the original was forwarded by the Queen Dowager to the Emperor) there is a short holograph private letter from Van der Delft to the Queen Dowager. He prays her Majesty most urgently to bear his needs in mind. His expenses are so great that he can carry the fardel no longer without falling into utter ruin and desolation, unless their Majesties will take pity on him and withdraw him from here, or increase his pay. Attached to this letter there is a statement of 7 pages headed "Statement of the expenses which I, François Van der Delft, have to maintain in my post as ambassador from the Emperor to the King of England."

April 6.
Vienna.
Imp. Arch.

238. Scepperus to Loys Scors.

The Imperial Ambassador and myself received your letters of 1st April, and knowing how busy you must have been on that day we thank you the more heartily for them.

We are glad to learn that you had conversed with the English Ambassador on the previous evening, and had found him kinder, as, in good truth, was fitting. But sometimes the faults of such people, accustomed to presume unduly, are great, and can only be remedied by good discretion and well-founded arguments such as you used............ Pray consider whether a few lasts of wheat might not be given to Lord Cobham, Deputy of Calais, for the nourishment of his household. Some of the principal of the King's ministers who have always been well disposed towards the Emperor's service have spoken to us on this subject; and have pressed the request. They ask for forty lasts, which we know is a large number, but they suggest that at least some smaller quantity

---

* It is curious that this is the exact sum that was to be handed to Duke Philip as dowry with the Princess Mary, the pretended match being apparently merely a feint.

1546.

might be granted to him. Lord Cobham and his friends may be very useful. We have not mentioned the matter to the Queen (Dowager of Hungary).

(He recommends Van der Delft's brother-in-law Jacques Hertzen, doctor of laws of Antwerp, to be made burgomaster of that town.) I do not dare to write to you several rumours current here with regard to the feminine sex. Some change is suspected to be pending in this respect; but I can say no more for the present.°

London, 6 April 1546.

April 6.
Paris.
Archives
Nationales.
K. 1486.

239. ST. MAURIS to COBOS.

In addition to my other news, I may say that the man who opened the negotiations for peace with England has returned hither with the message that if the Admiral of France will go to the frontier of Boulogne the Admiral of England will be there to meet him, and they can then discuss the settlement of peace. The Admiral of France is already there; not having gone thither, however, with that object, but to drive away 8,000 Englishmen who recently crossed the sea for the purpose of holding the passage, and of forcing the port of Etaples, which the King of France has fortified. The King of England wishes to hold Boulogne and all its territory until the King of France has paid him his overdue pensions, etc., in four instalments, the failure to pay any one of which to render nugatory all previous payments. The King of England asks for hostages, to be the highest personages in France; and demands in addition an exorbitant sum as a war indemnity, and for his expenditure in the fortification of Boulogne. I do not know yet whether the King of France will continue the negotiations on these bases; although the English have sent to say that if he does not entrust the negotiations to his Admiral they beg he will send a churchman to represent him. My own opinion is that it will all end in smoke, for the French will not consent to the retention of Boulogne by England.

The commissioners who met at Cambrai have separated without doing anything; and it will therefore be advisable to safeguard Spanish navigation, instructing shipmasters not to violate the French regulations, or they may be captured and lose all their merchandise.

I have learnt that the Scottish corsairs are now in the Breton ports, after having captured some Spanish shipping. I have complained of this to the King and to the Dauphin, and they have written to the corsairs, ordering them immediately to surrender such captures, and to refrain in future from molesting the Emperor's subjects. Still it will be prudent for Spanish ships to take due precautions for their safety on their voyages to Brittany.

The Queen Dowager of Hungary is at Cambrai, whence she goes to Artois to visit the Flemish frontiers. All is tranquil there. Notwithstanding all this talk of peace between the English and French, both sides are preparing for continuing the war.

° This evidently refers to the rumours of the King's intention to divorce Queen Catharine Parr.

1546.

I may add that the Venetian who is the peace intermediary passed through here (*i.e.* Paris) on his way to Boulogne two days since. He is accompanied by Monluc, to represent the King of France in arranging the amount of the war indemnity and the works at Boulogne, and also to endeavour to bring about a meeting between the Admirals of France and England. There is at present a rumour at Court that the prospects of peace are hopeful.

April 7.
Simancas
E. F. 502.

240. The EMPEROR to JUAN DE VEGA.

Approves of his answer to the Pope, respecting the proposal made by Cardinal Gambara and the Bishop of Ancona that his Holiness should remain neutral.

The Pope has conceived the idea of sending a Legate to mediate a permanent peace (*i.e.* between the Emperor and France) but former experience has shown how fruitless such endeavours usually are. You may tell his Holiness that the treaty at present in force suffices to make the opening of the Council (of Trent) possible, and consequently there is no immediate need for a more intimate alliance.

Let us know very carefully all you can learn relative to the Council (of Trent), and see that nothing is changed from what has been agreed upon. Cardinal Farnese has declared that the Council might become a source of great trouble, both to the Pope and us: but it is clear that this language is only used for the purpose of extorting better conditions for themselves. The King of France, as you say, has asked the Pope's assistance against England, and has been granted tenths. It is now known that the King will not be satisfied unless he gets four tenths. The French, moreover, are pressing the Pope to succour the Scots in their contest with the King of England; and at the same time are endeavouring to bring about a marriage between the daughter of Scotland and the son of the King of England. This is an entire innovation in French policy. It is impossible for us to mention the source from which this knowledge is derived: but it is undoubted. We note that his Holiness is discussing with Cardinal Carpi the possibility of an enterprise against England; and that the Pope, considering the subjection of England to be easy, is endeavouring to persuade the Cardinal that it would be better to begin with England rather than with Germany. The Cardinal, in his reply at the time, and his subsequent extended answer, after conference with you, with the object of concealing from the Pope all inkling of our real designs, spoke wisely and judiciously. We approve of all your suggestions in this respect. The hatred of the Pope to the King of England will doubtless be diligently fomented by the French, in order to obtain his sanction and support for their plans; and so to make better terms for themselves with England, perhaps even to the prejudice of religion itself.

With regard to Scotland, we may inform you that the French have no intention of carrying on the war in that quarter this year, and have sent an envoy to Scotland for the purpose of persuading the Queen to consent to the marriage of her daughter with the son of the King of England.

1546.

You must be very vigilant in watching the Pope's proceedings, respecting the enterprise in Germany. Do not mention to his Holiness the Bull about Parma and Piacenza, but be careful to report to us everything you hear on the subject. We note that the Pope was displeased that in a letter written to Pier Luigi he was not given the title of Parma and Piacenza. Cardinal Farnese has already been informed that we cannot recognise his right to the title until his claims to the Duchies have been confirmed by the estates of the Empire.

The courier from Naples has just arrived, bringing your letter of 23 March. We are greatly astonished and grieved at the final declaration of the Pope, to the effect that he will not deliver the brief authorising the sale of the monastic manors until we have ratified the treaty of alliance for the enterprise (*i.e.* against the Protestants). We have explained to the Bishop of Caserta and the Papal Nuncios that, if we signed the treaty before taking measures for our security, both our own life and that of our brother the King of the Romans would be endangered. You had better speak to Cardinal Farnese again on the subject, and to the Pope as well; urging them most forcibly to despatch the brief.

Pier Luigi (Farnese) will have to wait for the order of the Golden Fleece. It cannot be given to him at present, or at least until we see how affairs progress.

Tanaberth, 7 April 1546.

No Date, but probably referred to in the preceding letter.
Simancas.
E. Flanders, 505.

241. M. DE GRANVELLE'S opinion on CARDINAL GAMBARA'S discourse.

As is the case with the proposals made by the Friar with regard to England, Cardinal Gambara's discourse must be considered in the light of the possible intentions and ends of the Pope and his friends, who have unquestionably prompted the suggestions with the idea of befooling the Emperor, and so either to delay or to shirk altogether doing anything with regard to the Council (of Trent) or against the Turk; perhaps even to have an opportunity of throwing obstacles in the way of peace and disturb the tranquillity of Italy. It may be confidently concluded that what is said about the Duke of Ferrara is true; and no doubt they (the Papal party) are as anxious as they say in this story they tell about the Duke, seeing their relationship and sympathy, and the negotiations we have already witnessed of Cardinals Ferrara and Farnese. But in the present circumstances I do not think it will be advisable to enter into this present proposal, both for the reasons above stated and for others contained in many of Juan de Vega's letters; in addition to which Don Diego de Mendoza writes from Trent that the only thing by which the Pope and his friends will be moved is fear and that the present is the best time for isolating them. But still it

---

* The Pope considered that improper use had been made prematurely of the authority to appropriate the half-first-fruits on Spanish ecclesiastical preferments, before the treaty binding the Emperor to employ the funds in the religious war had been ratified. His deep distrust of the Emperor is evident in this; and he was determined that no such course should be taken in the case of the brief for the sale of the Spanish monastic manors, which, as will be seen later, he subsequently refused to confirm.

1546.

will not be wise to break the thread of this negotiation entirely, as they are displeased with the French, and if we refrain from repulsing them (*i.e.* the Papal party) altogether, they will still hope to deal with his Majesty and, underhand, to serve their own purposes in respect of the proposals contained in this discourse, namely to invest the Duke of Camarino. A reply might be given to the effect that his Majesty thanks Cardinal Gambara for his information, knowing the devotion and goodwill he has always borne towards his Majesty; but the condition of affairs of Christendom such as it is at present, the first consideration must be religious uniformity and the resistance to the Turk. When these two points are attended to others may be considered, and suitable means devised for the public and private benefit; the matters brought forward by Cardinal Gambara will receive due attention. We ought not to go beyond this, nor at present refer anything to Juan de Vega or others, to avoid giving the idea that we are ready to enter deeply into this negotiation now, which will only hinder the two main points and prevent the Pope from agreeing to reason.

April 8.
Simancas.
E. R. 873.

242. JUAN DE VEGA to the EMPEROR.

About four days ago Cardinal Farnese had a long conversation with Madame* in which he suggested to her that it would be well to induce your Majesty to employ Duke Ottavio in the Milan command, failing the Marquis (Guasto). He (Farnese) thought that it would be better that the matter should proceed from her Excellency, and expressed the earnest wish of the Pope and all of them (*i.e.* the Farneses) for her aggrandisement—with much more to the same effect. He suggested to her that it would be well to send some person to your Majesty on the subject, and proposed Lope de Guzman. Madame was reticent, and the Cardinal seeing that she did not second the idea as he wished, called Lope de Guzman, who was out of the way, and told him what he had said to Madame. Lope hesitated a good deal, and the Cardinal became embarrassed, begging Lope to speak out frankly what was in his mind. Lope replied as cleverly as he could, that he thought they ought not to ask your Majesty anything of the kind, and he himself declined the mission with which they wished to entrust him. As these people (*i.e.* the Farneses) are so cunning, I thought the object of the manœuvre was to fill Madame's head with wind rather than with any idea of being able to bring about what they suggested, and I therefore did not consider it worth while to report the matter to your Majesty in the other letter. But after I had closed the latter Cardinal Carpi informed me that Alexander Vitello† came to him this morning with a similar suggestion, about which he made a long discourse, and begged Carpi to give his opinion of it, and also as to the person who should

---

* This was the Emperor's illegitimate daughter, the wife of Octavio Farnese the Pope's grandson. It was one of the plans of Paul III. to aggrandise his family that the vacant duchy of Milan might be given to Octavio, but this did not suit the Emperor, who sent Ferrante Gonzaga there as Governor in succession to the Marquis del Guasto and in the following year granted the duchy to Prince Philip.

† The Commander of the Pope's forces and a confidential agent.

1546.

be sent to your Majesty. The Cardinal replied as modestly as he could, raising some difficulty about the matter, and refraining from expressing any approval of it. It is evident, therefore, that they are in earnest about the business. I learn also from a trustworthy source that the Pope is determined to make Cardinals at the four seasons of the Holy Ghost. The Pope has news that Barbarossa has lost his sight and hearing, and that Lufti Pasha had consequently been put in his place. Lufti is the son-in-law of the Turk, and it is said that an army is being raised to send against the Georgians; but I have received letters from the Secretary whom Don Diego (Hurtado de Mendoza) left in Venice, and from Don Diego himself, making no mention of this.

Rome, 8 April 1546.

April 12.
Vienna
Imp. Arch.

243. SCEPPERUS and VAN DER DELFT to the EMPEROR.

We have refrained from writing to your Majesty up to the present time because since our letters of 27th ultimo we have had nothing to say, having had no communication with the King's Ministers, except on the matter of passage of Penninck's troops through your Majesty's territory; and also that of a quantity of wheat. We found the ministers vehement in their language on these points, complaining that we gave them nothing but fine words without effect. We did not let this reproach pass without a fitting reply, as we have related in our letter to the Queen (Dowager). They made no mention whatever about the marriage or the aid: but as the Duke Palatine Philip has taken his leave, and starts to-day for Germany accompanied by one of the King's secretaries named Mason,[*] a man well esteemed, we have thought necessary to report to your Majesty what we have been able to gather about the mission of the Duke Palatine. We cannot affirm the correctness of our intelligence, as nothing has been said to us about the matter on the King's behalf. We hear, however, that the Duke's principal objects were three; first to concert with the King a league between him and the Protestants; secondly to offer him some troops if he needed them; and thirdly to treat with the marriage of Lady Mary, which has been under discussion for so long. The King has decided to enter into the negotiation for the league, and with that object is sending Secretary Mason; secondly to authorise the Duke Palatine to hire 10,000 infantry, including six standards of Low Germans, and two or three thousand horse; and thirdly to defer the marriage referred to for some time longer.

Although our advices from several quarters agree on these points, and, so far as regards the league, they are to some extent confirmed by the remarks of the ministers, to the effect that we wanted to put our foot on their necks, and were pressing them too far, so they must take care of themselves, and other similar bitter expressions, showing their discontent; still we cannot believe that the King has decided to accept the league, seeing that the majority of his Council are against it, and that he would thus be violating his alliance with your Majesty. With regard to the second point; as they (the

---

[*] Sir John Mason, who was subsequently English Ambassador to the Emperor.

1546.

English) have no hope whatever of gaining any more French territory, since the French have fortified Etaples and Hardelot, we perceive that they are growing tired of the war, and are inclined to a peace or a truce after they have finished the new fort of Maraise, which is very important to them. Besides, they must know that 10,000 infantry and two or three thousand horse would not be able one by one to enter France, and without your Majesty's permission they cannot pass through Flanders; and in addition to this they do not trust Germans over much, provisions are extremely dear, and it is clear that they have not time this season to put an army in the field. All these and other reasons well known to your Majesty make us think (under correction) that their action is simply ostentation and buckler-play for the purpose of deceiving the French and Germans. We cannot believe that they are anxious thus to hazard their money.

As to the marriage of the Duke Palatine, we know that when he took leave of the Queen, he went to Lady Mary, and conversed with her for more than an hour, although she was indisposed. She received him well, but some of the principal people in the realm, clergy and others, exhibit displeasure at the Duke's public remark to them that he had never heard mass until he came hither. For this and other reasons the marriage is not liked, which may well frustrate the object, whatever it may be. Your Majesty will be better able to learn the truth about the coming of the Duke and the mission of Secretary Mason; and also of the understanding the King may have with the Duke Maurice of Saxony and the Marquis Albert of Brandenburg, with whom we are informed he has his agents, although the latter are not persons of importance.

We have entered into conference with the King's Commissioners with regard to the customs tariff* (tonlieux) and the claims of your Majesty's subjects. The Commissioners are Sir William Petre, one of the principal secretaries of the King, and Nicholas Wotton, formerly ambassador to your Majesty; and we have found them ready to adopt a reasonable and equitable view. We are, however, afraid that the embargo of their ships in Spain, of which the release is refused, even against security, will render our task extremely difficult; the more so, as they say they were told in Spain that the ships would not be released on security for your Majesty's ambassador, or even for your Majesty yourself. This gave to Paget, who was authorised to settle Renegat's affair, the opportunity of saying to us that he would have no more to do with it; and that the only way for them was to make peace (*i.e.* with France).

London, 12 April.

April 12.
Vienna.
Imp. Arch.

244. SCEPPERUS and VAN DER DELFT to the QUEEN DOWAGER.

Your Majesty will learn from our letters to the Emperor what has passed here with regard to the Duke Philip, Count Palatine. It is said that he will cross the sea as soon as the wind serves, and if

---

* The question of the tariff arose from a complaint made by the Flemings that duties were imposed on goods in England in violation of old commercial agreements. For the purpose of deciding this question the old Customs books and agreements on both sides were to be inspected; the result being, as will be seen, that the English were justified in their action.

1546.

not he will go by way of Calais. To-day we shall inspect the Customs registers and tax accounts, and, so far as we can judge, these people are proceeding honestly in the matter. We have every hope of settling the first point, in accordance with equity and reason.

We have not been able to speak to Paget on the two points touching the bailiwick of Hesdin, and the cattle taken by Lord Grey, as he, Paget, has been much occupied—we know not whether with the affairs of Duke Philip or others. We also think that they (the English Councillors) are awaiting your Majesty's reply about the passage of Penninck and his men, and also the transit of some grain. Bread is becoming very scarce here, and all the grain they can collect is sent across the sea to feed their troops. We have heard nothing fresh about Francisco Bernardi, or anything else, and we are leaving these ministers alone, except the commissioners for the settlement of the two points.

The King is still at Westminster, but is returning to Greenwich this week. He will not leave this neighbourhood until Whitsuntide. He has taken measures against the depredations and robberies, which are of daily occurrence, but we do not know whether this will be effectual in suppressing them. London, 12 April 1546.

April 13.
Vienna.
Imp. Arch.

245. SCEPPERUS TO LOYS SCORS.

I remind you that when I was at Utrecht last I spoke to you, in accordance with a request from the English Council, with regard to some harquebusses belonging to the King of England seized in the Netherlands. You asked me at the time at what place the seizure of these harquebusses had been made, as certain harquebusses had been stopped at Dunkirk, which were said to belong to the King; but which, you were well informed, were really the property of a private merchant, if I recollect aright one Erasmus Schetz. I was unable to answer the question then as to who had made the seizure, or why it had been made, but since my return hither we have been informed for certain that the harquebusses in question were seized in the Zeeland Custom House at Antwerp. The Council here have accordingly requested us to ask for their release, and permission for other harquebusses which the King has ordered from Italy to pass through the Emperor's territories. These latter harquebusses are those that the Landgrave of Hesse seized on the Rhine, as you will see by the enclosed note signed by the first Secretary, Sir William Paget.[°]

London, 13 April 1546.

[°] The note, in Latin, still accompanies the letter. It sets forth that 2,500 harquebusses bought by the King in Italy had been stopped, part by the Landgrave of Hesse and part by the Duke of Wurtemburg. Some of them had been released and sent to Antwerp for shipment by Philip Suerz and his partners, but were seized there by the Prefect in July 1545. Paget begs for their release, and authority to export the rest, as they were all purchased in Italy for the King, and were merely in transit through the Emperor's dominions.

1546.
April 16.
Vienna.
Imp. Arch.

246. SCEPPERUS and VAN DER DELFT to the EMPEROR.

By your Majesty's letter to me, Van der Delft, written on the 5th instant at Dunkelspiel,° we learn that your Majesty was under the impression that I, Scepperus, had returned to the Queen (Dowager of Hungary). I should have done so if in the interim I had not received the Queen's instructions, dated the 1st instant, to remain here longer. Having signified to this King that I desired to know when I might take leave of him we had audience of him to-day. He received us graciously, and after he had given me leave to depart he expressed a hope that I would use my best offices in all things, and asked if we had no reply with regard to the matter we knew of, meaning the marriage. We answered, saying that the letters we had received made no mention whatever of it, and expressed our opinion that it would be extremely advisable that he should instruct his ambassador with your Majesty to represent his views, as the King of the Romans would be with your Majesty. The King made no reply to this, but changed the subject by saying that he had no desire but to remain friendly with your Majesty, although he knew that there had been misrepresentations made with regard to him in two or three quarters; but he paid no attention to them, and would not allow himself to be alienated from the friendship, alliance and pledges that bound him to your Majesty. He added that the contrivers of these intrigues would some day be known to your Majesty, and would receive their due reward. He wished us, he said, to inform your Majesty how he had been solicited by the French to enter into negotiations with them, and that if he would employ his Lord Admiral in the business the Admiral of France would meet him. In order to hear what the French had to say he was sending Secretary Paget to Calais, knowing very well at the same time that the object of the French was only to arouse distrust between your Majesty and him. In this, however, they would fail. If they proposed reasonable conditions he would listen to them, but otherwise he would stand his ground, neither doubting nor fearing anything; and with that he repeated very heartily his promise towards your Majesty, charging me, Scepperus, to convey his regards to the Queen (Dowager), who, as Regent of your Majesty's Netherlands, would always find him a good friend and brother. He then dismissed us graciously. So far as we can ascertain, this Duke Palatine Philip's business is nothing but buckler-play, as we wrote your Majesty previously. The Duke left here at three o'clock yesterday afternoon, and will go by Antwerp, where, it is said, he is to receive a large sum of money. The statement is made also that he is a pensioner of this King, with an allowance of 10,000 florins a year.

I, Scepperus, had decided to start for Flanders immediately, but the King's commissioners will come to-morrow to settle about the first of two points agreed upon at Utrecht, namely that respecting the Customs dues and imposts here, of which the Flemings complain; although we have seen that the English are fully justified by

---

° Vandenesse in his "Itinerary" says that Charles V. was at Dunkelspiel on the 3rd and 4th April, arriving at Ratisbon on the 10th.

1546.

their old registers, charters and controls, which we have inspected, for hundreds of years back up to the present time, as we have written to the Queen (Dowager). I have therefore decided to remain for to-morrow's conference.

London, 16 April 1546.

April 16.
Vienna.
Imp. Arch.

247. SCEPPERUS and VAN DER DELFT to the QUEEN DOWAGER.

Your Majesty will see by our letters to the Emperor the details of our interview with the King to-day; and I, Scepperus, hope to give a further personal relation to your Majesty as soon as God enables me to return, which will be as soon as possible. I have decided to take the sea route, though on the journey hither I did not find it so convenient as formerly. I wish, however, to avoid the annoyances of Calais, and also not to be obliged, out of civility, to salute the Duke Philip, Count Palatine, who is to stay at Calais for some days. We are anxious to pray your Majesty to order the captain of Gravelines to allow some fresh poultry, fish, and other similar things to pass for the Lord Admiral of England and Secretary Paget, who we find willing to exert themselves in favour of the settlement of the complaints made by the subjects of the Emperor. Paget has asked us to write to the captain of Gravelines on the subject.

London, 16 April 1546.

April (17?)
Vienna.
Imp. Arch.

248. The QUEEN DOWAGER to VAN DER DELFT and SCEPPERUS.

Your three letters of 5th and 6th instant to hand, the two of the latter date reaching us two days before the English Ambassador handed us the earlier letter. From them we learn of all that had passed between the English Councillors and yourselves, and the harsh words addressed to you with respect to the obstacles offered to the passage of Conrad Penninck's infantry; and also touching the wheat that had been shipped at Dortrecht. Penninck has since come hither; and after conferring with him we have consented to the passage of the soldiers, and the English Ambassador has undertaken to send word to the King etc.; and we have no doubt they will be mollified thereat, although if they would well consider the facts of the case they would have no cause for resentment against us, but should be grateful to us for the arrangements we have made. But still, since they maintain that we do nothing out of consideration for the King, but only give fine words without effect, and they are constantly blaming us for this, we wish you, on the first opportunity you can get, to ask for audience of the King, and assure him in our name that we have heard what the Councillors had said to you; and are extremely sorry that the King and they should have formed such an impression of us; although we think that up to the present we have done everything for him that could reasonably be expected of us. We intend in the future to act similarly, and to exert ourself to the utmost to preserve the good and sincere friendship between the Emperor and himself and between the respective countries and subjects. We will try to please and assist the King in all things, and can assure him that he will find no shortcoming on our part if his

1546.

ministers will reciprocate and do their duty by us. In order to prove to him that we have great and just cause to be offended with his officers, who entirely disregard the conditions on which concessions are made to them, we request the King to remember that from the first time that he asked for permission for Penninck's men to pass the Emperor's territory his ambassadors had been informed of the great injury that had already been inflicted on his Majesty's subjects, and those of Liège, by the troops raised for the King's service during the last two years, on the excuse of passing through the territories merely, although the King never received any efficient service from either of these levies. In order to avoid a similar evil in future, the Emperor decided that before he gave consent to the passage of Conrad Penninck's levies the said captain should come and confer with us, as was fitting; and we clearly signified to the ambassadors that if we could agree with Penninck about the details of the transit, permission would be given for the men to pass in small bands and not in a body; the condition also being that they must be assembled and mustered outside the Emperor's territories. Otherwise his Majesty the Emperor could not allow the men to pass at all, in order to avoid a repetition of the unpleasantness of the previous years. The ambassadors undertook to communicate this to Conrad Penninck, in order that he might proceed accordingly. And yet the muster-masters of the King have since tried to act entirely contrary, having in the first place wanted to make out that the consent to the passing had already been given, on condition that Penninck came to us, which the latter could not do (as he told us) before the muster; and subsequently they led the troops into the Emperor's dominions, and there passed the muster in direct violation of their undertaking. This gave us ample reason for adopting the measures necessary for preventing the passage of the men, in order to avoid falling into the same annoyances that were suffered previously. If the English muster-masters had listened to us the King would perhaps have received more efficient service from Landenberger and Von Reissenberg, or at least he would not have been so much cheated by them. As soon as Conrad Penninck came to us we attended to his business and granted the passport for the men so quickly that he could not say that he was delayed for two days. We sincerely hope that the King will be better served by these men than by the others; and, although we have been obliged by our duty to look to the protection of the subjects under our rule, the King should not take it in bad part, having regard to past events, and to the fact that his service has not been delayed in consequence. The King's officers state that the Abbess of Alten consented to the musters being taken there; but we have the letters of the Abbess denying this and complaining that the soldiers came boasting that they were going to muster there; and she says that if she consented that they should do so afterwards it was only because she was afraid, and wished to avoid still greater inconveniences. The King may be assured that we will not fail to do our best in this matter to maintain the friendship; but we resent the attempt on the part of his officers to do as they like here, as if they had the right to command us, which we do not at all under-

1546.

stand. We shall have enough to do on this occasion in hiding the transit of these troops from the French, who are already extremely offended; and if the matter is carefully considered it will really be seen that we are not treating the English and French equally, but are doing all we can to favour the English, whilst temporising as well as we may with the French.

With regard to the grain coming from Cleves and Julliers, which the King's officers say they wish to pass through the Emperor's territories, we should like to be able to meet the King's request as to this grain, and also that grown in this country, but the scarcity here is so very great as to be beyond expression, several poor people having died of famine; and great numbers for a long time past having eaten no bread but that made of wheat gleanings or beans, peas, barley or oats. We have had an enquiry made in various towns and find that the wheat in stock is not sufficient to feed the population until August; and we can see no other way of sustaining the subjects until the new wheat crop is ready except by retaining the wheat grown in Cleves and Julliers, which can only be exported through these territories, the expense of carrying it by land to any other place being so great as to be prohibitory. This course is the only one by which we can avert the impending famine. For the King's officers to say, as they do, that if we will allow the sailing of the wheat they have loaded they will bring an equivalent quantity more from Cleves and Julliers, may at first sight appear a not unreasonable proposition, but it is certain that the great scarcity and dearness of food here will not be remedied by such means; because by allowing the grain in question to leave, and afterwards supplying its place by bringing in a similar quantity, will not bring down the price at all. This is already so excessive that the poor people cannot pay it; the quantity usually sold for three (sous?) being now worth ten, and during the last fortnight even thirteen. The clamour of the people is so great as would move any heart to pity, and, as we say, there seems no way of helping them but by withholding the wheat coming from Cleves and Julliers. In addition to these facts we are informed that some of the merchants, seeing the close watch kept on the exportation of wheat here, have since devised a new scheme. They are usually in the habit of bringing the grain from Thilmont, which is the granary of Brabant, by way of Louvain and Antwerp to Holland; but they have now taken to carrying the wheat from Thilmont to Maestricht, where it is embarked on the Meuse and carried to Dortrecht and is there represented as grain from Cleves and Julliers. By this means it will be easy for them to denude Brabant of wheat. The English contend that by the terms of the last agreement we are bound to give free passage through these dominions for all they wish to send, victuals, horses, munitions or other things, but on consideration of the fourth clause of the treaty of Cambrai, together with the last agreement, we are of opinion that we are not so bound as regards such food as is urgently needed for the sustenance of the people here, but that our first duty is to provide that no famine should occur here before allowing any foodstuffs to go out for the nourishment of other people. We have fully stated all this to the English Ambassador here, who has promised to write it to England and to describe the great scarcity which he knows to exist here. You may also lay the facts before the English Council as you may consider fitting; but, notwithstanding all this, our anxiety to please the King has led us to give permission to the Ambassador to export from Amsterdam 100 lasts of wheat from Oestlandt, besides the 100 lasts previously authorised. This quantity will be sufficient to provision the fortresses and feed the troops in the field; and if we can obtain supplies of wheat from Oestlandt, as we hope to do, we will not fail to provide a further reasonable quantity for the King and his people. The King's officers talk about their having loaded 400 lasts at Dortrecht, but we have been unable to discover that they have ever shipped more than 80 lasts, in lieu of which we authorised the first 100 lasts from Oestlandt.

The deputies of the City of Antwerp, with a great number of merchants of various nations established in Antwerp, have been to Brussels for the purpose of laying before the Privy Council serious complaints of the depredations committed at sea by the armed forces in the service of the King of England. These attacks are of constant occurrence upon the merchant ships navigating between these countries and Spain and Italy; and the deputation stated that since the month of February last merchandise has been taken from such ships to the amount of 35,000 Flemish crowns. Not a ship is allowed to pass without the English pillaging something from her, and when the victims go to England to claim the restoration of their property they are ill-treated and personally attacked. The deputation demanded that some remedy should be adopted for this, or traffic in merchandise by sea must be abandoned. The President of the Council having referred the deputation to a subsequent consideration at this place (Binche) the representatives came hither and repeated their statements in the presence of the English Ambassador resident. We have requested the latter to convey the substance thereof to the King, in order that some measure may be adopted to avoid the abuses complained of, or otherwise his imperial Majesty would be forced to take the matter in hand himself, since the English armed forces are doing more damage to his subjects than to their enemies. We informed the deputation also that we were writing to you with instructions for you to press the matter upon the King, and recommended them to send some person to England thoroughly informed on the whole subject, who would be able to give you the information you required. The deputation, however, were not satisfied with this, but urged that we should decree the seizure of all English subjects and goods. We informed them that we were unable to do this, until we had first demanded from the King due restitution, and at last, although not without some regret, they agreed to this; and are sending thither a man with full instructions, and such proofs as they can obtain of the depredations. In the meanwhile we are forwarding to you the statement of claims to be made, and it has been handed to us, and request that you will forthwith lay it before the King and his Council, in order that reparation for the losses suffered by the merchants may be made on the presentation of proofs on their behalf, and that proper provision may be made in future for carrying out the agreement entered into last year with Secretary Paget,

1546.

providing that the subjects of these countries shall freely navigate without molestation from the King's forces, as is fitting for the observance and continuance of the existing friendship. Failing this it will be quite impossible for the people on this side to tolerate such injuries, and his imperial Majesty will have to provide other remedies, which may result in further trouble; as the merchants are pressing us urgently to decree a seizure, and we are willing to do so. You will handle this matter dexterously, in order that the persons despoiled, who are mostly Spaniards, may obtain some recompense for their losses: otherwise we see that we shall have another change of relations with the English. In order to provide for the future prevention of such trouble the King might insist that all of his ships of war that put to sea should give security that they will not injure his allies, who are of course the subjects of the Emperor, and that they will make proper declaration of all the prizes they capture at sea, as is the usual course when the intention is to act justly to everyone.

We asked the merchants if they were able to identify the men who plundered them, to which they replied that they were unable to do this: because when the merchantmen are overhauled by a man-of-war the mariners of the former have no means of knowing who their plunderers are. They only know that they are Englishmen. If the usual and proper course in similar cases be followed all prizes captured at sea are inspected by the Admiralty officers and an inventory taken of them; and the Councillors here think that this should be mentioned, though the sailors themselves would not bring it forward. Besides which they (the merchants, etc.) say that there are always dealers waiting in all the English ports to buy the plunder, and thus the goods arriving cannot well be traced. Nevertheless they will do their best to present their proofs as convincingly as possible.

The Antwerp deputation have handed us a letter setting forth the injuries and wrongs that people here have suffered at the hands of English sailors, and we are forwarding the document to you for consideration, and in order that you may see whether there is anything in it contrary to the treaty of alliance that is not included in the two preceding instructions taken thither by Councillor Van der Burgh. If such be the case you will embody it in your statement, and demand a fitting redress as with the other points contained in the instructions.

Binche, 17 (?) April 1546.

April 18.
Vienna.
Imp. Arch.

249. The EMPEROR to SCEPPERUS and VAN DER DELFT.

We wrote to you, Van der Delft, from Dunkelspiel under the impression that you, M. D'Eick, had returned to the Queen Dowager, as you wrote to M. de Granvelle that you intended to do. We have since received your letters of 26th ultimo. With regard to the request made to you by the Bishop of Winchester, the Master of the Horse and Secretary Paget, that you would write to our sister about the passage of Penninck's troops and the licence to export 400 lasts of grain, you will follow the Queen Dowager's instructions sent in reply to your letters. To these instructions we have nothing to add.

1546

We are likewise unable to add anything to the contents of M. D'Eick's instructions respecting the aid requested; and when you are again spoken to on the subject you will adhere closely to the directions there given for your guidance. If the English Councillors are not satisfied with this you will undertake to write to us and the Queen Dowager about it, but you will not go beyond.

Touching the observations which have been addressed to both of you separately by the Councillors, respecting the marriage, you have answered them admirably and quite as we wished. You will always be very careful to listen to all they have to say and try to understand their aim, but without going any further than you have hitherto done, in accordance with your instructions.

With regard to the going thither of the Duke Palatine Philip; according to what the English Ambassador told M. de Granvelle the object is to offer his services. There is, however, small likelihood of his being able to negotiate anything of consequence; though it will be advisable for you to discover all you can. Our Ambassador in France informs us that he hears that the English are negotiating a peace with the French: the matter being so far advanced that the only question still pending was that of the war indemnity and the fortifications of Boulogne. Monluc, he tells us, was to go to England about the business with a Venetian named Mafeo, and the Admirals of England and France were to meet and confer. You will do well to enquire into this and let us know what you can learn.

Regensburg (Ratisbon), 17 April 1546.

April 18.
Vienna
Imp. Arch.

250. The QUEEN DOWAGER to SCEPPERUS.

The object of the present is to reply specially to the remarks addressed to you by Paget respecting the esteem entertained for us by the King (of England), and repeated in your letter of 27th ultimo. It will be advisable for you, on the return thither of the gentleman who brought the present to us from the King, to visit the latter, and, under the pretext of the letters we write instructing you to thank him for his gift, to signify to him our ardent wish to preserve the ancient friendship between his house and ours. We desire nothing better than to be able to consolidate and perpetuate it to his successors: and we would not have failed to have given you letters of credence to the King, offering him the assurance of our continued kindness towards the advancement of the marriage which was under discussion between his son the prince and the daughter of my brother the King (of the Romans), only that when your instructions were drawn up we were absent from the Court. As the instructions were sent to you the instant of the Emperor's departure, and we were very busy taking leave of him etc., we had no leisure to send you the credence. Nevertheless, the King may rest assured that we shall do all we can to favour the matter (i.e. of the marriage) in accordance with what we may learn as to his wishes. You will confine yourself to these general terms until you receive a reply from his imperial Majesty to your letters of 27th ultimo, which should reach you soon.

1546.

The imperial Ambasssador in France writes that the French are misrepresenting your stay in England, saying that you were only sent to persuade the King not to make terms with the French and that next year the Emperor will join the King of England to invade France together. We have thought well to inform you of what they are saying, so that you may make some other pretence for your stay in England; such as that of watching the outcome of the present negotiations on private claims. The Venetian Ambassador might be informed of this, as he probably communicates his intelligence to the Venetian Ambassador in France.

Binche, 18 April 1546.

April 24.
Vienna.
Imp. Arch.

251. SCEPPERUS to the QUEEN DOWAGER.

(Sends copies of two letters from the Emperor to his ambassador in England, which the Queen had not received, dated Dunkelspiel, 5th April and Regensburg, 18 April.)

For the last ten or twelve days there is no appearance that the King of England or his Councillors are willing to settle any affairs, unless they be such that delay will prejudice the English.

Brussels, 24 April 1546.

April 24.
Simancas.
E. A. 642.

252. Document headed "Points of the private letter from his Majesty (the Emperor) to his Highness (Prince Philip) 24 April 1546."

His resolution with regard to the German enterprise has been adopted in consequence of the extreme need for redressing existing evils, in the interests of religion, and of the preservation of his Majesty's dominions and the House of Austria. The Emperor thinks of leaving Ratisbon and going to some place in the territory of the Duke of Bavaria. (Note for reply. "Since his Majesty has maturely considered what will be for the best, we can only pray to God that the affair may be as successful as his Majesty's zeal and devotion deserve.)

The Emperor hopes to have gathered his forces by the end of June; 40,000 men, with 12,000 Italians to be contributed by the Pope. The Emperor intends to obtain full security from his Holiness for the fulfilment of his promises.

The bills of exchange for the funds for the enterprise are to be obtained from Fuggers or Belzares; 150,000 or 200,000 ducats, and are to be made payable, if possible, at Augsburg or Nuremburg. They may be payable at sight or usance; but must be due before the enterprise is declared. (Note for reply. "The Grand Commander (*i.e.* Cobos) will write to his Majesty about the bills." A similar note is appended to all the financial paragraphs of the letter.) The Emperor will send to Genoa, and endeavour to obtain another bill for 150,000 ducats, to be covered by the proceeds of the half-first-fruits and the revenues of the military orders; the bills to fall due by the middle of June and to be paid in current money.

A further sum of 200,000 ducats will have to be placed in Flanders, to defray the expenses of the levy of 10,000 Low Germans and the 3,000 horse. This must be obtained on security of funds to be raised in Spain, and the bills of exchange be made

1546.

payable at Antwerp. No money should be obtained in Venice, as no sufficient amount will be found there. It is recapitulated that the bills of exchange above referred to, for 500,000 ducats, must be covered by the proceeds of the sources mentioned, and by the gold from the Indies, though the amount will be increased by the accruing interest. We are to obtain here (*i.e.* in Spain) from Fuggers, Belzares and the Genoese two bills for 300,000 or 400,000 ducats, on account of the items of supply already referred to and of the German revenues, payable by the beginning of June. With regard to the Genoese bills, it will be stipulated that they are to be covered by the first funds collected (*i.e.* from the half-first-fruits), in order that they (the Genoese) may not embarrass our negotiations. Arrangements must be made at once with regard to the realisation of the half-first-fruits, as the treaty will be signed (by the Pope) immediately. In order that he may be able to withdraw the Spanish troops from Piedmont for this enterprise the Emperor orders that 2,000 more men are to be raised in Spain, properly qualified captains being appointed to command them. They are to be sent (*i.e.* to Italy) in the galleys. Don Bernardino (de Mendoza) is to be instructed to have the latter ready. In addition to the 500,000 ducats above mentioned, as much more money as possible is to be raised on the Bull for the sale of the monastic manors when it is received.

April 30.
Simancas.
E. R. 873.

253. JUAN DE VEGA to the EMPEROR.

(In the course of a very long dispatch, mainly referring to ecclesiastical affairs in Spain, the dispute of the Pope with the Duke of Florence (Cosmo de Medici), and the subject of the Italian duchies, the following paragraphs alone refer to English matters.)[*]

Cardinal Farnese sent for my perusal a letter dated 10th instant written from the French Court by the Nuncio there, giving full particulars of the peace negotiations that are still in progress between the Kings of France and England. The opinion there is, and people here even have come to the same conclusion, that, if the matter is brought down to question of money, and the French offer a good round sum, in addition to the overdue pensions, whilst an arrangement be made for the King of France to arbitrate in the matter of Scotland, within certain limits, peace may be looked upon

---

[*] A somewhat curious series of paragraphs is contained in the letter, and may be mentioned as an instance of the manner in which ecclesiastical appointments were made to suit political ends. In November 1544 the Emperor had given instructions that a certain Friar Francisco Salazar should be detained in Rome, on any pretext, to prevent him from returning to France. Vega relates that the Friar, in complete ignorance of the reasons for his detention, has since been kept by the instrumentality of Cardinal Carpi, a creature of the Emperor's, in the Franciscan monastery of St. Peter of Montoro. This, Vega explains, had only been done at the cost of great trouble, as no valid excuse could be given for the Friar's detention. For the last six months, however, the Franciscan friars had complained bitterly of the expense of keeping him, although they were greatly edified by his sanctity. The prisoner also had begun to suspect that he was being detained for reasons of State. Matters, said Vega, could not go on much longer in this way, or a scandal would result, and:—"as persons are being sought for the ecclesiastical posts in the Indies, he might be given one of the churches that are being erected there; and thus we should all of us be relieved from this anxiety about him."

HENRY VIII.

1546.

as assured. What with this hope, and the Pope's view that the Protestant princes will not attend the Diet, where consequently nothing important will be done, his Holiness is, as I have said, easier in his mind.

Rome, 30 April 1546.

April 29.
Vienna.
Imp. Arch.

254. VAN DER DELFT to the EMPEROR.

Being at Court yesterday respecting some claims made by subjects of your Majesty I was summoned by the King, who asked me whether I had not received any letter from your Majesty since the departure of M. D'Eick (Scepperus). I replied that I had received nothing but a letter from the Queen (Dowager of Hungary), your sister, informing me that Penninck had been to her, and she had arranged with him for the passage of his troops, whereby she doubted not that he (Henry) would be better served by them than he had been by the Landenberger's and Von Reissenberg's men; and that he (Henry) should feel no misgiving that everything that your Majesty could honestly do to please him should be done without fail. He took this in good part; and, after some little vague grumbling about past events, he broached the subject of the meeting between his envoys and the French, saying that M. de Monluc, who had been sent by the King of France to the Turk in company with your Majesty's ambassador, had now gone to Calais, and had entered into communication with his Secretary (Paget), to whom he had expressed the inclination of the King of France towards peace and tranquillity, and a desire to find some means of ending this war, regretting that the Lord Admiral was not present to carry the matter further. Paget had replied that his master, the King of England, was no less desirous of the repose and tranquillity of Christendom, but that with regard to the remark about the presence of the Lord Admiral he could only say that when the Admiral of France came the Lord Admiral of England would not fail to attend also and discuss matters with him, as the distance was not great. Monluc had thereupon assured him (*i.e.* Paget) that the Admiral of France would come, and the latter was now daily expected at Calais. When the King had finished this relation he continued that, notwithstanding this, he did not mean to slacken in his efforts. He had, he said, already taken such measures that he did not fear the enemy. I then took my leave; but, Sire, whatever happens, I can see that all these people are very desirous of peace.

The Lords of the Council related to me that their troops on the Border of Scotland had seven or eight days ago entered the enemy's country, and had taken and burned a small town, capturing or killing during the engagement 400 men, without losing a single one of theirs, only three of their men being wounded; and they had brought back a great booty of cattle.

They also told me that the King had at the present time fully 10,000 combatants at sea. Certain it is that during the last three days 18 pinnaces, newly built in the form of foysts,° have sailed from here. They have on each side fifteen or sixteen oars, and are all

---

* *See* Note page 232.

1546.

well and similarly equipped both with regard to the size of their artillery and to their crews. The English also depend greatly upon their fort near Boulogne, which they say is now sufficiently advanced for defence.

Since Duke Philip the Palatine left here a courier has been despatched to Secretary Mason, who accompanied him, as we wrote to your Majesty. Some people who presume to know say that the despatch is to stop Mason's mission. As the courier started as soon as it was decided to negotiate with the French, I, too, am of that opinion. London, 29 April 1546.

April 29.
Vienna.
Imp. Arch.

255. VAN DER DELFT to the QUEEN DOWAGER.

I received your Majesty's letters of the 17th instant, and I was yesterday at Court, at Greenwich, where the King is passing Eastertide. As the Queen (Catharine Parr) came out from mass I had an opportunity of saluting her on behalf of the Emperor and your Majesty. She was very gracious, and seemed much pleased at the good health of your Majesties. I afterwards saw the Lords of the Council, and laid before them fully that which your Majesty wrote to me in your said letters, about the plundering of the Emperor's subjects. They (the Councillors) replied that they had already taken such measures as would, they thought, prevent any further depredations being committed: but, nevertheless, I did not omit to suggest to them the procedure advised by your Majesty with that object. They approved of it, but gave me no further reply. I then placed before them the statement of the particulars of the property which had quite recently been plundered; although they were already well informed on that point, as the merchants had made their complaints to your Majesty in the presence of their (*i.e.* the English) ambassador resident. They (the Councillors) expressed their annoyance and disapproval (*i.e.* of the pillage), but said that all the complaints and allegations of the merchants must not be accepted as just, as many abuses and exaggerations would be found in them, both as to sheltering French property under their names and nationality, and in the supply of provisions and other things prohibited by the treaties to the French. Nevertheless, they (the Councillors) promised to do justice in every case. In good truth, Madame, some of the complaints are open to objection, as also are the contentions of the sailors presented by the Antwerp people, with regard to the imposition of Customs dues, and the bad treatment they allege they suffered when they asked for payment for their services. These claims are not at all well founded, and M. d'Eick was of the same opinion after we had examined here the documents in support of them. I do not know of one of the claimants, moreover, who has come to me for his due who has not at once been paid. The only claimants now remaining are those who have lost their ships whilst they were in the King's service, and I urged the claims of these men for redress again yesterday. I was told in reply that the promises made to them should be fulfilled; and that they would be treated as was customary by other sovereigns in similar cases, but that these claimants must have patience until a more convenient occasion. In conversation with them (the Councillors) I dwelt on

1546.

the apathy of the King's ministers on the other side (*i.e.* Flanders) in the conduct of his affairs there, and their indifference to the good advice given to them which, indeed, they reverse rather than follow; but the Councillors made no reply to this, although I thought that they liked my reasoning.

After dining with the Council I was summoned to the King's presence. Having saluted him on behalf of your Majesty, I repeated to him your desire and good will towards the continuance of the sincere amity and alliance between the Emperor and him; and assured him that he might depend that your Majesty would not fail in the future, as you had not in the past, to do everything possible to please and favour him. I sincerely trusted that he would not allow anything to produce in him a contrary impression. He took this in good part, saying that he had no doubt of it: though he displayed some resentment for past events, but without going into particulars. Then, changing the subject, he entered into the conversation, which is reported fully in the letter to the Emperor, copy of which is enclosed for your Majesty's information.

London, 29 April 1546.

April 30.
Vienna.
Imp. Arch.

256. VAN DER DELFT to the QUEEN DOWAGER.

When this courier was ready to start the Lords of the Council sent a secretary to me with the enclosed note, saying that the King, having learnt of the seizure by his Vice-Admiral of the ships named in the schedule, he desired me to inform your Majesty that he had detained them, for the purpose of inspecting them and making use of those which might be found fitting for his service, to prevent his enemy from reinforcing himself with them. He alleged that the passage of such ships, exceeding 150 or 200 tons burden, was against the agreement between the Emperor and himself. I replied that I was ignorant of any such agreement, and asked for information as to the clause containing it. He (*i.e.* the Secretary) said he knew nothing of that, and had no instructions on the subject. I thought, therefore, best to detain this courier until I could obtain a further declaration on the subject. With this object I sent early this morning to Secretary Petre, and from him received a message to the effect that he thought the agreement was not in writing; but that he recollected well that when Secretary Paget was last in Brussels, the King (Henry), hearing that the King of France intended to make use of some Flemish ships, called the Emperor's attention thereto. Paget had thereupon written that the Emperor had agreed not to allow any ships to sail of a greater tonnage than six score to 150 tons. I beg for your Majesty's instructions.

London, 30 April 1546.

April (n.d.)
Simancas.
E. 73.

257. COBOS to the EMPEROR.

(Acknowledges Emperor's letters of 17th March. Refers to the Prince's letters for details of the financial situation.) I can only add, that every possible effort shall be made to raise and forward funds to your Majesty (for the enterprise against the Protestants). I will work with all needful diligence, but the demands that exist are very great, and the expenses we are obliged to incur here

1546.

unavoidable. His Highness is writing fully as to the only remaining sources from which money can be obtained, and I must refer you to his letter, only adding on my own account that I am more pained than anyone that every means of obtaining funds has been exhausted by previous demands. I know not how it will end, unless God in His goodness deigns to help us with a remedy. The bill for 32,000 crowns, which with the interest now amount to 35,520, shall be provided for as your Majesty orders; and also that which was to cover the amount advanced, to be made payable at Antwerp. With regard to Anthony Fuggers' claim for interest paid yearly on the loan arranged with him by M. de Granvelle etc., your Majesty knows our opinion: but as the Fuggers have on former occasions requested that the question should be referred to a legal decision, we have commissioned the bishop of Lugo, Dr. Guevara and Licentiate Galeaça to examine it. When we see how the matter stands legally we shall perhaps be able to come to a compromise; for believe me, your Majesty, when I repeat, that this would be a thing of most disastrous consequences and very damaging to us.

May 1.
Paris.
Archives
Nationales.
K. 1486.

258. St. Mauris to Cobos.

The negotiations for peace with England still continue, and have progressed so far that three days ago the Admiral went to Ardres to meet the Lord Admiral of England. He is authorised to give 1,200,000 crowns in cash for the arrears, and a million in gold for the war indemnity and the expense incurred in the fortification of Boulogne. This million in gold will be paid within 6 years, in addition to the payments falling due; the amount being deposited in the hands of a third party. On the expiry of the six years the English will be bound to surrender Boulogne etc., which they are to hold until that time; the King of France to retain in the meanwhile his new fort. As these conditions are decidedly favourable to the English, it is presumed that they will be accepted. We shall soon learn the result of the negotiations, and I will report to you from time to time. Notwithstanding the negotiations the English continue to strengthen themselves on this side of the sea, where they have some ten or twelve thousand men in the field; but without having as yet attempted any exploit except to throw themselves upon the garrison of Ardres. It is understood that if the peace is concluded the galleys will very shortly go to the Mediterranean, of which I think well to advise you. You requested me to keep my eye open to see whether anything is being planned here to the prejudice of Spain; and in reply I may say for certain that nothing fresh will be undertaken this year; as these people will have to find money to pay the English, they will hardly raise war elsewhere, even next year. The people are in great distress.

Melun, 1 May 1546.

May 1.
Paris.
Archives
Nationales.
K. 1486.

259. St. Mauris to Prince Philip.

Letters of 31 March received. No reply needed. I will only add that the infant daughter of the Dauphiness has not yet been christened; and it is said, I know not with what truth, that if the

1546.

peace is made with England the King of England will be godfather. The Queen (of France), it is said, will be one of the godmothers.

Melun, 1 May 1546.

May 9.
Simancas.
E. 73.

260. PRINCE PHILIP to the EMPEROR.

(Acknowledges receipt of letter of 17 March from Luxemburg, most of the points of which were anticipated by the writer's letter despatched immediately before receipt. After many dutiful expressions of rejoicing at the Emperor's good health etc. the letter proceeds to deal in detail with the subjects referred to in the Emperor's abovementioned letter (*q.r.*). As in most cases conformity is expressed, the paragraphs, with exception of the following, do not call for reproduction.) The Commissaries at Cambrai for the settlement of maritime questions (between the Emperor and France) having separated without coming to any decision, warning has been sent to all the Spanish ports for vigilance and care to be exercised, in order that shipping may escape molestation. This, however, seems but a small remedy for so great an evil at the hands both of French and English, and also from the Scottish corsairs. We are of opinion that your Majesty should have the matter considered, to see whether some means cannot be devised to avoid these attacks. In the meanwhile we will discuss here the adoption of the suggestions made by the Burgos people that ships should only sail armed and in flotillas.° With regard to the projected passage of the French galleys now in the western sea to Marseilles, due notice was sent to all the ports to hold themselves in readiness for defence; but in the matter of your Majesty's recommendation that they should be told not to supply provisions to the French or to receive them well, in consequence of the damage they committed on their outward voyage, we wish to make the following remarks: as your Majesty notices in your letter, there are very few ports on our coasts which would be able successfully to refuse to supply provisions to the French, or treat them otherwise than well, whilst there are many that might suffer much for doing so, being merely open roadsteads. From these the French upon such a pretext, or any other, might take anything they liked, even if it were refused to them, and this would be a greater loss of prestige for us than giving it to them. We have therefore thought prudent to moderate somewhat your Majesty's instructions on this point.

Madrid, 9 May 1546.

May 14.
Vienna.
Imp. Arch.

261. The EMPEROR to VAN DER DELFT.

We have received your letters of 29 April, and have noted the conversation you had with the King of England respecting his satisfaction with the course taken by our sister the Queen Dowager in the matter of Penninck, and also touching the communication between Secretary Paget and M. de Monluc, for the conclusion of

---

° *See* document No. 356.

1546.

peace with France etc. We thank you for your repeated advices; and, although we see no great indication as yet that the peace negotiations will be finally successful, you will do well to discover as much as possible of what is done, and inform us and our sister.

As to events here: we are daily expecting the arrival of our brother the King of the Romans; and in the meanwhile we have come to this place for a few days' rest.° On the arrival of our brother and the other princes and estates, who are already appearing, we will see how best we can set the Diet to work.

Strowbynge (Ströwingen), 14 May 1546.

May 14.
Vienna.
Imp. Arch.

262. VAN DER DELFT to the EMPEROR.

Since my last, of 29th April, nothing of importance has happened here, as all depends upon the issue of the Conference between the English and French, which is still proceeding; although the Lord Admiral when he learnt that the French galleys were at sea and had captured two pinnaces and some boats, left the Conference and put to sea. It is said here that he has had an encounter with the said galleys, and that some of the latter have had to seek refuge in Dunkirk, whilst the others fled into French harbours.† The expectation that these people entertained of peace seems therefore to have cooled, though I heard to-day from a man coming from Calais that Franciso Bernardi, who is managing this Conference, declares that he is certain that an arrangement will be arrived at. I have also been informed that this King is now more disposed to peace than he was, in consequence of his desire to lead personally a large force against Scotland. Whether anything will come of this I do not know, and I have had no opportunity of seeing the King to sound him on the subject. He came to Westminster a few days ago, leaving his Council at Greenwich, where I am told they are constantly busy against those suspected of holding forbidden opinions; by which it is evident that the authority of the bishops and churchmen is on the increase, and is more favoured by the King than formerly was the case. They (i.e. the churchmen) have so managed that a grave old doctor ‡ much liked by the King, who had preached about the sacrifice of the Mass in accordance with the new opinions, was severely rebuked and ordered to retract publicly. As he did not do this so thoroughly and explicitly as he ought to have done I am told that he will be in peril of losing his life if he persists. The Conference (between the English and French) has somewhat delayed the settlement of the business entrusted to Councillor Van der Burgh, who we hope will soon be able to return.

London, 14 May 1546.

---

* The Emperor was now settled at Ratisbon, where he remained until the 4th August.

† This appears to have been the fight off Ambleteuse, where eight French galleys attacked a similar number of English, four of which appear to have been ships or galleasses and four pinnaces. Stow mentions that there was much heavy firing and finally the Blancard galley with 230 French soldiers and 130 oarsmen was captured by the English.

‡ This would appear from a subsequent letter to be Dr. Edward Crome, vicar of St. Mary Aldermary, in the city of London.

HENRY VIII.

1546.
May 14.
*Vienna.
Imp. Arch.*

263. VAN DER DELFT and VAN DER BURGH to the QUEEN DOWAGER.

The Bishop and the Dean of London, who have been appointed to communicate with the writers instead of Dr. Petre and Nicholas Wotton, have hitherto been detained by other duties, and no further progress has therefore been made. London, 14 May 1546.*

May 18.
*Simancas.
E. 73.*

264. Draft of a private letter to de Granvelle apparently from Cobos. Referring to a quarrel that had taken place between de Granvelle and the Duke (of Alba?) the writer beseeches de Granvelle to overlook the matter in the interests of the Emperor's service. He assures him that de Granvelle's fears that the Duke's report of the matter will prejudice Prince Philip against de Granvelle are groundless. Expresses much dissatisfaction at the way that the Emperor's affairs are dealt with in Rome.† It would be worse if the Ambassador were not with him (*i.e.* the Pope). The interests at stake, being so great, the effects are not immediately apparent: "but no more care is taken of his Majesty's affairs than if they are those of the Turk."—The writer thinks that the Ambassador (Juan de Vega) might be changed with advantage, and discusses the possibility of making him Viceroy of Sicily; or, if the Marquis de Aguilar accepts the latter post, Vega might be made Viceroy of Catalonia. Don Diego de Mendoza might be sent to Rome, but the Emperor is still strongly of opinion that the ambassador there should not be a priest. The writer regrets this greatly. The Viceroy of Aragon would also do well for Rome, and the writer begs de Granvelle to forward his nomination, failing Mendoza. Several other appointments to posts in Spain are discussed.

May 25.
*Simancas.
E. R. 873.*

265. JUAN DE VEGA to the EMPEROR. (Extracts.)

On the 11th instant I wrote that up to that time the Pope had kept the secret of the enterprise against the Protestants. Since then they decided to send Duke Ottavio (Farnese) to Piacenza; and the Pope even wished that Madame should accompany him, it is said, to win the hearts of the people of those cities.‡ The Duke (Ottavio) was ordered to warn the legates, as they call those who make the levies, and he was told of the enterprise. It then became public; but as we strenuously denied the truth of it—as we still do—it was not generally believed until the 19th, when it was announced by some persons of high position, and we hear from some of those near the Pope that Duke Ottavio was openly preparing for the war. The Ambassador of Ferrara, the agent of

---

* Another letter from Van der Delft to the Queen Dowager, dated 27 May, is to a similar effect to the above; the King's commissioners being still occupied with other business.

† That is to say by the Farneses and by the Cardinals supposed to be in the interests of Spain and the Empire.

‡ Octavio Farnese was Pier Luigi's son and heir, another son being the Cardinal; and "Madame" was Octavio's wife, Duchess of Camarino, afterwards the famous Margaret of Parma, Governess of the Netherlands, the Emperor's illegitimate daughter. Octavio was destined by his grandfather to the command of the Papal contingent in war against the Protestants.

1546.

the Cardinal of Mantua and others came to enquire of me about it, but I assured them that it was untrue, and, though the matter is much talked about, it is not believed. As soon as the first rumour spread I sent to Cardinal Farnese to say how many efforts we were making to stop it, and asking him to get the Pope to do the same. He did so, and the Pope apologised for the news being divulged, which he said had been done by some of his people whom he was obliged to tell. The Pope, to judge by appearances, will do all he promised towards the enterprise, and even more.

Messer Nicolo, the ambassador from Siena, left here on the 17th instant. He has had many long conferences with me, in which I strove to overcome his idea that your Majesty's measures were directed against liberty. He assured me that from our first interview he had written to the Republic repeating what I had said and urged strict obedience to your Majesty's commands. The Pope in his farewell interview with the said Ambassador gave him the same advice.

The Pope and his friends keep their news from Trent quite secret, and everything from there makes them very anxious. I learn from two sources that from the day he received the letters from the Augsburg and Trent people the Cardinal (Farnese) wished to go to your Majesty. Now that he learns the vacancy of Seville he is still more anxious to go.

A bishop called Cana, Nazarus, a friar who it is said spoke very freely in the Council (of Trent), has come hither and has been well received, although with dissimulation. It may therefore be concluded that what he did in the Council was planned beforehand in order to sound the prelates.

(Recommends the Cardinal of Burgos for the vacant Archbishopric of Seville. Begs for rewards also for his brother Antonio de Vega and Pedro Marquina.)

Some residents of Sicily have petitioned through the Genoese here for a papal Brief to the effect enclosed. We have asked the Pope not to concede it without your Majesty's consent, although he is desirous of doing so, as it will aid greatly the building of St. Peter's. It is true it will benefit to some extent your Majesty's treasury, but if a third of the confiscations are to be given to the building, a third to your Majesty and a third to the denouncers it may injure the Kingdom of Sicily to have so much money taken from it.*

Rome, 25 May 1546.

May 27.
Vienna.
Imp. Arch.

266. VAN DER DELFT to the EMPEROR.

Since I wrote my last letter, of 14th instant, I have received your Majesty's letter written at Stöwingen on the same day, in which your Majesty commands me to report from time to time what I can learn of the conference between the English and French with regard to peace. I have continued my vigilance in this respect, in order to discover how affairs were proceeding; and with this object I made the excuse of pressing some complaints and claims of your

---

* Although the draft Brief is not enclosed, it is evident from the context that the proposal was to denounce those who during the previous 20 years had misused the powers given by the crusade and building-fund faculties.

Majesty's subjects to go to Court and see the Councillors on Sunday last. They received me very well, and gave favourable replies to my complaints, after which they asked me whether I had any special mission from your Majesty upon which I wished to see the King. Although I was really anxious to obtain access to him I had no good reason to allege, and was obliged to reply that I had nothing particular to say to his Majesty, but was quite at his disposal. I therefore did not see the King; and could extract nothing from the Councillors, though I tried several devices on them, collectively and individually, to draw them into conversation about their Calais negotiations.

Since then the Venetian Francisco Bernardi, who managed the negotiation, has arrived in London, and has told a man, who repeated it to me in confidence, that peace was now assured and settled; though I can learn nothing of the conditions, as Bernardi declined to disclose them. The next day, which was yesterday, there was a rumour all over London that peace had been made, and that Boulogne was to be surrendered, in return for which and the expenses and over-due payments the French were to pay four millions in gold. Until this sum was paid the English were to hold Ardres, any fortification of that place which in the interim the English might construct being paid for by the King of France when he finally took the place over. Others say that the four millions will cover this contingency also; and another version speaks of only two millions, without saying anything about a pension. In order to ascertain what is true in these several rumours I immediately sent a man to Court, but there not a word was said about peace, either by those near the King or by the Council, who, however, received my man more amiably than usual. Nevertheless, Sire, I cannot believe that what Bernardi says about the certainty of peace is altogether vain, seeing his persistent affirmation of it, and the continuance of conference; and the silence and dissimulation of the English make me suspect very strongly that the conditions will not turn out to be much to their advantage. Still, I am confidently informed that Bernardi, who had an understanding with M. de Monluc, when he initiated the negotiations assured the King (of England) that he could obtain what terms he pleased from the French. I will relate to your Majesty how the negotiation was brought about. The Lords of the Council, hearing the assurances and offers of Bernardi, asked him if he knew what they (the English) demanded. He replied that he supposed they would demand the retention of Boulogne, the payment of the pensions and arrears, and the marriage of the daughter of Scotland; or, at least, the renunciation of the Scottish and French alliance. All these terms, he said, he could obtain for them, if they would consent to enter into negotiations. As he also told them that the Admiral of France and other personages would attend the Conference the English did not refuse; but when Paget had crossed the sea and the Lord Admiral of England had also arrived, they found that the French personages deferred their coming. This greatly annoyed and mortified them (the English), and they became very suspicious of Bernardi's intrigue, as well as puzzled by the numerous and contradictory

1546.

rumours which reached here (London), such as that a close alliance and marriage were arranged between your Majesty and France, and on the other hand that preparations were being made to assist the Duke of Savoy to recover his territory.° Nevertheless they (the English) continued the negotiations commenced, being much more desirous of peace than they pretended to be. It is said that the Dauphin wrote a letter to this King, but I do not know if this can be believed; and I also hear that it was proposed to the English in the course of the negotiations, that they should bind themselves to an offensive and defensive alliance (d'estre ennemy des ennemys), but the King (of England) would not listen to this.

Paget is expected to arrive here every day, without any rumour existing that the negotiations have been broken off. Some people say that he is coming to conclude the affair. As soon as I can ascertain I will report to your Majesty. The King's ships recently had an engagement with the galleys of France; and the latter, to the number of sixteen, were compelled to retire, one of them being captured† with Baron de Saint Blancard on board. This has greatly rejoiced the people here (in England), especially as they have re-captured the small pinnaces and boats which had been taken by the French, as I wrote to your Majesty recently. The captured French galley is to be brought to London in a day or two.

The rumour continues that in the event of peace being made (with France) the King's army, with both Spaniards and Germans, will be conveyed against Scotland, and that the King wishes to make the campaign in person, as I wrote previously.

The examinations in the matter of the faith still continue, and the multitude of new sectarians here have been greatly restrained since the retraction of the preacher Dr. Crome, who, however, on the very day that he was ordered to retract what he had preached declared that he was more convinced in his opinions than ever. He afterwards confessed that he had only maintained this at the instance of certain persons he named to the Council. These persons, he said, had urged him to persist in his opinions, as he would be in greater danger if he retracted than otherwise. The contrary has proved to be the case, for several of his accomplices have been placed in the Tower, and he is strictly guarded.‡

London, 27 May 1546.

Postscript.—As I was closing this letter I have been informed that it is publicly stated at Court that peace has been made; but nothing is known as to the conditions, except that the King of France renounces his confederation with Scotland. Some people maintain

---

° It will be remembered that the French still held a large portion of Savoy, which by the treaty of Crespy was to have been surrendered on certain conditions, which neither the Emperor nor Francis I. had shown any readiness to fulfil. The marriage of a princess of the House of Austria with the Duke of Orleans, with the Duchy of Milan as a dowry, had been rendered impossible by the death of the bridegroom, and as this marriage was to counterbalance the retrocession of Savoy, the latter still remained in abeyance.

† The battle of Ambleteuse. *See* note on page 394.

‡ Dr. Edward Crome, Rector of St. Mary Aldermary, in the city of London, had on a previous occasion, in 1540, been ordered by the King to recant publicly at St. Paul's Cross the doctrines he had expounded in a sermon with regard to the value of masses for the dead. In this judgment he was threatened that if he were accused again of similar doctrines no favour should be shown him.

HENRY VIII.

1546.

that it is only a truce for eight years, but Francisco Bernardi, who left Court to-day for Calais, continues to affirm to an intimate friend of his that peace has really been concluded; but that the terms being not yet signed he could not divulge them. They would be known, however, in four days, he said.

June 2.
Vienna.
Imp. Arch.

267. VAN DER DELFT to the EMPEROR.

Since writing to your Majesty recently respecting the rumours that peace had been concluded, the said rumours had continued unabated at Court and elsewhere, and the general opinion was that peace had certainly been made. As, however, I had been unable to learn for certain what the conditions were, I deferred writing to your Majesty until now. The rumours have since died down, and to such an extent that all the hope of peace that existed has turned to dread of a continuance of the war. The people, gentle and simple, are quite tired of war, as was well proved by the joy they evinced at the news of peace, without caring what the conditions were. Although the conference still continues the English are not slackening in their activity in providing everything necessary for the prosecution of hostilities, and despatching the things needed to Boulogne. I hear that this King has ordered 2,000 men to be raised here, in consequence, it is said, of the continued reinforcement of the French camp. I am therefore at a loss what to write to your Majesty, with so many divergent rumours afloat. My doubt is increased by seeing that affairs are not proceeding according to the assertions made by those who are conducting them. But withal, Sire, I cannot believe that these people will do anything against your Majesty, although they say that they have been solicited to do so. I will report to your Majesty all I can learn.

The King came to London to-day and the Queen yesterday, and they are to remain here until the peace conference comes to an end.

London, 2 June 1546.

June 2.
Vienna.
Imp. Arch.

268. VAN DER DELFT to the QUEEN DOWAGER.

After my recent letters to your Majesty respecting the peace rumours the latter continued general, both at Court and elsewhere for two days longer, peace being then considered by everyone as certain. As, however, I could obtain no trustworthy confirmation, or learn anything of the conditions, I refrained from writing further on the subject to your Majesty. The rumour has since died down to such an extent that the hopes of peace have now turned to fear of the continuance of the war, of which everyone, noble and simple, is tired; as was well shown by the great joy that was displayed at the mere talk of peace, irrespective of terms or conditions. Although the Commissioners are still deliberating, there is no slackening in the collection and despatch of warlike stores to Boulogne. I am informed that the King has ordered a levy of 2,000 men here (i.e. London) in consequence of the statement that the French army is daily being strengthened. With all this, Madame,

1546.

I know not what to write about it, being in the midst of so many changes: and especially as I find that affairs are not proceeding in accordance with the assertions of those who conduct them. But, whatever may happen, I cannot believe that these people (the English) will do anything against the Emperor, although they say that they have been requested to do so. I will not fail to report what I can learn. The King came to London to-day, the Queen having arrived yesterday. It is said they will remain here until the result of the negotiations is known.

London, 2 June 1546.

June 3.
Vienna.
Imp. Arch.

269. VAN DER DELFT to the EMPEROR.

After despatching my letter yesterday by the ordinary courier I learnt that the Bishop of Winchester and the Master of the Horse, Sir Anthony Browne, were to start the same day to cross the sea. They had kept this so secret that there was no whisper of it at Court until they were ready to depart. I have done my best to-day to find out the cause of their journey, and with this object I sent a man to the Lords of the Council on some other pretext, but still I have been unable to discover what they are going for. I sent to complain to the Lord Chancellor of the delay which was caused in the settlement of a claim made by a certain Biscayner, in consequence of the absence of the Bishop of Winchester, who had been appointed joint arbitrator with me on the matter; but the only thing the Lord Chancellor said was that the bishop had gone on the King's service and would be back in five or six days. People discourse variously of their going.

I also heard to-day from a man whom Bernardi had assured previously that peace was practically concluded that Bernardi had told him subsequently that he had but small hope of peace, and that a settlement seemed now improbable.

London, 3 June 1546.

June 7.
Simancas.
E. 73.

270. PRINCE PHILIP to the EMPEROR.

Congratulations on recovery from gout, and upon the great benefit derived from taking the China water, etc., etc.

Notes that the Emperor continues in his resolve to carry through the enterprise against the Protestants, and was making preparations for it. The writer has therefore no more to say, as he concludes that the Emperor will have considered all the objections. The writer can only pray to God to prosper an undertaking so entirely in His service. Nevertheless, it must not be forgotten that the season is far advanced, and winter lasts longer in Germany than elsewhere. Please God, however, your Majesty will overcome this difficulty by your celerity; and that He will supply all shortcomings.

Notes the Emperor's remark that money is the first thing needful for the raising of troops, and that the Emperor has drawn two bills of exchange. The High Commendador (Cobos) will write on these points, as he has already done in previous letters. The sum requested will already have reached his Majesty's hand.

"With regard to the indispensable supplies needed for Spain, we must consider what means can be devised for obtaining them. I am extremely anxious at the impossibility of supplying your Majesty with all that you require from here; and especially if the King of France makes any attempt on our frontiers, as we fear he will, as soon as the enterprise is made public and the English and French come to terms to your Majesty's prejudice. Our needs here are so great that we could hardly resist. I can only trust in God to aid your Majesty in frustrating your enemies."

Spanish prelates ordered to go to the Council of Trent. Excuses, old age, sickness, etc. alleged by some of them (named) for not going. Inquisitor for the Kingdom of Sicily, etc. Dr. Sebastian has been appointed, and has accepted only with much reluctance, as the salary is very small.

With regard to the 2,000 men for Lombardy, since our letter of 18th May, we have arranged that the five companies raised in Aragon and Valencia shall be embarked at Tortosa, and the two companies from Villena and Murcia at Cartagena, this being the advice of Don Bernardino de Mendoza, Captain General of the galleys of Spain. The 2,000 quintals of biscuit ordered to be made for them are promised for the 8th or 10th instant. The captains report that the men are assembled, and we ordered the paymasters with the money to hurry thither at once. We are confident that by the 20th or 25th the companies will be mustered and the first wage paid; so that they may be embarked by the end of the month. As your Majesty did not write to Prince Doria he only sent 12 of his galleys with John Doria to drive off the corsairs, who are infesting these coasts. Doubtless when Doria gets your Majesty's subsequent orders, he will send the rest of the galleys, as the 12 already here with our own will not suffice to convey these 2,000 men. The men will receive one wage in money, and one in stores. The arms they need will be served out to them, and part of the amount will be discounted from the first wage here. The statement of the deductions afterwards will be sent with the men. Details of the movements of galleys and troops ordered, to defend the Spanish ports and convey the troops, supply of barley for garrisons, etc.

The advance of the Sheriff of Morocco to conquer the Kingdom of Fez. The King of Portugal requests permission to raise troops in Andalusia for the purpose of sending succour thither. We will do our best to aid him in this, as it is important to Spain that the Sheriff should not dominate the fortresses on the coast.

Proposes several appointments to vacant pensioned knighthoods, one of which he desires should be given to "Don Alonso de Tovar my carver." "The prior and consuls of the Guild of Merchants of Burgos sent one of their members hither, respecting the means to be adopted to prevent the molestation of your Majesty's subjects at sea by the French, English and Scots. He handed to me a memorandum of these proposals which I have had discussed in the Royal Council and the Council of War. Although the memorandum was generally approved of it was decided to refer it to your Majesty's consideration before taking action upon it. I beg your

1546.

Majesty to have it examined and send orders.* In the meanwhile, in accordance with the Council we have despatched letters to the justices at the ports on the west coasts, ordering them to inspect all ships about to put to sea, and if they find them unprovided with means of defence to forbid their sailing, until others may accompany them better furnished."

Begs the Emperor's favour for a pensioned knighthood for Don Alonso Osorio, now in Germany in the Emperor's service. He is the brother of a gentleman in his Majesty's service who died in Ratisbon and of another, a knight of St. John, whom the Turks killed in Algiers.† Begs church preferment for the singers in his (Philip's) chapel, who serve so well, and receive so little.

Madrid, 7 June 1546.

271. St. Mauris to Prince Philip.

June 8.
Paris.
Archives
Nationales.
K. 1486.

Your Highness' letters of 10th and 18th ultimo received. I have diligently enquired into the proceedings of M. d'Albret‡ against (Spanish) Navarre, and I have been unable to learn from anyone that he can raise war this year. He has not a doit, nor the King of France either. The latter has been forced to try to make peace with England for absolute want of money. If any troops are being raised on the Bayonne frontier or in Gascony it is asserted here that they are simply to withstand the Spaniards. Your Highness will see by the statement enclosed that the King of France addressed me personally to this effect. This is confirmed by what a servant of the King of Portugal who came hither by post told me, and also a Spanish courier, to the effect that on the frontier and in Gascony all the talk was that a Spanish force was coming against them. They were all in great alarm; and the King of France had caused proclamation to be made by a herald that every person was to make ready to join M. d'Albret when he should summon them. This is as much as I have been able to ascertain up to the present. The same cry about the Spanish force is prevalent here (in Paris). Nevertheless, to prevent our being caught unawares by any such talk, I am of opinion that the most efficacious means of frustrating the design will be the knowledge that your Highness has placed the frontiers in a state of defence, supposing that the design exists. I will do my best to get to the bottom of the business and will report to your Highness.

With regard to the peace with England, the people here look upon it as settled. The substance of the arrangement is that Boulogne with the whole county of Boulognais remain in the hands of the English for eight years; after which time they are to be

---

* The document will be found on page 356.

† The Prince was attached to a lady named Isabel de Osorio, who is usually referred to as the daughter of the Marquis of Astorga. The editor has been unable to trace her identity as such; and has elsewhere questioned the fact of her being a daughter of the head of the house of Osorio. It is possible that she was the sister of the gentlemen mentioned in this letter, who are also not recognisable as near relations of either of the titled branches of the house.

‡ Philip had in several previous letters expressed apprehension at news that reached him to the effect that Henry d'Albret (titular King of Navarre) was planning an attack on the Spanish frontier, with the covert aid of the King of France.

surrendered to the King of France, on the payment by him of two millions in gold in one sum, besides the pensions of 120,000 crowns a year.* The peace is generally considered shameful and injurious to the King of France, but he was obliged to consent to it for want of money. He will therefore be quite unable to aid M. d'Albret with funds.

Since the peace has been regarded as concluded, these people here have spread the intelligence that the French galleys in the western sea will start for the Mediterranean with the first fine weather. I believe this is true. There are 86 of them, though it is said that the English recently captured one, which they may return, as a consequence of the conclusion of peace. They may sail by the 15th or 20th June.

The remedies to be adopted against attacks and robberies at sea are still in suspense: but as peace is made with the English all such troubles will cease for the future, and we may confine our attention to the redress of past injuries. I have written this hurriedly to convey the news to your Highness, and will shortly write again in fuller detail. I must not omit to mention, however, that since they have become confident of peace, they have announced that many Normans were putting to sea in armed ships for purposes of plunder, their pretence being to go to Brazil. They expect the gold from the Indies will soon be on the way.

Melun, 8 June 1546.

June 9.
Vienna.
Imp. Arch.

272. The QUEEN DOWAGER to VAN DER DELFT.

The English ambassador resident here has just come on behalf of the King's Commissioners at Calais for the negotiations with the French, to inform us that peace was concluded between the two kings on the 7th instant, the King of England having reserved intact the treaty existing between him and the Emperor, with whom he wishes to remain in perfect accord. The ambassador said that he had no information beyond this, as to the terms of the peace treaty, and we thanked him for his communication. You will at once request audience of the King on our behalf and thank him for the information he caused to be conveyed to us, and also for his desire that the friendship now existing should be maintained between the Emperor and himself, which desire shall fully be reciprocated by us. We asked the ambassador whether the King's army was dispersed; so that in such case we might give orders for the transit through these territories of the soldiers whose road home led this way. We were told that the army had not yet been dismissed. You will therefore enquire of the Council when the forces are to dispersed, as we shall require to take measures to prevent any damage being suffered by subjects here during the transit of the soldiers. You will communicate to us also from time to time what the English are saying, now that they are at peace: whether they bear any rancour towards the Emperor for leaving them alone in the war; and let us know

---

* This is a fairly correct summary of the treaty signed at Campen on the previous day, 7 June. The treaty will be found printed in extenso in Rymer's "Fœdera," Vol. 15, p. 93.

1546.

the conditions of the peace, which we hear are greatly to the honour and reputation of the King of England; in which case the English will be all the more ready to make them known.—9 June 1546.

June 10.
Vienna.
Imp. Arch.

273. VAN DER DELFT to the EMPEROR.

Yesterday a courier arrived here from Calais for the King (of England) bringing the news that peace had been concluded, and Secretary Paget arrived the same evening. Various statements are current as to the conditions, and consequently I can still only write to your Majesty that it is said that Boulogne with the territory to the river remains in possession of the King of England, although many persons assert that this is the case only for a given time, until the King of France has paid a great sum of money. This I think most likely to be true, as the plenipotentiaries at the conference have been so long disputing the point whether the Englishmen or Picards were to be allowed to cultivate the territory of Boulogne. Up to the present no communication has been made to me. I will use every effort to discover the particulars, and will not fail to advise your Majesty immediately. The rumour is that the Admiral of France is coming hither, and that the Lord Admiral is to go to France.

The intelligence current here recently of the death of the Cardinal of Scotland still continues, and the news is now regarded as true. It is said that he was killed by the relatives of a man who had been executed by his orders for heresy. Some people still assert that the Cardinal was only wounded.

London, 10 June 1546.

June 10.
Vienna.
Imp. Arch.

274. VAN DER DELFT to the QUEEN DOWAGER of HUNGARY.[*]

In accordance with the letters from M. de Bevres and M. D'Eick, respecting the passage of Magnus David with your Majesty's safe conduct to Scotland, I sent to the Lords of the Council, who expressed their surprise at this dealing with their enemies, and at the large number of safe conducts that are being granted. They (the Council) were shown that your Majesty was in no way infringing upon the treaties in what you did, and that they themselves (the English) acted similarly. They replied that they would consider the matter, and would communicate their decision to me in two or three days; but up to the present time I have received no message from them. Magnus David himself has since arrived in London with the captain who captured him, though I have not yet seen him. I will not fail to render him such aid as I can. (The writer begs for consideration in the matter of his pecuniary affairs.)

London, 10 June 1546.

---

[*] The first paragraphs of this letter are identical with those which comprise the letter to the Emperor of the same date, and they are consequently not repeated here.

1546.
June 12.
Vienna.
Imp. Arch.

275. The Duke of Alburquerque° to Henry VIII.

A soldier who was formerly a servant of mine arrived yesterday from England, and told me that when he left there, there was a Spaniard imprisoned in the Tower of London, who claimed to be a cousin or a nephew of mine, and who, to give colour to his falsehood, brought letters ostensibly from me begging your Majesty to favour him. These letters having been thought genuine, the man has been well received and admitted to your Majesty's presence. I am, and shall always remain, grateful that your Majesty considers me so faithful a servant as for you to extend your favour to anyone bearing a recommendation from me; but I can assure your Majesty that in this case I did not write the letter, which is a forgery effected in order to prejudice your Majesty. The greatest favour that can be done to me in the matter is that the man should be severely punished as a warning to others not to go to England as spies under cover of my name and signature. Your Majesty may be perfectly certain that such persons will never be accredited with genuine letters of mine, for I am the last man to countenance with my aid anyone capable of going to England to the disservice of so good a friend and brother of my King, by whose orders I served your Majesty to the best of my ability. I am not surprised that the French should have invented this device to deprive me of the reward that my service merited, for they have shown their resentment against me for my action in the campaign by their treatment of me in the matter of my property;† but I wonder that anyone in England should have so bad opinion of me, as to think that I could send a kinsman of mine on so evil an errand. As the Spaniard in question was rogue enough to bring a forged letter bearing an imitation of my signature, it is possible that others may have carried thither similar forgeries for various objects, and I therefore think necessary to assure your Majesty that the present is the first letter I have written to you since I left your realm. I have refrained from doing so, because I am aware that frequently monarchs are pestered with letters from those who have served them, even though the latter are as powerless, as I am, to serve them again; though in my case, to be sure, the will is not wanting, and no journey would seem too long for me to take, if I could be useful to your Majesty, and had permission of my own King to serve you.

I have received news of your Majesty's recent victories, which have rejoiced the hearts of your servants, etc. etc.

Cuellar, 12 June 1546.

Endorsed:—Copy of the letter that is being sent to the King.

° Beltran de la Cueva, third Duke of Alburquerque and Marquis of Cuellar, grandson of the favourite of Henry IV. of Castile.

† It will be recalled that after the peace between the Emperor and France had been agreed upon, the Duke, who had served as Henry's adviser at the siege of Boulogne, returned to England with the King; his horses and baggage being shipped in two English barges for England, Alburquerque's intention being to return to Spain by sea from Plymouth. The barges and their cargoes were captured at sea by the French; and Alburquerque fruitlessly claimed the return of his property on the ground that he had retired from the position of combatant as soon as his Sovereign was at peace with France.

1546.
June 12.
Vienna.
Imp. Arch.

276. VAN DER DELFT to the EMPEROR.

Since I despatched my letter to your Majesty announcing the conclusion of peace, the Bishop of Durham[*] came to me, as he said on behalf of the King and Council, to inform me that peace had been concluded between his master and the King of France, in which peace your Majesty had been included; and all the treaties existing between your Majesty and the King expressly reserved and maintained in force. This, he assured me, had only been effected with great difficulty, owing to the opposition of the French, who were not less troublesome on the question of Scotland. The King (Henry), however, had firmly refused to agree to anything to the prejudice of your Majesty, or in contravention of the treaties with you; and the negotiations were almost entirely broken off in consequence. The King therefore placed no trust or confidence in the offers and promises of the French, until he saw the peace treaty actually signed by them; this being the excuse for their not having informed me earlier of the progress of their negotiations. In confirmation of this he (Tunstall) said that, when the King saw that, whilst the French were raising these difficulties they were constantly strengthening their forces by land and sea, he had despaired of coming to terms; and had not slackened in his preparations to continue the war. The bishop, then, as if of his own accord, remarked that the French reinforcements still continued daily, he knew not with what object. I do not quite understand this, either, and think well to advise your Majesty of it. With regard to the Scots, he said they had been included in the peace, on condition that they fulfil their promises and obligations towards the King (Henry), failing which the English are not to be bound to anything with regard to them; and may deal with them as they please. As he (Dr. Tunstall) did not volunteer any further statement as to the conditions, I was somewhat at a loss how to reply; but merely said I thanked God for having allowed the peace to be made, which was so sorely needed by Christendom at large, and acknowledged the kindness of the King, the Council and himself, for carrying the auspicious news to me. I added that I had never had any apprehension that the King his master would consent to anything prejudicial to your Majesty; and I rejoiced greatly that my confidence in this respect had not been at fault. I had no doubt that the arrangement arrived at was an honourable one for the King. To this he made no other reply than that the French after the first conference had proposed very iniquitous conditions, injurious both to your Majesty and to the King of England. He (Dr. Tunstall) was then leaving, and I asked him if they were to retain Boulogne. After a pause he simply replied yes: and so left me.

Since then I have learnt from a sure and secret source that it is true that the French strenuously endeavoured to seduce this King from his alliance with your Majesty, and that when the King dispatched his plenipotentiaries he strictly enjoined them not to listen to any proposals whatever which were discordant with the

---

[*] Cuthbert Tunstall, appointed to the See in 1530.

1546.

friendship and alliance with your Majesty. He (Henry) moreover entirely struck out certain clauses submitted by the French which were directed against this friendship. With regard to Boulogne, the town and its territory on this side of the river remain in the hands of the King of England, and will be inhabited by Englishmen until the King of France provides a very large sum of money, the amount of which was not communicated to me, to cover the cost of the war and the arrears of pension, which is still to be paid. It is said that peace will be proclaimed here to-morrow, and that the Admiral of France is to come hither, the Lord Admiral going to France. The galleys and ships of both princes are being recalled from the sea.

London, 12 June 1546.

June 14.
Vienna.
Imp. Arch.

277. VAN DER DELFT to the EMPEROR.

I received yesterday letters from the Queen instructing me to thank the King (of England) for the announcement of the conclusion of peace conveyed to her by his ambassador, and also for the good desire he had shown to maintain the amity and alliance with your Majesty in the course of the negotiations. I had audience of the King to-day for the purpose, and was received by him very kindly and graciously. He said that on no account would he have consented to make peace, unless the treaties and alliances he had with your Majesty were reserved intact. The French insisted upon this being done in the same form in which he (the King of England) had been included in the treaty of peace they had made with your Majesty; and with this object produced a certain extract from the said treaty. He (Henry) had, however, considered that the wording of this extract was insufficient and unsatisfactory, and persisted in his demand that all the treaties between him and your Majesty should be expressly reserved in all their vigour and force. The French raised great difficulties to this, and it seemed as if the whole negotiation would fall through in consequence. This had been the reason why he had deferred informing me of the matter, since, he told me, he would rather have broken off the conference altogether than have waived his demand for the express reservation of the treaties. I replied that I had never doubted that the peace would redound to his honour and advantage; and he then said that by the conditions he was to retain Boulogne, with the territory lying between the river and Guisnes and Calais; the pension to continue payable as heretofore, the first payment falling due in December next. If at the end of eight years the French wish to recover Boulogne they are bound to pay two millions in gold, in a lump-sum on one day. I remarked that in that case the place would remain firmly attached to him, whereupon he smiled. I can perceive no tendency in him but towards great satisfaction at the position of affairs, and constant attachment to your Majesty. The same may be said of his principal courtiers. They had a great meeting to-day, and the Lord Chancellor (Wriothesley), amongst others, assured me that he would not fail to work for the maintenance of the old friendship and alliance. They (the Councillors) also asked me very

1546.

scrupulously if I had written advice of the peace to your Majesty; and they were much pleased to hear that I had sent a special courier with the news to the Queen (Dowager). They did not mention Scotland to me, and in order to gain information I asked them if the rumour of the Cardinal's assassination was true. They said yes, it was, and that the two men who had committed the deed were of good family and now held the Cardinal's house.[*] The crime, they said, was a lamentable one, and Scotland in a bad way (bien basse). A French gentleman has come hither to invite the King to stand sponsor to the Dauphin's child. I understand that with this object he is to send a member of his order (*i.e.* the Garter). It is said also that Councillor Wotton is destined to be the ambassador resident in France.

The Bishop of Winchester and the Master of the Horse have returned here.

At the proclamation of peace made yesterday both in London and at Court, where the said French gentleman was present, it was was announced that, jointly with this treaty, the friendship, alliance and confederation between your Majesty and this King remained intact and inviolate.

London, 14 June 1546.

June 14.
Vienna
Imp. Arch.

278. Van der Delft to the Queen Dowager.

(The information contained in the letter to the Emperor of the same date is repeated, with only a few unimportant verbal variations. The following additional paragraphs occur in the present letter.)

After dinner as I was taking leave of them (*i.e.* the Councillors) I asked them if the King's army was to disperse, in order that your Majesty might take measures if necessary for the passage of the dismissed men without damage being done to the subjects. They replied that the King intended to dismiss the greater part of his troops next week, and they therefore begged me to write to your Majesty, so that the men might be accorded permission to pass, as was given for their journey thither (*i.e.* to Boulogne). I promised to do this, and I expect they will write to a similar effect to their ambassador resident with your Majesty.

(The writer humbly thanks the Queen for the gratuity she has accorded him as some solace for the great expense he is obliged to incur in his office.)

London, 14 June 1546.

June 17.
Paris.
Archives
Nationales.
K. 1486.

279. St. Mauris to Prince Philip.

I have replied in duplicate to your Highness' letters of 10th and 18th May; and I will now only refer to the contents of my last, in order to say that the more I enquire about the principal point dealt with (*i.e.* the apprehended attack upon Spanish Navarre by Henri d'Albret) the more convinced I am of the improbability of

---

[*] Beatoun was murdered in his castle of St. Andrews on the 29th May. Norman Leslie, the leader of the assassins, had captured the castle and held it for five months against the forces of the Regent Arran, when a truce was effected.

1546.

anything of the sort being effected this season, for the reasons I have already set forth. And if due diligence be observed it would be impossible for preparations for it to be made without their being discovered on the Spanish side.

On the 8th instant the peace between France and England was finally concluded at a place between Ardres and Guisnes,* where the Admirals of both nations met to negotiate; the negotiations having occupied about two months.

So far as can be positively ascertained the main provisions of the agreement are that Boulogne and all its county, with the whole of the forts except that constructed by the French last year, are to remain in the hands of the English for eight years; at the end of which time the King of France undertakes to pay two millions in gold, for the overdue annual pensions, and for the war indemnity cost of forts of Boulogne, etc. These two millions, and the pensions due for the next eight years from the present time, which will amount to 800,000 crowns more, are to be paid at the end of the eight years, and not before; the whole amount to be paid in a lump-sum; and when this condition is carried out the King of England undertakes to surrender the Boulognais etc. to France, including the new fort he has constructed near Marquise a league and a half from Calais. The Scots are included in the peace. I shall be able to learn further particulars later, and will convey them to your Highness. The peace was proclaimed at Paris on Whitsunday with a solemn procession, the King himself being in Paris at the time. The King of England is to do likewise in London. The Lord Admiral of England is expected in Paris. He comes with two objects: first to obtain this King's signature to the peace and to receive his oath to preserve it; and secondly to stand sponsor, as proxy for the King of England, for the young Princess of France.

As soon as the peace was agreed upon, both sovereigns broke up their armies, and the French dismissed the Lansquenets they had, which did not exceed 2,000. The rest of the force were Frenchmen; and there were not more than 10,000 men-at-arms altogether. It is asserted that the Admiral of France is at present taking measures to distribute their men-at-arms in the border towns; and they will need some of them even in Picardy. He (the Admiral) will shortly arrive in Paris; and, after conferring with the King, he will proceed to England to receive the King's oath and ratify the peace there.

It is considered certain that with the first favourable wind the galleys of France will sail for the Mediterranean, as they have no more to do in the ocean. One of them, under the command of Baron de Blancard, was captured recently by the English. Shortly before the peace was concluded there was a great skirmish, in which several French nobles were taken prisoners.

There is a rumour that certain Normans and Bretons are making ready to go to Brazil. It will be necessary to watch these men closely, to prevent them from molesting the vessels homeward bound from Peru. Any such action on their part would, however, be contrary to the wishes of the King, as he has often assured me.

---

* The peace was dated 7 June at Campen, the place referred to.

1546.

It is nearly six weeks since I have received any letters from the Emperor; so that I am at a loss what to write to your Highness about the Diet of Ratisbon.

Paris, 17 June 1546.

June 21.
Vienna.
Imp. Arch.

280. The EMPEROR to VAN DER DELFT.

We have received your letters of 15th and 27th ultimo and 3rd current, and have learnt therefrom all that had passed in the peace negotiations between the English and French, etc., for which information we thank you. We subsequently received a letter from our sister the Queen Dowager, enclosing a copy of one from the Admiral of France to her of 16 June, saying that peace was concluded; the English Ambassador having also assured her to the same effect. We have not yet been informed of the conditions in detail, but no doubt you will send us this information in your next letters, etc.

With regard to the return of their (*i.e.* the French) galleys to Marseilles; we have been in doubt as to whether we will let them pass by our Spanish dominions or not; having regard to the pillage and injury they will commit there on their way; in addition to the molestation which our subjects already constantly suffer at sea at the hands of the French. If you are spoken to about the voyage of these galleys by the Spanish coast, you may set forth the robberies and damage referred to, and say that in your opinion, since they are asking for this free passage, they had better begin by making restitution and redress to our subjects, and so take from the latter any reason for resenting the passage of the galleys by our coasts. You will go thus far; but will neither refuse nor accede to the request, and will report to us at once what was said in reply to you.

You will as soon as possible seek audience of the King (of England) and inform him on our behalf of the pleasure and satisfaction with which we have learnt of the conclusion of peace; and especially that, by the terms thereof, our treaty of alliance has been preserved intact; as we have been specially assured by the English Ambassador; and, indeed, as we fully expected would be the case. You will enlarge upon this point, as you see the opportunity affords, and the circumstances render desirable, in order to let the King understand that we were anxious for the agreement to be made, whilst observing duly our friendship and alliance.

We presume that rumours will have reached England that we are mustering an army; and perhaps the Protestants, even those who are ignorant of the object we have in view, may use great efforts to persuade the King of England to help them. You will therefore be very vigilant to obtain information of what goes on; so that when a fitting opportunity occurs, and in the way you think best, you may inform the King that it is impossible for us to ignore the proffered support and exhortations of the Catholics and honest folk of Germany, urging us to bring to reason certain princes who wish to prevent the common peace and justice of this country; and who wish to tyrannise over and oppress ecclesiastics and nobles, on the pretext of religion. We trust that, in regard of our friendship, the King will refuse to lend ear to such people, or to countenance

1546.

them. By so doing he will demonstrate the affection that he has always so emphatically professed towards us: and the frequent promises made through his own ministers, and through you, of his intention to act in all things cordially and fraternally, as we will always act towards him. We send you a letter of credence in case you should find it useful in making your statement more emphatic, etc.

Ratisbon, 21 June 1546.

June 21.
Vienna.
Imp. Arch.

281. The QUEEN DOWAGER to VAN DER DELFT.

Since yours of 10, 12 and 13 instant came to hand, we have received letters from the Emperor, informing us that, after having made every possible effort to bring the affairs of Germany to concord and tranquillity by a policy of conciliation and an avoidance of force, his Majesty, recognising that the Duke of Saxony and the Landgrave incessantly oppose his authority by keeping Duke Henry of Brunswick and his son prisoners, and occupying their territories, whilst refusing to attend the Diet or to obey his Majesty, which as vassals of the empire they are bound to do, has come to the conclusion that no further hope can be entertained that the two princes mentioned will be brought to submission by mildness; and the Emperor has consequently raised his forces of horse and foot to reduce them to obedience.* The Emperor will shortly inform you of this, for communication to the King of England; but as the letters may meet with some mishap on the road, and the information is already known, we have thought well to anticipate your receipt of the Emperor's letters, and to send you this direct, so that you may convey the intelligence to the King. As many people are trying to make out that this enterprise is not directed only against the Duke and the Landgrave, but is really undertaken on religious grounds, you may assure the King that his Majesty's intention is not to meddle with the religious question at all, but simply to punish the disobedience of the Duke and the Landgrave in the hope that he may thus bring Germany to unity. You will report what answer the King makes, what he seems to think of the enterprise; and also the rumours current about it in England.

We have not yet been able to learn the particulars of the articles of peace between the English and French; and it is important that we should know as soon as possible if the Scots are included in the treaty unconditionally, and if, consequently, the war with them is at an end. We have interrogated the English Ambassador here on the point, and he professes to know nothing. You will therefore inform the King or his Council that we, having, as they know, declared war against the Scots at the request of the English, the

---

* Philip of Hesse and John Frederick, Duke of Saxony, head of the Ernestine or senior branch of the house, with other members of the Smalkaldic league, absented themselves from the Diet of Ratisbon, recognising that, notwithstanding the elaborate efforts of the Emperor to deceive them, an attack upon religious liberty was impending. It will be seen in the course of the letters that the news of the Emperor's intentions were divulged earlier than he had intended, thanks mainly to the papal preparations and the gossip in Rome. By the above letter it is clear that even so late as this Charles was deliberately lying to Henry of England as to his intentions and protesting that the object of the war was not religious but political.

1546.

Emperor having for this reason refused to include them (the Scots) in his peace treaty with the French, notwithstanding all the persuasions of the French that he would do so; it is highly important that we should know whether the war with the Scots still continues, so that we may treat them accordingly. You will ask them (*i.e.* the English) to inform us of the true state of affairs. The French assert that the Scots are included unconditionally in the treaty; and that they (the French) would never have accepted peace without the inclusion of their allies. Others say that some condition was attached to the inclusion. No doubt if the Scots are included the King (of England) will have taken measures to prevent them from molesting the subjects of these dominions, in accordance with the treaty of alliance between the Emperor and the King (of England). Although the Bishop of Durham told you that the Scots were included, on condition that they fulfilled the treaties they have with the King of England, we should like to have some elucidation of the meaning of this condition, and whether it carries with it the cessation of war on the part of England and ourselves against the Scots. We having entered into the contest with the Scots solely by virtue of the treaty of alliance with England, we ought to be included in any negotiations or peace treaty with them. You will learn this as dexterously as you can.

With regard to the transit of soldiers who have left the English service, I have given permission that they should be allowed to pass, on condition that they pay for what they have and refrain from pilfering: otherwise they will be punished, in accordance with their offence. You can inform the Council of this, though probably the English Ambassador will have done so.

Brussels, 22 June 1546.

June 22.
Simancas.
E. R. 873.

282. CARDINAL OF CORIA to the EMPEROR.

The Archbishop of Cologne to be condemned for heterodoxy by the Pope.°

The capitulation which your Majesty signed on the 6th instant for the enterprise against the Protestants was considered to-day; and his Holiness has decided, in accordance with the opinion of the Sacred College, that it shall be heartily and sincerely accepted. We have all thanked God for guiding your Majesty to this holy and necessary resolution; and pray Him to give life and victory to your Majesty, etc. etc. . . . The enterprise is a great one; and some (*i.e.* of the Cardinals) were of opinion that grave difficulties would be encountered, through the danger of trusting Germans to fight against their own countrymen; and perhaps even against those who think like themselves.† They (*i.e.* the dissentient Cardinals)

° Hermann of Weid, Archbishop of Cologne had been deprived and excommunicated by the Pope for heresy. This was the principal cause for the premature unmasking of the Emperor's plans, and to some extent forced Charles' hand, as will be seen in the correspondence.

† This was actually the case. Not only did the famous Maurice of Saxony subsequently side with the Emperor to his own great worldly advantage, but the protestant Brandenburgs did so likewise, whilst the Count Palatine stood aside neutral.

1546.

also fear that the Protestants may enlist the aid of the Turk; and even that some Christian princes may help them openly or covertly. Others are of opinion that, Italy being divested of men and money, your Majesty's influence would increase unduly in the country; which, moreover, would be exposed to Protestant wars, in addition to those which usually afflict it. Other arguments were raised by those who desired to bring about a final settlement between your Majesty and the King of France before the enterprise was proceeded with. All these questions were satisfactorily met; as was also that which set forth the importance of the concession for the alienation of the monastic manors (in Spain), and of the league between the Pope and your Majesty against those who may seek to frustrate the object in view. The Cardinal of Trent especially gave great satisfaction by his prudence and reason. As he and the ambassador will write to you fully on the matter, and upon the appointment last Friday of a legate, I must refer your Majesty to their letters.

Before the arrival of the Cardinal (of Trent) the Pope discussed the business with some of the Cardinals, and dwelt upon the difficulties which occurred, by reason of the short time apparently available for warlike operations; and he also complained of certain encroachments upon the apostolic prerogatives over the temporalities etc. in Spain and Naples. He likewise expressed his dissatisfaction that so little information had been furnished to him, with regard to the preliminary steps which had led up to the decision. He had, he said, simply been told of the conclusion arrived at. On these and other points the ambassador will no doubt write to your Majesty; but so far as can be judged they were only raised in order that the value of the aid given to your Majesty may be enhanced.

Rome, 22 June 1546.

June 23.
Simancas.
E. R. 873.
Italian.

283. CARDINAL FARNESE to the EMPEROR.

I doubt not your Majesty will be informed by Señor Juan de la Vega of the readiness with which his Holiness has resolved to carry out everything that remains to be done on this side to aid the German enterprise. I have, nevertheless, thought well to convey the same intelligence to the Nuncio, in order that he may repeat it on my behalf to your Majesty. This testimony of mine will the more convince your Majesty that you may depend upon his Holiness. I also pray your Majesty to believe that never in my life have I experienced a consolation equal to this; both on account of the effects to be expected from the enterprise itself, and on account of the opportunity which God has thus afforded me personally of serving your Majesty.

Rome, 23 June 1546.

June 23.
Simancas.
E. R. 873.

284. JUAN DE VEGA to the EMPEROR.

Thanks to the diligence and laboriousness of the Cardinal of Trent he arrived there after dinner on Saturday 19th instant, notwithstanding his detention awaiting your Majesty's courier. I sent Pedro Marquina as far as Viterbo to meet him, and give him

1546.

a detailed account of the state of affairs here; and I also went out to meet him a mile or so before Cardinal Farnese, in order that I might confer with him as to the best course to take in your Majesty's interests.

Seeing how well Cardinal Farnese has behaved in the business of the German enterprise, which, thanks be to God, he has brought to a happy conclusion, Cardinal Trent and myself, after full consideration, thought it would be well that he (Farnese) should be informed of the main points of Cardinal Trent's mission; and that with a show of confidence in him, we might ask his advice.* He (Farnese) accepted the request with great satisfaction, and expressed an opinion that before anything else was done we should get the capitulation signed and ratified, and the troops sent off. After that, he thought, we could broach the other matters to the Pope. This opinion was given in a way that anyone would have come to the conclusion that its only object was the success of the enterprise. He (Farnese) also begged the Cardinal and myself to make influence with his Holiness that he (Farnese) should in any case be sent as legate, to serve God and your Majesty in this undertaking. He deplored that the French, the Venetian ambassadors and other private persons had striven, and were still striving, against the enterprise. It is quite true that they are doing so; and especially as regards Farnese's going thither (to Germany) suggesting to the Pope great distrust of your Majesty.

The first day of Cardinal Trent's arrival passed thus, and the next day he, and I in his company, went to see the Pope. We also thought well to ask Cardinal Farnese to go with us, which he did. After Cardinal Trent had kissed his Holiness' foot, delivered his letters of credit, and answered the usual ceremonial questions, he thanked his Holiness for the aid he had extended to the enterprise, and presented to him the signed capitulation. He explained the reason for the delay, and prayed his Holiness that no time should be lost, etc. His Holiness spoke at length, though not quite so long as usual, recapitulating certain complaints he had previously made to me personally. He raised difficulties to the enterprise, in consequence of a definite peace not having been made with France, and the English matter being in its present position. The season, he continued, was very far advanced, but he ended by saying that, so far as he was concerned, there should be no failure in fulfilling his promises.

Although he did not pledge himself so definitely as was to be desired with regard to the present steps, it was evident that he had no intention of breaking his word, but only raised these questions for the purpose of magnifying the importance of the undertaking, and its risks; and so of enhancing the value of his own share in it. We therefore let him say what he liked, without attempting entirely to upset his arguments. The next day the Pope held a council; and it was decided to issue the marching orders for the 12,000 infantry and 700 horse, adding to the cavalry men stipulated in the treaty 200 more, who will go

---

* Cardinal Trent's mission was principally to induce the Pope to grant to the Emperor the half first fruits on the ecclesiastical preferments in Flanders.

1546.

under command of John Baptist Savello; Alexander Vitello will have charge of the infantry, and the Duke Octavio will command in chief, in addition to the legate, whose name was not announced. Cardinal Farnese told Trent that, over and above the 700 horse above mentioned, he would have in his own train 300 mounted gentlemen and others, to bring up the number of cavalry in all to nearly 1,000. A good choice of officers has been made; and I think the force will be the best that has left Italy for a long time. Farnese also said that 200 mounted harquebussiers would be given to Captain Nicolo Seco, as your Majesty ordered, though it would be done with difficulty, a hundred being knocked off of the 300 requested.

The day following a congregation of Cardinals was held, which lasted for a long time. The enterprise was discussed, and it was resolved to sign the capitulation and furnish the money for the despatch of the troops. This has been done; and there is much drumming and rejoicing about the streets. But the matter was not carried through without a good deal of opposition on the part of many Cardinals, as your Majesty will learn from Cardinal Trent, who was present. I will only add, for my own part, that I have been informed by persons in high authority who were present at the congregation, that Cardinal Trent, both in his statement on behalf of your Majesty and in the way he met the various objections, bore himself so bravely and prudently as to fulfil the best wishes of your Majesty's servants. In addition to the other good parts he possesses, he proved that Teuton eloquence is in no whit inferior to the Italian. This is, in substance, what has been done since the Cardinals' arrival up to-day, Tuesday, 22 June. Later, with God's help, we will attend to the carrying out of the rest of the Cardinals' mission. I will give due advice of this, and of other things that I have omitted to mention, in order that the bearer of this may depart the more speedily.

Rome, 23 June 1546.

June 27.
Simancas.
E. B. 873.

285. JUAN DE VEGA to the EMPEROR.

Cardinal Trent sends a person to your Majesty with his report of all that has happened since his coming hither; and when, please God, the Cardinal himself arrives in your Majesty's presence, you will be in possession of full particulars, he having been present throughout, and having omitted no effort or skill in serving your Majesty efficaciously.

The capitulation, duly signed by the Pope, is being sent. His Holiness would much like to delay it, in consequence of the concession of sale of monastic manors. The Cardinal (Trent) says that when this point was discussed in the Consistory all the Cardinals were greatly against this concession. It would be better, they said, that the monasteries should contribute the 500,000 ducats in money, jewels, or loans on revenue, than to alienate their manors: and a satisfactory Brief should be drawn up to this effect. It was stated that the Pope would be very much obliged to your Majesty if you would consent to this.

1546.

It is quite true that the money could be obtained much more quickly and readily by the method proposed, than by the sale of the manors; with the additional advantage that your Majesty would not have to pledge your revenue to pay to the monasteries the income represented by the manors alienated. It looked a favourable suggestion but we did not accept it, but requested the Pope to sign the capitulation in its present form; and promised to lay the suggestion before your Majesty, as we now do. Cardinal Trent will write more at length on the same question. If your Majesty approves of the change, it will be necessary to send advice as quickly as possible. It will greatly please the Pope and the Sacred College, which I am sure will raise great difficulty about confirming the capitulation with the alienation clause in it. If your Majesty decides to keep things as they are, you might utilise the Brief which is in the hands of the Nuncio there (*i.e.* in Spain) and afterwards send advice hither as to the course to be pursued. Cardinal Trent has urged very strongly the matter of 100,000 crowns° in addition to the first 200,000; and even more strongly the request about the half first fruits in the Netherlands. There has been much discussion on these points, but they have declined to come to any decision at present, though it seems as if in the end they will consent, as the Pope signifies that if the enterprise begins well as he hopes, and he sees it going on favourably, he will do much more for it than he has promised. Until that time comes, he says, we must be satisfied with what he has already done. Your Majesty will have learnt that nothing was attempted in the way of suspending the Council (of Trent), as was feared would be the case, but that the date for the next session was fixed. For this and other reasons which will be conveyed by Cardinal Trent, the clause in the instructions relative to this point was not read to the Pope. The matter is left in my hands to be dealt with if any fresh suggestion of suspension is made or until all the other points of the instructions have been successfully carried out in a way that they cannot be undone. Cardinal Trent very cleverly managed to get the Secretary of the Duke of Florence out of prison. He did not request his release on behalf of your Majesty or the Duke of Florence; on the contrary, he swore to the Pope that not a word had been said to him on the matter; but that he made the request entirely of his own accord. He pressed the point so strongly and so eagerly, that, although the Pope alleged many reasons against it, the man was ultimately liberated.

Rome, 27 June 1546.

June 28.
Simancas.
E. B. 873.

286. JUAN DE VEGA to the EMPEROR.

I spoke to the Pope respecting the 30,000 crowns which Don Fernando wrote to me would be needed for bringing the Spanish infantry out of Piedmont and sending it to Germany, and also about the 50,000 crowns, and the 100,000 crowns deposited in

---

° Paul III. had given a half promise through Cardinal Farnese to contribute a further subsidy of 100,000 crowns in addition to the first 200,000 promised for the religious war. It will be seen that the Pope successfully evaded the payment of the additional subvention.

1546.

Augsburg. The steps directed by your Majesty were also taken concerning the money necessary for the cavalry to be raised by the Prince of Sulmona. We have made use of Farnese for these negotiations, but his Holiness has not come to any decision on the matter yet. He wishes to keep to the letter of the capitulation without doing any more for the present, but holds out hopes for the future.

In confirmation of this resolution, Farnese sent me word by Marquina that he thought it would be better not to press his Holiness further on these matters just now; and I have written in accordance with this to the Viceroy of Naples and to Don Fernando.[°] All diligence is being employed with regard to the fulfilment of the capitulation, and the carrying through of Cardinal Trent's instructions. Cardinal Farnese sent me last night a letter to read. It had been written by one of the Fuggers[†] to some merchants here, through whom the deposit of those 100,000 crowns was made in Fugger's house at Augsburg. They write giving the merchants notice that the time has already expired during which they were bound to furnish the money. There is, they say, a rumour of impending war in Germany; and they (the Fuggers) being no longer able to undertake to pay the sum in question there, they request that his Holiness should be informed of this. Farnese asked me what I thought should be done in the matter, in order that the Pope might at once do what was necessary. As it was a matter that allowed of no delay, and your Majesty had instructed Cardinal Trent that the deposits of funds should not be made in Augsburg, which was a suspicious place; nor in Venice, as it was too far off, I replied that the money might be transferred to Trent; and I sent Marquina to Cardinal Farnese this morning to make arrangements for this to be done; and the same in the case of the other 100,000 crowns, which are to be deposited. Farnese approved of this; saying that the 100,000 crowns that were in Augsburg should be transferred at once to Trent, and the other 100,000 he (Farnese) would carry to Germany himself. Rome, 28 June, 1546.

July 3.
Vienna
Imp. Arch.

287. The Emperor to Van der Delft.

We have received your letters of 10, 12 and 14th ultimo, and have been much pleased to read of the conversation between the King of England and yourself respecting the peace he has concluded with the King of France, in which peace the treaty of alliance between the former and us has been expressly reserved. We have already written to you instructions to thank him on our behalf, and to assure him of the great pleasure we have felt at hearing the news of peace. We have also instructed you to explain to him the reason why we are assembling forces, and we need not enlarge again upon that point; only saying that if on the receipt of this you have not

---

[°] Don Fernando Gonzaga, formerly Viceroy of Sicily had recently been appointed Governor of Milan for the Emperor.

[†] The Fuggers were the great German bankers, the Rothschilds of their day, whose financial ramification extended all over Europe, the principal seat of their business being at Augsburg.

already done so, you should lose no time in making the declaration on the first opportunity, using the kindest expressions possible; and reporting to us, as secretly as you can, what is going on there.

We send you enclosed the report we have received from Spain, as to the money and other property that was in the ship from the Indies pillaged by Renegat and other Englishmen. It will be necessary for you to take up the matter and claim restitution; letting us know as soon as possible what you obtain, in order that we may take the necessary measures in Spain respecting the claims made by Englishmen there.

Ratisbon, 3 July, 1546.

288. JUAN DE VEGA to the EMPEROR.

His Holiness has been asked for the money for the cavalry to be raised by the Prince of Sulmona, but he refused to give it, as he also did that required to bring the Spanish infantry out of Piedmont. To-morrow Sunday, Cardinal Farnese will receive the cross* of legate, and his brother the Duke (Octavio Farnese) the staff. The Cardinal says he will leave the same evening or on Monday, the Duke departing on Tuesday or Wednesday. Rome, 3 July, 1546.

289. ST. MAURIS to PRINCE PHILIP.

I have already informed your Highness of all I had been able to learn about the conditions of peace between France and England; and, as something fresh has come out here every day since, I have done my best to ascertain the true particulars for your Highness' information. First: I find that everyone agrees here that Boulogne and the forts are to remain in the hands of the English for eight years. The English also retain the territory of Boulogne on the Calais side; which they define as that on the other side of the river near Boulogne; the territory on this side (*i.e.* the South side) of the river to remain in the hands of the French. The English insisted on keeping the territory in question, on the ground that if the money they demand was not paid they should at least hold a valuable pledge to represent it, and in the meanwhile that the revenue derived would remunerate them for the loss of interest on the sum which should have been paid down. Some dispute was raised as to the ownership of the river itself, but it was finally arranged that it should be held in common. At the same time it was settled that the owners of property situated in the English zone might return to their homes, and retain their possessions, on taking the oath of allegiance to the King of England. It is true, Sire, that many persons asserted that the owners were not to be allowed to retain their possessions until the eight years of English occupation had expired; but I am positively assured that the conditions are really as I have stated them.

It has also been agreed that the King of England is to be bound to restore Boulogne at the end of the eight years, and not before, on

---

* That is to say of papal legate to the Emperor for the purposes of the religious war: Octavio Farnese (Duke of Camarino), the son-in-law of the Emperor, being given at the same time the baton of Commander of the Papal contingent.

1546.

the King of France paying him in current legal money of full weight the sum of 2,000,000 sun-crowns in gold, to represent the overdue pensions and the works on the fortifications of Boulogne, and the other neighbouring forts. The French assert that no mention whatever is made of a war-indemnity; and that they would never have consented to the shame of such a thing as to have paid an indemnity in a war where their own expenses have exceeded those of the English. The King of France is furthermore bound to pay at the expiry of the eight years the pensions then due. They say here now that the King of England is bound to accept the money and evacuate Boulogne before the end of the eight years, if the French wish to pay it: but it is believed for certain that he is not so bound.

The King of England has promised the King of France that when he receives the money, at the end of the eight years, he will give up Boulogne and the forts with the territory adjacent etc., as well as the other forts which the King of England has enormously strengthened. The Admiral of France is making very much of this point; as he says that the King of France could not have fortified these places for a million in gold.

Both sides are to be allowed to strengthen or finish the new forts they have made. The Holy See has not been included in the peace, but it is looked upon as certain that, by common consent, your Highness (*i.e.* Spain) has been included: the King of France I am assured, especially, having brought this point forward. On his part it was insisted, not only that he could not make peace without the consent of your Highness, but that you must be expressly included in it, and great demonstration of a desire to retain your friendship was made. In any case both of them are bound to this effect.

Cardinal Ferrara positively assured Mme. D'Etampes that the King of England binds himself by this peace to aid the King of France, if your Highness first violates the treaty of peace, the King of France being desirous of preventing your Highness from raising war against him, as he wishes to live in peace until his people have recovered. I have not heard this detail from any other quarter. When I was conversing recently with the Chancellor (Olivier), he told me that the Scots had been included unconditionally in the peace; and I have also heard this from the Queen of France,[a] she having learnt it from Châtillon, a friend of the Keeper of the Seals. When her Majesty told me this she said that the King of France undertook by the treaty to aid, so far as he could, the marriage of the young Queen of Scots with the Prince of England. He the (keeper of the seals) had divulged (to Châtillon) that during the negotiations the King of England had insisted that this clause was, in effect, an agreement that the marriage should take place, as everything, he said, depended upon the King of France. The latter, however, replied that the maiden was not yet at liberty, nor was she of an age when any definite talk about her marriage could be undertaken. Two gentlemen had thereupon been sent to Scotland, one French and the other English, to learn

---

[a] It must not be forgotten that the Queen was Eleanor of Austria, the sister of the Emperor.

the views of the Regent (Arran). The Regent and all the Scottish Council replied that they submitted the matter entirely to the decision of the King of France. The latter had expected another answer; but in the face of it he could not avoid making a promise that when the Princess of Scotland reached a proper age he would do his best to incline her to such a marriage. The people here, Sire, insist that these promises and purposes do not really bind them to anything: but the truth is that they themselves confess that the English will endeavour to hold them to them; and they add that the King of England has not taken the eight years for the purpose of restoring Boulogne, but because at the end of that time the Princess of Scotland will be marriageable; and if the King of France fails to promote the marriage, the King of England will refuse to fulfil his part of the treaty. This means that the King of England not only aims at obtaining the payment of his money, but to be able at the same time to allege the excuse of the marriage for making war upon Scotland, which he will easily subdue, unless France aids the Scots. If such aid is given he will pretend that the King of France has failed to promote the marriage, as he undertook to do. On the other hand, it is argued that the King of France might assist the Scots, as the latter are included in the peace.

We also learn through Châtillon that the Keeper of the Seals told him that he held a secret clause in the treaty, which is not included in the main document, mutually binding the Kings of France and England and the Protestants to aid each other if any of them be assailed. Châtillon told this in confidence to the Queen of France, adding that the Admiral had suggested that the Protestants deserved to have something done for them; as they had been the intermediaries who had brought about the peace. This, he said, would also be another cut at the Pope, to whom, he continued, the King of France bore no great love. No more, Sire, was learnt on this point, Châtillon being unable to say whether the mutual aid was to be furnished only in case of religious war, or in case of any attack whatever. Châtillon, however confirms that the King of France bound himself to help the Protestants if they were asssailed; and the agreement was repeated when the Duke of Lunenburg was here, as Châtillon says he was told by the Keeper of the Seals, who was theprin cipal instrument of the King of France in the negotiation of this mutual assistance clause. I can give no further assurance than this to your Highness of the truth.

The King of France recently informed the Queen that he had communicated to your Highness all the conditions of the peace treaty, as he had also done to the Queen of Hungary.[*] He had, no doubt, he said, that people would try to represent them otherwise. Your Highness will therefore be able to compare his version with mine; but these facts make me suspect that he has acted, or at least has endeavoured to act, sincerely towards your Highness in the negotiations.

---

[*] Mary of Austria Regent of the Netherlands, the Emperor's sister.

1546.

People here are not well pleased with the peace, seeing that the detention of Boulogne by the English will cause them a greater pest than before. And in good truth, Sire, the encroachments that will result are obvious.

In conclusion, I may say that public opinion is firm in the belief that the King of France has not negotiated the peace for the purpose of traversing your Highness' affairs, but out of sheer necessity, his realm being so exhausted and the people so impoverished that they can hardly maintain themselves. I am assured that, unless he is attacked, the King intends to preserve peace for some time.

With regard to the collection of the money to be paid to the English, it is asserted that the King of France, with the approval of his Council, has decided to impose during the next eight years four tithes each year, and to shut up the money in some place, so that his Church will pay the whole amount agreed upon. The people, however, are saying that the ladies will oppose this, as they would like to be recompensed and treated with this money.*

Melun, 4 July.

Another letter, of the same date, from St. Mauris to the Prince, refers to the embargo of a French ship in Spain. No complaint has been made yet to him about it. He is of opinion that the French Government may have addressed the Emperor direct about it; but he has been told that the French are keeping quiet, in order suddenly to embargo Spanish ships in France. "Truly the Admiral is very unjust. He openly declares his desire to enrich himself at the expense of others, under the pretence of his office." "Sire, the principal object of this letter is to inform your Highness that the King of France has received intelligence of the death of the Cardinal of Scotland. He was killed by two of his servants, at the solicitation of certain Scottish enemies of his, who are partisans of the King of England. The French are certain that the King of England himself caused the murder to be committed; as he hated the Cardinal mortally, because the latter opposed the marriage of the Princess of Scotland with the Prince of England. The worst of it is that after the deed was done the aforesaid Scots threw themselves into a very strong Scottish fortress, and the Cardinal's friends say that they will have them expelled by the Regent's forces, whilst possibly the King of England may help the other party, and thus a fresh conflict may arise through these Scotsmen, even before the time comes for the restitution of Boulogne. It is certain that the King of England will do all he can to keep the territory (*i.e.* the Boulognais), whilst the French will make every effort to prevent him; for they will not consent on any account that it shall remain English.

Melun, 4 July, 1546.

---

* The sentence is somewhat obscure. It runs thus, "Mas, el pueblo, Syre, dizen que las damas se oppornan porque estan en possession de ser recompensadas y gratificadas de los dichos dineros." The translation from the original French to Spanish for Philip's use has evidently not been made by a Spaniard, and there are several instances of similar obscurity in the text.

1546.
July 4.
Paris.
Archives
Nationales.
K. 1486.

290. ST. MAURIS to COBOS.

I reply to your enquiry of 20 June as to how the King of France and his ministers speak of the Emperor's undertaking in Germany. When they first heard of it, they rejoiced exceedingly, as they thought it would mean a perpetual war between his Majesty and his own people; the King himself saying at table that the Protestants would fight a hundred battles, and the Emperor was now just in the place that he (the King of France) had wished him in for a long time past. But afterwards, when they saw that Catholic Germany would rally to his Majesty's aid, and that the Lutheran towns and cities had not yet declared themselves against him, they began to say that as his Majesty had only to deal with a few individuals, he would carry through the enterprise as he liked. They are very downhearted at this, as they always believed that his Majesty would not put his foot down; and they are now saying that he is acting very cruelly in declaring war against a few princes who had risen against the Empire, but without touching the question of religion. I spoke two days since with the King of France on his Majesty's behalf, for the purpose of requesting him to refrain from helping those against whom his Majesty was making war. His answer was that he was not in any way bound to, or allied with, Germany or the Princes; and would not give any such help as that referred to, which, moreover, had not even been requested. Certainly all good people greatly esteem his Majesty for taking up arms in such a good cause. I took the opportunity to congratulate the King of France on the peace he had recently made. He replied that he was very much pleased at it, as the English had undertaken to return Boulogne to him. The Pope is moving the King of France to set on foot a reconciliation between the Holy See and the King of England, and he (the Pope) offers that, on condition that the King of England recognises the papacy, he (the Pope) will deal with all other matters to the King's satisfaction. The Pope also promises the King of France, in return for his good offices in this matter, that he (the Pope) will personally visit the Emperor, and intercede with him about Piedmont, and will use every effort to bring about a marriage between our Prince and Madame Marguérite.[*] The King of France has replied that he would most willingly intervene in the way desired, but that he is unable to do so at the present time, as he has recently been in negotiation with the King of England, and the latter had refused to allow the envoy sent by the Holy Father to France to go to England with the ordinary French ambassador sent thither.[†] The Pope, however, still persisted in his endeavours to find some means of bringing about a reconciliation, and intends to employ for the purpose a Venetian[‡] who took part in the recent peace negotiations, as he is popular in England.

The ordinary Nuncio here only a week ago again begged the King of France to send his prelates to the Council (of Trent) setting

---

[*] Between the recently widowed Philip and Margaret of France, afterwards the wife of Emanuel Philibert of Savoy.

[†] Odet de Selve, who had just been sent as ambassador to England, where he remained until 1549.

[‡] Francisco de Bernardi.

1546.

forth that the said Council will now commence to deal with the settlement of the faith (*conclusiones de la fe*). The King of France replied that he was astonished that the Holy Father should so continually exhort him to send his prelates to the Council, as he himself was acting in a way that impaired its completeness (*hacia actos contrarios a la perfeccion del Concilio*). He (the Pope) was assisting the Emperor with 10,000 men against the Dukes of Saxony and the Landgrave of Hesse. This was a great responsibility for him to take, as it was promoting war during the continuance of the Council, where he should have endeavoured to avoid it, and so have rendered its deliberations safe. There was good reason for not sending the prelates to the Council, even without this. Thus he (the King of France) showed himself extremely displeased at the Pope's aid being sent to the war, and excused himself from sending representatives to the Council.

I have already served here for a year and seven months, and have only received 500 crowns from Spain and 600 from Italy, much less than is due to me. Please send me 500 crowns as soon as possible. The Emperor decided that my salary of 5 sun-crowns per day should be paid by Spain; and promised me that the crowns should be sent hither in specie. They now want to pay me in Spanish crowns. Please let me be paid the difference, which will be 3½ sueldos per crown. I will send you a recently published decree, fixing the value of the Spanish crowns at 46½ sueldos and the French crowns are worth 45; so that in addition to my back pay I should be credited with 3½ sueldos for each crown that I have received.* Melun, 4 July, 1546.

July 6.
Vienna.
Imp. Arch.

291. VAN DER DELFT to the QUEEN DOWAGER.

I have received your Majesty's letter of 22nd ultimo; having on the previous day received that of the Emperor, dated 20th of the same month at Regensburg (Ratisbon), with a letter of credence for the King on the same subject as that sent by your Majesty. I sent to the Court at Greenwich to ask for audience, for the purpose of presenting the letter, and I was duly received by the King on Sunday, the day before yesterday. It happened that, at the same instant, the French Ambassador (son of the late first President of Paris) who had arrived here the previous day, and myself, entered the Court together. I should have preferred for him to have had audience first, so that I might have sounded the King as to how things were going: but I was preferred, and was accorded first admission. The King received me very graciously; and after having handed him the letter of credence, I assured him of the great pleasure that his Majesty had experienced at learning of the conclusion of peace between him (Henry) and France, with the

---

* The nominal value of the sun-crown was thus 50 sueldos. The complaints of the ambassadors and other officers of non-payment or short payment of their salaries are continually repeated in their letters to Cobos, but they are not usually reproduced in the Calendar, as they are only interesting as marking the general penury and the almost exclusive dependence of Charles upon Castile for his resources. The above paragraph, however, is printed in full, as it is important in fixing the somewhat disputed value of the current coinage at the time.

1546.

reservation of the treaties of amity between the Emperor and himself, which was in accordance with the confident expectation that his Imperial Majesty had always felt in him. He took this in good part; and I then stated to him the causes and reasons of the enterprise of his Majesty against certain princes of the Empire, who were disobedient, and perturbers of the general tranquillity of Germany, to the detriment of the imperial authority. The King appeared much displeased at this, and, interrupting me, he said that he had heard something of the enterprise; but he could not well believe that his Majesty would take up arms against his own people, especially in such times as these. Was the matter definitely decided? he asked. I replied that I believed so, and that the Emperor could not do otherwise than he had done, having endured so long the injuries, threats, and wrongs that they (the princes) had committed against the Duke of Brunswick and his sons, who were kept prisoners, without any regard to the fact that they were the Emperor's vassals; and, indeed, against all the Catholic nobles and ecclesiastics, forcing them by threats and other evil means to join their confederations. This, I said, was directed to the weakening of the imperial authority and the oppression of all Germany; where, although the Protestants were powerful, the party of those that desired tranquillity, union, justice, and keeping of everyone in his proper place, was not less so. These had long yearned for a remedy for the evil, which increased every day, and his Majesty had hitherto sought by gentleness to overcome the trouble. Since, however, no result had been attained by this means; but, on the contrary, things had gone from bad to worse, his Majesty had listened to the exhortation of his subjects, and for the maintenance of his authority and justice had been obliged to adopt extreme measures to reduce the disobedient elements to reason. The King repeated that he was displeased with this enterprise, and said that, if his Majesty had taken his advice, he would have postponed it. The reasons alleged by me, he said, were mere shadows: it was really the Pope's money that had induced the Emperor to do as he had done; and he much feared that his Majesty would find himself deceived after all; for the real origin of the war was perfectly well understood, and it was quite probable that those who pretended to be on his Majesty's side now would be against him some day. I replied that there was nothing shadowy in what I said as to the causes of the war but the plain truth; and the Emperor trusted that he (Henry) would see the matter in the same light, and not lend ear to those who would otherwise disguise it. So far as regarded the religious question, his Majesty would refer that to the Council. "What Council?" asked the King. I replied, "the Council of Trent"; whereupon he seemed not much pleased, and I thought necessary to repeat the words about his Majesty's trust that he would not listen to those who would endeavour to represent matters otherwise. I besought him to reflect on and consider the question sincerely, for he knew, I said, better than I, how much the Emperor had endured from some of his vassal princes. He replied that he had nothing to do with them; but that if he could do anything to avoid or pacify such a pitiable war, he would very willingly

1546.

do it. He then asked me if M. de Buren had set out with the troops it was said he had raised in Flanders. I replied that I did not know anything about that; and the King then questioned the wisdom of denuding Flanders of troops at the present time, with such a neighbour as we had. Although it seemed to me that this remark referred to the French, I am not sure that he had not Denmark in his mind, as some people here tell me that the Danes are arming to invade Holland. I therefore answered that the cavalry raised by Buren were foreigners, with the exception of one or two bands, and that the Netherlands were well guarded. He did not follow up this; but again expressed his displeasure that his Majesty should have entered upon this war. The French ambassador (Odet de Selve) was afterwards led into the King's presence by the Lord Admiral. He remained a considerable time with the King, and in the meanwhile I had several conversations with Winchester and Paget, whom I found very favourable to the public good, and to the interests of his Majesty. As these are the Councillors most in favour with the King, I doubt not that they will be good instruments for maintaining the existing friendship, and for preventing the Protestants from gaining footing or favour here. They (Gardiner and Paget) have confidently promised me this.

With regard to the peace conditions between the English and the French, I have been unable to ascertain anything beyond what I have already written to your Majesty. The Scots are, it appears, comprised in the peace, on the conditions mentioned to me by the Bishop of Durham, namely that they have to comply with all the treaties and engagements that they have entered into with the King of England; though I have not been informed what these engagements are. As your Majesty desires further enlightenment on the point, I asked the Councillors what was the position between them and the Scots; and if they were at peace or at war. I said it was necessary for us to know, because we were at war with the Scots for their (the English) sake, and for that reason the Emperor had declined to include the Scots in his treaty of peace with France, notwithstanding all the efforts made with that end by the French. They (the English Councillors) replied that the Scots were included on the condition I have mentioned; and that they (the English) had sent to Scotland to learn what the intention of the Scots was. A reply, they said, was expected shortly.

When I was conversing yesterday with Paget on the same subject, he told me that in the course of the recent peace negotiations, the Admiral of France and others had affirmed that the Scots were included in the peace between the Emperor and the French, although on the advice of those who conducted the business the point was not included formally in the capitulations, for certain reasons. On his (Paget's) asking them if he might state this fact confidently, they replied in the affirmative; and said that they would confirm him. As I saw that Paget made this assertion in good faith, I said that, although it was not true, I could easily believe that the French had told him so, for they had dared to tell us that the Scots were included absolutely unconditionally in this new peace (between England and France) in opposition to what the Council had told me last Sunday. I said it seemed very strange to me that he should

1546.

take for gospel what the French told him, whilst he would not believe what we said. He ended by assuring me that the Scots were only included on the condition mentioned, and promised that, as soon as their reply was received, he would advise me. Immediately he does so I will report to your Majesty.

I have heard from a secret source that since the French Ambassador and I have spoken with the King, the latter has continued melancholy. It is certain that he was on that day fully dressed and ready to go to mass, but did not go; nor did he go into his gardens, as he is in the habit of doing in the summer months. The coming of the Admiral of France is also deferred, and this is arousing suspicion on the part of the King: the Earl of Hertford, who was at Boulogne ready to come hither, having been ordered to remain there. The Admiral of England (Dudley) was ready to set out (for France), but now remains uncertain from day to-day; so I fancy that affairs are not yet entirely settled. Many persons say that the French have accepted the peace, because they saw that the Emperor was gathering his forces, and they thought it was in order to attack them (the French).

There is a great examination and punishment of the heretics here, no class being spared; and as those who have retracted have been pardoned, the principal doctors have publicly revoked the condemned doctrines, and this has had a very good effect upon the common people, who are greatly infected. The King comes to Westminster to-morrow. He is very well.

London, 6 July, 1546.

Postscript.—After having written the above I have heard from a trustworthy informant that great difficulty is foreseen here from the delay in the coming of the Admiral of France; and they (the English) are much chagrined that they have dismissed the Germans, since the King of France has not entirely broken up his army. The King (of England) is making ready all his ships, it is said to go against Scotland, but I suspect rather that it is to guard against surprise at any point.

July 15.
Simancas.
E. 1318

292. Advices from Venice.

Ludovico delle Arme had arrived at Venice, and the next day, he was with the chiefs for a long time, greatly alarming the country and the Cardinal of England, who is 15 miles away.[*] Delle Arme told Montesa that he had first been with the chiefs on private business for friends of his; and as the chiefs knew he had come from here (Germany) they had asked him what news he had. He had thereupon greatly magnified your Majesty's forces, and told them that you could do as you liked in the war, which would end

---

[*] It will be recollected that Ludovico delle Arme was an Italian condottiere in the service of England. The fear with which his negotiations with the Seigniory inspired Cardinal Pole arose probably from the idea that an alliance between Venice and the Protestants might lead to the Cardinal's surrender to the English King. Arme had gone to Monferrat on his way to Venice for the purpose of bespeaking mercenary troops for the English service from his house in Castelgoffredo. The Cardinal Regent of Mantua was greatly alarmed at his presence in Monferrat-Mantuan territory and refused to receive him, and finally requested him to leave the duchy. *See* Venetian Calendar.

1546.

sooner than was thought. He told the chiefs of the Council of Ten that he had gone to Ratisbon to see what your Majesty was doing, and had then taken a tour through the country to obtain information. He had found your Majesty the master of all. It was, he said, agreed upon by your Majesty and the Pope that on the passage of the Papal troops they were to steal a large stretch of territory belonging to the Seigniory, and stay there; aided by the Neapolitan and Milanese troops, as well as by those which were being raised in the neighbourhood of Trent, and others raised by the King of the Romans. If they, the Seigniory, were thus taken unaware before they could move, they would lose most of their territory on the mainland. The Seigniory were much alarmed at this, and they immediately sent the Duke of Urbino to Verona, and ordered the guards to be doubled everywhere. Cardinal Cornaro, a true and devoted servant of your Majesty, advised us of this.

A similar paper of advices from Venice of the same date states that the Seigniory was very indignant at a rumour, said to have been set afloat in Rome by the Cardinal of Trent, to the effect that they had been endeavouring to dissuade the Pope from aiding the Emperor. The Seigniory had emphatically declared that they were innocent of such an "infamous" proceeding. In order to clear the Cardinal of Trent of the blame, Cardinal Cornaro had published some letters he had received from Rome, saying that the Venetian ambassador there had brought great pressure upon the Pope and his friends to dissuade them from aiding in the war against the Protestants. The Seigniory had thereupon sent for these letters, and after reading them had published that their ambassador in Rome had acted thus without instructions and should be punished.

July 16.
Simancas.
E. R. 873.

293. JUAN DE VEGA to the EMPEROR.

(Details of letters received and despatched. Refers to previous letters with regard to the raising and despatch of the Papal contingent under the Farneses. All activity has been, and shall be, employed.) Not hearing any talk, or seeing any such attempts as your Majesty was informed from Trent would be made here to suspend the Council; and thinking that this arose from the Pope's desire to banish all cause for suspicion on your Majesty's part, I spoke to his Holiness about it. I said that your Majesty had heard of the rumours of the suspension of the Council on the occasion of the armed troops being sent; and I added that as such rumours might militate against the good intentions of his Holiness and your Majesty, in the matter of the Council I should be glad if he would cause the legates (of Trent) to be requested to make known that there was no thought or idea of suspending the Council. He replied that he had also heard the rumours in question, and had written to the legates on the same day that Cardinal Farnese left here, requesting them to address the prelates to the effect suggested by your Majesty. The prelates were to be told that these soldiers, being Papal troops, and not enemies, they should be regarded rather as an additional security than as a menace to the Council. So that six days before your Majesty's letter arrived here, your orders had been anticipated. We have been pressing for the Brief for the half-first fruits in Spain. His Holiness has ordered it to be dispatched, as it would have been already if the Pope had not been away at Frascati, twelve miles away. He returned yesterday, and the matter shall be closely followed up until the Brief is despatched. The Briefs directed to the prince-bishops and other ecclesiastics of Germany, respecting the aid due to your Majesty, are also being sent off.

Seven or eight days after the publication here of the Treaty with your Majesty, a secretary of the King of France named Aubespine arrived here. He had heard the news of the treaty as soon as he crossed the mountains ; and believing that in the circumstances his mission was unadvisable, he tarried on the road until he received a reply from the King. The day before he arrived in Rome, and subsequently, the couriers from France reached him, it is believed instructing him to refrain from carrying out his mission. The first time he saw his Holiness, he simply told him in general terms that peace had been concluded with England, giving a confused idea only of the terms. He also asked for a Cardinal's hat for a nephew of M. de Bourbon, and begged the Pope's pardon for some crimes committed by a certain bishop. He expressed dissatisfaction at the aid being given by the Pope to the war ; saying that the same should have been done for the King of France in his contest with England. The Turk, he said, would come ; and he raised other objections, not only to the Pope but also in conversation with other persons. He speaks very violently and passionately about it, and is full of threats of what the King of France will do. No doubt the Pope gave him a fit answer ; so I will only mention one point. He said that when aid had been requested against England, the King of France had resolutely declined to do what the Emperor had done without the slightest difficulty, namely to enter into agreement with the enemies of the Holy See without the co-operation and consent of the Pope.* He (the envoy) showed them the agreement (with England) which he said was honourable and proper : and then announced his departure for Venice, apparently very little pleased.

I am assured that his original mission was to negotiate a marriage between the Dauphin's daughter and Horatio (Farnese) and to deal with a still more important matter, these being the words used by the Secretary (Aubespine), who imparted the information to a confidant, but no further details were given as to what the affair was.

The Pope was troubled about it ; and I am informed also that in a conversation he had with Trivulciis he endeavoured through him to bring the French to a better frame of mind. The French who are here have, however, made very little account of Cardinal Trivulciis lately ; and he is much disatisfied with them. He says they do not know what they are about. †

The Secretary (Aubespine) afterwards remained here, whilst the Pope was at Frascati ; and sent to ask permission to go thither and take leave of his Holiness. It was however deferred until the Pope's return ; and yesterday the (French) Ambassador and the Secretary

---

* Referring to the Emperor's alliance with the King of England against France.
† Cardinal Trivulzio (Trivulciis) was the "protector" of French interests at Rome.

1546.

had an interview with the Pope, in which more amiability was shown than before. The marriage of the daughter of the Dauphin already mentioned was finally broached; and they said that the peace they had made with England included your Majesty. Trivulciis remarked to a certain person that, affairs between your Majesty and the King of France being in their present position, it is not decent of the latter to show resentment at this German enterprise, either by word or deed. The Secretary left here yesterday evening.

The Pope has been talking lately of sending a legate to France, to treat of a confirmation of the peace (*i.e.* between Charles and Francis), and prior to the coming of the Secretary they were very warm about it. Since then, however, the matter has cooled, and I suspect they wish to learn more about the progress of events in France from Dandino, who had gone thither as Nuncio; and at the same time to sound your Majesty's intentions through Cardinal Farnese.

I understand that the Pope's financiers are devising means for raising the money he will spend in this enterprise, without touching the funds he had by him. His Holiness says he will not use any of the latter money, except for some great enterprise against the Turk. The Pope had news from Bologna yesterday that his troops were mustered on the 11th instant, in larger numbers than had been expected, so that a good proportion of the whole force is now ready, and a muster is to be taken at once. They will then start on their march, and it is expected that by the 17th they will be on the way. In good truth, they have not lost a moment in this. The cavalry was also ready, and would start at the same time, or earlier if desired. The Pope was told that your Majesty desired to be informed every four days where the troops were, and the road they were following. His Holiness has written to the legate to this effect.

I wrote to your Majesty on the 28th ultimo about the deposit of funds in Augsburg and Venice. Since then we have been busy in the matter; for the Pope, in truth, has had some difficulty with the merchants with regard to the mode in which the funds are to be transferred. We have been much annoyed by the delay; and were not at first without some suspicion that there might be something behind it. I am told that it is now arranged that the 100,000 ducats payable in Augsburg are to be made available at Trent, and will be handed to the Cardinal (Farnese) there, or elsewhere as he may please, in certain instalments. The other 100,000 at Venice are also to be paid to the Cardinal (Farnese) or to his order. Seeing the need for the money I am sorry that it is to be paid in instalments; and that it will be necessary to await the arrival of the Cardinal there before any of it is paid. But as he is already on the road, and they tell me that when he arrives the money will be paid as your Majesty may require, I thought better to let them make their own arrangements with the merchants; even at the cost of some delay, rather than risk losing the money by insisting upon their sending it in specie. Besides which I noticed that when they were pressed much on this point they grew suspicious. I have taken the liberty to suspend my efforts with the Pope about the half-first

1546.

fruits in Flanders, and the additional 100,000 ducats, until the treaty obligations have been fully complied with and Cardinal Farnese is with your Majesty. My experience of the Pope has shown me that he will never do many things at a time; even though he may have decided upon them in principle. Besides this, he is always thinking or fearing that your Majesty will come to terms with the Lutherans. But if the hostilities begin, as the Pope is now beginning to believe that they will, and he knows that his troops and his grandsons are there, I believe that he will not only do what we now ask but even more. For my part, I can guarantee your Majesty that not a moment shall be lost.

Alexander Vitello came to take leave of me, and said in effect that he was delighted to be going, for it would afford him an opportunity of serving your Majesty, as he yearned to do. Cardinal Farnese and Octavio, he said, also meant well, but they were young; and, considering their station, he was obliged to be careful how he treated them: but he begged me to write to your Majesty how devoted he was, and to say that in any important matter in which your Majesty thought proper to make use of him and the troops, he would take care to manage things as your Majesty might indicate. John Baptist Savello spoke to the same effect, though not so definitely. He probably thought it unnecessary, as his command is a small one. His Holiness has expressed to me and others his tenderness at sending his two grandsons to the war, and I have made much of it and praised him greatly for the sacrifice. If your Majesty thinks well, you might also do the same, as his Holiness is fond of glory, etc.

When the cross was given to the legate (Cardinal Farnese) and the staff to Octavio, the two ceremonies were arranged by his Holiness, in accordance with what was clearly indicated by the stars. This caused murmuring amongst the people, and gave some trouble to the Cardinals; for it kept them from ten o'clock till nearly seven in the ceremonial.

Rome, 16 July, 1546.

(The rest of the above letter is occupied by questions of Spanish ecclesiastical appointments, etc.)

July 16.
Paris.
Archives
Nationales.
K. 1486.

294. ST. MAURIS to PRINCE PHILIP.

On the 5th instant I wrote a full account of events here; and mentioned the arrival of an English envoy, sent by the King to stand sponsor for the infant princess. The King of France met him half way between Fontainebleau and this place, on the pretence that he was returning from the chase. I mention this to your Majesty, because many persons of importance are quite at a loss to understand such a reception as this being accorded to the envoy; and that the King of France should have condescended to go out and meet him in person. As soon as the envoy (Sir Thomas Cheyney) had presented his respects to the King of France, the latter went on his road to Fontainebleau conversing with the Admiral of France, being followed by the English envoy who was chatting with the Dauphiness, and after them rode the whole company. As they neared the castle at about four o'clock in the afternoon, they were

1546.

received by salvos of artillery. The envoy supped that evening in the apartments prepared for him, being accompanied by Messieurs Laval and Canapé, who had come with him from Paris. The next day the envoy dined with the King of France, and supped with the ladies. After dinner he had a very long conversation with the King of France; to whom he handed the letters from the King of England. The conference lasted two hours, the King of France talking very much and using his hands freely in gestures of affection, in which he was liberally seconded by the Englishman; who, however, used but very few words. So far as can be ascertained the King set forth at length the former friendship between him and the King of England. It had, he said, been so firmly cemented by their interviews and other means that he was quite sure the King of England would never have departed from it, but for the exhortations and contrivance of your Highness. He (Francis) hoped, however, now that the friendship had been re-established, that the King of England and his people would never allow themselves to be deceived again, but would always rest in the security which was afforded to them by a close, constant, and sincere friendship with France. For his part, no disturbance of the friendship should come on any account whatever, and he would fulfil the agreement to the very letter. By means of this agreement their disputes were so fully settled that a perpetual friendship would henceforward exist between the two countries. The envoy replied that the King of England was similarly moved by a sincere and earnest wish to maintain the existing amity firmly; and he would fulfil to the utmost the treaty which had been made, on condition that the King of France also did the same. He added that he was himself fully aware that the breach in the old friendship had originated with the repudiation of the pensions and the non-payment of the amounts overdue, and with certain other causes; but, since the two princes had again become reconciled, he believed that all occasions for future disputes would disappear. He always repeated that if the King of France fulfilled the treaty, the King of England would do the same. This passed on the third instant, and on the following day, the fourth, the baptism was solemnised at four o'clock in the afternoon, the order of the ceremony being as follows. First marched the heralds of France and England, followed by M. de Longueville bearing the taper, after whom came M. de Guise with the cushion. M. de Montpensier then came carrying the cup, Saint Pol the basin, and the youthful M. d'Enghien the chrism. After them came the envoy of the King of England, carrying the infant princess in his arms, the babe wearing the royal mantle, of which the train was carried by Mme. de Montpensier and the Duchess de Nemours. Then came the Queen, whose train was borne by Mme. d'Etampes as lady of honour, and who was followed by Mme. Marguèrite of France, the Princess d'Albret and Mme. de Vendome walking together. In addition to these there was such an infinity of other ladies, and so great a multitude, that description would be difficult. The infant was christened Isabel de Valois, the King of England being godfather and the Queen of France and Princess d'Albret godmothers. As soon as the baptism was over the people began to shout " *Vive Madame Isabelle de Valois.*" It is said that the name of Isabel was chosen on purpose, because of the hope they have that at a future time a marriage may be arranged between the Princess and the Infante of Spain, where such names appear to be desired. When the ceremony was finished, all the company went to the King, who awaited them on a floor which had been specially constructed in the courtyard of the castle. The floor was covered with cloths and rushes for the dances, which began as soon as the company arrived.

The crowd being very great the King himself with a halberd turned all the men off the floor, except some who took part in the ball. After the ball had continued for some time supper was served in a hall specially made new for the purpose, and all covered with cloth of gold, both the ceiling and the walls, the rest of the apartments in the castle being richly decorated. There was a buffet of gold and silver plate, which was considered very magnificent; and the supper was served by the Admiral of France, as high-steward, accompanied by the rest of the King's household, the dances afterwards continuing until midnight. The next day there was a tournament, where the first prize was given to the Dauphin (afterwards Henry II.) as he broke more shafts than any other competitor; although some difficulty was raised about it, as some of the judges maintained that the prize should rightly have been awarded to M. 'd'Aumale, because he had broken a lance every time he had run, although his aggregate number was not so large as that of the Dauphin. The following day the English envoy handed to the Dauphiness the presents sent by the King his master. They comprised a jasper cup, a clock with a crystal cover, and a gold saltcellar on a chased gold stand, and with a chased gold cover upon which stags and other animals were carved. The envoy presented at the same time to the two nurses a gold chain each and a sum of money.

The 8th instant was fixed for the combat between the two Spanish Captains,* both of whom were at Fontainebleau, but at dinner time on that day a courier from England arrived with letters for the English Ambassador, instructing him to request the King of France to postpone the combat for five days, during which the English second chosen by the Spanish Captain on their side would arrive at this court. The request was granted and a postponement for eight days ordered, during which time the King will not budge from Fontainebleau, unless it be to some of the chateaux in the neighbourhood.

The day following that which had been originally fixed for the combat, the English special convoy departed from Court, after taking his leave of the King, who, it is said, presented him with a

---

* A very full and interesting account of this fight between Julian Romero and Captain Mora, evidently from the relation of the former, will be found in the Spanish Chronicle of Henry VIII. The duel arose out of the desertion from the English to the French service of some of the Spanish mercenaries at Boulogne. The English second mentioned in this letter, Sir Henry Knyvet, who had been sent specially from England for the purpose, appears to have been prevented from arriving at Fontainebleau until the morning of the fight—15 July (*see* his interesting letter to the King of 17th in State Papers of Henry VIII). He died before his return to England at Corbeuil, and was buried at the church of St. Paul in Paris. (*See* Holingshead.)

1546.

sideboard of plate worth five or six thousand crowns. In good truth, everything possible has been done here to welcome him, and to show the ardent desire they have to be friendly with the King of England. Whatever was most likely to gratify the envoy was that which best pleased the King, who ordered incessantly that every attention should be paid to him. This, Sire, is an evident sign of the wish they have to preserve their new friendship, which, as they say, they hope to utilise by and bye.

It is announced that after the combat the King will go to Paris to await the arrival of the Lord Admiral of England, in whose presence he will take the oath to fulfil the new treaty with all solemnity in the church of Notre Dame de Paris. The King of England will act similarly in London; this having been agreed between their Majesties, in order to please their respective peoples, who can only learn the results of princely negotiations by outward demonstrations. The rumour is that from Paris the King will proceed to Blois, Chambord and Remorantin, and thence to Moulins; but things change so frequently here that I can only report what is current at the moment.

The Dauphiness left for Blois immediately after the christening, carrying with her the baby-princess to be brought up with the Duke of Brittany.° She will await at Blois the arrival of the King there.

These people (*i.e.* the French) are getting rid of many of their soldiers, and they have already dismissed more than 2,000 of French veterans; who it is said are about to enter your Majesty's service. There is no news of any men being sent towards Bayonne. I send this information to your Majesty, because I have again been requested from Spain to make enquiries respecting the alleged enterprise against Navarre intended by M. d'Albret. I can hear no confirmation whatever of this: and I do not believe that anything will be done this year. In future we shall see from time to time what will happen. I have very dexterously enquired through Mme. D'Etampes, of a secretary of M. d'Albret what the latter, who is coming hither with his daughter, has been doing during his long absence. The secretary told Mme. D'Etampes that M. d'Albret's whole thought was to strengthen his town of Pau, as he had previously told me. The secretary added that his master had little enough money to do even this; which is a very different thing from making preparations for war. With regard to the rumour that M. d'Albret was secretly raising troops, the secretary affirms that nothing of the sort was being done: it was a gross invention without any particle of truth.

16 July, 1546.

21 July.
Vienna.
Imp. Arch.

295. VAN DER DELFT to the EMPEROR.

I have received your Majesty's letters of the 3rd instant, with the information sent from Spain respecting the Renegat affair. Your Majesty will have learnt from my last letters of 6th instant what

---

° The eldest son of the Dauphin Henry and Catharine de Medici, afterwards Francis II. He was at this time 3 years old, and became the first husband of Mary Queen of Scots.

1546.

had passed between the Bishop of Winchester, Paget and myself, and also with the King in relation to this matter, and the rest of your Majesty's instructions contained in your said letter.* Nothing of importance has since occurred to my knowledge. The Admiral of France is expected here within a week. The Lord Admiral (Dudley) left London six days since, and is now at Boulogne, waiting until the other is on the road. Several communications have already taken place here with the French Ambassador, with regard to which I can only conjecture that the postponement from day to day of the coming of the Admiral of France is arousing some distrust here, and the friends are now in doubt of a lasting peace being made. It is even asserted that the French are retaining a considerable number of troops under arms, notwithstanding that they have been ostensibly dismissed. I am doing my best to discover if there is any intrigue afoot with the French, to the prejudice of your Majesty, on account of the Protestants; but I have been unable as yet to see any signs of such a thing, or that any confederation exists with them (i.e. the Protestants) on this side. I hear, however, that Secretary Mason, who was sent with Duke Philip of Bavaria to Germany and was recalled hither when he had arrived as far as Flanders, has now again been dispatched thither, and this was after the news became current of your Majesty's enterprise. The Queen (Dowager of Hungary) instructed me to learn from the Council how matters stood between them and the Scots; as I had written that the latter were included in the peace concluded between France and England, on condition that they (the Scots) fulfilled the treaties existing between them and this King, whilst the French asserted that the Scots were included unconditionally. If such were the case it was considered (by the Queen Dowager) that your Majesty ought to be informed of it, since the state of war between your Majesty and the Scots existed solely in accordance with the clauses of your treaty of alliance with England, and you consequently should be included in any pacific arrangement with them. The Lords of the Council replied that it was true that the Scots had only been included in the peace on the condition above mentioned; and that in order to learn what their (i.e., Scots') intention was, an envoy had been sent from here to Scotland, a reply from whom was daily expected, and would be communicated to me. Since then I have continued to press for information as to their decision, but have been assured that no news has yet been received from the French gentleman who had been sent on the mission.

London, 21 July, 1546.

21 July.
Vienna.
Imp. Arch.

296. VAN DER DELFT to the QUEEN DOWAGER.

I have nothing of importance to write at present. The Admiral of France is expected here shortly, the Lord Admiral of England having left six days since, and still remaining in Boulogne until the French Admiral is on the road to come hither. There have been several conferences here with the French Ambassador, of the details

---

* This letter cannot now be found in the Imperial Archives, but the substance of it will be seen in the letter to the Queen Dowager of Hungary of the same date, 6 July.

1546.

of which I know nothing; but I cannot help suspecting that the delay from day to day in the coming of the Admiral of France is causing distrust on the part of the English, and is making them doubt as to the conclusion of an assured peace. This doubt is increased by the statement made that the French still retained a considerable force under arms, after the English had dismissed their troops. I am doing my best to discover if there was any intrigue or arrangement with the French prejudicial to the Emperor, or in the interests of the Protestants, but I can see no signs of anything of the sort, nor of any confederation between the English and them (*i.e.* the Protestants); although I hear that Secretary Mason, who had been sent with Duke Philip of Bavaria to Germany and was recalled when he had arrived as far as Antwerp, has again been despatched (to Germany) since the news was received here of the Emperor's undertaking.

The Lords of the Council have sent to complain to me of the ill-treatment experienced by English subjects in the town of Antwerp. In order to save their lives it is necessary for them to go armed and in bodies through the streets, as they are constantly assaulted and outraged by our people, and no measures are taken to remedy this state of things. Injurious words are also allowed to be used about this King, without any punishment of the offenders. As difficulties may arise out of this, the Councillors beg me to write on the subject to your Majesty, and to request you to give the matter your attention, as otherwise they (the English in Antwerp) will be obliged to withdraw. They (the Councillors) add, that the Emperor and the King being in perfect friendship and alliance, they hoped that your Majesty would take such steps as were fitting to keep subjects in good neighbourship and concord. I assured them that this would be done. I pray your Majesty to look to this, as to-day, again, complaints on the same subject have been made to me, and there is a strong rumour amongst the merchants here that English factors and merchants (in Antwerp) are to be recalled.

Since my last I have made several attempts to learn the reply that the English have received from the Scots, with regard to the inclusion of the latter in the peace between France and England. They say, however, that no reply has been received from the French gentleman who has gone to Scotland on this matter.

London, 21 July, 1546.

27 July.
Simancas.
E. Milan,
1192.
Italian.

297. Intelligence from TURIN, forwarded to the EMPEROR by FERNANDO DE GONZAGA (Governor of Milan).

It is improbable that the King of France will make any warlike movement this year. He has no money, few soldiers, and the season is already far advanced. He is, moreover, not at all sure of England; as the difficulties between them are not yet settled. The King of France is bound to pay by next Christmas day an instalment of the amount due by him to the King of England; and Boulogne is to be restored, some people say in six, others in eight years. The fact is that it will never be given back.

Negotiations are progressing for a marriage between the son of the King of England and the daughter of the King of Scotland.

The King of England offers to him of France, not only Boulogne but also Calais and the other places in France now held by the English, on condition that the French support this marriage. Whatever course the King of France adopts, his position is a bad one. If he accepts the King of England's offer Scotland will in the course of time be united with England; and in such case there is no doubt that the French will always be exposed to great danger from that quarter. It is the fact that France can at any time bring about war on the Scottish Border that renders England weak. On the other hand if the Scottish marriage does not take place, it will be evident that France has stood in the way and hostilities between the two Kings will promptly result. It is well known that the King (Queen?) of Scots will act as the King of France advises him to do. War between France and England being therefore still possible, the King of France will avoid a rupture with the Emperor, unless the Lutherans be willing to provide the former with large subsidies in money. If this were done, he might consider himself strong enough with help of the Turks to offer a successful opposition to the Emperor.

27 July, 1546.

30 July.
Simancas.
E. R. 873.

298. JUAN DE VEGA to the EMPEROR.

(Acknowledges letters brought by Catanio, the Secretary of Cardinal of Trent, and others. Refers the Emperor to previous letters, to show that instructions as to the Papal contingent and payment of Papal subsidy have all been anticipated.)

(Note for reply on margin. "He will have seen by the fresh letters taken by Aurelio (Catanio) what has been said about the 200,000 crowns, and that his Majesty is much displeased that this money is to be paid in deferred instalments. His Majesty expressed his displeasure in the presence of the Nuncio and of the Cardinal of Augsburg; but no remedy has been provided, especially by Cardinal Farnese, who shelters himself behind the Pope. His Majesty therefore trusts that he (i.e. Vega) will use every effort in the matter, which is of great importance. The Papal contingent has arrived here. It is very good, and his Majesty is satisfied with it.")

Before receiving the last letter I took advantage of the news of the troops leaving Augsburg* &c., to go to his Holiness, and submitted to him that as he saw now how urgent the need for resources was he should expedite the dispatch of the Brief for the half first fruits of the Netherlands. I said that I had no doubt that his Holiness on consideration would do this and more; and the delay that had already taken place in granting this concession was due to the circumstances not being ripe for it, as they now were, &c. His Holiness admitted the truth of what I said, and most graciously

---

* This refers to the first move of the Protestant forces against the Emperor. A large body of troops raised by the city of Augsburg under Schertel had left that city and was marching rapidly towards the Tyrol for the purpose of intercepting the Papal contingent in the mountain passes and so prevent it from reaching the Emperor. The latter was therefore in a most perilous position in Ratisbon, as he only had with him there about 3,000 Spaniards and 5,000 Germans, neither the Flemish contingent under Buren nor the troops from Italy having yet joined him. Unfortunately for the Protestant cause Schertel was summoned by the Landgrave of Hesse to join the main body of the Protestant army, and to this fatal error was mainly due the final victory of the Emperor.

1546.

made the concession requested, ordering that the Briefs should be authorised. They have been occupied in the matter for the last fortnight, and as soon as the Briefs are ready they shall be sent without delay; although all official documents here have to be so carefully considered, and pass through so many hands that things are done more slowly than could be wished.

(Marginal note. "It is well that these half first fruits have been granted, and that the documents are to be drawn up, but the delay and the reason given for it are perfectly incomprehensible. They have the precedents and forms of similar concessions; especially that of 1542. The delay is extremely prejudicial, as the Queen (Mary of Hungary) complains that for lack of this source of supply many things in favour of the enterprise cannot be done. A copy is sent with this (reply) of the petition presented for the previous concession referred to. This is not a matter which will brook delay; and the documents must be sent as soon as possible.")

The Briefs for the half first fruits of Spain directed to the Cardinals and to the Nuncio Poggio, who is granted the commission previously held in the matter by the Cardinal of Seville,[*] with the right of subdelegation, will be sent to the Prince (Philip) within four or five days. As neither your Majesty nor the Prince has nominated any fresh person to undertake the execution of the Briefs in Spain, the Pope has authorised the Nuncio to delegate his powers in this respect to the person to be appointed by your Majesty.

The only point now outstanding is that of the commutation of sale of the monastic manors, by the concession of other means for obtaining the funds. Your Majesty's consent to this, on the conditions and limitations set forth in your Majesty's instructions, has been conveyed to the Pope, who was extremely rejoiced thereat. He said it was important in your Majesty's interests that the matter should be so arranged, in addition to the difficulties which would thus be overcome, because it would deprive the King of France and others of a precedent for making a similar demand. The Pope has ordered the documents to be prepared.

(Note in margin. "The Pope will have to bear in mind that his Majesty only requires the resources that may be necessary for carrying out the enterprise; and these may be raised in the manner most agreeable to his Holiness. The affair is so important that he (the Pope) should accommodate himself readily to the adoption of the means that depend upon him. This matter must also be pushed on actively, and the conditions and modifications upon which his Majesty has consented to the change must be kept in view.")

With regard to the additional 100,000 crowns beyond the 200,000 already provided, I calculate that it will be time enough to urge this point when the various above-mentioned documents have been sent off. I will not fail to bring it forward actively then, and will not lose sight of it. I will duly report what progress is made. This completes all the points of your Majesty's instructions.

(Note in margin. "There is no time more convenient than the present for the 100,000 crowns; but the best opportunity for

---

[*] Cardinal Loaysa, Inquisitor General of Spain, who had recently died.

1546.

bringing it forward must be chosen. The need is great, and however actively the matter is dealt with, the money will come too late.")

(The rest of the letter is occupied with the question of the transfer of Cardinal Carpi's benefices in France, which was still pending. The writer urges Carpi's merits, his devotion, and his poverty, his abbacies in France producing him nothing; and prays the Emperor to allow the permutation.)

Rome, 30 July, 1546.

30 July.
Simancas.
E. 1318.

299. DIEGO HURTADO DE MENDOZA to the EMPEROR.

(A long relation of his mission to Venice for the purpose of expressing the Emperor's grave displeasure at the rumours that the Seigniory were in negotiation with the Lutherans and the Turks to his detriment.° The Seigniory emphatically deny the truth of the intelligence, and express their great devotion to the Emperor; and a circular letter from the Seigniory to its various ambassadors to this effect dated 27 July is enclosed. An extremely lengthy explanation is given of the communications that had taken place with the Protestants and the Turks; which are declared to have been perfectly innocent of offence towards the Emperor. Reference is made by Mendoza to the endeavours of the Protestants and English King's agents in Venice to arouse the distrust of the Seigniory against the Emperor: and the following marginal note on this subject is affixed:—"Memorandum : to speak to the English Ambassador who remained in Ratisbon about this Secretary, and to complain of the levity of Ludovico delle Arme.† The Ambassador in England must also be written to about it."

Venice, 30 July, 1546.

Attached to the above letter there is a copy of the instructions apparently given by Mendoza to Captain Pero Diaz de Corcuera, who carried the letter to the Emperor, with the verbal message set forth in the document. He is to say that the rumours of the Venetian intrigues with the Lutherans and Turks against the Emperor were originated by Ludovico delle Arme, "a light man with little brains and no goodwill."

The following clause in the instructions to Corcuera may be transcribed in full. "I have heard that the agent of the King of England and Ludovico delle Arme are endeavouring to bring about a league between the Seigniory, the King their master, and the King of France. They also promise on behalf of the King of England, the friendship of the Protestants, and on behalf of the

---

° Although he was still the Emperor's ambassador accredited to the Seigniory he had been at Trent, since the opening of the Council, watching the interests of his master. Thence he was recalled, as will be seen by this and subsequent letters, for the purpose of extending his diplomatic missions to Venice and Rome.

† The Italian condottiere in the English service, who had been sent to Venice on this mission and to raise troops if required. When the Venetian ambassador with the Emperor (Capilupo) told de Granvelle of delle Arme's proceedings in Mantua and Monferrat in April Granvelle had laughed and said that delle Arme was a light fellow who could do nothing. He seems, in fact, to have betrayed everybody, and the dramatic story of his turbulent end, his arrest for murder, his flight and return in the belief that his diplomatic character would protect him is told in the Venetian Calendar. The "English" secretary referred to was Balthasar Altieri.

1546.

King of France the friendship of the Turk. They propose to begin by getting the Seigniory to send an Ambassador to England, or else to manage the affair through a Venetian gentleman called Francisco Bernardi who intervened in the peace negotiations between France and England, and who receives from the King of England an allowance of 1,200 ducats a year. I suspect that this man did not take so active a part in the said negotiations without the knowledge and encouragement of the Seigniory; because all of them (the Venetians) are very timid, and this man is heir to an estate worth more than 80,000 crowns; which he would have imperilled if he had undertaken such a task entirely on his own responsibility. They also wish the King of England to send an Ambassador hither; and they nominate Ludovico delle Arme for the post. All the above intelligence about embassies proceeds from Ludovico himself.

I have been obliged to communicate all this to the Seigniory and give my authority, either to warn them not to enter into any such league against us, as was done when Cardinals Grimano and Ferrara came hither, or else to hinder it, if anything had already been done in the matter. I plied them with the arguments which I thought appropriate, and I think I convinced them, and that they will make no move.

I also divulged to them the trick that Ludovico delle Arme had played in giving the intelligence to the Cardinal (*i.e.* of Trent) although without naming his Eminence or giving them the least suspicion that it was he. My object was that in future they might give to the words of this fool only so much credit as they deserve; and that they might punish him if they liked, and prevent him from doing us any more injury. It is suspected that the Secretary or agent (*i.e.* Altieri) that the King of England has here, is, both privately and publicly, doing as much mischief as he can about Fernando de Gonzaga. I remind his Majesty that it may be well to write to his Ambassador in England about this.

I have many times assured his Majesty that he may proceed on his way without the slightest suspicion that the Seigniory can do him any harm, league or no league, for they have neither men, money nor victuals. As to their feelings towards us, they are as vile as can be; and the intensity increases or diminishes as his Majesty appears warlike or tranquil. Everything they do proceeds from fear, and some day utter shame will overwhelm them (que un dia ha de cargar sobre ellos el bochorno). If they saw an opportunity, and could deal secretly with powerful persons, they are capable of attempting any villainy. But they do not trust Turks nor Frenchmen, because they see that your Majesty is informed of everything; and they also distrust the Lutherans, because they are convinced that your Majesty has undertaken this enterprise with the concurrence of some of them*. They (the Seigniory) have therefore

---

* The Seigniory had ample reason for their distrust; for during the month Maurice of Saxony had thrown in his lot with the Emperor, being elevated to the position of Imperial Elector, in the place of his senior cousin, John Frederick the Magnanimous, who was in arms against the Catholics. The Duke of Cleves had just been married to the daughter of the King of the Romans, and was thenceforward an impossible ally to the Confederates. John and Albert of Brandenburg stood on the Emperor's side, Protestants though they were; whilst the Elector head of their house, and the Count Palatine himself were, at least for a time, frightened into neutrality.

1546.

decided that the safest course for them is to keep quiet, whilst they show, more by indications than by plain words, their bad dispositions to both sides. I remind his Majesty of the advisability of sending hither some fully authorised person, as I have to leave again for Trent. Captain Corcuera is provided with what is necessary for his journey, coming and going, both for himself and the two men he takes with him. I pray your Majesty to grant me a knighthood for a gentleman related to me who has served your Majesty."

Venice, 30 July, 1546.

31 July.
Vienna.
Imp. Arch.

300. The QUEEN DOWAGER to VAN DER DELFT.

Since writing our letter to you of 22nd ultimo, we have received yours of the 6th and 21st instant; by which we learn the small progress you are making in the settlement of the questions respecting the traffic and intercourse between the respective peoples, about which Councillor Van der Burgh was sent thither. The English ambassador and the special envoy sent hither to deal in the same matter are urging us strongly to bring our negotiations with them to a conclusion; as if they wished to have a solution of the matter on this side before dealing with it in England through you. For this reason we have given instructions that the conclusion of the business is not to be hurried here; and you will do well to press for a settlement of the points raised by you, since the excuse that the war prevented the Council from dealing with them will no longer hold water. If the English answer you by saying that their commissioners on this side are making but little progress, you may say that it must be recollected that when Councillor Van der Burgh arrived in London they kept you a long time waiting before dealing with the affairs in hand, their excuse being that they were busy with the war; whereas when their special envoy came hither we began negotiating with him at once. It is true that since then the wars in Germany have occurred, and have prevented the negotiations from proceeding so rapidly as before. But they (the English) ought not longer to delay the dispatch of Van der Burgh, who has remained there too long already. If you find it impossible to obtain a prompt decision, you had better send us a precise statement of all your proceedings, and attach to it your opinion upon the principal points. We will then consider what had better be done.

We have not yet been able to discover, from France or elsewhere, the true facts respecting the inclusion of the Scots. The latter still continue constantly to treat as enemies the Emperor's subjects whom they encounter at sea; and we have been consequently obliged to send to Scotland Secretary Strick, in order that he may learn there how matters are considered to stand. But notwithstanding this; as the period during which the Scots were to make their declaration has now expired, you had better ask the Council again to be good enough to let you know clearly what are their present relations with the Scots; if they are at peace with them, and whether these dominions have been included or not in any arrangement that may have been made. For the reasons already stated,

1546.

it is necessary that we should know this, so that we may act accordingly towards the Scots. You will also ask the Council to inform you of the details of the agreements they have made with the Scots. This can hardly be refused to you, as our quarrel with the Scots is solely on account of the English; and the terms of the treaty of alliance (*i.e.* between England and the Emperor) provide that the English should communicate such particulars to us, in order to show that the Emperor and his subjects have been included, as they had a right to be. You will also lay before the King and his Council the fact that several gentlemen of Artois, subjects of the Emperor possessing property in the Boulognais, have requested us to direct them as to how they are to proceed to recover the enjoyment of their estates as before the commencement of the war. We have been unable to answer them, as we are ignorant of the capitulations made between the English and French in the recent peace treaty.

Now that the war has ceased it is only reasonable to ask that private citizens should again enjoy the possession of their property; and you will ask them (the English) in our name to be good enough to state to you the conditions of the peace touching this part of the question, in order that these gentlemen may know how to proceed in satisfying their honour and duty. If on this pretext, or any other, you can procure a copy of the treaty between England and France we should be very glad.

As it is possible that the news from Germany may be misrepresented in England, we think advisable to inform you of the true facts, as we have heard them by letters from Augsburg, and we enclose copies of those sent to the imperial ambassador in France with the intelligence. With regard to Secretary Paget's assertion to you that the Admiral of France had affirmed that in the peace made between the Emperor and France, the Scots had been included, although it had not been set forth in the text of the treaty, we may say that the subsequent events have proved that the contrary was the case, and this must carry more conviction than the words of Frenchmen, who always try to disguise facts to please themselves. But in addition to this, we may inform you that it was *after* the peace was concluded that the Scottish secretary called Alexander (?) Paniter was here endeavouring to see his imperial Majesty, for the purpose of claiming the addition to the treaty of a clause including the Scots, in accordance with advice sent to the latter by the French. The secretary was refused an audience, whereat the French Ambassador was much scandalized, and gave out that the Scots were actually included. The Scottish secretary was shown a copy of the clauses of the treaty which provided for the inclusion of other princes; and seeing that he had been deceived by the French, made a great ado about it to the French ambassador. The latter at first tried to stand out that, although the text of the treaty did not contain the inclusion, the latter had really been agreed upon verbally. This was flatly contradicted by the Viceroy of Naples (Gonzaga) and M. de Granvelle; and then the French ambassador wanted to maintain that the inclusion of the Scots depended upon the provisions of previous treaties that had been confirmed by the treaty of peace. This assertion also was shown to be unfounded; and he then brought forward a third contention, namely that the Emperor was bound by the terms of the treaty to include the Scots on the demand of the King of France. This the (Scottish) Secretary also found to be untrue, and openly declared that the French had led them (the Scots) astray with words. The Admiral of France being afterwards at Bruges endeavoured to take the same ground as the ambassador had done, but M. de Granvelle answered him so plainly that he was obliged to hold his tongue. He was reminded that they (the French) had pressed for the inclusion of the Scots, but had been distinctly told that, even at the risk of breaking off the negotiations, they would not be included, except with the full consent of the King of England. When a good opportunity offers you may confidentially tell Paget of this.

With reference to the complaints made by the Council to you of the ill treatment of English merchants in Antwerp, we can only say that we have heard nothing of it; but on the contrary that the Antwerp authorities have executed one of their burgesses for having committed violence against an Englishman. It is true that several Italian and Spanish soldiers who have returned from the English camp have been misbehaving themselves somewhat in Antwerp, but they have been sent away, and we have had no complaints since.

We have likewise heard no complaints that anything is being said here to the disrespect of the King of England; but if we do hear of anything of the sort we will punish it in such a way as will satisfy the King. You may assure the Lords of the Council of this; but you may say also that what we do hear is that the people on the English frontier are saying every kind of evil thing about the Emperor. They hope, they say, that they will soon be at war with him again: but as we know that this does not proceed from the King we take no notice of it.

The French are spreading the rumour that a German gentleman sent by the Protestants to the King of England told the King of France that the former had agreed to help the Protestants against the Emperor. He (King Henry) was even trying to persuade the merchants, to whom he owed 400,000 crowns, to allow this sum to be lent to the Protestants; and he wished to arrange an interview with the King of France, for the purpose of making plans injurious to the Emperor, but the King of France declined to help the Germans, in order not to violate the treaty with his Majesty. Although we do not believe any of this, but quite the contrary, we have thought well to inform you of it, that you may secretly communicate it to Secretary Paget when you see fitting; letting him know that we have no doubt whatever of the King's goodwill, no matter what the French may say.

Brussels, 31 July, 1546.

31 July.
Simancas.
E. A. 642.

301. Extracts from a letter of the EMPEROR to PRINCE PHILIP.

With regard to the injuries inflicted upon our subjects by the English, French and Scots, I have read what you say and the letters written to you by Juan Martinez de Recalde[*] about the six ships,

---
[*] General of the galleys of Biscay. *See* note page 115.

1546.

two of which were sunk; and also the Scotch version of the matter. The Council have also sent us several letters and consultations on these subjects, advising us to arm some zabras (Biscay sloops) to prevent these attacks. Being naturally desirous of finding a remedy for the such outrages, we have taken the steps which have been communicated to you; this being all that could possibly be done short of declaring war or adopting privateering reprisals. With affairs in their present condition, we think it would be unwise to go beyond this. As regards the zabras, you will have the question considered in Spain, and see what can be done, in view of the attitude adopted by the French and English, now that they have made peace. So far as we are concerned here (*i.e.* in Germany) we can do no more than we have done.

Ratisbon, 31 July, 1546.

31 July.
Simancas.
E. A. 642.

302. The EMPEROR to JUAN DE VEGA.

This morning the Secretary of Cardinal Trent arrived with the account of the arrangement made with Cardinal Farnese, especially* with respect to the 200,000 ducats.* We send you copy of the document he brought, by which you will see how very far it differs from what we had expected from his Holiness, with regard to the resources he was to provide. We had entirely trusted in the Pope's furnishing the amount promised immediately, and we are quite scandalised at this not being done, as the whole affair depends upon it. Trusting in the Pope's undertaking, and believing, at least, that we should receive this money within a month, we had arranged to take all the other funds in various places at long instalments. Besides this, we have already spent large sums on the troops we now have here and those coming from Italy, as well as on the army under Count de Buren: a great expenditure, moreover, has had to be met for artillery and other necessaries for the undertaking, the calculation being that the present month's expenses could be met and partly covered by the Papal subsidy of 200,000 crowns, although it would fall far short of being sufficient for the purpose. Something must be done to find a remedy for this great difficulty by persuading his Holiness to provide the money at once. We have fully stated this to Cardinal Augsburg and the Nuncio who conducted the negotiation with Farnese at Worms; and who have been employed in the whole business; but it is in the highest degree necessary that you should make the Pope understand the position clearly and unequivocally. You will tell him that we cannot bring ourselves to believe that he means to imperil both the undertaking and ourselves in this way; and we are extremely astonished that the papal officers with Cardinal Farnese should say as they do, that you had approved of these bills at long usance. We must tell you, also, that you have behaved with great laxity in this matter. In a recent letter you merely mention these bills, without saying anything about the periods for which they were drawn. You should not have been satisfied, unless you knew when they were payable; and if they were

---

* That is to say the main subsidy which it had been understood was to be paid down in cash as soon as the enterprise was entered upon.

drawn at such usance as was undesirable, you ought to have objected strongly until the point was settled to your liking. It was not a matter that could be lightly passed over, or conceded to please the Pope; and we may tell you that so important is it, that we were never in such anxiety as on the present occasion. There is positively no way out of it but to get this money, and get it at once. It will be no easy matter for us to keep afloat until we get the most speedy reply possible. In an affair of such vital concern, in which the success of the whole enterprise is involved, his Holiness should consider deeply, and lay hands on the surest money he possesses, in order that not a moment may be lost in providing us with the cash. In order that no delay should occur, and that no other business should clash with this, we avoid mentioning anything in this letter but the money we need so much; this being the principal thing of all, and to remind you of the dispatch of the Flemish half first fruits. You will also urge his Holiness on this point, telling him that this is the time for him to show his goodwill to the enterprise and to ourselves, bearing in mind the troubles that would result from failure. I am confident that every other branch of the undertaking is progressing favourably; and that when the Spaniards and Italians arrive, which we expect will be soon, we will, with our forces already here and Buren's army teach our enemies a lesson. You will send your answer flying, for until we hear from you we shall be in the greatest anxiety.

Since writing the above the Nuncio has shown us a letter from Cardinal Farnese saying that he has communicated to Cardinal Trent the means by which the payment of the first 100,000 crowns may be anticipated, this being the sum payable by the merchants in Trent.* Farnese thinks that the amount may be discounted here (*i.e.* in Ratisbon) but that is impossible, as there are no merchants here with money or credit to that extent, and we have therefore thought well to send back Cardinal Trent's secretary immediately, to see whether some arrangement cannot be made with the said merchants (*i.e.* in Trent) and others in order that we may get the monies at once, and the payments to be made in Venice also discounted.† In order to meet instant need in the meanwhile, Cardinal Farnese is to be asked to send hither at once 100,000 crowns, or as much as he can, of the money he brings to pay the Italian troops, the sum to be repaid to him out of the bills. As all this is so uncertain, and we know not what will be done, we are writing to the Cardinal (Farnese) asking him to let you know speedily, so that you may take such steps as may be necessary by virtue of the letter of credence we now send you.

We have heard several times lately that Cardinal Santa Cruz (Santa Croce) who is one of the legates in the Council (of Trent) is

---

* This was the amount that the Pope's bankers had arranged for the Fuggers to pay at Augsburg, but which the latter subsequently had explained they could not undertake to pay in that place after the expiry of the period during which they had bound themselves to do so. The amount had then been made payable to the Pope's order at Trent, and Juan de Vega had agreed to this change without enquiring into the usance of the bills. Hence the Emperor's quite unwonted anger.

† The second half of the subsidy of 200,000 crowns

1546.

acting very badly; and has always aimed at breaking up the Council and moving it from Trent. I now hear that he is acting worse than ever; his pretext being that the troops now passing Trent, and the enemies who are approaching our brother's territories, are intimidating the prelates and others in the Council. As this action is so contrary to the authority and dignity of the Pope, and to the success of the enterprise, from which we hope so much, we were obliged to speak to Cardinal Augsburg and the Nuncio about it. We said that we could not believe that it was the Pope's wish to break up the Council or transfer it elsewhere, and that if he did not punish Cardinal Santa Cruz we should have to take the matter in hand ourselves. We have also instructed Cardinal Trent's secretary to give Santa Cruz a plain intimation of this. The Nuncio may write to Rome on the subject, or perhaps Santa Cruz, even, may do so; and for that reason we have mentioned it to you, in in order that you may explain to his Holiness that we are moved to be so angry with Cardinal Santa Cruz mainly by a desire to safeguard his (the Pope's) authority and to silence the scandal that otherwise would arise from this matter. Ratisbon, 31 July, 1546.

July (?)
Simancas.
E. A. 642.

303. MEMORANDUM to be sent to SPAIN.

One of the clauses in the treaty between the Pope and the Emperor permitted the sale of monastic manors in Spain, to the amount of 500,000 ducats, to be employed in the enterprise against the Protestants; the Emperor guaranteeing to the monasteries an income equal to that produced by the manors alienated. After the treaty was signed, the clause being discussed in Consistory was objected to by some of the Cardinals; and his Majesty was urgently requested to allow these 500,000 ducats to be procured from other sources. In order to please the Pope his Majesty consented to this.

His Holiness thereupon sent by Marquina the Bull providing that a sum of 300,000 ducats might be raised out of the property of the monasteries, the pledging of their rents, their silver, the fabrics of the Castilian cathedrals, and parish churches, etc., 200,000 to be raised out of the monastic property, and 100,000 out of the said church fabrics. The Pope explained that he had no doubt the Emperor would prefer this plan, as he would not be bound to provide an equivalent, as he would be if the manors had been sold, and thus the said 300,000 ducats would be a nett contribution easily and speedily realisable.

The arrangement made in Worms, however, with Farnese, and afterwards with Dandino, always contemplated that the monastic manors were to be sold to an amount which would leave the Emperor a clear 500,000 ducats, after providing for the recompense to be given to the monasteries; and his Majesty has consequently refused to accept the 300,000 ducats offered, or to allow the Bull to be promulgated. He has sent Don Juan de Mendoza to Rome, to urge the Pope to add to the documents authorising the raising of the 300,000, another 200,000 to complete the nett half million ducats promised in the treaty. He is to request that the greater proportion of the additional amount shall be placed rather upon the

446 SPANISH STATE PAPERS.

1546.

church fabrics than upon the monasteries, as it is thought that the money will be more easily raised from the former source than the latter.

This having been conveyed to the Pope by Juan de Vega, his Holiness insists that he has fulfilled the letter of the treaty, in what he has done; and if anything further is required of him in this respect, it must be asked as a favour, and not as an obligation. The result of Don Juan de Mendoza's negotiations is awaited.

1 Aug.
Simancas.
E. 806.
French.

304. PRINCESS MARY of England to the DUKE OF ALBURQUERQUE.

Monseigneur. I have received your letters dated 12th June, and have learnt from them, and from the report of your messenger, your position and good health; whereat I am much rejoiced. I am myself so afflicted by illness, as to be unable to answer your letters with my own hand: and I therefore must beg you to excuse this short letter, written by another for me. With regard to the Spaniard of whom you write,* I think that your servant will be well informed of the case: and will take you a faithful account of it. I end my letter praying God to give you a long and happy life. Written at the palace of the King, my sovereign lord and father, at Westminster, 1 August, 1546.

Signed, Mary, Daughter of England.

5 Aug.
Simancas.
E. R. 873

305. JUAN DE VEGA to the EMPEROR.

(Letter mainly concerned with Spanish ecclesiastical affairs, but containing the following paragraphs of interest respecting the Council of Trent.)

Your Majesty has been frequently informed that in our opinion the Pope would like if he could to break up the Council, by moving it or otherwise. It appears that the deputies of the Council and the Pope have been very busy lately, in strict secrecy, discussing the removal of the Council; and it was decided to issue a Bull ordering its transfer to Lucca, the Bull having been taken yesterday by the deputies who left to go to the legates (i.e. at Trent).

I learnt that this had been done from a very safe and secret source, and consequently I decided to request audience of the Pope immediately. I saw him yesterday, and I represented to him rather under the guise of kindliness and zeal for the public good, and for that of his Holiness, that such a course as that which he had adopted, might, if it were not promptly altered, deprive him of the fair fame he had gained by his resolution to aid the enterprise. It might also place in grave danger the interests of religion, and might imperil your Majesty. To promise the Lutherans a Council,

---

* It will be recollected that the Duke of Alburquerque had been in Henry's service during the war; and that a soi-disant Comendador Don Pedro Pacheco had come to England at the end of 1545, with a forged letter purporting to be signed by the Duke in his recommendation. The man called himself a relative of the Cuevas: and the Duke appears to have written to Princess Mary asking for information as to the Comendador's fate. Unfortunately the final result of the affair is not set forth in this correspondence.

HENRY VIII.   447

1546.

as he had done, would certainly lead them to clamour for it; and they would make use of it maliciously for evil ends. Whatever was done in this matter should only be decided upon in concurrence with your Majesty; and yet I, who was here as your representative, had not been informed of the step which he had now taken. I laid the matter before him in this tone, and answered as well as I could the many, and evidently carefully considered, objections to my view urged by the Pope. His Holiness finally answered me somewhat indefinitely that the legates would inform your Majesty of it, thus attributing to them and the deputies more importance than they have hitherto enjoyed. Next Friday, he said, there would be a Consistory, and he would then bring the matter forward. It seemed to me that, although he did not grow angry at what I said, he was much distressed about it.

In the absence of Don Diego de Mendoza from Trent I have advised the Cardinal of Jaen[*] of this, in order that he may take the necessary steps for carrying out your Majesty's wishes, and stop any talk about removing the Council. I am keeping my hand on the matter here to a similar end, and have told the Cardinals of Burgos, Carpi and Coria, what is to be discussed in the Consistory to-morrow, so that they may act as their consciences dictate. The same advice shall be given to other cardinals. Your Majesty shall be duly informed of what is done.

The Bull of the half first fruits of Flanders is being kept back, whilst they hunt for precedents. They have found portions of a draft amongst Andrés del Castillo's papers, but they require a complete copy of one of the former concessions, and they are looking for it everywhere.

Rome, 5 August, 1546.

11 Aug.
Simancas.
E. 73.

306. Document headed Decipher of letter in his Majesty's own hand to the High Comendador.

Cobos: I should like to write you a long letter, but business will not allow me the time to do so. I have therefore taken the course of writing at length to my son, and he will show the letter to you. By this you will learn what I wanted to say to you, especially about the loans. I commend all the financial arrangements to your care, and the circumstances in which I find myself must be my excuse for doing what is necessary in this respect. God, however, has taken away many of those who formerly murmured.[†] Although you have lost the Cardinal of Seville who at all events helped you with his tongue, you have, on the other hand, gained the Marquis de Mondejar, who will aid you in every way, as I well know that he is able and I hope willing to do. Read that letter to my son, in

---

[*] Cardinal Pacheco, who represented the Emperor in the Council whilst Diego de Mendoza was absent from Trent.

[†] Referring doubtless to those who in the beginning of the reign had endeavoured to maintain the right of the Commons of Castile to discuss and withhold supply until grievances had been remedied. The Cortes of Castile had now lost financial control, though those of Aragon, etc., preserved it, and consequently the main burden of the Emperor's vast expenditure fell upon Castile.

448   SPANISH STATE PAPERS.

1546.

case God should call me to himself.* I know that, though this may draw tears from your eyes, it will not dismay you; for in many other similar occasions you have served me well, and you have seen that God has brought me forth triumphant, as I trust He will do now, with increased honour; for the cause is His alone, and I have taken it in hand for His faith and service.

I have told my son in my letter to him about going to his sisters, and I have asked him to show you the letter; and also what I have written to him respecting the Duke of Alba. You will see by this what has happened in his business and how much he has lost by it. With regard to his (Philip's) sisters he is to do as I have written to him, and in other things also, I refer him generally to what I have written; because I do not know whether you have given him the letter or not. It is true that I have already been advised of some of the things mentioned: and I think they should be attended to. If there is anything in what they say, you must not fail to let me know in obscure words that I shall understand.† I wrote this letter so far last Sunday: you will see by the letters to my son that affairs are now very much more favourable than they have hitherto been, and I trust that every day they will grow better‡; if only the money does not fail us. I am quite sure you will act as you always do. If the enemy were more rapid I should be further pressed than I wish to be. There is however now no reason to fear them.—Burgh, near Landshut. 11 August, 1546.

P.S.—This letter was written with my own hand, but an inkstand was upset over it, and as I was too lazy to write it again, I have told Eraso to put it in cipher. Regard it as having been written by me.

15 Aug.
Vienna.
Imp. Arch.

307. The QUEEN DOWAGER to VAN DER DELFT.

Since we wrote our last letter of 31 July, the English Ambassador resident has addressed us on the subjects of the inclusion of the Scots in the treaty of peace between England and France; and the restoration to the enjoyment of their properties of the Emperor's subjects possessing estates in the Boulognais; we having previously communicated to the ambassador what we had written to you on both of those points. He informed us that he had been instructed by the English Council to reply with regard to them. The Scots, he said, had been included in the late treaty between England and France, in accordance with a clause, of which he exhibited a certified copy to the President of the (Flemish) Privy Council, but would not leave it with him, though he has since given us a

---

* The Emperor's words are extremely obscure, perhaps purposely so. Apparently this paragraph refers to another letter addressed to Philip, but sent to Cobos giving directions and instructions in case the Emperor should fall in the war.

† This would seem to refer to some information that had reached the Emperor as to the young widower's proceedings, probably with regard to his liaison and, it was asserted, secret marriage with Doña Isabel de Osorio which took place at this time.

‡ The Emperor had left Ratisbon, where he had been since April, on the 3rd August arriving at Landshut the next day, where, to his intense relief, Octavio Farnese and the Papal contingent joined him on the 14th. It was doubtless the proximity of this force which formed the reason for the improvement in the position mentioned in the paragraph.

1546.

copy of it, which we now enclose herewith. You will see that it sets forth that the English and Scots shall make peace and cease hostilities on both sides. With regard to the second point, he said that the King of England had 'taken the city and county of Boulogne in warfare, and possessed them by right of conquest. He was consequently proprietor and lord of all the lands comprised within the limits agreed upon between him and the French, without any obligation to restore anything; such being the custom of England. If any of the Emperor's subjects had interests that had suffered from this, their remedy was to appeal to the King of France, who had been the cause of their loss, through his inability to defend his subjects effectually. This had been the course adopted when the King of England had conquered Guisnes. This reply was considered far from reasonable; and much too prejudicial to the Emperor's subjects. You will consequently address the Council to the following effect. With regard to the inclusion of the Scots in the peace treaty; the Emperor went to war with them entirely out of consideration for the King of England; and the latter was consequently debarred by the 18th clause of the treaty of alliance, confirmed and explained subsequently at Utrecht, from entering into negotiations with the Scots, except with the knowledge and participation of the Emperor. As the latter has never been informed up to the present of the arrangements made with regard to the Scots in the peace treaty between England and France, and the Scots incessantly treat his Flemish subjects as enemies, the King of England cannot properly hold the Scots as friends without the consent of his Imperial Majesty; or at least the latter should be informed officially of the terms of the agreement, as touching the inclusion of the Scots, that such consent may be given, or the Scots brought to book for breaking the said agreement. We have no desire to prevent a friendship between the English and Scots, but it is necessary by the said 18th clause that the Emperor's consent should be given to the agreement with regard to them. He will give this consent willingly, provided that he sees his subjects properly indemnified; but it is impossible for the English to refuse his Majesty an official statement of the terms respecting the Scots, and you will demand the same for transmission to him.

Touching the reintegration in their estates and property in the Boulognais of the subjects of the Emperor, you will point out that, if the King keeps the property of such subjects, many of whom were in his own service before Boulogne, it may perchance turn to his future disadvantage: because not only would the course indicated be contrary to all justice, but also because in the war against France the Emperor's subjects were his friends and allies, and thus to deprive them of their properties would ensure that in any future war he would never find a single gentleman on this side of the sea to enter his service, knowing, as they would, that his victory would mean their own ruin. If such has been the custom in England itself, it cannot be allowed to extend to this side of the sea, where a different custom prevails. It is not true, moreover, that this was the course followed when the King of England conquered Guisnes; for the territory was acquired by him by a capitulation, in which it

1546.

was clearly expressed that the King of France should recompense the private citizens who possessed lands in the lordship of Guisnes. If such a provision as this had been included in the recent peace treaty, the Emperor's subjects would have obtained some redress, with the King of England's support. Now, however, these subjects have no remedy whatever against the King of France; and cannot even claim satisfaction without an official copy of the capitulation of Boulogne, which you will also demand, unless the King of England shall previously have listened to the request for reintegration. If this latter could be arranged with the King, on condition that the subjects in question take the oath of fidelity to him, you will reply that they will willingly do this, in the same form as they have hitherto done to the King of France; if it be shown to them by the terms of the treaty that they can take the oath without sacrificing their honour, or incurring reproach from the French that they have violated their previous oath. The French claim that the subjects in question cannot rightly take the oath to the King of England, who, they allege, is not the lord of the territory of Boulogne, but only holds possession of it for a time, as security for the money they (the French) have to pay him. You will inform us what answer is given to you on this subject.

We have received letters from the Emperor of 31st ultimo. You will see by the copies of the letters to the ambassador in France the news contained in them.

Brussels, 15 August, 1546.

16 Aug.
Vienna.
Imp. Arch.

308. VAN DER DELFT to the EMPEROR.

I am reporting fully to the Queen (Dowager of Hungary) the discourse I have had to-day with Secretary Paget, and I repeat to your Majesty only the substance thereof. Paget came to me on the King's behalf to state that the Duke Philip of Bavaria, Count Palatine, being again on his way hither to see the King, was stopped at Gravelines, where he still remains, forbidden to proceed further. The King was much annoyed and astonished at this, and requested me to write to the Queen, asking her to release the Duke and his followers, as he (the Duke) is in the King's pay and service. I replied that I had received no advice of the matter, but the King might be quite sure that the step had not been taken without just and urgent reasons. The plots and intrigues being carried on in Germany against your Majesty were perfectly well known. Paget replied that he knew nothing of such plots; but the King having been cheated by von Reissenberg during the war with France, had decided to utilise the services of a renowned and trustworthy person; and had, consequently, taken into his pay the said Duke Philip, who in accepting service under the King had not forgotten his duty towards your Majesty, as his Sovereign lord, from whom he and his house had received great favour. This, if it were necessary, could be proved by the letters and agreements concerning his engagement by the King. It should not be thought that either the Germans or the French had any understanding with them (the English) to the prejudice of your Majesty, for they (the English) would never listen to

HENRY VIII. 451

1546.

any such suggestions.[*] He (Paget) assured me most emphatically of this, and brought forward several reasons in support of it. Continuing the conversation, he remarked that he heard and believed for certain that the French had already a large number of troops with the intention of entering Italy. I asked him whether this was for the purpose of commencing war against your Majesty. "You know very well," he said, "that the French are always desirous of throwing obstacles in the way of the Emperor's enterprises; and I see plainly, that, as we began the war in alliance with the Emperor (although we were left in the lurch by him) so we shall finish it in alliance with him." After much other discourse, I quite convinced myself that what I have always said is the fact; namely that the King and the principal members of his Council, of whom the Lord Chancellor (Wriothesley), Paget, and the Bishop of Winchester (Gardiner) are the leaders, are entirely devoted to your Majesty's interests. It is true that they make no secret of their objection to see any increase in the power of our holy father the Pope, who is their enemy; but I can perceive no indication of their having any understanding with the Protestants; except that they (the English) will not conform or submit to a Council presided over by the Pope; which is easily understood, for the reason already mentioned. Apparently all their opposition would cease if your Majesty were yourself to convoke and preside over the Council (*i.e.* the Council of Trent), and this Paget himself told me in confidence. Our conversation then turned to the war in Germany, and I did not fail to set forth the just causes and reasons which had moved your Majesty to take the course you had done, and to commence the war; which really had nothing whatever to do with religion, but was solely to reduce to obedience those who continually defied your Majesty's imperial authority. He replied: "We are not so lacking in sense as not to recognise that if the Emperor is beaten in this war (which God forbid) all Christendom will suffer from the consequent confusion"; and that he (Paget) could only hope that matters might be settled by some peaceful agreement. With that he left me. I hear from a secret source that an envoy of the King of France, coming from Italy, has had an interview with the King (Henry), for the purpose of conducting some intrigues against our holy father the Pope and your Majesty; the proposal being to surprise some strong places in Italy, which are now in the Pope's hands, but of which some have been promised by his Holiness to your Majesty. I am, however, firmly of opinion that this King (Henry) will do nothing to your Majesty's detriment, however desirous he may be to annoy the Pope.

The Admiral of France has not yet arrived here, though he is looked for from day to day. The Lord Admiral of England returned here four days ago.

London, 16th August, 1546.

16 Aug.
Vienna.
Imp. Arch.

309. VAN DER DELFT to the QUEEN DOWAGER.

(The first portion of this letter is substantially identical with the paragraphs contained in the letter to the Emperor of the same date,

---

[*] With regard to the visits of Duke Philip, *see* note, page 348.

1546.

detailing Paget's complaint to the ambassador of the detention of Duke Philip of Bavaria at Gravelines. This portion is consequently omitted from the present letter.)

At this juncture I thought it would be appropriate to speak to him (Sir William Paget) about the rumours current in Flanders of a request having been made by the English for an interview with the King of France, for the purpose of planning something against the Emperor. Paget assured me that it was a mere dream: he had never heard such a thing mentioned, except that their ambassador with the Queen Dowager had written that she had spoken of it to him. I replied that I had been informed of it also by your Majesty, who, however, had never believed it, although the French proclaimed it very loudly. Your Majesty, I said, had quite a different opinion, and fully trusted that the King (of England) would not fail to preserve his good friendship and alliance with the Emperor. He (Paget) replied that we ought not to doubt that. They (the English) had, moreover, sufficient experience of war to prevent them from again entering into it lightly. I thought well to ask him if he recollected a Spanish letter sent by the Emperor, and brought and shown to the King by M. d' Eick.* He replied yes, the letter had not been lost sight of; but he thought that the French aimed at a different object, as he had heard, and fully believed, that they had already a large force to enter Italy. (The rest of the conversation on this subject, and on the Council of Trent, is the same as in the letter to the Emperor of this date, and is therefore not repeated here.) He (Paget) also asked me to write to your Majesty begging you to order the Captain of Gravelines to allow the King's servant to converse with Duke Philip, and, above all, to release the latter. He (Paget) thought that it was very desirable, as you would never find Duke Philip culpable in anything, that your Majesty should write a letter to the King (of England) excusing and softening this matter of the Duke's detention; and saying that it was done in ignorance that the Duke was in the King's service.

This seemed a good opportunity for asking Paget how they stood with the Scots. It was, I said, needful for us to know; for they (the Scots) were constantly injuring us, who were only at enmity with them on account of the English, in accordance with the treaty of alliance. If they (the English) were at peace with the Scots we ought to be included. He replied: "We also are suffering a great deal from them, and we do not know yet how it will end. We have sent the clause respecting the inclusion of Scotland to the English ambassador there, with instructions for him to exhibit it." He (Paget) also promised to send me a copy of the clause. I then related to him what your Majesty wrote to me in your last letters, as to the proceedings of Alexander Paniter in Brussels,† and also as to the subsequent interviews between M. de Granvelle and the Admiral of France at Bruges, with regard to the inclusion of Scotland; my object being to weaken the effect of what the Admiral of

---

* Referring apparently to the alleged plan of the French to deceive Henry by a feigned agreement with regard to the marriage of Prince Edward to Mary of Scotland mentioned in the Emperor's letter to Scepperus of 26 Feb., 1546, and subsequently.

† Paniter was the Secretary of Arran, who had been sent to Flanders to negotiate.

1546.

France had recently told him.* Paget replied that he perfectly recollected what had passed with Paniter, he (Paget) being there at the same time; but he knew nothing about the matter having been discussed at Bruges. With regard, however, to the positive statement of the Admiral of France, made in the presence of the English Ambassador in Brussels, and of Paniter himself, he (Paget) did not know what to believe. He (Paget) had asked the Admiral of France before several gentlemen if he might positively repeat the assertion; whereupon the Admiral had said yes, and that those who had negotiated the treaty (*i.e.* between the Emperor and France) would never deny it. Even, he said, if the Viceroy of Sicily (*i.e.* Gonzaga), who was of similar standing to himself (the Admiral of France), maintained that what he said was not true, he (the Admiral of France) would uphold it. To end the subject, I said that all this was but talk, and events would prove the truth: and Paget agreed with me in this. In order to see whether I could not get a copy of their treaty with France, I remarked that the Emperor's subjects who had property in Boulogne were asking how they were to proceed to obtain possession of what belonged to them. Paget replied that the property had been gained by right of conquest, and the King consequently regarded it as his own. Those, therefore, who wished to obtain it should address themselves to the King. This, he said, was one of the difficulties raised by the French on behalf of their own subjects, when the peace treaty had been practically concluded. The treaty had indeed almost fallen through on this point, as the King of England would not listen to any limitation of his right of conquest. When I pressed for a copy of the treaty, Paget told me plainly that the clause referring to the point simply stated, in substance, that such property remained absolutely to the King. As he was leaving me, Paget begged me urgently to use my best efforts to accelerate the release of Duke Philip; and not to forget to suggest to your Majesty to write a letter on the subject to the King (Henry). Your Majesty will know better than I how important it is at the present juncture to keep these people in as good a humour as possible, and to confirm in their attachment those who are well disposed to us. Finally Paget told me that Secretary Dr. Petre and the Dean of St. Paul's were going to Calais to settle a dispute they have with regard to the amount of a debt, which the French allege to be smaller than that which they (the English) claim. I do not think there is any other reason for their journey; having regard to the persons who are going.

(The next paragraph, with regard to the alleged attempt of the French to draw Henry into intrigues against the Emperor and the Pope in Italy, is the same as in the letter to the Emperor of the same date.)

See letter of 16 July, from Van der Delft to the Queen Dowager, in which it is related that Paget had assured the writer that the Admiral of France had positively asserted, that in the peace treaty between the Emperor and France, the Scots had been included by a tacit agreement, not set forth in the formal capitulations. The statement to the contrary is contained in the Queen Dowager's reply to Van der Delft of 31 July.

1546.

The Admiral of France has not yet arrived, but he is expected from one day to another, and is coming in his galleys. Great preparations are being made for him, the King being at Hampton Court, where he will receive him. The Lord Admiral returned from France four days ago.

London, 16 August, 1546.

17 Aug.
Simancas.
E. 1192.
Italian.

310. ADVICES FROM PIEDMONT.

The King of France has sent to the King of England, complaining that the latter has fortified Boulogne in violation of the treaty, and has begged him not to continue in this course. The answer was that the King of France ought to be very much obliged to him for doing it, because when the territory was restored to him he would have the advantage. The King of England sent his Lord Admiral to the King of France. He remained with the latter for five days, and was received with great rejoicing and pomp.

It appears that a brother of Count Fiesco was recently at the Court of France, and he too has been much caressed, especially by the Admiral. When he left the rumour was current at Court that he had gone to England, and he is publicly blamed for it; but in reality the rumour was only set afloat for the purpose of showing that they were not satisfied with him in the Court, and not because he had gone to England. Some people believe that whithersoever he may have gone he has an understanding with the King (of France).*

20 Aug.
Vienna.
Imp. Arch.

311. THE EMPEROR TO VAN DER DELFT.

We have received your letters and have heard what you wrote to M. de Granvelle. We thank you for your advices and especially for the news that the sacramentarians and other schismatics are being punished in England. Make all the enquiries you can on this point, and on the tendency of the King and his ministers in the matter. But especially try to discover their feeling towards the German Protestants, and whether there is any appearance of a desire to aid or favour the latter. Let us know also if the Protestants are making effort to obtain support in England; and what people are saying there about our enterprise. We may remark that we have heard from France that the King of England was carrying on some negotiations there, with the object of helping them (the Protestants), but we do not believe it; and, certainly, if the King continues to punish so actively the schismatics in England, it does not appear probable that he will help those in Germany. But, nevertheless, it is certain that a Secretary with the English ambassador in Venice has opened a negotiation with the Seigniory in favour of the Protestants; and is urging with much persistence that their (the Protestants') ambassadors should be received by the Seigniory. Letters also have been intercepted from the Elector of

---

* Giovanni Luigi Fiesco Count di Lavagna, the head of the great Genoese conspiracy against the Dorias and the Imperial interest, was naturally bidding for French and Papal support for his desperate scheme; and it will be seen by the above and other letters in this Calendar (page 112), that the Imperial agents were suspicious of him.

1546.

Saxony and the Landgrave of Hesse addressed to him (the Secretary) and we have made representations about this to the English ambassador here, who says he has written expressly to his master on the subject in letters that accompany the present, which letters you will forward as addressed. With regard to affairs between England and France, and those concerning Scotland, you will find out everything you can and will report to us from time to time. All we can say at present about affairs here is that we have assembled our forces, both German and Italian, and we are marching against the Elector of Saxony and the Landgrave of Hesse, hoping, with God's help, to punish them.° We send you the declaration of the grievances which we have against them, and which, in addition to other grave and intolerable causes, have led us to take the step we are taking.† It will be well for you to read this declaration to the King and his Council. Camp of Ratisbon, 20 August, 1546.

20 Aug.
Simancas.
E. R. 873.

312. JUAN DE VEGA to the EMPEROR.

By a papal courier I wrote on the 17th instant, saying that the Bull for the Flemish half-first-fruits had been despatched.‡

After many consultations, and much sorrow at your Majesty's message about the proposed removal of the Council, the Pope has resolved not to cause the removal for the present; and has ordered that none of the prelates are to leave Trent, and those who may have done so are to return.

The Pope had me approached by means of the person who had first spoken to me on the matter; namely Cardinal de Gambara, who said that, since the Pope had consented not to remove the Council, he hoped I would not make a noise about it, as the Pope was much grieved; and more to the same effect. I replied that it was impossible to help making a noise about it, as it was a matter for great regret, and most inconvenient and injurious to the public weal, besides being quite contrary to your Majesty's views. Many other similar attempts were made by them, their case being strengthened by such arguments as they thought would appeal to us.

The question of the commutation of the sale of the monastic manors is being actively dealt with, and is near a decision.

° The Emperor moved the following day towards Neuberg, crossing the Danube on the 24th, and being met by Cardinal Farnese and the Prince de Sulmone's contingent on the 25th. He remained before Ingolstadt in close proximity to the Protestant forces from the 27th to the 31st, when a desultory engagement lasting four days began, the Protestant forces being unskilfully led, and allowing the superior generalship of the Emperor to delay a decisive fight, until the arrival of the Flemings under Buren (15 September) and the inevitable divisions occurred in the heterogeneous Protestant army, made the victory of the Imperialists a foregone conclusion.

† Doubtless the famous, but illegal, ban of the Empire by which the Landgrave and John Frederick of Saxony were declared rebels and outlaws, and divested of all their privileges and possessions on the authority of the Emperor alone.

‡ This letter (wrongly dated 27th in the decipher) is in the archives, but it contains nothing more than a repetition of the news given in other communications; with respect to the Bull for the Flemish half-first-fruits, the commutation of the concession for the sale of the monastic manors in Spain, and the Pope's sorrow at the Emperor's firm rebuke of his underhand attempt to transfer the sittings of the Council of Trent to Lucca. As all these points are dealt with more fully in other letters, it has not been considered necessary to transcribe here the despatch referred to.

1546.

I have been informed by a person of quality as a fact that one of the Cardinals in the Pope's Council said to another Cardinal: "We know now what hitherto we have never been able to understand, namely what are the final aims of the Emperor with regard to the Council."*

Rome, 20 August, 1546.

20 Aug.
Simancas.
E. Milan.
1192.
Italian.

313. News from PIEDMONT sent to the EMPEROR by FERNANDO DE GONZAGA (Governor of Milan).

The King of France has raised a protest against the fortification of Boulogne by the English and has requested that the works be demolished, as they are in violation of the treaty. The King of England has replied that the fortifications will be for the benefit of the French as they will remain when the place is restored to them. The Admiral of England has been sent on a mission to the King of France and for five days was very splendidly entertained. The Admiral of France will accompany him to England.

20 August, 1546.

23 Aug.
Vienna.
Imp. Arch.

314. THE QUEEN DOWAGER to VAN DER DELFT.

We have received your letters of 16th instant; and we are much surprised that at that date no notice had been received in London that the Duke Palatine Philip had crossed over. As soon as we were informed of his detention we had orders written to the Lieutenant of Gravelines, who in the absence of the Captain had stopped the Duke, to allow him to continue his voyage. The King of England and his Council, however, have no just cause for resentment at the detention of the Duke, as he attempted to pass incognito and disguised his name; so that, if the Lieutenant had not noticed that he wore the order of the Golden Fleece (we ourselves having learnt that the Duke had passed through Antwerp), we should probably have considered it necessary to send and investigate who it was before we let him go. We cannot imagine what motive this Count Philip can have in going over to England so often, without once making himself known. This is not customary in Germany, as you may tell the King and his Council, whilst letting them know that we have no intention whatever of hindering the passage of those who wish to go over to see the King. But the passengers themselves are often the cause of their own detention by their adoption of devices which arouse suspicion against them. Affairs in Germany being in their present condition, it is in the highest degree necessary that we should keep a sharp eye on Germans passing through here; as is done in Germany itself, in the case of those leaving the country.† Nevertheless we should not have thought for a moment that Duke Philip, or anyone else, would have tried to hatch any plots in England against the Emperor, believing firmly that the friendship of the King is so sincere that he would never listen to such a thing.

---

* A marginal note against this paragraph says: "If this is notma de clearer further on it is not very easy to understand."

† The Bavarian family generally were neutral in the struggle, although inclining to the Catholic side. The Count Palatine, however, the young man's uncle, was a Lutheran and his sympathies at least were strongly favourable to the Confederates.

HENRY VIII.

1546.

As we released the Duke Philip before any request for us to do so was made by the King, we do not think there is any need for us to make a special excuse by letter. It will be sufficient for you to explain to them how the affair happened, which is really as is written above; but you will notice carefully whether the Duke shows any resentment at his having been stopped, or wishes to throw the blame for it upon us; and you will likewise discover what he is doing or soliciting in England, for our information.

You will have learnt from our letters of the 15th instant, which doubtless have ere this reached you, how the English Ambassador here replied to the two points referred to in the previous correspondence, namely the inclusion of the Scots in the peace treaty; and the reintegration in their estates of the Emperor's subjects in the Boulognais. The replies on both points agreed with what had been said to you on the other side; and we are unable sufficiently to express our surprise at the position taken up with regard to the second point—the restitution of the estates; as it seems to us utterly unreasonable that the Emperor's subjects, who have never served the King of France, but had sided with the English, should be deprived of their property by the failure of the King of France to retain his hold on Boulogne. We cannot believe that the King of England will persist in his present attitude, particularly as Paget appears to have remarked that the subjects should address their petitions to the King of England; and you will consequently press the King to allow the said claimants to be restored to the enjoyment of their estates, in the same way as before the war, on taking their feudatory oath to the King, as they are bound to do, according to the value of their respective fiefs. They will make no difficulty in doing this, if the King will consent to their returning to their possessions. Let us know the King's intentions in this matter.

Brussels, 23 August, 1546.

30 Aug.
Simancas.
E. B. 642.

315. THE EMPEROR to JUAN DE VEGA.

Pending receipt of your report as to what has been done about the 200,000 crowns and the other questions you have in hand, we defer answering yours of the 17th and 20th instant, and limit ourselves in the present to giving you an account, for your guidance, of the interviews with Cardinal Farnese here; since the matter discussed was that of money, of which you know the importance.

The Cardinal arrived at our camp (*i.e.* Ingolstadt) on St. Bartholomew's day (24 August) in the evening, and having been informed of his coming an hour before he arrived, we sent Prince Maximilian and the Prince of Piedmont to go and receive him with the Bishop of Arras.° They met him on a bridge, and accompanied him to our tent, outside of which we welcomed him with great demonstrations of affection, rejoicing at his coming in good health, and asking after the Pope, with other such general compliments as

---

° Prince Maximilian of Austria, son of Ferdinand King of the Romans and afterwards the Emperor Maximilian II., son-in-law of Charles. The Prince of Piedmont was Emmanuel Philibert, afterwards Duke of Savoy. The Bishop of Arras was Antoine de Perrenot, the younger de Granvelle, subsequently Cardinal de Granvelle.

1546.

are usual in first interviews. After a day or two the Cardinal wished to converse with us, and we were equally desirous of doing so with him; but as we were constantly worried, having the enemy so near to us and being uncertain of his design, we were unable to receive the Cardinal until the day before yesterday. He handed us a letter of credence from his Holiness; and, on the Pope's behalf, expressed his pleasure at witnessing the great goodwill we had displayed in this undertaking. He praised very highly what we had done and were doing, said how glad his Holiness would be to learn the present position of affairs, and that the armies had been mustered in such good form, etc. He then handed us the Bull for the half-first-fruits of Flanders; excusing the delay in its dispatch by saying that they had been unable to find the form for the concession, as a similar Bull had only once been granted previously by Pope Clement. In reply we gave him a general account of what had been done about the enterprise; and the gathering of forces previous to the arrival of the Duke of Camarino (Octavio Farnese), to whom, and to Alexander Vitello, we referred him for what had since been done in that respect.* We then proceeded to say that when the enterprise was first decided upon our intention was to employ all our strength and resources in its prosecution, and to carry it through if possible to a successful issue. This we had done so far, and we then re-stated the various reasons why it had been impossible to undertake the execution last year (the reasons in question are here set forth at great length); touching subsequently upon the allegations that had been made about our going to Landshut, which we said was now evident to everyone was for the purpose of collecting and concentrating the troops coming from Italy, and preventing the enemy from interposing between us and them, as was his intention if possible.† Our aims, we said, in this enterprise, were simply to serve God and redress the troubles of His Church, whilst increasing the power of his Holiness; and consequently we cared little what judgments men passed upon us. They had seen that when our troops were collected we had come in search of the enemy; ‡ and this subject led us to say how appropriately the Bull for the half-first-fruits had come, for we should need them, and all else, to carry through what we had begun. We then reminded him that when Granvelle went thither (to Rome) these Flemish half-first-fruits were conceded for

---

* The main body of the Papal contingent under Octavio had joined the Imperial camp at Landshut a fortnight previously.
† The Emperor had been criticised severely for his apparently rash move of abandoning Ratisbon, and advancing to Landshut, a town on the Iser, where he remained for 10 days, from the 4th to the 15th August. If Philip of Hesse had been an alert general the Emperor's movement might have been made a disastrous one, either by the Protestant capture of Ratisbon, which had been left with a small, weak garrison, or by a bold attack upon the Imperial camp before the arrival of the Papal contingent. The Emperor's tactics were, however, quite sound, as the first consideration for him was at any risk to prevent the Protestants from intercepting the Papal force and beating it before it could reach him. If this had been done the main body of Charles' army might have been dealt with before Buren arrived with the Dutch troops; in which case the Emperor's cause would have been ruined.
‡ The Emperor had marched to Neuberg and Ingolstadt as soon as Octavio and the Papal troops joined him; though he avoided taking the offensive for a decisive engagement pending the arrival of Buren.

1546.

a very much less important purpose than the present, and without so much loss of time. But still, we said, we could not avoid thanking his Holiness very earnestly for having sent us the Bull now, and especially since the Cardinal himself had brought it. All this, however, we continued, was absolutely useless if the payment of the 200,000 crowns was to be further delayed. The money was urgently needed, because we had arranged for the payment of our other bills in deferred instalments, in the full confidence that the Papal subsidy would meet the demands for August; and that it would provide the first ready money wanted to pay the many necessary expenses of the beginning of a campaign. We had always understood that this money would be forthcoming promptly, and reminded him of what had passed about it during the Worms negotiations,* and the promises subsequently made by his Holiness' ministers at Utrecht. It was then clearly stated that the expenses of the enterprise were to be drawn from the half-first-fruits of Spain, and the sale of the monastic manors; and as the Bulls for these concessions were unexpectedly delayed we could not obtain the money so promptly as was anticipated. It was always expressly understood that if we agreed (with the Pope) we ourselves would obtain the funds for the first month's disbursements, which we only succeeded in doing by paying heavy interest, and that the Papal subsidy of 200,000 crowns would be ready to provide for the second month; the succeeding month's expenses being met by us. In consequence of the delay that has occurred we have been obliged to seek money for the first and second months as well; at an interest so onerous, and in places so inconvenient, that we have been put to great trouble. In order the further to enforce this, we added that even if the 200,000 crowns had been paid in time it would not have been nearly sufficient to cover the month's expenditure; for not a month passes in which the payments do not exceed 300,000. This brought us to mention the hope we had that his Holiness would at a later date further aid us to the extent of the 100,000 additional, which he had always hinted that he would do. We pointed out the grave responsibility incurred if any reverse happened owing to want of money. We were staking our own lives and position in the business for the good of God's service, and the defence of the Pope's authority; and his Holiness on his part should use every effort to forward the enterprise as his own, touching, as it did, his dignity and interest. He well knew that we could, if we pleased, settle the questions concerning our own authority without an appeal to force; but, seeing that for the above reasons we had embarked ourselves so far in the business, we would leave to his Holiness' judgment what would be proper for him to do, if we were the commander-in-chief of his forces: bearing in mind that if the result should be different from that which we hope, by God's help, to attain, the Protestants would not satisfy themselves by simply destroying our rule in Germany, but would come down to Italy and to Rome, in order to do the same towards his Holiness. We again dwelt upon the trouble and risk we had incurred in staking our person and resources in the cause of God and religion,

---

* See page 213 et seq.

for although the enterprise had not been commenced ostensibly on that ground, we had always heartily wished that no other pretext than religion should be given for it. But on consulting with our brother the King of the Romans, the Duke of Bavaria and other Catholics, especially ecclesiastics, it was considered advisable to call it a war against rebels. His Holiness, however, would see that when we had punished the latter the religious question would be easily settled, this having always been our intention. The Cardinal (Farnese) in reply to this, spoke at length on the good offices he had performed, with the object of avoiding further delay in the payment of the subsidy; and finally promised that on the 6th proximo he would provide on account 80,000 ccowns, including the 30,000 now here. He had done no little thing, he said, in getting the Pope to take out of the Castle (*i.e.* St. Angelo) over 100,000 crowns, and contribute jewels and other valuables worth 60,000 more. We smiled at this; and could not help retorting that his Beatitude might have taken it all out of the Castle, and more besides; only that perhaps he expected to get the money elsewhere. After much discussion about the money, during which we again repeated the trouble and risk that would be caused by the delay, we could succeed in getting nothing further from him, except he would again write to the Pope on the subject, explaining the position to him, etc.; and the other questions, such as the valuation of the specie, etc., would be settled between him (Cardinal Farnese) and our ministers; in order that no loss on exchange should be incurred by us and that the nett sum of 200,000 crowns stipulated should reach our coffers. In this, and in all things, he promised his best offices.

After this matter was disposed of, he enlarged upon the Pope's great satisfaction that we had consented to the commutation of the concession for the sale of the monastic manors (in Spain) and the substitution of other means for raising the money in accordance with the wish of the College of Cardinals. He thanked us very cordially for this. We replied that, after considering your account of the Pope's views on the subject, we had agreed willingly to please his Holiness, with the conditions and limitations stated by us: but it would be necessary that the funds should be forthcoming promptly; as the promises we had made to the merchants must of course be fulfilled. His Holiness must therefore see that the matter is concluded without delay; as he had always been told that this was one of the principal sources upon which we depended for supply. The Cardinal replied that the Pope was very willing that the necessary documents should be despatched at once: and added that it behoved us also to take steps for carrying the authorisation into effect promptly. We tried to excuse ourselves from this by referring to what the Pope had said to you (de Vega), and suggested that the best way would be for his Holiness to send orders to all the monasteries, to the effect that means must at once be adopted to fulfil the command, and supply us with the sum of 500,000 in aid of the enterprise. These orders should be enforced by the obvious arguments; and the Pope should warn the monasteries that if they failed he would be unable to avoid authorising us to sell their manors and rents to the extent of 800,000 ducats.* In reference to this we told the Cardinal that although our intention was not to take more than 500,000 ducats, it would be advisable to give another turn to the screw, and frighten them into providing the sum required, by hinting that they otherwise might have to pay more. The Cardinal was quite satisfied with this, and said he would convey it to the Pope, begging us also to instruct our ministers in Rome to a similar effect, so that by their united efforts we might receive the funds without delay. You (de Vega) will keep the matter in hand, and see that no time be lost.

The Cardinal then turned to the subject of the Council (of Trent). The Pope, he said, had never been willing to listen to any talk of removing it elsewhere. He had, indeed, been very angry when he heard that some of the prelates had left Trent. The rumour of removal had been raised by the prelates themselves, in consequence of the bad air and unhealthiness of the place, the dearness of provisions, and the fear that the Protestants and Grisons might make a descent upon the town. But, after his Holiness had heard of the threats (braverias) of the Cardinal of Trent, and what had happened at the meetings; together with the message we had sent to Cardinal Santa Cruz,† it seemed to him that the intention existed of depriving the Council of its liberty; and then, at the request of a majority of the prelates, he had granted a Bull for the removal of the Council elsewhere, Lucca, Ferrara or other place to our satisfaction being suggested. The Cardinal tried to persuade us to this course, using the same arguments as those alleged by the prelates, with the addition of a new one; namely that if the Pope were to die, as he might, being so old, whilst the Council was pending, it might result in schism. We replied that the unhealthiness of Trent was not so great as was alleged, nor were victuals at an immoderate price, for the measures adopted by Cardinal Trent and the Consuls had kept the place abundantly supplied. With regard to the fear expressed that the enemy might come down upon the city, we said there might have been some reason for alarm when the country people attacked it; but that now, with our armies near at hand, it was absurd to be afraid, or that the Grisons would venture to move. The message we had sent to Cardinal Santa Cruz was only intended to apply in case he should propose the removal or suspension of the Council without the express order of his Holiness, as it was understood that he wished to do. We answered the Cardinal's argument about the danger of schism, by saying that if schism was to be the outcome of the Council, it would happen if the meetings were held in Lucca, Ferrara or anywhere else. The reasons advanced therefore were, we said, insufficient for removing the Council from Trent. The Cardinal ended by saying that as this point was one that appertained to the Council, he would not discuss it further, but would refer it to the consideration of the Nuncio, who had charge of such matters, and

---

* The meaning of this appears to be that both the Pope and the Emperor were desirous that the odium of first moving in the spoliation of the monasteries, etc. should be borne by the other.

† *See* the Emperor's letter to Vega of 31st July, page 443.

1546.

of our ministers. There has been much to do to-day in consequence of the approach of the enemy's headquarters towards our own, and our forces have been always in order of battle. For this reason, we have been unable to confer again with the Cardinal, but will do so on the first opportunity. (Urges Vega to activity in obtaining the despatch of the money questions by the Pope.)

Camp near Ingolstadt, 30 August, 1546.

NOTE.—In the reply from Vega to the above letter, dated Viterbo, 12 September, Vega informs the Emperor that Cardinal Farnese had not written to the Pope about the money, etc. until the 2nd September; but that the matters in question have since been actively dealt with. He has been unable to induce the Pope to increase the sum to be obtained from the monasteries beyond the 300,000 ducats, for which the Briefs will soon be despatched. He (Vega) has not ventured to mention the additional 100,000 crowns subsidy, for fear of delaying the matter in hand. Has frequently urged the Pope about the prompt payment of the 200,000, but his Holiness always replies that he has already disbursed the money; and has done his best to get the merchants to shorten the instalments. He says that he has fulfilled the treaty, and is surprised that the writer should hint otherwise. Orders, moreover, had been sent for 83,000 crowns of the amount to be paid forthwith in Germany, and in addition to this the legate, Cardinal Trent, and Don Diego de Mendoza have been in negotiation with the merchants. The Pope's ministers say that your Majesty might easily have discounted the whole of the money, and they thought you would have done so. Learns that Cardinal Farnese has now been given a free hand in the matter.

3 Sept.
Vienna.
Imp. Arch.

316. VAN DER DELFT to the QUEEN DOWAGER.

Since my last letters, carried by one of my own people, I have received three letters from your Majesty: the first dated 16th ultimo, respecting the two points of the inclusion of the Scots, and the restitution of property situated in Boulogne belonging to subjects of the Emperor: the second dated the 17th, about the deliverance of Magnus David: and the third, dated 23rd, brought by my said servant on his return hither.

As the Councillors have been fully occupied with the Admiral of France, I had no earlier opportunity of conferring with them; but on the morning of the day he left (Monday last) I sent to Hampton Court to learn when they would receive me. Paget returned a reply, saying that several of the Councillors had already left for London, and the King himself was starting on the following day for his progress. If, therefore, I had anything to communicate to the Council I could do so conveniently in London, but if I liked to go to Court I should give early notice in order that lodgings might be provided for me, as the King was going to houses of his away from populous places.

As I wished first to hear what the Councillors would say about the two principal points, especially as I knew that the Bishop of Winchester and the Chancellor would be there, I sent to ask the

1546.

latter when he would be at leisure to discuss them. He excused himself, on the ground of other occupations, and said that the Council was not meeting until Friday, which is to-day, but added that, if the matter was so pressing as to forbid delay, he would summon his colleagues earlier. I thought better, however, not to hurry them for the sake of a day or two; and consequently went to-day to dine with them at Westminster, laying before them the two statements about the Scots and Boulogne, in accordance with your Majesty's letter.

As regards the Scots, they replied that they were only included in the peace in so far as was expressed in the extract which your Majesty sent to me. I observed, that, according to my reading of the extract, I could only understand it as including the Scots absolutely in the peace treaty with France; and, consequently, that in compliance with the provisions of the treaty of alliance (*i.e.* between Henry and the Emperor) the Emperor should be duly informed of the exact settlement arranged. By the same treaty (of alliance), I said, the Emperor's consent was necessary, and should be requested; since his Majesty had entered into war with the Scots, solely in fulfilment of the treaty. His Majesty had no wish to obstruct the peace with the Scots, but it was unreasonable that the English should be at peace with them, as the English ambassador asserted, whilst the Emperor remained at war with them. They (the Lords of the Council) replied that their ambassador had been instructed to hand to your Majesty an authentic copy of the agreement made, and they had no doubt that this had already been done. They had, they said, no peace with the Scots, who since the treaty with France had continued to do them (the English) great damage. The King had consequently been obliged to fit out some of his ships to ensure navigation from their attacks, upon both the English and ourselves (*i.e.* the subjects of the Emperor); and one of the principal armed ships of the Scots had already been captured. It is true that the King had sent to Scotland the clause by which the Scots were included; but they would only agree to it with such additional conditions and limitations as the King (of England) had not accepted, and never would accept. The Regent of Scotland had written to the King (of England) in the name of the Queen of Scotland, asking for safe-conduct for the Scottish Privy Seal, a great master, and a secretary, to come to England, accompanied by a train of 50 horsemen, to treat for peace. In showing me this letter, which they (the Councillors) had received this morning, they read it out to me, word for word, and also their draft reply, consenting to grant the safe-conduct requested; and they finally assured me that nothing whatever should be concluded with the Scots, without his Majesty, the Emperor, being informed thereof, in accordance with the treaty.

This gave me an opportunity of introducing the subject of Magnus David, for whose deliverance I pressed. They raised great difficulties about this; but the Chancellor said that he had spoken to the King of the various requests I had made to that end; and although the King and his Council considered the charge against Magnus very suspicious, still, out of consideration for your Majesty, the King had consented to the man's surrender. When I spoke of his expenses they made light of them; but when the man is released I will insist upon this point.

We then came to the matter of the property owned by the subjects of the Emperor in the Boulognais, who had not served against the King of England, but of whom many had been on his side when he was before the town. Your Majesty, I said, was not satisfied with the reply given to you by the English Ambassador, or with that conveyed to me by Paget; and if they, the Councillors, thought they could give me no better reply now, I had decided to appeal to the King. They simply repeated the answer already given to your Majesty, and after some discussion between us on the matter they said that everything depended upon the King's benignity; and therewith they made a move to go to dinner. But, as I saw that this was a good opportunity for speaking frankly; the only three Councillors present being attached to the Emperor's interests—namely the Bishop of Winchester, the Grand Master, Lord St. John, and the Chancellor—I pressed my answer to their question, as to how the Emperor's affairs were progressing. His Majesty, I said, was very well, and M. de Buren had already, as they knew, crossed the Rhine without opposition. His Majesty was so well armed that, with the help of God, I hoped that he would overcome his enemies, who in addition to their rebellious inobedience, had invaded the Emperor's patrimonial territory in the Tyrol. News had arrived here yesterday that the enemy had taken the town of Ingolstadt, and had killed the Spaniards and Italians there, and the people who had received the news were very active in sending it to the King, but I thought that he (Henry) would not rejoice over it so much as they expected; believing, as I firmly did, that he desired nothing but the prosperity of the Emperor. Still, seeing that the Emperor's enemies, Sturmius and Dr. Brun, had obtained audience, and, as was asserted, had received aid in money here, I did not know what to think of it; except that everything in this world is mutable. I had even learnt that certain persons had come into great favour with the King, who I wished were as far away as they were last year. I did not mention the names of those I had in my mind, who were the Earl of Hertford (Seymour) and the Lord Admiral (Dudley). The councillors returned no answer to this remark, but they displayed, as usual, their great devotion and goodwill towards the Emperor's interests; only expressing apprehension that, in case of his Majesty being victorious, he had made a treaty with the Pope against the King. I told them that they should not believe such a thing; the Emperor would never do anything contrary to his treaty of friendship with the King. They might, I said, be sure of that, for there was no sovereign in the world who more earnestly desired long life to the King than his imperial Majesty. They expressed pleasure at this, and then we went to dinner, after which, seeing how busy they were, I took my leave.

It did not appear to me to be necessary to make any statement about what had happened with Duke Philip at Gravelines, as these three Councillors did not have much to do with his affairs. I cannot ascertain anything about these affairs, except that I

1546.

hear that he does not appear so well pleased here as he was before. I will not fail to take the first opportunity of going to Court, to learn the King's final decision respecting the Boulognais property, for your Majesty's information.

The Admiral of France was very magnificently treated here. He was met on his way to Hampton Court by the Prince (Edward) accompanied by more than 8 (80?) horsemen, most of them dressed in cloth of gold.*

The present made to him here was a sideboard of gold plate, with other gifts, such as horses, dogs, silver cups, etc. The formal signature of the treaty was, I understand, publicly performed. At this assembly the French spread a rumour that the King of France was gathering an armed force to invade the country of Liège; others say Lorraine: but I hope there is nothing in this.

London, 3 September, 1546.

3 Sep.
Vienna.
Imp. Arch.

317. Van der Delft to Loys Scors.

The reason why I have asked for letters from the Queen (Dowager of Hungary) to explain the detention of Duke Philip was because those (of the Council) who are in chief authority, and are devoted to the Emperor's interests, were desirous of thus satisfying the King, in order to maintain their own influence, and be the better able to work for the continuance of friendly relations. The letters would also give me an opportunity for a conference with the King, during which I might ascertain better than by any other means what is going on. There are people here endeavouring to get into favour, and to obtain power in the Government; but as they are not such as will suit our purposes I should like to be in a position to oppose them as much as possible.

I have forgotten to mention in the letter to the Queen that M. de Morette who came with the Admiral of France remains here, it is said, for the purpose of arranging for the restitution by the English of the galley captured by them before peace was signed; † the French contention being that the promise given by the Lord Admiral when the peace treaty was signed, of full restitution, covers the return of the galley as it stood when it was captured, whereas the Lord Admiral maintains that he only promised to restore the hull of the galley. The King, moreover, refuses to give back the slaves, to whom he has given their liberty. Nevertheless I do not know whether there is any other intrigue being conducted under this pretext. I will do my duty in trying to discover.

London, 3 September, 1546.

---

* Foxe quotes a curious account given by Cranmer of the discussions between the Admiral of France, Annebaut, and the King of England after the banquet at Hampton Court respecting the simultaneous adoption of the Protestant Reformation in England and France, changing the Mass into a Communion, and finally renouncing all dependence on the See of Rome. This was probably a feint on the part of Francis to deceive Henry.

† The galley of Baron de Blancard captured off Ambleteuse.

1546.
12 Sep.
Simancas.
E. A. 642.

318. The Emperor to Diego Hurtado de Mendoza.

(In a letter mainly occupied by the details of proceedings in the Council of Trent and by the instructions for Mendoza's mission to the Pope the following passage occurs.)

We have been informed that an Englishman and a Lutheran are in Venice endeavouring to negotiate with the Seigniory, to whom they are offering the county of Tyrol. God having granted us such signal advantages in the present war these intrigues do not disturb us much: it will, however, be well that you keep a vigilant watch. It would be well also if you could lay hold of the four men from Venice, Switzerland, and the Grisons, who went to solicit the County of Tyrol. The Lutheran has discovered what you had planned against him. Camp near Ingolstadt, 12 September, 1546.

12 Sep.
Simancas.
E. Milan.
1192.
Italian.

319. News from Piedmont enclosed in a letter from Fernando de Gonzaga to the Emperor.

A brother of Count Fiesco went some time since to the King of France, and was very graciously received, especially by the Admiral. It was generally asserted at the French Court that Fiesco had left and gone to the King of England. I am, however, of opinion that he is still in France, and that this false news is circulated in order to spread the belief that he has not been favourably entertained there. However that may be, it is quite evident that whatever Fiesco has done has been with the acquiescence of the King of France.

13 Sep.
Vienna.
Imp. Arch.

320. Van der Delft to the Emperor.

The Admiral of France has left here, after having been very magnificently entertained by the King during the few days of his stay. After his departure I went to the Lords of the Council, who were here in London, for the purpose of setting forth to them the instructions I had received from the Queen (Dowager); namely to press them for information as to the position of affairs between the English and the Scots, the latter of whom still continued to injure your Majesty's subjects; and also for the purpose of procuring the restitution of certain property in the Boulognais, which previous to the war was in possession of subjects of your Majesty. With regard to the first point they replied that they (the English) also were not at peace with the Scots, who had only accepted their inclusion in the peace treaty under great protests and conditions, which the King had considered altogether too prejudicial for him to concede, and he had consequently protested on his side. It is true that on the same day a letter had been received here from the Regent of Scotland in the name of the Queen, requesting safe-conducts for the Scottish Privy Seal, another great officer, and a secretary with a train of 40 horsemen, to come hither and treat for peace with the King. This letter the Lords of the Council read to me word for word, and also their draft reply; at the same time telling me that they would grant the safe-conducts requested, but would make no arrangement with the Scots without giving your Majesty due notice. I replied that this course was imperative upon them in fulfilment of the treaty of alliance.

Touching the second point, they repeated what they had told me on other occasions, namely that the King had won Boulogne by the sword, and consequently that he was by all rules the sole lord and master thereof. I showed them how unreasonable it would be for the subjects of your Majesty to be deprived of their property, whilst the Emperor and the King were on terms of close friendship; many of such subjects, moreover, having been in the King's service during the campaign, and if they were thus deprived of their property, their services in aiding the King in his conquest would redound to their prejudice instead of to their advantage. After much discussion they (the Councillors) ended by saying that they had no authority to give any other reply than the abovementioned, and the matter depended upon the King. I can plainly see, therefore, that it will have to be urged upon him personally; and I should already have been to see him about it, only that he is taking his pleasure, travelling from one house to another with a very small train, in consequence of the lack of lodging accommodation. I understand, however, that he will be at Guildford in three days, and I will not fail to seek him there and urge the matter diligently. Finding myself in a position to converse freely with the Councillors, in consequence of there being present only the Bishop of Winchester, the Lord Chancellor, and Lord St. John, the Grand Master (of the Household), who are entirely devoted to your Majesty's interests, I took the opportunity of acquainting them with the fact that suspicions are being conveyed to us with regard to the coming and going of one Sturmius and Dr. Brun, who were considered to be your Majesty's enemies. Your Majesty, however, I said, had no distrust, but depended so entirely upon the King's friendship as to be sure that he would not lend ear to such apostles, or, indeed, to anything at all prejudicial to your Majesty. For my own part, seeing the diversity of sects that existed in this country, the Protestants themselves having their openly declared champions, I did not quite know what to think of it, but to suppose that all things in this world are mutable. I had even heard that some of them (*i.e.* the Protestants) had gained great favour with the King; and I could only wish that they were as far away from the Court as they were last year. I did not mention the names of those to whom I wished to refer; but they were the Earl of Hertford and the Lord Admiral. The Councillors made no reply, although they clearly showed that they understood me, and continued in their great devotion towards your Majesty and their ardent wishes for your welfare, notwithstanding that they heard that, in the event of your Majesty's being victorious, you had made a treaty with the Pope against the King, their master. I told them that they should not believe such a thing. Your Majesty would never do anything against the treaty and friendship now existing with the King; and of this they might rest assured. They seemed much pleased at this, and we parted.

Since then I have received your Majesty's letters of 20th ultimo from Regensburg (Ratisbon), and the day after their receipt I was invited to dine with the Council. When I arrived they told me that they had written to the King an account of the conversation they had had with me, and his Majesty had replied to them without mentioning the two points referred to above, the consideration of which had been postponed until I appeared at Court. With regard, however, to Sturmius and Brun, they said that the King had not seen Sturmius for years, and did not know that he had been in England. It was true that Dr. Brun had been here, for the purpose of arranging with the King for the Strasburg people to hinder the passage of German troops for the service of the King of France, which was very convenient for them (*i.e.* the English) as they were at war with him. Dr. Brun had wished to place his son with the King, but the latter had declined, and certainly had no league or federation with these people to your Majesty's prejudice. The King, indeed, was much annoyed that suspicion should be cast upon him in this way, as he heard was the case, by words uttered at Venice by your ministers. Your Majesty, moreover, did not send him any information as to your affairs, which he was naturally anxious to know, as well as other people; especially as your Majesty had so great an enterprise in hand. He could not understand how it was that your Majesty failed to send him any notice of your success, either by letter or otherwise. They seemed to take this to heart more than anything else; for the Councillors added that your Majesty had made two treaties with France, one of which was kept strictly secret, although the purport of it was known to them. They also repeated their remark about the treaty with the Pope, though they did not persist in that, and it seemed to me also quite inappropriate to the occasion.

In the matter of Sturmius, I replied that my remarks on the subject were entirely unofficial, and were prompted solely by my devotion to the King, who, I thought, should be made acquainted with the stuff that these people were made of who were trying to draw him into their intrigues; they having first abandoned their schoolmaster's gowns, were now busying themselves in sowing trouble in Christendom. It was evident, I said, that these sects only tended to sedition, and to the abolition of superiors, both ecclesiastic and secular. They showed quite openly that all their plots were for the oppression of the goodly, and to bring confusion into the world. They (the English Councillors) were quite of the same opinion, saying amongst themselves in their own language that my words were true. With regard to the complaint as to the suspicion cast (upon the King), and the expressions said to have been used (in Venice) with regard to the King's inclinations; I said that they had been very ill-informed, as I was quite sure that your Majesty's ambassador in Venice (whom they had mentioned as Don Diego de Mendoza) or any other of your Majesty's ministers, would never say anything in derogation of the fair fame of the King; as it was perfectly certain that your Majesty had the most complete confidence in the King's friendship. It is true, I said, that their people (*i.e.* the English) in Venice had an understanding with your Majesty's enemies, and that a secretary who was with the English ambassador resident there, had solicited the post of ambassador of the Protestants to the Seigniory. This could be proved by certain intercepted letters, and your Majesty had caused a statement of the matter to be made to the English ambassador at the Imperial Court. They (the Councillors) expressed surprise at this and thanked me for the information.

Touching their remarks about the paucity of news that had been conveyed to them as to your Majesty's affairs, I pointed out to them that I had not failed to inform the King from the commencement of your Majesty's undertaking, and of the just causes which moved your Majesty in your action. Whilst I was saying this the Chancellor interrupted me with the remark that, as the King is a true friend of the Emperor, the latter might occasionally write a word to promote the continuance of kindly feeling and amity; whereupon the whole of them together begged me to ask your Majesty to bear this in mind for the future. In the matter of the treaties with France, I told them that I only knew of one treaty; and the only mention I had ever heard of a secret treaty in addition was that made by the King last year to M. D'Eick and myself. If the French had started a fresh rumour to this effect they (the English) ought not to believe it, but just the contrary, knowing, as they did, that the French said anything to serve their own ends. This was the case, I said, with the statement that they made the English believe, of their (the French) intention to commence war against your Majesty in Italy, for which I thanked them for informing me through Secretary Paget (as I wrote to your Majesty). It was quite evident now, I said, that what the French had then told them in apparent confidence had no object but to mislead and deceive them (the English), whilst they (the French) constructed a fort which might command the entrance into Boulogne harbour, at which task over the three thousand men were set to work on the very day that the Admiral of France left England. They (the Councillors) appeared very much displeased at this, though they tried to convince me that the work in question would not be so prejudicial to them as I supposed. We then spoke of the treaty with the Pope, and I repeated what I had previously said about it, adding that I was quite sure that none of those present, who knew well your Majesty's loyalty and virtue, could be of opinion that you would abuse your treaties or break your promise to anyone in the world, and least of all to their King, with whom your friendship and alliance were so ancient and so close. They admitted this warmly, but repeated to me that an occasional letter from your Majesty would do a great deal of good. I can see from this, Sire, that those who, with Secretary Paget, are most in favour would much like some confirmation or proof in support of their views, in order the better to rebut those who seek to bring about a change in religion and to incline the King to innovations disadvantageous to your Majesty.

After finishing this conversation I exhibited to them the contents of the Imperial ban against the Duke of Saxony and the Landgrave of Hesse, which they (the English Councillors) considered good and reasonable. Whilst we were in discourse about German affairs I divulged to them something of the acts, life and conduct of the Protestants, and their objects. The efforts they (the Protestants) were making here, I said, to obtain an alliance or assistance, were only for the purpose of submitting this

1546.

King and his realm to servitude and subjection to them, as I had told them on previous occasions; and if I had thought that the King was attached to the Protestants I should not have failed to intervene, moved by my affection for this country, although I had no authority to do so. But I should have given my opinion about it to the King, who I did not think would have taken it in evil part. They (the Councillors) thanked me, and said that anything proceeding from such good intentions could not be otherwise than agreeable to the King. With this we went to dinner, and the Chancellor asked me to mention the purport of our conversation to the King as soon as I had an opportunity. I will do so, Sire, to the best of my ability. I understand that two thousand men are to be sent from here across the sea. It is said also that the French, in addition to their sappers, have a good number of troops to assist and defend them. They (the sappers) are working continuously, according to French reports, constructing a haven where small boats may enter; but the English fear that their object may be to build a fort. Opinions vary on the subject, and many people think it may cause a re-commencement of the war. The Duke Philip, Count Palatine, and the Rhingrave are still here, but they do not seem to be made so much of as formerly. I hear, also, that they themselves are not so well pleased as they were, recognising perhaps that their marriage plans will not succeed.

Great activity is still displayed here in the inquisition against the sectarians, but the results are not so satisfactory as at first.º

London, 13 September, 1546.

13 Sep.
Vienna.
Imp. Arch.

321. VAN DER DELFT to the QUEEN DOWAGER.

I am now writing to the Emperor a portion of what I recently wrote to your Majesty, and also full particulars of what has since passed between me and the Lords of the Council, as your Majesty will see by the duplicates herewith.

Two days ago the Chancellor sent begging me to write to your Majesty, asking you to be pleased to allow the rest of the cannon-powder that the King has at Antwerp in the hands of one of his officers, named Mr. Dammesel [*sic*], and Erasmus Schetz to be sent hither without hindrance. This powder is only the remains of the parcel of which the rest has already been received, and the Chancellor trusts that your Majesty will raise no difficulty. I have encouraged this hope in him and refer the matter to your Majesty's judgment.

London, 13 September, 1546.

14 Sep.
Vienna.
Imp. Arch.

322. SOEPPERUS to the QUEEN DOWAGER.

I received yesterday your Majesty's letter of the 11th instant, and with regard to the Scottish affair, as soon as the States of Zeeland are assembled here in Walcheren, M. de Béures† and myself will use our best efforts to induce and persuade them to

---

º The highly "satisfactory results," at first, here referred to were the martyrdoms of Anne Askew, John Lascelles, Nicholas Belenian and John Adams, in July.

† Or Bèvres, Admiral of Flanders.

1546.

undertake the arming and equipment of some ships of war, to oppose the attacks of the Admiral of Scotland and his adherents; hoping that the storm which constantly rages at sea will prevent the Scots from carrying out their designs. We have thoroughly examined this island and all the approaches to it. M. Donas proposes that a bulwark should be constructed on a commanding point between Middleburg and Flushing. The point is called Blanckartshoek . . . . (Further details of the proposed fortification of Walcheren.)

Veere, 14 September, 1546.

14 Sep.
Vienna.
Imp. Arch.

323. The QUEEN DOWAGER to VAN DER DELFT.

We have learned by your letter of 3rd instant what had passed between you and the English Council respecting the two points discussed in previous letters, the inclusion of the Scots and the restitution of estates in the Boulognais to the Emperor's subjects. We have already informed you of the despatch of Secretary Strick to Scotland, for the purpose of claiming the restitution of the ships captured by the Scots since the conclusion of the peace treaty between England and France; and to learn how the Scots intended to behave towards the Emperor's subjects for the future. The Secretary has now given us an account of his negotiations, as you will see by copies enclosed: and he writes that the Scots consider that their inclusion in the treaty makes them at peace with England on their fulfilment of the conditions governing the inclusion. Having regard to the state of their affairs and the trouble still existing in their country, the Scots will not at present raise any difficulty in complying with the conditions; but they say, nevertheless, that they still remain at war with the Emperor and his subjects because, in the clause of the peace treaty providing for the inclusion of the Scots, no mention is made of the war between the Emperor and them. They say that, even if the Emperor be included in the treaty generally, he is not so in regard to the Scots, with whom his Majesty has come to no agreement, but only in regard to the two directly contracting parties, England and France, now both allies of the Emperor; and consequently that all captures made by the Scots from the Emperor's subjects are fair prizes. To tell the pure truth, we do not consider this contention altogether unreasonable; and by the same rule the English ought to admit that in consenting to the inclusion of the Scots on certain conditions to be fulfilled by the latter they (the English) were violating the terms of their treaty of alliance with the Emperor; inasmuch as they were making peace with the Scots and leaving the Emperor at war, whilst neglecting to inform the latter of their inclusion of the Scots in their treaty. This is in direct violation of clause 13 of the alliance treaty, as interpreted and agreed upon recently at Utrecht. You will accordingly declare to the English Council that, having regard to the contention advanced by the Scots to the Secretary from here (Strick), the inclusion of the Scots in the peace treaty with France is a contravention of the treaty of alliance between the Emperor and the King of England, and that we have no doubt that the King will prefer to stand by the latter rather than by the former. That being the case, the English ought not, and and indeed cannot by the terms of the alliance, admit the Scots to the benefit of their inclusion in the peace treaty until the Emperor has negotiated a peace with them. You will keep a sharp look out when the Scottish ambassadors arrive, that you may be fully informed of their dealings; and if you find that the commissioners appointed on the English side to negotiate with them do not give you an account of their proceedings you will insist strongly upon your being kept informed from day to day of what is done : and you can make this demand boldly without dissimulation. You will give us prompt notice of the coming of the Scots, in order that we may send you instructions as to the conditions we must obtain from them before we consent to a peace treaty.

We may inform you that we have heard that the dispatch of this Scottish mission to the King of England is mainly for the purpose of temporising and gaining time, and so preventing the King of England from sending succour to those who are holding the castle of St. Andrews; and you may, as if of your own motion, communicate this confidentially to some of the members of the Council who side with the Emperor; so that they may know how to deal with the Scots if they see that the latter are more inclined to drag matters out than to come to a settlement.

The Secretary (Strick) writes that the Scots are boasting that, now that they are at peace with the English, they want no peace with the Emperor; but you will take care to avoid all reference to such an attitude in conversation with the English : and will, on the contrary, say that the Scots are only too desirous of treating with us, as representing his Imperial Majesty, and if we liked to deal with them without the English, peace would already have been made; the reason that no better reply was given in Scotland to the Secretary having been simply this.

With reference to the restitution to the Emperor's subjects of their estates in the Boulognais; as the English Councillors will give no other reply than that already sent, we are sending you letters of credence for the King. In virtue of them you will, if you have not already done so, lay before him the facts of the case; and state what has passed in regard to it between you and the Council, with the reply they gave you, and that presented to us, by their orders, by the English ambassador here. Our duty towards the Emperor's subjects will not allow us to be satisfied with these replies; and as we cannot believe that it is the King's wish to treat these subjects worse than they are treated by the King of France, who has made no difficulty in restoring to such subjects the estates they possessed in that part of the Boulognais retained by him, the King of England should raise no difficulty. And especially considering that these subjects took no part against him; but many of them, on the contrary, were in his service under Count de Buren. They do not therefore deserve to be deprived of their property; and if this injustice is done the King will lose the adhesion of many good gentlemen, who only desire to do him faithful service when an opportunity may arise.

It is possible that the English may justly contend that in conquering the Boulognais they conquered all the lands appertaining

1546.

to French subjects within it. This may be, but it cannot be held equitably that they have conquered the lands of their own allies, who were never in arms against them or aided their enemies in any way, but, on the contrary, fought by the side of the English. The English have no right to depend upon the fact that these subjects were vassals of the King of France, in regard to the lands they held in the Boulognais, since they declined to side with him in the war, and prepared to abandon their estates rather than be obliged to serve him. For this reason the English cannot allege conquest over them; the right of conquest only existing over enemies, and not over allies. These should be allowed to retain their properties, as if they were the King of England's own subjects. With these and other arguments that will occur to you you will endeavour to persuade the King, as gently and kindly as you can, to make the restoration requested of him.

If the King remains firm and insists that he is not bound to restore these estates, but will consent to do so as a matter of grace and favour, you will not debate the point further, but will accept the concession as a favour; and will thank him from us so warmly as to ensure the concession being absolute, so that the claimants may be restored to the enjoyment of their properties in the same way as before the war, on condition of their taking a similar oath of fidelity to him as they formerly took to the King of France. If, however, the King offers to re-instate the claimants conditionally, either during his pleasure or on their taking an oath different from that which they are accustomed to take, you will not accept the offer, but will communicate it to us for our decision. If you find the King inclined to make the restitution in question you may say that we do not solicit it for the subjects of France but only for those who during the war have resided in these dominions as neutral subjects. You will use every possible effort in this matter, as it is of great importance, and may give rise at some future time to other difficulties unless a favourable settlement be arrived at. You will, however, deal with the King very gently, and employ the sweetest words you can, showing no signs of annoyance, until you receive further orders from us after we have learnt the King's final decision. We have managed to obtain from a trustworthy source the copy of the late peace treaty between England and France, of which we send you a transcript. As we are uncertain whether the copy is exactly in accord with the original, you will do well to take an opportunity of speaking to Secretary Paget about it, letting him know that you possess the copy, though begging him to keep the fact secret. By this means you may be able to draw from him whether the copy is in exact conformity with the original treaty or not. We believe that it is; because the clause relating to the inclusion of the Scots which was furnished to us by the English ambassador precisely agrees with our copy. You may also assure the Councillors that his Imperial Majesty has made no arrangement with the Pope to the prejudice of the King, and has no intention of doing anything of the sort, although perhaps there be certain persons who would like to persuade him to do so. We, however, consider the King to be so prudent and experienced as to refuse to credit such statements from them, knowing, as he does, that they bring them forward to serve their own ends, and with the hope of inducing the King to act in opposition to the Emperor. Some of the Protestants have even published an alleged treaty between the Pope and the Emperor to serve their own purposes, and quite different from the genuine treaty, hoping by this means to obtain assistance in money and otherwise. Touching the news of the capture of the town of Ingolstadt, of which some rumours have also been current here, we do not believe a word of it. According to the intelligence we have the enemies have never laid siege to the place, and if they had done so the Emperor had well provided for its defence, the fortress itself being naturally very strong. The people who first set this news afloat have since received contrary information, saying that when the rumour was spread nothing of the sort had happened. Subsequently the Emperor took the field not far from the enemies' quarters, and the enemies have now something to think of very different from capturing towns. His Majesty in the meanwhile is awaiting the arrival of the Count de Buren, who, as you will have learnt, has already crossed the Rhine; and since then has gone past Frankfort and the Meuse, in spite of the enemy, who endeavoured to stop him. His way is now clear to join the Emperor, unless, indeed, he has already effected a junction, as we have no news of him since the 28th ultimo. We are anxiously expecting the settlement of the affairs about which M. Adrien Van der Burgh was sent to England. His stay there has been quite long enough to have concluded the matters in question; and if you see no appearance of a prompt settlement it will be best for him to say that he has been recalled, as he has been unable to carry through his mission, and must return to his duties here.

Brussels, 14 September, 1546.

16 Sep.
Vienna.
Imp. Arch.

324. The EMPEROR to VAN DER DELFT.

We have received your letters of 16th August, relating what had passed between Secretary Paget and you respecting the detention of the Duke Palatine Philip; and also touching our enterprise and the French designs in Italy. With regard to the first point, of the detention of the Duke Philip, we can only say that up to the present we have heard nothing whatever about it from our sister, the Queen Dowager; but we suppose that the Queen will have written to you with instruction to explain it to the King of England: the reason for the detention being ample, seeing that the principal efforts of the enemy against us here are made from the territories and places owing allegiance to his brother though subject to us, and the King has no reason to complain on the ground that the Duke is in his service. As, however, we are in ignorance of what has happened since, we can only refer you to the instructions that our sister may send you on the subject, though you may employ the arguments mentioned above if you find convenient or necessary.

You will see by the document enclosed the course of events relative to our enterprise up to the present, and you may communicate the same to whomever you think well, paying no attention to any attempts that may be made to represent matters differently.

With regard to French intrigues, Italian affairs are being carefully watched. There seems, however, at present, no appearance that the French intend to make any move there, though we thank you for the intelligence you send, and hope you will continue to report all you hear: and particularly, as secretly as you can, what happens in England. Camp near Ratisbon, 16 September, 1546.

21 Sep.
Vienna.
Imp. Arch.

325. VAN DER DELFT to the QUEEN DOWAGER.

I have at this instant received your Majesty's letters of 14th, with enclosures, but as I have been unable to detain this courier, even a half-hour, whilst they are being deciphered I cannot now answer them.

I have, nevertheless, considered it advisable to inform your Majesty the reason that has prevented me from going to see the King, as I wrote in my last letters that it was my intention to do. When I was ready to start I was secretly informed that the King was very ill, and in great danger; the physicians giving very little hope of his recovery. As this was kept so secret it was evident that I should not obtain access to him, so that I remained here (in London), where the Council still is, until a better opportunity presented itself. As I hear now, however, that he is convalescent, I shall be ready to go to Court as soon as I have read your Majesty's letters, the contents of which shall guide my action.

The rumour is prevalent here that the French have demolished the fort they had begun to construct near Boulogne Harbour, but I do not know what truth there is in this. I heard previously that the King of France had recently sent an answer to this King on the subject to the effect that he did not wish to lose his friendship, but would do all he could to preserve it, and would consequently consent to refer to commissioners the point at issue (*i.e.* respecting the demolition of the fort). But still the French continued the construction. The Earl of Hertford since left here, so I am in doubt about the demolition.

London, 21 September, 1546.

22 Sep.
Simancas.
E. A. 642.

326. The EMPEROR to JUAN DE VEGA.

Recapitulates the points in Vega's letter of 12 Sep.; especially concerning the impossibility of inducing the Pope to increase the amount to be derived from the monasteries, etc., in Spain beyond 300,000 ducats. The Emperor then severely blames and rebukes Vega for accepting such a concession, knowing, as he does, that the original grant to be derived from the sale of the manors was 500,000. The whole history of the grant and the Emperor's consent to the substitution for it of a contribution of money of equal amount is repeated, but as the previous letters give the whole particulars, it is unnecessary to transcribe them again in this place. As soon as Vega's letter was received the Emperor sent the Regent Figueroa[*] from the Imperial camp to Ingolstadt to see Cardinal

---

[*] Juan de Figueroa, formerly Regent of Aragon, and subsequently special ambassador in England, was, with Granvelle and Cobos, one of the Emperor's most trusted confidants.

Farnese, who had remained there owing to indisposition. His mission was to express the Emperor's displeasure, and to say that his Majesty would accept nothing less than 500,000 ducats nett from this source. The Cardinal expressed surprise, and acknowledged the justice of the Emperor's complaint; but endeavoured to induce him to accept the 300,000 on account, promising that he (Farnese) would endeavour to bring his Holiness to reason with regard to the rest. The argument of the Pope and Sacred College was that, as the Emperor was not to guarantee any equivalent income for the second concession, as he was bound to do for the first, it was thought that he would be satisfied with 300,000 ducats nett. Figueroa insisted upon the whole 500,000 being granted. Vega is most emphatically ordered to insist upon a grant of the whole amount, not a maravedi less: and he is to hint that this sum, and much more, will have to be spent by the Emperor, in consequence of the copy of the clauses (of the treaty with the Emperor?) having been sent by the Pope to the Switzers; as this has caused the latter to dissemble and to allow their people to join the enemy. Many Switzers have recently arrived at the enemy's camp, and they are making great use of the copy of the treaty, which they have even sent to Bohemia to induce people there to take up arms against the Duke of Saxony.* The King of the Romans is much embarrassed about this. The Pope was told from the first that it was not desirable to publish more about the treaty than that the enterprise was directed solely to the punishment of the Elector of Saxony and the Landgrave of Hesse, under which pretext the religious question might be settled without arousing so much enmity.

Deplores the loss and inconvenience incurred by the insistence of the Pope upon the previously-made arrangements for paying the subsidy. But since his Holiness remains obdurate no more is to be said about it, though the money has had to be raised hastily and at onerous rates elsewhere.

Camp near Neuburg, 22 September, 1546.

25 Sep.
Simancas.
E. F. 502.

327. The QUEEN DOWAGER to the EMPEROR.

Secretary Strick, whom we sent to Scotland, has now returned; but the report he has furnished of his proceedings there is so prolix that we think it will be necessary only to send your Majesty an abstract of it.

He found it impossible to obtain restitution of the vessels and merchandise plundered by the Scots from your Majesty's subjects, Flemish and Spanish. The Scots, however, have promised to administer prompt and impartial justice, in accordance with the agreement concluded by Secretary Paniter and sent last year to your Majesty; all prizes that have been captured in violation of that agreement being restored. Strick, however, is of opinion that they will restore nothing, especially as it is said that the Regent (Arran) and other great personages share in the profits of the plunder.

---

* That is to say against Duke Maurice, who had now accepted the position of Imperial nominee to his cousin's dignity.

1546.

The Scots declare that, in their opinion, they are not at peace with your Majesty; their contention being that, although the Emperor, as well as themselves, be included in the recent peace treaty between France and England, they have always understood the inclusion clause only actually established a state of peace between them and the two contracting parties, but not between them (the Scots) and another party also included like themselves. They have, however, declared themselves ready to renew their former treaties with the house of Burgundy, without mentioning Spain, adding that they would renew the old treaties only on condition that their peace with your Majesty should be quite independent of their peace with the English. Otherwise they would be at the mercy of the King of England.

The Scots are not disinclined to send commissioners or ambassadors for the purpose of renewing the old treaties of peace with us, but they demand first to know whether your Majesty will be willing to negotiate with them without the prior restitution of the ships, etc. they have captured. We doubt not that the pillage and robberies at sea will be continued by the Scots, as the profit to them is very considerable. It is even said that the French will co-operate with them in this, and that a society is being formed for the express purpose of plundering the vessels homeward bound from the Indies. It will be necessary for us to arm a number of ships to prevent the spoliation of your Majesty's subjects thus: we have conferred with several persons well acquainted with mariners and maritime affairs, and we are assured that there will be no difficulty in fitting out and manning ships. The owners, however, would expect that the cost of so doing should be deducted from the taxes they have to pay. We should be glad to receive your Majesty's instructions on some doubtful points, in case the Scots send an ambassador to conclude peace.

1. According to the last treaty of alliance between your Majesty and the King of England you are not at liberty to deal with the Scots without the consent and inclusion of the King of England. But, on the other hand, the Scots are included in the recent peace treaty between France and England, and are consequently at peace with the latter, whilst still remaining at war with your Majesty. It appears, therefore, only reasonable that, as we remain alone at war with them, we should also be able to make a peace alone with the Scots, without the intervention of the King of England. As, however, the King of England would probably resent our entering into any negotiations with the Scots without his knowledge and acquiescence, we propose to instruct your Majesty's ambassador in England to broach the matter there to the King.

2. We shall be glad of your Majesty's direction as to whether we should treat with the Scots, if they persist in their demand to make peace with Flanders alone, without including Spain.

3. Also, does your Majesty wish us to enter into negotiations with the Scots at all prior to the restoration of the ships and merchandise they have stolen?

4. If the King of England concludes a peace with the Scots, including in the treaty with them your Majesty and all your dominions generally, will such an inclusion be sufficient for us

1546.

without further direct guarantees? Your Majesty would in such case be at peace with the Scot only so long as it suited the King of England to remain at peace with them. We shall be thankful for your Majesty's replies on these points for our guidance.

25 September, 1546.

27 Sep.
Simancas.
E. 73.

328. PRINCE PHILIP to the EMPEROR.

Letters of 10th August and others received. Notes the Emperor's good health, and the readiness of the armies, which only awaited the arrival of the Flemings under Buren. Prays for prompt advice of events. Cobos dangerously ill, but, nevertheless, "He summoned the Marques de Mondejar° and the Council of Finance, to discuss your Majesty's letter about the loans. Much difficulty was raised, and the opinion was that the affair would cause a great uproar and produce very little; but the Council, in order not to incur the disgrace of refusing your Majesty's request, of which they saw the need, decided to carry out your Majesty's wishes. The letters were accordingly drawn up and entrusted to proper people to execute, with instructions as to how they were to proceed. Replies have already been received in some instances; the Prior and Consuls of the merchants of Burgos especially at once agreeing to lend the 20,000 ducats. A list of the replies shall be sent; and every diligence shall be used in the matter.†

Seeing that the result of these loans was likely to be uncertain and small, as well as tardy, the Comendador Mayor (Cobos) suggested a means by which your Majesty might be supplied with funds more speedily. He had considered the matter for some time, but had only divulged it to me, the idea being to carry it out without consulting anyone. The proposal was to lay hands upon all the money that could be got, even though it was already pledged, and to send it in galleys to Genoa, and thence to your Majesty. The object of this was to avoid the loss and delay in exchange, and the inconvenience of the tightness of money at present existing in the Genoese market; whilst at the same time furnishing your Majesty with means at once, as the bills of exchange in any case would have to be drawn at long usance. Alonso del Castillo, your Majesty's chamberlain, was accordingly sent to Seville to expedite the collection of 150,000 ducats in gold, or as much as could be got in gold and the rest in silver, which specie he was directed to carry to Gibraltar, or any other place indicated by Don Bernardino de Mendoza. The latter officer was instructed to proceed with the galleys to the most convenient place for the shipping of the coin;

° Don Luis Hurtado de Mendoza, third Count de Tendilla, second Marquis de Mondejar, hereditary Governor of Granada. He had been Viceroy of Navarre and President of the Council of the Indies. He was now appointed President of the Supreme Council of State. One of his brothers was the famous Diego Hurtado de Mendoza, the ambassador to Venice and man of letters, and another Don Bernardino, General of the Spanish Galleys in the Mediterranean so frequently mentioned in these letters.

† This was the expedient of forced loans by individuals and Corporations which had been suggested by the Emperor as a means of raising funds. It will be seen that in the desperate financial condition of Castile Cobos considered the Emperor's suggestion inadequate, and proposed what was a most dishonest and violent remedy.

1546.

and to accompany it, either with the whole flotilla or to arm two galleys sufficiently to make the voyage with complete security. All this has been done with the utmost secrecy and dissimulation, for these realms are so utterly short of money that not a crown is to be seen, and great complaints and lamentations would be made if the matter were known. The greatest possible speed shall be employed in sending the money to Genoa; and it will be advisable for your Majesty to send instructions thither as to how it is to be forwarded to you. If on its arrival at Genoa no orders are there from your Majesty Mendoza is instructed to go on with the money in accordance with directions we now send to the Regent Figueroa and Don Fernando Gonzaga.[*] The latter is to provide an escort to protect the specie, if necessary. We also await the bill of exchange that the Ambassador Figueroa is instructed to obtain from the merchants of Genoa of 150,000 crowns. He writes that he was negotiating the business, which he found extremely difficult, though he still hoped to effect it. When the bill comes we will make every possible effort to give to the merchants the securities assigned to them, though it will be hard work to do it. If when this is done any balance is left to us, or we have anything remaining from the (forced) loans, we will try to get other bills of exchange." (Thanks the Emperor earnestly for his favour in the Milan matter, *i.e.* the grant of the Duchy of Milan to Philip. The illness of Cobos preventing him from being present at the taking of the oath, the Marquis de Mondejar and Gonzalo Perez attended, and the ceremony was carried out as the Emperor directed. As the testimony is drawn up in clear writing—*i.e.* not in cipher—it is considered advisable to send it by the galleys to Genoa. The provisioning of the fortress of Bugia, Goletta, etc. The Brief directing the Cardinals holding benefices in Spain to contribute the half-first-fruits has arrived, and Poggio the Nuncio has delegated to the Bishop of Lugo the authority to enforce the Pope's order. The authorities of the cathedral of Toledo have requested permission to meet and discuss matters in the interest of the churches. Permission given. Other Spanish ecclesiastical matters of secondary interest communicated.)

Guadalajara, 27 September, 1546.

1 Oct.
Simancas.
E. R. 873.

329. JUAN DE VEGA to the EMPEROR.

Emperor's letters received 20th, 21st, and 27th September. The writer defends himself with spirit against the Emperor's blame for accepting from the Pope the grant for 300,000 ducats instead of 500,000 from the Spanish monasteries, etc. He has accepted nothing unconditionally. On the day that the Emperor's letter was received the writer sought audience of the Pope, and laid before him his Majesty's complaint. "His Holiness replied very respectfully with regard to the 500,000 ducats. He was not so long-winded as usual, saying that he had thought he was fulfilling his

---

[*] Don Fernando de Gonzaga was the Governor of Milan, through which territory the specie would have to pass, and Figueroa was now representing the Emperor at Genoa, where a strong and sagacious statesman was needed owing to the threatening condition of affairs in the Republic and the impending attempt to overthrow the Dorias and the Imperial influence.

treaty obligation, taking into consideration the guaranteed income your Majesty would have had to give the monasteries in exchange for the monastic manors. He complained, though mildly, that he should be accused of having failed to fulfil his promises. I replied that the treaty laid down that he was to grant 500,000 out of the manors of the Castilian monasteries, and although these alternative means of raising the money had been discussed it had always been expressed that the treaty as it stood remained in full force until your Majesty received the whole amount stipulated. But still, I continued, I did not desire to wrangle over details; and I was sure that his Holiness, seeing the greatness of the cause at issue, would grant the full amount of 500,000 ducats from the same alternative sources as provided the 300,000. I pressed this as urgently as I could. He replied that it was sometimes advisable to do things in separate halves or quarters, rather than at one time, and what he had already done he thought was sufficient. He did not refuse to do more because he lacked good will, for he desired greatly the success of the enterprise and to please your Majesty. What was not done one day might be done another. "You discuss the matter," he said, "with Santa Flor: we will see what the Legate and the Nuncio write, and will set about considering some other means of getting the money." I replied that your Majesty only complained of the amount, not of the means for getting it; and if his Holiness would grant the 500,000 from the sources already agreed upon it could be done at once. In reply to this he only repeated his remark about consulting Santa Flor. (Here follows an account of a long discussion with the Pope about the Italian princes: their differences, projected marriages, etc., having no connection with English affairs or the Protestant Reformation.)

He did not reply a word to the complaint of his sending the heads of the treaty to the Swiss: but it is certain that he made the clauses public, and attributed the enterprise to religious causes, in order to exculpate himself with the French and Venetians. I believe he did so to the extent of writing to the King of France, even before the treaty was put into operation. He showed no signs that Cardinal Farnese had written anything about the 500,000 ducats; and even expressed some doubt that your Majesty had done so, as I said. I accordingly afterwards showed your Majesty's letter to Santa Flor, omitting a portion of it, however, when it was read over to him. . . . Santa Flor then admitted that the Legate (Farnese) had written in the same sense. I hear also from a trustworthy source that the Pope is angry with Farnese for having written to him so strongly on the matter. The day after I had seen his Holiness, and had shown a part of the letters to Santa Flor, I went to discuss with the latter, as his Holiness had directed, the question of the amount to be paid by the Spanish monasteries. He repeated nearly everything that the Pope had said, and announced that his Holiness would grant the whole 500,000 from the sources already agreed upon, conditionally upon your Majesty recompensing the monasteries for the property they might have to sell in order to pay the amount. I replied that this was no concession at all, because if they did not sell any of their manors the income from any other source which they might

HENRY VIII.

1546.

alienate would be worth only as much as the recompense your Majesty would have to give for it, so that nothing would be gained by your Majesty. He disputed this, saying that your Majesty might give them warrants at twenty or five and twenty, whilst they sold property up to a million for forty. This, he said, was what the Pope did in the case of certain house property sold by the monasteries. I told him that I did not see how this was to be done in Spain, unless they sold manors. This, in pure truth, is the very thing they wish to avoid, as they fear that it may form a precedent for attacking any church temporalities; and they would rather the Pope gave the 500,000 ducats from the sources suggested than they should be embarrassed in this way. I suggested to his Eminence that he should talk to the Pope again about it, and try to persuade his Holiness simply to increase the grant, as I did not like to send so hesitating and inconclusive an answer to your Majesty. He (Santa Flor) promised to do so, but assured me that the Pope had looked upon his reply as conclusive. He then let slip, but at once withdrew it, that the Pope was upset and worried, and he was glad that I gave him time to think the matter over again. On the same day I met the Pope as he was walking, and I turned back to accompany him. He asked me when I was writing to your Majesty, to which I replied that I had conferred with Cardinal Santa Flor, who would communicate to him the details of our interview. I was, I said, desirous of writing something definite in the interests of his Holiness and your Majesty, and even in the interests of God Himself. He replied that he hoped it would be so. He was returning to Rome on Saturday or Sunday, which seemed almost to mean that I should not write before then. I replied that if for any particular reason his Holiness desired this I would refrain from doing so; but that your Majesty was very anxious to know his decision on the matter. He made no answer to this, except to thank me. I will urge them for an answer and send it to your Majesty with all speed; because this delay is no doubt in order to see how affairs proceed, that they may act accordingly. They are more respectful than they were previous to the receipt of this last news.[o]

Burgueto, 1 October, 1546.

5 Oct.
Simancas
E. R. 873.

330. JUAN DE VEGA to the EMPEROR.

His Holiness arrived here on the 3rd instant, and the next day, as I was on my way to Mass at the Populo, I was met, as if by chance but in my opinion purposely, by Maffei, the Secretary of Farnese, who is at present conducting business here. After asking me for news about the war and other things, he remarked that his Holiness would do something in the matter of the documents (*i.e.* for obtaining funds from ecclesiastical sources in Spain) in order to

---

[o] Doubtless the capture of Neuburg by the Emperor, who entered the city on the 19th September. Buren and the Dutch contingent had joined on the 15th, and Maurice of Saxony's forces were now with the Imperial army. It was already evident that the Landgrave of Hesse and the Protestants had made a fatal mistake in allowing the complete concentration of the Emperor's army, instead of attacking the contingents separately.

please your Majesty, but that the Pope was still offended that it should have been said that he had failed to carry out his treaty obligations. Maffei wasted some words and time in justification of the Pope on this point; and I replied that I was glad to hear of his Holiness' good intention, but the "something" he mentioned must not fall short of the 500,000 ducats; and I repeated to him the various arguments in support of this. The same afternoon I sent to ask Cardinal Santa Flor to beg for an answer, and to urge him in your Majesty's name to use his best influence with the Pope. The Cardinal told my man (Juan Luis de Aragonia) the same as Maffei had told me; but Juan Luis was prepared for this, and is a sensible, businesslike man, so he replied that we must have the whole 500,000 ducats. He exhorted the Cardinal to this end very eagerly, and repudiated the suggestion that we should give to the monasteries equal compensation for the income they sold, as he said that if the manors were not sold the course suggested would neither benefit your Majesty nor the monasteries themselves. He pointed out that the Pope should bear in mind the present need for carrying out the terms of the treaty. The monasteries, he said, could easily find the 500,000 ducats by the aid of the Pope's authority; and he thus enforced my points, taking his stand firmly upon the 500,000 ducats and repudiating any compromise whatever.

Santa Flor promised to obtain the reply promptly, and to do his best in the matter; as it was only just that your Majesty should be satisfied. He would, he said, repeat to the Pope what I had recently observed, namely that his Holiness should bear in mind how the King of France, by his own authority, had made use of the ecclesiastical funds in his realm for his own ends. On the other hand, your Majesty's modesty and reverence for his Holiness and the apostolic See were always so great that, even when you had in hand so vast and sacred an enterprise, upon which the whole future of religion depended, you refrained from touching anything belonging to the Church without his Holiness' authority and consent.

I have thought well to let your Majesty know exactly what has passed up to the present, although the matter is not yet settled, in order that you may see how the affair is going to end: it being evident that their intention is to increase the amount but still to fall short of the half-million ducats. In accordance with your resolution and the state of affairs, your Majesty will therefore please instruct me how I am to proceed. In the last letters of 17th and 20th September your Majesty orders me not to accept anything less than the half-million, and if his Holiness will not grant that amount I will, pending further orders, refuse to accept anything short of that.

Peter Strozzi, it appears, is to go to the Turk accompanied by a French gentleman called Chatillon, and I am assured by a person of position that the Pope has been informed that they are going mainly at the instance of the Dauphin, who considers that his father's life will not last long; and wishes these men to be in Turkey when the King dies. I am also told for certain that the Pope recently remarked that he was determined to make no change in the Council (of Trent), in order to show the world that he, for

1546.

his part, gives no cause for dissension one way or the other; but that he will send to point out to your Majesty the inadvisability of allowing things to remain in their present position, and hoped that your Majesty would let him know your pleasure. In any case, he said, he would have done his duty. He talked much in this strain, as if to justify himself and to give the idea that he was not forced to desist from the attempt he made, but did so for good reasons. The Pope himself at first, and subsequently all the courtiers, are casting much blame upon Farnese and Duke Octavio for the bad order amongst their troops. The Pope, they say, always found the money required in good time, and to spare, whilst they (*i.e.* the brothers Farnese) had scattered and spent it, and find themselves now without the month's wage.* For this reason, they say, many of the troops have returned, and those that remain are not so well disciplined as they would have been if they were paid. By these means they (the courtiers) are exculpating their nation at the expense of the Legate and the Duke. They are all deeply mortified that their troops, from whom they expected such great things, should have made such an exhibition of themselves. A rumour was current here lately, though I know not whence originating, that the reason why the money to pay the Italian troops was lacking was that some of the funds destined for that purpose had been supplied to your Majesty for the purpose of paying the Germans. Now, however, they hear from private sources that, on the contrary, your Majesty provided 16,000 crowns towards the pay of the Italians; so that they are now without any excuse; and his Holiness and the rest of them are much put out. I am assured even that the Legate will be recalled.

Rome, 4 October, 1546.

Since writing the above I decided to hold it back until to-day (5th October at night) whilst I pressed Santa Flor for a reply. After much pro and contra, he sent word that his Holiness would not settle the matter with me until he heard from Cardinal Farnese, who was to discuss it with your Majesty, following the interview between Farnese and the Regent Figueroa at Ingoldstadt. My own belief is that their principal reason for delay is to see what will happen to the enemy, as they have just received advice that your Majesty came into touch with them on the 28th. I will continue to urge his Holiness for a decision.

The King of France has sent a reply about the Council (of Trent) to the effect that he is against its being moved. This has doubtless caused the Pope to be less anxious on this point than he was.

5 October, 1546.

---

* Contemporary historians of the campaign attribute the disorganization and indiscipline of the Italian troops to the climate and food of Germany having caused sickness amongst them, whilst the weakness of Cardinal Farnese in allowing himself to be frightened and cajoled into parting with his ready money to the Emperor as soon as he arrived at the Imperial camp deprived the Papal troops of their pay and naturally increased their insubordination.

1546.
7 Oct.
Vienna.
Imp. Arch.

331. VAN DER DELFT to the EMPEROR.

I have received your Majesty's letters of 17th ultimo from the camp at Dinglestadt (Ingoldstadt), and of 3rd instant. I was at Windsor when they reached me, having gone thither with a letter of credence from the Queen (Dowager of Hungary) to request this King to restore to your Majesty's subjects the property that belonged to them in the Boulognais. I found the King unwilling to grant this, and somewhat irritated by the embargoes, which are still maintained in Spain upon the property belonging to his subjects, the latter being refused possession of their belongings, even on their giving security. The King used the following words in relation to this : " I am being very badly treated in Spain. I have released all their ships here, and you people will do nothing for me." I mollified him as well as I could with fair words, but I could get no satisfactory reply from him; and I therefore thought best to defer pressing him further, until a better opportunity occurred. As he summoned me to the presence the moment I arrived, it appeared as if he expected some good news from me, or a letter from your Majesty; and when he was disappointed in this, our claims were less welcome to him than ever. He enquired very minutely as to your Majesty's success, saying that I could bear witness that your Majesty would never have undertaken this war by his advice, and he did not know what the end of it would be. I replied that your Majesty was forced to do as you had done in defence of your honour and authority. " Well, God grant that good may come of it," he said ; " but you Flemings are quite sure of your country, whatever happens." I replied that I trusted God would help your Majesty's just cause, and with regard to the Netherlands, I said, it was not badly off; especially as the alliance and friendship between your Majesty and himself (*i.e.* Henry) were assured. He welcomed me very graciously, and bade me be seated and covered; and when I took my leave he was similarly polite, placing his court, etc. at my disposal. Hearing the next morning that I was not very well, he repeated his kind messages, and offered me the service of all his physicians.

I afterwards asked for audience, to obtain his reply about the restitution in the Boulognais, and, as the King was passing in his chair, he sent Paget to tell me that it was being arranged to send commissioners from himself and the King of France to examine the various claims made by gentlemen and others to the possession of property in the Boulognais ; after which he would do whatever was just to your Majesty's satisfaction. I replied that this would cause a very long delay; but he assured me to the contrary, and promised that, without fail, the matter should be promptly and justly dealt with to our contentment. He (Paget) asked me to write to your Majesty, requesting you to order that the embargoes in Spain should be raised, for the satisfaction of the King, who in full confidence had freely released the Spanish property embargoed here last year. I told him it was all Renegat's fault, and I had ample documents to prove what had happened. He (Paget) still pressed for the release which, he said, should be effected, at least against security, since Renegat had offered to restore everything that was

1546.

found to be illegally captured. He also impressed upon me the irritation of the King when he heard what was said about the treaty with the Pope; and although I assured him that there was nothing to the prejudice of the King, all being false inventions of the enemy, set afloat for their own ends, I could not change his (Paget's) opinion of the matter, namely, that the Protestants had in their hands a treaty signed by the Pope himself.

Upon my asking him (Paget) what terms they were on with the Scots, who boasted that they were at peace with the English, and were correspondingly insolent to us, he replied that no peace had been settled with them. On the contrary, the King had fitted out a naval force to send against them, and to assure the safety of navigation, both for the English and for the Flemings. I have reported this fully to the Queen (Dowager) but I cannot omit to repeat to your Majesty my opinion, so far as I can ascertain, that they (the English) will never arrange a peace (with the Scots) without your Majesty's knowledge and consent. The Scottish ambassadors, of whom I wrote to your Majesty recently, have not arrived, and I have no news of them. The good news sent to me by your Majesty of the arrival of M. de Buren was the first intimation of the fact received here,[*] and greatly rejoiced those who are in the closest confidence of the King, as well as many other goodly personages to whom I communicated it.

Captain Paulin, general of the galleys of France, has been at Windsor, and Secretary Paget told me that the purpose of his visit was to settle the differences about the fortifications, of which the last commenced at the mouth of Boulogne has been demolished by the French themselves.[†] But he (Paget) frankly told me that the pretext for Paulin's coming was principally to obtain the restitution of St. Blancard's captured galley with the slaves. (*See* page 465.) On my way from the court yesterday I met the French M. de St. Germain, and later in the day the French ambassador (Odet de Selve). I am returning to court to-morrow, to learn what is going on, for your Majesty's information.

Duke Philip is here in London in ill case, and I cannot see that much favour is being shown to him, beyond the payment of his pension. London, 7 October, 1546.

7 Oct.
Vienna.
Imp. Arch.

332. Van der Delft to the Queen Dowager.

In order to learn the King's decision on the points of the property in the Boulognais, and of Scotland, in accordance with your Majesty's renewed instructions, I went to Windsor to see him. He

---

[*] Count de Buren with the Dutch forces had joined the Emperor at Ingoldstadt on the 15th September, and the Imperial army then being complete Charles immediately crossed the Danube, captured Neuberg (17th September) and proceeded on the triumphal campaign which for a time crushed the hopes of the German Protestants.

[†] This appears to have been a fortification on the south side of Boulogne harbour opposite to where an ancient tower had formerly stood. This latter had been captured by the English, and partly demolished, and the Duke of Alberquerque urged Henry to build a strong fortress on the other bank, or, he told the King, the French would certainly do it later, and would effectually threaten the town. Henry laughed at the Duke's counsel: but though the French frequently pretended or promised to dismantle their fort they did not do so, and it finally made Boulogne untenable.

summoned me to his presence the moment I arrived, without even allowing me time to change my clothes. After I had duly presented my letters of credence, I stated my case for the reintegration of the Emperor's subjects in the enjoyment of their property situated in the Boulognais, hoping to convince the King by the reasons in favour thereof fully set forth in your Majesty's letters. I found him, however, somewhat hard; and he was less inclined to listen to my demand than to complain at great length of the bad treatment suffered by his subjects in Spain, whose property still remained under embargo; release being refused, even against security. He also repeated other past grievances, and, in order to soften him a little, I said that I had no doubt that, with regard to the Spanish question, he would be satisfied in accordance with justice. He suddenly replied: "You give me nothing but words, and you are for ever making demands of me. At your solicitation and intercession I released all the Spanish ships that were under arrest here last year, and yet my people's property is still retained. This is not in accordance with the understanding. You have also continued to urge on behalf of the Spaniards the restitution of goods legally seized as the property of Frenchmen." I answered that I should be very sorry to do such a thing, which would be outside of my duty and my instructions, and I believed that he would never find that I had done so. "Yes, you have," he said, "and you have urged the claim upon me personally." As I could not understand to what he was referring, I asked him; and he replied that he referred to the goods captured off the Isle of Wight. I confessed the truth of my having urged this claim. It was, I said, the first commission I had fulfilled towards his Majesty: and the person interested, namely Lope de Carrion, was here, hoping that he would obtain restitution; which I doubted not that he would, if his Majesty had seen the proofs of the justice of his claim: but he (the King) was unfortunately ill-informed on the matter. "No, I am not," he replied. "I know all the allegations on both sides." Whereupon I told him that I had inspected all the papers and proofs produced by Carrion, and had found them so clear and evident that no doubt whatever could exist as to the justice of his claim, if right was to be done. As if to make light of the papers and proofs, the King asked: "What papers and proofs?" I replied: "Such as in accordance with all right and justice should have full credit given to them." I avoided continuing this subject, and endeavoured to obtain a favourable reply to my first demand, pointing out to him that the gentlemen thus denuded and deprived of their property had not fought against him, and in many cases even had served under him in the conquest of the Boulognais; and I exhorted him in the softest words I could choose to continue to do justice to all, especially as I heard that the King of France had restored the property of the Emperor's subjects in that portion of the Boulognais which he still retained in his possession. The King replied: "That is not true; what I have won by the sword is mine, and I will hold it with my own people for the period agreed upon in the treaties, without putting it into the hands of those whom I cannot trust." I observed that he had no just cause

1546.

for suspicion, nor should he raise any difficulty against the subjects of the Emperor, with whom he was on such good terms, becoming his vassals, as they would serve him as loyally as his own subjects, and even more effectively. But it was all of no avail. He said: "Speak no more to me about it," and he then began to repeat his former complaints about the treatment of his subjects in Spain. I continued to insist upon a final reply, that I might communicate to your Majesty, and at length he said: "The Queen will be satisfied in reason." I did not consider this to be a decided answer, and as I saw that no good fortune would attend my efforts on this occasion, I took my leave of him, saying that I hoped I should receive a more favourable reply some other day. As I was going out he called me back, and asked me what news I had of the Emperor and of the Count de Buren. As I had nothing fresh to say to him on that point, he continued: "You know well that it was not by my advice that the Emperor undertook this war. I do not know how it is going to finish, for I hear that Count de Buren has had an engagement, in which M. de Brabançon and several others have fallen; and are you Flemings fully prepared against possible attack?". I replied that we were, and especially as we were such good friends and allies of his Majesty (*i.e.* of the King of England). He then bade me farewell, having throughout the conversation been very condescending to me, causing me to be covered and seated near him. I could think of no other reason for his changed demeanour than that he may have been disappointed in his expectation, thinking, perhaps, that I had come to court with some news or letters from the Emperor, which he greatly desires, as I have been informed by his most confidential councillors.

On my departure I was conducted by Secretary Paget, who, although he was called to the King, asked me how I had got on. I replied that I was greatly astonished that so good a prince as the King had not given me a more favourable answer. That which he gave me, though I had heard it perfectly well, I had now quite forgotten, and he (Paget) might tell the King that I should not write to your Majesty, or indeed to anyone, until I received a better reply.

Paget and I had several discussions on this first point, but he finally promised me to do his best to bring the matter to a favourable issue. With regard to the second point, namely Scotland, he assured me that they were by no means at peace with the Scots, as would soon be evident. He told me in confidence that the King was preparing a naval force to attack the Scots, which would ensure the safety of navigation, both for the English and for us.

As I was very unwell on the following day, the King sent to say that his physicians and everything in his court were at my disposal; as indeed he had done as soon as I left him on the previous day. Three or four days afterwards, feeling myself somewhat better, I asked to see Secretary Paget, with whom I had much conversation. He told me that the moment after he left me he had repeated to the King what I had said. The King told him in reply that he did not know what he had said to displease me: it was not his intention to do so. Finally I expressed my intention to leave for London for a day, and write to your Majesty by the courier, and I desired to know what would be the most convenient opportunity for the King to inform me of his good pleasure and final reply. Paget undertook to convey this to the King.

The next day he came and told me that the King, who was about to start for his hunting, had instructed him (Paget) to say that it was intended to appoint commissioners on behalf of England and France, for the purpose of considering all claims on the part of gentlemen and private persons to the enjoyment of properties in the Boulognais; and when this had been done he would do everything that was reasonable to satisfy your Majesty. Paget then added these words: "There is nothing the King would not do for the Queen: and I do wish she would not be so chary of pleasing him in these little things, like the gunpowder, the harquebusses, the pikes, etc." I undertook to write to your Majesty and to the Emperor, as I had done previously about the Spanish question:· but, as to the reply brought to the Boulognais claim, I said that the course proposed meant a delay for ever. Paget assured me that this was not so, and that it would all be favourably settled. He afterwards told me how offended the King was at the talk of a treaty between the Pope and the Emperor; and although I assured him that there was nothing to the prejudice of the King, all this talk being merely false inventions of enemies, who spread it for their own ends, I could not shake him in his belief that the Protestants have in their hands a treaty signed with the Pope's own hand.

Touching the Scots, he said that on that same day seven or eight great ships well armed and equipped had sailed against them. I said that that was an alarming thing for us; for the English only knew how to despoil their friends. In the course of the conversation respecting the inclusion of the Scots (in the treaty of peace between England and France) he told me that I did not well understand the clause. There was, he said, no inclusion contrary to the treaty of alliance (*i.e.* between England and the Emperor), the wording being: "*Sine prejudicio tractatuum quos alteruter princeps habere pretendit, etc.*," signifying that it was without prejudice to the treaty between the Emperor and the King of England. This, he continued, was his intention when these words were inserted. I said that the words, in any case, were very obscure.

Madame: So far as I can judge, they will not treat with the Scots without the knowledge and consent of your Majesties, nor will they contravene the treaty of alliance. The (Scottish) ambassadors have not yet arrived, nor is there any news of their coming; but I will keep my eye on events.

Captain Paulin, general of the galleys of France, arrived on the same day that I was at court; and Secretary Paget told me that his coming was quite unexpected. His pretext was to moderate the disputes that have arisen about the fortifications; but Paget thought the real object of his visit was to recover the galley with the slaves belonging to St. Blancard. On my way from court yesterday morning I met M. de St. Germain, and in the afternoon the French ambassador. I shall return to-morrow to learn what is going on.

London, 7 October, 1546.

HENRY VIII. 489

1546.
10 Oct.
Vienna.
Imp. Arch.

333. Van der Delft to the Queen Dowager.

I received to-day your Majesty's letters written on the 27th ultimo, respecting the departure of the English Commissioner sent from here to settle the disputes about the Customs dues (*tonlieux*) and others. As he has withdrawn, your Majesty considers it unnecessary that Councillor Van der Burgh should remain here any longer, unless other affairs should need his continued presence. Whether such be the case or not, your Majesty will be better able to judge by the letters which Van der Burgh and myself have written to your Majesty by the last courier, three days since. For my own part, as Van der Burgh has got matters into such a good train, I think, saving your Majesty's good pleasure, that he could still be usefully employed here in advancing them further, especially as henceforward the more important claims, such as that of Lope de Carrion and the jewels, are to be discussed and settled. Van der Burgh will therefore await here your Majesty's further orders. I am leaving for the court to-day, and will duly report to your Majesty all I can learn.

London, 10 October, 1546.

10 Oct.
Simancas.
E. R. 873.

334. Juan de Vega to the Emperor.

Maffei[*] came to me yesterday with a great deal of talk about how sorry his Holiness was (as I have written previously) that anyone should say he had not fulfilled his treaty obligations. Cardinal Santa Flor, he said, had done his very best to appease his Holiness, but had not succeeded in doing so, as his Holiness said that he would not be asked to do a favour as if it were a debt. I replied that I had expected him to bring me a better message than that, which was quite true, and that his Holiness would have raised the amount to 500,000 ducats, either as an obligation or a favour: whichever he chose to call it. Maffei said that such a favour had never been requested of his Holiness. The latter wished first to prove that he had fulfilled all he was bound to: and subsequently to grant the favour, if it was asked of him. I enquired what other request could be made beyond that which I had already addressed to his Holiness, to which he (Maffei) replied that your Majesty would have to ask the favour and not I. After some discussion on this point I said that I would go myself to his Holiness the next day, in order to settle this business and advise your Majesty. Maffei begged me earnestly not to go until Monday, as they would as sure to have received letters from the Legate on that day, and a decision could then be arrived at; whereas if I went previously my visit would be fruitless. I saw plainly that the object was simply to delay matters until they learnt how things had turned out; but I thought best to wait as they asked, for fear the Pope might take the bit between the teeth and decide flatly in the negative; especially as they go up and down with extraordinary fickleness at any piece of good or bad news. When, for instance, intelligence came that

---

[*] Cardinal Farnese's Secretary, who was acting as the Pope's factotum during his grandson's absence.

M. de Buren had arrived and that Neuburg had been captured, they were as respectful as can be imagined, and looked upon the enemy's cause as utterly lost, quite contrary to their previous view. Now, however, they have news dated 28th and 29th September, saying that it was impossible for your Majesty's forces to reach the enemy's camp,* and giving an account of I know not what wretched little skirmish where 15 or 20 Italian horse had been lost, to which they add your Majesty had a touch of gout: and they are now no doubt on the other side. I suspect that they will not give us any decision until they see how affairs are going, but no effort shall be spared to urge them to give a reply, whilst I avoid furnishing them with an opportunity of saying decidedly no. God grant your Majesty prosperity and victory, and frustrate the arts and devices of those who depend upon events for their loyalty. A Cardinal of the Congregation, speaking of the Council (of Trent), says that, in conversation with the Nuncio in France, the King of France said recently that if the Pope did not submit to the Council all that the latter did would be worthless. I expect that the Pope will keep this secret as long as he can.

Rome, 10 October, 1546.

10 Oct.
Simancas.
E. 73.

335. Prince Philip to the Emperor.

(Has received no news of the enterprise. Is very anxious, and prays God for victory, etc.)

Since the last courier left rapid steps were taken about the money which was sent from Seville to your Majesty by sea. They write from there that they have already collected 180,000 crowns, and efforts were being made to bring the amount up to 200,000. It will shortly be shipped in two galleys, which Don Bernadino de Mendoza is fitting out for the voyage. He is going to command them in person, as he thinks that the voyage will be expedited, and be safer, by his taking only two galleys instead of the whole fleet, the other vessels being very much damaged by their voyages this summer. The season, moreover, is already advanced, and he writes that as some corsair vessels may be lying in wait for him at Isladeras it will be well for Andrea Doria's galleys, or some of them, to come out to meet him and ensure his safety. This courier is being despatched to advise Prince Doria of this, and to direct him, in case he has laid up his galleys for the winter, to send some of them, as many as he thinks necessary for the purpose, to Isladeras. We are also directing the Ambassador Figueroa to request the Prince to do this, and so to avoid all risk and difficulty. The present courier is also taking the acceptance of the merchants for the 80,000 crowns bill that Figueroa recently drew in Genoa. It has been no small difficulty to get the merchants to give their acceptance to this bill, and to consent to the matter of the loans and to the fresh bill we are sending to your Majesty. You will see all this in full detail in

---

* The Emperor had remained before the town of Nördlingen from the 24th September till the 2nd October in a fruitless attempt to subdue it, when he had been forced for a time to abandon his strategical position owing to the movement of the main body of the enemy to relieve the town.

1546.

the High Comendador's letter, and I do not repeat it here. He (Cobos) is still seriously ill; but he has been very diligent and careful in these matters. (Sends the official testimony of his oath as Duke of Milan by Alonso Castillo, who is going in the money galleys to Genoa. Defence and provision of the fortresses of Goletta and Bugia and other purely Spanish matters; health of the Infanta Doña Maria, etc.)

Guadalajara, 10 October, 1546.

12 Oct.
Vienna.
Imp. Arch.

336. The Emperor to Van der Delft.

We have duly received your letters of 18th ultimo, and note the conversations that had taken place between the King of England and some of his councillors; as also your other information and the contents of your letters to M. de Granvelle. Touching the desire of the King and his Council to be informed of the progress of our army, you will have learnt by our last letters of 14th ultimo what had happened up to that date, and we have trusted also to the English ambassador here writing home from time to time, on some occasions indeed his letters being enclosed in our despatches to you. We are now sending you copy of a note written to our sister the Queen Dowager, and to our son the Prince of Spain, giving a perfectly true account of events. If the English ambassador writes otherwise, it must be from information given to him by the French ambassador, as they are nearly always together. You will, however, make no reference to this, as their familiarity is believed to arise rather from the persistence of the French ambassador than from any desire of the other. We write you also a letter of credence for the King, which you give him to assure him of the truth of our account of events; and, if you see a good opportunity, you may tell him that we have written informing you that we hear that attempts were being made to persuade him that we had entered into some agreement with the Pope to his (Henry's) disadvantage. You may assure him on our word of honour that this is quite untrue; and, on the contrary, we have always repulsed any such suggestion. With regard to the assertion that we had made a secret treaty with France you gave a very good answer in saying that the French would not stick at inventing anything that seemed favourable to their designs, good or evil, and that they are not to be believed except on indisputable evidence. It would not be honest or in accordance with our natural bent to use such coin as this, and we do not choose further to discuss this point, though we have often been solicited thereto. It suffices for us that the King of England has always found us his true and faithful friend, who has never done anything to his prejudice with anybody, and we trust that he will not allow himself to be misled by such suggestions, as we ourselves will not. He may judge what honesty can be alleged by those who pretend to divulge things that passed in secrecy, and how far such people can be believed in anything.

1546.

With regard to the Scots we have recently written, and are now doing so again to the Queen our sister, to whom we refer you for instructions.

Camp, near Donauwerth.* 12 October, 1546.

14 Oct.
Simancas.
E. A. 642.

337. The EMPEROR to PRINCE PHILIP.

(In a letter dealing mainly with the circumstances of the war with the Protestants the following passage occurs.)

Our sister the Queen Dowager of Hungary has informed us of what she is negotiating with the Scots, respecting the Spanish and Flemish ships and merchandise which have been captured by them. We enclose you a copy of her letter†; to which we have replied on each point, and have ordered that no treaty is to be concluded with the Scots, except it be a general one in which all our dominions and territories without exception be included. Means must be found for preventing the molestation of Spanish vessels whilst these negotiations are progressing.

Camp (at Dunkelspeil?), 14 October, 1546.

16 Oct.
Simancas.
E. R. 873.

338. JUAN DE VEGA to the EMPEROR.

(Since his last has continued to press the Pope about the 500,000 ducats; but can get no further reply beyond a profession of desire to satisfy the Emperor, and a promise to decide the question when the expected reply comes from the Legate. They say that this reply has not yet arrived.) I sent to complain of the delay to Cardinal Santa Flor, as I had heard that a long conference with the Pope had taken place on the subject. He replied that his Holiness still insisted upon the elucidation of the point as to whether or no he had fulfilled his treaty obligations. When it had been decided that he had done so—as doubtless it would be—and he was asked to grant the rest as a favour, he would satisfy your Majesty. Notwithstanding all my subsequent efforts, I can get nothing beyond this. I expect he is waiting to see how things will turn out.

On the day of the Creation, the 13th instant, at which festivity the ambassadors of France and Venice, as well as myself, were present, the Pope called me to him whilst he was at table; and, after asking me for news of your Majesty, he summoned the French and Venetian ambassadors. He then made a long speech about peace, and spoke of the Venetians and their friendship with the Turk. Everyone was silent at this, and his Holiness turned to me and asked what I thought of it. I praised his suggestion, and remarked that peace at present existed between your Majesty and the Christian King; and I was quite sure when it was considered desirable to cement it further your Majesty would show the same goodwill as ever and offer no obstacle. The French ambassador spoke more at length, dwelling upon the need for prompt efforts,

---

* The town of Donauwerth had surrendered to Octavio Farnese and Schomberg on the 9th. The Emperor arrived there on the 11th, and on the 12th, the day this letter was written, he appeared before Dunkelspiel, which at once surrendered.

† See letter No. 327, page 476.

HENRY VIII.

1546.

with the object of pacifying still further the relations between your Majesty and the King of France; and said that by some mutual sacrifice peace might be made. I replied that your Majesty was already pacified towards the King of France, as you had shown on several occasions, and I had no doubt that a similar feeling was entertained by the King of France, etc. The Venetian said not a word, although the Pope pressed him several times to do so. He simply replied that he approved of what I said.

I am told that the Pope has fallen out with the Venetians, and is much dissatisfied with the French, in consequence of what I wrote to your Majesty before about the Council (*see* letter, Vega to the Emperor, 10 October, p. 489). I am again assured that the King of France spoke as reported, and with much warmth. The man who brings me the news also says that the King of France has sent to the Pope to say that if the latter wishes to transfer the sittings to Avignon the King will cause the Prelates from England and the Lutherans to go thither. My own belief is that this would not at all suit the Pope, even if the King of France could do it. It is reported in two letters from your Majesty's camp that Peter Strozzi had gone to the rebel headquarters. The Pope spoke in disapproval of this, and remarked to me that if the King (of France) had ordered this it was badly and unwisely done.* I replied, agreeing with him. The Pope also explained at length his reasons for recalling the Legate. It was, he said, mainly owing to his (*i.e.* Farnese's) bad disposition and the belief that he would be rather a hindrance than a help. But as he learnt by the last letters that he was behaving better, and that your Majesty wished him to stay he (the Pope) had rejoiced at it.† He spoke much and with great respect for your Majesty on this point; and I expressed my pleasure that the Legate was to remain. We are here in great anxiety to hear of your Majesty's progress, nothing having been received since the news of the camp having left the neighbourhood of Neuburg on the 2nd instant.

Rome, 16 October, 1546.

17 Oct.
Vienna.
Imp. Arch.

339. VAN DER DELFT to the EMPEROR.

Whilst I was in conversation to-day with Paget, on questions of private claims, he told me, in confidence, that, when he reported to the King what their ambassador, the Bishop of Westminster, had recently written, to the effect that M. de Granvelle had assured him

---

* Peter Strozzi was one of the two brothers, famous Italian galley commanders in the service of France.

† The young Cardinal's recall by his grandfather was probably mainly in consequence of his and the Pope's disappointment when they found that the Emperor's war was less of a crusade than had been represented to them when the Papal subsidy was requested. Farnese had expected to lead the host with elevated crucifix, like another Saint Dominic, but, as these letters show, the Emperor treated him and the Pope as mere instruments of his Imperial policy, and the granting of the dukedom of Milan to Prince Philip must have proved to the Farneses. that, whatever happened, the Emperor did not intend to reward them as bountifully as they had hoped. The murder of Pier Luigi a few months later, by the Emperor's close friend and Viceroy Gonzaga. finally completed the breach, of which the commencement may be traced in Juan de Vega's letters.

1546.

of the Emperor's entire trust in the King's friendship; notwithstanding all the attempts made to breed suspicion of him, he (Paget) had not failed to impress upon the King the advisability of giving to the Emperor further reason for continuing to entertain this confidence. With this end the King wrote to his ambassador to expose to your Majesty the intrigues and plots designed against you, and your Majesty will receive the details of these from the said ambassador. Paget afterwards urged me to beg your Majesty to have the embargoes raised in Spain; the release of the property there still being refused, even against security. The King's subjects are constantly complaining of this, and the King could not avoid great annoyance at treatment which he considered altogether unendurable, whilst every effort was being made here to do justice to your subjects. The latter have really been to a large extent favourably dealt with, and those whose cases are still pending would be more hopeful if the embargoes (in Spain) were modified. As I have on several occasions written fully to your Majesty on this subject, I will not dwell upon it further now; but, as this King takes it very much to heart, and is frequently bringing it up in his interviews with me, I crave your Majesty's instructions as to how I am to satisfy him.

Windsor, 17 October, 1546.

25 Oct.
Simancas.
E. R. 873.

340. JUAN DE VEGA to the EMPEROR.

(The resolution about the 500,000 ducats still being delayed, on the pretence that they had not received a reply from the Legate, the writer had again urgently pressed the Pope for a decision. His Holiness had only repeated his former reply, insisting that what he had already done was an equivalent to his original promise. After much pressure the Pope had promised to have the matter considered by his councillors. The writer had prayed that the amount granted should not be less than 500,000 ducats, and that the decision should be prompt, whereupon the Pope promised that no time should be lost but would pledge himself no further as to the amount. The decision will certainly depend upon the Emperor's success in the war. The Pope spoke at length on the war, which he hoped would be successful, and referred to the event on St. Francis' day,[*] an account of which had been sent to Rome, with the inconsiderate suggestion that the enemy might have been engaged with advantage.) I replied that your Majesty was wise and experienced and that the course you had adopted was doubtless the best. People, I said, frequently talked about what they did not understand. His Holiness then referred to the rebuke he had administered to the

---

[*] i.e. 4th October. Vandenesse says—"On the 4th October the army was in the village of Dettingen near Bestertrey. During the whole of this night the Protestants were marching away from Donauwerth through the mountains to Nordlingen, in sight of the Imperial army, which on the 5th encamped just opposite to them." Juan de Vega was quite correct in his comment. The Emperor's tactics were able and successful. He temporarily raised the siege of Nordlingen and drew off on the approach of the Landgrave from Donauwerth. As soon as the Protestant army arrived at Nordlingen the Emperor placed himself between it and Donauwerth, detaching a strong force under Octavio Farnese to seize the latter place, which the Landgrave was powerless now to aid.

1546.

French ambassador (who had preceded me in an interview with him) about the going of Peter Strozzi to the enemy's headquarters. The ambassador had excused it by saying that Strozzi had gone thither in a private capacity, and that the King of France had not supplied him with money, as had been reported here, but had simply given him a warrant for the amount he owed him. He said also that Strozzi would not go to the Turk, as was rumoured in Rome, etc. The Pope appeared to some extent to accept the French excuses, rather because he understands the character of the people than because he thought the excuses themselves sufficient. He enlarged upon their defectiveness and praised your Majesty highly, continuing his speech by saying that the best remedy for all the evil would be a good peace. In order that he (the Pope) might, at some time or another, be instrumental in bringing this about, he had done his best to banish the distrust which the French had sometimes entertained of him; not because he wavered in his desire to remain closely united to your Majesty, towards whom he had many causes of attachment, which he mentioned, besides the personal contrast between your Majesty and the King (of France). He would, he said, continue in this course, and requested my opinion. I accepted his kindly professions towards your Majesty, and approved to some extent of his procedure with the French; hinting lightly, however, that in the matters touching the enterprise that did not infringe neutrality, his Holiness might, without scruple, go further than he did. The French, I said, were not people to whom so much respect need be paid. I praised his desire for peace; but remarked that your Majesty had never deviated from it, either in acts or words, although the King (of France) had not always reciprocated fittingly, etc. . . . The Pope is very much pleased that your Majesty has given to Duke Octavio the command at Donauwerth. His Holiness is sending anew to the Council (of Trent) some of the confidential Prelates of the Roman Court, and ordering those who are in the neighbourhood of Trent to go thither, his intention being to suspend the sittings. As this is the object they are always aiming at they are constantly planning this or the other scheme to carry it out. Rome, 25 October, 1546.

25 Oct.
Simancas.
E. 1192.

341. EXTRACT from a CIPHERED DOCUMENT headed ADVICES FROM PIEDMONT, 25 October, 1546.

English affairs are proceeding in a way which gives small hope of a permanent settlement, although negotiations are being bravely pushed forward. It is feared that no success will attend the efforts, because the King of England wishes to have the daughter of Scotland, and the King of France will not consent to this. The King of France greatly fears an agreement between the Emperor and the Lutherans. He has recently sent a Frenchman called M. de Villarand to the Landgrave to disturb any such agreement.

8 Nov.
Vienna.
Imp. Arch.

342. The EMPEROR to VAN DER DELFT.

Your letters of 7th and 17th ultimo have been duly received. We note the conversation you had with the King of England, and subsequently with Secretary Paget, on his behalf, in which he expressed his

1546.

intention to continue in his friendship and alliance with us. His ambassador here has addressed us to a similar effect in very handsome terms, such as Paget used to you. We have been much gratified at this; and have requested the ambassador to convey to his master our very cordial thanks. You will also thank the King warmly on our behalf, on the first opportunity, assuring him of our entire and sincere reciprocity by the truest and most perfect friendship on our side. In order the more fully to testify this, we have consented, entirely out of consideration for him and in spite of the frequent statements we have received from Spain of the maltreatment of our subjects in England, to relax, against security, the embargoes placed on English property in Spain, in accordance with the request made to you by Secretary Paget. We are sending orders to this effect with all possible speed by special courier, although Renegat has not yet restored that which he has unjustly taken from us. You will continue your efforts to obtain restitution of the latter, and will not slacken in your demands until it be given. You may also tell the King that those who told him those stories would have ventured to question directly the sincere and perfect friendship between the King and ourselves, only that by so doing they would have made it known that they do not consider their friendship in England secure, and that they are seeking every opportunity for gaining what they desire without making any return for it. But we consider the King, our good brother, to be so extremely prudent and experienced, that he will remain constantly vigilant and on his guard.

Nothing of importance has happened here since our last, except some skirmishes of little effect. The enemy remains still in the same place, whilst we, more for convenience in obtaining supplies than anything else, decided not to remain any longer at the place where we were, but to pitch our camp here. You will be informed of what else may happen. Camp at Laningen,* 8 November, 1546.

12 Nov.
Vienna.
Imp. Arch.

343. The QUEEN DOWAGER to VAN DER DELFT.

We informed you by our letter of 14th September of the action of Secretary Strick in Scotland, and sent you a duplicate of his letters. He has since returned hither, and has handed us a report of his mission, of which we also enclose copy herewith. You will see that the Scots are extremely anxious to treat with us; their wish being, however, to negotiate quite independently, without any reference to the English. We do not intend to consent to this, in order not to contravene clause 18 of the treaty of alliance; although the English in their treaty with France have included the Scots on the conditions stated, without the slightest reference to the rights of the Emperor and his subjects, who went to war with the Scots entirely on account of the King of England, as we explained to you fully in our letter of 15th August. We are informed that the Scots are deferring the doing of justice to the Emperor's subjects until a reply is received from us on the subject, and we have consequently

---

* After the fall of Donauwerth (9th October) Dunkelspeil had surrendered and on the 13th Laningen had done the same, whereupon the Landgrave's troops had been seized with panic, and had fled with great loss. The Confederate army was now in rapid process of disintegration within a mile of the Emperor's position near Laningen.

1546.

despatched the bearer of this letter to Scotland with our answer, of which we send you herewith a copy. You will, in his Majesty's name, request the King of England to grant a passport for this bearer to proceed through England to Scotland, without being searched. This is the more important, as he is carrying with him several safe-conducts for Scotsmen; and we are very anxious that they should not fall into the hands of the English officers. If the English ministers wish to know the reason for the sending of this bearer, you will tell them that he is carrying letters to the Regent of Scotland, asking for a raising of the embargo, and the restoration to the owners, of the property belonging to the Emperor's subjects seized by the Scots; this demand being in conformity with the recent peace treaty between England and France. You may say that the man is a mere messenger, and that no difficulty should be raised to letting him pass, any more than we raise to the passage of the King of England's messengers sent through these territories to Italy and Germany. If, as we can hardly believe, you meet with any real difficulty in obtaining these passports you will order the messenger to deliver the safe-conducts to you, and will write to Mr. David Paniter, Bishop-elect of Ross, secretary and councillor to the Queen of Scotland, telling him that the bearer was instructed to hand to him 70 safe-conducts, sixty of which were to be distributed at the discretion of the Regent, and ten at the pleasure of the said bishop; with certain private letters from us to the latter, explaining this more fully. In consequence, however, of the difficulty you have encountered in obtaining the passports for the messenger, and to prevent the said safe-conducts being taken from him on the English and Scottish border, you have retained the safe-conducts for the purpose of returning them hither and having them sent to Scotland by sea. You will in such case return them to us, and we will send them to Scotland. We see by your letters to the Emperor in September that the Scots had sent to ask the King of England for safe-conducts for the Scottish privy seal, a great master and a secretary, with a train of 40 horsemen, to come on an embassy to the King of England; but you have said nothing to us about it since. We request you to inform us if this embassy has arrived, or if any change has occurred; and if you have not discovered the reason why the embassy has tarried so long: seeing that Secretary Strick has informed us that so long ago as when he was in Scotland he heard of the intention to send it to England; rather with the object of temporising than anything else.

Please also let us know how the English are bearing themselves towards the Scots, and if there is free intercourse between the two countries, or an appearance of enmity is still kept up; and if so, on what pretext, since the Scots have accepted the conditions imposed on their inclusion in the treaty of peace. One of these conditions was that the English should not again commence war against them, unless fresh cause was given. Has any new dispute arisen, or has war on either side been reopened since the signing of the treaty?

We are fully informed by your letter of 6th ultimo of the particulars of your interview with the King of England, respecting the reinstatement in their estates in the Boulognais of such subjects of the Emperor as possessed them before the war; and we note that Secretary Paget told you that it was the King's intention to refer the investigation of such claims to deputies chosen by himself and the King of France respectively; and that after hearing the evidence he would deal with the matter justly, to our satisfaction. You will do well to refer to the subject again in conversation with Paget, and get to know whether the King has appointed any representatives yet. Inform us of what you can learn, as we are daily being importuned by the gentlemen interested, who, grieved as they are at their losses, will not have patience. Some of them, moreover, are very angry that they aided the King in his conquest of Boulogne, as they expected a very different recompense from being despoiled of their property. Ascertain from Paget whether it would be well to stir up the King about it again; so that he may understand that the matter cannot be allowed to remain in its present condition. Perhaps you may have better luck next time than when you spoke to him before on the subject. Advise us fully of what you do. We do not know whether Paget informed you that he spoke by the King's orders when he communicated to you the proposal advanced by the French and the Rheingrave, about which you sent to us your Secretary, who has recently returned to England.[*] If Paget spoke for the King it would be courteous to thank the latter on our behalf; and to tell him that we have already conveyed the information to the Emperor, who will also be certainly very much obliged to him; and that it is by such good offices as these that the King proves his sincere friendship for the Emperor and his subjects. You may tell him that our absence has prevented us from writing about it previously; but you will be governed by what you may learn, or have learnt, from Paget, and by your knowledge, as to whether the King wishes to know if we have been informed or not. Of course if Paget gave his information in a way which signified that the King did not desire to know that it was communicated to us, you will not say anything about it to the King.

Brussels, 12 November, 1546.

12 Nov.
Vienna.
Imp. Arch.

344. The Queen Dowager to Van der Delft and Van der Burgh.

We have caused the Council here to consider the report of the negotiations you have been conducting in England with the King's Commissioners, respecting the general and specified complaints made by the Emperor's subjects; and the conclusion has been arrived at here that the English have no great desire to mend matters, but would prefer to continue in the old way. They are conceding less now than they did at the Bourbourg conference, and there seems no probability that Van der Burgh's further stay in

---

[*] This would appear to have been a secret communication made by Paget to Van der Delft, to the effect that a project had been broached to the King for a joint attack upon the Dutch coast by the French and Protestants, in order to divert the Emperor's forces from the seat of war in Germany. The intelligence appeared sufficiently important for Van der Delft to send his Secretary Jean du Bois to Flanders to convey it to the Queen Dowager.

1546.

England will produce any good fruit. We therefore think that it will be better for him to announce that he has orders to return hither, asking them (the English Commissioners) to give him a written statement of the points, so far agreed upon, as set forth in your report to us. The English should also be requested to give a reply on the points which they undertook to lay before the King or Council, in order that they also may be put in writing and settled as soon as possible. You (Van der Burgh) will promise to report to us the points still in dispute, and to write afterwards to Van der Delft the further steps to be taken about them. If you find that the English Commissioners wish still longer to delay the matter, in consequence of your request for the written agreement on the points already settled, you will, with all possible politeness and kindness, tell them that they should recollect that you, Van der Burgh, were in England a long while before the English envoys were sent hither; that these envoys have some time since returned home, and yet you are unable to obtain a decision or despatch. You are afraid, therefore, that the intention is to concede less to you than was conceded by the English Commissioners at Bourbourg. But, nevertheless, you must content yourself with what answers they choose to give you, for the purpose of going and reporting the same to us; and you may tell them that you will wait three or four days longer, if they will work at the affair during that period; but at the end thereof you intend to obey our orders and return hither, since the English Commissioners sent to us have been recalled. You will act accordingly, and stay there no longer: and we may remark that, when the English Commissioners took leave here they did so with a sufficiently bad grace, saying that they were going; and would tarry no more. When they were begged to stay until our return from Hainault, whither we had gone hunting, they refused, but asked to be allowed to go to us thither, without the ambassador, to take their leave, which, in consideration of their importunity, we allowed them to do.

With regard to the complaints of the merchants here against those of the Staple at Calais, which complaints the English Commissioners wish to palliate, on the ground that these complaints are all covered by the commercial treaties of 1499 and 1522,* you may see by the advices received from Lille, Armentiers, etc., that, although certain points are covered by the provisions of these commercial treaties, the English fail to observe the treaties; and continually defraud the merchants here, for which no redress whatever can be obtained. You will endeavour, by urging for a final reply on this matter, to obtain some sort of remedy for the systematic evasion of the treaties in question; but you must not on this account delay the return of Van der Burgh, unless you see that the English are disposed to deal more freely than they have hitherto done.

---

* Although 1522 appears to be the date in the document the relations between oreign merchants and the members of the Staple were ruled at this time by the regulation dated 13 July, 1527, of which a copy will be found in the Harl. MSS. 442, and printed in *extenso* by the Camden Society in "The Chronicle of Calais."

1546.

We observe the excuse made by the English Commissioners to your first complaint on account of the merchants here against those of the Staple, and we find it very tame (sobre). No doubt you will have given them a suitable answer, to the effect that the proceedings of those of the Staple do not accord, as they allege, with freedom of trade, but constitute a veritable monopoly in favour of the members of the Staple, who have a statute amongst themselves that no one may have a sample of wool (avoir montre de laines) unless he buys. Otherwise he is not again admitted to the Staple. When they sell new wools, moreover, they must also sell old wools, and the merchants are not allowed to buy otherwise. This is a violation of the free intercourse in merchandise established by the treaties. They (the members of the Staple) also compel the merchants here to take old wools when they desire to buy new; and when the purchasers, after they have bought, wish to abandon the old wools and only to transport the new, they are not allowed to do so, but are forced to despatch and pay the imposts on the old wool. This is quite unreasonable. If on this side we liked to set up a rival monopoly they would soon find a way to redress matters; but this would be inadvisable, as a violation of the commercial treaties, and would militate against the perfect friendship between the two sovereigns; who ask that their respective subjects should be well and fairly treated. You will therefore endeavour to obtain some remedy for the evils complained of.

Having regard to the fact that the English commissioner who was here did not make any great effort to obtain a settlement of the various private claims presented formerly by the English Commissioners at Bourbourg, we fear there is no hope that they (the English) intend to make any favourable settlement of similar claims of ours. You, Van der Burgh, will consequently not delay your departure on this account. After we have considered here your report on the questions still pending, we will send to you (Van der Delft) instructions for future proceedings.—Brussels, 12 November, 1546.

13 Nov.
Vienna.
Imp. Arch.

345. VAN DER DELFT to the QUEEN DOWAGER.

I arrived here to-day from Windsor, and the Lords of the Council have just sent one of their Secretaries to me to inform me that two ambassadors from Scotland have come hither. These ambassadors have not yet had access to the King or to the Council; and consequently the purport of their mission is not known: but as soon as the King is in possession of the information, it shall be communicated to me, together with his decision upon the matter, before the latter is conveyed to the said ambassadors, this being in accordance with the terms of the Treaty of Alliance (i.e., between Henry and the Emperor). They (the Councillors) assure me that nothing shall be negotiated with them (the Scots) without my knowledge, in order that the Treaty may be kept inviolate and the King's friendship maintained. I have thanked the Lords of the Council through their secretary, who also told me that the King had expressly ordered that a special messenger should be sent to Windsor with the information, in case I had not arrived in London.

1546.

As your Majesty wrote to me that when these ambassadors arrived you would send me instructions as to what you require of the Scots before consenting to a peace with them, I shall be glad to learn your Majesty's pleasure. In the meanwhile I will do my best to learn what is being done.

London, 13 November, 1546.

13 Nov.
Vienna.
Imp. Arch.

346. VAN DER DELFT to LOYS SCORS.

I received from Jehan du Bois the packet from the Emperor, and, as regards the letter of credence sent to me to enable me to declare to this King the progress of events in Germany, I have had no opportunity of doing this, in consequence of the King's having left Windsor to visit some private houses; besides which they have already received fresher news here from that quarter. I have, however, given an account of such intelligence as I had to the Council. (Thanks Scors for the good news he sends with regard to the writer's private affairs, etc.)

I am expecting the arrival of the envoy the Queen (Dowager) was sending to Scotland. I do not write to her Majesty, as there is nothing particular to say at present. It is said that two ambassadors have arrived here from Scotland; but as I have only just arrived myself at Windsor, I have not had time to ascertain the truth of it. I will find out to-morrow.

My brother, Fernando de Bernuy, has not received the money advanced for the Emperor's service. Pray favour me by endeavouring to get the assignment he holds on the Naples revenue rendered effective.

Just as I was closing this, one of the Secretaries of the Council came to me, and I have therefore written a few words to the Queen (Dowager) which you will see.

Windsor, 13 November, 1546.

15 Nov.
Paris.
Archives
Nationales.
K. 1486.

347. ST. MAURIS to the EMPEROR.

(A long recapitulation of previous letters sent and details of couriers, etc. The ardent desire of the King of France and all his Court to bring about the marriage (*i.e.* of Prince Philip and the French Princess Margaret). Details of the various conversations with the Duchess of Lorraine, Cardinal Lorraine and many other personages on this subject. St. Mauris, whilst professing great sympathy with the proposed marriage, had replied to the French ladies who had urged the matter upon him that he declined to address the Emperor on the subject, unless the King of France himself or his Ministers asked him to do so. The French do not mention the matter to the Queen, being distrustful of her Majesty, in consequence of her daughter the Infanta.[*] They think that her Majesty has dissuaded the Emperor from the match, and say so openly. She has consequently held herself quite aloof from all these importunities lately, whilst doing her duty, and taking every

---

[*] It must be recollected that the Queen Eleanor wife of Francis I. was a sister of the Emperor Charles V. It was proposed to marry Philip to his Portuguese cousin, daughter of Eleanor by her first husband.

1546.

opportunity of showing her goodwill to the proposed match. She will, when occasion offers, converse with those who may assure the King and the Dauphin that their suspicions against her are unfounded. She has requested the writer to convey this to the Emperor, and to say that she hears from Mme. de Montpensier, who is the close confidante of Mme. d'Etampes, that the King is bringing forward this marriage now, in the belief that the Emperor will the more easily accept it, as he still at war with the Protestants and the latter are unsubdued. In order further to strengthen his hands in this business, the King of France has caused the Ambassadors from the Levant to arrive at this juncture, with the object of spreading the idea that the Turk may attack Germany this year. The writer gives, at great length, reasons for believing this view to be true. The French wish to see the Emperor in difficulties in the war, in order that they may come to his aid and so forward the marriage. When they heard from the writer recently the news of the Emperor's success they were much alarmed, as they had previously learnt that the Imperialists had retired with great loss, whereupon they rejoiced exceedingly.[*] The writer confirms his previous report that the King of France had secretly sent commissions to raise men in Burgundy, in case he should need them. He is also amassing money: retaining all the crowns he can get and paying his outgoings in French money. Some people say that this is to pay the King of England; but many believe that it is to attack the Emperor if he will not come to terms with them. There are still a great number of Protestants at Court who are favoured as if they were brothers, etc. Even Mme. d'Etampes in order to please the Protestants calls them her brother evangelists, and says that she has good reason for doing so, as they are doing a truly fraternal act towards France by opposing the Emperor. The writer is assured of this by the Queen, and quite believes it, as Mme. d'Etampes greatly inclines to the Lutheran discipline. When Barbarossa was in Provence the King of France called the Turks his brothers, so no surprise need be felt at this fraternising with Protestants.)

"With regard to the King of England, I may add that the French, in view of his recent promises, are convinced that things cannot continue very long as they are. They (and especially the Admiral of France) say that no opportunity for regaining Boulogne would be so propitious as shortly after the decease of the King of England; their claims would continue against the Princess, his elder daughter. They count upon dissensions occurring upon the King's death; and consider that this will be their opportunity. Indeed they have already taken measures to prepare for war against England when the expected death of the King takes place; unless in the meanwhile they manage to recapture Boulogne, as they will endeavour to do. The King of England is well aware of this. As the French are so desirous of attacking England when the King dies, I am of opinion that their present policy is to draw your Majesty to a close alliance, in order the better to carry out their object. The fact is that they

---

[*] The retirement from before Nördlingen was, as has already been explained in another note, a feint by means of which Donauwerth was seized by a coup de main.

1546.

are all in such trouble about Boulogne that they will leave no stone unturned to recover the place. I hear from the Nuncio that the King of France has ordered the first instalment of the half of the last pension to be paid in England on the 1st instant, 50,000 crowns." (Rumours that the King of France is supplying money to the German Protestants. Movements of the King of France. To pass Lent in Paris, and then go to Fontainebleau. He is travelling rapidly; as, notwithstanding the excessive rains, he went on some days seven or eight leagues, rising quite early, contrary to his custom. His haste on the road, accompanied by a large train, caused the death from cold of more than ———— persons, who were travelling on foot; and being unable to reach a lodging by day, an enormous number of baggage horses, etc., were left behind, as was the Dauphin himself. A large number of Lutherans have been burnt by the Court of Paris at Meaux, some of the principal people of the place, and as a permanent memorial of this they have demolished certain houses where the false doctrine was preached. A great storm at sea, which has destroyed much shipping belonging to the port of Dieppe. The godly say that this is a just judgment of God, as they were all corsairs, whose only resource was what they stole at sea. Gives particulars of certain Protestant spies in the Emperor's camp.)

18 Nov.
Simancas.
E. R. 873.

348. JUAN DE VEGA to the EMPEROR.

(Don Juan Hurtado de Mendoza arrived, and after consultation with the writer respecting his mission,* they went together to see the Pope on the 12th instant.)

After Don Juan had kissed the Pope's foot, and performed the usual ceremonies, etc., he told his Holiness the object of his coming, and referred him to his written instructions. He exhorted his Holiness to accede to the requests contained in it, and consequently my own action was limited to praying the Pope to give a speedy answer; necessary as it was, in the circumstances, and consonant with the dignity of his Holiness and your Majesty that, the greater the difficulty which presented itself, the greater the effort should be made to overcome it. The Pope gave a fair but general reply, and expressed a desire to see the instructions which Don Juan held in his hand, and thereupon gave to his Holiness to read.

---

* The mission of Don Juan de Mendoza was to request a prolongation of the treaty with the Pope and to insist upon the concession by Paul III. of the whole amount of 500.000 ducats, nett, to be paid by the Spanish monasteries, etc., towards the cost of the war. The amount was originally to have been raised by the sale of monastic manors, the Emperor undertaking to pay to the monasteries a yearly equivalent of the revenue derived from the alienated manors. When the College of Cardinals objected to the sale of the lands, Charles had consented to the ecclesiastical subsidy being raised by the monasteries from their moveable possessions, or by loan; and the Pope considered that, as no equivalent revenue would in this case be paid by the Emperor, the latter should be content with 300,000, instead of 500,000 ducats. This view the Emperor indignantly refuted; he would have the 500,000 nett, or nothing. It is plain from Vega's letters that he was no match in subtlety for the Pope and Cardinals; and Juan de Mendoza was accordingly sent with a hint that, if the Pope would not grant what was requested, Charles would seize the monastic property without Papal consent, as sovereign of Spain. It will be seen later that Don Juan de Toledo was subsequently sent with a much more strongly worded demand.

1546.

Don Juan afterwards visited various Cardinals, for whom he had letters and messages. He found a general disposition amongst them to await the arrival of Cardinal Farnese, which they were convinced would be the best course. Don Juan told the Pope that his (Don Juan's) coming was for the very purpose of avoiding the loss of time from now until the Cardinal's arrival here. (The rest of the letter concerns the Italian duchies, the projected marriage of Victoria Farnese, the Pope's granddaughter, with the Marquis of Pescara, the transfer of the writer, Juan de Vega, to the Viceroyalty of Sicily, the Pope's desire to bring about a permanent agreement between the Emperor and France, and other points of little or no interest in connection with England or the Protestant Reformation.)

Rome, 18 November, 1546.

20 Nov.
Simancas.
E. R. 873.

349. JUAN DE VEGA to the EMPEROR.

Since writing the accompanying letter I hear from a trustworthy source that the Legates will return from Trent after having first issued the decree of "justification," for which purpose the prelates were recently sent to Trent by the Pope. They (the Legates at the Council) say that, even if the Pope orders them to remain at Trent, they will not do so, as their continuance there would obviously imperil their lives. At the same time news arrived here of the defeat of the Saxons by the army of the King of the Romans, and that the Duke of Saxony had begged for a safe conduct to go to your Majesty; the Swiss having also deserted the enemy's camp, some joining your Majesty's forces. It is also reported that the Count Palatine has recalled the troops he had with the Protestants: and in face of all this I think it probable that the decision of the Legates to return may be changed.

Rome, 20 November, 1546.

20 Nov.
Simancas.
E. R. 873.

350. JUAN DE VEGA to the EMPEROR.

(Efforts of the French party to prevent a prolongation of the alliance between the Pope and the Emperor.)

It is quite certain that the French are insisting that the Council of Trent should settle certain articles touching religion, such as "justification," etc.; the object being that, in such case, your Majesty will have more difficulty in subduing the Germans to your wishes. Some people, however, think that the real difficulties arise from the annoyance of his Holiness that the sittings of the Council are not to be removed elsewhere, and from his perturbation at what happened in Trent with regard to the war at the beginning; as well as the dissatisfaction expressed by your Majesty at the failure to fulfil the Treaty. To this must be added the fact that certain things which were expected to happen after the Legate had arrived have not taken place, whereby many persons are hinting to his Holiness that he will not obtain after all what he had looked for in

1546.

joining your Majesty.° They are saying that it is now desired to deprive the Pope of all the rest of his forces; and finally to declare as enemies all those who oppose the alliance; and they therefore urge that some recompense ought to be given to the Pope for what he does both in the matter of the transfer of the Council, and in other private matters. All this is merely the judgment of people; but it is to be supposed that the Pope understands that it will be to the public interest to carry to a successful issue that which has been commenced with his assistance, and not to desert your Majesty at such a crisis as this. As this truth cannot be overcome, those to whom it is unwelcome, or who have their own ends, to serve, dwell much upon the difficulty which would arise if the Holy See should become vacant whilst the Council was in session, and schism were to be the result. They also urge the need for settling on a permanent footing the peace between your Majesty and France, which they say will be easy. But as this matter would evidently occupy more time than the present crisis allows, they take their principal stand on the question of the Council. Some of your Majesty's adherents here, who have opposed the transfer of the sittings, are asking whether your Majesty would be content that arrangements should be made in the Council for the election of a new Pope in case the See should fall vacant, by which means schism would be avoided. They say that it would be well to fix some period during which it might be seen how the war turned out: and if it was seen that no further advantage could be gained by the continuance of the Council, the difficulties which they fear from the latter might be obviated (i.e. by its suspension or transference). They are moved to this opinion by zeal in the cause of God and your Majesty: especially as they know the great anxiety of the Pope to remove the Council; and that his Holiness will not decide the question until Farnese arrives.

Rome, 20 November, 1546.

22 Nov.
Simancas.
E. V. 1318.

351. DIEGO HURTADO DE MENDOZA to the EMPEROR.

(Has pressed Cardinal Farnese about the rest of the 200,000 crowns, and the Cardinal promises faithfully that they shall be paid when he arrives in Rome.)†

"Cardinal Farnese has instructed me how I should bear myself in Rome with regard to three principal points. First, I must make

---

° Farnese's recall from the Imperial camp had been largely owing to the disappointment of the Pope and his party at finding that they were after all to be used only as instruments of the Emperor's policy, whilst the rewards expected by the Farneses were either placed in the back-ground altogether, or else once more made conditional on further concessions from the Pope. Pier Luigi's dukedoms of Parma and Piacenza were still unrecognised by the Emperor. Octavio's hopes of Milan were now seen to be unrealisable, as the duchy had been given to Prince Philip; and even the Golden Fleece which Pier Luigi had asked for was withheld. From this time Paul III. drifted further away from the Emperor; though his grandson Octavio saw that his best policy was to adhere humbly to the side of his father-in-law, which he did.

† Farnese had arrived in Venice on his way back to Rome from the Imperial camp. Diego Hurtado de Mendoza, the first diplomatist in the Emperor's service, was now to go to Rome to endeavour to attain the ends that Juan de Mendoza and Juan de Vega had failed to extort from the Pope.

1546.

friends with the Pope and avoid speaking roughly to him. He complained greatly of the rudeness with which the Pope had hitherto been treated by your Majesty's ministers. Secondly, he advised me not to be closely intimate with any of the Cardinals, because the Spaniards were odious to Italians, and *vice versa*. All of them, he said, gave themselves airs as being employed in your Majesty's affairs; but if anyone could be of any service it was he himself, as he had placed himself under your Majesty's protection, and filled the position he did towards the Pope. Thirdly, he said that *Madame** was offended because she was not consulted and employed by your Majesty's ministers. I said I quite agreed with him on all points and would follow your Majesty's orders.

He, Farnese, also spoke of the desire of the Pope to marry the bastard daughter of the Dauphin to Horatio (Farnese); but that he, Cardinal Farnese, was strongly opposed to it. The King of France, he said, was urging the proclamation of the decree respecting "justification." He had certain news that the Lutherans had offered to make the King of France emperor on the sole condition that the Swiss Cantons which he influenced should join the Protestants. The King declined the offer; but the Dauphin is strongly in favour of it, and they are negotiating with him.

The Pope is of opinion that until your Majesty makes friends with the King of France not much will be done in German affairs, and, unless a peace can be arranged, he does not wish to find any more money for the war, nor to keep his troops in the field longer than he is obliged. Farnese received letters from the Pope last night, directing him to hurry to Rome, as he wishes to send him to France about the peace. Farnese says, however, that he is tired, and wishes to avoid the mission; but if he cannot do so he will send persons ahead to negotiate whilst he will go only for the conclusion. I used what arguments I could to show him that the Pope ought, in any case, to continue his subventions, etc. to the war, especially as the negotiations with France were a Lutheran device to frighten the Pope to withdraw. I praised his design of avoiding the French mission. He will leave here on Friday, and Cardinal Trent also. I shall accompany the latter until I get outside Venetian territory; where I shall await your Majesty's orders as to my successor here, as it is not desirable for us to abandon Venetian affairs. Farnese says he wishes to bring Peter Strozzi to your Majesty's service. I have approved of this, as the negotiation will be useful to us in any case. Peter Strozzi and Count Mirandola arrived here to-night and the former has seen Farnese, who tells me that Peter is discontented with the French service and wishes to remain either with the Pope or your Majesty.—Venice, 22nd and 27th November, 1546.

28 Nov.
Simancas.
E. A. 642.

352. The EMPEROR to PRINCE PHILIP.

(Gives an account of the difficulty encountered in obtaining in due form the Papal Bull for the sale of the monastic manors in Spain in accordance with the treaty, and recapitulates the lengthened

---

* The Duchess of Camarino, Octavio Farnese's wife, daughter of the Emperor.

1546.

discussions which have taken place in Rome, and with Farnese, on the subject. Finding the Bull finally granted by the Pope to be unsatisfactory, the writer had sent Don Juan de Mendoza to try and obtain a better one. Copy of his instruction enclosed, and details of his negotiations. Seeing the vital necessity, in the interests of God, the good of Christianity, etc., that the enterprise against the Protestants should be prosecuted, and the Imperial army kept in the field as long as possible—the enemy being already exhausted, disheartened and short of supplies—it is more urgent now than ever it was that every effort should be employed to that end, especially having regard to the success of the King of the Romans and Duke Maurice in Saxony. Otherwise all that has hitherto been gained would be lost, and the great expenditure wasted, whilst the interests of religion would be imperilled, as well as the writer's prestige and position, especially if another army has to be raised next year. In addition to the impossibility of doing this, owing to the great cost already incurred, and the Imperial resources being exhausted, the opportunity might be taken by the enemies to form new combinations and consolidate their forces, as they are even now attempting to do with the cities, etc. The French also are beginning to show their hand everywhere.) "With the resources we have now in hand, although they are much divided, we can keep our army afoot until the end of December next, a very much larger sum however being needed for us to hold out until the enemy either break up or are forced to risk an engagement in unfavourable conditions for them. All this has caused us to discuss and consider various means by which money may be raised plentifully, without casting the burden upon the poor or asking for further supplies from the Spanish Cortes, our desire truly being to relieve Spain as much as possible. Bearing in mind that the Bull about which Don Juan has gone to Rome (*i.e.* for the grant of Spanish ecclesiastical funds) will produce quite an insufficient sum for our needs, we have decided that if the Pope declines or delays to grant what is requested of him, or even if he concedes it, he shall be pressed most urgently as follows. Since we have entered upon this undertaking for the reasons of which he is aware, and matters are in the present critical state, it is most undesirable that everything should be endangered by want of money; and for this reason we request that he will not only do his part towards the prosecution of the enterprise, but will consent to our obtaining the funds needful from other sources. We therefore ask that, in addition to the contributions to be furnished by the monasteries, he will immediately issue a Bull authorising us to take from cathedrals, churches, hermitages, monasteries and convents, of all orders even mendicants (except in Castile*), in every part of our dominions, contributions for the purpose in hand. All these, in addition to the quota they may have to pay (for the previous Bull), must pay a half of all the gold, silver or jewels that they possess, retaining the other half and the ornaments, etc. for divine service.

---

* The wording of the clause is exceedingly involved and inverted: but the meaning is that the Mendicant Orders of Castile alone shall be excepted, all other orders and every sort of ecclesiastical establishment being included.

They must all further pay a half of the yearly revenue of the ecclesiastical fabrics. With this mission we have despatched Don Juan de Toledo. He had been instructed to stay at Trent, to assist in the Council, but we have now ordered him to go straight to Florence, and reside there for the present; attending to other affairs of ours there, until he learns how matters are going in Rome, keeping in the meanwhile in close correspondence with Juan de Vega and Don Juan de Mendoza. In case of the Pope's declining or delaying the granting of the amended Bull, or even if he concedes it, Don Juan de Toledo is to proceed at once to Rome, and, jointly with Juan de Vega, make his request of his Holiness; both of them thenceforward using all their dexterity and persuasion to bring the Pope to consent promptly to our requirements, and grant the Bull mentioned above. They are instructed to assure his Holiness that we shall hold such concession in the highest esteem, and, if it be necessary, they are to say that we cannot possibly avoid (*i.e.* in any case) ordering the steps mentioned to be adopted, having no conscientious scruples in the matter, as we have been assured by our Confessor that the funds to be thus raised being destined for an object so exclusively in the interests of God and the Catholic faith, the mode indicated for obtaining them may be justly adopted. They are to point out, moreover, that the King of France on several occasions, for his own purposes, and not for such an enterprise as this, has raised funds by similar means without any authority from the Pope. The lukewarmness and hesitation of the Pope towards the prosecution of our enterprise has hitherto been evident, but we are confident that, for the reasons set forth above and others, he will make the concession we request without delay or difficulty, and that there will be no need for us to act as we have hinted, as we would very much rather proceed by virtue of his concession than without it. We most earnestly and urgently desire that this may be the case, as we should be most reluctant to touch the ecclesiastical funds without his authority. We have thought well to communicate all this to you, in order that you may secretly convey it to the Council of State, and any other persons you may desire, and discuss with them the best means to carry out our intention; because it is our firm determination, as soon as we hear what the Pope's attitude is, without delay to take possession of a half of all the gold, silver, and jewels in the cathedrals, parish churches and other hermitages, monasteries of friars and nuns, etc., of all our dominions, depending upon the crowns of Castile, Aragon, Valencia and Cataluña, except those which will have to contribute to the first Bull. These will only have to furnish a sum sufficient to bring up their respective contributions to the same as the rest, namely one-half of their treasure.* In addition to this all will have to subscribe one-half of the year's revenue of their fabrics. Similar notice is being sent to

---

* The sum of 500,000 ducats to be raised from the monasteries, etc., by the previous Bull only applied to the kingdoms of Castile, and the amount to be paid under this new project by them was to be one-half of their treasure minus what they had provided under the previous Bull.

1546.

Flanders, Naples, Sicily, Milan and the islands. In order to lose no time you will have everything made ready, so that we may get the money with the necessary rapidity.

28th November, 1546.

29 Nov.
Vienna.
Imp. Arch.

353. VAN DER DELFT to the QUEEN DOWAGER.*

In my last letter of 13th instant, I informed your Majesty of the coming hither of the Scottish ambassadors; and that the Lords of the Council had, by the King's orders, sent to assure me that nothing should be negotiated with them except with my knowledge and in my presence. Seven or eight days afterwards the Ambassadors saw the King at Oatlands. One of them is the Bishop of Ross,† and the other Dr. Whittingham. They stated their mission as follows: According to the Treaty of Peace recently made between the King and the King of France, in which the Scots are included, they desire to enjoy the benefit of such inclusion, which they have accepted, and now accept, in order to be at peace with the King of England. The King heard them, but entered into no discussion with them, simply referring them to his Council. The Councillors met here in London, the number of them being large, and they gave me notice of the day, the day before yesterday, they had fixed for the communication with the Scots' ambassadors, and requested me to be present, which invitation I accepted. When they were all assembled they (the Councillors) spoke to me apart, repeating to me what had passed between the ambassadors and the King, as I have reported it above, and said that they had desired my presence in fulfilment of the conditions of the Treaty of Alliance. They also asked me whether I had full instructions as to all the damage suffered by the subjects of the Emperor at the hands of the Scots. I replied that the amount of injury inflicted was inestimable, and they said the same on their side, besides the great obligations under which the Scots were to the King, they having signed, sealed and confirmed by parliament, conditions with which they did not comply. We then went to dinner, after which the French ambassador came, and the Scots set forth the object of their mission, in the same way that they had done to the King: demanding that their inclusion in the peace treaty should take effect, or that a reason to the contrary should be given to them. The Lord Chancellor told them that a full reply should be given to them in my presence, since we were partners in the war; and with that the Council retired. I remained alone with the French ambassador and the Scotsmen; and the Bishop of Ross asked me whether I admitted the correctness of what the Chancellor had said. He thought (he said) that I had no instructions to say that the Emperor and the English had common cause against them. I replied that I had no instructions to say so, but it was quite true that we were

---

* The decipher of this letter is not now in the Imperial Archives, but by the aid of a key which exists there it was re-deciphered by the writer. This is also the case with most of the letters of this year from the Emperor to Van der Delft.

† This was David Paniter, Regent Arran's Secretary, who had gone backwards and forwards several times to Flanders. He had recently been appointed Bishop of Ross.

both at war, which was what the Chancellor had said. "Well," said he, "I do not think you are aware of it, but I may tell you that we are in negotiation and understanding with your side; and I do so in order that you may know that we are not at war, as you seem to think; and we have nothing to do with you here, being simply here to treat with the English." I replied that with regard to a Treaty (of peace with the Emperor) I knew nothing; but if there was one, they had better produce it for my guidance. If they did not, I was unable as yet to treat them otherwise than as enemies. He caught up the last word and asked me very sourly if I was instructed to call them enemies.

In order not to submit tamely to so rude a question, I replied that I did not know about instructions, but those who were at all times and places despoiling and injuring the subjects of the Emperor, as they (the Scots) were, must of necessity be either enemies or pirates. I then recounted several examples, and cited cases where the French themselves had compelled them to restore the ships and men taken from the Emperor's subjects as they were leaving French havens. With regard to their mission, I said I very well understood from their relation whom they were addressing. To this they replied that it would not be proper for them to produce the Treaty they had with us. As, Madame, I had learnt from the letters and documents that your Majesty sent me whilst Secretary Strick was still in Scotland, that he had found them impervious to reason, and had but little hope of coming to an arrangement; whilst I was also aware of the outrages suffered daily by the subjects of the Emperor at the hands of the Scots, and I had no knowledge of any treaty having been made with them, I can only suppose that the Bishop (of Ross) wished to bandy words with me, and deal with me as he did with Secretary Strick, with the object of breeding distrust between us (i.e. between the English and the Emperor).

When the Lords of the Council returned, the Scots were told that, with regard to their inclusion in the Treaty of peace, it was understood to be subject to the words employed in the clause, namely:—"Saving the treaties which each of the contracting princes claimed to have." This on the part of the English meant their Treaty with the Emperor. The Scots maintained that the words quoted only referred to the Treaties that had been made with them; but they were told that this view of the clause was untenable, because the words originally drafted by the French had run thus: "Saving the Treaties which each of the contracting princes claimed to have with the Scots"; and this draft had been refused by the English, who struck out the words "with the Scots": the King having given orders that the negotiations should be broken off, rather than that the Treaty with the Emperor should be vitiated. The words struck out were therefore omitted from the clause, which stood as at present, the Treaty with the Emperor being thus safe-guarded. The Council then continued that, even without going beyond the first point of the inclusion, it was obvious that the Scots could not claim to benefit by the inclusion clause, because they had since given several fresh occasions

1546.

for continuing the war. It would be sufficient to instance the evil treatment and great damage inflicted by the Scots on the subjects of the Emperor, the King's good brother and perpetual ally. The Scots had therefore not shown themselves worthy of the friendship of the English; besides which, the former had also given fresh offence to the English themselves, having raided, despoiled and burnt their lands on the borders, and injured and seized English subjects. This alone was more than sufficient to annul the inclusion clause. With regard to the damage inflicted upon the Emperor's subjects, the Scots gave no answer; but with respect to the English claims, they expressed themselves ready to make restitution of all that might be decided to have been unduly taken. The Council, however, continued to dwell upon the violations of English territory; which the Scots maintained had taken place before the proclamation of peace and their inclusion therein. The Council thereupon told them that the amount of good will and honesty on the part of the Scots was demonstrated by their having postponed the declaration of peace until the day after the exploit in question. Even, however, if no fresh offence had been given, the inclusion clause was conditional upon the consent of the Emperor, which consent the King would have used his influence to obtain if the Scots had shown themselves worthy of his good offices.

The Scots, with the French ambassador, who spoke in favour of their view of the inclusion, then brought forward sundry subtleties with regard to the words "*nova occasione data*" referring to the Treaty made in the year '15; but the Council told them that this was plainly contrary to the context, as the words could only refer to the interpretation of the inclusion clause: "et encore, *ce caso quo.*"

During these disputes the ardent desire of the English to hold inviolate their Treaty with the Emperor was very plainly apparent. The Council remarked that the King of France, having sought peace, greatly wished to include the Scots (unconditionally), but the King of England had refused, although the Admiral of France had assured the English that the Scots had been already included in the Treaty between the Emperor and France. They (the English Council) at the time believed this to be true; but still they so worded the clause for the inclusion of the Scots in their own treaty as not to prejudice their Treaties with the Emperor. They had since learnt that what the Admiral of France told them was not true; and they called me to witness that I had assured them that this was the case. I thereupon thought it advisable to repeat what your Majesty wrote to me formerly, and assure them that neither verbally, as the French averred, nor in writing, had the Scots been included by the Emperor. I was, I said, also certain that this had been clearly stated to the Bishop (of Ross) when he was in Flanders in 1544, and also to the Admiral of France at Bruges afterwards. At last the matter went so far, Madame, that we told them (the Scots) plainly that they might produce the signatures and seals if they liked, for we had had and still possessed them all, but found none of them genuine. The Scots, seeing that their arguments did not avail them, requested that the reasons against them should be

512   SPANISH STATE PAPERS.

1546.

handed them in writing. This was agreed to, and we separated until the next conference. The English consider these two Scottish ambassadors very cunning; and understand that they have come hither to gain time, for reasons which will be obvious. This is the reason why they wish to cajole me about the existence of a treaty, and I quite expect they will reap all the advantage they can from it with the English, so as to breed distrust of us. In order to provide against this, I related to the Lord Chancellor before I left what had passed between the Bishop (of Ross) and myself. The Chancellor said I had answered excellently, and begged me to report everything fully to your Majesty.

I recently received letters from the Emperor dated the 8th instant, which came with the King's despatches through the enemies' camp, and consequently were not signed. The originals will come through Italy and France by his Majesty's courier. I spoke to Paget about this; and he thinks I had better address a few words to the King on the subject. He has undertaken to let me know when the best opportunity occurs for doing so. I am anxious for such an opportunity, the better to learn what is going on.—London, 29 November, 1546.

29 Nov.
Vienna.
Imp. Arch.

354. VAN DER DELFT to LOYS SCORS.

You will see by my letter to the Queen what passed between me and the Scottish ambassadors.

The other day one of the King's heralds came here to bring me a disguised letter (lettre deguisée) from the Emperor, which had come into their hands by chance. It came very appropriately to confound those who falsely reported here that a great part of the Emperor's forces had been lost, as in this letter, which is dated the 8th of this month, his Majesty says that nothing had happened but a few unimportant skirmishes since his last letter.* The Emperor also said that out of consideration for this King he had expressly ordered that the embargoes effected in Spain on English property were to be immediately raised, against security, which release has hitherto been refused there. His Majesty also instructs me to thank the King for the information which he had caused to be conveyed to him, respecting the intrigue about which I sent Jehan du Bois thither.

London, 29 November, 1546.

30 Nov.
Vienna.
Imp. Arch.

355. VAN DER DELFT to the QUEEN DOWAGER.

After I had handed to this courier the letters herewith, your Majesty's courier arrived here with your letters of 12th instant, on his way to Scotland. Scottish affairs having changed, as your Majesty will see by my said letters, I have judged it advisable to detain your courier, and to refrain from attempting to carry out his mission, whilst concealing his arrival, until your Majesty deigns to send me further orders. The Bishop of Ross, to whom the courier is addressed, is here, as

---

* This letter will be found on page 491.

your Majesty will learn, and it appears to me extremely dangerous to confide over much in him, as he is considered here a double-faced person. It may be feared that, if he were to perceive here any signs of a treaty with your Majesty, he would turn them to the advantage of the Scots, and to our prejudice; and I presume that your Majesty does not desire at this juncture to give any reason for offence to the English. I await your Majesty's commands.

London, 30 November, 1546.

30 Nov.
Vienna.
Imp. Arch.

356. VAN DER DELFT to LOYS SCORS.

Yesterday I handed the enclosed letters for conveyance to a merchants' courier going to Antwerp, with whom I had agreed, in accordance with the note written to you. This courier, however, secretly tarried here in town, to gain another silver-piece from the merchants; and in the interim the Queen's courier on his way to Scotland arrived here. I therefore demanded my letters back from the first man, for the purpose of sending them by some other special courier, and so avoiding any further delay on the part of this man. But as I could find no other who would go for less than 18 ducats, I have been obliged, after all, to let the first man take the letters. You will see, however, that, through his fault, I am able to advise at less cost the receipt of the Queen's letter; and also that I have thought best to detain the Queen's courier and conceal his coming, both from the English and the Scots, until I receive further orders from her Majesty. When the Queen receives my said letters she will learn what has passed here, and that no great dependence can be placed on the inclusion of the Scots in the peace between France and England. If these people (the English), moreover, learn that negotiations are going on between us and the Scots, I am not sure that it will be advantageous to the Emperor's interests.

London, 30 November, 1546.

7 & 24 Nov.
5 & 12 Dec.
Simancas.
E.R. 873.

357. Document headed :—"Account of letters from Juan de Vega 7 and 24 November and 5 and 12 December, 1546. Answered from Heilbronn 16 January, 1547."

Decision on the points at issue had been delayed until the arrival of Cardinal Farnese on the 11th. Vega had spoken to the latter, and he had promised to use every effort to obtain a prompt and favourable decision. Before Farnese arrived it had been suggested to Vega through Cardinal Santa Flor that the Pope would grant the whole 500,000 ducats, on condition that this concession should cover the supplementary grant of 100,000 crowns, of which hopes had always been given. Vega had refused this, taking his stand on the instructions.

(Marginal note for reply: He did very well in this. Let him keep to it.)

Vega says that if the Pope is once convinced of your Majesty's success, he has no doubt that he will do all that is required of him; although it is evident that he is ill pleased. On the contrary, he and his friends cannot conceal the favourable progress of events,

1546.

and never cease their confessions of the enemy's weakness. Cardinal Farnese had expressed his great satisfaction and devotion to your Majesty, but some people do not believe the truth of it. Still every appearance of confidence in him shall be shown. The Pope has had many conferences with the French Ambassador, concerning peace and with reference to this enterprise. They are employing every sort of artifice to persuade Vega of the difficulty they (i.e. the Pope and his Counsellors) will have in continuing the subvention, etc., though the Bishop of Ancona assures him of the Pope's desire to satisfy your Majesty, on condition that Vega will use his good offices in the matter of peace between your Majesty and France.

(Marginal note for reply : He must persist in pressing the mission of Don Juan de Mendoza, pointing out the perplexity of the Emperor at the long delay in sending the reply and furnishing the subsidy. His Holiness must remember how earnestly the Emperor has written about it, and how urgently the help is required. With regard to the question of peace (i.e. the confirmation of the peace between the Emperor and France) it has no connection whatever with the main point at issue, and Juan de Vega will not make any move in this respect as they request. The Nuncio recently told de Granvelle that he had received letters from Rome referring exclusively to this question of peace, and that as the time had arrived for sending the troops into winter quarters, he thought it would be advisable to endeavour to conclude peace (with France). Granvelle asked him if he had any communication to make about Don Juan de Mendoza's mission, to which question he replied in the negative. Granvelle then told him to consider what the Emperor would think of his having nothing to say about the principal business in hand. To this he only answered that he hoped shortly to have a reply on that point.)

Don Juan de Mendoza writes that he had spoken to Cardinal Farnese as soon as he arrived, and the latter had promised all his aid, saying that he was no longer Legate, but only a servant of your Majesty. Mendoza desires instructions as to how long he should remain in Rome if the Pope delays his decision, and also if his Holiness should raise difficulties about the other subsidies which are justly payable, especially the 500,000 ducats.

With regard to the Council, no advice had come from Trent nor any reply to the letter written lately from Rothenburg with regard to the suspension and the other points discussed there between Cardinals Farnese and Trent and others.

(The rest of this document refers to the Italian princes and Spanish ecclesiastical appointments of no interest.)

5 Dec.
Simancas.
E.R. 873.

358. JUAN DE VEGA to the EMPEROR.

(Congratulations on the victories of the King of the Romans in Saxony, the retirement of the Landgrave and the weakness of the enemy.)

"I am of opinion that this news will do more in favour of the affairs now being negotiated than Cardinal Farnese's promised efforts, as he has delayed so long before coming to keep his word. He has indeed not yet arrived ; nor is it known for certain when he

1546.

is coming, though I am informed that he is not passing by way of Piacenza, as was previously announced. Since the good news has been received they have written asking him to hurry, but I suspect that their real object was further to delay his coming, in order that the Pope might utilise the delay for his own ends. Since my last letters of 18 and 20 ultimo Don Juan Hurtado de Mendoza and I have been with the Cardinal ministers, and once with the Pope. It would be tedious and useless to detail all that has passed in these interviews; the substance of it all was that they replied to Don Juan's requests, raising difficulties, especially in the prolongation of the treaty and in the matter of the 500,000 ducats. They said that they must await the arrival of Cardinal Farnese for the other points. When we pressed the Pope urgently for a decision so that Don Juan might return, it was arranged that we should meet the ministers again, and discuss the matters dependent upon the existing treaty,* since we could do that without the Legate (i.e. Farnese), but that the questions touching future action must await Farnese's arrival.

This was four days ago, and although we have asked for an appointment with the ministers we have been unable to obtain one: nor can we quite make out what their decision will be, though I have always been of opinion that the Pope will not dare to refrain from aiding your Majesty. Since the news above-mentioned (i.e. of the victories in Saxony) we have been informed that the Pope would satisfy your Majesty in the matter of the 500,000 ducats; and also in the increase of his contingent, as well as providing money for the rest. I am also privately informed by a trustworthy person that Maffeo told him to-day that the Pope would do as your Majesty asked; as, under the circumstances, no other course was possible. I am pressing them for a decision, and Cardinal Santa Flor to-day sent me excuses for not having met us, the Pope having been unwell, but promised to see his Holiness and arrange.

I have not been able to understand what is the Pope's decision about the Council (of Trent), but I expect that your Majesty will have learnt from Trent. But I know that before the news (of the victories) arrived, they were not satisfied with the proposals for the prorogation which were brought forward by your Majesty's representatives; and I am told that they are still very much discontented on the point; although when the letters of 22nd ultimo arrived the Pope sent a message to Trent in a great hurry.

Rome, 5 December, 1546.

5 Dec.
Simancas.
E. 1192

359. Document headed:— "Account of the letters of Don Diego (Hurtado de Mendoza) respecting the Council (i.e. of Trent) for consideration of his Majesty. Discussed at Rothenburg, 5 December, 1546."

Cardinal Farnese having arrived at Trent, to all appearance determined to live and die in his Majesty's service, a meeting was held of the Legates, Cardinals Farnese and Trent, and Don Diego.

---

* That is to say the completion of the grant of 500,000 ducats from the Castilian monasteries, and the payment of the supplementary 100,000 direct Papal subvention.

The three following points comprising the future action with regard to the Council were brought forward for discussion:—

1. The article of "Justification" being now on the point of final decision, is it to the benefit of Christendom and of the "enterprise" that it should be promulgated at once or suspended for a month or two?

2. Would it be better to bring forward in the Council the article touching the residence of bishops, or for his Holiness himself to issue a Bull voluntarily granting to the bishops all he honestly could do in order that they might be able to reside in their churches?

3. Since your Majesty had not consented to the transfer of the Council elsewhere, what was to be done with it? (*i.e.* the Council.)

With regard to the first point, the arguments for and against the promulgation of the article are set forth at length, the final decision of the five persons present being that the inconvenience that would result from the suspension of the article would be more easily dealt with and remedied than the difficulty that would be caused by its promulgation; and it was determined that the promulgation should be delayed for the present. At the same time it was recommended that the substance of the article should be quietly spread throughout the Church by the bishops, etc. Don Diego wrote privately that a doctrine spread in this way would lack authority, as it would be necessary for the Council to reserve the right of abolishing, supplying or changing what it might consider necessary, according to circumstances.

With regard to the second point, of the residence of prelates, the question was so difficult and dangerous, owing to the fact that each prelate would interpret it according to his own interests, disregarding the larger interests of Christendom. The decision of the point might give rise to divisions between the Pope and the Council, or between the Princes and the Roman Church, which might end in schism. It was therefore thought best that the Pope should at once issue a Bull allowing to the prelates who would live in their churches all the concessions proposed recently to the legates, and even more amply still, especially abolishing the exemptions to priests, friars and chapters. Don Diego was anxious to learn from the legates exactly what concessions the Pope intended to grant to the bishops; but he was told that the matter was purely one of ecclesiastical discipline.

On the third point, it was considered that no question of removing the sittings elsewhere was to be discussed, and that the best course would be to announce a recess or suspension for six months. This would avoid many difficulties: amongst others that, as the Council is to sit during the war and the latter is suspended during the winter, the Council should also be similarly suspended. If the Council continued to sit during a suspension of hostilities, it would be necessary to close it very shortly; because after the publication of the "Justification" article, there would be nothing further to occupy the Council, all the other articles being either dependent upon that of Justification, or already settled by previous resolutions. The objects to be gained jointly by the Council and the war together would therefore fail; and at the same time it was recollected that if

1546.

an attempt was made to deal with matters slowly the Council would dissolve of itself, which would be the most dangerous eventuality of all; seeing that the idea of consulting the Universities on the article of Justification had been rejected by the whole of the Council, in consequence of the scandal and loss of prestige that would result as well as the bad example it would set to posterity. Each party present therefore decided to lay these views respectively before the Pope, the Emperor, etc.

After discussion with the Emperor, the following answer was ordered to be sent to Don Diego (de Mendoza).

It will be well to defer the publication of the decision that may be adopted respecting "Justification," even if the decision itself is adopted secretly, in order to avoid the dissemination of the discord and bad feeling that have arisen over this article. These have already caused the ungodly to print an account of what has passed, and to allege that the Council came to fisticuffs about the article. If the Papal party desire to act otherwise let them do so without consulting us, in order that they may have no excuse for saying that his Majesty and his ministers have openly or tacitly consented to the resolution of the article, or their action regarding it without full consideration; especially as the Papal party objected to consulting the Universities and other learned persons outside the Council; their objection being founded on their own interests, and on the Pope's claim to superiority over the Council. With regard to the dissemination of the doctrine contained in the article by means of preachers, perhaps it would be best not to do this, but to follow the usual course in the Church before these innovations were heard of. With regard to the second point, of remedying the grievances of the bishops, as these grievances are against the Pope and the Roman court the Emperor does not desire to interfere at all in the matter; but to leave it entirely to the Pope, whom he refers to the articles forwarded to the Council from Spain on the subject. On the points there indicated a remedy must be provided in the interests of the good government of his Majesty's dominions. His Majesty hopes that these matters will be settled without the necessity of discussing them in the Council. Don Diego did well in declining to consent to the suspension of the Council. Nothing further should be done on this point, but a stand should be made upon the instructions given to Don Juan de Mendoza[*] and communicated to Don Juan de Toledo, as similar reasons to those stated therein have moved his Majesty to refuse to allow the Council to be moved. The chief of these reasons is the continuance of his obligation to secure the holding of the Council on German territory, an obligation now greater than ever, seeing that the Emperor is engaged in the war, and affairs are in their present condition.

---

[*] It will be recollected that Don Juan de Mendoza's principal mission to Rome was to negotiate a prolongation of the treaty—now expiring by effluxion of time—between the Pope and the Emperor. The employment of the Council of Trent as an auxiliary in the religious policy of the Emperor was one of the main objects of the treaty, and Don Juan was to insist that in the renewed treaty the points relating to the Council should remain intact; although, as these letters show, the Pope and his party had long before grown alarmed at their powerlessness to control the Council being held in the Emperor's territories and dominated by his creatures.

518   SPANISH STATE PAPERS.

1546.

If in these circumstances we were to consent to a suspension, it would furnish a pretext for its entire dissolution. With all due moderation, therefore, the suspension or recess, which is almost the same thing, should be avoided. They must be made to understand that his Majesty cannot consent to it.

6 Dec.
Paris.
Archives
Nationales.
K. 1486.

360. ST. MAURIS to PRINCE PHILIP.

(Sends letters he has received giving an account of the defeat of the Protestants in Saxony, "whom God for ever confound.") I cannot omit to tell your Highness one thing: that the King of France, the Dauphin and all this court are dreadfully alarmed at this defeat of the Protestants; fearing that as they have aided our enemies, they (the French) may now feel the smart.

The Commissioners of France and England have been assembled in Calais for a long time past to settle their difficulties; but, so far as I can learn, they will fail to come to an agreement, and will separate without doing anything. The King of France has lost hope of an arrangement, and hates the King of England worse than ever, whilst the King of England as deeply distrusts him, as I am told by his ambassador here. He says that the King of England is offended that the King of France should still maintain his galleys at sea (*i.e.* outside the Mediterranean). These galleys are now near Rouen etc., and it is said that in the spring they will go to the east (*i.e.* into the Mediterranean). I will keep myself informed on the matter. The King of France has renewed his edicts against the exportation of wheat or barley.

Angers, 6 December, 1546.

8 Dec.
Vienna.
Imp. Arch.

361. THE QUEEN DOWAGER to VAN DER DELFT.

We last wrote to you on the 2nd instant, sending you the instructions and documents touching the Scottish affairs; and we have since received your letters of 30 and 31 November, informing us of what had passed between the King of England's ministers and the Scottish ambassadors, and also of the statement made to you by the Bishop of Ross, to the effect that the kingdom of Scotland had another treaty with the Emperor; and was not at war with his Majesty, as with the English. We note the reply that you gave him. The English ministers having so explicitly declared in your presence that they do not regard the Scots as having been included in the peace with France, except by the consent of his Imperial Majesty, there will be no necessity for you to make the representation contained in our last letters; but when you see a fitting opportunity you may enforce and confirm the declaration of the English ministers, by stating to the Scottish ambassadors that we, as Regent of these dominions for the Emperor, have been informed by the King of France, by letters from his admiral, of the treaty of peace made between the two Kings, each of whom had included in the treaty the Emperor, his territories and subjects, and we have also learnt that the Scots were likewise included, in accordance with an extract of the treaty furnished to us. We see, nevertheless, that the Scots have not ceased to assail, plunder, and rob the

HENRY VIII.

1546.

subjects of his Imperial Majesty; and consequently we sent to Scotland his Majesty's ordinary secretary, M. Matthew Strick, to learn on what pretext the Scots still continued thus to attack his Majesty's subjects, since we understood that by virtue of the inclusion referred to we were at peace with Scotland. Secretary Strick also demanded the restoration of all prizes captured since the treaty of peace; but he was informed by the Scots that they considered themselves included in the peace between England and France, on conditions which they said they had accepted; and that, consequently, they were at peace with England. They were not, however, they said, at peace with the Emperor and his subjects, because the clauses of the treaty of peace were only binding on the contracting parties. As such an interpretation as this is directly at variance with the treaty of alliance between the Emperor and the King of England, and the latter could not include the Scots in the peace except on the condition that the Emperor consented, we are unable to accept this statement of the Scots. We have conveyed this through you to the ministers of the King of England, who have always assured us that the Scots were only included in the peace provided they were at peace with the Emperor: this, indeed, being clearly expressed in the text of the inclusion clause. The Bishop of Ross therefore had no reason for asking you so pointedly whether you were instructed to confirm what the English Chancellor had said, namely, that we were jointly with the English at war with the Scots; since he himself (the Bishop of Ross) had said the same thing in Scotland to Secretary Strick, for the purpose of arousing distrust between the King of England and ourselves. He (the bishop) must also know very well that he was plainly told, when he was in Brussels, that we had no intention of negotiating with the Scots except with the co-operation of the King of England. This was the sole reason why the Emperor refused to include the Scots in the treaty of Créspy. Although the French endeavoured, by means of several contentions proposed by the bishop, to maintain that the Scots were included in that treaty, the bishop was perfectly well aware, and finally admitted, that such was not the case.

If, perchance, the Scottish ambassadors should again say anything, in the presence of the English ministers, about our having another treaty with Scotland, but without further particularising it, you will say that you cannot speak of that, as you have never heard of such a treaty; but that you do not believe that they can show that any treaty has been made with them that could weaken the treaty of alliance existing between the Emperor and the King of England; which alliance we wish to observe faithfully and sincerely. You will not go beyond this, unless your hand be forced by the production or quotation from the agreement of Antwerp.[*] If this be done by the Scots, you will give satisfaction to the English ministers by using the arguments contained in the

---

[*] This appears to have been an arrangement made after the return of Secretary Strick to Flanders from Scotland, and is referred to in the Queen Dowager's letter to Van der Delft of 12 November. It provided for the giving of security for all Flemish property embargoed in Scotland and the carrying on of commerce between Scotland and Flanders by means of a liberal concession of safe-conducts on both sides.

1546.

instructions sent you; but you will take great care not to be drawn into any dispute about the said agreement, if you can avoid it, in the presence of the English ministers. If the Scots waive the inclusion clause, as they will be obliged to do if the English stand firm, and begin to negotiate anew, you will intervene in the negotiations, and insist with the English that the Scots must first restore everything they have captured since the treaty of peace between France and England, both from the Emperor's subjects and the English. You must keep firm on this point.

If the Scots undertake to do this you must tell them at the same time that they must immediately release everything they have stopped, and call in the sureties given by their subjects at the instance of Secretary Strick and since for the captures effected by the Scots from the Emperor's subjects. There must be no delay in this respect; and with regard to the rest of the property, which may have already been scattered or made away with, a joint committee will have to meet and clear up the matter, after which restitution must be made; the persons and property of Scottish subjects being made answerable for the same. But you must take care not to mention the property embargoed, or now on security in Scotland, until the Scottish ambassadors have agreed in principle to the restitution, for fear that if the matter is mentioned before they may seize the opportunity of scattering the whole of the property. If, moreover, you see a disposition on the part of the English to make their own profit out of the business in their new treaty, by abandoning the claims for captures and damages committed by the Scots on their subjects, and they ask you to make similar concessions, in the interests of peace, you will answer that you have no authority to do so, and you cannot consent without communicating with us, as in such case you will do. You will, at the same time, let us know what you can learn of the probable tenour of any treaty the English may make with the Scots. You may signify to the English ministers that, in your opinion, we ought not to forego the restitution referred to, as it is the principal point at issue. As to the rest, you will proceed in accordance with the instructions sent you previously. Touching the messenger we sent to Scotland, you did right in detaining him in England, and you had better send him back hither, retaining his packet until you see what you can settle with the Scots. If, perchance, they do not agree to anything, you had better consider whether it would not be advisable to speak privately to the Bishop of Ross respecting the prolongation of the agreement of Antwerp; but make no mention of this, unless you see that the negotiations for peace are entirely broken off.

You have not yet sent us any reply respecting the matter we instructed you to press, as to the reinstatement of the Emperor's subjects possessing properties in the Boulognais. What have you done respecting Paget's observations to you on the subject? We are desirous of knowing what has passed in the matter, which must be actively dealt with, as it is of the highest importance.

Tournai, 8 December, 1546.

HENRY VIII. 521

1546.
9 Dec.
Simancas.
E.V. 1318.

362. DIEGO HURTADO DE MENDOZA to the EMPEROR.

I have come hither (Venice) because Peter Strozzi is secretly here, apparently negotiating something, and also because of this peace the Pope is so bent upon making between your Majesty and France; it even being said that he will give no more money for the war (*i.e.* with the Protestants) unless your Majesty will consent to a peace with France.

The Republic (of Venice) carries it crest high, and people are very indignant that the German war is stopping their trade. Still, as I have often written, the Republic will not adopt any course to your Majesty's detriment in the present state of things. I only refer to it again to clear my conscience.*

I have written freely to your Majesty on other occasions how passionately the presidents and prelates (*i.e.* in the Council of Trent) deal with religious questions, and how confusedly, how disorderly, and how regardfully to private interests such matters are discussed. This is proved by the manner in which the article of "Justification" was proceeded with; but it was first exhibited in the original plan for business, and then in the question of the conception of the Virgin.

In that of the justification, respecting the certainty of grace, so much passion and corruption have been exhibited on both sides, and so little devotion in essential things, that it is easy to judge how everything has been, and will be, dealt with in this Council.

From head to foot selfish interests are supreme, and they (*i.e.* the prelates) have no other God, and no other law, than their own advantage, in accordance with which their every decision is ruled.† All this being true, as it is, if they hurry to settle the articles of "Justification," and the residence (of the bishops), everything will be over; and the Council will be wound up in four days. From this two inconveniences will arise. First the abuses will be fixed, whilst we who have seen how things have been done, and have heard what has passed, will be bound to abide by the determinations arrived at. Secondly: in case it should be desired to amend matters by another Council it will be almost impossible to do so; as the abuses have been approved of by this Council, and the Pope remains the perpetual head of the Council which will defend such abuses.

I hear from Juan de Vega that the Pope does not approve of the suggestion of suspending the sittings. This may arise from an idea that everything is bad for him which appears even tolerably good to your Majesty's ministers, for in matters of religion a man must

---

* The nervous desire of the Seigniory to avoid offending the Emperor whilst smiling upon his enemies will be seen by a perusal of the various letters written to the Venetian ambassadors during this period and published in the Venetian Calendar of the Rolls Series.

† This extraordinary denunciation of the Council of Trent by the statesman who above all others had forced it to the policy of his master proves how arrogantly the Emperor's ministers resented the slightest attempt on the part of the prelates, or of the Pope, to look upon the assembly from an ecclesiastical point of view; and how completely the Emperor—and his son after him—used religion and the Church as an instrument for their political ends; uniformity of religious profession being vital to the maintenance of their political preponderance in Europe.

1546.

say what he thinks without being asked. As I am now leaving my duties in the Council to serve your Majesty elsewhere, I feel conscientiously obliged to write to your Majesty. I did so before in all sincerity, and I now point out, as I did in my letters from Trent, the difficulties I foresee in the resolution of the articles upon "Justification," the residence of prelates, and the hasty action of the Council in the matter of suspension of the sittings, in case your Majesty cannot spin matters out, or other difficulties occur which may render these necessary.

(The rest of this letter, 2 pages, is occupied by Venetian affairs and rumours of Turkish movements in the Mediterranean of no interest.)

Venice, 9 December, 1546.

12 Dec.
Simancas.
E.B. 873.

363. JUAN DE VEGA to the EMPEROR.

(Letter received detailing the Emperor's progress. His Holiness had received news of the dispersal of the enemy, which had caused much sensation. The Pope spoke of holding rejoicings; but as the Emperor's last letter is not very definite the rejoicings have been postponed. Much talk on the matter. Cardinal Farnese has arrived. He and Juan de Mendoza saw his Holiness this morning. No decision arrived at yet, but indications tend to the belief that a favourable result will be obtained, especially about the 500,000 ducats. They wish, however, to make this concession cover the supplement due for the troops sent short, and the extra 100,000 ducats. We will not accept this. The other matter ordered by the Emperor must be dealt with in another letter, as the present is not going by a private courrier.

The writer is now ready to start for his new Viceroyalty of Naples, when his orders arrive. Thanks the Emperor for sending galleys to convey him.)

As a more certain messenger is now taking this letter, I can write the rest more clearly. When his Holiness is quite convinced of your Majesty's success, I believe he will do what is asked of him; although he is much chagrined, and his people are so to an extent that they are unable to conceal, at your Majesty's success. They are most unwilling to admit the weakness of the enemy. In public Cardinal Farnese has expressed his great devotion to your Majesty; but those who see beneath the surface are not so certain of this. But still every mark of confidence shall be shown to him here to see whether it will expedite matters, which are being delayed in an extraordinary manner. That other business[*] shall be kept quite secret; as if they knew that it was to be broached they would throw every obstacle in the way of those now under discussion. I am of opinion that their design is to make these

---

[*] That is to say the secret instruction to Don Juan de Toledo, mentioned in the Emperor's letter to his son (28 November) to press the Pope to grant permission for the Emperor to take a half of all the treasure owned by the churches, etc., in his dominions. It will be seen that though the permission of the Pope was to be asked, yet the Emperor had decided, whether his Holiness consented or not, to take these ecclesiastical treasures for his own purposes.

1546.

latter affairs a means of forming a new alliance with your Majesty. If this be the case, they will afterwards be less inclined to turn back than at present when they are perhaps partly undecided.

Rome, 12 December, 1546.

14 Dec.
Vienna.
Imp. Arch.

364. VAN DER DELFT to the EMPEROR.

After the receipt of your Majesty's letters of 10th October, containing a letter of credence for me to communicate to the King what had happened up to that time to your Majesty's enemies, I demanded audience. As, however, the King was not very well I was referred to the Council, to whom I conveyed the contents of your Majesty's note. Since then I have received an unsigned letter of the 8th November, of which the original reached me on the 6th instant, as I was coming from Oatlands, where on the previous day I had spoken to the King and had communicated to him the intelligence contained in the said unsigned letter. He took in good part your Majesty's assurance of your Majesty's reciprocity of his good and perfect friendship; and, with regard to the French efforts to make out that the friendship on his side was not sincere, and their continued intrigues to re-gain what they claim, and your Majesty's confidence that he (the King of England) would understand these plans and be on his guard, he replied; "I believe, and am quite aware, that they (the French) are not only trying to intrigue with me against the Emperor, but even to a greater extent are seeking to intrigue with the Emperor against me. With this object they have used every possible means, both with the Protestants and with the Pope; but, with God's help, I hope to be able to guard my realm and my possessions across the sea, in spite of them." He then bade me be seated, and said: "I wish to chat with you touching your Master's affairs, which are giving me frequent matter for reflection. I think it very strange that, considering the intimate friendship existing between us, he should give me no account of his undertakings; and that I should know nothing of his affairs, towards the success of which I have every goodwill, not only in the public interest but also because of my affection for one, to whom I am, and always was, a good friend and brother. But I am afraid he will allow himself to be seduced by the Pope." I thought well, Sire, to reply (as your Majesty had written to me) that you had negotiated nothing with the Pope to his (Henry's) disadvantage; but that, on the contrary, you had always rebutted such suggestions. He seemed pleased at this, but nevertheless said: "I know that the Pope has not fulfilled the promises he made to the Emperor": and to judge from the discourse he then held with regard to your Majesty's affairs, I could gather that he wished to see the war in Germany appeased by an accord honourable and glorious to your Majesty, and your Majesty's arms turned against those who, he said, always endeavour to frustrate your enterprises. After he had given me an account of the condition of your Majesty's army, and of that of the enemy, which was not to your Majesty's advantage, as he heard from a man who had recently arrived from the seat of war, he expressed his unfeigned regret that such was the case:

and then resumed the subject of a peaceful arrangement. He would, he said, willingly act on your Majesty's behalf in the matter as a true and sincere friend; and when a settlement was concluded he would join your Majesty against the French, for the purpose of checking their power, and that of their allies, which latter are only awaiting an opportunity to play their own game. He would, he said, also bring into the league the Protestants and the King of Denmark; but this was said in the strictest confidence, and he forbade me to mention that I had heard it from him, in case I communicated it in any of my letters to the Queen (Dowager). I was pleased with this conversation, Sire, both because I could discern clearly the desire he possesses to preserve perfect friendship with your Majesty, and because it is evident that he has no secret understanding with, or trust in, the French. I did my best to prove to him that your Majesty was not making war against the Protestants (*i.e.* as such) but I could not convince him of this; and then set forth how your Majesty had written to me, saying that solely out of consideration for him you had ordered the release of his subjects' property embargoed in Spain, on security being given. He asked me why security was exacted, to which I replied, in order to obtain redress for what Renegat had unjustly seized. He (Henry) replied that he had refused to do justice to no one; and that no claim had been made (on account of Renegat's seizures), the embargoes in Spain being a violation of the treaties. I said that I held a letter of credence from the Prince of Spain in favour of the merchants whose property had been plundered by Renegat; and that these merchants had sent a special representative hither with powers to recover the property. This man, Sire, has only come to me just recently. There was previously no one that I could help against Renegat; and the representative of the merchants who has now appeared expressly states that he knows of nothing belonging to your Majesty.° I will urge the matter actively with the Lords of the Council, to whom the King has referred the matter. In the discussions with the King's Commissioners lately, the claims of certain of your Majesty's subjects, merchants of Burgos, were urged. One of these was made by Lope de Carrion, who has been prosecuting it for a long time unsuccessfully; and the commissioners persisted in their opinion that the prize was a good one. I thought well to take the opportunity of gently urging the King himself to order redress to be given to Carrion by some arrangement, and so to end, once for all, the merchants' claims, of which Carrion's was the principal and a possible source of future dispute between the Princes. But the moment the King heard the name of this case, he said: "I pray you not to speak to me of that again. The affairs of the Emperor

---

* It will be recalled that the claims on account of merchants and that on account of the Emperor in this matter did not run on all fours. Renegat had seized certain property and specie from a Spanish ship from America, in revenge for the detention in a Spanish port of a French prize captured by him. The specie having been embarked without the legal registration was claimed by the Emperor as his, the owners having forfeited it by their violation of the law. The merchandise being still private property was claimed by the merchants, but its value was small in comparison with that of the specie, which was lost to them in any case, and their claim was urged timidly.

1546.

and myself do not depend upon the merchants, who can prosecute their claims before my Council." I begged him to pardon me if I urged the matter upon him; but he had been kind enough when I first came here to make me judge of the case, and I believed that I had given him no reason to trust me less now than he did then. I prayed him to believe that I had no other object to gain in pressing this case than my great desire to banish all occasion for discord between your Majesties. He replied: "Let my subjects receive redress as well." I said that redress should be accorded on both sides, and I would not mention the matter to him again until after the embargoes had been raised in Spain. He laughed and replied: "Well; we will talk about it then," and with that he dismissed me very amiably, the whole court welcoming me more warmly than ever before.

The next day as I was returning to London I met a courier on the road, sent by the Queen Regent (Mary of Hungary) with the original of your Majesty's letter of the 8th ultimo; and as I learnt also from private letters of the success of your Majesty's army, and the good exploit of the King of the Romans and Duke Maurice of Saxony, in addition to the information contained in your Majesty's letter, I immediately wrote to the first Secretary (*i.e.* Paget) asking him to communicate my good news to the King. The Councillors here are delighted with the intelligence.

I have informed the Queen (Dowager) of the coming hither of two ambassadors from Scotland. One of them is the Bishop of Ross, whose name is Paniter, and who went in 1544 to your Majesty at Brussels. The object of their mission was to seek the inclusion of Scotland in the peace between France and England; and of this, and the answer they received, in my presence, I also duly informed the Queen (Dowager). This answer was to the effect that there was no inclusion of Scotland in the peace except that all treaties existing in the case of both contracting sovereigns were specially reserved. This meant, in the case of the English, the treaty of alliance with your Majesty, with which the King (of England) would on no account interfere, and they (the English) had firmly adhered to this. The Scots thereupon pressed the point of the consequent inclusion of Scotland, saying that they had since given no motive for invalidating such inclusion. The English replied that, on the contrary, they (the Scots) had given several fresh and serious motives for the continued prosecution of the war against them. If no other existed, their (the Scots) attacks since the peace upon the subjects of your Majesty, the King of England's friend and ally, were sufficient. The subject of the inclusion of Scotland was very vigorously opposed by the English, as I have fully reported to the Queen (Dowager), from whom I have received instructions how I am to proceed, in case a peace or another arrangement (*i.e.* with the Scots) is negotiated here. I am daily awaiting an opportunity to converse with the Council on this matter, in accordance with the Queen (Dowager's) instructions, and also on the subject of Renegat's captures, but they (the Councillors) are much hindered by their own affairs, both those connected with the last parliament (which placed in the King's hands all the

1546.

chantries) and those concerning the coming parliament, which will deal with the distribution and employment of the proceeds. It may be feared also that the bishops will suffer in their revenues.

The principal subject of their deliberations was seen afterwards: for the day before yesterday the Duke of Norfolk[*] was taken to the Tower, he having arrived here (*i.e.* in London) the same day. His son, the Earl of Surrey, had been detained for five or six days previously in the house of the Lord Chancellor. The reason for this is still unknown; but some people who assume to know assert that they (*i.e.* the Duke and his son) held secretly some ambiguous discourse against the King, whilst the latter was ill at Windsor six weeks ago; the object being to obtain the government of the Prince. Some other Englishmen say that the hope of their liberation is very small, as the father (*i.e.* the Duke of Norfolk) was deprived of his staff of office and of his Garter before he was taken to the Tower by water; the son (*i.e.* the Earl of Surrey) being led thither publicly through the streets.

Paulin, General of the galleys of France, has been here for the last two days. He is the commissioner for France to settle the delimitation of the territories in the Boulognais, and the questions about the fortifications. As Master Seymour,[†] brother of the Earl of Hertford, who was the English Commissioner, arrived a day before Paulin, it is said that they have been unable to agree on the said question on the spot, and have come hither about it. The French, it appears, insist upon completing the fortifications they have commenced, which the English will by no means allow, and intended to make it impossible by so arranging the delimitation that an entire portion of the fortification would be included in the English boundary. It is, however, quite possible that Paulin's coming may be more for the purpose of promoting the intrigue of which your Majesty has been informed, and of which I have also advised the Queen (Dowager) by my own secretary, in order to avoid the risk of letters. I have given information of this to the King, who was very glad to know it. So far as I can judge, Sire, the coming of Paulin and the Scottish ambassadors is merely for the purpose of temporising; the French, finding the opportunity gone by to carry out their previous desires, and being now anxious to seek other means on this side. These people (the English councillors) are of the same opinion, and are consequently on their guard, having made great provision of biscuit and other things necessary for their fleet.

London, 14 December, 1546.

14 Dec.
Vienna.
Imp. Arch.

365. VAN DER DELFT to the QUEEN DOWAGER.

I went to the King at Oatlands for the purpose of fulfilling my mission to him from the Emperor, and also to present a letter of credence from your nephew the Prince of Spain, to enable me to claim satisfaction for the property seized by Renegat: and I took

---

[*] Thomas Howard, third duke, 1473-1554.
[†] Afterwards Thomas Lord Seymour of Sudeley, Lord Admiral, and husband of Queen Catharine Parr. He was beheaded by his brother Somerset 20 March, 1549.

1546.

the opportunity of mentioning Lope de Carrion's claim, and the rest of them. I was referred to the Council, and on my way back to London the next day I met this courier with your Majesty's letters. As soon as I arrived I sent to ask the Lords of the Council when it would be convenient for them to receive me. They excused themselves, by saying that they were extremely busy, and begged me to have patience until the King came to London. Still, they said, if the matter was very pressing they would thank me to let them know. I send a reply to the effect that I wished to see them not on private affairs alone, which could wait, and which, as they had doubtless heard, had been referred to them by the King, but because I had been instructed by your Majesty to make a communication, and I wished to fulfil my duty in this respect, and to be able to send an answer to your Majesty. To this they replied that, within two or three days, they would let me know when they could receive me, and yesterday morning they sent word that they could do so. When I arrived at the Council they apologised greatly for delaying the interview for so long, in consequence, they said, of their many great affairs; which, indeed, Madame, were public enough, the Duke of Norfolk having been taken to the Tower the day before yesterday, the same day that he arrived in London, and also the Earl of Surrey, his son, who for five or six days previously had been under arrest in the Lord Chancellor's house. The cause of this is at present unknown, though it is asserted that they entertained some ambiguous designs against the King, when he was ill at Windsor some six weeks ago; the plan being to obtain control of the Prince, and, as some people say, of the country; though I know not with what truth. The chance of their liberation is very small, for the Garter and his staff of office were taken from the father before he was sent to the Tower, and the son was led thither publicly through the streets.

After hearing the apologies of the Council I stated my mission, though not without letting them know that I was at a loss to understand the rumour that the Scottish ambassadors had sent their herald back to Scotland and that a French gentleman named Oysif had also passed through here on his way thither. I added that I had fully reported to your Majesty all that had passed at the first conference; and that they (the English councillors) had rejected the inclusion clause, by virtue of the treaty with the Emperor, which treaty they insisted upon safeguarding, and had no intention of contravening. Your Majesty had, I said, thereupon written to me that, as the Emperor was at war with the Scots by reason of the said treaty of alliance, he had not only declined to include them in his peace treaty with France, but had also refused to listen since to their requests for a peace with his Majesty, who had taken this course in order not to contravene his treaty of alliance with England. The Councillors replied that they could not prevent the King of France from sending to Scotland whomsoever he pleased; and they then begun to say laughingly, in their own language, as I understood, that passengers from France would not bring any benefit to them. They afterwards turned to me, and said that the letters carried by him (Oysif) with regard to us, might be called letters of Bellerophon; "and as for the Scottish ambassadors, affairs remained in exactly the same position as they were when you yourself were present at the conference and saw how lovingly we treated them." Nothing, they said, of importance should be done without my knowledge. With this, Madame, they rose and went to dinner, the whole Council being present, except Secretary Paget, who was with the King. For this reason I had no opportunity of renewing the discussion of the Boulognais claims, the Council having already referred that question to the King himself, upon whose benignity, they said, it entirely depended. The commissioners appointed by the King to settle the limits of the Boulognais arrived this morning, and are now with the King, without having first seen the Council. On the first opportunity I will speak to Paget about it, as I can get more from him in this matter than from the others.

In my conversation with the King I thanked him, by the Emperor's orders, for the information he had sent to his Majesty through his (Henry's) ambassador, and also on your Majesty's behalf for having sent the same intelligence through his Secretary to me for your Majesty's information. I told him that, for certain reasons, I had not sent the intelligence by letter, but by my Secretary, and the King seemed pleased at this. Continuing my mission from the Emperor, I said that although the French thought to carry on this intrigue with him, they make it perfectly evident that they have no intention of remaining true to their friendship with him, but will seek every opportunity to recover what they claim, without any cost to themselves; but I was sure that the King (of England), with his great prudence, was well aware of that, and would be on his guard. He replied, that he would hold tight his own country and his territory in France against them. He knew well that the French not only endeavoured to treat with him or with the Emperor, but had made advances to the Protestants, and even to the Pope. He ended his discourse by saying that he wished the Emperor all prosperity, but still would like to see him in good and honourable accord with the Protestants, and that afterwards he should come and help him (Henry) to attack those who stood in his path. I was glad, Madame, throughout all this conversation, to see his unfeigned desire and determination to preserve his friendship with the Emperor, especially as the news then current here was not at all to our advantage. As I heard nothing more from the King about the intrigue, I mentioned it to Paget, saying that the trick that the King had told the Emperor and your Majesty about was not very secret, for I had learnt from another quarter also, besides what Paget had told me, that, in anticipation of the exploit, the French galleys had not been dismissed, and that all the hulks coming to France after Candlemas were to be seized for the invasion of Holland.* He laughed at this, and whilst we were at table, hearing that I was about sending for a supply of French wines for my own use, he said openly "Take care you do so before Candlemas." I had no opportunity of speaking more fully with him, but will diligently seek one, not only on account of this

---

* See note page 498.

1546.

question but also with relation to the Boulognais claims, about which it is said that Paulin, Captain of the galleys of France, arrived here the day before yesterday, he having been entrusted with this commission. It may be that he hopes, by one means or another, to bring these people to his plans. I will report all I can learn to your Majesty.

With regard to the safe-conducts for Scotland, I will keep the packet here, in accordance with your Majesty's orders written from Tournai. I think this will be the wisest course under the circumstances.

London, 14 December, 1546.

16 Dec.
Simancas.
E. 1318.

366. DIEGO HURTADO DE MENDOZA to the EMPEROR.

I received your Majesty's letter of the 5th instant, approving of the opinion that it would be better to postpone the publication of the article on "Justification," which, being of so much importance in its treatment, might give rise to many more things being printed than the schismatics (*desviados*) have already issued. When I discussed the matter with the Legates, however, they had decided to publish it at Advent, and immediately to conclude the Council. Now that things have changed they may alter their minds with regard to the latter point.

As to keeping matters secret that is impossible, for there are many bishops in the assembly more Lutheran than they are Christian, and some of them are entirely Lutheran.

Not another word has been spoken in your Majesty's name, except to find fault with their manner of proceeding, and to advise them to act with due gravity.

With regard to submitting this point ("Justification") to the consideration of the Universities, your Majesty says that it has not been approved of for private reasons, *and as touching the superiority of the Pope*. The ecclesiastics say that the reason is to safeguard the prestige and authority of the Council itself, and those on your Majesty's side and the Pope's friends are at one on this point. When the intention (*i.e.* to submit the question to the Universities) was made public from Rome, I am informed that they were all dissatisfied with it. There is no doubt that the expedient of spreading the doctrine respecting "Justification" by means of the Generals (of orders) and preachers is nothing but wind. Touching the Bull on the question of prelates' residence, the matter is much discussed between them, and they are agreed that when the Council closes the Bull will either be granted in the terms they (the prelates) desire, or nothing will be conceded.

I have not seen the heads of the demands sent by the Spanish churches, but I understand that there are many things concerning not only these churches but others also, which are necessary, and may be justly granted by Sovereigns, in case they are not conceded by the Pope: and I am informed by learned men that this may be done without the princes being guilty of disobedience. Your Majesty will have seen by my former letter the discussion we held respecting the suspension of the Council; and that no suggestion was made by us that we had any knowledge of your Majesty's wishes on

1546.

the subject. Having regard to the past and present circumstances and needs, I wish to remind your Majesty that in the Cardinal of Trent's instructions there is a clause, saying that, in the event of the removal of the Council being urged, we are to endeavour at least to obtain a vacation or suspension. Coupling this instruction with the above-mentioned facts, and the evil way they were proceeding with the "Justification" article, it seemed to us that it would be a worse thing for the Council to end badly even than to consent to its removal or dissolution; whilst the least disagreeable alternative would be a suspension. I have informed the Cardinals of Trent and Jaen* of your Majesty's wishes, in order that they may manage affairs accordingly.

Venice, 16 December, 1546.

17 Dec.
Vienna.
Imp. Arch.

367. VAN DER DELFT to LOYS SCORS.

I have taken possession of the eleven packets brought by the bearer,† and will deal with them as directed. I am still of opinion, under correction, that on no account is it advisable that the Scots here should receive any fresh information as to a new arrangement (with the Emperor), in order to avoid arousing any distrust of us on the part of the English. It appears as if the Scots intended by dissimulation to lead things to their advantage on both sides; for, notwithstanding the agreement arrived at with them in Antwerp, you will learn how they have treated us. During the last four or five days they have captured an Antwerp ship and full cargo from London; and, to judge by their attitude during the first conference about it, it does not appear very desirable that we should agree with these people here; who, in my opinion, have simply come hither for the purpose of temporising. The King of France, who, as I wrote to the Queen (Dowager), has sent M. d'Oysif to Scotland, also, no doubt, thinks to work his way the better whilst these ambassadors are here. The English (Councillors) are fully of this opinion, as I have learnt since I wrote my letter to the Queen.

The English are secretly making great naval preparations, and those here who are supposed to know inform me that the King of France also is making great preparations to enter into the Emperor's Flanders dominions. My own opinion is that it is the English who will be those to feel it most. I have, however, been unable to ascertain anything further about the intrigue which is being carried on, beyond what I have written to her Majesty. Paulin, with the French ambassador, is still at Oatlands with the King, who is to come to Greenwich for the Christmas holidays. I will seek every opportunity to communicate with Secretary Paget. I can see not the slightest reason for fear or doubt on this side; but still it is well that the Netherlands are well provided, for the French galleys have not been kept together for nothing. It may well happen, however, that the blow may fall entirely on this coast, the chance of attacking us having failed, and the King (of England)

---

* Don Pedro Pacheco, Bishop of Jaen.
† The safe-conducts under cover of which commerce was to be carried on, pending a permanent arrangement between Scotland and Flanders.

1546.

resisting all their persuasions to aid their plans. I sent yesterday to the Lord Chancellor for some private business, and he returned a message to me, to the effect that he had forgotten when I was in the Council to speak to me about the case of the Duke of Norfolk and his son. It was, he said, pitiable that persons of such high and noble lineage should have undertaken so shameful a business as to plan the seizure of the government of the King by sinister means. The King, he said, was too old to allow himself to be governed; and in order absolutely to usurp the government, they (the Duke and his son) intended to kill all the Council, whilst they alone obtained complete control over the prince.

London, 17 December, 1546.

20 Dec.
Simancas.
E. R. 873.

368. JUAN HURTADO DE MENDOZA to the EMPEROR.

On the 19th instant Cardinal Farnese sent for me; and although I expected some elucidation of the progress of affairs, I was not prepared to find, as I did, that Cardinals Sfondrato and Ardinguello would be there with Farnese and Santa Flor. In the presence of Maffei they began to expound the reply to my mission. With regard to the Council, they had nothing to say, as affairs had changed since I left. Touching the 500,000 crowns, they said that the Pope and the Consistory had always understood that the grant was to be conditional, and that unless your Majesty gave a recompense the utmost they could do was to concede a Bull for 400,000 on the fabrics and the monasteries, in view of the above-mentioned fact, and also that the Pope had granted other favours charged upon Spanish ecclesiastical possessions. With respect to the 100,000 crowns, his Holiness had not undertaken to furnish the sum. Touching our claim that, since the Pope had not sent the full number of men or amount of wages agreed upon, the proportion lacking to comply with the terms of the treaty should be provided; namely that his Holiness should send and pay 12,000 infantry: they replied that the Pope thought he had fulfilled the undertaking, but if this was disputed the matter might be discussed in a friendly way, as he is anxious that the treaty obligations should be carried out scrupulously. With regard to the prolongation (of the existing treaty) they said, seeing the differences that might arise (judging from the past) on that subject, and considering that in the present circumstances the need was not so pressing as at first, it would suffice for his Holiness, who has hitherto not failed in his duty, to say that he would not fail in the future: doing what he could, having regard to the expenses already incurred, and this they now declared in his Holiness' name.

I replied at length to all these points; expressing dissatisfaction at the decisions, and ended by saying that my instructions were so drafted that I could not depart a hairsbreadth from them, Juan de Vega's instructions being conceived in the same way. I would discuss the matter with Vega, and we would together see the Pope; who, we still hoped, would consent to all that we asked of him, as we thought your Majesty's labours and goodwill deserved.

(The writer then relates that the Cardinals complained of various, stated, points of no present importance).

1546.

When the interview was ended I went out in company with Secretary Maffei, who I fancied had something to add. I therefore began to deplore that after so long a delay such an answer should have been given to me, and he comforted me by saying that they would do better than they had promised. What I could gather from him was this: that if the 100,000 ducats lacking to make up the 500,000 were requested to be charged on the ecclesiastical property in the kingdom of Naples it might be granted, but in such case we should have to give way on the question of the supplementary grant. He said this was simply his own advice to me, and he spoke without instructions. I beg your Majesty's orders, and in the meanwhile Vega and I will not cease to gain what ground we may, whilst adhering to my instructions and your Majesty's letter of 5th instant.—Rome, 20 December, 1546.

20 Dec.
Simancas,
K. 73.

369. PRINCE PHILIP to the EMPEROR.

(Letter of 24 October received, and later indirect news of Emperor's good health; prays the Emperor relieve their anxiety by sending further intelligence, etc.)

Your Majesty will have learnt that the galleys carried from Spain 200,000 crowns in gold, but no silver, and we doubt not that your Majesty will ere this have had it forwarded from Genoa, where we hope that it arrived some time ago. With regard to the loans, your Majesty will see by the enclosed statement how much we have been able to collect.[*] With these funds we have completed the payments to Andrea Doria, and two instalments of wages to the jewel-keepers, for which purposes the money that was taken to send to your Majesty in the galleys was intended.

I have learnt from your Majesty's letters that Queen Mary (of Hungary) had sent to arrange with the Scots respecting the ships belonging to your Majesty's subjects which they had captured. Your Majesty's reply on the matter was wise. The Council here has discussed it, and they have agreed again to warn the mariners to sail well protected, so that no damage may be done to them. They have been warned to this effect twice already, but it has not much effect. I have communicated also with the Council of the Indies what your Majesty writes, in order that they may consider and provide what can be done to safeguard the ships coming from the Indies. I will report the result to your Majesty, but as these things cannot be done without money, the same difficulty occurs in this as in all else.

(The rest of the letter (two pages) is occupied with Spanish internal questions of no present interest.)—Madrid, 20 December, 1546.

24 Dec.
Vienna.
Imp. Arch

370. VAN DER DELFT to the EMPEROR.

My last letter to your Majesty was dated 14th instant; and since then I went to see the Councillors, to whom the King had referred me to make my statement of the complaints of your subjects.

---

[*] That is the forced loans levied at the orders of the Emperor, before Cobos had devised his scheme for seizing all the specie obtainable, regardless of prior claims, and sending it to Genoa.

1546.

After I had laid before them several instances of wrong and injury they had suffered, I complained of the small results obtained by your Majesty's commissioner and myself; we having been delayed not only the forty days provided in the agreement of Utrecht, but nearly eight months. I found them (the Councillors) more obstinate than I have ever known them to be, and they finally postponed the whole matter until the return of the King to London. The assembly of Councillors was a large one, as they were occupied in the question of the Duke of Norfolk and his son, who are prisoners, but they made no mention whatever to me of the subject. The next day, however, the Lord Chancellor sent me a message by my man saying that the cause of their arrest was that they had planned by sinister means to obtain the government of the King, who was too old now to allow himself to be governed. Their (*i.e.* Norfolk and Surrey's) intention was to usurp authority by means of the murder of all the members of the Council, and the control of the prince by them alone. The Earl of Surrey, however, had not been under arrest in his (the Chancellor's) house for this plot, but in consequence of a letter of his, full of threats, written to a gentleman. Two other gentlemen of faith and honour subsequently came forward and charged them with this conspiracy. With regard to the son, though he has always been so generous to his countrymen, there is not one of them, however, devoted to him, but regards him as suspect; and the earl appeared much downcast on his way to the house. The feeling against the father is less severe. The Duke, both in the barge and on entering the Tower, publicly declared that no person had ever been carried thither before who was a more loyal servant of his prince than he was, and always had been. The fate of both of them will soon be known, as the King, who has now arrived here, is keeping himself very secluded at Court, all persons, but his Councillors and three or four gentlemen of his chamber, being denied entrance; the King, it is said, being deeply engaged, and much perplexed in the consideration of this affair. It is understood that he will be thus occupied during the holidays and some days in addition, the Queen and all the courtiers having gone to Greenwich, though she (*i.e.* Queen Catherine Parr) has never been known before to leave him on solemn occasions like this. I do not know what to think or suspect. Although the King recently told me, as an excuse for not receiving me when I sought audience, that he had suffered from a sharp attack of fever, which had lasted in its burning stage for thirty hours, but that he was now quite restored, his colour does not bear out the latter statement, and he looks to me greatly fallen away. In order to discover whether, under the pretext of considering the affair of these prisoners, an attempt was being made to conceal any indisposition of the King, I found means to send my man to the Lord Admiral. Whilst he was at Court, where he slept that night, he learnt from a friend that the King was not at all well, though he had seen him dressed on the previous day. But, Sire, I do not think, in any case, that I ought to conceal my opinion from your Majesty of affairs here, which change almost daily.

Four or five months ago great enquiries and prosecutions were carried out against the heretics and sacramentarians, but they have

1546.

now ceased, since the Earl of Hertford and the Lord Admiral have resided at court. The publicly expressed opinion, therefore, that these two nobles are in favour of the sects may be accepted as true, and also that they have obtained such influence over the King as to lead him according to their fancy. In order to avoid this, some of the principal Councillors to whom I had pointed out the evils and dangers threatened by these sects, unless they were vigorously opposed, requested me some time ago to address the King to a similar effect, as I wrote to your Majesty at the time. I find them (the Councillors) now of a different aspect, and much inclined to please and entertain the Earl and the Admiral; neither of whom has ever been very favourably disposed towards your Majesty's subjects. This being the case, and since those who were well disposed have changed, it may be assumed that these two have entirely obtained the favour and authority of the King. A proof of this is, that nothing is now done at court without their intervention, and the meetings of the Council are mostly held in the Earl of Hertford's house. It is even asserted here that the custody of the prince and the government of the realm will be entrusted to them; and the misfortunes that have befallen the house of Norfolk may well have come from the same quarter. As regards the diversity of religion, the people at large are to a great extent on their (*i.e.* Seymour and Dudley's) side, the majority being of these perverse sects, and in favour of getting rid of the bishops. They do not, indeed, conceal their wish to see the Bishop of Winchester and other adherents of the ancient faith sent to the Tower to keep company with the Duke of Norfolk. All this makes it probable that in the parliament which begins next month some strange acts and constitutions will be passed. I have always found the King personally strongly in favour of preserving the friendship with your Majesty, and I understand that he will never change in this respect; but it is to be feared that if God take him, which I trust will not be the case for many years, the change will cause trouble, and plunge everything here into confusion. For the reasons stated above, therefore, I am the less surprised, Sire, that the better the news that reaches here of the progress of your Majesty's affairs in Germany, the more difficult do I find the Council in my negotiations with them. Your Majesty will be better able to judge than anyone of the significance and tendency of all this; and I pray for pardon if I have ventured too far in laying before you my suspicions and opinions, which I would far rather prove false than true.

Captain Paulin is still here, awaiting a reply to his demands both as to the prisoners and the galley, and as to the delimitation proceedings in the Boulognais. There is no doubt that he hoped to carry through the intrigue already commenced (of which your Majesty has been informed), under the cloak of settling the old quarrels; but he did not find these people responsive.* I hear from a secret and perfectly trustworthy source that they (*i.e.* the English Councillors) look upon him as a cunning blade (*fin gallant*) whose coming is simply for the purpose of deceiving and playing

---

* That is to say the suggestion for a joint *coup de main* of England, France, and the Protestants on the Dutch coast to divert the Emperor's forces from Germany.

1546.

with them, until the Scots are thoroughly well supplied with provisions and munitions of war from France. The French and Scots are very active in this matter, and doubtless the Scottish embassy is directed to the same end, since the ambassadors are tarrying here so long without doing anything. It is said here that the Castle of St. Andrews is well provided with food, and remains firm for the King of England; although those who killed the Cardinal and held the castle have now come hither to the King.

London, 24 December, 1546.

24 Dec.
Vienna.
Imp. Arch.

371. VAN DER DELFT to the QUEEN DOWAGER.

I am writing to the Emperor to say that the King is so unwell that, considering his age and corpulence, fears are entertained that he will be unable to survive further attacks, such as he recently suffered at Windsor. God preserve him! for if he should succumb there is but slight hope of the change being for the better. The King is here in London; the Queen being at Greenwich. It is an innovation for them to be thus separated during the festivities. The common rumour is that he is occupied in the matter of the Duke of Norfolk and his son, who are prisoners, and he does not wish to be disturbed. The only persons allowed at Court are his Privy Council and some of his Gentlemen of the Chamber. I requested audience of the Council lately, but they deferred the interview for two or three days, on the pretext that they were very busy, but said that they would send me word when they could see me. I have, however, up to the present, not received any summons from them, and, to judge by appearances, there does not seem much chance of my having a prompt opportunity of questioning them, as they are extremely busy about these prisoners, for reasons which I have stated in my letter to the President (*i.e.* Scors).

Captain Paulin is also still here, and cannot obtain the despatch of the claims on behalf of private persons, the captured galley, and the delimitation of the Bonlognais. There is no doubt that he had the idea of carrying through the intrigue of which your Majesty knows, under cover of negotiations for the settlement of old disputes and claims, but he did not find these people so compliant as he hoped. I learn from a secret, but perfectly trustworthy source, that the English look upon him as a cunning blade (fin gallant) who has only come hither to deceive and entertain them, whilst the Scots are being supplied from France with the stores and munitions necessary for war, in which provision both the French and the Scots will be diligent. The Scottish embassy here is doubtless to serve the same object, seeing that it has remained here so long without doing anything. It is asserted here that the castle of St. Andrews is well supplied with victuals, and remains firm for the King of England; although those who killed the Cardinal and held St. Andrews have come hither to the King.

London, 24 December, 1546.

24 Dec.
Vienna.
Imp. Arch.

372. The QUEEN DOWAGER to VAN DER DELFT.

The ambassador resident here from the King of England handed to us on the 19th instant your letter of the 14th; and afterwards

1546.

informed us by the King's orders of the arrest of the Duke of Norfolk and his son, the Earl of Surrey; adding that God had been very merciful to the King in having preserved him from the treason of the duke and the earl. They had, he said, so influenced a large number of those surrounding the King as to bring them to their side, and had planned to depose (defaire) the King and seize the government of the young prince, and of the realm, perhaps with the intention of subsequently dealing with the prince in the same way as with his father, and taking possession of the kingdom. Although they were at first only suspected of a plan for seizing the control of the prince and the realm, yet the Earl of Surrey, upon being interrogated, had confessed the whole treason. We thanked the ambassador for his communication, saying that we rejoiced that God had preserved the King from such a danger: and we advise you in order that you may know what passed, since you say in your letters that you did not know the reason of the arrest.

The French ambassador here, some time since, expressed to us his master's sincere wish that some means could be found for establishing harmony and friendship between the Emperor, his dominions and subjects, and Scotland and the Scots; adding that, if we wished it, he would be very glad to exert his good offices with this object. He signified that the King (of France) would be much gratified if he were requested to act as an intermediary. Being uncertain of the object they had in so openly expressing this desire, and fearing that perhaps they were aiming at arousing distrust between the King of England and us, we replied to the ambassador, that after the treaty of Crespy the Scottish ambassador had very urgently solicited, through the ministers of the King of France, their inclusion in the said treaty. This was decidedly refused, and the Scottish ambassador was plainly told that no peace negotiations would be entered into with them, except in accord with the King of England. We were subsequently informed, both by the King of France and the King of England, that in their recent peace treaty they had included the Emperor and the Scots; and we consequently sent an envoy to Scotland for the purpose of learning from the Scots whether they considered that this inclusion made them at peace with his Imperial Majesty and his subjects. The Scots replied to our envoy (Strick) that they did not consider themselves at peace with us, but would send an envoy to us to negotiate. Since then they had sent an embassy to England, to discuss the inclusion referred to, and you had intervened in the discussion on behalf of the Emperor. We were, however, as yet ignorant of the result that might be attained by the discussions; but if the Scots chose to send a mission to us we would willingly listen to what they had to say; and if we found them amenable to reason we would readily reciprocate. We did not go beyond this, as we have no intention whatever of negotiating with them, except with the co-operation and consent of the King of England in accordance with the provisions of the treaty of alliance. Subsequent to this the King of France again signified his ardent desire to be useful in the matter, and sent an envoy to Scotland, for the purpose, as he told us, of persuading the Scottish Government, unless it desired to forfeit the friendship of France, to become reconciled

1546.

to us. The French envoy came hither on his way to Scotland, to ask us if we had anything we desired to send thither, but we let him go without confiding any message to him. The imperial ambassador in France writes that the principal object of the envoy is to inform the Scottish Government that the King of France wishes them to send ambassadors to us, to induce us to include the Scots in the treaty of Crespy, which we have no intention whatever of doing. You may communicate this to the English ministers, so that they may, as soon as possible, settle what terms they can make with the Scottish ambassadors. You may tell the latter, if the English wish you to do so, that we do not intend to enter into any negotiation with them, except conjointly with the King of England; and, if the French try to represent their embassy to Scotland in any other light than that set forth above, you may assure the English ministers that affairs are exactly as we have represented them.

The Count-Elector Palatine is sending some wines to the King of England, which have passed through here.* They are in charge of a young man, a son of M. Antoine de Metz. You may let some of your people address him, on the pretext that you know his father, and show him attention, in order to discover from him—if you cannot do so from the English ministers—whether he has been instructed to carry on any other plot; as he was formerly sent to France on some mission from his master. Let us know what you can learn. We hear that the young man is a pretty good tippler, and when in his cups he blurts out all he knows.

We send you the latest news we have from Germany, not from the Emperor's camp, but by private letters from Spires and Mayence, and you can communicate it to the English ministers.

Please push forward the claims of the Emperor's subjects having estates in the Boulognais, that we may know at once what the King intends to do about it.

Binche, 24 December, 1546.

27 Dec.
Vienna.
Imp. Arch.

373. VAN DER DELFT to LOYS SCORS.

I gave the enclosed packet for the Queen to a sailor who was ready to leave, but he and several others were seized for the King's service, it is said in the revictualling of Boulogne. Councillor Van der Burgh afterwards went to Paget, as he reports to her Majesty in his letter enclosed. I hear that the Councillors have been several times, and indeed go daily, to the Tower to examine the two prisoners.† The King is said to be better, and intends in a day or two to accord an audience to the French ambassador, who has insisted upon seeing him. I will use every effort to discover with what satisfaction Paulin will leave here.—London, 27 December, 1546.

29 Dec.
Simancas.
E. 1318.

374. DIEGO HURTADO DE MENDOZA to the EMPEROR.

The Seigniory has appointed Navagero, formerly ambassador to your Majesty, to be ambassador in England. I may remind your

---

* The Elector Palatine Frederick had now become reconciled with the Emperor and had withdrawn his troops.
† The Duke of Norfolk and the Earl of Surrey.

1546.

Majesty that I have twice reported that they were discussing this, and that it was a joint trick of the English and French to which it was suspected the Pope was a party. I may also remind your Majesty that I said that Cardinal Farnese had told me that the Pope intended to send him to France to negotiate a peace between the King and your Majesty.

It may be concluded that this ambassador (Navagero) is going to negotiate some league between France and England and this Seigniory. I will do my utmost here to learn what is afoot, and your Majesty will instruct your ambassador in England on the subject.*

I think from this that the government (of Venice) is in the hands of persons ill affected towards your Majesty. Most of them are young and with little experience: some very poor and some very rich. The poor wish for novelty, in order to make themselves rich, whilst the rich are afraid and distrustful of your Majesty. So that by different roads they both travel to the same goal, notwithstanding the lack of money.

Your Majesty must know that there are two councils here; one, called the Council of Petitions, where everything is finally settled, and which does not desire war with your Majesty; and the other the Council of Ten, where matters are discussed and prepared for decision. This latter Council is ill disposed towards your Majesty's interests and frequently deceives the other Council.

Venice, 29 December, 1546.

No date.
Simancas.
E. 1318.

375. Details of an interview between DIEGO HURTADO DE MENDOZA and the VENETIAN SEIGNIORY.

(Whilst professing a desire on the part of the Emperor to be friendly with Venice, Mendoza complained specifically of the unfriendly attitude of the Seigniory. The following are the heads of the complaint.

Their ministers had done their utmost to dissuade the Pope from joining in the league against the Lutherans.

They had advised the Protestants to hold out for four months, after which the Seigniory would help them to a settlement or otherwise.

They were in close communications with the Lutherans.

They were negotiating with the Turk to attack Hungary, and thus impede the war against the Lutherans.

His Majesty was greatly surprised at all this, as he had given no cause for such action.

The Seigniory expressed much surprise at such allegations; which were the invention of enemies, and defended themselves specifically against them.)

---

* Secretary Zambon had thitherto represented the Seigniory in London as agent. Repeated requests had been made by Henry, through his resident minister in Venice, Sigismund Harvel, and his special envoy, Ludovico delle Arme, that a regularly accredited ambassador from Venice should be sent. The deliberations of the Council of Ten on the subject and the appointment of Navagero will be found in the Venetian Calendar of the date. Ludovico delle Arme was at this period accused of the murder of Mafio Bernardo, a Venetian noble, but was spared from prosecution until the consent of the King of England was obtained. He was soon afterwards beheaded for the crime.

1546.

"With regard to the third point, they said that a certain Baltasar Altieri, Secretary of the English ambassador, had presented to them some letters from the Protestant German legates, but they contained nothing beyond a recommendation of the person of the bearer.* He had subsequently presented to them other letters from the legates of the Protestants at Ulm praying them not to allow free passage through Venetian territory nor victuals, etc., to the Papal troops being sent to Germany. The Seigniory had paid no attention to these letters, as had been proved by the fact that they had allowed passage and victuals to the said troops. They had had no further communications with these Protestants."

(They deny emphatically and at length that they had negotiated with the Turk anything to the Emperor's prejudice.†)

1547.
1 Jan.
Simancas.
E. B. 874.

376. JUAN DE VEGA to the EMPEROR.

Your Majesty will learn from Don Juan de Mendoza's letters the progress of the commission entrusted to him, in accordance with the instructions given to him, and sent to me in your Majesty's letters to me of 28 October and 5 December last.

It is quite evident that the reason for the Pope's recent efforts for peace is his idea that if peace be secured he may avoid helping your Majesty any further; employing for the purpose his usual artifices and arguments twisted to his own ends. The last time Don Juan and I went to see him, which was on Wednesday, 29th December, Don Juan politely and respectfully urged upon him the need for promptitude in settling the business upon which he had come, at the same time deploring the delay that had already taken place, and the little progress made since Cardinal Farnese's return, which we had always been assured was the only thing they were waiting for. The Pope, in his reply to this, founded his excuses and his avoidance of further aiding your Majesty upon the talk of the necessity for peace. He dwelt so long on this point that to repeat it would be prolix, and his arguments were to a great extent too irrelevant for me to reproduce in writing, though I had a good mind to tell his Holiness that they were so. The gist of all his talk was that he had always desired peace, and following the footsteps of Christ, he had always striven to bring it about, as occupying His place on earth, however unworthily. If peace had been hitherto desirable, it was now more urgently needed than ever, in order that German affairs might be successfully settled. He set forth that, though your Majesty was now on the top (supra), this being the expression he used, much still remained to be done. The Turks, he said, were arming, and the King of France would unite with the Lutherans; and the best remedy for it all was to make peace, especially since the French appeared now to desire it, and his Holiness hinted thus that he had recently been informed of this

---

* Details of the negotiations carried on between "Balthasar Alterius" and the Seigniory will be found in the Venetian Calendar. In an earlier page of the present volume there is an account of his having sought the position of representative of the confederate princes of Germany to the Seigniory. Van der Delft had complained of this to the English Council.

† Similar protestations were sent by the Seigniory to their agent with the Emperor, Alvise Mocenigo, who had in October informed his Government of what was being said on the subject in the Emperor's chamber.

tendency anew. He said that he, having always kept himself neutral by the best means in his power, now found himself in the thirteenth year of his Pontificate. The French were suspicious and rash, and he did not wish to give them cause for believing that he fed and promoted wars by providing resources to your Majesty, which would make them think that he would be a bad instrument for arranging peace, now, he said, vitally necessary. I replied that peace in the abstract was good for its own sake, and praised him for his efforts at pacification, and for the prudent considerations he had set forth, especially about the Turk and the King of France, but I thought it would even be more prudent to prevent the occurrence of the dangers suggested, which might be done by aiding your Majesty liberally, so that you might promptly subjugate the Germans and impose peace in that part of the world. I said that your Majesty was rather more than "on the top" in the struggle, for the principal ringleader, both in point of position and criminality, the late Duke of Saxony, had been soundly punished, and the Landgrave partially so, the former having lost his territories and electoral dignity, and the latter his assumed authority, since he had taken to flight. As to the rest of Germany, some of the insurgents had surrendered and others were seeking your Majesty's mercy. As soon as this German matter was settled, the Turk would take care what he did and peace would be then so much the nearer. The signs of it were, I said, already visible; for the King (of France) was more inclined to it than before, now that your Majesty's affairs were more prosperous. His Holiness, I said, no doubt meant well; and we all wished for peace, but we differed as to the process by which it might be attained; and I could not avoid saying that it was an indecent and reprehensible action for the King of France to ask the Pope, out of consideration for him, to cease helping your Majesty in an enterprise so advantageous to the faith and the interests of religion. He immediately denied that the French had made any such request to him. But as I have written to your Majesty, I have positive knowledge that, not only have they done so, but his Holiness has promised them to withhold assistance to your Majesty. His Holiness again turned to the subject of peace, endeavouring to refute the arguments I had used, although he spoke more moderately than before. I replied as before; praising peace in principle, and saying that your Majesty had always loved it, and still did so; but I had no authority, nor had Don Juan, to deal in the matter. I urged the Pope to settle the matter entrusted to us, and to write to your Majesty as he pleased about peace.

The day before we saw the Pope, I had a letter of advice from the Cardinals of Trent and Jaen, of which copy is enclosed, saying, that the day previously a meeting of the Cardinals who are appointed a Commission on the matters of the Council, had been held, where it was decided, Cardinal Morone alone dissenting, that the decree on the article of justification should be published. Morone set forth the many difficulties and disagreed with the rest. In view of your Majesty's letter to Don Diego de Mendoza, and the instructions to Don Juan, I thought that, unless the Pope was spoken to on the subject—which he seemed himself to wish to

1547.

keep secret—he might allege later that not even your Majesty's ambassador, or anyone else, had referred to it or pointed out the need for deep consideration in the matter; and I therefore decided to take action.

After disposing of the questions referred to above, I told his Holiness that I had to mention a matter of the highest importance, and I only did so in the best interests of himself and your Majesty. In order to mollify and prevent him from getting angry at what I had to say, I continued that from Cardinals Trent and Jaen, and Don Diego de Mendoza, I had learnt that the Council intended to declare and publish the article on Justification; and from your Majesty's communications I knew the many objections that existed to the publication of the article at present; or indeed that anything should be done in the Council hurriedly, before your Majesty had time to bring the Germans to agree to it, and for the prelates and others to remedy the religious troubles; the state of religion being such that the only cure possible was by means of the Council. If this article were published, I said, it would look like a condemnation of these people (*i.e.* the German dissentients) without hearing them. Don Juan added some words to the same effect, and concluded by saying that we spoke in all love and charity—convinced that his Holiness would act for the best. He replied that he was ignorant of what your Majesty had written on the subject, or else he had forgotten it, thus hinting that he was under the impression that the objections we had brought forth were founded on the article itself, and passing over the arguments we had used to prove that our objection was to the time and manner of promulgating it. I replied that there was no objection to the article being adopted; for we believed what the Church believed; but the objection was to the mode of procedure, as we had submitted to his Holiness, and your Majesty had pointed out in Don Juan's instructions, &c.

He seemed to take note of what I said, and we thought that he would act cautiously, avoiding publishing the article so soon as the people thought. But the matter remained doubtful, and the Pope told us to show what the instructions said on the point, and Don Diego's communication, to Cardinals Cresentio, Sfrondrato and Ardinguello, after which the question would be considered.

Don Juan and Marquina afterwards went to see these Cardinals, and read the instructions etc. and your Majesty's letter to Don Diego, saying that your Majesty wished the matter to be dealt with in a way that would enable the best results for religion to be obtained from what had been done by force of arms in Germany. Cresentio discussed the question at great length with Don Juan, and the impression left upon us is that they are still undecided how they shall act. They seem, indeed, to be frightened, and this confirms what I have said before to your Majesty, that the more boldly they are spoken to about the Council the more tractable they are, and, to say the truth, I think that the same course might be adopted in other matters as well. The Pope hinted—and the Cardinal afterwards told Don Juan plainly—that he intends to send an envoy to your Majesty respecting the peace (*i.e.* with France), and also, as it seems, respecting the continuance of the enterprise

1547.

(against the Protestants). He is acting in accord with the French ambassador and his adherents here, and I learn from two trustworthy sources that the French do not believe that the Pope really desires peace or that he will be a means of bringing it about. They think his present action in the matter is mainly prompted by a desire to find a pretext for avoiding the giving of further aid to your Majesty. These same people, however, say that the King of France is more anxious for peace than ever, a sure sign that he dreads what may happen if it be not made.

Soon after the news came of the rout and flight of the enemy, the King of France wrote to his ambassador, instructing him to assure the Pope that it had not been a flight, but simply a strategical retreat, and that he must not imagine that the Smalkaldic league was weak. The French party in Rome are still saying the same thing.

Rome, 1 January, 1547.

Note.—A letter from Don Juan de Mendoza to the Emperor of the same date gives similar information to the above. He dwells at great length upon the various excuses and devices adopted by the Pope, Cardinal Farnese, etc., for the purpose of delaying the granting the additional subventions which the Emperor requested. The letter is not reproduced here, as all the points are more clearly set forth in Vega's letter and in Don Juan's previous letter (page 531).

9 Jan.
Vienna.
Imp. Arch.

377. VAN DER DELFT to the QUEEN DOWAGER.

My last letters were dated 24th ultimo, and I received your Majesty's letters with those from the Emperor on the 4th instant, an hour after those from Secretary Bave of 25th ultimo came to hand with good news from his Majesty. When I have an opportunity of access to the King, I will not fail to fulfil your Majesty's orders. There is however at present no possibility of my obtaining audience, owing to his indisposition. Captain Paulin has been unable to see him, and is far from pleased thereat. Some of the principal members of his suite, even, do not hide their suspicion that on the pretence that the King wishes to see and speak to Paulin before he leaves they have been kept here for two months out of artfulness. Nevertheless it is said that as soon as the courier they have sent to the King of France returns, they will have audience here. I have made most diligent enquiries to discover what it means, but have only been able to learn that it all depends upon the differences existing between them (*i.e.* the English and French). It is certain that a very intimate friend of his said "If Paulin had only listened to me he would not have pushed his negotiations so far as he has done, but would have left the ambassador to do it, and thus would have avoided this annoyance. It would be much more advisable that he (Paulin) should be by the side of our master (*i.e.* the King of France), who is making a port between Dieppe and Havre Neuf at a place called Fécamp, for the shelter of his galleys. The galleys, too, are being repaired, and 20 new ones being built at Marseilles."[*]

---

[*] Baron de la Garde (Captain Paulin) was commander of the galleys of France, and the meaning of the passage is that he would be more useful there than wasting time in England.

1547.

Yesterday a gentleman of the Chamber named Morrison* left here for Denmark. I understand that the object of his going is to keep the Danes friendly, and prevent them from giving assistance to the Scots. He also wishes to take measures for being able to raise troops there when they want them. I learn that they (the English) are taking the Scottish war very much to heart. They are making great preparations; but I perceive very clearly that they do not feel at all sure of the French. They are extremely suspicious of the French galleys, especially as fresh supplies are constantly being sent to Boulogne. And as in this last war England lost the flower of her men, they are obliged to employ foreigners. If the French attempt anything against them whilst the Emperor is in Germany, they (the English) will have no chance of obtaining either Germans or Spaniards. I believe also that they are thinking of getting men in Oestlandt and Neumark, and they are trying in Italy.

Parliament is to open next week and the oath of allegiance as successor to the crown will be taken to the Prince, the son of this King, as soon as possible. The discourse here about it is variable.

I received some time ago a letter from your Majesty ordering me to speak to the King in favour of a gentleman of Moravia called Stephen d'Assenberg, said to be a pensioner of the King, and directing me to aid the gentleman to the best of my ability. I would, of course, never willingly fail to do all that your Majesty may please to command; but nevertheless I have thought best to defer complying with your orders in this respect, until your Majesty is made aware of the difficulty I find in it. Before my first coming hither d'Assenberg had fallen into disgrace with the King and all the Councillors, for certain evil acts of his which they say injured them to the extent of several thousands of pounds sterling. After absenting himself for some time he returned, in hope that the late Duke of Suffolk would befriend him. When I first arrived here I found him in the midst of his suit, which in the end turned out completely fruitless; and he then departed from here for Oestlandt, and nothing has been heard of him for two years. I therefore doubt if the King would take in good part any attempt at intercession for a person with whom he is so deeply offended. I have also ascertained that all the members of the Council are against him, and for this he has only himself to thank; because whilst he was in favour with the King he was not sufficiently respectful to the Council, which was imprudent in a foreigner, and his business therefore offers many difficulties. I pray your Majesty to instruct me as to whether you desire me to importune at the present time in so unpleasant an affair.

London, 9 January, 1547.

10 Jan.
Vienna.
Imp. Arch.

378. THE QUEEN DOWAGER to VAN DER DELFT.

By the enclosed extract, you will see the discourse addressed to us by the French ambassador, and our reply to him. The only object seems to be to stir up a fresh war; and we think well to inform you of this, so that you may know what is going on here; redoubling your vigilance to investigate the proceedings adopted by the French

---
* Sir Richard Moryson, afterwards ambassador in Germany.

1547.

ministers towards the King of England, and to sound the feelings of the King and his ministers as regards the Emperor's interests. If you learn that Paulin has taken leave of the King dissatisfied with the outcome of his negociations, you may tell Secretary Paget, in confidence, that the French ambassador here has given us notice of the retention of the Swiss and their captains, whom the King of France is raising in Germany for his service. These troops have been mustered and reviewed, and other mercenaries are being raised, though on the emphatic assurance of the King of France that they are not intended for service against his Imperial Majesty or his dominions. We are not inclined to give too much credence to these assurances; but still we should like the King of England and his ministers to know what is being done; though we do not believe that the preparations referred to are directed to his injury. But, nevertheless, the French are very cunning and cautious; and it is prudent not to depend implicitly on their words.

Do not go beyond this.

Be very careful to discover what the Protestant ambassadors who have gone by France to England are doing, and let us know. We have no fresh news from Germany, except that the Emperor has been reconciled to the Duke of Wurtemburg, who will be reinstated on conditions. Do not forget the Boulognais claims.

Binche, 10 January, 1547.

31 Jan.
Vienna.
Imp. Arch.

379. The QUEEN DOWAGER to VAN DER DELFT.

We have received from the hand of your Secretary, who is the bearer of the present, your letter of 23rd instant; and have heard what Secretary Paget proposed to you, as a means of pacifying German affairs: that the King would willingly act as intermediary if he had reason to believe that the Emperor would accept his help towards a settlement, but that he (the King of England) is anxious not to expose himself to the slight of a rebuff. We have no doubt that this proceeds from the sincere affection which the King bears to the Emperor, and from a desire that the affairs of the latter may prosper; and you will accordingly thank him for it, in our name, when opportunity offers. We know well that the intervention of no prince in Christendom would be so welcome to the Emperor as that of the King of England; but since your wish for our opinion as to whether his Imperial Majesty would at present accept his intercession, and Paget reposed confidence in you, we will inform you of the present state of affairs in Germany, according to our advices. Since the submission of the Duke of Wurtemburg and the cities of Ulm and Frankfort, the people of Augsburg have become reconciled, submitting themselves to his Majesty's clemency, and accepting the conditions prescribed to them. The Strasburg people have also sent their representatives to make a similar arrangement; although some have striven to prevent them from doing so. The ex-Elector of Saxony and the Landgrave of Hesse are seeking by every possible means to become reconciled with his Majesty; the Landgrave having even prayed our brother the King of the Romans through the Landgrave's son-in-law, Duke Maurice, to agree to an an arrangement; but as our brother the Emperor has no intention of treating these two (*i.e.* the Landgrave and the Elector of Saxony) as princes; regarding them as his vassals, and rebels who, by means of false libels and other writings, have declared him to have forfeited the Imperial crown, and to be no longer their liege lord and sovereign, with many other shameful insolences, too execrable and hateful to be repeated, his Majesty has caused them to be informed that he will not deal with them unless they submit to his mercy, or as it is called in their language, "*ingnade.*" In such case, his Majesty will make known his pleasure to them. Others whose offence has been less grave than theirs have thus made their submission: and, having regard to their great transgression and injury towards their sovereign, we do not see how his Majesty can possibly act otherwise, without a sacrifice of his dignity. Now that the cities that supported them have submitted, it may be hoped that it will be easy to punish their great insolence; and although we know that the intercession of the King of England for the Landgrave and the Saxon would be very agreeable to the Emperor, yet we are not without fear that the latter would decline to enter into any capitulations with them if they did not first submit to his good pleasure. We do not believe that, considering the King's sincere friendship for the Emperor, he would advise him to act otherwise, particularly bearing in mind the condition and quality of the offenders; who are but rebel vassals. You will communicate this to Secretary Paget, in the same strict confidence with which he addressed you, assuring him that, beyond what we have said, we are quite ignorant of the Emperor's intentions, but if we can discover anything further with regard to it, we will, with due secrecy, inform you of it. Thank him also for the good offices he performs in his Majesty's affairs.

If the French attempt to sustain the rebels, or mix themselves in this war, we trust that the Emperor will find means to resist them, and that they will be unable to avail themselves of the aid of the Turk, who, during the coming year, will not invade Hungary. According to the latest news we have from the east, the third son of the Turk, who had been sent against the Persians with a great force, was defeated, and consequently the Turk, who had come from Constantinople to Adrianople for the purpose of preparing his army for the attack of Hungary, had returned to Constantinople, and had thrown the whole of his forces against the Persian and his adherents. The Turk had also immediately sent back the ambassador of the King of the Romans, with most gracious messages, whereas before the said ambassador had the greatest of trouble even to obtain an audience. This gives us hope that, by this means, God may afford time and opportunity for a beneficent union of Christian princes, for the purpose of jointly directing their forces against the Turk.

The Emperor, in his latest letters to us, repeats what you wrote to him about the impending change of government in England, in order that we may consider what can be done to improve the way in which his interests are dealt with there and to preserve the good friendship now existing. It is desired also to know whether it would be advisable to take any fresh or special steps in this direction, for the purpose of influencing those who are at present

546 SPANISH STATE PAPERS.

1547.

in the Government, or those who may succeed to the charge of the young prince and the realm after the death of the King. You will please send us your opinion on this point, as soon as possible, and all else that may occur to you, with the object of keeping England friendly, and if there is any way of preventing the country from further surrendering itself to sectarianism.

Binche, 31 January, 1547.

17 Jan.
Vienna.
Imp. Arch.

380. The EMPEROR to VAN DER DELFT.

We have received your letters of 14th and 24th ultimo and have noted what you say, especially in the latter, with regard to the probability of changes taking place in England. You have done us very acceptable service in writing this, and as the matter is of the highest importance, needing mature consideration, we have sent a copy of your letters to the Queen Dowager, although doubtless you will already have done so. After the question has been fully discussed by the Queen Dowager and our Flemish Council, the former will instruct you as to how you are to proceed. You will carefully fulfil the orders the Queen may send you; and as the matter is referred to her, we need not deal with it at length here.

With regard to events in Germany, you will have already heard that, since our last letters, Ulm has surrendered unconditionally to our clemency and that the Frankforters have done the same. We have lodged in the latter city 4,000 foot and 300 horse. We have also pardoned the Duke of Würtemburg, who submitted absolutely to us, and has promised every assistance to us. He has, moreover, pledged himself never to allow any subject of his to serve against us in any way, and to punish rigorously those who dare to do so; he will not permit any of our enemies to oppose us in his dominion; and has undertaken all this on behalf of both himself and his son. He has bound himself to pay us within forty days (of which some have already expired) a sum of 40,000 ducats. In order that we may be still further secured in the land we have retained in our own hands the three principal fortresses in his territory chosen by ourselves. The other towns in Germany are rapidly surrendering themselves. This week Kempen, Meiningen, Ravensburg, Vivrac, and others, have done so, and we have forgiven them. We are now preparing to leave here and go to Ulm, where we shall be in touch with all affairs, and shall be able from thence to attack and bring the Augsburg people to reason; our army having already marched on the way thither. Having news that the ex-Elector had still an armed force with him in the territories of Duke Maurice of Saxony, with the intention of attempting to regain what the King of the Romans, our brother, and Duke Maurice have taken from him, we have sent reinforcements thither, which with those contributed to Duke Maurice by the King of the Romans, and the contingent of Marquis Albert of Brandenburg consisting of 1,200 horse and 8 standards of German foot, all excellent troops, will, we are confident, be sufficient to defeat the enemy entirely, and to deal with him in such a way as will render him incapable of further mischief there.

1547.

Duke Maurice will also be aided by the troops we are mustering in Westphalia, whither we have sent M. de Grüningen to prevent the towns there from aiding our enemies.

We will continue to give you an account of all that happens, so that you may convey the information to the King, and to such other persons as you consider advisable. It is also of the highest importance that you should keep us constantly informed of occurrences in England.

Heilbron, 17 January, 1547.

17 Jan.
Simancas.
E. R. 874.

381. JUAN DE VEGA to the EMPEROR.

(The Turk's general, Belerbey of Babylonia, defeated by the Sophi and the Georgians, which will give the Turk plenty to do for the present and prevent him from interfering elsewhere.)

I am informed that the publication of the decree of "Justification" will not at present be ordered, as the Pope received this news a week ago, but as the period he had spoken of for the publication will have expired by the time the present letter is received, we shall soon see if my advices are correct or not. My principal reason for writing this to your Majesty is that it should be understood that if he does not publish the decree it will probably be in consequence of this news having been added to the doubts already entertained about it, and having together brought him to a better state of mind. God grant that it may be so.

A letter has been received here from Antonio Bocio, a Genoese adherent of Count Fiesco, in which he relates to one Franco de Achavari, also a Genoese and Fiesco's agent in this Court, a remark of the Count (Fiesco) shortly before he made his attempt. He was urging upon his hearers how easy of execution the plan would be, and said in confirmation of this that Pier Luigi (Farnese) would send him from Placencia (Piacenza) a thousand foot soldiers before any other troops could arrive in Genoa to oppose him. Adding this expression to several other indications and words that have fallen, especially from Cardinal Farnese, my suspicions daily increase that the events that have happened in Genoa (Fiesco's conspiracy) were connived at by the Pope.

His Holiness has been in the country for some days, but it is said that he will soon return to Rome; and I will then endeavour to ascertain his intentions, with regard to sending the aid that he seemed inclined to contribute when the news of the surrender of Ulm was received. I will also try to expedite the other points contained in Don Juan de Mendoza's instructions. I am very sorry for the delay that has taken place in this respect; because it is causing Don Francisco de Toledo's arrival here to be deferred, and especially as no instructions have been received from your Majesty since Don Juan's arrival, as to what course should be taken in the matters at issue. Cardinal Farnese declares that he is entirely devoted to your Majesty, but at the same time he says that he has no influence whatever over his grandfather, at least so far as regards recent affairs. This appears to be the case, for nothing has been obtained through him. In addition to the fact that the Cardinal is a person upon whom small reliance can be placed, I am

1547.

of opinion that his professions of devotion to your Majesty increased recently, in proportion with the Pope's intentions to act in a way displeasing to your Majesty. As an instance of the small influence of the Cardinal, he has been unable even to obtain any settlement of the trifling sum of five or six thousand ducats, representing the exchange on the monies deposited with D. Diego de Mendoza.

Rome, 17 January, 1547.

17 Jan.
Simancas.
E.R. 644.

382. THE EMPEROR to JUAN DE VEGA.

(Notes that no progress has been made in settling the points entrusted to Don Juan de Mendoza, and can only hope that a resolution will be arrived at after the arrival (in Rome) of Cardinal Farnese, as it is hardly to be believed that they (the Papal ministers) will continue their procrastination in the face of recent events here, a summary of which is sent herewith for publication, as may be considered most advisable.)

If matters are still pending when you receive this, you will not fail to let his Holiness know how perplexed we are by the delay in the sending of his decision. He may well consider what has been written on this subject, and the great need we are now experiencing, more than ever before, for a prompt reply and the means for finishing so important a business, which by God's grace has been auspiciously commenced.

We note your information, to the effect that previous to the arrival of Cardinal Farnese, Cardinal Santa Flor intimated that the Pope would concede the 500,000 crowns demanded (on the Spanish ecclesiastical property), on condition that this should also cover the amount for the supplementary troops, and the additional 100,000 crowns that he had always given us hopes of our receiving if the enterprise went forward. You did quite right in refusing to accept this offer and in adhering to the instructions, and we feel sure you will have acted similarly in the other pending matters, whilst doing your best to obtain the prompt decision which we so much need. From what we know of the Pope's feelings, and the small amount of satisfaction at our success displayed by him and his friends (the exact opposite of what their attitude should be, considering that our principal object is God's service and the interests of religion) it will be best to appear not to notice his attitude, but to dissemble and hide your feelings until the pending questions are settled. At the same time you will express great confidence in Cardinal Farnese, in order to encourage him to aid us, as he promised us when he was here.

With regard to their talk about the peace with France, and the difficulty in continuing the assistance (*i.e.* the Papal aid to the Emperor) if the peace question is not settled, this has nothing whatever to do with our present request to his Holiness, supported by such powerful reasons; and you need say little about it, but will adhere to the answers you have already given on the point. Since we are mentioning this, we may also say, for your own information, and for use as you may find advisable, that the Nuncio came the other day to Granvelle, and told him that he had received letters from Rome, entirely on this matter of peace; adding that,

1547.

as the troops would now go into quarters, it was a good time for peace to be settled. Granvelle then asked him whether he had anything to say with regard to the points contained in Don Juan (de Mendoza's) instructions, to which he replied that he had not; and Granvelle then remarked that he (the Nuncio), being so acute as he was, might easily guess what we must think of this, and what good reason we had to be offended that he should come to us expressly to talk about the peace (with France), without mentioning a word as to the business now in hand, important as it was. He had not a word to say to this, except that he hoped a reply would soon come from his Holiness.

17 January, 1547.

23 Jan.
Vienna.
Imp. Arch.

383. THE QUEEN DOWAGER to VAN DER DELFT.

Since writing our letter of 10th instant, we have received yours of the 9th. We learn from Germany that the Duke of Würtemburg has accepted the terms arranged by his envoys, who have publicly asked the Emperor's pardon for their master's misdeeds, and have promised that in future he will be a good and loyal vassal to his Imperial Majesty. The Duke will have to pay 300,000 florins as a penalty, and the Emperor retains in his own hands four of his principal fortresses. The towns of Ulm and Frankfort have also, through their representatives, prayed for mercy, and have obtained the grace of his Imperial Majesty, and thus the whole of Upper Germany, from Frankfort towards Italy, is at the present time submissive to the Emperor, except the towns of Strasburg and Augsburg, which (latter) has sent Fugger to intercede with the Emperor, and to pray for his forgiveness. We think that Strasburg would do the same but for the intrigues of the French. The King of Denmark has sent to inform the Emperor of the endeavours that the rebels have been making to induce him (the King of Denmark) to take up arms against his Majesty. This he resolutely refused to do, but, on the contrary, had restored two vessels which had been captured from the Emperor's subjects by a pirate, on the pretext of bearing the authority of the Landgrave. The Emperor was much gratified at this, and has sent back the King of Denmark's envoy very graciously, requesting, amongst other things, that the Scots should not be allowed to frequent Denmark, or to sell their booty there until they have satisfied the Emperor and the King of England for the injuries they (the Scots) have done to their subjects. When you have an opportunity you may communicate this to the English ministers.

We are sending you herewith duplicate of a letter sent to us by Olaus, Chancellor of our brother the King of the Romans, and formerly our Councillor, from which you will learn what is being said in the East, and that the King of France divulges to the Turk everything that passes in Christendom. He has even communicated to him what has been done about Boulogne; and it will be advisable for you to let some of the English ministers know the first paragraph of the letter touching Constantinople.

The French also report that, owing to a rising at Genoa, all of Prince Doria's galleys have been lost. We have since received another account of the affair which represents it as not so bad as was represented by the French.

1547.

We again recommend you to follow up actively the question of the reinstatement of the Emperor's subjects in their properties in the Boulognais. Do not allow the affair to drag, but make every possible effort to obtain the reinstatement.

If Councillor Van der Burgh has not yet set out, let him return at once, with or without farewell audience of the King. This is necessary to safeguard our dignity, as he has remained in England too long already since their Commissioner went back, and the present procrastination is only for the purpose of delaying his departure.

We have previously written to you, as also has M. d'Eick several times, instructing you to complain to the King's Council that a certain Cornelius Bellin, residing at Calais, is daily robbing the subjects of these dominions. This man's accomplices have been executed in the town for the depredations they have committed at sea. You have never sent us any reply on this subject, and we send you herewith a memorandum from the Zeelanders, complaining of the constant menaces of this Bellin, which we order you expressly to communicate to the English Council. Inform us when you have done so.

Binche, 23 January, 1547.

25 Jan.
Simancas.
E. 75.

384. PRINCE PHILIP to the EMPEROR.

(Letter of 28 November received, and also one from F. Gonzaga of 26 December, giving an account of events. His rejoicing at the favourable progress is tempered at his sorrow to hear that the Emperor is again suffering from gout. Begs for constant news of the Emperor's health. He is very anxious.) I note your Majesty's observations, with regard to the necessity for carrying forward the enterprise upon which you are engaged, and of keeping afoot a part of the army, for the purpose of completing matters as your Majesty desires and the interests of Christendom demand. I also note the mission of Don Juan de Mendoza to his Holiness, to request the latter to complete the sum of 500,000 ducats he had granted on the Spanish monasteries, etc. Even this amount being so inadequate to the needs, I note that another means of obtaining further funds had been discussed; namely, to request the Pope to consent to your Majesty's appropriating half the gold, silver, and jewels of all the churches and monasteries of these realms, and half (the value) the cathedral fabrics; the churches, etc., that have already contributed being only called upon to pay as much as will bring up their share to the same as the rest. If his Holiness refuses this concession, I note that your Majesty's Confessor is of opinion that in so good and holy a cause you would be justified in taking this contribution on your own authority, and that your Majesty wishes us here to discuss secretly the best means for putting this plan into execution, pending the receipt of instructions from your Majesty after you had learnt the Pope's decision. In accordance with this I summoned to my presence the Marquis de Mondejar, the Archbishop of Seville, and the Council of Finance; and informed them of the substance of what had been written to Rome, at the same time informing them of your Majesty's need of help, instructing them secretly to consider the matter well, and report to me for

1547

your Majesty's information. They met several times in a room in the palace; and, finding the matter so weighty, they wished to consult the Royal Council, which, in any case, would have to intervene before the matter could be executed, and might at that juncture object because they had not been informed previously. The Archbishop of Seville therefore undertook to convey the matter to the Royal Council, and the whole of them fully discussed it in my presence, with the following result. They recognise the great importance of the enterprise in which your Majesty is engaged, and the urgent need of maintaining the army, for the purpose of completing the settlement of Germany; and the whole of them wish that your Majesty should receive the aid you require. But, though this appropriation of the treasure of the churches may be justifiable on the ground that the aid is required for the extirpation of heresy and the defence of the faith, the Council are of opinion that the measure proposed offers so many grave objections and difficulties as to render it almost impossible. Even if the Pope were to concede the permission to your Majesty, the Council believe that it would not be advantageous to your Majesty's service to adopt the course suggested, nor would it redound to the benefit of these realms, for several reasons which they submitted. Much less would this be the case if his Holiness refused his consent, seeing the evil name it would bring to your Majesty throughout Christendom, especially bearing in mind the action of the King of England towards the churches in his realm. The example cited of the King of France was not considered a sufficient justification for your Majesty's proposed step; since throughout the world your Majesty's devotion and fidelity to religion are notorious, and the difference between the actions of the one monarch and the other is recognised everywhere. In addition to this much scandal would be caused throughout Spain to see that, even before the collection of the half first fruits granted by the Pope, and whilst the clergymen who came about the congregation were still here, and so soon after the execution of the Bull expected for the 300,000 or 500,000, ducats, another for taking half the treasure should arrive. Consider, your Majesty, what perturbation would thus be caused in all people's minds, not only to the clergy, who are so influential (*que son tanta parte*) in these realms, as your Majesty knows, but still greater trouble would be caused to laymen, who would conclude that no security existed anywhere; since even sacred property devoted to divine service was not spared from attack. Charity and devotion, too, would be lost, and the people would discontinue to benefit the church, in the belief that whenever pressing need occurred a similar course to this would again be adopted. The measure moreover would be impossible of execution, because it would have to be carried out on the authority either of the Pope or of your Majesty and the Pope jointly, for your Majesty's authority alone would not be sufficient. Directly they (the clergy?) knew that the step was pending on your Majesty's authority only, not a single church or monastery in Spain would fail to hide, bury or transport everything valuable they possessed; and the clergy would claim great credit for doing so. There would be no means of compelling them to reveal what they had, or discover the treasure, and they would not hesitate to perjure themselves, if necessary, to protect it. This would result in the arrest and imprisonment of ecclesiastics, the maltreatment of religious persons, and the commission of violent and grievous acts by the officers entrusted with the execution of the measure; and it would be impossible to prevent it. Much disturbance would thus be caused in all religious circles, and perhaps even greater dangers.

In France people may tolerate such things, owing to the fact that the King of France rules rather as a despot than as a natural overlord (*señor natural*) and follows his whim rather than his reason, which your Majesty will not do; and, besides this, the French people, as your Majesty knows, are willing to put up with anything, and the difference between the two nations in this respect is very great. These realms and your subjects in them expect to be treated in a different fashion, in accordance with their character, their valour and their merits in your Majesty's service. The amount that would be obtained by executing the proposal would, moreover, be small, for the reasons stated above, as it would be quite impossible to prevent the treasure from being hidden or transported; and also in consequence of the extreme poverty and want in these realms, which would render the execution even more impossible. With affairs in their present condition here, the country so utterly exhausted, and every device or means for raising money even for daily needs and for defence being at an end, as your Majesty was recently informed, there being insufficient even to pay the officers of justice, galleys, guards, etc., the adoption of the measure proposed would drive the people to complete desperation. It is true that the enterprise in which your Majesty is engaged concerns all Christendom and the general public zeal, but it is thought that your Majesty ought to look first to the preservation of your Spanish dominions, that have served you so generously, so constantly, and so well, even though only out of obedience to our holy mother church and respect for the Holy See. For these and other reasons which were fully discussed, but need not be repeated here, although they would be manifest if an attempt were made to carry the proposal into execution, it was the unanimous opinion of all present that even if the measure were much more justifiable than it appears to be, the difficulties and obstacles to it were so many and grave as to make its execution almost, if not quite, impossible; and none of those present at the conference could see any honest way of adopting it.

It was resolved that your Majesty should be advised of this with all speed, in order that you should not continue to depend upon this means of obtaining funds. The reason that the matter has not been dealt with earlier is that the proposal, being a novel one and of grave importance, it was necessary that it should be maturely discussed and considered from all points of view; so that a decided opinion should be sent to your Majesty. It was also desired that the clergyman who came to settle with the churches about the subsidy should depart from here before the question was settled. We do not set forth here the means by which it might be possible to carry the proposal into effect, because after thus placing before you the difficulties and objections to the proposal itself, we shall be

1547.

satisfied to obey your Majesty's further orders in this respect. We pray your Majesty to consider it well, in view of the state of things here, and send your instructions. Your Majesty, it is true, did not request advice from Spain on the matter; but the whole of the persons consulted, as faithful servants and subjects, deemed necessary thus to lay before you what they thought, in order that your Majesty, in view of all the facts, and having consideration to what is due to your repute, your Christian character, your respect to the Apostolic See, and the preservation of these realms, might arrive at a final resolution worthy of your Catholic spirit. Whilst all those present were of this opinion, they desire, nevertheless, to say that they cannot imagine the reason why the Pope did not grant to your Majesty the concession for the sale of the monastic manors, since they (the monasteries) were to receive an equivalent revenue, and they would thenceforth be free from the jurisdictions and lawsuits attached to the possession of the manors; and would thus be more at liberty to attend to their sacred duties. It is thought that your Majesty should urgently renew your request for this concession; since the intention was already known in Spain, and no objection was raised to it. It was, moreover, a better looking way of obtaining funds, and touched the interests of fewer people in general; besides which an equivalent was to be given, and even though the net amount to be got by this means might not be great, it would to some extent meet your Majesty's needs.

Having in view the urgent necessity that your Majesty should be relieved somehow, I summoned the Council of Finance, to consider what other means they could devise for raising money. They have met for this purpose several times, and their recommendations are contained in a separate report. There are objections to the means they suggest, but still some funds may be got together by them. Your Majesty will please consider the whole question, and send us your commands. In order to prevent the church property from being appropriated, any other device should be welcomed, though it may not of itself be without objection.

(The Papal brief recently sent for the pardon of the Moriscoes of Granada is not worded as requested. Prays the Emperor to write to Rome, in order that it may be drafted as was required. This may be a means of raising money.)—Madrid, 25 January, 1547.

25 Jan.
Simancas.
E. 75.

385. COBOS to the EMPEROR.

(Has had a relapse and has been at death's door. His successive attacks of fever have lasted five months, during which he has hardly left his bed. Is now better, but so weak as to be unable even to sign a letter. The doctors tell him he may be strong enough soon to move from Madrid, which he does not wish to do, but the physicians say he will not recover until he has a change. He has never ceased from labouring in the Emperor's service during his sickness, and Juan de Vargas has worked well and zealously in his place, and will do so in his absence from Madrid. Congratulates the Emperor on his successful campaign, especially the surrender of Ulm, of which he had recently heard from Fernando Gonzaga, and previously from the Queen of France. Is glad the 200,000 crowns and the other funds arrived so opportunely. He has done his best in this respect, and to hear of his success is the best medicine for him.)

With regard to your Majesty's last letter respecting the fabrics of the churches, etc., his Highness (Prince Philip) has consulted the Council of Finance and the Royal Council, etc., and writes separately to your Majesty on the subject. I therefore can only refer your Majesty to his letter, though I cannot help confirming the opinions there set forth; for in good truth affairs here are in such a condition that I do not see how it would be possible to carry out the proposal. Great pains are being taken to devise some other means for obtaining money; and your Majesty may rest assured that no point shall be overlooked.

A report is being sent to-day of an agreement for a loan from Arias Pardo. If it is carried through I expect it will be possible to get from that quarter over 160,000 ducats payable at short notice. Other sales are also being attempted, and I pray your Majesty to reply promptly on the point, as it will not be a bad way to obtain some relief by this means. Efforts should also be made there (in Germany) to get the Bull for the monasteries (i.e. the sale of the monastic manors) despatched, as there will be no great difficulty in putting that into execution. . . . . Since the Prince (Philip) came from Guadalajara I have been so ill as to prevent me from seeing him and talking to him about the business your Majesty knows of. What I said and agreed with him previously I should like to write to your Majesty, but I have been, and still am, unable to do so in my own handwriting, and I must leave it until I am better. As soon as I can write, I will, before I leave here, let your Majesty know all that has passed; but I may say here only, that I trust in God that all will go well, and that nothing bad has taken place really. It was all simply boyishness, as I wrote to your Majesty.

The Infantas are well, and I hear that the Marquis Don Bernardo treats them well. As your Majesty knows, it is usual at the end of the year to check the cost of their establishment, in order that if the estimate has been exceeded the amount required may be provided. Owing to the great dearness of everything during the past year, and the cost of the Prince's maintenance for the four months he has stayed there (i.e. with the Infantas), the estimate has been exceeded in the steward's department by 50,000 ducats, and the Infantas' own expenses, with their dresses, etc., which were estimated at 2,000 ducats have risen to 24,000, because as they abandoned their mourning they were obliged to spend money on new dresses, in addition to their usual expenditure. The choristers in the chapel have also to be paid out of this account, and several extraordinary charges have fallen upon it, so that altogether the estimate for this establishment has been exceeded by 74,000 ducats. This sum must be obtained from a ready-money source, as it cannot be avoided. If your Majesty had replied about the wheat, the amount, or part of it, might have been raised from that. I expect the Prince and the Marquis will write separately to your Majesty on these points, and in the meanwhile I am urging the Marquis to be very careful not to incur any avoidable expense. As soon as the

HENRY VIII. 555

1547.

Queen (Dowager of Hungary's) letters arrived measures were taken to meet the Flemish bills. It was hoped that, as they were secured on the half first fruits, they would be met as all the others had been, but it seems that this is a fresh arrangement, and the holders claim to receive the amount there in money and will not accept consignments of revenues. The two merchants interested have been sent for, as they are not here. Every effort shall be made to get the bills met somehow, as I expect they will be.

Madrid, 25 January, 1547.

29 Jan.
Vienna.
Imp. Arch.

386. CHAPUYS to the QUEEN DOWAGER.

I received yesterday afternoon your Majesty's letters of the 27th instant, commanding me to give my poor opinion on the subjects dealt with in the two extracts sent to me. These subjects from their nature and importance demand far more wit and activity of mind than I possess at present, tormented and unhinged, as I am, with the gout, which has again attacked me in the last two days. To give a valuable opinion on them, moreover, needs recent communication with the people concerned (*i.e.* the English), who are so changeable and inconsistent that they vary, I will not say from year to year, but every moment; and no other set of affairs, in my opinion, so urgently needs personal consideration on the spot, or upon which an opinion is so likely to be wrong if given without recent observation. This your Majesty has foreseen by sending thither (*i.e.* to England) the present ambassador resident, a discreet and prudent man, who must now know the English well. Still, in obedience to your Majesty's orders, I will give my humble opinion, under the due correction of your Majesty and your Council. If the King of England gives his countenance to his stirrers-up of heresy, the Earl of Hertford and the Lord Admiral (which may be feared for the reasons mentioned by the ambassador, and because, according to report, the Queen, instigated thereto by the Duchess of Suffolk,° the Countess of Hertford,† and the Admiral's wife,‡ is infected by the sect, which she would not be likely to favour, at least openly, unless she knew the King's feeling) it would be quite useless to attempt to turn him from his fancy by words and exhortations, even if they were addressed to him in the name of the Emperor. On the contrary, they would be more likely to give him a pretext for hurrying on the enterprise and harden him in his obstinacy, in order that he might show his absolute power and his independence of anyone. This again might bring about a certain irritation or coolness on his part towards the Emperor, which at the present time is undesirable in the interests of Christendom.

° Catharine. Baroness Willoughby D'Eresby, widow of Charles Brandon, Duke of Suffolk, who, although a goddaughter of Catharine of Aragon and daughter of a Spanish lady, Maria de Sarmiento, was a devoted adherent of the Protestant reformation, for which she and her second husband, Francis Bertie, suffered exile and confiscation under Mary.

† Anne Stanhope, also a devoted Protestant.

‡ Jane, daughter of Sir Edward Guildford, wife of John Dudley, Earl of Warwick.

Nevertheless, in case of any doubtful tendency or change on the part of the King, it would not be bad for the ambassador to speak to him, as if of his own accord; praising and reminding him of the decrees promulgated by him some months ago for the extinction of heresy, and expressing the belief that he intended to persevere in the same virtuous direction. He (the ambassador) might say that so sharp and dangerous a malady (as heresy) needed to be well watched with ceaseless vigilance on the part of those whose duty it was, since everything could not be brought to his (the King's) personal cognisance. He (the ambassador) might then proceed to lay before the King the evils that may grow out of religious innovations, as he (the ambassador) writes that he has already stated to some of the Councillors. As the King is in the habit of at once communicating to his council what is said to him, the ambassador might confer on the subject with some of the members, with whom he is on most confidential terms. Although several of the councillors are well inclined, I much doubt, however, that that he will find many of them disposed to join in the dance or to undertake anything against the earl (Seymour) and the admiral (Dudley), seeing the violent and injurious words used recently by the former towards the Lord Chancellor (Wriothesley) and by the Admiral towards Winchester (Paulet). When I was last in England Winchester would have been sent to the Tower by the orders of the earl and the admiral, if the Duke of Norfolk had not interceded, and informed the King, to whom Winchester justified himself and escaped for the time. In order, as the saying is, to hold a candle to the devil, the ambassador, after he has spoken to the King, might communicate his discourse to the earl and the admiral. It is out of the question, of course, that he could convert them from their accursed affection; the malady being one of those incurable mental ones into which they have fallen by natural inclination, and besides this, they are the further confirmed in it by their plans to obtain the government of the prince. As they lack league or assistance they have determined to drag the whole country into this damnable error, to which there exists no counteracting influence amongst the secular nobility, except the Duke of Norfolk, who is against them and enjoys great power amongst the people of the north; this being, in my opinion the reason for his detention and that of his son, who also is considered a man of great courage. There is nothing else to stand in their way except the wealth and authority of the bishops, who are men of wit and experience. It is therefore to be feared that in this coming parliament the bishops will be divested of their property and authority, and will thenceforward receive nothing but certain pensions from the King's coffers. The Earl of Hertford first conceived this plan through the teaching of Cromwell, who, as soon as he doubted his ability to reconcile the Emperor with the King, adopted the expedient of entering into this heresy, and so to place the whole of the realm at issue with his Imperial Majesty. But for this plan, the whole country was so devoted to the Emperor that anything he had cared to undertake there in favour of the Queen (Catharine of Aragon) would have succeeded almost without effort. They (the English) fear no other force than that of his Majesty; neither French nor Scots, owing to the natural hate of Englishmen towards the latter; and recollecting, as they do, the ample cause that the Emperor had to attack them for the advancement of the Princess (*i.e.* Mary) nothing his Majesty says now will have any effect upon them. On the contrary, they will turn it to their own profit and advantage. It is, moreover, not proposed to employ other than fair or cool words to them; and we may well fear as Seneca says "*Qui frigide rogat docet negare.*" And if (which God forbid) the King should die, which would be more inopportune for us than it would have been twenty years ago, it is probable that these two men (*i.e.* Seymour and Dudley) will have the management of affairs, because, apart from the King's affection for them, and other reasons, there are no other nobles of a fit age and ability for the task. It is quite true, and probable from appearances, that disturbances might take place; and in that case the ambassador should employ his dexterity according to the circumstances, which, as one cannot forsee, one cannot now advise upon. I will, however, just hazard one remark. If the King's decease should happen before the injuries inflicted by Englishmen on his Majesty's subjects have been redressed, a perfectly licit, honest, and just means will be ready at hand, not only to secure compensation but also to arouse the ire of a portion of the (English) people against the Governors; and consequently to hold affairs somewhat in check. This would be to decree an embargo similar to that effected by his Majesty two years ago; and, with this end, it will be advisable to avoid arousing any distrust or doubt amongst the English merchants as to the safety of their coming hither to trade, and to show them the usual favour and kindness. There is no doubt that the Governors would be much perplexed by such a seizure, since the King himself the last time was so much upset by it, and by the complaints of the people.

With regard to the question of whether it will be advisable to take any fresh steps in English affairs, I can only say that, after what I have written above, I think not. It is true that if the parliament were celebrated with the same amount of liberty as was anciently enjoyed, when the parliament met to punish the Kings, some remonstrances might be addressed to Parliament. But at the present time there is no way of doing this; for if St. Peter and St. Paul were to return to earth, and seek to enter, the King would not allow them to do so. He openly told me this himself once, at the time that I was insisting upon entering the House, when the legitimacy of the Princess Mary was under discussion. No man present at the sittings dare for his life's sake open his mouth, or say a word, without watching the will of the King and his Council. Still it seems to me that no harm could be done by M. de Granvelle addressing a remonstrance to the Bishop of Winchester, in the sense I have mentioned above, to be employed by the Emperor's ambassador in England, with whatever additions his (de Granvelle's) great experience and ability may dictate.

In conclusion, Madame, I beg to say that I am of opinion that at present it would be advisable for his Majesty to avoid any further action, either spiritual or temporal. Our doctors tell us that, even if the Pope or other prelate is right in fulminating censures against anyone, in cases where the adoption of such a course threatens to aggravate the malady the censure should be withheld, and if already issued should be revoked. The aphorism of physicians with regard

1547.

to certain maladies should be borne in mind. They say that the best and quickest cure that can be adopted is to leave the evil untouched to avoid irritating it further.

Louvain, 29th January, 1547.

1546-7 (?)
S. D.°
Vienna.
Imp. Arch.

387. From the QUEEN DOWAGER. Document headed: "Draft memorandum for Van der Delft."

Disputes and differences having formerly arisen between the Governing body of the English merchants in Flanders, etc., on the one hand, and the Burgomasters, Sheriffs, and Town Council of Antwerp on the other, the said merchants complained that the Antwerp authorities failed to observe the privileges, contracts and agreements existing between the said parties. The Antwerp authorities denied that this was the case, and as a consequence of the dispute the English merchants by order of their Governor withdrew from the city of Antwerp and refused to return. Certain communications thereupon took place; but as the matter touched the authority of our brother the Emperor, and the English merchants contended that reparation was due to them for certain dues which they had paid, not for the profit of the city of Antwerp but for the Emperor's treasury, we, the Queen Dowager of Hungary and Bohemia, Regent, ordered the Antwerp authorities not to enter into any negotiation with the Governor and merchants of England without our consent. Dr. Smith was then sent with the said Governor of the merchants, bearing letters of credence from the King of England to the Queen Regent, and instructions to settle the points in dispute. Her Majesty had several conferences held with them, and finally, in the interests of the perfect and sincere amity between the Emperor and the King and with the object of avoiding similar disputes for the future, it was agreed that the Queen should give strict orders to the Burgomasters, Sheriffs and Council of the city of Antwerp to observe scrupulously the agreements and conventions that they had with the English merchants. The first of these agreements is dated 1 June, 1543 (?) and the second 22 December, 1537. These treaties were ordered to be strictly carried out, and reparation made for any attempt that might be discovered to evade them in the past; the English on their side also being pledged to fulfil the same treaties without fraud or malfeisance. The Governor of the English merchants, moreover, is not to be allowed, in case of any similar dispute in the future, to compel the merchants of his nation to withdraw from the city of Antwerp, or to cease their operations there, without first giving

---

* Although this document bears no date it is apparently of the period here assigned to it, as it marks the conclusion of one point of the long-drawn negotiations for the elucidation of Paget's agreement made at Utrecht in April, 1545, which had kept Councillor Van den Burgh in London until the end of January, 1547. The special point dealt with in this document is the unauthorised levying of dues on English goods by the Antwerpers, in violation of the treaties of commerce. Although in one of his letters Van der Delft expresses an opinion that the English complaint was justified, it will be seen that the President of the Court of English merchants in Antwerp, Thomas Chamberlain, was made a scapegoat to save appearances.

1547.

notice to his Imperial Majesty, the Queen Regent or the Governor General of these dominions, or else to the King of England's ambassador here resident for communication to the aforesaid, in order that measures may be taken for settling the question at issue before it reaches the extreme stage which the recent dispute has done; the same being inconvenient, as between friendly and allied sovereigns. It must be understood, however, that no hindrance must, by reason of this agreement, be offered to the English merchants to frequent the fairs of other towns in these dominions whenever they please, nor must they be prevented from carrying on their business anywhere in accordance with the commercial treaties existing; which treaties are in nowise prejudiced or abrogated. As the principal blame for the recent trouble is attributed to the new Court-master or Governor, Thomas Chamberlain, the King of England will remove him from the position of Court-master, and will appoint thereto a peaceful, discreet man, who will seek the welfare, repose and tranquillity of business.

ADDENDA.

1530.

May 7.
Simancas.
E.V. 1557.

388. The EMPEROR to CAROCCIOLO and RODRIGO NIÑO.*

Approves of their action in speaking to the Doge about the divorce proceedings against the Queen of England, showing him the justice of the Queen's contention. They are to continue in the same course, and in the event of the King of England further communicating with the Seigniory respecting the divorce they are to take care that nothing be done prejudicial to the interests of the Queen. Shortly after the Emperor's arrival at Innspruck the English ambassador asked leave to go to Rome to fulfil a mission from his master. He said that another ambassador would shortly arrive to fill his place. Has no doubt that the ambassador is going to Rome to negotiate with the Pope about the Queen of England's case. The Bishop of London has also left Lyons for Rouen. The Doge may be informed of their movements if it be considered desirable.

Innspruck, 7 May, 1530.

23 May.
Simancas.
E. 1557.

389. The EMPEROR to RODRIGO NIÑO.

Thanks him for his action with the Doge and Seigniory respecting the divorce case of the Queen of England. The Seigniory behaved as was to be expected in the matter,† and Niño is to tell them that the matter of the divorce is not a private affair of the Emperor's only, but deeply concerns the interests of all Christendom. Niño will therefore be vigilant to neglect nothing that touches the matter; and the Emperor trusts that the Seigniory will continue in their favourable attitude. All information to be sent to the Emperor and to Mai in Rome.

Innspruck, 22 May.

4 June.
Paris.
Archives
Nationales.
K. 1641.

390. SIR FRANCIS BRIAN to the IMPERIAL COMMISSIONERS.

He hereby delivers into the hands of the Imperial Commissary in the house of Anglade at Bayonne the power of the King of England dated 19 February, 1529, and declares in the name of his master and in the presence of Guillaume de Barrés, the Imperial Commissary, that all debts and questions between the Emperor and the King of England are now settled, in accordance with the treaty of Madrid and Cambrai.

---

* The Emperor's Ambassadors in Venice.
† This refers to the news contained in a letter of 17 May from Rodrigo Niño to the Emperor (Henry VIII. Calendar, Gairdner) to the effect that the Seigniory had ordered the University of Padua to decline the King of England's request that an opinion should be pronounced as to the validity of his marriage with Queen Catharine. Another letter written on the same day as the above from the Emperor to Mai in Rome is to a similar effect.

1530.

He delivers to Guillaume de Barrés
1. A bond of the Emperor dated 18 July, 1517, for 100,000 gold florins and 40,000 gold nobles.
2. A bond of the Emperor dated 21 June, 1522, for 150,000 sun crowns.
3. The power of the Emperor to Bernard de Misa and Jehan de la Sauch to receive from the King of England 20,000 nobles.
4. The bond of the Seigneur de Ravenstein and others, dated 17 July, 1517.
5. A letter from the Emperor dated 2 July, 1517, promising that the documents respecting his debts to the King of England will be duly despatched and delivered by Chancellor Sauvaige.
6. A letter from the Emperor dated 21 August, 1517, pledging his person and property for the repayment of the 40,000 nobles.
8. (?) A letter of the Emperor dated 22 July, 1517, acknowledging receipt of 30,000 gold crowns.
9. The document dated Windsor, 19 July, 1522, by which the Emperor binds himself to pay every year to the King of England 133,305 sun crowns.

Power of the Emperor to Louis de Flanders, Seigneur de Praet and Guillaume de Barrés to receive the said documents, etc., dated Bologna, 19 December, 1529.

The parchment (in Latin) is signed by Brian and witnessed by notaries.

Bayonne, 4 June, 1530.

NOTE.—A letter (Simancas C. de C. 14) from Alvaro de Lugo to the Empress, 4 April, 1530, advises the arrival of Brian at Bayonne with the Fleur de Lys, and relates that he accompanied the French Commissioners to Fuenterrabia where he was much feasted. "When they returned the tide was low, and the ambassadors had to be carried ashore on the backs of sailors. The sailor who carried the English ambassador tripped and fell down, letting the ambassador drop in the water. Some boats at once came to rescue him from his unpleasant dilemma, and no harm was done except that he was thoroughly drenched." It is not quite clear what the fleur de lys referred to was—perhaps some pledge or token: but Chapuys in a letter to the Emperor of 6 February, 1530, mentions the arrival in England of a French ambassador "Johan Jocquin" to pay the pensions paid by King Francis in England: "mais il me dit . . . que la chose que l'avoyt plus hasté d'y venir estait le recouvrement de la Fleur de Lys." A little later Chapuys says: "Sire hier arriva icy ung lapidayre serviteur de Madame qu'elle a icy envoyé pour recognoystre les pieces de la fleur de lys. Il assisterat quant l'on la lui monstrerat et la pourrat visiter sans autre semblant. Car si le Roy continue au propos qu'ay dernièrement ecris a votre Majesté de l'envoyer par son homme et bien cacheté il n'est besoin d'icy faire scrupuleuse visitation. Cela appertiendrat a ceux qui seront commis de la part de Votre Majesté pour la recevoir."

HENRY VIII. 563

1530.

14 June.
Simancas.
E. V. 1557.

391. The EMPEROR to RODRIGO NIÑO. (Venice.)

Directs him to thank the Seigniory very heartily in his name for their good will and action respecting the cause of the Queen of England. He is to assure the Venetians that it will not be the Emperor's fault if the good understanding which at present exists between them be interrupted.

Niño's relations with the English ambassador are approved of. He is to continue these negotiations in order to learn what the English intend to do, and he is to thank the Bishop of Quienta for his zeal in the service of the Queen of England. He is not yet to speak to the Venetians about the measures to be adopted against the Lutherans. The Bishop of Quienta is doing well, but he must continue to act in his own name only.

Innspruck, 14 June, 1530.

14 June.
Simancas.
E. V. 1557.

392. The EMPEROR to MICER MICHAEL MAI. (Extract.)

Thanks him for his diligence and prudence in the negotiations respecting the case of the Queen of England, and instructs him to continue in the same course exactly as if the matter was one concerning the Emperor's own person. The Emperor approves of the Pope's proposal that he shall write to the King of France asking him not to allow the doctors of Paris to assemble for the purpose of arriving at an opinion against the Queen of England. If the Pope has not already written to this effect, he must be asked to do so soon. Mai did right in exercising his influence with his Holiness to obtain the brief requested by the Queen of England. The Emperor has already been advised by Rodrigo Niño of what had passed there (i.e. at Venice) and has instructed Niño to keep Mai informed of all that passes. The Bishop of Vaison has rendered good service to the Queen of England in Venice. He is always a true friend and Mai is to thank him. When the Bishop of London and Dr. Bennet arrive (in Rome) Mai is to employ all means in order to learn what they are doing and their objects. He is to keep the Emperor fully advised of their negotiations, and he is likewise to enquire very carefully concerning the marriages, which according to the Pope are being arranged in England. The Emperor is glad that Cardinal Cajetano is favourable to the Queen of England, and Mai is to gain over to her cause as many cardinals as may be won by honest means. Dr. Ortiz is to go to Rome as soon as possible, as well as Count de Mirandula and Montes de Oca to serve the Queen of England.

Munich, 14 June, 1530.

18 June.
Simancas.
E.V. 1308.

393. RODRIGO NIÑO to the EMPEROR. (Extract.)

Three days ago the Bishop of London[*] arrived here for the purpose of requesting the Seigniory to convoke a meeting of the doctors of law and obtain their opinion, and also that of the

---

[*] Dr. John Stokesley, who had recently been elevated to the See of London on the translation of Cuthbert Tonstall to Durham vice Wolsey. Dr. Stokesley died in 1539, and was succeeded in the See of London by Dr. Bonner.

1530.

University of Padua on the divorce case between the King and Queen of England. The Bishop has not yet been to the College. I am persuaded that he will not succeed in obtaining what he asks.

Venice, 18 June, 1530.

27 June.
Simancas.
E. V. 1557.

394. The EMPEROR to MICHAEL MAI. (Extract.)

Approves of Mai's action with regard to the Spanish friar who volunteered to dispute the cause of the Queen of England in the general chapter of the Dominican Order. The Imperial ambassador (in Siena) Don Lope de Soria informs the Emperor that he has spoken to Master Philip Decio, respecting his advocating the Queen of England's cause.* He had already been engaged by the English, but promised to render good service to the Queen. The Emperor has written to Lope de Soria instructing him to secure Master Philip. It would be a great victory if a learned doctor of so much fame, after already accepting a brief for the King of England, were to abandon his case and pronounce himself in favour of the Queen.

Augsburg, 27 June, 1530.

27 June.
Simancas.
E. V. 1557.

395. The EMPEROR to the CARDINAL OF RAVENNA.

Thanks him warmly for the good services he is rendering to the Queen of England. The cause is regarded by the Emperor as a personal one of his own. Although it is well known that the Cardinal is influenced in his advocacy by no other considerations than those of justice, the Emperor nevertheless begs him to accept a more substantial token of his gratitude.

Augsburg, 27 June, 1530.

22 July.
Simancas.
E. V. 1557.

396. The EMPEROR to MICHAEL MAI. (Extract.)

Approves of all the steps taken by Mai with regard to the cause of the Queen of England. Even if he cannot obtain a commission from the Pope authorising the case to be proceeded with throughout the vacation, no opportunity must be missed of urging his Holiness to have the case accelerated as much as possible. The Pope must never for a moment suspect that the Emperor looks upon the Queen of England's affair with lukewarmness or indifference. The Emperor is of opinion that it well becomes a good Pope to send a person to England for the purpose of persuading the King not to persist further in his divorce proceedings, and he approves of the steps taken by Mai with the person selected for the mission before he left Rome.† Mai also acted judiciously in writing to the Queen and the Imperial ambassador in England, informing them of the Pope's intention in this respect. The Emperor also writes to them to the same effect.

Augsburg, 22 July, 1530.

---

* *See* letter from Michael Mai to the Emperor, 14 June, Calendar Henry VIII., Vol. 4, part 3, p. 2900.
† *i.e.* the Baron di Borgo, a Neapolitan nobleman, sent as Nuncio. *See* letter, Mai to the Emperor, 18 July, Calendar Henry VIII, Vol. 4, part 3, p. 2935.

HENRY VIII. 565

1530.

6 July.
Simancas.
E. V. 1308.

397. RODRIGO NIÑO to the EMPEROR.

The Bishop of London has returned from Padua, and the writer has been informed by the Seigniory that he has not succeeded in his mission there with the doctors and professors of the University.* The Bishop of London (*i.e.* Stokesley) only associates with the Prior of St. John and Pole of the Order of St. Dominic. The writer has spoken to Pole and has warned him that he should consider carefully what he is doing.† It is dangerous at this time to call into question and discuss the power of the Pope. Pole replied that he had hitherto been mistaken, and that the Bishop of London had informed him that the Pope wished the question to be discussed and decided in favour of the King of England. The writer disabused Pole's mind, assuring him that this was not true. The result of the conversation was that Pole promised to do as the Pope wished. His Holiness has sent for another friar, with whom the English were in negotiation. His name is Francis George. When this friar returns to Venice the Prior of St. John and all the others will do as he tells them.

Venice, 6 July, 1530.

31 July.
Simancas.
E. R. 850.

398. FRAY GARCIA DE LOAISA, CARDINAL of OSMA, to COBOS.

Although I recently wrote to you it would be a crime of *lesæ majestatis* to omit any opportunity of doing so again. . . I cannot accept the pension which the Emperor has deigned to confer upon me. Part of the amount would be better employed in buying the goodwill of the Cardinals in Rome. I fear you will not come out of the affair of the Diet in Germany so clean as you enter it. If only the Council could be sent to the devil, and a compromise with the heretics be brought about, permitting them to retain some of the errors but remedying those which are most damnable, the affairs of the Emperor would not remain long in their present bad condition. I have very frequently expressed this opinion in my letters, but my advice seems to be overlooked. Pray do your best to effect an arrangement with the heretics.‡

Rome, 31 July, 1530.

2 Aug.
Simancas.
E. V. 1557.

399. The EMPEROR to MAI. (Extracts.)

Unsatisfactory state of religion in Germany. Nothing will be of any use but a general Council. A national Council would do more harm than good. Thanks for his services in the matter of the Queen of England. It is time that the brief promised by the Pope was despatched, forbidding the universities to give their opinions in

---

* *See* letter from the Same to the Same, 13 July, Calendar Henry VIII., Vol. 4, part 3. p. 2930.

† This would appear to refer to the proposal of Henry VIII. to Pole for the acceptance by the latter of some of Wolsley's great preferments.

‡ Although this letter does not directly touch upon English affairs, it is reproduced here in order to show that the first Spanish ecclesiastic of his day, the tutor and mentor later of Prince Philip, and trusted adviser of the Emperor, was in favour of a compromise which would, if it had been adopted, probably have maintained the unity of the Christian Church. There are many other letters of Loaisa in the packet to a similar effect.

1530.

the matter of the divorce. These opinions are prejudicial to the authority of his Holiness. There is nothing to be said with regard to the other brief, in which the Pope orders the Universities to pronounce their judgment in acccordance with their consciences and the canon law. If the small alterations they wish to make in the brief are not prejudicial to the Queen's cause they may be made. It is also meet that his Holiness should take steps to stop the custom of buying "votes." The English purchase them as if they were merchandise in a shop. The Emperor is sending a full statement of the divorce case to Sicily and Majorca, in order to obtain from those places also opinions on the divorce case. More "Imperial" opinions on the case enclosed. Urge the Pope to accelerate proceedings.

Augsburg, 2 August, 1530.

NOTE.—Accompanying this letter are others to Cardinals San Sisto and Grimaldo, thanking them for their services in the Queen of England's case. Mai will speak more fully to them on the subject.

8 Aug.
Simancas.
E. V. 1306.

400. RODRIGO NIÑO to the EMPEROR. (Extract.)

The Bishop of London (Stokesley) is still in Venice, doing his utmost to persuade the Seigniory to order the University of Padua to pronounce an opinion on the merits of the divorce case in England. The Seigniory have twice assured him that they could not do so, and the question has now degenerated to a paper wrangle between the Venetians and the English. Things have gone so far, indeed, that the Venetians are afraid to send out the three galleasses, which are ready to sail for England and Flanders, unless the King of England will grant them a safe-conduct. At this moment the Pregai is assembled to consider the matter.

Venice, 8 August, 1530.

16 Aug.
Simancas.
L. Sueltos, 3.

401. The EMPRESS to the EMPEROR. (Extract.)

Before she received his last letter, containing a statement of the case of the Queen of England, a similar statement had reached her from Micer Mai in Rome. The Queen of England herself has also written to her a full account of the case, of which copies are being made to be sent to the Universities of Castile, Aragon, Valencia and Catalonia, with the orders of the Empress that the Universities are to study the case very carefully and send their opinions to her. Originals of the same shall be sent to the Emperor, and copies to Micer Mai in Rome. She does not believe that a single University in Spain will pronounce against the Queen of England, seeing that law and equity are all on her side. The Empress rejoices that the Emperor is so determined to defend the right of the injured Queen, which, indeed, it is his duty to do; not only because she is his aunt but also because the case closely concerns the Christian religion itself. Dr. Ortiz is reputed to be a very learned man, but he is somewhat narrow minded and crabbed. It would therefore be desirable to associate with him in his mission another scholar, such

HENRY VIII. 567

1530.

a person, for instance, as the Licentiate de Miranda, Canon of Seville, who is also a man of high repute and profound learning.

Madrid, 16 August, 1530.

Simancas.
T. c. I., 4.

402. The Divorce.

Opinion of Licentiate Illescas on the marriage of Henry VIII. and Queen Catharine. Although at first sight it would appear that the Pope had no authority to dispense in this case, because dispensations may only be granted in certain circumstances, set forth in the law, and because this dispensation was obtained surreptitiously, yet, on consideration, the Pope's dispensation will be found to be valid, because his Holiness, being endowed with the power of God on earth, his pronouncements being divine, are not ruled by earthly law. To doubt this would be impious and sacrilegious.

NOTE.—In the same bundle as the above there is a lengthy and strongly-worded opinion in favour of the Queen's contention by another learned jurist, the Licentiate Curiel. (T. c. I. 4, 125.) Simancas.

Attached to this paper (p. 126) there is the Latin draft of the "protest of the Attorney of the Queen of England," setting forth that the marriage of Arthur and Catharine was arranged for the purpose of ending the wars between Spain and England, and in the interests of a national alliance; that the marriage was never consummated. Evidence of this given. The Papal dispensations vindicated. The wedding (with Henry) was legal both in common and canon law, and must be maintained in the interests of public honesty.

A number of similar opinions by various Spanish jurists and ecclesiastics are in the same bundle.

12 Sept.
Simancas.
E. V. 1308.

403. Rodrigo Niño to the Emperor.

The Bishop of London when he departed from Venice left money with a friar from Padua, with instructions that he was to go to all the libraries in Italy and search for books which might be quoted as authorities in favour of the King of England's contention. The General of the Augustinian Order, to which the friar belongs, has forbidden him to do this. No affair has ever been pushed with so much zeal as the Bishop of London shows in this. The Emperor will in future be informed from Rome of the Bishop's movements.

Venice, 12 September, 1530.

23 Sept.
Simancas.
E. V. 1557.

404. The Emperor to Rodrigo Niño.

Many thanks for his good services in the case of the Queen of England by means of Paulo Torellas. Rejoices that Raphael de Como has declared himself in favour of the Queen, revoking what he had formerly written to the contrary. One of the printed copies of his retraction sent shall be forwarded to England, the other copy being reserved for future use. Niño did well in sending another copy to Micer Mai in Rome. Thank Don Raphael, and give him the enclosed letter. Letters are also being written to the Bishop of

1530.

Quienta, the Prior of St. John and to Dr. Parisius, which are to be delivered to them by Niño.* The English pretend that the University of Paris has pronounced an opinion in favour of the King's contention. The truth is, however, that certain members of the University, having been bribed by money and other means, or intimidated by threats, have given a private opinion in the King's favour. But they are the least learned and the least esteemed members of the University. The principal scholars, those who enjoy the highest reputation, 48 in number, declared spontaneously that justice was on the side of the Queen. Although the English are much favoured in France, and have made extraordinary efforts there, they did not succeed in obtaining the seal of the University upon the opinion given by the King's partisans, although the latter were in a majority. The reason why the attachment of the University seal was refused was that those who had voted in favour of the King were held in little esteem, whilst the great scholars whose influence was all powerful in the University were on the other side. The University of Poitiers also has declared in favour of the Queen. It is therefore evident that all those who pretend that the King of England has the law on his side are bought and bribed, either by money or some equally lawless means.

Niño did well in writing to Mai in Rome that the Bishop of London was procuring opinions in favour of his King in Bologna. Mai has been ordered to request his Holiness to prevent the Bishop of London from continuing his intrigues. The Emperor does no believe that the Pope has really granted to the Bishop of London the brief which the latter pretends he has received. If it had been the fact Mai would certainly have informed the Emperor, and in no case would his Holiness have granted the brief in such a form as the English allege.

Augsburg, 23 September, 1530.

13 Oct
Simancas
E. B. 849

405. RODRIGO NIÑO to the EMPEROR. (Extract.)

Dr. Parisius† has come to see him. The Emperor's letter delivered to him, and the writer had a long conversation with him respecting the Queen of England's divorce case. The doctor assures him that the law is on the side of the Queen, and he promises to study the case more closely than he has done; although he says that he cannot in any case give his opinion formally in writing, as the Seigniory have strictly forbidden him to do so on either side. If, however, this prohibition be removed he will gladly pronounce his opinion; his most ardent desire being to render service to the Emperor. Begs instructions as to whether he is to request the Seigniory to remove the prohibition. As Mariano Surin, who is also a professor of the University of Padua, has given his judgment in favour of the King of England it is only just that Dr. Parisius be at liberty to give his in favour of the Queen. Believes that the opinion of Mariano Surin is strongly in favour of the King of England, as he is very intimate with Richard (i.e., Dr. Richard

---

* These letters of thanks for their aid in the Queen's favour are attached.
† Rector of the University of Padua.

1530.

Croke, English ambassador in Venice), and no doctor of law will ever allow the writing of a sheet of paper to stand in the way of a hundred ducats coming to his house. Dr. Parisius seems to be a man of sound judgment, and he has a reputation for very great learning. He says that what the theologians say about the case is all nonsense. It is a simple question of law, not of theology.

Venice, 18 October, 1530.

30 Oct.
Simancas.
E. V. 1557.

406. The EMPEROR to MAI. (Extract.)

If it be possible to obtain a copy of the bulls, which he writes that the Auditor de la Camera has bought and sent to England, he would be glad of them; but it must be managed in such a way as not to offend the Pope. There is no remark necessary with regard to the going of the Duke of Albany to Rome.

Mai's action in the case of the Queen of England is approved of. He is always to act with the greatest zeal and diligence, in order that the ends of justice be not defeated to the prejudice of the Queen. He is especially to avoid, and to nip in the bud, any suggestion that may be made with the object of referring the divorce question to the King of France, or to bring about a compromise through his intervention, which could not fail to be highly injurious to the Queen, the Pope, and the Emperor himself.

Augsburg, 30 October, 1530.

11 Nov.
Simancas.
E. V. 1557.

407. The EMPEROR to MAI.

Notes from his letters that the Pope wishes to postpone the proceedings in the divorce case of the Queen of England for twenty days, and that Cardinals Osma and Santa Croce were of opinion that the Emperor should consent to such postponement. The justice of their reasons is fully acknowledged, but if the postponement be allowed, it must be on the express condition that no further delay shall take place, but that in future all diligence shall be exercised in securing the rights of the Queen of England. The cause must on no account be proceeded with in any other place than Rome, or before any other judge than the Pope. Mai is to be very careful that the negotiations between the Pope and the King of France are discountenanced, the object of them being to refer the divorce question to the arbitration of the King of France.

He is to dissuade the Pope from giving the Cardinal's hat to the Auditor de la Camera and to Casale.* They would reflect little credit on the Holy See, and the cause of the Queen of England would be much prejudiced, as they are known to be enemies.

Augsburg, 12 November, 1530.

25 Nov.
Simancas.
E. R. 850.

408. CARDINAL GADDI to the EMPEROR.

Complains that the Emperor has been liberal towards other Cardinals and various persons in the papal court who have done far less for him than Gaddi has done. Gaddi has even suffered imprisonment in times past in Naples in the Emperor's service; and yet no

---

* Sir Gregory Casale, the King of England's agent in Venice, and afterwards in Rome.

1530.

favour has been extended to him. Offers to serve the Emperor in every way that may be desired, but he expects to be rewarded, and prays that money may be sent to him.*

Rome, 25 November, 1530.

Extract from folio Diary of Consistories.

9 Dec.
Simancas.
E. 2015.

409. MINUTES of a SECRET CONSISTORY OF CARDINALS, held in the Apostolic Palace at Rome, Friday, 9 December, 1530.

Cardinal Cibo read a letter from the King of England asking that two Cardinals' hats should be granted, respectively to the Bishop of Worcester, his ambassador in Rome, and to the Protonotary Casale, his ambassador in Venice. The King declared in this letter that a negative answer to this request would be regarded by him as a personal insult, so many Cardinals having been created during the last few months at the instance of other princes. The Consistory being but thinly attended, the consideration of the King of England's request was postponed.

NOTE.—In a letter from Mai to the Emperor, of 14 December (partly summarised in the Calendar of Henry VIII., Vol. 4, part 3), the writer rejoices to hear what passed at the Consistory, and thanks God that no English Cardinals are to be made. The separation of the King of England, he says, from his mistress Anne remains to be dealt with in the next Consistory.

22 Dec.
Simancas.
E. V. 1308.

410. RODRIGO NIÑO to the EMPEROR. (Extract.)

Dr. Parisius, who is a very great scholar, has refused to pronounce an opinion in favour of the Queen of England, unless the Emperor expressly orders him to do so. If such an order be given to him, he will return the thirty ducats he has received from the King of England, and say that, being a subject of the Emperor, he cannot do what has been requested of him.† Niño thinks that it would be well that the doctor should be written to. He has divulged to the writer the means and ways by which the English procure opinions in favour of their King's case, and Niño proposes to send the information to Micer Mai. The Seigniory has handed to the writer the copy of an opinion given by a certain doctor of canon law in favour of the King of England; and this also will be sent to Mai. It will be advisable likewise to send to Mai the opinions of the Prior of St. John and Pole. The General of the Augustines has forwarded to the writer an opinion favourable to the Queen, but he has not signed it, as he fears that the King of England would confiscate the property of the Order in England if he did so.

Venice, 22 December, 1530.

---

* In the same bundle as the above are three letters, dated 14th November, from Cardinals Santa Croce, Cesarini, and Egidio to the Emperor, thanking him in fulsome terms for his liberal rewards to them.

† In answer to this the Emperor writes (Aix la Chapelle, 15 January, 1531) that he does not think it will be wise to ask Dr. Parisius in plain words in writing to give an opinion in favour of the Queen; but he encloses a general letter to the doctor expressing a hope that the latter will do as the ambassador will ask him.

1530.

No date.
Simancas.
E. 2016.

411. POPE CLEMENT VII. to HENRY VIII.

If he followed the King's example he would fall into a similar error and allow himself to be led captive by his passions. But mindful of his high position he prefers to imitate the greater example of Christ Jesus, whose vicar on earth he is.

In all things that depend upon his will, he is ready to gratify the King of England, but in matters touching justice he is forced to be guided only by the law of God.

The Pope is unable to give the King an answer with regard to the matrimonial cause, because he (the Pope) being the judge of the case, he considers it unbecoming for a judge to declare before hand his opinion in a cause upon which he will presently have to pronounce judgment. But, however willing he might be to tell the King his opinion, it would be impossible now for him to do so, as he has ordered Paulus de Capisurciis, one of the Apostolic auditors, to draw up and present a report on the case to him in Consistory. This report is not yet finished, nor are the proceedings in England before the papal legates yet produced, or the witnesses' evidence taken. It is therefore impossible at present to say which party in the case is in the right. When he first authorised the legates to proceed with the cause in England he was perfectly right, as it was in the interests of the Queen that the proceedings should take place in her presence. But as subsequently the Queen declined to recognise the authority of the legates, and appealed from them to himself (the Pope), his only course was to instruct the auditor of the Rota to furnish him with a full report of the case for the Consistory of Cardinals. The auditor is instructed to enquire into the facts and circumstances of the case, and to deliberate with his assistant auditors on the matter; after which he (the Pope) and the Cardinals will decide in accordance with justice, which in Rome must be equal for all men, even though they be Emperors and Kings. The Pontiffs derive their authority from God and not from men. The laws of England are not violated by the relegation of the cause to Rome, because they deal with temporal matters and not spiritual questions, such as this. If, however, a General Council were assembled the Pope would willingly refer the decision of the cause to such a tribunal.

NOTE.—This document, like many others of the Roman papers of similar date included in this Calendar, forms part of a series of transcripts of the Roman Archives procured by Juan Berzosa by order of Phillp II., and now at Simancas.

1531.
15 and 17 Jan.
Simancas.
E. V. 1557.

412. The EMPEROR to MAI. (Extract.)

(The Council (of Trent) necessary. The Pope's insincerity in the matter. He is to be treated very cautiously.)

Mai is to continue in his efforts to obtain justice for the Queen of England, and to prevent the Pope from being intimidated by the English. It is to be hoped that Dr. Ortiz has ere this arrived in Rome; as he had been informed by letters from Spain that the doctor had started on his journey; and he also learns that all the papers relative to the Queen of England's marriage, together with

1531.

the opinions of several learned corporations, have been sent to the doctor. More opinions of the same kind will follow; and Cardinal Colonna has sent the opinions of the learned doctors in Naples, to which the writer has added one drawn up by Master Sigismund Lafredo. Rodrigo Niño is of the same opinion as that expressed by Mai, that a brief should not be sent to Venice. It would probably do more harm than good, and he is not to ask the Pope to send it, nor is he to ask for the despatch of a brief to the Procurators of the University of Paris. The doctors of that University are so much terrorised by the King's ministers, and have been dealt with by such dishonest and corrupt means that no good result can be expected from them. It would make a very bad impression on the public if the Queen of England were to request their opinion, and that they should be divided on the subject.

Is much surprised that Cardinal Santi Quatri declines the pension of 2,000 ducats. He is to be told that he renders himself suspicious thereby.

Notes Mai's report that it was known in Rome that there had been a beginning of ill feeling between the Kings of France and England. All that is known in the Imperial Court is that they had quarrelled about the money which was to be paid to England, but that they had now made it up and had become friends again. Mai is to learn as much as possible on this subject. It is possible that the Duke of Albany, who hates the King of England, might be induced to speak out about it.

As the Pope has already promised to send to England a formal inhibition, commanding that the cause of the Queen be no further proceeded with in that realm, Mai is to take care that his Holiness fulfils his promise in this respect. He is to tell his Holiness that the affair does not only concern the Queen of England, but also the authority of the Holy See. It is important that the inhibition should be sent without delay, because the King of England intends very shortly to carry some very prejudicial measures in his Parliament, which has already been convoked for the purpose. The Emperor has sent special authority to his ambassador in England, with instructions to protest in the Emperor's name against any measures which may be turned to the Queen's prejudice. The ambassador in England will inform Mai direct of what is going on there.

Liege, 17 January, 1531.

2 Feb.
Simancas.
E. V. 1308.

413. RODRIGO NIÑO to the EMPEROR. (Extracts.)

Agrees that the marriage spoken of, between the Duke of Milan and the Princess of England, is not likely to take place. Has already reported that the Protonotary Casale, the King of England's ambassador in Venice, had gone to England for the purpose of arranging this marriage if possible, but Niño now learns that Casale is still staying with the Duke of Milan, although he has had time to have travelled to England and back. No doubt the Protonotary Carocciolo has sent fuller information to the Emperor on this point. The Emperor's letters delivered to the Prior of St. John and Pole, asking them to revoke and annul the opinions they had given in the

Queen's divorce case: but he (Niño) fears that this and all similar measures will have very little effect, as the King of England is determined to divorce the Queen *de facto*, and to contract a marriage with another woman. The matter must, indeed, have gone very far, as Micer Mai writes the same news from Rome as that current in Venice. The writer will nevertheless send the Emperor's letter to Dr. Parisius, and ask him personally to study the question carefully, in order that he may be prepared to pronounce an opinion as soon as the Emperor's order arrives. There is no doubt that when Dr. Parisius does deliver his opinion it will be the weightiest of any given in the cause.

Yesterday whilst going to Mass with the Doge, the latter told him that the Protonotary Casale, ambassador from the King of England to Venice, had returned hither, and during the celebration of Mass the English ambassador himself came up to speak to the writer, and to convey to him the compliments of the Protonotary Carocciolo, saying that he (Casale) had been staying for some time with the Duke of Milan at Vigevano. He denied that he had been to England, but confesses that he sent a special messenger to the King, with letters concerning the marriage, adding that he was expecting an answer from day to day. The writer, however, is still of opinion that Casale himself has been to England, as he has been absent from Venice three months.

Venice, 2 February, 1531.

10 Feb.
Simancas.
E. V. 1558.

414. The EMPEROR to BARON DEL BORGO, Papal Nuncio for England.

Hears that the Pope has commanded him to execute a certain mission in England, touching the divorce case of the Queen. Is persuaded that he will do his duty, as on all other occasions. Nevertheless, as the Emperor regards the interests of his aunt, the Queen of England, as his own, and is convinced that Borgo will be mindful of his allegiance and his customary devotion to the Emperor's affairs, he commands him not only to execute carefully the instructions of his Holiness, but also in general to exert himself to the utmost to defend the good cause of the Queen. The Imperial ambassador in England will further discourse with him on this subject.

Brussels, 10 February, 1531.

16 Feb.
Simancas.
E. V. 1558.

415. The EMPEROR to MAI.

Concerning the Council (of Trent). Cardinal Osma, Don Pedro de la Cueva, and J. A. Muxetula are to explain to the Pope the need for a Council. Thanks to Pope for information about Duke of Albany's mission. The Emperor's interview with King of France not yet settled; but the Pope need not fear that anything to his prejudice will be done. Mai is to do nothing in the matter of the Duke of Albany's mission, but is to watch what is negotiated with the Pope. Italian and Swiss affairs. With respect to the divorce of the Queen of England, Mai's letters to the Emperor and Granvelle have been read, and also copies of those sent to Cobos.

1531.

They are approved of. The briefs containing the inhibition came just in time, and he has decided to send them to England with letters of his own (the Emperor's) although it is not easy to deliver them to the persons for whom they are destined with safety to the latter, as the King of England has appointed guards to watch closely that no letter from the Pope to his Nuncio passes the frontier. The letters to the Nuncio cannot but exercise a favourable influence. The Emperor has read the copy of the King of England's letter to the Pope and his Holiness' answer. The Pope is to be earnestly thanked for it. Mai is to endeavour to obtain a brief for the separation.* As it has already been proposed in Consistory to grant such a brief, and the measure is one of simple justice, it is to be hoped that no delay will occur. The Emperor notes Mai's advice that some arrangement should be effected with the King of England about the divorce, if the King should be present at the intended meeting between the Emperor and the King of France. This is, however, no time to talk about arrangements and compromises. What must be demanded is justice, full and honest, and nothing must be omitted that may procure it. If they (the English) see that justice is demanded boldly, and the demand is pressed, they will grow not a little alarmed, and will not dare to disregard their plain duty or refuse obedience to the Church and the Apostolic See. The Emperor has written to his ambassador in England, ordering him to have search made for all the documents relating to the proceedings in England. He has also instructed the ambassador (in France ?) to obtain for him, if possible, the book in the library of the Dominican friars in Paris, mentioned by the ambassador in his letters. Mai is to send to the Emperor and also to Spain a copy of the questions upon which evidence is to be given by the witnesses (*i.e.*, in the proceedings in the divorce case in Rome).

Brussels, 16 February, 1531.

22 April.
Simancas.
E. V. 1558.

416. The EMPEROR to MAI. (Extract.)

Mai's action about the divorce case approved of.

The Emperor is much astonished to learn that the Cardinal of Utrecht has written that the only alternatives are either to settle the English affair by a compromise, or else to let the proceedings continue for the three or four years necessary before a decision can be given in the ordinary course of law. Mai is to tell the Cardinal not to entertain such ideas, or at least not to declare them.

Ghent, 22 April, 1531.

29 April &
14 Aug.
Simancas.
Latin.

417. Proceedings before Pedro Zapata, Abbot of the Monastery of the Holy Sepulchre in Calatayud, and Miguel Ximenez Dembun, Abbot of Veruela, in the Cloisters of the Cathedral of Zaragoza, authorised by the Papal Auditor, to enquire in the matter of the divorce case of the Queen of England. The notarial documents set forth at great length (102 pages) the facts of the case, the

---

* Apparently the separation of Henry from Anne Boleyn.

1531.

depositions of many witnesses, and the certificate that the King of England had been duly summoned to appear before the tribunal (14 July, 1531).

The judges declare the King of England contumacious.

Notarial certificate signed in Zaragoza Cathedral, 14 August, 1531.

4 June.
Simancas.
E. V. 1558.

418. The EMPEROR to MAI. (Extracts.)

(Need for the General Council.)

The Emperor reserves his final decision with regard to the proposed Scottish marriage, until a reply comes (from Scotland?). He is not disinclined to consent to a match between the King of Scotland and one of his nieces, a daughter of the King of the Romans, and it would be desirable if the affair could be settled before the Emperor left Flanders. Mai is to speak to the Cardinal of Ravenna, and push on the negotiations as much as may be possible or seemly in so delicate a matter. Above all, Mai must constantly urge energetically upon the Pope the need for speedy justice being done in the case of the Queen of England. The Emperor is not disinclined to reward fittingly the person to whose care the case of the Queen of England is entrusted. He thinks, however, that the present is an inconvenient time to give such a reward, both on account of the auditor and in view of the present state of the business. If the Emperor were to treat this person liberally at this juncture he would be obliged to do the same for Simoneta and other persons. Mai is directed to speak to the individual in question and ask him what kind of reward he would like best.

Ghent, 4 June, 1531.

21 Sept.
Simancas.
T. c. I.
Latin.

419. NOTARIAL CERTIFICATE of the Judgment of the Rector and Doctors of the University of Alcalá upon the questions submitted to them respecting the divorce case.

They unanimously agree that:—
1. It is not against natural law for a man to marry the childless widow of his deceased brother.
2. That it is not against the divine law as promulgated by Moses.
3. That it is not against the Scriptures.
4. That such marriages are only forbidden by human legislation.
5. That the Pope has power to dispense with prohibitions depending upon human legislation.

Signed by the Rector Egidio and nineteen doctors.

25 Nov.
Simancas.
E. V. 1558.

420. The EMPEROR to MAI.

The greatest diligence and energy must be exercised at this juncture to obtain justice for the Queen of England. The negotiations at present are in a most dangerous position, and the Queen is being more hardly pressed and worse treated than ever. The Emperor is writing a letter to the Pope on the subject, and he adds

1531.

also a paragraph to the present letter which may be shown to his Holiness. The English pronouncements are only idle threats, which are intended to frighten the Pope, but which they dare not carry out. A letter from the Queen of England and some opinions on her cause are enclosed.

(The following paragraph intended for the Pope's eye is not to be put into cipher.)

The Emperor is extremely astonished at the manner in which the proceedings relative to the divorce case of his dear aunt the Queen of England are being conducted. It would indeed be strange if it were otherwise, for the justice of the Queen's case is so clear, and the injustice done to her so evident, that an entirely different handling of the case (in Rome) was to have been expected. The Emperor has no doubt that Mai has frequently urged his Holiness to pronounce judgment; but still his Majesty cannot avoid thinking that Mai has not shown so much zeal in the matter as was his duty and he has been expressly instructed to do. Had he done so the Emperor is persuaded that the Pope could not have failed to accede to his request, that a simple and evident act of justice should be done, such as every person of whatever station has a right to demand. The Emperor is writing to his Holiness,* begging him to pronounce judgment without further delay, and thus release the good Queen from the trouble which she has suffered so long. The poor Queen, whose wrongs have made her the subject of the pity and commiseration of the world, is now being treated worse than ever, and Mai is to supplicate his Holiness over and over again not to protract the proceedings in her case, but to give judgment promptly. Mai is to write by every courier to the Emperor on the subject.

Brussels, 25 November, 1531.

NOTE.—On the same day as the above letter was written, but later, the Emperor writes again to Mai, mainly about other matters, but containing the following paragraph relating to the English affair. "Is glad to see that Mai has been pressing with so much zeal and good effect the matter of the divorce case. He is to take care that the Pope does not relapse into his former state of indecision. With this object Mai must deliver the letter which is enclosed in the other despatch."

No date.
Simancas.
T. c. I., 4.

421. THE EMPEROR to POPE CLEMENT VII.

The Emperor begs to give the following reply to the remarks of his Holiness through the Legate on the question of the Queen of England's affair.

He thanks him both in his own name and in that of his aunt the Queen for treating her cause in a manner befitting their common father, and such as justifies the hope that the matter may end well. The Emperor has constituted himself the defender of the marriage, in order to preserve the prestige and honour of the Pope and the Apostolic See from the calumnies of those who endeavour to assail it. This he does in fulfilment of his duty as champion of the Holy

---

* The letter to the Pope found in another bundle, and without date, printed below, is no doubt that referred to.

1531 ?

Church; but in addition he is led thereto by his obligation to defend from injustice so near a kinswoman of his own as the Queen. The marriage was solemnised by the sanction of the Holy See and cannot be dissolved. The matter is of such great importance and touches the rights of so many persons that the Emperor fails to understand how it could be disposed of in the town of Cambrai or in any place but Rome, and at the Court of the Pope, whose authority all Christians recognise and whose judgment all must obey. The Emperor therefore most earnestly prays the Pope to decide the case in his own court at Rome. The Queen is now, and will remain until her cause be decided, almost divorced from the King, and suffers thereby the gravest injustice. The Emperor therefore earnestly begs his Holiness to pronounce judgment with the least possible delay.

S. D.
Simancas.
E. 2016.
Latin.

422. Report presented to POPE CLEMENT VII., with a summary of the facts connected with the English Divorce.

In the year 1527, when the Pope was staying at the Castle of St. Angelo, there came to him a Secretary of the King of England to beg for a brief, which was granted.

Subsequently, in the year 1528, the Pope being then at Orvieto, Dr. Stephen and Dr. Fox came to him praying that he would declare null and void the dispensation granted by Pope Julius II. The reason they alleged for their request was that the dispensation had been obtained by false representations, namely that it had been untruly stated that the marriage was necessary in order to bring about peace between the Sovereigns of England and Spain and prevent war; and also that the King (then Prince of Wales) was desirous of the marriage. They alleged that the King had afterwards protested against the marriage, and thereby rendered the dispensation invalid. When the wedding took place, moreover, the reason alleged for it, upon which the dispensation had been given, had ceased to exist, as Queen Isabel was dead, and the marriage could not secure peace between her and England.

The Pope explained to the English ambassadors how unreasonable their request was, and that it was contrary to both law and justice that a decision upon so important a point should be arrived at without both parties being heard. The ambassadors insisted upon the Pope's consulting the Cardinals and the doctors of Perugia, who unanimously agreed that the demands of the English ambassadors could not properly be complied with.

The ambassadors thereupon requested the Pope to ratify and approve in anticipation a decree of divorce; and the Pope refused to do this, on the ground that it was unreasonable to ask him to approve of a judgment that had not yet been pronounced, and before he could know whether or not the judges had decided in accordance with the law, especially as the Pope himself would be the judge of any appeal that might be lodged against the judgment.

The ambassadors then asked that the case might be referred to Legates authorised to proceed to England. This request was granted, and the ambassadors selected the Cardinals whom they wished to be appointed. The Pope was disinclined himself to take cognisance of the case because his many other occupations fully employed him.

Cardinal Campeggio then proceeded to England.

The Queen presented a copy of the brief of dispensation, which in some points differed from the brief in the possession of the King. The King thereupon sent three ambassadors, Dr. Stephen, Dr. Peter Vannius and Dr. Drianus to the Pope, asking his Holiness to declare the brief, of which a copy had been produced by the Queen, to be false. The Pope promised them to request the Emperor to send the original of his brief to Rome, in order that his Holiness might decide which was the false and which the genuine one.

At this juncture there arrived in Rome ambassadors from the Emperor, who claimed that his Holiness should hear what they had to say in the matter of the Queen; but as they did not produce their powers or credentials the Pope refused to do so, notwithstanding their vehement protest that it was impious and cruel that the cause of so saintly a person as the Queen should be denied a hearing. Subsequently these ambassadors produced credentials in their favour from the Queen herself, and it was then impossible to refuse to give them audience.

The Queen declared through them that the legates were notoriously partial, and protested against all proceedings in her case in England. This protest was duly lodged at the *Signatura*, and copies of it were handed to the (English) ambassadors, with a notification of a period during which they might show cause why the Queen's contention should not be complied with. When the formalities were fulfilled, the question was debated and the decision unanimously adopted that the conduct of the legates was open to suspicion of partiality; the further proceedings in the case being thereupon ordered to be carried on by the Rota in Rome.

At the instance of the King of England the proceedings were then suspended for six months. The King of England has no just reason to complain that the powers granted to Cardinal Campeggio were limited, in so far that he was ordered not to deliver judgment (in England) until the Pope had been consulted on the matter. Such limitations are frequently made in similar cases.

N. D.
Simancas.
E. 2016.
Latin.

423. Consultation furnished by a MINISTER (unknown) to POPE CLEMENT VII. on the divorce case.

The present paper will be limited to a consideration of the expediency of enquiring into the reasons adduced by the King of England in support of the alleged nullity of his marriage, or whether it would be wiser to bury the affair in entire oblivion.

First, with regard to the King's alleged conscientious objection to his marriage. He says that he considers himself related in the first degree of affinity to the Queen; and that assuming in such case that the Pope had no power to grant dispensation the King fears that he may suffer for his marriage at the Day of Judgment. But the King here only *assumes* what it is necessary that he should *prove*; namely that his Holiness has not the power to dispense in

1531 ? such cases. If the dispensation is thought to be invalidated merely by errors in it, this can easily be remedied by asking for a new dispensation.

But the true reasons for the King's request for a divorce are not to be sought in his pretended scruples of conscience, but in his carnal lust. It is well known that he has already chosen the lady he intends to marry, and it is currently asserted that his proposed bride is related to him in the same degree of affinity as the Queen, and the objection to the legality of a marriage with her is consequently the same. The only difference is that, in the case of the Queen, the obstacle is said to have arisen from a legitimate union; whereas in the case of the other lady, it arises from an adulterous connection. But canon law in this respect makes no distinction between lawful cohabitation and fornication, and recognises the same impediment in both cases. The King of England may reply that he has obtained dispensation from such an obstacle in one case, and may therefore in another marry the sister of a lady with whom he has cohabited; but he should be begged to consider how gravely his reputation would suffer from such a proceeding.

If the King is of opinion that marriage between persons in the first degree of affinity cannot be made lawful by dispensation he certainly cannot lawfully marry his intended bride; and if he thinks that a new dispensation may remove the obstacles raised by his scruples, such new dispensation should be requested for his marriage with the Queen, rather than for the new projected marriage.

If honour has not sufficient hold over the King of England, at least he should avoid the open scandal created in England and elsewhere by his divorce, and should not expose his posterity to the calamities of a disputed succession. The example of the sons of Henry III. should surely warn him against such a course.

The King alleges a desire to have more children, but experience tends to show that his designated bride is probably sterile.

It is probable that the Queen may predecease the King, who in such case may lawfully marry again. There are instances where God has vouchsafed children to patriachs even in extreme old age.

If in the present circumstances the King marries another wife, the husband of the Princess (Mary) will probably dispute the right of succession of any children of such marriage, with the result that wars and contention will be caused.

The divorce of the King of England from the Queen is an affront to the Emperor and all his family; the consequence will be not only ill-feeling between them, but also wars between their respective subjects, and rebellion in England. The position of the King of England is one of the most influential in Europe. The power of the Emperor and the King of France is so nearly equal that the King of England is in most cases able to decide questions between them by siding with one or the other. He is honoured, and his friendship is therefore sought by both; but if for any reason the Emperor becomes his implacable enemy the King of England thenceforward will be dependent upon the King of France, and it would be wise for him to remember that the French do not love the English any more than the English love the French.

1531?

The King of England owes his title of Defender of the Faith to his marriage with the Queen.

NOTE.—There is in the same bundle a similar disquisition addressed to the Pope apparently by the same Minister, but as no fresh facts are adduced and the diffuse arguments are mainly legal, based upon the marriage laws of the ancients, there appears to be no need for reproducing the document here.

1532.
16 Jan.
Simancas.
E. B. 858.
Latin.

424. PROTEST of the Excusator of the KING OF ENGLAND against the proceedings in the divorce case before the POPE and the Roman tribunals, sent by Dr. ORTIZ to the EMPEROR.

Protests in his own name and in that of the King and people of England against all writs, articles, depositions of witnesses, and in general against all proceedings which have taken place, or which may hereafter take place, before his Holiness or the Papal courts touching the matrimonial cause of the King of England and Queen Catharine, his pretended wife.

The matter at issue is of the highest importance, both on account of the holiness of the sacrament of marriage, and of the exalted position of the interested parties.

It is therefore of the highest importance that the King of England should be personally present at the proceedings, especially as it would be impossible for him to instruct any other person so perfectly that the latter could faithfully represent his scruples and sentiments.

The ancestors of the King, and the King himself, have been, and are, sovereign lords of the realm of England, and they possessed, as he possesses, many fortresses, towns, cities, and lordships bordering other countries, especially Scotland and France. Experience has proved that whenever Kings, and especially Kings of England, are absent from their realms in distant lands, rebellions, seditions and other troubles break out at home, to the great suffering of rulers and peoples. It is probable that if the present King of England were absent from his country for any length of time, rebellion, civil war, and other calamities would take place, and that on his return it would be difficult for him to restore peace and order. Rome is distant from England more than 1,000 Italian miles. The King is owner in England of many possessions and privileges, and he is the supreme chief of the Government. If he went to Rome, therefore, he would expose his own person and his Kingdom to grave danger, as he would be obliged to travel through foreign dominions. It is directly opposed to the established custom in England, and to the King's interest, for him thus to imperil his life and realm; and it is consequently evident that the King cannot come to Rome without incurring these dangers.

From the facts here set forth, which are, moreover, notorious, it is clear that the King of England cannot be expected to attend personally any proceedings in the divorce case that may take place in Rome; and still less can he be bound to send a proxy or attorney.

The *excusator* therefore declares that the citation of the King of England before the Roman courts is null and void; and he protests against all further proceedings in Rome in the matrimonial cause referred to.

1532.

NOTE.—The above document is incorrectly calendared by Señor Gayangos, Vol. 4, part 2, p. 363, as "Dr. Ortiz's allegation in favour of the marriage."

8 Feb.
Simancas.
E. B. 858.

425. CARDINAL OF OSMA (LOAISA) to COBOS.

The English affair is very uphill work. They (the English) do not scruple to make use of the worst artifices of the devil himself to cause delay. The College of Cardinals, bearing in mind the importance of the matter, are likewise inclined to deal slowly with it, and so favour the English objects. The writer is deeply grieved to see how the affair drags, and it is still more painful for him to hint that, in his opinion, the Spanish ambassador (in Rome) is not doing all that he might. It is true that he makes a great show of activity, and, in fact, has done something of late, but he is lacking in knowledge, and above all, in diligence. When he addresses the Pope he speaks without energy, and in a manner to suggest that the matter has no interest for him. Lawyers and members of the Rota say that it is his (Mai's) fault that the divorce case was not finished a year ago. Had not the writer been in Rome the cause would hardly have been commenced, and what the ambassador has done recently has only been in consequence of the writer's energy putting him to shame. The ambassador would make a good Vice-Chancellor, as in that post he would work under the eyes of his master, but he is a very indifferent ambassador. J. A. Muxetula, on the other hand, is an excellent servant of the Emperor.° Rome, 8 February, 1532.

26 Feb.
Simancas.
E. V. 1559.

426. The EMPEROR to MAI. (Extract.)

The affair of the Queen of England has been so often delayed that it is impossible to consent to any further postponement. Now that the Pope has given his promise, Mai is to take care that judgment is speedily pronounced. The Emperor has not yet received a copy of the brief from the Pope which is to be delivered to the King of England, having missed the bearer on the road, but it will no doubt be delivered to the writer at Ratisbon. The ambassador in England has written, saying that the King has sent a certain Dr. Boner to Italy, in order to solicit the Universities and learned corporations to endorse the opinion pronounced by the doctors of canon law in Paris, that the divorce case should be carried through in England. Begs the Pope not to permit the English to obtain such opinions by bribery and other unlawful means.

Postscript.—After receiving Mai's letters of 9th and 10th February, it seems to me that fresh delay is intended in the divorce case, and that dishonest means are being employed to delay the decision. You must speak earnestly to the Pope about it.
Augsburg, 26 February, 1532.

26 Feb.
Simancas.
E. V. 1559.

427. The EMPEROR to RODRIGO NIÑO. (Extract.)

Niño is in the Emperor's name warmly to thank the Seigniory of Venice for not having permitted the Professors of the University of

---

° Juan Antonio Muxetula was the special envoy from the Emperor to Rome in connection with the divorce proceedings.

1532.

Padua to proceed to Rome and plead the cause of the King of England, although the English ambassador had requested them to do so. The Seigniory acted perfectly rightly in refusing permission to them. The whole object of the English is to delay the final decision of the case. He has been informed by his ambassador in England that the King has again sent a person from England to solicit the Universities and other learned bodies to give an approval of the opinion of the canonists of Paris. This agent of the King is a Dr. Boner. Niño is to watch and oppose his proceedings.

Augsburg, 26 February, 1532.

12 March.
Simancas.
E. B. 860.

428. CARDINAL LOAISA* to the EMPEROR.

The Pope convoked a congregation of Cardinals, in which it was decided to send a Cardinal Legate to the Kings of France and England, for the purpose of requesting their aid against the Turks. If the King of France be disinclined to engage in open warfare with the Turk, the Legate is to beg him to remain quiet and neutral in his own country, and to avoid taking the opportunity of the war to raise trouble in Italy or to occupy Genoa and Milan. The writer thinks that the sending of such a Legate to France and England would be prejudicial to the interests of the Emperor, and he therefore spoke to the Pope to this effect. His Holiness thereupon promised to let the matter drop. (Note in the handwriting of Cobos, on the margin of the above, "Very Good!") The Secretary of the Voyvode who went to England has returned. He reports that the King of England has promised to aid the Voyvode in such a manner as the King of France may consider advisable. The letters that have come to hand from England state, however, that King Henry is not really much disposed to help the Voyode. (Note in margin, by Cobos, "He must continue to send information on this subject.")

Rome, 12 March, 1532.

12 March.
Simancas.
E. B. 858.

429. CARDINAL LOAISA (Bishop of Sigüenza) to COBOS.

News from Venice that the Turks are preparing for war. The writer accompanied Juan Antonio Muxetula and the Imperial ambassador (Mai) to see the Pope, who informed them that, according to the news he had received by Venice and Ancona from Constantinople, war was inevitable. His Holiness summoned a convocation of twelve Cardinals for the next day, in order to discuss the means of resistance. When they had assembled, the Pope declared that little assistance could be looked for from France or England. The Nuncio in England had spoken to the King on the subject, but the King had exclaimed in reply that he would not help the Pope against the Turk to the extent of a *Carlino*, unless the matrimonial cause were delegated to the consideration and decision of French judges. From the Christian King even less can be expected. If he can be prevented from helping the Turks it is all

---

* Cardinal Loaisa had just been promoted from the bishopric of Osma to that of Sigüenza.

HENRY VIII. 583

1532.

that can be hoped for. The Pope concluded by saying that he would aid the Emperor in defending Sicily, and that he was ready to send a Cardinal Legate to the Kings of France and England, in order to endeavour once more to persuade them to do their duty as Christian princes. If they were unwilling to give active assistance they might at least be induced to remain neutral. The writer considered that the sending of a Legate to France and England would be useless, because before he could arrive in England hostilities with the Turk would have commenced. Besides, both these Kings are so busy with their own dishonest schemes that nothing could possibly be got from them, unless the Pope stooped to do their bidding. Moreover the French and English between them would put so much idle stuff into the head of the Cardinal who might be sent to them, that he might become friendly to them and return to Rome an opponent of the Emperor. The contentions of the Kings of France and England would also assume a more plausible appearance in the eyes of people in general if a Legate was sent to them by his Holiness.

The writer is anxious to know what measures are contemplated to prevent the King of France from occupying Milan and Genoa whilst the Emperor is occupied with the war against the Turk.

Rome, 12 March, 1532.

NOTE.—In a letter of the same date as the above Mai sends somewhat similar information to the Emperor. Muxetula, the special envoy, also writes in the same strain.

22 March.
Simancas.
E. R. 858.

430. CARDINAL LOAISA to COBOS. (Extract.)

Don Antonio Enriquez has written a book on the divorce case of the Queen of England. Although the book is a weak production, its Latin being as faulty as its arguments, the author has stolen every sentence of it from other writers. It is the same thing with this book as with the songs of Gabriel, which the uncle of Don Antonio, the Admiral, copied and called his own.

Rome, 22 March, 1532.

26 May.
Simancas.
E. R. 858.

431. IÑIGO LOPEZ DE MENDOZA, Cardinal of Burgos, to the EMPEROR.

The English matter does not make much progress, and the writer fears that such will be the case for some time to come. There are many persons in Rome who care little for what is said, but who are in great fear of what might be done. He has spoken very strongly and openly with the Pope about it, but doubts if it will be of much use. If the pace be not quickened somehow those who have begun the business will never live to see the ending.

Rome, 26 May, 1532.

4 July.
Simancas.
E. R. 859.

432. MAI to the EMPEROR.

It has been strictly forbidden under heavy penalty to speak of what has been decided in the Queen of England's case. He has, however, contrived to hear that the decision is in favour of the Queen, as it has been resolved that the King of England must send

1532.

his power of attorney, and in default of his doing so the proceedings are to be continued at the beginning of next year, without regard for the English *excusator*, or for what may be written from England. This resolution is considered by people in Rome to be very satisfactory, although no judgment on the main case has been pronounced. It is to be hoped that the decree will be issued before the beginning of the vacation. In order to gain time it would be advisable to have recourse to the bribery usual in Rome in such cases.*

Rome, 4 July, 1532.

Note.—Similar information was written to the Emperor on the same day by Dr. Ortiz and Cardinal Loaisa. (*See* Calendar Henry VIII.)

N. D.
Simancas.
T. e I. 4.
Latin.

433. Draft of an Address from the English Ambassador to the Emperor.

The Emperor and the King of England have been, and are, united by true love and friendship. There is however now unfortunately some reason to fear that this holy union may be disturbed by suspicion, and in order to avoid such an eventuality the King of England has ordered me to address to his Imperial Majesty the following observations.

The King of England sent his ambassadors to the Pope for the purpose of complaining of the injustice and evil treatment which he (the King) had received at the hands of the papal legates; they having summoned him to appear in Rome either personally or by a resident ambassador. This citation is not justified by law, as has been confirmed by the decisions of the Universities of Paris and Orleans, by the Chancellor of France, the most learned Cardinals and the presidents of the Parliament of Paris, the highest authorities in canon law. The Pope answered the King of England's complaint by saying that the Emperor did not wish the cause of the divorce to be decided in any other place than Rome; but the King cannot forget the Emperor's promise not to do anything in this affair that could obstruct the ends of justice. The King of England, who has always favoured the policy of the Emperor, is convinced that the latter has no reason to deal otherwise than justly towards him, and trusts that the Pope may have misunderstood the Emperor or have gone beyond his authority in saying that "the Emperor did not wish it" (imperator non vult). If the Emperor has been mistaken with regard to the law, he will, the King is sure, allow the latter to demonstrate the truth to him; and he hopes that after his Imperial Majesty has read the opinion of the Universities of Paris and Orleans, of the Chancellor of France and other councillors, he will no longer entertain any doubt in the matter, and will abstain from intervening in the manner suggested by the Pope.

---

* Marginal note for reply by Cobos. "He is to do all he can, and to write, with the greatest secrecy."

1532.
2 Aug.
Simancas.
E. V. 1559.

434. The Emperor to Cardinal Loaisa.

To continue to persuade the Pope to remain friendly and give up his negotiations with France.

Disapproves of the arrest of the Secretary of the late Cardinal Colonna.* Begs his Holiness to release him. The decision adopted in the Queen of England's case does not appear to the Emperor to be so favourable as to arouse the suspicion that it may have been arrived at for the purpose of avoiding the execution of it. He has instructed the ambassador (Mai) to see that the sentence be duly registered in the form prescribed by the law. The Cardinal also must look to this.

Ratisbon, 2 August, 1532.

18 Sept.
Simancas.
E. R. 860.

435. Muxetula† to the Emperor.

Letters from France and England report that the Kings of the two countries are on very cordial terms, and intend to have an interview at Boulogne. They declare they will make war next year, the King of France attacking Milan and the King of England Flanders. The writer is not of opinion that these threats have any real foundation, as if the two Kings had any real intention of commencing war they would certainly not talk so much about it. There is, however, no doubt that if the Turks attack Christendom the Kings of France and England will do their best to profit by the opportunity. Rincon, who has treated with the Turks, is a great scoundrel (bribon). The pope is in unfeigned alarm, though the writer is doing his best to comfort him, and to assure him that the threats of England and France are but empty boasting.

Rome, 18 September, 1532.

Oct.
Simancas.
E. 1457.

436. News from Italy. (Extract.)

The divorce case of the King and Queen of England will be proceeded with in November, and it is reported that it will be speedily concluded.

The Kings of France and England were to have an interview on the 20 October. The King of England intends to bring with him his concubine, Anne, whom he has lately created Marchioness of Pembroke. It is said that her marquisate is endowed with five thousand ducats a year, and that it will enable her to make an advantageous match. The French and English threaten much, not only the Pope but all the world, with this interview and the agreements to be made therein. They say that they will convoke a Council, but it is very improbable that they will do so; and, indeed, it is quite likely that, as happened on a previous occasion, the two Kings will meet and separate without working any miracles.

---

* In a letter to the Emperor, dated a few days previously, Mai had sent news that the man had been arrested with others, accused of a plot to poison the Pope. In a marginal note for reply Cobos somewhat indignantly suggests that the accusation is a calumny, and directs Mai to favour the house of Colonna in all ways, but in a manner that will not arouse suspicion against the Emperor.

† Juan Antonio Muxetula or Musetula, Special Envoy from the Emperor of Rome.

1533.
30 April.
Simancas
E. R. 860.

437. Cardinal Palmerio° to Cobos.

The King of England has married his concubine Anne. The Pope is very indignant at his disobedience. Many people believe that the interview between his Holiness and the King of France will not now take place, but the writer is of a different opinion, and regards the marriage in question to be an additional reason for the interview. The Emperor, however, may rest assured that the Pope will do nothing at the interview to prejudice the interests of his Majesty. It is the Pope's own interest to avoid embarassing the Emperor, and the writer hopes that complete success may attend the enterprise of his Majesty against England.

Rome, 30 April, 1533.

6 May.
Simancas.
E. V. 1560.

438. The Emperor to Count Cifuentes.† (Extract.)

Approves the declaration of the Count to his Holiness respecting the Queen of England's case, requesting that judgment should be promptly pronounced. The Imperial ambassador in England confirms what Cifuentes writes; namely that, according to common report, the King of England has really married his concubine, Anne. The King of France also has conveyed the same intelligence to the Imperial ambassador in his court; but, withal, the Emperor is not quite convinced that the marriage has taken place. As soon as it is known beyond doubt that the King and his concubine are married the Emperor will send fresh instructions to Cifuentes. The latter in his last despatch says that the Pope asked him what the Emperor would do if the King of England did marry his concubine, to which Cifuentes had replied that the Pope should first do what he was in duty bound to do, and the Emperor would afterwards consider what ought to be done on his part. This answer was a very good one. Cifuentes is not to say that he has received any answer to the Pope's question, but he is to continue to press with the greatest energy that a judgment in the case shall be delivered without further delay. The more confirmed becomes the apprehension that the King will marry his concubine, the more urgent is it that the judgment should be pronounced promptly. The delay emboldens the King and helps him to persevere in his object. If he succeeds the Pope will be responsible.

Barcelona, 6 May, 1533.

21 May.
Simancas.
E. R. 860.

439. Cardinal of Jaen‡ to the Emperor. (Extract.)

Not much to say about the proposed interview between the Pope and the King of France at Nice, as the ambassador (Count Cifuentes)

°Andrea Matteo, Bishop of Matera, frequently called Cardinal Matteo or Cardinal of Matera.
† Now Imperial ambassador in Rome.
‡ Gabriel Merino, Archbishop of Bari and Bishop of Jaen, in Spain.

1533.

has not communicated any instructions on the subject.° The same is the case with respect to the English matter. The writer deals with the Pope through Jacopo Salviati and the Archbishop of Capua. His principal object is to paint the nefarious and heretical act of the King of England in the darkest possible colours (afeando el hecho hasta el cielo), and to fill the Pope with disgust of it. None of the other heresies is as heinous as that of the King of England, and it appears to the writer that the Pope cannot avoid issuing a brief in the strongest terms, and pronouncing a separation *a mensa et thoro*. At the same time the proceedings of the principal cause must be carried through. Prays the Emperor to send the most emphatic instructions, in order to silence those who are always inclined to stand aloof until they see how his Majesty will take the affair.

Rome, 21 May, 1533.

29 May.
Simancas.
E. V. 1560.

440. The EMPEROR to ANTONIO DE LEYVA, Prince of Ascoli.

The Pope declares that his intended interview with the King of France will be greatly advantageous to the welfare of Christendom. The Emperor on the contrary believes that it will cause great calamities.

The King of England has behaved very badly towards him in separating from the Queen, his lawful wife, and even going to the length of marrying his concubine. Has sent Rodrigo Davalos to Rome, to co-operate with the ambassador in the matter of the divorce.

Barcelona, 29 May, 1533.

31 May.
Simancas.
E. V. 1560.

441. The EMPEROR to the POPE (CLEMENT VII.).

His Holiness is well aware of all that has passed concerning the matter of the Queen of England. The Emperor has never ceased to supplicate him, both personally and through his ambassadors, to deliver judgment in the divorce case. When after their last interview the Emperor took leave of his Holiness the latter promised him faithfully that he would allow no more delay in the matter. Since then events have taken place that have shocked the feelings of the whole world, and constitute a scandal and an affront to the Holy See and an evil precedent for others.† The Emperor is of opinion that the delays to which the Pope has consented have been the principal cause of these evils. Being so nearly concerned in the affair, in his two-fold capacity, namely as natural protector of the Holy Church and See, and as a near kinsman of the Queen of England, the Emperor has decided to send Rodrigo Davalos, a gentleman of his household, in order that, conjointly with his ambassador, he may address his Holiness on the Emperor's behalf, and ask that justice may be done.

Barcelona, 31 May, 1533.

° There was great jealousy between Cifuentes and the Cardinal, and in a letter written by the latter to the Emperor on the 22nd May, he says that the Ambassador threatens to leave Rome if the Cardinal meddles with diplomatic matters.

† That is to say, the marriage of Henry VIII. and Anne Boleyn and the disinheriting of the Princess Mary.

588   SPANISH STATE PAPERS.

1533.

NOTE.—The instructions to Davalos and Cifuentes will be found calendared in Henry VIII. Vol. 6, p. 254.

31 May.
Simancas.
E. V. 1560.

442. The EMPEROR to COUNT CIFUENTES.

Has carefully and minutely considered what is to be done in the cause of the Queen of England, and has come to the conclusion that the proceedings at law must be continued.* The reasons that have moved him to this decision are set forth in the instructions which will be handed to Cifuentes by Rodrigo Davalos, a gentleman of the Emperor's household, together with this dispatch. Although fully convinced of the ability and diligence of Cifuentes, the Emperor has thought well to commission Rodrigo Davalos conjointly with him to conduct the negotiations concerning the cause of the Queen of England. He has done this in order that the Pope may see how much importance he attaches to the subject.†

(The rest of this letter is concerned with subjects unconnected with England, and of no present importance.)

Barcelona, 31 May, 1533.

3 June.
Simancas.
E. R. 860.

443. CARDINAL OF JAEN to COBOS.

Spoke with the Pope after his last letter of 28th ultimo left. It is now settled that the interview between his Holiness and the King of France is to take place at Nice in September. As the time is so far ahead perhaps some circumstance may intervene to prevent the meeting after all. In the meanwhile, the Bishop of Faenza is sent to France, in order to settle beforehand the various subjects which are to be touched upon, and the concessions to be made on each side. The writer spoke with the Pope about the Scottish marriage. His Holiness said that it would be a good thing if the Emperor could bring it to pass. His Nuncio, however, had written that the King of France had already almost formally concluded a marriage treaty between the King of Scots and a daughter of the King of Navarre.

With regard to the Queen of England, the Pope has already signed the duplicate briefs, but they are not yet despatched to France, England, Flanders, and other countries where they are likely to be read by the English. It is in the highest degree necessary that the English, as well as Christians in general, should know that the Pope resents the unspeakable crime against the Holy See and the Christian religion committed by the King of England. The person sent by that King to Rome, and who, although not duly authorised, is called the "*Defensor*," has requested the Pope to refer the question to English judges. His Holiness listened to all the arguments brought forward in favour of this demand, and when the speaker had finished said that he was astonished at such a request being made, seeing the disrespectful manner in which the King of England had behaved towards the

---

* The minutes of the deliberations in the Emperor's Council in this matter are calendered in Henry VIII., Vol. 6, p. 252.

† Letters of a similar tenour to the above were also sent on the same date to Dr. Ortiz and the Cardinal of Jaen.

Holy See. He then dismissed the so-called Defensor with very angry words. The writer has obtained this information from his Holiness himself, and it has since been confirmed by the Papal chamberlains. The writer is of opinion that the Emperor should condemn in very strong terms the misdeeds of the King of England.

Count de Cifuentes has informed the writer that he resents that he (Cardinal of Jaen) or anyone else should meddle with diplomatic affairs.

Rome, 3 June, 1533.

16 July.
Simancas.
E B. 860.
Italian.

444. CARDINAL CAMPEGGIO to the EMPEROR.

Has not written to him since he returned to Italy, but has always been, and still remains, his sincere and devoted servant. Now that Rodrigo Davalos is about to return to him he cannot allow the opportunity to pass without repeating his promise to do all in his power to serve him in the English affairs, and on all other occasions that may offer.*

Rome, 16 July, 1533.

18 July.
Simancas.
Guerra, 3.

445. COUNT CIFUENTES to COBOS. (Extracts.)

Begs that presents be made to Cardinals De la Valle, Monte and Matera. If Cardinal of Jaen is to take part in the negotiations with Rome, Cifuentes wishes to be relieved of his post as ambassador. If Micer Mai consented for reasons of his own to share his diplomatic authority with a Cardinal, it is no reason why the writer also should submit to such a humiliation.

Has given to Secretary Blasio 300 ducats for the judgment. The judgment, although it is not so favourable as could be wished, is not altogether bad. Has not taken the 300 ducats from the Emperor's funds, but on bills of Exchange on Colardi, which the Queen of England will pay. The Sentence cannot yet be printed, as a preamble must first be written to it, and a bull drafted from it.

Rome, 18 July, 1533.

29 July.
Simancas.
E. V. 1560.

446. The EMPEROR to COUNT CIFUENTES. (Extracts.)

Nothing to add about the interview between the Pope and the King of France. Refers him also to the other letters with regard to the affairs of England. He must do all he can to bring the Queen's cause to a speedy conclusion, and Rodrigo Davalos is to return to Spain. The Emperor carefully notes all Cifuentes writes about the communications made by the Pope to him to the effect that the Emperor might now easily gain the friendship of the King of France if the former were instrumental in obtaining Calais for the latter. The Pope is confident that in such case the King of France would renounce his friendship with England, and abandon his plans in Italy. The King of England would be deservedly punished. The Emperor notes likewise Cifuentes' answer to the Pope

---

* By the same courier that carried this letter were sent others of similar tenour from Cardinals San Severino, Del Monte, etc.

on this subject. The case is a very delicate one, and must be maturely considered, but the Emperor thinks that at the present time no negotiations should on any account be opened with the King of France, as in such case the latter King would be the first person to make capital out of them by divulging them to the King of England. The latter would then have good reason for resentment and for alleging that the Emperor contemplated making war upon him, and disturbing the peace of Christendom, which is quite contrary to the Emperor's intention. Besides, if the King of France added Calais to Boulogne and his other dominions in that part of Europe, the French would at once look upon themselves as the masters of Flanders, and would in all probability begin war there. For these and many other reasons the Emperor desires that the matter broached by the Pope be dropped, and be no more spoken of. If the Pope should again mention the project Cifuentes is adroitly to avoid giving any answer. Cifuentes is also to avoid discourse with regard to the Pope's other suggestion, namely that of marrying the daughter of the Queen of England with the Duke of Norfolk. It is undesirable that any decided answer should be given to this project until the Queen's cause is concluded. The Pope avers that the Duke of Norfolk is married in England, but that the marriage is invalid as it is only a marriage *per verba de futuro*, and the Duke was only brought to consent to it by intimidation. If it is true that the marriage is only covenanted by *verba de futuro*, the Pope may entertain the negotiations with regard to this proposed match between the Princess and the Duke until the final sentence is pronounced in the divorce case of the Queen.* The Duke of Norfolk has already gone to France with a numerous train in order to be present at the interview between the Pope and King Francis, the object of the embassy being to increase the authority and prestige of the King of England. Cifuentes is directed to accompany his Holiness to the interview, if it takes place, but he is not to increase his household or incur any extraordinary expenses. The Emperor's authority and prestige happily do not depend upon such futile things.

The Emperor notes Cifuentes' remark that many people are of opinion that the Queen (Catharine of Aragon) should leave England, as her life is considered in danger. He has already considered this question, as Cifuentes will have noticed by the instructions given to Rodrigo Davalos; his decided opinion being that, on no account, ought the Queen to leave England, in order that she may preserve the attachment towards her of the English people, which she would sacrifice by leaving the country.

With regard to the Pope's question to Cifuentes, as to what he (the Emperor) would do if, and when, his Holiness pronounced judgment in favour of the Queen of England, the answer is contained in the instructions sent by Rodrigo Davalos, and the

---

* Thomas Howard, third Duke of Norfolk, was at this time a widower of 60 years of age, his first wife having been the Princess Anne, third daughter of Edward IV, and his second Elizabeth, second daughter of Edward Stafford Duke of Buckingham, by whom he had two sons and three daughters. The Princess Mary at the time was 17 years of age.

1533.

Emperor notes that when Cifuentes read the clause in the instructions to the Pope, the latter, whilst praising it for its prudence, said that it was not an answer to his question. If the Pope again touches upon this subject Cifuentes is to repeat what he has already declared, namely that it is the Pope's business first to pronounce the judgment, and the Emperor will then consider the steps necessary to enforce it. The Pope ought to be satisfied with this answer. He may rest assured that the Emperor will not fail in his duty.

If the Pope will not send him the bull to levy the *cruzada* he (the Emperor) will levy it without the bull, as the cruzada was promised to him, and he intends to employ the proceeds against the infidels.°

Monzon, 29 July, 1533.

25 Aug.
Simancas.
Milan, 1177.

447. ANTONIO DE LEYVA to the EMPEROR. (Extract.)

The Marquis of Saluzzo writes that the King of England is making great efforts to dissuade the King of France from going to meet the Pope and from further entertaining the idea of the marriage (*i.e.* of the Duke of Orleans) with the niece of the Pope.† The King of England offers him (Francis) large sums of money to be spent in his enterprise against Milan, on condition that he abandons the proposed interview with his Holiness. Would to God this interview could in truth be prevented. It bodes no good.—Frasinet, 25 August, 1533.

30 Aug.
Simancas.
E. V. 1560.

448. The EMPEROR to COUNT CIFUENTES. (Extracts.)

Does not believe that the Pope would go with his niece to meet the King of France, if the various subjects to be dealt with, including the marriage, had not been settled beforehand.

The Emperor approves of the Pope's decree ordering the King of England to produce before the end of September all the documents concerning the proceedings in the divorce which may have taken place in England, in case he (the King) intends to refer to such proceedings in Rome. He also approves of the manner in which the judgment is to be communicated to the King of England, and thanks Cifuentes for the zeal he has shown in the matter. He must continue to do all in his power to obtain the final decision on the main case without delay. The decree ordering the judgment to be carried into effect must also be despatched speedily. The Emperor has read, and caused others to read, the memorandum forwarded by Cifuentes on the question as to whether "the Anne" to whom the King of England is married should be cited to appear or not. He is of the same opinion as the scholars who compiled the memorandum, namely that Anne should not be summoned to appear before the tribunal at Rome.

° The Crusada was a Bull conceded and renewed periodically to Spanish Sovereigns, authorising them to sell ecclesiastical indulgencies to their subjects, the proceeds—which formed a considerable portion of the Spanish revenue—being ostensibly applied to the wars against the infidels.

† This was the marriage that afterwards took place between the future Henry II. of France and Catharine de Medici.

The Imperial ambassador in England has written that the King of England trusts most implicitly in the Pope's Nuncio now resident in England. The confidence of the King in this Nuncio is so great that he has begged the latter to accompany the English ambassador to the interview between his Holiness and the King of France. The Emperor informs Cifuentes of this in order that he may be very cautious in his dealings with the Nuncio, and that he may secretly inform the Pope or Salviati of the sentiments of the Nuncio in England.

The Emperor notes in Cifuentes' last letter that the Pope had received news from the person whom he had sent to England for the purpose of entering into the negotiations about the Council (of Trent), and that the Archbishop of Reggio, who was in Germany on the same business, had written that the Germans are strongly of opinion that the Council should be held in a German, and not an Italian, town. The agent sent by the King of the Romans to remonstrate with the Pope about the English affair writes to the same effect. Notes Cifuentes' observation that this agent had also been negotiating with the Pope about the Lutheran question, and had declared that there was no remedy but armed force; of which declaration the Pope had warmly approved. Cifuentes had hesitated to express an opinion on the subject. The Emperor had since received news from the Archbishop of Reggio and the President of Malines that the Catholic Prince Electors had not yet given their final answer, but that the Duke of Saxony and his followers insist that the Council should be held in a German town, and on no account in Italy. The Emperor is therefore not yet in a position to announce his will as to whether armed force may be employed against the Lutherans or not. If the agent of the King of the Romans expressed himself in the affirmative on the question he must presumably have done so without authority, as there is no army by which the Lutherans could be subjected. The answer of the Duke of Saxony and his adherents is very discourteous to the Pope, for which the Emperor is sorry. He believes that the reply was drawn up by Melancthon, at least it was written in his hand. A copy of it is enclosed.

Cifuentes' letter of 14th instant just to hand, and the Emperor notes that as soon as the King of England was informed of the last sentence in the divorce case he recalled his ambassadors from Rome, and ordered the return to England of the Duke of Norfolk, who was to have been present at the interview between the Pope and the King of France. The Emperor learns with great pleasure that when the Pope announced in the Consistory the steps decided upon by the King of England (*i.e.* in withdrawing his ambassadors) all the Cardinals declared that the Pope had simply done his duty, and that the King of England had no cause for complaint. Approves of the decision not to recall immediately the Papal Nuncio in England, but to order him to follow the lead of the Imperial ambassador. The Emperor notes that, although the Pope appears publicly sorry for the steps the King of England has taken, he is secretly glad of them, because he thinks that they may prove an obstacle to the meeting with the King of France. The Pope likes the idea of the interview much less than formerly, and would be

1533.

glad to be able to avoid it without incurring the responsibility of himself declining it. Cifuentes is to be careful to keep the Emperor well informed of what he can learn in Rome about this, as the news from France appears to contradict what Cifuentes says as to the probability of the interview not taking place. The King of France is continuing his journey to Marseilles; and the galleys have already put to sea from that port for the purpose of escorting the Pope. The Duke of Norfolk has taken his leave of the King of France, and is now on his way back to England. It is said that the marriage of the Duke of Orleans* and the niece of the Pope is not yet to be consummated, on account of the youth of the Duke. Cifuentes is to enquire into the truth of this.

Monzon, 30 August, 1533.

24 Sept.
Simancas.
E. R. 860.

449. POPE CLEMENT VII. to the EMPEROR. (Extract.)

Has no longer any doubts or scruples in the matrimonial cause of England, and is fully decided to do what the laws provide; being convinced that the Emperor on his side will use every effort in his power to carry his judgment into effect.

Gratefully accepts the abbacy of Monserrat for "his Cardinal." Intends to speak with him about the Council and the affairs of Germany, and hopes that the Emperor will be satisfied with him. Intends shortly to convoke the Council.

Pisa, 24 September, 1533.

1534.
28 Jan.
Simancas.
E. R. 860.

450. COUNT CIFUENTES to COBOS.

Aponte arrived. Not his fault that he was somewhat later than expected, as the roads are very bad.

Aponte's credentials are drawn with great skill. The Pope will be obliged either to send aid against the Turk or show his hand. Cifuentes asked the Pope some time ago what secret matter had been settled at the Marseilles interview. His reason for doing so was that he did not wish to appear distrustful, or to show over confidence. Has again, in the presence of Aponte, conveyed to the Pope in the mildest form what the Emperor wrote about the Marseilles interview and the affairs of Germany. The Pope appeared very frightened (medroso), a sure sign that he has concluded something that he wishes not to be known.

About a month since he pressed the Pope very urgently to give at once his final sentence on the principal point of the divorce case. His Holiness said on that occasion that last year at Belvedere Rodrigo Davalos told him that the Emperor declared that he would bind himself to execute the final sentence as soon as the Pope pronounced it, and his Holiness asked Cifuentes if he was authorised to make such a pledge for the Emperor. Cifuentes has refrained hitherto from mentioning this point, as he did not wish to injure Davalos. Even now he has not mentioned the matter in his letters to the Emperor, and leaves to the discretion of Cobos whether or not Davalos' blunder shall be communicated to his Majesty.

---

* Henry Duke of Orleans was born in March, 1519, so that at this time he was but fourteen and a half years old.

1534.

Cifuentes told the Pope that he was not authorised to make the declaration referred to, and that Rodrigo Davalos could not have been instructed to say what he had done, as he had been strictly enjoined in his credentials to make no declaration or pledge of any sort without the knowledge and consent of Cifuentes. The latter repeated to the Pope what he had told him so often; namely that the Emperor would do his duty, but that his Majesty would bind himself to nothing explicitly before he had seen the sentence itself. The Cardinal of Santa Croce and the Archbishop of Capua also told Cifuentes that they had heard the Pope declare that Davalos had made the promise referred to in the name of the Emperor.—Rome, 23 January, 1534.

4 March.
Simancas.
E. V. 1561.

451. The EMPEROR to COUNT CIFUENTES. (Extracts.)

The King of the Romans has written saying that the negotiations carried on at the Marseilles interview were wholly directed against the Emperor's and the King of the Romans' interests.

Notes Cifuentes' information with regard to the Queen of England's case, and approves of his answer to the Pope's question as to what the Emperor would do in order to carry the final sentence into effect when it was pronounced. He can make no further declaration than that already made on this point, and the Pope must have confidence in him. The Emperor likewise approves of what Cifuentes said when the Pope proposed to nominate a person to defend the interests of the King of England in the divorce proceedings in Rome, and considers that the steps taken by Cifuentes to obtain a delivery of the final sentence on the main case without further delay have been judicious. As, notwithstanding the decision of the Pope not to appoint any person to represent the King of England's interests in the suit, the Consistory has resolved that the whole proceedings in the case are to be recited again, there is nothing for it but to submit, but Cifuentes must continue to urge most forcibly that a speedy decision on the main point shall be arrived at. Cifuentes did quite right in these circumstances to refrain from bringing up the executorial decrees that were sent to him from Flanders. In order to convince the Pope and the Cardinals how necessary it is that the affair shall be brought to a prompt conclusion nothing will be more efficacious than to point out to them the indignities to which the Queen is being subjected. Enclosed is the copy of a declaration made by the King of England's Privy Council in contempt of the authority of the Pope and the Church. Let this be seen in Rome.—Toledo, 4 March, 1534.

N. D.
June (?)
Simancas.
T. e I. 4.

452. COUNT CIFUENTES to the EMPEROR.

After the sentence in the divorce case of the Queen of England was pronounced, declaring the marriage of the King of England with her perfectly lawful and valid, communications were held with the learned doctors engaged in the case with regard to the minatory clause which should be added to the letters of execution. The authorities were of opinion that the King of England should be ordered to obey the sentence *sub pena* of being deprived of his Kingdom if he is contumacious. This opinion seems only right and

1534.

just. There is, however, one circumstance to be considered, which may raise some doubt. The Pope claims that the realm of England is a feud of the Church, and that the Pontiff possesses the right, conceded by former Kings, of investiture. Many learned doctors share this opinion. It is furthermore alleged that the King of England by acts he has already committed to the prejudice of the Holy See is, in fact, at present schismatic and heretical, and that the Pope has the right to confiscate and dispose of the Kingdom of England as an ecclesiastical fief, the Princess being incapacitated from succeeding by reason of the heresy of her father.

Cifuentes has doubted the advisability of demanding that the King of England should be deprived of his Kingdom as stated. If the King were declared to have forfeited his realm, as a consequence merely of his contumacy in regard of the sentence in the suit, the Princess would not thereby be deprived, especially if it were stated in the executorial decree that the confiscation of the King's right to the Kingdom was to be executed in favour of the Princess. If that were done no dispute could arise afterwards on the question of whether the feud reverted to the Church in prejudice to the rights of the Princess or not. It is not, however, sure if the Pope and the Cardinals would insert such a clause in the decree, and Cifuentes has thought best to say nothing at present about the forfeiture of the Kingdom. He awaits the Emperor's instructions on the subject.*

It has also been considered that if the forfeiture of the realm in favour of the Princess were demanded the King would be greatly irritated, and both the Queen and the Princess would be placed in great peril for their lives. Cifuentes begs for instructions as to his action, in the case of the realm of England being declared forfeited to the Holy See. (In a marginal note Cobos says that this is not yet needed. Cifuentes must first ask for the executorial decrees to be issued.) In the meanwhile Cifuentes, in order to lose no time, has asked for the decrees to be issued in the usual form. If necessary the forfeiture clause may be asked for later, if the Emperor so orders.

We have already the executorial decrees that were issued in consequence of the former attempted proceedings (*i.e.* those before the Archbishop of Canterbury), and on these decrees the aid of secular force might be invoked, as well as on the decrees that are now to be granted. It was therefore discussed whether it would be advisable to proceed on the former decrees or wait for the latter to be issued as a consequence of the judgment on the main point in the case; or whether it would be better to proceed jointly in virtue of both decrees. The reason for this discussion was that, before the later executorial decrees can be issued, promulgated, and reproduced with the usual formalities, the secular force invokable under the first decree might be collected and organised, this decree being directed to the Emperor, Kings, Princes, Barons, etc. ordering them to seize the person and property of the King of England pending his submission.†

---

* In a marginal note Cobos expresses his approval of these considerations, and similar approval is marked at the end of each paragraph.

† Cobos writes with reference to this: They are to proceed in the ordinary manner, for reasons which will be explained. They must be told that if the business is precipitated the King of England would have reason to complain and to quash the proceedings altogether.

1534.

In order that the interdict placed upon England may not deprive the country of commerce with other nations, it has been debated if it would not be well to ask the Pope to order all Englishmen on pain of excommunication to respect the said interdict, and that they should regard the Queen as their Queen instead of Anne. It is true that it is impossible to excommunicate a whole people, but all English persons who do not obey may be excommunicated for disobeying the Pope's commands, and this will come to the same thing. It is not yet known whether his Holiness will consent to pronounce the general excommunication when he sees that his commands are not obeyed.[*] After the sentence had been pronounced, the Archbishop of Paris[†] came to Rome for the purpose of forwarding the interests of the King of England; alleging that he was duly accredited by the King. He said that his instructions enjoined him to give full credit to what the French ambassador in England might write to him. The ambassador, he said, had written to him to the effect that he had in his possession a paper signed by the King of England, in which he professes his willingness to obey the sentence with regard to his proceedings,[‡] but that he wished his case to be decided in a place other than Rome. A copy of this paper was sent to the Archbishop of Paris; and in full Consistory, at which the Pope was present, it was resolved that the sentence already pronounced could not be revoked, as the Queen had acquired rights by it. This is the present condition of the business. (Marginal note by Cobos: This is good. He must do his best and see that the sentence be not annulled, as he says it was decided in the Consistory.)

1 May.
Simancas.
E. V. 1563.

453. The Emperor to Count-Cifuentes. (Extracts.)

Has ordered the collector of the Pope to be spoken to about the English affair, and enclosed a memorandum of the discourse with him. The Emperor thanked his Holiness for all he had done in the case, and, since the Emperor has been directly asked to state what steps he intended to take for the purpose of carrying the sentence into effect, he answered that he would not be found remiss in performing his duty in this particular, as he had already explained by letter to his ambassador. The Emperor begged that his Holiness would not omit to do all that strict justice demanded from fear that his sentences would not be enforced. Has written more fully on this subject in the despatches taken by Tello de Guzman.

Cifuentes' letter of 2nd instant now to hand.

There is nothing to add with regard to the Queen of England's case. The answer given to the Archbishop of Paris was good, when the latter told Cifuentes that he had not come to oppose the just cause of the Queen of England, but only to explain how matters stood in England. Approves also of what Cifuentes said when he was told by the Pope and Cardinals that the King of France is by no means pleased with what the King of England has done, and

---

[*] Marginal note by Cobos: They may ask for it. If difficulties are raised, the King, Anne, and their abettors may be excommunicated.
[†] Cardinal Jean du Bellay.
[‡] That is to say, the illegal proceedings before Archbishop Cranmer.

1534.

that he (Francis) still hopes to be able to persuade him (Henry) to again recognise the authority of the Pope. He notes without further comment the answer given by Cifuentes to the Archbishop of Paris when the latter said that the promulgation of the sentence seemed to him very inopportune at the present time, as the King of England was willing to revoke his late action and become once more an obedient son of the Church, if his matrimonial suit were heard at Cambrai. All these suggestions are merely for the purpose of delaying the Queen's case. If any arrangement of this sort was to have been brought forward, it should have been done at the Marseilles interview.

As Cifuentes considers it necessary to make presents to those who have the management of the business, and he has discounted bills for 2,500 ducats for this purpose, his bills shall be duly met when presented. The Emperor doubts not that the money will be distributed in a way that will produce the greatest amount of good. The memorandum drawn up by the learned doctors who are acting for the Queen will be carefully considered. The manner of proceeding proposed by them has been approved of, as will be seen by the marginal notes against each clause. These notes are to be kept secret, and not even the lawyers must see them. The due accomplishment of the Emperor's plans will be greatly aided by secrecy.

Notes that the Pope told Cifuentes that the King of France intended to marry his eldest daughter to the King of Scots[*]; and that the King of England, as soon as he learned of the project, brought forward a plan to marry his own daughter (Princess Mary) to the King of Scots, promising in such event to pay a great sum of money and to return to Scotland certain territories he had conquered from him; on condition, however, that the Princess was to renounce her claims to the English throne. Cifuentes had replied that this seemed a very improbable story, as the King of England would not dare to marry his daughter in Scotland even though she did renounce her English inheritance. This answer was judicious.

Toledo, 1 May, 1534.

27 July.
Simancas.
E. V. 1561.

454. The Emperor to Count Cifuentes.

Notes the intention of the Pope to send a person to the King of England for the purpose of endeavouring once more to persuade him to do his duty and to obey the sentence that has been delivered. After all the efforts that have been made to dissuade the Pope from this course, there is nothing more to be said about it.

The Emperor is decidedly of opinion that, at all events, it would be unbecoming for the Pope to fulfil his expressed intention of sending an ambassador to be present at the meeting between the Kings of France and England, as most certainly nothing of benefit for Christendom will be discussed at such a meeting. But if his Holiness persists in his intention of sending an ambassador, Cifuentes must urge upon him to give special instructions to his envoy to

---

[*] The eldest daughter of Francis who survived her childhood, Princess Madeleine, who at the date of the letter was fourteen years of age, married James V. of Scotland three years later (1 January, 1537).

1534.

oppose and contradict everything that may be proposed prejudicial to the Queen of England. The very least that the Emperor expects of the Pope is that he will not be a party to any such attempts. The Emperor does not yet know whether his ambassador to England will be present at the meeting. On the occasion of the last meeting between the Kings, the King of England objected to his presence; but if the Imperial ambassadors to France and England are to attend, due instructions will be sent to them on no account to countenance any negotiations that may injure the Queen's rights. Begs the Pope to instruct his envoy to follow the lead of the Imperial ambassadors if these be present at the interview.

The measures taken by Cifuentes with regard to the despatch of the executorial decrees are approved of. He is to follow his instructions closely. The Pope must be made to see that his prestige is deeply concerned in the prompt execution, whilst, on the other hand, it will be convenient for some time to elapse before the decrees are delivered to the Emperor, in order that the latter may be the better able to consider the steps to be taken.

Palencia, 27 July, 1534.

16 Aug.
Simancas.
E. V. 1561.

455. The EMPEROR to COUNT CIFUENTES. (Extracts.)

Conversation of Cifuentes with Carnisera about Kings of France and England and the Voyvode, Cifuentes' reply to Carnisera's question, as to whether the Emperor would give his niece, the daughter of the King of Denmark, in marriage to the King of Scots was excellent.* If Carnisera repeats the question, the same answer must be given, namely that Cifuentes is ignorant of the Emperor's wishes on the subject. The Emperor desires to know all that can be learnt about this.

Cifuentes' account of his conversation with the Pope is carefully noted, the subject being a reconciliation between the Emperor and the King of France in opposition to the King of England. The Pope said that the King of France would be very willing to join the Emperor in some enterprise against England, but that he fears the Emperor would betray the negotiations to King Henry, enter into a close alliance with him and abandon the friendship of France. Cifuentes did well in not entering into details on this point, but simply observed that it was not the Emperor's custom to break his word and betray his friends. Cifuentes is to try all he can to discover from the Pope the particulars of this suggestion, and write very fully about it to the Emperor.

Cifuentes is not to make any opposition to the Pope with respect to the sending of a person to England for the purpose of exhorting the King to submit to the sentence.

Palencia, 16 August, 1534.

---

* It is not clear which of the two daughters of Elizabeth of Austria and Christian II. is referred to. The elder, Dorothea, married in the following year, 1535, the Prince Palatine Frederick; the younger, the famous Christina, who afterwards refused the hand of Henry VIII., married in 1534 Francis Sforza Duke of Milan, who died in the following year. She married in 1541 Francis Duke of Lorraine. The elder daughter is probably the one meant.

HENRY VIII. 599

1535.
N. D.
(Feb. 1, 1535?)
Simancas
E. I. 806.
Italian.

456. NEWS from ENGLAND sent by COUNT DE CIFUENTES.

The King of England has summoned the Steward of the Queen to the Palace, and has behaved with greater moderation towards her than previously.* He has even spoken of sending back to her her old servants, and it is said that orders had already been given to that effect. The reason for this more moderate attitude is that the Emperor has treated, and is treating, the English ambassadors at the Imperial court with great courtesy, and tells them in gentler words than he formerly employed that the Queen ought to be restored to her former dignity. Good results are to be hoped from this line of conduct. It will certainly be more successful than any other method of proceeding. It is said that Anne is not popular with the English, in consequence of her pride, and because of the insolence and evil carriage of her brothers and other relatives. The King himself does not love her so much as he formerly did, and it is said that he is paying court to another lady of whom he is enamoured. Many of the nobility favour this new passion of the King in order to lead him away from Anne.

10 May.
Simancas.
E. V. 1563.

457. The EMPEROR to COUNT CIFUENTES. (Extract.)

If a favourable opportunity offers he is to speak to the Pope about the business of Ireland, and to persuade his Holiness, with the greatest dexterity possible, that the enterprise would serve his interests and enhance his prestige. Cifuentes is to entertain the person who spoke to him on the subject of Ireland, by saying that, as some time has passed since the person left that island, and the present condition of affairs there is not known, Cifuentes is somewhat at a loss how to answer, but that the Emperor is always ready to help them as soon as his present enterprise is brought to a conclusion, and he is able better to judge what is best to be done with regard to Ireland.

Barcelona, 10 May, 1535.

15 Oct.
Simancas.
Genoa, 1368.

458. CHAPUYS to GOMEZ SUAREZ DE FIGUEROA.†

A certain Irish gentleman had in former years done much to oppose those of his countrymen who submitted to the King of England, because, being, as he said, a dutiful son of the Holy Father, he felt it to be his duty to prevent if possible Ireland following the evil example of England and separating from the Church. This gentleman, however, seeing that the Pope, unmindful of the struggles of the faithful in Ireland, did nothing to support or help them, has thought it best to crave the pardon of the King of England. Without previously requesting a safe conduct, or any other guarantee, he went personally to London to implore the clemency of the King, who, however, cast him into the Tower of London, from which place few indeed of those who are consigned to it leave it except for the scaffold.

---

* The Steward in question was doubtless Francisco Felipe, particulars of whom will be found in the Spanish Chronicle of Henry VIII., edited by the present writer. See also the letters of Chapuys to the Emperor in February, 1535, in Henry VIII. Calendar.
† Imperial Ambassador in Genoa.

The Commissioners of the King are visiting the monasteries and turning out all the inmates under twenty-five years of age, the rest of the monks who remain being forbidden ever to leave the cloister. The King's ministers hope that the monks thus imprisoned will find the life intolerable, and therefore abandon their monasteries, and they (the King's ministers) hope that great sums of money will accrue to the King in this way. The same policy is being followed with regard to convents of nuns if they are rich. Worse things still may be expected from the next Parliament. (Mutual confiscations of vessels and goods by the King of England and King of Sweden and Duke of Holstein.)

London, 15 October, 1535.

22 Dec.
Simancas.
E. V. 1563.

459. The Emperor to Count Cifuentes. (Extract.)

The King of France continues the same. He has not abandoned his pretensions to Milan, and is still bent on extending his dominions. There is no doubt that he and the King of England are carrying on very close and secret negotiations, each with his own end in view. If it be true, as it is reported, that the King of England offers to the French money and troops for the purpose of attacking the Emperor's interests, the value to be attached to the offers of the King of France to assist in the execution of the Papal sentence against him of England may be judged. Even if the King of England has not made the offers attributed to him, the King of France, being so intimate with him as he is, cannot be trusted. The Emperor is credibly informed that the Cardinal of Paris* endeavoured to interrupt the sitting of the Consistory when this matter was brought forward.

Naples, 22 December, 1535.

1536.
6 Jan.
Simancas.
E. V. 1564.

460. The Emperor to Count Cifuentes. (Extract from two letters of same date.)

Will follow his advice and enter Rome unarmed. His Court and household will also come without arms, although the men-at-arms, the light-horse and infantry, which form his escort, will of course carry their arms as usual. The Emperor is astonished to hear that Pier Luigi† is not satisfied with him. When he was in Naples he expressed himself as perfectly satisfied, and ready to do all that was contained in the instructions given to him. He is to be told that the best way for him to obtain fresh favours will be to fulfil his promises.‡

---

* Jean Cardinal du Bellay.
† Pier Luigi Farnese, son of the Pope Paul III. (Alessandro Farnese).
‡ It will be recollected that Charles on his return from Tunis at this period had summoned at Naples the representatives of Sicily and Naples for the purpose of obtaining supplies to seize Milan, the last Sforza Duke of which had recently died without heirs. The entry of the Emperor in Rome for the first time during the pontificate of the Farnese Paul III. was of unexampled magnificence. Du Bellay gives a spirited account of the Emperor's haughty speech before the Pope, challenging Francis to personal combat or to national war for the Duchy of Milan. He could now afford to take this bold course because the greedy Farneses were ready to do his bidding. The Emperor remained at Naples until the 22 March, when he proceeded to Rome and defied France as mentioned above.

1536.

The Legates proposed to the Emperor to come to terms with the King of France about the Duchy of Milan, the measures necessary for the preservation of religion, an offensive and defensive league against the Turk, and the affairs of the King of England. This, they said, would ensure the general peace of Christendom. The Pope proposed to act as mediator. As the French ambassador has likewise informed the Emperor that the King is desirous of entering into negotiations with him on the subjects mentioned, the Emperor could not well reject the approaches, and declared that he would consent to reasonable conditions of peace with the King of France. The General of the Franciscan Order also approached him in a similar way.

The Emperor notes Cifuentes' information that, through the negligence of the Portuguese ambassador, the brief (granting the Pope's pardon and absolution to the converted Portuguese Jews) was conceded on the petition of the newly converted. Pier Luigi writes to the same effect. Cifuentes is to press the Pope most urgently to grant to Portugal the same form of Inquisition as that in Spain, and to revoke his brief granting pardon to these reconciled converts, in order that our Holy Faith may be exalted and God's cause served. If men who had been converted for years, and had been baptised and openly professed Christianity, whilst secretly remaining Jews, and had perhaps already been condemned and burned in effigy in Spain, were to be thus pardoned in Portugal, heresy would be encouraged and God and his Holy Faith prejudiced. Cifuentes is not to leave this affair in the hands of the Portuguese ambassadors, but himself carry on the negotiations about it.

Naples, 6 January, 1536.

14 Jan.
Simancas.
E. V. 1564.

461. The EMPEROR to COUNT CIFUENTES.

Glad to hear from Giovanni Pietro Cafarello and Pier Luigi that the Pope is so favourably disposed.

The Imperial ambassador in France writes that the King says the Emperor's declarations concerning the Duchy of Milan and the peace are extremely vague and general. Cifuentes is to use every effort to learn what is going on between the Kings of France and England. The Emperor is quite convinced that the former has not only no intention of aiding in the execution of the papal sentence to be launched against the King of England, but has made up his mind to oppose any attempt to execute the same. His reasons are, in the first place, his close friendship with the King of England, and in the second place his apprehension that the authority of the Pope might become greater than would suit him if the sentence were carried with effect. Cifuentes is to tell the Pope this.

Naples, 14 January, 1536.

16 Jan.
Simancas.
E. V. 1564.

462. The EMPEROR to COUNT CIFUENTES.

Learns from Cifuentes' letters that in spite of all the opposition of the Cardinal of Paris, the Pope had until recently persisted in his determination to grant and despatch the Bulls depriving the King of England of his realm; but that his Holiness had now

1536.

changed his mind, and had suspended the despatch of the Bulls. It is possible that the reason for this change of front may be found in the negotiations which the Pope is carrying on with France concerning the arrangement of a general peace. The Emperor would like the forfeiture of the King of England to be declared before he (the Emperor) came to Rome, and Cifuentes is to use every means with his Holiness to have this business concluded before his Majesty meets his Holiness. Notes that Cifuentes says that the executorial decrees of the judgment given in favour of the Queen and Princess of England can be despatched secretly and with the knowledge of very few persons. Cifuentes is to desire that the decree be thus despatched with the utmost secrecy; but it must be kept distinct from the Bull depriving the King of England of his crown, in order that it may be employed as circumstances may render desirable.

Naples, 16 January, 1536.

29 Jan.
Simancas.
E. V. 1564.

463. The EMPEROR to COUNT CIFUENTES. (Extract.)

The executorial decrees against the King of England to be asked for.

The Imperial Ambassador in France writes news of the death of the Queen of England; but as the ambassador in England has said nothing about it, the Emperor hopes the report is false.[*] The Emperor cannot consent to the French demand that his rights in the Duchy of Milan should be settled on the Duke of Orleans. The Nuncio has received news that the French will first try to get Milan by peaceful means, but that if they fail they are determined to conquer it by force of arms, for which purpose a numerous army is being raised. Thinks this is only a French move to get better terms, but the Emperor has thought well to levy German and Italian troops.

Naples, 29 January, 1536.

29 Feb.
Simancas.
C. de C., 33.

464. The EMPRESS to the EMPEROR. (Extract.)

She and her Council are persuaded that the Emperor ought to make peace with France if acceptable conditions can be obtained. Even if no other reasons for this existed it would avoid a ruinous war. It is true that the King of France cannot be trusted much, but if good securities could be devised, the policy would be worth trying.[†]

The Empress is greatly grieved to hear of the death of the Queen of England, both on account of what is current with regard to the circumstances of her death, and on account of the grief of the Princess. Does not consider it necessary to perform funeral obsequies in Spain for her, as the Emperor has ordered such to be solemnised in his own Court. But if the Emperor wishes the funeral service to take place in Spain as well, she will order it at once.

Madrid, 29 February, 1536.

---

[*] Queen Catharine had died on the 7th January.

[†] It will be noted that in every case the representatives whom the Emperor left to govern Spain in his absence urged a pacific policy, as they were brought into contact with the misery and ruin of the Castilian realms which were called upon to support the main cost of the Emperor's wars.

1536.

15 July.
Simancas.
C. de C., 70.

465. The EMPRESS to the EMPEROR.

The surprises of England are the work of the Almighty, who has thus avenged the injustice done to our aunt, the Queen.°

With regard to the Emperor's project to marry the King of England with her sister, the Infanta, and the Infante Don Luis with the Princess of England, supposes the plan is now to be abandoned, as the King of England is already married again.† Before this latter marriage was known in Spain, she had written to her brother the King (of Portugal) in conformity with what the Emperor had written to her on the subject, but she has now written again to her brother saying that the King of England was already married.

Valladolid, 15 July, 1536.

31 Aug.
Simancas.
E. V. 1564.

466. The EMPEROR to COUNT CIFUENTES. (Extract.)

With regard to your report of what our ambassador in England writes to you touching the Princess (of England) our niece, the ambassador has also conveyed the same information to us.‡ We have maturely considered it and have written to the ambassador in reply that if the death of the Princess can by no other means be avoided she should submit to her father with regard to the statutes and the succession, since any such submission extorted from her by extreme peril of death could not prejudice her in any way. As regards the dispensation or absolution which the ambassador thinks should be obtained from the Pope, if you think that his Holiness would not look favourably upon such a request, or that if it were asked of him in this form it might become publicly known, we are of opinion that no harm will be done, either to the question of conscience or to the succession, by leaving the matter pending for the present, until we see what may happen in England. The affair is of such a nature that, if it were to become known, the life of the Princess would obviously be placed in great danger; and our ambassador has been instructed to make the necessary protests in England. In the meantime you may keep the letter he has written to you on the matter, in order to be able to show it to his Holiness if he should happen to mention the matter to you, or exhibit any displeasure at the course the Princess has taken; so that in any case she may be justified. We note in your letter that Sir (Gregory) Casale is still urging you to speak to the Pope in our name asking his Holiness to send a Nuncio to the King of England for the purpose of persuading the latter to abandon his present opinions. You have done quite right in refraining from all action to this effect until you obtained our instructions. We are of opinion that it will be undesirable to speak to the Pope on the matter until we know what will become of the Princess. To judge by the manner in which she is being treated at present not much good can be expected from them (*i.e.* the English).

Aix, 31 August, 1536.

° The trial and execution of Anne Boleyn, 19 May, 1536.
† *i.e.* to Jane Seymour, 20 May, 1536.
‡ With reference to the renunciation of her allegiance to Rome, wrung by Cromwell from Mary, see the letters from Chapuys to the Emperor, 1st July, 1536, *et seq.*, and Mary's Correspondence with Cromwell in Cotton M.S., Otho X.

1536.
21 Sept.
R.A. of History
Madrid.
Salazar A. 42.

467. JUAN MARTINEZ DE RECALDE to JUAN VASQUEZ DE MOLINA.

A vessel belonging to Antibes has arrived in Bilbao from England in nine days. The passengers in her report that the Duke of Wales, commonly called the Great Talbot, and three other English nobles, have risen against the King of England, and have killed eight or ten of his servants. The King has retired to the Tower of London, where he is besieged by the populace, the greater part of the common people having declared themselves against him. The passengers in the ship say that when they sailed from England the bells were being rung all day and night in the town, and the people took seven prisoners. The vessel also brings news that the King of England intended to crown his present wife, but that the nobles did not like it. God grant them peace.

Bilbao, 21 September, 1536.

NOTE.—In a report on affairs in England written to the Emperor from Brussels on the 15 October, 1536 (Simancas Guerra, Mar y Tierra, 9) it is mentioned that Chapuys' nephew had just arrived from England bringing the news that the people there were in great commotion against the King, who not content with devastating all the monasteries, had now committed fresh spoliation. It is said (continues the report) that 50,000 men are in arms, though what they intend to do is not known. They are in want of a leader to command them and sustain the courage of "my people of Israel."

26 Sept.
Simancas.
C de C., 33.

468. The EMPRESS to the EMPEROR. (Extract.)

Is extremely glad to hear that the negotiations with England are so promising, both with regard to the marriage of the Princess with the writer's brother (the Portuguese Infante Luis), as with regard to other subjects. Prays God not to forsake the Emperor.

Madrid, 26 September, 1536.

28 Oct.
Simancas.
E. V. 1564.

469. The EMPEROR to COUNT CIFUENTES.

(Negotiations with France through the Pope. Duke of Orleans, Duke of Angouleme, Duchy of Milan, the Infante Luis, the Pope's grandsons, etc.)

As the affair of the Princess of England is no longer a secret, the Pope is to be asked to take any steps in her favour which may appear advisable. As the circumstances which obliged her to act as she has done were so imperative, it cannot be believed that the Pope will raise any difficulties (i.e. in granting to the Princess Mary an absolution from her promise of submission to her father).

Genoa, 28 October, 1536.

1537.
June.
Madrid.
Bib. Nat.

470. REPORT of the reception of the new ENGLISH AMBASSADORS by the EMPEROR at Valladolid.

On Friday, the 22nd June, the English ambassadors were introduced to the Emperor by Don Pedro de la Cueva, the Cardinal of Toledo being present. The Emperor was informed

1537.

by order of the King of England that four noblemen of the north (of England) had been beheaded as rebels, namely Lords Darcy and Hussey, Lord Giles (Pole), Constable and Bigod; and that the Queen was pregnant (which, however, the Emperor already knew).

At the bull fight Don Luis de Avila y Zuñiga was caught by one of the bulls and badly gored, but was saved by a soldier. The Emperor himself dealt a skilful lance-thrust to the same bull. The Emperor left Valladolid on the 10th July.

1539.
12 May.
Simancas.
Sueltos, 3.

471. CARDINAL POLE to the EMPEROR.

The death of the Empress, a dreadful misfortune, but God has been pleased to endow the Emperor with strength of character to bear it. With respect to his business, he need only say here that he has written fully to M. de Granvelle and to the Nuncio, explaining the reasons which have moved him to go no further on his way to England but to stay at Carpentras.

Carpentras, 12 May, 1539.

NOTE.—On the margin of this letter Idiaquez has written "Condolence answered. As for the business mentioned by him, the Nuncio and Cardinal Farnese must be spoken to about it. His Holiness will instruct him as to the course he should pursue."

19 May.
Simancas.
E. 2005.
7.

472. INSTRUCTIONS from PAUL III. to CARDINAL FARNESE sent to the Emperor primarily to condole with him on the death of the Empress.

The instructions mainly concern the Pope's efforts to bring the King of France into the league against the Turk, the intentions of the Lutherans as to assembling a Diet at Nuremburg, etc.; but the following clause relates to England. "His Holiness is desirous that the Emperor and the King of France should send special ambassadors to the King of England, for the purpose of inducing him to return to his former obedience to the Holy Church and to God; and if he refuses, to tell him that in such case the Emperor and the King of France would be obliged to fulfil the commands of the Apostolic See, and execute by force the sentence of excommunication and deprivation against him."

NOTE.—In the same bundle, fols. 11 and 17, there is another sheet of instructions to Farnese from his grandfather, dated 28 November, for his guidance in his new mission to the Emperor and the King of France with similar objects to those mentioned above. "Without peace, a Council is impossible, without a Council the great calamities caused by the Turks, the disobedience of the King of England, and the heresy in Germany, cannot be effectually remedied. The enterprise against the Turk cannot be successfully undertaken unless the house is first cleansed, and therefore the Council, the English affair and those of the Lutherans must first be satisfactorily dealt with." In the separate instructions to Farnese with regard to the French portion of his mission the following clauses are contained. "With respect to the affairs of England, it will be necessary to be very pressing and emphatic with him (*i.e.* King Francis). Farnese is to watch closely both the

1539.

King of France and the Emperor in this matter, and to endeavour by every means to ascertain whether either or both of them are carrying on secret negotiations with the King of England. If he finds such to be the case, he (Farnese) is to make the intelligence known, saying that he has obtained his information from England or Scotland. He is to beg both the Emperor and the King of France not to grant a safe-conduct to the Princess of Cleves, the wife of the King of England, if it be true that she is a Lutheran."

S. D.
Simancas.
E. 2016.
88.

473. MEMORANDUM from MARCELLO CERVINI, Bishop of Nicastro,[*] nominated to proceed to England, to CARDINAL FARNESE.

Being asked to give his opinion as to the manner in which he would propose to proceed in his business with the King of England, his first impulse would be to say: "As your Reverence and the King of France may direct." But being in duty bound to give a fuller reply, he does so in all sincerity.

In the first place he would tell the King of England that the Pope having been informed by the writer of the various acts of injustice done to the King by Pope Clement (VII.) and his advisers, has expressed his readiness to arrange in a satisfactory manner all the differences that exist between Rome and England. His Holiness, recognising that he could not bring about peace upon terms so equitable as he wished, had sent the writer to the King of France to assure him of his continued willingness to do all good offices towards him (Henry). The first time the writer conveyed this message from his Holiness to the King of France the latter heard it with expressions of doubt upon his face, fearing, perchance, that the real object might be to create dissensions between the princes. But when the Pope's own brief was handed to him, and he had again discoursed with the writer upon his mission, the King of France consented to inform the King of England of the Pope's advances, leaving the said King to take what further steps in the matter he might consider advisable. The King of France graciously said that he not only wished, himself, to take advantage of the Pope's good disposition, but that the benefit of it might also accrue to his ally (*i.e.* King Henry). This is all, so far, in accord with the wishes both of the Pope and the King of France. The writer would then dwell upon the good intentions of his Holiness towards him (the King of England) so long as the latter is animated by friendly sentiments towards the Pope; although it is not yet possible to set down the precise words the writer would employ: but this much he can say positively, that he will be as careful to safeguard the honour and interests of the King of France as of the Pope himself. He trusts the Cardinal (Farnese) and the King of France will help him.

There is no doubt that the King of England will carefully weigh every word he (the writer) says, and the latter will lose credit if in any particular he differs from that which the Cardinal and the King of France may write to England. The writer therefore proposes

---

[*] He was made Bishop of Reggio in 1540, and Cardinal of Santa Croce in December, 1539, and became Pope Marcellus II. in 1555 for a few weeks.

to follow as nearly as possible the wording of their communications. This is what he proposes to do in the first audience. If, however, the King of France directs him to proceed otherwise, he is quite willing to do so; his only desire being to bring about a durable peace between all the Princes of Christendom.

It is possible that the King of England will not be satisfied with merely general professions of friendship, and will seek to know in what manner the Pope proposes to reconcile him on the various subjects in dispute. In such case the writer intends to ask him (the King) what his demands are. If the King of England speaks of his honour, and is not satisfied with the brief sent by the Pope to the King of France, the writer proposes to promise him another brief, addressed to him personally, and to the prelates and nobles of England, in which his honour will be entirely safeguarded, always on condition that he will consent to accept the King of France as arbitrator upon all points which cannot be amicably settled directly. The Pope has promised the writer to grant such a brief.

The King of England will in the second place ask for absolution for all his past offences, and that the sentences passed upon him be quashed. There will be little difficulty about this. The writer is willing to do all that the King of France desires. The King of England may request absolution, either in person or by proxy, or even by brief; and he can be absolved by the Pope or the Cardinal in any way which may seem most advisable. However it be done it must be kept secret, as the Emperor would perhaps oppose it; though that would not be of vital consequence.

Another question upon which the King of England would seek enlightenment, is that of the monasteries which have been suppressed by him. This is a grave point. The writer proposes to address the King of England with regard to it in the name of the King of France, saying that the latter is of opinion that the Pope might be asked to give "a cross" for the greater part of the amount thus obtained;[*] and the King of France might consent to the rest, on the ground that the King was moved to commit the depredations referred to by such reasons as the disorder of the friars, the poverty of the kingdom, and similar reasons that will occur to his Majesty (the King of France). The King of England will ask that the Bishops created by him be confirmed by the Pope. The decision on this point must also be left to the King of France. The writer is sure that the Pope will consent to this course; and it must be left to the conscience of the King of England whether he elevated these Bishops to the Bench because of their qualifications for good prelates, or because they promised him to serve his interests in disregard for the Pope.

If the King of England refers to the annatas (first-fruits) the writer proposes to tell him that it is universally known that these are not the property of the Pope himself, but are applied to making war on infidels and heretics. Although all other Christian princes pay them without hesitation the Pope is ready to meet the wishes of

[*] The permissions given by the Popes to the temporal sovereigns to raise funds from ecclesiastical sources were called "Crociate" or crusades, and giving "a cross" (croce) was a familiar variant.

the King of England in this respect if the King of France desires him to do so, and the King of England can show good reasons why he should be relieved from the payment of this revenue, which is a general obligation on all Christian countries. It is true that this question offers very great difficulties, as the first-fruit Bulls have to be issued in Rome by officials who would probably object to the compromise made with the King of England. But still the writer does not consider these difficulties to be insuperable. The King of England will no doubt argue in favour of his demand for exemption that England is a very remote country, that his bishoprics are overburdened, and that their revenues are much smaller than is believed. The decision in this matter can be left to the King of France.

If the writer be commissioned by the Cardinal and the King of France to treat with the King of England, he would not open out to him all at once what he has written above. For if the King of England saw all the cards on the table at the beginning he would probably raise difficulties, and say that the relations of England with Rome are satisfactory to him at present and that he desired no change. Before, therefore, entering into detail, the writer would endeavour to obtain from the King a written statement of the concessions he (the King) is willing to make, on the writer's assuring him that at the instance of the King of France the Pope was willing to grant all his reasonable demands. If the Cardinal does not approve of his proposal, the writer begs him to give his own views on the subject, which he will faithfully follow in his negotiations with the King of England.

The writer has always been on friendly terms with the King of England, and has served him faithfully. He promises to remind the King of his past services, and hopes to be able to exercise some influence upon him. The King of England would have no reason to complain of the King of France, even if the former did not get all he wanted, provided that his real interests did not suffer.

The writer prays the Cardinal to read and consider this memorandum very carefully and to discuss with him any points which appear doubtful, as the writer is anxious to be well informed of the Cardinal's wishes before he leaves for England. The writer requests permission to speak to the King of England about the Emperor in the terms he thinks most advisable, even if it be not in favour of the Emperor, as he knows that the King of England hates the Emperor.

The King of England will probably ask that the matrimonial cause be compromised, and that the decision shall be left to the King of France. This demand should not be conceded, as if the King of France were to accept the task of arbitrating on the question, he would expose himself and the Pope to great inconvenience, inasmuch as it is certain that the King of England is of opinion that the whole world should be exactly as he wishes it to be, and he would ask for what was quite impossible to grant. The King of France would therefore be obliged either to decide unjustly or lose his friends. The writer will try to induce the King of England to give up his infatuation, by telling him that the Pope cannot bind himself beforehand on this point.

1540.

It is impossible for the writer to set forth in detail all he proposes to say to the King, as he is in the dark as yet with regard to the points touching the Pope or the Council that the King may start. The writer begs earnestly that this memorandum may not be sent to England, but preserved most strictly secret. The writer is convinced that it would be impossible to induce the King of England to make any concessions unless he is allowed to believe that he makes them of his own free will. It is quite possible, even, that he will make sport of the writer, and of his Holiness as well.

The writer thinks necessary to write first to the King of France, and beg him to use his influence with the King of England to dispose him to reconcile himself with the Pope. The King of England must be moved to promise that the writer's life shall not be in peril during his stay in England.

The writer assures the Cardinal that his object in writing this memorandum is solely for the purpose of informing him of his views with regard to the English affair.

29 July.
Simancas.
E.E. 806.
Latin.

474. THE EMPEROR to the KING OF SCOTS.

Has heard by his letters that requests have been urged in Germany for permission to carry into execution the letters of marque and reprisal against the subjects of the King of Portugal, which had been granted by the Emperor's father (Philip) and grandfather (sic) Charles Duke of Burgundy, but have since been formally revoked. The Emperor begs that the King of Scots will not importune him with demands of such nature. The letters of marque referred to were granted when circumstances were entirely different from the present, and the reasons for granting them now no longer exist. The Emperor hopes that the King of Portugal will do all justice to the King of Scots, and remove the need for reprisals. At the same time the Emperor requests that the King of Scots will prohibit his subjects from committing acts of piracy in the Holland, Zeeland and other parts of Lower Germany.

The Hague, 29 July 1540.

1541.
25 Feb.
Simancas.
E.A. 638.

475. IDIAQUEZ to COBOS.

(In a letter of advice from the one Secretary in Germany to the other in Spain, the following passage relating to England occurs:) "The relations with England continue without change. Although the new English ambassador has made no formal proposal, he hints that if the Emperor would consent to marry the Princess (i.e., Mary Tudor) great advantages might accrue to him."[*]

Ratisbon, 25 February 1541.

---

[*] Bishop Stephen Gardiner, the ambassador in question, had on this occasion hinted to Granvelle that a reconciliation between Charles and Henry was desirable. Granvelle had somewhat roughly replied that Henry had outraged and wounded the Emperor deeply by his divorce and his repudiation of Rome, and that reparation must first come from him. *See* letter from the Nuncio Poggio to Cardinal Santa Croce (Marcello Cervini), Calendar Henry VIII. Vol. XVI. *p.* 260.

1541.
4 July.
Simancas.
E.A. 638.

476. IDIAQUEZ to COBOS.

(In another letter of advice similar to the above, the following passage occurs:) "We are now on friendly terms with England, and it would be quite easy now, if the Emperor thought advisable, to enter into negotiations. His Imperial Majesty has, however, postponed for the present the opening of such negotiations, although he has been assured that the English will treat with no other power without the Emperor."

Ratisbon, 4 July 1541.

1543.
10 Oct.
Simancas.
C. de C. 60.

477. PRINCE PHILIP to the EMPEROR. (Extract.)

The Imperial Ambassador in England (Chapuys) has written him news respecting the negotiations of M. de Chantonnay* and the King of England, and M. de Chantonnay himself confirms them. The Prince rejoices greatly at the assurance of this good news contained in the Emperor's letter, the agreement with England being so important.

Valladolid, 10 October 1543.

1544.
14 Feb.
Simancas.
F.A. 640.

478. The EMPEROR to PRINCE PHILIP.

Has had no letter from him for the last four months, and would be in great uneasiness in consequence had he not been informed that the Prince had gone from Salamanca to Valladolid to pass the winter with his young wife. The affairs of Italy, and especially those of Piedmont, are in a very critical state, the French having a large army collected there. The Prince must procure money in Spain by any means. The security of our dominions depends upon the success of the invasion which the Emperor intends to make of France during the present year, and he hopes thereby to compel the King of France, at last, to accept reasonable conditions of peace. The King of England has promised to join the Emperor with an army of 37,000 foot and 7,000 horse with the necessary artillery and munitions of war, whilst the Emperor is bound by the treaty to supplement the English force by sending to it 2,000 horse and 2,000 Germans: the Emperor and King Henry agreeing to help each other in all ways and in all places. In order to do so great sums of money will be needed, as well as a large number of soldiers. Every effort must be made to raise money in Spain and to send it promptly.†

Spires, 14 February, 1544.

---

* The news of the Emperor's alliance with the excommunicated Henry was not so favourably received by the papal interest. In a letter from the Emperor to Juan de Vega, his ambassador in Rome, 15 November 1543 (Simancas E.F. 505), not calendared here as being of insufficient importance, the following passage occurs :—" With reference to what you report as to the saying of the Pope that our alliance with the King of England is on a par with the alliance of the King of France with the Turk, your reply thereto was very judicious and you will lose no opportunity of showing his Holiness how widely different is our conduct from that of the French King." Chantonnay, the brother of the Bishop of Arras (afterwards Cardinal de Granvelle) had been sent to sound Henry on the formation of the league between the Emperor and England against France.

† The letter from Cobos to the Emperor, 14 May, in Spanish Calendar, Vol. VII. p. 154, is an answer to the above. In it Cobos says that after the money then sent be spent, there will be no means of getting one "real" more out of the Spanish people.

1544.

Postscript in the handwriting of the Emperor :—

"My boy. I have written to you by Juan Zapata about these affairs. The way by which this letter is sent is not very safe, and it is not advisable to write much except in cipher. I will therefore say nothing beyond these words : try to be a good son, and get for me as much money as I have asked for and more if possible. My, and your, fortune is at stake. Help me promptly ; for delay would be almost as detrimental as failure. If I should break down now it would be hard in future to remedy our misfortune. Employ all the means at which I have hinted, and others if you think they would be more feasible."

14 May.
Simancas.
O. de C. 69.

479. PRINCE PHILIP to the EMPEROR.

Is glad to hear that Martin Alonso has arrived in England with his despatches. Hopes the Emperor has ere this received the letters the Prince sent by him. Wishes to know what the German Princes will do at the Diet. The conditions of peace proposed by the French are not acceptable. The Prince is convinced that the instructions taken by Fernando de Gonzaga to England have been very maturely considered and could not be improved. Is rejoiced to hear that the answer given by the King of England is so satisfactory. If both the Emperor and the King jointly attack the King of France vigorously the latter will be forced to make peace on reasonable conditions ; or at least he will be paralysed in his attempts against Spain and Italy. News reaches the writer from all sides that the King of France intends to fortify strongly the frontier places on the borders of Picardy and Champagne, and to make his principal move on Italy, as he has already attacked Catalonia, with the help of the Turkish fleet. The Prince notes the Emperor's intentions to invade France on one side whilst the King of England makes a vigorous attack on the other. It is impossible for the Prince, who is distant from the scene of action, to express an opinion upon the plans, but the Emperor being upon the spot, is with his great wisdom the best judge as to the most desirable course to be adopted.

Andrea Doria and Figueroa are both of opinion that it would be a good thing to gain over Barbarossa to the Emperor's side, but the terms asked by the former are out of the question.

Valladolid, 14 May 1544.

6 July.
Simancas.
E.P. 500.

480. The EMPEROR to COBOS.

Juan Zapata has come to him with a message from Count Cifuentes* to the effect that the Infanta Maria is now so grown that it is time to think of a husband for her. The Emperor, being her father, would naturally be delighted to see her well married, but no good match seems at present available for her. The Prince of England is still a child ; the Prince of Portugal is already betrothed

---

* Count Cifuentes, formerly ambassador in Rome, had now become governor of the young Princesses. The Infanta Maria subsequently married her cousin Maximilian, afterwards Emperor, the eldest son of Ferdinand.

1544.

to the Princess Juana*; the Dauphin is married and has children; whilst as to the Duke of Orleans, Cobos knows well the turn that negotiations have taken in that direction. The King of France and his sons, moreover, have not deserved that any of the latter should be married to the Infanta Maria. There only remain therefore the sons of the King of the Romans to whom the Infanta could be married; but, in any case, it will be necessary to postpone the decision as to the person until children have been born to the Prince (Philip).

Metz, 6 July 1544.

6 July.
Simancas.
E.F. 500.

481. The EMPEROR to PRINCE PHILIP.

Is glad to be able to say that the States of the Empire have voted aid for him in his war with France. This assistance came most opportunely. There is not much fresh to say about the English. Their vanguard and rearguard have already left Calais and are entering French territory; the King of England himself with the main attacking force being expected at Calais on the 8th instant. The Emperor thinks that the English will do all they can to injure the French; at least, so they say; though he doubts whether they will advance far into France, as they are encumbered with a great number of heavy baggage-wagons. Still they will help the Emperor to bring about a favourable peace with France, since if the latter is attacked at different points she will have to divide her forces.

Metz, 6 July 1544.

14 Aug.
Simancas.
E.F. 500.

482. The EMPEROR to PRINCE PHILIP.

Monsieur de Longueville, who is with the Duke of Orleans, and who possesses the confidence of Mme. d'Etampes, approached M. de Granvelle through a physician when they were at Spires and offered terms of peace. The Emperor at the time took no notice of these offers, as he thought that the only result would be to arouse the distrust of the English towards him. The Cardinal of Lorraine afterwards sent the Bailif of Dijon, who stayed for a day in M. de Granvelle's house.† He asked for the Infanta Maria in marriage for the Duke of Orleans with Flanders and Milan as a dowry. The Emperor replied that he had already disposed of the hand of his daughter otherwise; but that he would be pleased that the Duke of Orleans should marry the second daughter of the King of the Romans, to whom he would give a good dower.

Camp before Landrecy, 14 and 18 August 1544.

18 Aug.
Simancas.
E.F. 500.

483. IDIAQUEZ to COBOS.

The Emperor is writing more fully about the negotiations for peace. The Admiral of France is expected in three or four days.

---

* The Princess Juana, eldest daughter of Charles, married soon afterwards Don John of Portugal, heir to the crown. He died in 1554.
† The details of these peace negotiations are fully discussed in the Introduction to Vol. VII. of the Spanish Calendar.

1544.

The King of England is raising no difficulties with regard to these proposed negotiations, mainly because the French have also entered into negotiations with him. The King of England would like to mediate between the Emperor and France. The writer wishes him success. Peace is most desirable for many reasons, and especially because the war is being conducted so badly; the accounts received by the Emperor being very unfavourable.[*] The King of England is besieging Boulogne and Montreuil, two places not far from Calais. The possession of Boulogne would be of great advantage to the English.

Before Landrecy, 18 August 1544.

---

[*] A description of the military position of the Emperor and his forces at this time will be found on page 308, Vol. VII. Spanish Calendar.

ERRATA.

Page 97, fifth line from the bottom; Danvers should read Chamberlain; the person referred to being Sir Thomas Chamberlain, Governor, or Master, of the Court of English Merchants in Antwerp.

„ 100, tenth line from the bottom; the name suggested in brackets should be Furstenberg, not Nassau.

„ 141, twentieth line from the bottom; the same alteration should be made.

„ 226, eleventh line from the bottom, for Camerino read Camarino. Both forms are used in the manuscripts, but the latter form is preferred.

„ 556, twenty-second line from the top, the name suggested in brackets should be Gardiner, not Paulet.

GENERAL INDEX.

GENERAL INDEX.

A

Achavari, Agent in Rome for Count Fiesco, 547.
Admiral of England. *See* Dudley.
Admiral of France. *See* Annebaut.
Admiralty Court, English, 118, 120, 121, 122, 123-125, 130, 223.
Adventures of a mercenary in England and France. *See* Ortiz de la Rea.
Agreement between Henry and Charles for arbitration. 53-57, 60, 64-70.
Aguilar, Marques de, 395.
Alba, Duke of, 72, 74, 228, 229, 278, 395.
Alburquerque, Duke of, letter from, to Henry VIII., 405.
Alburquerque, Duke of, letter from, to Princess Mary, 446.
Alburquerque, Duke of, with Henry at Boulogne, 5, 32, 79, 98n, 151, 223, 281, 282-286, 288, 289, 310, 405, 446.
Alciate, the scholar, 340.
Alliance between Henry and the Emperor. *See* Subsidy demanded and Sicily, Viceroy of.
Alliance, alleged, between France and England, 419, 420, 431, 432, 452, 453, 465.
Alten, passage of mercenaries in the English service through, 362, 363, 365-369, 382.
Altieri, Balthasar, English agent in Venice, 438, 439, 454, 468, 469, 539.
Ambleteuse, naval engagement between the English and French at, 394.
Ancona, Bishop of, 374, 514.
Anne of Cleves, at the English Court, 348.
Annebaut, Claude, Admiral of France, 87-88, 99, 149, 197, 198, 206, 207, 222, 223, 225, 229, 238, 244, 245, 250, 255, 256, 259, 265, 269, 272, 273, 274, 275, 278, 284, 302, 364, 373, 374, 380, 386, 389, 404, 409, 419, 420, 425, 426, 430, 431, 434, 441, 442, 451-453, 454. His reception in England, 465, 466, 502, 511.
Antenori, Genoese merchant in Antwerp, 64, 168.
Antwerp, orders for the seizure of all English property at, 21, 23-26, 123, 130, 138, 166, 189.

Antwerp, embargo in, of Henry's funds, 248, 251.
Antwerp, arms for the English seized there, 379.
Antwerp, English merchants in, their alleged withdrawal from Flanders with their property, 138-142, 157, 163, 166, 558.
Antwerp, financial arrangements in. *See* Loans.
Antwerp, ill-treatment of English subjects in, 435, 442, 558, 559.
Antwerp, merchants demand reprisals for English depredations on shipping, 384, 385, 390.
Aragon, Catharine of, 556.
Aragon, Cortes of, 308.
Arbitration with regard to the Commercial claims (*see also* Seizures), 53-57, 63, 64, 65-69, 70, 86, 91, 93, 97, 105, 111, 112, 114, 115, 116, 117. Chapuys' conferences at, 132-138, 139, 140, 144, 159, 160, 163. Failure of the arbitration, 170, 171-174. Renewed attempts, 298, 299, 311, 317, 319, 326, 334, 335, 342, 349, 362, 371. Fresh Commissions appointed, 378, 380, 381, 385, 387, 390, 391, 394, 395, 400, 440, 474, 484, 485-488, 489, 498-500, 518, 524, 527, 533, 537, 550, 558.
Arce, Captain, a Spanish mercenary, 295n.
Arschot, Duke of, 15.
Arsinguelo, Cardinal, 321, 531, 541.
Ardres, 12, 25, 77, 98, 111, 143, 148, 242; Skirmish near, 247, 251, 279, 314, 320, 344, 392.
Arles, Bishop of, 101.
Armaments and Convoy to be enforced upon Spanish shipping as a protection against attack, 356-359, 365, 393, 401.
Arme, Luigi delle, a mercenary leader, 17, 71, 310, 368, 426, 427, 438, 538.
Armignac, Cardinal, 183.
Arms and munitions, etc., export of from Flanders for England (*see also* Seizures), 107, 121-122, 163, 180, 230, 313, 319, 320, 325, 341, 342, 343, 344, 379, 470.
Arran, the Regent, 1, 89, 325, 420, 463, 466, 497.
Arras, M. de, Antoine de Perrenot, afterwards Cardinal de Granvelle, 4, 5, 6, 9, 11, 13, 14, 19, 21, 34n, 45, 60, 61, 63, 66, 72, 112, 170, 179, 219, 236, 262, 457.
Aubespine, French Secretary of State, 5, 80, 428.
Aubyn, Philip, his action with regard to the Spanish mercenaries, 57.

Augsburg, Cardinal of, 436, 443, 445.
Aumale, M. d' (Duke d'Aumale), 255, 432.
Auto de Fe in Seville, 139.
Avila, Don Juan, his intelligence from Flanders, 247.

B

Baptism of Elizabeth de Valois. *See* Elizabeth of France.
Bar, Duchy of, 102, 149, 195, 209.
Barbain, Thomas, his ship embargoed by the English, 91.
Barbarossa, Turkish Admiral, 182, 209, 215, 222, 337, 502.
Barbe, Dr., death of, 371.
Bartlett (of the King's Chamber), visits Chapuys and Vander Delft, 1.
Bavaria, Duke of, 102, 307.
Bavaria, Duke Philip of, Count Palatine. *See* Philip.
Bave Joos, Secretary of the Flemish Council, letters to from Chapuys, 54, 111.
Bave Joos, 54, 71, 94, 294, 299, 301, 542.
Bellay, Cardinal du, his negotiations for peace with England, 5, 6, 7, 45, 60, 97, 101.
Bellin, Cornelius, a pirate of Calais, 550.
Belsares, bankers, 387, 388.
Bergh. *See* Vander Bergh.
Bernardi, Francesco, Venetian peace intermediary between England and France, 364, 368, 372, 374, 379, 394, 397, 398, 399, 400, 422, 439.
Bernuy, F. de, Vander Delft's brother, 501.
Bertheuille, M. de, otherwise Fontenay, 232, 233, 239, 293, 294, 309, 310.
Beton, Cardinal, 165. Murdered, 404, 406, 421.
Bevres, Flemish Admiral, 404, 470.
Beyler, Bey, Turkish officer defeated by the Persians, 547.
Bezana, Pedro Paulo, an English agent in Antwerp, 230.
Bies, M. de, at Boulogne, 173, 223, 334, 349.
Bishops, English, their prerogatives, 279, 291.
Bishops, residence of in the dioceses, 516-518, 521, 522.
Blancard galley, captured by the English, 394, 398, 409, 465, 488, 535.
Bocio, Antonio, an adherent of Count Fiesco in Genoa, 547.
Boissot, Charles, Master of Requests in Flanders, letters patent from the Emperor to seize all English property in Antwerp, etc., 21.
Boissy, M. de, 255.
Bombach, Ludwig von, a Protestant envoy to England, 249, 266.

Bonvise, M. de, 138, 171.
Bossu, M. de, Admiral of Flanders, 24.
Boulognais, possession of the lands therein conquered by the English, 407, 421, 441, 449, 450, 453, 457, 462-464, 465-467, 471-473, 484, 485-488, 497, 498, 520, 528, 529, 534, 535, 537, 550.
Boulogne (the English at), 12, 13, 14, 16, 17, 25, 26, 33, 40, 66, 67, 68, 78, 87, 94, 95, 96, 97, 98, 99, 100, 106, 111, 114, 126, 127, 129, 133, 135, 136, 137, 145-146, 148, 152, 165, 170 172, 173, 186-189, 192, 198, 200, 204, 206 209, 215, 220, 223, 224, 229, 231, 232, 236, 239, 241-244, 247, 248, 250, 251, 255, 259, 265, 269, 276, 277, 282, 283, 287, 292, 295, 296, 311, 314, 318, 320, 328, 329, 333, 334, 336, 345, 349, 361, 362, 364, 371, 373, 374, 386, 390, 392, 397, 402, 405-409, 418, 419, 421, 435, 449, 454, 456, 469, 475, 485, 488 502, 543, 549.
Boulogne, French Captain of (Vervins), accused of treachery, 223.
Boulogne, night surprise of, by the French, 292, 294, 295.
Boulogne, ransom for. *See* Peace negotiations and Scepperus.
Bourbon, Constable de, 16.
Bourbon, Cardinal, 428.
Bourbourg, arbitration commission at, 69, 91, 93, 97, 116, 117, 132-138, 139, 141-146, 159, 160, 170, 171-174, 218, 296, 408.
Brabançon, M. de, 487.
Brabant, Chancellor of, letter to, from Chapuys, 141.
Brabant, Chancellor of, to embargo English property in Flanders, 138, 139, 141-142, 166, 189.
Brandenburg, Albert of, 371, 378, 439n, 546.
Brandenburg, the Elector of, 326, 439n.
Brazil, French expedition to, 351, 403, 409.
Bread, price of, in Spain, 212.
Brederode, Sieur, to prevent the passage of Conrad Penninck's mercenaries by Gueldres, 363.
Brienne, Count of, 222.
Brittany, Duke of, Francis de Valois, afterwards Francis II, 433.
Browne, Sir Anthony, Master of the Horse, 20, 35, 39, 123, 124, 135, 230, 345, 346, 347, 385, 400, 408.
Bruges, Burgomaster of, letter to, from Vander Delft, 131.
Bruges, merchants of, their request to be allowed to trade with Scotland, 125, 131.
Brun, Dr., 464, 467, 468.
Brunswick, Duke of, 209, 210, 271, 277, 279, 292, 301, 354, 411, 424.
Brusquet, Erasmus, 107.
Bucharest, Prince Philip of, a mercenary leader, 17.
Buda, the Vaivode of, 210.

GENERAL INDEX.   619

Buren, Count de, commands Imperial contingent with Henry's army, 59, 366. Commands the Flemish contingent in the Schmalkaldic war, 425, 443, 455n, 464, 474, 478, 485, 487, 490.

Burgos, Bishop of, 244, 245.

Burgos, merchants of, plundered by the English, 15, 30-31, 33, 36, 38, 91, 93, 117-124, 132, 138, 140, 141, 142, 144, 152-157, 160, 168, 169, 172, 176, 189, 203, 356-359, 393, 401, 442, 486, 524.

Bury, M., French agent in Scotland, 151.

Butler, Richard, Secretary of Queen Katharine Parr, 17, 130.

Butts, Dr., the King's physician, death of, 320.

C

Caceres, a Spanish spy, 105, 107, 108, 158.

Cahors in Piedmont, dispute about the possession of, 224.

Calais, 12, 25, 129, 279, 389, 394, 399, 403, 404, 499, 500.

Calais, Censier (Farmer), at, detained by the English, 54, 56.

Calais, Deputy of, 25, 54.

Calais, the Staple at, 334-336. Flemish complaints of, 499-500.

Camarino, Duchess of (Margaret of Austria, wife of Ottavio Farnese), 197, 208, 213, 226, 227, 323, 324, 376, 377, 395, 506.

Cambuskenneth, Abbot of. *See* Paniter, David.

Campen, peace treaty of, 406-409, 410, 411, 418, 419, 420, 421, 425, 428, 430-433, 434, 435, 441, 452, 453, 454, 456, 463, 465, 471-472, 510-523, 526.

Cana of Nazarus, Bishop of, at the Council of Trent, 396.

Canapé, M. de, French Courtier, 431.

Carulero, Gerard, 310.

Carew, Sir George, drowned in the Mary Rose, 190.

Carlo Giovanni (Jehan Carlo), Genoese merchant in Flanders, 29, 174.

Carlos, Don, his birth, 174, 199, 303, proposed betrothal with Elisabeth of Valois, 364.

Carne, Dr., English ambassador in Flanders, 93, 97, 195, 272, 319, 320, 341, 359, 361, 363, 371, 372, 403, 448, 457.

Carpi, Cardinal, 197, 256, 374, 376, 377, 388, 438, 447.

Carrion, Lope de, Spanish merchant in London, 138, 169, 170, 218, 486, 489, 524, 527.

Carvajal, Don Diego, special Spanish envoy to France, 150, 151, 205, 216, 270.

Casimbrot, Leonard, proposed Flemish Commissioner to settle the commercial claims, 298, 299.

Castello, Alcalde, deposition before, 282.

Castillo, Alonso del, 478, 491.

Castro, Duke of. *See* Pier Lingi Farnese.

Catharine, Princess, daughter of Ferdinand, King of the Romans, proposed marriage with the Duke of Orleans, 41-43, 79, 80.

Catharine de Medici. *See* the Dauphiness.

Catanio Aurelio, Secretary to Cardinal Trent, 436.

Chapuys, Eustace, Imperial ambassador in England, letter from, to the Chancellor of Brabant, 141.

Chapuys, Eustace, letters from, to Joos Bave, 54, 111.

Chapuys, letters from, to the Emperor, 17, 103, 115, 131, 140, 143, 159, 171.

Chapuys, letters from, to Secretary de Granvelle, 142, 143, 217.

Chapuys, Eustace, letters from, to Mary of Hungary, 110, 161, 555.

Chapuys, Eustace, letters from, to Loys Scoys, the Secretary of the Imperial Council, 62, 161.

Chapuys, letters from, to Vander Delft, 136, 162, 168, 134.

Chapuys and Vander Delft, letters from, to the Emperor, 1, 23, 29, 35, 37.

Chapuys and Vander Delft, letters from, to Mary of Hungary, 23, 44, 55, 57, 63, 90, 93.

Chapuys, letters to, from the Emperor, 93, 115, 129, 138, 164.

Chapuys and Vander Delft, letters to, from Mary of Hungary, 44, 83.

Chapuys, Eustace, letters to, from Vander Delft, 167.

Chapuys and Vander Delft, letters to, from the Emperor, 26, 35.

Chapuys, Eustace, Imperial Ambassador (*see also* Chapuys and Vander Delft), to represent the Emperor in the arbitration on the Seizures, 93. His last interview with Henry, etc., 104-110, 113, 114, 115. At the arbitration conference, 116, 126, 127, 128. His advice to the Emperor and Vander Delft on English affairs, 131-138, 140-142. His conversations with Thirlby and Petre, 141, 143-146, 159, 160. His advice on English affairs, 161, 162, 164, 168-171. His discourse with Thirlby and Petre, 171-174, 178, 179, 185, 195, 205, 215, 217, 336. His opinion on the condition of England, 555-558.

Chapuys and Vander Delft, their arrival in England and reception, 1. Their conversation with the King, 2-9. Discourse with the Councillors, 9, 10-16, 17-20, 29-31, 33. Interview with the King, 33-34. With Paget, etc. 39 With the Councillors, 57-62, 91, 92, 96, 97. Chapuys' farewell to England, 106-110.

Charlerois, its cession to France claimed, 43, 196.

Charles V. letters from, to Chapuys, 93, 115, 129, 138, 164.

Charles V. letter from, to the Chancellor of Brabant, 138.

Charles V. Emperor, letters from, to Chapuys and Vander Delft, 26, 35.

Charles V. Emperor, letters from, to Cobos, 34, 63, 211, 280, 447.

Charles V. letter from, to Andrea Doria, 112.

Charles V. letters from, to Figneroa, his ambassador in Genoa, 89, 112.

Charles V. letters from, to Henry VIII. 241, 252, 272.

Charles V. letter from, to Diego Hurtado de Mendoza, 466.

Charles V. letters from, to Prince Philip, 213, 269, 297, 303, 304, 305, 326, 350, 387, 442, 445, 492, 506.

Charles V. letters from, to St. Mauris, 275, 277.

Charles V. letters from, to Scepperus, 243, 245, 258, 263, 274, 312, 385.

Charles V. letters from, to Vander Delft, 114, 125, 162, 175, 219, 243, 245, 258, 263, 273, 274, 281, 288, 293, 312, 385, 398, 410, 417, 454, 475, 491, 495, 546.

Charles V. Emperor, letters from, to Juan de Vega, 41 (2), 273, 374, 443, 457, 475, 548.

Charles V. letter from, to the Bishop of Winchester, 272.

Charles V. Emperor, letters to from Chapuys, 17, 103, 115, 131, 140, 143, 159, 171.

Charles V. Emperor, letters to (from Chapuys and Vander Delft), 1, 23, 29, 35, 37.

Charles V. letters to, from Cobos, 174, 229, 391, 553.

Charles V. letter to, from Cardinal Coria, 412.

Charles V. letter to, from Cardinal Farnese, 413.

Charles V. letters to, from Henry VIII. 140, 195, 247, 262, 267, 275, 277.

Charles V. letter to, from Mary, Queen Dowager of Hungary, 476.

Charles V. letters to, from Diego Hurtado de Mendoza, 258, 311, 438, 505, 513, 521, 529, 537, 538.

Charles V. letter to, from Juan Hurtado de Mendoza, 531.

Charles V. letter to, from Dr. Molon, Inquisitor of Seville, 139.

Charles V. letters to, from Prince Philip, 72, 228, 352, 393, 400, 478, 490, 532, 550.

Charles V. letters to, from St. Mauris, 87, 206, 501.

Charles V. letters to, from Scepperus, 82, 273, 329, 345, 377, 380.

Charles V. letters to, from Loys Scors, 81, 82.

Charles V letter to, from Titian, 258.

Charles V. letters to, from Vander Delft, 171, 129, 130, 152, 164, 185, 199, 230, 246, 249, 250, 262, 264, 268, 275, 279, 281, 292, 293, 295, 309, 312, 317, 320, 329, 345, 377, 380, 389, 394, 396, 399, 400, 404, 406, 407, 433, 450, 466, 484, 493, 523, 532.

Charles V. letters to, from Juan de Vega, 321, 337, 376, 388, 395, 413, 415, 416, 418, 427, 436, 445, 446, 455, 479, 481, 489, 492, 494, 503, 504 (2), 513, 514, 522, 539, 547.

Charles V. his alliance with the Pope, 113, 183, 184, 210, 213, 214, 225, 244, 268, 269, 292, 297, 305-308, 321-324, 337, 352, 354, 355. 374, 375, 387, 386, 395, 400, 412-417, 424, 427-430, 436, 437, 443-446, 457-462, 464, 469, 473, 474-476, 479-483, 485, 489, 490, 491-493, 494, 495, 503, 506-508, 513, 514, 515, 523, 531, 538, 539-542.

Charles V. his views on the religious war in Germany, 305-308, 326, 328, 329. 350, 387, 388, 400, 410-412, 424, 458. 459, 507, 524, 544, 545, 550.

Charles V. Emperor, his peace with France, 4-9, 11, 12. 13, 14, 15, 19, 20, 27, 40, 45-46, 49-50, 60-61, 62, 65, 75-80, 89, 100, 103, 109, 110, 125-128, 132, 134, 154, 161, 178-182, 185, 190, 200-202, 215, 218, 222, 223, 224, 231, 236, 240, 245, 252-254, 257, 262, 273, 276, 278, 279, 280, 286, 292, 302, 313, 318, 321, 327, 351, 364, 374, 383, 398, 413, 425, 429, 436, 442, 469, 492, 493, 495, 505, 506, 514, 521, 538, 539, 541, 548.

Charles V. his intervention to secure peace between England and France, 53-57, 60, 64-69, 82, 85, 96, 97, 106, 109, 110, 116, 132, 144-146, 161, 163, 164, 169, 170-174, 181, 186-190, 191, 192, 195, 202, 204, 206-207, 215, 219, 231, 232, 235-240, 241-244, 253, 259-262, 264, 265-267, 269, 270-272, 273, 274-280, 286, 298.

Charles V. condemns Henry's conduct of the war in France, 179, 215.

Charles V. Emperor, his health and movements, 71, 72, 76, 101a, 181, 211, 214, 260, 266a, 271, 277, 297, 298, 303, 304, 310, 312, 314, 331, 350, 380, 387, 393, 400, 447, 490, 532, 550.

Charles V. his warlike preparations, 224, 226, 303, 307, 387, 401, 410, 411, 426, 448.

Charles V. at the Schmalkaldic war, 448, 455, 457-462, 475, 476, 490, 491-404, 496, 502, 507, 512, 524, 525, 540-542, 544, 545-547, 548.

Charles V. his anxiety for his son Philip, 447, 448, 554.

Charles V. his relations with the Lutherans. *See* Germany, Religious affairs in.

Charles V. his instructions regarding the Council of Trent, 515-518, 529.

Charles V. his financial measures. *See* Finance.

Charles V. his message to his son and daughters, 446, 447.

GENERAL INDEX.

Chastillon, French Minister, 77, 78, 99, 419, 420, 482.
Chamberlain, Mr. Thomas, English Consul at Antwerp, 91, 93, 97, 141. His dismissal demanded by the Flemish authorities, 558, 559.
Chancellor, the. *See* Wriothesley.
Chancellor of Brabant, letter to, from the Emperor, 138.
Chantries in England, suppression of, 291.
Cheyney, Sir Thomas, 7n. Sent to France to ratify the peace, 430-433.
Christophe, German Secretary in Flanders, 299.
Church revenues in England to be seized by the King, 136, 279, 291, 293, 531, 556.
Cifuentes, Count, illness and death of, 212. (*See also* Addenda Index.)
Claims, Commercial. *See* Seizures, and arbitration.
Clairmont, M. de, a French bishop at the Council of Trent, 253.
Cleves and Julliers. Grain from for export. *See* Wheat.
Cleves, Duke of, 16, 19, 101, 223, 224, 291.
Cobham, Lord, Deputy of Calais, 372.
Cobos, Francisco de los, letters from, to the Emperor, 174, 229, 391, 553.
Cobos, Francisco de los. letter from, to Secretary Granvelle, 71.
Cobos, Francisco, letters to, from Charles V. 34, 63, 211, 280, 447.
Cobos, Francisco de los, letter to, from Secretary Idiaquez, 268.
Cobos, Francisco de los, letter to, from de Granvelle, 327.
Cobos, Francisco de los, letters to, from St. Mauris, 31, 76, 80, 97, 147, 195, 205, 206, 229, 294, 373, 392, 422.
Cobos, Francisco de los, letters to, from Vargas, 34, 63, 71.
Cobos, Francisco de los, Spanish Minister, 31, 103, 175, 211, 303, 304, 307, 352, 387, 391, 392, 400, 447, 478, 553. His views on Spanish Finance, 553-555.
Cobos, his opinions on the Wars of Religion, 72, 74, 229.
Coinage, debasement of, by Henry VIII. 136.
Coinage, debasement of, in France, 147.
Cologne, Bishop of, 102, 183, 326, 328, 331, 412.
Combat between two Spanish Captains at Fontainebleau, 432, 433.
Comendador Mayor. *See* Cobos.
Comendador the, mysterious Spaniard in England. *See* Pacheco.
Commercial relations between France and Spain, 199.
Commercial claims and disputes. *See* Seizures.
Compagni, Bartolome, a peace intermediary, 232, 239, 244.
Confessor. *See* Guevara.

Conrad, Penninck, a German mercenary leader, 291, 294, 296, 300, 310, 311-314, 320, 329, 330, 334, 342, 343, 345, 359, 360, 362, 363, 365-367, 368, 369, 370, 377, 379, 381, 382, 385, 389, 393.
Conspiracy, alleged, against Henry VIII. 526, 527, 531, 533, 534, 535, 536, 537.
Contraband of War, agreement between Henry and the Emperor with regard to (*see also* Paget and Seizures), 81-86.
Cordova, Don Alvaro de, 175.
Coria, the Cardinal of, letter from, to the Emperor, 412.
Cornaro, Cardinal, 427.
Crépy, terms of the Peace of, 41-43, 71, 72, 79, 80, 98, 102, 150, 196, 197, 213, 214, 221, 224, 245, 257, 276, 278, 286, 302, 364, 398n, 536, 537.
Crescencius, Cardinal, 321, 541.
Crome, Dr. Edward, Vicar of St. Mary Aldermary, forced to retract reformed opinions, 394, 398, 426.
Cromwell, Thomas, Earl of Essex, 556.
Council, the English Secretary of, 55, 57, 62, 391, 501.
Councillors, Privy. *See* Hertford, Winchester, and Paget.
Courrières, M. de, 4, 5, 7, 14, 15, 61, 185.
Cueva, Pedro de la, otherwise Pacheco, 282, 288, 289.
Custom house records of England and Flanders (tollieux), 170, 378, 379, 380, 381, 390, 489.

D

D'Albret, Jeanne, 99, 101, 221, 223, 224, 225, 280, 431.
D'Albret, Margaret of France, Queen of Navarre, 221, 224, 225.
D'Albret, M., titular King of Navarre, 99, 101, 151, 221-224, 254, 402, 408, 433.
Damesell, Sir William, English factor at Antwerp, 470.
Dampierre, Governor of Ardres, 148. Killed in a skirmish, 247.
Dandino, Bishop of Caserta, Papal envoy to the Emperor, 268, 269, 321, 322, 339, 375, 429, 445.
Dandolo sent by the Emperor to Pope Paul III. 184, 197, 208, 210, 213, 226.
D'ansell, Sir William. *See* Damesell.
Danvers, Court Master of. *See* Chamberlain, Thomas.
D'Assenberg, Stephen, 543.
Dauphin, the (Henry of Valois), 68, 88, 99, 100, 112, 199, 220, 301, 373, 432, 502, 503, 506.
Dauphiness of France (Catharine de Medici), 302, 364, 392, 431, 433.

D'Aux of Provence, Chevalier, killed in the French invasion of the Isle of Wight, 194, 198.
Declaration of war demanded from the Emperor against France. *See* Subsidy demanded.
D'Eick, M. de. *See* Scepperus.
Delft, Van der. *See* Van der Delft.
Denmark, King of, 19, 249, 291, 372, 549.
Dias de Coruera, Captain, sent by Hurtado de Mendoza to the Emperor, 433, 440.
Dimock, John, English Commissioner in Flanders, 325.
Dolci, Gasparo (Jaspar Duchy), Genoese merchant in Flanders, 29, 57, 64, 159, 232, 248.
Doria, Andrea, letters from, to Prince Philip, 111, 277.
Doria, Andrea, letters to, from the Emperor, 112.
Doria, Prince Andrea, 75, 89-90, 100, 112, 183, 210, 213, 401, 490, 532, 549.
Doria, John Antonio, 183, 401.
Dorset, Marquis of (Henry Grey), 318, 320.
Douglas, Earl (*sic*), said to have defeated the English, 54.
Dragut Reis, Moslem corsair, 183. Reported killed, 210.
Du Bois, Jehan, Secretary, sent by Van der Delft to Flanders to divulge the proposed French and Lutheran design against the Emperor's Dutch coast, 498, 501, 512.
Dudley, Lady Catharine, her christening, 280.
Dudley, Lady. *See* Lisle.
Dudley, Lord Lisle, Lord Admiral, 99, 124, 158, 187, 238, 241, 249, 280, 311, 320, 334, 364, 373, 374, 380. His mission to France, 381, 386, 389, 394, 397, 404, 409, 425, 426, 433, 434, 451, 454, 456, 465, 467, 533. In favour with Henry, 534, 555, 556, 557.
Dudley, Lord Lisle. His brother sent with a present to Flanders, 345, 386.
Durham, Bishop of, Cuthbert Tunstall. His peace mission to France, 279, 344, 345, 406, 412, 425.

E

Ecclesiastical discipline at Trent, 515-518, 521.
Ecclesiastical revenues in Spain, their appropriation for the war. *See* Spain's contribution.
Edward Prince of Wales, 78. Suggested marriage with Margaret of France, 198. Suggested marriage with a niece of the Emperor, 300, 313, 315-317, 326, 330-334, 344-347, 362, 367, 368, 371, 380, 386. Suggested marriage with Mary Stuart, 207, 221, 287, 303, 374, 419, 420, 421, 435, 436, 452, 495, 545, 546.

Elizabeth, Empress, her portrait by Titian, 258.
Elizabeth of France (afterwards Queen of Spain), 302, 364, 392. Her christening, 408, 409, 428, 429, 431.
Emperor, the. *See* Charles V.
Embargoes. *See* Seizures.
Enghein, M. de, 94, 220, 431.
England, invasion of, by France, 76-77, 98, 124, 126, 128, 132, 135, 136, 140, 147, 151, 153, 162, 165, 190, 191, 197, 204, 220, 261, 279.
England stated to be a refuge for Flemish malefactors, 349.
England, scarcity in. *See* Scarcity.
England, condition of, at the time of Henry VIII.'s fatal illness, 555-558.
English subjects ill-treated in Antwerp. *See* Antwerp.
English troops, complaints of their conduct in Flanders, 18, 25, 31, 44, 341, 360, 362, 382, 442.
Essex, Earl of (William Parr), 318.
Este, Don Francisco de, 148, 197.
Étampes, Duchess d'. Her attempts to negotiate peace with England, 92, 96, 102, 103, 105, 110, 147, 165, 183, 223n, 232, 237, 239, 301, 419, 431, 433, 572.
Étampes, M. de, 88, 89.
Étaples, English attack upon, 373, 378.

F

Falmouth, Spanish mercenary troops at, 58.
Fane, Sir Ralph, Lieutenant of the Gentlemen pensioners, his mission to Flanders, 230, 241, 274.
Farnese, Cardinal, letter from, to the Emperor, 413.
Farnese, Cardinal, 98, 113, 213, 225, 226, 227, 244, 273, 321, 322, 323, 327, 337-339, 374, 375, 376, 388, 396, 413-416, 417, 427, 429-430, 436, 443, 444, 455, 457-462, 476, 480, 483, 493, 505, 506, 513, 514, 515, 522, 531, 532, 538, 539, 542, 547, 548.
Farnese, Constance, daughter of Paul III., her death, 183.
Farnese, Horatio, 428, 506.
Farnese, Ottavio, Duke of Camarino, 90, 213, 223, 227, 257, 322, 323, 376, 395. Commands the papal contingent, 418, 430, 458-462, 483, 495, 505n.
Farnese, Victoria, granddaughter of Paul III., 504.
Farnese, the. *See also* Paul III., Pier Luigi, and Parma.
Ferdinand, Archduke of Austria, 211.
Ferdinand, King of the Romans, letters to, from St. Mauris, 254, 286.

GENERAL INDEX.

Ferdinand, King of the Romans, 41-43, 71, 211, 267, 302, 315, 316, 329, 346, 347, 350, 394, 476, 507, 514, 525, 545.

Fernando, Duke of Aragon, 75-76.

Ferrandina, Duke of, 211.

Ferrara, Cardinal, 149, 183, 375, 419, 439.

Ferrara, dispute with Florence, 196.

Ferrara, Duke of, 340, 375.

Fiesco, a Genoese, 87, 100, 112, 322, 454, 466, 547.

Figueroa, Imperial Ambassador in Genoa, letters to, from the Emperor, 89. 112.

Figueroa, Don Juan de, 211, 476, 479, 483, 490.

Finance, the Emperor's, 35, 41, 72-75, 184, 212, 213, 215, 226, 268, 295, 301, 303, 304, 305, 317, 321, 352, 353, 387, 388, 391, 392, 400, 401, 414-416, 417, 423, 429, 436, 437, 443-446, 457-462, 475, 476, 478, 479-483, 507, 508, 513, 514, 515, 522, 531, 548, 550-555.

First fruits, ecclesiastical, in Spain, to be taken for the Lutheran war. *See* Spain's contribution.

Flanders, passage of mercenaries through, for the English service. *See also* mercenaries, 235, 240, 241, 246, 263, 299, 300, 312-314, 320, 330, 342, 343, 345, 359, 360, 365-367, 368, 369, 377, 378, 379, 381, 382, 385, 389, 408, 412.

Flanders, ecclesiastical first fruits of, to be appropriated for the Lutheran war. 414, 436, 437, 447, 455, 458.

Flanders, proposed cession as a dower, 42.

Flanders, intelligence from, 247.

Flanders, scarcity in, 384.

Flemings, oppression of, by the English, 92, 126, 138, 141, 349, 360, 363, 378, 384, 385, 390.

Florence, Duke of (Cosmo de Medici), 328, 337, 349, 350, 388, 416.

Florence, dispute with Ferrara for precedence, 196.

Food stuffs, export of, from Flanders. *See* Wheat, etc.

Framoiselle, a French peace envoy to Henry VIII. 173.

France, statements of occurrences in, 31, 76-79, 80, 87-88, 97-100, 147-152, 195, 205-206, 209, 219, 286, 302, 364, 373, 402, 409, 419, 430-433, 501-503.

France, Queen of, Eleanor of Austria, 77, 199, 301, 302, 393, 419, 420, 431, 501, 502, 553.

France, distress in, 221, 236, 242, 421.

France, taxation in, 257, 287, 288, 421, 552.

France, tumults in, 257, 288.

France, Spanish distrust of, 286, 287, 292, 302, 402, 421, 502, 503, 530.

Francis I. 32, 40, 42, 43, 63, 68, 76-79, 80, 87, 97-100, 109, 110, 149, 196, 199, 206, 219-220, 225, 243, 257, 250, 286, 295, 301, 315, 364, 430-433, 502, 503, 549.

Francis I. his relations with the Pope, 78, 98, 100, 196, 256, 257, 292, 315, 321, 365, 374, 419, 420, 422, 428, 482, 492, 493, 495, 528, 540, 551, 552.

Francis I. his relations with the German Protestants, 102, 148, 149, 197, 221, 256, 302, 420, 422, 428, 434, 442, 495, 498, 502, 503, 506, 518, 528, 539, 545.

Francis I. his malady, 1, 76, 196, 219, 220, 223, 225, 295, 301, 482.

Frankfort, surrender of, 544, 546.

Frederick, Count Palatine, 183, 210, 326, 350, 371, 412, 537.

French naval and military movements, (*see also* Galleys, French), 135, 142, 143, 147-152, 172, 199, 205, 209, 220, 224, 229, 247, 255, 256, 257, 265, 320, 324, 329, 350, 351, 394, 530, 542.

French depredation upon Spanish shipping, etc., 88, 98, 103, 115, 199, 209, 211, 314, 216, 257, 270, 320, 329, 351, 365, 373, 393, 403, 409, 410, 421.

French violation of Imperial territory, 197, 211, 214, 216.

French expeditions to Scotland. *See* Montgomerie.

French fears of a renewed offensive alliance between Henry and the Emperor, 387.

French invasion of the isle of Wight. *See* Invasion.

French property to be sequestrated in Spain, 216, 421.

French Protestants, 102, 149, 197, 221, 502, 503.

French ships captured by the English, 94, 109, 111, 209, 220, 394n, 409, 465.

Fuentarrabia, horses from, 80.

Fuggers, German bankers, 146, 248, 387, 388, 392, 417, 549.

Funds for the Lutheran war. *See* Spain's contribution to.

Furstenberg, Count William of, a prisoner in France, 100, 101, 148, 196, 197, 221, 256, 282, 288, 310.

G

Galeaçn, Dr., Spanish jurist, 392.

Galleasses, preferred by Henry VIII. to galleys, 317, 335.

Gallego Francisco, his ship captured by Renegat, 212. (*See also* Renegat.)

Galley slaves, dispute between France and Spain about the possession of, 199, 205.

Galleys, French, 77, 79, 87, 103, 109, 111, 114, 130, 135, 142, 143, 147, 149, 172, 199, 205, 209, 211, 216, 218, 220, 256, 257, 350, 392, 393, 394, 403, 409, 410, 454, 518, 528, 542, 543.

Galleys, Spanish, movements of, in Mediterranean, 113, 183, 199, 210, 215, 216, 277, 351, 388, 401, 478, 479, 490, 549.
Gamay, Thomas, at the Bourbourg arbitration, 140.
Gambara, Cardinal, his proposal that the Pope should mediate between the Emperor and France, 374-376, 455.
Gamboa, Pedro de, mercenary colonel in the English service, 55, 69, 294, 300.
Gandia, Duke of (Borgia), 76.
Garbrand, Henry, letters from, to Jehan Lobel and Gerard Has, merchants, 139.
Gardiner, Stephen. See Winchester, Bishop of.
Genoa, Fiesco's plot in, 100, 112, 454n, 466, 547, 549.
Gerard, Secretary, French Envoy to the Turk, 197, 210.
German mercenaries. See Mercenaries.
Germany, religious affairs in (see also War of Religion), 102, 114, 183-184, 196, 208, 214, 225-227, 228, 249, 250, 267, 271, 279, 305-308, 314, 326, 328, 329, 331, 350, 353-356, 371, 372, 377, 378, 387, 394, 396, 411-413, 420, 422, 424, 425, 428, 434, 435, 436, 439n, 450, 455, 456, 464, 466-470, 474-476, 483-485, 494, 495, 503, 504, 506, 507, 508, 518, 523, 525, 529, 537-539, 541, 542, 544-546, 549.
Golden Fleece, chapter of, held, 294, 304.
Gomez de Silva, Ruy, 174.
Gonzaga, Fernando de, Governor of Milan, intelligence sent by him from Turin, etc., 435, 454, 456, 466, 495, 550.
Gonzaga, Fernando de, Viceroy of Sicily, and afterwards of Milan, 13, 30, 111, 200, 416, 417, 439, 441, 478, 479, 493n, 553.
Gonzaga, Luis, Lord of Castiglione, to enter the English service, 183, 311.
Gragnan (or Grignan), M. de, French Envoy to Worms, 102, 149, 208.
Granvelle, Secretary, letter from, to Cobos, 327.
Granvelle, Secretary de, letters from, to Van der Delft, 266.
Granvelle, Secretary de, letters to, from Chapuys, 142, 143, 217.
Granvelle, Secretary, letter to, from Cobos, 71.
Granvelle, Secretary de, letters to, from Scepperus, 273, 300, 335.
Granvelle, Secretary de, letters to, from Van der Delft, 296, 309.
Granvelle, M. de, Imperial Secretary of State, 31, 41, 71, 72, 102, 112, 131, 164, 170, 175, 266, 268, 278, 296, 297, 312, 370, 395, 441, 548, 549, 557.
Granvelle, Secretary de. His opinion on Cardinal Gambara's discourse, 375.
Grain, export from France prohibited, 518.
Gravelines, prohibition of food being sent, from there to the English camp, 317, 381.

Gravelines, conference at. See Bourbourg.
Great Harry, flagship of the English fleet, 187.
Greenwich, interviews at, 2-9, 23, 309, 380, 390, 423-426.
Grey de Wilton, Lord, 148n, 172, 247n, 361, 362, 379.
Grimano, Cardinal, 439.
Grüningen, M. de, Imperial commander in the Schmalkaldic war. 547.
Guaras Antonio, a Spanish merchant in London. His claims, 117, 117n, 118, 168.
Guasto, Marquis del, Governor of Milan, 89-90, 102, 112, 113, 183, 210, 211, 215, 323, 327, 376.
Gueldres, passage of mercenaries through. See Alten.
Gueldres, the bastard of (Martin Varotten), 101, 234.
Gueldres, Marshal of, 363.
Guevara, Antonio de, the Emperor's confessor, etc., 74. His opinion on the war against Lutheranism, 353-356, 392, 550.
Guevara, Colonel Carlos de, a Spanish mercenary captain in England, 289.
Guildford, Henry VIII. at, 230, 467.
Guise, Duke of, 102, 209, 252, 431.
Guisnes, 26, 111, 133, 148, 177, 172, 185, 220, 247, 336.
Guzman, Captain, 32, 222, 225.
Guzman, Don Pedro, otherwise Don Pedro de Noche, 284, 285.
Guzman, Friar Gabriel, an intermediary for peace between France and the Emperor, 281, 292.
Guzman, Lope de, 376.
Guzman, Friar Martin de, 223, 255.

H

Hall, Francis, Controller of Calais, 230.
Hampton Court, 295, 309, 454, 462, 465n.
Hard, Martin von, of Guedelenbourg, a captain of mercenaries, 334.
Hardelot (Ardellot), capture of, by the English, 111, 148. Fortified by the French, 378.
Haro, Juan de, a Spanish mercenary captain, his desertion to the French, 69, 295n.
Harvel, Sigismund, English minister in Venice, 538n.
Heilly, Mlle. de. See Étampes.
Henriox, Gheert, a captain of mercenaries, 334.
Henry VIII. letters from, to the Emperor, 140, 195, 247, 262, 267, 275, 277.
Henry VIII. letters from, to the Queen Dowager of Hungary, 230, 268.
Henry VIII. letters to, from the Emperor, 241, 252, 272.

GENERAL INDEX. 625

Henry VIII. letter to, from the Duke of Alburquerque, 405.

Henry VIII. his reception of Chapuys and Van der Delft, 2. In broken health, 2. His indignation at the Emperor's peace with France, 5. Calls Chapuys a liar, 5. Defends his conduct of the war, 6, 7, 8, 13, 14. His rudeness excused by the Councillors, 18. Interview with the Ambassadors, 33. His contention with regard to the peace between Charles and Francis, 60-61. His determination to hold Boulogne, 66-67. His arrangement with Charles respecting liberty of navigation, 81-86. His alleged agreement with the Duke of Savoy against France, 89. His last interview with Chapuys, 107-110, 129, 131, 140. His anger with the Emperor, 153-157. His journey to Portsmouth, 162, 165, 167, 168, 173, 186. His interview with Van der Delft there, 186-190. Witnesses the naval fight off Portsmouth, 191. Demands the Emperor's aid afresh, 200-202, 205, 231. Reception of the Emperor's peace intervention, 235-240. Seeks interview with the Emperor, 246, 247, 249-255. His reply to the peace proposals, 259-262, 265. Present in Parliament, 279. Receives Van der Delft, 310. Rumours of his intention to divorce Katharine Parr and marry again, 318. His illness, 320, 324, 329, 330. His interview with Scepperus and Van der Delft, 330-333. His rumoured leaning towards Catholicism, 339, 394. His regard for Mary of Hungary, 344, 345, 346, 386. Comes to Westminster, 349, 365, 379, 380, 394. His views on the peace with France, 407, 426. To stand sponsor to the Dauphin's child, 408, 409, 428-431. His views on the peace, 436, 467. Serious illness of, 475, 484. His indignant protest at the Emperor's treatment of him, 486, 487, 488. Receives the Scottish envoys, 509. His opinion of the French, 523. His distrust of the Pope, 523, 528. Conspiracy against him, 526, 527, 531, 533, 534. His illness, 535, 537, 542, 545, 546, 555-558.

Henry VIII. his relations with the German Protestants, 126, 127, 130, 134, 240, 249, 250, 251, 276, 279, 287, 290, 331, 371, 377, 380, 410-412, 420, 424, 425, 434, 438, 439, 442, 450, 451, 454, 455, 464, 466-470, 484, 487, 523, 524, 528, 537, 539, 544, 545.

Henry VIII. his views on the marriage of his son to a niece of the Emperor, 331-333, 346-348, 362, 367, 368.

Henry VIII. his offer to mediate between the Emperor and the Lutherans, 544, 545.

Henry VIII. his proposed interview with the Emperor. *See* Interview *and* Scepperus.

Henry VIII. suggests an offensive league against France, 524.

Henry VIII. his treaty of alliance with the Emperor. *See* Subsidy demanded.

Hesdin, its restitution to France claimed, 43, 72, 150, 196, 276, 363, 364.

Hesse, the Landgrave of, 102, 209, 210, 234, 249, 277, 279, 328, 350, 354, 379, 410, 411, 455, 469, 476, 514, 540, 544, 545, 549.

Hermes, Dr., proposed Flemish Commissioner to regulate the commercial claims, 298.

Herrera, otherwise the Comendador Pacheco, 282, 288.

Hertford, Earl of, Edward Seymour, 3. Conference with the Ambassadors, 9-16, 17-20, 23, 24-26, 57-62. To command the army in Scotland, 95, 124, 135, 165. In London, 233, 294, 300. To go to Boulogne, 329, 333, 345, 426. In favour with Henry, 464, 467, 475, 526, 534, 555, 556, 557.

Hertford and Gardiner, their mission to demand the aid of the Emperor against France, 3-4, 17, 26, 35, 37, 39, 45, 48, 49, 60, 64, 83, 86, 92, 126-128, 138, 154, 177, 178, 201.

Hertford, Countess of (Ann Stanhope), a Protestant partisan, 555.

Hertzen, Jacques, recommended by Van der Delft as Burgomaster of Antwerp, 373.

Hochstadt, Count, to prevent the passage of Conrad Penninck's mercenaries by Gueldres, 363, 365, 366.

Hôpital, Chancellor of France, 275.

Horses, export of, from Flanders, 16, 361.

Horses, scarcity of, in Spain, 327.

Huesca, Pedro, his news from the imperial court sent to Gonzalo Perez in Spain, 208.

Hungary, Queen Dowager of. *See* Mary.

Hurtado de Mendoza, Diego. *See* Mendoza.

I

Idiaquez, Secretary, letter from, to Cobos, 268.

Idiaquez, Spanish Secretary of State, 71. His account of affairs at Worms, etc., sent to Spain, 225, 278, 280.

Infantas, the, their domestic expenditure, 554, 555.

Inquisition in Spain, English complaints of, 291, 293, 333.

Inquisition in Seville, statement by Dr. Molon of Jews and Lutherans punished by, 139.

Inquisition in Sicily, 352, 401.

Interview proposed between Henry and the Emperor, 246, 247, 251-254, 260-262, 266, 268, 270-272, 273, 298.

Invasion of England. *See* England, invasion of.

Irish troops to be sent to Boulogne, 318, 320.

J

Jaen, Bishop of. *See* Pacheco, Cardinal.
Jean, Jaques, a German secretary, 256.
Jedburgh justice (Corinthian justice), 24.
Joan, Queen of Spain, 304.
Justification, article of, at the Council of Trent, 515-518, 521, 522, 529, 530, 541, 547.

K

Katharine, Queen. *See* Parr, Katharine, *and also* Aragon.
Knyvett, Sir Henry, 124, 283-286, 432.

L

Landenberger, a mercenary captain in the English service, 37, 126, 234, 241, 342, 360, 382, 389.
Lange, a French peace envoy to Henry VIII., 173.
Lauenberg, Duke of, 158, 291.
Lantree, M. de. 16.
Laval, M. de, French courtier, 431.
Lent, strict observance of, in England, 349.
Leyton, Dr., English ambassador in France, 100.
Liege, territory of the Bishop of, passage of mercenaries through, 263, 300, 363, 382.
Lisle, Lady (Jane Guildford). A Protestant partisan, 555.
Loans raised by Henry VIII. in Antwerp, 24, 29, 136, 146, 248, 319, 340.
Lobel, Jehan, and Has Gerard, merchants of Lille, their claims against the English, 139, 144.
Lodge, Thomas, his peace negotiations in France, 77, 99.
Lolme de, of Antwerp, his son, a defaulter, arrested in England, 348.
London, Bishop of, 395.
Longueville, Duke of, 79, 431.
L'Orge, M. de. *See* Montgomerie.
Lorraine, Cardinal Charles, 102, 195, 501.
Lorraine, Duchess of, 102, 195, 209, 501.
Lorraine, Duke Francis of, 32, 78, 102. His death, 195, 208, 224, 227.
Louvain, Chapuys at, 184, 195, 205.
Ludeña, Friar Juan de, 284.

Lufti, Pasha, 377.
Lugo, Bishop of, 392, 479.
Luna, Don Juan de, Spanish commander in Siena, 323, 324, 327.
Lunenburg, Duke of, 420.
Lutherans, massacre of, near Avignon, 148.
Lutherans. *See* "Germany, religious affairs in," and "War of religion in Germany."
Luxemburg, Duke of, expected in England, 241.

M

Mafeo, a Venetian peace intermediary, 386.
Maffei, or Maffeo, Secretary to Cardinal Farnese, 481, 482, 489, 515, 531, 532.
Magnus, David, Imperial Envoy to Scotland, 404, 462, 463.
Margaret of Austria, afterwards Duchess of Parma. *See* Camarino, Duchess of.
Margaret of France, 32. Proposed marriage with Emmanuel Philibert of Savoy. 99. Proposed marriage with Edward Prince of Wales, 198. Proposed marriage with Emmanuel Philibert, 221. With Prince Philip, 229, 275, 276, 278, 280, 287, 301, 422, 431, 501.
Maria, Infanta, of Spain. Proposed marriage with the Duke of Orleans, 41, 71, 79, 197, 303. Her father's wishes with regard to her, 448. Her domestic expenditure, 554.
Marquina, Pedro, envoy to the Pope, 268, 279, 292, 305, 321, 327, 338, 396, 413, 417, 445, 541.
Marriages stipulated for in the peace of Crepy, 41-43, 71, 79, 80, 90, 98, 102, 112, 214, 215, 228, 244, 295.
Marriage proposed between Edward Prince of Wales and a niece of the Emperor. *See* Edward Prince of Wales.
Marseilles, French galleys at. *See* Galleys.
Mary, Princess, of England, letter from, to the Duke of Alburquerque, 446.
Mary, Princess, 2, 32, 78, 104. Suggested marriage with the Duke of Orleans, 198. Suggested marriage with the Duke of Vendome, 255. Present at Lady Catharine Dudley's baptism, 280. Rumours of her intended marriage with the King of Poland, 318. Betrothed to Duke Philip of Bavaria, Count Palatine, 348, 377, 378. Letter from, 446. Her position at her father's death, 557.
Mary, Queen, Dowager of Hungary, letter from, to Van der Bergh, 498.
Mary, Queen, Dowager of Hungary, letters from, to Chapuys and Van der Delft, 44, 83.

GENERAL INDEX.

Mary, Queen, Dowager of Hungary, letter from, to the Emperor, 476.

Mary, Queen, Dowager of Hungary, letters from, to Van der Delft, 319, 340, 381, 386, 403, 411, 440, 448, 456, 471, 496, 498, 518, 535, 543, 544, 549, 558.

Mary, Queen, Dowager of Hungary, letters to, from Adrian Van der Bergh, 395.

Mary, Queen, Dowager of Hungary, letters to, from Chapuys, 110, 161, 555.

Mary, Queen, Dowager of Hungary, Stadtholderinn, letters to, from Chapuys and Van der Delft, 23, 44, 55, 57, 63, 90, 93, 95.

Mary, Queen, Dowager of Hungary, letters to, from Henry VIII. 230, 268.

Mary, Queen, Dowager of Hungary, letters to, from Scepperus, 234, 235, 324, 325, 329, 334 (2), 343, 344, 371, 378, 381, 387, 470.

Mary, Queen, Dowager of Hungary, letters to, from Van der Delft, 113, 125, 130, 158, 167, 194, 205, 230, 235, 248, 249, 263, 325, 334, 343, 344, 371, 378, 381, 390, 391, 395, 399, 404, 408, 423, 434, 451, 462, 470, 475, 485, 489, 500, 512, 526, 535, 542.

Mary, Queen, Dowager of Hungary, Stadtholderinn, 2, 5, 6, 7, 8, 15, 16, 18, 23, 33, 41, 82, 83, 99, 105, 117, 138, 170, 209, 212, 298, 317, 345, 347, 373, 386, 434, 452, 488, 524, 522.

Mary of Guise, Queen, Dowager of Scotland, 315, 436.

Mary, Queen of Scots, letter from, 1.

Mary, Queen of Scots, suggested marriage with a son of the King of the Romans, 108, 113, 114. Suggested marriage with Edward, Prince of Wales, 207, 221, 303, 315. Suggested marriage with the son of the Regent Arran, 325. With Edward, Prince of Wales, 330, 331, 347, 374, 419, 420, 421, 435, 436, 462, 495.

Mary Rose, the, founders in Portsmouth harbour, 190.

Mason, Secretary Sir John, King's postmaster, 371, 372, 377, 378, 390, 434, 435.

Master of the Horse. See Browne, Sir Anthony.

Mayence, Bishop of, death of, 271, 350.

Maximilian, Archduke, of Austria, 211, 221, 475.

Massini, Ipolito (Ypolitus Masinus), an envoy of the Duchess d'Etampes to England, 165.

Mendoza, Bernardino de, General of the Spanish galleys in the Mediterranean, 72, 199, 215, 228, 351, 388, 401, 478, 479, 490.

Mendoza, Diego Hurtado de, letters from, to the Emperor, 258, 311, 438, 505, 513, 521, 529, 537, 538.

Mendoza, Diego Hurtado de, letters to, from the Emperor, 466.

Mendoza, Diego Hurtado de, summary of his interview with the Venetian Seigniory, 538.

Mendoza, Don Diego Hurtado de, Spanish ambassador in Venice, 210, 258. His opinion of the Council of Trent, 311, 375, 377, 395, 438, 439, 447, 462, 466, 468, 505, 515-518, 521, 529, 537-539, 540, 548.

Mendoza, Juan Hurtado de, letter from, to the Emperor, 531.

Mendoza, Don Juan de, his mission to Rome, 445, 446, 503, 504, 505-508, 514, 515, 517, 522, 531, 532, 539-542, 547, 548, 550.

Mendoza, Lope Hurtado de, Spanish ambassador in Portugal, letter from, to Prince Philip, 318.

Mendoza, Maitre d'Hotel to Francois I. 198.

Mercenaries, German, Italian and Spanish, in the English service, 15, 17, 26, 28, 31, 37, 38, 45, 53, 55-57, 59-62, 68, 70, 71, 95, 101, 108, 122, 124, 126, 158, 165, 180, 183, 204, 208, 209, 222, 234, 235, 240, 241, 244, 246, 250, 262, 263, 269, 273, 274, 277, 283-286, 291, 292-294, 295, 296, 300, 301, 310, 311-314, 318, 320, 329, 330, 334, 342, 343, 345, 349, 359, 360-363, 365-367, 368, 371, 377, 381, 382, 386, 389, 398, 408, 409, 412, 426, 543.

Mercenaries in the French service, 58, 63, 69, 76, 80, 100, 143, 149, 180, 183, 198, 203, 222, 225, 258, 283-286, 409, 468, 503, 544.

Metz, Antoine de, his son sent to London with a present of wine, 537.

Metz, Bishop of, Jean de Lorraine, 102, 195.

Meunier, Cornelius, 319.

Meudon, Cardinal, 147.

Milan, proposed cession as a dower to Princess Catharine, 42, 72, 79, 80, 90, 135, 197, 244, 257, 362.

Mirandola, Count de la, 148, 224, 506.

Molon, Dr., letter from, to the Emperor, 139.

Monastic manors, proposed sale of, in Spain to pay for the Lutheran war. See Spain's contribution.

Mondejar, Marquis of, 447, 428, 479, 550.

Monluc, M. de, French envoy to the Turk, 197, 302. Peace intermediary sent to Boulogne, 374, 386, 389, 393, 397.

Montgomerie, Jacques Sieur de l'Orge, 77, 88, 103, 147, 150, 198.

Monti, Cardinal, 71.

Montpensier, M. de. (Duke de Montpensier), 431.

Montpensier, Mme. de, 431.

Montreuil, siege of, 12, 13, 14, 179.

Mora, Captain, a Spanish mercenary, 295. His duel, 432, 433.

Morette, Charles Solier de. French ambassador to the Emperor, 54, 66-69, 80, 82, 89-90, 109, 267, 274, 277, 278, 465.

Moriscos of Granada, 75.

Morocco, Sheriff of, attacks the Kingdom of Fez, 401.

Morone, Cardinal, 540.

Morrison (Moryson), Sir Richard, goes to Denmark, 543.
Mortlake, Van der Delft's residence at, 240, 241.
Munitions of war. *See* Arms, etc.
Musica, Antonio, suspected of spying, 241.
Mustapha Pasha, the son of Soliman the Magnificent, 183, 209.

N

Navagero, to go as Venetian ambassador to England, 537, 538.
Naval battles between the English and French, 147, 158, 172, 190, 191, 194, 197, 198, 204, 211, 229, 232, 234, 238, 244, 248, 255, 256, 394, 398.
Naval preparations, etc., in England, 124, 130, 135, 158, 187, 209, 220, 232, 240, 248, 255, 295, 317, 320, 325, 329, 334, 335, 336, 349, 371, 389, 390, 394, 463, 485, 488, 530, 543.
Navarre, the Kingdom of, 99, 151, 402, 408, 433.
Naves, Flemish Vice-Chancellor, 299.
Navigation freedom of. *See* Seizures.
Nemours, Mme. de, 431.
Neuburg, capture of by the Emperor, 481, 490, 493.
Neutrality of the Emperor in the war between England and France. *See* Subsidy demanded.
Nevers, M. de (Duke de Nevers), 255.
Nicholas, a French negotiator in Rome, 321.
Nicolo, Messer Sienese Envoy to Rome, 396.
Noirthoudt, letters written jointly with St. Mauris to the Emperor, 206.
Noirthoudt, M. de, special Imperial Envoy to France to negotiate peace with England, 207, 235, 238, 243, 254, 264.
Norfolk, Duke of, 124, 130, 135, 147, 148, 349. His arrest, 526, 527, 531, 533, 534, 535, 536, 537, 556.
Nuncios. *See* Poggio, Sfondrato, etc.

O

Oatlands, Henry VIII. at, 509.
Odet, de Selve, French ambassador to England, 322n. 423, 424, 425, 485, 488, 511, 530, 537.
Olaus, Chancellor to Ferdinand, King of the Romans, 549.
"Old Man, the," a tower on Boulogne harbour, 98, 148.

Olivier, Chancellor of France, 419.
Orange, William of, 150.
Orleans, Duke of, 32. Negotiations for his marriage with a niece or daughter of the Emperor, 41-43, 71, 78, 79, 80, 98, 101, 108, 109, 173, 183, 197, 208, 222, 244. Suggested marriage with Mary Tudor, 78, 198. Death of, 245, 247, 250, 255, 257, 275, 362.
Ortiz, de Melgaredo, imprisonment of, 76.
Ortiz, de la Rea Juan, a prisoner. His deposition with regard to his service in England and France, 283-286.
Osorio, Don Alonso de, 402.
Osorio, Dona Isabel de, 402n, 448n.
Otañez, Gaspar de, 285, 286.
Oysip, M. de, French envoy to Scotland, 527, 528, 530, 536, 537.

P

Pacheco, Bishop of Jaen, afterwards Cardinal, 41, 329, 396, 447, 530, 540, 541.
Pacheco, Don Pedro, a mysterious personage so called, 282, 288, 289, 290, 293, 294, 295, 309, 310, 312, 405.
Paget, Sir William, Secretary of State. Conferences with the ambassadors, 9-16, 17-20, 23, 24, 29. His mission to the Emperor, 35, 39, 41, 44-47, 48-52. His draft agreement respecting the seizures, etc., 53, 55-57, 60, 64, 65-69, 70, 71. His agreement with regard to contraband of war, etc., 81-82, 83-86, 91-92, 93, 95-96, 97. Farewell interview with Chapuys, 107, 109. Sends a thoroughbred dog to Mary of Hungary. Referred to, 111-116, 119, 120, 121, 131, 132, 133, 144, 155, 162, 163, 165, 168, 169, 172, 178, 185-187, 193, 194, 203, 218, 230, 231, 235, 239, 248, 250, 252, 279, 290, 309, 325, 329, 330, 344-348, 364, 368, 371, 378-380, 381, 385, 386, 389, 393, 404, 425, 434, 442, 450-453, 464, 473, 484, 485, 487, 493, 496, 498, 512, 520, 525, 528, 530, 544.
Palavicini, opposed by Pier Luigi Farnese, 329.
Palavicini, Marquis de, an Italian mercenary captain, 95.
Palmer, Sir Thomas, 148n, 256.
Palatine, Count. *See* Frederick.
Pamele, Adolf van. Proposed Flemish Commissioner to settle the commercial claims, 298.
Paniter, David, Bishop of Ross, 1, 47, 54, 56, 65, 86, 91, 94, 106, 107, 108, 109, 113, 441, 452, 453, 476, 497, 509-512, 518-520, 525.

GENERAL INDEX.

Papal contingent for the Schmalkaldic war, 226, 268, 322, 387, 395, 414, 415, 418, 427-430, 436, 437, 455, 457, 458-462, 483, 493, 495, 504, 505, 506, 514, 515, 531. (*See also* War of Religion.)

Pardo Albroz, his ship detained by the English, 91.

Pardo Diego, Spanish merchant, 138.

Parliament, English, 279, 291, 293, 534, 543, 556, 557.

Parma and Piacenza, Duchies of, 197, 208, 213, 226, 227, 244, 257, 258, 297, 322, 323, 368, 375, 395, 505n, 547.

Parr, Katharine, Queen. Her interview with the Imperial ambassador, 2. Her kindness to Princess Mary, 2. Farewell to Chapuys, 104-105, 111. Negotiations of her Secretary with the German Protestants, 130, 163, 232. 310. Rumours of her divorce, 319, 373, 378, 390, 400, 534, 535. Favours the Protestant party. 555.

Parr, Queen Katharine, her Secretary. *See* Butler, Richard.

Paul III., Pope (Farnese). 32. 34. 63, 183, 213, 225-228, 244, 321-324, 337-339, 349, 350, 368, 395, 412-417, 436, 437-481, 503-504.

Paul III., Pope. His alliance with the Emperor to suppress Lutheranism, 34, 35, 41, 72. 74, 75. 113, 183, 210, 213, 225-228, 244, 268, 269, 273, 292, 297, 305-308, 321-324. 327. 337-339, 352, 354, 355, 375, 387. 388, 395, 412-417, 427-430. 436, 437, 443-446, 457-462. 475, 476-483. 503-505, 513, 514, 531. 539-542, 548, 550-555.

Paul III., Pope. Spanish distrust of him, 374, 375, 376, 439, 436, 437, 443, 475, 476, 480, 481, 489, 490, 492, 493, 539-541, 547, 548, 550.

Paul III., Pope. Suggested aid to France against England. 41. 42, 63, 71, 78, 98, 100, 119, 196, 255-257. 374.

Paul III., Pope, and the Council of Trent, 41, 71, 100, 101, 113, 210, 269, 292, 311, 321. 322, 327. 329, 339, 349, 374, 375, 396, 422, 423, 427. 445, 446, 447, 455, 461, 483, 490, 493, 495, 504, 505, 515-518, 521, 529, 540, 541, 547.

Paul III. His attempt to reconcile Henry VIII. to the Papacy, 422.

Paul III, Pope. His violent temper, 337. 338.

Paulin, Baron de la Garde, General of the galleys of France, 77, 148, 199, 220, 256n, 485, 526, 529, 530, 534, 535, 542, 544.

Peace negotiations between England and France, 47, 49, 54. 56, 65-69, 77, 82-86, 94. 96, 97, 100, 106, 109. 115, 116, 126, 129, 135. 144-146, 147, 165, 170, 173, 186-192, 195, 198, 206-207, 209, 219, 220, 231, 233, 235-240, 241 244, 250-251. 255, 259-262, 264, 265, 266-272, 273, 274-280, 286, 287, 290, 293, 295, 314, 315, 325, 328, 334, 364, 368, 373, 380, 386, 388, 389, 392, 394, 397, 398-400, 402, 403.

Peace, proposed terms of, 241, 242, 250, 251, 259-262, 276, 277, 290, 373, 392, 397, 398, 402, 403, 404, 406-409.

Peace, concluded between England and France, 403, 404, 406-409, 410, 418, 419, 425, 430-433, 434, 435, 463-465, 495, 518, 526.

Penninck. *See* Conrad Penninck.

Peralta, Iñigo de, Quartermaster, 210.

Perez, Gonzalo, Imperial Secretary of State, 103.

Perkin, Warbeck, 16.

Peru, French ships destined for, 205, 217

Pescara, Marquis of, 504.

Petre, Sir William, Secretary of State, 91. At the arbitration conference, 116, 131, 133, 134, 143, 144-146, 159, 171-174, 218, 250, 371, 378, 391, 394, 453.

Philip, Prince of Spain, letters from, to the Emperor, 72, 228, 352, 393, 400, 478, 490, 532, 550.

Philip, Prince, letters to, from Andrea Doria, 111, 277.

Philip, Prince, letters to, from the Emperor, 213, 269, 297, 303, 304, 305, 326, 350, 387, 442, 445, 492, 506.

Philip, Prince, letters to, from Lope Hurtado de Mendoza, 318.

Philip, Prince, letter to, from Juan Martinez de Recalde, 115.

Philip, Prince, letters to, from St. Mauris, 103, 199, 219, 301, 392, 402, 408, 418, 430, 518.

Philip, Prince of Spain, letters to, from Juan de Vega, 183, 292, 349.

Philip, Prince of Spain, 32, 34, 41, 99, 111, 143, 150, 174. Birth of his son and death of his wife, 175, 211. Intelligence sent to, from Worms, 182, 269. Suggestions for his marriage, 275, 278, 280, 303, 422. His father's anxiety for him, 448, 554. His efforts to raise money, 478, 479, 490, 532, 550-555. Proposals for his marriage, 501.

Philip, Prince of Spain, his views on Spanish finance, etc., 72-75, 353, 387, 400, 401, 478, 479, 490, 532, 550-553.

Philip, Prince of Spain, his views on the Lutheran war, 228, 352, 387, 400, 550-553.

Philip, Prince of Spain, takes the oath as Duke of Milan, 491.

Philip. Count Palatine, Duke of Bavaria, his visit to England as a suitor for Princess Mary, 348, 349, 370, 371, 372, 377, 378, 380, 381, 386, 390, 434, 435, 450, 451-453, 456, 457, 464, 465, 470, 474, 485.

Philip, a Protestant envoy, 249.

Piacenza, Duchy of. *See* Parma and Piacenza.

Piedmont, Prince of, Emmanuel Philibert, of Savoy, 32, 99, 150, 183, 198, 210, 221, 225, 281, 287, 457.

Piedmont, intelligence from, 435, 454, 456, 466, 495.

630 GENERAL INDEX.

Piedmont, occupation of, by the French, 286, 302, 328, 364, 398, 422.
Pier Luigi, Farnese, 227, 257. 258, 322, 323, 363, 375. 395, 493n, 505n. 547.
Piracy in the Mediterranean, 210, 401.
Piracy. *See* Seizures *and also* Renegat.
Pirates, Scottish, 88, 150, 196, 365, 373. 393, 466, 476. 485, 492, 510, 530, 532, 549.
Plague, at Boulogne, etc., 173, 253, 265.
Plan suggested for the protection of Spanish shipping against pirates, 356-359, 393, 401, 442, 443, 532.
Plot of the French against the Emperor, divulged by Paget, 526, 528, 529, 530, 534, 535, 542. 544.
Plymouth, Mayor of, imprisoned for plundering Spaniards, 203.
Plymouth, Spanish mercenary troop at, 58.
Poggio, Giovanni, Bishop of Tropea, Nuncio, 34, 305, 375, 436, 437, 443, 444, 445, 479, 514, 548, 549.
Poland, Queen of, daughter of Ferdinand, King of the Romans, death of, 211.
Poland, Embassy from, 310, 318.
Poland, King of, a suitor to Princess Mary, 318.
Pole, Reginald, Cardinal, 71, 426.
Pope, the. *See* Paul III.
Portocarrero, Don Pedro, 288, 289, 290, 293, 309, 310, 312, 405.
Portrait of the Empress Elizabeth, by Titian, 258.
Portuguese envoy to England, dies in Paris, 281, 289, 293, 318.
Portugal, King of, wishes to succour the Kingdom of, Fez, 401.
Portuguese ships captured by France, 80, 101, 150, 205, 223, 318.
Poyet, Chancellor of France, 101, 102.
Poyns, Lord, Governor of Boulogne, 94. In a skirmish, 172.
Praet, M. de, Imperial Councillor, 64, 278, 335, 363.
Privy Council of England, their dealings with Van der Delft about the Spanish Commercial claims, 117-124, 125, 155-157, 164-5, 203, 263, 275, 309, 385, 387, 390, 391, 379, 498-500, 524, 533.
Proclamation of peace between England and France. *See* Peace concluded.
Protestant negotiations to secure peace between England and France, 249, 252, 265, 276, 279, 287, 290.
Protestant envoys. *See* Soledanus, etc.
Protestant cities in Germany, surrender to the Emperor, 544-546, 549.
Protestants in France. *See* French Protestants.
Protestantism in England, 394, 398, 426, 454, 464, 465, 467, 470, 470n, 534, 555-558.
Puñonrostro, Count, 76.

Q

Queen of England, the. *See* Parr, Katharine.
Quintana, Dueñas (Quintana, Done), Spanish merchant plundered, 132, 142, 144, 176, 203.

R

Ratisbon, Diet of, 211, 214, 237, 260, 271, 302, 304-306, 314, 316. 317, 322, 326, 328, 329, 333, 346, 350, 365, 386, 389, 394, 410, 411, 423, 444, 467.
Real, Bartolomé del, mercenary captain, 225.
Recalde, Juan Martines de, Spanish admiral, letter from, to Prince Philip, 115.
Recalde, Juan Martines de, 442.
Reissenberg, Frederick von, Captain of German mercenaries, 234, 235, 245, 273, 274, 299, 310 342, 382, 389.
Religion in England. *See* Protestantism in England.
Religious revenues in Spain, appropriated for the Lutheran war. *See* Spain's contribution.
Religious wars in Germany. *See* War of religion, and Germany religious affairs in.
René of Nassau, death of, 150.
Renegat (or Reniger), an English sea captain accused of piracy, 95, 96, 105, 117-120, 141, 143, 160, 169, 175, 176, 177, 182, 203, 212, 263, 275, 290, 293, 296, 297, 309, 312, 317, 378, 418, 433, 434, 484, 496, 524, 526.
Reniger. *See* Renegat.
Reseta, William de, his ship plundered at Plymouth, 139.
Rhinegrave, the, in England, 470, 498.
Ringolt, an Antwerp peace intermediary, 239.
Rithberg, Count, 301.
Roche sur Yonne, Prince, 148, 197, 221, 256.
Rojas Don, Antonio de, 175.
Rœulx, Count de, Adrian de Croy, 15, 136, 142, 147, 361, 363, 364.
Rome, intelligence from. *See also* Juan de Vegas' letters, 244, 321, 337, 376, 436, 437, 479-483, 503, 504, 513, 539-542.
Rome, financial affairs of, 324, 429, 436, 437, 443-446, 475, 476, 479-481, 507, 508, 533, 550.
Romero, Julian, a Spanish mercenary captain, 69, 295n. His public duel in France, 432, 433.
Ronquillo, Alcalde, deposition before, 282.
Ross, Bishop of. *See* Paniter, David.
Rossem, Martin van, mercenary captain, 235, 313.
Roussy, Count of, 222.
Rouse, Anthony, merchant, his claims against the English, 139.
Russell, John, Lord, Lord Privy Seal, 16, 135, 309.

GENERAL INDEX.

S

St. Andrews, castle of, still held by Beton's murderers, 535.

Saint Blancard, Baron de (*see also* Blancard Galley), 398, 409, 465n, 488.

Saint Boniface, Count de, a Veronese mercenary leader, 17.

Saint Disier, the Emperor's attack upon, 13, 14, 76, 150n, 282, 289, 293, 309.

St. Germain, M. de. 485, 488.

St. John, Lord (Paulet), Master of the Household, 124, 145, 464, 467.

St. Mauris *or* St. Maurice, Imperial ambassador in France, letter from, to Francisco de los Cobos, 31, 76, 80, 97, 147, 195, 205, 206, 229, 294, 373, 392, 422.

St. Mauris. Imperial ambassador in France, letters from, to the Emperor, 87, 206, 501.

St. Mauris, Imperial ambassador in France, letters from, to Ferdinand King of the Romans, 254, 286.

St. Maurice, Imperial ambassador in France, letters from, to Prince Philip, 103, 199, 219, 301, 392, 402, 408, 418, 430, 518.

St. Mauris, Imperial ambassador in France, letters to, from the Emperor, 275, 277.

St. Mauris, Imperial ambassador in France, his interview with Francis I. respecting the peace with England, 207, 259, 365, 386, 419-423, 501-503.

St. Paul's, Dean of, 453.

Saint Pol, M. de, 431.

Safe Conducts. *See* Seizures.

Salazar, Friar Francisco, detained in Rome, 388.

Salcedo, 100.

Salvaglio, Angelon, 29, 38.

Salviati. Cardinal, a French partizan in Rome, 321, 337, 338.

Sangentes, Juan, of Somorrostro, 282.

Sanches de Miranda, Martin, his claims against England, 117-119, 176, 309.

San Salvador, the ship captured by Renegat, 212. (*See also* Renegal.)

Santa Croce, Cardinal, 71, 414, 445, 461.

Santa Flor, Cardinal, 479-482, 483, 489, 513, 515, 531, 548.

Savello, John Baptist, Papal officer. 430,

Savoy, Duke of, 276, 278, 287, 302, 364, 398.

Savoy, Duke of, alleged agreement with Henry VIII. against France, 89, 90, 99, 101, 151.

Savoy, French occupation of. (*See also* Piedmont), 78.

Saxony. Duke John Frederick of, 102, 210, 249, 326, 411, 439, 455, 469, 476, 540, 544, 545, 546.

Saxony, Maurice of, 101, 354, 371, 378, 412, 439, 476, 507, 525, 544, 546, 547.

Scarcity of food in England, 336, 349, 370, 378, 379.

Scepperus, Cornelius, M. d'Eick, letters from, to the Emperor, 82, 273, 329, 345, 377, 380.

Scepperus, Cornelius, letters from, to Granvelle, 273, 300, 335.

Scepperus, Cornelius, letters from, to the Queen Dowager of Hungary, 234, 235, 324, 325, 329, 334 (2), 343, 344, 371, 378, 381, 387, 470.

Scepperus, Cornelius (M. d'Eick), letters from, to Loys Scors, 233, 239, 241, 297, 298, 311, 319, 325, 336, 348, 372, 379.

Scepperus, Cornelius, letters to, from the Emperor, 243, 245, 258, 263, 274, 312, 385.

Scepperus, Cornelius, letters to, from the Queen Dowager, 319, 340, 381.

Scepperus, Cornelius (M. d'Eick), 66, 67, 71, 83. His mission to England, 209. Incidents of his voyage and arrival in London, 233. Interviews with Henry VIII. and his Council at Guildford, 235-240. Fresh instructions to, 252. His mission from Henry to the Emperor, 246, 247, 251. Sent back to England with reply, 252-254. Fresh instructions, 270. His peace negotiations, 258. The proposed interview between the monarchs, 260-262. Returns to Flanders, 263, 264, 265, 266. Fresh reply, 270-272, 273-275, 297, 298, 300-301, 309. His new mission to England, 312-317, 319, 324, 325, 326, 328-335, 343-348, 365-369-372, 377, 380, 385, 386, 387, 404, 452, 469, 550.

Schetz, Erasmus, merchant in Antwerp, 343, 370, 379, 470.

Schmalkaldic war. *See* War of Religion.

Schore, L., President of the Council of Flanders. *See* Scors Loys.

Soledanus Johannes, of Strasburg, a Protestant Envoy to England, 249, 252, 265, 276.

Scors Loys, President of the Council of Flanders, letters from, to the Emperor, 81, 82.

Scors Loys, letters to, from Van der Delft, 325, 465, 501, 512, 513, 530, 537.

Scors Loys. President of the Council of Flanders, letters to, from Cornelius Scepperus (M. d'Eick), 233, 239, 241, 297, 298, 311, 319, 325, 336, 348, 372, 379.

Scors Loys, President of the Flemish Council, letters to, from Chapuys, 62, 161.

Scors Loys, President of the Flemish Council, 66-69, 71, 81, 83, 234, 266, 301, 312, 370, 501, 535.

Scotland. statements of affairs in, 221, 240, 374, 408.

Scotland, relations of, with England, 347, 348, 388, 398, 404, 406, 419, 420, 434, 436, 440, 441, 442, 449, 452, 453, 462-464, 466, 467, 471-473, 476, 477, 485, 488, 489, 496-498, 500, 501, 509-512, 513, 518-520, 525, 527, 528, 543, 549.

Scotland, relations with the Emperor, 47, 54, 62, 65, 86, 91, 92, 94, 102, 106, 107, 108, 109, 113, 124, 148, 202, 206, 333, 404, 411, 412, 425, 440-442, 462-464, 466-467, 471-473, 476, 477, 492, 496-498, 500, 501, 509-512, 513, 518-520, 525, 527, 530, 536, 537, 549.

Scotland, its inclusion in the Peace treaty with France, 12, 19, 47, 54, 62, 102, 148, 206, 207, 224, 232, 243, 263, 276, 368, 406, 409, 411, 412, 419, 420, 425, 434, 435, 440-442, 448, 449, 452, 453, 457, 462-464, 466, 467, 471-473, 476, 477, 485, 488, 489, 492, 496-498, 500, 501, 509-512, 513, 518, 520, 525, 527, 528, 530, 536, 537.

Scotland, warlike movements in, 95, 124, 135, 165, 209, 211, 220, 232, 240, 242, 243, 255, 292, 294, 339, 543.

Scotland, alleged defeat of the English in, 54, 103.

Scotland, Queen of. See Mary, Queen of Scots.

Scots in the French service (see also Montgomerie), 77, 92, 103, 147, 158, 198, 220.

Scottish embassy to England, 463, 466, 471, 472, 485, 497, 500, 501, 509-512, 513, 518-520, 525, 527, 530, 535, 536.

Scottish depredations on Spanish and Flemish shipping. See Pirates, Scottish.

Sebastian, Dr., appointed Inquisitor of Sicily, 401.

Seco Nicolo, Imperial ambassador to Turkey, 210.

Secretary of the English Privy Council. See Council.

Sedan, M. de, seeks inclusion in the peace, 224.

Seizures of ships and merchandise by England, 3, 4, 11-12, 15, 18, 21, 23-26, 27, 28, 29-31, 33, 34, 36, 38, 44-47, 48-53, 54, 55-57, 63-64, 65-69, 70, 76, 81-86, 91-92, 93, 94, 95, 96, 105, 111, 112, 114, 115, 117, 118, 119, 120, 121, 124, 125, 126, 127, 132, 134, 138, 140, 141, 142, 143, 144, 152-157, 159, 160, 161, 164, 165, 166, 168-171, 172-174, 175, 176, 177, 184, 185, 189, 194, 195, 196, 203, 209, 211, 212, 216, 217, 218, 219, 224, 228, 263, 270, 275, 290, 293, 296, 297, 298, 299, 300, 301, 309, 311, 317, 318, 326, 329, 334, 336, 348, 349, 361, 362-378, 379, 384, 385, 390, 391, 393, 397, 400, 401-418, 433, 434, 440, 442, 443, 485, 486-488, 496, 524, 526, 527, 533.

Seizures of English property in Spain, 114, 116, 117, 134, 141, 143, 153, 160, 161, 168-171, 172, 176, 182, 184, 189, 203, 216, 217, 275, 296, 297, 309, 333, 378, 418, 485, 486-488, 494, 496, 524, 526.

Seizures of English property in Flanders, etc. (see also Antwerp), 21, 22, 23-26, 27, 28, 29-31, 33, 34, 36, 38, 44-53, 54, 55-57, 63, 64, 65, 69-70, 90-92, 107, 130, 138, 141-143, 153, 160, 168-171, 184, 216, 224, 248, 249.

Sempy, M. de, Flemish Councillor, 83.

Seristori, Everado Florentine, envoy to Rome, arrested by the Pope, 338, 350, 416.

Seville, Archbishop of, Cardinal Garcia de Loaysa, 74, 75, 352. Death of, 396, 447.

Seymour, Edward, Earl of Hertford. See Hertford.

Seymour, Sir Thomas, 526.

Sfondrato, Francisco, Cardinal Nuncio, 34, 321, 375, 531, 541.

Sicily, ecclesiastical revenues in, 396.

Sicily, Lutheranism in, 351.

Sicily, Viceroy of, F. Gonzaga. See Gonzaga.

Siena, revolution in, 323, 324, 327, 339, 396.

Silly, M. de, 31.

Soissons, Bishop of, 279.

Soliman, the Sultan. See Turk.

Sophi, the, of Persia, 209, 547.

Smith, Dr. (Sir Thomas Smith), sent to Antwerp to present the English complaints, 558.

Spain, condition of, 73-75, 212, 304, 308, 392, 401, 479, 551-555.

Spain, Princess of (Maria of Portugal, wife of Prince Philip), 32, 73, 111. Her death, 175, 211, 229, 232.

Spain, Prince of. See Philip.

Spain, seizure of specie in, for the Emperor, 478, 479, 490, 532, 554.

Spain's contributions to the Lutheran war, 35, 72-75, 184, 212, 213, 225, 226, 268, 297, 303-304, 305-308, 321, 337, 375, 387, 388, 392, 400, 401, 413-417, 428, 430, 431, 436, 437, 443-446, 457-462, 475, 476, 478, 479-483, 489, 490, 492, 494, 503, 504, 507, 508, 513-515, 522, 531, 532, 548, 550-555.

Spanish Council, its report on the Emperor's financial demands, 550-555.

Spanish commercial claims. See Seizures, Privy Council and Renegat.

Spanish fears of an alliance between France and England, 254, 304, 315, 328, 352, 368, 392, 434, 435, 442, 452, 526, 530, 537, 538, 544.

Spanish finance. See Finance.

Spanish mercenaries. See Mercenaries.

Spanish merchants and shipmasters plundered. See Burgos merchants and Seizures.

Spanish shipping, plan for the protection of, against the depredation of English and French pirates, 356-359, 365.

Specie, seizure of, in Spain, for the war. See Spain.

Stadtholderinn. See Mary, Queen Dowager of Hungary.

Stenay, its restoration to Lorraine claimed by France, 43, 73, 79, 224.

Strick, Flemish Secretary sent to Scotland, 440, 471-473, 476, 477, 496, 497, 510, 519, 536.

Strozzi, Leone, prior of Capua, 77, 256, 322.

Strozzi, Pietro, 111, 149, 256, 257, 322, 482, 493, 495, 506, 521.

Sturmius, a Protestant envoy, 249, 265, 276, 464, 467, 468.

GENERAL INDEX.

Subsidy demanded by Henry for his war against France, 3, 4-5, 6, 11-13, 19, 20, 26, 37, 39, 45-47, 49-50, 64, 65, 83-86, 92, 105, 109, 110. The Emperor's conditions, 125-128, 129, 132-138, 140, 142, 152-157, 158, 163, 166, 171, 173, 177-182, 185, 190, 193, 200-204, 215, 218, 231, 251, 254, 262, 297, 300, 316, 319, 330, 333, 346, 371, 386.

Subsidy from the Pope for the Lutheran war. *See* "War of religion, Papal aid to."

Suffolk, Duchess of (Lady Willoughby D'Eresby) 280. Rumoured intention of the King to marry her, 318. A Protestant partisan, 555.

Suffolk, Duke of (Charles Brandon), 5, 25, 33, 105, 106, 107, 130, 135. Illness of, 235. Death of, 241.

Surrey, Earl of, 233, 292, 349, 361. Arrested, 526, 527, 531, 533, 534, 535, 536, 537.

Sussex, invaded by the French, 204.

Symon, Jehan, his ship seized, 168.

T

Tallies (tollieux) for Customs dues. *See* Custom house records.

Tassis, Spanish Postmaster General, 303, 304.

Taxation in England, 158, 291.

Taxation in Spain as compared to France, 551, 552.

Thirlby, Dr., Bishop of Westminster, to take part in the arbitration conference, 97, 116, 132, 134, 141, 143, 144-146, 159, 171-174. Appointed Ambassador to the Emperor, 195, 212, 215, 218, 219, 241, 260, 262, 264, 265, 266, 277, 293, 310-314, 346, 386, 491, 493, 496, 557.

Titian (Titianno Vercelli), letter from, to the Emperor, 258.

Titian, his portrait of the Empress, 258. Reward to be granted to him, 258. A "fancy picture" by him; "his best work," 258.

Toledo, Archbishop of, Cardinal Tavera, 74, 75. Death of, 228.

Toledo, Don Garcia de, 183, 210. His disgrace and arrest, 211.

Toledo, Don Enrique de, in France, 103.

Toledo, Don Juan, his mission to Rome, 508, 517, 522.

Toledo, Don Francisco, his mission to Rome, 547.

Torre, Antonio de, his ship taken by the English, 56.

Tourcoing, Sieur de, Baudoin de Lanoy, his missions to England, 21-23, 24-26, 27, 51.

Tournament and ball at Fontainebleau to celebrate the peace, 432.

Tournon, Cardinal, 103, 206, 207, 208, 244, 245, 250, 259.

Tovar, Don Alonso de, 401.

Treasure claimed by the Emperor from England. *See* Renegat.

Trent, Cardinal of, 413-416, 417, 427, 436, 439, 443, 444, 461, 506, 514, 515, 530, 540, 541.

Trent, Council of, 32, 41, 63, 71, 75, 78, 98, 100, 101, 110, 113, 114, 149, 152, 183, 197, 210, 214, 225, 256, 258, 269, 292, 297, 311-312, 314, 317, 321, 322, 327, 329, 339, 349, 365, 374, 375, 396, 413, 423, 424, 427, 440, 445-447, 451, 455, 461, 482, 483, 490, 493, 495, 504-506, 514-518, 521-522, 529, 530, 540, 541, 547.

Tréport, attack upon, by the English, 255.

Trigway, Dr., 91.

Trivulciis, Cardinal, 244, 321, 428, 429.

Truce, proposed between England and France. *See* Peace negotiations.

Tunstall, Dr. Cuthbert. *See* Durham, Bishop of.

Turk, relations with, 34-5, 72, 74, 75, 79, 99, 100, 101, 110, 113, 114, 151, 182, 183, 189, 197, 209, 210, 212, 214, 222, 227, 246, 271, 302, 375, 438, 439, 482, 502, 539, 540, 545, 549.

U

Ulm, surrender of, 544, 546, 547, 549, 553.

Urbino, Duke of, 323, 427.

V

Vaivode, the *See* Buda.

Van der Bergh, Adrian, letters from, to the Queen Dowager, 395.

Van der Bergh, Adrian, letter to, from the Queen Dowager, 498.

Van der Bergh, Adrian, Flemish Commissioner to England to settle the commercial claims, 311, 334, 335, 336, 342, 349, 362, 371, 385, 394, 400, 474, 498, 499, 500, 537, 550.

Van der Delft, François, letter from, to the Burgomaster, etc., of Bruges, 131.

Van der Delft, François, letters from, to Chapuys, 167.

Van der Delft, François, letters from, to the Emperor, 32, 117, 129, 130, 152, 164, 185, 199, 230, 246, 249, 250, 262, 264, 268, 275, 279, 281, 292, 293, 295, 309, 312, 317, 320, 329, 345, 377, 380, 389, 394, 396, 399, 400, 404, 406, 407, 433, 450, 466, 484, 493, 523, 532. (*See also* Chapuys *and* Van der Delft.)

Van der Delft, François, letters from, to Granvelle, 296, 309.

Van der Delft, ambassador in England, letters from, to the Queen Mary Dowager of Hungary, 113, 125, 130, 158, 167, 194, 205, 230, 235, 248, 249, 263, 325, 334, 343, 344, 371, 373, 381, 390, 391, 395, 399, 404, 408, 423, 434, 451, 462, 470, 475, 485, 489, 500, 509, 512, 526, 535, 542.

Van der Delft, François, letters from, to Loys Scors, 325, 465, 501, 512, 513, 530, 537.

Van der Delft, letters to, from Chapuys, 136, 162, 168, 184.

Van der Delft, François, Imperial ambassador in England, letters to, from the Emperor, 114, 125, 162, 175, 219, 243, 245, 258, 263, 273, 274, 281, 288, 293, 312, 385, 393, 410, 417, 454, 475, 491, 495, 546.

Van der Delft, François, letter to, from Granvelle, 266.

Van der Delft, François, letters to, from the Queen Dowager of Hungary, 319, 340, 381, 386, 403, 411, 440, 448, 456, 471, 496, 498, 518, 535, 543, 544, 549, 558.

Van der Delft, François, Imperial ambassador in England (see also "Chapuys and Van der Delft"), 115, 116, 125, 131. His interview with Henry VIII., 153-157. Joins the Court at Portsmouth, 165, 167, 186. His interview there with Henry VIII., 187-193, 200-203, 205, 215-218. With Henry VIII. in his progress, 231; His peace negotiations with Scepperus, 235-240. Interview with Henry VIII., 250, 251. Fresh instructions jointly with Scepperus, 270, 275. Stands sponsor for Lady Catherine Dudley, 280. His interview with Renegat, 290, 299, 309. Interview with Henry VIII., 311, 330-333. His position in England, 336. Interview with English ministers, 343-348, 365-367-372, 377. Interviews with Henry VIII., 380, 389, 407, 423-426, 485-488, 523, 526, 527.

Van der Delft, François, Imperial ambassador in England. (See also Chapuys and Van der Delft.)

Vargas, Licentiate Juan de, 34n, 553.

Vargas, Licentiate, letters to, from Cobos, 63.

Vargas, Licentiate, letters from, to Cobos, 34, 71.

Vaughan, Dr. Stephen, 91, 93, 97.

Vega, Antonio de, 396.

Vega, Juan de, letters from, to the Emperor, 321, 337, 376, 388, 395, 413, 415, 416, 418, 427, 436, 445, 446, 455, 479, 481, 489, 492, 494, 503, 504 (2), 513, 514-522, 539, 547.

Vega, Juan de, Spanish ambassador in Rome, letters from, to Prince Philip, 183, 292, 349.

Vega, Juan de, letters to, from the Emperor, 41 (2), 273, 374, 443, 457, 475, 548.

Vega, Juan de, Spanish ambassador in Rome, 34, 226, 273, 274, 305, 321-324, 375-377, 395, 413, 436, 437, 457-462, 481, 489, 492, 493, 503-505, 508, 513-515, 522, 531, 539.

Veltwych, Secretary, sent as an envoy from the Emperor to the Turk, 189.

Vendome, M. de (Antoine de Bourbon), 221, 221n. Suggested marriage with Mary Tudor, 255.

Vendome, Mme. de, 431.

Venice, advices from, 426.

Venice, English relations with, 438, 439, 454, 455, 466, 468, 538, 539.

Venice, description of its Government, 538.

Venice, Seigniory of, 210, 245, 258, 368, 426, 427, 438, 439, 454, 455, 466, 521, 537-539.

Vervins. See Boulogne, Captain of.

Viglius, Dr., 299.

Villarand, M. de, 495.

Vincent, M., Imperial Financial Commissioner in Flanders, 301.

Vitello, Alessandro, Papal officer, 376, 430, 458.

W

Walcheren, island of, threatened Scottish attack upon, 471.

Wales, Prince of. See Edward.

War with France, 5-16, 17-20, 32, 33, 40, 45, 46, 58, 60, 61, 63, 65-69, 77, 78, 81, 84-86, 87-90, 92, 94-95, 96, 97, 105, 109, 111, 115, 116, 124-128, 129, 130, 132-135, 136, 140, 142, 145-146, 147-152, 161, 162, 165, 173, 178-182, 187-190, 191-194, 196, 200-204, 206, 209, 214, 218, 220, 222, 223, 237, 229, 235-240, 247, 248, 255, 265, 267, 269, 271, 274, 282, 283, 287, 292, 295, 296, 310, 314, 317, 318, 319, 320, 324, 328, 329, 333, 335, 336, 345, 349, 361, 371, 373, 378, 389, 398, 399.

War of Religion in Germany, 102, 183, 184, 196, 209, 225, 226, 227, 228, 268, 271, 279, 305-308, 310, 353-356, 387, 400, 411-413, 416, 422, 424-425, 436, 448, 451, 455, 457-462, 464, 469, 474, 481-485, 491-493, 494, 502, 504, 505, 507, 512, 514, 515, 522, 523, 525, 540-542, 544, 545-547, 549.

War of Religion. The Papal aid to the Emperor, 34-5, 72, 74, 75, 113, 183, 184, 213, 225, 226, 227, 228, 268, 269, 273, 305-308, 321-324, 327, 337, 352, 355, 356, 375, 387, 388, 395, 412-417, 424, 427-430, 436, 437, 443-446, 457-462, 475, 476-483, 489, 490, 492, 494, 503, 504, 505, 506-508, 513, 514, 515, 521, 522, 523, 531, 538, 539-542, 547, 548, 550-555.

GENERAL INDEX.

War indemnity from France to England, 373, 374, 386, 392, 397, 403, 404, 406-409, 418, 419, 421, 435, 503.

Westminster, Bishop of. *See* Thirlby, Dr.

Wheat, etc., export of, from Flanders, 325, 341, 342, 343, 345-348, 360, 361, 365-367, 368, 370, 372, 377, 383, 385.

Whittingham, Dr., Scottish envoy to England, 509-512.

Wight, Isle of, invaded by the French, 191, 194, 198, 204, 205.

Winchester, Bishop of (Stephen Gardiner), letter to, from the Emperor, 272.

Winchester, Bishop of (Stephen Gardiner), visits Chapuys and Van der Delft, 1. Discusses the seizures with them, 3. At Boulogne, 7. Conferences with the ambassadors, 9-16, 17-20, 23, 24-26, 57-62, 63, 95, 96, 193, 194, 201, 230, 235, 248, 250, 252, 265, 345-348, 365, 366, 367, 368-370, 385, 408, 425, 434, 451, 462, 464, 467-470, 534, 556.

Winchester, Bishop of (Stephen Gardiner), his negotiations in Flanders, 265, 267, 268, 272, 273, 274-280, 281, 300, 301, 312-314, 315-317, 319, 320, 326, 328, 329. His return, 330, 340, 342.

Winchester, Bishop of (Stephen Gardiner), his peace mission to France, 400.

Winchester, Bishop of, his mission with Hertford to the Emperor, to demand aid against France. *See* Hertford.

Windham, Captain, an alleged pirate, 105, 118.

Winter, Master, ships seized by, 168.

Worms, the Diet of, 41, 63, 71, 100, 102, 113, 114, 149, 196, 197, 208, 209, 210, 211, 227, 306, 340, 445.

Wotton, Dr. Nicholas, English ambassador with the Emperor, 21, 26, 31, 34, 36, 37, 44-47, 55, 56, 66, 71, 125, 126, 129, 140, 159, 162, 175, 180. His recall, 195, 241, 300, 371. A Commissioner to settle the Commercial claims, 378, 395. To go as ambassador to France, 408.

Wriothesley, Lord Chancellor, 25, 33, 105, 106, 107, 118, 119, 120, 166, 168, 174, 186, 187, 235, 249, 279, 290, 291, 309, 400, 407, 451, 462, 464, 467-470, 509, 519, 526, 527, 531, 533, 556.

Wurtemberg, Duke of, 249, 544, 546, 549.

Z

Zorilla, Dr., Imperial agent at Trent, 258.

Zapata de Cardenas, Juan, sent to arrest Don Gorcia de Toledo, 211.

Zambon, Venetian, agent in London, 538.

INDEX TO ADDENDA.

A

Albany, Duke of, 569, 572, 573.
Alcala, Rector and Doctors of the University of, Certificate of their decisions on points submitted to them relative to the English divorce, 575.
Annebaut, Admiral of France, to negotiate the peace of Crépy, 612.
Aponte, Imperial envoy to Rome, 593.
Auditor de la Camera. *See* Worcester, Bishop of.
Augustine Friar, of Padua, forbidden to seek authorities favourable to Henry's case in the Divorce proceedings, 567.
Augustines, General of the, 567, 570.
Avila y Zuñiga, Don Luis, gored at a bull fight in honour of the English embassy, 605.

B

Barbarossa, suggestion to gain him for the Emperor against France, 611.
Barrés Guillaume, Imperial Commissioner to receive the Emperor's bonds of indebtedness to England, 561, 562.
Bellay, du, Archbishop of Paris, 596, 597, 600, 601.
Bennnet, Dr., English envoy to Rome, 563.
Bigod, Lord (*sic*), 605.
Blasio Secretary, in Rome, to be paid for the judgment against Henry VIII. 589.
Boleyn, Anne, Marchioness of Pembroke, 585, 586, 591. 595. Executed, 603.
Bologna, University of, 568.
Boner, Dr., sent to Italy to obtain decisions of Universities in favour of Henry's case, 581, 582.
Borgo, Baron del, papal envoy to England, 564, 573, 574.
Boulogne, besieged by the English, 613.
Brian, Sir Francis, letter from, to the Imperial Commissioners for ratifying the agreement between England and the Emperor, 561.
Brian, Sir Francis, his arrival at Bayonne and Fuenterrabia to deliver to the Imperial Commissioners the Emperor's bonds for various sums advanced by Henry VIII. 561. His mishap on landing at Fuenterrabia, 562.
Bull fight in honour of the English ambassadors (1537), 605.
Bulls, papal, bought and sent to England by the Auditor de la Camera, 589. (*See also* Worcester, Bishop of.)
Burgos, Cardinal of (Mendoza), letter from, to the Emperor, 583.

C

Cajetano, Cardinal, a partisan of Queen Catharine in Rome, 563.
Calais, the English army leaves to invade France, 612.
Calais, suggested cession to France, 589, 590.
Campeggio, Cardinal, letter from, to Cobos, 589.
Campeggio, Cardinal, 578.
Capisuroiis, Paulus, Apostolic Auditor to draft a report on the Divorce case, 571.
Capua, Archbishop of, 587, 594.
Cardinals, etc., rewarded for their advocacy of Queen Catharine's case, 570, 575, 589, 597.
Carne, Dr. *See* Excusator.
Carnisera, Papal official in Rome, 598.
Carrociolo, Imperial Ambassador in Milan, letter to, from the Emperor, 561.
Carrociolo, Protonotary, Imperial Ambassador in Milan, 561, 572, 573.
Casale, Gregorio, English representative in Venice, proposed for a Cardinal's hat by Henry VIII. 569, 570, 572, 573, 608.
Catharine of Aragon, Queen. 561, 563, 564, 565, 566, 567, 568, 569, 570, 571, 572, 573, 575, 576, 577, 578, 585, 586, 587, 590, 591, 594, 595, 598, 599, 602. Her death, 602.
Catharine of Aragon, proposal that she should leave England, 590.
Catharine de Medici, her marriage with the Duke of Orleans, 591, 593.
Cervini Marcello, Bishop of Nicastro, his memorandum on his proposed mission to England, 606.

INDEX TO ADDENDA.

Chapuys, Eustace, Imperial Ambassador in England, letter from, to Gomez Suarez de Figueroa, 599.
Chapuys, Eustace, Imperial Ambassador in England, 592, 610.
Chantonnay, M. de, his mission to England (1543), 610.
Charles V. letter from, to Baron del Borgo, designated as Papal envoy to England, 573.
Charles V. letter from, to Carrociolo, Imperial Ambassador in Venice, 561.
Charles V. letters from, to Count Cifuentes, his Ambassador in Rome, 586, 588, 589, 591, 594, 596, 597, 598, 599, 600, 601, 602, 603, 604.
Charles V. letters from, to Pope Clement VII. 576, 587.
Charles V. letter from, to Cobos, 611.
Charles V. letter from, to James V. King of Scots, 609.
Charles V. letter from, to Antonio de Leyva, Prince of Ascoli, 587.
Charles V. letter from, to Cardinal Loaisa, 585.
Charles V. letters from, to Michael Mai, his Ambassador in Rome, 563, 564, 565, 569, 571, 573, 574, 575, 581.
Charles V. letters from, to Prince Philip, 610, 612 (2).
Charles V. letters from, to Rodrigo Niño, Imperial Ambassador in Venice, 561, 563, 567, 581.
Charles V. letter from, to the Cardinal of Ravenna, 564.
Charles V. letter to, from the Cardinal Archbishop of Burgos (Mendoza), 583.
Charles V. letter to, from Count Cifuentes, 594.
Charles V. letter to, from Pope Clement VII. 593.
Charles V. letter to, from Cardinal Gaddi, 569.
Charles V. letters to, from the Empress, 566, 602, 604.
Charles V. letter to, from the Cardinal Bishop of Jaen, 586.
Charles V. letter to, from Antonio de Leyva, 591.
Charles V. letter to, from Cardinal Loaisa, 582.
Charles V. letter to, from Michael Mai, 583.
Charles V. letter to, from Juan Antonio Muxetula, 585.
Charles V. letters to, from Rodrigo Niño, 563, 565, 566, 567, 568, 570, 572.
Charles V. letters to, from Prince Philip, 610, 611.
Charles V. letter to, from Cardinal Pole, 605.
Charles V. his attitude towards the divorce proceedings, 563, 564, 567, 569, 572, 573, 574, 575, 576, 577, 581, 584, 585, 586, 587, 588, 590, 591, 593, 594, 595, 596, 601, 602.
Charles V. his alliance with Henry VIII. against France, 610, 611, 612, 613.

Charles V. his indebtedness in England, discharge of, 562.
Charles V. his proposed interview with Francis I., 574.
Charles V. his visit to Rome, 600, 601, 602.
Charles V. levies troops to defend Milan, 602.
Charles V. receives the English ambassadors, 604.
Charles V. suggested marriage with Mary Tudor, 609.
Charles V. refuses to allow the King of Scots to use the revoked letters of marque against Portugal, 609.
Cibo, Cardinal, 570.
Cifuentes, Count, Imperial ambassador in Rome, letters from, to Cobos, 589, 593.
Cifuentes, Count, Imperial ambassador in Rome, letters from, to the Emperor, 594.
Cifuentes, Count, Imperial ambassador in Rome, letters to, from the Emperor, 586, 588, 589, 591, 594, 596, 597, 599, 600 (2), 601 (2), 603, 604.
Cifuentes, Count, Imperial ambassador, his negotiations in Rome, 586, 587, 588, 589, 590, 591, 592, 593, 594, 595, 597, 598, 599, 600, 601, 602. In Spain, 611.
Cifuentes, Count, his jealousy of the Cardinal of Jaen, 587, 589.
Clement VII. Pope, letter from, to the Emperor, 593.
Clement VII. Pope, letter from, to Henry VIII. 571.
Clement VII. Pope, letters to, from the Emperor, 576, 587.
Clement VII. his action relative to the English divorce, 563, 564, 565, 566, 569, 570, 571, 572, 574, 576, 578, 580, 581, 582, 583, 584, 585, 586, 587, 588, 590, 591, 592, 593, 594, 595, 596, 597.
Clement VII. his determination to send an envoy to be present at the meeting of Henry VIII. and Francis I. 597, 598.
Clement VII. Pope, his interview with Francis I. 586, 587, 588, 589, 590, 591, 592, 593.
Clement VII. his plan to alienate France from England, 589, 590, 598.
Clement VII. Pope, proposes to send Legates to England and France, to beg for aid in a crusade against the Turk, 582, 583.
Clement VII. Pope, his fears of Turkish aggression, 585, 593.
Clement VII. his plan to reconcile Henry VIII. 597, 598.
Clement VII. and a proposed Council of the Church, 571, 573, 593.
Cleves, Anne of, 606.
Cobos, Francisco de los, letters to, from Count Cifuentes, 589, 593.
Cobos, Francisco de los, letter to, from the Emperor, 611.
Cobos, Francisco de los, letters to, from Idiaquez, 609, 610, 612.

Cobos, Francisco de los, letter to, from the Cardinal Bishop of Jaen, 588.
Cobos, Francisco de los, letter to, from Cardinal Campeggio, 589.
Cobos, Francisco de los, letters to, from Cardinal Louisa, 565, 581, 582, 583.
Cobos, Francisco de los, letter to, from Cardinal Palmerio, 586.
Colonna, Cardinal, 572. His Secretary arrested, accused of a plot to poison the Pope, 585.
Como Rafael, Italian jurist in favour of Queen Catharine, 567.
Concubine, the. See Boleyn, Anne.
Consistory of Cardinals. Minutes of a secret discussion at, relative to creating two Cardinals on the nomination of Henry VIII., 570.
Constable, Lord (sic), 605.
Council of the Church suggested, 565, 571, 573, 575, 592, 593, 605, 609.
Cranmer, Archbishop of Canterbury, 595.
Crépy, preliminaries of the peace of, 612, 613.
Croke, Dr. Richard, English ambassador in Venice, 569.
Crusade Bulls. Charles V. threatens to levy the tax himself unless the Pope promptly renews the Bulls, 591.
Cueva, Don Pedro de, 573, 604.
Curiel, Licentiate, gives an opinion favourable to Queen Catharine, 567.

D

Darcy, Lord, 605.
Davalos, Rodrigo, his mission to Rome on the divorce case, 587, 588, 589, 590, 593, 594.
Decio, Master Philip, a Sienese jurist engaged in the divorce proceedings, 564
Divorce, the, Imperial action in Rome, relative thereto, 563, 564, 565, 566, 567, 570, 571, 572, 573, 574, 576, 577, 578, 583, 584, 585, 586, 587, 588, 589, 590, 593, 594, 595, 596, 597.
Divorce, proceedings in Rome in Henry's absence, 584, 585, 588, 589, 591, 592, 594, 595, 597.
Divorce proceedings, Venetian action relative thereto, 561, 563, 565, 566, 567, 568.
Divorce, the, arguments presented to the Pope against Henry's contentions, 578-580.
Divorce, certificate of the decisions arrived at by the University of Alcalá thereupon, 575.
Divorce, summary account of the proceedings drawn up for the information of the Pope, Clement VII. 577.
Divorce, the, decision in Rome that Henry must be present in person or proxy, 583, 584, 585, 589.

Doria, Prince Andrea, 611.
Drianus, Dr., sent to Rome by Henry VIII. 578.

E

Elizabeth of Portugal, wife of Charles V. See Empress.
Empress, the, letters from, to the Emperor Charles V. 566, 602, 604.
Empress, the, her action in favour of Queen Catharine, 566. Her opinion of Dr. Ortiz, 566. Grief for her death, 602. Advocates a pacific policy towards France, 602. Her remark respecting the execution of Anne Boleyn, 603. Death of, 605. Her portrait. See Titian.
England, news of, transmitted from Italy, 585, 599.
England, news from, sent from Bilbao by Juan Martinez de Recalde, 604.
English ambassador, reception of, by Charles V. at Valladolid (1537), 604.
Englishmen, proposed excommunication of, 596.
England, reported revolution in, 604, 605.
Enriquez, Don Antonio, writes a "weak book" in favour of the Queen's case in the divorce, 583.
Étampes, Mme. de, her efforts to obtain peace, 612.
Excusator (Dr. Carne), for Henry VIII. at Rome, his protest, 580.

F

Faenza, Bishop of, sent to France by the Pope, 588.
Farnese, Cardinal, 605, 606, 607, 609.
Farnese, Cardinal, instructions to him on his mission to the Emperor (1539), 605.
Farnese, Pier Luigi. See Pier Luigi.
Farnese. See also Paul III., Pope.
Felipe, Francis, steward to Queen Catharine, 599.
Ferdinand, King of the Romans, 594.
Figueroa, Gomes Suarez de, Imperial ambassador in Genoa, letter to, from Chapuys, 599.
Financial arrangements between the Emperor and Henry VIII. 562.
Fleur de lys, a jewel pledged by the Emperor in England, 562.
Fox, Dr., sent to Rome in 1528, 577, 578.
Francis I. his relations with the Emperor, 582, 583, 585, 589, 590, 594, 596, 600, 601, 602, 604, 605, 606, 607, 610, 611.

Francis I. his relations with the Pope, 582, 583, 585, 586, 587, 588, 589, 590, 591, 592, 593, 600, 601, 602, 604, 605, 606, 607.

Francis I. his attitude in the English divorce proceedings, 563, 569, 596, 597, 600, 601.

Francis I. his pretensions in Italy. *See* Francis I. his relations with the Emperor.

Francis, George, Friar, 565.

G

Gaddi, Cardinal, letter from, to the Emperor, 569.

Gaddi, Cardinal, discontented with his reward, 569.

Germany, the Protestants in, 563, 592, 593.

Gonzaga, Fernando de, his mission to England, 611.

Granvelle, Secretary, approached by French peace intermediaries (1544), 612.

Grimaldo, Cardinal, a partisan of Queen Catharine in Rome, 566.

H

Henry VIII. letter to, from Pope Clement VII. 571.

Henry VIII. his negotiations in Rome relative to the divorce proceedings, 565, 569, 570, 571, 574, 575, 576, 577, 578, 580, 581, 584, 588, 589. Withdraws his ambassador from Rome, 592. Negotiates through du Bellay, 596, 597.

Henry VIII. his negotiations with the Seigniory of Venice relative to the divorce, 561, 563, 564, 566, 567, 569, 570, 582.

Henry VIII. declared contumacious by the Tribunal at Zaragosa, 575.

Henry VIII. his demand in 1528 for the nullification of his marriage, 577.

Henry VIII. summoned to Rome in person or proxy, 584. His ambassadors protest to the Emperor thereupon, 584, 585. Summoned to produce all documents of the proceedings in England, 588, 589, 591, 592. Decision given against him on the main question, 594, 595, 597, 600, 601.

Henry VIII. his determination to divorce Catharine and marry another woman, 573, 579, 585.

Henry VIII. his marriage with Anne Boleyn, 586, 587. His love for her waning, 599.

Henry VIII. protest of his excusator at Rome against the proceedings in the divorce case before the Pope, 580.

Henry VIII. treats Queen Catharine with greater moderation, 599.

Henry VIII. said to have taken refuge in the Tower of London, 604.

Henry VIII. proposed forfeiture of his realm by the Pope, 595, 596, 601, 602.

Henry VIII. his relations with the Emperor, 561, 562, 572, 574, 579, 584, 586, 589, 590, 599, 604.

Henry VIII. the Emperor's proposal for a marriage between him and the Infanta of Portugal, 603, 604.

Henry VIII., his alliance with the Emperor against France, 610, 611, 612, 613.

Henry VIII. said to be raising no difficulties with regard to the peace negotiations between the Emperor and France, 613.

Henry VIII. his relations with the Turk, 582, 583.

Henry VIII. his relations with France, 572, 574, 579, 582, 585, 586, 589, 590, 591, 596, 600, 601, 609, 610, 611, 612, 613.

Henry VIII. projected interview with Francis I. 585, 586, 597.

Henry VIII. accompanies his army to invade France, 612. Besieges Boulogne and Montreuil, 613.

Henry VIII. his ecclesiastical depredations, 600, 604.

Henry VIII. marriage with Jane Seymour, 603, 605.

Henry VIII. Marcello Cervini's plan to reconcile him to the Papacy, 606-608.

Hussey, Lord, 605.

I

Idiaques, Secretary, letters from, to Cobos, 609, 610, 612.

Illescas, Licentiate, his legal opinion upon the question of the English divorce, 567.

Ireland, projected enterprise against, 599.

Italy, English news sent therefrom, 585.

J

Jaen, Cardinal Bishop of, letter from, to Cobos, 588.

Jaen, Cardinal Bishop of (Merino), letter from, to the Emperor, 586.

Jaen, Cardinal of, his action in Rome, and Cifuentes' jealousy of him, 587, 589.

James V. King of Scots, letter to, from the Emperor, 609.
Jews, reconciliation of. *See* Portuguese Jews.
Juana, Princess of Spain, 612.
Julius II. Pope, 577.

L

Lafredo, Sigismund, gives an opinion in favour of Queen Catharine, 572.
Leyva, Antonio de, Prince of Ascoli, letter from, to the Emperor, 591.
Leyva, Antonio de, Prince of Ascoli, letter to, from the Emperor, 587.
Loaisa Fray, Garcia de, Cardinal Bishop of Osma, letters from, to Cobors, 565, 581, 582, 583.
Loaisa Fray, Gracia de, Cardinal Bishop of Osma, letter from, to the Emperor, 582.
Loaisa, Cardinal Bishop of Osma, letter to, from the Emperor, 585.
Loaisa, Cardinal, his opinions on Papal policy, 582, 583.
Loaisa, Cardinal, his opinion on religious reform, 565, 573, 583.
Loaisa, Cardinal, his action in the divorce proceedings, 569, 581.
Loaisa, Cardinal, his complaint of Mai's inactivity, 581.
London, Bishop of (Dr. John Stokesley), Ambassador to the Emperor, his mission to Rome and Venice relative to the divorce proceedings, 561, 563, 564, 565, 566, 567, 568.
Longueville, M. de, a peace intermediary between Mme. D'Etampes and the Emperor, 612.
Lorraine, Cardinal, intervenes in the peace negotiations (1544), 612.
Lutherans, intended action against them, 563. Their feeling towards the Council of the Church, 592.

M

Mai, Michael, Imperial Ambassador in Rome, letter from, to the Emperor, 583.
Mai, Micer, Michael, Imperial Ambassador in Rome, letters to, from the Emperor, 563, 564, 565, 569, 571, 573, 574, 575, 581.
Mai, Michael, Imperial Ambassador in Rome, his negotiations relative to the English divorce, etc., 563, 564, 566, 569, 571, 572, 573, 575, 576, 581, 583, 585, 589.
Maria, Princess, of Spain, suggestions for her marriage, 611, 612.

Mary Tudor, Princess, reported plan to marry her to the Duke of Milan, 572, 573. To the Duke of Norfolk, 590. To James V. of Scotland, 597. To the Infante Luis of Portugal, 603, 604.
Mary Tudor, Princess, 595, 602. The Emperor advises her to submit to her father, 603. Papal absolution promised to her, 604.
Matera, Cardinal, to be rewarded by the Emperor, 589.
Melancthon, writes the Duke of Saxony's reply to the Pope relative to the proposed Council of the Church, 592.
Mendoza, Iñigo Lopez de, Cardinal Archbishop of Burgos. *See* Burgos.
Milan, Duke of, reported matrimonial engagement with Princess Mary Tudor, 572, 573.
Milan, French pretensions to. *See* Francis I. his relations with the Emperor.
Miranda, Licentiate, Canon of Seville, the Empress suggests that he should go to Rome to advocate Queen Catharine's cause, 567.
Mirandola, Count de la (Mirandula), Spanish special envoy to Rome in the divorce proceedings, 563.
Molina, Juan Vasquez, news from England sent to him by Juan Martinez de Recalde, 604.
Monasteries, suppression of, in England, 600, 604.
Monte, Cardinal, to be rewarded by the Emperor, 589.
Montes de Oca, Spanish jurist sent to Rome in the divorce proceedings, 563.
Muxetula, Juan Antonio, Imperial envoy to Rome, letter from, to the Emperor, 585.
Muxetula, Juan Antonio, 573, 581.

N

Niño, Rodrigo, Imperial ambassador in Venice, letters from, to the Emperor, 563, 565, 566, 567, 568, 570, 572.
Niño, Rodrigo, letters to, from the Emperor, 561, 563, 567, 581.
Niño, Rodrigo, Imperial ambassador in Venice, his action relative to the English divorce, 561, 563, 566, 567, 568, 572, 581.
Norfolk, Duke of, suggested marriage with Princess Mary Tudor, 590.
Norfolk, Duke of, intended to be present at the interview between the Pope and Francis I, 592. Recalled to England, 592-593.
Northern Lords, beheaded for rebellion by Henry VIII, 605.
Nuncio, the, in England, friendship of Henry VIII. for him, 572.

INDEX TO ADDENDA.

O

Orleans, Duke of (Henry de Valois), his marriage with the niece of the Pope (Catharine de Medici), 591, 593.
Orleans, Duke of (Charles de Valois), stipulations for his marriage in the Treaty of Crépy, 612.
Orleans, University of, 584.
Ortiz, Dr., Spanish jurist sent to Rome in the divorce proceedings, 563, 566, 571, 580, 584, 588.
Osuna, Cardinal, Bishop of. *See* Loaisa.

P

Padua, University of, its action relative to the English divorce, 561, 564, 565, 566, 568, 581, 582.
Palmerio, Cardinal, letter from, to Cobos, 586.
Papal briefs surreptitiously sent to England, 574.
Papal briefs issued against Henry VIII, 588, 591, 592, 594, 595.
Paris, the University of, and the English divorce, 563, 568, 572, 581, 582, 584.
Parisius, Dr., Rector of the University of Padua, 568, 569, 570, 573.
Paul III. Pope, 600, 601, 605.
Paul III. Pope, his action in the divorce case, 602.
Paul III. Pope, his attempts to reconcile Henry VIII. 605-606.
Paul III. Pope, his instructions to Cardinal Farnese on his mission to the Emperor (1539), 605.
Philip, Prince, letters from, to the Emperor, 610, 611.
Philip, Prince, letters to, from the Emperor, 610, 612 (2).
Philip, Prince, 610. His father's exhortation to him, 611, 612.
Poitiers, University of, 568.
Pole, Cardinal, letter from, to the Emperor, 605.
Pole, Cardinal, 565, 570, 572. His condolence on the death of the Empress, 605. His reasons for not proceeding to England, 605.
Pole, Giles, 605.
Portuguese Jews converted, their pardon by the Pope opposed by the Emperor, 601.
Pier Luigi, Farnese, 600, 601.
Pirates, Scottish, 609.
Praet, M. de (Louis de Flandres), Imperial minister, 562.
Protest of Henry VIII. against the divorce proceedings in Rome, 580.

Q

Queen of England. *See* Catharine of Aragon.
Quienta, Bishop of, 563, 568.

R

Ravenna, Cardinal of, letter to, from the Emperor, 564.
Ravenna, Cardinal, a partisan of Queen Catharine in Rome, 564, 576.
Recalde, Juan Martinez de, news from England, transmitted by him to Juan Vasquez de Molina, 604.
Reggio, Archbishop of, 592.
Rincon, envoy to the Turk, 585.
Rome, visit of Charles V. to, 600, 601, 602.
Rome, negotiations in. *See* Mai and Cifuentes.

S

St. John, Prior of, Ecclesiastic at Venice, 565, 568, 570, 572, 573.
Salusso, Marquis of, 591.
Salviati, Jacopo (afterwards Cardinal), 587, 592.
Santa Croce, Cardinal, 569, 570, 594.
San Sisto, Cardinal, a partisan of Queen Catharine in Rome, 566.
Santi Quatri, declines an Imperial pension, 572.
Saxony, Duke of, his attitude towards the proposed Council of the Church, 592.
Scotland, King of, James V. proposed marriage with a daughter of the King of the Romans, 575, 588. Proposed marriage with Jeanne D'Albret, 588. Proposed marriage with Princess Madeleine of France, 597. Proposed marriage with Princess Mary Tudor, 597. Proposed marriage with the daughter of the King of Denmark, 598. (*See also* James V.)
Scotland, King of, James V. requests permission of the Emperor to use letters of marque against Portuguese shipping, 609.
Seville, Archbishop of. *See also* Loaisa.
Sigüenza, Bishop of. *See* Loaisa.
Soria, Lope de, Imperial Ambassador in Siena, 564.

Spain, money to be raised in, for the war against France, 610, 611.
Spanish ecclesiastical revenues. *See* Crusade, Bull.
Stephen (Gardiner), Dr., sent to Rome in 1528, 577, 578.
Stokesley, Dr. John. *See* London, Bishop of.
Surin, Mariano, Professor at the University of Padua, 568.
Sweden and Holstein, English ships and goods confiscated in, 600.

T

Torellas, Paulo, Venetian Jurist favourable to Queen Catharine, 567.
Turk, the, Christian relations with, 582, 583, 585, 593, 601, 605, 611.

U

Universities, the competition for their decisions on the divorce matter (*see also* Padua, Paris, etc.), 565, 566, 568, 570, 572, 581.
Utrecht, Cardinal of, favours a compromise with Henry on the divorce proceedings, 574.

V

Vaison, Bishop of, a partisan of Queen Catharine in Venice, 563.
Vannius, Peter, sent to Rome by Henry VIII. 578.
Valle, Cardinal de la, to be rewarded by the Emperor, 569.

Venice, the Doge of, addressed on the subject of the English divorce, 561.
Venice, Seigniory of, their attitude towards the English divorce, 561, 563, 564, 565, 566, 568, 570, 572, 581.
Voyvode, the (of Buda?), Henry VIII. promises to help him, 582, 598.

W

War against France by Henry VIII. and the Emperor, 610, 612, 613.
Winchester, Bishop of (Gardiner), his efforts to reconcile the Emperor and Henry VIII. (1541), 609. (*See also* Stephen, Dr.)
Worcester, Bishop of, English Envoy to Rome, proposed as a Cardinal by Henry VIII. 569, 570.

X

Ximenes, Dembrun Miguel, Abbot, holds an enquiry at Zaragoza in the divorce allegations, 574.

Z

Zapata, Juan, 611.
Zapata, Pedro de, abbot of the monastery of the Holy Sepulchre at Calatayud, inquiry held by him at Zaragoza in the divorce allegations, 575.

CATALOGUE

(Revised to 30th November, 1903),

OF

ENGLISH, SCOTCH, AND IRISH RECORD PUBLICATIONS,

REPORTS OF THE HISTORICAL MANUSCRIPTS COMMISSION,

AND

ANNUAL REPORTS OF THE DEPUTY KEEPERS OF THE PUBLIC RECORDS, ENGLAND AND IRELAND,

Printed for

HIS MAJESTY'S STATIONERY OFFICE,

And to be purchased,

Either directly or through any Bookseller, from

EYRE AND SPOTTISWOODE, EAST HARDING STREET, FLEET STREET, E.C., and 32, ABINGDON STREET, WESTMINSTER, S.W.; or

OLIVER & BOYD, EDINBURGH; or

EDWARD PONSONBY, 116, GRAFTON STREET, DUBLIN.

CONTENTS.

	Page
CALENDARS OF STATE PAPERS, &c.	3
PUBLIC RECORD OFFICE, LISTS AND INDEXES	9
CHRONICLES AND MEMORIALS OF GREAT BRITAIN AND IRELAND DURING THE MIDDLE AGES	10
PUBLICATIONS OF THE RECORD COMMISSIONERS, &c.	20
WORKS PUBLISHED IN PHOTOZINCOGRAPHY	22
HISTORICAL MANUSCRIPTS COMMISSION	24
REPORTS OF THE DEPUTY KEEPER OF THE PUBLIC RECORDS	31
SCOTCH RECORD PUBLICATIONS	35
IRISH RECORD PUBLICATIONS	36
REPORTS OF THE DEPUTY KEEPER OF THE PUBLIC RECORDS, IRELAND	37

CALENDARS OF STATE PAPERS, &C.

[IMPERIAL 8vo., cloth. *Price 15s. each Volume or Part.*]

Subsequent to recommendations of Committees of the House of Commons in 1800 and 1836, the Master of the Rolls, in 1865, stated to the Lords of the Treasury that although "the Records, State Papers, "and Documents in his charge constitute the most complete and perfect "series of their kind in the civilized world," and although "they are "of the greatest value in a historical and constitutional point of view, yet "they are comparatively useless to the public, from the want of proper "Calendars and Indexes." Whereupon their Lordships assented to the necessity of having Calendars prepared, and empowered the Master of the Rolls to take such steps as might be necessary for this purpose.

The following Works have been already published in this Series:—

CALENDARIUM GENEALOGICUM; for the Reigns of Henry III. and Edward I. Edited by CHARLES ROBERTS. 2 Vols. 1865.

SYLLABUS, IN ENGLISH, OF RYMER'S FŒDERA. By Sir THOMAS DUFFUS HARDY, D.C.L. 1869-1885. Vol. I.—1066-1377. (*Out of print.*) Vol. II.—1377-1654. Vol. III., Appendix and Index.

DESCRIPTIVE CATALOGUE OF ANCIENT DEEDS, preserved in the Public Record Office. 1890-1902. Vols. I., II., III. and IV.

CALENDAR OF THE PATENT ROLLS, prepared under the superintendence of the Deputy Keeper of the Records. 1891-1903:—

HENRY III. (*Latin text*)
   Vol. I.—1216-1225. | Vol. II.—1225-1232.

EDWARD I.
   Vol. I.— 1272-1281. | Vol. III.—1292-1301.
   Vol. II.— 1281-1292. | Vol. IV.—1301-1307.

EDWARD II.
   Vol. I.—1307-1313. | Vol. III.—1317-1321.
   Vol. II.—1313-1317.

EDWARD III.
   Vol. I.— 1327-1330. | Vol. V.— 1340-1343.
   Vol. II.— 1330-1334. | Vol. VI.— 1343-1345.
   Vol. III.—1334-1338. | Vol. VII.—1345-1348.
   Vol. IV.—1338-1340.

RICHARD II.
   Vol. I.— 1377-1381. | Vol. III.—1385-1389.
   Vol. II.—1381-1385. | Vol. IV.—1388-1392.

HENRY IV.
   Vol. I.—1399-1401.

HENRY VI.
   Vol. I.—1422-1429.

EDWARD IV.
   Vol. I.— 1461-1467. | Vol. II.—1467-1477.

EDWARD IV., EDWARD V., RICHARD III., 1476-1485.

CALENDAR OF THE CLOSE ROLLS, prepared under the superintendence of the Deputy Keeper of the Records. 1892-1902:—

Henry III. (*Latin text*). N.S.
   Vol. I.—1227-1231.

EDWARD I.
   Vol. I.— 1272-1279. | Vol. II.—1279-1288.

EDWARD II.
   Vol. I.— 1307-1313. | Vol. III.—1318-1323.
   Vol. II.—1313-1318. | Vol. IV.—1323-1327.

EDWARD III.
   Vol. I.— 1327-1330. | Vol. IV.—1337-1339.
   Vol. II.— 1330-1333. | Vol. V.—1339-1341.
   Vol. III.—1333-1337. | Vol. VI.—1341-1343.

CALENDAR OF THE CHARTER ROLLS, prepared under the superintendence of the Deputy Keeper of the Records. 1903.
   Vol. I.—1226-1257.

CALENDAR OF INQUISITIONS POST MORTEM and other analogous documents, prepared under the superintendence of the Deputy Keeper of the Records. 1898.
   HENRY VII.—Vol. I.

A. 407. Wt. 2/2208. 2,000.—18/11/03. M.

INQUISITIONS AND ASSESSMENTS relating to FEUDAL AIDS, etc., prepared under the superintendence of the Deputy Keeper of the Records. 1284-1431. Vol. I. Bedford to Devon. 1899. Vol. II. Dorset to Huntingdon. 1900.

CALENDAR OF LETTERS AND PAPERS, FOREIGN AND DOMESTIC, OF THE REIGN OF HENRY VIII, preserved in the Public Record Office, the British Museum, and elsewhere in England. *Edited by* J. S. BREWER, M.A. (Vols. I.-IV.); *by* JAMES GAIRDNER (Vols. V.-XIII.); *and by* JAMES GAIRDNER, C.B., and R. H. BRODIE (Vols. XIV-XVIII.). 1862-1902.

Vol. I.—1509-1514. (*Out of print.*)
Vol. II. (in two parts)—1515-1518. (*Part I out of print.*)
Vol. III. (in two parts)—1519-1523.
Vol. IV.—Introduction.
Vol. IV., Part 1.—1524-1526.
Vol. IV., Part 2.—1526-1528.
Vol. IV., Part 3.—1529-1530.
Vol. V.—1531-1532.
Vol. VI.—1533.
Vol. VII.—1534.
Vol. VIII.—1535, to July.
Vol. IX.—1535, Aug. to Dec.
Vol. X.—1536, Jan. to June.
Vol. XI.—1536, July to Dec.
Vol. XII., Part 1.—1537, Jan. to May.
Vol. XII., Part 2.—1537, June to Dec.
Vol. XIII., Part 1.—1538, Jan. to July.
Vol. XIII., Part 2.—1538, Aug. to Dec.
Vol. XIV., Part 1.—1539, Jan. to July.
Vol. XIV., Part 2.—1539, Aug. to Dec.
Vol. XV.—1540, Jan. to Aug.
Vol. XVI.—1540, Sept. to 1541, Dec.
Vol. XVII.—1542.
Vol. XVIII., Part 1.—1543, Jan. to July.
Vol. XVIII., Part 2.—1543, Aug to Dec.
Vol. XIX., Part I.—1544, Jan. to July.

CALENDAR OF STATE PAPERS, DOMESTIC SERIES, OF THE REIGNS OF EDWARD VI., MARY, ELIZABETH, and JAMES I. *Edited by* ROBERT LEMON, F.S.A. (Vols. I. and II.) *and by* MARY ANNE EVERETT GREEN (Vols. III.-XII.). 1856-1872.

Vol. I.— 1547-1580.
Vol. II.— 1581-1590.
Vol. III.—1591-1594. (*Out of print.*)
Vol. IV.—1595-1597.
Vol. V.— 1598-1601.
Vol. VI.—1601-1603, with Addenda, 1547-1565.
Vol. VII.— Addenda, 1566-1579.
Vol. VIII.—1603-1610.
Vol. IX.— 1611-1618.
Vol. X.— 1619-1623.
Vol. XI.— 1623-1625, with Addenda, 1603-1625.
Vol. XII.— Addenda, 1580-1625.

CALENDAR OF STATE PAPERS, DOMESTIC SERIES, OF THE REIGN OF CHARLES I. *Edited by* JOHN BRUCE, F.S.A. (Vols. I.-XII.); *by* JOHN BRUCE, F.S.A., and WILLIAM DOUGLAS HAMILTON, F.S.A. (Vol. XIII.); *by* WILLIAM DOUGLAS HAMILTON, F.S.A. (Vols. XIV.-XXII.); *by* WILLIAM DOUGLAS HAMILTON, F.S.A., and SOPHIE C. LOMAS (Vol. XXIII.). 1858-1897.

Vol. I.— 1625-1626.
Vol. II.— 1627-1628.
Vol. III.— 1628-1629.
Vol. IV.— 1629-1631.
Vol. V.— 1631-1633.
Vol. VI.— 1633-1634.
Vol. VII.— 1634-1635.
Vol. VIII.— 1635.
Vol. IX.— 1635-1636.
Vol. X.— 1636-1637.
Vol. XI.— 1637.
Vol. XII.— 1637-1638.
Vol. XIII.— 1638-1639.
Vol. XIV.— 1639.
Vol. XV.— 1639-1640.
Vol. XVI.— 1640.
Vol. XVII.— 1640-1641.
Vol. XVIII.—1641-1643.
Vol. XIX.— 1644.
Vol. XX.— 1644-1645.
Vol. XXI.— 1645-1647.
Vol. XXII.— 1648-1649.
Vol. XXIII.—Addenda, 1625-1649.

CALENDAR OF STATE PAPERS, DOMESTIC SERIES, DURING THE COMMONWEALTH. *Edited by* MARY ANNE EVERETT GREEN. 1875-1885.

Vol. I.— 1649-1650.
Vol. II.— 1650.
Vol. III.— 1651.
Vol. IV.— 1651-1652.
Vol. V.— 1652-1653.
Vol. VI.— 1653-1654.
Vol. VII.—1654.
Vol. VIII.—1655.
Vol. IX.— 1655-1656.
Vol. X.— 1656-1657.
Vol. XI.— 1657-1658.
Vol. XII.— 1658-1659.
Vol. XIII.—1659-1660.

CALENDAR OF STATE PAPERS:—COMMITTEE FOR THE ADVANCE OF MONEY.
1642-1656. *Edited by* MARY ANNE EVERETT GREEN. Parts I.-III., 1888.

CALENDAR OF STATE PAPERS:—COMMITTEE FOR COMPOUNDING, &c., 1643-1660. *Edited by* MARY ANNE EVERETT GREEN. Parts I.-V., 1889-1892.

CALENDAR OF STATE PAPERS, DOMESTIC SERIES, OF THE REIGN OF CHARLES II. *Edited by* MARY ANNE EVERETT GREEN (Vol. I.-X.); *and by* F. H. BLACKBURNE DANIELL, M.A. (Vols. XI.-XIII.) 1860-1902.

  Vol. I.— 1660-1661.
  Vol. II.— 1661-1662.
  Vol. III.— 1663-1664.
  Vol. IV.— 1664-1665.
  Vol. V.— 1665-1666.
  Vol. VI.— 1666-1667.
  Vol. VII.— 1667.
  Vol. VIII.— 1667-1668.
  Vol. IX.— 1668-1669.
  Vol. X.— 1670 and Addenda, 1660-1670.
  Vol. XI.— 1671.
  Vol. XII.— 1671-1672.
  Vol. XIII.— 1672.
  Vol. XIV.— 1672-1673.
  Vol. XV.— 1673.

CALENDAR OF STATE PAPERS, DOMESTIC SERIES, OF THE REIGN OF WILLIAM III. *Edited by* WILLIAM JOHN HARDY, F.S.A. 1895-1901.

  Vol. I.— 1689-1690.
  Vol. II.—1690-1691.
  Vol. III.—1691-1692.

CALENDAR OF HOME OFFICE PAPERS OF THE REIGN OF GEORGE III. Vols. I. and II. *Edited by* JOSEPH REDINGTON. 1878-1879. Vols. III. and IV. *Edited by* RICHARD ARTHUR ROBERTS, Barrister-at-Law. 1881, 1899.

  Vol. I.— 1760 (25 Oct.)-1765.
  Vol. II.—1766-1769.
  Vol. III.—1770-1772.
  Vol. IV.—1773-1775.

CALENDAR OF TREASURY PAPERS. *Edited by* JOSEPH REDINGTON. 1868-1889.

  Vol. I.— 1557-1696.
  Vol. II.— 1697-1702.
  Vol. III.—1702-1707.
  Vol. IV.—1708-1714.
  Vol. V.— 1714-1719.
  Vol. VI.—1720-1728.

CALENDAR OF TREASURY BOOKS AND PAPERS. *Edited by* W. A. SHAW, M.A. 1897-1903.

  Vol. I.— 1729-1730.
  Vol. II.— 1731-1734.
  Vol. III.—1735-1738.
  Vol. IV.—1739-1741.
  Vol. V.— 1742-1745.

CALENDAR OF STATE PAPERS relating to SCOTLAND. *Edited by* MARKHAM JOHN THORPE. 1858.

  Vol. I.— 1509-1589.
  Vol. II.—1589-1603; an Appendix, 1543-1592; and State Papers relating to Mary Queen of Scots.

CALENDAR OF DOCUMENTS relating to IRELAND, in the Public Record Office, London. *Edited by* HENRY SAVAGE SWEETMAN, B.A., Barrister-at-Law (Ireland); *and by* GUSTAVUS FREDERICK HANDCOCK. 1875-1886.

  Vol. I.— 1171-1251.
  Vol. II.— 1252-1284.
  Vol. III.—1285-1292.
  Vol. IV.—1293-1301.
  Vol. V.— 1302-1307.

CALENDAR OF STATE PAPERS relating to IRELAND. *Edited by* HANS CLAUDE HAMILTON, F.S.A.; 1860-1890, and by E. G. ATKINSON, 1893-1903.

  Vol. I.— 1509-1573.
  Vol. II.— 1574-1585.
  Vol. III.—1586-1588.
  Vol. IV.—1588-1592.
  Vol. V.— 1592-1596.
  Vol. VI.— 1596-1597.
  Vol. VII.—1598-1599.
  Vol. VIII.—1599-1600.
  Vol. IX.— 1600.

CALENDAR OF STATE PAPERS relating to IRELAND, preserved in the Public Record Office, and elsewhere. *Edited by* the Rev. C. W. RUSSELL, D.D., and JOHN P. PRENDERGAST, Barrister-at-Law. 1872-1880.

    Vol. I.— 1603-1606.   Vol. IV.—1611-1614.
    Vol. II.— 1606-1608.   Vol. V.— 1615-1625.
    Vol. III.—1608-1610.

CALENDAR OF STATE PAPERS relating to IRELAND. *Edited by* R. P. MAHAFFY, B.A. 1901-1903.

    Vol. I.—1625-1632.   Vol. II.—1633-1647.
    Adventurers for Land, 1642-1659.

CALENDAR OF THE CAREW PAPERS, preserved in the Lambeth Library. *Edited by* J. S. BREWER, M.A., *and* WILLIAM BULLEN. 1867-1873.

    Vol. I.— 1515-1574. (*Out of print.*)   Vol. IV.—1601-1603.
    Vol. II.— 1575-1588.   Vol. V.— Book of Howth. Miscellaneous.
    Vol. III.—1589-1600.   Vol. VI.—1603-1624.

CALENDAR OF STATE PAPERS, COLONIAL SERIES. *Edited by* W. NOEL SAINSBURY, *and by* the Hon. J. W. FORTESCUE. 1860-1903.

    Vol. I.—America and West Indies, 1574-1660.
    Vol. II.—East Indies, China, and Japan, 1513-1616. (*Out of print.*)
    Vol. III.—   „   „   „   1617-1621. (*Out of print.*)
    Vol. IV.—   „   „   „   1622-1624.
    Vol. V.—America and West Indies, 1661-1668.
    Vol. VI.—East Indies, 1625-1629.
    Vol. VII.—America and West Indies, 1669-1674.
    Vol. VIII.—East Indies and Persia, 1630-1634.
    Vol. IX.—America and West Indies, 1675-1676, and Addenda 1574-1674.
    Vol. X.—America and West Indies, 1677-1680.
    Vol. XI.—   „   „   1681-1685.
    Vol. XII.—   „   „   1685-1688.
    Vol. XIII.—   „   „   1689-1692.
    Vol. XIV.—   „   „   1693-1696.

CALENDAR OF STATE PAPERS, FOREIGN SERIES, OF THE REIGN OF EDWARD VI., preserved in the Public Record Office. 1547-1553. *Edited by* W. B. TURNBULL, Barrister-at-Law, &c. 1861.

Ditto—MARY. 1553-1558.

CALENDAR OF STATE PAPERS, FOREIGN SERIES, OF THE REIGN OF ELIZABETH, preserved in the Public Record Office, &c. *Edited by* the Rev. JOSEPH STEVENSON, M.A. (Vols. I.-VII.); ALLAN JAMES CROSBY, M.A., Barrister-at-Law (Vols. VIII.-XI.), *and* ARTHUR JOHN BUTLER, M.A. 1863-1903.

    Vol. I.— 1558-1559.   Vol. VIII.—1566-1568.
    Vol. II.— 1559-1560.   Vol. IX.— 1569-1571.
    Vol. III. 1560-1561.   Vol. X.— 1572-1574.
    Vol. IV.—1561-1562.   Vol. XI.— 1575-1577.
    Vol. V.— 1562.   Vol. XII.— 1577-1578.
    Vol. VI.— 1563.   Vol. XIII.—1578-1579.
    Vol. VII.—1564-1565.

CALENDAR OF DOCUMENTS IN FRANCE, illustrative of the History of Great Britain and Ireland, Vol. I. A.D. 918-1206. *Edited by* J. HORACE ROUND, M.A. 1899.

CALENDAR OF LETTERS, DESPATCHES, AND STATE PAPERS, relating to the Negotiations between England and Spain, preserved at Simancas, and elsewhere. *Edited by* G. A. BERGENROTH (Vols. I. and II.); *by* DON PASCUAL DE GAYANGOS (Vols. III. to VI.); *and by* DON PASCUAL DE GAYANGOS *and* MARTIN A. S. HUME (Vol. VII.) 1862–1899.

Vol. I.— 1485–1509.
Vol. II.— 1509–1525.
Supplement to Vol. I. and Vol. II.
Vol. III. Part 1.—1525–1526.
Vol. III. Part 2.—1527–1529.
Vol. IV. Part 1.—1529–1530.
Vol. IV. Part 2.—1531–1533.
Vol. IV. Part 2.—1531–1533, *continued.*
Vol. V. Part 1.—1534–1535.
Vol. V. Part 2.—1536–1538.
Vol. VI. Part 1.—1538–1542.
Vol. VI. Part 2.—1542–1543.
Vol. VII. Part 1.—1544.

CALENDAR OF LETTERS AND STATE PAPERS, relating to ENGLISH AFFAIRS, preserved principally in the Archives of Simancas. *Edited by* MARTIN A. S. HUME, F.R.Hist.S. 1892–1899.

Vol. I. —1558–1567.
Vol. II.—1568–1579.
Vol. III.—1580–1586.
Vol. IV.—1587–1603.

CALENDAR OF STATE PAPERS AND MANUSCRIPTS, relating to ENGLISH AFFAIRS, preserved in the Archives of Venice, &c. *Edited by* RAWDON BROWN, 1864–1884, *by* RAWDON BROWN *and the* Right Hon. G. CAVENDISH BENTINCK, M.P., 1890, *and by* HORATIO F. BROWN, 1895–1900.

Vol. I.— 1202–1509.
Vol. II.— 1509–1519.
Vol. III.—1520–1526.
Vol. IV.—1527–1533.
Vol. V.— 1534–1554.
Vol. VI., Part I.—1555–1556.
Vol. VI., Part II.— 1556–1557.
Vol. VI., Part III.—1557–1558.
Vol. VII.— 1558–1580.
Vol. VIII.— 1581–1591.
Vol. IX.— 1592–1603.
Vol. X.— 1603–1607.

CALENDAR of entries in the PAPAL REGISTERS, illustrating the history of Great Britain and Ireland. *Edited by* W. H. BLISS, B.C.L. (Vols. I. and II.); *by* W. H. BLISS *and* C. JOHNSON, M.A. (Vol. III.); *and by* W. H. BLISS *and* J. A. TWEMLOW, B.A. (Vol IV.)

PAPAL LETTERS. 1893–1902.
Vol. I.— 1198–1304.
Vol. II.—1305–1342.
Vol. III.—1342–1362.
Vol. IV.—1362–1404.

PETITIONS TO THE POPE. 1896.
Vol. I.—1342–1419.

REPORT OF THE DEPUTY KEEPER OF THE RECORDS AND THE REV. J. S. BREWER upon the Carte and Carew Papers in the Bodleian and Lambeth Libraries. 1864. *Price* 2s. 6d.

REPORT OF THE DEPUTY KEEPER OF THE RECORDS upon the Documents in the Archives and Public Libraries of Venice. 1866. *Price* 2s. 6d.

GUIDE TO THE PRINCIPAL CLASSES OF DOCUMENTS IN THE PUBLIC RECORD OFFICE. *By* S. R. SCARGILL-BIRD, F.S.A. *Second Edition.* 1896. *Price* 7s.

ACTS OF THE PRIVY COUNCIL OF ENGLAND, New Series. *Edited by* JOHN ROCHE DASENT, C.B., M.A., Barrister-at-Law. 1890–1903. *Price* 10s. *each.*

Vol. I.— 1542–1547.
Vol. II.— 1547–1550.
Vol. III.— 1550–1552.
Vol. IV.— 1552–1554.
Vol. V.— 1554–1556.
Vol. VI.— 1556–1558.
Vol. VII.— 1558–1570.
Vol. VIII.—1571–1575.
Vol. IX.— 1575–1577.
Vol. X.— 1577–1578.
Vol. XI.— 1578–1580.
Vol. XII.— 1580–1581.
Vol. XIII.—1581–1582.
Vol. XIV.—1586–1587.
Vol. XV.— 1587–1588.
Vol. XVI.— 1588.
Vol. XVII.— 1588–1589.
Vol. XVIII.—1589–1590.
Vol. XIX.— 1590.
Vol. XX.— 1590–1591.
Vol XXI.— 1591.
Vol. XXII.— 1591–1592.
Vol. XXIII.—1592.
Vol. XXIV.— 1592–1593.
Vol. XXV.— 1595–1596.
Vol. XXVI.— 1596–1597.
Vol. XXVII.—1597.

CATALOGUE OF MANUSCRIPTS and other objects in the MUSEUM of the PUBLIC RECORD OFFICE, *by* SIR H. C. MAXWELL LYTE, K.C.B. 1902. *Price* 6d.

In the Press.

DESCRIPTIVE CATALOGUE OF ANCIENT DEEDS, preserved in the Public Record Office. Vol. V.

CALENDAR OF THE PATENT ROLLS OF THE REIGN OF EDWARD II. Vols. IV. and V. 1321, &c.

CALENDAR OF THE PATENT ROLLS OF THE REIGN OF EDWARD III. Vol. VIII. 1348, &c.

CALENDAR OF THE PATENT ROLLS OF THE REIGN OF RICHARD II. Vol. V. 1390, &c.

CALENDAR OF THE PATENT ROLLS OF THE REIGN OF HENRY IV. Vol. II.

CALENDAR OF THE PATENT ROLLS OF THE REIGN OF HENRY VI. Vol. II.

CALENDAR OF THE CLOSE ROLLS OF THE REIGN OF EDWARD III. Vol. VII.

CALENDAR OF THE CHARTER ROLLS. Vol. II.

INQUISITIONS AND ASSESSMENTS relating to FEUDAL AIDS. Vol. III. Kent to Norfolk.

CALENDAR OF STATE PAPERS, relating to ENGLISH AFFAIRS, preserved in the Archives of Venice, &c. *Edited by* HORATIO F. BROWN. Vol. XI.

CALENDAR of entries in the PAPAL REGISTERS, illustrating the History of Great Britain and Ireland. *Edited by* W. H. BLISS, B.C.L., and J. A. TWEMLOW, B.A. Papal Letters. Vols. V. and VI. 1404, &c.

CALENDAR OF STATE PAPERS, DOMESTIC SERIES, OF THE REIGN OF WILLIAM III. Vol. IV. *Edited by* W. J. HARDY, F.S.A.

CALENDAR OF STATE PAPERS, COLONIAL SERIES. Vol. XV. *Edited by* the Hon. J. W. FORTESCUE.

CALENDAR OF STATE PAPERS, FOREIGN AND DOMESTIC; HENRY VIII. Vol. XIX. Part II.

CALENDAR OF TREASURY BOOKS. Vols. I. and II.

CALENDAR OF STATE PAPERS, FOREIGN. Vol. XIV.

CALENDAR OF STATE PAPERS, DOMESTIC SERIES, OF THE REIGN OF CHARLES II. Vol. XVI.

PUBLIC RECORD OFFICE.

LISTS AND INDEXES.

The object of these publications is to make the contents of the Public Record Office more easily available. In conjunction with the Calendars, they will, in course of time, form a catalogue of the National Archives, as explained in the Fifty-first Report of the Deputy Keeper of the Records (page 10).

No. I. Index of ANCIENT PETITIONS of the Chancery and the Exchequer. 1892. Price 9s. 6d.

No. II. List and Index of DECLARED ACCOUNTS from the Pipe Office and the Audit Office. 1893. Price 15s.

No. III. List of volumes of STATE PAPERS (Great Britain and Ireland). Part I., A.D. 1547-1760. 1894. Price 6s. 6d.

No. IV. List of PLEA ROLLS. 1894. Price 7s.

No. V. List of MINISTERS' ACCOUNTS preserved in the Public Record Office. Part I. 1894. Price 16s.

No. VI. List and Index of COURT ROLLS preserved in the Public Record Office. Part I. 1896. Price 15s.

No. VII. Index of CHANCERY PROCEEDINGS, Series II. A.D. 1558-1579. 1896. Price 14s.

No. VIII. List and Index of MINISTERS' ACCOUNTS. Appendix, Corrigenda and Index to Part I. 1897. Price 3s.

No. IX. List of SHERIFFS from the earliest times to A.D. 1831. 1898. Price 9s.

No. X. List of proceedings with regard to CHARITABLE USES. 1899. Price 5s.

No. XI. List of FOREIGN ACCOUNTS enrolled on the Great Rolls of the Exchequer. 1900. Price 10s.

No. XII. List of EARLY CHANCERY PROCEEDINGS. Vol. I. 1901. Price 12s.

No. XIII. List of STAR-CHAMBER PROCEEDINGS. Vol. I. 1485-1558. Price 10s.

No. XIV. List of records of the DUCHY OF LANCASTER. 1901. Price 5s.

No. XV. List of ANCIENT CORRESPONDENCE of the Chancery and Exchequer. 1902. Price 12s.

In the Press.

No. XVI. List of EARLY CHANCERY PROCEEDINGS. Vol. II.

No. XVII. List of INQUISITIONS AD QUOD DAMNUM. Part I.

List of ADMIRALTY RECORDS.

In Progress.

List of ANCIENT ACCOUNTS.

List of SURVEYS, RENTALS, &c.

THE CHRONICLES AND MEMORIALS OF GREAT BRITAIN AND IRELAND DURING THE MIDDLE AGES.

[ROYAL 8vo. *Price* 10s. *each Volume or Part.*]

1. THE CHRONICLE OF ENGLAND, by JOHN CAPGRAVE. *Edited by* the Rev. F. C. HINGESTON, M.A. 1858.

    Capgrave's Chronicle extends from the creation of the world to the year 1417. Being written in English, it is of value as a record of the language spoken in Norfolk.

2. CHRONICON MONASTERII DE ABINGDON. Vols. I. and II. *Edited by* the Rev. JOSEPH STEPHENSON, M.A., Vicar of Leighton Buzzard. 1858.

    This Chronicle traces the history of the monastery from its foundation by King Ina of Wessex, to the reign of Richard I. The author incorporates into his history various charters of the Saxon kings, as illustrating not only the history of the locality but that of the kingdom.

3. LIVES OF EDWARD THE CONFESSOR. I.—La Estoire de Seint Aedward le Rei. II.—Vita Beati Edvardi Regis et Confessoris. III.—Vita Æduuardi Regis qui apud Westmonasterium requiescit. *Edited by* HENRY RICHARDS LUARD, M.A., Fellow and Assistant Tutor of Trinity College, Cambridge. 1858.

    The first is a poem in French, probably written in 1245. The second is an anonymous poem, written between 1440 and 1450, which is mainly valuable as a specimen of the Latin poetry of the time. The third, also by an anonymous author, was apparently written between 1066 and 1074.

4. MONUMENTA FRANCISCANA.

    Vol. I.—Thomas de Eccleston de Adventu Fratrum Minorum in Angliam. Adæ de Marisco Epistolæ. Registrum Fratrum Minorum Londoniæ. *Edited by* J. S. BREWER, M.A., Professor of English Literature, King's College, London.

    Vol. II.—De Adventu Minorum; re-edited with additions. Chronicle of the Grey Friars. The ancient English version of the Rule of St. Francis. Abbreviatio Statutorum, 1451, &c. *Edited by* RICHARD HOWLETT, Barrister-at-Law. 1858, 1882.

5. FASCICULI ZIZANIORUM MAGISTRI JOHANNIS WYCLIF CUM TRITICO. Ascribed to THOMAS NETTER, of WALDEN, Provincial of the Carmelite Order in England, and Confessor to King Henry the Fifth. *Edited by* the Rev. W. W. SHIRLEY, M.A., Tutor and late Fellow of Wadham College, Oxford. 1858.

    This work gives the only contemporaneous account of the rise of the Lollards.

6. THE BUIK OF THE CRONICLIS OF SCOTLAND; or, A Metrical Version of the History of Hector Boece; by WILLIAM STEWART. Vols. I.-III. *Edited by* W. B. TURNBULL, Barrister-at-Law. 1858.

    This is a metrical translation of a Latin Prose Chronicle, written in the first half of the 16th century. The narrative begins with the earliest legends and ends with the death of James I. of Scotland, and the "evil ending of the traitors that slew him." The peculiarities of the Scottish dialect are well illustrated in this version.

7. JOHANNIS CAPGRAVE LIBER DE ILLUSTRIBUS HENRICIS. *Edited by* the Rev. F. C. HINGESTON, M.A. 1858.

    The first part relates only to the history of the Empire from the election of Henry I. the Fowler, to the end of the reign of the Emperor Henry VI. The second part is devoted to English history, from the accession of Henry I. in 1100, to 1446, which was the twenty-fourth year of the reign of Henry VI. The third part contains the lives of illustrious men who have borne the name of Henry in various parts of the world.

8. HISTORIA MONASTERII S. AUGUSTINI CANTUARIENSIS by THOMAS OF ELMHAM, formerly Monk and Treasurer of that Foundation. *Edited by* CHARLES HARDWICK, M.A., Fellow of St. Catherine's Hall, and Christian Advocate in the University of Cambridge. 1858.

This history extends from the arrival of St. Augustine in Kent until 1191.

9. EULOGIUM (HISTORIARUM SIVE TEMPORIS): Chronicon ab Orbe condito usque ad Annum Domini 1366; a monacho quodam Malmesbiriensi exaratum. Vols. I.-III. *Edited by* F. S. HAYDON, B.A. 1858-1863.

This is a Latin Chronicle extending from the Creation to the latter part of the reign of Edward III., with a continuation to the year 1413.

10. MEMORIALS OF HENRY THE SEVENTH; Bernardi Andreæ Tholosatis Vita Regis Henrici Septimi; necnon alia quædam ad eundem Regem Spectantia. *Edited by* JAMES GAIRDNER. 1858.

The contents of this volume are—(1) a life of Henry VII., by his poet Laureate and historiographer, Bernard André, of Toulouse, with some compositions in verse, of which he is supposed to have been the author; (2) the journals of Roger Machado during certain embassies to Spain and Brittany, the first of which had reference to the marriage of the King's son, Arthur, with Catharine of Arragon; (3) two curious reports by envoys sent to Spain in 1505 touching the succession to the Crown of Castile, and a project of marriage between Henry VII. and the Queen of Naples; and (4) an account of Philip of Castile's reception in England in 1506. Other documents of interest are given in an appendix.

11. MEMORIALS OF HENRY THE FIFTH. I.—Vita Henrici Quinti, Roberto Redmanno auctore. II.—Versus Rhythmici in laudem Regis Henrici Quinti. III.—Elmhami Liber Metricus de Henrico V. *Edited by* CHARLES A. COLE. 1858.

12. MUNIMENTA GILDHALLÆ LONDONIENSIS; Liber Albus, Liber Custumarum, et Liber Horn, in archivis Gildhallæ asservati.

   Vol. I., Liber Albus.

   Vol. II. (in Two Parts), Liber Custumarum.

   Vol. III., Translation of the Anglo-Norman Passages in Liber Albus, Glossaries, Appendices, and Index.

   Edited by HENRY THOMAS RILEY, M.A., Barrister-at-Law. 1859-1862.

The *Liber Albus*, compiled by John Carpenter, Common Clerk of the City of London in the year 1419, gives an account of the laws, regulations, and institutions of that City in the 12th, 13th, 14th, and early part of the 15th centuries. The *Liber Custumarum* was compiled in the early part of the 14th century during the reign of Edward II. It also gives an account of the laws, regulations, and institutions of the City of London in the 12th, 13th, and early part of the 14th centuries.

13. CHRONICA JOHANNIS DE OXENEDES. *Edited by* SIR HENRY ELLIS, K.H. 1859.

Although this Chronicle tells of the arrival of Hengist and Horsa, it substantially begins with the reign of King Alfred, and comes down to 1292. It is particularly valuable for notices of events in the eastern portions of the kingdom.

14. A COLLECTION OF POLITICAL POEMS AND SONGS RELATING TO ENGLISH HISTORY, FROM THE ACCESSION OF EDWARD III. TO THE REIGN OF HENRY VIII. Vols. I. and II. *Edited by* THOMAS WRIGHT, M.A. 1859-1861.

15. The "OPUS TERTIUM," "OPUS MINUS," &c. of ROGER BACON. *Edited by* J. S. BREWER, M.A., Professor of English Literature, King's College, London. 1859.

16. BARTHOLOMÆI DE COTTON, MONACHI NORWICENSIS, HISTORIA ANGLICANA; 449-1298; necnon ejusdem Liber de Archiepiscopis et Episcopis Angliæ. *Edited by* HENRY RICHARDS LUARD, M.A., Fellow and Assistant Tutor of Trinty College, Cambridge, 1859.

17. BRUT Y TYWYSOGION; or, The Chronicle of the Princes of Wales. *Edited by* the Rev. JOHN WILLIAMS AB ITHEL, M.A. 1860.

This work, written in the ancient Welsh language, begins with the abdication and death of Caedwala at Rome, in the year 681, and continues the history down to the subjugation of Wales by Edward I., about the year 1282.

18. A COLLECTION OF ROYAL AND HISTORICAL LETTERS DURING THE REIGN OF HENRY IV. 1399-1404. *Edited by* the Rev. F. C. HINGESTON, M.A., of Exeter College, Oxford. 1860.

19. THE REPRESSOR OF OVER MUCH BLAMING OF THE CLERGY. By REGINALD PECOCK, sometime Bishop of Chichester. Vols. I. and II. *Edited by* the Rev. CHURCHILL BABINGTON, B.D., Fellow of St. John's College, Cambridge. 1860.

> The author was born about the end of the fourteenth century, consecrated Bishop of St. Asaph in the year 1444, and translated to the see of Chichester in 1450. His work gives a full account of the views of the Lollards, and has great value for the philologist.

20. ANNALES CAMBRIÆ. *Edited by* the Rev. JOHN WILLIAMS AB ITHEL, M.A. 1860.

> These annals, which are in Latin, commence in 447, and come down to 1288. The earlier portion appears to be taken from an Irish Chronicle used by Tigernach, and by the compiler of the Annals of Ulster.

21. THE WORKS OF GIRALDUS CAMBRENSIS. Vols. I.-IV. *Edited by* the Rev. J. S. BREWER, M.A., Professor of English Literature, King's College, London. Vols. V.-VII. *Edited by* the Rev. JAMES F. DIMOCK, M.A., Rector of Barnburgh, Yorkshire. Vol. VIII. *Edited by* GEORGE F. WARNER, M.A., of the Department of MSS., British Museum. 1861-1891.

> These volumes contain the historical works of Gerald du Barry, who lived in the reigns of Henry II., Richard I., and John.
> The *Topographia Hibernica* (in Vol. V.) is the result of Giraldus' two visits to Ireland, the first in 1183, the second in 1185-6, when he accompanied Prince John into that country. The *Expugnatio Hibernica* was written about 1188. Vol. VI. contains the *Itinerarium Kambriæ et Descriptio Kambriæ*, and Vol. VII., the lives of S. Remigius and S. Hugh. Vol. VIII. contains the Treatise *De Principum Instructione*, and an index to Vols. I.-IV. and VIII.

22. LETTERS AND PAPERS ILLUSTRATIVE OF THE WARS OF THE ENGLISH IN FRANCE DURING THE REIGN OF HENRY THE SIXTH, KING OF ENGLAND, Vol. I., and Vol. II. (in Two Parts). *Edited by* the Rev. JOSEPH STEVENSON, M.A., Vicar of Leighton Buzzard. 1861-1864.

23. THE ANGLO-SAXON CHRONICLE, ACCORDING TO THE SEVERAL ORIGINAL AUTHORITIES. Vol. I., Original Texts. Vol. II., Translation. *Edited and translated by* BENJAMIN THORPE, Member of the Royal Academy of Sciences at Munich, and of the Society of Netherlandish Literature at Leyden. 1861.

> There are at present six independent manuscripts of the Saxon Chronicle, ending in different years, and written in different parts of the country. In this edition, the text of each manuscript is printed in columns on the same page, so that the student may see at a glance the various changes which occur in orthography.

24. LETTERS AND PAPERS ILLUSTRATIVE OF THE REIGNS OF RICHARD III. AND HENRY VII. Vols. I. and II. *Edited by* JAMES GAIRDNER, 1861-1863.

> The principal contents of the volumes are some diplomatic Papers of Richard III., correspondence between Henry VII. and Ferdinand and Isabella of Spain; documents relating to Edmund de la Pole, Earl of Suffolk; and a portion of the correspondence of James IV of Scotland.

25. LETTERS OF BISHOP GROSSETESTE. *Edited by* the Rev. HENRY RICHARDS LUARD, M.A., Fellow and Assistant Tutor of Trinity College, Cambridge. 1861.

> The letters of Robert Grosseteste range in date from about 1210 to 1253. They refer especially to the diocese of Lincoln, of which Grosseteste was bishop.

26. DESCRIPTIVE CATALOGUE OF MANUSCRIPTS RELATING TO THE HISTORY OF GREAT BRITAIN AND IRELAND. Vol. I. (in Two Parts); Anterior to the Norman Invasion. *(Out of print.)* Vol. II.; 1066-1200. Vol. III.; 1200-1327. *By* Sir THOMAS DUFFUS HARDY, D.C.L., Deputy Keeper of the Records. 1862-1871.

27. ROYAL AND OTHER HISTORICAL LETTERS ILLUSTRATIVE OF THE REIGN OF HENRY III. Vol. I. 1216-1235. Vol. II. 1236-1272. *Selected and edited by* the Rev. W. W. SHIRLEY, D.D., Regius Professor of Ecclesiastical History, and Canon of Christ Church, Oxford. 1862-1866.

28. CHRONICA MONASTERII S. ALBANI:—

    1. THOMÆ WALSINGHAM HISTORIA ANGLICANA; Vol. I., 1272-1381 Vol. II., 1381-1422.

    2. WILLELMI RISHANGER CHRONICA ET ANNALES, 1259-1307.

    3. JOHANNIS DE TROKELOWE ET HENRICI DE BLANEFORDE CHRONICA ET ANNALES 1259-1296; 1307-1324; 1392-1406.

    4. GESTA ABBATUM MONASTERII S. ALBANI, A THOMA WALSINGHAM, REGNANTE RICARDO SECUNDO, EJUSDEM ECCLESIÆ PRÆCENTORE, COMPILATA; Vol. I., 793-1290: Vol. II., 1290-1349: Vol. III., 1349-1411.

    5. JOHANNIS AMUNDESHAM, MONACHI MONASTERII S. ALBANI, UT VIDETUR, ANNALES; Vols. I. and II.

    6. REGISTRA QUORUNDAM ABBATUM MONASTERII S. ALBANI, QUI SÆCULO XV^{mo} FLORUERE; Vol. I., REGISTRUM ABBATIÆ JOHANNIS WHETHAMSTEDE, ABBATIS MONASTERII SANCTI ALBANI, ITERUM SUSCEPTÆ; ROBERTO BLAKENEY, CAPELLANO, QUONDAM ADSCRIPTUM: Vol. II., REGISTRA JOHANNIS WHETHAMSTEDE, WILLELMI ALBON, ET WILLELMI WALINGFORDE, ABBATUM MONASTERII SANCTI ALBANI, CUM APPENDICE CONTINENTE QUASDAM EPISTOLAS A JOHANNE WHETHAMSTEDE CONSCRIPTAS.

    7. YPODIGMA NEUSTRIÆ A THOMA WALSINGHAM, QUONDAM MONACHO MONASTERII S. ALBANI, CONSCRIPTUM.

Edited by HENRY THOMAS RILEY, M.A., Barrister-at-Law. 1863-1876.

    In the first two volumes is a History of England, from the death of Henry III. to the death of Henry V., by Thomas Walsingham, Precentor of St. Albans.
    In the 3rd volume is a Chronicle of English History, attributed to William Rishanger, who lived in the reign of Edward I.: an account of transactions attending the award of the kingdom of Scotland to John Balliol, 1291-1292, also attributed to William Rishanger, but on no sufficient ground: a short Chronicle of English History, 1292 to 1300, by an unknown hand: a short Chronicle, Willelmi Rishanger Gesta Edwardi Primi, Regis Angliæ, probably by the same hand: and fragments of three Chronicles of English History, 1285 to 1307.
    In the 4th volume is a Chronicle of English History, 1259 to 1296: Annals of Edward II., 1307 to 1323, by John de Trokelowe, a monk of St. Albans, and a continuation of Trokelowe's Annals, 1323, 1324, by Henry de Blaneforde: a full Chronicle of English History, 1392 to 1406. and an account of the benefactors of St. Albans, written in the early part of the 15th century.
    The 5th, 6th, and 7th volumes contain a history of the Abbots of St. Albans, 793 to 1411, mainly compiled by Thomas Walsingham, with a Continuation.
    The 8th and 9th volumes, in continuation of the Annals, contain a Chronicle probably of John Amundesham, a monk of St. Albans.
    The 10th and 11th volumes relate especially to the acts and proceedings of Abbots Whethamstede, Albon, and Wallingford.
    The 12th volume contains a compendious History of England to the reign of Henry V. and of Normandy in early times, also by Thomas Walsingham, and dedicated to Henry V.

29. CHRONICON ABBATIÆ EVESHAMENSIS, AUCTORIBUS DOMINICO PRIORE EVESHAMIÆ ET THOMA DE MARLEBERGE ABBATE, A FUNDATIONE AD ANNUM 1213, UNA CUM CONTINUATIONE AD ANNUM 1418. *Edited by* the Rev. W. D. MACRAY, Bodleian Library, Oxford. 1863.

    The Chronicle of Evesham illustrates the history of that important monastery from 690 to 1418. Its chief feature is an autobiography, which makes us acquainted with the inner daily life of a great abbey. Interspersed are many notices of general, personal, and local history.

30. RICARDI DE CIRENCESTRIA SPECULUM HISTORIALE DE GESTIS REGUM ANGLIÆ. Vol. I., 447-871. Vol. II., 872-1066. *Edited by* JOHN E. B. MAYOR, M.A., Fellow of St. John's College, Cambridge. 1863-1869.

    Richard of Cirencester's history is in four books, and gives many charters in favour of Westminster Abbey, and a very full account of the lives and miracles of the saints, especially of Edward the Confessor, whose reign occupies the fourth book. A treatise on the Coronation, by William of Sudbury, a monk of Westminster, fills book ii. c. 3.

31. YEAR BOOKS OF THE REIGNS OF EDWARD THE FIRST AND EDWARD THE THIRD. Years 20-21, 21-22, 30-31, 32-33, and 33-35 Edw. I; and 11-12 Edw. III. *Edited and translated by* ALFRED JOHN HORWOOD, Barrister-at-Law. Years 12-13, 13-14, 14, 14-15, 15, 16, 17, and 17-18, Edward III. *Edited and translated by* LUKE OWEN PIKE, M.A., Barrister-at-Law. 1863-1903.

32. NARRATIVES OF THE EXPULSION OF THE ENGLISH FROM NORMANDY, 1449-1450.—Robertus Blondelli de Reductione Normanniæ: Le Recouvrement de Normendie, par Berry, Hérault du Roy: Conferences between the Ambassadors of France and England. *Edited by* the Rev. JOSEPH STEVENSON, M.A. 1863.

33. HISTORIA ET CARTULARIUM MONASTERII S. PETRI GLOUCESTRIÆ. Vols. I.-III. *Edited by* W. H. HART, F.S.A., Membre Correspondant de la Société des Antiquaires de Normandie. 1863-1867.

34. ALEXANDRI NECKAM DE NATURIS RERUM LIBRI DUO; with NECKAM's POEM, DE LAUDIBUS DIVINÆ SAPIENTIÆ. *Edited by* THOMAS WRIGHT, M.A. 1863.

35. LEECHDOMS, WORTCUNNING, AND STARCRAFT OF EARLY ENGLAND; being a Collection of Documents illustrating the History of Science in this Country before the Norman Conquest. Vols. I.-III. *Collected and edited by* the Rev. T. OSWALD COCKAYNE, M.A. 1864-1866.

36. ANNALES MONASTICI.

Vol. I.:—Annales de Margan, 1066-1232; Annales de Theokesberia, 1066-1263; Annales de Burton, 1004-1263.

Vol. II.:—Annales Monasterii de Wintonia, 519-1277; Annales Monasterii de Waverleia, 1-1291.

Vol. III.:—Annales Prioratus de Dunstaplia, 1-1297. Annales Monasterii de Bermundeseia, 1042-1432.

Vol. IV.:—Annales Monasterii de Oseneia, 1016-1347; Chronicon vulgo dictum Chronicon Thomæ Wykes, 1066-1289; Annales Prioratus de Wigornia, 1-1377.

Vol. V.:—Index and Glossary.

Edited by HENRY RICHARDS LUARDS, M.A., Fellow and Assistant Tutor of Trinity College, and Registrary of the University, Cambridge. 1864-1869.

37. MAGNA VITA S. HUGONIS EPISCOPI LINCOLNIENSIS. *Edited by* the Rev. JAMES F. DIMOCK, M.A., Rector of Barnburgh, Yorkshire. 1864.

38. CHRONICLES AND MEMORIALS OF THE REIGN OF RICHARD THE FIRST.

Vol. I.:—ITINERARIUM PEREGRINORUM ET GESTA REGIS RICARDI.

Vol. II.:—EPISTOLÆ CANTUARIENSES; the Letters of the Prior and Convent of Christ Church, Canterbury; 1187 to 1199.

Edited by the Rev. WILLIAM STUBBS, M.A., Vicar of Navestock, Essex, and Lambeth Librarian. 1864-1865.

The authorship of the Chronicle in Vol. I., hitherto ascribed to Geoffrey Vinesauf, is now more correctly ascribed to Richard, Canon of the Holy Trinity of London.
The letters in Vol. II., written between 1187 and 1199, had their origin in a dispute which arose from the attempts of Baldwin and Hubert, archbishops of Canterbury, to found a college of secular canons, a project which gave great umbrage to the monks of Canterbury.

39. RECUEIL DES CRONIQUES ET ANCHIENNES ISTORIES DE LA GRANT BRETAIGNE A PRESENT NOMME ENGLETERRE, par JEHAN DE WAURIN. Vol. I., Albina to 683. Vol. II., 1399-1422. Vol. III., 1422-1431. *Edited by* WILLIAM HARDY, F.S.A. 1864-1879. Vol. IV., 1431-1447. Vol. V., 1447-1471. *Edited by* Sir WILLIAM HARDY, F.S.A., and EDWARD L. C. P. HARDY, F.S.A. 1884-1891.

40. A COLLECTION OF THE CHRONICLES AND ANCIENT HISTORIES OF GREAT BRITAIN, NOW CALLED ENGLAND, by JOHN DE WAURIN. Vol. I., Albina to 688. Vol. II., 1399-1422. Vol. III., 1422-1431. (Translations of the preceding Vols. I., II., and III.) *Edited and translated by* Sir WILLIAM HARDY, F.S.A., and EDWARD L. C. P. HARDY, F.S.A. 1864-1891.

41. POLYCHRONICON RANULPHI HIGDEN, with Trevisa's Translation. Vols. I and II. *Edited by* CHURCHILL BABINGTON, B.D., Senior Fellow of St. John's College, Cambridge. Vols. III.-IX. *Edited by* the Rev. JOSEPH RAWSON LUMBY, D.D., Norrisian Professor of Divinity, Vicar of St. Edward's, Fellow of St. Catharine's College, and late Fellow of Magdalene College, Cambridge. 1865-1886.

This chronicle begins with the Creation, and is brought down to the reign of Edward III. The two English translations, which are printed with the original Latin, afford interesting illustrations of the gradual change of our language, for one was made in the fourteenth century, the other in the fifteenth.

42. LE LIVERE DE REIS DE BRITTANIE E LE LIVERE DE REIS DE ENGLETERE. *Edited by* the Rev. JOHN GLOVER, M.A., Vicar of Brading, Isle of Wight, formerly Librarian of Trinity College, Cambridge. 1865.

These two treatises are valuable as careful abstracts of previous historians.

43. CHRONICA MONASTERII DE MELSA AB ANNO 1150 USQUE AD ANNUM 1406, Vols. I.-III. *Edited by* EDWARD AUGUSTUS BOND, Assistant Keeper of Manuscripts, and Egerton Librarian, British Museum. 1866-1868.

44. MATTHÆI PARISIENSIS HISTORIA ANGLORUM, SIVE UT VULGO DICITUR HISTORIA MINOR. Vols. I.,-III. 1067-1253. *Edited by* Sir FREDERICK MADDEN, K.H., Keeper of the Manuscript Department of the British Museum. 1866-1869.

45. LIBER MONASTERII DE HYDA: A CHRONICLE AND CHARTULARY OF HYDE ABBEY, WINCHESTER, 455-1023. *Edited by* EDWARD EDWARDS. 1866.

The "Book of Hyde" is a compilation from much earlier sources, which are usually indicated with considerable care and precision. In many cases, however, the Hyde Chronicler appears to correct, to qualify, or to amplify the statements which, in substance, he adopts.
There is to be found, in the "Book of Hyde," much information relating to the reign of King Alfred which is not known to exist elsewhere. The volume contains some curious specimens of Anglo-Saxon and mediæval English.

46. CHRONICON SCOTORUM. A CHRONICLE OF IRISH AFFAIRS, from the earliest times to 1135; and SUPPLEMENT, containing the events from 1141 to 1150. *Edited, with Translation, by* WILLIAM MAUNSELL HENNESSY, M.R.I.A. 1866.

47. THE CHRONICLE OF PIERRE DE LANGTOFT, IN FRENCH VERSE, FROM THE EARLIEST PERIOD TO THE DEATH OF EDWARD I. Vols. I. and II. *Edited by* THOMAS WRIGHT, M.A. 1866-1868.

It is probable that Pierre de Langtoft was a canon of Bridlington, in Yorkshire and lived in the reign of Edward I., and during a portion of the reign of Edward II. This chronicle is divided into three parts; in the first, is an abridgment of Geoffrey of Monmouth's "Historia Britonum"; in the second, a history of the Anglo-Saxon and Norman kings, to the death of Henry III.; in the third, a history of the reign of Edward I. The language is a specimen of the French of Yorkshire.

48. THE WAR OF THE GAEDHIL WITH THE GAILL, or THE INVASIONS OF IRELAND BY THE DANES AND OTHER NORSEMEN. *Edited, with a Translation, by* the Rev. JAMES HENTHORN TODD, D.D., Senior Fellow of Trinity College, and Regius Professor of Hebrew in the University of Dublin. 1867.

49. GESTA REGIS HENRICI SECUNDI BENEDICTI ABBATIS. CHRONICLE OF THE REIGNS OF HENRY II. AND RICHARD I., 1169-1192, known under the name of BENEDICT OF PETERBOROUGH. Vols. I. and II. *Edited by* the Rev. WILLIAM STUBBS, M.A., Regius Professor of Modern History, Oxford, and Lambeth Librarian. 1867.

50. MUNIMENTA ACADEMICA, OR, DOCUMENTS ILLUSTRATIVE OF ACADEMICAL LIFE AND STUDIES AT OXFORD (in Two Parts). *Edited by* the Rev. HENRY ANSTEY, M.A., Vicar of St. Wendron, Cornwall, and late Vice-Principal of St. Mary Hall, Oxford. 1868.

51. CHRONICA MAGISTRI ROGERI DE HOUEDENE. Vols. I.-IV. *Edited by* the Rev. WILLIAM STUBBS, M.A., Regius Professor of Modern History and Fellow of Oriel College, Oxford. 1868-1871.

> The earlier portion, extending from 732 to 1148, appears to be a copy of a compilation made in Northumbria about 1161, to which Hoveden added little. From 1148 to 1169—a very valuable portion of this work—the matter is derived from another source, to which Hoveden appears to have supplied little. From 1170 to 1192 is the portion which corresponds to some extent with the Chronicle known under the name of Benedict of Peterborough (*see* No. 49). From 1192 to 1201 may be said to be wholly Hoveden's work.

52. WILLELMI MALMESBIRIENSIS MONACHI DE GESTIS PONTIFICUM ANGLORUM LIBRI QUINQUE. *Edited by* N. E. S. A. HAMILTON, of the Department of Manuscripts, British Museum. 1870.

53. HISTORIC AND MUNICIPAL DOCUMENTS OF IRELAND, FROM THE ARCHIVES OF THE CITY OF DUBLIN, &c. 1172-1320. *Edited by* JOHN T. GILBERT, F.S.A., Secretary of the Public Record Office of Ireland. 1870.

54. THE ANNALS OF LOCH CÉ. A CHRONICLE OF IRISH AFFAIRS, FROM 1041 to 1590. Vols. I. and II. *Edited, with a Translation, by* WILLIAM MAUNSELL HENNESSY, M.R.I.A. 1871.

55. MONUMENTA JURIDICA. THE BLACK BOOK OF THE ADMIRALTY, WITH APPENDICES, Vols. I.-IV. *Edited by* Sir TRAVERS TWISS, Q.C., D.C.L. 1871-1876.

> This book contains the ancient ordinances and laws relating to the navy.

56. MEMORIALS OF THE REIGN OF HENRY VI.:—OFFICIAL CORRESPONDENCE OF THOMAS BEKYNTON, SECRETARY TO HENRY VI., AND BISHOP OF BATH AND WELLS. *Edited by* the Rev. GEORGE WILLIAMS, B.D., Vicar of Ringwood, late Fellow of King's College, Cambridge. Vols. I. and II. 1872.

57. MATTHÆI PARISIENSIS, MONACHI SANCTI ALBANI, CHRONICA MAJORA. Vol. I. The Creation to A.D. 1066. Vol. II. 1067 to 1216. Vol. III. 1216 to 1239. Vol. IV. 1240 to 1247. Vol. V. 1248 to 1259. Vol. VI. Additamenta. Vol. VII. Index. *Edited by* the Rev. HENRY RICHARDS LUARD, D.D., Fellow of Trinity College, Registrary of the University, and Vicar of Great St. Mary's, Cambridge. 1872-1884.

58. MEMORIALE FRATRIS WALTERI DE COVENTRIA.—THE HISTORICAL COLLECTIONS OF WALTER OF COVENTRY. Vols. I. and II. *Edited by* the Rev. WILLIAM STUBBS, M.A., Regius Professor of Modern History, and Fellow of Oriel College, Oxford. 1872-1873.

59. THE ANGLO-LATIN SATIRICAL POETS AND EPIGRAMMATISTS OF THE TWELFTH CENTURY. Vols. I. and II. *Collected and edited by* THOMAS WRIGHT, M.A., Corresponding Member of the National Institute of France (Académie des Inscriptions et Belles-Lettres). 1872.

60. MATERIALS FOR A HISTORY OF THE REIGN OF HENRY VII., FROM ORIGINAL DOCUMENTS PRESERVED IN THE PUBLIC RECORD OFFICE. Vols. I. and II. *Edited by* the Rev. WILLIAM CAMPBELL, M.A., one of Her Majesty's Inspectors of Schools. 1873-1877.

61. HISTORICAL PAPERS AND LETTERS FROM THE NORTHERN REGISTERS. *Edited by* the Rev. JAMES RAINE, M.A., Canon of York, and Secretary of the Surtees Society. 1873.

62. REGISTRUM PALATINUM DUNELMENSE. THE REGISTER OF RICHARD DE KELLAWE, LORD PALATINE AND BISHOP OF DURHAM; 1311-1316. Vols. I.-IV. *Edited by* Sir THOMAS DUFFUS HARDY, D.C.L., Deputy Keeper of the Records. 1873-1878.

63. MEMORIALS OF ST. DUNSTAN, ARCHBISHOP OF CANTERBURY. *Edited by* the Rev. WILLIAM STUBBS, M.A., Regius Professor of Modern History and Fellow of Oriel College, Oxford. 1874.

64. CHRONICON ANGLIÆ, AB ANNO DOMINI 1328 USQUE AD ANNUM 1388, AUCTORE MONACHO QUODAM SANCTI ALBANI. *Edited by* EDWARD MAUNDE THOMPSON, Barrister-at-Law, Assistant Keeper of the Manuscripts in the British Museum. 1874.

65. THÓMAS SAGA ERKIBYSKUPS. A LIFE OF ARCHBISHOP THOMAS BECKET IN ICELANDIC. Vols. I. and II., *Edited, with English Translation, Notes, and Glossary,* by M. EIRIKR MAGNUSSON, M.A., Sub-Librarian, of the University Library, Cambridge. 1875-1884.

66. RADULPHI DE COGGESHALL CHRONICON ANGLICANUM. *Edited by* the Rev. JOSEPH STEVENSON, M.A. 1875.

67. MATERIALS FOR THE HISTORY OF THOMAS BECKET, ARCHBISHOP OF CANTERBURY. Vols. I.-VI. *Edited by* the Rev. JAMES CRAIGIE ROBERTSON, M.A., Canon of Canterbury. 1875-1883. Vol. VII. *Edited by* JOSEPH BRIGSTOCKE SHEPPARD, LL.D. 1885.

The first volume contains the life of that celebrated man, and the miracles after his death, by William, a monk of Canterbury. The second, the life by Benedict of Peterborough; John of Salisbury; Alan of Tewkesbury; and Edward Grim. The third, the life by William Fitzstephen; and Herbert of Bosham. The fourth, anonymous lives, Quadrilogus, &c. The fifth, sixth, and seventh, the Epistles, and known letters.

68. RADULFI DE DICETO, DECANI LUNDONIENSIS, OPERA HISTORICA. THE HISTORICAL WORKS OF MASTER RALPH DE DICETO, DEAN OF LONDON. Vols. I. and II. *Edited by* the Rev. WILLIAM STUBBS, M.A., Regius Professor of Modern History, and Fellow of Oriel College, Oxford. 1876.

The Abbreviationes Chronicorum extend to 1147 and the Ymagines Historiarum to 1201.

69. ROLL OF THE PROCEEDINGS OF THE KING'S COUNCIL IN IRELAND, FOR A PORTION OF THE 16TH YEAR OF THE REIGN OF RICHARD II. 1392-93. *Edited by* the Rev. JAMES GRAVES, B.A. 1877.

70. HENRICI DE BRACTON DE LEGIBUS ET CONSUETUDINIBUS ANGLIÆ LIBRI QUINQUE IN VARIOS TRACTATUS DISTINCTI. Vols. I.-VI. *Edited by* SIR TRAVERS TWISS, Q.C., D.C.L. 1878-1883.

71. THE HISTORIANS OF THE CHURCH OF YORK, AND ITS ARCHBISHOPS. Vols. I.-III. *Edited by* the Rev. JAMES RAINE, M.A., Canon of York, and Secretary of the Surtees Society. 1879-1894.

72. REGISTRUM MALMESBURIENSE. THE REGISTER OF MALMESBURY ABBEY, PRESERVED IN THE PUBLIC RECORD OFFICE. Vols. I. and II. *Edited by* the Rev. J. S. BREWER, M.A., Preacher at the Rolls, and Rector of Toppesfield; *and* CHARLES TRICE MARTIN, B.A. 1879-1880.

73. HISTORICAL WORKS OF GERVASE OF CANTERBURY. Vols. I. and II. *Edited by* the Rev. WILLIAM STUBBS, D.D., Canon Residentiary of St. Paul's, London; Regius Professor of Modern History and Fellow of Oriel College, Oxford, &c. 1879, 1880.

74. HENRICI ARCHIDIACONI HUNTENDUNENSIS HISTORIA ANGLORUM. THE HISTORY OF THE ENGLISH, BY HENRY, ARCHDEACON OF HUNTINGDON, from A.D. 55 to A.D. 1154, in Eight Books. *Edited by* THOMAS ARNOLD, M.A., 1879.

75. THE HISTORICAL WORKS OF SYMEON OF DURHAM. Vols. I. and II. *Edited by* THOMAS ARNOLD, M.A. 1882-1885.

76. CHRONICLE OF THE REIGNS OF EDWARD I. AND EDWARD II. Vols. I and II. *Edited by* the Rev. WILLIAM STUBBS, D.D., Canon Residentiary of St. Paul's, London; Regius Professor of Modern History, and Fellow of Oriel College, Oxford, &c 1882-1883.

The first volume of these Chronicles contains the *Annales Londonienses,* and the *Annales Paulini*: the second, I.—*Commendatio Lamentabilis in Transitu magni Regis Edwardi.* II.—*Gesta Edwardi de Carnarvan Auctore Canonico Bridlingtonensi.* III.—*Monachi cujusdam Malmesberiensis Vita Edwardi II.* IV.—*Vita et Mors Edwardi II., conscripta a Thoma de la Moore.*

77. REGISTRUM EPISTOLARUM FRATRIS JOHANNIS PECKHAM, ARCHIEPISCOPI CANTUARIENSIS. Vols. I.-III. *Edited by* CHARLES TRICE MARTIN, B.A., F.S.A., 1882-1886.

78. REGISTER OF S. OSMUND. Vols. I. and II. *Edited by* the Rev. W. H. RICH JONES, M.A., F.S.A., Canon of Salisbury, Vicar of Bradford-on-Avon. 1883, 1884.

   This Register derives its name from containing the statutes, rules, and orders made or compiled by S. Osmund, to be observed in the Cathedral and diocese of Salisbury.

79. CHARTULARY OF THE ABBEY OF RAMSEY. Vols. I.-III. *Edited by* WILLIAM HENRY HART, F.S.A., and the Rev. PONSONBY ANNESLEY LYONS. 1884-1893.

80. CHARTULARIES OF ST. MARY'S ABBEY, DUBLIN, WITH THE REGISTER OF ITS HOUSE AT DUNBRODY, COUNTY OF WEXFORD, AND ANNALS OF IRELAND, 1162-1370. Vols. I. and II. *Edited by* JOHN THOMAS GILBERT, F.S.A., M.R.I.A. 1884, 1885.

81. EADMERI HISTORIA NOVORUM IN ANGLIA, ET OPUSCULA DUO DE VITA SANCTI ANSELMI ET QUIBUSDAM MIRACULIS EJUS. *Edited by* the Rev. MARTIN RULE, M.A. 1884.

82. CHRONICLES OF THE REIGNS OF STEPHEN, HENRY II., AND RICHARD I. Vols. I.-IV. *Edited by* RICHARD HOWLETT, Barrister-at-Law. 1884-1889.

   Vol. I. contains Books I.-IV. of the *Historia Rerum Anglicarum* of William of Newburgh.
   Vol. II. contains Book V. of that work, the continuation of the same to A.D. 1298, and the *Draco Normannicus* of Etienne de Rouen.
   Vol. III. contains the *Gesta Stephani Regis*, the Chronicle of Richard of Hexham, the *Relatio de Standardo* of St. Aelred of Rievaulx, the poem of Jordan Fantosme, and the Chronicle of Richard of Devizes.
   Vol. IV. contains the Chronicle of Robert of Torigni.

83. CHRONICLE OF THE ABBEY OF RAMSEY. *Edited by* the Rev. WILLIAM DUNN MACRAY, M.A., F.S.A., Rector of Ducklington, Oxon. 1886.

84. CHRONICA ROGERI DE WENDOVER, SIVE FLORES HISTORIARUM. Vols. I.-III. *Edited by* HENRY GAY HEWLETT, Keeper of the Records of the Land Revenue. 1886-1889.

   This edition gives that portion only of Roger of Wendover's Chronicle which can be accounted an original authority.

85. THE LETTER BOOKS OF THE MONASTERY OF CHRIST CHURCH, CANTERBURY. Vols. I.-III. *Edited by* JOSEPH BRIGSTOCKE SHEPPARD, LL.D. 1887-1889.

   The Letters printed in these volumes were chiefly written between 1296 and 1298.

86. THE METRICAL CHRONICLE OF ROBERT OF GLOUCESTER. *Edited by* WILLIAM ALDIS WRIGHT, M.A., Senior Fellow of Trinity College, Cambridge. Parts I. and II., 1887.

   The date of the composition of this Chronicle is placed about the year 1300. The writer appears to have been an eye witness of many events of which he describes. The language in which it is written was the dialect of Gloucestershire at that time.

87. CHRONICLE OF ROBERT OF BRUNNE. *Edited by* FREDERICK JAMES FURNIVALL, M.A., Barrister-at-Law. Parts I. and II. 1887.

   Robert of Brunne, or Bourne, co. Lincoln, was a member of the Gilbertine Order established at Sempringham. His Chronicle is described by its editor as a work of fiction, a contribution not to English history, but to the history of English.

88. ICELANDIC SAGAS AND OTHER HISTORICAL DOCUMENTS relating to the Settlements and Descents of the Northmen on the British Isles. Vol. I. Orkneyinga Saga, and Magnus Saga. Vol. II. Hakonar Saga, and Magnus Saga. *Edited by* GUDBRAND VIGFUSSON, M.A. 1887. Vols. III. and IV. Translations of the above by Sir GEORGE WEBBE DASENT, D.C.L. 1894.

89. THE TRIPARTITE LIFE OF ST. PATRICK, with other documents relating to that Saint. *Edited by* WHITLEY STOKES, LL.D., D.C.L., Honorary Fellow of Jesus College, Oxford; and Corresponding Member of the Institute of France. Parts I. and II. 1887.

90. Willelmi monachi Malmesbiriensis de Regum Gestis Anglorum libri V.; et Historiæ Novellæ, libri III. *Edited by* William Stubbs, D.D., Bishop of Oxford. Vols. I. and II. 1887-1889.

91. Lestorie des Engles solum Geffrei Gaimar. *Edited by* the late Sir Thomas Duffus Hardy, D.C.L., Deputy Keeper of the Records; *continued and translated by* Charles Trice Martin, B.A., F.S.A. Vols. I. and II. 1888-1889.

92. Chronicle of Henry Knighton, Canon of Leicester. Vols. I. and II. *Edited by* the Rev. Joseph Rawson Lumby, D.D., Norrisian Professor of Divinity. 1889-1895.

93. Chronicle of Adam Murimuth, with the Chronicle of Robert of Avesbury. *Edited by* Edward Maunde Thompson, LL.D., F.S.A., Principal Librarian and Secretary of the British Museum. 1889.

94. Register of the Abbey of St. Thomas the Martyr, Dublin. *Edited by* John Thomas Gilbert, F.S.A., M.R.I.A. 1889.

95. Flores Historiarum. *Edited by* the Rev. H. R. Luard, D.D., Fellow of Trinity College and Registrary of the University, Cambridge. Vol. I., The Creation to A.D. 1066. Vol. II. A.D. 1067-1264. Vol. III. A.D. 1265-1326. 1890.

96. Memorials of St. Edmund's Abbey. *Edited by* Thomas Arnold, M.A., Fellow of the Royal University of Ireland. Vols. I.-III. 1890-1896.

97. Charters and Documents, illustrating the History of the Cathedral and City of Sarum, 1100-1300; forming an Appendix to the Register of S. Osmund. *Selected by* the late Rev. W. H. Rich Jones, M.A., F.S.A., *and edited by* the Rev. W. D. Macray, M.A., F.S.A., Rector of Ducklington. 1891.

98. Memoranda de Parliamento, 25 Edward I. 1305. *Edited by* F. W. Maitland, M.A. 1893.

99. The Red Book of the Exchequer. *Edited by* Hubert Hall, F.S.A. of the Public Record Office. Parts I.-III. 1896.

PUBLICATIONS
OF THE RECORD COMMISSIONERS, &c.

In boards or cloth. Volumes not mentioned in this list are out of print.

ROTULORUM ORIGINALIUM IN CURIA SCACCARII ABBREVIATIO. Hen. III.—Edw. III. Edited by HENRY PLAYFORD. 2 Vols. folio (1805-1810). 12s. 6d. each.

LIBRORUM MANUSCRIPTORUM BIBLIOTHECÆ HARLEIANÆ CATALOGUS. Vol. 4. Edited by the Rev. T. HARTWELL HORNE. Folio (1812), 18s.

ABBREVIATIO PLACITORUM. Richard I.—Edward II. Edited by the Right Hon. GEORGE ROSE and W. ILLINGWORTH. 1 Vol. folio (1811), 18s.

LIBRI CENSUALIS vocati, DOMESDAY-BOOK, INDICES. Edited by Sir HENRY ELLIS. Folio (1816), (Domesday-Book, Vol. 3). 21s.

LIBRI CENSUALIS vocati DOMESDAY-BOOK, ADDITAMENTA EX CODIC. ANTIQUISS. Edited by Sir HENRY ELLIS. Folio (1816), (Domesday-Book, Vol. 4). 21s.

STATUTES OF THE REALM. Edited by Sir T. E. TOMLINS, JOHN RAITHBY, JOHN CALEY and WM. ELLIOTT. Vols. 10 and 11, Folios (1824-1828) Indices, 30s. each.

VALOR ECCLESIASTICUS, temp. Hen. VIII., Auctoritate Regia institutus. Edited by JOHN CALEY and the Rev. JOSEPH HUNTER. Vols. 5 to 6, folio (1825-1834). 25s. each. The Introduction, separately, 8vo. 2s. 6d.

FŒDERA, CONVENTIONES, LITTERÆ, &c.; or, RYMER'S FŒDERA. New Edition, folio. Edited by JOHN CALEY and FRED HOLBROOKE. Vol. 4, 1377-1383 (1869). 6s.

DUCATUS LANCASTRIÆ CALENDARIUM INQUISITIONUM POST MORTEM, &c. Part 3, Calendar to Pleadings, &c., Hen. VII.—13 Eliz. Part 4, Calendar to Pleadings, to end of Eliz. (1827-1834). Edited by R. J. HARPER, JOHN CALEY, and WM. MINCHIN. Folio. Part 4 (or Vol. 3), 21s.

CALENDARS OF THE PROCEEDINGS IN CHANCERY, ELIZ.; with Examples of Proceedings from Ric. II. Edited by JOHN BAYLEY. Vol. 3. (1832), folio, 21s.

ROTULI LITTERARUM CLAUSARUM IN TURRI LONDINENSI ASSERVATI. 2 Vols. folio (1833, 1844). Edited by THOMAS DUFFUS HARDY. Vol. 2, 1224-1227. 18s.

PROCEEDINGS AND ORDINANCES OF THE PRIVY COUNCIL OF ENGLAND. 10 Ric. II.—33 Hen. VIII. Edited by Sir NICHOLAS HARRIS NICOLAS. 7 Vols. royal 8vo. (1834-1837). 14s. each. (Vol. 1 out of print.)

ROTULI LITTERARUM PATENTIUM IN TURRI LOND. ASSERVATI. 1201-1216. Edited by T. DUFFUS HARDY. 1 Vol. folio (1835), 31s. 6d. The Introduction, separately, 8vo. 9s.

ROTULI CURIÆ REGIS. Rolls and Records of the Court held before the King's Justiciars or Justices. 6 Richard 1.—1 John. Edited by Sir FRANCIS PALGRAVE. Vol. 2, royal 8vo. (1835). 14s.

ROTULI NORMANNIÆ IN TURRI LOND. ASSERVATI. 1200-1205; 1417-1418. Edited by THOMAS DUFFUS HARDY. 1 Vol. royal 8vo. (1835). 12s. 6d.

ROTULI DE OBLATIS ET FINIBUS IN TURRI LOND. ASSERVATI, temp. Regis Johannis. Edited by THOMAS DUFFUS HARDY. 1 Vol. royal 8vo. (1835). 18s.

EXCERPTA E ROTULIS FINIUM IN TURRI LONDINENSI ASSERVATIS. Henry III. 1216-1272. Edited by CHARLES ROBERTS. 2 Vols. royal 8vo. (1835, 1836). Vol. 1, 14s. Vol. 2, 18s.

FINES, SIVE PEDES FINIUM: SIVE FINALES CONCORDIÆ IN CURIA DOMINI REGIS. 7 Richard 1.—16 John, 1195—1214. Edited by the Rev. JOSEPH HUNTER. In Counties. 2 Vols. royal 8vo. (1835-1844); Vol. 1, 8s. 6d.; Vol. 2, 2s. 6d.

ANCIENT KALENDARS AND INVENTORIES OF THE TREASURY OF HIS MAJESTY'S EXCHEQUER; with Documents illustrating its History. Edited by Sir FRANCIS PALGRAVE. 3 Vols. royal 8vo. (1836). 42s.

DOCUMENTS AND RECORDS illustrating the History of Scotland, and Transactions between Scotland and England; preserved in the Treasury of Her Majesty's Exchequer. Edited by Sir FRANCIS PALGRAVE. 1 Vol. royal 8vo. (1837).

ROTULI CHARTARUM IN TURRI LONDINENSI ASSERVATI. 1190-1216. Edited by THOMAS DUFFUS HARDY. 1 Vol. folio (1837). 30s.

REPORT OF THE PROCEEDINGS OF THE RECORD COMMISSIONERS, 1831-1837. 1 Vol. fol. (1837). 8s.

REGISTRUM vulgariter nuncupatum "The Record of Caernarvon," e codice MS. Harleiano, 696, descriptum. Edited by Sir HENRY ELLIS. 1 Vol. folio (1838). 31s. 6d.

ANCIENT LAWS AND INSTITUTES OF ENGLAND; comprising Laws enacted under the Anglo-Saxon Kings, with translation of the Saxon; the Laws called Edward the Confessor's; the laws of William the Conqueror, and those ascribed to Henry I.; Monumenta Ecclesiastica Anglicana, from 7th to 10th century; and Ancient Latin Version of the Anglo-Saxon Laws. *Edited by* BENJAMIN THORPE. 1 Vol. folio, 40s. 2 Vols. royal 8vo., 30s. *(Vol. 1 is out of print.)*

ANCIENT LAWS AND INSTITUTES OF WALES; comprising Laws supposed to be enacted by Howel the Good, modified by Regulations prior to the Conquest by Edward I.; and anomalous Laws, principally of Institutions which continued in force. With translation. Also, Latin Transcripts, containing Digests of Laws, principally of the Dimetian Code. *Edited by* ANEURIN OWEN. 1 Vol. folio (1841), 44s. 2 Vols. royal 8vo., 36s.

ROTULI DE LIBERATE AC DE MISIS ET PRÆSTITIS, Regnante Johanne. *Edited by* THOMAS DUFFUS HARDY. 1 Vol royal 8vo. (1844). 6s.

THE GREAT ROLLS OF THE PIPE, 2, 4, Hen. II., 1155-1158. *Edited by* the Rev. JOSEPH HUNTER. 1 Vol. royal 8vo. (1844). 4s. 6d.

THE GREAT ROLL OF THE PIPE, 1 Ric. I., 1189-1190. *Edited by* the Rev. JOSEPH HUNTER. 1 Vol. royal 8vo. (1844). 6s.

DOCUMENTS ILLUSTRATIVE OF ENGLISH HISTORY in the 13th and 14th centuries, from the Records of the Queen's Remembrancer in the Exchequer. *Edited by* HENRY COLE. 1 Vol. fcp. folio (1844). 45s. 6d.

MODUS TENENDI PARLIAMENTUM. An Ancient Treatise on the Mode of holding the Parliament in England. *Edited by* THOMAS DUFFUS HARDY. 1 Vol. 8vo. (1846). 2s. 6d.

REGISTRUM MAGNI SIGILLI REG. SCOT. in Archivis Publicis asservatum. Vol. 1, 1306-1424. *(For continuation see page 33.) Edited by* THOMAS THOMSON. Folio (1814). 10s. 6d.

ACTS OF THE PARLIAMENTS OF SCOTLAND. Folio (1814-1875). *Edited by* THOMAS THOMSON and COSMO INNES. Vol. 1, 42s. Vols. 5 and 6 (in three Parts), 21s. each Part; Vols. 7, 8, 9, 10, and 11, 10s. 6d. each; Vol. 12 (Index), 63s. Or, 12 Vols. in 13, 12l. 12s.

ACTS OF THE LORDS AUDITORS OF CAUSES AND COMPLAINTS (ACTA DOMINORUM AUDITORUM). 1466-1494. *Edited by* THOMAS THOMSON. Folio (1839). 10s. 6d.

ACTS OF THE LORDS OF COUNCIL IN CIVIL CAUSES (ACTA DOMINORUM CONCILII). 1478-1495. *Edited by* THOMAS THOMSON. Folio (1839). 10s. 6d.

ISSUE ROLL OF THOMAS DE BRANTINGHAM, Bishop of Exeter, Lord High Treasurer, containing Payments out of the Revenue, 44 Edw. III., 1376. *Edited by* FREDERICK DEVON. 1 Vol. royal 8vo., 25s.

ISSUES OF THE EXCHEQUER, James I.; from the Pell Records. *Edited by* FREDERICK DEVON, Esq. 1 Vol. 4to. (1836), 30s. Or, royal 8vo. 21s.

ISSUES OF THE EXCHEQUER, Henry III.—Henry VI.; from the Pell Records. *Edited by* FREDERICK DEVON. 1 Vol. royal 8vo., 30s.

HANDBOOK TO THE PUBLIC RECORDS. By F. S. THOMAS, Secretary of the Public Record Office. 1 Vol. royal 8vo., (1853). 12s.

HISTORICAL NOTES RELATIVE TO THE HISTORY OF ENGLAND. Henry VIII.—Anne (1509-1714). A Book of Reference for ascertaining the Dates of Events. *By* F. S. THOMAS. 3 Vols. 8vo. (1856). 40s.

STATE PAPERS, DURING THE REIGN OF HENRY THE EIGHTH: with Indices of Persons and Places. 11 Vols. 4to. (1830-1852), 10s. 6d. each.
Vol. I.—Domestic Correspondence.
Vols. II. & III.—Correspondence relating to Ireland.
Vols. IV. & V.—Correspondence relating to Scotland.
Vols. VI. to XI.—Correspondence between England and Foreign Courts.

REPORTS ON THE UTRECHT PSALTER.

THE ATHANASIAN CREED IN CONNEXION WITH THE UTRECHT PSALTER; being a Report to the Right Honourable Lord Romilly, Master of the Rolls, on a Manuscript in the University of Utrecht, by Sir Thomas Duffus Hardy, D.C.L., Deputy Keeper of the Public Records. 1872. 4to. 44pp. 2 fac-similes half bound. *Price* 20s.

FURTHER REPORT ON THE UTRECHT PSALTER; in answer to the Eighth Report made to the Trustees of the British Museum, and edited by the Dean of Westminster. By Sir Thomas Duffus Hardy, D.C.L., Deputy Keeper of the Public Records 1874. 4to. 80 pp. half bound. *Price* 10s.

WORKS PUBLISHED IN PHOTOZINCOGRAPHY.

DOMESDAY BOOK, or the GREAT SURVEY OF ENGLAND OF WILLIAM THE CONQUEROR, 1086; fac-simile of the Part relating to each county, separately (with a few exceptions of double counties). Photozincographed at the Ordnance Survey Office, Southampton, by Colonel Sir HENRY JAMES, R.E., F.R.S., DIRECTOR-GENERAL of the ORDNANCE SURVEY, under the superintendence of W. BASEVI SANDERS, an Assistant Record Keeper. 35 Parts, imperial quarto and demy quarto (1861-1863), boards.

Domesday Survey is in two parts or volumes. The first, in folio, contains the counties of Bedford, Berks, Bucks, Cambridge, Chester, and Lancaster, Cornwall, Derby, Devon, Dorset, Gloucester, Hants, Hereford, Herts, Huntingdon, Kent, Leicester and Rutland, Lincoln, Middlesex, Northampton, Nottingham, Oxford, Salop, Somerset, Stafford, Surrey, Sussex, Warwick, Wilts, Worcester, and York. The second volume, in quarto, contains the counties of Essex, Norfolk, and Suffolk.

Domesday Book was printed *verbatim et literatim* during the last century, in consequence of an address of the House of Lords to King George III. in 1767. It was not, however, commenced until 1773, and was completed early in 1783. In 1860, Her Majesty's Government, with the concurrence of the Master of the Rolls, determined to apply the art of photozincography in the production of a fac-simile of Domesday Book.

Title.	Price.	Title.	Price.
	£ s. d.		£ s. d.
In Great Domesday Book.		Brought forward	7 17 0
		Middlesex	0 8 0
Bedfordshire	0 8 0	Nottinghamshire	0 10 0
Berkshire	0 8 0	Northamptonshire	0 8 0
Buckingham	0 8 0	Oxfordshire	0 8 0
Cambridge	0 10 0	Rutlandshire (bound with	
Cheshire and Lancashire	0 8 0	Leicestershire)	
Cornwall	0 8 0	Shropshire (*out of print*)	0 8 0
Derbyshire	0 8 0	Somersetshire	0 10 0
Devonshire	0 10 0	Staffordshire	0 8 0
Dorsetshire	0 8 0	Surrey	0 8 0
Gloucestershire (*out of print*)	0 8 0	Sussex	0 10 0
Hampshire	0 10 0	Warwickshire	0 8 0
Herefordshire	0 8 0	Wiltshire	0 10 0
Hertfordshire	0 10 0	Worcestershire	0 8 0
Huntingdonshire	0 8 0	Yorkshire (*out of print*)	1 1 0
Kent (*out of print*)	0 8 0		
Lancashire (*see Cheshire and Lancashire*)	—	*In Little Domesday Book.*	
Leicestershire and Rutlandshire	0 8 0	Norfolk	1 3 0
		Suffolk	1 2 0
Lincolnshire	1 1 0	Essex	0 16 0
Carried forward	7 17 0	Total	£17 3 0

FAC-SIMILES OF NATIONAL MANUSCRIPTS, from WILLIAM THE CONQUEROR to QUEEN ANNE, selected under the direction of the Master of the Rolls and Photozincographed, by Command of Her Majesty, by Colonel Sir HENRY JAMES, R.E., F.R.S., DIRECTOR-GENERAL of the ORDNANCE SURVEY, and edited by W. BASEVI SANDERS, an Assistant Record Keeper. Price, each Part, with translations and notes, double foolscap folio, 16s.

Part I. (William the Conqueror to Henry VII.). 1865. (*Out of print.*)

Part II. (Henry VII. and Edward VI.). 1866.

Part III. (Mary and Elizabeth). 1867.

Part IV. (James I. to Anne). 1868.

> The first Part extends from William the Conqueror to Henry VII., and contains autographs of the kings of England, as well as of many other illustrious personages famous in history, and some interesting charters, letters patent, and state papers. The second Part, for the reigns of Henry VIII. and Edward VI., consists principally of holograph letters, and autographs of kings, princes, statesmen, and other persons of great historical interest, who lived during those reigns. The third Part contains similar documents for the reigns of Mary and Elizabeth, including a signed bill of Lady Jane Grey. The fourth Part concludes the series, and comprises a number of documents taken from the originals belonging to the Constable of the Tower of London; also several records illustrative of the Gunpowder Plot, and a woodcut containing portraits of Mary Queen of Scots and James VI., circulated by their adherents in England, 1580-3.

FAC-SIMILES OF ANGLO-SAXON MANUSCRIPTS. Photozincographed, by Command of Her Majesty, upon the recommendation of the Master of the Rolls, by the DIRECTOR-GENERAL of the ORDNANCE SURVEY, Lieut.-General J. CAMERON, R.E., C.B., F.R.S., and edited by W. BASEVI SANDERS, an Assistant Record Keeper. Part I. *Price 2l. 10s.*

> The Anglo-Saxon MSS. represented in this volume form the earlier portions of the collection of archives belonging to the Dean and Chapter of Canterbury, and consist of a series of 25 charters, deeds, and wills, commencing with a record of proceedings at the first Synodal Council of Clovesho in 742, and terminating with the first part of a tripartite chirograph of the sixth year of the reign of Edward the Confessor.

FAC-SIMILES OF ANGLO-SAXON MANUSCRIPTS. Photozincographed, by Command of Her Majesty, upon the recommendation of the Master of the Rolls, by the DIRECTOR-GENERAL of the ORDNANCE SURVEY, Major-General A. COOK, R.E., C.B., and collected and edited by W. BASEVI SANDERS, an Assistant Record Keeper. Part II. *Price 3l. 10s.* (Also, separately. Edward the Confessor's Charter. *Price 2s.*)

> The originals of the fac-similes contained in this volume belong to the Deans and Chapters of Westminster, Exeter, Wells, Winchester, and Worcester; the Marquis of Bath, the Earl of Ilchester, Winchester College, Her Majesty's Public Record Office, Bodleian Library, Somersetshire Archæological and National History Society's Museum in Taunton Castle, and William Salt Library at Stafford. They consist of charters and other documents granted by, or during the reigns of, Baldred, Æthelred, Offa, and Burgred, Kings of Mercia; Uhtred of the Huiccas, Caedwalla and Ini of Wessex; Æthelwulf, Eadward the Elder, Æthelstan, Eadmund the First, Eadred, Eadwig, Eadgar, Eadward the Second, Æthelred the Second, Cnut, Eadward the Confessor, and William the Conqueror, embracing altogether a period of nearly four hundred years.

FAC-SIMILES OF ANGLO-SAXON MANUSCRIPTS. Photozincographed, by Command of Her Majesty, upon the recommendation of the Master of the Rolls, by the DIRECTOR-GENERAL of the ORDNANCE SURVEY, Colonel R. H. STOTHERD, R.E., C.B., and collected and edited by W. BASEVI SANDERS, an Assistant Record Keeper. Part III. *Price 6l. 6s.*

> This volume contains fac-similes of the Ashburnham Collection of Anglo-Saxon Charters, &c., including King Alfred's Will. The MSS. represented in it range from A.D. 697 to A.D. 1161, being charters, wills, deeds, and reports of Synodal transactions during the reigns of Kings Wihtred of Kent, Offa, Eardwulf, Coenwulf, Cuthred, Beornwulf, Æthelwulf, Ælfred, Eadward the Elder, Eadmund, Eadred, Queen Eadgifu, and Kings Eadgar, Æthelred the Second, Cnut, Henry the First, and Henry the Second. In addition to these are two belonging to the Marquis of Anglesey, one of them being the Foundation Charter of Burton Abbey by Æthelred the Second, with the testament of its great benefactor Wulfric.

HISTORICAL MANUSCRIPTS COMMISSION.

REPORTS OF THE ROYAL COMMISSIONERS APPOINTED TO INQUIRE WHAT PAPERS AND MANUSCRIPTS BELONGING TO PRIVATE FAMILIES AND INSTITUTIONS ARE EXTANT WHICH WOULD BE OF UTILITY IN THE ILLUSTRATION OF HISTORY, CONSTITUTIONAL LAW, SCIENCE, AND GENERAL LITERATURE.

Date.	—	Size.	Sessional Paper.	Price.

1870 (Reprinted 1874.)	FIRST REPORT, WITH APPENDIX
	Contents:—
	  ENGLAND. House of Lords; Cambridge Colleges; Abingdon and other Corporations, &c.
	  SCOTLAND. Advocates' Library, Glasgow Corporation, &c.
	  IRELAND. Dublin, Cork, and other Corporations, &c.
		f'cap	[C. 55]	s. d.
				1 6

1871	SECOND REPORT WITH APPENDIX AND INDEX TO THE FIRST AND SECOND REPORTS
	Contents:—
	  ENGLAND. House of Lords; Cambridge Colleges; Oxford Colleges; Monastery of Dominican Friars at Woodchester, Duke of Bedford, Earl Spencer, &c.
	  SCOTLAND. Aberdeen and St. Andrew's Universities, &c.
	  IRELAND. Marquis of Ormonde; Dr. Lyons, &c.
		,,	[C. 441]	3 10

1872 (Reprinted 1895.)	THIRD REPORT WITH APPENDIX AND INDEX
	Contents:—
	  ENGLAND. House of Lords; Cambridge Colleges; Stonyhurst College; Bridgwater and other Corporations; Duke of Northumberland, Marquis of Lansdowne, Marquis of Bath, &c.
	  SCOTLAND. University of Glasgow: Duke of Montrose, &c.
	  IRELAND. Marquis of Ormonde; Black Book of Limerick, &c.
		,,	[C. 673]	6 0

1873	FOURTH REPORT, WITH APPENDIX. PART I.
	Contents:—
	  ENGLAND. House of Lords. Westminster Abbey; Cambridge and Oxford Colleges; Cinque Ports, Hythe, and other Corporations, Marquis of Bath, Earl of Denbigh, &c.
	  SCOTLAND. Duke of Argyll, &c.
	  IRELAND. Trinity College, Dublin Marquis of Ormonde.
		,,	[C. 857]	6 8

Date.		Size.	Sessional Paper.	Price.
				s. d.
1873	FOURTH REPORT. PART II. INDEX	f'cap	[C. 857 i.]	2 6

1876	FIFTH REPORT, WITH APPENDIX. PART I.
	Contents :—
	  ENGLAND. House of Lords; Oxford and Cambridge Colleges; Dean and Chapter of Canterbury; Rye, Lydd, and other Corporations. Duke of Sutherland, Marquis of Lansdowne, Reginald Cholmondeley, Esq., &c.
	  SCOTLAND. Earl of Aberdeen, &c.
		,,	[C.1432]	7 0

,,	DITTO. PART II. INDEX	,,	[C.1432 i.]	3 6

1877	SIXTH REPORT, WITH APPENDIX. PART I.
	Contents :—
	  ENGLAND. House of Lords; Oxford and Cambridge Colleges; Lambeth Palace; Black Book of the Archdeacon of Canterbury; Bridport, Wallingford, and other Corporations; Lord Leconfield, Sir Reginald Graham, Sir Henry Ingilby, &c.
	  SCOTLAND. Duke of Argyll, Earl of Moray, &c.
	  IRELAND. Marquis of Ormonde.
		,,	[C.1745]	8 6

(Reprinted 1893.)	DITTO. PART II. INDEX	,,	[C.2102]	1 10
1879 (Reprinted 1895.)	SEVENTH REPORT, WITH APPENDIX. PART I. Contents :— House of Lords; County of Somerset; Earl of Egmont, Sir Frederick Graham, Sir Harry Verney, &c.	,,	[C.2340]	7 6
(Reprinted 1895.)	DITTO. PART II. APPENDIX AND INDEX Contents :— Duke of Athole, Marquis of Ormonde, S. F. Livingstone, Esq., &c.	,,	[C. 2340 i.]	3 6

1881	EIGHTH REPORT, WITH APPENDIX AND INDEX. PART I.
	Contents :—
	  List of collections examined, 1869-1880.
	  ENGLAND. House of Lords; Duke of Marlborough; Magdalen College, Oxford; Royal College of Physicians; Queen Anne's Bounty Office; Corporations of Chester, Leicester, &c.
	  IRELAND. Marquis of Ormonde, Lord Emly, The O'Conor Don, Trinity College, Dublin, &c.
		,,	[C.3040]	[Out of print.]

1881	DITTO. PART II. APPENDIX AND INDEX Contents :— Duke of Manchester.	,,	[C. 3040 i.]	[Out of print.]
1881	DITTO. PART III. APPENDIX AND INDEX Contents :— Earl of Ashburnham.	,,	[C. 3040 ii.]	[Out of print.]

Date.		Size.	Sessional Paper.	Price.
1883 (Reprinted 1895.)	NINTH REPORT, WITH APPENDIX AND INDEX. PART I. Contents:— St. Paul's and Canterbury Cathedrals; Eton College; Carlisle, Yarmouth, Canterbury, and Barnstaple Corporations, &c.	f'cap	[C.3773]	s. d. 5 2
1884 (Reprinted 1895.)	DITTO. PART II. APPENDIX AND INDEX Contents:— ENGLAND. House of Lords. Earl of Leicester; C. Pole Gell, Alfred Morrison, Esqs., &c. SCOTLAND. Lord Elphinstone, H. C. Maxwell Stuart, Esq., &c. IRELAND. Duke of Leinster, Marquis of Drogheda, &c.	„	[C.3773 i.]	6 3
1884	DITTO. PART III. APPENDIX AND INDEX Contents:— Mrs. Stopford Sackville.	„	[C.3773 ii.]	[Out of Print.]
1883 (Reprinted 1895.)	CALENDAR OF THE MANUSCRIPTS OF THE MARQUIS OF SALISBURY, K.G. (or CECIL MSS.). PART I. 1306-1571.	8vo.	[C.3777]	3 5
1888	DITTO. PART II. 1572-1582.	„	[C.5463]	3 5
1889	DITTO. PART III. 1583-1589.	„	[C.5889 v.]	2 1
1892	DITTO. PART IV. 1590-1594.	„	[C.6823]	2 11
1894	DITTO. PART V. 1594-1596.	„	[C.7574]	2 6
1896	DITTO. PART VI. 1596.	„	[C.7884]	2 8
1899	DITTO. PART VII. 1597.	„	[C.9246]	2 8
1899	DITTO. PART VIII. 1598.	„	[C.9467]	2 8
1902	DITTO. PART IX. 1599.	„	[Cd.928]	2 3
1885	TENTH REPORT This is introductory to the following.		[C.4548]	[Out of Print.]
1885 (Reprinted 1895.)	(1.) APPENDIX AND INDEX Earl of Eglinton. Sir J. S. Maxwell, Bart., and C. S. H. D. Moray, C. F. Weston Underwood. G. W. Digby. Esqs.	„	[C.4575]	3 7
1885	(2.) APPENDIX AND INDEX The Family of Gawdy.	„	[C.4576 iii.]	1 4
1885	(3.) APPENDIX AND INDEX Wells Cathedral.	„	[C.4576 ii.]	[Out of Print.]
1885	(4.) APPENDIX AND INDEX Earl of Westmorland; Capt. Stewart; Lord Stafford; Sir N. W. Throckmorton; Sir P. T. Mainwaring, Lord Muncaster, M.P., Capt. J. F. Bagot, Earl of Kilmorey, Earl of Powis, and others, the Corporations of Kendal, Wenlock, Bridgnorth, Eye, Plymouth, and the County of Essex; and Stonyhurst College.	„	[C.4576]	[Out of Print.]
1885 (Reprinted 1895.)	(5.) APPENDIX AND INDEX Marquis of Ormonde, Earl of Fingall, Corporations of Galway, Waterford, the Sees of Dublin and Ossory, the Jesuits in Ireland.	„	[4576 i.]	2 10

Date.		Size.	Sessional Paper.	Price.
				s. d.
1887	(6.) APPENDIX AND INDEX Marquis of Abergavenny; Lord Braye; G. F. Luttrell; P. P. Bouverie; W. Bromley Davenport; R. T. Balfour, Esquires.	8vo.	[C.5242]	1 7
1887	ELEVENTH REPORT This is introductory to the following:—	,,	[C.5060 vi.]	0 3
1887	(1.) APPENDIX AND INDEX H. D. Skrine, Esq., Salvetti Correspondence.	,,	[C.5060]	1 1
1887	(2.) APPENDIX AND INDEX House of Lords. 1678-1688.	,,	[C.5060 i.]	2 0
1887	(3.) APPENDIX AND INDEX Corporations of Southampton and Lynn.	,,	[C.5060 ii.]	1 8
1887	(4.) APPENDIX AND INDEX Marquess Townshend.	,,	[C.5060 iii.]	2 6
1887	(5.) APPENDIX AND INDEX Earl of Dartmouth.	,,	[C.5060 iv.]	2 8
1887	(6.) APPENDIX AND INDEX Duke of Hamilton.	,,	[C.5060 v.]	1 6
1888	(7.) APPENDIX AND INDEX Duke of Leeds, Marchioness of Waterford, Lord Hothfield, &c.; Bridgwater Trust Office, Reading Corporation, Inner Temple Library.	,,	[C.5612]	2 0
1890	TWELFTH REPORT This is introductory to the following:—	,,	[C.5889]	0 3
1888	(1.) APPENDIX Earl Cowper, K.G. (Coke MSS., at Melbourne Hall, Derby). Vol. I.	,,	[C.5472]	2 7
1888	(2.) APPENDIX Ditto. Vol. II	,,	[C.5613]	2 5
1889	(3.) APPENDIX AND INDEX Ditto. Vol. III.	,,	[C.5889 i.]	1 4
1888	(4.) APPENDIX Duke of Rutland, G.C.B. Vol. I.	,,	[C.5614]	[Out of Print.]
1891	(5.) APPENDIX AND INDEX Ditto. Vol. II.	,,	[C.5889 ii.]	2 0
1889	(6.) APPENDIX AND INDEX House of Lords, 1689-1690.	,,	[C.5889 iii.]	2 1
1890	(7.) APPENDIX AND INDEX S. H. le Fleming, Esq., of Rydal.	,,	[C.5889 iv.]	1 11
1891	(8.) APPENDIX AND INDEX Duke of Athole, K.T., and Earl of Home.	,,	[C.6338]	1 0
1891	(9.) APPENDIX AND INDEX Duke of Beaufort, K.G., Earl of Donoughmore, J. H. Gurney, W. W. B. Hulton, R. W. Ketton, G. A. Aitken, P. V. Smith, Esqs.; Bishop of Ely; Cathedrals of Ely, Gloucester, Lincoln, and Peterborough, Corporations of Gloucester, Higham Ferrers, and Newark; Southwell Minster; Lincoln District Registry.	,,	[C.6338 i.]	2 6

Date.		Size.	Sessional Paper.	Price.
				s. d.
1891	(10.) APPENDIX The First Earl of Charlemont. Vol. I.	8vo.	[C. 6338 ii.]	1 11
1892	THIRTEENTH REPORT This is introductory to the following:—	,,	[C.6827]	0 3
1891	(1.) APPENDIX Duke of Portland. Vol. I.	,,	[C.6474]	3 0
	(2.) APPENDIX AND INDEX. Ditto. Vol. II.	,,	[C. 6827 i.]	2 0
1892	(3.) APPENDIX. J. B. Fortescue, Esq., of Dropmore. Vol. I.	,,	[C.6660]	2 7
1892	(4.) APPENDIX AND INDEX Corporations of Rye, Hastings, and Hereford. Capt. F. C. Loder-Symonds, E. R. Wodehouse, M.P., J. Dovaston, Esqs., Sir T. B. Lennard, Bart., Rev. W. D. Macray, and Earl of Dartmouth (Supplementary Report).	,,	[C.6810]	2 4
1892	(5.) APPENDIX AND INDEX. House of Lords, 1690-1691	,,	[C.6822]	2 4
1893	(6.) APPENDIX AND INDEX. Sir W. Fitzherbert, Bart.; The Delaval Family, of Seaton Delaval; Earl of Ancaster; and Gen. Lyttelton-Annesley.	,,	[C.7166]	1 4
1893	(7.) APPENDIX AND INDEX. Earl of Lonsdale	,,	[C.7241]	1 3
1893	(8.) APPENDIX AND INDEX. The First Earl of Charlemont. Vol. II.	,,	[C.7424]	1 11
1896	FOURTEENTH REPORT This is introductory to the following:—	,,	[C.7983]	0 3
1894	(1.) APPENDIX AND INDEX. Duke of Rutland, G.C.B. Vol. III.	,,	[C.7476]	1 11
1894	(2.) APPENDIX. Duke of Portland. Vol. III.	,,	[C.7569]	2 8
1894	(3.) APPENDIX AND INDEX. Duke of Roxburghe; Sir H. H. Campbell, Bart.; Earl of Strathmore; and Countess Dowager of Seafield.	,,	[C.7570]	1 2
1894	(4.) APPENDIX AND INDEX. Lord Kenyon	,,	[C.7571]	2 10
1896	(5.) APPENDIX. J. B. Fortescue, Esq., of Dropmore. Vol. II.	,,	[C.7572]	2 8
1895	(6.) APPENDIX AND INDEX. House of Lords, 1692-1693	,,	[C.7573]	1 11
	(Manuscripts of the House of Lords, 1693-1695, Vol. I. (New Series.) See H.L. No. 5 of 1900. Price 2/9). *Ditto. 1695-1697. Vol. II. See H.L. No. 18. 1903. Price 2/9.*			
1895	(7.) APPENDIX. Marquis of Ormonde	,,	[C.7678]	1 10

Date.		Size.	Sessional Paper.	Price.
1895	(8.) APPENDIX AND INDEX. Lincoln, Bury St. Edmunds, Hertford, and Great Grimsby Corporations; The Dean and Chapter of Worcester, and of Lichfield; The Bishop's Registry of Worcester.	8vo.	[C.7881]	s. d. 1 5
1896	(9.) APPENDIX AND INDEX. Earl of Buckinghamshire; Earl of Lindsey; Earl of Onslow; Lord Emly; T. J. Hare, Esq.; and J. Round, Esq., M.P.	,,	[C.7882]	2 6
1895	(10.) APPENDIX AND INDEX. Earl of Dartmouth. Vol. II. American Papers.	,,	[C.7883]	2 9
1899	FIFTEENTH REPORT - - - - - This is introductory to the following:—	,,	[C.9295]	0 4
1896	(1.) APPENDIX AND INDEX. Earl of Dartmouth. Vol. III.	,,	[C.8156]	1 5
1897	(2.) APPENDIX. J. Eliot Hodgkin, Esq.	,,	[C.8327]	1 8
1897	(3.) APPENDIX AND INDEX. Charles Haliday, Esq., of Dublin; Acts of the Privy Council in Ireland, 1556-1571; Sir William Ussher's Table to the Council Book; Table to the Red Council Book.	,,	[C.8364]	1 4
1897	(4.) APPENDIX. Duke of Portland. Vol. IV.	,,	[C.8497]	2 11
1897	(5.) APPENDIX AND INDEX. The Right Hon. F. J. Savile Foljambe	,,	[C.8550]	0 10
1897	(6.) APPENDIX AND INDEX. Earl of Carlisle, Castle Howard	,,	[C.8551]	3 6
1897	(7.) APPENDIX AND INDEX. Duke of Somerset; Marquis of Ailesbury; and Sir F.G. Puleston, Bart.	,,	[C.8552]	1 9
1897	(8.) APPENDIX AND INDEX. Duke of Buccleuch and Queensberry, at Drumlanrig.	,,	[C.8553]	1 4
1897	(9.) APPENDIX AND INDEX. J. J. Hope Johnstone, Esq., of Annandale	,,	[C.8554]	1 0
1899	10.) Shrewsbury and Coventry Corporations; Sir H. O. Corbet, Bart., Earl of Radnor. P.T. Tillard; J.R Carr-Ellison; Andrew Kingsmill, Esqrs.		[C.9472]	1 0

Date.		Size.	Sessional Paper.	Price.
				s. d.
1898	MANUSCRIPTS IN THE WELSH LANGUAGE. Vol. I.—Lord Mostyn, at Mostyn Hall.	8vo.	[C.8829]	1 4
1899	Vol. I. Part II.—W. R. M. Wynne, Esq. of Peniarth.	,,	[C.9468]	2 11
1902	Vol. II. Part I.—Jesus College, Oxford; Free Library, Cardiff; Havod; Wrexham; Llanwrin; Merthyr; Aberdâr.		[Cd.1100]	1 9
1903	Vol. II. Part II.—Plas Llan Stephan; Free Library, Cardiff.	,,	[Cd.1692]	1 8
1899	Manuscripts of the Duke of Buccleuch and Queensberry, K.G., K.T., at Montagu House, Whitehall. Vol. I.	,,	[C.9244]	2 7
1899	Ditto Marquess of Ormonde, K.P., at Kilkenny Castle. Vol. II.	,,	[C.9245]	2 0
1899	Ditto Duke of Portland, K.G. Vol. V.	,,	[C.9466]	2 9
1899	Ditto J. M. Heathcote, Esq.	,,	[C.9469]	1 3
1899	Ditto J. B. Fortescue, Esq. Vol. III.	,,	[C.9470]	3 1
1899	Ditto F. W. Leyborne-Popham, Esq.	,,	[C.9471]	1 6
1900	Ditto Mrs. Frankland-Russell-Astley	,,	[Cd.282]	2 0
1900	Ditto Lord Montagu of Beaulieu	,,	[Cd.283]	1 1
1900	Ditto Beverley Corporation	,,	[Cd.284]	1 0
1901	Ditto Duke of Portland, K.G. Vol. VI., with Index to Vols. III.-VI.	,,	[Cd.676]	1 9
1901	Ditto. Vol. VII.	,,	[Cd.783]	2 3
1901	Ditto Various Collections. Vol. I. Corporations of Berwick-on-Tweed, Burford and Lostwithiel; the Counties of Wilts and Worcester; the Bishop of Chichester; and the Dean and Chapters of Chichester, Canterbury and Salisbury.	,,	[Cd.784]	2 0
1902	Ditto Calendar of the Stuart Manuscripts at Windsor Castle, belonging to His Majesty the King. Vol. I.	,,	[Cd.927]	2 11
1902	Ditto Marquess of Ormonde, K.P., at Kilkenny Castle. New Series. Vol. I.	,,	[Cd.929]	1 7
1902	Ditto Colonel David Milne-Home of Wedderburn Castle, N.B.	,,	[Cd.931]	1 4
1903	Ditto Various Collections. Vol. II. Sir Geo. Wombwell; Duke of Norfolk; Lord Edmund Talbot (the Shrewsbury papers); Miss Buxton, Mrs. Harford and Mrs. Wentworth of Woolley.	,,	[Cd.932]	2 4
1903	Ditto Duke of Buccleuch and Queensberry, K.G., K.T., at Montagu House, Whitehall. Vol. II. (Part I.)	,,	[Cd.930]	1 10
1903	Ditto Vol. II. (Part II.)	,,	[Cd.930-i]	1 11
1903	Ditto Marquess of Ormonde, K.P., at Kilkenny Castle. New Series. Vol. II.	,,	[Cd.1691]	1 10

ANNUAL REPORTS OF THE DEPUTY KEEPER OF THE PUBLIC RECORDS.

REPORTS NOS. 1-22, IN FOLIO, PUBLISHED BETWEEN 1840 AND 1861, ARE NO LONGER ON SALE. SUBSEQUENT REPORTS ARE IN OCTAVO.

Date.	Number of Report.	Chief Contents.	Sessional No.	Price.
1862	23	Proceedings	[C.2970]	s. d. 0 4
1863	24	Ditto	[C.3142]	[Out of print.]
1864	25	Calendar of Crown Leases, 33-38 Hen. VIII.—Calendar of Bills and Answers, &c., Hen. VIII.—Ph. & Mary, for Cheshire and Flintshire.—List of Lords High Treasurers and Chief Commissioners of the Treasury, from Hen. VII.	[C.3318]	[Out of print.]
1865	26	List of Plans annexed to Inclosure Awards, 31 Geo. II.-7 Will. IV.—Calendar of Privy Seals, &c., for Cheshire and Flintshire, Hen. VI.-Eliz.—Calendar of Writs of General Livery, &c., for Cheshire, Eliz.-Charles I.—Calendar of Deeds, &c., on the Chester Plea Rolls, Hen. III. and Edw. I.	[C.3492]	[Out of print.]
1866	27	List of Awards of Inclosure Commissioners.—References to Charters in the Cartæ Antiquæ and the Confirmation Rolls of Chancery, Ethelbert of Kent-James I.—Calendar of Deeds, &c., on the Chester Plea Rolls. Edw. II.	[C.3717]	[Out of print.]
1867	28	Calendar of Fines, Cheshire and Flintshire, Edw. I.—Calendar of Deeds, &c., on the Chester Plea Rolls, Edw. III. Table of Law Terms, from the Norman Conquest to 1 Will. IV.	[C.3839]	[Out of print.]
1868	29	Calendar of Royal Charters.—Calendar of Deeds, &c., on the Chester Plea Rolls Richard II.-Henry VII.—Durham Records, Letter and Report.	[C.4012]	[Out of print.]
1869	30	Duchy of Lancaster, Records, Inventory—Durham Records, Inventory.—Calendar of Deeds, &c., on the Chester Plea Rolls, Hen. VIII.—Calendar of Decrees of Court of General Surveyors, 34-38 Hen. VIII.—Calendar of Royal Charters.—State Paper Office, Calendar of Documents relating to the History of, to 1800.—Tower of London. Index to Documents in custody of the Constable of.—Calendar of Dockets, &c., for Privy Seals, 1634-1711.—Report of the Commissioners on Carte Papers.—Venetian Ciphers.	C.4165	[Out of print.]

Date.	Number of Report.	Chief Contents.	Sessional No.	Price.
				s. d.
1870	31	Duchy of Lancaster Records, Calendar of Royal Charters.—Durham Records, Calendar of Chancery Enrolments; Cursitor's Records.—List of Officers of Palatinate of Chester, in Cheshire and Flintshire, and North Wales.—List of Sheriffs of England, 13 Hen I. to 4 Edw. III.	C.187	[Out of print.]
1871	32	Part I.—Report of the Commissioners on Carte Papers.—Calendarium Genealogicum, 1 & 2 Edw. II.—Durham Records, Calendar of Cursitor's Records, Chancery Enrolments.—Duchy of Lancaster Records, Calendar of Rolls of the Chancery of the County Palatine.	C.374	[Out of print.]
1871	—	Part II.—Charities; Calendar of Trust Deeds enrolled on the Close Rolls of Chancery, subsequent to 9 Geo. II.	C.374 i.]	[Out of print.]
1872	33	Duchy of Lancaster Records, Calendar of Rolls of the Chancery of the County Palatine.—Durham Records, Calendar of the Cursitor's Records, Chancery Enrolments.—Report on the Shaftesbury Papers. Venetian Transcripts.—Greek Copies of the Athanasian Creed.	C.620	[Out of print.]
1873	34	Durham Records, Calendar of the Cursitor's Records, Chancery Enrolments.—Supplementary Report on the Shaftesbury Papers.	[C.728]	1 9
1874	35	Duchy of Lancaster Records, Calendar of Ancient Charters or Grants.—Palatinate of Lancaster; Inventory and Lists of Documents transferred to the Public Record Office.—Durham Records, Calendar of Cursitor's Records.—Chancery Enrolments.—Second Supplementary Report on the Shaftesbury Papers.	C.1043	[Out of print.]
1875	6	Durham Records, Calendar of the Cursitor's Records, Chancery Enrolments.—Duchy of Lancaster Records; Calendar of Ancient Charters or Grants.—Report upon Documents in French Archives relating to British History.—Calendar of Recognizance Rolls of the Palatinate of Chester, to end of reign of Hen. IV.	[C.1301]	[Out of print.]
1876	37	Part I.—Durham Records, Calendar of the Cursitor's Records, Chancery Enrolments.—Duchy of Lancaster Records, Calendar of Ancient Rolls of the Chancery of the County Palatine.—List of French Ambassadors, &c. in England, 1509-1714.	C.1514	[Out of print.]

Date.	Number of Report.	Chief Contents.	Sessional No.	Price.
				s. d.
1876	—	Part II.—Calendar of Recognizance Rolls of the Palatinate of Chester; Hen. V.—Hen. VII.	[C.1544 i.]	[Out of print.]
1877	38	Exchequer Records, Catalogue of Special Commissions, 1 Eliz. to 10 Vict., Calendar of Depositions taken by Commission, 1 Eliz. to end of James I.—List of Representative Peers for Scotland and Ireland.	[C.1747]	[Out of print.]
1878	39	Calendar of Recognizance Rolls of the Palatinate of Chester, 1 Hen. VIII.—11 Geo. IV.—Exchequer Records, Calendar of Depositions taken by Commission, Charles I.—Duchy of Lancaster Records; Calendar of Lancashire Inquisitions post Mortem, &c.—Third Supplementary Report on the Shaftesbury Papers.—List of Despatches of French Ambassadors to England 1509-1714.	[C.2128]	[Out of print.]
1879	40	Calendar of Depositions taken by Commission, Commonwealth—James II.—Miscellaneous Records of Queen's Remembrancer in the Exchequer.—Durham Records, Calendar of the Cursitors' Records, Chancery Enrolments.—Calendar of Duchy of Lancaster Patent Rolls, 5 Ric. II.—21 Hen. VII.	[C.2377]	[Out of print.]
1880	41	Calendar of Depositions taken by Commission, William and Mary to George I.—Calendar of Norman Rolls, Hen. V., Part I.—List of Calendars, Indexes, &c., in the Public Record Office on 31st December, 1879.	[C.2658]	4 8
1881	42	Calendar of Depositions taken by Commission, George II.—Calendar of Norman Rolls, Hen. V., Part II. and Glossary.—Calendar of Patent Rolls, 1 Edw. I. Transcripts from Paris.	[C.2972]	4 0
1882	43	Calendar of Privy Seals, &c., 1-7 Charles I.—Duchy of Lancaster Records, Inventory of Court Rolls, Hen. III.—Geo. IV. Calendar of Privy Seals, Ric. II.—Calendar of Patent Rolls, 2 Edw. I.—Fourth Supplementary Report on the Shaftesbury Papers.—Transcripts from Paris.—Report on Libraries in Sweden.—Report on Papers relating to English History in the State Archives, Stockholm.—Report on Canadian Archives.	[C.3425]	3 10
1883	44	Calendar of Patent Rolls, 3 Edw. I.—Durham Records, Cursitors' Records, Inquisitions post Mortem, &c.—Calendar of French Rolls, 1-10 Hen. V.—Report from Venice.—Transcripts from Paris.—Report from Rome.	[C.3771]	3 6

Date.	Number of Report.	Chief Contents.	Sessional No.	Price.
				s. d.
1884	45	Duchy of Lancaster Records, Inventory of Ministers' and Receivers' Accounts, Edw. I.—Geo. III.—Durham Records, Cursitors' Records, Inquisitions post Mortem, &c.—Calendar of Diplomatic Documents.—Transcripts from Paris.—Reports from Rome and Stockholm.—Report on Archives of Denmark, &c.—Transcripts from Venice.—Calendar of Patent Rolls, 4 Edw. I.	[C.4425]	4 3
1885	46	Presentations to Offices on the Patent Rolls, Charles II.—Transcripts from Paris.—Reports from Rome.—Second Report on Archives of Denmark, &c.—Calendar of Patent Rolls, 5 Edw. I.—Catalogue of Venetian Manuscripts bequeathed by Mr. Rawdon Brown to the Public Record Office.	[C.4746]	2 10
1886	47	Transcripts from Paris—Third Report on Archives of Denmark, &c.—List of Creations of Peers and Baronets, 1483-1646.—Calendar of Patent Rolls, 6 Edw. I.	[C.4888]	2 2
1887	48	Calendar of Patent Rolls, 7 Edw. I.—Calendar of French Rolls, Henry VI.—Calendar of Privy Seals, &c., 8-11 Charles I.—Calendar of Diplomatic Documents.—Schedules of Valueless Documents.	[C.5234]	3 6
1888	49	Calendar of Patent Rolls, 8 Edw. I.—Index to Leases and Pensions (Augmentation Office).—Calendar of Star Chamber Proceedings.	[C.5596]	3 3
1889	50	Calendar of Patent Rolls, 9 Edw. I.	[C.5847]	1 2
1890	51	Proceedings	[C.6108]	0 2
1891	52	Ditto	[C.6528]	0 1½
1892	53	Ditto	[C.6804]	0 2½
1893	54	Ditto	[C.7079]	0 1½
1894	55	Ditto	[C.7444]	0 1½
1895	56	Ditto	[C.7841]	0 1½
1896	57	Ditto. Account of the Rolls Chapel with eight plates of the Chapel.	[C.8271]	1 0
1897	58	Ditto	[C.8543]	0 1½
1898	59	Ditto	[C.8906]	0 1
1899	60	Ditto	[C.9366]	0 1
1900	61	Ditto	[Cd.245]	0 1
1901	62	Ditto	[Cd.617]	0 1
1902	63	Ditto	[Cd.1141]	0 1
1903	64	Ditto	[Cd.1620]	0 1
		Indexes to Printed Reports, viz.:— Reports 1-22 (1840-1861) " 23-39 (1862-1878)	— —	4 0 2 0

SCOTLAND.

CATALOGUE OF SCOTTISH RECORD PUBLICATIONS.

PUBLISHED UNDER THE DIRECTION OF

THE LORD CLERK REGISTER OF SCOTLAND.

[OTHER WORKS RELATING TO SCOTLAND WILL BE FOUND AMONG THE PUBLICATIONS OF THE RECORD COMMISSIONERS, *see* pp. 21-22.]

1. CHRONICLES OF THE PICTS AND SCOTS, AND OTHER EARLY MEMORIALS OF SCOTTISH HISTORY. Royal 8vo., half bound (1867). *Edited by* WILLIAM F. SKENE, LL.D. (*Out of print.*)
2. LEDGER OF ANDREW HALYBURTON, CONSERVATOR OF THE PRIVILEGES OF THE SCOTCH NATION IN THE NETHERLANDS (1492-1503); TOGETHER WITH THE BOOKS OF CUSTOMS AND VALUATION OF MERCHANDISES IN SCOTLAND. *Edited by* COSMO INNES. Royal 8vo., half bound (1867). *Price* 10s.
3. DOCUMENTS ILLUSTRATIVE OF THE HISTORY OF SCOTLAND FROM THE DEATH OF KING ALEXANDER THE THIRD TO THE ACCESSION OF ROBERT BRUCE, from original and authentic copies in London, Paris, Brussels, Lille, and Ghent. In 2 Vols. royal 8vo., half bound (1870). *Edited by the* Rev. JOSEPH STEVENSON. (*Out of print.*)
4. ACCOUNTS OF THE LORD HIGH TREASURER OF SCOTLAND. Vol. I., A.D. 1473-1498. *Edited by* THOMAS DICKSON. 1877. *Price* 10s. (*Out of Print.*) Vol. II., A.D. 1500-1504. *Edited by* SIR J. B. PAUL. 1900. *Price* 10s. Vol. III. A.D. 1506-1507. Vol. IV. 1507-1583. *Edited by* SIR J. B. PAUL. *Price* 10s.
5. REGISTER OF THE PRIVY COUNCIL OF SCOTLAND. *Edited and arranged by* J. H. BURTON, LL.D. Vol. I., 1545-1569. Vol. II., 1569-1578. Vol. III., A.D. 1578-1585. Vol. IV., A.D., 1585-1592. Vol. V., 1592-1599. Vol. VI., 1599-1604. Vol. VII., 1604-1607. Vol. VIII., 1607-1610. Vol. IX., 1610-1613. Vol. X., 1613-1616. Vol. XI., 1616-1619. Vol. XII. 1619-1622. Vol. XIII. 1622-1625. Vol. XIV., Addenda, 1545-1625. *Edited by* DAVID MASSON, LL.D., 1877-1895. *Price* 15s. *each.* Ditto, Second Series. Vol. I., 1625-1627. Vol. II., 1627-1628. Vol. III., 1629-1630. *Edited by* D. MASSON, LL.D. *Price* 15s.
6. ROTULI SCACCARII REGUM SCOTORUM. THE EXCHEQUER ROLLS OF SCOTLAND. Vol. I., A.D. 1264-1359. Vol. II., A.D. 1359-1379. 1880. Vol. III., A.D. 1379-1406. Vol. IV., A.D. 1406-1436. Vol. V., A.D. 1437-1454. Vol. VI., 1455-1460. Vol. VII., 1460-1469. Vol. VIII., A.D. 1470-1479. Vol. IX., 1480-1487. Addenda, 1437-1487. Vol. X., 1488-1496. Vol. XI., 1497-1501. Vol. XII., 1502-1507. Vol. XIII., 1508-1513. Vol. XIV., 1513-1522. Vol. XV., 1523-1529. Vol. XVI., 1529-1536. Vol. XVII., 1537-1542. Vol. XVIII., 1543-1556. Vol. XIX., 1557-1567. Vol. XX., 1568-1579. Vol. XXI., 1580-1588. *Edited by* JOHN STUART, LL.D. (Vol. I.); GEORGE BURNETT (Vols. II. to XII.); GEORGE BURNETT and Æ. J. G. MACKAY (Vols. XIII. to XX.); and G. P. MCNEIL (Vols. XV. to XXI.) 1878-1898. *Price* 10s. *each.*
7. CALENDAR OF DOCUMENTS RELATING TO SCOTLAND, preserved in the Public Record Office. *Edited by* JOSEPH BAIN. Vol. I. (1881). Vol. II., 1272-1307 (1884). Vol. III., 1307-1357 (1887). Vol. IV., 1357-1509 (1888). *Price* 15s. *each.*
8. REGISTER OF THE GREAT SEAL OF SCOTLAND. Vol. I., A.D. 1306-1424 (*see* p. 21). Vol. II., A.D. 1424-1513. Vol. III., A.D. 1513-1546. Vol. IV., A.D. 1546-1580. Vol. V., A.D. 1580-1593. Vol. VI., A.D. 1593-1609. Vol. VII., A.D. 1609-1620. Vol. VIII., A.D. 1620-1623. Vol. IX., A.D. 1634-1651. *Edited by* JAMES BALFOUR PAUL and J. M. THOMSON, 1882-1894. *Price* 15s. *each.*
9. THE HAMILTON PAPERS. Letters and Papers illustrating the Political Relations of England and Scotland in the XVIth century. Formerly in the Possession of the Duke of Hamilton, now in the British Museum. *Edited by* JOSEPH BAIN, F.S.A. Scot. Vol. I., A.D. 1532-1543 (1890). Vol. II., A.D. 1543-1590. *Price* 15s. *each.*
10. BORDERS OF ENGLAND AND SCOTLAND. Calendar of. Letters and Papers relating to the Affairs of the. Preserved in Her Majesty's Public Record Office, London. *Edited by* JOSEPH BAIN. Vol. I., A.D. 1560-1594. Vol. II., A.D. 1595-1603. *Price* 15s. *each.*
11. STATE PAPERS RELATING TO SCOTLAND AND MARY QUEEN OF SCOTS. Calendar of A.D. 1547-1603. Vol. I., 1547-1563. Vol. II., A.D. 1563-1569. Vol. III., 1569-1571. *Edited by* JOSEPH BAIN. *Price* 15s.

FAC-SIMILES OF THE NATIONAL MSS. OF SCOTLAND. Parts I., II., and III. (*Out of print.*)

IRELAND.

CATALOGUE OF IRISH RECORD PUBLICATIONS.

1. CALENDAR OF THE PATENT AND CLOSE ROLLS OF CHANCERY IN IRELAND, HENRY VIII., EDWARD VI., MARY AND ELIZABETH, AND FOR THE 1ST TO THE 7TH YEAR OF CHARLES I. *Edited by* JAMES MORRIN. Royal 8vo. (1861-3). Vols. I., II., and III. *Price* 11s. *each.*

2. ANCIENT LAWS AND INSTITUTES OF IRELAND. Senchus Mor. (1865-1880.) Vols. I., II., III., IV., V., and VI. *Price* 10s. *each.*

3. ABSTRACTS OF THE IRISH PATENT ROLLS OF JAMES I. (*Out of print.*)

4. ANNALS OF ULSTER. Otherwise Annals of Senate, a Chronicle of Irish Affairs from A.D. 431-1131, 1155-1541. With a translation and Notes, Vol. I., A.D. 431-1056. Vol. II., A.D. 1057-1131; 1155-1378. Vol. III., A.D. 1379-1541. Vol. IV., Introduction and Index. Half morocco. *Price* 10s. *each.*

5. CHARTÆ PRIVILEGIA ET IMMUNITATES, being transcripts of Charters and Privileges to Cities, Towns, Abbeys, and other Bodies Corporate. 18 Henry II. to 18 Richard II. (1171-1395.) Printed by the Irish Record Commission, 1829-1830. Folio, 92pp. Boards (1889). *Price* 5s.

FAC-SIMILES OF NATIONAL MANUSCRIPTS OF IRELAND, FROM THE EARLIEST EXTANT SPECIMENS TO A.D. 1719. *Edited by* JOHN T. GILBERT, F.S.A., M.R.I.A. Part I. is out of print. Parts II. and III. *Price* 42s. *each.* Part IV. 1. *Price* 5l. 5s. Part IV. 2. *Price* 4l. 10s.

> This work forms a comprehensive Palæographic Series for Ireland. It furnishes characteristic specimens of the documents which have come down from each of the classes which, in past ages, formed principal elements in the population of Ireland, or exercised an influence in her affairs. With these reproductions are combined facsimiles of writings connected with eminent personages or transactions of importance in the annals of the country to the early part of the eighteenth century.
>
> The specimens have been reproduced as nearly as possible in accordance with the originals, in dimensions, colouring, and general appearance. Characteristic examples of styles of writing and caligraphic ornamentation are, as far as practicable, associated with subjects of historic and linguistic interest. Descriptions of the various manuscripts are given by the Editor in the Introduction. The contents of the specimens are fully elucidated and printed in the original languages, opposite to the Fac-similes—line for line—without contractions—thus facilitating reference and aiding effectively those interested in palæographic studies.
>
> In the work are also printed in full, for the first time, many original and important historical documents.
>
> Part I. commences with the earliest Irish MSS. extant.
> Part II.: From the Twelfth Century to A.D. 1299.
> Part III.: From A.D. 1300 to end of reign of Henry VIII.
> Part IV. 1: From reign of Edward VI. to that of James I.
> In part IV. 2 the work is carried down to the early part of the eighteenth century, with Index to the entire publication.

ACCOUNT OF FAC-SIMILES OF NATIONAL MANUSCRIPTS OF IRELAND. In one Volume 8vo., with Index. *Price* 10s. Parts I. and II. together. *Price* 2s. 6d. Part II. *Price* 1s. 6d. Part III. *Price* 1s. Part IV. 1. *Price* 2s. Part IV. 2. *Price* 2s. 6d.

ANNUAL REPORTS OF THE DEPUTY KEEPER OF THE PUBLIC RECORDS, IRELAND.

Date.	Number of Report.	Chief Contents of Appendices.	Sessional No.	Price.
				s. d.
1869	1	Contents of the principal Record Repositories of Ireland in 1864.—Notices of Records transferred from Chancery Offices.—Irish State Papers presented by Philadelphia Library Company.	[C.4157]	[Out of print.]
1870	2	Notices of Records transferred from Chancery, Queen's Bench, and Exchequer Offices.—Index to Original Deeds received from Master Litton's Office.	[C.137]	[Out of print.]
1871	3	Notices of Records transferred from Queen's Bench, Common Pleas, and Exchequer Offices.—Report on J. F. Furguson's MSS.—Exchequer Indices, &c.	[C.329]	[Out of print.]
1872	4	Records of Probate Registries	[C.515]	[Out of print.]
1873	5	Notices of Records from Queen's Bench Calendar of Fines and Recoveries of the Palatinate of Tipperary, 1664-1715.—Index to Reports to date.	[C.760]	0 8
1874	6	Notices of Records transferred from Chancery, Queen's Bench, and Common Pleas Offices.—Report respecting "Facsimiles of National MSS. of Ireland."—List of Chancery Pleadings (1662-1690) and Calendar to Chancery Rolls (1662-1713) of Palatinate of Tipperary.	[C.963]	[Out of print.]
1875	7	Notices of Records from Exchequer and Admiralty Offices.—Calendar and Index to Fiants of Henry VIII.	[C.1175]	[Out of print.]
1876	8	Calendar and Index to Fiants of Edward VI.	[C.1469]	[Out of print.]
1877	9	Index to the Liber Munerum Publicorum Hiberniæ.—Calendar and Index to Fiants of Philip and Mary.	[C.1702]	[Out of print.]
1878	10	Index to Deputy Keeper's 6th, 7th, 8th, 9th, and 10th Reports.	[C.2034]	[Out of print.]
1879	11	Calendar to Fiants of Elizabeth (1558-1570).	[C.2311]	[Out of print.]
1880	12	Calendar to Fiants of Elizabeth, continued (1570-1576).	[C.2583]	[Out of print.]
1881	13	Calendar to Fiants of Elizabeth, continued (1576-1583).	[C.2929]	1 5
1882	14	Report of Keeper of State Papers containing Catalogue of Commonwealth Books transferred from Bermingham Tower.	[C.3215]	0 6½
1883	15	Calendar to Fiants of Elizabeth, continued (1583-1586).—Index to Deputy Keeper's 11th, 12th, 13th, 14th, and 15th Reports.	[C.3676]	1 0
1884	16	Calendar to Fiants of Elizabeth, continued (1586-1595).	[C.4062]	1 6
1885	17	Report on Iron Chest of attainders following after 1641 and 1688.—Queen's Bench Calendar to Fiants of Elizabeth continued (1596-1601).	[C.4487]	1 6
1886	18	Calendar to Fiants of Elizabeth, continued (1601-1603).—Memorandum on Statements (1702) and Declarons (1713-14) of Huguenot Pensioners.	[C.4755]	1 1

Date.	Number of Report.	Chief Contents of Appendices.	Sessional No.	Price.
				s. d.
1887	19	Notice of Records of Incumbered and Landed Estates Courts.—Report of Keeper of State Papers, containing Table of Abstracts of Decrees of Innocence (1663), with Index.	[C.5185]	0 6
1888	20	Calendar to Christ Church Deeds in Novum Registrum, 1174-1684. Index to Deputy Keeper's 16th, 17th, 18th, 19th, and 20th Reports.	[C.5535]	0 8½
1889	21	Index to Calendars of Fiants of the reign of Queen Elizabeth. Letters A—C.	[C.5835]	1 0
1890	22	Catalogue of Proclamations, 1618-1660	[C.6180]	0 2½
		Index to Fiants of Elizabeth. D—Z	[C.6180 i.]	2 0
1891	23	Catalogue of Proclamations, 1661-1767.—Calendar to Christ Church Deeds, 1177-1462.	[C.6504]	1 1
1892	24	Catalogue of Proclamations, 1767-1875. Contents of the Red Book of the Exchequer. Calendar to Christ Church Deeds, 1462-1602.	[C.6765]	0 9½
1893	25	Regulations respecting State Papers. Instructions for Parochial Custodians. Index to Twenty-first to Twenty-fifth Reports.	[C.7170]	0 3
1894	26	Abstract of Antrim Inquisition, 3 James I., Bankruptcy Records, 1857-1872; Early Plea Rolls to 51 Edward III.	[C.7488]	0 3½
		Index to the Act or Grant Books, and to Original Wills, of the Diocese of Dublin to the year 1800.	[C.7488 i.]	[Out of print.]
1895	27	Records from Courts and Offices transferred to, and deposited at the Public Record Office in Ireland.	[C.7802]	0 2½
1896	—	Index to Calendars of Christ Church Deeds 1174-1684, contained in Appendices to 20th, 23rd, and 24th Reports.	[C.8080]	0 5½
1896	28	(1.) Report on the Early Plea Rolls, continued from 51 Edward III.	[C.8163]	0 5½
		(2.) Table showing present Custodies of Parochial Records.	—	—
1897	29	Copy and Translation of Five Instruments of Record in the Public Record Office of Ireland, written in the Irish Character and Tongue, 1584-1606.	[C.8567]	0 3
1898	30	Report on M.S.S. of Sir T. Phillipps' Library; Index to Deputy Keeper's Reports, 26th to 30th, incl.	[C.9030]	0 3½
1899	31	Report of Proceedings, and Appendix (1) Corrections to the Addenda to the Dublin Grants Index in Appendix to the 26th Report; (2.) Notes on the Departmental Letters and Official Papers, 1760-89.	[C.9478]	0 5½
1900	—	Index to the Act or Grant Book and Original Wills of the Diocese of Dublin from 1800-1858.	[Cd. 4]	4 7
1900	32	Report of Proceedings and Appendix.—Report on the Records of the Clerks of the Crown and Peace transferred prior to 1900.	[Cd. 274]	0 6
1901	33	Report of Proceedings and Appendix (1) Notes on Manuscript Volumes connected with the Irish Revenue, the Court of Trustees of Forfeited Estates, &c., in the possession of Earl Annesley; (2) Report on the Books of the Treasury and Accounting Departments in Ireland.	[Cd. 729]	0 5

Date.	Number of Report	Chief Contents of Appendices.	Sessional No.	Price.
				s. d.
1902	34	Report of Proceedings and Appendix (1) List of Maps presented by Commissioners of Woods and Forests; (2) Report on Register of Irregular Marriages, 1799-1844.	[Cd.1176]	0 2½
1903	35	Report of Proceedings and Appendix (1) Regulations as to access to Military Records; (2) Records found in former Record Office; (3) Catalogue of Accounts on the Pipe Rolls of Irish Exchequer, Henry III	[Cd.1504]	0 3